13e

Anthropology
The Human Challenge

WILLIAM A. HAVILAND
University of Vermont

HARALD E. L. PRINS
Kansas State University

DANA WALRATH
University of Vermont

BUNNY McBRIDE
Kansas State University

WADSWORTH
CENGAGE Learning

Australia • Brazil • Japan • Korea • Mexico • Singapore • Spain • United Kingdom • United States

WADSWORTH
CENGAGE Learning™

Anthropology: The Human Challenge,
Thirteenth Edition
William A. Haviland, Harald E. L. Prins, Dana Walrath, Bunny McBride

Anthropology Editor: Erin Mitchell

Developmental Editor: Lin Marshall Gaylord

Assistant Editor: Rachael Krapf

Editorial Assistant: Pamela Simon

Media Editor: Melanie Cregger

Marketing Manager: Andrew Keay

Marketing Coordinator: Dimitri Hagnéré

Marketing Communications Manager:
   Tami Strang

Content Project Manager: Samen Iqbal

Creative Director: Rob Hugel

Art Director: Caryl Gorska

Print Buyer: Karen Hunt

Rights Acquisitions Account Manager, Text:
   Roberta Broyer

Rights Acquisitions Account Manager, Image:
   Robyn Young

Production Service: Joan Keyes,
   Dovetail Publishing Services

Text Designer: Lisa Buckley

Photo Researchers: Billie Porter, Susan Kaprov

Copy Editor: Jennifer Gordon

Cover Designer: Lawrence R. Didona

Cover Image, clockwise from top: © Skyscan/
Corbis, © Werner Forman/HIP/The Image
Works, © Keren Su/Corbis, © Nancy Brown/
Getty Images, © E & E Image Library/HIP/The
Image Works, © DLILLC/Corbis, © Z. Radovan/
Lebrecht/The Image Works

Compositor: Pre-PressPMG

For product information and technology assistance, contact us at
Cengage Learning Customer & Sales Support, 1-800-354-9706

For permission to use material from this text or product,
submit all requests online at **cengage.com/permissions**
Further permissions questions can be emailed to
permissionrequest@cengage.com

Library of Congress Control Number: 2009941337

Student Edition:

ISBN-13: 978-0-495-81084-1

ISBN-10: 0-495-81084-3

Loose-leaf Edition:

ISBN-13: 978-0-8400-3331-4

ISBN-10: 0-8400-3331-1

Wadsworth
20 Davis Drive
Belmont, CA 94002-3098
USA

Cengage Learning is a leading provider of customized learning solutions with office locations around the globe, including Singapore, the United Kingdom, Australia, Mexico, Brazil, and Japan. Locate your local office at **www.cengage.com/global.**

Cengage Learning products are represented in Canada by Nelson Education, Ltd.

To learn more about Wadsworth, visit **www.cengage.com/wadsworth**

Purchase any of our products at your local college store or at our preferred online store **www.CengageBrain.com.**

Printed in the United States of America
2 3 4 5 6 7 14 13 12 11 10

Dedicated to our parents who provided each of us with a nourishing environment, inspiring guidance, and an appreciation for cultural heritage. All of them fostered in all of us an eagerness to explore, experience, and enjoy other cultures, past and present.

Putting the World in Perspective

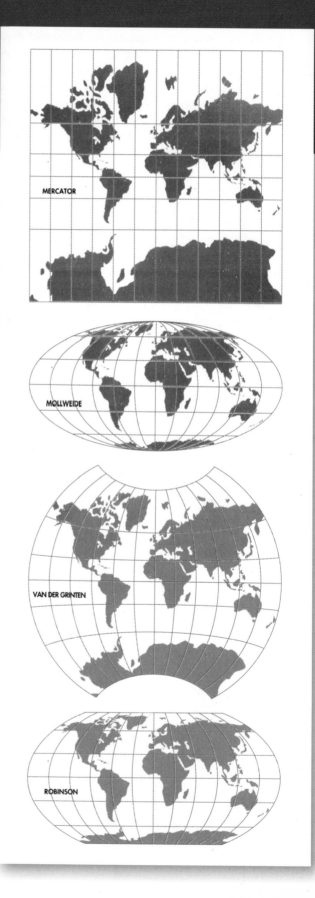

Although all humans that we know about are capable of producing accurate sketches of localities and regions with which they are familiar, **cartography** (the craft of map making as we know it today) had its beginnings in 16th-century Europe, and its subsequent development is related to the expansion of Europeans to all parts of the globe. From the beginning, there have been two problems with maps: the technical one of how to depict on a two-dimensional, flat surface a three-dimensional spherical object, and the cultural one of whose worldview they reflect. In fact, the two issues are inseparable, for the particular projection one uses inevitably makes a statement about how one views one's own people and their place in the world. Indeed, maps often shape our perception of reality as much as they reflect it.

In cartography, a **projection** refers to the system of intersecting lines (of longitude and latitude) by which part or all of the globe is represented on a flat surface. There are more than a hundred different projections in use today, ranging from polar perspectives to interrupted "butterflies" to rectangles to heart shapes. Each projection causes distortion in size, shape, or distance in some way or another. A map that correctly shows the shape of a landmass will of necessity misrepresent the size. A map that is accurate along the equator will be deceptive at the poles.

Perhaps no projection has had more influence on the way we see the world than that of Gerhardus Mercator, who devised his map in 1569 as a navigational aid for mariners. So well suited was Mercator's map for this purpose that it continues to be used for navigational charts today. At the same time, the Mercator projection became a standard for depicting landmasses, something for which it was never intended. Although an accurate navigational tool, the Mercator projection greatly exaggerates the size of landmasses in higher latitudes, giving about two thirds of the map's surface to the northern hemisphere. Thus the lands occupied by Europeans and European descendants appear far larger than those of other people. For example, North America (19 million square kilometers) appears almost twice the size of Africa (30 million square kilometers), while Europe is shown as equal in size to South America, which actually has nearly twice the landmass of Europe.

A map developed in 1805 by Karl B. Mollweide was one of the earlier *equal-area projections* of the world. Equal-area projections portray landmasses in correct relative size, but, as a result, distort the shape of continents more than other projections. They most often compress and warp lands in the higher latitudes and vertically stretch landmasses close to the equator. Other equal-area projections include the Lambert Cylindrical Equal-Area Projection (1772), the Hammer Equal-Area Projection (1892), and the Eckert Equal-Area Projection (1906).

The Van der Grinten Projection (1904) was a compromise aimed at minimizing both the distortions of size in the Mercator and the distortion of shape in equal-area maps such as the Mollweide. Although an improvement, the lands of the northern hemisphere are still emphasized at the expense of the southern. For example, in the Van der Grinten, the Commonwealth of Independent States (the former Soviet Union) and Canada are shown at more than twice their relative size.

The Robinson Projection, which was adopted by the National Geographic Society in 1988 to replace the Van der Grinten, is one of the best compromises to date between the distortions of size and shape. Although an improvement over the Van der Grinten, the Robinson Projection still depicts lands in the northern latitudes as proportionally larger at the same time that it depicts lands in the lower latitudes (representing most Third World nations) as proportionally smaller. Like European maps before it, the Robinson Projection places Europe at the center of the map with the Atlantic Ocean and the Americas to the left, emphasizing the cultural connection between Europe and North America, while neglecting the geographic closeness of northwestern North America to northeastern Asia.

The following pages show four maps that each convey quite different cultural messages. Included among them is the Peters Projection, an equal-area map that has been adopted as the official map of UNESCO (the United Nations Educational, Scientific, and Cultural Organization), and a map made in Japan, showing us how the world looks from the other side.

The Robinson Projection

The map below is based on the Robinson Projection, which is used today by the National Geographic Society and Rand McNally. Although the Robinson Projection distorts the relative size of landmasses, it does so much less than most other projections. Still, it places Europe at the center of the map. This particular view of the world has been used to identify the location of many of the cultures discussed in this text.

The Peters Projection

The map below is based on the Peters Projection, which has been adopted as the official map of UNESCO. While it distorts the shape of continents (countries near the equator are vertically elongated by a ratio of 2 to 1), the Peters Projection does show all continents according to their correct relative size. Though Europe is still at the center, it is not shown as larger and more extensive than the Third World.

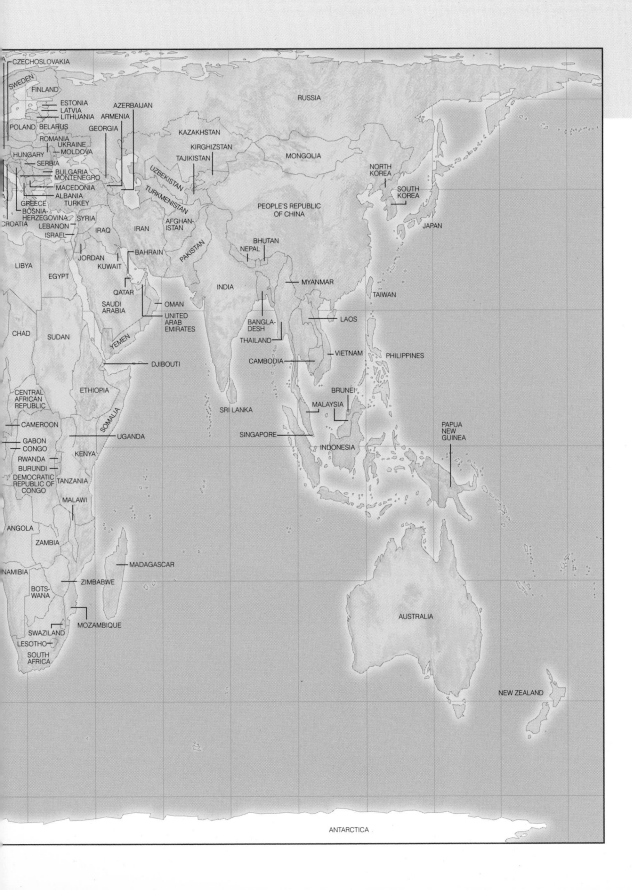

CZECHOSLOVAKIA
SWEDEN
FINLAND
ESTONIA
LATVIA
LITHUANIA
POLAND BELARUS
ROMANIA
UKRAINE
MOLDOVA
HUNGARY
SERBIA
BULGARIA
MONTENEGRO
MACEDONIA
GREECE ALBANIA
BOSNIA- TURKEY
HERZEGOVINA
CROATIA
LEBANON
ISRAEL
LIBYA
EGYPT
CHAD
SUDAN
CENTRAL
AFRICAN
REPUBLIC
CAMEROON
GABON
CONGO
RWANDA
BURUNDI
DEMOCRATIC
REPUBLIC OF
CONGO
MALAWI
ANGOLA
ZAMBIA
NAMIBIA
BOTS-
WANA
SWAZILAND
LESOTHO
SOUTH
AFRICA

AZERBAIJAN
ARMENIA
GEORGIA
UZBEKISTAN
TURKMENISTAN
SYRIA
IRAQ
IRAN
AFGHAN-
ISTAN
JORDAN
KUWAIT
BAHRAIN
QATAR
SAUDI
ARABIA
YEMEN
OMAN
UNITED
ARAB
EMIRATES
DJIBOUTI
ETHIOPIA
SOMALIA
UGANDA
KENYA
TANZANIA
ZIMBABWE
MADAGASCAR
MOZAMBIQUE

RUSSIA
KAZAKHSTAN
MONGOLIA
KIRGHIZSTAN
TAJIKISTAN
PAKISTAN
INDIA
SRI LANKA
PEOPLE'S REPUBLIC
OF CHINA
NORTH
KOREA
SOUTH
KOREA
JAPAN
TAIWAN
BHUTAN
NEPAL
MYANMAR
BANGLA-
DESH
THAILAND
LAOS
VIETNAM
CAMBODIA
PHILIPPINES
BRUNEI
MALAYSIA
SINGAPORE
INDONESIA
PAPUA
NEW
GUINEA
AUSTRALIA
NEW ZEALAND
ANTARCTICA

Japanese Map

Not all maps place Europe at the center of the world, as this Japanese map illustrates. Besides reflecting the importance the Japanese attach to themselves in the world, this map has the virtue of showing the geographic proximity of North America to Asia, a fact easily overlooked when maps place Europe at their center.

GREENLAND

UNITED
STATES

CANADA

UNITED STATES

MEXICO

THE
BAHAMAS

HAITI

CUBA

DOMINICAN REPUBLIC

JAMAICA

NICARAGUA

BELIZE
GUATEMALA
EL SALVADOR
HONDURAS
COSTA RICA
PANAMA

VENEZUELA

FRENCH GUIANA

COLOMBIA

GUYANA

SURINAM

ECUADOR

BRAZIL

PERU

BOLIVIA

PARAGUAY

CHILE

ARGENTINA

URUGUAY

NEW ZEALAND

ANTARCTICA

The Turnabout Map

The way maps may reflect (and influence) our thinking is exemplified by the Turnabout Map, which places the South Pole at the top and the North Pole at the bottom. Words and phrases such as "on top," "over," and "above" tend to be equated by some people with superiority. Turning things upside-down may cause us to rethink the way North Americans regard themselves in relation to the people of Central America. © 1982 by Jesse Levine Turnabout Map™—Dist. by Laguna Sales, Inc., 7040 Via Valverde, San Jose, CA 95135

A NEW WORLD
of Understanding

Ever since maps were first drawn, certain countries have been located at the top, others below. Since "on top," "over," and "above" are equated with superiority, while "down there," "beneath," and "below" imply the reverse, these wholly arbitrary placements, over the years, have led to misconceptions and misjudgments.

This Turnabout Map of the Americas serves to correct the imbalance. It focuses attention in new directions toward areas of exploding populations, energies, and potentialities. It is geographically correct. Only the perspective has been changed.

Brief Contents

Features Contents

Contents

© Steve Bloom Images/Alamy

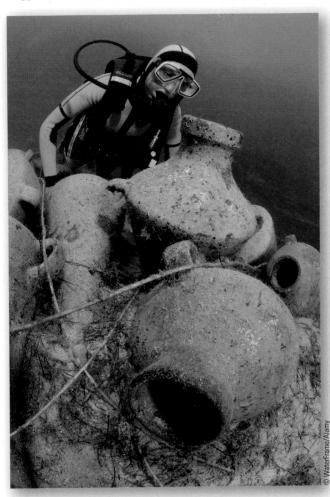

Chapter 10 The Neolithic Revolution: The Domestication of Plants and Animals   228

Chapter 11 The Emergence of Cities and States   252

© Michael Conye/Getty Images

Chapter 12 Modern Human Diversity: Race and Racism   276

© Julia Jean

Chapter 15 Ethnographic Research: Its
History, Methods, and Theories   342

Gai Ming-sheng/HK China Tourism Press

Jochen Tack/Photo Library

Preface

Lucky 13. Working on this thirteenth edition of *Anthropology: The Human Challenge* has proved to us how fortunate we are to have the opportunity to revisit our textbook multiple times with the ambition of reaching well beyond mere updating to making the narrative and images ever-more compelling, informative, and relevant to readers. Our efforts continue to be fueled by vital feedback from our students and from anthropology professors who have reviewed and used previous editions. Their input—combined with our own ongoing research and the surprisingly delightful task of rethinking familiar concepts that appear self-evident—has helped us bring fresh insight to classical themes.

With each new edition, we look anew at the archetypal examples of our discipline and weigh them against the latest innovative research methodologies, archaeological discoveries, genetic and other biological findings, linguistic insights, and ethnographic descriptions, theoretical revelations, and significant examples of applied anthropology. These considerations, combined with attention to compelling issues in our global theater, go toward fashioning a thought-provoking textbook that presents both classical and fresh material in ways that stimulate students' interest, stir critical reflection, and prompt "ah-ha" moments.

Our Mission

Time and time again, we have observed that most students enter an introductory anthropology class intrigued by the general subject but with little more than a vague sense of what it is all about. Thus the first and most obvious task of our text is to provide a thorough introduction to the discipline—its foundations as a domain of knowledge and its major insights into the rich diversity of humans as a culture-making species.

In doing this, we draw from the research and ideas of a number of traditions of anthropological thought, exposing students to a mix of theoretical perspectives and methodologies. Such inclusiveness reflects our conviction that different approaches offer distinctly important insights about human biology, behavior, and beliefs.

If most students start out with a vague sense of what anthropology is, they often have less clear and potentially more problematic views of the superiority of their own species and culture. A second task for this text, then, is to prod students to appreciate the richness and complexity of human diversity. Along with this is the aim of helping them understand why there are so many differences and similarities in the human condition, past and present.

Debates regarding globalization and notions of progress, the "naturalness" of the mother/father/child(ren) nuclear family, new genetic technologies, and how gender roles relate to biological variation all benefit greatly from the fresh and often fascinating insights gained through anthropology. This probing aspect of our discipline is perhaps the most valuable gift we can pass on to those who take our classes. If we, as teachers (and textbook authors), do our jobs well, students will gain a wider and more open-minded outlook on the world and a critical but constructive perspective on human origins and on their own biology and culture today. To borrow a favorite line from the famous poet T. S. Eliot, "the end of all our exploring will be to arrive where we started and know the place for the first time" (*Four Quartets*).

There has never been as great a need for students to acquire the anthropological tools to help them escape culture-bound ways of thinking and acting and to gain more tolerance for other ways of life. Thus we have written this text, in large part, to help students make sense of our increasingly complex world and to navigate through its interrelated biological and cultural networks with knowledge and skill, whatever professional path they take. We see the book as a guide for people entering the often bewildering maze of global crossroads in the 21st century.

A Distinctive Approach

Two key factors distinguish *Anthropology: The Human Challenge* from other introductory anthropology texts: our integrative presentation of the discipline's four fields and a trio of unifying themes that tie the book together.

Integration of the Four Fields

Unlike traditional texts that present anthropology's four fields—archaeology, linguistics, cultural anthropology, and physical anthropology—as if they were relatively separate or independent, our book takes an integrative approach. This reflects the comprehensive character of our discipline, a domain of knowledge where members of our species are studied in their totality—as social creatures biologically evolved with the inherent capacity of learning and sharing culture by means of symbolic communication. This approach also reflects our collective experience as practicing anthropologists who recognize that we cannot fully understand humanity in all its fascinating complexity unless we appreciate the systemic interplay among environmental, physiological, material, social, ideological, psychological, and symbolic factors, both past and present.

For analytical purposes, of course, we have no choice but to discuss physical anthropology as distinct from archaeology, linguistics, and sociocultural anthropology. Accordingly, there are separate chapters that focus primarily on each field, but the links among them are shown repeatedly. Among many examples of this integrative approach, Chapter 12, "Modern Human Diversity: Race and Racism," discusses the social context of "race" and recent cultural practices that have impacted the human genome. Similarly, material concerning linguistics appears not only in Chapter 16, "Language and Communication," but also in the chapters on primate behavior (Chapter 4), on early *Homo* and the origins of culture (Chapter 8), and on the emergence of cities and states (Chapter 11). These chapters include material on the linguistic capabilities of apes, the emergence of human language, and the origin of writing. In addition, every chapter includes a Biocultural Connection feature to further illustrate the interplay of biological and cultural processes in shaping the human experience.

Unifying Themes

In our own teaching, we have come to recognize the value of marking out unifying themes that help students see the big picture as they grapple with the vast array of material involved with the study of human beings. In *Anthropology* we employ three such themes:

1. We present anthropology as a study of human-kind's responses through time to the fundamental challenges of survival. Each chapter is framed by this theme, opening with a Challenge Issue paragraph and photograph and ending with Questions for Reflection tied to that particular challenge.

2. We emphasize the integration of human culture and biology in the steps humans take to meet these challenges. The **Biocultural Connection** theme appears throughout the text—as a thread in the main narrative and in boxed features that highlight this connection with a topical example for each chapter.

3. We track the emergence of **globalization and its disparate impact on various peoples and cultures around the world.** While European colonization was a global force for centuries—leaving a significant, often devastating, footprint on the affected peoples in Asia, Africa, and the Americas—decolonization began about 200 years ago and became a worldwide wave in the mid-1900s. Since the 1960s, however, political and economic hegemony has taken a new and fast-paced form—namely, globalization (in many ways a concept that expands or builds on imperialism). Attention to both forms of global domination—colonialism and globalization—runs through *Anthropology,* culminating in the final chapter where we apply the concept of structural power to globalization, discussing it in terms of hard and soft power and linking it to structural violence.

Pedagogy

Anthropology: The Human Challenge features a range of learning aids, in addition to the three unifying themes described above. Each pedagogical piece plays an important role in the learning process—from clarifying and enlivening the material to revealing relevancy and aiding recall.

Accessible Language and a Cross-Cultural Voice

What could be more basic to pedagogy than clear communication? In addition to our standing as professional anthropologists, all four co-authors have made a specialty of speaking to audiences outside of our profession. Using that experience in the writing of this text, we consciously cut through unnecessary jargon to speak directly to students. Manuscript reviewers have recognized this, noting that even the most difficult concepts are presented in prose that is straightforward and understandable for today's first- and second-year college students. Where technical terms are necessary, they appear in bold-faced type, are carefully defined in the narrative, and are presented again in the running glossary in simple, clear language; these terms also appear in the glossary at the end of the book.

To make the narrative more accessible to students, we have broken it up into smaller bites, shortening the length of the paragraphs. We have also inserted additional subheads to provide visual cues to help students track what has been read and what is coming next.

Accessibility involves not only clear writing enhanced by visual cues but also a broadly engaging voice or style. The voice of *Anthropology* is distinct among introductory texts in the discipline, for it has been written from a cross-cultural perspective. We avoid the typical Western "we/they" voice in favor of a more inclusive one that will resonate with both Western and non-Western students and professors. Also, we highlight the theories and work of anthropologists from all over the world. Finally, we have drawn the text's cultural examples from industrial and postindustrial societies as well as nonindustrial ones. No doubt these efforts have played a role in the book's international appeal, evident in various translations and international editions.

Compelling Visuals

Haviland et al. texts repeatedly garner high praise from students and faculty for having a rich array of visuals, including maps, photographs, and figures. This is important since humans—like all primates—are visually oriented, and a well-chosen image may serve to "fix" key information in a student's mind. Unlike some competing texts, all of our visuals are in color, enhancing their appeal and impact. Notably, all maps and figures (many new to this edition) have been created with a color-blind sensitive palette.

PHOTOGRAPHS

Our pages feature a hard-sought collection of new and meaningful photographs. Large in size, many of them feature substantial captions that help students do a "deep read" of the image. Each chapter features at least fourteen pictures, and many chapters contain one of our popular Visual Counterpoints—side-by-side photos that effectively compare and contrast biological or cultural features.

MAPS

Map features include our "Putting the World in Perspective" map series, locator maps, and distribution maps that provide overviews of key issues such as pollution, endangered species, and energy consumption. Of special note are the Globalscape maps and stories, described in the boxed features section a bit further on.

Challenge Issues and Questions for Reflection

Each chapter opens with a Challenge Issue and accompanying photograph, which together carry forward the book's theme of humankind's responses through time to the fundamental challenges of survival within the context of the particular chapter. And each chapter closes with five Questions for Reflection, including one that relates back to the Challenge Issue presented in the chapter's opening. These questions are designed to stimulate and deepen thought, trigger class discussion, and link the material to the students' own lives.

Chapter Preview

Every chapter opening also presents three or four preview questions that mark out the key issues covered in the chapter. Beyond orienting students to the chapter contents, these questions provide study points useful when preparing for exams.

Barrel Model of Culture

Past and present, every culture is an integrated and dynamic system of adaptation that responds to a combination of internal and external factors. This is illustrated by a pedagogical device we refer to as the "barrel model" of culture. Depicted in a simple but telling drawing (Figure 14.2), the barrel model shows the interrelatedness of social, ideological, and economic factors within a cultural system along with outside influences of environment, climate, and other societies. Throughout the book examples are linked to this point and this image.

Integrated Gender Coverage

In contrast to many introductory texts, *Anthropology* integrates rather than separates gender coverage. Thus material on gender-related issues is included in *every* chapter. The result of this approach is a measure of gender-related material that far exceeds the single chapter that most books contain.

Why is the gender-related material integrated? Because concepts and issues surrounding gender are almost always too complicated to remove from their context. Moreover, spreading this material through all of the chapters has a pedagogical purpose, for it emphasizes how considerations of gender enter into virtually everything people do. Further, integration of gender into the book's "biological" chapters allows students to grasp the analytic distinction between sex and gender, illustrating the subtle influence of gender norms on biological theories about sex difference. Gender-related material ranges from discussions of gender roles in evolutionary discourse and studies of nonhuman primates, to intersexuality, homosexual identity, same-sex marriage, and female genital mutilation. Through a steady drumbeat of such coverage, this edition avoids ghettoizing gender to a single chapter that is preceded and followed by resounding silence.

Glossary as You Go

The running glossary is designed to catch the student's eye, reinforcing the meaning of each newly introduced term. It is also useful for chapter review, as the student may readily isolate the new terms from those introduced in earlier chapters. A complete glossary is also included at the back of the book. In the glossaries, each term is defined in clear, understandable language. As a result, less class time is required for going over terms, leaving instructors free to pursue other matters of interest.

Special Boxed Features

Our text includes five types of special boxed features. Every chapter contains a Biocultural Connection, along with two of the following three features: an Original Study, Anthropology Applied, and Anthropologist of Note. In addition, about half of the chapters include a Globalscape. All of these boxed features are carefully placed and introduced within the main narrative to alert students to their importance and relevance.

BIOCULTURAL CONNECTIONS

Appearing in every chapter, this signature feature of the Haviland et al. textbooks illustrates how cultural and biological processes interact to shape human biology, beliefs, and behavior. It reflects the integrated biocultural approach central to the field of anthropology today. New to this edition is a critical thinking question to accompany each topic explored. The twenty-seven Biocultural Connection titles hint at the intriguing array of topics covered by this feature:

- "The Anthropology of Organ Transplantation"
- "The Social Impact of Genetics on Reproduction"
- "Why Red Is Such a Potent Color," by Meredith F. Small
- "Disturbing Behaviors of the Orangutan," by Anne Nacey Maggioncaldo and Robert M. Sapolsky
- "Kennewick Man"
- "Why 'Ida' Inspires Navel-Gazing at Our Ancestry," by Meredith F. Small
- "Evolution and Human Birth"
- "Sex, Gender, and Female Paleoanthropologists"
- "Paleolithic Prescriptions for the Diseases of Civilization"
- "Breastfeeding, Fertility, and Beliefs"
- "Perilous Pigs: The Introduction of Swine-Borne Disease to the Americas," by Charles C. Mann
- "Beans, Enzymes, and Adaptation to Malaria"
- "Picturing Pesticides"
- "Adult Human Stature and the Effects of Culture: An Archaeological Example"
- "Pig Lovers and Pig Haters," by Marvin Harris
- "The Biology of Human Speech"
- "A Cross-Cultural Perspective on Psychosomatic Symptoms and Mental Health"
- "Surviving in the Andes: Aymara Adaptation to High Altitude"
- "Cacao: The Love Bean in the Money Tree"
- "Marriage Prohibitions in the United States," by Martin Ottenheimer
- "Maori Origins: Ancestral Genes and Mythical Canoes"
- "African Burial Ground Project," by Michael Blakey
- "Sex, Gender, and Human Violence"
- "Change Your Karma and Change Your Sex?," by Hillary Crane
- "Peyote Art: Divine Visions among the Huichol"
- "Studying the Emergence of New Diseases"
- "Toxic Breast Milk Threatens Arctic Culture"

ORIGINAL STUDIES

Written expressly for this text, or selected from ethnographies and other original works by anthropologists, these studies present concrete examples that bring specific concepts to life and convey the passion of the authors. Each study sheds additional light on an important anthropological concept or subject area found in the chapter where it appears. Notably, these boxes are carefully integrated within the flow of the chapter narrative, signaling students that their content is not extraneous or supplemental. Appearing in twenty-three chapters, Original Studies cover a wide range of topics, evident from their titles:

- "Fighting HIV/AIDS in Africa: Traditional Healers on the Front Line," by Suzanne Leclerc-Madlala
- "Ninety-Eight Percent Alike: What Our Similarity to Apes Tells Us about Our Understanding of Genetics," by Jonathan Marks
- "Ethics of Great Ape Habituation and Conservation: The Costs and Benefits of Ecotourism," by Michele Goldsmith
- "Reconciliation and Its Cultural Modification in Primates," by Frans B. M. de Waal
- "Whispers from the Ice," by Sherry Simpson
- "Melding Heart and Head," by Sir Robert May
- "Ankles of the Australopithecines," by John Hawks
- "Humans as Prey," by Donna Hart
- "Paleolithic Paint Job," by Roger Lewin
- "History of Mortality and Physiological Stress," by Anna Roosevelt
- "Action Archaeology and the community at El Pilar," by Anabel Ford
- "A Feckless Quest for the Basketball Gene," by Jonathan Marks
- "Dancing Skeletons: Life and Death in West Africa," by Katherine Dettwyler
- "The Importance of Trobriand Women," by Annette B. Weiner

- "Language and the Intellectual Abilities of Orangutans," by H. Lyn White Miles
- "The Blessed Curse," by R. K. Williamson
- "Gardens of the Mekranoti Kayapo," by Dennis Werner
- "Arranging Marriage in India," by Serena Nanda
- "Honor Killings in the Netherlands," by Clementine van Eck
- "The Jewish *Eruv*: Symbolic Place in Public Space," by Susan Lees
- "Sacred Law in Global Capitalism," by Bill Maurer
- "The Modern Tattoo Community," by Margo DeMello
- "Standardizing the Body: The Question of Choice," by Laura Nader

ANTHROPOLOGY APPLIED

These succinct and compelling profiles illustrate anthropology's wide-ranging relevance in today's world and give students a glimpse into a variety of the careers anthropologists enjoy. Featured in seventeen chapters, they include

- "Forensic Anthropology: Voices for the Dead"
- "What It Means to Be a Woman: How Women Around the World Cope with Infertility," by Karen Springen
- "The Congo Heartland Project"
- "Cultural Resource Management," by John Crock
- "Stone Tools for Modern Surgeons"
- "The Real Dirt on Rainforest Fertility," by Charles C. Mann
- "Tell It to the Marines: Teaching the Troops about Cultural Heritage," by Jane C. Waldbaum
- "New Houses for Apache Indians," by George S. Esber
- "When Bambi Spoke Arapaho: Preserving Indigenous Languages," by S. Neyooxet Greymorning
- "Agricultural Development and the Anthropologist"
- "Global Ecotourism and Local Indigenous Culture in Bolivia," by Amanda Stronza
- "Resolving a Native American Tribal Membership Dispute," by Harald E. L. Prins
- "Anthropologists and Social Impact Assessment"
- "Dispute Resolution and the Anthropologist"
- "Reconciling Modern Medicine with Traditional Beliefs in Swaziland," by Edward C. Green
- "Bringing Back the Past," by Jennifer Sapiel Neptune
- "Development Anthropology and Dams"

ANTHROPOLOGISTS OF NOTE

Profiling pioneering and contemporary anthropologists from many corners of the world, this feature puts the work of noted anthropologists in historical perspective and draws attention to the international nature of the discipline in terms of both subject matter and practitioners. This edition highlights twenty distinct anthropologists

from all four fields of the discipline: Berhane Asfaw, Gregory Bateson, Ruth Fulton Benedict, Franz Boas, Peter Ellison, Paul Farmer, Jane Goodall, Kinji Imanishi, Fatimah Jackson, Louis S. B. Leakey, Mary Leakey, Claude Lévi-Strauss, Bronislaw Malinowski, Margaret Mead, Laura Nader, Matilda Coxe Stevenson, Allan Wilson, Eric R. Wolf, Rosita Worl, and Xinzhi Wu.

GLOBALSCAPES

Appearing in about half of the chapters, this unique feature charts the global flow of people, goods, and services, as well as pollutants and pathogens. With a map, a story, and a photo highlighting a topic geared toward student interests, every Globalscape shows how the world is interconnected through human activity. Each one ends with a Global Twister—a question that prods students to think critically about globalization. Globalscapes in this edition are:

- "A Global Body Shop?," investigating human organ trafficking around the world
- "Gorilla Hand Ashtrays?," showing how mining for the cell phone component coltan is linked to gorilla habitat destruction
- "Whose Lakes Are These?," exploring the global and local impact of efforts to preserve places of shared cultural and natural importance through UNESCO's World Heritage List
- "Factory Farming Fiasco?," investigating the global industrial farming practices that have led to the current swine flu pandemic
- "Iraqi Artifacts in New York City?," exploring the effects of the Iraq War on the precious Mesopotamian artifacts that were housed in the National Museum in Baghdad
- "From Soap Opera to Clinic?," chronicling pioneering methods to disseminate life-changing public health information through radio and television dramas
- "Chicken Out: Bush's Legs or Phoenix Talons?," following the far-flung distribution of chicken parts in today's large-scale poultry industry
- "How Much for a Red Delicious?," describing Jamaican migrant laborers working in Maine and Florida
- "Transnational Child Exchange?," chronicling international adoption
- "Football Diplomacy?" tracing the life of an Ivory Coast soccer star and the numerous countries in which he has trained and played
- "Pirate Pursuits in Puntland?," unveiling the complex economics behind piracy off the coast of Somalia
- "Do Coffins Fly?," highlighting the work of a Ghanaian custom coffin maker gaining global recognition as art
- "*Probo Koala's* Dirty Secrets?," investigating the dumping of First World toxic waste in Third World countries

Changes and Highlights in the Thirteenth Edition

The pedagogical features described above strengthen each of the twenty-seven chapters in *Anthropology,* serving as threads that tie the text together and help students feel the holistic nature of the discipline. In addition, the engagingly presented concepts themselves provide students with a solid foundation in the principles and practices of anthropology today.

The text in hand has a significantly different feel to it than previous editions. All chapters have been revised extensively—the data, examples, and Suggested Readings updated, the chapter openers refreshed with new, up-to-date Challenge Issues and related photographs, and the writing further chiseled to make it all the more clear, lively, and engaging. Also, in addition to providing at least one new entry in the much-used Questions for Reflection at the end of the chapter, we have introduced a new question in each Biocultural Connection box.

Beyond these overall changes, each chapter has undergone specific modifications and additions. The inventory presented below provides brief previews of the chapter contents and changes in this edition.

CHAPTER 1: THE ESSENCE OF ANTHROPOLOGY

The book's opening chapter introduces students to the holistic discipline of anthropology, the unique focus of each of its fields, and the common philosophical perspective and methodological approaches they share. Touching briefly on fieldwork and the comparative method, along with ethical issues and examples of applied anthropology in all four fields, this chapter provides a foundation for our two methods chapters—one exploring field methods in cultural anthropology and the other explaining the methods for studying the past shared by archaeology and paleoanthropology.

A new Challenge Issue dealing with global aspects of surrogate births demonstrates the ways that an integrated holistic anthropological perspective contributes to the ability to negotiate the new technologies and practices of our ever-more interconnected world. The updated descriptions of the anthropological fields that follow take into account the excellent suggestions of our reviewers. The section on linguistic anthropology has been expanded to include linguistic relativity, sociolinguistics, the work to save endangered languages, and the ways that languages continually change. The overview of physical anthropology was reorganized to improve the flow and includes an expanded discussion of developmental and physiological adaptation. Primate conservation issues are also highlighted. The archaeology section now includes

historical archaeology and the work of James Deetz along with mention of other archaeological subspecializations. Technological innovations in archaeology such as GIS and GPR are included. Philippe Bourgois's work on the urban drug scene is included to illustrate range of the field sites open to ethnographers today.

The chapter also rejects the characterization of a liberal bias in anthropology, identifying instead the discipline's critical evaluation of the status quo. The ideological diversity among anthropologists is explored while emphasizing their shared methodology that avoids ethnocentrism. An expanded section on ethics includes the history of ethics, the changes of the AAA Code in response to classified or corporate fieldwork, and the effects of emergent technology. We emphasize the shared global environment in the section on globalization, with an updated Globalscape on organ trafficking.

CHAPTER 2: GENETICS AND EVOLUTION

This revised chapter on genetics and evolution grounds students in basic human biological processes including the evolutionary forces that worked over millennia to shape us into the species we are today. By moving some material to later chapters, we are able to add new concepts and diagrams that will serve to clarify and simplify the genetic mechanisms at work. The new Challenge Issue focusing on DNA fingerprinting, genetic determinism, and identity captures students' attention regarding the relevancy of genetics. The Chapter Preview questions have been expanded to make the genetic material more accessible. Sections on hominin taxonomy and altruism and other models of behavior have been moved to other chapters to make room for a more detailed but accessible discussion of genetics and evolution. This includes more on the background of the development of evolutionary theory including Cuvier's catastrophism, Lamarck's inheritance of acquired characteristics, and Lyell's principles of geology.

This edition includes a discussion of chromatids to clarify students' understanding of DNA replication, mitosis, and meiosis. Examples of classic Mendelian traits that students can explore with their relatives and thought questions accompanying the figures will help students master this material. New figures on Punnett squares, a karyotype illustrating the locus of a variety of common genes, and the alleles using sickle-cell disease as an example will make these concepts more accessible. The discussion of the forces of evolution includes a new section illustrating genetic drift and founder effects featuring the achromotopsia on Pingelap Island in Micronesia. A new section on adaptation and physical variation introduces the concept of clines. Finally, a new Anthropology Applied feature on global infertility as a human rights issue features the work of Marcia Inhorn.

CHAPTER 3: LIVING PRIMATES

With this edition, our original chapter on the living primates was expanded into two separate chapters. This allowed for more material on the vital issue of primate conservation as we survey the living primates and the place of humans among them. Our expanded section on primate conservation includes the scope of the threat, description of diverse conservation methods, along with coverage of some of the successes such as the recovery of golden lion tamarin populations. A new Anthropology Applied on primate conservation features the work of bonobo specialist Jef Dupain and the Congo Heartland Project of the African Wildlife Foundation. Michele Goldsmith explores the ethics of field research in the chapter's Original Study. The chapter's Globalscape connects cell phone recycling to the preservation of endangered gorilla habitats. A new figure presenting the biogeography of the primates includes the twenty-five most endangered primate species.

In terms of our survey of living primates, we include an in-depth discussion of primate taxonomy including the hot spots, alternate taxonomies, and controversies (tarsier question and hominid/hominin question). The clade/grade distinction is described, and the term *clade* is added to the discussion and running glossary. Our figure comparing the skeletons of bison and gorilla has been revised to help students understand how skeletal analyses are conducted. Moving primate behavior to its own chapter has allowed for more coverage of non-hominoid living primates (lemurs/lorises, tarsiers, Old and New World monkeys). Notably, Karen Strier's work with the muriqui is included in the discussion of New World monkeys that provides insights into field methods and primate demographics. A new Biocultural Connection by Meredith Small focuses on primate vision and the human affinity for the color red.

CHAPTER 4: PRIMATE BEHAVIOR

This new, beautifully illustrated chapter is devoted exclusively to primate behavior, allowing for an expanded treatment of the topic. The sophistication of primate behavior is framed by ethical questions regarding the use of primates in medical research that open and close the chapter. While the chapter emphasizes the great apes, examples from other anthropoid primates are included in this discussion. A new section critically discusses the use of baboon studies to reconstruct lifeways of our ancestors. New material on primate communication includes syntax in vervet monkeys and dialect in marmosets, along with new material on social learning among macaques. Our discussion of communication also includes a discussion of altruism and an expanded section on the communication abilities of the bonobo Kanzi. Various forms of primate social organization are outlined along with their proposed links to biological features such as sexual dimorphism.

These and other theories about primate reproductive biology are analyzed in terms of the potential influence of contemporary gender norms, an approach pioneered by primatologist Linda Fedigan. A new Biocultural Connection on arrested development in male orangutans by Anne Nacey Maggioncaldo and Robert M. Sapolsky complements this discussion. Along with many new, updated, and classic references, this chapter contains all new Questions for Reflection and Suggested Readings.

CHAPTER 5: FIELD METHODS IN ARCHAEOLOGY AND PALEOANTHROPOLOGY

This methods chapter clearly conveys the key methodological techniques employed by archaeologists and paleoanthropologists as they study human prehistory. We open with the question of shared cultural heritage and ownership of the past through a new Challenge Issue on the Bamiyan Buddhas of Afghanistan destroyed by the Taliban in 2001. We have streamlined this comprehensive chapter with this edition to make room for technological advances and the ethical issues that have arisen from these new technologies. The chapter contains a new figure to illustrate the concept of stratification and a complete description of the ecofacts and features used to study the past. We cover new technologies such as ground-penetrating radar (GPR), geographic information systems (GIS), remote sensing techniques, and an expanded section on underwater archaeology. We describe the use of CT scans in bioarchaeology, forensics, and paleoanthropology and make explicit the links between bioarchaeology and forensics. The chapter includes more coverage on the purpose of NAGPRA. We also explore the issues surrounding the digitization of human remains and aboriginal responses to museum efforts to do this in contexts without NAGPRA, as seen in the current controversy between the University of Vienna and the Ju/'hoansi people.

An Anthropology Applied box on cultural resource management by John Crock, an Original Study on the chance discovery of the skeleton of a young girl frozen in the ice of Barrow, Alaska, and a Biocultural Connection on Kennewick Man all provide insights into the complexities involved in investigating the past. They also explore the philosophical approach necessary for successful collaboration between scientists and local people.

CHAPTER 6: MACROEVOLUTION AND THE EARLY PRIMATES

Building on the evolutionary principles laid out in Chapter 2, this chapter provides an excellent overview of macroevolutionary mechanisms along with a concise discussion of mammalian primate evolution. While introducing students to concepts such as heterochrony, homeobox genes, anagenesis, and cladogenesis, through clear descriptions and diagrams, we also discuss the comparative approach employed by evolutionary scientists.

The Eocene specimen "Ida" (*Darwinius masillae*) discovered in 2009 is featured in a variety of contexts. The chapter's Challenge Issue discusses the recent popularity of human evolutionary studies in the media, asking how the self-correcting nature of science can function against a backdrop of "tweets," Google logos, and unprecedented prices for fossil specimens paid by museums to private collectors. A new Biocultural Connection by Meredith Small explores the significance of the "Ida" specimen.

Another chapter theme is the importance of understanding evolutionary processes for the survival of the planet. In a new Original Study, leading global ecologist Sir Robert May explores the relationship between human practices and the extinction of other species. Against this philosophical backdrop, we also consider the mechanics of the molecular regulation of variational change as well as punctuated change using recent discoveries regarding Darwin's finches. A new figure accompanies this discussion. Another new figure compares the skull shape and size of fossil prosimians and fossil anthropoids. A revised timeline and figure of the evolutionary relationships among the anthropoid primates take into account the potential new fossil gorilla evidence discovered in 2007 (*Chororapithecus abyssinicus*). More images of fossil specimens are included in the chapter compared to previous editions so that students can "see" as well as read about our mammalian primate heritage.

CHAPTER 7: THE FIRST BIPEDS

This up-to-date chapter explores bipedalism, the distinctive feature of the human evolutionary line, concentrating on the australopithecines and other species that inhabited Africa before the appearance of the genus *Homo*. It contains the new evidence and analyses published in 2009 suggesting that forest-dwelling *Ardipithecus* is the common ancestor to all later bipeds. It also integrates this notion into the hypotheses regarding the savannah adaptation of our ancestors. We introduce students to how paleoanthropologists go about reconstructing human evolutionary history. A new Original Study, "Ankles of the Australopithecines" by John Hawks, exemplifies how paleoanthropologists use comparative morphological studies to reconstruct the past. Chapter figures and glossary terms are linked to this Original Study.

Current ethical issues also find their way into the chapter, such as the controversy regarding the current U.S. tour of the 3.2-million-year-old "Lucy" fossils. A new figure compares gracile and robust australopithecines, and a revised figure also indicates all the major australopithecine sites. The Biocultural Connection on evolution and human birth explores the ways that contemporary Western practices influenced the paleoanthropological reconstruction of the human birth pattern. The Anthropologists of Note feature explores the extraordinary contributions of Louis and Mary Leakey to the discipline of paleoanthropology.

CHAPTER 8: EARLY *HOMO* AND THE ORIGINS OF CULTURE

This chapter traces the genus *Homo* from its origins 2.5 or so million years ago up until the Upper Paleolithic. Taking a "lumping" approach, it divides the fossil record into the three divisions of *Homo habilis*, *Homo erectus*, and archaic *Homo sapiens*. At the same time we explore the differences between lumping and splitting fossil specimens into numerous taxa and discuss the relationship between biological change and cultural change in human evolutionary history. The place of the Neandertals in this history closes the chapter. The chapter contains sufficient detail for an introductory course on human origins while streamlining the presentation from previous editions and avoiding redundancy.

Many new figures allow for material to be communicated clearly and efficiently. For example, the new figure comparing KNM ER 1470 and KNM ER 1813 illustrates the taxonomic issue of lumping or splitting in early *Homo*. The new discoveries from Gona, including the well-preserved pelvis, are included as is the newly discovered *Homo erectus* footprint trail from Kenya. Middle Paleolithic *Homo* from throughout the world is surveyed in this chapter while the question of modern human origins is saved for Chapter 9. A nuanced discussion of sex and gender in the fossil record is supported by a Biocultural Connection on the contributions of female paleoanthropologists to the discipline, along with the recent revisioning of the "man the hunter" hypothesis as "man the hunted" in the chapter's Original Study. The Anthropology Applied box demonstrates the unique strengths of stone tools through their use by modern-day surgeons.

CHAPTER 9: THE GLOBAL EXPANSION OF *HOMO SAPIENS* AND THEIR TECHNOLOGY

This chapter explores the fossil, genetic, and cultural evidence used in theories to account for modern human origins. It also explores the cultural explosion characteristic of the Upper Paleolithic and the spread of humans throughout the globe. To make space for an in-depth discussion of the multiregional continuity versus out of Africa models of modern human origins, we have streamlined and reorganized material to avoid redundancy. Rich with new and revised figures, the chapter also includes the latest discoveries such as the Venus figurine from Hohle Fels Cave as well as the flute from the same site. New research on cooking and brain metabolism is included as is recent research on the peopling of the Americas. A new section on gender and archaeology features Margaret Conkey's work as a feminist practicing archaeology and the contemporary projections of gender norms onto Venus figurines.

The chapter's boxed features chronicle paleoanthropology from throughout the globe. The Anthropologists of Note features Ethiopian paleoanthropologist Berhane Asfaw and Chinese paleoanthropologist Xinzhi Wu. The Biocultural Connection looks to contemporary hunter-gatherers, whose lifeways have not departed as glaringly from our Paleolithic template, in order to promote human health. The Original Study details the methods used by prehistoric artists to paint cave walls in southwestern France. A new Globalscape on World Heritage sites focuses on Willandra Lakes in Australia and the importance of this place to the Aboriginal people of the region, as well as to paleoanthropologists and the global community.

CHAPTER 10: THE NEOLITHIC REVOLUTION: THE DOMESTICATION OF PLANTS AND ANIMALS

Chapter 10 concentrates on the drastic cultural changes that occurred at the Neolithic transition with the domestication of plants and animals along with the development of permanent settlements in villages. The unexpected deleterious health consequences of this "Neolithic revolution" are explored throughout the chapter along with the complex relationship between food production and population growth.

The new Challenge Issue featuring a contemporary Hmong embroidery depicting the mythical origins of agriculture opens the chapter. The art illustrates that global food flows have a long history. We include a new section on primary and secondary innovation, as well as the recent discovery of the earliest pottery from Yuchanyan Cave, located in China's Hunan Province, and current research providing new dates for earliest dairying. Several revised figures, such as ones on the Fertile Crescent and the domestication of corn from teosinte, improve clarity and provide richer content.

Several sections of the chapter have been expanded. These include the contemporary application of *terra preta*, the rich black earth produced by Amazonian farmers and described in the chapter's Anthropology Applied box; the impact of colonialism on American Indian cultures; and the ongoing health consequences of the Neolithic transition. Table 10.1 has been updated to show the incidence of selected zoonotic diseases globally along with prevention strategies. A new Globalscape on swine flu and industrial farming practices illustrates the consequences of these large-scale operations.

CHAPTER 11: THE EMERGENCE OF CITIES AND STATES

This chapter draws parallels between ancient and modern cities and states while exploring the origins of this very human way of life. It contains a variety of new figures and examples that drive home the points about the beginnings of cities and states and the many facets, both positive and negative, of these social organizations that have endured to the present. Continuity is shown through factors ranging from social stratification, to the social distribution of sickness and health, to artisanal techniques.

Carneiro's theory on the development of states is described in more detail in this revised chapter. In terms of ancient sites, the figure of Teotihuacan is revised for clarity, and a new figure of Tikal shows the major monuments and causeways. The chapter's Original Study on El Pilar is revised and updated. We discuss the Cahokia mounds as an example of the both the presence of cities and the conscious choice by North American Indians not to engage in conquest relationships.

New figures on cuneiform writing and bronze lost-wax casting illustrate the details of these innovations. Sections on social stratification and disease are expanded to include both the impact within a given society and the effects of conquest. This expanded coverage included the impact of infectious disease brought about by European colonizers of the Americas, we include a new Biocultural Connection from Charles Mann's book *1491*. The chapter's Anthropology Applied box and Globalscape both feature the link between contemporary military action and preservation of ancient cultural heritage.

CHAPTER 12: MODERN HUMAN DIVERSITY: RACE AND RACISM

This chapter gives an overview of race and racism, in the science of the past as well as current problems. With the politics of diversity changing globally, an understanding of the true nature of biological variation has become indispensable. The contributions of anthropology to debunking race as a biological category—starting with the work of Franz Boas and Ashley Montagu—are complemented by the contemporary work of cutting-edge biological anthropologists such as Jonathan Marks (Original Study) and Fatimah Jackson (Anthropologist of Note). We emphasize the interaction of the cultural and biological throughout the chapter in topics ranging from skin color to intelligence to G-6-PD deficiency as detailed in the Biocultural Connection.

With this edition, we include the history of the Mexican *casta* system and the contemporary tragedy of Rwandan genocide. The section on race and human evolution is expanded and includes a discussion of scientific and pseudo-scientific attempts to predict behavior by physical phenotypic characteristics. The section concludes with neurological research dealing with the brain and stereotypical thinking. Informative new illustrations include a demonstration of the differences between a normal female pelvis and one deformed by bone disease and a contemporary graphic artist's views on 19th- and early 20th-century racial hierarchies.

CHAPTER 13: HUMAN ADAPTATION TO A CHANGING WORLD

From battles between local farmers and multinational corporations for water rights in India to new findings on the toxic effects of plastics, this chapter continues to engage with the ways humans adapt to the human-made environment. The chapter weaves together the anthropological study of adaptation by biological and medical anthropologists with advanced work in evolutionary medicine and the political ecology of health and disease. It examines the way that human alteration of the environment is leading to disease in our species and how political and social forces impact the distribution of health and disease in human populations.

New to this chapter are global flows of HIV/AIDS and prevention strategies and a Globalscape concerning an initiative incorporating public health education into radio and television soap operas. This edition features a significantly expanded section on the impact of environmental estrogens on human disease. Our emphasis on the relationship between economics and fertility in women continues. Several of the straightforward biological adaptations also explored in this chapter are now supported with new figures, including an illustration of the relationship between altitude and partial pressure of oxygen and illustrations of Bergmann's rule and Allen's rule. In addition, a new section explores the highly topical issue of vaccinations and so-called pox parties.

The work of reproductive ecologist Peter Ellison linking human fertility to the environment is featured in the Anthropologist of Note box. Cross-cultural differences in sickness categories are featured in Katherine Dettwyler's stirring piece on infection, malnutrition, and Down syndrome. The Biocultural Connection features the impact of industrial farming pesticides on child development. Throughout this chapter, we explore the biocultural theme characteristic of the entire text as connections are drawn between human health and political and economic forces both globally and locally.

CHAPTER 14: CHARACTERISTICS OF CULTURE

This foundational chapter addresses anthropology's core concept of culture, exploring the term and its significance for human individuals and societies. Elaborating on culture as the medium through which humans handle the problems of existence, we mark out its characteristics as something that is learned, shared, based on symbols, integrated, and dynamic. This chapter discusses ethnocentrism and cultural relativism, as well as culture and adaptation; the functions of culture; culture, society, and the individual; and culture and change. Ethnographic examples include a general look at the Amish of North America and a particular sketch of cremation rituals in Bali. We present a new figure showing China's ethnic groups, which accompanies a discussion about and photo of the Uyghur, a Turkish-speaking Muslim ethnic minority living in China's northwestern province of Xinjiang.

The section on culture and adaptation illustrates with several examples that what is adaptive in the short run may be maladaptive over time, including the fast-shrinking Ogallala aquifer in the U.S. Central Plains. The overhauled section on culture change features a wide-ranging discussion on topics from sustainability to fashion. A new Visual Counterpoint in the section on ethnocentrism compares the anti-immigration protests of Russian Nationalists with those of the American right-wing Minutemen Civil Defense Corps. Special features include a Biocultural Connection on adult stature and the effects of culture, an expanded Anthropologist of Note profile on Bronislaw Malinowski, and George Esber's Anthropology Applied box on new housing for Apache Indians. This chapter also presents the "barrel model" illustration, conveying the key concepts of the integration of cultural infrastructure, social structure, and superstructure.

CHAPTER 15: ETHNOGRAPHIC RESEARCH: ITS HISTORY, METHODS, AND THEORIES

This chapter takes a unique approach to discussing ethnographic research. It begins with a historical overview on the subject—from the colonial era and salvage ethnography to acculturation studies, advocacy anthropology, and multi-sited ethnography in the era of globalization. The work of numerous anthropologists, past and present, is used to illustrate this historical journey. The chapter continues with an overview of research methods—marking out what is involved in choosing a research question and site and how one goes about doing preparatory research and participant observation. This section also covers ethnographic tools and aids, data-gathering methods, fieldwork challenges, and the creation of an ethnography in written, film, or digital formats.

The chapter also offers an overview of anthropology's theoretical perspectives, discusses the comparative method and the Human Relations Area Files, and explores the moral dilemmas and ethical responsibilities encountered in anthropological research. Special features include the Biocultural Connection "Pig Lovers and Pig Haters" by Marvin Harris, Annette Weiner's Original Study on Trobriand women, and an Anthropologists of Note box that profiles the pioneering visual anthropology work of Gregory Bateson and Margaret Mead. The chapter features new photographs of indigenous assistants trained by anthropologists collecting GPS data in the field and reviewing the downloaded data, alongside a map that is the result of their efforts. In addition, we have developed the section on advocacy anthropology and studying up, clarifying the link between the two, as well as the section on fieldwork challenges—especially the discussion of subjectivity and reflexivity. A new conclusion explores the ethical responsibilities of anthropological research in light of the idea that "knowledge is power."

CHAPTER 16: LANGUAGE AND COMMUNICATION

This chapter investigates the nature of language and the three branches of linguistic anthropology—descriptive linguistics, historical linguistics, and the study of language in its social and cultural settings (ethnolinguistics and sociolinguistics). The latter features new discussions of linguistic relativity and linguistic determinism. Also found here are sections on paralanguage and tonal languages and a fascinating new exploration of talking drums and whistled speech. We have retained and refined the sections on language and gender and body language (proxemics and kinesics) and provided updated material on the impact of electronic media on language and communication worldwide. A historical sketch about writing takes readers from traditional speech performatives and memory devices to Egyptian hieroglyphics to the conception and spread of the alphabet to the 2003 to 2012 Literacy Decade established by the United Nations. A revised and expanded discussion of language loss and revival features an intriguing look at new technology used by linguistic anthropologists collaborating on field research with speakers of endangered Khoisan "click" languages in southern Africa. That section also includes the latest data on the digital divide and its impact on ethnic minority languages—plus an updated chart showing Internet language populations.

This edition includes a revised Biocultural Connection on the biology of human speech, an updated Original Study on the language and intellectual abilities of orangutans, and a new and compelling Anthropology Applied piece, "When Bambi Spoke Arapaho: Preserving Indigenous Languages," by S. Neyooxet Greymorning.

A new conclusion recounts how the telecommunication revolution of the last two decades—mobile phones in particular—are transforming everything from social relations to economic dealings, even in the most remote corners of the world.

CHAPTER 17: SOCIAL IDENTITY, PERSONALITY, AND GENDER

Looking at individual identity within a sociocultural context, this chapter surveys the concept of self, enculturation and the behavioral environment, social identity through personal naming, the development of personality, the concepts of group and modal personality, and the idea of national character. Ethnographic examples include a Navajo naming and First Laugh Ceremony and a description of *sadhus* (ascetic Hindu monks). Our discussion on naming includes a new subsection describing name loss by Brule Sioux Luther Standing Bear and a brief recounting of how President Obama and his father both changed their given names and later reverted back to them. The revised discussion on normal and abnormal personality in a social context includes sobering statistics from a new global report on state-sponsored homophobia.

A substantial section of the chapter provides a thought-provoking historical overview of intersexuality, transsexuality, and transgendering, including current statistics on the incidence of intersexuality worldwide and a revised Original Study on intersexuality. In conjunction with the latter is a new photograph of the intersexed South African track star Caster Semenya, whose 2009 international championship was marred by accusations that she was not "fully female." Other special features include an Anthropologist of Note on Ruth Fulton Benedict and a Biocultural Connection about cross-cultural perspectives on psychosomatic symptoms and mental health. A new concluding section drives home the need for medical pluralism with a variety of healing modalities fit for humanity caught up in the worldwide dynamics of the 21st century.

CHAPTER 18: PATTERNS OF SUBSISTENCE

Here we investigate the various ways humans meet their basic needs and how societies adapt through culture to the environment. We begin with a discussion of adaptation, followed by profiles on modes of subsistence in which we look at food-foraging and food-producing societies—pastoralism, crop cultivation, and industrialization. In this edition, chapter headings, along with the narratives they introduce, have been significantly revised to provide greater clarity and a consistent focus on how—across time, space, and cultures—food is obtained, produced, and distributed. The section on adaptation and cultural evolution includes a new ethnohistorical example—the precontact Easter Island ecosystem collapse cause by deforestation. A new discussion of peasantry has been added, along with an extensive narrative about large-scale industrial food production, using chickens as an example.

The chapter's boxed features include a new Biocultural Connection on "Surviving in the Andes: Aymara Adaptation to High Altitude," along with an Original Study on swidden gardening in the Amazon basin in Brazil. We have included a newly illustrated Anthropology Applied piece about reviving ancient farming practices in Peru. Also in this chapter is a new Globalscape chronicling the international poultry industry.

A new conclusion summarizes the pros and cons of new subsistence strategies and technological innovations—how they impact different members of a society in the short and long run.

CHAPTER 19: ECONOMIC SYSTEMS

This chapter delves into such matters as the control of resources (natural, technological, labor) and types of labor division (gender, age, cooperative, task specialization). A section on distribution and exchange defines various forms of reciprocity (with a detailed and illustrated description of the Kula ring and a revised definition and new discussion of silent trade), along with redistribution and market exchange. The discussion on leveling mechanisms has been revised and expanded, with new narratives on cargos and the potlatch (including a rare and remarkable contemporary potlatch photograph). Our much revised concluding section, "Local Economies and Global Capitalism," includes a new discussion on guest laborers, the global tourism industry, the impact of mobile phones on small producers in remote areas, and genetically modified seeds developed and marketed worldwide—all indicating the economic opportunities and challenges of our era.

The chapter presents two new boxed features: Amanda Stronza's Anthropology Applied piece, "Global Ecotourism and Local Indigenous Culture in Bolivia," and an Anthropologist of Note profile on Rosita Worl, a Tlingit activist.

CHAPTER 20: SEX, MARRIAGE, AND FAMILY

Exploring the close interconnection among sexual reproductive practices, marriage, family, and household, we discuss the household as the basic building block in a culture's social structure, the center where childrearing as well as shelter, economic production, consumption, and inheritance are commonly organized. Particulars addressed in this chapter include the incest taboo, endogamy and exogamy, dowry and bride-price, cousin marriage, same-sex marriage, divorce, residence patterns, and non-family households. Updated definitions of marriage, family, nuclear family, and extended family encompass current real-life situations around the world.

Among the various ethnographic examples, the presentation on the Nayar has been significantly revised to, among other things, clarify traditional practices from those of today. Updates include the most recent available figures concerning the makeup of U.S. households today and same-sex marriage around the world. The section on divorce has been expanded, with additional commentary on common cross-cultural reasons for ending marriages. Our revised concluding section discusses how transnationalism, growing numbers of migrant laborers, international adoptions, and modern reproductive technologies are all impacting the ways humans think about and form families.

Boxed features include Serena Nanda's engaging Original Study on arranged marriage in India and a revised version of Martin Ottenheimer's Biocultural Connection on marriage prohibitions in the United States. The new Anthropologist of Note box commemorates the life and contributions of Claude Lévi-Strauss, who passed away at age 100 while this book was in production. Also, a new Globalscape investigates the blessings and issues of international adoption.

CHAPTER 21: KINSHIP AND DESCENT

This chapter marks out the various forms of descent groups and the roles descent plays as an integrated feature in a cultural system. Details and examples are presented concerning lineages, clans, phratries, and moieties (highlighting Hopi Indian matriclans and Scottish highland patriclans, among others), followed by illustrated examples of a representative range of kinship systems and their kinship terminologies.

The chapter includes a look at diasporic communities in today's globalized world and ethnographic examples from the Han Chinese, Maori of New Zealand, and Canela Indians of Brazil. A new section, "Making Relatives," features two subsections. The first is on fictive kin and ritual adoption, illustrating how, across cultures, people have developed ideas about how someone becomes "one of us," whether by birth, paternal recognition, or some other means. Examples include compadrazgo or "co-parenthood," established through a Roman Catholic baptismal ceremony and especially common in Latin America. The second part discusses kinship and new reproductive technologies, touching on the mind-boggling array of reproductive possibilities and how they are impacting humanity's conceptions of what it means to be biologically related.

This chapter includes an Anthropology Applied box on resolving Native American tribal membership disputes, a thought-provoking Original Study on honor killings among Turkish immigrants in the Netherlands, and a Biocultural Connection piece about ancient Maori mythical traditions that are now supported by genetic research.

CHAPTER 22: GROUPING BY GENDER, AGE, COMMON INTEREST, AND SOCIAL CLASS

This much-refined chapter includes discussions of grouping by gender, age, common interest, and social class. The section on age grouping features ethnographic material from the Mundurucu of Brazil and the Tiriki and Maasai of East Africa. Common-interest group examples range from the Shriners to the Crips to the Jewish diaspora. Also included is a new subsection describing the social networking platforms available to Internet and mobile phone users. In addition, we have expanded our discussion of women's organizations, profiling various groups such as SEWA, India's far-reaching Self-Employed Women's Association, which is having an enormous impact on the economic contributions of women. Our revised section on social class and caste includes three historical case studies:

one on caste and its role in India's Hindu culture (accompanied by a new figure illustrating the traditional Hindu caste system) and two concerning racial segregation in South Africa and the United States.

Boxed features include Michael Blakey's Biocultural Connection on the African Burial Ground Project—the archaeological dig in New York City that revealed the physical stress of an entire community brought on by the social institution of slavery—and a shorter, punchier version of Susan Lees's Original Study on the Jewish *eruv*. Also included in this chapter is an updated version of our Globalscape about an Ivory Coast soccer star and the political impact of sports.

We conclude the chapter with a much-revised section on social mobility, noting that while great disparities in wealth, power, and prestige persist in many parts of the world, there are notable social changes in the opposite direction. Among them is a growing social justice movement among India's lowest castes and Untouchables, including a group of women known as the Pink Vigilantes.

CHAPTER 23: POLITICS, POWER, AND VIOLENCE

Looking at a range of uncentralized and centralized political systems—from kin-ordered bands and tribes to chiefdoms and states—this chapter explores the question of power, the intersection of politics and religion, and issues of political leadership and gender. Discussing the maintenance of order, we look at internalized and externalized controls (including a section on gossip's role in curbing socially unacceptable behavior), along with social control through witchcraft and through law. We mark the functions of law and the ways different societies deal with crime, including sentencing laws in Canada based on traditional Native American restorative justice techniques such as the Talking Circle.

Next, we shift our focus from maintaining order within a society to external affairs, including a discussion of violent conflict and warfare. In addition to a revised subsection that gives an overview of the 5,000-year history of armed conflicts among humans, we include material on current ideological and political conflicts and genocide, along with a map showing the frequency of armed conflicts in multinational states where one group suppresses other(s).

Special features include a Biocultural Connection exploring the relationship of sex, gender, and violence; an updated Anthropology Applied box on dispute resolution; and a new Globalscape profiling the surprising and complex economics behind piracy off the coast of Somalia. The revised final section of this chapter includes a new historical narrative on the concept of "crimes against humanity" and the International Criminal Court established in the Netherlands in 2002, which now has 110 member states.

CHAPTER 24: SPIRITUALITY, RELIGION, AND THE SUPERNATURAL

This chapter opens with a description of the anthropological approach to religion and the current distinctions between religion and spirituality, followed by an overview of the status of religion and spirituality today. The latter includes a chart showing the major religions of the world with their percentages of believers, along with a new world map depicting the global distribution of major religions that indicates where each is the majority. We then discuss beliefs concerning supernatural beings and spiritual forces (gods and goddesses, ancestral spirits, animism, and animatism), religious specialists (priests and priestesses, as well as shamans), and rituals and ceremonies (rites of passage and rites of intensification). The section on shamanism explores the origins of the term and presents our "shamanic complex" model of how shamanic healings take place. Ethnographic examples include the vision quests of Penobscot Indians of New England and the trance dancing and healing of Ju/'hoansi healers in southern Africa. We include a new subsection on taboos that discusses Mary Douglas's rituals of purity and impurity, along with a much-revised section on rites of passage, highlighting the original work of van Gennep.

A section on religion, magic, and witchcraft highlights Ibibio witchcraft, while another passage marks out religion's psychological and social functions, including efforts to heal physical, emotional, and social ills. Touching on religion and cultural change, this chapter looks at revitalization movements and new material on indigenous Christian churches in Africa.

Among other highlights in this chapter are discussions on sacred places and women's roles in religious leadership. Boxed features include Hillary Crane's arresting Biocultural Connection about Taiwanese Buddhist nuns, along with an Anthropology Applied piece on the mix of traditional beliefs and modern medicine in Swaziland. The chapter closes with a newly crafted section on the enduring nature of religion and spirituality that includes Bill Maurer's timely new Original Study on Shariah law and banking, "Sacred Law in Global Capitalism."

CHAPTER 25: THE ARTS

This chapter explores in detail three key categories of art—visual, verbal, and musical—illustrating what they reveal about and what functions they play in societies. It describes the distinctly holistic approach anthropologists bring to the study of art, noting the range of cultural insights art reveals—from kinship structures to social values, religious beliefs, and political ideas. Various approaches to analyzing art (such as aesthetic and interpretive) are applied to rock art in southern Africa. Ethnographic examples in the section on verbal arts include the Abenaki creation myth of Tabaldak, one of many versions of the classic and culturally widespread father/son/donkey tale, as well as samples of modern urban legends in the United States.

The revised section on music now begins by stepping back in time to 40,000-year-old bone flutes and whistles unearthed by archaeologists and then marches forward to Abenaki shamans playing cedar flutes to summon game animals, traditional and New Age shamans playing drums to evoke trances, laborers on the edge of the Sahara working to the beat of a drum, and West African *griots* who recount their people's history through percussion and lyrics. Beyond such examples, this chapter discusses the elements of music, including tonality, rhythm, and melody. The chapter includes a Biocultural Connection about the role of peyote in Huichol art, along with a shorter, sharper version of Margo DeMello's Original Study, on the modern tattoo community.

The chapter's revised conclusion describes how endangered indigenous groups use aesthetic traditions as part of their cultural and economic survival strategy. It features a moving example of this in a new Applied Anthropology piece, "Bringing Back the Past," by Penobscot Indian anthropologist and master beader, Jennifer Sapiel Neptune.

CHAPTER 26: PROCESSES OF CHANGE

The themes and terminology of globalization are woven through this chapter, which includes definitions that distinguish *progress* from *modernization, rebellion* from *revolution,* and *acculturation* from *enculturation.* Here, we discuss mechanisms of change—innovation, diffusion, and cultural loss, as well as repressive change. Two new and very different examples have been added to the section on diffusion: We trace the spread of maize/corn and of the metric system. Our exploration of culture change and loss covers acculturation and ethnocide, citing a range of examples of repressive change from around the world—including a discussion of ethnocide in Tibet. This chapter also looks at reactions to such change, including revitalization movements, rebellions, and revolutions. A discussion on modernization touches on the issue of self-determination among indigenous peoples and highlights two contrasting cases: Skolt Lapp reindeer herders of Finland and Shuar Indians of Ecuador. Also featured are the historical profile of applied or practical anthropology and the emergence of action or advocacy anthropology in collaboration with indigenous societies, ethnic minorities, and other besieged or repressed groups. Among the many images in this chapter is a new United Nations Refugee Agency map showing the numbers and home countries of the 42 million forcibly displaced people in the world today.

Boxed features include a Biocultural Connection on the emergence of new diseases, an Anthropologist of Note profile on Eric R. Wolf, and an Anthropology Applied piece on development anthropology and dams, with a new and fascinating satellite image of China's Three Gorges Dam. The chapter concludes with a discussion of globalization as a worldwide process of accelerated modernization in which all parts of the earth are becoming interconnected in one vast, interrelated, and all-encompassing system.

CHAPTER 27: GLOBAL CHALLENGES, LOCAL RESPONSES, AND THE ROLE OF ANTHROPOLOGY

Our final chapter zeroes in on numerous global challenges confronting the human species today. We ask students to use the anthropological tools they have learned to think critically about these issues and take informed steps to help bring about a future in which humans live harmoniously with one another and with the natural world that sustains us. Sections on global culture and ethnic resurgence look at Westernization and its counterforce of growing nationalism and the breakup of multi-ethnic states. We present examples of resistance to globalization and discuss pluralism and multiculturalism.

We also recount the ever-widening gap between those who have wealth and power and those who do not. We define and illustrate the term *structural power* and its two branches—hard power (military and economic might) and soft power (media might that gains control through ideological influence). A substantial section about the rise of global corporations places this phenomenon in historical context and highlights the largest corporations (making particular note of media corporations and the emergence of the global "mediascape"). A new chart showing global distribution of military expenditure appears in this section, along with a graph comparing corporate profits to country GDPs.

We then address problems of structural violence—from pollution to epidemics of hunger and obesity. We also touch on the psychological problems that derive from powerful marketing messages shaping cultural standards concerning the ideal human body.

Special box features include an updated version of Laura Nader's Original Study "Standardizing the Body: The Question of Choice"; a Biocultural Connection about the threat to Arctic cultures from outside contamination; and an updated Globalscape on the practice of dumping toxic waste in the Third World.

We close with a summary of the meaning of this chapter's vast and sometimes troubling content—and discuss the role anthropology can play in helping to solve practical problems on local and global levels. Featured in this concluding section is a heartening new Anthropologist of Note on Paul Farmer, world-renowned anthropologist, medical doctor, and human rights activist.

Supplements

Anthropology comes with a comprehensive supplements program to help instructors create an effective learning environment both inside and outside the classroom and to aid students in mastering the material.

Supplements for Instructors

ONLINE INSTRUCTOR'S MANUAL AND TEST BANK

The Instructor's Manual offers detailed chapter outlines, lecture suggestions, key terms, and student activities such as video exercises and Internet exercises. In addition, there are over seventy-five chapter test questions including multiple choice, true/false, fill-in-the-blank, short answer, and essay.

POWERLECTURE WITH JOININ™ AND EXAMVIEW®

On CD or DVD, this one-stop class preparation tool contains ready-to-use Microsoft PowerPoint slides, enabling you to assemble, edit, publish, and present custom lectures with ease. PowerLecture helps you bring together text-specific lecture outlines and art from Haviland's text along with videos and your own materials—culminating in powerful, personalized, media-enhanced presentations. The **JoinIn**™ content (for use with most "clicker" systems) available within PowerLecture delivers instant classroom assessment and active learning. Take polls and attendance, quiz, and invite students to actively participate while they learn. Featuring automatic grading, **ExamView**® is also available within PowerLecture, allowing you to create, deliver, and customize tests and study guides (both print and online) in minutes. See assessments onscreen exactly as they will print or display online. Build tests of up to 250 questions using up to twelve question types and enter an unlimited number of new questions or edit existing questions. PowerLecture also includes the text's Instructor's Resource Manual and Test Bank as Word documents.

WEBTUTOR ON BLACKBOARD AND WEBCT

Jumpstart your course with customizable, rich, text-specific content within your course management system. Simply load a content cartridge into your course management system to easily blend, add, edit, reorganize, or delete content, all of which is specific to Haviland et al.'s *Anthropology: The Human Challenge*, 13th edition, and includes media resources, quizzing, weblinks, discussion topics, and interactive games and exercises.

WADSWORTH ANTHROPOLOGY VIDEO LIBRARY

Qualified adopters may select full-length videos from an extensive library of offerings drawn from such excellent educational video sources as *Films for the Humanities and Sciences*.

ABC ANTHROPOLOGY VIDEO SERIES

This exclusive video series was created jointly by Wadsworth and ABC for the anthropology course. Each video contains approximately 60 minutes of footage originally broadcast on ABC within the past several years. The videos are broken into short 2- to 7-minute segments, perfect for classroom use as lecture launchers or to illustrate key anthropological concepts. An annotated table of contents accompanies each video, providing descriptions of the segments and suggestions for their possible use within the course.

AIDS IN AFRICA DVD

Southern Africa has been overcome by a pandemic of unparalleled proportions. This documentary series focuses on the new democracy of Namibia and the many actions there to control HIV/AIDS. Included in this series are four documentary films created by the Periclean Scholars at Elon University: (1) *Young Struggles, Eternal Faith,* which focuses on caregivers in the faith community; (2) *The Shining Lights of Opuwo,* which shows how young people share their messages of hope through song and dance; (3) *A Measure of Our Humanity,* which describes HIV/AIDS as an issue related to gender, poverty, stigma, education, and justice; and (4) *You Wake Me Up,* a story of two HIV-positive women and their acts of courage helping other women learn to survive. Cengage/Wadsworth is excited to offer these award-winning films to instructors for use in class. When presenting topics such as gender, faith, culture, poverty, and so on, the films will be enlightening for students and will expand their global perspective of HIV/AIDS.

Online Resources for Instructors and Students

ANTHROPOLOGY RESOURCE CENTER

This online center offers a wealth of information and useful tools for both instructors and students in all four fields of anthropology. It includes interactive maps, learning modules, video exercises, and breaking news in anthropology. For instructors, the Resource Center includes a gateway to time-saving teaching tools, such as image banks, sample syllabi, and more. Access to the website is available free when bundled with the text or for purchase at a nominal fee.

THE HAVILAND ET AL. COMPANION WEBSITE

The book's companion site includes chapter-specific resources for instructors and students. For instructors, the site offers a password-protected Instructor's Manual, Microsoft PowerPoint presentation slides, and more. For students, there are a multitude of text-specific study aids:

tutorial practice quizzes that can be scored and e-mailed to the instructor, weblinks, flash cards, crossword puzzles, and much more.

INFOTRAC® COLLEGE EDITION

InfoTrac College Edition is an online library that offers full-length articles from thousands of scholarly and popular publications. Among the journals available are *American Anthropologist, Current Anthropology,* and *Canadian Review of Sociology and Anthropology.* Contact your local Cengage sales representative for details.

Supplements for Students

TELECOURSE STUDY GUIDE

The new distance learning course, **Anthropology: The Four Fields,** provides online and print companion study guide options that include study aids, interactive exercises, videos, and more.

Additional Student Resources

BASIC GENETICS FOR ANTHROPOLOGY CD-ROM: PRINCIPLES AND APPLICATIONS (STAND-ALONE VERSION), BY ROBERT JURMAIN AND LYNN KILGORE

This student CD-ROM expands on such biological concepts as biological inheritance (genes, DNA sequencing, and so on) and applications of that to modern human populations at the molecular level (human variation and adaptation—to disease, diet, growth, and development). Interactive animations and simulations bring these important concepts to life for students so they can fully understand the essential biological principles required for physical anthropology. Also available are quizzes and interactive flashcards for further study.

HOMINID FOSSILS CD-ROM: AN INTERACTIVE ATLAS, BY JAMES AHERN

The interactive atlas CD-ROM includes over seventy-five key fossils important for a clear understanding of human evolution. The QuickTime Virtual Reality (QTVR) "object" movie format for each fossil enables students to have a near-authentic experience of working with these important finds, by allowing them to rotate the fossil 360 degrees. Unlike some VR media, QTVR objects are made using actual photographs of the real objects and thus better preserve details of color and texture. The fossils used are high-quality research casts and real fossils. The organization of the atlas is nonlinear, with three levels and multiple paths, enabling students to see how the fossil fits into the map of human evolution in terms of geography, time, and evolution. The CD-ROM offers students an inviting,

authentic learning environment, one that also contains a dynamic quizzing feature that will allow students to test their knowledge of fossil and species identification, as well as provide more detailed information about the fossil record.

VIRTUAL LABORATORIES FOR PHYSICAL ANTHROPOLOGY CD-ROM, FOURTH EDITION, BY JOHN KAPPELMAN

The new edition of this full-color, interactive CD-ROM provides students with a hands-on computer component for completing lab assignments at school or at home. Through the use of video clips, 3-D animations, sound, and digital images, students can actively participate in twelve labs as part of their physical anthropology and archaeology course. The labs and assignments teach students how to formulate and test hypotheses with exercises that include how to measure, plot, interpret, and evaluate a variety of data drawn from osteological, behavioral, and fossil materials.

Readings and Case Studies

CLASSIC AND CONTEMPORARY READINGS IN PHYSICAL ANTHROPOLOGY, EDITED BY M. K. SANDFORD WITH EILEEN M. JACKSON

This highly accessible reader emphasizes science—its principles and methods—as well as the historical development of physical anthropology and the applications of new technology to the discipline. The editors provide an introduction to the reader as well as a brief overview of the article so students know what to look for. Each article also includes discussion questions and Internet resources.

CLASSIC READINGS IN CULTURAL ANTHROPOLOGY, 2ND EDITION, EDITED BY GARY FERRARO

Now in its second edition, this reader includes historical and recent articles that have had a profound effect on the field of anthropology. Organized according to the major topic areas found in most cultural anthropology courses, this reader includes an introduction to the material as well as a brief overview of each article, discussion questions, and InfoTrac College Edition key search terms.

GLOBALIZATION AND CHANGE IN FIFTEEN CULTURES: BORN IN ONE WORLD, LIVING IN ANOTHER, EDITED BY GEORGE SPINDLER AND JANICE E. STOCKARD

In this volume, fifteen case study authors write about culture change in today's diverse settings around the world. Each original article provides insight into the dynamics and meanings of change, as well as the effects of globalization at the local level.

CASE STUDIES IN CULTURAL ANTHROPOLOGY, EDITED BY GEORGE SPINDLER AND JANICE E. STOCKARD

Select from more than sixty classic and contemporary ethnographies representing geographic and topical diversity. Newer case studies focus on cultural change and cultural continuity, reflecting the globalization of the world.

CASE STUDIES IN CONTEMPORARY SOCIAL ISSUES, EDITED BY JOHN A. YOUNG

Framed around social issues, these new contemporary case studies are globally comparative and represent the cutting-edge work of anthropologists today.

CASE STUDIES IN ARCHAEOLOGY, EDITED BY JEFFREY QUILTER

These engaging accounts of new archaeological techniques, issues, and solutions—as well as studies discussing the collection of material remains—range from site-specific excavations to types of archaeology practiced.

EVOLUTION OF THE BRAIN MODULE: NEUROANATOMY, DEVELOPMENT, AND PALEONTOLOGY, BY DANIEL D. WHITE

The human species is the only species that has ever created a symphony, written a poem, developed a mathematical equation, or studied its own origins. The biological structure that has enabled humans to perform these feats of intelligence is the human brain. This module explores the basics of neuroanatomy, brain development, lateralization, and sexual dimorphism and provides the fossil evidence for hominid brain evolution. This module in chapter-like print format can be packaged free with the text.

FORENSIC ANTHROPOLOGY MODULE: A BRIEF REVIEW, BY DIANE FRANCE

Diane France explores the myths and realities of forensic anthropology: the search for human remains in crime scenes, forensic anthropology in the courtroom, special challenges in mass fatality incident responses (such as plane crashes and terrorist acts), and what students should consider if they want to pursue a career in forensic anthropology.

MOLECULAR ANTHROPOLOGY MODULE, BY LESLIE KNAPP

Leslie Knapp explores how molecular genetic methods are used to understand the organization and expression of genetic information in humans and nonhuman primates. Students will learn about the common laboratory methods used to study genetic variation and evolution in molecular anthropology. Examples are drawn from up-to-date research on human evolutionary origins and comparative primate genomics to demonstrate that scientific research is an ongoing process with theories frequently being questioned and reevaluated.

HUMAN ENVIRONMENT INTERACTIONS: NEW DIRECTIONS IN HUMAN ECOLOGY, BY CATHY GALVIN

Cathy Galvin provides students with an introduction to the basic concepts in human ecology before discussing cultural ecology, human adaptation studies, human behavioral ecology, and political ecology. The module concludes with a discussion of resilience and global change as a result of human–environment interactions today.

Acknowledgments

In this day and age, no textbook comes to fruition without extensive collaboration. Beyond the shared endeavors of our author team, this book owes its completion to a wide range of individuals, from colleagues in the discipline to those involved in the production process. We are particularly grateful for the comments received through an electronic survey as well as the remarkable group of manuscript reviewers listed below. They provided unusually detailed and thoughtful feedback that helped us to hone and re-hone our narrative.

Stewart Brewer, Dana College
Kendall Campbell, Washington State University
Jennifer Coe, Jamestown Community College
Julie David, Orange Coast College and California
    Baptist University
Rene M. Descartes, State University of New York at
    Cobleskill
Sylvia Grider, Texas A&M University
Susan H. Krook, Normandale Community College
Barbara J. Michael, University of North Carolina,
    Wilmington
Renee B. Walker, SUNY College at Oneonta
Linda F. Whitmer, Hope International University
Holly E. Yatros, Oakland Community College and
    Macomb Community College

We carefully considered and made use of the wide range of comments provided by these individuals. Our decisions on how to utilize their suggestions were influenced by our own perspectives on anthropology and teaching, combined with the priorities and page limits of this text. Neither our reviewers nor any of the other anthropologists mentioned here should be held responsible for any shortcomings in this book. They should, however, be credited as contributors to many of the book's strengths.

Thanks, too, go to colleagues who provided material for some of the Original Study, Biocultural Connection, and Anthropology Applied boxes in this text: Michael Blakey, Hillary Crane, John Crock, Margo DeMello, Katherine Dettwyler, Frans B. M. de Waal, George S. Esber, Anabel Ford, Michele Goldsmith, Edward C. Green, S. Neyooxet Greymorning, Marvin Harris, Donna Hart, John Hawks, Michael M. Horowitz, Suzanne Leclerc-Madlala, Susan Lees, Roger Lewin, Anne Nacey Maggioncalda, Charles C. Mann, Jonathan Marks, Bill Maurer, Sir Robert May, H. Lyn White Miles, Laura Nader, Serena Nanda, Jennifer Sapiel Neptune, Martin Ottenheimer, Anna Roosevelt, Robert M. Sapolsky, Sherry Simpson, Meredith F. Small, Karen Springen, Amanda Stronza, William Ury, Clementine van Eck, Annette B. Weiner, Dennis Werner, R. K. Williamson, and Jane C. Waldbaum. Among these individuals we particularly want to acknowledge our admiration, affection, and appreciation for our mutual friend and colleague Jim Petersen, whose life came to an abrupt and tragic end while returning from fieldwork in the Brazilian Amazon. Jim's work is featured in one of the pieces by Charles C. Mann.

We have debts of gratitude to office workers in our departments for their cheerful help in clerical matters: Karen Rundquist, Emira Smailagic, Katie Weaver, and Sheri Youngberg. And to research librarian extraordinaire Nancy Bianchi and colleagues Yvette Pigeon, Paula Duncan, Lajiri Van Ness-Otunnu, and Michael Wesch for engaging in lively discussions of anthropological and pedagogical approaches. Also worthy of note here are the introductory anthropology teaching assistants who, through the years, have shed light for us on effective ways to reach new generations of students.

Our thanksgiving inventory would be incomplete without mentioning individuals at Wadsworth Publishing who helped conceive this text and bring it to fruition. Special gratitude goes to acquisitions editor Erin Mitchell and to senior development editor Lin Marshall Gaylord for her vision, vigor, and anthropological knowledge. Our thanks also go out to Wadsworth's skilled and enthusiastic editorial, marketing, design, and production team: Andrew Keay (marketing manager), Melanie Cregger (media editor), Pamela Simon (editorial assistant), Rachel Krapf (assistant editor), as well as Jerilyn Emori (content project manager) and Caryl Gorska (art director).

In addition to all of the above, we have had the invaluable aid of several most able freelancers, including our photo researchers Billie Porter and Susan Kaprov, who were always willing to go the extra mile to find the most telling and compelling photographs, and our skilled graphic designer Lisa Buckley. We are especially thankful to have had the opportunity to work once again with copy editor Jennifer Gordon and production coordinator Joan Keyes of Dovetail Publishing Services. Consummate professionals and generous souls, both of them keep track of countless details and bring calm efficiency and grace to the demands of meeting difficult deadlines. Their efforts and skills play a major role in making our work doable and pleasurable.

And finally, all of us are indebted to family members who have not only put up with our textbook preoccupation but cheered us on in the endeavor. Dana had the tireless support and keen eye of husband Peter Bingham—along with the varied contributions of their three sons Nishan, Tavid, and Aram Bingham. As co-author spouses under the same roof, Harald and Bunny have picked up slack for each other on every front to help this project move along smoothly. But the biggest debt of gratitude may be in Bill's corner for initiating this book more than three decades ago, building it into a leading introductory text used by hundreds of thousands of students around the world, and having the foresight to bring a trio of co-authors on board about a decade ago to maintain and build upon the established strengths of this long-term educational endeavor. Before putting together a team of co-authors several editions ago, he relied on the know-how of his spouse Anita de Laguna Haviland, whose varied skills played a vital role in this book's success.

About the Authors

Authors Bunny McBride, Dana Walrath, Harald Prins, and William Haviland

All four members of this author team share overlapping research interests and a similar vision of what anthropology is (and should be) about. For example, all are true believers in the four-field approach to anthropology and all have some involvement in applied work.

WILLIAM A. HAVILAND is Professor Emeritus at the University of Vermont, where he founded the Department of Anthropology and taught for thirty-two years. He holds a PhD in anthropology from the University of Pennsylvania.

He has carried out original research in archaeology in Guatemala and Vermont; ethnography in Maine and Vermont; and physical anthropology in Guatemala. This work has been the basis of numerous publications in various national and international books and journals, as well as in media intended for the general public. His books include *The Original Vermonters*, co-authored with Marjorie Power, and a technical monograph on ancient Maya settlement. He also served as consultant for the award-winning telecourse, *Faces of Culture*, and is co-editor of the series *Tikal Reports*, published by the University of Pennsylvania Museum of Archaeology and Anthropology.

Besides his teaching and writing, Dr. Haviland has lectured to numerous professional as well as non-professional audiences in Canada, Mexico, Lesotho, South Africa, and Spain, as well as in the United States. A staunch supporter of indigenous rights, he served as expert witness for the Missisquoi Abenakis of Vermont in an important court case over aboriginal fishing rights.

Awards received by Dr. Haviland include being named University Scholar by the Graduate School of the University of Vermont in 1990; a Certificate of Appreciation from the Sovereign Republic of the Abenaki Nation of Missisquoi, St. Francis/Sokoki Band in 1996; and a Lifetime Achievement Award from the Center for Research on Vermont in 2006. Now retired from teaching, he continues his research, writing, and lecturing from the coast of Maine. His most recent book is *At the Place of the Lobsters and Crabs* (2009).

HARALD E. L. PRINS is a University Distinguished Professor of Anthropology at Kansas State University. Born in the Netherlands, he studied at universities in Europe and the United States. He has done extensive fieldwork among indigenous peoples in South and North America, published many dozens of articles in seven languages, authored *The Mi'kmaq: Resistance, Accommodation, and Cultural Survival* (1996), co-authored *Indians in Eden* (2009), and co-edited *American Beginnings* (1994) and other books. Also trained in film, he has made award-winning documentaries and served as president of the Society for Visual Anthropology and visual anthropology editor of the *American Anthropologist*. Dr. Prins has won his university's most prestigious undergraduate teaching awards, held the Coffman Chair for University Distinguished Teaching Scholars (2004–2005), and was selected as Professor of the Year for the State of Kansas by the Carnegie Foundation for the Advancement of Teaching in 2008. Active in human rights, he served as expert witness in Native rights cases in the U.S. Senate and various Canadian courts, and was instrumental in the successful federal recognition and land claims of the Aroostook Band of Micmacs (1991). Dr. Prins was appointed Research Associate at the National Museum of Natural History, Smithsonian Institution (2008–2011), and served as guest professor at Lund University in Sweden (2010).

DANA WALRATH is Assistant Professor of Family Medicine at the University of Vermont and a Women's Studies-affiliated faculty member. She earned her PhD in anthropology from the University of Pennsylvania and is a medical and biological anthropologist with principal interests in biocultural aspects of reproduction, the cultural context of biomedicine, genetics, and evolutionary medicine. She co-founded and directed an innovative educational program at the University of Vermont's College of Medicine that brings anthropological theory and practice to first-year medical students. Before joining the faculty at the University of Vermont in 2000, she taught at the University of Pennsylvania and Temple University. Her research has been supported by the National Science Foundation, Health Resources and Services Administration, the Centers for Disease Control, and the Templeton Foundation. Dr. Walrath's publications have appeared in *Current Anthropology, American Anthropologist,* and *American Journal of Physical Anthropology.* An active member of the Council on the Anthropology of Reproduction, she has also served on a national committee to develop women's health-care learning objectives for medical education and works locally to improve health care for refugees and immigrants.

BUNNY MCBRIDE is an award-winning author specializing in cultural anthropology, indigenous peoples, international tourism, and nature conservation issues. Published in dozens of national and international print media, she has reported from Africa, Europe, China, and the Indian Ocean. Highly rated as a teacher, she served as visiting anthropology faculty at Principia College, the Salt Institute for Documentary Field Studies, and since 1996 as adjunct lecturer of anthropology at Kansas State University. McBride's many publications include *Women of the Dawn* (1999), *Molly Spotted Elk: A Penobscot in Paris* (1995), and *Indians in Eden: Wabanakis and Rusticators on Maine's Mount Desert Island, 1850s–1920s* (co-authored, 2009). The Maine State legislature awarded her a special commendation for significant contributions to Native women's history (1999). A community activist and researcher for the Aroostook Band of Micmacs (1981–1991), McBride assisted this Maine Indian community in its successful efforts to reclaim lands, gain tribal status, and revitalize cultural traditions. She has curated various museum exhibits based on her research, most recently *Journeys West: The David & Peggy Rockefeller American Indian Art Collection* for the Abbe Museum in Bar Harbor, Maine. Currently she is working on a new book co-authored with Harald Prins (*From Indian Island to Omaha Beach: The Story of Charles Shay, Penobscot Indian War Hero,* 2010) and a series of museum exhibitions based on a two-volume study co-authored with Harald Prins for the National Park Service (*Asticou's Island Domain,* 2007). McBride also serves as oral history advisor for the Kansas Humanities Council and as board member and vice president of the Women's World Summit Foundation, based in Geneva, Switzerland.

Challenge Issue   It is a challenge to make sense of who we are. Where did we come from? Why are we so radically different from some animals and so surprisingly similar to others? Why do our bodies look the way they do? How do we explain so many different beliefs, languages, and customs? Why do we act in certain ways? What makes us tick? While some people answer these questions with biological mechanisms and others with social or spiritual explanations, scholars in the discipline of anthropology address them through a holistic, integrated approach. Anthropology considers human culture and biology, in all times and places, as inextricably intertwined, each affecting the other in important ways. This photograph, taken in a specialized maternity clinic in Gujarat, India, provides a case in point. Since commercial surrogacy—the practice of paying a woman to carry another's fetus to term—was legalized in 2002, wealthy childless parents from all over the globe have traveled to India for this service. Chosen by foreigners because of their healthy drug-free lifestyle and lower fees, Indian women take on extra biological risk to make it possible for others to reproduce their genes. Global politics and local cultural practices interact with the seemingly purely biological process of birth. Understanding humanity in all its biological and cultural variety, past and present, is the fundamental contribution of anthropology. In the era of globalization, this contribution is all the more important. Indeed, the holistic and integrative anthropological perspective has become essential to human survival.

CHAPTER 1

The Essence of Anthropology

Chapter Preview

What Is Anthropology?

Anthropology, the study of humankind everywhere throughout time, produces knowledge about what makes people different from one another and what we all have in common. Anthropologists work within four fields of the discipline. While physical anthropologists focus on humans as biological organisms (tracing evolutionary development and looking at biological variations), cultural anthropologists investigate the contrasting ways groups of humans think, feel, and behave. Archaeologists try to recover information about human cultures—usually from the past—by studying material objects, skeletal remains, and settlements. Meanwhile, linguists study languages—communication systems by which cultures are maintained and passed on to succeeding generations. Practitioners in all four fields are informed by one another's findings and united by a common anthropological perspective on the human condition.

How Does Anthropology Compare to Other Disciplines?

In studying humankind, early anthropologists came to the conclusion that to fully understand the complexities of human thought, feelings, behavior, and biology, it was necessary to study and compare all humans, wherever and whenever. More than any other feature, this comparative, cross-cultural, long-term perspective distinguishes anthropology from other social sciences. Anthropologists are not the only scholars who study people, but they are uniquely holistic in their approach, focusing on the interconnections and interdependence of all aspects of the human experience, past and present. This holistic and integrative outlook equips anthropologists to grapple with an issue of overriding importance for all of us today: globalization.

How Do Anthropologists Do What They Do?

Anthropologists, like other scholars, are concerned with the description and explanation of reality. They formulate and test hypotheses—tentative explanations of observed phenomena—concerning humankind. Their aim is to develop reliable theories—interpretations or explanations supported by bodies of data—about our species. These data are usually collected through fieldwork—a particular kind of hands-on research that gives anthropologists enough familiarity with a situation that they can begin to recognize patterns, regularities, and exceptions. It is also through careful observation, combined with comparison, that anthropologists test their theories.

For as long as we have been on earth, people have sought to understand who we are, where we come from, and why we act as we do. Throughout most of human history, though, people relied on myth and folklore for answers, rather than on the systematic testing of data obtained through careful observation. Anthropology, over the last 150 years, has emerged as a tradition of scientific inquiry with its own approaches to answering these questions. Simply stated, **anthropology** is the study of humankind in all times and places. While focusing primarily on *Homo sapiens*—the human species—anthropologists also study our ancestors and close animal relatives for clues about what it means to be human.

The Development of Anthropology

Although works of anthropological significance have a considerable antiquity—about 2,500 years ago the Greek historian Herodotus chronicled the many different cultures he encountered during extensive journeys through territories surrounding the Mediterranean Sea and beyond, and nearly 700 years ago far-roving North African Arab scholar Ibn Khaldun wrote a "universal history"—anthropology as a distinct field of inquiry is a relatively recent product of Western civilization. The first anthropology program in the United States, for example, was established at the University of Pennsylvania in 1886, and the first doctorate in anthropology was granted by Clark University in 1892. If people have always been concerned about their origins and those of others, then why did it take such a long time for a systematic discipline of anthropology to appear?

The answer to this is as complex as human history. In part, it relates to the limits of human technology. Throughout most of history, the geographic horizons of people have been restricted. Without ways to travel to distant parts of the world, observation of cultures and peoples far from one's own was a difficult—if not impossible—undertaking. Extensive travel was usually the privilege of an exclusive few; the study of foreign peoples and cultures could not flourish until improved modes of transportation and communication developed.

This is not to say that people have been unaware of the existence of others in the world who look and act differently from themselves. The Old and New Testaments of the Bible, for example, are full of references to diverse ancient peoples, among them Babylonians, Egyptians, Greeks,

anthropology The study of humankind in all times and places.

Anthropologists come from many corners of the world and carry out research in a huge variety of cultures all around the globe. Dr. Jayasinhji Jhala, pictured here, hails from the old city of Dhrangadhra in Gujarat, northwestern India. A member of the Jhala clan of Rajputs, an aristocratic caste of warriors, he grew up in the royal palace of his father, the maharaja. After earning a bachelor of arts degree in India, he came to the United States and earned a master's in visual studies from MIT, followed by a doctorate in anthropology from Harvard. Currently a professor and director of the programs of Visual Anthropology and the Visual Anthropology Media Laboratory at Temple University, he returns regularly to India with students to film cultural traditions in his own caste-stratified society.

© Documentary Educational Resources

Jews, and Syrians. However, the differences among these people are slight in comparison to those among peoples of arctic Siberia, the Amazon rainforest, and the Kalahari Desert of southern Africa.

The invention of the magnetic compass allowed seafarers on better-equipped sailing ships to travel to truly faraway places and to meet people who differed radically from themselves. The massive encounter with previously unknown peoples—which began 500 years ago as Europeans sought to extend their trade and political domination to all parts of the world—focused attention on human differences in all their amazing variety. With this attention, Europeans gradually came to recognize that despite all the differences, they might share a basic humanity with people everywhere. Initially, Europeans labeled these societies "savage" or "barbarian" because they did not share the same cultural values. Over time, however, Europeans acknowledged such highly diverse groups as fellow members of one species and therefore as relevant to an understanding of what it is to be human. This growing interest in human diversity coincided with increasing efforts to explain findings in scientific terms. It cast doubts on the traditional explanations based on religious texts such as the Torah, Bible, or Koran and helped set the stage for the birth of anthropology.

Although anthropology originated within the historical context of European cultures, it has long since gone global. Today, it is an exciting, transnational discipline whose practitioners come from diverse societies all around the world. Many professional anthropologists born and raised in Asian, African, Latin American, or American Indian cultures traditionally studied by European and North American anthropologists contribute substantially to the discipline. Their distinct non-Western perspectives shed new light not only on their own cultures but on those of others. It is noteworthy that in one regard diversity has long been a hallmark of the discipline: From its earliest days, women as well as men have entered the field. Throughout this text, we will be spotlighting individual anthropologists, illustrating the diversity of these practitioners and their work.

Anthropological Perspectives

Many academic disciplines are concerned in one way or another with our species. For example, biology focuses on the genetic, anatomical, and physiological aspects of organisms. Psychology is concerned primarily with cognitive, mental, and emotional issues, while economics examines the production, distribution, and management of material resources. And various disciplines in the humanities look into the historic, artistic, and philosophic achievements of human cultures. But anthropology is distinct because of its focus on the interconnections and interdependence of all aspects of the human experience in all places and times—both biological and cultural, past and present. It is this **holistic perspective** that best equips anthropologists to broadly address that elusive phenomenon we call human nature.

Anthropologists welcome the contributions of researchers from other disciplines and in return offer the benefit of their own findings. Anthropologists do not

expect, for example, to know as much about the structure of the human eye as anatomists or as much about the perception of color as psychologists. As synthesizers, however, anthropologists are prepared to understand how these bodies of knowledge relate to color-naming practices in different human societies. Because they look for the broad basis of human ideas and practices without limiting themselves to any single social or biological aspect, anthropologists can acquire an especially expansive and inclusive overview of the complex biological and cultural organism that is the human being.

The holistic perspective also helps anthropologists stay keenly aware of ways that their own cultural ideas and values may impact their research. As the old saying goes, people often see what they believe, rather than what appears before their eyes. By maintaining a critical awareness of their own assumptions about human nature—checking and rechecking the ways their beliefs and actions might be shaping their research—anthropologists strive to gain objective knowledge about people. With this in mind, anthropologists aim to avoid the pitfalls of **ethnocentrism**, a belief that the ways of one's own culture are the only proper ones. Thus anthropologists have contributed uniquely to our understanding of diversity in human thought, biology, and behavior, as well as to our understanding of the many shared characteristics of humans.

To some, an inclusive, holistic perspective that emphasizes the inherent diversity within and among human cultures can be mistaken as shorthand for uniform liberal politics among anthropologists. This is not the case. Individual anthropologists are quite varied in their personal, political, and religious beliefs. At the same time, they apply a rigorous methodology for researching cultural practices from the perspective of the culture being studied—a methodology that requires them to check for the influences of their own biases. This is as true for an anthropologist analyzing the culture of the global banking industry as it is for one investigating trance dancing among contemporary hunter-gatherers. We might say that anthropology is a discipline concerned with unbiased evaluation of diverse human systems, including one's own. At times this requires challenging the status quo that is maintained and defended by the power elites of the system under study. This is true regardless of whether anthropologists focus on aspects of their own culture or on distant and different cultures.

holistic perspective A fundamental principle of anthropology: that the various parts of human culture and biology must be viewed in the broadest possible context in order to understand their interconnections and interdependence.

ethnocentrism The belief that the ways of one's own culture are the only proper ones.

Visual Counterpoint

Although infants in the United States typically sleep apart from their parents, cross-cultural research shows that co-sleeping, of mother and baby in particular, is the rule. Without the breathing cues provided by someone sleeping nearby, an infant is more susceptible to sudden infant death syndrome (SIDS), a phenomenon in which a 4- to 6-month-old baby stops breathing and dies while asleep. The highest rates of SIDS are found among infants in the United States. The photo on the right shows a Nenet family sleeping together in their *chum* (reindeer-skin tent). Nenet people are arctic reindeer pastoralists living in Siberia.

While other social sciences have concentrated predominantly on contemporary peoples living in North American and European (Western) societies, historically anthropologists have focused primarily on non-Western peoples and cultures. Anthropologists work with the understanding that to fully access the complexities of human ideas, behavior, and biology, *all* humans, wherever and whenever, must be studied. Anthropologists work with a time depth that extends back millions of years to our pre-human ancestors. A cross-cultural, comparative, and long-term evolutionary perspective distinguishes anthropology from other social sciences. This all-encompassing approach also guards against **culture-bound** theories of human behavior: that is, theories based on assumptions about the world and reality that come from the researcher's own particular culture.

As a case in point, consider the fact that infants in the United States typically sleep apart from their parents. To people accustomed to multi-bedroom houses, cribs, and car seats, this may seem normal, but cross-cultural research shows that co-sleeping, of mother and baby in particular, is the norm. Further, the practice of sleeping apart favored in the United States dates back only about 200 years.

Recent studies have shown that separation of mother and infant has important biological and cultural consequences. For one thing, it increases the length of the infant's crying

bouts. Some mothers incorrectly interpret the crying as indicating that the babies are receiving insufficient breast milk and consequently switch to feeding them bottled formula, proven to be less healthy. In extreme cases, a baby's cries may provoke physical abuse. But the benefits of co-sleeping go beyond significant reductions in crying: Infants who are breastfed receive more stimulation important for brain development, and they are apparently less susceptible to sudden infant death syndrome (SIDS or "crib death"). There are benefits to the mother as well: Frequent nursing prevents early ovulation after childbirth, it promotes loss of weight gained during pregnancy, and nursing mothers get at least as much sleep as mothers who sleep apart from their infants.[1]

Why do so many mothers continue to sleep separately from their infants? In the United States the cultural values of independence and consumerism come into play. To begin building individual identities, babies are provided with rooms (or at least space) of their own. This room also provides parents with a place for the toys, furniture, and other paraphernalia associated with "good" and "caring" childrearing in the United States.

Anthropology's historical emphasis on studying traditional, non-Western peoples has often led to findings that run

culture-bound Looking at the world and reality based on the assumptions and values of one's own culture.

[1] Barr, R. G. (1997, October). The crying game. *Natural History*, 47. Also, McKenna, J. J. (2002, September–October). Breastfeeding and bedsharing. *Mothering*, 28–37; and McKenna, J. J., & McDade, T. (2005, June). Why babies should never sleep alone: A review of the co-sleeping controversy in relation to SIDS, bedsharing, and breast feeding. *Pediatric Respiratory Reviews 6* (2), 134–152.

counter to generally accepted opinions derived from Western studies. Thus anthropologists were the first to demonstrate

> that the world does not divide into the pious and the superstitious; that there are sculptures in jungles and paintings in deserts; that political order is possible without centralized power and principled justice without codified rules; that the norms of reason were not fixed in Greece, the evolution of morality not consummated in England.... We have, with no little success, sought to keep the world off balance; pulling out rugs, upsetting tea tables, setting off firecrackers. It has been the office of others to reassure; ours to unsettle.[2]

Although the findings of anthropologists have often challenged the conclusions of sociologists, psychologists, and economists, anthropology is absolutely indispensable to them, as it is the only consistent check against culture-bound assertions. In a sense, anthropology is to these disciplines what the laboratory is to physics and chemistry: an essential testing ground for their theories.

Anthropology and Its Fields

Individual anthropologists tend to specialize in one of four fields or subdisciplines: physical (biological) anthropology, archaeology, linguistic anthropology, or cultural anthropology (Figure 1.1). Some anthropologists consider archaeology and linguistics as part of the broader study of human cultures, but archaeology and linguistics also have close ties to biological anthropology. For example, while linguistic anthropology focuses on the cultural aspects of language, it has deep connections to the evolution of human language and to the biological basis of speech and language studied within physical anthropology.

Each of anthropology's fields may take a distinct approach to the study of humans, but all gather and analyze data that are essential to explaining similarities and differences among humans, across time and space. Moreover, all of them generate knowledge that has numerous practical applications. Many scholars within each of the four fields practice **applied anthropology,** which entails using anthropological knowledge and methods to solve practical problems. Applied anthropologists do not offer their perspectives from the sidelines. Instead, they actively collaborate with the communities in which they work—setting goals, solving problems, and conducting research together. In this book, numerous specific examples of how anthropology contributes to solving a wide range of challenges appear in Anthropology Applied features.

[2] Geertz, C. (1984). Distinguished lecture: Anti anti-relativism. *American Anthropologist 86,* 275.

Figure 1.1 The four fields of anthropology. Note that the divisions among them are not sharp, indicating that their boundaries overlap.

One of the earliest contexts in which anthropological knowledge was applied to a practical problem was the international public health movement that began in the 1920s. This marked the beginning of **medical anthropology**—a specialization that combines theoretical and applied approaches from the fields of cultural and biological anthropology with the study of human health and disease. The work of medical anthropologists sheds light on the connections between human health and political and economic forces, both locally and globally. Examples of this specialization appear in many of the Biocultural Connections featured in this text, including the one presented in this chapter, "The Anthropology of Organ Transplantation."

Physical Anthropology

Physical anthropology, also called *biological anthropology,* focuses on humans as biological organisms. Traditionally, biological anthropologists concentrated on human evolution, primatology, growth and development, human adaptation, and forensics. Today, **molecular anthropology,** or the anthropological study of genes and genetic relationships, contributes significantly to the contemporary study of human biological diversity. Comparisons among groups

applied anthropology The use of anthropological knowledge and methods to solve practical problems, often for a specific client.

medical anthropology A specialization in anthropology that combines theoretical and applied approaches from cultural and biological anthropology with the study of human health and disease.

physical anthropology The systematic study of humans as biological organisms; also known as biological anthropology.

molecular anthropology A branch of biological anthropology that uses genetic and biochemical techniques to test hypotheses about human evolution, adaptation, and variation.

The Anthropology of Organ Transplantation

In 1954, the first organ transplant occurred in Boston when surgeons removed a kidney from one identical twin to place it inside his sick brother. Though some transplants rely upon living donors, routine organ transplantation depends largely upon the availability of organs obtained from individuals who have died.

From an anthropological perspective, the meanings of death and the body vary cross-culturally. While death could be said to represent a particular biological state, social agreement about this state's significance is of paramount importance. Anthropologist Margaret Lock has explored differences between Japanese and North American acceptance of the biological state of "brain death" and how it affects the practice of organ transplants.

Brain death relies upon the absence of measurable electrical currents in the brain and the inability to breathe without technological assistance. The brain-dead individual, though attached to machines, still seems alive with a beating heart and pink cheeks. North Americans find brain death acceptable, in part, because personhood and individuality are culturally located in the brain. North American comfort with brain death has allowed for the "gift of life" through organ donation and subsequent transplantation.

By contrast, in Japan, the concept of brain death is hotly contested and organ transplants are rarely performed. The Japanese do not incorporate a mind–body split into their models of themselves and locate personhood throughout the body rather than in the brain. They resist accepting a warm pink body as a corpse from which organs can be harvested. Further, organs cannot be transformed into "gifts" because anonymous donation is not compatible with Japanese social patterns of reciprocal exchange.

Organ transplantation carries far greater social meaning than the purely biological movement of an organ from one individual to another. Cultural and biological processes are tightly woven into every aspect of this new social practice.

BIOCULTURAL QUESTION

What criteria do you use for death, and is it compatible with the idea of organ donation? Do you think that donated organs are fairly distributed in your society or throughout the globe?

(For more on this subject, see Lock, M. (2001). Twice dead: Organ transplants and the reinvention of death. *Berkeley: University of California Press.)*

---

separated by time, geography, or the frequency of a particular gene can reveal how humans have adapted and where they have migrated. As experts in the anatomy of human bones and tissues, physical anthropologists lend their knowledge about the body to applied areas such as gross anatomy laboratories, public health, and criminal investigations.

PALEOANTHROPOLOGY

Paleoanthropology is the study of the origins and predecessors of the present human species; in other words, it is the study of human evolution. Paleoanthropologists focus on biological changes through time to understand how, when, and why we became the kind of organisms we are today. In biological terms, we humans are primates, one of the many kinds of mammals. Because we share a common ancestry with other primates, most specifically apes, paleoanthropologists look back to the earliest primates (65 or so million years ago) or even the earliest mammals (225 million years ago) to reconstruct the complex path of human evolution. Paleoanthropology, unlike other evolutionary studies, takes a **biocultural** approach, focusing on the interaction of biology and culture.

The fossilized skeletons of our ancestors allow paleoanthropologists to reconstruct the course of human evolutionary history. To do this, paleoanthropologists compare the size and shape of these fossils to one another and to the bones of living species. Each new fossil discovery brings another piece to add to the puzzle of human evolutionary history. Biochemical and genetic studies add considerably to the fossil evidence. As we will see in later chapters, genetic evidence establishes the close relationship between humans and ape species—chimpanzees, bonobos, and gorillas. Genetic analyses indicate that the distinctive human line originated 5 to 8 million years ago. Physical anthropology therefore deals with much greater time spans than the other branches of anthropology.

PRIMATOLOGY

Studying the anatomy and behavior of the other primates helps us understand what we share with our closest living relatives and what makes humans unique. Therefore, **primatology,** or the study of living and fossil primates, is a vital part of physical anthropology. Primates include the Asian and African apes, as well as monkeys, lemurs, lorises, and tarsiers.

Biologically, humans are members of the ape family—large-bodied, broad-shouldered primates with no tail. Detailed studies of ape behavior in the wild indicate that the sharing of learned behavior is a significant part of their social life. Increasingly, primatologists designate the shared, learned behavior of nonhuman apes as *culture.* For example, tool use and communication systems indicate the elementary basis of language in some ape societies. Primate studies offer scientifically grounded perspectives on the behavior of our ancestors, as well as greater appreciation and respect for the abilities of our closest

paleoanthropology The study of the origins and predecessors of the present human species; the study of human evolution.
biocultural Focusing on the interaction of biology and culture.
primatology The study of living and fossil primates.

Though Jane Goodall originally began her studies of chimpanzees to shed light on the behavior of our distant ancestors, the knowledge she has amassed through over forty years in the field has reinforced how similar we are. In turn, she has devoted her career to championing the rights of our closest living relatives.

living relatives. As human activity encroaches on all parts of the world, the habitats of many primate species are endangered, thereby threatening the survival of the species themselves. Primatologists often advocate for the preservation of primate habitats so that these remarkable animals will be able to continue to inhabit the earth with us.

HUMAN GROWTH, ADAPTATION, AND VARIATION

Another specialty of physical anthropologists is the study of human growth and development. Anthropologists examine biological mechanisms of growth as well as the impact of the environment on the growth process. For example, Franz Boas, a pioneer of American anthropology of the early 20th century (see the Anthropologists of Note feature in this chapter) compared the heights of immigrants who spent their childhood in the "old country" (Europe) to the increased heights reached by their children who grew up in the United States. Today, physical anthropologists study the impact of disease, pollution, and poverty on growth. Comparisons between human and nonhuman primate growth patterns can provide clues to the evolutionary history of humans. Detailed anthropological studies of the hormonal, genetic, and physiological bases of healthy growth in living humans also contribute significantly to the health of children today.

Studies of human adaptation focus on the capacity of humans to adapt or adjust to their material environment—biologically and culturally. This branch of physical anthropology takes a comparative approach to humans living today in a variety of environments. Humans are remarkable among the primates in that they now inhabit the entire earth. Though cultural adaptations make it possible for humans to live in some environmental extremes, biological adaptations also contribute to survival in extreme cold, heat, and high altitude.

Some of these biological adaptations are built into the genetic makeup of populations. The long period of human growth and development provides ample opportunity for the environment to shape the human body. *Developmental adaptations* are responsible for some features of human variation, such as the enlargement of the right ventricle of the heart to help push blood to the lungs among the Quechua Indians of the Andean highlands known as the *altiplano*. In contrast, *physiological adaptations* are short-term changes in response to a particular environmental stimulus. For example, a woman who normally lives at sea level will undergo a series of physiological responses, such as increased production of oxygen-carrying red blood cells, if she suddenly moves to a high altitude. All of these kinds of biological adaptation contribute to present-day human variation.

Human differences include visible traits such as height, body build, and skin color, as well as biochemical factors such as blood type and susceptibility to certain diseases. Still, we remain members of a single species. Physical anthropology applies all the techniques of modern biology to achieve fuller understanding of human variation and its relationship to the different environments in which people have lived. Physical anthropologists' research on human variation has debunked false notions of biologically defined races, a belief based on widespread misinterpretation of human variation.

Forensic Anthropology: Voices for the Dead

Forensic anthropology is the analysis of skeletal remains for legal purposes. Law enforcement authorities call upon forensic anthropologists to use skeletal remains to identify murder victims, missing persons, or people who have died in disasters, such as plane crashes. Forensic anthropologists have also contributed substantially to the investigation of human rights abuses in all parts of the world by identifying victims and documenting the cause of their death.

Among the best-known forensic anthropologists is Clyde C. Snow. He has been practicing in this field for over forty years—first for the Federal Aviation Administration and more recently as a freelance consultant. In addition to the usual police work, Snow has studied the remains of General George Armstrong Custer and his men from the 1876 battle at Little Big Horn, and in 1985 he went to Brazil, where he identified the remains of the notorious Nazi war criminal Josef Mengele.

He was also instrumental in establishing the first forensic team devoted to documenting cases of human rights abuses around the world. This began in 1984 when he went to Argentina at the request of a newly elected civilian government to help with the identification of remains of the *desaparecidos,* or "disappeared ones," the 9,000 or more people who were eliminated by death squads during seven years of military rule. A year later, he returned to give expert testimony at the trial of nine junta members and to teach Argentineans how to recover, clean, repair, preserve, photograph, x-ray, and analyze bones. Besides providing factual accounts of the fate of victims to their surviving kin and refuting the assertions of revisionists that the massacres never happened, the work of Snow and his Argentinean associates was crucial in convicting several military officers of kidnapping, torture, and murder.

Since Snow's pioneering work, forensic anthropologists have become increasingly involved in the investigation of human rights abuses in all parts of the world, from Chile to Guatemala, Haiti, the Philippines, Rwanda, Iraq, Bosnia, and Kosovo. Meanwhile, they continue to do important work for more typical clients. In the United States these clients include the Federal Bureau of Investigation and city, state, and county medical examiners' offices.

Forensic anthropologists specializing in skeletal remains commonly work closely with forensic archaeologists. The relation between them is rather like that between a forensic pathologist, who examines a corpse to establish time and manner of death, and a crime scene

© AP Photo/Rodrigo Abd

The excavation of mass graves by the Guatemalan Foundation for Forensic Anthropology (Fernando Moscoso Moller, director) documents the human rights abuses committed during Guatemala's bloody civil war, a conflict that left 200,000 people dead and another 40,000 missing. In 2009, in a mass grave in the Quiche region, Diego Lux Tzunux uses his cell phone to photograph the skeletal remains believed to belong to his brother Manuel who disappeared in 1980. Genetic analyses allow forensic anthropologists to confirm the identity of individuals so that family members can know the fate of their loved ones. The analysis of skeletal remains provides evidence of the torture and massacre sustained by these individuals.

FORENSIC ANTHROPOLOGY

One of the many practical applications of physical anthropology is **forensic anthropology:** the identification of human skeletal remains for legal purposes. Although they are called upon by law enforcement authorities to identify murder victims, forensic anthropologists also investigate human rights abuses such as systematic genocide,

forensic anthropology Applied subfield of physical anthropology that specializes in the identification of human skeletal remains for legal purposes.

terrorism, and war crimes. These specialists use details of skeletal anatomy to establish the age, sex, population affiliation, and stature of the deceased. Forensic anthropologists can also determine whether the person was right- or left-handed, exhibited any physical abnormalities, or had experienced trauma. While forensics relies upon differing frequencies of certain skeletal characteristics to establish population affiliation, it is nevertheless false to say that all people from a given population have a particular type of skeleton. (See the Anthropology Applied feature to read about the work of several forensic anthropologists and forensic archaeologists.)

investigator, who searches the site for clues. While the forensic anthropologist deals with the human remains—often only bones and teeth—the forensic archaeologist controls the site, recording the position of all relevant finds and recovering any clues associated with the remains. In 1995, for example, a team was assembled by the United Nations to investigate a mass atrocity in Rwanda; this group included archaeologists from the U.S. National Park Service's Midwest Archaeological Center. They performed the standard archaeological procedures of mapping the site; determining its boundaries; photographing and recording all surface finds; and excavating, photographing, and recording buried skeletons and associated materials in mass graves.[a]

In another example, Karen Burns of the University of Georgia was part of a team sent to northern Iraq after the 1991 Gulf War to investigate alleged atrocities. On a military base where there had been many executions, she excavated the remains of a man's body found lying on its side facing Mecca, conforming to Islamic practice. Although no intact clothing existed, two polyester threads typically used in sewing were found along the sides of both legs. Although the threads survived, the clothing, because it was made of natural fiber, had decayed. "Those two threads at each side of the leg just shouted that his family didn't bury him," said Burns.[b] Proper though his position was, no Islamic family would bury their own in a garment sewn with polyester thread; proper ritual would require a simple shroud.

In recent years New York City has been the site of two major anthropological analyses of skeletal remains. To deal with a present-day atrocity, Amy Zelson Mundorff, a forensic anthropologist for New York City's Office of the Chief Medical Examiner, supervised and coordinated the management, treatment, and cataloguing of people who lost their lives in the September 11 terrorist attack on the World Trade Center. Mundorff herself had been injured in the attack, but she was able to return to work two days after the towers fell.

And in 1991, just a short distance from the World Trade Center site, construction workers in lower Manhattan discovered an African burial ground from the 17th and 18th centuries. A bioarchaeological rather than strictly forensic approach allowed researchers to examine the complete cultural and historical context and lifeways of the entire population buried there. The African Burial Ground Project provided incontrovertible evidence of the horror of slavery in North America, in the busy northern port of New York City. The more than 400 individuals buried there, many of them children, were worked so far beyond their ability to endure that their spines were fractured. African American biological archaeologist Michael Blakey, who led the research team, noted the social impact of this work:

> Descendants of the enslaved in different parts of the world have the right to know about the past and the right to memorialize history so that it might not happen again. With the project, we knew that we were peeling off layers of obscurity. We were also doing something that scholars within the African diaspora have been

doing for about 150 years and that is realizing that history has political implications of empowerment and disempowerment. That history is not just to be discovered but to be re-discovered, to be corrected, and that African-American history is distorted. Omissions are made in order to create a convenient view of national and white identity at the expense of our understanding our world and also at the expense of African-American identity. So that the project of history—in this case using archaeology and skeletal biology—is a project meant to help us understand something that has been systematically hidden from us.[c]

Thus several kinds of anthropologists analyze human remains for a variety of purposes, contributing to the documentation and correction of violence committed by humans of the past and present.

---

[a] Haglund, W. D., Conner, M., & Scott, D. D. (2001). The archaeology of contemporary mass graves. *Historical Archaeology* 35 (1), 57–69.

[b] Cornwell, T. (1995, November 10). Skeleton staff. *Times Higher Education*, 20. http://www.timeshighereducation. co.uk/story.asp?storyCode=96035& sectioncode=26.

[c] "Return to the African Burial Ground: An interview with physical anthropologist Michael L. Blakey." (2003, November 20). *Archaeology*. http://www.archaeology.org/ online/interviews/blakey/.

Cultural Anthropology

Cultural anthropology (also called *social* or *sociocultural anthropology*) is the study of patterns of human behavior, thought, and feelings. It focuses on humans as culture-producing and culture-reproducing creatures. Thus in order to understand the work of the cultural anthropologist, we must clarify what we mean by **culture**—a society's shared and socially transmitted ideas, values, and perceptions, which are used to make sense of experience and generate behavior and are reflected in that behavior. These standards are socially learned, rather than acquired through biological inheritance. The manifestations of culture may vary considerably from place to place, but no person is "more cultured" in the anthropological sense than any other.

cultural anthropology Also known as social or sociocultural anthropology. The study of customary patterns in human behavior, thought, and feelings. It focuses on humans as culture-producing and culture-reproducing creatures.

culture A society's shared and socially transmitted ideas, values, and perceptions, which are used to make sense of experience and generate behavior and are reflected in that behavior.

Through his pioneering ethnographic studies of the culture of drug addicts and dealers, cultural anthropologist Philippe Bourgois opened up a new range of edgy field sites for cultural anthropologists. The insights from his detailed ethnographies about this world have been important not only for anthropological literature but for those concerned with the health of individuals and communities. Here Bourgois is pictured in one of his more recent field sites, a homeless encampment in North Philadelphia.

© Jeff Schonberg 2009

Cultural anthropology has two main components: ethnography and ethnology. An **ethnography** is a detailed description of a particular culture primarily based on **fieldwork,** which is the term all anthropologists use for on-location research. Because the hallmark of ethnographic fieldwork is a combination of social participation and personal observation within the community being studied, as well as interviews and discussions with individual members of a group, the ethnographic method is commonly referred to as **participant observation.** Ethnographies provide the information used to make systematic comparisons among cultures all across the world. Known as **ethnology,** such cross-cultural research allows anthropologists to develop anthropological theories that help explain why certain important differences or similarities occur among groups.

ETHNOGRAPHY

Through participant observation—eating a people's food, sleeping under their roof, learning how to speak and

ethnography A detailed description of a particular culture primarily based on fieldwork.

fieldwork The term anthropologists use for on-location research.

participant observation In ethnography, the technique of learning a people's culture through social participation and personal observation within the community being studied, as well as interviews and discussion with individual members of the group over an extended period of time.

ethnology The study and analysis of different cultures from a comparative or historical point of view, utilizing ethnographic accounts and developing anthropological theories that help explain why certain important differences or similarities occur among groups.

behave acceptably, and personally experiencing their habits and customs—the ethnographer seeks to gain the best possible understanding of a particular way of life. Being a participant observer does not mean that the anthropologist must join in battles to study a culture in which warfare is prominent; but by living among a warlike people, the ethnographer should be able to understand how warfare fits into the overall cultural framework. She or he must observe carefully to gain an overview without placing too much emphasis on one part at the expense of another. Only by discovering how *all* aspects of a culture—its social, political, economic, and religious practices and institutions—relate to one another can the ethnographer begin to understand the cultural system. This is the holistic perspective so basic to the discipline.

The popular image of ethnographic fieldwork is that it occurs among people who live in far-off, isolated places. To be sure, much ethnographic work has been done in the remote villages of Africa or South America, the islands of the Pacific Ocean, the Indian reservations of North America, the deserts of Australia, and so on. However, as the discipline has developed, Western industrialized societies have also become the focus of anthropological study. Some of this shift occurred as scholars from non-Western cultures became anthropologists. Ethnographic fieldwork has transformed from having expert Western anthropologists study people in "other" places to collaboration among anthropologists and the varied communities in which they work. Today, anthropologists from all around the globe employ the same research techniques that were used in the study of non-Western peoples to explore such diverse subjects as religious movements, street gangs, land rights, schools, marriage practices, conflict resolution, corporate bureaucracies, and health-care systems in Western cultures.

ETHNOLOGY

Largely descriptive in nature, ethnography provides the raw data needed for ethnology—the branch of cultural anthropology that involves cross-cultural comparisons and theories that explain differences or similarities among groups. Intriguing insights into one's own beliefs and practices may come from cross-cultural comparisons. Consider, for example, the amount of time spent on domestic chores by industrialized peoples and traditional food foragers (people who rely on wild plant and animal resources for subsistence). Anthropological research has shown that food foragers work far less time at domestic tasks and other subsistence pursuits compared to people in industrialized societies. Urban women in the United States who were not working for wages outside their homes put 55 hours a week into their housework—this despite all the "labor-saving" dishwashers, washing machines, clothes dryers, vacuum cleaners, food processors, and microwave ovens. In contrast, aboriginal women in Australia devoted 20 hours a week to their chores.[3] Nevertheless, consumer appliances have become important indicators of a high standard of living in the United States due to the widespread belief that household appliances reduce housework and increase leisure time.

By making systematic comparisons, ethnologists seek to arrive at scientific explanations concerning the function and operation of social practices and cultural features and patterns in all times and places. Today cultural anthropologists contribute to applied research in a variety of contexts—ranging from business to education to health care to government intervention to humanitarian aid.

Linguistic Anthropology

Perhaps the most distinctive feature of the human species is language. Although the sounds and gestures made by some other animals—especially apes—may serve functions comparable to those of human language, no other animal has developed a system of symbolic communication as complex as that of humans. Language allows people to preserve and transmit countless details of their culture from generation to generation.

The branch of anthropology that studies human languages is called **linguistic anthropology.** Although it shares data and methods with the more general discipline of linguistics, it differs in that it uses these to answer anthropological questions related to society and culture, such as language use within speech communities. When this field began, it emphasized the documentation of languages of cultures under ethnographic study—particularly those

whose future seemed precarious. Mastery of Native American languages—with grammatical structures so different from the Indo-European and Semitic languages to which Euramerican scholars were accustomed—prompted the notion of *linguistic relativity.* This refers to the idea that linguistic diversity reflects not just differences in sounds and grammar but differences in ways of looking at the world. For example, the observation that the language of the Hopi Indians of the American Southwest had no words for *past, present,* and *future* led the early proponents of linguistic relativity to suggest that the Hopi people had a different conception of time.[4] Similarly, the observation that English-speaking North Americans use a number of slang words—such as *dough, greenback, dust, loot, bucks, change, paper, cake, moolah, benjamins,* and *bread*—to refer to money could be a product of linguistic relativity. The profusion of names helps to identify a thing of special importance to a culture. For instance, the importance of money within North American culture is evident in the association between money and time, production, and capital in phrases such as "time is money" and "spend some time."

Complex ideas and practices integral to a culture's survival can also be reflected in language. For example, among the Nuer, a nomadic group that travels with grazing animals throughout southern Sudan, a baby born with a visible deformity is not considered a human baby. Instead it is called a baby hippopotamus. This name allows for the safe return of the hippopotamus to the river where it belongs. Such infants would not be able to survive in this society, and so linguistic practice is compatible with the compassionate choice the Nuer have had to make.

The notion of linguistic relativity has been challenged by theorists who propose that the human capacity for language is based on biological universals that underlie all human thought. Recently, Canadian cognitive scientist Stephen Pinker has even suggested that, at a fundamental

---

[3] Bodley, J. H. (1985). *Anthropology and contemporary human problems* (2nd ed., p. 69). Palo Alto, CA: Mayfield.

[4] Whorf, B. (1941). The relation of habitual thought and behavior to language. In L. Spier, A. I. Hallowell, & S. S. Newman (Eds.), *Language, culture, and personality: Essays in memory of Edward Sapir* (pp. 75–93). Menasha, WI: Sapir Memorial Publication Fund.

linguistic anthropology The study of human languages—looking at their structure, history, and relation to social and cultural contexts.

Linguistic anthropologist Gregory Anderson has devoted his career to saving indigenous languages. He founded and heads the Living Tongues Institute of Endangered Languages and works throughout the globe to preserve languages that are dying out at a shocking rate of about one every two weeks. Here he is working with Don Francisco Ninacondis and Ariel Ninacondis in Charazani, Bolivia, to preserve their language Kallawaya.

© Living Tongues Institute

level, thought is nonverbal.[5] A holistic anthropological approach considers language to have both a universal biological basis and specific cultural patterning.

Researching questions about human relations through language can involve focusing on specific speech events.[6] Such events form a **discourse** or an extended communication on a particular subject. These speech events reveal how social factors such as financial status, age, or gender affect the way an individual uses its culture's language. The linguistic anthropologist might examine whether the tendency for females in the United States to end statements with an upward inflection, as though the statement were a question, reflects a pattern of male dominance in this society. Because members of any culture may use a variety of different registers and inflections, the ones they choose to use at a specific instance convey particular meanings.

As with the anthropological perspective on culture, language is similarly regarded as alive, malleable, and changing. Online tools such as Urban Dictionary track the changes in North American slang, and traditional dictionaries include new words and usages each year. The implications of these language changes help increase our understanding of the human past. By working out relationships among languages and examining their spatial

distributions, linguistic anthropologists may estimate how long the speakers of those languages have lived where they do. By identifying those words in related languages that have survived from an ancient ancestral tongue, these linguistic anthropologists can also suggest not only where, but how, the speakers of the ancestral language lived. Such work has shown, for example, linguistic ties between geographically distant groups such as the people of Finland and Turkey.

Linguistic anthropology is practiced in a number of applied settings. For example, linguistic anthropologists have collaborated with ethnic minorities in the revival of languages suppressed or lost during periods of oppression by another ethnic group. This work has included helping to create written forms of languages that previously existed only orally. This sort of applied linguistic anthropology represents the true collaboration that is characteristic of anthropological research today.

Archaeology

Archaeology is the branch of anthropology that studies human cultures through the recovery and analysis of material remains and environmental data. Such material products include tools, pottery, hearths, and enclosures that remain as traces of cultural practices in the past, as well as human, plant, and marine remains, some of which date back 2.5 million years. The arrangement of these traces when recovered reflects specific human ideas and behavior. For example, shallow, restricted concentrations of charcoal that include oxidized earth, bone fragments, and charred plant remains, located near pieces of fire-cracked rock, pottery, and tools suitable for food preparation, indicate cooking and food processing. Such remains can reveal much about

---

[5] Pinker, S. (1994). *The language instinct: How the mind creates language.* New York: Morrow.

[6] Hymes, D. (1974). *Foundations in sociolinguistics: An ethnographic approach.* Philadelphia: University of Pennsylvania Press.

discourse An extended communication on a particular subject.
archaeology The study of human cultures through the recovery and analysis of material remains and environmental data.

a people's diet and subsistence practices. Together with skeletal remains, these material remains help archaeologists reconstruct the biocultural context of past human lifeways. Archaeologists organize this material and use it to explain cultural variability and culture change through time.

Because archaeology is explicitly tied to unearthing material remains in particular environmental contexts, a variety of innovations in the geographic and geologic sciences have been readily incorporated into archaeological research. Innovations such as geographic information systems (GIS), remote sensing, and ground penetrating radar (GPR) complement traditional explorations of the past through archaeological digs.

Archaeologists can reach back for clues to human behavior far beyond the mere 5,000 years to which historians are confined by their reliance on written records. Calling this time period "prehistoric" does not mean that these societies were less interested in their history or that they did not have ways of recording and transmitting history. It simply means that written records do not exist. That said, archaeologists are not limited to the study of societies without written records; they may study those for which historic documents are available to supplement the material remains. In most literate societies, written records are associated with governing elites rather than with farmers, fishers, laborers, or slaves, and therefore they include the biases of the ruling classes. In fact, according to James Deetz, a pioneer in historical archaeology of the Americas, in many historical contexts, "material culture may be the most objective source of information we have."[7]

ARCHAEOLOGICAL SUBSPECIALTIES

While archaeologists tend to specialize in particular culture zones or time periods, connected with particular regions of the world, a number of topical subspecialties also exist. **Bioarchaeology,** for instance, is the archaeological study of human remains, emphasizing the preservation of cultural and social processes in the skeleton. For example, mummified skeletal remains from the Andean highlands in South America not only preserve this burial practice but also provide evidence of some of the earliest brain surgery ever documented. In addition, these bioarchaeological remains exhibit skull deformation techniques that distinguish nobility from other members of society. Other archaeologists specialize in *ethnobotany,* studying how people of a given culture made use of indigenous plants. Still others specialize in *zooarchaeology,* tracking the animal remains recovered in archaeological excavations.

Although most archaeologists concentrate on the past, some of them study material objects in contemporary settings. One example is the Garbage Project, founded by William Rathje at the University of Arizona in 1973. This anthropological study of household waste of Tucson residents produced a wide range of thought-provoking information about contemporary social issues. For example, when surveyed by questionnaires, only 15 percent of households reported consuming beer, and no household reported consuming more than eight cans a week. Analysis of garbage from the same area showed that some beer was consumed in over 80 percent of the households, and 50 percent of households discarded more than eight cans per week.

In addition to providing actual data on beer consumption, the Garbage Project has tested the validity of research survey techniques, upon which sociologists, economists, other social scientists and policymakers rely heavily. The tests show a significant difference between what people *say* they do and what the garbage analysis shows they *actually* do. Therefore, ideas about human behavior based on simple survey techniques may be seriously in error.

In 1987, the Garbage Project began a program of excavating landfills in different parts of the United States and Canada. From this work came the first reliable data on what materials actually go into landfills and what happens to them there. And once again, common beliefs turned out to be at odds with the actual situation. For example, when buried in deep compost landfills, biodegradable materials such as newspapers take far longer to decay than anyone had expected. This kind of information is a vital step toward solving waste disposal problems.[8]

Ranging from technical to philosophical, the impact of the Garbage Project has been profound. Data from its landfill studies on hazardous waste and rates of decay of various materials play a major role in landfill regulation and management today. In terms of philosophy, the data gathered from the Garbage Project underscored the dire need for public recycling and composting that is now an accepted part of mainstream U.S. culture.

CULTURAL RESOURCE MANAGEMENT

While archaeology may conjure up images of ancient pyramids and the like, much archaeological fieldwork is carried out as **cultural resource management**. What

---

[7] Deetz, J. (1977). *In small things forgotten: The archaeology of early American life* (p. 160). Garden City, NY: Anchor/Doubleday.

[8] Details regarding the Garbage Project's history and legacy can be found at http://traumwerk.stanford.edu:3455/17/174.

---

bioarchaeology The archaeological study of human remains, emphasizing the preservation of cultural and social processes in the skeleton.

cultural resource management A branch of archaeology tied to government policies for the protection of cultural resources and involving surveying and/or excavating archaeological and historical remains threatened by construction or development.

distinguishes this work from traditional archaeological research is that it is specifically charged with preserving important aspects of a country's prehistoric and historic heritage. For example, in the United States, if the transportation department of a state government plans to replace an inadequate highway bridge, the state must first contract with archaeologists to identify and protect any significant prehistoric or historic resources that might be affected.

Since passage of the Historic Preservation Act of 1966, the National Environmental Policy Act of 1969, the Archaeological and Historical Preservation Act of 1974, and the Archaeological Resources Protection Act of 1979, cultural resource management is required for any construction project that is partially funded or licensed by the U.S. government. As a result, the field of cultural resource management has flourished. Many archaeologists are employed by such agencies as the Army Corps of Engineers, the National Park Service, the U.S. Forest Service, and the U.S. Natural Resource Conservation Service to assist in the preservation, restoration, and salvage of archaeological resources. Countries such as Canada and the United Kingdom have programs very similar to that of the United States, and from Chile to China, various governments use archaeological expertise to protect and manage their cultural heritage.

When cultural resource management work or other archaeological investigation unearths Native American cultural items or human remains, federal laws come into the picture again. The Native American Graves Protection and Repatriation Act (NAGPRA), passed in 1990, provides a process for the return of these remains to lineal descendants, culturally affiliated Indian tribes, and Native Hawaiian organizations. NAGPRA has become central to the work of anthropologists who study Paleo-Indian cultures in the United States. It has also been the source of controversy, such as that regarding Kennewick Man, a 9,300-year-old skeleton discovered near Kennewick, Washington, in 1996.

In addition to working in all the capacities mentioned, archaeologists also consult for engineering firms to help them prepare environmental impact statements. Some of these archaeologists operate out of universities and colleges, while others are on the staff of independent consulting firms. When state legislation sponsors any kind of archaeological work, it is referred to as *contract archaeology*.

empirical Based on observations of the world rather than on intuition or faith.
hypothesis A tentative explanation of the relationships between certain phenomena.

Anthropology, Science, and the Humanities

With its broad scope of subjects and methods, anthropology has sometimes been called the most humane of the sciences and the most scientific of the humanities—a designation that most anthropologists accept with pride. Given their intense involvement with people of all times and places, anthropologists have amassed considerable information about human failure and success, weakness and greatness—the real stuff of the humanities. While anthropologists steer clear of a cold, impersonal scientific approach that reduces people and the things they do and think to mere numbers, their quantitative studies have contributed substantially to the scientific study of the human condition. But even the most scientific anthropologists always keep in mind that human societies are made up of individuals with rich assortments of emotions and aspirations that demand respect.

Beyond this, anthropologists remain committed to the proposition that one cannot fully understand another culture by simply observing it; as the term *participant observation* implies, one must *experience* it as well. This same commitment to fieldwork and to the systematic collection of data, whether qualitative or quantitative, is also evidence of the scientific side of anthropology. Anthropology is an **empirical** social science based on observations or information about humans taken in through the senses and verified by others rather than on intuition or faith. But anthropology is distinguished from other sciences by the diverse ways in which scientific research is conducted within the discipline.

Science, a carefully honed way of producing knowledge, aims to reveal and explain the underlying logic, the structural processes that make the world tick. In their search for explanations, scientists do not assume that things are always as they appear on the surface. After all, what could be more obvious to the scientifically uninformed observer than the earth staying still while the sun travels around it every day? The creative scientific endeavor seeks testable explanations for observed phenomena, ideally in terms of the workings of hidden but unchanging principles or laws. Two basic ingredients are essential for this: imagination and skepticism. Imagination, though having the potential to lead us astray, helps us recognize unexpected ways phenomena might be ordered and to think of old things in new ways. Without it, there can be no science. Skepticism allows us to distinguish fact (an observation verified by others) from fancy, to test our speculations, and to prevent our imaginations from running wild.

Like other scientists, anthropologists often begin their research with a **hypothesis** (a tentative explanation or hunch) about the possible relationships between certain observed facts or events. By gathering various kinds of data that seem

Franz Boas (1858–1942) ■ *Matilda Coxe Stevenson (1849–1915)*

Franz Boas was not the first to teach anthropology in the United States, but it was Boas and his students, with their insistence on scientific rigor, who made anthropology courses common in college and university curricula. Born and raised in Germany where he studied physics, mathematics, and geography, Boas did his first ethnographic research among the Inuit (Eskimos) in arctic Canada in 1883 and 1884. After a brief academic career in Berlin, he came to the United States where he worked in museums interspersed with ethnographic research among the Kwakiutl (Kwakwaka'wakw) Indians in the Canadian Pacific. In 1896, he became a professor at Columbia University in New York City. He authored an incredible number of publications, founded professional organizations and journals, and taught two generations of great anthropologists, including numerous women and ethnic minorities.

As a Jewish immigrant, Boas recognized the dangers of ethnocentrism and especially racism. Through ethnographic fieldwork and comparative analysis, he demonstrated that white supremacy theories and other schemes ranking non-European peoples and cultures as inferior were biased, ill-informed, and unscientific. Throughout his long and illustrious academic career, he promoted anthropology not only as a human science but also as an instrument to combat racism and prejudice in the world.

Among the founders of North American anthropology were a number of women who were highly influential among women's rights advocates in the late 1800s. One such pioneering anthropologist was **Matilda Coxe Stevenson,** who did fieldwork among the Zuni Indians of Arizona. In 1885, she founded the Women's Anthropological Society in Washington, DC, the first professional association for women scientists. Three years later, hired by the Smithsonian's Bureau of American Ethnology, she became one of the first women in the world to receive a full-time official position in science.

The tradition of women being active in anthropology continues. In fact, since World War II more than half the presidents of the now 12,000-member American Anthropological Association have been women.

Recording observations on film as well as in notebooks, Stevenson and Boas were also pioneers in visual anthropology. Stevenson used an early box camera to document Pueblo Indian religious ceremonies and material culture, while Boas photographed Inuit (Eskimos) in northern Canada in 1883 and Kwakiutl Indians from the early 1890s for cultural as well as physical anthropological documentation. Today, these old photographs are greatly valued not only by anthropologists and historians, but also by indigenous peoples themselves.

Mathilda Cox Stevenson in New Mexico about 1895.

National Anthropological Archives Smithsonian 1895 Neg02871000

Franz Boas on a sailing ship circa 1925.

© Bildarchiv Preussischer Kulturbesitz/Art Resource, NY

to ground such suggested explanations on evidence, anthropologists come up with a **theory**—an explanation supported by a reliable body of data. In their effort to demonstrate links between *known* facts or events, anthropologists may discover *unexpected* facts, events, or relationships. An important function of theory is that it guides us in our explorations and may result in new knowledge. Equally important, the newly discovered facts may provide evidence that certain explanations, however popular or firmly believed, are unfounded. When the evidence is lacking or fails to support the suggested explanations, promising hypotheses or attractive hunches must be dropped. In other words, anthropology relies on empirical evidence. Moreover, no scientific theory—no matter how widely accepted by the international community of scholars—is beyond challenge.

It is important to distinguish between scientific theories—which are always open to future challenges born of new evidence or insights—and doctrine. A **doctrine**, or dogma, is an assertion of opinion or belief formally handed down by an authority as true and indisputable. For instance, those who accept a creationist doctrine on the origin of the human species as recounted in sacred texts or myths do so on the basis of religious authority;

theory In science, an explanation of natural phenomena, supported by a reliable body of data.

doctrine An assertion of opinion or belief formally handed down by an authority as true and indisputable.

they concede that their views may be contrary to explanations derived from genetics, geology, biology, or other sciences. Such doctrines cannot be tested or proved one way or another: They are accepted as matters of faith.

Straightforward though the scientific approach may seem, its application is not always easy. For instance, once a hypothesis has been proposed, the person who suggested it is strongly motivated to verify it, and this can cause one to unwittingly overlook negative evidence and unanticipated findings. This is a familiar problem in all science as noted by paleontologist Stephen Jay Gould: "The greatest impediment to scientific innovation is usually a conceptual lock, not a factual lock."[9] Because culture provides and shapes our very thoughts, it can be challenging to frame hypotheses or to develop interpretations that are not culture-bound. But by encompassing both humanism and science, the discipline of anthropology can draw on its internal diversity to overcome conceptual locks.

Fieldwork

All anthropologists think about whether their culture may have shaped the scientific questions they ask. In so doing, they rely heavily on a technique that has been successful in other disciplines: They immerse themselves in the data to the fullest extent possible. In the process, anthropologists become so thoroughly familiar with even the smallest details that they begin to recognize underlying patterns in the data, many of which might have been overlooked. Recognition of such patterns enables the anthropologist to frame meaningful hypotheses, which then may be subjected to further testing or validation in the field. Within anthropology, fieldwork provides additional rigor to the concept of total immersion in the data.

While fieldwork was introduced above in connection with cultural anthropology, it is characteristic of *all* the anthropological subdisciplines. Archaeologists and paleoanthropologists excavate in the field. A biological anthropologist interested in the effects of globalization on nutrition and growth will live in the field among a community of people to study this question. A primatologist might live among a group of chimpanzees or baboons just as a linguist would study the language of a culture by living in that community. Fieldwork, being fully immersed in another culture, challenges the anthropologist to be aware of the ways that cultural factors influence the research questions. Anthropological researchers monitor themselves by constantly checking their own biases and assumptions as they work; they present these self-reflections along with their observations, a practice known as *reflexivity*.

The validity or the reliability of a researcher's conclusions is established through the replication of observations and/or experiments by another researcher. Thus it becomes obvious if one's colleague has "gotten it right." But traditional validation by others is uniquely challenging in anthropology because observational access is often limited. Contact with a particular research site can be constrained by a number of factors. Difficulties of travel, obtaining permits, insufficient funding, or other conditions can interfere with access; also, what may be observed in a certain context at a certain time may not be observable at others. Thus one researcher cannot easily confirm the reliability or completeness of another's account. For this reason, anthropologists bear a special responsibility for accurate reporting. In the final research report, she or he must be clear about several basic issues: Why was a particular location selected as a research site? What were the research objectives? What were the local conditions during fieldwork? Which local individuals played a role in conducting the research? How were the data collected and recorded? How did the researcher check his or her own biases? Without such background information, it is difficult for others to judge the validity of the account and the soundness of the researcher's conclusions.

On a personal level, fieldwork requires the researcher to step out of his or her cultural comfort zone into a world that is unfamiliar and sometimes unsettling. Anthropologists in the field are likely to face a host of challenges—physical, social, mental, political, and ethical. They may have to deal with the physical challenge of adjusting to unaccustomed food, climate, and hygiene conditions. Typically, anthropologists in the field struggle with such mental challenges as being lonely, feeling like a perpetual outsider, being socially clumsy and clueless in their new cultural setting, and having to be alert around the clock because anything that is happening or being said may be significant to their research. Political challenges include the possibility of unwittingly letting oneself be used by factions within the community, or being viewed with suspicion by government authorities who may suspect the anthropologist is a spy. And there are ethical dilemmas as well: What does the anthropologist do if faced with a cultural practice he or she finds troubling, such as female circumcision? How does one deal with demands for food supplies and/or medicine? And is the fieldworker ever justified in using deception to gain vital information? Many such ethical questions arise in anthropological fieldwork.

At the same time, fieldwork often leads to tangible and meaningful personal, professional, and social rewards, ranging from lasting friendships to vital knowledge and insights concerning the human condition that make positive contributions to people's lives. Something of the meaning of anthropological fieldwork—its usefulness and its impact

---

[9] Gould, S. J. (1989). *Wonderful life* (p. 226). New York: Norton.

on researcher and subject—is conveyed in the following Original Study by Suzanne Leclerc-Madlala, an anthropologist who left her familiar New England surroundings about twenty-five years ago to do AIDS research among Zulu-speaking people in South Africa. Her research interest has changed the course of her own life, not to mention the lives of individuals who have AIDS/HIV and the type of treatment they receive.

Original Study

Fighting HIV/AIDS in Africa: Traditional Healers on the Front Line

by Suzanne Leclerc-Madlala

In the 1980s, as a North American anthropology graduate student at George Washington University, I met and married a Zulu-speaking student from South Africa. It was the height of apartheid, and upon moving to that country I was classified as "honorary black" and forced to live in a segregated township with my husband. The AIDS epidemic was in its

infancy, but it was clear from the start that an anthropological understanding of how people perceive and engage with this disease would be crucial for developing interventions. I wanted to learn all that I could to make a difference, and this culminated in earning a PhD from the University of Natal on the cultural construction of AIDS among the Zulu. The HIV/AIDS pandemic in Africa became my professional passion.

Faced with overwhelming global health-care needs, the World Health Organization passed a series of resolutions in the 1970s promoting collaboration between traditional and modern medicine. Such moves held a special relevance for Africa where traditional healers typically outnumber practitioners of modern medicine by a ratio of 100 to 1 or more. Given Africa's disproportionate burden of disease, supporting partnership efforts with traditional healers makes sense. But what sounds sensible today was once considered absurd, even heretical. For centuries Westerners generally viewed traditional healing as a whole lot

of primitive mumbo jumbo practiced by witchdoctors with demonic powers who perpetuated superstition. Yet, its practice survived. Today, as the African continent grapples with an HIV/AIDS epidemic of crisis proportion, millions of sick people who are either too poor or too distant to access modern health care are proving that traditional healers are an invaluable resource in the fight against AIDS.

Of the world's estimated 40 million people currently infected by HIV, 70 percent live in sub-Saharan Africa, and the vast majority of children left orphaned by AIDS are African. From the 1980s onward, as Africa became synonymous with the rapid spread of HIV/AIDS, a number of prevention programs involved traditional healers. My initial research in South Africa's KwaZulu-Natal province—where it is estimated that 36 percent of the population is HIV infected—revealed that traditional Zulu healers were regularly consulted for the treatment of sexually transmitted disease (STD). I found that such diseases, along with HIV/AIDS, were usually attributed to transgressions of taboos related to birth, pregnancy, marriage, and death. Moreover, these diseases were often understood within a framework of pollution and contagion, and like most serious illnesses, ultimately believed to have their causal roots in witchcraft.

In the course of my research, I investigated a pioneer program in STD and HIV education for traditional healers in the province. The program aimed to provide basic biomedical knowledge about the various modes of disease transmission, the means available for prevention, the diagnosing of symptoms, the keeping of records, and the making of patient referrals to local clinics and hospitals.

Interviews with the healers showed that many maintained a deep suspicion of modern medicine. They perceived AIDS education as a one-way street intended to press them into formal health structures and convince them of the superiority of modern medicine. Yet, today, few of the 6,000-plus KwaZulu-Natal

Medical anthropologist Suzanne Leclerc-Madlala visits with "Doctor" Koloko in KwaZulu-Natal, South Africa. This Zulu traditional healer proudly displays her official AIDS training certificate.

CONTINUED

CONTINUED

healers who have been trained in AIDS education say they would opt for less collaboration; most want to have more.

Treatments by Zulu healers for HIV/AIDS often take the form of infusions of bitter herbs to "cleanse" the body, strengthen the blood, and remove misfortune and "pollution." Some treatments provide effective relief from common ailments associated with AIDS such as itchy skin rashes, oral thrush, persistent diarrhea, and general debility. Indigenous plants such as unwele (Sutherlandia frutescens) and African potato (Hypoxis hemerocallidea) are well-known traditional medicines that have proven immuno-boosting properties.

Both have recently become available in modern pharmacies packaged in tablet form. With modern anti-retroviral treatments still well beyond the reach of most South Africans, indigenous medicines that can delay or alleviate some of the suffering caused by AIDS are proving to be valuable and popular treatments.

Knowledge about potentially infectious bodily fluids has led healers to change some of their practices. Where porcupine quills were once used to give a type of indigenous injection, patients are now advised to bring their own sewing needles to consultations. Patients provide their own individual razor blades for making incisions on their skin, where previously healers reused the same razor on many clients. Some healers claim they have given up the practice of biting

clients' skin to remove foreign objects from the body. It is not uncommon today, especially in urban centers like Durban, to find healers proudly displaying AIDS training certificates in their inner-city "surgeries" where they don white jackets and wear protective latex gloves.

Politics and controversy have dogged South Africa's official response to HIV/AIDS. But back home in the waddle-and-daub, animal-skin-draped herbariums and divining huts of traditional healers, the politics of AIDS holds little relevance. Here the sick and dying are coming in droves to be treated by healers who have been part and parcel of community life (and death) since time immemorial. In many cases traditional healers have transformed their homes into hospices for AIDS patients. Because of the strong stigma that still plagues the disease, those with AIDS symptoms are often abandoned or sometimes chased away from their homes by family members. They seek refuge with healers who provide them with comfort in their final days. Healers' homes are also becoming orphanages as healers respond to what has been called the "third wave" of AIDS destruction: the growing legions of orphaned children.

The practice of traditional healing in Africa is adapting to the changing face of health and illness in the context of HIV/AIDS. But those who are suffering go to traditional healers not only in search of relief for physical symptoms. They go to learn about the ultimate cause of their disease—something other than the

immediate cause of a sexually transmitted "germ" or "virus." They go to find answers to the "why me and not him" questions, the "why now" and "why this." As with most traditional healing systems worldwide, healing among the Zulu and most all African ethnic groups cannot be separated from the spiritual concerns of the individual and the cosmological beliefs of the community at large. Traditional healers help to restore a sense of balance between the individual and the community, on one hand, and between the individual and the cosmos, or ancestors, on the other hand. They provide health care that is personalized, culturally appropriate, holistic, and tailored to meet the needs and expectations of the patient. In many ways it is a far more satisfactory form of healing than that offered by modern medicine.

Traditional healing in Africa is flourishing in the era of AIDS, and understanding why this is so requires a shift in the conceptual framework by which we understand, explain, and interpret health. Anthropological methods and its comparative and holistic perspective can facilitate, like no other discipline, the type of understanding that is urgently needed to address the AIDS crisis.

Adapted from: Leclerc-Madlala, S. (2002). Bodies and politics: Healing rituals in the democratic South Africa. In V. Faure (Ed.), Les cahiers de 'l'IFAS, no. 2. Johannesburg: The French Institute. (Leclerc-Madlala now works for USAID.)

Anthropology's Comparative Method

The end product of anthropological research, if properly carried out, is a coherent statement about a people that provides an explanatory framework for understanding the beliefs, behavior, or biology of those who have been studied. And this, in turn, is what permits the anthropologist to frame broader hypotheses about human beliefs, behavior, and biology. A single instance of any phenomenon is generally insufficient for supporting a plausible hypothesis. Without some basis for comparison, the hypothesis grounded in a single case may be no more than a particular historical coincidence. On the other hand, a single case may be enough to cast doubt on, if not refute, a theory that had previously been held to be valid. For example, the discovery in 1948 that Aborigines living in Australia's northern Arnhem Land put in an average workday of less than

6 hours, while living well above a bare-sufficiency level, was enough to call into question the widely accepted notion that food-foraging peoples are so preoccupied with finding scarce food that they lack time for any of life's more pleasurable activities. The observations made in the Arnhem Land study have since been confirmed many times over in various parts of the world.

To test hypothetical explanations of cultural and biological phenomena, researchers compare data gathered from several societies found in a region; these data are derived from a variety of approaches, including archaeology, biology, linguistics, history, and ethnography. Carefully controlled comparison provides a broader basis for drawing general conclusions about humans than does the study of a single culture or population.

Ideally, theories in anthropology are generated from worldwide comparisons or comparisons across species or through time. The cross-cultural researcher examines a global sample of societies in order to discover whether hypotheses proposed to explain cultural phenomena or biological variation are universally applicable. The cross-cultural researcher depends upon data gathered by other scholars as well as his or her own. These data can be in the form of written accounts, artifacts and skeletal collections housed in museums, published descriptions of these collections, or recently constructed databases that allow for cross-species comparisons of the molecular structure of specific genes or proteins.

Questions of Ethics

The kinds of research carried out by anthropologists, and the settings within which they work, raise a number of important moral questions about the potential uses and abuses of our knowledge. In the early years of the discipline, many anthropologists documented traditional cultures they assumed would disappear due to disease, warfare, or acculturation imposed by colonialism, growing state power, or international market expansion. Some worked as government anthropologists, gathering data used to formulate policies concerning indigenous peoples or even to help predict the behavior of enemies during wartime. After the colonial era ended in the 1960s, anthropologists began to establish a code of ethics to ensure their research did not harm the groups they studied.

Today, this code grapples with serious questions: Who will utilize our findings and for what purposes? Who decides what research questions are asked? Who, if anyone, will profit from the research? For example, in the case of research on an ethnic or religious minority whose values may be at odds with the dominant mainstream society, will government or corporate interests use anthropological data to suppress that group? And what of traditional communities around the world? Who is to decide what changes should, or should not, be introduced for community "betterment"? And who defines what constitutes betterment—the community, a national government, or an international agency like the World Health Organization? What are the limits of cultural relativism when a traditional practice is considered a human rights abuse globally?

Today, many universities require that anthropologists, like other researchers, communicate in advance the nature, purpose, and potential impact of the planned study to individuals who provide information—and obtain their **informed consent,** or formal recorded agreement to participate in the research. Of course, this requirement is easier to fulfill in some societies or cultures than in others. When it is a challenge to obtain informed consent, or even impossible to precisely explain the meaning and purpose of this concept and its actual consequences, anthropologists may protect the identities of individuals, families, or even entire communities by altering their names and locations. For example, when Dutch anthropologist Anton Blok studied the Sicilian mafia, he did not obtain the informed consent of this violent secret group but opted not to disclose their real identities.[10]

Anthropologists deal with matters that are private and sensitive, including things that individuals would prefer not to have generally known about them. How does one write about such important but delicate issues and at the same time protect the privacy of the individuals who have shared their stories?

The dilemma facing anthropologists is also recognized in the preamble to the code of ethics of the American Anthropological Association (AAA), which was formalized in 1971 and revised in 1998 and again in 2009. This document outlines the various ethical responsibilities and moral obligations of anthropologists, including this central maxim: "Anthropological researchers must do everything in their power to ensure that their research does not harm the safety, dignity, or privacy of the people with whom they work, conduct research, or perform other professional activities." The recent healthy round of debates regarding this code has focused on the potential ethical breaches if anthropologists undertake classified contract work for the military, as some have in Afghanistan, or work for corporations. Some argue that in both cases the required transparency to the people studied cannot be maintained under these circumstances.

The AAA ethics statement is an educational document that lays out the rules and ideals applicable to anthropologists in all the subdisciplines. While the AAA has no legal authority, it does issue policy statements on research ethics questions as they come up. For example, recently the AAA recommended that field notes from medical settings should be protected and not subject to subpoena in malpractice lawsuits. This honors the ethical imperative to protect the privacy of individuals who have shared their stories with anthropologists.

---

[10] Blok, A. (1974). *The mafia of a Sicilian village 1860–1960: A study of violent peasant entrepreneurs.* New York: Harper & Row.

informed consent Formal recorded agreement to participate in research; federally mandated for all research in the United States and Europe.

The consumption habits of people in more temperate parts of the world are threatening the lifestyle of people from circumpolar regions. As global warming melts the polar ice caps, traditional ways of life, such as building an igloo, may become impossible. This Inuit man—in Iqaluit, the capital of the Canadian territory of Nunavut—may not be able to construct an igloo much longer. Therefore, the Inuit people consider global warming a human rights issue.

© The Canadian Press (Kevin Frayer)

Emerging technologies have ethical implications that impact anthropological inquiry. For example, the ability to sequence and patent particular genes has led to debates about who has the right to hold a patent—the individuals from whom the particular genes were obtained or the researcher who studies the genes? Given the radical changes taking place in the world today, a scientific understanding of the past has never been more important. Do ancient remains belong to the scientist, to the people living in the region under scientific investigation, or to whoever happens to have possession of them? Market forces convert these remains into very expensive collectibles and lead to systematic mining of archaeological and fossil sites. Collaboration between local people and scientists not only preserves the ancient remains from market forces but also honors the connections of indigenous people to the places and remains under study.

To sort out the answers to the all of the above questions, anthropologists recognize that they have special obligations to three sets of people: those whom they study, those who fund the research, and those in the profession who rely on published findings to increase our collective knowledge. Because fieldwork requires a relationship of trust between fieldworkers and the community in which they work, the anthropologist's first responsibility clearly is to the people who have shared their stories and the greater community. Everything possible must be done to protect their physical, social, and psychological welfare and to honor their dignity and privacy.

This task is frequently complex. For example, telling the story of a people gives information both to relief agencies who might help them and to others who might take advantage of them. While anthropologists regard a people's right to maintain their own culture as a basic premise, any connections with outsiders can endanger the cultural identity of the community being studied. To surmount these obstacles, anthropologists frequently collaborate with and contribute to the communities in which they are working, allowing the people being studied to have some say about how their stories are told.

Anthropology and Globalization

A holistic perspective and a long-term commitment to understanding the human species in all its variety are the essence of anthropology. Thus anthropology is well equipped to grapple with an issue that has overriding importance for all of us at the beginning of the 21st century: **globalization.** This term refers to worldwide interconnectedness, evidenced in global movements of natural resources, trade goods, human labor, finance capital, information, and infectious diseases. Although worldwide travel, trade relations, and information flow have existed for several centuries, the pace and magnitude of these

globalization Worldwide interconnectedness, evidenced in global movements of natural resources, trade goods, human labor, finance capital, information, and infectious diseases.

Globalscape

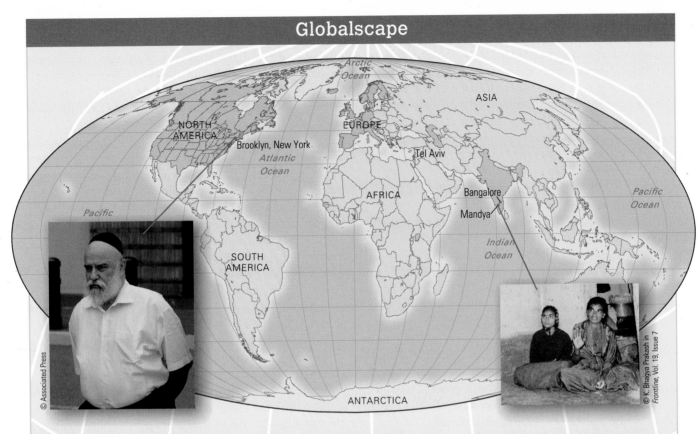

© Associated Press

© K. Bhagya Prakash in *Frontline*, Vol. 19, Issue 7

A Global Body Shop?

Lakshmamma, a mother in southern India's rural village of Holalu, near Mandya, has sold one of her kidneys for about 30,000 rupees ($650). This is far below the average going rate of $6,000 per kidney in the global organ transplant business. But the broker took his commission, and corrupt officials needed to be paid as well. Although India passed a law in 1994 prohibiting the buying and selling of human organs, the business is booming. In Europe and North America, kidney transplants can cost $200,000 or more, plus the waiting list for donor kidneys is long, and dialysis is expensive. Thus "transplant tourism," in India and several other countries, caters to affluent patients in search of "fresh" kidneys to be harvested from poor people like Lakshmamma, pictured here with her daughter.

The global trade network in organs has been documented by Israeli filmmaker Nick Rosen, who sold his own kidney for $15,000 through a broker in Tel Aviv to a Brooklyn, New York, dialysis patient. Rosen explained to the physicians at Mt. Sinai Hospital in New York City that he was donating his kidney altruistically. Medical anthropologist Nancy Scheper-Hughes has taken on the criminal and medical aspects of global organ trafficking for the past twenty years or so. She also co-founded Organs Watch in Berkeley, California, an organization working to stop the illegal traffic in organs.

The well-publicized arrest of Brooklyn-based organ broker Levy Izhak Rosenbaum in July 2009—part of an FBI sting operation that also led to the arrest of forty-three other individuals, including several public officials in New Jersey—represents progress made in combating illegal trafficking of body parts. According to Scheper-Hughes, "Rosenbaum wasn't the tip of an iceberg, but the end of something."[a] International crackdowns and changes in local laws are beginning to bring down these illegal global networks.

Global Twister   Considering that $650 is a fortune in a poor village like Holalu, does medical globalization benefit or exploit people like Lakshmamma who are looked upon as human commodities? What factors account for the different values placed on the two donated kidneys?

---

[a] http://www.npr.org/templates/story/story.php?storyId=106997368.

long-distance exchanges have picked up enormously in recent decades; the Internet, in particular, has greatly expanded information exchange capacities.

The powerful forces driving globalization are technological innovations, cost differences among countries, faster knowledge transfers, and increased trade and financial integration among countries. Touching almost everybody's life on the planet, globalization is about economics as much as politics, and it changes human relations and ideas as well as our natural environments. Even geographically remote communities are quickly becoming interdependent through globalization.

Doing research in all corners of the world, anthropologists are confronted with the impact of globalization on human communities wherever they are located. As participant observers, they describe and try to explain how individuals and organizations respond to the massive changes confronting them. Anthropologists may also find out how local responses sometimes change the global flows directed at them. Dramatically increasing every year, globalization can be a two-edged sword. It may generate economic growth and prosperity, but it also undermines long-established institutions. Generally, globalization has brought significant gains to higher-educated groups in wealthier countries, while doing little to boost developing countries and actually contributing to the erosion of traditional cultures. Upheavals due to globalization are key causes for rising levels of ethnic and religious conflict throughout the world.

Since all of us now live in a global village, we can no longer afford the luxury of ignoring our neighbors, no matter how distant they may seem. In this age of globalization, anthropology may not only provide humanity with useful insights concerning diversity, but it may also assist us in avoiding or overcoming significant problems born of that diversity. In countless social arenas, from schools to businesses to hospitals to emergency centers, anthropologists have done cross-cultural research that makes it possible for educators, businesspeople, doctors, and humanitarians to do their work more effectively.

For example, in the United States today, discrimination based on notions of race continues to be a serious issue affecting economic, political, and social relations. Far from being the biological reality it is supposed to be, anthropologists have shown that the concept of race (and the classification of human groups into higher and lower racial types) emerged in the 18th century as an ideological vehicle for justifying European dominance over Africans and American Indians. In fact, differences of skin color are simply surface adaptations to different climactic zones and have nothing to do with physical or mental capabilities. Indeed, geneticists find far more biologic variation *within* any given human population than *among* them. In short, human "races" are divisive categories based on prejudice, false ideas of differences, and erroneous notions of the superiority of one's own group. Given the importance of this issue, race and other aspects of biologic variation will be discussed further in upcoming sections of the text.

A second example of the impact of globalization involves the issue of same-sex marriage. In 1989, Denmark became the first country to enact a comprehensive set of legal protections for same-sex couples, known as the Registered Partnership Act. At this writing, more than a half-dozen other countries and a growing number of individual U.S. states have passed similar laws, variously named, and numerous countries around the world are considering or have passed legislation providing people in homosexual unions the benefits and protections

afforded by marriage.[11] In some societies—including Belgium, Canada, the Netherlands, Norway, South Africa, Spain, and Sweden—same-sex marriages are considered socially acceptable and allowed by law, even though opposite-sex marriages are far more common. The same is true for several U.S. states including Connecticut, Iowa, Massachusetts, New Hampshire, and Vermont.

As individuals, countries, and states struggle to define the boundaries of legal protections they will grant to same-sex couples, the anthropological perspective on marriage is useful. Anthropologists have documented same-sex marriages in human societies in various parts of the world, where they are regarded as acceptable under appropriate circumstances. Homosexual behavior occurs in the animal world just as it does among humans.[12] The key difference between people and other animals is that human societies possess beliefs regarding homosexual behavior, just as they do for heterosexual behavior. An understanding of global variation in marriage patterns and sexual behavior does not dictate that one pattern is more right than another. It simply illustrates that all human societies define the boundaries for social relationships.

A final example relates to the common confusion of *nation* with *state*. Anthropology makes an important distinction between these two: States are politically organized territories that are internationally recognized, whereas nations are socially organized bodies of people who share ethnicity—a common origin, language, and cultural heritage. For example, the Kurds constitute a nation, but their homeland is divided among several states: Iran, Iraq, Turkey, and Syria. The international boundaries among these states were drawn up after World War I, with little regard for the region's ethnic groups or nations. Similar processes have taken place throughout the world, especially in Asia and Africa, often making political conditions in these countries inherently unstable. As we will see in later chapters, states and nations rarely coincide—nations being split among different states, and states typically being controlled by members of one nation who commonly use their control to gain access to the land, resources, and labor of other nationalities within the state. Most of the armed conflicts in the world today, such as the many-layered conflicts in the Caucasus Mountains of Russia's

[11] Merin, Y. (2002). *Equality for same-sex couples: The legal recognition of gay partnerships in Europe and the United States.* Chicago: University of Chicago Press; "Court says same-sex marriage is a right." (2004, February 5). *San Francisco Chronicle;* current overviews and updates on the global status of same-sex marriage are posted on the Internet by the Partners Task Force for Gay & Lesbian Couples at www.buddybuddy.com.

[12] Kirkpatrick, R. C. (2000). The evolution of human homosexual behavior. *Current Anthropology 41,* 384.

southern borderlands, are of this sort and are not mere acts of "tribalism" or "terrorism," as commonly asserted.

As these examples show, ignorance about other cultures and their ways is a cause of serious problems throughout the world, especially now that our interactions and interdependence have been transformed by global information exchange and transportation advances. Anthropology offers a way of looking at and understanding the world's peoples—insights that are nothing less than basic skills for survival in this age of globalization.

Questions for Reflection

1. Anthropology uses a holistic approach to explain all aspects of human beliefs, behavior, and biology. How might anthropology challenge your personal perspective on the following questions: Where did we come from? Why do we act in certain ways? Does the example of legalized paid surrogacy, featured in the chapter opener, challenge your worldview?

2. From the holistic anthropological perspective, humans have one leg in culture and the other in nature. Are there examples from your life that illustrate the interconnectedness of human biology and culture?

3. Globalization can be described as a two-edged sword. How does it foster growth and destruction simultaneously?

4. The textbook definitions of *state* and *nation* are based on scientific distinctions between both organizational types. However, this distinction is commonly lost in everyday language. Consider, for instance, the names *United States of America* and *United Nations*. How does confusing the terms contribute to political conflict?

5. The Biocultural Connection in this chapter contrasts different cultural perspectives on brain death, while the Original Study features a discussion about traditional Zulu healers and their role in dealing with AIDS victims. What do these two accounts suggest about the role of applied anthropology in dealing with cross-cultural health issues around the world?

Suggested Readings

Bonvillain, N. (2007). *Language, culture, and communication: The meaning of messages* (5th ed.). Upper Saddle River, NJ: Prentice-Hall.

An up-to-date text on language and communication in a cultural context.

Fagan, B. M. (2005). *Archaeology: A brief introduction* (9th ed.). New York: Longman.

This primer offers an overview of archaeological theory and methodology, from field survey techniques to excavation to analysis of materials.

Kedia, S., & Van Willigen, J. (2005). *Applied anthropology: Domains of application.* New York: Praeger.

Compelling essays by prominent scholars on the potential, accomplishments, and methods of applied anthropology in domains including development, agriculture, environment, health and medicine, nutrition, population displacement and resettlement, business and industry, education, and aging. The contributors show how anthropology can be used to address today's social, economic, health, and technical challenges.

Marks, J. (2009). *Why I am not a scientist: Anthropology and modern knowledge.* Berkeley: University of California Press.

With his inimitable wit and deep philosophical insights, biological anthropologist Jonathan Marks shows the immense power of bringing an anthropological perspective to the culture of science.

Peacock, J. L. (2002). *The anthropological lens: Harsh light, soft focus* (2nd ed.). New York: Cambridge University Press.

This lively and innovative book gives the reader a good understanding of the diversity of activities undertaken by cultural anthropologists, while at the same time identifying the unifying themes that hold the discipline together. Additions to the second edition include such topics as globalization, gender, and postmodernism.

Challenge Issue The genetics revolution has given new meaning to human identity. Police identify criminals through DNA fingerprinting and maintain DNA databases of convicts and suspects for solving crimes in the future. Others wrongfully imprisoned for many years have been freed after genetic testing. But the thornier issue in genetics is whether genes can predispose an individual to criminal behavior. Do our genes determine our actions? Some scientists argue that biology controls behavior because of hints found in the genome, the complete sequence of human DNA. These new theories are dangerously similar to those proposed in the late 19th and early 20th centuries, as they do not take into account the social and political environments in which genes are ultimately expressed. As we learn more about the human genetic code, will we reshape our understanding of what it means to be human? How much of our lives are dictated by the structure of DNA? And what will be the social consequences of depicting people as beings programmed by their DNA? Individuals and societies can answer these challenging questions using an anthropological perspective, which emphasizes the connections between human biology and culture.

CHAPTER 2

Genetics and Evolution

Chapter Preview

What Is Evolution?

Although all living creatures ultimately share a common ancestry, they have come to differ from one another through the process of evolution. Biological evolution refers to genetic change over successive generations. The process of change is characterized by descent with modification, as descendant populations diverge from ancestral ones. As a population's genetic variation changes from one generation to another, genetic change is reflected in visible differences between organisms. With sufficient genetic change, a new species can appear. Thus, the process of evolution provides a mechanism to account for the diversity of life on earth.

What Is the Molecular Basis of Evolution?

Scientists began to understand the mechanics of heredity and how evolution works in populations long before molecular biologists identified the genetic basis of evolutionary change. With the discovery of DNA (deoxyribonucleic acid) molecules in 1953, scientists came to understand how genetic information is stored in the chromosomes of a cell. Genes, specific portions of DNA molecules, direct the synthesis of the protein molecules upon which all living organisms depend. Through the process of biological reproduction, each of us inherits a combination of genes from our biological parents that creates a unique new individual.

What Are the Forces Responsible for Evolution?

Four evolutionary forces—mutation, genetic drift, gene flow, and natural selection—account for change in the genetic composition of populations. Random mutations introduce new genetic variation into individual organisms. Gene flow (the introduction of new gene variants from other populations), genetic drift (random changes in frequencies of gene variants in a population), and natural selection shape genetic variation at the population level. Natural selection is the mechanism of evolution that results in adaptive change, favoring individuals with genetic variants relatively better adapted to the conditions of local environments.

The mythology of most peoples includes a story explaining the appearance of humans on earth. The account of creation recorded in Genesis in the Bible, for example, explains human origins. A vastly different example, serving the same function, is the traditional belief of the Nez Perce, American Indians native to eastern Oregon and Idaho. For the Nez Perce, humanity is the creation of Coyote, a trickster-transformer inhabiting the earth before humans. Coyote chased the giant beaver monster Wishpoosh over the earth, leaving a trail to form the Columbia River. When Coyote caught Wishpoosh, he killed him, dragged his body to the riverbank, and cut it into pieces, each body part transforming into one of the various peoples of this region. The Nez Perce were made from Wishpoosh's head, thus conferring on them great intelligence and horsemanship.[1]

Creation stories depict the relationship between humans and the rest of the natural world, sometimes reflecting a deep connection among people, other animals, and the earth. In the traditional Nez Perce creation story, groups of people derive from specific body parts—each possessing a special talent and relationship with a particular animal. By contrast, the story of creation in the Book of Genesis emphasizes human uniqueness and the concept of time. Creation is depicted as a series of actions occurring over the course of six days. God's final act of creation is to fashion the first human from the earth in his own image before the seventh day of rest.

This linear creation story from Genesis—shared by Jews, Christians, and Muslims—differs from the cyclical creation stories characteristic of Hinduism, which emphasize reincarnation and the cycle of life, including creation and destruction. For Hindus, the diversity of life on earth comes from three gods—Lord Brahma, the creator; Lord Vishnu, the preserver; and Lord Shiva, the destroyer and re-creator—all of whom are part of the Supreme One. When Lord Brahma sleeps the world is destroyed, then re-created again when he awakes. Similarly, according to the Intelligent Design movement—proposed by a conservative think tank called the Discovery Institute in Seattle, Washington—creation is the result of some sort of supreme intelligent being.

Like creation stories, evolution, the major organizing principle of the biological sciences, accounts for the diversity of life on earth. Theories of evolution provide explanations for how it works and for how the variety of organisms, both in the past and today, came into being. However, evolution differs from creation stories in that it explains the diversity of life in consistent scientific language, using testable ideas (hypotheses). Contemporary scientists make comparisons among living organisms to test hypotheses drawn from evolutionary theory. Through their research, scientists have deciphered the molecular basis of evolution and the mechanisms through which evolutionary forces work on populations of organisms. Though scientific theories of evolution treat humans as biological organisms, at the same time historical and cultural processes also shape evolutionary theory and our understanding of it.

The Classification of Living Things

Examining the development of biology and its central concept, evolution, provides an excellent example of the ways that historical and cultural processes can shape scientific thought. As the exploration of foreign lands by European seafarers, including Columbus, changed the prevailing European approach to the natural world, the discovery of new life forms challenged the previously held notion of fixed, unchanging life on earth. As well, the invention of instruments, such as the microscope to study the previously invisible interior of cells, led to new appreciation of life's diversity.

Before this time, Europeans organized living things and inanimate objects alike into a ladder or hierarchy known as the Great Chain of Being—an approach to nature first developed by the great philosopher Aristotle in ancient Greece over 2,000 years ago. The categories were based upon visible similarities, and one member of each category was considered its "primate" (from the Latin *primus*), meaning the first or best of the group. For example, the primate of rocks was the diamond, and the primate of birds was the eagle, and so forth. Humans were at the very top of the ladder, just below the angels.

This classificatory system was in place until Carl von Linné (using the Latin-form name Carolus Linnaeus) developed the *Systema Naturae,* or system of nature, in the 18th century to classify the living things that were being brought back to Europe on seafaring vessels from all parts of the globe. Linnaeus's compendium reflected a new understanding of life on earth and of the place of humanity among the animals.

Linnaeus noted the similarity among humans, monkeys, and apes, classifying them together as **primates.** Not the first or the best of the animals on earth, primates are just one of several kinds of **mammal,** animals having body hair or fur who suckle or nurse their young. In other

---

[1] Clark, E. E. (1966). *Indian legends of the Pacific Northwest* (p. 174). Berkeley: University of California Press.

primate   The group of mammals that includes lemurs, lorises, tarsiers, monkeys, apes, and humans.

mammal   The class of vertebrate animals distinguished by bodies covered with fur, self-regulating temperature, and, in females, milk-producing mammary glands.

Lindauer Bilderbogen no 5, edited by Friedrich Boer. Jan Thorbecke Verlag. Sigmaringen, West Germany

A professor of medicine and botany in Sweden, Carolus Linnaeus, who created the first comprehensive system of living things, also prepared and prescribed medicinal plants, as did other physicians of the time. He arranged for his students to join the major European voyages, such as Captain James Cook's first round-the-world voyage, so they could bring back new medicinal plants and other life forms. Through his observation of the bloom times of some plant species, Linnaeus proposed a "flower clock" that could show the time of day according to whether blossoms of particular species were open or shut.

words, Linnaeus classified living things into a series of categories that are progressively more inclusive on the basis of internal and external visual similarities. **Species**, the smallest working units in biological classificatory systems, are reproductively isolated populations or groups of populations capable of interbreeding to produce fertile offspring. Species are subdivisions of a larger, more inclusive group, called a **genus** (plural, **genera**). Humans, for example, are classified in the genus *Homo* and species *sapiens*. This binomial nomenclature, or two-part naming system, mirrors the naming patterns in many European societies where individuals possess two names—one personal and the other reflecting their membership in a larger group of related individuals.

Linnaeus based his classificatory system on the following criteria:

1. *Body structure:* A Guernsey cow and a Holstein cow are the same species because, unlike a cow and a horse, they have identical body structure.
2. *Body function:* Cows and horses give birth to live young. Although they are different species, they are

closer than either cows or horses are to chickens, which lay eggs and have no mammary glands.
3. *Sequence of bodily growth:* At the time of birth—or hatching out of the egg—young cows and chickens resemble their parents in their body plan. They are therefore more closely related to each other than either one is to the frog, whose tadpoles undergo a series of changes before attaining the basic adult form.

Modern **taxonomy,** or the science of classification (from the Greek for naming divisions), while retaining the structure of the Linnaean system, is based on more than body structure, function, and growth. Today, scientists also compare protein structure and genetic material to construct the relationships among living things. Such molecular comparisons can even be aimed at parasites, bacteria, and viruses, allowing scientists to classify or trace the origins of particular diseases, such as swine flu, SARS (sudden acute respiratory syndrome), or HIV (human immunodeficiency virus). An emphasis on genetics rather than morphology has led to a reworking of taxonomic designation in the human family, among others, as is described in Table 2.1. Alternative taxonomies based on genetics compared to body form in the primate order will be discussed in detail in the next chapter.

Cross-species comparisons identify anatomical features of similar function as **analogies,** while anatomical features that have evolved from a common ancestral feature are called **homologies.** For example, the hand of a human and the wing of a bat evolved from the forelimb of a common ancestor, though they have acquired different functions: The human hand and bat wing are homologous structures. During their early embryonic development, homologous structures arise in a similar fashion and pass through similar stages before differentiating. The wings of birds and butterflies look similar and have a similar function (flying): These are analogous, but not homologous, structures because they do not follow the same

species The smallest working units in the system of classification. Among living organisms, species are populations or groups of populations capable of interbreeding and producing fertile viable offspring.

genus (genera, pl.) In the system of plant and animal classification, a group of like species.

taxonomy The science of classification.

analogies In biology, structures possessed by different organisms that are superficially similar due to similar function, without sharing a common developmental pathway or structure.

homologies In biology, structures possessed by two different organisms that arise in similar fashion and pass through similar stages during embryonic development though they may possess different functions.

Table 2.1 Classification of Humans

Taxonomic Category	Category to Which Humans Belong	Biological Features Used to Define and Place Humans in This Category
Kingdom	Animalia	Humans are animals. We do not make our own food (as plants do) but depend upon the consumption of other organisms.
Phylum	Chordata	Humans are chordates. We have a **notochord** (a rodlike structure of cartilage) and nerve chord running along the back of the body as well as gill slits in the embryonic stage of our life cycle.
Subphylum*	Vertebrata	Humans are vertebrates possessing an internal backbone, with a segmented spinal column.
Class	Mammalia	Humans are mammals, warm-blooded animals covered with fur, possessing mammary glands for nourishing their young after birth.
Order	Primates	Humans are primates, a kind of mammal with a generalized anatomy, relatively large brains, and grasping hands and feet.
Suborder	Anthropoidea	Humans are anthropoids—social, daylight-active primates. (An alternative suborder taxonomic system is discussed in Chapter 3.)
Superfamily	Hominoidea	Humans are hominoids with broad flexible shoulders and no tail. Chimps, bonobos, gorillas, orangutans, gibbons, and siamangs are also hominoids.
Family Subfamily	Hominidae Homininae	Humans are hominids. We are hominoids from Africa, genetically more closely related to chimps, bonobos, and gorillas than to hominoids from Asia. Some scientists use "hominid" to refer only to humans and their ancestors. Others include chimps and gorillas in this category, using the subfamily "hominin" to distinguish humans and their ancestors from chimps and gorillas and their ancestors. (The alternative taxonomies at the subfamily level are explored further in Chapter 3.)
Genus Species	*Homo sapiens*	Humans have large brains and rely on cultural adaptations to survive. Ancestral fossils are placed in this genus and species depending upon details of the skull shape and interpretations of their cultural capabilities. Genus and species names are always italicized.

*Most categories can be expanded or narrowed by adding the prefix "sub" or "super." A family could thus be part of a superfamily and in turn contain two or more subfamilies.

Visual Counterpoint

An example of homology: The same bones of the mammalian forelimb differentiate into the human arm and hand and the bat wing. These structures have the same embryonic origin but come to take on different functions.

Visual Counterpoint

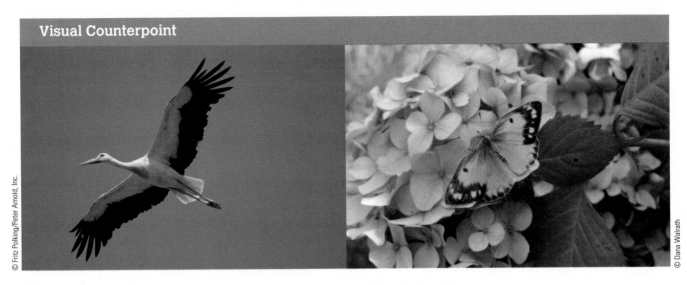

An example of analogy: The wings of birds and butterflies are both used for flight and share similar appearance due to their common function. However, the course of their development and their structure differ.

developmental sequence. Only homologies are relevant for constructing evolutionary relationships.

Through careful comparison and analysis of organisms, Linnaeus and his successors have grouped species into genera and into even larger groups such as families, orders, classes, phyla, and kingdoms. Each taxonomic level is distinguished by characteristics shared by all the organisms in the group.

The Discovery of Evolution

Just as European seafaring and exploration brought about an awareness of the diversity of life across the earth, construction and mining, which came with the onset of industrialization in Europe, led to an awareness of change in life forms through time. As work like cutting railway lines or quarrying limestone became commonplace, fossils, or preserved remains, of past life forms were brought into the light.

At first, the fossilized remains of elephants and giant saber-toothed tigers in Europe were interpreted according to religious doctrine. For example, the early 19th-century theory of *catastrophism*, championed by French paleontologist and anatomist Georges Cuvier, invoked natural events like the supposed Great Flood chronicled in Genesis to account for the disappearance of these species in European lands. Another French scientist, Jean-Baptiste Lamarck, was among the first to suggest a mechanism to account for diversity among living creatures that did not rely upon scriptures. His theory of the

"inheritance of acquired characteristics" proposed that behavior brought about changes in organisms' forms. The famed example was that the first giraffe gained its long neck by stretching to reach the leaves on the highest treetop branches and in turn passed this acquired long neck onto its offspring. While Lamarck's theory has long since been disproved as a mechanism to account for biological change, his proposal seems likely as a change mechanism for cultural inheritance, and he is credited with making the connection between organisms and the environments they inhabit.

During this same time, British geologist Sir Charles Lyell championed *uniformitarianism*—a theory that accounts for variation in the earth's surface. According to Lyell, these variations are the result of gradual changes over extremely long periods of time; although the changes are not obvious at the moment, they are caused by the same natural processes, such as erosion, that are immediately observable. Because the time span required for uniformitarianism is so long, this theory was incompatible with literal interpretations of the Bible, in which the earth is believed to be only about 6,000 years old.

With industrialization, however, Europeans became generally more comfortable with the ideas of change and progress. In hindsight, it seems inevitable that someone would hit upon the scientific concept of evolution. So it was that, by the start of the 19th century, many naturalists

notochord A rodlike structure of cartilage that, in vertebrates, is replaced by the vertebral column.

had come to accept the idea that life had evolved, even though they were not clear about how it happened. It remained for Charles Darwin (1809–1882) to formulate a theory that has withstood the test of time.

Grandson of Erasmus Darwin (a physician, scientist, poet, and originator of a theory of evolution himself), Charles Darwin began studying medicine at the University of Edinburgh, Scotland. Finding himself unfit for this profession, he went to Christ's College, Cambridge University, to study theology. He then left Cambridge to take the position of companion to British Royal Navy Captain Robert FitzRoy on the *H.M.S. Beagle*, which was about to embark on a scientific expedition to explore various poorly mapped parts of the world. The voyage lasted for almost five years, taking Darwin along the coasts of South America, to the Galapagos Islands, across the Pacific to Australia, and then across the Indian and Atlantic Oceans to South America before returning to England in 1836.

Observing the tremendous diversity of living creatures as well as the astounding fossils of extinct animals, Darwin began to note that species varied according to the environments they inhabited. The observations he made on this voyage, his readings of Lyell's *Principles of Geology* (1830), and the arguments he had with the orthodox and dogmatic FitzRoy all contributed to the ideas culminating in Darwin's most famous book, *On the Origin of Species*. This book, published in 1859, over twenty years after he returned from his voyage, described a theory of evolution accounting for change within species and for the emergence of new species in purely naturalistic terms.

Darwin added observations from English farm life and intellectual thought to the ideas he began to develop on the *Beagle*. He paid particular attention to domesticated animals and farmers' practice of breeding their stock to select for specific traits. Darwin's theoretical breakthrough derived from an essay by economist Thomas Malthus (1766–1834), which warned of the potential consequences of increased human population, particularly of the poor. Malthus observed that animal populations, unlike human populations, remained stable, due to an overproduction of young followed by a large proportion of animal offspring not surviving to maturity. Darwin wrote in his autobiography, "It at once struck me that under these circumstances favourable variations would tend to be preserved, and unfavourable ones to be destroyed. The results of this would be the formation of a new species. Here, then I had at last got a theory by which to work."[2]

Today Darwinian **natural selection** can be defined as the evolutionary process through which factors in the environment exert pressure, favoring some individuals over others to produce the next generation. Darwin combined his observations into the theory of evolution as follows: All species display a range of variation, and all have the ability to expand beyond their means of subsistence. It follows that, in their "struggle for existence," organisms with variations to help them survive in a particular environment will reproduce with greater success than others. Thus, as generation succeeds generation, nature selects the most advantageous variations and species evolve. So obvious did the idea seem in hindsight that Thomas Henry Huxley, one of the era's most prominent scientists, remarked, "How extremely stupid of me not to have thought of that."[3]

As often happens in the history of science, Darwin was not alone in authoring the theory of natural selection. A Welshman, Alfred Russel Wallace, independently came up with the same idea at the same time while on a voyage to the Malay Archipelago in Southeast Asia to collect specimens for European zoos and museums. According to his autobiography, a theory came to Wallace while he was in a feverish delirium from malaria. He shared excitedly his idea with other scientists in England, including Darwin, whose own theory was yet unpublished. The two scientists jointly presented their findings.

However straightforward the idea of evolution by natural selection may appear, the theory was (and has continued to be) a source of considerable controversy. Darwin avoided the most contentious question of human origins, limiting his commentary in the original work to a single sentence near the end: "much light will be thrown on the origin of man and his history." The feisty Thomas Henry Huxley, however, took up the subject of human origins explicitly through comparative anatomy of apes and humans and an examination of the fossils in his book, *On Man's Place in Nature*, published in 1863.

Two problems plagued Darwin's theory throughout his career: First, how did variation arise in the first place? Second, what was the mechanism of heredity by which variable traits could be passed from one generation to the next? Ironically, some of the information Darwin needed, the basic laws of heredity, were available by 1866, through the experimental work of Gregor Mendel (1822–1884), a Roman Catholic monk, working in the monastery gardens in Brno, a city in today's Czech Republic.

Mendel, who was raised on a farm, possessed two particular talents: a flair for mathematics and a passion for gardening. As with all farmers of his time, Mendel had an intuitive

---

[2] Darwin, C. (1887). *Autobiography.* Reprinted in F. Darwin (Ed.). (1902), *The life and letters of Charles Darwin.* London: John Murray.

natural selection The evolutionary process through which factors in the environment exert pressure, favoring some individuals over others to produce the next generation.

---

[3] Darwin, C. (1887). *Autobiography.* Reprinted in F. Darwin (Ed.). (1902), *The life and letters of Charles Darwin.* London: John Murray. [3] Quoted in Durant, J. C. (2000, April 23). Everybody into the gene pool. *New York Times Book Review,* 11.

understanding of biological inheritance. He went a step farther, though, in that he recognized the need for theoretical explanations, so at age 34, he began careful breeding experiments in the monastery garden, starting with pea plants.

Over eight years, Mendel planted over 30,000 plants—controlling their pollination, observing the results, and figuring out the mathematics behind it all. This allowed him to predict the outcome of hybridization, or breeding that combined distinct varieties of the same species, over successive generations, in terms of basic laws of heredity. Though his findings were published in 1866 in a respected scientific journal, no one seemed to recognize the importance of Mendel's work during his lifetime.

Interestingly, a copy of this journal was found in Darwin's own library with the pages still uncut (journals were printed on long continuous sheets of paper and then folded into pages to be cut by the reader), an indication that the journal had never been read. In 1900, cell biology had advanced to the point where appreciation of Mendel's laws was inevitable, and in that year three European botanists, working independently of one another, rediscovered not only the laws but also Mendel's original paper. With this recognition, the science of genetics began. Still, it would be another fifty-three years before the molecular mechanisms of heredity and the discrete units of inheritance would be discovered. Today, a comprehensive understanding of heredity, molecular genetics, and population genetics supports evolutionary theory.

Heredity

In order to understand how evolution works, one has to have some understanding of the mechanics of heredity, because heritable variation constitutes the raw material for evolution. Our knowledge of the mechanisms of heredity is fairly recent; most of the fruitful research into the molecular level of inheritance has taken place in the past five decades. Although some aspects remain puzzling, the outlines by now are reasonably clear.

The Transmission of Genes

Today we define a **gene** as a portion of the DNA molecule containing a sequence of base pairs that encodes a particular protein; however, the molecular basis of the gene was not known at the turn of the 20th century when biologists coined the term from the Greek word for "birth." Mendel had deduced the presence and activity of genes by experimenting with garden peas to determine how various traits are passed from one generation to the next. Specifically, he discovered that inheritance was *particulate*, rather than *blending*, as Darwin and many others thought. That is, the units controlling the expression of visible traits come in pairs, one from each parent, and retain their separate identities over the generations rather than blending into a combination of parental traits in offspring. This was the basis of Mendel's first

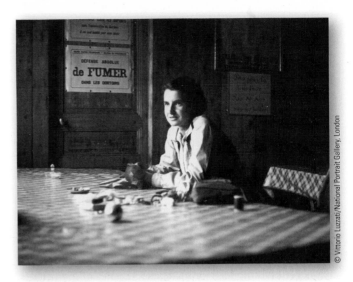

British scientist Rosalind Franklin's pioneering work in x-ray crystal photography played a vital role in unlocking the secret of the genetic code in 1953. Without her permission, Franklin's colleague Maurice Wilkins showed one of her images to James Watson. In his book *The Double Helix*, Watson wrote, "The instant I saw the picture my mouth fell open and my pulse began to race." While her research was published simultaneously in the prestigious journal *Nature* in 1953 alongside that of James Watson, Francis Crick, and Maurice Wilkins, only the gentlemen received the Nobel Prize for the double-helix model of DNA in 1962.

law of segregation, which states that pairs of genes separate and keep their individuality and are passed on to the next generation, unaltered. Another of his laws—**independent assortment**—states that different traits (under the control of distinct genes) are inherited independently of one another.

Mendel based his laws on statistical frequencies of observed characteristics, such as color and texture in generations of plants. His inferences about the mechanisms of inheritance were confirmed through the discovery of the cellular and molecular basis of inheritance in the first half of the 20th century. When **chromosomes,** the cellular structures containing the genetic information, were discovered at the start of the 20th century, they provided a visible vehicle for transmission of traits proposed in Mendel's laws.

It was not until 1953 that James Watson and Francis Crick found that genes are actually portions of molecules

gene A portion of the DNA molecule containing a sequence of base pairs that is the fundamental physical and functional unit of heredity.

law of segregation The Mendelian principle that variants of genes for a particular trait retain their separate identities through the generations.

law of independent assortment The Mendelian principle that genes controlling different traits are inherited independently of one another.

chromosomes In the cell nucleus, the structures visible during cellular division containing long strands of DNA combined with a protein.

of deoxyribonucleic acid (**DNA**)—long strands of which form chromosomes. DNA is a complex molecule with an unusual shape, rather like two strands of a rope twisted around each other with ladderlike steps between the two strands. X-ray crystallographic photographs of the DNA molecule created by British scientist Rosalind Franklin contributed significantly to deciphering the molecule's structure. Alternating sugar and phosphate molecules form the backbone of these strands connected to each other by four base pairs: adenine, thymine, guanine, and cytosine (usually written as A, T, G, and C). Connections between the strands occur between so-called complementary pairs of bases (A to T, G to C; Figure 2.1). Sequences of three complementary bases specify the sequence of amino acids in protein synthesis. This arrangement allows genes to replicate or make exact copies of themselves. The term **chromatid** refers to one half of the "X" shape of chromosomes visible once replication is complete. Sister chromatids are exact copies of each other.

How is the DNA recipe converted into a protein? Through a series of intervening steps, each three-base sequence of a gene, called a **codon,** specifies production of a particular amino acid, strings of which build proteins. Because DNA cannot leave the cell's nucleus (Figures 2.2), the

DNA Deoxyribonucleic acid. The genetic material consisting of a complex molecule whose base structure directs the synthesis of proteins.

chromatid One half of the "X" shape of chromosomes visible once replication is complete. Sister chromatids are exact copies of each other.

codon Three-base sequence of a gene that specifies a particular amino acid for inclusion in a protein.

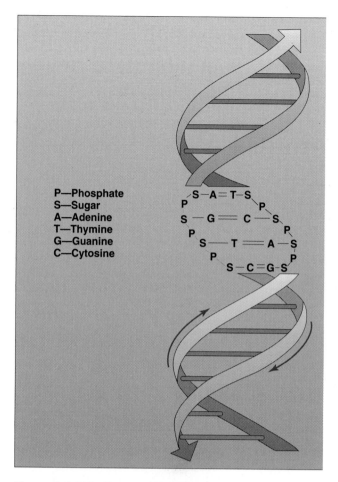

P—Phosphate
S—Sugar
A—Adenine
T—Thymine
G—Guanine
C—Cytosine

Figure 2.1 This diagrammatic representation of a portion of deoxyribonucleic acid (DNA) illustrates its twisted ladderlike structure. Alternating sugar and phosphate groups form the structural sides of the ladder. The connecting "rungs" are formed by pairings between complementary bases—adenine with thymine and cytosine with guanine.

Figure 2.2 Structure of a generalized eukaryotic, or nucleated, cell, illustrating the cell's three-dimensional nature. DNA is located in the nucleus. Because DNA cannot leave the nucleus, genes must first be transcribed into RNA, which carries genetic information to the ribosomes, where protein synthesis occurs. Note also the mitochondria, which contain their own circular chromosomes and mitochondrial DNA.

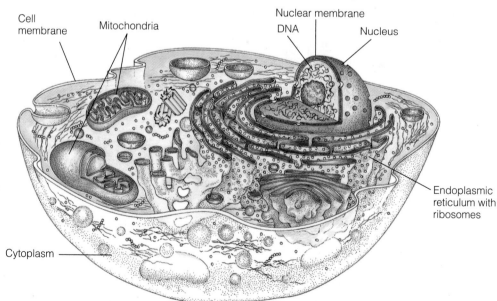

Cell membrane

Mitochondria

Nuclear membrane

DNA

Nucleus

Endoplasmic reticulum with ribosomes

Cytoplasm

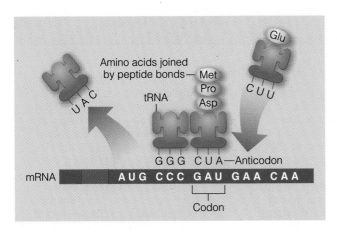

Figure 2.3 Codons of DNA (a sequence of three bases) are transcribed into the complementary codons of a kind of RNA called messenger RNA (mRNA) in order to leave the nucleus. In the ribosomes, these codons are translated into proteins by transfer RNA (tRNA), which strings the amino acids together into particular chains. Can you think of the bases that would have been found in the DNA that correspond to the section of mRNA pictured here?

directions for a specific protein are first converted into ribonucleic acid or **RNA** in a process called **transcription**. RNA differs from DNA in the structure of its sugar phosphate backbone and in the presence of the base uracil rather than thymine. Next, the RNA (called *messenger RNA* or *mRNA*) travels to the **ribosomes**, the cellular structure (Figure 2.3) where **translation** of the directions found in the codons into proteins occurs. Anti-codons of transfer RNA (tRNA) transport the individual amino acids to the corresponding mRNA codons, and the amino acids are joined together by peptide bonds to form polypeptide chains. For example, the sequence of AUG specifies the amino acid methionine, CCC proline, GAU aspartic acid, and so on.

There are twenty amino acids, which are strung together in different amounts and sequences to produce an almost infinite number of different proteins. This is the so-called **genetic code**, and it is the same for every living thing, whether a worm or a human being. In addition to the genetic information stored in the chromosomes of the nucleus, complex organisms also possess cellular structures called *mitochondria*, each of which has a single circular chromosome. The genetic material known as *mitochondrial DNA* or *mtDNA* has figured prominently in human evolutionary studies. On the other end of the spectrum, simple living things without nucleated cells, such as the retrovirus that causes AIDS, contain their genetic information only as RNA.

Genes and Alleles

A sequence of chemical bases on a molecule of DNA (a gene) constitutes a recipe for making proteins. As science writer Matt Ridley puts it, "Proteins . . . do almost every chemical, structural, and regulatory thing that is done in the body: they generate energy, fight infection, digest food, form hair, carry oxygen, and so on and on."[4] Almost everything in the body is made of or by proteins.

There are alternate forms of genes, known as **alleles.** For example, the gene for a human blood type in the A-B-O system refers to a specific portion of a DNA molecule on chromosome 9 that in this case is 1,062 letters long (a medium-sized gene). This gene specifies the production of an **enzyme,** a kind of protein that initiates and directs a chemical reaction. This particular enzyme causes molecules involved in immune responses to attach to the surface of red blood cells. Alleles correspond to alternate forms of this gene (changes in the base pairs of the DNA) that determine the specific blood type (the A allele and B allele). Genes, then, are not really separate structures, as had once been imagined, but locations, like dots on a map. These genes provide the recipe for the many proteins that keep us alive and healthy.

The human **genome**—the complete sequence of human DNA—contains 3 billion chemical bases, with 20,000 to 25,000 genes, a number similar to that found in most mammals. Of the 3 billion bases, humans and mice are about 90 percent identical. Both species have three times as many genes as does the fruit fly but half the number of genes found in the rice plant. In other words, the number of genes or base pairs does not explain every difference among organisms. At the same time, those 20,000 to 25,000 human genes account for only 1 to 1.5 percent of the entire genome, indicating that scientists still have far more to learn about how genes work. Frequently, genes themselves are split by long stretches of DNA that is not part of the known protein code; for example, the 1,062 bases of the A-B-O blood-group gene are interrupted by five such stretches. In the course of protein production,

---

[4] Ridley, M. (1999). *Genome: The autobiography of a species in 23 chapters* (p. 40). New York: HarperCollins.

RNA Ribonucleic acid; similar to DNA but with uracil substituted for the base thymine. Transcribes and carries instructions from DNA from the nucleus to the ribosomes, where it directs protein synthesis. Some simple life forms contain RNA only.

transcription Process of conversion of instructions from DNA into RNA.

ribosomes Structures in the cell where translation occurs.

translation Process of conversion of RNA instructions into proteins.

genetic code The sequence of three bases (a codon) that specifies the sequence of amino acids in protein synthesis.

alleles Alternate forms of a single gene.

enzyme Protein that initiates and directs chemical reactions.

genome The complete structure sequence of DNA for a species.

The Social Impact of Genetics on Reproduction

While pregnancy and childbirth have been traditional subjects for cultural anthropology, the advances in genetics are raising new questions for the biocultural study of reproduction. At first glance, the genetics revolution has simply expanded biological knowledge. Individuals today, compared to a hundred years ago, can see their own genetic makeup, even down to the base-pair sequence level. But this new biological knowledge also has the capacity to profoundly transform cultures, and in many places new genetic information has dramatically affected the social experience of pregnancy and childbirth.

New reproductive technologies allow for the genetic assessment of fertilized eggs and embryos (the earliest stage of animal development), with far-reaching social consequences. These technologies have also become of interest to cultural anthropologists who are studying the social impact of biological knowledge. For nearly twenty-five years, anthropologist Rayna Rapp has examined the social influence of prenatal genetic testing in North America.[a] Her work illustrates that biological facts pertaining to reproduction do not exist outside of an interpretive framework provided by the culture.

Prenatal genetic testing is conducted most frequently through amniocentesis, a technique developed in the 1960s through which fluid, containing cells from the developing embryo, is drawn from the womb of a pregnant woman. The chromosomes and specific genes are then analyzed for abnormalities. Rapp has traced the development of amniocentesis from an experimental procedure to one routinely used in pregnancy in North America. For example, today pregnant women over the age of 35 routinely undergo this test because certain genetic conditions are associated with older maternal age. Trisomy 21 or Down syndrome, in which individuals have an extra 21st chromosome, can be easily identified through amniocentesis.

Through ethnographic study, Rapp has shown that a biological fact (such as an extra 21st chromosome) is open to diverse interpretations and reproductive choices by "potential parents." She also illustrates how genetic testing may lead to the labeling of certain people as "undesirable," pitting women's reproductive rights against the rights of the disabled—born or unborn. Generally, during the first two trimesters, women in the United States have a constitutionally protected right to decide whether to terminate or continue a pregnancy for any reason at all, including the diagnosis of a genetic anomaly. Following this window, federal law protects the rights of disabled individuals with these same anomalies.

Individual women must negotiate a terrain in which few rules exist to guide them. New reproductive technology, which reveals genetic anomalies, has created an utterly novel social situation. Rapp's anthropological investigation of the social impact of amniocentesis illustrates the complex interplay between biological knowledge and cultural practices.

BIOCULTURAL QUESTION

What do you think about prenatal genetic testing for diseases? Would you like to know if you carry the recessive allele for a harmful condition?

[a]Rapp, R. (1999). *Testing women, testing the fetus: The social impact of amniocentesis in America.* New York: Routledge.

Courtesy of Rayna Rapp

Medical anthropologist Rayna Rapp has conducted fieldwork in genetics laboratories and genetic counseling centers as part of her ethnographic study of the social impact of genetic testing.

these stretches of DNA are metaphorically snipped out and left on the cutting room floor.

Some of this seemingly useless, noncoding DNA (often called *junk DNA*) has been inserted by retroviruses. *Retroviruses* are some of the most diverse and widespread infectious entities of vertebrates—responsible for AIDS, hepatitis, anemias, and some neurological disorders.[5] Other junk DNA consists of decaying hulks of once-useful but now functionless genes: damaged genes that have been "turned off." As cells divide and reproduce, junk DNA, like known genes, also replicates. Mistakes can occur in the replication process, adding or subtracting repeats of the four bases: A, C, G, and T. This happens with some frequency and differently in every individual. As these "mistakes" accumulate over time, each person develops his or her unique DNA fingerprint.

Cell Division

In order to grow and maintain good health, the cells of an organism must divide and produce new cells. Cell division is initiated when the chromosomes replicate, forming a second pair that duplicates the original pair of chromosomes in the nucleus. To do this, the DNA "unzips" between the base pairs—adenine from thymine and

[5] Amábile-Cuevas, C. F., & Chicurel, M. E. (1993). Horizontal gene transfer. *American Scientist 81*, 338.

guanine from cytosine—and then each base on each now-single strand attracts its complementary base, reconstituting the second half of the double helix. Each new pair is surrounded by a membrane and becomes the nucleus that directs the activities of a new cell. This kind of cell division is called **mitosis.** As long as no errors are made in this replication process, cells within organisms can divide to form daughter cells that are exact genetic copies of the parent cell.

Like most animals, humans reproduce sexually. One reason sex is so popular, from an evolutionary perspective, is that it provides opportunity for genetic variation. All animals contain two copies of each chromosome, having inherited one from each parent. In humans this involves twenty-three pairs of chromosomes. Sexual reproduction can bring beneficial alleles together, purge the genome of harmful ones, and allow beneficial alleles to spread without being held back by the baggage of disadvantageous variants of other genes. While human societies have always regulated sexual reproduction in some ways, the science of genetics has had a tremendous impact on social aspects of reproduction, as seen in this chapter's Biocultural Connection.

Sexual reproduction increases genetic diversity, which in turn has contributed to a multitude of adaptations among sexually reproducing species such as humans. When new individuals are produced through sexual reproduction, the process involves the merging of two cells, one from each parent. If two regular body cells, each containing twenty-three pairs of chromosomes, were to merge, the result would be a new individual with forty-six pairs of chromosomes; such an individual surely could not survive. But this increase in chromosome number does not occur, because the sex cells that join to form a new individual are the product of a different kind of cell division, called **meiosis.**

Although meiosis begins like mitosis, with the replication and doubling of the original genes in chromosomes through the formation of sister chromatids, it proceeds to divide that number into four new cells rather than two (Figure 2.4). Thus each new cell has only half the number of chromosomes compared to the parent cell. Human eggs and sperm, for example, have twenty-three single chromosomes (half of a pair), whereas body cells have twenty-three pairs, or forty-six chromosomes.

mitosis A kind of cell division that produces new cells having exactly the same number of chromosome pairs, and hence copies of genes, as the parent cell.

meiosis A kind of cell division that produces the sex cells, each of which has half the number of chromosomes found in other cells of the organism.

Figure 2.4 Each chromosome consists of two sister chromatids, which are exact copies of each other. During mitosis, these sister chromatids separate into two identical daughter cells. In meiosis, the cell division responsible for the formation of gametes, the first division halves the chromosome number. The second meiotic division is essentially like mitosis and involves the separation of sister chromatids. Chromosomes in red came from one parent; those in blue came from the other. Meiosis results in four daughter cells that are not identical.

Karyotype with a Few Genetic Loci

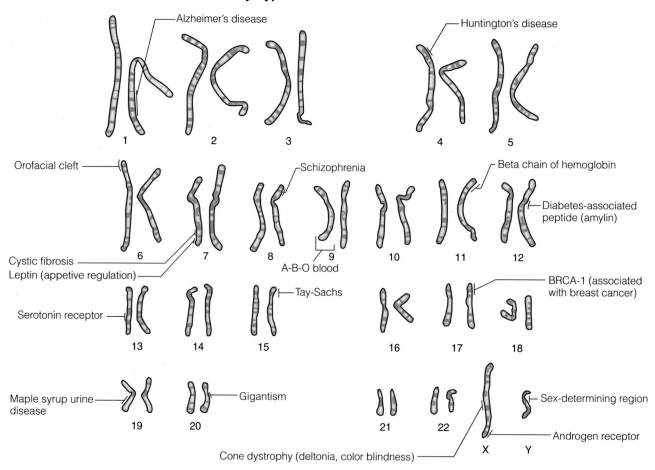

Figure 2.5 **The twenty-three pairs of chromosomes humans possess include twenty-two pairs of somatic or body chromosomes plus one pair of sex chromosomes for a total of forty-six chromosomes. Of each pair, one is inherited from the individual's mother and the other from the father. Each pair of chromosomes has a characteristic size and shape. The genes coding for specific traits are located on specified places on each chromosome as indicated here. In the lower right corner is the pair of sex chromosomes typically found in males: a larger X chromosome (left) and smaller Y. Females typically possess two X chromosomes. Offspring inherit an X chromosome from their mother but either an X or a Y from their father, resulting in approximately equal numbers of male and female offspring in subsequent generations. Though the Y chromosome is critical for differentiation into a male phenotype, compared to other chromosomes the Y is tiny and carries little genetic information.**

The process of meiotic division has important implications for genetics. Because paired chromosomes are separated, two different types of new cells will be formed; two of the four new cells will have one half of a pair of chromosomes, and the other two will have the second half of the original chromosome pair. At the same time, corresponding portions of one chromosome may "cross over" to the other one, somewhat scrambling the genetic material compared to the original chromosomes.

Sometimes the original pair is **homozygous,** possessing identical alleles for a specific gene. For example, if in both chromosomes of the original pair the gene for A-B-O blood type is represented by the allele for type A blood, then all new cells will have the A allele. But if the original pair is **heterozygous,** with the A allele on one chromosome and the allele for type B blood on the other, then half of the new cells will contain only the B allele; the offspring have a 50-50 chance of getting either one. It is impossible to predict any single individual's **genotype,** or genetic composition, but (as Mendel originally discovered) statistical probabilities can be established (see Figure 2.5).

homozygous Refers to a chromosome pair that bears identical alleles for a single gene.

heterozygous Refers to a chromosome pair that bears different alleles for a single gene.

genotype The alleles possessed for a particular gene.

What happens when a child inherits the allele for type O blood from one parent and that for type A from the other? Will the child have blood of type A, O, or some mixture of the two? Figure 2.6 illustrates some of the possible outcomes. Many of these questions were answered by Mendel's original experiments.

Mendel discovered that certain alleles are able to mask the presence of others; one allele is dominant, whereas the other is recessive. Actually, it is the traits that are dominant or recessive, rather than the alleles themselves; geneticists merely speak of dominant and recessive alleles for the sake of convenience. Among your biological relatives you can trace classic examples of visible traits governed by simple dominance such as a widow's peak (dominant), attached earlobes (recessive), or the presence of hair on the back of the middle section of each finger (dominant). A person with a widow's peak may be either homozygous or heterozygous because the presence of one allele will mask the allele for an un-peaked hairline. Similarly, one might speak of the allele for type A blood as being dominant to the one for type O. An individual whose blood-type genes are heterozygous, with one A and one O allele, will have type A blood. In other words, the heterozygous condition (AO) will show exactly the same physical characteristic, or **phenotype,** as the homozygous (AA), even though the two have a somewhat different genetic composition, or genotype. Only the homozygous recessive genotype (OO) will show the phenotype of type O blood.

The **dominance** of one allele does not mean that the **recessive** one is lost or in some way blended. A type A heterozygous parent (AO) will produce sex cells containing both A and O alleles. (This is an example of Mendel's law of segregation—that alleles retain their separate identities.) Recessive alleles can be handed down for generations before they are matched with another recessive in the process of sexual reproduction and show up in the phenotype. The presence of the dominant allele simply masks the expression of the recessive allele.

All of the traits Mendel studied in garden peas showed this dominant–recessive relationship, and so for some years it was believed that this was the only relationship possible. Later studies, however, have indicated that patterns of inheritance are not always so simple. In some cases, neither allele is dominant; they are both co-dominant. An example of co-dominance in human heredity can be seen in the inheritance of blood types. Type A is produced by one allele; type B by another. A heterozygous individual will have a phenotype of AB, because neither allele can dominate the other.

The inheritance of blood types points out another complexity of heredity. Although each of us has at most two alleles for any given gene, the number of *possible* alleles is by no means limited to two. Certain traits have three or more allelic forms. For example, over a hundred alleles exist for **hemoglobin,** the blood protein that carries oxygen. Only one allele can appear on each of the two homologous chromosomes, so each individual is limited to two genetic alleles.

Polygenetic Inheritance

So far, we have spoken as if all the traits of organisms are determined by just one gene. However, most physical traits—such as height, skin color, or liability to disease—are controlled by multiple genes. In such cases, we speak of **polygenetic inheritance,** where the

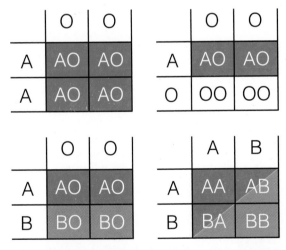

Figure 2.6 These four Punnett squares (named for British geneticist Reginald Punnett) illustrate some of the possible phenotypes and genotypes of offspring within the A-B-O system. Each individual possesses two alleles within this system, and together these two alleles constitute the individual's genotype. "Phenotype" refers to the physical characteristics expressed by the individual. The alleles of one parent are listed on the left-hand side of the square while the other parent's alleles are listed across the top. The potential genotypes of offspring are listed in the colored squares by letter. Phenotypes are indicated by color: Blue indicates the type A phenotype; orange indicates the B phenotype. Individuals with one A and one B allele have the AB phenotype and make both blood antigens. Individuals with the O phenotype have two O alleles.

phenotype The observable characteristic of an organism that may or may not reflect a particular genotype due to the variable expression of dominant and recessive alleles.

dominance The ability of one allele for a trait to mask the presence of another allele.

recessive An allele for a trait whose expression is masked by the presence of a dominant allele.

hemoglobin The protein that carries oxygen in red blood cells.

polygenetic inheritance When two or more genes contribute to the phenotypic expression of a single characteristic.

respective alleles of two or more genes influence phenotype. For example, several individuals may have the exact same height, but because there is no single gene for determining an individual's height, we cannot neatly unravel the genetic underpinnings of 5 feet 3 inches or 160 centimeters.

Characteristics subject to polygenetic inheritance exhibit a continuous range of variation in their phenotypic expression that does not correspond to simple Mendelian rules. As biological anthropologist Jonathan Marks demonstrates in the following Original Study, the relationship between genetics and continuous traits remains a mystery.

Original Study

Ninety-Eight Percent Alike: What Our Similarity to Apes Tells Us about Our Understanding of Genetics   *by Jonathan Marks*

It's not too hard to tell Jane Goodall from a chimpanzee. Goodall is the one with long legs and short arms, a prominent forehead, and whites in her eyes. She's the one with a significant amount of hair only on her head, not all over her body. She's the one who walks, talks, and wears clothing.

A few decades ago, however, the nascent field of molecular genetics recognized an apparent paradox: However easy it may be to tell Jane Goodall from a chimpanzee on the basis of physical characteristics, it is considerably harder to tell them apart according to their genes.

More recently, geneticists have been able to determine with precision that humans and chimpanzees are over 98 percent identical genetically, and that figure has become one of the most well-known factoids in the popular scientific literature. It has been invoked to argue that we are simply a third kind of chimpanzee, together with the common chimp and the rarer bonobo; to claim human rights for nonhuman apes; and to explain the roots of male aggression.

Using the figure in those ways, however, ignores the context necessary to make sense of it. Actually, our amazing genetic similarity to chimpanzees is a scientific fact constructed from two rather more mundane facts: our familiarity with the apes and our unfamiliarity with genetic comparisons.

To begin with, it is unfair to juxtapose the differences between the bodies of people and apes with the similarities in their genes. After all, we have been comparing the bodies of humans and chimpanzees for 300 years, and we have been comparing DNA sequences for less than 20 years.

Now that we are familiar with chimpanzees, we quickly see how different they look from us. But when the chimpanzee was a novelty, in the 18th

century, scholars were struck by the overwhelming similarity of human and ape bodies. And why not? Bone for bone, muscle for muscle, organ for organ, the bodies of humans and apes differ only in subtle ways. And yet, it is impossible to say just how physically similar they are. Forty percent? Sixty percent? Ninety-eight percent? Three-dimensional beings that develop over their lifetimes don't lend themselves to a simple scale of similarity.

Genetics brings something different to the comparison. A DNA sequence is a one-dimensional entity, a long series of A, G, C, and T subunits. Align two sequences from different species and you can simply tabulate their similarities; if they match 98 out of 100 times, then the species are 98 percent genetically identical.

But is that more or less than their bodies match? We have no easy way

A true four-fielder, biological anthropologist Jonathan Marks is at the grave of Emile Durkheim, the French sociologist who profoundly influenced the founding of cultural anthropology.

By Jonathan Marks (2000)

to tell, for making sense of the question "How similar are a human and a chimp?" requires a frame of reference. In other words, we should be asking: "How similar are a human and a chimp, compared to what?" Let's try and answer the question. How similar are a human and a chimp, compared to, say, a sea urchin? The human and chimpanzee have limbs, skeletons, bilateral symmetry, a central nervous system; each bone, muscle, and organ matches. For all intents and purposes, the human and chimpanzee aren't 98 percent identical, they're 100 percent identical.

On the other hand, when we compare the DNA of humans and chimps, what does the percentage of similarity mean? We conceptualize it on a linear scale, on which 100 percent is perfectly identical, and 0 percent is totally different. But the structure of DNA gives the scale a statistical idiosyncrasy.

Because DNA is a linear array of those four bases—A, G, C, and T—only four possibilities exist at any specific point in a DNA sequence. The laws of chance tell us that two random sequences from species that have no ancestry in common will match at about one in every four sites.

Thus, even two unrelated DNA sequences will be 25 percent identical, not 0 percent identical. (You can, of course, generate sequences more different than that, but greater differences would not occur randomly.) The most different two DNA sequences can be, then, is 75 percent different.

Now consider that all multicellular life on earth is related. A human, a chimpanzee, and the banana the chimpanzee is eating share a remote common ancestry, but a common ancestry nevertheless. Therefore, if we compare any particular DNA sequence in a human and a banana, the sequence would have to be more than 25 percent identical.

For the sake of argument, let's say 35 percent. In other words, your DNA is over one-third the same as a banana's. Yet, of course, there are few ways other than genetically in which a human could be shown to be one-third identical to a banana.

That context may help us to assess the 98 percent DNA similarity of humans and chimpanzees. The fact that our DNA is 98 percent identical to that of a chimp is not a transcendent statement about our natures, but merely a decontextualized and culturally interpreted datum.

Moreover, the genetic comparison is misleading because it ignores qualitative differences among genomes. Genetic evolution involves much more than simply replacing one base with another. Thus, even among such close relatives as human and chimpanzee, we find that the chimp's genome is estimated to be about 10 percent larger than the human's; that one human chromosome contains a fusion of two small chimpanzee chromosomes; and that the tips of each chimpanzee chromosome contain a DNA sequence that is not present in humans.

In other words, the pattern we encounter genetically is actually quite close to the pattern we encounter anatomically. In spite of the shock the figure of 98 percent may give us, humans are obviously identifiably different from, as well as very similar to, chimpanzees. The apparent paradox is simply a result of how mundane the apes have become, and how exotic DNA still is.

Evolution, Individuals, and Populations

At the level of the individual, the study of genetics shows how traits are transmitted from parent to offspring, enabling a prediction about the chances that any given individual will display some phenotypic characteristic. At the level of the group, the study of genetics takes on additional significance, revealing how evolutionary processes account for the diversity of life on earth.

A key concept in genetics is that of the **population,** or a group of individuals within which breeding takes place. **Gene pool** refers to all the genetic variants possessed by members of a population. It is within populations that natural selection takes place, as some members contribute a disproportionate share of the next generation. Over generations, the relative proportions of alleles in a population change (biological evolution) according to the varying reproductive success of individuals within that population. In other words, at the level of population genetics, **evolution** can be defined as changes in allele frequencies in populations. This is also known as *microevolution.* Four evolutionary forces—mutation, gene flow, genetic drift, and natural selection—are responsible for the genetic changes that underlie the biological variation present in species today. As we shall see, variation is at the heart of evolution. These evolutionary forces create and pattern diversity.

In theory, the characteristics of any given population should remain stable. For example, generation after generation, the bullfrogs in a farm pond look much alike, have the same calls, and exhibit the same behavior when breeding. The gene pool of the population—the genetic variation available to that population—appears to remain stable over time.

Although some alleles may be dominant over others, recessive alleles are not just lost or destroyed. Statistically, an individual who is heterozygous for a particular gene with one dominant (A) and one recessive (a) allele has a 50 percent chance of passing on the dominant allele and a 50 percent chance of passing on the recessive allele. Even if another dominant allele masks the presence of the recessive allele in the next generation, the recessive allele nonetheless will continue to be a part of the gene pool.

Because alleles are not "lost" in the process of reproduction, the frequency of the different alleles within a population should remain exactly the same from one generation to the next in the absence of evolution. In 1908, the English mathematician G. H. Hardy (1877–1947) and the German obstetrician W. Weinberg (1862–1937) worked this idea into a mathematical formula called the **Hardy-Weinberg principle.** The principle algebraically demonstrates that the percentages of individuals homozygous for the dominant allele, homozygous for the recessive allele, and heterozygous will remain the same from one generation to the next provided that certain specified conditions are met. Among the conditions are these: Mating is entirely random; the population is sufficiently

population In biology, a group of similar individuals that can and do interbreed.

gene pool All the genetic variants possessed by members of a population.

evolution Changes in allele frequencies in populations; also known as microevolution.

Hardy-Weinberg principle Demonstrates algebraically that the percentages of individuals that are homozygous for the dominant allele, homozygous for the recessive allele, and heterozygous should remain constant from one generation to the next, provided that certain specified conditions are met.

In evolutionary terms, mutations serve as the ultimate source of all new genetic variation. A generally positive force, most mutations have minimal effect or are neutral. Nevertheless, human-produced mutagens—such as pollutants, preservatives, cigarette smoke, radiation, and even some medicines—increasingly threaten people in industrial societies. While the negative effects of mutation are evident in the clear link between cigarette smoke and cancer, the positive side of mutation has been fictionalized in the special talents of the X-Men.

20th Century Fox/The Kobal Collection/Hayes, Kerry

large for a statistical average to express itself; no new variants will be introduced into the population's gene pool; and all individuals are equally successful at surviving and reproducing. These four conditions are equivalent to the absence of evolution. Geographic, physiologic, and social factors may favor mating between certain individuals over others.

Thus changes in the gene pools of populations, without which there could be no evolution, can and do take place. The mechanisms by which these changes might lead to the formation of new species will be discussed in detail in Chapter 6.

Evolutionary Forces

Mutation

The ultimate source of evolutionary change is **mutation** of genes because mutation constantly introduces new variation. Although some mutations may be harmful or beneficial to individuals, most mutations are neutral. But in an evolutionary sense, random mutation is inherently positive, as it provides the ultimate source of new genetic variation. New body plans—such as walking on two legs compared to knuckle-walking like our closest relatives, chimpanzees and gorillas—ultimately depended on genetic mutation. A random mutation might create a new allele that creates a modified

mutation Chance alteration of genetic material that produces new variation.

protein making a new biological task possible. Without the variation brought in through random mutation, populations could not change over time in response to changing environments.

For sexually reproducing species like humans, the only mutations of any *evolutionary* consequence are those occurring in sex cells, since these cells form future generations. Mutations may arise whenever copying mistakes are made during cell division. This may involve a change in a single base of a DNA sequence or, at the other extreme, relocation of large segments of DNA, including entire chromosomes. As you read this page, the DNA in each cell of your body is being damaged.[6] Fortunately, DNA repair enzymes constantly scan for mistakes, slicing out damaged segments and patching up gaps. These repair mechanisms prevent diseases like cancer and ensure that we get a faithful copy of our parental inheritance. Genes controlling DNA repair therefore form a critical part of any species' genetic makeup.

Because no species has perfect DNA repair, new mutations arise continuously, so that all species continue to evolve. Geneticists have calculated the rate at which various types of mutant genes appear. In human populations, they run from a low of about five mutations per million sex cells formed, in the case of a gene abnormality that leads to the absence of an iris in the eye, to a high of about a hundred per million, in the case of a gene involved in a form of muscular dystrophy. The average is about thirty mutants per million. Environmental factors may increase the rate at which mutations occur. These include certain dyes,

[6]Culotta, E., & Koshland, D. E., Jr. (1994). DNA repair works its way to the top. *Science 266*, 1926.

antibiotics, and chemicals used in the preservation of food. Radiation, whether industrial or solar, represents another important cause of mutation. There is even evidence that stress can raise mutation rates, increasing the diversity necessary for selection if successful adaptation is to occur.[7]

In humans, as in all multicellular animals, the very nature of genetic material ensures that mutations will occur. For instance, the fact that a gene can be split by stretches of DNA that are not part of that gene increases the chances that a mistake in the process of copying DNA will cause mutations. To cite one example, no fewer than fifty such segments of DNA fragment the gene for collagen—the main structural protein of the skin, bones, and cartilage. One possible benefit of this seemingly inefficient situation is that it allows the gene segments themselves to be shuffled like a deck of cards, sometimes creating new proteins with new functions. So although individuals may suffer as a result, mutations also confer versatility at the population level, making it possible for an evolving species to adapt more quickly to environmental changes. Remember, however, that mutations occur randomly and thus do not arise out of need for some new adaptation.

Genetic Drift

Another evolutionary force is **genetic drift,** or the chance fluctuations of allele frequencies in the gene pool of a population. These changes at the population level come about due to random events at the individual level. Over the course of its lifetime, each individual is subject to a number of random events affecting its survival. For example, an individual squirrel in good health and possessed of a number of advantageous traits may be killed in a chance forest fire; a genetically well-adapted baby cougar may not live longer than a day if its mother gets caught in an avalanche, whereas the weaker offspring of a mother that does not die may survive. In a large population, such accidents of nature are unimportant; the accidents that preserve individuals with certain alleles will be balanced out by the accidents that destroy them. However, in small populations such averaging out may not be possible. Some alleles may become overrepresented in a population due to chance events.

Because today human populations are large, we might suppose that human beings are unaffected by genetic drift. But a chance event, like a rock slide that kills five people from a small town, say a population of 1,000, could significantly alter the frequencies of alleles in the local gene pool.

A particular kind of genetic drift, known as **founder effects,** may occur when an existing population splits up into two or more new ones, especially if one of these new populations is founded by a small number of individuals.

In such cases, it is unlikely that the gene frequencies of the smaller population will be representative of those of the larger one. Isolated island populations may possess limited variability due to founder effects.

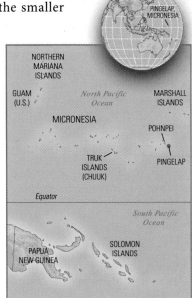

An interesting example can be seen on the Pacific Ocean island of Pingelap in Micronesia, where 5 percent of the population is completely color-blind, a condition known as *achromotopsia*. This is not the "normal" red-green color blindness that affects 8 to 20 percent of males in most populations but rather a complete inability to see color. The high frequency of achromotopsia occurred sometime around 1775 after a typhoon swept through the island, reducing its total population to only twenty individuals. Among the survivors was a single individual who was heterozygous for this condition. After a few generations, this gene became fully embedded in the expanding population. Today a full 30 percent of the island's inhabitants are carriers compared to a mere .003 percent seen in the United States.[8]

Genetic drift is likely to have been an important factor in human evolution, because until 10,000 years ago all humans were food foragers generally living in relatively small communities. Whenever biological variation is observed, whether it is the distant past or the present, it is always possible that chance events of genetic drift are responsible for it.

Gene Flow

Another factor that brings change to the gene pool of a population is **gene flow,** or the introduction of new alleles from nearby populations. Interbreeding allows

---

[7]Chicurel, M. (2001). Can organisms speed their own evolution? *Science* 292, 1824–1827.

[8]Sacks, O. (1998). *Island of the colorblind.* New York: Knopf.

genetic drift Chance fluctuations of allele frequencies in the gene pool of a population.

founder effects A particular form of genetic drift deriving from a small founding population not possessing all the alleles present in the original population.

gene flow The introduction of alleles from the gene pool of one population into that of another.

What It Means to Be a Woman: How Women Around the World Cope with Infertility   *by Karen Springen*

As anthropologists study the social consequences of infertility throughout the globe, their findings help reduce the social stigma surrounding this condition and make new biomedical technologies more available. In some developing countries, the consequences of infertility—which can include ostracism, physical abuse, and even suicide—are heartbreaking. "If you are infertile in some cultures, you are less than a dog," says Willem Ombelet of the Genk Institute for Fertility Technology in Belgium. Women are often uneducated, so their only identity comes from being moms. "It [infertility] is an issue of profound human suffering, particularly for women," says Marcia Inhorn, professor of anthropology and international affairs at Yale University. "It's a human-rights issue."

Marcia C. Inhorn at one of her research site—an IVF clinic in the United Arab Emirates—where she studies reproductive tourism in the Arab world.

The stigma that infertile women face can infiltrate every aspect of life. They may not even be invited to weddings or other important gatherings. "People see them as having a 'bad eye' that will make you infertile, too. Infertile women are considered inauspicious," says Inhorn. Other people simply "don't want to have them around at joyous occasions," says Frank van Balen, co-author (with Inhorn) of "Infertility Around the Globe" and a professor in the department of social and behavioral sciences at the University of Amsterdam. Their reasoning: "they could spoil it," he says.

Often the female takes the blame even when the problem lies with the man, says Inhorn. The women often keep their husband's secret and bear the insults. In Chad, a proverb says, "A woman without children is like a tree without leaves." If women don't bear children, their husbands may leave them or take new wives with society's blessing. In some Muslim places, women can't go on the street on their own. "If they have a child with them, they can do their errands," says van Balen.

Childlessness can also be an enormous economic problem in developing countries where Social Security, pensions, and retirement-savings plans are not the norm. "If you don't have your children, no one looks after you," says Guido Pennings, professor of philosophy and moral science at Belgium's Ghent University. Religion shapes attitudes, too. In the Hindu religion, a woman without a child,

particularly a son, can't go to heaven. Sons perform death rituals. Infertile couples worry that without a child, who will mourn for them and bury them? In China and Vietnam, the traditional belief is that the souls of childless people can't easily rest. In India, the eldest son traditionally lights the funeral pyre. In Muslim cultures, the stigma follows childless women even after death: Women without children aren't always allowed to be buried in graveyards or sacred grounds.

In Western countries, it has become much more socially acceptable to be childless, and more American women are hitting their 40s without kids, according to the latest census data. By contrast, in many developing countries, women have no careers—just motherhood—to give them their identity. "The notion of child-free living is not considered an acceptable thing for a married couple," says Inhorn. And particularly in Muslim and Hindu areas, she says, adoption "is not an immediate second path."

Legal adoption is "bureaucratically onerous" and often not socially acceptable, says Elizabeth Roberts, assistant professor of anthropology at the University of Michigan, who studied the people of Ecuador. So it's not surprising that even extremely poor people may go into debt trying to conceive. "A family is only a family if there are children, basically," says Roberts. "The biggest stumbling block is money."

Many couples may waste valuable years resorting to "black magic," says

---

"road-tested" genes to flow into and out of populations, thus increasing the total amount of variation present within the population. Migration of individuals or groups into the territory occupied by others may lead to gene flow.

Geographic factors also can affect gene flow. For example, if a river separates two populations of small mammals, preventing interbreeding, these populations will begin to accrue random genetic differences due to their isolation. If the river changes course and the two populations can interbreed freely, new alleles that may have been present in only one population will now be present in both populations due to gene flow.

Among humans, social factors—such as mating rules, intergroup conflict, and our ability to travel great

distances—affect gene flow. For example, the last 500 years have seen the introduction of Spanish and African alleles into Central and South American populations from Spanish colonists and African slaves. More recent migrations of people from East Asia have added to this mix. When gene flow is present, variation within populations increases. Throughout the history of life on earth, gene flow has kept human populations from developing into separate species.

Natural Selection

Although gene flow and genetic drift may produce changes in the allele frequency in a population, that change would not necessarily make the population better adapted to its

Aravinda Guntupalli, a professor at the University of Tübingen in Germany who studied infertility in India. The couples ask so-called sacred people what days they should fast, and they journey to spiritual places. In the tribal area of India where Guntupalli worked, women dry up umbilical cords and sneak them into infertile women's food to try to help them. "They think it creates some fertility juice in the body," she says.

Not surprisingly, infertility treatments are rarely covered by insurance or by government aid. "How do you provide what is clearly a highly technological, sophisticated procedure in a place that doesn't have a lot of money?" says Adamson, a member of the not-for-profit International Committee Monitoring Assisted Reproductive Technologies, a technical adviser to the World Health Organization. Leaders of countries struggling with dirty drinking water, tuberculosis, malaria, and AIDS may find IVF expenditures hard to justify.

Infertile couples in developing countries don't publicize the fact that they need help even if they can afford treatment. Children are seen as a gift of the gods, so failure to conceive may be perceived as an indication that someone has sinned or is unworthy. "People aren't willing to go up on [the equivalent of] Oprah Winfrey and say, 'Yes, I'm infertile, and I'm getting treatment,'" says Dr. Aniruddha Malpani, an Ob-Gyn who runs the Malpani Infertility Clinic in Mumbai with his wife. "People have

actually traveled [for treatment], telling people they're going on holiday," says Inhorn.

Even for couples who do have access to fertility clinics, there are challenges. For example, some cultures consider masturbation evil. Yet it's traditionally the way doctors get semen samples to check a man's sperm count and then to perform IVF. In some cases, doctors can offer condoms that allow a couple to have intercourse and save the sperm. Another cultural hurdle: The Muslim world does not accept egg or sperm donation. "Each child should have a known father and a known mother," explains Inhorn. "Every child must know his own heritage." Adds Adamson: "It's very important to honor and respect the fact that people have these values."

One important approach is to focus on preventing, rather than curing, infertility. A major cause of infertility is untreated reproductive tract infections such as chlamydia and gonorrhea. In places like Africa, the cost of condoms, and taboos against them, contribute to the STD problem. Infection from female genital mutilation adds to the problem. And in some countries, 90 percent of women do not deliver in hospitals, which can also cause complications. And the hospitals they use for birth or abortions aren't always sanitary. Some doctors also believe sperm quality has suffered from toxins like lead, high in Mexico City and Cairo, and dioxin sprayed on crops.

In the developed world, there's sometimes little sympathy for the problem, since the common view is that developing countries are suffering from overpopulation and don't need any more babies. The United Nations projects that the world population will balloon from its current 6.7 billion to 9.1 billion by 2050. But the picture is more complicated than it seems. "We have a fertility paradox in Africa—high fertility rates and high infertility rates," says Dr. Silke Dyer, an Ob-Gyn in Cape Town and a member of the European Society for Human Reproduction and Embryology task force on developing countries and infertility. (Infertility treatment proponents note that IVF doesn't contribute to overpopulation any more than saving lives with vaccinations does. And both alleviate suffering.)

The good news is that interest in treating infertility around the globe is growing. In 2004, the World Health Organization said people should have access to high-quality services for family planning, including infertility services. Doctors hope to provide $200 to $500 IVF cycles, with cheaper drugs and simplified laboratories, by the end of the year in places like Cape Town and Cairo. Their goal: more happy birth stories.

Adapted from Springen, K. (2008, September 15). What it means to be a woman: How women around the world cope with infertility. *Newsweek Web Exclusive. http://www.newsweek.com/id/158625.*

biological and social environment. Natural selection, the evolutionary force described by Darwin, accounts for adaptive change. **Adaptation** is a series of beneficial adjustments to the environment. Adaptation is not an active process but rather the outcome of natural selection. As we will explore throughout this textbook, humans can adapt to their environment through culture as well as biology. When biological adaptation occurs at a genetic level, natural selection is at work.

As described earlier in the chapter, natural selection refers to the evolutionary process through which genetic variation at the population level is shaped to fit local environmental conditions. In other words, instead of a completely random selection of individuals whose traits will be passed on to the next generation, there is selection by the

forces of nature. In the process, the frequency of genetic variants for harmful or nonadaptive traits within the population is reduced while the frequency of genetic variants for adaptive traits is increased. Over time, changes in the genetic structure of the population are visible in the biology or behavior of a population, and such genetic changes can result in the formation of new species.

In popular writing, natural selection is often thought of as "survival of the fittest," a phrase coined by British philosopher Herbert Spencer (1820–1903). The phrase implies that the physically weak, being unfit, are

adaptation A series of beneficial adjustments to the environment.

Across the globe, newborn babies weigh on average between 5 and 8 pounds. Stabilizing selection seems to be operating here to keep infant size well matched to the size of the human birth canal for successful childbirth. Natural selection can promote stability as well as change.

© Camille Tokerud/Getty Images

eliminated from the population by disease, predation, or starvation. Obviously, the survival of the fittest has some bearing on natural selection. But there are many cases in which "less fit" individuals survive, and even do quite well, but do not reproduce. They may be incapable of attracting mates, or they may be sterile, or they may produce offspring that do not survive after birth. For example, among the Uganda kob, a kind of antelope native to East Africa, males that are unable to attract females form bachelor herds in which they live out their lives. As members of a herd, they are reasonably well protected against predators, and so they may survive to relatively old ages. They do not, however, pass on their genes to succeeding generations.

Ultimately, all natural selection is measured in terms of **reproductive success**—mating and production of viable offspring who will in turn carry on one's genes. Reproductive success is also a powerful social phenomenon in some human societies where a woman's social worth is assessed in terms of her ability to bear children. In these contexts infertility becomes a human rights issue, as described in the Anthropology Applied feature.

The change in genetic variants in human populations can be very slow. For example, if an environment changed such that a recessive allele that had been present in humans at a modest frequency suddenly became

lethal, this allele's frequency would still decrease only gradually. Even with complete selection against those homozygous for this allele, the allele would persist in the offspring of heterozygotes. In the first several generations, the frequency of the allele would decrease at a relatively rapid rate. However, with time, as the frequency of the recessive allele drops, the probability of forming a recessive homozygote also drops, so that it would take many generations to realize even a small decrease in allele frequency. This is compounded by the fact that a human generation takes about twenty-five years (forty generations would span over a thousand years). Nevertheless, even such small and slow changes can have a significant cumulative impact on both the genotypes and phenotypes of any population.

As a consequence of the process of natural selection, populations generally become well adapted to their environments. For example, consider the plants and animals that survive in the deserts of the western United States. Members of the cactus family have extensive root networks close to the surface of the soil, enabling them to soak up the slightest bit of moisture; they are able to store large quantities of water whenever it is available; they are shaped so as to expose the smallest possible surface to the dry air and are generally leafless as mature plants, thereby preventing water loss through evaporation; and a covering of spines discourages animals from chewing into the juicy flesh of the plant. Desert animals are also adapted to their environment. The kangaroo rat can survive without drinking water; many reptiles live in burrows where the temperature is lower; most animals are nocturnal or active only in the cool of the night. By

reproductive success The relative production of fertile offspring by a genotype. In practical terms, the number of offspring produced by individual members of a population is tallied and compared to that of others.

extrapolation, biologists assume that the same adaptive mechanisms also work on behavioral traits. These theories and how they influence the evolution of humans will be discussed in Chapter 4.

Natural selection may also promote stability, rather than change. **Stabilizing selection** occurs in populations that are already well adapted or where change would be disadvantageous. In cases where change is disadvantageous, natural selection will favor the retention of allele frequencies more or less as they are. However, the evolutionary history of most life forms is not one of constant change, proceeding as a steady, stately progression over vast periods of time; rather, it is one of prolonged periods of relative stability or gradual change punctuated by shorter periods of more rapid change (or extinction) when altered conditions require new adaptations or when a new mutation produces an opportunity to adapt to some other available environment. According to the fossil record, most species survive between 3 and 5 million years.[9]

Although it is true that all living organisms have many adaptive characteristics, it is not true that all characteristics are adaptive. All male mammals, for example, possess nipples, even though they serve no useful purpose. To female mammals, however, nipples are essential to reproductive success, which is why males have them. The two sexes are not separate entities, shaped independently by natural selection, but are variants upon a single body plan, elaborated in later embryology. Precursors of mammary glands are built in all mammalian fetuses, enlarging later in the development of females, but remaining small and without function in males.

Nor is it true that current utility is a reliable guide to historical origin or future use. For one thing, traits that seem nonadaptive may be co-opted for later use, and traits that appear adaptive might have come about due to unrelated changes in the pattern of growth and development. For instance, the unusually large size of a kiwi's egg enhances the survivability of kiwi chicks, in that they are particularly large and capable when hatched. Nevertheless, kiwi eggs probably did not evolve to this large size because the size is adaptive. Rather, kiwis evolved from an ancestor that was the size of an ostrich, and in birds, egg size reduces at a slower rate than does body size. Therefore, the outsized eggs of kiwi birds seem to be no more than a developmental byproduct of a reduction in body size.[10]

Similarly, an existing adaptation may come under strong selective pressure for some new purpose, as did

This x-ray showing the unusually large size of a kiwi egg illustrates that evolution does not continue by preplanned design but rather by a process of tinkering with preexisting body forms.

insect wings. These did not arise so that insects might fly, but rather as structures that were used to "row," and later skim, across the surface of the water.[11] Later, the larger ones by chance proved useful for purposes of flight. In both the kiwi eggs and the insect wings, what we see is natural selection operating as "a creative scavenger, taking what is available and putting it to new use."[12]

The adaptability of organic structures and functions, no matter how much a source of wonder and fascination, nevertheless falls short of perfection. This is so because natural selection can only work with what the existing store of genetic variation provides; it cannot create something entirely new. In the words of one evolutionary biologist, evolution is a process of tinkering, rather than design. Often tinkering involves balancing beneficial and harmful effects of a specific allele, as the case of sickle-cell anemia illustrates.

The Case of Sickle-Cell Anemia

Among human beings, **sickle-cell anemia** is a particularly well-studied case of adaptation (Figure 2.7). This painful disease, in which the oxygen-carrying red blood cells

[9] Thompson, K. S. (1997). Natural selection and evolution's smoking gun. *American Scientist 85*, 516.

[10] Gould, S. J. (1991). *Bully for brontosaurus* (pp. 109–123). New York: Norton.

[11] Kaiser, J. (1994). A new theory of insect wing origins takes off. *Science 266*, 363.

[12] Dorit, R. (1997). Molecular evolution and scientific inquiry, misperceived. *American Scientist 85*, 475.

stabilizing selection Natural selection acting to promote stability rather than change in a population's gene pool.

Normal Allele

Codon	CTG	ACT	CCT	GAG	GAG	AAG	TCT
Amino acid	Leucine	Thr	Proline	Glutamic acid	Glutamic acid	Lysine	Serine
Position	3	4	5	6	7	8	9

Sickle Cell Allele

Codon	CTG	ACT	CCT	GTG	GAG	AAG	TCT
Amino acid	Leucine	Thr	Proline	Valine	Glutamic acid	Lysine	Serine

Figure 2.7 Mutation of a single base of DNA can result in a dramatically different protein. Pictured here are codons 3 through 9 for the beta chain of hemoglobin, the protein that carries oxygen in red blood cells and the amino acids these codons specify. The top row depicts the normal allele, and in the bottom row is the single substitution that makes the red blood cells bend into a sickle shape (clogging the capillary beds and causing great pain, which is what occurs with sickle-cell anemia). Sickling occurs because the amino acid valine, compared to glutamic acid in the normal allele, gives the hemoglobin molecule different properties. The beta chain is 146 amino acids long. A simple mutation (the substitution of thymine for adenine in position 6 as indicated in red) has dramatic and tragic consequences.

change shape (sickle) and clog the finest parts of the circulatory system, is caused by a mutation in the gene coding for hemoglobin, the protein responsible for oxygen transport. This disorder first came to the attention of geneticists in Chicago when it was observed that most North Americans who suffer from it are of African ancestry. Investigation traced the abnormality to populations that live in a clearly defined belt across tropical Central Africa where the sickle-cell allele is found at surprisingly high frequencies. Geneticists were curious about why such a harmful hereditary disability persisted in these populations.

According to the theory of natural selection, any alleles that are harmful will tend to disappear from the group, because the individuals who are homozygous for the abnormality generally die—are "selected out"—before they are able to reproduce. Why, then, had this seemingly harmful condition remained in populations from tropical Central Africa?

The answer to this mystery began to emerge when it was noticed that the areas with high rates of sickle-cell anemia are also areas in which a particularly deadly form of malaria (falciparum) is common (Figure 2.8). This severe form of malaria causes many deaths or, in those who survive, high fever that significantly interferes with the victims' reproductive abilities. Moreover, it was discovered that hemoglobin abnormalities are also found in people living in parts of the Arabian Peninsula, Greece, Algeria, Syria, and India, all regions where malaria is (or was) common.

Further research established that while individuals with hemoglobin abnormalities can still contract malaria, hemoglobin abnormalities are associated with an

© Meckes/Ottawa/Photo Researchers, Inc.

Sickle-cell anemia is caused by a genetic mutation in a single base of the hemoglobin gene resulting in abnormal hemoglobin, called hemoglobin S. Those afflicted by the disease are homozygous for the S allele, and all their red blood cells "sickle." Co-dominance is observable with the sickle and normal alleles. Heterozygotes make 50 percent normal hemoglobin and 50 percent sickle hemoglobin. Shown here is a sickle hemoglobin red blood cell among normal red blood cells.

increased ability to survive the effects of the malarial parasite; it seems that the effects of the abnormal hemoglobin in limited amounts were less injurious than the effects of the malarial parasite. Thus selection favored heterozygous individuals with normal and sickling hemoglobin (Hb^AHb^S). The loss of alleles for abnormal hemoglobin

sickle-cell anemia An inherited form of anemia caused by a mutation in the hemoglobin protein that causes the red blood cells to assume a sickle shape.

Why Red Is Such a Potent Color   *by Meredith F. Small*

The Olympic athletes have been parading around like fashionistas in an array of colorful outfits, and we, their adoring public, can't resist commenting on the style and color of their high-end athletic wear. My favorite was the faux silk, faux embroidered, slinky red leotards of the Chinese women's gymnasts.

Apparently, as researchers have recently discovered, the choice of red for those leotards might also have given the Chinese gymnasts an advantage. But why is the color red so impressive?

The answer lies in our tree-living past.

© Cheng Min/Xinhua/Landov

The human response to the color red may well be rooted in our anthropoid heritage. Could this have given the Chinese gymnastic team an edge? It is certain that our ape ancestry contributes to the human range of motion. While we are all not able to move in the same ways that these talented gymnasts can, the human ability to grasp, swing, stretch, and throw things derives from characteristics of the hands and shoulders inherited from our ape ancestors.

In the back of the vertebrate eyeball are two kinds of cells called rods and cones that respond to light. Cones take in a wide range of light, which means they recognize colors, and they are stimulated best during daylight. Rods respond to a narrower range of light (meaning only white light) but notice that light from far away and at night.

Isaac Newton was the first person to hold up a prism and refract white light into a rainbow of colors and realize that there might be variation in what the eye can see. Color comes at us in electromagnetic waves. When the wavelength of light is short we perceive purple or blue. Medium wavelengths of lights tickle the cones in another way and we think green. Short light wavelengths make those cones stand up and dance as bright spots of yellow, orange, and red.

Various animals distinguish only parts of that rainbow because their cones respond in different ways. Butterflies, for example, see into the ultraviolet end of the rainbow, which allows them to see their own complex markings better than we can. Foxes and owls are basically color-blind and it doesn't matter because they are awake at night when the light spectrum is limited anyway.

Humans are lucky enough to be primates, animals with decent color vision, and we can thank monkeys for this special ability.

Long ago, primitive primates that resemble today's lemurs and lorises saw only green and blue, the longer wavelengths of color. But when monkeys evolved, around 34 million years ago, their cones became sensitive to even shorter wavelengths of color and they saw red.

And what a difference. With red, the forest comes alive. Instead of a blanket of bluish-green leaves, the world is suddenly accented with ripe red, yellow, and orange fruits, and even the leaves look different.

For a monkey leaping through the forest canopy, color vision would be an essential advantage. Unripe fruit doesn't have enough carbs to sustain a hungry primate and they taste really sour. Unripe leaves not only taste bad, they are toxic and indigestible.

For the first humans foraging about the forest and savannah around 5 million years ago, it would have been be much more efficient to spot a ripe fruit or tuber than bite into a zillion just to get the right one. And so humans ended up with color vision even though we no longer live in trees.

But color is more than wavelengths, more than an indicator of ripeness, to us.

Color has become symbolic, meaning it has meaning, and that meaning is highly cultural.

Chinese athletes and Chinese brides wear red because red is considered lucky. The U.S. athletes also wear red because that bright color is in the U.S. flag, and because designers of athletic wear, as well as scientists, know that red gets you noticed.

BIOCULTURAL QUESTION

While the vast majority of humans see color as described here, 8 to 20 percent of human males have red-green color blindness. Do you know someone who is color-blind? What could a conversation with a color-blind person reveal about the anthropological perspective? What colors besides red have particular meanings? Do these meanings derive from biology or culture?

Adapted from Small, M. F. (2008, August 15). Why red is such a potent color. Live Science. http://www. livescience.com/culture/080815-hn-color-red.html.

By contrast, monkeys, apes, and humans possess both color and stereoscopic vision. Color vision markedly improves the diet of these primates compared to most other mammals. The ability to distinguish colors allows anthropoid primates to choose ripe fruits or tender immature leaves due to their red rather than green coloration. See this chapter's Biocultural Connection to see how our primate ancestry affects our response to color.

In addition to color vision, anthropoid primates possess a unique structure called the **fovea centralis,** or central pit, in the retina of each eye. Like a camera lens, this feature enables the animal to focus on a particular object

fovea centralis A shallow pit in the retina of the eye that enables an animal to focus on an object while maintaining visual contact with its surroundings.

for acutely clear perception without sacrificing visual contact with the object's surroundings.

The primates' emphasis on visual acuity came at the expense of their sense of smell. Smells are processed in the forebrain, a part of the brain that projects into the snout of animals depending upon smells. A large protruding snout, however, may interfere with stereoscopic vision. But smell is an expendable sense to diurnal tree-dwelling animals in search of insects; they no longer needed to live a "nose to the ground" existence, sniffing the ground in search of food. The anthropoids especially have the least-developed sense of smell of all land animals. Though our sense of smell allows humans to distinguish perfumes, and even to distinguish family members from strangers, our brains have come to emphasize vision rather than smell. Prosimians, by contrast, still rely more on smell than on vision, possessing numerous scent glands for marking objects in their territories.

Arboreal primates also possess an acute sense of touch. An effective feeling and grasping mechanism helps prevent them from falling and tumbling while speeding through the trees. The early mammals from which primates evolved possessed tiny touch-sensitive hairs at the tips of their hands and feet. In primates, sensitive pads backed up by nails on the tips of the animals' fingers and toes replaced these hairs.

The Primate Brain

These changes in sensory organs have corresponding changes to the primate brain. In addition, an increase in brain size, particularly in the cerebral hemispheres—the areas supporting conscious thought—occurred in the course of primate evolution. In monkeys, apes, and humans, the cerebral hemispheres completely cover the cerebellum, the part of the brain that coordinates the muscles and maintains body balance.

One of the most significant outcomes of this development is the flexibility seen in primate behavior. Rather than relying on reflexes controlled by the cerebellum, primates constantly react to a variety of features in the environment. Messages from the hands and feet, eyes and ears, as well as from the sensors of balance, movement, heat, touch, and pain, are simultaneously relayed to the cerebral cortex. Obviously the cortex had to evolve considerably in order to receive, analyze, and coordinate these impressions

and transmit the appropriate response back down to the motor nerves. The enlarged, responsive cerebral cortex provides the biological basis for flexible behavior patterns found in all primates, including humans.

There are many reasons for the increased learning capacity of the primate brain, but it likely started as the earliest primates, along with many other mammals, began to carry out their activities in the daylight hours. Prior to 65 million years ago, mammals seem to have been nocturnal in their habits. The extinction of the dinosaurs and climate change at that time opened new **ecological niches**—a species' way of life considered in the full context of its environment, including other species, geology, climate, and so on. With the change to a diurnal life, the sense of vision took on greater importance, and so visual acuity was favored by natural selection. Unlike reptile vision, where the information-processing neurons are in the retina, mammalian vision is processed in the brain, permitting integration with information received through other senses such as sound, touch, taste, and smell.

If the evolution of visual acuity led to larger brains, it is likely that the primates' insect predation in an arboreal setting also played a role in enlargement of the brain. This would have required great agility and muscular coordination, favoring development of the brain centers. Thus it is of interest that much of the higher mental faculties are apparently developed in an area alongside the motor centers of the brain.[3]

Another related hypothesis that may help account for primate brain enlargement involves the use of hands as tactile instruments to replace the teeth and jaws or snout. The hands assumed some of the grasping, tearing, and dividing functions of the jaws, again requiring development of the brain centers for more complete coordination.

The Primate Skeleton

The skeleton gives animals with internal backbones, or **vertebrates,** their basic shape or silhouette, supports the soft tissues, and helps protect vital internal organs (Figure 3.6). In primates, for example, the skull protects the brain and the eyes. A number of factors are responsible for the shape of the primate skull as compared with those of most other mammals: changes in dentition, changes in the sensory organs of sight and smell, and increased brain size.

The primate braincase, or **cranium,** tends to be high and vaulted. A solid partition exists in anthropoid primates between the eye and the temple, affording maximum protection to the eyes from the contraction of the chewing muscles positioned directly next to the eyes.

---

ecological niche A species' way of life considered in the full context of its environment, including factors such as diet, activity, terrain, vegetation, predators, prey, and climate.

vertebrate An animal with a backbone, including fish, amphibians, reptiles, birds, and mammals.

cranium The braincase of the skull.

---

[3]Romer, A. S. (1945). *Vertebrate paleontology* (p. 103). Chicago: University of Chicago Press.

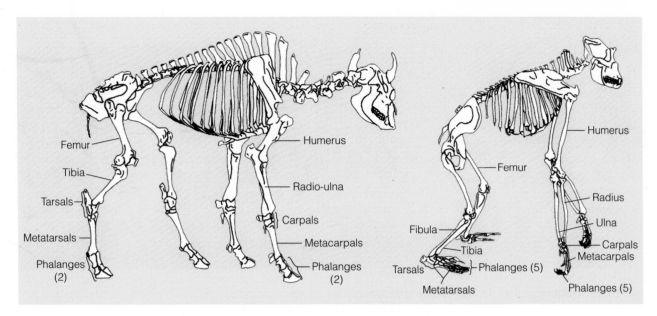

Figure 3.6 All primates possess the same ancestral vertebrate limb pattern seen in reptiles and amphibians, consisting of a single upper long bone, two lower long bones, and five radiating digits (fingers and toes), as seen in this gorilla (right) skeleton. Other mammals such as bison (left) have a modified version of this pattern. In the course of evolution, bison have lost all but two of their digits, which form their hooves. The second long bone in the lower part of the limb is reduced. Note also the joining of the skull and vertebral column in these skeletons. In bison (as in most mammals) the skull projects forward from the vertebral column, but in semi-erect gorillas, the vertebral column is further beneath the skull.

The **foramen magnum** (the large opening at the base of the skull through which the spinal cord passes and connects to the brain) is an important clue to evolutionary relationships. In most mammals, as in dogs and horses, this opening faces directly backward, with the skull projecting forward from the vertebral column. In humans, by contrast, the vertebral column joins the skull toward the center of its base, thereby placing the skull in a balanced position as required for habitual upright posture. Other primates, though they frequently cling, sit, or hang with their bodies upright, are not as fully committed to upright posture as humans, and so their foramen magnum is not as far forward.

In anthropoid primates, the snout or muzzle portion of the skull reduced as the acuity of the sense of smell declined. The smaller snout offers less interference with stereoscopic vision; it also enables the eyes to take a frontal position. As a result, primates have flatter faces than some other mammals.

Below the primate skull and the neck is the **clavicle,** or collarbone, a bone found in ancestral mammals though lost in mammals such as cats. The size of the clavicle is reduced in quadrupedal primates like monkeys that possess a narrow sturdy body plan. In the apes, by contrast, it is broad, orienting the arms at the side rather than at the front of the body and forming part of the **suspensory hanging apparatus** of this group (see Table 3.2). The clavicle also supports the **scapula** (shoulder blade) and allows for the muscle development that is required for flexible yet powerful arm movement—permitting large-bodied apes to hang suspended below tree branches and to **brachiate**, or swing from tree to tree.

The limbs of the primate skeleton follow the same basic ancestral plan seen in the earliest vertebrates. Other animals possess limbs specialized to optimize a particular behavior, such as speed. In each primate arm or leg, the upper portion of the limb has a single long bone, the lower portion two long bones, and then hands or feet with five radiating digits (phalanges). Their grasping feet and hands have sensitive pads at the tips of their digits, backed up (except in some prosimians) by flattened nails. This unique

foramen magnum A large opening in the skull through which the spinal cord passes and connects to the brain.

clavicle The collarbone connecting the sternum (breastbone) with the scapula (shoulder blade).

suspensory hanging apparatus The broad powerful shoulder joints and muscles found in all the hominoids, allowing these large-bodied primates to hang suspended below the tree branches.

scapula The shoulder blade.

brachiation Using the arms to move from branch to branch, with the body hanging suspended beneath the arms.

Visual Counterpoint

© blickwinkel/Alamy

© Kevin Schafer/Peter Arnold, Inc.

Wherever there is competition from the anthropoid primates, prosimian species, such as this loris on the right, retain the arboreal nocturnal patterns of the earliest fossil primates. Notice its large eyes, long snout, and moist split nose—all useful in its relatively solitary search for food in the trees at night. In contrast, only on the large island of Madagascar off the eastern coast of Africa, where no anthropoids existed until humans arrived, have prosimians come to occupy the diurnal ground-dwelling niche as do these ring-tailed lemurs. While all prosimians still rely on scent, marking their territory and communicating through smelly messages, daytime activity allowed the prosimians on Madagascar to become far less solitary. Also notice the difference in the size of the eyes in these two groups. Just as it would be incorrect to think of prosimians as "less evolved" than anthropoid primates because they bear a closer resemblance to the ancestral primate condition, it is also incorrect to think of lorises as less evolved compared to lemurs.

combination of pad and nail provides the animal with an excellent **prehensile** (grasping) device for use when moving from branch to branch. The structural characteristics of the primate foot and hand make grasping possible; the digits are extremely flexible, the big toe is fully **opposable** to the other digits in all but humans and their immediate ancestors, and the thumb is opposable to the other digits to varying degrees.

The retention of the flexible vertebrate limb pattern in primates was a valuable asset to evolving humans. It was, in part, having hands capable of grasping that enabled our own ancestors to manufacture and use tools and to embark on the evolutionary pathway that led to the revolutionary ability to adapt through culture.

To sum up, what becomes apparent when humans are compared to other primates is how many of the characteristics we consider distinctly human are not in fact uniquely ours; rather, they are variants of typical primate traits. We humans look the way we do because we are primates, and the differences between us and others of this order—especially the apes—are more differences of degree than differences of kind.

Living Primates

Except for a few species of Old World monkeys who live in temperate climates and humans who inhabit the entire globe, living primates inhabit warm areas of the world. We will briefly explore the diversity of the five natural groupings of living primates: lemurs and lorises, tarsiers, New World monkeys, Old World monkeys, and apes. We will examine each group's distinctive habitat, biological features, and behavior.

Lemurs and Lorises

Although the natural habitat of lemurs is restricted to the large island of Madagascar (off the east coast of Africa), lorises range from Africa to southern and eastern Asia. Only on Madagascar, where there was no competition from anthropoid primates until humans arrived, are lemurs diurnal, or active during the day; lorises, by contrast, are all nocturnal and arboreal.

All these animals are small, with none larger than a good-sized dog. In general body outline, they resemble

> **prehensile** Having the ability to grasp.
> **opposable** Able to bring the thumb or big toe in contact with the tips of the other digits on the same hand or foot in order to grasp objects.

rodents and insectivores, with short pointed snouts, large pointed ears, and big eyes. In the anatomy of the upper lip and snout, lemurs and lorises resemble nonprimate mammals in that the upper lip is bound down to the gums, thus limiting their range of facial expression. The naked skin on the nose around the nostrils is moist and split, which facilitates a keen sense of smell. Most also have long tails, with that of a ring-tail lemur somewhat like the tail of a raccoon.

Lemurs and lorises have typical primate "hands," although they use them in pairs, rather than one at a time. Their fingers and toes are particularly strong. Sensitive pads and flattened nails are located at the tips of the fingers and toes, although they retain a claw on their second toe, sometimes called a grooming claw, which they use for scratching and cleaning. Lemurs and lorises possess another unique structure for grooming: a dental comb made up of the lower incisors and canines that projects forward from the jaw and that can be run through the fur. Behind the incisors and canines, lemurs and lorises have three premolars and molars, resulting in a dental formula of 2-1-3-3.

Lemurs and lorises have scent glands at their wrists, under their arms, and/or in their anal regions that they use for communication. Individuals leave smelly messages for one another by rubbing their scent glands on tree branches or some other fixture of the environment. Through such olfactory clues, lemurs and lorises can recognize distinct individuals within their own group as well as pinpoint their location and physical state. They also use scent to mark their territory, thus communicating to members of other groups.

The hind legs of lemurs and lorises are longer than their front legs, and when they move on all fours, the forelimbs are in a palms-down position. Some species can also move from tree to tree by vertical clinging and leaping. First they hang onto the trunk of one tree in an upright position, with their long legs curled up tightly like springs and their heads twisted to look in the direction they are moving. They propel themselves into the air, do a "180," and land facing the trunk on their tree of choice.

With their distinctive mix of characteristics, lemurs and lorises appear to occupy a place between the anthropoid primates and insectivores, the mammalian order that includes moles and shrews.

Tarsiers

Outwardly, tarsiers resemble lemurs and lorises. Molecular evidence, however, indicates a closer relationship to monkeys, apes, and humans. The head, eyes, and ears of these kitten-sized arboreal creatures are huge in proportion to the body. They have the remarkable ability to turn their heads 180 degrees, so they can see where they have been as well as where they are going. Their digits end in platelike adhesive discs.

Tarsiers are named for the elongated tarsal, or foot bone, that provides leverage for jumps of 6 feet or more. Tarsiers are mainly nocturnal insect eaters and so occupy a niche that is similar to that of the earliest ancestral primates. In the structure of the nose and lips and in the part of the brain governing vision, tarsiers resemble monkeys.

With their large eyes, tarsiers are well adapted for nocturnal life. If humans possessed eyes proportionally the same size as tarsiers relative to the size of our faces, our eyes would be approximately the size of oranges. In their nocturnal habit and outward appearance, tarsiers resemble lemurs and lorises. Genetically, however, they are more closed related to monkeys and apes, causing scientists to rework the suborder divisions in primate taxonomy to reflect this evolutionary relationship.

Grasping hands and three-dimensional vision enable primates like this South American monkey to lead an active life in the trees. In some New World monkey species, a grasping or prehensile tail makes tree life even easier. The naked skin on the underside of the tail resembles the sensitive skin found at the tips of our fingers and is even covered with whorls like fingerprints. This sensory skin allows New World monkeys to use their tails as a fifth limb.

New World Monkeys

New World monkeys live in tropical forests of South and Central America. In outward body plan they closely resemble Old World monkeys, except that New World monkeys are characterized by flat noses with widely separated, outward-flaring nostrils. Their infraorder name platyrrhine (from the Greek for "flat-nosed") comes from this characteristic. There are five different families of New World monkeys, and they range in size from less than a pound to over 30 pounds.

There are two reasons why New World monkeys have not been studied as extensively as other primates. The first is that an emphasis on human origins in primatology meant that Old World species were favored by researchers. The second is that nearly all New World species are arboreal, which makes it more difficult for researchers to observe them. In recent decades, however, primatologists have conducted numerous long-range field studies on a variety of species.

For example, anthropologist Karen Strier has studied the woolly spider monkey, or muriqui, in the state of Minas Gerais, Brazil, for close to three decades. Her field studies progressed from examining muriqui diet, social structure, and **demographics** (population characteristics such as the number of individuals of each age and sex) to tracking the reproductive cycles and health of these large, peaceful forest dwellers. She pioneered a noninvasive method to measure reproductive hormone levels and the presence of parasites through analysis of the feces of individual animals. Her fieldwork included waiting to catch feces (in a gloved hand) the moment it was dropping from the trees or quickly retrieving it from the ground. Through analysis of these samples, Strier was able to document correlations between diet and fertility.

Strier also documented a reduced parasite load in muriquis that consumed certain plants—apparently for their medicinal/therapeutic value. Amazonian peoples have been known to use some of these plants for the same reason. As these human populations become increasingly removed from their traditional lifeways due to globalization and modernization, the muriqui may become a valuable source to reclaim knowledge of the forest. According to Strier, "While traditional peoples of the Amazon have survived long enough to impart some of their knowledge of forest plants, the indigenous human societies of the Atlantic forest are long gone. The muriqui and other monkeys may provide humans with their best guides to the forest's medicinal values."[4] Field studies like Strier's not only have contributed to our understanding of the behavior and biology of New World monkeys but have also played a major role in bringing back a number of species from the brink of extinction.

New World monkeys—unlike Old World monkeys, apes, and humans—possess a 2-1-3-3 dental formula (three, rather than two, premolars on each

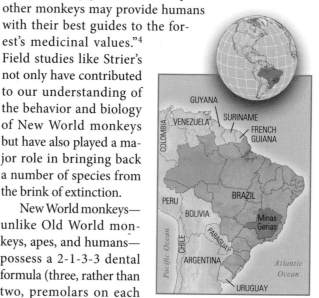

demographics Population characteristics such as the number of individuals of each age and sex.

4 Strier, K. (1993, March). Menu for a monkey. *Natural History*, 42.

© dbimages/Alamy

While all Old World monkeys share certain features like a narrow body plan, a non-prehensile tail, and a 2-1-2-3 dental formula, some unusual specializations are also seen. The proboscis monkey, found in the mangrove swamps of Borneo, is known for its unusual protruding nose, which provides a chamber for extra resonance for its vocalizations. When a monkey is alarmed, the nose fills with blood so that the resonating chamber becomes even more enlarged.

side of each jaw). This is not as much a functional distinction as it is a difference in evolutionary path. The common ancestor of Old World anthropoids and New World anthropoids possessed this 2-1-3-3 dental pattern. In the New World this pattern remained, while in Old World species a molar was lost.

Like Old World monkeys, New World monkeys have long tails. All members of one group, the family Atelidae, possess prehensile or grasping tails that they use as a fifth limb. The naked skin on the underside of their tail resembles the sensitive skin found at the tips of our fingers and is even covered with whorls like fingerprints.

Platyrrhines walk on all fours with their palms down and scamper along tree branches in search of fruit, which they eat sitting upright. Although New World monkeys spend much of their time in the trees, they rarely hang suspended below the branches or swing from limb to limb by their arms and have not developed the extremely long forelimbs and broad shoulders characteristic of the apes.

Old World Monkeys

Old World or catarrhine (from the Greek for "sharp-nosed") primates are divided from the apes at the superfamily taxonomic level. They resemble New World monkeys in their basic body plan, but their noses are distinctive, with closely spaced, downward-pointing nostrils. Divided into two subfamilies, the Cercopithecinae and the Colobinae, which contain eleven and ten genera, respectively, Old World monkeys are very diverse and occupy a broader range of habitats compared to New World monkey species, which occupy only tropical forests.

Some Old World monkeys are known for their unusual coloring, such as mandrills (pictured on page 62) with their brightly colored faces and genitals. Others, like proboscis monkeys, have long droopy noses. They all possess a 2-1-2-3 dental formula (two, rather than three, premolars on each side of each jaw) and tails that are never prehensile. They may be either arboreal or terrestrial, using a quadrupedal pattern of locomotion on the ground or in the trees in a palms-down position. Their body plan is narrow with hind limbs and forelimbs of equal length, a reduced clavicle (collarbone), and relatively fixed and sturdy shoulder, elbow, and wrist joints.

The arboreal species include the colubus guereza monkey—a species known to have been hunted by chimpanzees. Some are equally at home on the ground and in the trees, such as the macaques, of which some nineteen species range from tropical Africa and Asia to Gibraltar on the southern coast of Spain to Japan. At the northernmost portions of their range, these primates are living in temperate rather than strictly tropical environments.

Baboons, a kind of Old World monkey, have been of particular interest to paleoanthropologists because they live in environments similar to those in which humans may have originated. These baboons have abandoned trees (except for sleeping and refuge) and are largely terrestrial, living in the savannahs, deserts, and highlands of Africa. Somewhat dog-faced, they have long muzzles and a fierce look and eat a diet of leaves, seeds, insects, lizards, and small mammals. They live in large, well-organized troops comprised of related females and adult males that have transferred out of other troops.

Other Old World species also have much to tell us. For example, over the past several decades primatologists

© Gerard Lacz/Peter Arnold, Inc.

While all apes or hominoids possess a suspensory hanging apparatus that allows them to hang from the branches of the forest canopy, only the gibbon is a master of brachiation—swinging from branch to branch. The nonhuman hominoids can also walk bipedally for brief periods of time when they need their arms free for carrying, but they cannot sustain bipedal locomotion for more than 50 to 100 yards. Hominoid anatomy is better adapted to knuckle-walking and hanging in the trees.

have documented primate social learning and innovation in colonies of macaques in Japan. Similarly, field studies of vervet monkeys in eastern and southern Africa have revealed that these Old World monkeys possess sophisticated communication abilities. In short, wherever primatologists study primates they make fascinating new discoveries. These discoveries contribute not only to the disciplines of primatology, evolutionary biology, and ecology but also to deepening our understanding of who we are as primates. Chapter 4 includes more on the behavior of baboons and a variety of other Old World monkey species.

Small and Great Apes

The apes of the hominoid superfamily are our closest cousins in the animal world. Like us, apes are large, wide-bodied primates with no tails. As described earlier, apes possess a shoulder anatomy specialized for hanging suspended below tree branches. All apes have this suspensory

hanging apparatus, though among apes only small, lithe gibbons and talented gymnasts swing from branch to branch in the pattern known as *brachiation*. At the opposite extreme are gorillas, which generally climb trees, using their prehensile hands and feet to grip the trunk and branches. While smaller gorillas may swing between branches, in large individuals swinging is limited to leaning outward while reaching for fruit and clasping a limb for support. Still, most of their time is spent on the ground. All apes except humans and their immediate ancestors possess arms that are longer than their legs.

In moving on the ground, African apes "knuckle-walk" on the backs of their hands, resting their weight on the middle joints of the fingers. They stand erect when reaching for fruit, looking over tall grass, or doing any activity where they find an erect position advantageous. The semi-erect position is natural in apes when on the ground because the curvature of their vertebral column places their center of gravity, which is high in their bodies, in front of their hip joint. Thus they are both "top heavy" and "front heavy." Though apes can walk on two legs, or bipedally, for short distances, the structure of the ape pelvis is not well suited to support the weight of the torso and limbs for more than several minutes.

Gibbons and siamangs, the small apes that are native to Southeast Asia and Malaya, have compact, slim bodies with extraordinarily long arms compared to their short legs and stand about 3 feet high. Although their usual form of locomotion is brachiation, they can run erect, holding their arms out for balance. Gibbon and siamang males and females are similar in size, living in family groups of two parents and offspring.

Orangutans, found in Borneo and Sumatra, are divided into two distinct species. They are considerably taller than gibbons and siamangs and are much heavier, with the bulk characteristic of the great apes. In the closeness of the eyes and facial prominence, an orangutan looks very human-like. The people of Sumatra gave orangutans their name, "person of the forest," using the Malay term *oran,* which means "person." On the ground, orangutans walk with their forelimbs in a fists-sideways or a palms-down position. They are, however, more arboreal than the African apes. Although sociable by nature, the orangutans of upland Borneo spend most of their time alone (except in the case of females with young), as they have to forage over a wide area to obtain sufficient food. By contrast, fruits and insects are sufficiently abundant in the swamps of Sumatra to sustain groups of adults and permit coordinated group travel. Thus gregariousness is a function of habitat productivity.[5]

_____

[5] Normile, D. (1998). Habitat seen as playing larger role in shaping behavior. *Science 279,* 1454.

© Jay Ullal

This male orangutan was photographed along the Gohong River on the island of Kaja, Borneo. A resident of a preserve where captive animals are rehabituated into the wild, the young male copied this hunting behavior by watching humans spear fishing along the same river. Although so far the orangutan has been unable to nab a fish with his spear tip, his intent is clear. This rare photograph, along with the first photograph of a swimming orangutan, appears in the beautiful book titled *Thinkers of the Jungle,* by Gerd Schuster, Willie Smits, and photographer Jay Ullal.

Gorillas, found in equatorial Africa, are the largest of the apes; an adult male can weigh over 450 pounds, with females about half that size. Scientists distinguish between two gorilla species: the lowland and mountain varieties. The body is covered with a thick coat of glossy black hair, and mature males have a silvery gray upper back. There is a strikingly human look about the face, and like humans, gorillas focus on things in their field of vision by directing the eyes rather than moving the head.

Gorillas are mostly ground dwellers, but the lighter females and young may sleep in trees in carefully constructed nests. Because of their weight, adult males spend less time in the trees but raise and lower themselves among the tree branches when searching for fruit. Gorillas knuckle-walk, using all four limbs with the fingers of the hand flexed, placing the knuckles instead of the palm of the hand on the ground. They stand erect to reach for fruit, to see something more easily, or to threaten perceived sources of danger with their famous chest-beating displays. Though known for these displays to protect the members of their troop, adult male silverback gorillas are the gentle giants of the forest. As vegetarians, gorillas devote a major portion of each day to eating volumes of plant matter to sustain their massive bodies. Although gorillas are gentle and tolerant, bluffing aggression is an important part of their behavioral repertoire.

Chimpanzees and bonobos are two closely related species of the same genus (*Pan*), pictured frequently throughout this chapter. Bonobos are restricted in their distribution to the rainforests of the Democratic Republic of Congo. The common chimpanzee, by contrast, is widely distributed in the forested portions of sub-Saharan Africa. Chimpanzees and bonobos are probably the best known of the apes and have long been favorites in zoos and circuses.

In the past, bonobos were thought to be the same species. When bonobos were recognized as a distinct species in 1929, their common name was "pygmy chimpanzee." "Bonobo" replaced this term because not only does their size range overlap with that of chimpanzees, but as we will explore in the next chapter, this feature is not the most characteristic difference between the two groups.

Although thought of as particularly quick and clever, all four great apes are of equal intelligence, despite some differences in cognitive styles. More arboreal than gorillas but less so than orangutans, chimpanzees and bonobos forage on the ground much of the day, knuckle-walking like gorillas. At sunset, they return to the trees, where they build their nests.

Primate Conservation

The above survey of living primates illustrates the diversity of our closest living relatives. To ensure that they will continue to share the planet with us, primate conservation has become an issue of vital importance. Nearly 50 percent of the known primate species and subspecies face extinction in the next decade.[6]

In Asia, the statistics are even more alarming, with more than 70 percent of species threatened and at least 80 percent at risk in Indonesia and Vietnam. Included among them are all of the great apes, as well as such formerly widespread and adaptable species as rhesus macaques. In the wild these animals are threatened by habitat destruction caused by

[6] Kaplan, M. (2008, August 5). Almost half of primate species face extinction. doi:10.1038/news.2008.1013.

Globalscape

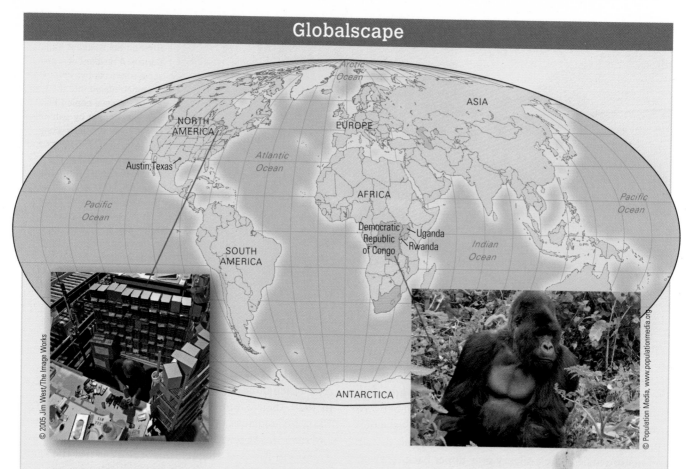

© 2005 Jim West/The Image Works

© Population Media, www.populationmedia.org

Gorilla Hand Ashtrays?

Tricia, a 20-year-old from Austin, Texas, blogs: "At that party did you meet the guy from South Africa that looked like an exact replica of Dave Matthews (only skinnier) who was talking about gorilla hand ashtrays?"[a] The unnamed guy was talking about one of the many real threats to gorillas in the wild. With no natural enemies, human actions alone are responsible for the shrinking population of gorillas in their natural habitats in Rwanda, Uganda, and the Democratic Republic of Congo. Despite conservation work, begun by the late primatologist Dian Fossey, who pioneered field studies of the gorillas in the 1970s, gorilla hand ashtrays

and heads remain coveted souvenirs for unsavory tourists. A poacher can sell these body parts and the remaining bushmeat for a handsome profit.

Today, not only do logging and mining in gorilla habitats destroy these forests, but roads make it easier for poachers to access the gorillas. Local governments of Rwanda and Uganda in partnership with the Fossey Fund and the Bush Meat Project have set up poaching patrols and community partnerships to protect the endangered gorillas. Thousands of miles away, Tricia and her friends can also help by recycling their cell phones. The mineral coltan that is found in cell phones is mined primarily from gorilla habitats in

the Democratic Republic of Congo. Recycling, as pictured here in a Michigan cell phone recycling plant, will reduce the amount of new coltan needed.

Global Twister   Encouraging recycling of cell phones and discouraging poaching both will impact gorilla survival. How would you go about convincing average cell phone users or poachers to change their habits or livelihood to protect endangered gorillas?

---

[a]http://profile.myspace.com/index.cfm?fuseaction=user.viewprofile&friendid=40312227. (accessed July 3, 2006)

economic development (farming, lumbering, cattle ranching, rubber tapping), as well as by hunters and trappers who pursue them for food, trophies, research, or as exotic pets. Primatologists have long known the devastating effects of habitat destruction through slash-and-burn agriculture.

Further, it is not just traditional practices, such as the burning and clearing of tropical forests, that are destroying primate habitats. War also impacts primate habitats significantly, even after a war has ended. Hunters may use the

automatic weapons left over from human conflicts in their pursuit of bushmeat. Also, because monkeys and apes are so closely related to humans, they are regarded as essential for biomedical research. While most primates in laboratories are bred in captivity, an active trade in live primates still threatens their local extinction. Globalization also exerts a profound impact on local conditions. This chapter's Globalscape illustrates how cell phones are impacting gorilla habitats and the survival of this species.

Because of their vulnerability, the conservation of primates has become a matter of urgency. Traditional conservation efforts have emphasized habitat preservation above all else, but primatologists are now expanding their efforts to include educating local communities and discouraging the hunting of primates for food and medical purposes. Some primatologists are even looking for alternative economic strategies for local peoples so that human and primate populations can return to the successful coexistence that prevailed before colonialism and globalization contributed to the destabilization of tradition homelands. This chapter's Anthropology Applied looks at these economic development efforts in the Democratic Republic of Congo.

In direct conservation efforts, primatologists work to maintain some populations in the wild, either by establishing preserves where animals are already living or by moving populations to suitable habitats. These approaches require constant monitoring and management to ensure that sufficient space and resources remain available. As humans encroach on primate habitats, translocation of primates to protected areas is an viable strategy for primate conservation, and the field studies by primatologists for such relocations are invaluable.

For example, when the troop of free-ranging baboons that primatologist Shirley Strum had been studying for fifteen years in Kenya began raiding people's crops and garbage on newly established farms, she was instrumental in successfully moving this troop and two other local troops—130 animals in all—to more sparsely inhabited country 150 miles away. Knowing their habits, Strum was able to trap, tranquilize, and transport the animals to their new home while preserving the baboons' vital social relationships. Strum's careful work allowed for a smooth transition. With social relations intact, the baboons did not abandon their new homes nor did they block the transfer of new males, with their all-important knowledge of local resources, into the troop. The success of her effort, which had never been tried with baboons, proves that translocation is a realistic technique for saving endangered primate species. However, this conservation effort depends first on available land, where preserves can be established to provide habitats for endangered primates.

A second strategy has been developed to help primates that have been illegally trapped—either for market as pets or for biomedical research. This approach involves returning these recovered animals to their natural habitats. Researchers have established orphanages in which specially trained human substitute mothers support the young primates so that they can gain enough social skills to return to living with their own species.

A third strategy to preventing primate extinction is to maintain breeding colonies in captivity. These colonies encourage psychological and physical well-being, as well as reproductive success. Primates in zoos and laboratories do not successfully reproduce when deprived of such

Because of their exceptional beauty, golden lion tamarin monkeys (or golden marmosets) have been kept as pets since colonial times. More recently, they have also been threatened by development, as they reside in the tropical forest habitats around the popular tourist destination of Rio de Janeiro, Brazil. A major conservation effort, initiated in the 1980s to save these monkeys, included planting wildlife corridors to connect the remaining forest patches and releasing animals bred in captivity into these newly created environments. Today live wild births have increased steadily, and the golden lion tamarin population is recovering from the threat of extinction.

amenities as opportunities for climbing, materials for nest building, others with whom to socialize, and places for privacy. While such features contribute to the success of breeding colonies in captivity, ensuring the survival of our primate cousins in suitable natural habitats is a far greater challenge that humans must meet in the years to come.

The good news is the results of conservation efforts are beginning to show. For example, due to intense conservation programs, the population size of the mountain gorilla (*Gorilla beringei beringei*) is increasing, even with the political chaos of Rwanda, Uganda, and the Democratic Republic of Congo. Western lowland gorilla populations (*Gorilla gorilla*) are also on the rise. Similarly, tamarin monkey populations in Brazil have stabilized despite being on the brink of extinction thirty years ago, demonstrating the effectiveness of the conservation initiatives put into place. According to primatologist Sylvia Atsalis, "The presence alone of scientists has been shown to protect primates, acting as a deterrent to habitat destruction and hunting. The more people we can send, the more we can help to protect endangered primates."[7]

---

[7] Ibid.

The Congo Heartland Project

Under the leadership of Belgian primatologist Jef Dupain, the African Wildlife Foundation has embarked on a number of projects to support the continued survival of bonobos and mountain gorillas in the Democratic Republic of Congo (DRC). Called the Congo Heartland Project, this work is designed to support the local human populations devastated by a decade of civil war in the Congo itself as well as the impact of the massive influx of refugees from war and genocide in neighboring Rwanda.

The rich rainforest habitats of the tributaries of the mighty Congo River in the DRC are the only natural habitats for bonobos in the world. Mountain gorillas can be found in the DRC and in neighboring Uganda and Rwanda. Primatological fieldwork thrived in sites established during the 1970s until the mid-1990s when war and genocide led to the forced removal of primatologists. While many left the region, Dupain stayed and monitored the kinds of bushmeat brought into the markets in Kinshasa. With the human population desperate and starving and the poachers armed with automatic weapons outnumbering the few park rangers charged with protecting the

great apes, many primates perished. Since a fragile peace was achieved in 2003, initiatives of the Congo Heartland Project have been reestablished, including involving local communities in agricultural practices to protecting the Congo River and its tributaries and to preserve their precious animal populations.

Congo Heartland Project initiatives typically empower local communities in development efforts using a participative, interactive, and transparent approach. For example, a range of different ethnic groups, including those who are marginalized such as Pygmies and women, met with local authorities to reestablish the management policies of Dupain's field site (the Lomako Yokokala Faunal Reserve) as it reopened for researchers and ecotourists. Forty percent of the income generated in park revenues is to return to the local communities. According to Dupain, success for these projects is defined as follows:

> Local communities take part in decision making on how the protected area will be managed, on how revenue will be shared, and as a result, local communities take up the defense of their protected area. In time, densities of bonobo, bongo, forest elephant, Congo peacock, leopard, Allen's swamp monkey, black and white colobus, and many others will increase, more tourists and researchers will come and will be willing to pay for this environmental service, local communities will have increased access to education, medical treatment, electricity, clean water . . . the list goes on.

Mange Bofaso put it best: "In Katanga they have diamonds. Here in Lomako, we have bonobos."[a]

The Congo Heartland Project also includes encouraging a variety of alternative economic practices in communities bordering existing wildlife preserves. For example, around the Virunga National Park, home to the endangered mountain gorilla, Congolese Enterprise Officer Wellard Makambo encourages and monitors bee keeping and a women's mushroom farm collective. He also advises members of a conflict resolution team dealing with gorillas that have left the wildlife preserve to raid human crops. Local communities require reassurance and restitution, while gorillas need to be returned safely to the park. When Makambo made his first trip back to the Bukima Ranger Station after the war, he wrote,

> While I was standing on the hill surveying the amazing Bukima view I felt like a mighty silverback gorilla looking at his bountiful bamboo kingdom. One whose life would be hopeless if this kingdom is destroyed. I tried to measure the effects of the war on people and on our activities and projects. It was tough getting my head around it: how to re-start things when you realise effort alone is not sufficient. You need stability as well, which is slowly coming back to this area.

These economic development projects are playing a crucial role in restoring the stability in the region required for the continued survival of bonobos and mountain gorillas.

© AWF/Paul Thomson

The African Wildlife Foundation team in the Congo Heartland. The Lomako Conservation Research Center provides jobs for local families and serves as an anchor for research, conservation, and microenterprise activities in the largely undisturbed Lomako Forest while also securing the habitat of the bonobo, a rare great ape that lives in the Lomako Forest.

[a]African Wildlife Foundation, Facebook blog. http://www.facebook.com/pages/African-Wildlife-Foundation/11918108948. (accessed June 13, 2009)

[b]Ibid.

Questions for Reflection

1. Does knowing more about the numerous similarities among the primates including humans motivate you personally to want to meet the challenge of preventing the extinction of our primate cousins? How would you go about doing this?

2. Considering some of the trends seen among the primates, such as increased brain size or reduced tooth number, why is it that we cannot say that some primates are more evolved than others? What is wrong with the statement that humans are more evolved than chimpanzees?

3. Two systems exist for dividing the primate order into suborders because of difficulties with classifying tarsiers.

Should classification systems be based on genetic relationships or based on the biological concept of grade? Is the continued use of the older terminology an instance of inertia or a difference in philosophy? How do the issues brought up by the "tarsier problem" translate to the hominoids?

4. What aspects of mammalian primate biology do you see reflected in yourself or in other humans you know?

5. Many primate species are endangered today. What human factors are causing endangerment of primates, and how can we prevent the extinction of our closest living relatives?

Suggested Readings

de Waal, F.B.M. (2001). *The ape and the sushi master*. New York: Basic.

This masterful discussion of the presence of culture among apes moves this concept from an anthropocentric realm and ties it instead to communication and social organization. In an accessible style, Frans de Waal, one of the world's foremost experts on bonobos, demonstrates ape culture while challenging human intellectual theories designed to exclude animals from the "culture club."

de Waal, F.B.M. (2003). *My family album: Thirty years of primate photography*. Berkeley: University of California Press.

This book expertly blends scientific theories with photographs. De Waal illustrates the emotional intelligence, personality, and diverse social behaviors of the apes and Old World monkeys he has encountered in the field.

Fossey, D. (1983). *Gorillas in the mist*. Burlington, MA: Houghton Mifflin.

The late Dian Fossey is to gorillas what Jane Goodall is to chimpanzees. Fossey devoted years to the study of gorilla behavior in the field. This book is about the first thirteen years of her study; as well as being readable and informative, it is well illustrated.

Galdikas, B. (1995). *Reflections on Eden: My years with the orangutans of Borneo*. New York: Little, Brown.

Biruté Galdikas is the least known of the trio of young women sent by Louis Leakey in 1971 to study apes in the wild. Her work with the orangutans of Borneo, however, is magnificent. In this book she presents rich scientific information as well as her personal reflections on a life spent fully integrated with orangutans and the culture of Borneo.

Goodall, J. (1990). *Through a window: My thirty years with the chimpanzees of Gombe*. Boston: Houghton Mifflin.

This fascinating book is a personal account of Jane Goodall's early experiences studying wild chimpanzees in Tanzania. A pleasure to read and a fount of information on the behavior of these apes, the book is profusely illustrated as well.

Goodall, J. (2000). *Reason for hope: A spiritual journey*. New York: Warner.

Jane Goodall's memoir linking her monumental life's work with the chimpanzees of Gombe to her spiritual convictions. She clearly states her commitment to conferring on chimpanzees the same rights and respect experienced by humans through the exploration of difficult topics such as environmental destruction, animal abuse, and genocide. She expands the concept of humanity while providing us with powerful reasons to maintain hope.

Rowe, N., & Mittermeier, R. A. (1996). *The pictorial guide to the living primates*. East Hampton, NY: Pogonias.

Filled with dynamic photographs of primates in nature, this book also provides concise descriptions (including anatomy, taxonomy, diet, social structure, maps, and so on) for 234 species of primates. The book is useful for students and primatologists alike.

Challenge Issue Biological similarities among humans, apes, and Old World monkeys have led to the extensive use of nonhuman primate species in biomedical research aimed at preventing or curing disease in humans. These research animals are subjected to procedures that would be considered morally questionable if done on humans. Mickey, for example, was one of the hundreds of chimps who spent decades of her life alone in a concrete-and-steel windowless cage in a private research facility in New Mexico run by Frederick Coulston. After years of testing the effects of various infectious diseases, cosmetics, drugs, and pesticides on chimps like Mickey, the Coulston laboratory finally closed in 2002 when government research funding was withdrawn due to repeated violations of the Animal Welfare Act. But after years of abuse and neglect, research chimpanzees lack the skills to participate in chimpanzee social life. Furthermore, research animals have often been infected with deadly diseases such as HIV or hepatitis and cannot be released into the wild. Fortunately, Mickey and the other research chimps were given sanctuary through Save the Chimps, one of several organizations that rescue research animals. The human challenge for the future will be to use our abundant intelligence and social conscience, traits that our closest relatives also possess, to make the development of alternative research methods a top priority, so that nonhuman primates no longer have to be victimized by biomedical research.

CHAPTER 4

Primate Behavior

Chapter Preview

Why Do Anthropologists Study the Social Behavior of Primates?

The study of the social behavior of primates has contributed significantly to ecology and evolutionary theory. In addition, analysis of the behavior of monkeys and apes living today—especially those most closely related to us—provides important clues from which to reconstruct the adaptations and behavior patterns involved in the emergence of our earliest ancestors. The more we know about our nearest living relatives, the more it becomes clear that many of the differences between apes and humans reflect differences in degree of expression of shared characteristics.

What Determines the Behavior of Nonhuman Primates?

Diet, type of social organization, reproductive patterning, differences between the sexes, and the particular ecosystem a group of primates inhabits all contribute to the behavior of nonhuman primates. For many years primate behavior was seen as environmentally determined and tied to a certain diet and characteristics of the ecosystem. Today primatologists have established a strong socially learned component to primate behavior. Compared to other mammals, primates are characterized by a relatively long growth and development period that allows young primates to learn the behaviors of their social group. Some of these behaviors are influenced by the biology of the species while other behaviors derive from the traditions of the group.

Do Nonhuman Primates Possess Culture?

The more we learn of the behavior of our nearest primate cousins, the more we become aware of the importance of learned, socially shared practices and knowledge among the homonoids. This raises the question of whether chimpanzees, bonobos, and the other apes have culture. The answer appears to be yes. Detailed study of ape behavior has revealed variation among groups in use of tools and patterns of social engagement; these differences seem to derive from the traditions of the group rather than a biologically determined script. Humans share with the other apes an ability to learn the complex but flexible patterns of behavior particular to a social group during a long period of childhood dependency.

In October 1960, the young Jane Goodall sent word back to her mentor, paleoanthropologist Louis Leakey, that she had observed two chimps turning sticks into tools for fishing termites out of nesting mounds (or termitarias). Leakey replied, "Now we must redefine tool, redefine Man, or accept chimpanzees as humans."[1] Field studies of primates by Western scientists have always contained a degree of anthropocentrism and a focus on what nonhuman primates can tell us about ourselves. How and why did humans develop as we did during the course of our evolutionary history? Because culture, tool use, and language were thought to be uniquely human, perhaps studies of primate behavior might unravel an old nature–nurture question: How much of human behavior is biologically determined and how much of it derives from culture?

Research into primate behavior has shown again and again the behavioral sophistication of our closest living relatives—the anthropoid primates in general and the hominoids in particular. Certainly, biology plays a role in primate behavior, but there are times that behavior is determined by the social traditions of the groups. Of course, as with humans, nature and nurture are linked. Primates require more time to reach adulthood compared to many other mammals. During their lengthy growth and development, young primates learn the behaviors of their social group.

While Goodall was originally criticized for giving names to the chimps she studied (David Greybeard and Goliath were the two chimps she first observed stripping twigs of their leaves to fish for termites), field studies have documented that primates know one another as individuals and can vary their behavior accordingly. The same is true of many other long-lived social mammals, such as elephants and dolphins. Observations of primates in their natural habitats over the past decades have shown that social interaction, organization, learning, reproduction, care of the young, and communication among our primate relatives are similar to human behavior.

Primates as Models for Human Evolution

As we will explore in the human evolution chapters to come, the human line split from a common ancestor that we share with the African apes. Although this split occurred millions of years ago, paleoanthropologists in the mid-20th century were hopeful that observations made among the living apes might shed light on the lifeways of the fossil species they were discovering. Louis Leakey encouraged Jane Goodall to begin her research with chimpanzees in

Gombe Stream Chimpanzee Reserve (now a national park) on the eastern shores of Lake Tanganyika in Tanzania for this reason.

But the forest ape behavior model appeared flawed to the paleoanthropologists of the past. The fossil evidence indicated that the earliest human ancestors inhabited a grassy savannah environment rather than the tropical forests inhabited by the apes. Instead, paleoanthropologists turned to baboons: a group of Old World monkey species that inhabit the savannah environments of eastern Africa where the richest fossil evidence of our ancestors had also been found. While the savannah environment has certainly been important in human evolution, recent fossil discoveries and analyses have lead paleoanthropologists back into the forest. The earliest two-legged ancestors inhabited a forested environment and have lead paleoanthropologists to investigate the human origins in terms of the transition from forest to savannah.

Though baboons differ considerably from our two-legged ancestors, their survival strategies provide some clues as to how our ancestors adapted to the savannah environment. Members of the genus *Papio*, baboons are among the largest of the Old World monkeys. Fully terrestrial, troops of baboons can be seen sitting together on the dry savannah earth to forage for corms (thick, nutritious underground reproductive parts of plants). They keep a watchful eye out for predators while feeding. At the first sight or sound of danger, alarm calls by members of the troop will signal for all the individuals to retreat to safety.

Baboons live in groups that vary dramatically in size, from under ten to hundreds of individuals. In some species the groups are multi-male multi-female while others are made up of a series of harems—one male with several females that he dominates. Sexual dimorphism—anatomical differences between males and females—is high in baboons, and therefore males can use their physical advantages to overpower females easily. But the degree to which males choose to do so varies from group to group.

Extrapolating from baboons to theories about our ancestors poses problems. To use the words of primatologists Shirley Strum and William Mitchell, these baboon "models" often became baboon "muddles."[2] Paleoanthropologists

---

[1] Jane Goodall Institute. http://www.janegoodall.org/jane/study-corner/Jane/bio.asp. (accessed June 16, 2009)

[2] Strum, S., & Mitchell, W. (1987). Baboon models and muddles. In W. Kinsey (Ed.), *The evolution of human behavior: Primate models*. Albany: State University of New York Press.

The behavior of baboons, a type of Old World monkey, has been particularly well studied. There are several distinct species of baboon, each with their own social rules. In troops of hamadryas baboons (pictured), the sacred baboons of ancient Egypt, each male has a harem of females over which he dominates. Female hamadryas baboons, if transferred to a troop of olive baboons, where females are less submissive, maintain the passive behaviors learned in their original troop. But a female olive baboon placed in the hamadryas troop quickly learns submissive behaviors in order to survive.

did not expect our ancestors to possess tails or **ischial callosities**—the hardened, nerveless buttock pads that allow baboons to sit for long periods of time. Tails are strictly a monkey characteristic, not an ape one, and among the hominoids, only gibbons and siamangs possess ischial callosities. Instead, paleoanthropologists looking for evolutionary information were trying to piece together examples of *convergence*—of behaviors that might appear in large-bodied, dimorphic primates living in large multi-male multi-female groups in a savannah environment.

The upside of paleoanthropology's "baboon hypothesis" is that it led to many excellent long-term field studies of baboons that have yielded fascinating data on their social organization, omnivorous diet, mating patterns and other reproductive strategies, communication, and so forth. As with most primate field studies, the evolutionary questions remain in the background while the rich repertoire of primate behavior takes center stage.

Primate Social Organization

Primates are social animals, living and traveling in groups that vary in size and composition from species to species. Different environmental and biological factors have been linked to the group's size, and all the possible organizational forms appear in various primate species.

For example, gibbons live in small nuclear family units consisting of a pair of bonded adults and their offspring. Orangutans tend to lead solitary existences, males and females coming together only to mate. Young orangutans stay with their mothers until they reach adult status.

Chimps and bonobos live in large multi-male multi-female groups. Among chimps and bonobos, the largest social organizational unit is the **community,** composed of fifty or more individuals who collectively inhabit a large geographic area. Rarely, however, are all these animals together at one time. Instead, they are usually found ranging singly or in small subgroups consisting of adult males together, females with their young, or males and females together with young. In the course of their travels, subgroups may join forces and forage together, but sooner or later these subgroups break up again into smaller units. When they do, some individuals split off and others join, so that the new subunits may be different in their composition from the ones that initially came together.

ischial callosities Hardened, nerveless pads on the buttocks that allow baboons and other primates to sit for long periods of time.

community A unit of primate social organization composed of fifty or more individuals who inhabit a large geographic area together.

The gorilla group is a "family" of five to thirty individuals led by a mature silver-backed male and including younger (black-backed) males, females, the young, and occasionally other silverbacks. Subordinate males, however, are usually prevented by the dominant male from mating with the group's females. Thus young, sexually mature males, who take on the characteristic silver color at the end of the sexual maturation process (about 11 to 13 years of age), are forced to leave their **natal group**—the community they have known since birth—by the dominant silverback. After some time as a solitary male in the forest, a young silverback may find the opportunity to start his own social group by winning outside females. In the natal group, if the dominant male is weakening with age, one of his sons may remain with the group to succeed to his father's position. Alternatively, an outside male may take over the group. With the dominant male controlling the group, gorillas rarely fight over food, territory, or sex, but they will fight fiercely to maintain the integrity of the group.

In many primate species, including humans, adolescence is a time during which individuals change the relationships they have had with their natal group. Among primates this change takes the form of migration to new social groups. In many species, females constitute the core of the social system. For example, offspring tend to remain with the group to which their mother, rather than their father, belongs. Among gorillas, male adolescents leave their natal groups more frequently than females. However, adolescent female chimpanzees and bonobos are frequently the ones to migrate.

In two Tanzanian chimpanzee communities studied, about half the females may leave the community they have known since birth to join another group.[3] Other females may also temporarily leave their group to mate with males of another group. Among bonobos, adolescent females appear to always transfer to another group, where they promptly establish bonds with females of their new group. While biological factors such as the hormonal influences on sexual maturity play a role in adolescent migration, the variation across species, and within the chimpanzees in dispersal patterns, indicates that differences may also derive from the learned social traditions of the group.

Home Range

Primates usually move about within a circumscribed area, or **home range,** which varies in size depending on the group and on ecological factors such as availability of food. Ranges often change seasonally, and the number of miles traveled by a group in a day varies. Some areas, known as *core areas,* are used more often than others. Core areas typically contain water, food sources, resting places, and sleeping trees. The ranges of different groups may overlap, as among bonobos, where 65 percent of one community's range may overlap with that of another.[4] By contrast, chimpanzee territories, at least in some regions, are exclusively occupied and will be defended from intrusion (Figure 4.1).

Gorillas do not defend their home range against incursions of others of their kind, although they will defend their group if it is in any way threatened. In the lowlands of Central Africa, it is not uncommon to find several families feeding in close proximity to one another.[5] In encounters with other communities, bonobos will defend their immediate space through vocalizations and displays but rarely through fighting. Usually, they settle down and feed side by side, not infrequently grooming, playing, and engaging in sexual activity between groups as well.

Chimpanzees, by contrast, have been observed patrolling their territories to ward off potential trespassers. Moreover, Jane Goodall (see Anthropologists of Note) has recorded the destruction of one chimpanzee community by another invading group. This sort of deadly intercommunity interaction has never been observed among bonobos. Some have interpreted the apparent territorial behavior as an expression of the supposedly violent nature of chimpanzees. However, another interpretation is that the violence that Goodall witnessed was a response to crowding as a consequence of human activity.[6]

[4] Parish, A. R. (1998). Comment. *Current Anthropology 39,* 414.

[5] Parnell, R. (1999). Gorilla exposé. *Natural History 108* (8), 43.

[6] Power, M. G. (1995). Gombe revisited: Are chimpanzees violent and hierarchical in the "free" state? *General Anthropology 2* (1), 5–9.

[3] Moore, J. (1998). Comment. *Current Anthropology 39,* 412.

natal group The group or the community an animal has inhabited since birth.

home range The geographic area within which a group of primates usually moves.

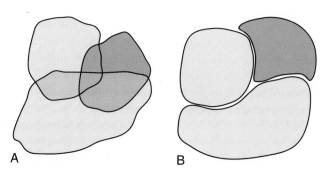

Figure 4.1 Home ranges illustrated in A can be overlapping. When members of the same species meet one another in the shared parts of the range, there might be some tension, deference, or peaceful mingling. Some groups maintain clear territories (B) that are strictly defended from any intrusion by members of the same species.

Jane Goodall (b. 1934) ▪ Kinji Imanishi (1902–1992)

In July 1960, **Jane Goodall** arrived with her mother at the Gombe Chimpanzee Reserve on the shores of Lake Tanganyika in Tanzania. Goodall was the first of three women Kenyan anthropologist Louis Leakey sent out to study great apes in the wild (the others were Dian Fossey and Biruté Galdikas, who studied gorillas and orangutans, respectively); her task was to begin a long-term study of chimpanzees. Little did she realize that, more than forty years later, she would still be at it.

Born in London, Goodall grew up and was schooled in Bournemouth, England. As a child, she dreamed of going to live in Africa, so when an invitation arrived to visit a friend in Kenya, she jumped at the opportunity. While in Kenya, she met Leakey, who gave her a job as an assistant secretary. Before long, she was on her way to Gombe. Within a year, the outside world began to hear the most extraordinary things about this pioneering woman: tales of tool-making apes, cooperative hunts by chimpanzees, and what seemed like exotic chimpanzee rain dances. By the mid-1960s, her work had earned her a doctorate from Cambridge University, and Gombe was

on its way to becoming one of the most dynamic field stations for the study of animal behavior anywhere in the world.

Although Goodall is still very much involved with chimpanzees, she spends a good deal of time these days lecturing, writing, and overseeing the work of other researchers. She is heavily committed to primate con-servation. Goodall is also passionately dedicated to halting illegal trafficking in chimps as well as fighting for the humane treatment of captive chimps.

Kinji Imanishi—naturalist, explorer, and mountain climber—profoundly influenced primatology in Japan and throughout the world. Like all Japanese scholars, he was fully aware of Western

methods and theories but developed a radically different approach to the scientific study of the natural world.

He dates his transformation to a youthful encounter with a grasshopper: "I was walking along a path in a valley, and there was a grasshopper on a leaf in a shrubbery. Until that moment I had happily caught insects, killed them with chloroform, impaled them on pins, and looked up their names, but I realized I

knew nothing at all about how this grasshopper lived in the wild."[a] In his most important work, *The World of Living Things*, first published in 1941, Imanishi developed a comprehensive theory about the natural world rooted in Japanese cultural beliefs and practices.

Imanishi's work challenged Western evolutionary theory in several ways. First, Imanishi's theory, like Japanese culture, does not emphasize differences between humans and other animals. Second, rather than focusing on the biology of individual organisms, Imanishi suggested that naturalists examine "specia" (a species society) to which individuals belong as the unit of analysis. Rather than focusing on time, Imanishi emphasized space in his approach to the natural world. He highlighted the harmony of all living things rather than conflict and competition among individual organisms.

Imanishi's research techniques, now standard worldwide, developed directly from his theories: long-term field study of primates in their natural societies using methods from ethnography. With his students, Imanishi conducted pioneering field studies of African apes and Japanese and Tibetan macaques, long before Louis Leakey sent the first Western primatologists into the field. Japanese primatologists were the first to document the importance of kinship, the complexity of primate societies, patterns of social learning, and the unique char-acter of each primate social group. Because of the work by Imanishi and his students, we now think about the distinct cultures of primate societies.

[a] Heita, K. (1999). Imanishi's world view. *Journal of Japanese Trade and Industry* 18 (2), 15.

Social Hierarchy

Relationships among individuals within ape communities are relatively harmonious. In the past, primatologists believed that male **dominance hierarchies** (the pattern seen in baboons), in which some animals outrank and may dominate others, formed the basis of primate social structures. The researchers noted that physical strength and size play a role in determining an animal's rank. By this measure males generally outrank females. However, the gender bias of the humans studying these animals may have contributed disproportionately to this theory, with its emphasis

on domination through superior size and strength. Male dominance hierarchies seemed "natural" to the early primatologists who, after all, were coming from human social systems organized according to similar principles.

With the benefit of detailed field studies over the last forty years, many of which were pioneered by female primatologists

dominance hierarchies Observed ranking systems in primate societies ordering individuals from high (alpha) to low standing corresponding to predictable behavioral interactions including domination.

like Goodall, the nuances of primate social behavior and the importance of female primates have been documented. High-ranking (alpha) females may dominate low-ranking males. In groups such as bonobos, females dominate overall. While strength and size contribute to an animal's rank, other important factors include the rank of its mother and effectiveness at creating alliances with other individuals. For males, drive or motivation to achieve high status also influences rank. For example, in the community studied by Goodall, one male chimp hit upon the idea of incorporating noisy kerosene cans into his charging displays, thereby intimidating all the other males.[7] As a result, he rose from relatively low status to the number one (alpha) position.

Among bonobos, female–female bonds play an important role in determining rank. Further, the strength of the bond between mother and son may interfere with the ranking among males. Not only do bonobo males defer to females in feeding, but alpha females have been observed chasing high-ranking males. Alpha males even yield to low-ranking females, and groups of females form alliances in which they may cooperatively attack males, to the point of inflicting blood-drawing injuries.[8] Thus instead of the male dominance characteristic of chimps, one sees female dominance.

Western primatologists' focus on social rank and attack behavior may be a legacy of the individualistic, competitive nature of the societies in which evolutionary theory originated. To a certain degree, natural selection relies upon a struggle among living creatures rather than peaceful coexistence. By contrast, noted Japanese primatologist Kinji Imanishi (see Anthropologists of Note) developed a harmonious theory of evolution and initiated field studies of bonobos that have demonstrated the importance of social cooperation rather than competition. As the work of Dutch primatologist Frans de Waal illustrates in the following Original Study, reconciliation after an attack may be even more important from an evolutionary perspective than the actual attack.

---

[7] Goodall, J. (1986). *The chimpanzees of Gombe: Patterns of behavior* (p. 424). Cambridge, MA: Belknap.

[8] de Waal, F. B. M., Kano, T., & Parish, A. R. (1998). Comments. *Current Anthropology 39*, 408, 410, 413.

Original Study

Reconciliation and Its Cultural Modification in Primates *by Frans B. M. de Waal*

Despite the continuing popularity of the struggle-for-life metaphor, it is increasingly recognized that there are drawbacks to open competition, hence that there are sound evolutionary reasons for curbing it. The dependency of social animals on group life and cooperation makes aggression a socially costly strategy. The basic dilemma facing many animals, including humans, is that they sometimes cannot win a fight without losing a friend.

This photo shows what may happen after a conflict—in this case between two female bonobos. About 10 minutes after their fight, the two females approach each other, with one clinging to the other and both rubbing their clitorises and genital swellings together in a pattern known as genito-genital rubbing, or GG-rubbing. This sexual contact, typical

of bonobos, constitutes a so-called reconciliation. Chimpanzees, which are closely related to bonobos (and to us:

Two adult female bonobos engage in so-called GG-rubbing, a sexual form of reconciliation typical of this species.

bonobos and chimpanzees are our closest animal relatives), usually reconcile in a less sexual fashion, with an embrace and mouth-to-mouth kiss.

There is now evidence for reconciliation in more than twenty-five different primate species, not just in apes but also in many monkeys. The same sorts of studies have been conducted on human children in the schoolyard, and of course children show reconciliation as well. Researchers have even found reconciliation in dolphins, spotted hyenas, and some other nonprimates. Reconciliation seems widespread: a common mechanism found whenever relationships need to be maintained despite occasional conflict.[a,b]

The definition of reconciliation used in animal research is a friendly reunion between former opponents not long after a conflict. This is somewhat different from definitions in the dictionary, primarily because we look for an empirical definition that is useful in observational studies—in our case, the stipulation that the reunion happen not long after the conflict. There is no intrinsic reason that a reconciliation could not occur after hours or days, or, in the case of humans, generations.

Let me describe two interesting elaborations on the mechanism of reconciliation. One is *mediation*. Chimpanzees are the only animals to use mediators in conflict resolution. In order to be able to mediate conflict, one needs to understand relationships outside of oneself, which may be the reason why other animals fail to show this aspect of conflict resolution. For example, if two male chimpanzees have been involved in a fight, even on a very large island as where I did my studies, they can easily avoid each other, but instead they will sit opposite from each other, not too far apart, and avoid eye contact. They can sit like this for a long time. In this situation, a third party, such as an older female, may move in and try to solve the issue. The female will approach one of the males and groom him for a brief while. She then gets up and walks slowly to the other male, and the first male walks right behind her.

We have seen situations in which, if the first male failed to follow, the female turned around to grab his arm and make him follow. So the process of getting the two males in proximity seems intentional on the part of the female. She then begins grooming the other male, and the first male grooms her. Before long, the female disappears from the scene, and the males continue grooming: She has in effect brought the two parties together.

There exists a limited anthropological literature on the role of conflict resolution, a process absolutely crucial for the maintenance of the human social fabric in the same way that it is crucial for our primate relatives. In human society, mediation is often done by high-ranking or senior members of the community, sometimes culminating in feasts in which the restoration of harmony is celebrated.[c]

The second elaboration on the reconciliation concept is that it is not purely instinctive, not even in our animal relatives. It is a learned social skill subject to what primatologists now increasingly call "culture" (meaning that the behavior is subject to learning from others as opposed to genetic transmission).[d] To test the learnability of reconciliation, I conducted an experiment with young rhesus and stumptail monkeys. Not nearly as conciliatory as stumptail monkeys, rhesus monkeys have the reputation of being rather aggressive and despotic. Stumptails are considered more laid-back and tolerant. We housed members of the two species together for 5 months. By the end of this period, they were a fully integrated group: They slept, played, and groomed together.

After 5 months, we separated them again, and measured the effect of their time together on conciliatory behavior. The research controls—rhesus monkeys who had lived with one another, without any stumptails—showed absolutely no change in the tendency to reconcile. Stumptails showed a high rate of reconciliation, which was also expected, because they also do so if living together. The most interesting group was the experimental rhesus monkeys, those who had lived with stumptails. These monkeys started out at the same low level of reconciliation as the rhesus controls, but after they had lived with the stumptails, and after we had segregated them again so that they were now housed only with other rhesus monkeys who had gone through the same experience, these rhesus monkeys reconciled as much as stumptails do. This means that we created a "new and improved" rhesus monkey, one that made up with its opponents far more easily than a regular rhesus monkey.[e]

This was in effect an experiment on social culture: We changed the culture of a group of rhesus monkeys and made it more similar to that of stumptail monkeys by exposing them to the practices of this other species. This experiment also shows that there exists a great deal of flexibility in primate behavior. We humans come from a long lineage of primates with great social sophistication and a well-developed potential for behavioral modification and learning from others.

---

[a]de Waal, F.B.M. (2000). Primates: A natural heritage of conflict resolution. *Science 28,* 586–590.

[b]Aureli, F., & de Waal, F.B.M. (2000). *Natural conflict resolution.* Berkeley: University of California Press.

[c]Reviewed by Frye, D. P. (2000). Conflict management in cross-cultural perspective. In F. Aureli & F.B.M. de Waal, *Natural conflict resolution* (pp. 334–351). Berkeley: University of California Press.

[d]For a discussion of the animal culture concept, see de Waal, F.B.M. (2001). *The ape and the sushi master.* New York: Basic.

[e]de Waal, F.B.M., & Johanowicz, D. L. (1993). Modification of reconciliation behavior through social experience: An experiment with two macaque species. *Child Development 64,* 897–908.

Individual Interaction and Bonding

The social sophistication characteristic of primates is evident in behaviors that at first glance might seem wholly practical. For example, **grooming,** the ritual cleaning of another animal to remove parasites and other matter from its skin or coat, is a common pastime for both chimpanzees and bonobos. The grooming animal deftly parts the hair of the one being groomed and removes any foreign object, often eating it. But besides serving hygienic purposes, it can be a social gesture of friendliness, closeness, appeasement, reconciliation, or even submission.

Bonobos and chimpanzees have favorite grooming partners. Group sociability, an important behavioral trait undoubtedly also found among human ancestors, is further expressed in embracing, touching, and the joyous welcoming of other members of the ape community.

Interestingly, different chimp communities have different styles of grooming. In one East African group, for example, the two chimps groom each other face to face, with one hand, while clasping their partner's free hand. In another group 90 miles distant, the hand clasp is unknown. In East Africa, all communities incorporate leaves in their grooming, but in West Africa they do not.

Gorillas, though gentle and tolerant, are also aloof and independent, and individual interaction among

grooming The ritual cleaning of another animal's coat to remove parasites and other matter.

Grooming is an important activity among all catarrhine primates, as shown here in a group of chimps grooming each other in a pattern known as the Domino Effect. Such activity is important for strengthening bonds among individual members of the group.

adults tends to be quite restrained. Friendship or closeness between adults and infants is more evident. Among bonobos, chimpanzees, gorillas, and orangutans, as among most other primates, the mother–infant bond is the strongest and longest lasting. It may endure for many years—commonly for the lifetime of the mother. Gorilla infants share their mothers' nests but have also been seen sharing nests with mature, childless females. Bonobo, chimpanzee, and gorilla males are attentive to juveniles and play a role in their socialization. Bonobo males even carry infants on occasion. Their interest in a youngster does not elicit the nervous reaction from the mother that it does among chimps; chimp mothers may be reacting to the occasional infanticide on the part of chimpanzee males, a behavior never observed among bonobos.

Sexual Behavior

Most mammals mate only during specified breeding seasons occurring once or twice a year. While some primates have a fixed breeding season tied to a simultaneous increase in body fat, or to the consumption of specific plant foods, many primate species are able to breed at any time during the course of the year. Among the African apes, as with humans, no fixed breeding season exists. In chimps,

estrus In some primate females, the time of sexual receptivity during which ovulation is visibly displayed.

ovulation Moment when an egg released from the ovaries into the womb is receptive for fertilization.

frequent sexual activity—initiated by either the male or the female—occurs during **estrus,** the period when the female is receptive to impregnation. In chimpanzees, estrus is signaled by vivid swelling of the skin around the genitals. Bonobo females, by contrast, appear as if they are fertile at all times due to their constantly swollen genitals and interest in sex. Gorillas appear to show less interest in sex compared to either chimps or bonobos.

By most human standards, the sexual behavior of chimps is promiscuous. A dozen or so males have been observed to have as many as fifty copulations in one day with a single female in estrus. For the most part, females mate with males of their own group. Dominant males try to monopolize females in full estrus, although cooperation from the female is usually required for this to succeed. In addition, an individual female and a lower-ranking male sometimes form a temporary bond, leaving the group together for a few "private" days during the female's fertile period. Interestingly, the relationship between reproductive success and social rank differs for males and females. In the chimpanzee community studied by Goodall, about half the infants were sired by low- or mid-level males. Although for females high rank is linked with successful reproduction, social success for males—achieving alpha status—does not translate neatly into the evolutionary currency of reproductive success.

In contrast to chimpanzees, bonobos (like humans) do not limit their sexual behavior to times of female fertility. The constant genital swelling of bonobos, in effect, conceals the females' **ovulation,** or moment when an egg released into the womb is receptive for fertilization.

to face from a branch and rubbing their erect penises together as if crossing swords. Among females, genital rubbing is particularly common.

As described in this chapter's Original Study, the primary function of most of this sex, both hetero- and homosexual, is to reduce tensions and resolve social conflicts. Bonobo sexual activity is very frequent but also very brief, lasting only 8 to 10 seconds. Since the documentation of sexual activities among bonobos, field studies by primatologists are now recording a variety of sexual behaviors among other species as well. This chapter's Biocultural Connection describes a variation on sexuality in orangutans that has been described as disturbing.

In gorilla families, the dominant silverback tends to have exclusive breeding rights with the females, although he will sometimes tolerate the presence of a young adult male and allow him occasional access to a low-ranking female. Generally by the time a young male becomes a silverback he must leave "home," luring partners away from other established groups, in order to have reproductive success.

Field studies have revealed variation in the typical gorilla pattern of a single dominant male. There are gorilla groups in Uganda and Rwanda in which there are multiple silverback males. Still, in one gorilla group with more than one adult male studied in Rwanda, a single dominant male fathered all but one of ten juveniles.[10]

Although the vast majority of primate species are not **monogamous**—bonded exclusively to a single sexual partner—in their mating habits, many smaller species of New World monkeys, a few island-dwelling populations of leaf-eating Old World monkeys, and all of the smaller apes (gibbons and siamangs) appear to mate for life with a single individual of the opposite sex. None of these species is closely related to human beings, nor do monogamous species ever display the degree of sexual dimorphism—anatomical differences between males and females—that is characteristic of our closest primate relatives or that was characteristic of our own ancient ancestors.

Evolutionary biologists, dating back to Charles Darwin himself,[11] have proposed that sexual dimorphism (for example, larger male size in apes, beautiful feathers in peacocks) relates to competition among males for access to females. Females only evolved by what Canadian primatologist Linda Fedigan has called the "coat-tails theory"

Because geladas spend far more time sitting than upright, signaling ovulation through genital swelling is nowhere near as practical as signaling it through the reddening of a patch of furless skin on their chests. This way it is easy for other members of the group to see that they are fertile even while they are foraging.

Ovulation is also concealed in humans, by the absence of genital swelling at all times.

Concealed ovulation in humans and bonobos may play a role in separating sexual activity for social and pleasurable reasons from the purely biological task of reproduction. In fact, among bonobos (as among humans) sexuality goes far beyond male–female mating for purposes of biological reproduction. Primatologists have observed virtually every possible combination of ages and sexes engaging in a remarkable array of sexual activities, including oral sex, tongue-kissing, and massaging each other's genitals.[9] Male bonobos may mount each other, or one may rub his scrotum against that of the other. They have also been observed "penis fencing"—hanging face

---

[9] de Waal, F. B. M. (2001). *The ape and the sushi master* (pp. 131–132). New York: Basic.

[10] Gibbons, A. (2001). Studying humans—and their cousins and parasites. *Science 292*, 627.

[11] Darwin, C. (1936). *The descent of man and selection in relation to sex.* New York: Random House (Modern Library). (orig. 1871)

monogamous Mating for life with a single individual of the opposite sex.

Disturbing Behaviors of the Orangutan   *by Anne Nacey Maggioncalda and Robert M. Sapolsky*

An adult male orangutan is an impressive sight. The animal has a pair of wide cheek pads, called flanges, and a well-developed throat sac used for emitting loud cries known as long calls. The mature male also has long, brightly colored hair on its body and face. These are secondary sexual characteristics, the flamboyant signals that male orangutans flaunt to proclaim their fertility and fitness to the opposite sex. The features emerge during orangutan adolescence: Males reach puberty at around 7 to 9 years of age, then spend a few years in a far-from-impressive "subadult" stage, during which they are about the same size as mature females. The males reach their adult size and develop secondary sexual traits by ages 12 to 14. Or at least that's what primate researchers used to think.

As stable social groups of orangutans were established in zoos, however, it became clear that an adolescent male could remain a subadult, in a state of arrested development, until his late teens. In the 1970s, studies of orangutans in the rainforests of Southeast Asia by Biruté M. F. Galdikas . . . and others produced the same finding: Sometimes males were arrested adolescents for a decade or more, about half their potential reproductive lives. Variability of this magnitude is fascinating—it is like finding a species in which pregnancy could last anywhere from six months to five years.

Biologists are keenly interested in studying cases of arrested development because they often shed light on the processes of growth and maturation. . . . Environmental factors can . . . slow or halt an organism's development. For instance, food shortages delay maturation in humans and many other animals. This response is logical from an evolutionary standpoint—if it is unclear whether you will survive another week, it makes no sense to waste calories by adding bone mass or developing secondary sexual characteristics. Gymnasts and ballet dancers who exercise to extremes and anorexics who starve themselves sometimes experience delayed onset of puberty.

Among male orangutans, though, the cause of arrested development seems to lie in the animals' social environment. The presence of dominant adult males appears to delay the maturation of adolescent males in the same vicinity. Until recently, researchers believed that they were observing a stress-induced pathology—that is, the adolescent orangutans stopped developing because the adult males bullied and frightened them. Over the past few years, however, we have conducted studies (by measuring stress, growth, and reproductive hormone levels in urine) suggesting that arrested development among orangutans is not a pathology but an adaptive evolutionary strategy. The arrested adolescent males are capable of impregnating females, and by staying small and immature (in terms of secondary sexual features) they minimize the amount of food they need and lower the

The male orangutan on the right has retained his adolescent physique even though his primary sex characteristics are fully mature, allowing him to father offspring. The male on the left has developed the secondary sexual characteristics typical of the adult male orangutan. These two individuals might be very close to the same age.

risk of serious conflict with adult males. But the strategy of these arrested adolescents has a disquieting aspect: They copulate forcibly with females. In other words, they rape.

These findings overturned some long-held assumptions about orangutans. Apparently, arrested adolescents are neither stressed nor reproductively suppressed. What is going on? It turns out that there is more than one way for a male orangutan to improve his chances of reproducing.

A cornerstone of modern evolutionary theory is that animal behavior has evolved not for the good of the species or the social group but to maximize the number of gene copies passed on by an individual and its close relatives. For a long time, the study of primates was dominated by simplistic models of how animals achieve this goal. According to these models, male behavior consists of virtually nothing but aggression and competition to gain access to females. If only one female is sexually receptive in a group with many males, this competition would result in the highest-ranking male mating with her; if two females are receptive, the males ranking first and second in the hierarchy would mate with them, and so on.

But this kind of behavior is rarely seen among social primates. Instead male primates can choose alternative strategies to maximize their reproductive success. Why should there be alternatives? Because the seemingly logical strategy—developing powerful muscles and dramatic secondary sexual characteristics to excel at male–male competition—has some serious drawbacks. In many species, maintaining those secondary characteristics requires elevated testosterone levels, which have a variety of adverse effects on health. The aggression that comes with such a strategy is not great for health either.

Furthermore, increased body mass means greater metabolic demands and more pressure for successful food acquisition. During famines, the bigger primates are less likely to survive. For an arboreal species such as the orangutan, the heavier body of the mature male also limits which trees and branches can be accessed for food. And the development of secondary sexual characteristics makes a male more conspicuous, both to predators and to other males that view those characteristics as a challenge.

In contrast, the key impression that a developmentally arrested male communicates to an adult male is a lack of threat or challenge, because the immature male looks like a kid. Arrested male orangutans are apparently inconspicuous enough to be spared a certain amount of social stress. What is more, the "low profile" of these animals may actually give them a competitive advantage when it comes to reproduction. In many primate species, the low-ranking males are actually doing a fair share of the mating. Genetic paternity testing of these primates has shown that the subordinate males are quite successful in passing on their genes. . . .

The great majority of adult female orangutans are sexually receptive only to mature males. So how do the arrested males mate? Observations of orangutans both in the wild and in captive populations have indicated that the arrested males forcibly copulate with females. Rape is an apt term for these copulations: The adult females usually resist the arrested adolescents fiercely, biting the males whenever they can and emitting loud, guttural sounds (called rape grunts) that are heard only under these circumstances. Adult males sometimes rape, too, but not nearly as often as the arrested males.

Thus, two reproductive strategies appear to have evolved for adolescent male orangutans. If no fully mature males are nearby, the adolescent will most likely develop quickly in the hopes of attracting female attention. When adult males are present, however, a strategy of arrested development has its advantages. If the social environment changes—say, if the nearby adult males die off or migrate—the arrested males will rapidly develop secondary sexual features and change their behavior patterns. Researchers are now trying to determine exactly how the presence or absence of adult males triggers hormonal changes in the adolescents.

What are the lessons we can learn from the male orangutan? First, a situation that seems stressful from a human's perspective may not necessarily be so. Second, the existence of alternative reproductive strategies shows that the optimal approach can vary dramatically in different social and ecological settings. There is no single blueprint for understanding the evolution of behavior. Third, although the recognition of alternative strategies built around female choice has generally met with a receptive audience among scientists, the rape-oriented strategy of arrested male orangutans is not so pleasing. But the study of primates has demonstrated time and again that the behavior of these animals is far from Disney-esque.

One must be cautious, however, in trying to gain insights into human behavior by extrapolating from animal studies. There is a temptation to leap to a wrongheaded conclusion: Because forcible copulation occurs in orangutans and something similar occurs in humans, rape has a natural basis and is therefore unstoppable. This argument ignores the fact that the orangutan is the only nonhuman primate to engage in forcible copulation as a routine means of siring offspring. Furthermore, close observations of orangutan rape show that it is very different from human rape: For example, researchers have never seen a male orangutan injure a female during copulation in an apparently intentional manner. Most important, the orangutan's physiology, life history, and social structure are completely unlike those of any other primate. Orangutans have evolved a unique set of adaptations to survive in their environment, and hence it would be the height of absurdity to draw simpleminded parallels between their behaviors and those of humans.

BIOCULTURAL QUESTION

While primatologists call the forced copulations by arrested male orangutans "rape," how does this differ from rape in humans?

Adapted from Maggioncalda, A. N., & Sapolsky, R. M. (2002). Disturbing behaviors of the orangutan. Scientific American 286 (6), 60–65.

of evolution.[12] She points out that evolutionary theories about sexual dimorphism and reproductive behaviors are particularly susceptible to becoming "gendered." That is, the gender norms of the scientists can easily creep their way (subconsciously, of course) into the theories they are creating. Darwin's era, despite the reign of Queen Victoria, was firmly patriarchal, and male–male competition prevailed in British society. Women of Darwin's time were denied basic rights like the right to vote and own property. Inheritance laws favored first-born male heirs. Feminist analyses such as Fedigan's have contributed substantially to the developing discipline of primatology.

Primate field studies have revealed that male–male competition is just one of many factors playing a role in primate reproduction. A broad range of social processes contribute to reproductive success, with as much variation as the numerous biological factors that contribute to body size. For example, in baboons, which are a very sexually dimorphic species, the female's choice of mate is as important as male–male competition. Females frequently choose to mate with lower-ranking males that show strong male–female **affiliative** actions (tending to promote social cohesion) and good parental behavior.[13]

In orangutans, the avoidance of male–male competition has become biologically evident in the male pattern of growth and development. Unlike gorillas that develop their silver backs at the same time as they become sexually active, orangutan males become sexually mature before they develop the secondary sex characteristics that would mark their adult status. Described in detail in this chapter's Biocultural Connection, this state of arrested development allows these lower-ranking males to have sexual alliances with females. Thus they optimize their personal reproductive success while simultaneously avoiding the stresses and costs of male–male competition.

Among baboons, paternal involvement has been shown to have distinct advantages for offspring, including more rapid growth in baboon infants if they receive attention from their fathers. In addition, adult males will also intercede on their offspring's behalf when the young ones are involved in fights. In short, choosing a good mate can optimize the reproductive success of female baboons.

Reproduction and Care of Young

The average adult female monkey or ape spends most of her adult life either pregnant or nursing her young, times at which she is not sexually receptive. Apes generally nurse

---

[12] Fedigan, L. M. (1992). *Primate paradigms: Sex roles and social bonds.* Chicago: University of Chicago Press.

[13] Sapolsky, R. (2002). *A primate's memoir: Love, death, and baboons in East Africa.* New York: Vintage.

affiliative Tending to promote social cohesion.

---

each of their young for about four to five years. After her infant is weaned, she will come into estrus periodically, until she becomes pregnant again.

Among primates, as among some other mammals, females generally give birth to one infant at a time. Natural selection may have favored single births among primate tree dwellers because the primate infant, which has a highly developed grasping ability (the grasping reflex can also be seen in human infants), must be transported about by its mother, and more than one clinging infant would interfere with movement in the trees. Only among the smaller nocturnal prosimians, the primates closest to the ancestral condition, are multiple births common. Among the anthropoids, only the true marmoset, a kind of New World monkey, has a pattern of habitual twinning. Other species like humans will twin occasionally. In marmosets, both parents share infant care, with fathers doing most of the carrying.

Primates follow a pattern of bearing few young but devoting more time and effort to the care of each individual offspring. Compared to other mammals such as mice, which pass from birth to adulthood in a matter of weeks, primates spend a great deal of time growing up. As a general rule, the more closely related to humans the species is, the longer the period of infant and childhood dependency (Figure 4.2). For example, a lemur is dependent upon its mother for only a few months after birth, while an ape is dependent for four or five years. A chimpanzee infant cannot survive if its mother dies before it reaches the age of 4 at the very least. During the juvenile period, young primates are still dependent on the larger social group rather than on their mothers alone, using this period for learning and refining a variety of behaviors. If a juvenile primate's mother dies, he or she may be adopted by an older male or female member of the social group. Among bonobos, a juvenile who has lost his or her mother has very little social standing in the group.

The long interval between births, particularly among the apes, results in small population size. A female chimpanzee, for example, does not reach sexual maturity until about the age of 10, and once she produces her first live offspring, there is a period of five or six years before she will bear another. So, assuming that none of her offspring die before adulthood, a female chimpanzee must survive for at least twenty or twenty-one years just to maintain the status quo in chimpanzee population. In fact, chimpanzee infants and juveniles do die from time to time, and not all females live full reproductive lives. This is one reason why apes are far less abundant in the world today than are monkeys.

A long slow period of growth and development, particularly among the hominoids, also provides opportunities. Born without built-in responses dictating specific behavior in complex situations, the young monkey or ape, like the young human, learns how to strategically interact

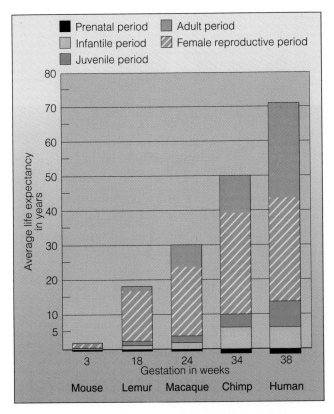

Figure 4.2 A long life cycle, including a long period of childhood dependency, is characteristic of the primates. In biological terms, infancy ends when young mammals are weaned, and adulthood is defined as sexual maturation. In many species, such as mice, animals become sexually mature as soon as they are weaned. Among primates, a juvenile period for social learning occurs between infancy and adulthood. For humans, the biological definitions of infancy and adulthood are modified according to cultural norms.

games, such as jostling for position on the top of a hillside or following and mimicking a single youngster. One juvenile, becoming annoyed at repeated harassment by an infant, picked it up, climbed a tree, and deposited it on a branch from which it was unable to get down on its own; eventually, its mother came to retrieve it.

Communication and Learning

Primates, like many animals, vocalize. They have a great range of calls that are often used together with movements of the face or body to convey a message. Observers have not yet established the meaning of all the sounds, but a good number have been distinguished, such as warning calls, threat calls, defense calls, and gathering calls. The behavioral reactions of other animals hearing the call have also been studied. Among bonobos, chimpanzees, and gorillas, most vocalizations communicate an emotional state rather than information. Much of the communication of these species takes place by using specific gestures and postures. Indeed, a number of these, such as kissing and embracing, are used universally among humans, as well as apes.

Primatologists have classified numerous chimpanzee vocalizations and visual communication signals. Facial expressions convey emotional states such as distress, fear, or excitement. Distinct vocalizations or calls have been associated with a variety of sensations. For example, chimps will smack their lips or clack their teeth to express

with others and even to manipulate them for his or her own benefit—by trial and error, observation, imitation, and practice. Young primates make mistakes along the way, learning to modify their behavior based on the reactions of other members of the group. Each member of the community has a unique physical appearance and personality. Youngsters learn to match their interactive behaviors according to each individual's social position and temperament. Anatomical features common to all monkeys and apes—such as a free upper lip (unlike lemurs and cats, for example)—allow for varied facial expression, contributing to communication between individuals. Much of this learning takes place through play.

For primate infants and juveniles, play is more than a way to pass the hours. It is a vital means of finding out about the environment, learning social skills, and testing a variety of behaviors. Chimpanzee infants mimic the food-getting activities of adults, "attack" dozing adults, and "harass" adolescents. Observers have watched young gorillas do somersaults, wrestle, and play various organized

Many ape nonverbal communications are easily recognized by humans, as we share the same gestures.

Athletes who have been blind since birth use the same body gestures to express victory and defeat as sighted athletes. Because they do this without ever having seen an "end zone" celebration, this indicates that these body gestures are hardwired into humans and presumably derive from our primate heritage.

pleasure with sociable body contact. Calls called "pant-hoots," which are used to announce the arrival of individuals or to inquire, can be differentiated into specific types. Together, these facilitate group protection, coordination of group efforts, and social interaction in general.

To what degree are various forms of communication universal and to what degree are they specific to a given group? On the group-specificity side, primatologists have recently documented within-species dialects of calls that appear as groups are isolated in their habitats. Social factors, genetic drift, and habitat acoustics could all contribute to the appearance of these distinct dialects.[14]

Smiles and embraces have long been understood to be universal among humans and our closest relatives. But recently some additional universals have been documented. Blind athletes use the same gestures to express submission or victory that sighted athletes use at the end of a match, though they have never seen such gestures themselves.[15] This raises interesting questions about whether primate communications are biologically hardwired or learned.

Visual communication can also take place through objects. Bonobos do so with trail markers. When foraging, the community breaks up into smaller groups, rejoining again in the evening to nest together. To keep track of each party's whereabouts, those in the lead, at the intersections of trails or where downed trees obscure the path, will deliberately stomp down the vegetation so as to indicate their direction or rip off large leaves and place them carefully for the same purpose. Thus they all know where to come together at the end of the day.[16]

Primatologists have also found that primates can communicate specific threats through their calls. Researchers have documented that vervet monkey alarm calls communicate on several levels of meaning to elicit specific responses from others in the group.[17] The calls designated types of predators (birds of prey, big cats, snakes) and where the threat might arise. Further, they have documented how young vervets go about learning the appropriate use of the calls. If the young individual has uttered the correct call, it will be repeated by adults, and the appropriate escape behavior will follow (heading into the trees to get away from a cat or into brush to be safe from an eagle). But if an infant utters the cry for an eagle in response to a leaf falling from the sky or in response to a nonthreatening bird, no adult calls will follow.

From an evolutionary perspective, scientists have been puzzled about behaviors such as these vervet alarm calls. Biologists assume that the forces of natural selection work on behavioral traits just as they do on genetic traits. It seems reasonable that individuals in a group of vervet

---

[14] de la Torre, S., & Snowden, C. T. (2009). Dialects in pygmy marmosets? Population variation in call structure. *American Journal of Primatology 71* (4), 333–342.

[15] Tracy, J. L., & Matsumoto, D. (2008). The spontaneous expression of pride and shame: Evidence for biologically innate nonverbal displays. *Proceedings of the National Academy of Sciences 105* (33), 11655–11660.

[16] Recer, P. (1998, February 16). Apes shown to communicate in the wild. *Burlington Free Press*, 12A.

[17] Seyfarth, R. M., Cheney, D. L., & Marler, P. (1980). Vervet monkey alarm calls: Semantic communication in a free-ranging primate. *Animal Behavior 28* (4), 1070–1094.

monkeys capable of warning one another of the presence of predators would have a significant survival advantage over those without this capability. However, these warning situations are enigmatic to evolutionary biologists because they would expect the animals to act in their own self-interest, with survival of self paramount. By giving an alarm call, an individual calls attention to itself, thereby becoming an obvious target for the predator. How, then, could **altruism,** or concern for the welfare of others, evolve so that individuals place themselves at risk for the good of the group? One biologist's solution substitutes money for reproductive fitness to illustrate how such cooperative behavior may have come about:

> You are given a choice. Either you can receive $10 and keep it all or you can receive $10 million if you give $6 million to your next door neighbor. Which would you do? Guessing that most selfish people would be happy with a net gain of $4 million, I consider the second option to be a form of selfish behavior in which a neighbor gains an incidental benefit. I have termed such selfish behavior benevolent.[18]

Natural selection of beneficial social traits was probably an important influence on human evolution, since in the primates some degree of cooperative social behavior became important for food-getting, defense, and mate attraction. Indeed, anthropologist Christopher Boehm argues, "If human nature were merely selfish, vigilant punishment of deviants would be expected, whereas the elaborate prosocial prescriptions that favor altruism would come as a surprise."[19]

Evolution has shaped primates to be social creatures, and communication is thus integral to our order. Experiments with captive apes, carried out over several decades, reveal that their communicative abilities exceed what they make use of in the wild. In some of these experiments, bonobos and chimpanzees have been taught to communicate using symbols, as in the case of Kanzi, a bonobo who uses a visual keyboard. Other chimpanzees, gorillas, and orangutans have been taught American Sign Language.

Although this research is controversial, in part because it challenges notions of human uniqueness, it has become evident that apes are capable of understanding language quite well, even using rudimentary grammar. They are able to generate original utterances, ask questions, distinguish naming something from asking for it, develop original ways to tell lies, coordinate their actions, and spontaneously teach language to others. Even though

The Great Ape Trust, photo courtesy of Sue Savage-Rumbaugh

Kanzi, the 23-year-old bonobo at the Great Ape Trust of Iowa, communicates with primatologist Sue Savage-Rumbaugh by pointing to visual images called lexigrams. With hundreds of lexigrams, Kanzi can communicate thoughts and feelings he wishes to express. He also understands spoken language and can reply in a conversation with the lexigrams. Kanzi began to learn this form of communication when he was a youngster, tagging along while his mother had language lessons. Though he showed no interest in the lessons, later he spontaneously began to use lexigrams himself.

they cannot literally *speak,* it is now clear that all of the great ape species can develop *language skills* to the level of a 2- to 3-year-old human child.[20] Interestingly, a Japanese research team led by primatologist Tetsuro Matsuzawa recently demonstrated that chimps can outperform college students at a computer-based memory game. The researchers propose that human brains have lost some of the spatial skill required to master this game to allow for more sophisticated human language.[21]

Observations of monkeys and apes have shown learning abilities remarkably similar to those of humans. Numerous examples of inventive behavior have been observed among monkeys, as well as among apes. The snow monkeys or macaques of the research colony on Koshima Island, Japan, are particularly famous for demonstrating that individuals can invent new behaviors that then get passed on to the group through imitation.

---

[18] Nunney, L. (1998). Are we selfish because are we nice, or are we nice because we are selfish? *Science 281,* 1619.

[19] Boehm, C. (2000). The evolution of moral communities. *School of American Research, 2000 Annual Report,* 7.

---

[20] Lestel, D. (1998). How chimpanzees have domesticated humans. *Anthropology Today 12* (3); Miles, H. L. W. (1993). Language and the orangutan: The "old person" of the forest. In P. Cavalieri & P. Singer (Eds.), *The Great Ape Project* (pp. 45–50). New York: St. Martin's.

[21] Inoue, S., Matsuzawa, T. (2007). "Working Memory of Numerals in Chimpanzees." *Current Biology, 17* (23), 1004–1005.

altruism Concern for the welfare of others expressed as increased risk undertaken by individuals for the good of the group.

In the 1950s and early 1960s, one particularly bright young female macaque named Imo (Japanese primatologists always considered it appropriate to name individual animals) started several innovative behaviors in her troop. She figured out that grain could be separated from sand if it was placed in water. The sand sank and the grain floated clean, making it much easier to eat. She also began the practice of washing the sweet potatoes that primatologists provided—first in fresh water but later in the ocean, presumably because of the pleasant taste the saltwater added. In each case, these innovations were initially imitated by other young animals; Imo's mother was the lone older macaque to embrace the innovations right away.

One newly discovered example is a technique of food manipulation on the part of captive chimpanzees in the

zoo of Madrid, Spain. It began when a 5-year-old female rubbed apples against a sharp corner of a concrete wall in order to lick the mashed pieces and juice left on the wall. From this youngster, the practice of "smearing" spread to her peers, and within five years most group members were performing the operation frequently and consistently. The innovation has become standardized and durable, having transcended two generations in the group.[22]

Another dramatic example of learning is afforded by the way chimpanzees in West Africa crack open oil-palm nuts. For this they use tools: an anvil stone with a level surface on which to place the nut and a good-sized hammer stone to crack it. Not any stone will do; it must be of the right shape and weight, and the anvil may require leveling by placing smaller stones beneath one or more edges. Nor does random banging away do the job; the nut has to be hit at the right speed and the right trajectory, or else the nut simply flies off into the forest. Last but not least, the apes must avoid mashing their fingers, rather than the nut. According to fieldworkers, the expertise of the chimps far exceeds that of any human who tries cracking these hardest nuts in the world.

Youngsters learn this process by staying near to adults who are cracking nuts, where their mothers share some of the food. This teaches them about the edibility of the nuts but not how to get at what is edible. This they learn by observing and by "aping" (copying) the adults. At first they play with a nut or stone alone; later they begin to randomly combine objects. They soon learn, however, that placing nuts on anvils and hitting them with a hand or foot gets them nowhere.

Only after three years of futile effort do they begin to coordinate all of the multiple actions and objects, but even then it is only after a great deal of practice, by the age of 6 or 7 years, that they become proficient in this task. They do this for over a thousand days. Evidently, it is social motivation that accounts for their perseverance after at least three years of failure, with no reward to reinforce their effort. At first, they are motivated by a desire to act like the

In the same way that young Imo got her troop to begin washing sweet potatoes in saltwater, at Kyoto University's Koshima Island Primatology Research Preserve another young female macaque recently taught other macaques to bathe in hot springs. In the Nagano Mountains of Japan, this macaque, named Mukbili, began bathing in the springs. Others followed her, and now this is an activity practiced by all members of the group.

[22] Fernandez-Carriba, S., & Loeches, A. (2001). Fruit smearing by captive chimpanzees: A newly observed food-processing behavior. *Current Anthropology 42*, 143–147.

mother; only later does the desire to feed on the tasty nut-meat take over.[23]

Use of Objects as Tools

A **tool** may be defined as an object used to facilitate some task or activity. The nut cracking just discussed is the most complex tool-use task observed by researchers in the wild, involving both hands, two tools, and exact coordination. It is not, however, the only case of tool use among apes in the wild. Chimpanzees, bonobos, and orangutans make and use tools.

Here, a distinction must be made between simple tool use, as when one pounds something with a convenient stone when a hammer is not available, and tool making, which involves deliberate modification of some material for its intended use. Thus otters that use unmodified stones to crack open clams may be tool users, but they are not toolmakers. Not only do chimpanzees modify objects to make them suitable for particular purposes, but chimps also modify these objects into regular and set patterns. They pick up and even prepare objects for future use at some other location, and they can use objects as tools to solve new problems. Thus chimps have been observed using stalks of grass, twigs that they have stripped of leaves, and even sticks up to 3 feet long that they have smoothed down to "fish" for termites. They insert the modified stick into a termite nest, wait a few minutes, pull the stick out, and eat the insects clinging to it, all of which requires considerable dexterity. Chimpanzees are equally deliberate in their own nest building. They test the vines and branches to make sure they are usable. If they are not, the animal moves to another site.

Other examples of chimpanzee use of tools involve leaves, used as wipes or as sponges, to get water out of a hollow to drink. Large sticks may serve as clubs or as missiles (as may stones) in aggressive or defensive displays. Twigs are used as toothpicks to clean teeth as well as to extract loose baby teeth. They use these dental tools not just on themselves but on other individuals as well.[24]

In the wild, bonobos have not been observed making and using tools to the extent seen in chimpanzees. However, the use of large leaves as trail markers may be considered a form of tool use. That these animals do have further capabilities is exemplified by a captive bonobo who has figured out how to make tools of stone that are remarkably like the earliest such tools made by our own ancestors.[25]

Chimps use a variety of tools in the wild. Here a chimp is using a long stick stripped of its side branches to fish for termites. Chimps will select a stick when still quite far from a termite mound and modify its shape on the way to the snacking spot.

Chimpanzees also use plants for medicinal purposes, illustrating their selectivity with raw materials, a quality related to tool manufacture. Chimps that are ill by outward appearance have been observed to seek out specific plants of the genus *Aspilia*. They will eat the leaves singly without chewing them, letting the leaves soften in their mouths for a long time before swallowing. Primatologists have discovered that the leaves pass through the chimp's digestive system whole and relatively intact, having scraped parasites off the intestine walls in the process.

---

[23] de Waal, *The ape and the sushi master.*

[24] McGrew, W. C. (2000). Dental care in chimps. *Science 288*, 1747.

[25] Toth, N., et al. (1993–2001). Pan the tool-maker: Investigations into the stone tool-making and tool-using capabilities of a bonobo (*Pan panisicus*). *Journal of Archaeological Science 20* (1), 81–91.

tool An object used to facilitate some task or activity. Although tool making involves intentional modification of the material of which it is made, tool use may involve objects either modified for some particular purpose or completely unmodified.

Although gorillas (like bonobos and chimps) build nests, they are the only one of the four great apes that have not been observed to make and use other tools in the wild. The reason for this is probably not that gorillas lack the intelligence or skill to do so; rather, their easy diet of leaves and nettles makes tools of no particular use.

Hunting

Prior to the 1980s most primates were thought to be vegetarian while humans alone were considered meat-eating hunters. Among the vegetarians, *folivores* were thought to eat only leaves while *frugivores* feasted on fruits. Though some primates do have specialized adaptations—such as a complex stomach and shearing teeth to aid in the digestion of leaves or an extra-long small intestine to slow the passage of juicy fruits so they can be readily absorbed—primate field studies have revealed that the diets of monkeys and apes are extremely varied.

Many primates are *omnivores* who eat a broad range of foods. Goodall's fieldwork among chimpanzees in their natural habitat at Gombe Stream demonstrates that these apes supplement their primary diet of fruits and other plant foods with insects and meat. Even more surprising, she found that in addition to killing small invertebrate animals for food, they also hunt and eat monkeys. Goodall observed chimpanzees grabbing adult red colobus monkeys and flailing them to death. Since her pioneering work, other primatologists have documented hunting behavior in baboons and capuchin monkeys, among others.

Chimpanzee females sometimes hunt, but males do so far more frequently. When on the hunt, they may spend hours watching, following, and chasing intended prey. Moreover, in contrast to the usual primate practice of each animal finding its own food, hunting frequently involves teamwork to trap and kill prey, particularly when hunting for baboons. Once a potential victim has been isolated from its troop, three or more adult chimps will carefully position themselves so as to block off escape routes while another pursues the prey. Following the kill, most who are present get a share of the meat, either by grabbing a piece as chance affords or by begging for it.

Whatever the nutritional value of meat, hunting is not done purely for dietary purposes, but for social and sexual reasons as well. Anthropologist Craig Stanford, who has been doing fieldwork among the chimpanzees of Gombe since the early 1990s, found that these sizable apes (100-pound males are common) frequently kill animals weighing up to 25 pounds and eat much more meat than previously believed. Their preferred prey is the red colobus monkey that shares their forested habitat.

Annually, chimpanzee hunting parties at Gombe kill about 20 percent of these monkeys, many of them babies, often shaking them out of the tops of 30-foot trees. They may capture and kill as many as seven victims in a raid. These hunts usually take place during the dry season when plant foods are less readily available and when females display genital swelling, which signals that they are ready to mate. On average, each chimp at Gombe eats about a quarter-pound of meat per day during the dry season. For female chimps, a supply of protein-rich food helps support the increased nutritional requirements of pregnancy and lactation.

Somewhat different chimpanzee hunting practices have been observed in West Africa. At Tai National Park in the Ivory Coast, for instance, chimpanzees engage in highly coordinated team efforts to chase monkeys hiding in very tall trees in the dense tropical forest. Individuals who have especially distinguished themselves in a successful hunt see their contributions rewarded with more meat.

Recent research shows that bonobos in Congo's rainforest also supplement their diet with meat obtained by means of hunting. Although their behavior resembles that of chimpanzees, there are crucial differences. Among bonobos, hunting is primarily a female activity. Also, female hunters regularly share carcasses with other females, but less often with males. Even when the most dominant male throws a tantrum nearby, he may still be denied a share of meat.[26] Female bonobos behave in much the same way when it comes to sharing other foods such as fruits.

While it had long been assumed that male chimpanzees were the primary hunters, primatologist Jill Pruetz and her colleagues researching in Fongoli, Senegal, documented habitual hunting by groups of young female and male chimpanzees using spears.[27] The chimps took spears they had previously prepared and sharpened to a point and jabbed them repeatedly into the hollow parts

[26] Ingmanson, E. J. (1998). Comment. *Current Anthropology 39*, 409.

[27] Pruetz, J. D., & Bertolani, P. (2007, March 6). Savanna chimpanzees, *Pan troglodytes verus*, hunt with tools. *Current Biology 17*, 412–417.

of trees where small animals, including primates, might be hiding. The primatologists even observed the chimps extract bush babies from tree hollows with the spears. Because this behavior is practiced primarily by young chimpanzees, with one adolescent female the most frequently exhibiting the behavior, spear hunting seems to be a relatively recent innovation in the group. Just as the young female Japanese macaques mentioned above were the innovators in those groups, this young female chimp seems to be leading this behavior in Senegal. Further, the savannah conditions of the Fongoli Reserve make these observations particularly interesting in terms of human evolutionary studies, which have tended to suggest that males hunted while females gathered.

The Question of Culture

The more we learn of the behavior of our nearest primate relatives, the more we become aware of the importance of learned, socially shared practices and knowledge in these creatures. Do chimpanzees, bonobos, and the other apes have culture? The answer appears to be yes. The detailed study of ape behavior has revealed varied use of tools and patterns of social engagement that seem to derive from the traditions of the specific group rather than a biologically determined script. Humans share with the other apes an ability to learn the complex but flexible patterns of behavior particular to a social group during a long period of childhood dependency.

If we agree that these other primates possess culture, does this demand a reorientation in how humans behave toward them, such as stopping the use of monkeys and apes in biomedical research? Jane Goodall argues vehemently for this change. She emphasizes that cultural processes determine the place of animals within biomedical research, and she advocates eliminating the cultural distinction between humans and our closest relatives for research purposes. Some governments are responding to her calls as seen by the 2008 approval by the Spanish Parliament of the "Declaration on Great Apes," which extends some human rights to gorillas, chimpanzees, bonobos, and orangutans.[28]

Some biomedical research disturbs animals minimally. For example, DNA can be extracted from the hair naturally shed by living primates, allowing for cross-species comparisons of disease genes. To facilitate this process, cell repositories have been established for researchers to obtain samples of primate DNA. Other biomedical research is far more invasive to the individual primate. For example, to document the infectious nature of kuru, a disease closely related to mad cow disease, extract from the brains of sick humans was injected into the brains of living chimpanzees. A year and a half later, the chimpanzees began to sicken. They had the same classic features of kuru—uncontrollable spasticity, seizures, dementia, and ultimately death.

The biological similarities of humans and other primates leading to such research practices derive from a long, shared evolutionary history. By comparison, the cultural rules that allow our closest relatives to be the subjects of biomedical research are relatively recent. As Goodall has said, "Surely it should be a matter of moral responsibility that we humans, differing from other animals mainly by virtue of our more highly developed intellect and, with it, our greater capacity for understanding and compassion, ensure that the medical progress slowly detaches its roots from the manure of non-human animal suffering and despair. Particularly when this involves the servitude of our closest relatives."[29]

But there are powerful social barriers that work against the well-being of our animal relatives. In Western societies there has been an unfortunate tendency to erect what paleontologist Stephen Jay Gould refers to as "golden barriers" that set us apart from the rest of the animal kingdom.[30] Sadly, this mindset blinds us to the fact that a continuum exists between "us" and "them" (animals). We have already seen that the physical differences between humans and apes are largely differences of degree, rather than kind. It now appears that the same is true with respect to behavior. As primatologist Richard Wrangham put it,

> Like humans, [chimpanzees] laugh, make up after a quarrel, support each other in times of trouble, medicate themselves with chemical and physical remedies, stop each other from eating poisonous foods, collaborate in the hunt, help each other over physical obstacles, raid neighboring groups, lose their tempers, get excited by dramatic weather, invent ways to show off, have family traditions and group traditions, make tools, devise plans, deceive, play tricks, grieve, and are cruel and are kind.[31]

---

[28] O'Carroll, E. (2008, June 27). Spain to grant some human rights to apes. *Christian Science Monitor.*

[29] Goodall, J. (1990). *Through a window: My thirty years with the chimpanzees of Gombe.* Boston: Houghton Mifflin.

[30] Quoted in de Waal, *The ape and the sushi master,* p. 235.

[31] Quoted in Mydens, S. (2001, August 12). He's not hairy, he's my brother. *New York Times,* sec. 4, 5.

This is not to say that we are "just" another ape; obviously, degree does make a difference. Nevertheless, the continuities between us and our primate kin reflect a common evolutionary heritage and a responsibility to help our cousins today. Because of our shared evolutionary heritage, the biology and behavior of the other living primates, like the contemporary study of genetics, provide valuable insight into our understanding of human origins. The methods scientists use to recover data directly from fossilized bones and preserved cultural remains in order to study the human past are the subject of the next chapter.

Questions for Reflection

1. Those who fully support the use of nonhuman primates in biomedical research argue that using a limited number of chimpanzees or rhesus macaques to lessen human suffering and spare human lives is justified. Do you agree or disagree? What kinds of alternatives might be developed to replace nonhuman primates in biomedical research?

2. What kinds of communication systems have been observed in primates? How do these differ from human language?

3. This chapter describes several instances of scientists revising their paradigms when it appeared that their work was overly influenced by their own cultural norms, such as prevailing gender roles. Can you think of ways that this might still be occurring? How do researchers prevent this from happening?

4. Given the variation seen in the specific behaviors of chimp, bonobo, and gorilla groups, is it fair to say that these primates possess culture?

5. As we explored in the previous chapter, many primate species are endangered today. What features of ape biology may be responsible for apes' limited population size? Do these biological limitations pertain to humans? Why or why not?

Suggested Readings

Cavalieri, P., & Singer, P. (1994). *The Great Ape Project: Equality beyond humanity.* New York: St. Martin's.

This edited volume brings together leading primatologists, ethicists, animal rights activists, field biologists, and psychologists to make the case for extending the rights guaranteed to humans to the other great apes. This book was the first initiative of the Great Ape Project, a worldwide initiative to protect chimpanzees, bonobos, gorillas, and orangutans.

Cheney, D. L., & Seyfarth, R. M. (2007). *Baboon metaphysics: The evolution of a social mind.* Chicago: University of Chicago Press.

Through in-depth field studies extending over years, primatologists Cheney and Seyfarth examine the degree to which baboon behavior indicates thought compared to instinct. Their fascinating analysis written in an engaging style responds to the statement Charles Darwin made: "He who understands baboons would do more towards metaphysics than Locke."

de Waal, F. B. M., & Lanting, F. (1998). *Bonobo: The forgotten ape.* Berkeley: University of California Press.

This book perfectly blends photographs and text to allow the reader to immediately see the inherent humanity of the bonobos.

Fedigan, L. (1992). *Primate paradigms: Sex roles and social bonds.* Chicago: University of Chicago Press.

Fedigan uses a broad intellectual framework to connect the study of sex differences in primates to feminist theory as well as to the sciences of psychology, neurobiology, endocrinology, and biology. Her perspectives have helped shape primatology as it is practiced today.

Sapolsky, R. (2002). *A primate's memoir: Love, death, and baboons in East Africa.* New York: Vintage.

This book will take the reader from Sapolsky's childhood in New York City to his years working with a troop of baboons in Kenya, with his fascinating work as a neuroendocrinologist thrown in for good measure. Sapolsky is witty, cynical, and emotional as he tells his story and that of the baboons and the other humans who were part of this journey.

Challenge Issue Given the radical changes taking place in the world today, a scientific understanding of the past has never been more important. But investigating ancient remains challenges us to solve the complex question of who owns the past. For example, pictured here is the Bamiyan Valley, located along a section of the ancient Silk Road, which was a network of trade routes that stretched from eastern Asia to the Mediterranean. Before the Islamic invasion of the 9th century, this place of great natural beauty, located within the Hazarajat region of central Afghanistan, was a Buddhist homeland. There were several Buddhist monasteries, thousands of painted caves, and two colossal statues of Buddha, carved into the cliffs at the valley's edge and dating back some 1,500 years. In March 2001, the Taliban destroyed these two Buddhas on the grounds that they were idolatrous and an insult to Islam. Today, the niches that once held these grand sculptures are hauntingly empty. A huge international outcry has led to cooperative efforts to rebuild and preserve this archaeological site, and already the results have been impressive. In 2008 a team of Japanese, European, and U.S. researchers demonstrated that the Bamiyan cave wall images are the oldest oil paintings in the world. To whom do such ancient remains belong—to the local government, to the global community, to researchers or scientific institutions, to people living in the region, to those who happen to have possession at the moment? The archaeological perspective holds that for the collective benefit of local peoples and the global community alike, these questions must be answered with an eye to long-term preservation, cooperation, and peace.

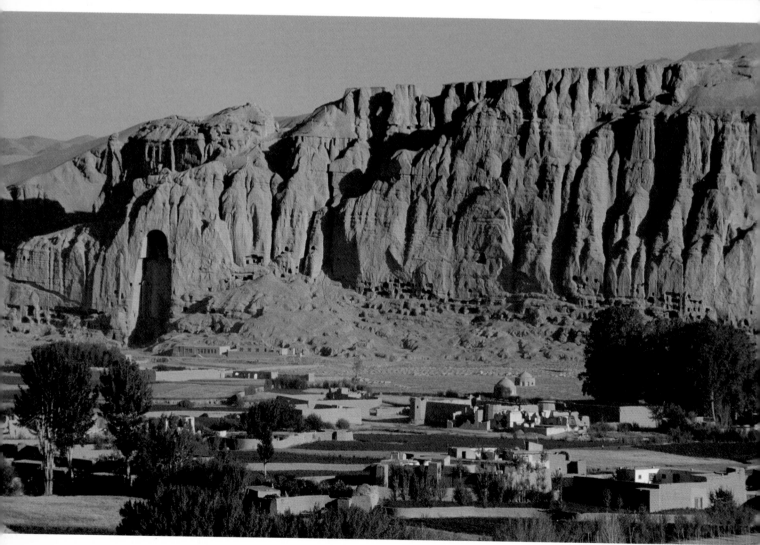

CHAPTER 5

Field Methods in Archaeology and Paleoanthropology

Chapter Preview

How Are the Physical and Cultural Remains of Past Humans Investigated?

Archaeologists and paleoanthropologists investigate the past by excavating sites where biological and cultural remains are found. Unfortunately, excavation results in the site's destruction. Thus every attempt is made to excavate in such a way that the location and context of everything recovered, no matter how small, are precisely recorded. Through careful analysis of the physical and cultural remains recovered through excavation, scientists make sense of the data and enhance our knowledge of the biology, behavior, and beliefs of our ancestors. The success of an excavation also depends upon cooperation and respect between anthropologists who are investigating the past and the living people connected to the sites and remains being studied.

Are Human Physical and Cultural Remains Always Found Together?

Archaeological sites are places containing the cultural remains of past human activity. Sites are revealed by the presence of artifacts as well as soil marks, changes in vegetation, and irregularities of the earth's surface. While skeletons of recent peoples are frequently associated with their cultural remains, as we go back in time, the association of physical and cultural remains becomes less likely. Fossils are defined as any surviving trace or impression of an organism from the past. Fossils sometimes accompany archaeological sites, but many of them predate the first stone tools or other cultural artifacts. The human cultural practice of burying the dead, starting about 100,000 years ago, changed the nature of the fossil record, providing relatively complete skeletons as well as information about this cultural practice.

How Are Archaeological or Fossil Remains Dated?

Calculating the age of physical and cultural remains is an essential aspect of interpreting the past. Remains can be dated by noting their stratigraphic position, by measuring the chemicals contained in fossil bones, or by association with other plant, animal, or cultural remains. More precise dating methods rely upon advances in the disciplines of chemistry and physics that use properties such as rates of decay of radioactive elements. These elements may be present in the remains themselves or in the surrounding soil. By comparing dates and remains across a variety of sites, anthropologists can make inferences about human origins, migrations, and technological developments. Sometimes the development of a new dating technique leads to an entirely new interpretation of physical and cultural remains.

Paleoanthropology and archaeology are the anthropological specialties most concerned with our past. They share a focus on **prehistory,** a conventional term used to refer to the period of time before written records. For some people, the term *prehistoric* might conjure up images of "primitive" cavemen and cavewomen, but it does not imply a lack of history or any inferiority—merely a lack of written history. Archaeologists also focus on the cultural remains of peoples living since the invention of writing, such as the makers of the Bamiyan Buddhas and the oil paintings buried in caves behind them as described in the chapter opener.[1] The next several chapters of this book focus on the past; this chapter examines the methods archaeologists and paleoanthropologists use to study that past.

Most of us are familiar with some kind of archaeological material: a coin dug out of the earth, a fragment of an ancient pot, a spear point used by some ancient hunter. Finding and cataloguing such objects are often thought to be the chief goal of archaeology. This was true up until the early 20th century, when professional and amateur archaeologists alike collected cultural treasures, but the situation changed by the mid-20th century. Today, the aim is to use archaeological remains to reconstruct the culture and worldview of past human societies. Archaeologists examine every recoverable detail from past societies, including all kinds of structures (not just palaces and temples), hearths, garbage dumps, bones, and plant remains. Although it may appear that archaeologists are digging up *things,* they are really digging up human biology, behavior, and beliefs.

Similarly, paleoanthropologists who study the physical remains of our ancestors and other ancient primates do more than find and catalogue old bones. Paleoanthropologists recover, describe, and organize these remains to see what they can tell us about human biological evolution. It is not so much a case of finding the ancient bones but finding out what the bones mean.

---

[1] Bonn-Muller, E. (2009). Oldest oil paintings: Bamiyan, Afghanistan. *Archaeology 62* (1); Cotte, M. (2008). *Journal of Analytical Atomic Spectrometry.* doi: 10.1039/b801358f.

---

prehistory A conventional term used to refer to the period of time before the appearance of written records; does not deny the existence of history, merely of *written* history.

artifact Any object fashioned or altered by humans.

material culture The durable aspects of culture, such as tools, structures, and art.

ecofact The natural remains of plants and animals found in the archaeological record.

feature A non-portable element such as a hearth or an architectural element such as a wall that is preserved in the archaeological record.

Recovering Cultural and Biological Remains

Archaeologists and paleoanthropologists face a dilemma. The only way to thoroughly investigate our past is to excavate sites where biological and cultural remains are found. Unfortunately, excavation results in the site's destruction. Thus researchers strive to excavate in such a way that the location and context of everything recovered, no matter how small, are precisely recorded. These records help scientists make sense of the data and enhance our knowledge of the past. Knowledge that can be derived from physical and cultural remains diminishes dramatically if accurate and detailed records of the excavation are not kept. As anthropologist Brian Fagan has put it,

> The fundamental premise of excavation is that all digging is destructive, even that done by experts. The archaeologist's primary responsibility, therefore, is to record a site for posterity as it is dug because there are no second chances.[2]

Archaeologists work with **artifacts,** any object fashioned or altered by humans—a flint scraper, a basket, an axe, or such things as house ruins or walls. An artifact expresses a facet of human culture. Because it is something that someone made, archaeologists like to say that an artifact is a product or representation of human behavior and beliefs, or, in more technical terms, artifacts are **material culture.**

Artifacts are not considered in isolation; rather, they are integrated with biological and ecological remains. Such **ecofacts,** the natural remains of plants and animals found in the archaeological record, convey much about associated artifacts. Archaeologists also focus on **features**—non-portable elements such as hearths and architectural elements such as walls—that are preserved in the archaeological record. Just as important as the artifacts and physical remains is the way they were left in the ground. For example, what people do with the things they have made, how they dispose of them, and how they lose them reflect important aspects of human culture. In other words, context allows archaeologists to understand the cultures of the past.

Similarly, context provides important information about biological remains. It provides information about which fossils are earlier or later in time than other fossils. Also, by noting the association of ancient human fossils with the remains of other species, the paleoanthropologist may make significant progress in reconstructing environmental settings of the past.

---

[2] Fagan, B. M. (1995). *People of the earth* (8th ed., p. 19). New York: HarperCollins.

In rare circumstances, human bodies are so well preserved that they could be mistaken for recent corpses. Such is the case of "Ötzi," the 5,200-year-old "Ice Man," exposed by the melting of an alpine glacier in the Tyrolean Alps in 1991. Both the Italian and the Austrian governments felt they had legitimate claims on this rare find, and they mounted legal, geographic, and taphonomic arguments for housing the body. These arguments continued as the specimen, just released from the ice, began to thaw.

Cultural and physical remains represent distinct kinds of data, but the fullest interpretation of the human past requires the integration of ancient human biology and culture. Often paleoanthropologists and archaeologists work together to systematically excavate and analyze fragmentary remains, placing scraps of bone, shattered pottery, and scattered campsites into broad interpretive contexts.

The Nature of Fossils

Broadly defined, a **fossil** is any mineralized trace or impression of an organism that has been preserved in the earth's crust from past geologic time. Fossilization typically involves the hard parts of an organism. Bones, teeth, shells, horns, and the woody tissues of plants are the most successfully fossilized materials. Although the soft parts of an organism are rarely fossilized, casts or impressions of footprints, brains, and even whole bodies are sometimes found. Because dead animals quickly attract meat-eating scavengers and bacteria that cause decomposition, they rarely survive long enough to become fossilized. For an organism to become a fossil, it must be covered by some protective substance soon after death.

An organism or part of an organism may be preserved in a number of ways. The whole animal may be frozen in ice, like the famous mammoths found in Siberia, safe from the forces of predators, weathering, and bacteria. Or it may be enclosed in a natural resin exuding from evergreen trees, later becoming hardened and fossilized as amber. Specimens of spiders and insects dating back millions of years have been preserved in the Baltic Sea area in northeastern Europe, which is rich in resin-producing evergreens such as pine, spruce, or fir trees.

fossil Any mineralized trace or impression of an organism that has been preserved in the earth's crust from past geologic time.

© Javier Trueba/Madrid Scientific Films

To excavate the ancient Stone Age site Sima de los Huesos or "Pit of Bones," Spanish paleoanthropologist Juan Luis Arsuaga and his team spend nearly an hour each day traveling underground through a narrow passage to a small enclosed space, rich with human remains. Here, fossils are excavated with great care and transported back to the laboratory, where the long process of interpretation and analysis begins.

An organism may be preserved in the bottoms of lakes and sea basins, where the body or body part may be quickly covered with sediment. An entire organism may also be mummified or preserved in tar pits, peat, oil, or asphalt bogs, in which the chemical environment prevents the growth of decay-producing bacteria.

It is especially rare to find an entire organism fossilized, let alone a human one. Fossils generally consist of scattered teeth and fragments of bones found embedded in rock deposits. Most have been altered in some way in the process of becoming fossilized. **Taphonomy** (from the Greek for "tomb"), the study of the biologic and geologic processes by which dead organisms become fossils, provides systematic understanding of the fossilization process vital for the scientific interpretations of the fossils themselves.

taphonomy The study of how bones and other materials come to be preserved in the earth as fossils.

Fossilization is most apt to occur among marine animals and other creatures living near water. Concentrations of shells and other parts of organisms are covered and completely enclosed by the soft waterborne sediments that eventually harden into shale and limestone in the following fashion: As the remains of organisms accumulate on shallow sea, river, or lake bottoms, they become covered by sediment and silt, or sand. These materials gradually harden, forming a protective shell around the skeleton of the organism. The internal cavities of bones or teeth and other parts of the skeleton fill in with mineral deposits from the sediment immediately surrounding the specimen. Then the external walls of the bone decay and are replaced by calcium carbonate or silica.

Unless protected in some way, the bones of a land dweller are generally scattered and exposed to the deteriorating influence of the elements, predators, and scavengers. Occasionally, terrestrial animals living near lakes or rivers become fossilized if they die next to or in the water. A land dweller may also become fossilized if it happens to die in a cave, or if some other meat-eating animal drags its remains to a site protected from erosion and decay. In caves, conditions are often excellent for fossilization, as minerals contained in water dripping from the ceiling may harden over bones left on the cave floor. In northern China, for example, many fossils of *Homo erectus* (discussed in Chapter 8) and other animals were found in a cave near a village called Zhoukoudian, in deposits of consolidated clay and rock that had fallen from the cave's limestone ceiling. The cave had been frequented by both humans and predatory animals, which left remains of many a meal there.

Burial of the Dead

It is quite rare to find entirely preserved fossil skeletons dating to before the cultural practice of burial began about 100,000 years ago. The human fossil record from before this time consists primarily of fragmentary remains. The fossil record for many other primates is even poorer, because organic materials decay rapidly in the tropical

forests where they lived. The records are much more complete for primates (such as evolving humans) that lived on the grassy plains or in savannah environments, where conditions were far more favorable to the formation of fossils. This was particularly true in places where ash deposited from volcanic eruptions or waterborne sediment along lakes and streams could quickly cover organisms that died there. At several localities in Ethiopia, Kenya, and Tanzania in East Africa, numerous fossils important for our understanding of human evolution have been found near ancient lakes and streams, often sandwiched between layers of volcanic ash.

In more recent times, such complete remains, although not common, are often quite spectacular and may be particularly informative. As an example, consider the recovery in 1994 of an Eskimo girl's remains in Barrow, Alaska, described in the Original Study. As seen in this case study, successful exploration of the past depends upon cooperation and respect between anthropologists and the living people with ancestral connections to the physical and cultural remains being studied.

Original Study

Whispers from the Ice   *by Sherry Simpson*

People grew excited when a summer rainstorm softened the bluff known as Ukkuqsi, sloughing off huge chunks of earth containing remains of historic and prehistoric houses, part of the old village that predates the modern community of Barrow. Left protruding from the slope was a human head. Archaeologist Anne Jensen happened to be in Barrow

buying strapping tape when the body appeared. Her firm, SJS Archaeological Services, Inc., was closing a field season at nearby Point Franklin, and Jensen offered the team's help in a kind of archaeological triage to remove the body before it eroded completely from the earth.

The North Slope Borough hired her and Glenn Sheehan, both associated with Pennsylvania's Bryn Mawr College, to conduct the work. The National Science Foundation, which supported the 3-year Point Franklin Project, agreed to fund the autopsy and subsequent analysis of the body and artifacts. The Ukkuqsi excavation quickly became a community event. In remarkably sunny and calm weather, volunteers troweled and picked through the thawing soil, finding trade beads, animal bones, and other items. Teenage boys worked alongside grandmothers. The smell of sea mammal oil, sweet at first then corrupt, mingled with ancient organic odors of decomposed vegetation. One man searched the beach for artifacts that had eroded from the bluff, discovering such treasures as two feather parkas. Elder Silas Negovanna, originally of

Wainwright, visited several times, "more or less out of curiosity to see what they have in mind," he said. George Leavitt, who lives in a house on the bluff, stopped by one day while carrying home groceries and suggested a way to spray water to thaw the soil without washing away valuable artifacts. Tour groups added the excavation to their rounds.

"This community has a great interest in archaeology up here just because it's so recent to their experience," says oral historian Karen Brewster, a tall young woman who interviews elders as part of her work with the North Slope Borough's division of Inupiat History, Language, and Culture. "The site's right in town, and everybody was really fascinated by it."

Slowly, as the workers scraped and shoveled, the earth surrendered its historical hoard: carved wooden bowls, ladles, and such clothing as a mitten made from polar bear hide, bird-skin parkas, and mukluks. The items spanned prehistoric times, dated in Barrow to before explorers first arrived in 1826.

The work prompted visiting elders to recall when they or their parents lived in traditional sod houses and relied wholly on the land and sea for sustenance.

CONTINUED

CONTINUED

Some remembered sliding down the hill as children, before the sea gnawed away the slope. Others described the site's use as a lookout for whales or ships. For the archaeologists, having elders stand beside them and identify items and historical context is like hearing the past whispering in their ears. Elders often know from experience, or from stories, the answers to the scientists' questions about how items were used or made. "In this instance, usually the only puzzled people are the archaeologists," jokes archaeologist Sheehan.

A modern town of 4,000, Barrow exists in a cultural continuum, where history is not detached or remote but still pulses through contemporary life. People live, hunt, and fish where their ancestors did, but they can also buy fresh vegetables at the store and jet to other places. Elementary school classes include computer and Inupiaq language studies. Caribou skins, still ruddy with blood, and black brant carcasses hang near late-model cars outside homes equipped with television antennas. A man uses power tools to work on his whaling boat. And those who appear from the earth are not just bodies, but relatives. "We're not a people frozen in time," says Jana Harcharek, an Inupiat Eskimo who teaches Inupiaq and nurtures her culture among young people. "There will always be that connection between us [and our ancestors]. They're not a separate entity."

The past drew still closer as the archaeologists neared the body. After several days of digging through thawed soil, they used water supplied by the local fire station's tanker truck to melt through permafrost until they reached the remains, about 3 feet below the surface. A shell of clear ice encased the body, which rested in what appeared to be a former meat cellar. With the low-pressure play of water from the tanker, the archaeologists teased the icy casket from the frozen earth, exposing a tiny foot. Only then did they realize they had uncovered a child. "That was kind of sad, because she was about my daughter's size," says archaeologist Jensen.

The girl was curled up beneath a baleen toboggan and part of a covering

that Inupiat elder Bertha Leavitt identified as a kayak skin by its stitching. The child, who appeared to be 5 or 6, remained remarkably intact after her dark passage through time. Her face was cloaked by a covering that puzzled some onlookers. It didn't look like human hair, or even fur, but something with a feathery residue. Finally they concluded it was a hood from a feather parka made of bird skins. The rest of her body was delineated muscle that had freeze-dried into a dark brick-red color. Her hands rested on her knees, which were drawn up to her chin. Frost particles coated the bends of her arms and legs.

"We decided we needed to go talk to the elders and see what they

In the long cool days of the Alaska summer, archaeologist Anne Jensen and her team excavate artifacts that will be exhibited at the Inupiat Heritage Center in Barrow, Alaska. In addition to traditional museum displays honoring the past, the center actively promotes the continuation of Inupiat Eskimo cultural traditions through innovations such as the elder-in-residence program.

© Courtesy of Anne Jensen and Glenn Sheehan

wanted, to get some kind of feeling as to whether they wanted to bury her right away, or whether they were willing to allow some studies in a respectful manner—studies that would be of some use to residents of the North Slope," Jensen says. Working with community elders is not a radical idea to Jensen or Sheehan, whose previous work in the Arctic has earned them high regard from local officials who appreciate their sensitivity. The researchers feel obligated not only to follow community wishes, but to invite villagers to sites and to share all information through public presentations. In fact, Jensen is reluctant to discuss findings with the press before the townspeople themselves hear it.

"It seems like it's a matter of simple common courtesy," she says. Such consideration can only help researchers, she points out. "If people don't get along with you, they're not going to talk to you, and they're liable to throw you out on your ear." In the past, scientists were not terribly sensitive about such matters, generally regarding human remains—and sometimes living natives—as artifacts themselves. Once, the girl's body would have been hauled off to the catacombs of some university or museum, and relics would have disappeared into exhibit drawers in what Sheehan describes as "hit-and-run archaeology."

"Grave robbers" is how Inupiat Jana Harcharek refers to early Arctic researchers. "They took human remains and their burial goods. It's pretty gruesome. But, of course, at the time they thought they were doing science a big favor. Thank goodness attitudes have changed."

Today, not only scientists but municipal officials confer with the Barrow Elders Council when local people find skeletons from traditional platform burials out on the tundra, or when bodies appear in the house mounds. The elders appreciate such consultations, says Samuel Simmonds, a tall, dignified man known for his carving. A retired Presbyterian minister, he presided at burial ceremonies of the famous "frozen family," ancient Inupiats discovered in Barrow [about twenty years ago]. "They were part of us, we know that," he says simply, as if the connection between old bones and bodies and living relatives is self-evident. In the case of the newly discovered body, he says, "We were concerned that it was reburied in a respectful manner. They were nice enough to come over and ask us."

The elders also wanted to restrict media attention and prevent photographs of the body except for a few showing her position at the site. They approved a limited autopsy to help answer questions about the body's sex, age, and state of health. She was placed in an orange plastic body bag in a stainless steel morgue with the temperature turned down to below freezing.

With the help of staff at the Indian Health Service Hospital, Jensen sent the girl's still-frozen body to Anchorage's

Providence Hospital. There she assisted with an autopsy performed by Dr. Michael Zimmerman of New York City's Mount Sinai Hospital. Zimmerman, an expert on prehistoric frozen bodies, had autopsied Barrow's frozen family in 1982, and was on his way to work on the prehistoric man recently discovered in the Alps.

The findings suggest the girl's life was very hard. She ultimately died of starvation, but also had emphysema caused by a rare congenital disease—the lack of an enzyme that protects the lungs. She probably was sickly and needed extra care all her brief life. The autopsy also found soot in her lungs from the family's sea mammal oil lamps, and she had osteoporosis, which was caused by a diet exclusively of meat from marine mammals. The girl's stomach was empty, but her intestinal tract contained dirt and animal fur. That remains a mystery and raises questions about the condition of the rest of the family. "It's not likely that she would be hungry and everyone else well fed," Jensen says.

That the girl appears to have been placed deliberately in the cellar provokes further questions about precontact burial practices, which the researchers hope Barrow elders can help answer. Historic accounts indicate the dead often were wrapped in skins and laid out on the tundra on wooden platforms, rather than buried in the frozen earth. But perhaps the entire family was starving and too weak to remove the dead girl from the house, Jensen speculates. "We probably won't ever be able to say, 'This is the way it was,'" she adds. "For that you need a time machine."

The scientific team reported to the elders that radiocarbon dating places the girl's death in about AD 1200. If correct—for dating is technically tricky in the Arctic—the date would set the girl's life about 100 years before her people formed settled whaling villages, Sheehan says.

Following the autopsy and the body's return to Barrow . . . , one last request by the elders was honored. The little girl, wrapped in her feather parka, was placed in a casket and buried in a small Christian ceremony next to the grave of the other prehistoric bodies. Hundreds of years after her death, an Inupiat daughter was welcomed back into the midst of her community.

The "rescue" of the little girl's body from the raw forces of time and nature means researchers and the Inupiat people will continue to learn still more about the region's culture. Sheehan and Jensen returned to Barrow in winter 1994 to explain their findings to townspeople. "We expect to learn just as much from them," Sheehan said before the trip. A North Slope Cultural Center . . . will store and display artifacts from the dig sites.

Laboratory tests and analyses also will contribute information. The archaeologists hope measurements of heavy metals in the girl's body will allow comparisons with modern-day pollution contaminating the sea mammals that Inupiats eat today. The soot damage in her lungs might offer health implications for Third World people who rely on oil lamps, dung fires, and charcoal for heat and light. Genetic tests could illuminate early population movements of Inupiats. The project also serves as a model for good relations between archaeologists and Native people. "The larger overall message from this work is that scientists and communities don't have to be at odds," Sheehan says. "In fact, there are mutual interests that we all have. Scientists have obligations to communities. And when more scientists realize that, and when more communities hold scientists to those standards, then everybody will be happier."

Adapted from Simpson, S. (1995, April). Whispers from the ice. Alaska, 23–28.

Searching for Artifacts and Fossils

Where are artifacts and fossils found? Places containing archaeological remains of previous human activity are known as *sites*. There are many kinds of sites, and sometimes it is difficult to define their boundaries, for remains may be strewn over large areas. Sites are even found under water. Some examples of sites identified by archaeologists and paleoanthropologists are hunting campsites, from which hunters went out to hunt game; kill sites, in which game was killed and butchered; village sites, in which domestic activities took place; and cemeteries, in which the dead, and sometimes their belongings, were buried.

While skeletons of recent peoples are frequently associated with their cultural remains, archaeological sites may or may not contain any physical remains. As we go back in time, the association of physical and cultural remains becomes less likely. Physical remains dating from before 2.5 to 2.6 million years ago are found in isolation. This is not proof of the absence of material culture. It simply indicates that the earliest forms of material culture were not preserved in the archaeological record. It is likely that the earliest tools were made of organic materials (such as the termiting sticks used by chimpanzees) that were much less likely to be preserved. Similarly, fossils are found only in geologic contexts where conditions are known to have been right for fossilization. By contrast, archaeological sites may be found just about anywhere, perhaps because many date from more recent periods.

Site Identification

The first task for the archaeologist is actually finding sites to investigate. Archaeological sites, particularly very old ones, frequently lie buried underground, covered by layers of sediment deposited since the site was in use. Most sites are revealed by the presence of artifacts. Chance may play a crucial role in the site's discovery, as in the case discussed in Barrow, Alaska. Usually, however, the archaeologist will have to survey a region in order to plot the sites available for excavation.

A survey can be made from the ground, but more territory can be covered from the air. Aerial photographs

Some archaeological features are best seen from the air, such as this massive figure of a monkey made in prehistoric times on the Nazca Desert of Peru. Ancient people selectively removed the top layer of reddish stones thus exposing the light-colored earth below.

have been used by archaeologists since the 1920s and are widely used today. Among other things, such photographs were used for the discovery and interpretation of the huge geometric and zoomorphic (from Latin for "animal-shaped") markings on the coastal desert of Peru. More recently a variety of innovations in the geographic and geologic sciences have been incorporated into archaeological surveys and other aspects of research. Innovations such as geographic information systems (GIS), remote sensing, and ground penetrating radar (GPR) complement traditional archaeological exploration methods.

High-resolution aerial photographs, including satellite imagery, resulted in the astonishing discovery of over 500 miles of prehistoric roadways connecting sites in the four-corners region of the United States (where Arizona, New Mexico, Colorado, and Utah meet) with other sites in ways that archaeologists had never suspected. This discovery led to a new understanding of prehistoric Pueblo Indian economic, social, and political organization. Evidently, large centers in this region governed a number of smaller satellite communities, mobilized labor for large public works, and allowed for the distribution of goods over substantial distances.

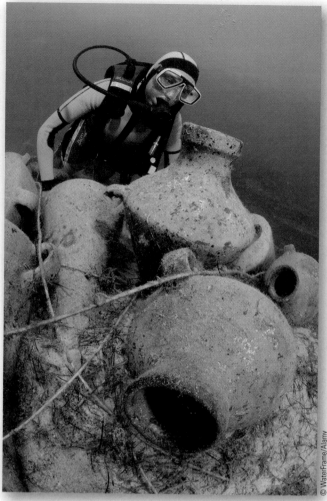

Here a diver recovers antique amphorae (the traditional containers for transporting wine, olives, olive oil, grain, and other commodities) from the site of a shipwreck in the Mediterranean Sea near the village of Kas, Turkey. The shipwreck dates back to the time of the Trojan War (over 3,000 years ago). Underwater archaeologists—led in this expedition by George Bass from the Institute of Nautical Archaeology of Texas A & M University collaborating with the Bodrum Museum of Underwater Archaeology in Istanbul, Turkey—can reconstruct facets of the past, ranging from ancient trade routes and and shipbuilding techniques, through the analysis of such remains.

More obvious sites, such as the human-made mounds or *tells* of the Middle East, are easier to spot from the ground, for the country is open. But it is more difficult to locate ruins, even those that are well above ground, where there is a heavy forest cover. Thus the discovery of archaeological sites is strongly affected by local geography and climate.

Some sites may be spotted by changes in vegetation. For example, the topsoil of ancient storage and refuse pits is often richer in organic matter than that of the surrounding areas, and so it grows distinctive vegetation. At Tikal, an ancient Maya site in Guatemala, breadnut trees usually grow near the remains of ancient houses, so archaeologists can use these trees as guideposts.

On the ground, sites can be spotted by **soil marks,** or stains, showing up on the surface of recently plowed fields. Soil marks led archaeologists to many of the Bronze Age burial mounds in northern Hertfordshire and southwestern Cambridgeshire, England. The mounds hardly rose out of the ground, yet each was circled at its core by chalky soil marks. Sometimes the very presence of a particular chalky rock is significant.

Documents, maps, and folklore are also useful to the archaeologist. Heinrich Schliemann, the famous and controversial 19th-century German archaeologist, was led to the discovery of Troy after a reading of Homer's *Iliad.* He assumed that the city described by Homer as Ilium was really Troy. Place names and local lore often are an indication that an archaeological site is to be found in the area. Archaeological surveys therefore often depend upon amateur collectors and local people who are usually familiar with the history of the land.

Sometimes natural processes, such as soil erosion or droughts, expose sites or fossils. For example, in eastern North America erosion along the coastlines and river banks has exposed prehistoric refuse mounds known as shell **middens** (the general term for a trash deposit), which are filled with the remains of mussels and/or oysters, indicating that shellfish consumption was common. Similarly, a whole village of stone huts was exposed at Skara Brae in Scotland's Orkney Islands by the action of wind as it blew away sand.

Though natural forces sometimes expose fossils and sites, human physical and cultural remains are more often accidentally discovered. In Chapter 2 we noted how construction and quarrying work in Europe led to the discovery of fossils of extinct animals, which then played a role in the development of evolutionary theory. Similarly, limestone quarrying at a variety of sites in South Africa early in the 20th century led to the discovery of the earliest humanlike fossils from millions of years ago (see Chapter 7). Disturbances of the earth on a smaller scale, such as plowing, sometimes turn up bones, fragments of pots, and other archaeological objects.

Because construction projects do uncover archaeological remains so frequently, in many countries, including the United States, construction projects require government approval in order to ensure the identification and protection of archaeological remains. Cultural resource management, introduced in Chapter 1, is routinely included in the environmental review process for federally funded or licensed construction projects in the United States, as it is in Europe. This chapter's Anthropology Applied feature takes a closer look at cultural resource management.

Archaeological Excavation

Once a researcher identifies a site likely to contribute to his or her research agenda, the next step is to plan and carry out excavation. Obtaining permission to excavate from a variety of local and national authorities is a critical part of this planning. To begin, the land is cleared, and the places to be excavated are plotted as a **grid system** (Figure 5.1). The surface of the site is divided into squares of equal size, and each square is numbered and marked with stakes. Each object found may then be located precisely in the square from which it came. (Remember, context is everything!) The starting point of a grid system, which is located precisely in three dimensions, may be a large rock, the edge of a stone wall, or an iron rod sunk into the ground; this point is also known as the reference or **datum point.**

At a large site covering several square miles, the plotting may be done in terms of individual structures, numbered according to the square of a "giant grid" in which they are found. In a gridded site, each square is dug separately with great care. (In the photo on page 106, note how the grid system is used even in underwater archaeology.) Trowels are used to scrape the soil, and screens are used to sift all the loose soil so that even the smallest artifacts, such as flint chips or beads, are recovered.

A technique employed when looking for very fine objects, such as fish scales or very small bones, is called **flotation.** Flotation consists of immersing soil in water, causing the particles to separate. Some will float, others will sink to the bottom, and the remains can be easily retrieved.

If the site is **stratified**—that is, if the remains lie in layers one upon the other—each layer, or stratum, will be dug separately. Each layer, having been settled during a particular span of time, will contain artifacts deposited at the same time and belonging to the same culture (Figure 5.2). Cultural change can be traced through the order in which artifacts were deposited—deeper layers reveal older artifacts. But, archaeologists Frank Hole and Robert F. Heizer suggest,

> because of difficulties in analyzing stratigraphy, archaeologists must use the greatest caution in drawing conclusions. Almost all interpretations of time, space, and culture contexts depend on stratigraphy. The refinements of laboratory techniques for

soil mark A stain that shows up on the surface of recently plowed fields that reveals an archaeological site.

middens A refuse or garbage disposal area in an archaeological site.

grid system A system for recording data in three dimensions for an archaeological excavation.

datum point The starting point, or reference, for a grid system.

flotation An archaeological technique employed to recover very tiny objects by immersion of soil samples in water to separate heavy from light particles.

stratified Layered; term used to describe archaeological sites where the remains lie in layers, one upon another.

Cultural Resource Management   *by John Crock*

In the United States and Europe, cultural resource management or "regulatory" archaeology employs more archaeologists than universities and museums combined. This work is mandated by laws like Section 106 of the National Historic Preservation Act, which requires a cultural resources review for federally funded or regulated development projects, like the construction of new highways. These federal requirements have provided the funds for me and many other archaeologists to do what we love the best: to reconstruct the lives of people in the past through excavation of the material traces they have left behind.

For example, the Vermont Agency of Transportation's Missisquoi Bay Bridge Project at the northern end of Lake Champlain resulted in the discovery of one of the most significant archaeological sites ever found in Vermont. The initial Phase I survey sampling for the project included the excavation of small shovel test pits across the level field that would one day become the new bridge approach. Seven of the initial fifty-seven pits contained evidence of an archaeological site, including a total of just eight artifacts. Fortunately, this limited evidence was enough to document the presence of a pre-contact Native American habitation, later named the Bohannon site after the landowner.

To determine its size and significance, we conducted a Phase II

evaluation of the site. Native American deposits were recovered from thirty-nine of the additional sixty-seven Phase II test pits excavated. The majority of the artifacts recovered are small fragments of clay pottery, including a portion of a turtle head effigy from a pipe or vessel. It was this artifact, the likes of which had never before been excavated in Vermont, which helped indicate the site was significant and eligible for the National Register of Historic Places. The effigy, and the style and thickness of pottery shards, indicated the site dated to the late pre-contact or contact period, between about 1400 and 1700. Since the site could not be avoided during construction, Phase III data recovery excavations were necessary to salvage a sample of the endangered site.

It was only during this final phase of work that the true size and significance of the Bohannon site was revealed. Excavation of large areas uncovered a substantial sample of decorated clay pipes and jars. Paleobotanist Nancy Sidell identified corn kernels and parts of corn plants in hearth and trash pit features at the site, indicating that the residents of the site grew corn close by. Zooarchaeologist Nanny Carder identified twenty-four different species in bone refuse from the same features, revealing a broad diet of animals ranging from flying squirrel to black bear. Living floors, trash pits, and the former location of house posts also were identified.

To salvage as much information as possible from the site before construction, an acre of the project area was stripped of topsoil to try to determine more about the layout of the site. Hundreds of post "mold" stains were revealed, from which portions of several longhouses have been reconstructed. A sample of corn kernels found was radiocarbon dated using accelerator

mass spectrometry (AMS) to around AD 1600. Other dates and their error ranges place the site occupation between 1450 and 1650.

We believe the site was occupied just prior to 1609, when the first Europeans entered the region, based on the style of the pottery, the radiocarbon dates, and the fact that no European artifacts were recovered. The decorated clay pipes and pottery jars from the site are identical to material that has been found at late pre-contact village sites along the St. Lawrence River in Quebec. The inventory of artifacts, food resources, and house patterns from the site all suggest that the people at the Bohannon site were closely related to the St. Lawrence Iroquoians, a First Nations people who lived in what is now Quebec and Ontario.

From its humble identification in the early stages of archaeological survey for the new bridge, the Bohannon site has yielded an incredible amount of information; it represents the first St. Lawrence Iroquoian village discovered in Vermont.

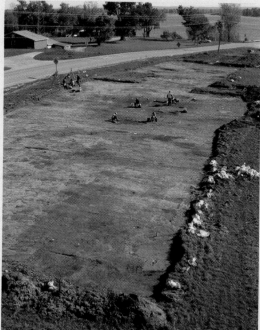

Located on a relatively unobtrusive piece of land along an existing road, the first St. Lawrence Iroquoian village was discovered only because federal law mandated archaeological exploration before a road and bridge expansion project.

Figure 5.1 At large sites covering several square miles, a giant grid is constructed, as shown in this map of the center of the ancient Maya city of Tikal. Each square of the grid is one quarter of a square kilometer; individual structures are numbered according to the square in which they are found.

analysis are wasted if archaeologists cannot specify the stratigraphic position of their artifacts.[3]

If no stratification is present, then the archaeologist digs by arbitrary levels. Each square must be dug so that its edges and profiles are straight; walls between squares are often left standing to serve as visual correlates of the grid system.

Fossil Excavation

Although fossil excavation is similar to archaeological excavation, there are some key differences. The paleoanthropologist must be particularly skilled in the techniques of geology, or have ready access to geologic expertise,

because a fossil is of little value unless its place in the sequence of rocks that contain it can be determined.

In order to provide all the necessary expertise, paleoanthropological expeditions today generally are made up of teams of experts in various fields in addition to physical anthropology. Surgical skill and caution are required to remove a fossil from its burial place without damage. Unusual tools and materials are found in the kit of the paleoanthropologist—pickaxes, dental instruments, enamel coating, burlap for bandages, and sculpting plaster.

To remove newly discovered bones, the paleoanthropologist begins uncovering the specimen, using pick and shovel for initial excavation, then small camel-hair brushes and dental picks to remove loose and easily detachable debris surrounding the bones. Once the entire specimen has been uncovered (a process that may take days of back-breaking, patient labor), the bones are covered with shellac

[3] Hole, F., & Heizer, R. F. (1969). *An introduction to prehistoric archeology* (p. 113). New York: Holt, Rinehart & Winston.

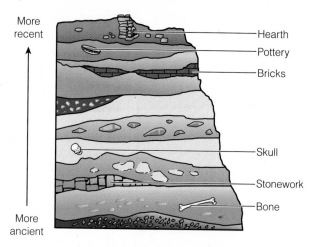

More recent ↑

More ancient ↓

- Hearth
- Pottery
- Bricks
- Skull
- Stonework
- Bone

Figure 5.2 Some sites are stratified, in that archaeological remains lie in layers stacked one on top of the other; older layers are lower down, and more recent layers are on top. Geologic processes will result in strata of different depths in different places. Careful mapping of each stratum using the grid system is essential for interpretation of the site.

and tissue paper to prevent cracking and damage during further excavation and handling.

Both the fossil and the earth immediately surrounding it, or the *matrix,* are prepared for removal as a single block. The bones and matrix are cut out of the earth (but not removed), and more shellac is applied to the entire block to harden it. The bones are covered with burlap bandages dipped in plaster. Then the block is enclosed in more plaster and burlap bandages, perhaps splinted with tree branches and allowed to dry overnight. After it has hardened, the entire block is carefully removed from the earth, ready for packing and transport to a laboratory. Before leaving the discovery area, the investigator makes a thorough sketch map of the terrain and pinpoints the find on geologic maps to aid future investigators.

State of Preservation of Archaeological and Fossil Evidence

The results of an excavation depend greatly on the condition of the remains. Inorganic materials such as stone

and metal are more resistant to decay than organic ones such as wood and bone. Sometimes the anthropologist discovers an assemblage—a collection of artifacts—made of durable inorganic materials, such as stone tools, and traces of organic ones long since decomposed, such as woodwork (Figure 5.3), textiles, or food.

Climate, local geologic conditions, and cultural practices also play a role in the state of preservation. For example, our knowledge of ancient Egyptian culture stems not only from their burial practices but from the effects of climate and soil on preservation. The ancient Egyptians believed that eternal life could be achieved only if the dead person were buried with his or her worldly possessions. Hence, their tombs are usually filled with a wealth of artifacts, including the skeletons of other humans owned by dynastic rulers.

Under favorable climatic conditions, even the most perishable objects may survive over vast periods of time. The earliest Egyptian burials, consisting of shallow pits in the sand with bodies buried long before mummification was practiced, often yield well-preserved corpses. Their preservation can only be the result of rapid desiccation, or complete drying out, in the warm desert climate. The elaborate tombs of the rulers of dynastic Egypt often contain wooden furniture, textiles, flowers, and written scrolls on paper made from papyrus reeds, barely touched by time, seemingly as fresh looking as they were when deposited in the tombs as long as 5,000 years ago—a consequence of the region's arid climatic conditions. Of course, the ancient Egyptian burial practices selectively preserved more information about the elite members of society than the average individual.

The dryness of certain caves is also a factor in the preservation of **coprolites,** the scientific term for fossilized human or animal feces. Coprolites provide information on prehistoric diet and health. From the analysis of elements preserved in coprolites such as seeds, insect skeletons, and tiny bones from fish or amphibians, archaeologists and paleoanthropologists can directly determine diets from the past. This information, in turn,

coprolites Preserved fecal material providing evidence of the diet and health of past organisms.

Figure 5.3 Although the wooden posts of a house may have long since decayed, their positions may still be marked by discoloration of the soil. The plan shown on the left—of an ancient post-hole pattern and depression at Snaketown, Arizona—permits the hypothetical house reconstruction on the right.

The preservation of archaeological remains is dependent upon the environment. Even before the invention of mummification technologies, buried bodies were very well preserved in Egypt because they dried so quickly in the extremely arid environment.

At the Maya site of Tikal, these intricately carved figures, originally made of wood, were recovered from a king's tomb by pouring plaster into a cavity in the soil, left when the original organic material decayed.

massive structures of stone—as a result of the pressure exerted upon them by the heavy forest vegetation. The rain and humidity soon destroy almost all traces of woodwork, textiles, or basketry. Fortunately, impressions of these artifacts can sometimes be preserved in plaster, and some objects made of wood or plant fibers are depicted in stone carvings and pottery figurines. Thus even in the face of substantial decay of organic substances, something may still be learned about them.

Sorting Out the Evidence

Excavation records include a scale map of all the features, the stratification of each excavated square, a description of the exact location and depth of every artifact or bone unearthed, and photographs and scale drawings of the objects. This is the only way archaeological evidence can later be pieced together so as to arrive at a plausible reconstruction of a culture. Although the archaeologist or paleoanthropologist may be interested only in certain kinds of remains, every aspect of the site must be recorded, whether it is relevant to the particular investigation or not, because such evidence may be useful to others and would otherwise be lost forever. In sum, archaeological sites are nonrenewable resources. The disturbance of the arrangement of artifacts, even by proper excavation, is permanent.

Sometimes sites are illegally looted, which can result in loss not only of the artifacts themselves but of the site. Although looting has long been a threat to the archaeological record, it has become a high-tech endeavor today. Avid collectors and fans of archaeological sites unwittingly

can shed light on overall health. Because many sources of food are available only in certain seasons, it is even possible to tell the time of year in which the food was eaten.

Certain climates can obliterate all evidence of organic remains. Maya ruins found in the tropical rainforests of Mesoamerica (the region encompassing central and southern Mexico and northern Central America) are often in a state of collapse—notwithstanding that many are

In September 2006, researchers announced the discovery of a spectacular new fossil—the skeleton of a young child dated to 3.3 million years ago. The fossil was actually discovered in the Dikika area of northern Ethiopia in 2000. Since then, researchers worked on careful recovery and analysis of the fossilized remains so that when the announcement was made, a great deal was already known about the specimen. Their analyses have determined that this child, a little girl about 3 years old who likely died in a flash flood, was a member of *Australopithecus afarensis,* the same species as the famous Lucy specimen (see Chapter 7). Due to the importance of this find, some scientists have referred to this child as "Lucy's baby" though the child lived about 150,000 years before Lucy.

© AFP/Getty Images

aid looting through sharing site and artifact location information on the Internet, which has also provided a market for artifacts.

Once the artifact or fossil has been freed from the surrounding matrix, a variety of other laboratory methods come into play. Generally, archaeologists and paleoanthropologists plan on at least three hours of laboratory work for each hour of fieldwork. In the lab, artifacts that have been recovered must first be cleaned and catalogued—often a tedious and time-consuming job—before they are ready for analysis. From the shapes of the artifacts as well as from the traces of manufacture and wear, archaeologists can usually determine their function. For example, the Russian archaeologist S. A. Semenov devoted many years to the study of prehistoric technology. In the case of a flint tool used as a scraper, he was able to determine, by examining the wear patterns of the tool under a microscope, that the prehistoric individuals who used it began to scrape from right to left and then scraped from left to right, and in so doing avoided straining the muscles of the hand.[4] From the work of Semenov and others, we now know that right-handed individuals made most stone tools preserved in the archaeological record, a fact that has implications for brain

structure. The relationships among populations can also be traced through material remains (Figure 5.4).

Dental specimens are frequently analyzed under the microscope to examine markings on teeth that might provide clues about diet in the past. Specimens are now regularly scanned using computed tomography (CT) to analyze structural details of the bone. Imprints or **endocasts** of the insides of skulls are taken to determine the size and shape of ancient brains.

Advances in genetic technology are now applied to ancient human remains. Anthropologists extract genetic material from skeletal remains in order to perform DNA comparisons among the specimen, other fossils, and living people. Small fragments of DNA are amplified or copied repeatedly using **polymerase chain reaction (PCR)**

S-twist (\ )   Z-twist (/)

Figure 5.4 In northern New England, prehistoric pottery was often decorated by impressing the damp clay with a cord-wrapped stick. Examination of cord impressions reveals that coastal people twisted fibers used to make cordage to the left (Z-twist), while those living inland did the opposite (S-twist). The nonfunctional differences reflect motor habits so deeply ingrained as to seem completely natural to the cordage makers. From this, we may infer two distinctively different populations.

---

[4] Semenov, S. A. (1964). *Prehistoric technology.* New York: Barnes & Noble.

endocast A cast of the inside of a skull; used to help determine the size and shape of the brain.

polymerase chain reaction (PCR) A technique for amplifying or creating multiple copies of fragments of DNA so that it can be studied in the laboratory.

technology to provide a sufficient amount of material to perform these analyses. However, unless DNA is preserved in a stable material such as amber, it will decay over time. Therefore, analyses of DNA extracted from specimens older than about 50,000 years become increasingly unreliable due to the decay of DNA.

As defined in Chapter 1, *bioarchaeology,* which seeks to understand past cultures through analysis of skeletal remains, is a growing area within anthropology. It combines the biological anthropologists' expertise in skeletal biology with the archaeological reconstruction of human cultures. Examination of human skeletal material provides important insights into ancient peoples' diets, gender roles, social status, and patterns of activity. For example, analysis of human skeletons shows that elite members of society had access to more nutritious foods, allowing them to reach their full growth potential.[5]

Gender roles in a given society can be assessed through skeletons as well. In fully preserved adult skeletons, the sex of the deceased individual can be determined with a high degree of accuracy, allowing for comparisons of male and female life expectancy, mortality, and health status (Figure 5.5). These analyses can help establish the social roles of men and women in past societies.

Forensics, bioarchaeology's cousin discipline, also examines skeletal remains to determine characteristics of a deceased or injured individual. As with archaeological research, this information is integrated with material remains. New biomedical technology also plays a role in the investigation of remains from both the past and the present. For example, CT scans have added new information

Figure 5.5 The complete male and female skeletons differ on average in some consistent ways that allow skeletal biologists to identify the sex of the deceased individual. In addition to noting some of these features labeled above, learning the basic skeleton will be useful in the chapters ahead as we trace the history of human evolution.

[5] Haviland, W. (1967). Stature at Tikal, Guatemala: Implications for ancient Maya, demography, and social organization. *American Antiquity 32,* 316–325.

Skulls from peoples of the Tiwanaku empire, who tightly bound the heads of their children. The shape of the skull distinguished people from various parts of the empire that flourished in the Andes mountains of South America between AD 550 and 950.

in forensic, bioarchaeological, and paleoanthropological contexts. While a CT scan cannot substitute for an autopsy in forensic contexts, it is useful for identification after mass disasters. It can provide evidence of past trauma that might not be revealed from an investigation aimed at determining the immediate cause of death.[6]

In archaeological contexts, CT technology has been particularly useful for determining whether damage to remains took place during excavation or whether it preceded death. For example, after the remains of Egyptian King Tut were scanned, scientists uniformly agreed that the young king did not die of a head injury as previously thought; some suggested that a broken femur may have been the cause of his death.[7] To minimize handling, these rare fossil specimens are scanned one at a time so that researchers can study the digital images.

Recently, skeletal analyses have become more difficult to carry out, especially in the United States, where American Indian communities now often request the return of skeletons from archaeological excavations for reburial, as required by federal law. Anthropologists find themselves in a quandary over this requirement. As scientists, anthropologists know the importance of the information that can be gleaned from studies of human skeletons, but as scholars subject to ethical principles, they are bound to respect the feelings of those for whom the skeletons possess cultural and spiritual significance.

New techniques, such as 3D digital images of Native American skeletons, help to resolve this conflict as they allow for both rapid repatriation and continued study of skeletal remains. But globally, aboriginal groups are questioning the practice of digitizing remains of their people without permission. For example, the University of Vienna in Austria has been challenged by representatives of the Ju/'hoansi people of southern Africa because the remains that its ethnological museum has in its possession were not donated; rather, they were taken early in the century by Rudolf Pöch, a Viennese anthropologist whose writings about racial hierarchies were used as part of Nazi Germany's eugenics movement. According to Roger Chennells, the South African legal advisor for the Ju/'hoansi, their position is: "We have not been consulted,

and we do not support any photographic archiving of our people's remains—we are opposed to it."[8]

By the standards of the 1990 Native American Graves Protection and Repatriation Act (NAGPRA), the Ju/'hoansi would have legal decision-making authority over the fate of these remains; but the equivalent of NAGPRA has not yet been codified as international law. Even with NAGPRA in place, the handling of remains is still often controversial. Scientists and American Indians sometimes have been unable to move beyond their conflicting views as seen with Kennewick Man, a 9,300-year-old skeleton that was dislodged by the Columbia River in Washington State in 1996. This chapter's Biocultural Connection focuses on how this controversy has been playing out in the federal courts.

Dating the Past

With accurate and detailed records of their excavations in hand, archaeologists and paleoanthropologists are able to deal with a crucial research issue: the question of age. As we have seen, analysis of physical and cultural remains is dependent on knowledge about the age of the artifacts or specimens. How, then, are the materials retrieved from excavations reliably dated? Calculating the age of physical and cultural remains is an essential aspect of interpreting the past. Because archaeologists and paleoanthropologists often deal with peoples and events from long ago, the traditional calendar of historic times is of little use to them.

Remains can be dated by noting their position in the earth, by measuring the amount of chemicals contained in fossil bones, or by association with other plant, animal, or cultural remains. These are known as **relative dating** techniques because they do not establish precise dates for specific remains but rather their relationship to a series of remains. Methods of **absolute** or **chronometric dating** (from the Latin for "measuring time") provide actual dates calculated in years "before the present" (BP). These methods rely on chemical and physical properties such as rates of decay of radioactive elements, which may be present in the remains themselves or in the surrounding soil. Absolute dating methods scientifically establish actual dates for the major events of geologic and evolutionary history. By comparing dates and remains across a variety of sites, anthropologists can reconstruct human origins, migrations, and technological developments.

Many relative and chronometric techniques are available. However, most of these techniques are applicable only for certain time spans and in certain environmental contexts. Bear in mind that each of the chronometric dating techniques also has a margin of error. Ideally, archaeologists

---

[6] Leth, P. M. (2007). The use of CT scanning in forensic autopsy. *Forensic Science, Medicine, and Pathology 3* (1), 65–69.

[7] Handwerk, B. (2005, March 8). King Tut not murdered violently, CT scans show. *National Geographic News, 2.*

relative dating In archaeology and paleoanthropology, designating an event, object, or fossil as being older or younger than another.

absolute or chronometric dating In archaeology and paleoanthropology, dating recovered material based on solar years, centuries, or other units of absolute time.

---

[8] Scully, T. (2008). Online anthropology draws protest from aboriginal group. *Nature 453,* 1155. doi:10.1038/4531155a.

Biocultural Connection

Kennewick Man

The "Ancient One" and "Kennewick Man" both refer to the 9,300-year-old skeletal remains that were found in 1996 below the surface of Lake Wallula, part of the Columbia River, in Kennewick, Washington State. This discovery has been the center of continuing controversy since it was made. Who owns these human remains? Who can determine what shall be done with them? Do the biological characteristics preserved in these remains play a role in determining their fate?

This particular conflict involves three major parties. Because the skeleton was found on a location for which the U.S. Army Corps of Engineers is responsible, this federal agency first took possession of the remains. Appealing to a 1990 federal law, the Native American Graves Protection and Repatriation Act (NAGPRA), a nearby American Indian group named the Confederated Tribes of the Umatilla Indian Reservation (representing the region's Umatilla, Cayuse, and Walla Walla nations) claimed the remains. Because Kennewick Man was found within their ancestral homeland, they argue that they are "culturally affiliated" with the individual they refer

to as the Ancient One. Viewing these human bones as belonging to an ancestor, they wish to return them to the earth in a respectful ceremony.

This claim was challenged in federal court by a group of scientists, including some archaeologists and biological anthropologists. They view these human remains, among the oldest ever discovered in the western hemisphere, as scientifically precious, with potential to shed light on the earliest population movements in the Americas. The scientists do not want to "own" the remains but want the opportunity to study them. By means of DNA analysis, for instance, these scientists expect to determine possible prehistoric linkages between this individual and ancient human remains found elsewhere, including Asia. Moreover, scientific analysis may determine whether there actually exists any biological connection between these remains and currently living Native peoples, including individuals residing on the Umatilla Indian Reservation.

Fearing the loss of a unique scientific specimen, the scientists filed a lawsuit in federal court to prevent reburial before these bones were researched and

analyzed. Their legal challenge is not based on "cultural affiliation," which is a very difficult concept when it concerns such ancient human remains, but focuses on the fact that the region's Native peoples cannot prove they are direct lineal descendants. Unless such ties have been objectively established, they argue, Kennewick Man should be released for scientific study.

In 2004 federal court rulings permitted initial scientific investigations. Just as these investigations were wrapping up in July 2005, the Senate Indian Affairs Committee heard testimony on a proposal by Arizona Senator John McCain to expand NAGPRA so that remains such as these would be once again prohibited from study. Congress adjourned without this bill becoming law, and the remains have been studied continually since then.

Doug Owsley, the forensic anthropologist from the Smithsonian Institution leading the research team, has said that scientific investigation is yielding even more information than expected. Because conflicting worldviews are at the center of this controversy, it is unlikely that it will be easily resolved.

© Eurelios/Photo Researchers, Inc.

and paleoanthropologists utilize as many methods as are appropriate, given the materials available and the funds at their disposal. By doing so, they significantly reduce the risk of error. Several of the most frequently employed dating techniques are presented in Table 5.1.

Relative Dating

Of the many relative dating techniques available, **stratigraphy** is probably the most reliable (recall Figure 5.2). Stratigraphy is based on the simple principle

that the oldest layer, or stratum, was deposited first (it is the deepest) whereas the newest layer was deposited last (in undisturbed situations, it lies at the top). Similarly, archaeological evidence is usually deposited in chronological order. The lowest stratum contains the oldest artifacts and/or fossils whereas the uppermost stratum contains the most recent ones. Thus even in the

stratigraphy In archaeology and paleoanthropology, the most reliable method of relative dating by means of strata.

Table 5.1 Absolute and Relative Dating Methods

Dating Method	Time Period	Method's Process	Drawbacks
Stratigraphy	Relative only	Based on the law of superposition, which states that lower layers or strata are older than higher layers	Site specific; natural forces, such as earthquakes, and human activity, such as burials, disturb stratigraphic relationships
Fluorine analysis	Relative only	Compares the amount of fluorine from surrounding soil absorbed by specimens after deposition	Site specific
Faunal and floral series	Relative only	Sequencing remains into relative chronological order based on an evolutionary sequence established in another region with reliable absolute dates; called *palynology* when done with pollen grains	Dependent upon known relationships established elsewhere
Seriation	Relative only	Sequencing cultural remains into relative chronological order based on stylistic features	Dependent upon known relationships established elsewhere
Dendrochronology	About 3,000 years BP maximum	Compares tree-growth rings preserved in a site with a tree of known age	Requires ancient trees of known age
Radiocarbon	Accurate less than 50,000 years BP	Compares the ratio of radioactive carbon 14 (^{14}C) (with a half-life of 5,730 years) to stable carbon 12 (^{12}C) in organic material	Increasingly inaccurate when assessing remains from more than 50,000 years ago
Potassium argon (K-Ar)	More than 200,000 years BP	Compares the amount of radioactive potassium (^{40}K) (with a half-life of 1.3 billion years) to stable argon (^{40}Ar)	Requires volcanic ash; requires cross-checking due to contamination from atmospheric argon
Amino acid racemization	40,000–180,000 years BP	Compares the change in the number of proteins in a right- versus left-sided three-dimensional structure	Amino acids leached out from soil variably cause error
Thermoluminescence	Possibly up to 200,000 years BP	Measures the amount of light given off due to radioactivity when sample heated to high temperatures	Technique developed for recent materials such as Greek pottery; not clear how accurate the dates are for older remains
Electron spin resonance	Possibly up to 200,000 years BP	Measures the resonance of trapped electrons in a magnetic field	Works with tooth enamel—not yet developed for bone; problems with accuracy
Fission track	Wide range of times	Measures the tracks left in crystals by uranium as it decays; good cross-check for K-Ar technique	Useful for dating crystals only
Paleomagnetic reversals	Wide range of times	Measures orientation of magnetic particles in stones and links them to whether magnetic field of earth pulled toward the north or south during their formation	Large periods of normal or reversed magnetic orientation require dating by some other method; some smaller events known to interrupt the sequence
Uranium series	40,000–180,000 years BP	Measures the amount of uranium decaying in cave sites	Large error range

absence of precise dates, one knows the *relative* age of objects in one stratum compared with the ages of those in other strata. However, defining the stratigraphy of a given site can be complicated by geologic activities such

fluorine dating In archaeology or paleoanthropology, a technique for relative dating based on the fact that the amount of fluorine in bones is proportional to their age.

as earthquakes that shift the position of stratigraphic layers.

Another method of relative dating is the **fluorine** method. It is based on the fact that the amount of fluorine deposited in bones is proportional to the amount of time they have been in the earth. The oldest bones contain the greatest amount of fluorine and vice versa. The fluorine test is useful in dating bones that cannot be ascribed with certainty to any particular stratum. A shortcoming of this culture areas, series have even been developed for particular styles of pottery.

Similar inferences are made with animal or faunal series. For example, very early North American Indian sites have yielded the remains of mastodons and mammoths—animals now extinct—and on this basis the sites can be dated to a time before these animals died out, roughly 10,000 years ago. For dating some of the earliest African fossils in human evolution, faunal series have been developed in regions where accurate chronometric dates can be established. These series can then be used to establish relative sequences in other regions. Similar series have been established for plants, particularly using grains of pollen. This approach has become known as **palynology.** The kind of pollen found in any geologic stratum depends on the kind of vegetation that existed at the time that stratum was deposited. A site or locality can therefore be dated by determining what kind of pollen was found associated with it. In addition, palynology also helps to reconstruct the environments in which prehistoric people lived.

Chronometric Dating

Chronometric dating methods apply chemistry and physics to calculate the ages of physical and cultural remains. Several methods use naturally occurring radioactive elements that are present either in the remains themselves or in the surrounding soil.

One of the most widely used methods of absolute dating is **radiocarbon dating.** This method uses the fact that while they are alive, all organisms absorb radioactive carbon (known as carbon 14 or ^{14}C) as well as ordinary carbon 12 (^{12}C) in proportions identical to those found in the atmosphere. Absorption of ^{14}C ceases at the time of death, and the ratio between the two forms of carbon begins to change as the unstable radioactive element ^{14}C begins to "decay." Each radioactive element decays, or transforms into a stable nonradioactive form, at a specific rate. The amount of time it takes for one half of the material originally present to decay is expressed as the "half-life." In the case of ^{14}C, it takes 5,730 years for half of the amount of ^{14}C present to decay to stable nitrogen 14. In another

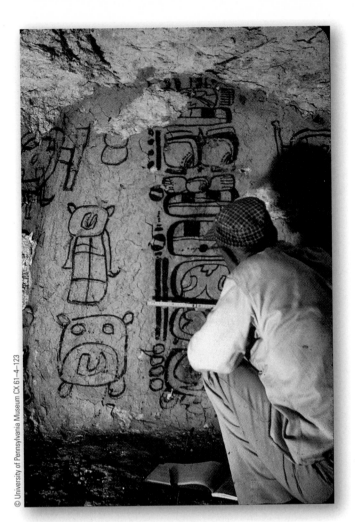

Some ancient societies devised precise ways of recording dates that archaeologists have been able to correlate with our own calendar. Here is the tomb of an important ruler, Siyaj Chan K'awil II, at the ancient Maya city of Tikal. The glyphs painted on the wall give the date of the burial in the Maya calendar, which is the same as March 18, AD 457, in the Gregorian calendar.

method is that the amount of naturally occurring fluorine is not constant but varies from region to region, making it difficult to validate cross-site comparisons of fluorine values. This method was vital for exposing the infamous Piltdown hoax in England, in which a human skull and orangutan jaw were placed together in the earth as false evidence for an early human ancestor (see Chapter 7).

Relative dating can also be done by **seriation,** a method of establishing sequences of plant, animal, or even cultural remains. With seriation, the order of appearance of a succession (or series) of plants, animals, or artifacts provides relative dates for a site based on a series established in another area. An example of seriation based on cultural artifacts is the Stone–Bronze–Iron Age series used by prehistorians (see Chapter 11). Within a given region, sites containing artifacts made of iron are generally more recent than sites containing only stone tools. In well-investigated

seriation In archaeology and paleoanthropology, a technique for relative dating based on putting groups of objects into a sequence in relation to one another.

palynology In archaeology and paleoanthropology, a technique of relative dating based on changes in fossil pollen over time.

radiocarbon dating In archaeology and paleoanthropology, a technique of chronometric dating based on measuring the amount of radioactive carbon (^{14}C) left in organic materials found in archaeological sites.

5,730 years (11,460 years total), half of the remaining amount will also decay to nitrogen 14 so that only one quarter of the original amount of ^{14}C will be present. Thus the age of an organic substance such as charcoal, wood, shell, or bone can be measured through determining the changing proportion of ^{14}C relative to the amount of stable ^{12}C.

Though scientists can measure the amount of radioactive carbon left in even a few milligrams of a given organic substance of a recent specimen, the amount of carbon 14 present in remains from the distant past is so small that accurate detection is difficult. The radiocarbon method can adequately date organic materials up to about 50,000 years old, but dating older material is far less reliable.

Of course, one has to be sure that the organic remains were truly contemporaneous with the archaeological materials. For example, charcoal found on a site may have gotten there from a recent forest fire rather than a more ancient activity, or wood found at a site may have been retrieved by the people who lived there from some older context.

Because there is always a certain amount of error involved, radiocarbon dates (like all chronometric dating methods) are not as absolute as is sometimes thought. This is why any stated date always has a plus-or-minus (±) factor attached to it corresponding to one standard deviation above and below the mean value. For example, a date of 5,200 ± 120 years ago means that there is about a 2 out of 3 chance (or a 67 percent chance) that the true date falls somewhere between 5,080 and 5,320 radiocarbon years ago. The qualification "radiocarbon years" is used because radiocarbon years are not precisely equivalent to calendar years.

The discovery that radiocarbon years are not precisely equivalent to calendar years was made possible by another method of absolute dating: **dendrochronology** (derived from *dendron*, a Greek word meaning "tree"). Originally devised for dating Pueblo Indian sites in the North American Southwest, this method is based on the fact that in the right kind of climate, trees add one (and only one) new growth ring to their trunks every year. The rings vary in thickness, depending upon the amount of rainfall received in a year, so that climatic fluctuation is registered in the growth ring. By taking a sample of wood, such as a beam from a Pueblo Indian house, and by comparing its pattern of rings with those in the trunk of a tree of known age, archaeologists can date the archaeological material.

Dendrochronology is applicable only to wooden objects. Furthermore, it can be used only in regions in which trees of great age, such as the giant sequoias and the bristlecone pine, are known to grow. Radiocarbon dating of wood from bristlecone pines dated by dendrochronology allows scientists to correct the carbon 14 dates so as to bring them into agreement with calendar dates.

Potassium-argon dating, another commonly used method of absolute dating, is based on a technique similar to that of radiocarbon analysis. Following intense heating, as from a volcanic eruption, radioactive potassium decays at a known rate to form argon—any previously existing argon having been released by the heating of the molten lava. The half-life of radioactive potassium is 1.3 billion years. Deposits that are millions of years old can now be dated by measuring the ratio of potassium to argon in a given rock.

Volcanic debris at various localities in East Africa is routinely dated by potassium-argon analysis, indicating when the volcanic eruption occurred. If fossils or artifacts are found sandwiched between layers of volcanic ash, as they are at Olduvai and other sites in East Africa, they can be dated with some precision. As with radiocarbon dates, there are limits to that precision, and potassium-argon dates are always stated with a plus-or-minus margin of error attached. The precision of this method is limited to time periods older than about 200,000 years ago.

Though radiocarbon and potassium-argon methods are extremely valuable, neither technique works well during the time period dating from about 50,000 years ago to about 200,000 years ago. Because this same time period happens to be very important in human evolutionary history, scientists have developed a number of other methods to obtain accurate dates during this critical period.

One such method, *amino acid racemization,* is based on the fact that amino acids trapped in organic materials gradually change, or racemize, after death, from left-handed forms to right-handed forms. Thus the ratio of left- to right-handed forms should indicate the specimen's age. Unfortunately, in substances like bone, moisture and acids in the soil can leach out the amino acids, thereby introducing a serious source of error. However, ostrich eggshells have proved immune to this problem, the amino acids being so effectively locked up in a tight mineral matrix that they are preserved for thousands of years. Because ostrich eggs were widely used as food and the shells were used as containers in Africa and the Middle East, they provide a powerful means of dating sites of the later parts of the Old Stone Age (Paleolithic), between 40,000 and 180,000 years ago.

dendrochronology In archaeology and paleoanthropology, a technique of chronometric dating based on the number of rings of growth found in a tree trunk.

potassium-argon dating In archaeology and paleoanthropology, a technique of chronometric dating that measures the ratio of radioactive potassium to argon in volcanic debris associated with human remains.

CHAPTER 6

Macroevolution and the Early Primates

Chapter Preview

What Is Macroevolution?

While microevolution refers to changes in the allele frequencies of populations, macroevolution focuses on the formation of new species (speciation) and on the evolutionary relationships among groups of species. Speciation may proceed in a branching manner, as when reproductive isolation of populations prevents gene flow between them, leading to the formation of separate species. Alternatively, in the absence of isolation, a species may evolve without branching in response to environmental changes. The accumulation of small changes from generation to generation may transform an ancestral species into a new one.

When and Where Did the First Primates Appear, and What Were They Like?

Fossil evidence indicates that the earliest primates began to develop around 65 million years ago (mya), when the mass extinction of the dinosaurs opened new ecological opportunities for mammals. By 55 mya, primates inhabited North America and Eurasia, which at that time were joined together as the supercontinent Laurasia and separated from Africa. The earliest primates were small nocturnal insect eaters adapted to life in the trees.

When Did the First Monkeys and Apes Appear, and What Were They Like?

By the late Eocene epoch, about 40 mya, diurnal anthropoid primates appeared. Many of the Old World anthropoid species became ground dwellers. By the Miocene epoch (beginning 23.5 mya), apes were widespread in Asia, Africa, and Europe. While some of these hominoids were relatively small, others were larger than present-day gorillas. Sometime between 5 and 8 mya, a branch of the African hominoid line became bipedal, beginning the evolutionary line that later produced humans.

Today, humans are the only primate existing globally. We inhabit every continent, including areas as inhospitable as the icy Antarctic or the scorching Sahara Desert. This extended geographic range reflects the adaptability of *Homo sapiens.* By comparison, our relatives in the hominoid superfamily live in very circumscribed areas of the Old World tropical rainforest. Chimpanzees, bonobos, and gorillas can be found only in portions of Central, East, and West Africa. Orangutans are limited to the trees on the Southeast Asian islands of Sumatra and Borneo. Gibbons and siamangs swing through the branches of a variety of Southeast Asian forests.

Such comparisons between humans and the other primates appear natural to biologists and anthropologists today, because they accept that modern humans, apes, and monkeys are descended from the same prehistoric ancestors. However, a century and a half ago, when Charles Darwin published *On the Origin of Species* (1859), this notion was so controversial that Darwin limited himself to a single sentence on the subject. Today, anthropologists, as well as the global scientific community in general, accept that human origins are revealed in the evolutionary history of the primates. We now know that much of who we are, as culture-bearing biological organisms, derives from our mammalian primate heritage.

Although many of the primates discussed in this chapter no longer exist, their descendants (as we discussed in Chapters 3 and 4) now live in South and Central America, Africa, Asia, and Gibraltar at the southern tip of Spain, and in zoos and laboratories all over the world. The successful adaptation of the primates largely reflects their intelligence, a characteristic that provides for behavioral flexibility. Other physical traits, such as stereoscopic vision and a grasping hand, have also been instrumental in the success of the primates.

Why do paleoanthropologists attempt to recreate primate evolutionary history from ancient evidence? The study of these ancestral primates gives us a better understanding of the physical forces that caused these early creatures to evolve into today's primates. It gives us a fuller knowledge of the processes through which an insect-eating, small-brained mammal evolved into a toolmaker, a thinker, a human being. In addition, the continued survival of our species and of our world now depends on understanding evolutionary processes and the way all organisms interact with their environment.

Macroevolution and the Process of Speciation

While microevolution refers to changes in the allele frequencies of populations, **macroevolution** focuses on the formation of new species (**speciation**) and on the evolutionary relationships among groups of species. To understand how the primates evolved, we must first look at how the evolutionary forces discussed in Chapter 2 can lead to macroevolutionary change. As noted in that chapter, the term *species* is usually defined as a population or group of populations that is capable of interbreeding and producing fertile, viable offspring. In other words, species are reproductively isolated. This definition, however, is not altogether satisfactory, because in nature isolated populations may be in the process of evolving into different species, and it is hard to tell exactly when they become biologically distinct without conducting breeding experiments. Furthermore, this definition can only be tested among living groups. Breeding experiments cannot be conducted with sets of fossilized bones.

Certain factors, known as **isolating mechanisms,** can separate breeding populations and lead to the appearance of new species. Because isolation prevents gene flow, changes that affect the gene pool of one population cannot be introduced into the gene pool of the other. Random mutation may introduce new alleles in one of the isolated populations but not in the other. Genetic drift and natural selection may affect the two populations in different ways. Over time, as the two populations come to differ from each other, speciation occurs in a branching fashion known as **cladogenesis** (Figure 6.1) (from the Greek *klados,* meaning "branch" or "shoot").

Some isolating mechanisms are geographic—preventing contact, hence gene flow, between members of separated populations. Biologic aspects of organisms can also serve as isolating mechanisms. For example, early miscarriage of the hybrid offspring or sterility of the hybrid offspring, as in the case of closely related species such as horses and donkeys (producing sterile mules), serve as mechanisms to keep populations reproductively isolated from one another.

Isolating mechanisms may also be social rather than physical. Speciation due to this mechanism is particularly common among birds. For example, cuckoos (birds that do not build nests of their own but lay their eggs in other birds' nests) attract mates by mimicking the song of the bird species in whose nests they place their eggs.

macroevolution Evolution above the species level.

speciation The process of forming new species.

isolating mechanism A factor that separates breeding populations, thereby preventing gene flow, creating divergent subspecies and ultimately (if maintained) divergent species.

cladogenesis Speciation through a branching mechanism whereby an ancestral population gives rise to two or more descendant populations.

Visual Counterpoint

Regulatory genes turn other genes on and off. A mere change in their timing can cause significant evolutionary change because these genes can alter the course of an individual organism's development. This may have played a role in differentiating chimps and humans; for example, adult humans retain the flat facial profile of juvenile chimps. Within primate species in which sexual dimorphism is high, females tend to retain the juvenile traits more than males.

Thus cuckoos that are physically capable of mating may be isolated due to differences in courtship song behavior, which effectively isolates them from other cuckoos singing different tunes. Though social rules about marriage might be said to impose reproductive isolation among humans,

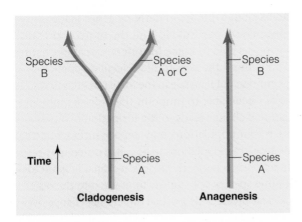

Figure 6.1 Cladogenesis occurs as different populations of an ancestral species become reproductively isolated. Through drift and differential selection, the number of descendant species increases. By contrast, anagenesis can occur through a process of variational change that takes place as small differences in traits that, by chance, are advantageous in a particular environment accumulate in a species' gene pool. Over time, this may produce sufficient change to transform an old species into a new one. Genetic drift may also account for anagenesis.

these social barriers have no biological counterpart. For humans, there are no sufficiently absolute or long-lasting barriers to gene flow.

Because speciation is a process, it can occur at various rates. Speciation through the process of adaptive change to the environment as proposed in Darwin's *Origin of Species* is generally considered to occur at a slow rate. In this model, speciation may occur as organisms become more adapted to their environmental niche. Sometimes, however, speciation can occur quite rapidly. For example, a genetic mutation, such as one involving a key regulatory gene, can lead to the formation of a new body plan. Such genetic accidents may involve material that is broken off, transposed, or transferred from one chromosome to another.

Genes that regulate the growth and development of an organism can have a major effect on its adult form. Developmental change in the timing of events, a phenomenon known as **heterochrony** (from Latin for "different time"), is often responsible for changes in the shape or size of a body part. A kind of heterochrony called *neotony,* in which juvenile traits are retained in the adult state, may be responsible for some of the visible differences between

heterochrony Change in the timing of developmental events that is often responsible for changes in the shape or size of a body part.

Sometimes mutations in a single gene can cause reorganization of an organism's body plan. Here the "bithorax" homeobox gene has caused this fruit fly to have two thoraxes and two sets of wings. Another homeobox gene, "antennepedia," caused legs to develop in the place of antennae on the heads of fruit flies.

humans and chimps. Scientists have discovered certain key genes called **homeobox genes** that are responsible for large-scale effects on the growth and development of the organism. If a new body plan happens to be adaptive, natural selection will maintain this new form for long periods of time rather than promoting change.

Paleontologists Stephen Jay Gould and Niles Eldred proposed that speciation occurs in a pattern of **punctuated equilibria**—the alternation between periods of rapid speciation and times of stability. Often this conception of evolutionary change is contrasted with speciation through adaptation, sometimes known as *Darwinian gradualism*. A close look at genetic mechanisms and the fossil record indicates that both models of evolutionary change are important.

homeobox gene A gene responsible for large-scale effects on growth and development that are frequently responsible for major reorganization of body plans in organisms.

punctuated equilibria A model of macroevolutionary change that suggests evolution occurs via long periods of stability or stasis punctuated by periods of rapid change.

anagenesis A sustained directional shift in a population's average characteristics.

All working evolutionary scientists—including Gould, the champion of the punctuated equilibrium model—recognize the importance of both rapid change and gradual Darwinian processes. Gould describes Darwinian evolution as *variational* change that occurs

> by the twofold process of producing copious and undirected variation within a population and then passing along only a biased (selected) portion of this variation to the next generation. In this manner, the variation within a population at any moment can be converted into differences in mean values (average size, average braininess) among successive populations through time.[1]

He states that this kind of change is unsettling because it is not predictable and does not proceed according to simple natural laws such as gravity. Instead,

> the sensible and explainable but quite unpredictable nature of the outcome (dependent upon complex and contingent changes in local environments), the nonprogressive character of the alteration (adaptive only to these unpredictable local circumstances and not inevitably building a "better" organism in any cosmic or general sense)—flow from the variational basis of natural selection.[2]

Genetic mechanisms underlie both rapid and gradual changes because mutations can have small or large effects. It is particularly interesting to see how molecular genetics supports Darwinian evolutionary change. For example, the tailoring of beak size and shape to diet among finches on the Galapagos Islands, in the Pacific Ocean west of Ecuador, constituted Darwin's classic example of natural selection (Figure 6.2). Recently scientists identified two proteins along with the underlying genes that control beak shape and size in birds. It is all the more impressive that Darwin was able to make his inferences about natural selection without the benefit of molecular genetics.

A fundamental puzzle in the fossil record is that scientists have not been able to pinpoint the precise moment when variational change leads to the formation of a new species. More recent populations may appear sufficiently changed from ancestral populations to be called different species. The difficulty arises because, given a reasonably good fossil record, one species will appear to grade into the other without a clear break. This gradual directional change over time, called **anagenesis,** can occur within a single line, without any evident branching (see Figure 6.1). Speciation is inferred as organisms take on a different appearance over time.

[1] Gould, S. J. (2000). What does the dreaded "E" word mean anyway? *Natural History 109* (1), 34–36.

[2] Ibid.

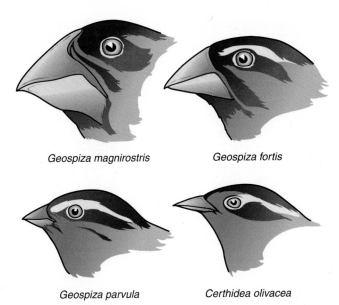

Geospiza magnirostris   *Geospiza fortis*

Geospiza parvula   *Certhidea olivacea*

Figure 6.2 Scientists have begun to unravel the genetic mechanisms controlling beak shape and size of finches studied by Darwin on the Galapagos Islands. Darwin noted how beak size and shape were related to each species' diet and used the birds to illustrate adaptation to a particular ecological niche. Finches with blunt crushing beaks are seed eaters while others with long probing beaks pick between cactus thorns for food or use the beaks to get insects.

It may be difficult to determine whether variation preserved in the fossil record presents evidence of separate species. How can we tell whether two sets of fossilized bones represent organisms capable of interbreeding and producing viable fertile offspring? Paleoanthropologists use as many data sources as possible, checking the proposed evolutionary relationships in order to approximate an answer to this question. Today, paleoanthropologists use genetic data as well as observations about the biology and behavior of living groups to support theories about speciation in the past. Thus reconstructing evolutionary relationships draws on much more than bones alone. Fossil finds are always interpreted against the backdrop of scientific discoveries as well as prevailing beliefs and biases. Fortunately, the self-correcting nature of scientific investigation allows evolutionary lines to be redrawn in light of all new discoveries and more compelling explanations.

Constructing Evolutionary Relationships

In addition to designating species in the fossil record, paleoanthropologists and paleontologists construct evolutionary relationships among fossil groups. Scientists pay particular attention to features appearing more recently in evolutionary history that are unique to a line, calling these features **derived.** The counterparts to derived traits are **ancestral** characteristics, which occur not only in the present-day species but in ancestral forms as well. For example,

bilateral symmetry, a body plan in which the right and left sides of the body are mirror images of each other, is an ancestral trait in humans. Because it is a characteristic of all vertebrates including fish, reptiles, birds, and mammals, bilateral symmetry does not contribute to the reconstruction of evolutionary relationships among fossil primates. Instead, paleoanthropologists pay particular attention to recently evolved derived features in order to construct evolutionary relationships among fossil groups. For example, because changes in bones associated with bipedalism are present only in the human line, these derived features can be used to separate humans and their ancestors from other hominoids.

Sorting out evolutionary relationships among fossil species may be complicated by a phenomenon called **convergent evolution,** in which two more distant forms develop greater similarities. The classic examples of convergence involve analogies discussed in Chapter 2, such as the wings of birds and butterflies, which resemble each other because these structures serve similar functions. Convergent evolution occurs when an environment exerts similar pressures on distantly related organisms causing these species to resemble each other. Distinguishing the physical similarities produced by convergent evolution from those resulting from shared ancestry may be difficult, complicating the reconstruction of the evolutionary history of any given species.

Among more closely related groups, convergence of homologous structures can occur, as when an identical structure present within several distinct species takes on a similar form in distantly related groups. Among the primates, an example is hind-leg dominance in both lemurs and humans. In most primates, the hind limbs are either shorter or of the same length as the forelimbs. Lemurs and humans are not as closely related to each other as are humans and chimps, for example, but both have longer hind limbs related to their patterns of locomotion. Humans are bipedal while lemurs use their long legs to push off and propel them from tree to tree. Hind-leg dominance appeared separately in these two groups and is not indicative of a close evolutionary relationship. Only shared derived features can be used to establish relationships among groups of species.

The Nondirectedness of Macroevolution

In the nonscientific community, evolution is often seen as leading in a predictable and determined way from one-celled organisms, through various multicelled forms, to

derived Characteristics that define a group of organisms and that did not exist in ancestral populations.

ancestral Characteristics that define a group of organisms that are due to shared ancestry.

convergent evolution In biological evolution, a process by which unrelated populations develop similarities to one another due to similar function rather than shared ancestry.

Visual Counterpoint

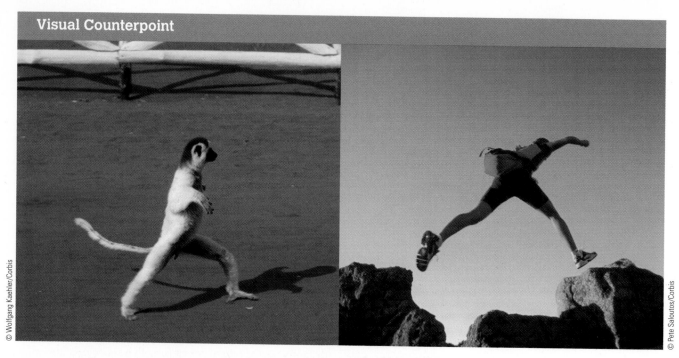

© Wolfgang Kaehler/Corbis

© Pete Saloutos/Corbis

The characteristic long legs of prosimians and humans are not the result of a close evolutionary relationship. This is instead the result of convergence of homologous structures. The long legs of prosimians allow them to follow their characteristic pattern of locomotion, called vertical clinging and leaping. On rare occasions for the briefest periods of time, they are also capable of taking a bipedal step or two.

humans, who occupy the top rung of a ladder of progress. However, even though one-celled organisms appeared long before multicellular forms, single-celled organisms were not replaced by multicellular descendants. Single-celled organisms exist in greater numbers and diversity than all forms of multicellular life and live in a greater variety of habitats.[3]

As for humans, we are indeed recent arrivals in the world (though not as recent as some new strains of bacteria). Our appearance—like that of any kind of organism—was made possible only as a consequence of a whole string of accidental happenings in the past. To cite but one example, about 65 million years ago the earth's climate changed drastically. Evidence suggests that a meteor or some other sort of extraterrestrial body slammed into earth where the Yucatan Peninsula of Mexico now exists, cooling global temperatures to such an extent as to cause the extinction of the dinosaurs (and numerous other species as well). For 100 million years, dinosaurs had dominated most terrestrial environments available for vertebrate animals and would probably have continued to do so were it not for this event. Although mammals appeared at about the same time as reptiles, they existed as small, inconspicuous creatures that an observer who came to earth from outer space would probably have dismissed as insignificant.

But with the demise of the dinosaurs, all sorts of opportunities became available, allowing mammals to begin their great expansion into a variety of species including our own ancestors, the earliest primates. Therefore, an essentially random event—the collision with a comet or asteroid—made our own existence possible. Had it not happened, or had it happened at some other time (before the existence of mammals), we would not be here.[4]

The history of any species is an outcome of many such occurrences. At any point in the chain of events, had any one element been different, the final result would be markedly different. As Gould puts it, "All evolutionary sequences include . . . a fortuitous series of accidents with respect to future evolutionary success. Human brains and bodies did not evolve along a direct and inevitable ladder, but by a circuitous and tortuous route carved by adaptations evolved for different reasons, and fortunately suited to later needs."[5]

Given that humans arrived here by chance relatively late in the history of life on earth, the drastic changes humans have imposed on the environment and on the other species with which we share this earth are particularly shocking. As described in this chapter's Original Study by Australian zoologist Sir Robert May, it is now time for humans to create solutions.

[3] Gould, S. J. (1996). *Full house: The spread of excellence from Plato to Darwin* (pp. 176–195). New York: Harmony.

[4] Gould, S. J. (1985). *The flamingo's smile: Reflections in natural history* (p. 409). New York: Norton.

[5] Ibid., p. 410.

Original Study

Melding Heart and Head   *by Sir Robert May*

Today we are living at a very special time in the history of the Earth. It is a time which might come in the history of any inhabited planet, when the activities of one particular species—in this case, ourselves—come to rival the scale and scope of the natural processes which built, and which maintain, the planet's biosphere.

It is easy to be skeptical of such dramatic claims, which are often voiced around millennia or other years with many zeros in them. But there are objective facts which demonstrate just how special our own time is. For one thing, humans today take for their own use somewhere between a quarter and a half of all plant material that grows on earth each year. For another—from the tropical rainforests, across the grain fields of America, Europe and Asia, to the Arctic tundra—fully half of all the atoms of nitrogen and of phosphorous annually fixed in new plants come from human intervention in the form of fertilizers rather than natural cycles. Turning to the sea, we take 10 percent of all its production each year, and larger amounts (around 30 percent) in rich areas of nutrient upwelling.

But all this represents bad news for the diverse populations of invertebrates, birds, and other creatures that share the countryside with us. *The State of the UK's Birds 1999*, recently published by the Royal Society for the Protection of Birds (RSPB) and the British Trust for Ornithology (BTO), for example, documents declines in populations of 41 species of woodland birds (on average down 20 percent from the mid-1970s) and of 20 species of farmland birds (down 40 percent over the same period).

More broadly, the outcome of intensification of agriculture, around the world, is an ever more Silent Spring. Documented extinctions of bird and mammal species over the past century or so are at a rate roughly 1,000 times faster than the rates seen, on average, over the half-billion-year sweep of the fossil record. The various causes are habitat destruction, unsustainably excessive harvesting and other exploitation, adverse impacts by introduced alien species, and—more often—combinations of all three.

Projections of future extinction rates are more difficult to make. Four different lines of argument, ranging from one which applies generally to all plants and animals, through to others which generalize from particular families of birds, reptiles, and mammals, all suggest a roughly tenfold increase in extinction rates over the coming few centuries. These are sober, analytic estimates, free of the rhetorical exaggerations which sometimes afflict the subject. These estimates make it clear that we are currently on the breaking tip of a sixth great wave of extinction in the history of life on Earth, fully comparable with the Big Five in the fossil record, such as the one that extinguished the dinosaurs.

Diminishing Gains

Toward the end of this century, estimates which I rate as rather optimistic suggest that—barring catastrophes—our descendants will live in a world of 10 billion people. How will they be fed? The Green Revolution, underpinned as it is by massive and unsustainable inputs of fossil fuel energy, already shows signs of diminishing gains. Just as we could not feed today's global population with yesterday's agriculture, I do not believe we can feed tomorrow's population with today's.

But if we seek only further intensification of agriculture—a further ratcheting up in the spirit of the Green Revolution—then we may feed tomorrow's world, but it will be biologically impoverished, and I doubt its sustainability. If, on the other hand, we use our increasing understanding of the molecular machinery of life, along with other cultural changes, to produce an agriculture that works with the grain of nature—rather than using fossil fuel subsidies to wrench nature to our crops—then I hope we can achieve Conway's Doubly Green Revolution.

Harnessing Impulse

Part of the motive for all this must be a more sustainable way of doing things. But a related part of the motive must come from our natural impulses of concern, and even affection, for the other creatures we share the world with. Too often, however, such concern expresses itself through a disproportionate focus on large mammals and colourful birds: "charismatic megafauna." Although understandable and effective in engaging a wider public, particularly in the developed world, these targets are not necessarily those that would be chosen in an analytic quest to preserve the maximum amount of the planet's evolutionary history, as written in the genetic richness and variability within today's living species. Although our emotions may relate most easily to the big mammals and the interesting birds, the smaller invertebrates and the diverse plant kingdom are more important for the functioning of many ecosystems, and they also carry more of the record of how life evolved on our planet. The justification that by saving charismatic megafauna we necessarily save large areas of habitat, and thence a host of less emotionally resonant invertebrates and plants, does not always survive close examination: such studies as do exist suggest that "hot spots" for birds are often weakly correlated with "hot spots" for particular plant and insect groups.

To summarize, I believe the challenge of the century is to emphasize valid emotional and ethical arguments for conserving biological diversity, but also to combine them with analytic approaches that ask questions—often cold and difficult ones—about which actions will, in the long run, be most effective in sustaining as much as possible of the biological riches and the unaccounted ecosystem services we have inherited. This melding of heart and head will, I think, pose tough challenges and choices. It is not an easy recipe for a new beginning to a new millennium.

Adapted from May, R. (2000). Melding heart and head. Beyond 2000. *New York: United Nations Environment Programme. http://www.unep.org/ourplanet/ imgversn/111/may.html*

Continental Drift and Geologic Time

As described in Chapter 5, context and dating are vital for the interpretation of fossils. Because primate evolution extends so far back in time, paleoanthropologists reconstruct this evolution in conjunction with information about the geologic history of the earth.

The geologic time scale is unfamiliar because few people deal with hundreds of millions of anything, let alone years, on a regular basis. To understand this type of scale, astronomer Carl Sagan correlated the geologic time scale for the history of the earth to a single calendar year. In this "cosmic calendar," the earth itself originates on January 1, the first organisms appear approximately 9 months later around September 25, followed by the earliest vertebrates around December 20, mammals on December 25, primates on December 29, hominoids at 10:15 AM on New Year's Eve, bipeds at 9:30 PM, with our species appearing in the last minutes before midnight. In this chapter, we will consider human evolutionary history beginning with the December 25 appearance of the mammals in the Mesozoic era, roughly 245 million years ago.

Over such vast amounts of time, the earth itself has changed considerably. During the past 200 million years, the position of the continents has shifted through a process called **continental drift,** which accounts for the rearrangement of adjacent landmasses through the theory of plate tectonics. According to this theory, the continents, embedded in platelike segments of the earth, move their positions as the edges of the underlying plates are created or destroyed (Figure 6.3). Plate movements are also responsible for geologic phenomena such as earthquakes, volcanic activity, and mountain formation. Continental drift is important for understanding the distribution of fossil primate groups whose history we will now explore.

Early Mammals

By 190 million years ago—the end of what geologists call the Triassic period—true mammals were on the scene. Mammals from the Triassic, Jurassic (135–190 mya), and Cretaceous (65–135 mya) periods are largely known from hundreds of fossils, especially teeth and jaw parts. Because

continental drift According to the theory of plate tectonics, the movement of continents embedded in underlying plates on the earth's surface in relation to one another over the history of life on earth.

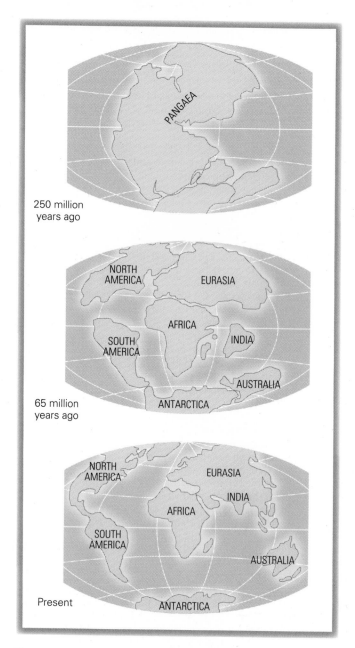

Figure 6.3 Continental drift is illustrated by the position of the continents during several geologic periods. At the time of the extinction of the dinosaurs 65 million years ago, the seas opened up by continental drift, creating isolating barriers between major landmasses. About 23 million years ago, at the start of the time period known as the Miocene epoch, African and Eurasian landmasses reconnected.

teeth are the hardest, most durable structures, they often outlast other parts of an animal's skeleton. Fortunately, investigators often are able to infer a good deal about the total animal on the basis of only a few teeth found lying in the earth.

For example, as described in Chapter 3, unlike the relatively homogeneous teeth of reptiles, mammals possess distinct tooth types, the structure of which varies by species. Knowledge of the way the teeth fit together indicates the arrangement of muscles needed to operate the jaws. Reconstruction of the jaw muscles, in turn, indicates how the skull must have been shaped to provide a place for these muscles to attach. The shape of the jaws and details of the teeth also suggest the type of food that these animals consumed. Thus a mere jawbone fragment with a few teeth contains a great deal of information about the animal from which it came.

An interesting observation about the evolution of the mammals is that the diverse forms with which we are familiar today, including the primates, are the products of an **adaptive radiation:** the rapid increase in number of related species following a change in their environment. This did not begin until after mammals had been present on the earth for over 100 million years. With the mass extinction of many reptiles at the end of the Cretaceous, however, a number of existing *ecological niches,* or functional positions in their habitats, became available to mammals. A species' niche incorporates factors such as diet, activity, terrain, vegetation, predators, prey, and climate.

The story of mammalian evolution starts as early as 230 to 280 mya (Figure 6.4). From deposits of this period, which geologists call the Permian, we have the remains of reptiles with features pointing in a distinctly mammalian direction. These mammal-like reptiles were slimmer than most other reptiles and were flesh eaters. Graded fossils demonstrate trends toward a mammalian pattern such as a reduction in the number of bones, the shifting of limbs underneath the body, the development of a separation between the mouth and nasal cavity, differentiation of the teeth, and so forth.

Eventually these creatures became extinct, but not before some of them developed into true mammals by the Triassic period. During the Jurassic period that followed, dinosaurs and other large reptiles dominated the earth, and mammals remained tiny, inconspicuous creatures occupying a nocturnal niche.

By chance, mammals were **preadapted**—possessing the biological equipment to take advantage of the new opportunities available to them through the mass extinction of the dinosaurs and other reptiles 65 million years ago. As **homeotherms,** mammals possess the ability to maintain a constant body temperature, a trait that appears to have promoted the adaptive radiation of the mammals. Mammals can be active at a wide range of environmental temperatures, whereas reptiles, as **isotherms** that take their body temperature from the surrounding environment, become progressively sluggish as the surrounding temperature drops. Cold global temperatures 65 mya appear to be responsible for the mass extinction of dinosaurs and some other reptiles, while mammals, as homeotherms, were preadapted for this climate change.

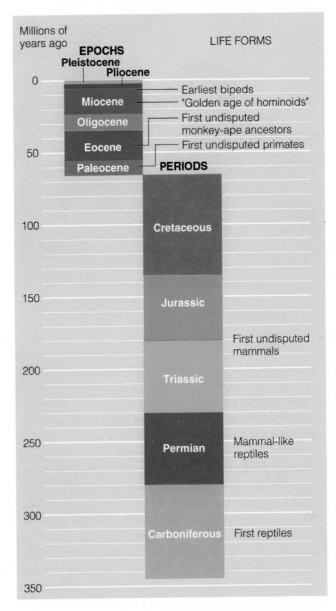

Figure 6.4 This timeline highlights some major milestones in the course of mammalian primate evolution that ultimately led to humans and their ancestors. The Paleocene, Eocene, Oligocene, and Miocene epochs are subsets of the Tertiary period. The Quaternary period begins with the Pleistocene and continues today.

adaptive radiation Rapid diversification of an evolving population as it adapts to a variety of available niches.

preadapted Possessing characteristics that, by chance, are advantageous in future environmental conditions.

homeotherm An animal that maintains a relatively constant body temperature despite environmental fluctuations.

isotherm An animal whose body temperature rises or falls according to the temperature of the surrounding environment.

Though popular media depict the coexistence of humans and dinosaurs, in reality the extinction of the dinosaurs occurred 65 mya, while the first bipeds ancestral to humans appeared between 5 and 8 mya.

The appearance of the true seed plants (the angiosperms) provided not only highly nutritious fruit seeds and flowers but also a host of habitats for numerous edible insects and worms—just the sorts of food required by mammals with their higher metabolism. For species like mammals to continue to survive, a wide diversity of plants, insects, and even single-celled organisms needs to be maintained. In ecosystems these organisms are dependent upon one another.

However, the mammalian trait of maintaining constant body temperature requires a diet high in calories. Based on evidence from their teeth, scientists know that early mammals ate foods such as insects, worms, and eggs. As animals with nocturnal habits, mammals have well-developed senses of smell and hearing relative to reptiles. Although things cannot be seen as well in the dark as they can in the light, they can still be heard and smelled.

The mammalian pattern also differs from reptiles in terms of how they care for their young. Compared to reptiles, mammalian species are **k-selected.** This means that they produce relatively few offspring at a time, providing them with considerable parental care. A universal feature of how mammals care for their young is the production of food (milk) via the mammary glands. Reptiles are relatively **r-selected,** which means that they produce many young at a time and invest little effort caring for their young after they are born. Though among mammals some species are relatively more k- or r-selected, the high energy requirements of mammals, entailed by parental investment and the maintenance of a constant body temperature, demand more nutrition than required by reptiles. During their adaptive radiation, the fruits, nuts, and seeds of flowering plants that became more common in the late Cretaceous period provided mammals with high-quality nutrition.

k-selected Reproduction involving the production of relatively few offspring with high parental investment in each.

r-selected Reproduction involving the production of large numbers of offspring with relatively low parental investment in each.

arboreal hypothesis A theory for primate evolution that proposes that life in the trees was responsible for enhanced visual acuity and manual dexterity in primates.

The Rise of the Primates

Early primates began to emerge during this time of great global change at the start of the Paleocene epoch. The distribution of fossil primates on earth makes sense only when one understands that the positions of the continents today differ tremendously from what was found in the past (see Figure 6.3). As noted earlier, during this period North America and Eurasia were connected in the supercontinent called Laurasia. South America, Africa, Antarctica, Australia, and the Indian subcontinent—previously joined together as the supercontinent Gondwanaland—were beginning to separate from one another through continental drift. Africa was separated from Eurasia by a narrow body of water.

On land, dinosaurs had become extinct, and mammals were undergoing the great adaptive radiation that ultimately led to the development of the diverse forms with which we are familiar today. At the same time, the newly evolved grasses, shrubs, and other flowering plants proliferated enormously. This diversification, along with a milder climate, favored the spread of dense, lush tropical and subtropical forests over the earth, including North and South America and much of Eurasia and Africa. With the spread of these huge belts of forest, the stage was set for the movement of some mammals into the trees. Forests would provide our early ancestors with the ecological niches in which they would flourish. Fossil evidence of primatelike mammals from the Paleocene forests has been found in North America and Eurasia. See Figure 6.5 for a full timeline of primate evolution.

One theory for primate evolution, the **arboreal hypothesis,** proposes that life in the trees was responsible for enhanced visual acuity and manual dexterity in primates. Misjudgments and errors of coordination, leading to

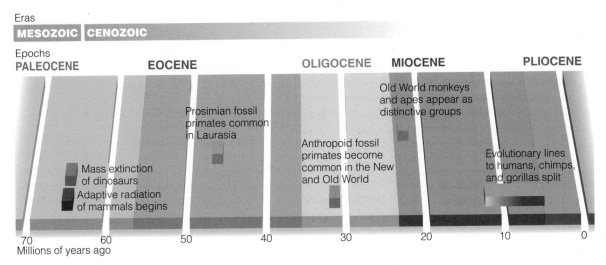

Figure 6.5 **This timeline depicts some of the major events of primate evolution.**

falls that injured or killed the individuals poorly adapted to arboreal life, may have been a part of initial forays into the trees. Natural selection would favor those that judged depth correctly and gripped the branches strongly. Early primates that took to the trees were probably in some measure pre-adapted by virtue of behavioral flexibility, better vision, and more dexterous fingers than their contemporaries.

Primatologist Matt Cartmill further suggests that primate visual and grasping abilities were also promoted through the activity of hunting for insects by sight. His **visual predation hypothesis** accounts for the observation that other tree-dwelling species and hunting species do not necessarily possess the same combination of visual and manual abilities possessed by the primates. The relatively small size of the early primates allowed them to make use of the smaller branches of trees; larger, heavier competitors, and most predators, could not follow. The move to the smaller branches also gave them access to an abundant food supply; the primates were able to gather insects, leaves, flowers, and fruits directly rather than waiting for them to fall to the ground.

The strong selection in a new environment led to an acceleration in the rate of change of primate characteristics. Paradoxically, these changes eventually made possible a return to the ground by some primates, including the ancestors of the genus *Homo*.

True Primates

The first well-preserved "true" primates appeared by about 55 mya at the start of the Eocene epoch. During this time period, an abrupt warming trend began on earth, causing many older forms of mammals to become extinct, to be replaced by recognizable forerunners of some of today's forms. Among the latter was an adaptive radiation of prosimian primates, of which over fifty fossil genera are known. Fossils of these creatures have been found in Africa, North America, Europe, and Asia, where the warm,

wet conditions of the Eocene sustained extensive rainforests. Relative to ancestral primatelike mammals, these early primate families had enlarged braincases, slightly reduced snouts, and a somewhat forward position of the eye orbits, which, though not completely walled in, are surrounded by a complete bony ring called a *postorbital bar* (Figure 6.6).

During the Eocene, the first signs of anthropoid primates also begin to appear in the fossil record. Until

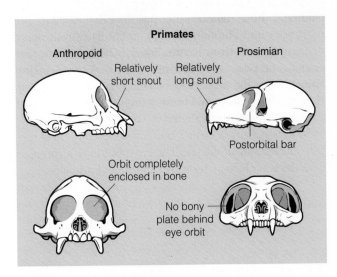

Figure 6.6 **Ancestral features seen in Eocene and Oligocene primates are still seen in prosimians today. Like modern lemurs, these fossil prosimians have a postorbital bar, a bony ring around the eye socket that is open in the back. Anthropoid primates have orbits completely enclosed in bone. Note also the difference in the relative size of the snout in these two groups. Paleoanthropologists make these kinds of comparisons as they reconstruct our evolutionary history.**

visual predation hypothesis A theory for primate evolution that proposes that hunting behavior in tree-dwelling primates was responsible for their enhanced visual acuity and manual dexterity.

recently, the earliest evidence consisted of the tiny species *Eosimias* (pronounced "ee-o-sim-ee-us"; Latin for "dawn of the monkeys"), represented by fossils from China, dated to about 45 mya. The Chinese fossils represent several species of tiny, insect-eating animals and are the smallest primates ever documented.[6] Some scientists have challenged whether these tiny fossils are truly anthropoids as they are reconstructed largely from foot bones rather than skulls or teeth. As described in the chapter opener, in 2009, controversy and media attention swirled around the spectacularly well-preserved 47-million-year-old potential anthropoid nicknamed "Ida."[7,8,9,10] Initially discovered thirty years ago through a mining and drilling operation at an old quarry near the southern German hamlet of Messel, Ida's remains were separated and sold to different collections. In Ida's time, the Messel region was a tropical forest with a lake and volcano. Fossils from this region are embedded into flaky layers of rock that split open into "plates." Now that the two plates that constitute Ida have been reunited, scientists can debate whether Ida is indeed the earliest anthropoid or not. This distinction, which would place her on the line leading to humans, captures our imaginations as described in this chapter's Biocultural Connection by anthropologist-primatologist Meredith Small.

More recent than Ida and well into the Oligocene epoch, rich deposits of primate fossils have been found in Fayum, Egypt. These fossils include a diverse range of species including some of the earliest to possess a dental comb. But more relevant to human ancestry are the early anthropoid primate species from Fayum, identified through dental, cranial, and postcranial (the rest of the skeleton) remains. Some possess the ancestral dental formula (2-1-3-3) seen in New World monkeys and prosimians, while others have the derived dental formula shared by Old World monkeys and apes: two incisors, a canine, two premolars, and three molars on each side of the jaw. The eye orbits have a complete wall, the latter being a feature of anthropoid primates.[11]

Although there is still much to be learned about the Eocene primates, it is clear that they were abundant, diverse, and widespread. Among them were ancestors of today's prosimians and anthropoids.[12] With the end of the Eocene, substantial changes took place among the primates, as among other mammals. In North America, now well isolated from Eurasia, primates became extinct, and elsewhere their range seems to have been reduced considerably.

Climate change affected primate and mammalian evolution. Through the late Eocene, climates were becoming somewhat cooler and drier, but then temperatures took a sudden dive, triggering the formation of an ice cap over previously forested Antarctica. The result was a marked reduction in the range of suitable environments for primates. At the same time, cold climate led to lower sea levels through the formation of ice caps, perhaps changing opportunities for migration of primates.

Oligocene Anthropoids

During the Oligocene epoch, from about 23 to 34 mya, the anthropoid primates diversified and expanded their range. Fossil evidence from Egypt's Fayum region has yielded sufficient fossils (more than 1,000) to reveal that by 33 mya, Old World anthropoid primates existed in considerable diversity. Moreover, the cast of characters is growing, as new fossils continue to be found in the Fayum, as well as in newly discovered localities in Algeria (North Africa) and Oman (Arabian Peninsula). At present, we have evidence of at least sixty genera included in two families. During the Oligocene, prosimian fossil forms became far less prominent than anthropoids. Only on the large island of Madagascar (off the coast of East Africa), which was devoid of anthropoids until humans arrived, is prosimian diversity still evident. In their isolation, they underwent a further adaptive radiation.

Fossil evidence indicates that these Old World anthropoids were quadrupeds who were diurnal, as evidenced by their smaller orbits (eyes). Many of these Oligocene species possess a mixture of monkey and ape features. Of particular interest is the genus *Aegyptopithecus* (pronounced "Egypt-o-pith-ee-kus"; Greek for "Egyptian ape"), an Oligocene anthropoid that has sometimes been called a monkey with an ape's teeth. *Aegyptopithecus* possessed a mosaic of monkey and ape features as well as features shared by both groups. Its lower molars have the five cusps of an ape, and the upper canine and lower first premolar exhibit the sort of shearing surfaces found in monkeys and apes. Its skull has eye sockets that are in a forward position and completely protected by a bony wall, as is typical of modern monkeys and apes. The endocast of its skull indicates that it had a larger visual cortex than that found in prosimians. Relative to its body

[6] Gebo, D. L., et al. (2001). Middle Eocene primate tarsals from China: Implications for haplorhine evolution. *American Journal of Physical Anthropology 116*, 83–107.

[7] Franzen, J. L., et al. (2009). Complete primate skeleton from the middle Eocene of Messel in Germany: Morphology and paleobiology. *PLoS ONE 4* (5), e5723.

[8] Dalton, R. (2009). Fossil primate challenges Ida's place: Controversial German specimen is related to lemurs, not humans, analysis of an Egyptian find suggests. Published online 21 October 2009, *Nature 461*, 1040, doi:10.1038/4611040a; Editorial. Media frenzy. *Nature 459*, 484, doi:10.1038/459484a; Published online 27 May 2009.

[9] Simons, E. L., et al. (2009). Outrage at high price paid for a fossil. *Correspondence Nature 460*, 456, doi:10.1038/460456a; Published online 22 July 2009.

[10] Seiffert, E. R., et al. (2009). Convergent evolution of anthropoid-like adaptations in Eocene adapiform primates. *Nature 461*, 1118–1121, doi:10.1038/nature08429; Received 11 July 2009; Accepted 18 August 2009.

[11] Simons, E. L. (1995). Skulls and anterior teeth of *Catopithecus* (Primates: Anthropoidea) from the Eocene and anthropoid origins. *Science 268*, 1885–1888.

[12] Kay, R. F., Ross, C., & Williams, B. A. (1997). Anthropoid origins. *Science 275*, 803–804.

Why "Ida" Inspires Navel-Gazing at Our Ancestry   *by Meredith F. Small*

One long line of evidence that supports evolution is the ongoing discovery of "transitional" fossils that bridge the gap between one obvious kind of species and another. Nowhere are these transitional animals more interesting than when looking backwards through time at the human lineage.

This week, scientists from the University of Oslo announced the discovery (or re-discovery since the fossil was dug up in 1983) of a 47-million-year-old female primate known as Ida. This almost complete female animal appears to represent the transition between what are often called "primitive" primates, such as lemurs and lorises (known as prosimians), and the more "lofty" monkey, apes, and humans. And even more interesting, this transition was in place long before anyone realized.

We love this stuff because humans are a self-interested species, and some of that navel-gazing has been directed toward our ancient past. Luckily for us, we have living examples of our history still with us today.

Usually, the cycle of life involves repeated speciation, extinction, and survival of modified forms, so that what we see today is not anything like what came before. But as the human lineage went through a prosimian phase, then a monkey phase, then an ape phase over time, those branches didn't completely die off. Instead, representatives of every historical stage can still be found in forests, savannahs, and zoos around the world.

The ancient forms, of course, have been modified by natural selection during the millions of years they have survived, and their reign is not what it used to be. Prosimian primates were once found all across North America and Europe, and now they have retreated to specialized niches in Africa (especially Madagascar) and Asia. Monkeys ruled the Earth 34 million years ago during the Oligocene, but now they mostly rule forests that cling to the equator. And during the Miocene, about 23 million years ago, apes were all over the place until they fell from grace leaving only four endangered species.

That kind of ancestral mirroring is not so common. If, for example, we were modern horses, we wouldn't be able to find decent representatives of the various stages of horse evolution galloping

Courtesy of PLoS

Plate A   10 cm   Plate B

Due to the fragility of Ida's remains, scientists have been using CT scan technology to study her. The radiographic image in Plate B reveals that parts of this image have been forged (compare it to the chapter opener photo). Only the true remains show up as white because the mineralized bones and teeth in fossils, as in living creatures, are opaque in an x-ray.

across a field. We'd have to deduce everything about our horsy past from the fossils that happened to be preserved and unearthed.

But we humans have these living primate templates and so we know something about how the long line of our ancestors not only looked in the flesh, we also have an idea of how they behaved, ate, socialized, and mated.

And that's also why Ida is such a special find. She seems to be covering the entire history of primate anatomical evolution all on her own. She was the size and build of modern lemurs but lacked the "tooth comb" that prosimians use to clear their fur, which makes her more like a monkey. Ida also had the flat face of monkey, and, oddly, she had the heel bone of a human.

Ida seems to be cobbled together by evolution and looks like she could take off in any and all species directions.

The mishmash of Ida's features is a reminder that although we have living examples of our past, the story might be more complicated than we think. Sometimes it takes an animal that was buried long ago, had the unusual experience of becoming a fossil, was unearthed in Germany in 1983, sold off in parts, put back together, and then presented as the biological Rosetta stone for the Primate Order to make us take another look, and revaluate, our past.

BIOCULTURAL QUESTION

What cultural factors make the biology of the Ida specimen capture our collective imaginations?

Adapted from Small, M. F. (2009, May 15). Why "Ida" inspires navel-gazing at our ancestry. Live Science. http://www.livescience.com/history/090520-hn-ida.html

size, the brain of *Aegyptopithecus* was smaller than that of more recent anthropoids. Still, this primate seems to have had a larger brain than any prosimian, past or present. Possessed of a monkeylike skull and body, and fingers and toes capable of powerful grasping, it evidently moved about in a quadrupedal, monkeylike manner.[13]

The teeth of *Aegyptopithecus* suggest that this species may be closely related to an ancestor of humans and modern apes. Although no bigger than a modern house cat, *Aegyptopithecus* was nonetheless one of the larger Oligocene primates. Differences between males and females include larger body size, more formidable canine teeth, and deeper mandibles (lower jaws) in the males. In modern anthropoids, such sexual dimorphism correlates with social systems in which competition among males is high.

New World Monkeys

The earliest evidence of primates in Central and South America dates from this time. These fossil primates are certainly anthropoid monkeys, with the eyes fully encased in bone and limb bones for quadrupedal locomotion. Scientists hypothesize that these primates came to South America from Africa, because the earliest fossil evidence of anthropoids is from the Old World.

Some of the African anthropoids arrived in South America, which at the time was not attached to any other landmass, probably by means of floating masses of vegetation of the sort that originate even today in the great rivers of West and Central Africa. In the Oligocene, the distance between the two continents was far less than it is today; favorable winds and currents could easily have carried "floating islands" of vegetation to South America within a period of time that New World monkey ancestors could have survived.[14] Nearly all living and fossil New World primates possess the ancestral dental formula (2-1-3-3) of prosimians compared to the derived pattern (2-1-2-3) found in Old World anthropoids.

Miocene Apes

True apes first appeared in the fossil record during the Miocene epoch, 5 to 23 mya. It was also during this time period that the African and Eurasian landmasses made direct contact. For most of the preceding 100 million years, the Tethys Sea—a continuous body of water that joined what are now the Mediterranean and Black Seas to the Indian Ocean—created a barrier to migration between Africa and Eurasia. Once joined through the region of what is now the Middle East and Gibraltar, Old World primates, such as the apes, could extend their range from Africa into Eurasia. Miocene ape fossil remains have been found everywhere from the caves of China, to the forests of France, to East Africa, where scientists have recovered the oldest fossil remains of bipeds.

So varied and ubiquitous were the fossil apes of this period that the Miocene has even been labeled by some as the "golden age of the hominoids." The word *hominoid* comes from the Latin roots *homo* and *homin* (meaning "human being") and the suffix *oïdes* ("resembling"). As a group, the hominoids get their name from their resemblance to humans.

In addition to the Old World anthropoid dental formula of 2-1-2-3 and Y5 molars, hominoids can be characterized by the derived characteristics of Y5 molars, having no tail, and having broad flexible shoulder joints. As described in Chapters 3 and 4, the likeness between humans and the other apes bespeaks an important evolutionary relationship that makes other living hominoids vulnerable to human needs in today's world. In the distant past, one of the Miocene apes is the direct ancestor of the human line. Exactly which one is a question still to be resolved.

An examination of the history of the contenders for direct human ancestor among the Miocene apes demonstrates how reconstruction of evolutionary relationships draws on much more than simply bones. Scientists interpret fossil finds by drawing on existing beliefs and knowledge. With new discoveries, interpretations change.

The first Miocene ape fossil remains were found in Africa in the 1930s and 1940s by the British archaeologist A. T. Hopwood and the renowned Kenyan paleoanthropologist Louis Leakey. These fossils turned up on one of the many islands in Lake Victoria, the 27,000-square-mile lake where Kenya, Tanzania, and Uganda meet. Impressed with the chimplike appearance of these fossil remains, Hopwood suggested that the new species be named *Proconsul*, combining the Latin root for "before" (*pro*) with the stage name of a chimpanzee who was performing in London at the time.

Dated to the early Miocene 17 to 21 million years ago, *Proconsul* has some of the classic hominoid features, lacking a tail and having the characteristic pattern of Y5 grooves in the lower molar teeth. However, the adaptations of the upper body seen in later apes (including humans) were absent. These included a skeletal structure adapted for hanging suspended below tree branches. In other words, *Proconsul* had some apelike features as well as some features of four-footed Old World monkeys (Figure 6.7). This mixture of ape and monkey features makes *Proconsul* a contender for a missing link between monkeys and apes but not as a connection between Miocene apes and later-appearing bipeds.

At least seven fossil hominoid groups besides *Proconsul* have been found in East Africa from the early to middle Miocene. But between 5 and 14 mya this fossil record thins out. It is not that all the apes suddenly moved from

[13] Ankel-Simons, F., Fleagle, J. G., & Chatrath, P. S. (1998). Femoral anatomy of *Aegyptopithecus zeuxis*, an early Oligocene anthropoid. *American Journal of Physical Anthropology 106*, 421–422.

[14] Houle, A. (1999). The origin of platyrrhines: An evaluation of the Antarctic scenario and the floating island model. *American Journal of Physical Anthropology 109*, 554–556.

Figure 6.7 Reconstructed skeleton of *Proconsul*. Note the apelike absence of a tail but monkeylike limb and body proportions. *Proconsul*, however, was capable of greater rotation of forelimbs than monkeys.

Africa to Eurasia, but that the environmental conditions made it less likely that any of the African remains would fossilize. Tropical forests inhabited by chimps and gorillas today constitute unfavorable conditions for the preservation of bones. As mentioned in Chapter 5, in order to become a fossil, bones must be quickly incorporated into the earth before any rotting or decomposition occurs. In tropical forests, the heat, humidity, and general abundance of life make this unlikely. The bones' organic matrix is consumed by other creatures before it can be fossilized.

Nevertheless, the scarcity of African fossil evidence from this time period fits well with notions about human origins that prevailed in the past. Two factors conspired to take the focus away from Africa. First, investigators initially did not consider that humans were any more closely related to the African apes than they were to the other intelligent great ape—the Asian orangutan. Chimps, bonobos, gorillas, and orangutans were thought to be more closely related to one another than any of them were to humans. The construction of evolutionary relationships still relied upon visual similarities among species, much as it did in the mid-1700s when Linnaeus developed the taxonomic scheme that grouped humans with other primates. Chimps, bonobos, gorillas, and orangutans all possess the same basic body plan, adapted to hanging by their arms from branches or knuckle-walking on the ground. Humans and their ancestors had an altogether different form of locomotion: walking upright on two legs. On an anatomical basis, the first Miocene ape to become bipedal could have come from any part of the vast Old World range of the Miocene apes.

The second factor drawing attention away from African origins was more subtle; it was not embedded in the bones from the earth but in the subconscious minds of the scientists: It was hard for these Eurocentric researchers to imagine

For many years paleoanthropologists considered the European wood ape *Dryopithecus* to be an important ancestor to humans. Fossil remains had been discovered in Europe as early as the 1850s. Eurocentrism allowed researchers to emphasize the European fossil record and to explain away the evidence from Africa.

that humans originated entirely in Africa. European scientists in the early 20th century therefore concentrated on the various species of European ape—all members of the genus *Dryopithecus* (pronounced "dry-o-pith-ee-kus"). They believed that humans evolved where "civilization" developed and that these apes could be the missing link to humans.

As we will see in the next chapter, it took many years for the first bipedal fossils discovered in South Africa in the 1920s to be accepted by the scientific community as key evidence of the human line. Instead, human origins were imagined to involve a close link between those who invented the first tools and those responsible for Western civilization.

During the 1960s, it appeared as though this Miocene human ancestor lived in the Siwaliks, the foothills of the majestic Himalayan Mountains along the northern borders of India and Pakistan, near the ruins of the later Indus Valley civilization. The Himalayas are some of the youngest mountains of the world. They began forming during the Miocene when the Indian subcontinent collided with the rest of Eurasia, and they have been becoming taller ever since.

In honor of the Hindu religion practiced in the region where the fossils were found, the contender was given the name *Ramapithecus*, after the Indian deity Rama and the Greek word for "ape," *pithekos*. Rama is the physical embodiment, or incarnation, of the major Hindu god Vishnu, the preserver. He is meant to portray what a perfect human can be. He is benevolent, protects the weak, and exemplifies all noble human characteristics. Features like the relative delicacy and curvature of the jaw and palate as well as thick tooth enamel led paleoanthropologists David Pilbeam and Elwyn Simons to suggest that this was the first hominoid to become part of the direct human line. They suggested that *Ramapithecus* was a bipedal tool user—the earliest human ancestor. With these qualities, *Ramapithecus* was perfectly named.

Other Miocene apes were also present in the foothills of the Himalayas. *Sivapithecus* was named after the Hindu deity Shiva, the god of destruction and regeneration. In the Hindu religion Lord Shiva is depicted as an asocial hermit who, when provoked, reduces his enemies to smoldering ashes in fits of rage. Though never considered a human ancestor, *Sivapithecus* also had the humanlike characteristic of thick molar tooth enamel (unlike the African apes but like the orangutans). *Sivapithecus* also had large projecting canine teeth more suitable to a destroyer than to a human ancestor. The *Sivapithecus* and *Ramapithecus* fossils were dated to between 7 and 12 mya.

The interpretation of these fossils changed with discoveries in the laboratory. By the 1970s, scientists had begun using biochemical and genetic evidence to establish evolutionary relationships among species. Vince Sarich, a biochemist at the University of California, Berkeley, was working in the laboratory of Allan Wilson (see Anthropologist of Note) and developed the revolutionary concept of a **molecular clock.** Such clocks help detect when the branching of related species from a common ancestor took place in the distant past.

Sarich used a molecular technique that had been around since the beginning of the 20th century: comparison of the blood proteins of living groups. He worked on serum albumin, a protein from the fluid portion of the blood (like the albumin that forms egg whites) that can be precipitated out of solution. *Precipitation* refers to the chemical transformation of a substance dissolved in a liquid back into its solid form. One of the forces that will cause such precipitation is contact of this protein with

The Natural History Museum, London

In the 1960s scientists identified two distinct species of Miocene ape from the foothills of the Himalayas: *Sivapithecus* and *Ramapithecus*. The smaller one, *Ramapithecus*, was proposed as a tool-using species ancestral to humans. Molecular investigations along with new fossil finds demonstrate that these specimens were actually the male and female of the same species and ancestral to orangutans. This well-preserved specimen from the Potwar Plateau of Pakistan proved that *Sivapithecus* was ancestral to the orangutan.

antibodies directed against it. Antibodies are proteins produced by organisms as part of an immune response to an infection. The technique relies on the notion that the stronger the biochemical reaction between the protein and the antibody (the more precipitate), the closer the evolutionary relationship. The antibodies and proteins of closely related species resemble one another more than the antibodies and proteins of distant species.

Sarich made immunological comparisons between a variety of species and suggested that he could establish dates for evolutionary events by calculating a molecular rate of change over time. By assuming a constant rate of change in the protein structure of each species over time, Sarich used these results to predict times of divergence between related groups. Each molecular clock needs to be set, or calibrated, by the dates associated with a known event, such as the divergence between prosimian and anthropoid primates or Old World monkeys and apes, as established by absolute dating methods.

Using this technique, Sarich proposed a sequence of divergence for the living hominoids showing that human, chimp, and gorilla lines split roughly 5 mya. He boldly stated

molecular clock The hypothesis that dates of divergences among related species can be calculated through an examination of the genetic mutations that have accrued since the divergence.

Anthropologist of Note

Allan Wilson (1934–1991)

Though a biochemist by training, New Zealander **Allan Wilson** has made key contributions to anthropology through his pioneering work in applying the principles of biochemistry to human evolutionary questions. Wilson forged

Allan Wilson (right) observes as a laboratory rabbit is injected.

a new "hybrid science," combining fossil and molecular evidence with groundbreaking results. Because the molecular evidence required rethinking long-held theories about the relationships among fossil groups, Wilson's work has been surrounded by controversy. According to those close to Wilson, he enjoyed his role as an outsider—being on the edges of anthropology and shaking things up.

Wilson was born in Ngaruwahia, New Zealand, and grew up on a farm in Pukekohe. After attending school in New Zealand and Australia, he was invited to study biochemistry at the University of California, Berkeley, in 1955. His father was reluctant to have his son travel so far from home, but his mother saw this as an opportunity for him and encouraged him to head to California.

Wilson stayed at Berkeley for the next thirty-five years, running one of the world's most creative biochemistry labs. In the 1960s, Berkeley was a center of academic liberalism and social protest. Wilson's highly original work was conducted with a similar revolutionary spirit, garnering him a MacArthur "genius"

award, two Guggenheim fellowships, and a place on the short list for the Nobel Prize.

He developed the notion of a "molecular clock" with his graduate student Vince Sarich and published the groundbreaking paper "Immunological Time-Scale for Human Evolution" in the journal *Science* in 1967. The molecular clock proposes that evolutionary events such as the split between humans and apes can be dated through an examination of the number of genetic mutations that accumulated since two species diverged from a common ancestor. In the 1980s, his laboratory (including Rebecca Cann and Mark Stoneking) was also responsible for seminal work with the mitochondrial Eve hypothesis that continues to be widely debated today (see Chapters 8 and 9).

Wilson died from leukemia at the age of 56. Joseph Felsenstein, one of his biographers, stated in his obituary in the journal *Nature,* "while others concentrated on what evolution could tell them about molecules, Wilson always looked for ways that molecules could say something about evolution."

---

that it was impossible to have a separate human line before 7 mya "no matter what it looked like." In other words, anything that old would also have to be ancestral to chimps and gorillas as well as humans. Because *Ramapithecus,* even with its humanlike jaws, was dated to between 7 and 12 mya, it could no longer be considered a human ancestor.

In the meantime, Pilbeam continued fossil hunting in the Himalayan foothills. Further specimens began to indicate that *Ramapithecus* was actually a smaller, perhaps female version of *Sivapithecus.*[15] Eventually all the specimens referred to as *Ramapithecus* were "sunk" or absorbed into the *Sivapithecus* group, so that today *Ramapithecus* no longer exists as a valid name for a Miocene ape. Instead of two distinct groups, one of which went on to evolve into humans, they are considered males and females of the sexually dimorphic genus *Sivapithecus.* Pilbeam found a spectacular complete specimen in the Potwar Plateau of Pakistan, showing that *Sivapithecus* was undoubtedly the ancestor of orangutans. This conclusion matched well with the molecular evidence that the separate line to orangutans originated 10 to 12 mya.

All of these changes reflect the fact that paleoanthropologists participate in an unusual kind of science. Paleoanthropology, like all paleontology, is a science of discovery. As new fossil discoveries come to light, interpretations inevitably change, making for better understanding of our evolutionary history. Today, discoveries can occur in the laboratory as easily as on the site of an excavation. Molecular studies since the 1970s provide a new line of evidence much the same way that fossils provide new data as they are unearthed. A discovery in the laboratory, like molecular clocks (now calibrating the split between 5 and 8 mya), can drastically change the interpretation of the fossil evidence.

The converse is also true. Fossil discoveries can raise new interpretations of the course of evolutionary history. The discovery of a 10-million-year-old ape in Ethiopia in 2007, thought to be ancestral to gorillas, provides a case in point.[16] Genetic evidence had pointed to a split between humans and the other African apes sometime between 5 and 8 mya. The scientists who found the nine fossil teeth that resulted in the naming of the species claim

---

[15] Pilbeam, D. R. (1987). Rethinking human origins. In R. L. Ciochon & J. G. Fleagle (Eds.), *Primate evolution and human origins* (p. 217). Hawthorne, NY: Aldine.

[16] Suwa, G., et al. (2007, August 23). A new species of great ape from the late Miocene epoch in Ethiopia. *Nature 448,* 921–924.

that it indicates that the gorilla lineage had become distinct 2 to 4 million years earlier than that. The species is called *Chororapithecus abyssinicus*, after Chorora, the local area where the fossil was found, and Abyssinia, the ancient name of Ethiopia. While Ethiopia has been the home for numerous spectacular fossil specimens that are part of the human lineage, this is the first fossil ape discovery from this region. Other scientists do not concur, however, and feel more fossil evidence is warranted before pushing back the timing of the split.

Miocene Apes and Human Origins

As described above, determining which Miocene apes were directly ancestral to humans is one of the key questions in primate evolution. Molecular evidence directs our attention to Africa between 5 and 8 mya (Figure 6.8). Though any fossil discoveries in Africa from this critical time period

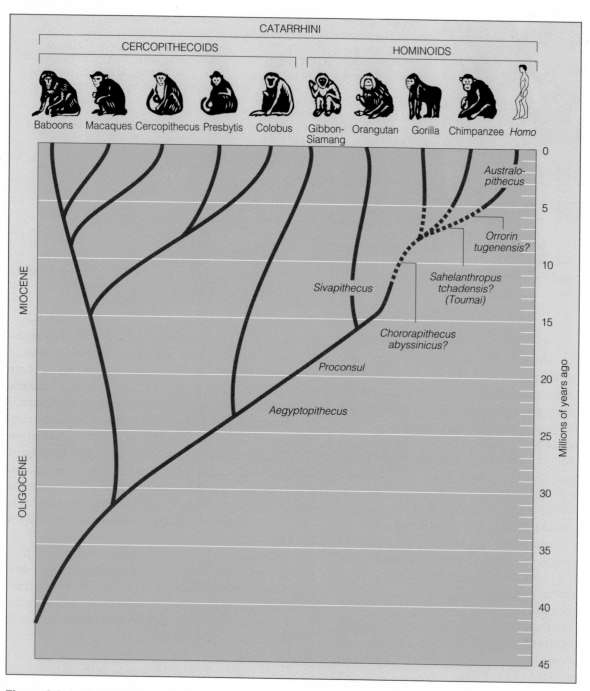

Figure 6.8 Although debate continues over details, this chart represents a reasonable reconstruction of evolutionary relationships among the Old World anthropoid primates. (Extinct evolutionary lines are not shown.) The 2007 discovery of a fossil ancestor to gorillas has suggested a new interpretation of the timing and nature of the split between humans and the African apes.

© Michael Brunet

The spectacular skull from Chad nicknamed "Toumai" ("hope for life") has been proposed as the earliest direct human ancestor. While the 6- to 7-million-year-old specimen is beautifully preserved and has some derived features, some paleoanthropologists feel that alone, it does not establish bipedalism, the derived trait characteristic of the human line.

© Orbin, Thierry/Corbis Sygma

These 6-million-year-old fossils, discovered in Kenya in 2001, represent a new species, *Orrorin tugenensis*, which has also been proposed as the earliest human ancestor. Like Toumai, these bones are surrounded by controversy. The thigh bones (femora) strongly suggest bipedalism, and the upper arm bone (humerus) may be more like that of humans than it is like some of the later bipeds. More discoveries and scientific comparisons will solve controversies surrounding both *Orrorin* and Toumai.

have the potential to be the missing link between humans and the other African ape species, the evidence from this period has been, until recently, particularly scrappy. Controversy surrounds the interpretation of many of these new fossil finds.

For example, in Chad in the summer of 2002, a team of international researchers led by Michel Brunet of France unearthed a well-preserved skull dated to between 6 and 7 mya.[17] Calling their find *Sahelanthropus tchadensis* ("Sahel man of Chad," referring to the Sahel—a belt of semi-arid land bordering the southern edge of the Sahara Desert)—the researchers suggested that this specimen represented the earliest known ancestor of humans, or earliest biped. Nicknamed "Toumai," from the region's Goran-language word meaning "hope for life" (a name typically given to babies born just before the dry season), this specimen is the only skull from this time period.

Considering that bipedalism is the derived characteristic that indicates inclusion in the human subfamily, some paleoanthropologists argue that the relationship of this specimen to humans cannot be established from skull bones alone. The research team argues that derived features, such as a reduced canine tooth, can be seen in the face of the Toumai specimen, indicating its status as a member of the human evolutionary line. Whether or not this specimen proves to be a direct human ancestor, as the only skull from this time period it is nevertheless a very important find.

In 2001, 6-million-year-old fossils discovered in Kenya by French and British researchers Brigitte Senut and Martin Pickford were also reported as human ancestors.[18] Officially given the species name *Orrorin tugenensis* (*Orrorin* meaning "original man" and *tugenensis* meaning "from the Tugen Hills") but nicknamed "Millennium Man," these specimens have also been surrounded by controversy.

The evidence for *Orrorin* consists of fragmentary arm and thigh bones, a finger bone, some jaw fragments, and teeth of at least five individuals. The thigh bones demonstrate possible but not definite bipedalism. Unfortunately, the distal or far ends of the thigh bone that would prove this are not fully preserved. The humerus (upper arm) appears to be more like that of humans than it is like the later bipedal species we will explore in the next chapter. Also *Orrorin* appears to be larger in size than some of these later bipeds. The methods that paleoanthropologists use to determine bipedalism from the fossil record will be fully described in Chapter 7.

---

[17] Brunet, M., et al. (2002). A new hominid from the Upper Miocene of Chad, Central Africa. *Nature 418*, 145–151.

[18] Senut, B., et al. (2001). First hominid from the Miocene (Lukeino Formation, Kenya). *Comptes Rendus de l'Académie de Sciences 332*, 137–144.

Questions for Reflection

1. How can evolutionary studies attract public attention while avoiding getting caught up in a media blitz? Did the current popularity of fossils in the media influence you personally?

2. Why are shared derived characteristics more important than shared ancestral characteristics in evolutionary reconstructions? Using the Miocene apes and humans, think about the ways that conclusions about evolution would change if ancestral rather than derived characteristics were used to figure out evolutionary relationships among species.

3. As we discussed, species are populations or groups of populations that are capable of interbreeding and producing fertile, viable offspring. Why is this biological definition of species difficult to apply to the fossil record?

4. The interpretation of fossil material changes with the discovery of new specimens and with findings in the laboratory. How has that happened? Can you imagine a different conception of human evolutionary history in the future?

5. An understanding of the changing position of the earth's continents through the past several hundred million years is important for the reconstruction of primate evolutionary history. Do you think the evolutionary history of the primates can be understood without knowledge of continental drift?

Suggested Readings

Carroll, S. B. (2005). *Endless forms most beautiful: The new science of evo devo.* New York: Norton.

The individual development of an organism from a single fertilized egg to its multibillion-celled complexity and its evolutionary history have been linked in the minds of scientists since Darwin's time. Today the burgeoning field of evolutionary development harnesses the power of molecular genetics to map out the ways that evolution and development are connected. Carroll's engaging book is an excellent introduction to one of the hottest areas of evolutionary biology.

Fleagle, J. (1998). *Primate adaptation and evolution.* New York: Academic.

This beautifully illustrated book is an excellent introduction to the field of primate evolution, synthesizing the fossil record with primate anatomical and behavioral variation.

Hartwig, W. C. (2002). *The primate fossil record.* New York: Cambridge University Press.

This book contains an up-to-date and comprehensive treatment of the discovery and interpretation of primate fossils.

Jones, S., Martin, R., & Pilbeam, D. (1994). *The Cambridge encyclopedia of human evolution.* New York: Cambridge University Press.

This comprehensive introduction to the human species covers genetics, primatology, and fossil evidence as well as a detailed exploration of contemporary human ecology, demography, and disease. Over seventy scholars from throughout the world contributed to this encyclopedia.

Mayr, E., & Diamond, J. (2002). *What evolution is.* New York: Basic.

Written for a general educated audience, this engaging book provides a comprehensive treatment of evolutionary theory.

Challenge Issue In the fall of 2009, a dramatic paleoanthropological find was announced: a remarkably complete skeleton of a putative human ancestor dated to 4.4 million years ago. Only a half-dozen partially complete fossil skeletons on the human line older than 1 million years have ever been discovered, and this one is the oldest. Nicknamed "Ardi," short for the new species, *Ardipithecus ramidus,* the fossil remains themselves were first discovered between 1992 and 1995. All the fine cracks visible in this close up of Ardi's lower jaw shows how fragile these ancient bones are. Features such as the small size of Ardi's canine tooth led paleoanthropologists to determine that she is a female. Early analyses of the Ardi remains in the early 1990s also established that there were forest rather than savannah dwellers on the human line. For the following fifteen-plus years, an international team of forty-seven scientists conducted painstaking excavation, reconstruction, and analysis to create a complete picture of the lifeways of this new species; through this process Ardi has become "personified." A series of research papers in the prestigious journal *Science,* along with a Discovery Channel documentary about how the scientists went about their work, reveal not only the importance of the find but how Ardi has captured our collective imagination. Sophisticated computer graphics allow scientists to simulate how regulatory genes might have shaped the development of Ardi's bones that caused her to move in a more humanlike fashion. Gymnasts were tapped to mimic her gait for scientific analysis, and advances in physics and chemistry were incorporated in the reconstruction of the ancient forested environment she inhabited. In the coming years, as scientists debate how the Ardi discovery influences theories about the human evolutionary line, these ancient bones that we know as the individual Ardi challenge us to think about what it means to be human.

© T. White

CHAPTER 7

The First Bipeds

Chapter Preview

What Is the Anatomy of Bipedalism, and How Is It Preserved in the Fossil Record?

Bipedalism is the shared derived characteristic used to establish whether a fossilized hominoid is part of the evolutionary line that produced humans. Evidence for bipedalism is preserved literally from head to toe. Bipedalism can be inferred from the forward position of the large opening in the base of the skull, a series of curves in the spinal column, the basin-shaped structure of the pelvis, the angle of the lower limbs from the hip joint to the knees, and the shape of the foot bones. Thus even fragmentary evidence can prove bipedalism, providing the right fragment is preserved. Several groups from between 4 and 7 million years ago (mya) have been proposed as the earliest bipedal human ancestor. Some of these, such as 4.4 mya *Ardipithecus* specimens, preserve evidence of facultative bipedalism, or an intermediate form of upright walking, and may be the link between earlier and later hominins.

What Role Did Bipedalism Play in Human Evolutionary History?

Numerous theories stressing adaptation have been proposed to account for the appearance of bipedalism in human evolutionary history. These theories range from the adaptive advantage of having hands free to carry young or wield weapons to adapting to the danger of too much heat in the brain from direct exposure to the sun in a hot, treeless environment. While bipedalism was present in the earliest forest-dwelling hominins, this way of movement may have conferred an adaptive advantage on bipeds as the environment became increasingly arid over the course of the Pliocene. Bipedalism appeared in human evolutionary history several million years before brain size expanded.

Who Were the First Bipeds, and What Were They Like?

The fossil record indicates that around the time of the Miocene to Pliocene transition, between 5 and 6 mya, the first confirmed bipeds appeared in Africa. The recently discovered genus *Ardipithecus* (4.4 to 5.8 mya) may be ancestral to the genus *Australopithecus,* a group of fossil bipeds known since the early 20th century. Australopithecines include a diverse group of fully bipedal species still possessing relatively small-sized brains in proportion to their body size. Some of the later australopithecines, known as "robust" forms, possessed particularly large teeth, jaws, and chewing muscles and represent an evolutionary dead end, disappearing from the fossil record completely by 1 mya. One of the other australopithecine species, though it is not clear which one, appears to be a direct ancestor of the genus *Homo*.

Though genetic evidence established that the human line diverged from those leading to chimpanzees and gorillas between 5 and 8 mya, for a long time the fossil evidence of the early stages of human evolution was both sparse and tenuous. Today, however, several interesting specimens from Africa fill in this important period. Inclusion of any fossil specimen in the human evolutionary line depends upon evidence for bipedalism (also called *bipedality*), the defining characteristic of the human line. The possible human ancestors from the Miocene recently found in Chad (*Sahelanthropus tchadensis*) and Kenya (*Orrorin tugenensis*), dated 6 to 7 mya, were described in the last chapter. In this chapter, we will pick up our story with a diverse array of fossil bipeds from the Pliocene—the geological epoch that began around 5 mya beginning with Ardipithecus from the chapter opener.[1]

Before focusing on the fossils, however, let's look at the anatomy of **bipedalism**—the shared derived characteristic distinguishing humans and their ancestors from the other African apes.

The Anatomy of Bipedalism

For a hominoid fossil to be definitively classified as part of the human evolutionary line, certain evidence of bipedalism is required. Bipedalism is associated with anatomical changes literally from head to toe.

Bipedalism can even be preserved in the skull (Figure 7.1) because balancing the head in an upright posture requires a skull position relatively centered above the spinal column. The spinal cord leaves the skull at its base through an opening called the *foramen magnum* (Latin for "big opening"). In a knuckle-walker like a chimp, the foramen magnum is placed more toward the back of the skull while in a biped it is in a more forward position.

Extending down from the skull of a biped, the spinal column makes a series of convex and concave curves that together maintain the body in an upright posture by positioning the body's center of gravity above the legs rather than forward. The curves correspond to the neck (cervical), chest (thoracic), lower back (lumbar), and pelvic (sacral) regions of the spine, respectively. In a chimp, the shape of the spine follows a single arching curve

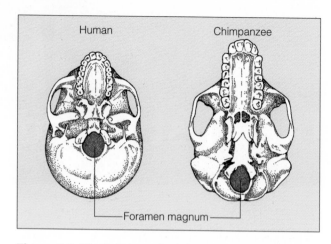

Figure 7.1 Bipedalism can be inferred from the position of the foramen magnum, the large opening at the base of the skull. Note its relatively forward position on the human skull (left) compared to the chimp skull.

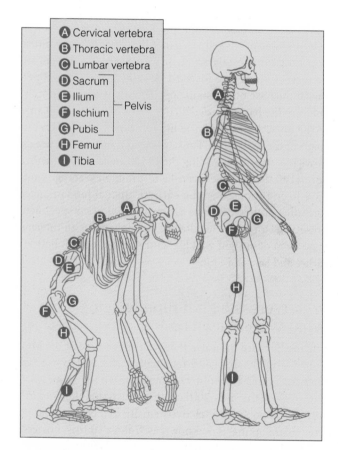

Figure 7.2 Differences between skeletons of chimps and humans reflect their mode of locomotion.

(Figure 7.2). Interestingly, at birth the spines of human babies have a single arching curve as seen in adult apes. As humans mature the curves characteristic of bipedalism appear, the cervical curve at about 3 months on average and the lumbar curve at around 12 months—a time when many babies begin to walk.

[1] White, T. D., et al. (2009, October). *Ardipithecus ramidus* and the paleobiology of early hominids. *Science 326* (5949), 64, 75–86; see also the entire October 2, 2009, issue of *Science*.

bipedalism The mode of locomotion in which an organism walks upright on its two hind legs, characteristic of humans and their ancestors; also called bipedality.

Fossilized footprints were preserved in volcanic ash at the 3.6-million-year-old Tanzanian site of Laetoli. As shown here, the foot of a living human fits right inside this ancient footprint, which shows the characteristic pattern of bipedal walking. The actual trail of footprints is 24 meters (80 feet) long.

The shape of the pelvis also differs considerably between bipeds and other apes. Rather than an elongated shape following the arch of the spine as seen in chimps, the biped pelvis is wider and foreshortened so that it can provide structural support for the upright body. With a wide bipedal pelvis, the lower limbs would be oriented away from the body's center of gravity if the thigh bones (femora) did not angle in toward each other from the hip to the knee, a phenomenon described as "kneeing-in." (Notice how your own knees and feet can touch when standing while your hip joints remain widely spaced.) This angling does not continue past the knee to the shin bones (tibia), which are oriented vertically. The resulting knee joint is not symmetrical, allowing the thigh and shin bones to meet despite their different orientations (Figure 7.3).

Another characteristic of bipeds is their stable arched feet and the absent opposable big toe. The ape big toe is in an **abducted** position (sticking out away from the midline) while the human big toe is pulled in toward the midline (**adducted**). In general, humans and their ancestors possess shorter toes than the other apes.

These anatomical features allow paleoanthropologists to "diagnose" bipedal locomotion even in fragmentary remains such as the top of the shin bone or the base of a skull. In addition, bipedal locomotion can also be established through fossilized footprints, preserving not so much the shape of foot bones but the characteristic stride used by humans and their ancestors. In fact, bipedal locomotion is a process of shifting the body's weight from one foot to the other as the nonsupporting foot swings forward. While the body is supported in a one-legged stance, a biped takes a stride by swinging the other leg forward. The heel of the foot is the first part of the swinging leg to hit the ground. Then as the biped

Homo sapiens   *Australopithecus*   Ape

Figure 7.3 Examination of the upper hip bones and lower limbs of (from left) *Homo sapiens*, *Australopithecus*, and an ape can be used to determine means of locomotion. The similarities between the human and australopithecine bones are striking and are indicative of bipedal locomotion.

continues to move forward, he or she rolls from the heel toward the toe, pushing or "toeing off" into the next swing phase of the stride (Figure 7.4). While one leg is moving from heel strike to toe off of the stance phase,

abduction Movement away from the midline of the body or from the center of the hand or foot.

adduction Movement toward the midline of the body or to the center of the hand or foot.

Figure 7.4 The bipedal gait in some regards is really "serial monopedalism" or locomotion one foot at a time through a series of controlled falls. Note how the body's weight shifts from one foot to the other as an individual moves through the swing phase to heel strike and toe off.

the other leg is moving forward through the swing phase of walking.

The most dramatic confirmation of our ancestors' walking ability comes from Laetoli, Tanzania, where, 3.6 mya, two (perhaps three) individuals walked across newly fallen volcanic ash. Because it was damp, the ash took the impressions of their feet, and these were sealed beneath subsequent ash falls until discovered by chemist Paul Abell in 1978. Abell was part of a team led by British paleoanthropologist Mary Leakey in search of human origins at Laetoli (see Anthropologists of Note). The shape of the footprints and the linear distance between the heel strikes and toe offs are quite human.

Once bipedalism is established in a fossil specimen, paleoanthropologists turn to other features, such as the skull or teeth, so that they can begin to establish relationships among the various fossil groups. Often scholars bring different interpretations to the fossil evidence.

Ardipithecus

Made famous through the partially complete 4.4-million-year-old skeleton specimen "Ardi," the genus *Ardipithecus* has dramatically changed what is known about the earliest bipeds. The genus is actually divided into two species, *Ardipithecus ramidus* and the older *Ardipithecus kadabba* dated to between 5.2 and 5.8 mya. The *Ardipithecus* remains show that some of the earliest bipeds inhabited a forested environment much like that of contemporary chimpanzees, bonobos, and gorillas; these remains were found in fossil-rich deposits along Ethiopia's Awash

© T. White

The remarkably complete remains of *Ardipithecus ramidus* have allowed paleoanthropologists to begin to reconstruct the biology and lifeways of the early forest dwelling hominins. When the first "Ardi" remains were discovered in the early 1990s she was placed on a side branch of human evolution but scientific investigation of this remarkable skeleton has lead paleoanthropologists to suggest she is a direct ancestor to the human line.

Louis S. B. Leakey (1903–1972) ▪ Mary Leakey (1913–1996)

Few figures in the history of paleoanthropology discovered so many key fossils, received so much public acclaim, or stirred up as much controversy as **Louis Leakey** and his second wife, **Mary Leakey.** Born in Kenya of missionary parents, Louis received his early education from an English governess and subsequently was sent to England for a university education. He returned to Kenya in the 1920s to begin his career there.

It was in 1931 that Louis and his research assistant from England, Mary Nicol (whom he married in 1936), began working in their spare time at Olduvai Gorge in Tanzania, searching patiently and persistently for remains of early human ancestors. It seemed a good place to look, for there were numerous animal fossils as well as crude stone tools lying scattered on the ground and eroding out of the walls of the gorge.

Their patience and persistence were not rewarded until 1959, when Mary found the first fossil. A year later, another skull was found, and Olduvai was on its way to being recognized as one of the most important sources of fossils relevant to human evolution in all of Africa. While Louis reconstructed,

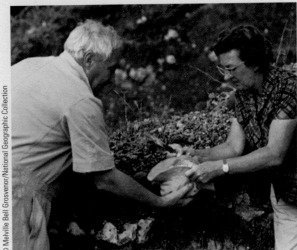

© Melville Bell Grosvenor/National Geographic Collection

described, and interpreted the fossil material, Mary made the definitive study of the Oldowan tools, a very early stone tool industry.

The Leakeys' important discoveries were not limited to those at Olduvai. In the early 1930s, they found the first fossils of Miocene apes in Africa at Rusinga Island in Lake Victoria. Also in the 1930s, Louis found a number of skulls at Kanjera, Kenya, that show a mixture of derived and more ancestral features. In 1948, at Fort Ternan, Kenya, the Leakeys found the remains of a late Miocene ape with features that seemed appropriate for an ancestor

of the bipeds. After Louis's death, Paul Abell, a member of an expedition led by Mary Leakey, found the first fossilized footprints of early bipeds at Laetoli, Tanzania.

In addition to their own work, Louis Leakey promoted a good deal of important work on the part of others. He made it possible for Jane Goodall to begin her landmark field studies of chimpanzees; later he was instrumental in setting up similar studies among gorillas (by Dian Fossey) and orangutans (by Biruté Galdikas). He set into motion the fellowship program responsible for the training of numerous paleoanthropologists from Africa. The Leakey tradition has been continued by son Richard, his wife Meave, and their daughter Louise.

Louis Leakey had a flamboyant personality and a way of interpreting fossil materials that frequently did not stand up well to careful scrutiny, but this did not stop him from publicly presenting his views as if they were the gospel truth. It was this aspect of the Leakeys' work that generated controversy. Nonetheless, the Leakeys produced a great deal of work that resulted in a much fuller understanding of human origins.

River accompanied by fossils of forest animals. The name **Ardipithecus ramidus** is fitting for an ultimate human ancestor as *Ardi* means "floor" and *ramid* means "root" in the local Afar language.

Now that the spectacular Ardi specimen has been sufficiently analyzed by the team who discovered her, paleoanthropologists are debating her exact place on the human line. Because the other African apes share a body plan similar to one another, many paleoanthropologists expected the earliest bipeds to resemble something halfway between chimps and humans. Instead, Ardi shows that these forest creatures moved in a combination of ways: They moved

across the tops of branches with the palms of their hands and feet facing downward, and they walked between the trees on the ground in an upright position. The other African apes, as we saw in previous chapters, knuckle-walk on the forest floor and hang suspended below the branches. In other words, Ardi resembles some of the early Miocene apes more than she does the living African apes.

This calls into question what the last common ancestor of humans and the other African apes looked like. Does Ardi represent the more ancestral form, with the other apes evolving independently after they split from the human line but still converging to the typical African ape body plan? Or does Ardi represent a new body plan, characteristic of the earliest bipeds that evolved away from the African ape plan shared by chimps and gorillas? And what of Ardi's relationship to the later bipeds? Until fall

Ardipithecus ramidus One of the earliest bipeds that lived in forested portions of eastern Africa about 4.4 million years ago.

2009, *Ardipithecus* was generally considered a side branch on the human evolutionary tree. Now, the international team has proposed that Ardi may be a direct ancestor to the later bipeds, including humans.

The famous Ardi specimen, at 120 centimeters tall and a weight of about 50 kilograms, is comparable in size to a female chimpanzee. The size and shape of this partial skeleton's brain and the enamel thickness of the specimen's teeth are similar to chimpanzees as well. Though possessing a grasping big toe, Ardi's locomotion, unlike that of a chimp, has been reconstructed as bipedal when on the ground.

The *Ardipithecus* finds, along with the *Orrorin* and Toumai specimens described in the previous chapter, have begun to provide evidence for the time period before the appearance of the ancient bipeds belonging to the genus *Australopithecus*. The first representatives of this group were discovered in the early 20th century, long before the majority of scientists were comfortable with the now-accepted notion that humans originated on the African continent.

The Taung child, discovered in South Africa in 1924, was the first fossil specimen placed in the genus *Australopithecus*. Though Raymond Dart correctly diagnosed the Taung child's bipedal mode of locomotion as well as its importance in human evolution, other scientists rejected Dart's claims that this small-brained biped with a humanlike face was a direct ancestor to humans. In the early 20th century, scientists expected the ancestors to humans to possess a large brain and an apelike face and to originate from Europe or Asia rather than Africa.

Australopithecus

Most of the early bipeds from the Pliocene are members of the genus **Australopithecus,** a genus that includes species from East, South, and Central Africa. The name for this group of fossils was coined back in 1924 when the first important fossil from Africa proposed to be a human ancestor came to light. This unusual fossil, consisting of a partial skull and natural brain cast of a young individual, was brought to the attention of anatomist Raymond Dart of the University of Witwatersrand in Johannesburg, South Africa. The "Taung child," named for the limestone quarry in the South African town of Taung (Tswana for "place of the lion") in which it was found, was unlike any creature Dart had seen before. Recognizing an intriguing mixture of ape and human characteristics in this unusual fossil, Dart proposed a new taxonomic category for his discovery— *Australopithecus africanus* or "southern ape of Africa"— suggesting that this specimen represented an extinct form that was ancestral to humans.

Although the anatomy of the base of the skull indicated that the Taung child was probably a biped,

Australopithecus The genus including several species of early bipeds from East, South, and Central Africa living between about 1.1 and 4.3 million years ago, one of whom was directly ancestral to humans.

the scientific community was not ready to accept the notion of a small-brained African ancestor to humans. Dart's original paper describing the Taung child was published in the February 1925 edition of the prestigious journal *Nature.* The next month's issue was filled with venomous critiques rejecting Dart's proposal that this specimen represented an ancestor to humans. Criticisms of Dart ranged from biased to fussy to sound. Some scholars chastised Dart for incorrectly combining Latin and Greek in the genus and species name he coined. Valid critics questioned the wisdom of making inferences made about the appearance of an adult of the species based only on the fossilized remains of a young individual.

However, ethnocentric bias was the biggest obstacle to Dart's proposed human ancestor. Paleoanthropologists of the early 20th century expected that the ancestor to humans already had a large brain. Moreover, most European scientists expected to find evidence of this large-brained ancestor in Europe or, barring that, Asia.

In fact, many scientists of the 1920s even believed that the ancestor to humans had already been found in the Piltdown gravels of Sussex, England, in 1910. The Piltdown specimens consisted of a humanlike skull and an apelike jaw that seemed to fit together, though the crucial joints connecting the two were missing. They were discovered along with the bones of some other animal species known to be extinct. Charles Dawson—the British amateur archaeologist,

Discovery of the Piltdown Man in 1911, Cooke, Arthur Clark (1867–1951)/Geographical Society, London, UK/The Bridgeman Art Library

The Piltdown forgery was widely accepted as ancestral to humans, in large part because it fit with conventional expectations that the missing link would have a large brain and an apelike face. No one knows with certainty how many of the "Piltdown Gang"—scientists supporting this specimen as the missing link—were actually involved in the forgery. It is likely that Charles Dawson had help from at least one scientist. Sir Arthur Conan Doyle, the author of the Sherlock Holmes detective stories, has also been implicated.

paleontologist, and practicing lawyer who found these remains—immodestly named them *Eoanthropus dawsoni* or "Dawson's dawn man." Until the 1950s the Piltdown remains were widely accepted as representing the missing link between apes and humans; today they are known as one of the biggest hoaxes in the history of science.

There were several reasons for widespread acceptance of Dawson's "dawn man." As Darwin's theory of evolution by natural selection began to gain acceptance in the early 20th century, intense interest developed in finding traces of prehistoric human ancestors. Accordingly, predictions were made as to what those ancestors looked like. Darwin himself, on the basis of his knowledge of embryology and the comparative anatomy of living apes and humans, suggested in his 1871 book *The Descent of Man* that early humans had, among other things, a large brain and an apelike face and jaw.

Although the tools made by prehistoric peoples were commonly found in Europe, their bones were not. A few fossilized skeletons had come to light in France and Germany, but they were not at all like the predicted missing link, nor had any human fossils been discovered in England ever before. Given this state of affairs, the Piltdown finds could not have come at a better time. Here at last was the long-awaited missing link, and it was almost exactly as predicted. Even better, so far as English-speaking scientists were concerned, it was found on English soil.

In the context of the evidence available in the early 1900s, it was easy to accept the idea of an ancient human with a large brain and an apelike face. Fortunately, the self-correcting nature of science has prevailed, exposing the Piltdown specimens as a forgery. The discoveries—primarily in South Africa, China, and Java—of fossils of smaller-brained bipeds from the distant past caused scientists to question Piltdown's authenticity. Ultimately, the application of the newly developed fluorine dating method (described in Chapter 5) by British physical anthropologist Kenneth Oakley and colleagues in 1953 proved conclusively that Piltdown was a forgery. The skull, which was indeed human, was approximately 600 years old, whereas the jaw, which proved to be from an orangutan, was even more recent. Finally, Dart and the Taung child were fully vindicated.

Today, genetic and fossil evidence indicates that the human evolutionary line begins with a small-brained bipedal ape from Africa. Numerous international expeditions—including researchers from Kenya, Ethiopia, Japan, Belgium, Great Britain, Canada, France, Israel, the Netherlands, South Africa, and the United States—have scoured East, South, and Central Africa, recovering unprecedented amounts of fossil material. This wealth of evidence has allowed scientists to continually refine our understanding of early human evolution. Even though debate continues over the details, today there is widespread agreement over its broad outline. Each new discovery, such as the Ardi skeleton, confirms our African origins and the importance of bipedalism to distinguishing humans and their ancestors from the other African apes.

The Pliocene Environment and Hominin Diversity

As described in the previous chapter, the Miocene epoch was a time of tremendous geologic change. The effects of these changes continued into the Pliocene. The steady movement of geologic plates supporting the African and Eurasian continents resulted in a collision of the two landmasses at either end of what now is the Mediterranean Sea (Figure 7.5). This contact allowed for the spread of species between these continents.

A suite of geologic changes, known as the Great Rift Valley system, are associated with this collision. This system consists of a separation between geologic plates, extending from the Middle East through the Red Sea and eastern Africa into southern Africa. Part of rifting involves the steady increase in the elevation of the eastern third of the African continent, which experienced a cooler and dryer climate and a transformation of vegetation from forest to dry grassy **savannah.**

The system also contributed to the volcanic activity in the region, which provides opportunities for accurate dating of fossil specimens. Also in the Miocene, the Indian subcontinent, which had been a solitary landmass for many millions of years, came into its present position through a collision with Eurasia, contributing further to cooler, dryer conditions globally. In addition to causing global climate change, these geologic events also provided excellent opportunities for the discovery of fossil specimens as layers of the earth became exposed through the rifting process.

Diverse Australopithecine Species

Since Dart's original find, hundreds of other fossil bipeds have been discovered, first in South Africa and later in Tanzania, Malawi, Kenya, Ethiopia, and Chad. As they were discovered, many were placed in a variety of different genera and species, but now usually all are considered to belong to the single genus *Australopithecus*. Anthropologists recognize up to eight species of the genus (Table 7.1). In addition, some other groups of fossil bipeds from the Pliocene epoch (1.6 to around 5 mya) have been discovered, including the earliest representatives of the genus *Homo*.

First we will describe the australopithecines and their contemporaries in the order in which they inhabited the earth up to the middle Pliocene (2.5 mya) when the genus

savannah Semi-arid plains environment as in eastern Africa.

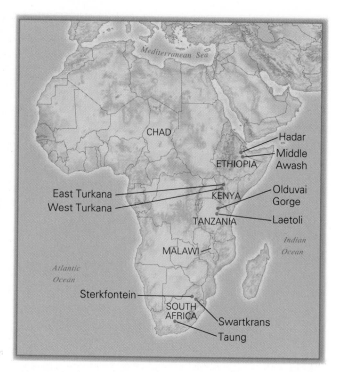

Figure 7.5 **Australopithecine fossils have been found in South Africa, Malawi, Tanzania, Kenya, Ethiopia, and Chad. In the Miocene the Eurasian and African continents made contact at the eastern and western ends of what now is the Mediterranean Sea. As these landmasses met, "rifting" also occurred, gradually raising the elevation of the eastern third of Africa. The dryer climates that resulted may have played a role in human evolution in the distant past. This rifting also gives us excellent geologic conditions for finding fossils today.**

Homo first appeared. The East African and South African evidence will be presented separately because the dating for East African sites is more reliable. Next we will examine late-appearing australopithecines, including a grade of australopithecine found in both eastern and southern Africa that coexisted with the genus *Homo*.

East Africa

The oldest australopithecine species known so far consists of some jaw and limb bones from Kenya that date to between 3.9 and 4.2 mya (see *Australopithecus anamensis* in Table 7.1). Meave and Louise Leakey, daughter-in-law and granddaughter of Louis and Mary Leakey, discovered these fossils in 1995 and decided to place them in a separate species from other known australopithecines. Its name means "ape-man of the lake," and it shows particularities in the teeth such as a true *sectorial*: a lower premolar tooth shaped to hone the upper canine as seen in apes. In humans and more recent ancestors, the premolar has a characteristic bicuspid shape and does not sharpen the canine each time the jaws come together. As

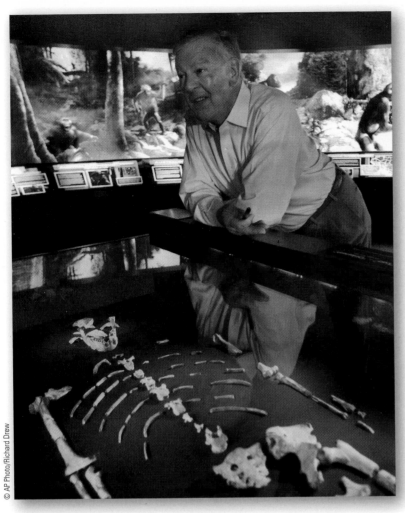

Lucy, the 3.2-million-year-old fossil specimen, is on a six-year U.S. tour as part of a traveling exhibit organized and curated by the Ethiopian government and the Houston Museum of Natural History. Though Lucy has done much to popularize paleoanthropology and evolutionary studies since her discovery in 1974, some paleoanthropologists—like C. Owen Lovejoy and Richard Leakey—have said that placing her fragile ancient skeleton on public display is far too risky. The Smithsonian Institution and the Cleveland Museum of Natural History have declined to host the show for this reason. Others—like her discoverer Donald Johanson, pictured here with Lucy in the exhibition space in Times Square, New York—feel that the benefits outweigh the risks. Benefits include the study of Lucy's remains via CT scans so that future generations of scientists can study them without actually handling the fragile bones. In addition, the revenues from the tour will be used to help modernize Ethiopia's museums. Finally, the exhibit will increase public awareness of human origins and the vital role of Africa and, in particular, Ethiopia in our evolutionary history.

in other australopithecines and humans, the enamel in the molar teeth is thick. The limb bone fragments indicate bipedalism.

Moving closer to the present, the next species defined in the fossil record is *Australopithecus afarensis.*

No longer the earliest australopithecine species, it still remains one of the best known due to the Laetoli footprints from Tanzania, the famous Lucy specimen, and the recent discovery of the 3.3-million-year-old remains of a young child called "Lucy's baby," both from Ethiopia.

Table 7.1 Species of *Australopithecus* and Other Pliocene Fossil Hominins*

Species	Location	Dates	Notable Features/Fossil Specimens
Ardipithecus ramidus	Ethiopia	4.4 mya[†]	Fossil remains of over thirty-five individuals including Ardi (another species, *Ardipithecus kadabba*, dates to 5.4–5.8 mya)
A. anamensis	Kenya	3.9–4.2 mya	Oldest australopithecine
Kenyanthropus platyops	Kenya	3.2–3.5 mya	Contemporary with australopithecines, believed by some to be a member of that genus
A. africanus	South Africa	2.3–3 mya	First discovered, gracile, well represented in fossil record (Taung)
A. aethiopicus	Kenya	2.5 mya	Oldest robust australopithecine (Black Skull)
A. bahrelghazali	Chad	3–3.5 mya	Only australopithecine from Central Africa
A. boisei	Kenya	1.2–2.3 mya	Later robust form coexisted with early *Homo* (Zinj)
A. garhi	Ethiopia	2.5 mya	Later East African australopithecine with humanlike dentition
A. robustus	South Africa	1–2 mya	Coexisted with early *Homo*

*Paleoanthropologists differ in the number of species they recognize, some suggesting separate genera.

[†]Million years ago.

Figure 7.6 Sexual dimorphism in canine teeth.

Figure 7.7 Trunk skeletons of modern human, *A. afarensis*, and chimpanzee, compared. In its pelvis, the australopithecine resembles the modern human, but its rib cage shows the pyramidal configuration of the ape.

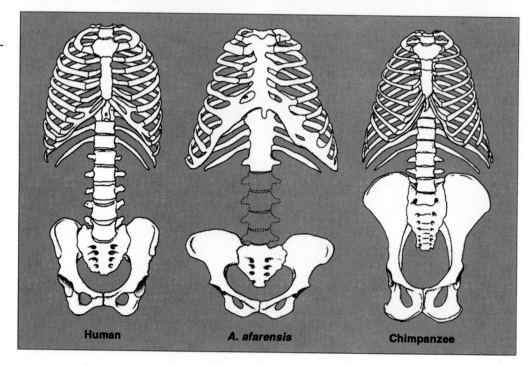

Lucy consists of bones from almost all parts of a single 3.2-million-year-old skeleton discovered in 1974 in the Afar Triangle of Ethiopia (hence the name *afarensis*). Standing only 3½ feet tall, this adult female was named after the Beatles song "Lucy in the Sky with Diamonds," which the paleoanthropologists listened to as they celebrated her discovery. The Afar region is also famous for the "First Family," a collection of bones from at least thirteen individuals, ranging in age from infancy to adulthood, who died together as a result of some single calamity.

At least sixty individuals from *A. afarensis* (once the name of a genus has been established, it can be abbreviated with the first letter followed by the complete species name) have been removed from fossil localities in Ethiopia and Tanzania. Specimens from Ethiopia's Afar region are securely dated by potassium argon to between 2.9 and 3.9 mya. Material from Laetoli, in Tanzania, is securely dated to 3.6 mya. Altogether, *A. afarensis* appears to be a sexually dimorphic bipedal species with estimates of body size and weight ranging between 1.1 and

1.6 meters (3½–5 feet) and 29 and 45 kilograms (64–100 pounds), respectively.[2]

If paleoanthropologists are correct in assuming that larger fossil specimens were males and smaller specimens females, males were about 1½ times the size of females. In this respect, they were somewhat like the Miocene African apes, with sexual dimorphism greater than one sees in a modern chimpanzee but less than one sees in gorillas and orangutans. Male canine teeth, too, are significantly larger than canine teeth of females, though canine size is reduced compared to that of chimps (Figure 7.6).

Nearly 40 percent complete, the Lucy specimen has provided invaluable information about the shape of the pelvis and torso of early human ancestors. The physical appearance of *A. afarensis* was unusual by human standards: They may be described as looking like an ape from the waist up and like a human from the waist down (Figure 7.7). In

---

[2] McHenry, H. M. (1992). Body size and proportions in early hominids. *American Journal of Physical Anthropology 87*, 407.

Fossil finds are rare enough, but a well-preserved juvenile specimen is especially unusual. The skull and skeleton of this young girl are actually tens of thousands of years older than Lucy, but due to her incredible preservation, she has been nicknamed "Lucy's baby." In addition to the skull pictured here, this specimen includes a torso, fingers, and a foot.

addition, a forearm bone from Lucy, which is relatively shorter than that of an ape, suggests that the upper limb was lighter and the center of gravity lower in the body than in apes. Still, the arms of Lucy and other early australopithecines are long in proportion to their legs when compared to the proportions seen in humans.

Though she lived about 150,000 years before her namesake, "Lucy's baby," the discovery from Ethiopia announced in 2006, will add considerably to our knowledge about *A. afarensis* once the analyses are complete.[3] These fossilized remains of a young child, dated to 3.3 mya, were discovered in the Dikika area of northern Ethiopia in 2000. Because the remains of this child, thought to have died in a flash flood, are particularly well preserved, scientists can investigate new aspects of this species' biology and behavior. For example, a preserved hyoid bone (located in the throat region) will allow scientists to reconstruct australopithecine patterns of vocalization. While the lower limbs clearly indicate bipedalism, the specimen's scapula and long curved finger bones are more apelike.

The curvature of the fingers and toes and the somewhat elevated position of the shoulder joint seen in adult specimens indicate that *A. afarensis* was more adapted to tree climbing compared to more recent human ancestors. In the following Original Study, paleoanthropologist John Hawks discusses the kinds of evidence used to reconstruct a behavior such as tree climbing in our ancestors.

---

[3] Zeresenay, A., et al. (2006). A juvenile early hominin skeleton from Dikika, Ethiopia. *Nature 443*, 296–301.

Original Study

Ankles of the Australopithecines   *by John Hawks*

Recent University of Michigan Ph.D. Jeremy DeSilva gets some nice press about his work demonstrating that fossil hominins didn't climb like chimpanzees.

"Frankly, I thought I was going to find that early humans would be quite capable, but their ankle morphology was decidedly maladaptive for the kind of climbing I was seeing in chimps," DeSilva told LiveScience. "It kind of reinvented in my mind what they were doing and how they could have survived in an African savannah without the ability to go up in the trees."[a]

This is a good example of the comparative method in paleoanthropology. We can't observe the behavior of extinct species; we can only observe

the behavior of their living relatives. We can observe the anatomy of fossil specimens, but testing hypotheses about their behavior requires us to understand the relationship between anatomy and behavior in living species. We've known about the anatomy of fossil hominid ankles for a long time, but it's not so obvious how the anatomical differences between them and chimpanzee ankles relates to behavior.

DeSilva studied the tibiae and ankle bones of early hominins and concludes "that if hominins included tree climbing as part of their locomotor repertoire, then they were performing this activity in a manner decidedly unlike modern chimpanzees."

DeSilva's conclusion is straightforward and easy to illustrate. Chimpanzees climb vertical tree trunks pretty much like a logger does. A logger slings a strap around the trunk and leans back on it. Friction from the strap holds him up as he moves his feet upward; spikes on his boots hold him while he moves the strap.

Of course, chimpanzees don't have spikes on their feet, and they don't use a strap. Instead, their arms are long enough to wrap around the trunk, and they can wedge a foot against the trunk by flexing their ankle upward—dorsiflexing it—or grip the trunk by bending the ankle sideways—inverting the foot—around it. The paper includes

CONTINUED

CONTINUED

a photo that shows the chimpanzee style of climbing clearly.

You might wonder, yeah so what? Isn't it obvious that chimpanzees climb this way?

Well, it wasn't so obvious which features of the ankle might adapt chimpanzees to this style of climbing. By watching the chimpanzees (and other apes) DeSilva was able to determine the average amount (and range) of dorsiflexion and inversion of the feet while climbing, and could also assess the extent to which dorsiflexion is accomplished at the ankle joint (as opposed to the midfoot). In this case, the observations were pretty obvious—chimpanzees were habitually flexing their ankles in ways that would damage a human ankle. Then, by examining the bony limits on human ankle flexibility, DeSilva showed that fossil hominins shared the same constraints on ankle movement as recent people. They couldn't have climbed like chimpanzees.

Human Climbing

I would say that the ankle-joint observations match the rest of the skeleton. It seems pretty obvious that *Australopithecus afarensis* and later hominids couldn't possibly have climbed in the chimpanzee-like manner described in DeSilva's paper, because the hominins' arms were too short. If a logger tried to climb with his arms instead of a strap, even spikes on his feet would be relatively ineffective holding him up. Dorsiflexion would be hopeless—the normal component of force against the tree trunk would be insufficient to prevent slipping.

Humans who *aren't* loggers use a different strategy to climb vertical tree trunks—they put a large fraction of the surface area of their legs directly in contact with the trunk. Wrapping legs around and pressing them together gives the necessary friction to hold the body up.

If you're like me, you'll remember this climbing strategy ruefully from gym class, where "rope

climbing" is the lowest common denominator of fitness tests. The sad fact is that many otherwise-normal humans fall on the wrong side of the line between mass and muscle power. Straining my groin muscles to the max, I still could never pull my way up a rope.

There's nothing magical about getting a human to climb. Ladders, after all, are relatively easy for the large fraction of the population who can't climb a rope or tree trunk. The trick with a ladder is that friction is organized in a more effective way for our ankle mechanics and arm length. But you don't need to schlep a ladder, if you can manage a little extra arm strength and a low enough body mass.

Early Hominin Climbing

Australopithecines were light in mass, and from what we can tell, they had

The amount of dorsiflexion in a chimpanzee's foot allows it to climb trees with the feet in a position that is impossible for humans. Comparisons like this between living species allow paleoanthropologists to reconstruct the pattern of locomotion in fossil groups.

strong arms. So they had what it takes for humans today to climb trees effectively—not like chimpanzees, but like humans. Up to *A. afarensis*, every early hominin we know about lived in an environment that was at least partially wooded.

In his comments about the paper, DeSilva hypothesizes a trade-off between climbing ability and effective bipedality, so that early hominins could not have effectively adapted to both. I don't think a chimpanzee-like ankle would have been any use with arms as short as australopithecines'. So I don't see the necessity of a trade-off in ankle morphology. *A. afarensis*—long before any evidence of stone tool manufacture—had very non-apelike arms, hands and thumbs.

But there's one significant question that DeSilva omits discussing—the footbones of a South African australopithecine: StW 573. Clarke and Tobias[b] describe the foot of StW 573 as having a big toe that is abducted (sticks out) from the foot, intermediate between the chimpanzee and human condition. They conclude:

> [W]e now have the best available evidence that the earliest South African australopithecine, while bipedal, was equipped to include arboreal, climbing activities in its locomotor repertoire. Its foot has departed to only a small degree from that of the chimpanzee. It is becoming clear that *Australopithecus* was not an obligate terrestrial biped, but rather a facultative biped and climber. (p. 524)

DeSilva studied the talus (an ankle bone), not the toe. StW 573 has a talus, and although it is not in DeSilva's sample, it probably would place very close to the other hominins in his comparison. Even Clarke and Tobias described its talus as humanlike—their argument for an intermediate form was based mostly on the toe.

But still, it's hard to believe that australopithecines would retain a chimpanzee-like big toe, if they couldn't use that big toe by inverting or dorsiflexing their foot in any significant way. By all other accounts, an abducted hallux (big toe) would only impede effective bipedality. It is of no use at all for a human-like pattern of climbing. The only remaining utility would be for small-branch grasping, but small branches would seem unlikely as a support for hominin arboreality.

One possibility is that Clarke and Tobias were simply mistaken. That appears to be the explanation favored by Harcourt-Smith and Aiello[c] and McHenry and Jones[d] who concluded that all known hominin feet appear to lack any "ape-like ability to oppose the big toe." They also point to the Laetoli footprint trails, most observers of which agree that the big toe was adducted, not abducted.

I tend to favor that explanation—australopithecines simply didn't have a grasping foot. But they may not have shared the medial longitudinal arch, at least not in the human configuration, and without it one might doubt that their gait featured as strong a toe-off as that of later humans. Who knows?

[a] DeSilva, J. M. (2009). Functional morphology of the ankle and the likelihood of climbing in early hominins. *Proceeding of the National Academy of Sciences, USA 106,* 6567–6572.
[b] Clarke, R. J., & Tobias, P. V. (1995). Sterkfontein Member 2 foot bones of the oldest South African hominid. *Science 269,* 521–524.
[c] Harcourt-Smith, W. E. H., & Aiello, L. C. (2004). Fossils, feet and the evolution of human bipedal locomotion. *Journal of Anatomy 204,* 403–416, at 412.
[d] McHenry, H. M., & Jones, A. L. (2006). Hallucial convergence in early hominids. *Journal of Human Evolution 50,* 534–539.

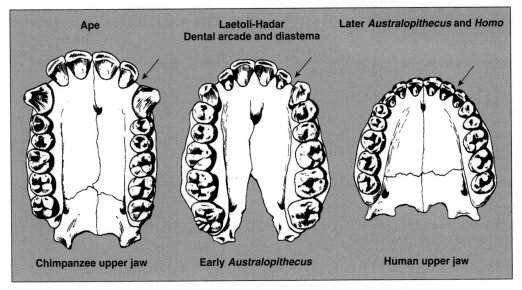

Ape

Laetoli-Hadar
Dental arcade and diastema

Later *Australopithecus* and *Homo*

Chimpanzee upper jaw   **Early *Australopithecus***   **Human upper jaw**

Figure 7.8 The upper jaws of an ape, *Australopithecus,* and modern human show important differences in the shape of the dental arch and the spacing between the canines and adjoining teeth. Only in the earliest australopithecines can a diastema (a large gap between the upper canine and incisor) be seen.

The skull bones are particularly important for reconstructing evolutionary relationships as well as for learning about the cognitive capacities of ancestral species. The skull of *A. afarensis* is relatively low, the forehead slopes backward, and the brow ridge that helps give apes such massive-looking foreheads is also present. The lower half of the face is chinless and accented by jaws that are quite large, relative to the size of the skull. The brain is small and apelike, and the general conformation of the skull seems nonhuman. Even the semicircular canal, a part of the ear crucial to maintenance of balance, is apelike. Cranial capacity, commonly used as an index of brain size for *A. afarensis,* averages about 420 cubic centimeters (cc), roughly equivalent to the size of a chimpanzee and about one-third the size of living humans.[4] Intelligence, however, is indicated not only by absolute brain size but also by the ratio of brain to body size. Unfortunately, with such a wide range of adult weights, it is not clear whether australopithecine brain size was larger than a modern ape's, relative to body size.

Much has been written about australopithecine teeth because they are one of the primary means for distinguishing among closely related groups. In *A. afarensis,* unlike humans, the teeth are all quite large, particularly the molars. The premolar is no longer fully sectorial as in *A. anamensis,* but most other features of the teeth represent a more ancestral rather than derived condition. For example, the rows of the teeth are more parallel (the ancestral ape condition) compared to the arch seen in the human tooth rows. The canines project slightly, and a slight space or gap known as a **diastema** remains between the upper incisors and canines as found in the apes (Figure 7.8).

[4] Grine, F. E. (1993). Australopithecine taxonomy and phylogeny: Historical background and recent interpretation. In R. L. Ciochon & J. G. Fleagle (Eds.), *The human evolution source book* (pp. 201–202). Englewood Cliffs, NJ: Prentice-Hall.

diastema A space between the canines and other teeth allowing the large projecting canines to fit within the jaw.

This 3- to 4-million-year-old skull could be another australopithecine or, as its discoverers suggest, a separate genus: *Kenyanthropus platyops*.

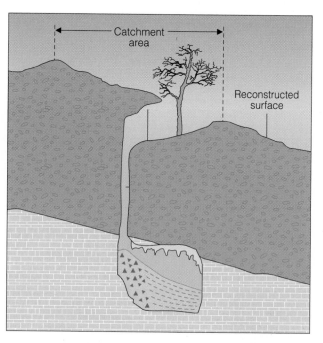

Figure 7.9 Many of the fossil sites in South Africa were limestone caverns connected to the surface by a shaft. Over time, dirt, bones, and other matter that fell down the shaft accumulated inside the cavern, becoming fossilized. In the Pliocene, the earth next to the shaft's opening provided a sheltered location for trees that, in turn, may have been used by predators for eating without being bothered by scavengers.

To further complicate the diversity seen in *A. afarensis*, in 2001 Meave and Louise Leakey announced the discovery of an almost complete cranium, parts of two upper jaws, and assorted teeth from a site in northern Kenya, dated to between 3.2 and 3.5 mya.[5] Contemporary with early East African *Australopithecus*, the Leakeys see this as a different genus named **Kenyanthropus platyops** ("flat-faced man of Kenya"). Unlike early australopithecines, *Kenyanthropus* is said to have a small braincase and small molars set in a large, humanlike, flat face. But again, there is controversy; the Leakeys see the fossils as ancestral to the genus *Homo*. Other paleoanthropologists are not convinced, suggesting that the Leakeys' interpretation rests on a questionable reconstruction of badly broken fossil specimens.[6]

Central Africa

Dated to the same time period as *Kenyanthropus platyops* is another recent discovery of an australopithecine from Chad in Central Africa. The name of the new species, *Australopithecus bahrelghazali,* is for a nearby riverbed and

consists of a jaw and several teeth dated to between 3 and 3.5 mya.[7] This is the first australopithecine discovered in Central Africa. With time, perhaps more discoveries from this region will give a fuller understanding of the role of *A. bahrelghazali* in human evolution and its relationship to the possible bipeds from the Miocene.

South Africa

Throughout the 20th century and into the present, paleoanthropologists have continued to recover australopithecine fossils from a variety of sites in South Africa. Included in this group are numerous fossils found beginning in the 1930s at Sterkfontein and Makapansgat, in addition to Dart's original find from Taung.

It is important to note, however, that South African sites, lacking the clear stratigraphy and volcanic ash of East African sites, are much more difficult to date and interpret (Figure 7.9). One unusually complete skull and skeleton has been dated by paleomagnetism to about 3.5 mya,[8]

---

[5] Leakey, M. G., et al. (2001). New hominin genus from eastern Africa shows diverse middle Pliocene lineages. *Nature 410*, 433–440.

[6] White, T. D. (2003). Early hominids—diversity or distortion? *Science 299,* 1994–1997.

Kenyanthropus platyops   A proposed genus and species of biped contemporary with early australopithecines; may not be a separate genus.

---

[7] Brunet, M., et al. (1995). The first australopithecine 2,500 kilometers west of the Rift Valley (Chad). *Nature 16*, 378 (6554), 273–275.

[8] Clarke, R. J. (1998). First ever discovery of a well preserved skull and associated skeleton of Australopithecus. *South African Journal of Science 94*, 460–464.

Figure 7.10 Drawing of the foot bones of a 3- to 3.5-million-year-old *Australopithecus* from Sterkfontein, South Africa, as they would have been in the complete foot. Note how long and flexible the first toe (at right) is. This is a drawing of the StW specimen referred to in this chapter's Original Study.

as was a partial foot skeleton (Figure 7.10) described in 1995.[9] The other South African remains are difficult to date. A faunal series established in East Africa places these specimens between 2.3 and 3 mya. These specimens are all classified in the australopithecine species named by Dart—*A. africanus,* also known as **gracile australopithecines.**

The reconstruction of australopithecine biology is controversial. Some researchers think they see evidence for some expansion of the brain in *A. africanus,* while others vigorously disagree. Paleoanthropologists also compare the outside appearance of the brain, as revealed by casts of the insides of skulls. Some researchers suggest that cerebral reorganization toward a human condition is present,[10] while others argue the organization of the brain is more apelike than human.[11] At the moment, the weight of the evidence favors mental capabilities for all gracile australopithecines as being comparable to those of modern great apes (chimps, bonobos, gorillas, orangutans).

Using patterns of tooth eruption in young australopithecines such as Taung, paleoanthropologist Alan Mann and colleagues suggest that the developmental pattern of australopithecines was more humanlike than apelike,[12] though some other paleoanthropologists do not agree. Evidence from the recent discovery of the young *A. afarensis* specimen (Lucy's baby) will help scientists to resolve this debate. Our current understanding of genetics and the macroevolutionary process indicates that a developmental shift is likely to have accompanied a change in body plan such as the emergence of bipedalism among the African hominoids.

Other South African sites have yielded fossils whose skulls and teeth looked quite different from the gracile australopithecines described above. These South African fossils are known as *Australopithecus robustus.* They are notable for having teeth, jaws, and chewing muscles that are massive (robust) relative to the size of the braincase. The gracile forms are slightly smaller on average and lack such robust chewing structures. Over the course of evolution, several distinct groups of **robust australopithecines** have appeared not only in South Africa, but throughout East Africa as well.

Robust Australopithecines

The remains of robust australopithecines were first found at Kromdraai and Swartkrans by South African paleoanthropologists Robert Broom and John Robinson in the 1930s in deposits that, unfortunately, cannot be securely dated. Current thinking puts them between 1 and 1.8 mya. Usually referred to as *A. robustus* (see Table 7.1), this species possessed a characteristic robust chewing apparatus including a **sagittal crest** running from front to back along the top of the skull (Figure 7.11). This feature provides sufficient area on a relatively small braincase for attachment of the huge temporal muscles required to operate powerful jaws. Present in robust australopithecines and gorillas today, the sagittal crest feature provides an example of convergent evolution.

[12] Mann, A., Lampl, M., & Monge, J. (1990). Patterns of ontogeny in human evolution: Evidence from dental development. *Yearbook of Physical Anthropology 33,* 111–150.

gracile australopithecines Members of the genus *Australopithecus* possessing a more lightly built chewing apparatus; likely had a diet that included more meat than that of the robust *australopithecines*; best represented by the South African species *A. africanus.*

robust australopithecines Several species within the genus *Australopithecus,* who lived from 2.5 to 1.1 million years ago in eastern and southern Africa; known for the rugged nature of their chewing apparatus (large back teeth, large chewing muscles, and a bony ridge on their skull tops for the insertion of these large muscles).

sagittal crest A crest running from front to back on the top of the skull along the midline to provide a surface of bone for the attachment of the large temporal muscles for chewing.

[9] Clarke, R. J., & Tobias, P. V. (1995). Sterkfontein member 2 foot bones of the oldest South African hominid. *Science 269,* 521–524.

[10] Holloway, R. L., & de LaCoste-Lareymondie, M. C. (1982). Brain endocast asymmetry in pongids and hominids: Some preliminary findings on the paleontology of cerebral dominance. *American Journal of Physical Anthropology 58,* 101–110.

[11] Falk, D. (1989). Apelike endocast of "ape-man" Taung. *American Journal of Physical Anthropology 80,* 335–339.

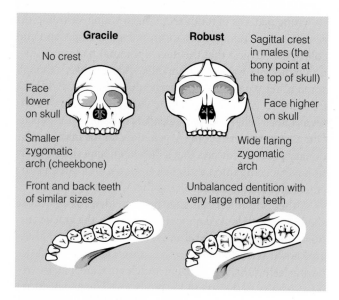

Figure 7.11 The differences between gracile and robust australopithecines are related primarily to their chewing apparatus. Robust species have extremely large cheek teeth, large chewing muscles, and a bony ridge on the top of their skulls for the attachment of large temporal muscles for chewing. The front and back teeth of gracile species are balanced in size, and their chewing muscles (reflected in a less massive skull) are more like those seen in the later genus *Homo*. If you place your own hands on the sides of your skull above your ears while opening and closing your jaw, you can feel where your temporal muscles attach to your skull. By moving your hands toward the top of your skull you can feel where these muscles end in humans.

The first robust australopithecine to be found in East Africa was discovered by Mary Leakey in the summer of 1959, the centennial year of the publication of Darwin's *On the Origin of Species*. She found it in Olduvai Gorge, a fossil-rich area near Ngorongoro Crater, on the Serengeti Plain of Tanzania. Olduvai is a huge gash in the earth, about 40 kilometers (25 miles) long and 91 meters (300 feet) deep, which cuts through Plio-Pleistocene and recent geologic strata revealing close to 2 million years of the earth's history.

Mary Leakey's discovery was reconstructed by her husband Louis, who gave it the name *Zinjanthropus boisei* (*Zinj*, an old Arabic name for "East Africa," *boisei* after the benefactor who funded their expedition). At first, he thought this ancient fossil seemed more humanlike than *Australopithecus* and extremely close to modern humans in evolutionary development, in part due to the stone tools found in association with this specimen. Further study, however, revealed that *Zinjanthropus*, the remains of which consisted of a skull and a few limb bones, was an East African species of robust australopithecine. Although similar in many ways to *A. robustus*, Zinj is now most commonly referred to as *Australopithecus boisei* (see Table 7.1). Potassium-argon dating places this early species at about 1.75 million years old.

Since the time of Mary Leakey's original *A. boisei* find, numerous other fossils of this robust species have been found at Olduvai, as well as north and east of Lake Turkana in Kenya.

© John Reader/Photo Researchers Inc.

The robust australopithecines and the earliest members of genus *Homo* inhabited the earth at the same time. These skulls and leg bones were all found along the eastern shores of Lake Turkana in Kenya and are dated to between 1.7 and 1.9 mya. The two specimens with the rounded skulls are classified by many paleoanthropologists as members of the species *Homo habilis*. The robust australopithecine at the top of the photograph has the bony ridge along the top of its skull.

Although one fossil specimen often referred to as the "Black Skull" (see *A. aethiopicus* in Table 7.1) is known to be as much as 2.5 million years old, some date to as recently as 1.1 mya.

Like robust australopithecines from South Africa, East African robust forms possessed enormous molars and premolars. Despite a large mandible and palate, the anterior teeth (canines and incisors) were often crowded, owing to the room needed for the massive molars.

The heavy skull, more massive even than seen in the robust forms from South Africa, has a sagittal crest and prominent brow ridges. Cranial capacity ranges from about 500 to 530 cubic centimeters. Body size, too, is somewhat larger; whereas the South African robust forms are estimated to have weighed between 32 and 40 kilograms, the East African robusts probably weighed from 34 to 49 kilograms.

Because the earliest robust skull from East Africa (2.5 million years old), the so-called Black Skull from Kenya, retains a number of ancestral features shared with earlier East African australopithecines, it is possible that it evolved from *A. afarensis*, giving rise to the later robust East African forms. Whether the South African robust australopithecines represent a southern offshoot of the East African line or

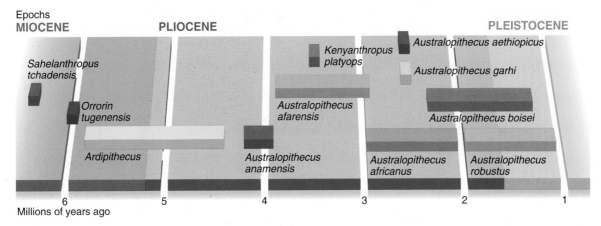

Epochs
MIOCENE **PLIOCENE** **PLEISTOCENE**

Sahelanthropus tchadensis

Orrorin tugenensis

Ardipithecus

Australopithecus anamensis

Australopithecus afarensis

Kenyanthropus platyops

Australopithecus aethiopicus

Australopithecus garhi

Australopithecus boisei

Australopithecus africanus

Australopithecus robustus

6   5   4   3   2   1

Millions of years ago

Figure 7.12 The Pliocene fossil bipeds and the scientific names by which they have been known, arranged according to when they lived. *A. aethiopicus*, *A. boisei*, and *A. robustus* are all robust australopithecines. Whether the different species names are warranted is a matter of debate.

convergent evolution from a South African ancestor has not been settled; arguments can be presented for both interpretations. In either case, what happened was that the later robust australopithecines developed molars and premolars that are both absolutely and relatively larger than those of earlier australopithecines who possessed front and back teeth more in proportion to those seen in the genus *Homo.*

Larger teeth require more bone to support them, hence the prominent jaws of the robust australopithecines. Larger jaws and heavy chewing activity require more jaw musculature that attaches to the skull. The marked crests seen on skulls of the late australopithecines provide for the attachment of chewing muscles on a skull that has increased very little in size. In effect, robust australopithecines had evolved into highly efficient chewing machines. Clearly, their immense cheek teeth and powerful chewing muscles bespeak the heavy chewing required for a diet of uncooked plant foods. This general level of biological organization shared by separate fossil groups as seen in the robust australopithecines is referred to as a *grade.*

Many anthropologists believe that, by becoming a specialized consumer of plant foods, the late australopithecines avoided competing for the same niche with early *Homo,* with which they were contemporaries. In the course of evolution, the **law of competitive exclusion** dictates that when two closely related species compete for the same niche, one will out-compete the other, bringing about the loser's extinction. That early *Homo* and late *Australopithecus* did not compete for the same niche is suggested by their coexistence for something like 1.5 million years from about 1 to 2.5 mya (Figure 7.12).

law of competitive exclusion When two closely related species compete for the same niche, one will out-compete the other, bringing about the latter's extinction.

Photographer David Brill, a specialist in images of fossils and paleoanthropologists at work, positions the upper jaw and the other skull fragments of *Australopithecus garhi* so that the fragments are aligned as they would be in a complete skull.

© T. White 1998

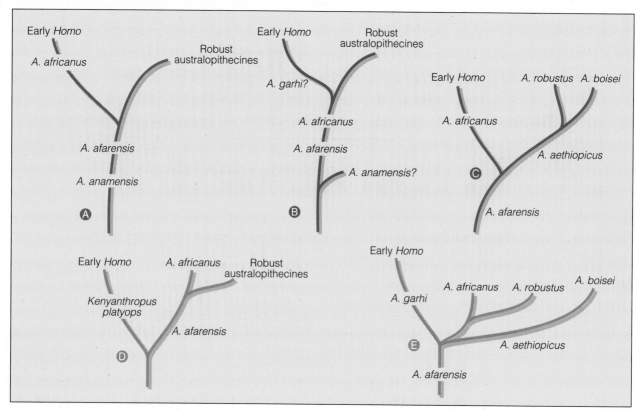

Figure 7.13 The relationship among the various australopithecine (and other) Pliocene groups, and the question of which group is ancestral to the genus *Homo*, are debated by anthropologists. Several alternative hypotheses are presented in these diagrams. Most agree, however, that the robust australopithecines represent an evolutionary side branch. *Ardipithecus ramidus* has been proposed as ancestral to the australopithecines.

Australopithecines and the Genus *Homo*

A variety of bipeds inhabited Africa about 2.5 mya, around the time the first evidence for the genus *Homo* begins to appear. In 1999, discoveries in East Africa added another australopithecine to the mix. Found in the Afar region of Ethiopia, these fossils were named *Australopithecus garhi* from the word for "surprise" in the local Afar language. Though the teeth were large, this australopithecine possessed an arched dental arcade and a ratio between front and back teeth more like humans and South African gracile australopithecines rather than like robust groups. For this reason, some have proposed that *A. garhi* is ancestral to the genus *Homo*. More evidence will be needed to prove whether or not this is true.

Precise relationships among all the australopithecine species (and other bipeds) that have been defined during the Pliocene are still not settled. In this mix, the question of which australopithecine was ancestral to humans remains particularly controversial. A variety of scenarios have been proposed, each one giving a different australopithecine group the starring role as the immediate human ancestor

(Figure 7.13). Though paleoanthropologists debate which species is ancestral to humans, they agree that the robust australopithecines, though successful in their time, ultimately represent an evolutionary side branch.

Environment, Diet, and Origins of the Human Line

Having described the fossil material, we may now consider how evolution transformed an early ape into a hominin. Generally, such paleoanthropological reconstructions and hypotheses about the origin of bipedalism rely heavily on the evolutionary role of natural selection. The question at hand is not so much *why* bipedalism developed as much as *how* bipedalism allowed these ancestors to adapt to their environment.

Hypotheses about adaptation begin with features evident in the fossil evidence. For example, the fossil record indicates that once bipedalism appeared, over the next several million years the shape of the face and teeth shifted from a more apelike to a humanlike condition. To refine their hypotheses, paleoanthropologists add to the fossil evidence through scientific reconstructions of environmental conditions and inferences made from data gathered on living nonhuman primates and humans. In this regard, evolutionary reconstructions involve piecing together a coherent story or narrative about the past. Sometimes these narratives are tenuous. But as paleoanthropologists consider their own biases and incorporate new evidence as it is discovered, the quality of the narrative improves.

For many years, the human evolutionary narrative has been tied to the emergence of the savannah environment in eastern Africa as the global climate changes of the Miocene led to increasingly cooler and dryer conditions. While the evidence from *Ardipithecus* shows that the earliest members of the human line were forest dwellers, over time the size of tropical forests decreased or, more commonly, broke up into mosaics where patches of forest were interspersed with savannah or other types of open country. The forebears of the human line are thought to have lived in places with access to both trees and open country. With the breaking up of forests, these early ancestors found themselves spending more and more time on the ground and had to adapt to this new, more open environment.

The most obvious problem facing these ancestors in their new situation, other than getting from one patch of trees to another, was getting food. As the forest thinned or shrank, the traditional ape-type foods found in trees became less available, especially in seasons of reduced rainfall. Therefore, it became more and more necessary to forage on the ground for foods such as seeds, grasses, and roots. With reduced canine teeth, early bipeds were relatively defenseless when down on the ground and were easy targets for numerous carnivorous predators. That predators were a problem is revealed by the South African fossils, most of which are from individuals that were dropped into rock fissures by leopards or, in the case of Dart's original find, by an eagle.

Many investigators have argued that the hands of early bipeds took over the weapon functions of the reduced canine teeth. Hands enabled them to threaten predators by using wooden objects as clubs and throwing stones. This quality is shared with many of the other hominoids. Recall the male chimpanzee (Chapter 4) who wielded objects as part of his display to obtain alpha status. In australopithecines the use of clubs and throwing stones may have set the stage for the much later manufacture of more efficient weapons from bone, wood, and stone.

Although the hands of the later australopithecines were suitable for tool making, no evidence exists that any of them actually *made* stone tools. Similarly, experiments with captive bonobos have shown that they are capable of making crude chipped stone tools, but they have never been known to do so outside of captivity. Thus to be able to do something is not necessarily equivalent to doing it.

In fact, the earliest known stone tools, dating to about 2.5 mya, are about 2 million years more recent than the oldest fossils of *Australopithecus*. However, *Australopithecus* certainly had no less intelligence and dexterity than do modern great apes, all of whom make use of tools when it is to their advantage to do so. Orangutans, bonobos, chimpanzees, and even gorillas have all been observed in the wild making and using simple tools such as those described in Chapter 4. Most likely, the ability to make and use simple tools is something that goes back to the last common ancestor of the Asian and African apes, before the appearance of the first bipeds.

It is reasonable to suppose, then, that australopithecine tool use was similar to that of the other great apes. Unfortunately, few tools that they used are likely to have survived for a million and more years, and any that did would be hard to recognize as such. Although we cannot be certain about this, in addition to clubs and objects thrown for defense, sturdy sticks may have been used to dig edible roots, and convenient stones may have been used (as some chimpanzees do) to crack open nuts. In fact, some animal bones from australopithecine sites in South Africa show microscopic wear patterns suggesting their use to dig edible roots from the ground. We may also allow the possibility that, like chimpanzees, females may have used tools more often to get and process food than males, but the latter may have used tools more often as "weapons."[13] The female chimpanzees who hunted with spears as described in Chapter 4 call into question these distinct roles for the sexes.

Humans Stand on Their Own Two Feet

From the broad-shouldered, long-armed, tailless ape body plan, the human line became fully bipedal. Our late Miocene forebears seem to have been primates that combined quadrupedal tree climbing with perhaps some swinging below the branches. On the ground, they were capable of assuming an upright stance, at least on occasion (optional, versus obligatory, bipedalism).

Paleoanthropologists generally take the negative aspects of bipedal locomotion into account when considering the advantages of this pattern of locomotion. For example, paleoanthropologists have suggested that bipedalism makes an animal more visible to predators, exposes its soft underbelly or gut, and interferes with the ability to instantly change direction while running. They also

[13] Goodall, J. (1986). *The chimpanzees of Gombe: Patterns of behavior* (pp. 552, 564). Cambridge, MA: Belknap.

emphasize that bipedalism does not result in particularly fast running; quadrupedal chimpanzees and baboons, for example, are 30 to 34 percent faster than we bipeds. For 100-meter distances, our best athletes today may attain speeds of 34 to 37 kilometers per hour, while the larger African carnivores from which bipeds might need to run can attain speeds up to 60 to 70 kilometers per hour. The consequences of a leg or foot injury are more serious for a biped while a quadruped can do amazingly well on three legs. A biped with only one functional leg is seriously hindered—an easy meal for some carnivore.

Because each of these drawbacks would have placed our early ancestors at risk from predators, paleoanthropologists have asked what made bipedal locomotion worth paying such a high price. It is hard to imagine bipedalism becoming a viable adaptation in the absence of strong selective pressure in its favor; therefore, a number of theories have been proposed to account for the adaptive advantages of bipedalism.

One once-popular suggestion is that bipedal locomotion allowed males to gather food on the savannah and transport it back to females, who were restricted from doing so by the dependence of their offspring.[14] This explanation is unlikely, however, because female apes, not to mention women among food-foraging peoples, routinely combine infant care with foraging for food. Indeed, among most food foragers, it is the women who commonly supply the bulk of the food eaten by both sexes.

Moreover, the pair bonding (one male attached to one female) presumed by this model is not characteristic of terrestrial primates, nor of those displaying the degree of sexual dimorphism that was characteristic of *Australopithecus*. Nor is it really characteristic of *Homo sapiens*. In a substantial majority of recent human societies, including those in which people forage for their food, some form of polygamy—marriage to two or more individuals at the same time—is not only permitted but preferred. And even in the supposedly monogamous United States, it is relatively common for an individual to marry (and hence mate with) two or more others (the only requirement is that he or she not be married to more than one mate at the same time).

Although we may reject as culture-bound the idea of male breadwinners provisioning stay-at-home moms, it is true that bipedal locomotion does make transport of bulky foods possible. (See the Biocultural Connection for another example of the influence of socially defined roles and theories about the evolution of human childbirth.) Nevertheless, a fully erect biped on the ground—whether male or female—has the ability to gather such foods for transport back to a tree or other place of safety for

consumption. The biped does not have to remain out in the open, exposed and vulnerable, to do all of its eating.

Besides making it possible to carry food, bipedalism could have facilitated the food quest in other ways. With their hands free and body upright, the animals could reach otherwise unobtainable food on thorny trees too flimsy and too spiny to climb. Furthermore, with both hands free, they could gather other small foods more quickly using both hands. And in times of scarcity, being able to see farther, with the head in an upright position, would have helped them locate food and water sources.

Food may not have been the only thing transported by early bipeds. As we saw in Chapters 3 and 4, primate infants must be able to cling to their mothers in order to be carried; because the mother is using her forelimbs in locomotion, to either walk or swing, she cannot hold her infant as well. Chimpanzee infants, for example, must cling by themselves to their mother, and even up to 4 years of age, they make long journeys on their mother's back. Injuries caused by falling from the mother are a significant cause of infant mortality among apes. Thus the ability to carry infants would have made a significant contribution to the survivorship of offspring, and the ancestors of *Australopithecus* would have been capable of doing just this.

Another suggestion—that bipedal locomotion arose as an adaptation for nonterritorial scavenging of meat[15]—is unlikely. Although it is true that a biped is able to travel long distances without tiring, and that a daily supply of dead animal carcasses would have been available to early bipeds only if they were capable of ranging over vast areas, no evidence exists to indicate that they did much in the way of scavenging prior to about 2.5 mya. Furthermore, the heavy wear seen on australopithecine teeth is indicative of a diet high in tough, fibrous plant foods. Thus scavenging was likely an unforeseen byproduct of bipedal locomotion, rather than a cause of it.

Although bipedalism appeared before our ancestors lived in the savannah, it is still possible that bipedalism served as a means to cope with heat stress out in the open as the forested environments disappeared. In addition to bipedalism, one of the most obvious differences between humans and other living hominoids is our relative nakedness. Body hair in humans is generally limited to a fine sparse layer over most of the body with a very dense cover of hair limited primarily to the head. Peter Wheeler, a British physiologist, has suggested that bipedalism and the human pattern of body hair growth are both adaptations to the heat stress of the savannah environment.[16] Building upon the earlier "radiator" theory of paleoanthropologist

[14] Lovejoy, C. O. (1981). The origin of man. *Science 211*, 341–350.

[15] Lewin, R. (1987). Four legs good, two legs bad. *Science 235*, 969–971.

[16] Quoted in Folger, T. (1993). The naked and bipedal. *Discover 14* (11), 34–35. Reprinted with permission.

Evolution and Human Birth

Because biology and culture have always shaped human experience, it can be a challenge to separate the influences of each of these factors on human practices. For example, in the 1950s, paleoanthropologists developed the theory that human childbirth is particularly difficult compared to birth in other mammals. This theory was based in part on the observation of a "tight fit" between the human mother's birth canal and the baby's head, though several other primates also possess similarly tight fits between the newborn's head or shoulders and the birth canal. Nevertheless, changes in the birth canal associated with bipedalism coupled with the evolution of large brains were held responsible for difficult birth in humans.

At the same historical moment, American childbirth practices were changing. In one generation from the 1920s to the 1950s, birth shifted from the home to the hospital. In the process childbirth transformed from something a woman normally accomplished at home, perhaps with the help of a midwife or relatives, into the high-tech delivery of a neonate (the medical term for a newborn) with the assistance of medically trained personnel. Women in the 1950s were generally fully anesthetized during the birth process.

Paleoanthropological theories mirrored the cultural norms, providing a scientific explanation for the change in American childbirth practices.

As a scientific theory, the idea of difficult human birth stands on shaky ground. No fossil neonates have ever been recovered, and only a handful of complete pelves (the bones forming the birth canal) exist. Instead, scientists must examine the birth process in living humans and nonhuman primates to reconstruct the evolution of the human birth pattern.

Cultural beliefs and practices, however, shape every aspect of birth. Cultural factors determine where a birth occurs, the actions of the individuals present, and beliefs about the nature of the experience. When paleoanthropologists of the 1950s and 1960s asserted that human childbirth is more difficult than birth in other mammals, they may have been drawing upon their own cultural beliefs that childbirth is dangerous and belongs in a hospital.

A quick look at global neonatal mortality statistics indicates that in countries such as the Netherlands and Sweden, healthy well-nourished women give birth successfully outside of hospitals, as they did throughout human evolutionary history. In other countries, deaths related to childbirth reflect malnutrition, infectious disease, and the low social status of women, rather than an inherently faulty biology.

Man Ray (1890–1976) © ARS, NY. Statuette of Ixcuina, Mexican Goddess of Maternity. 1890–1941. Gelatin silver print, 9-1/16 x 6-7/8". Gift of James Thrall Soby (204.1991). Digital Image © The Museum of Modern Art/Licensed by SCALA/Art Resource, NY/Artists Rights Society (ARS)

Tlazolteotl, the earth mother goddess of the Aztecs, is depicted here giving birth in a squatting position, which is favored by women throughout the world. For hospital births, women generally have to work against gravity to bring a child in the world, as they tend to be placed on their backs with their legs in stirrups for the benefit of attending physicians.

BIOCULTURAL QUESTION

Though well-nourished healthy women successfully birth their babies outside of hospital settings, Caesarean section (C-section) rates have been rising in industrialized societies. In the United States one in three births is by C-section. The C-section rates in many Latin American countries are greater than 50 percent of all births. What cultural factors have led to this practice? Would your personal approach to birth change with the knowledge that humans have successfully adapted to childbirth?

Dean Falk, Wheeler developed this hypothesis through comparative anatomy, experimental studies, and the observation that humans are the only apes to inhabit the savannah environment today.

Many other animals, however, inhabit the savannah, and each of them possesses some mechanism for coping with heat stress. Some animals, like many of the carnivores, are active only when the sun is low in the sky, early

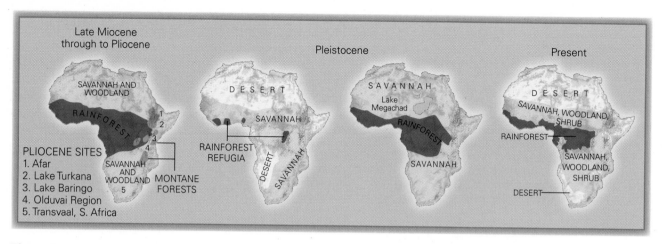

Figure 7.14 Since the late Miocene, the vegetation zones of Africa have changed considerably.

or late in the day, or when it is absent altogether at night. Some, like antelope, are evolved to tolerate high body temperatures that would kill humans due to overheating of the brain tissue. They accomplish this through cooling their blood in their muzzles through evaporation before it enters the vessels leading to the delicate tissues of the brain.

According to Wheeler, the interesting thing about humans and other primates is that

> We can't uncouple brain temperature from the rest of the body, the way an antelope does, so we've got to prevent any damaging elevations in body temperature. And of course the problem is even more acute for an ape, because in general, the larger and more complex the brain, the more easily it is damaged. So, there were incredible selective pressures on early hominids favoring adaptations that would reduce thermal stress-pressures that may have favored bipedalism.[17]

The idea that bipedal posture reduces the amount of heat to which humans are exposed is not completely new, but Wheeler has scientifically studied this phenomenon. He took a systematic series of measurements on the exposure of an early biped, like Lucy, to solar radiation in upright and quadrupedal stances. He found that the bipedal stance reduced exposure to solar radiation by 60 percent, indicating that a biped would require less water to stay cool in a savannah environment compared to a quadruped.

Wheeler further suggests that bipedalism made the human body hair pattern possible. Fur can keep out solar radiation as well as retaining heat. A biped, with reduced exposure to the sun everywhere except the head, would benefit from hair loss on the body surface to increase the efficiency of sweating to cool down. On the head, hair serves as a shield, blocking the solar radiation.

An objection to the above scenario might be that when bipedalism developed, savannah was not as extensive in Africa as it is today (Figure 7.14). In both East and South Africa, environments included closed and open bush and woodlands. Moreover, fossil flora and fauna found with *Ardipithecus* and the possible human ancestors from the Miocene are typical of a moist, closed, wooded habitat.

However, the presence of bipedalism in the fossil record without a savannah environment does not indicate that bipedalism was not adaptive to these conditions. It merely indicates that bipedalism appeared without any particular adaptive benefits at first, likely through a random macromutation. Bipedalism provided a body plan preadapted to the heat stress of the savannah environment.

In an earlier era of human evolutionary studies, larger brains were thought to have permitted the evolution of bipedalism. Around the mid-20th century, theories for the adaptability of bipedalism involved a feedback loop between tool use, brain expansion, and free hands brought about by bipedalism. We now know not only that bipedality preceded the evolution of larger brains by several million years, but we can also consider the possibility that bipedalism may have preadapted human ancestors for brain expansion. According to Wheeler,

> The brain is one of the most metabolically active tissues in the body. . . . In the case of humans it accounts for something like 20 percent of total energy consumption. So you've got an organ producing a lot of heat that you've got to dump. Once we'd become bipedal and naked and achieved this ability to dump heat, that may have allowed the expansion of the brain that took place later in human evolution. It didn't cause it, but you can't have a large brain unless you can cool it.[18]

[17] Ibid.

[18] Ibid.

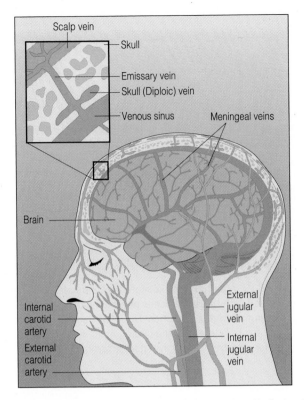

Figure 7.15 **In humans, blood from the face and scalp, instead of returning directly to the heart, may be directed instead into the braincase and then to the heart. Already cooled at the surface of the skin, blood is able to carry heat away from the brain.**

Consistent with Wheeler's hypothesis is the fact that the system for drainage of the blood from the cranium of the earlier australopithecines is significantly different from that of the genus *Homo* (Figure 7.15).

Though paleoanthropologists cannot resolve every detail of the course of human evolution from the available data, over time the narrative they have constructed has improved. Human evolution evidently took place in fits and starts, rather than at a steady pace. Today we know that bipedalism preceded brain expansion by several million years. Bipedalism likely occurred as a sudden shift in body plan, while the tempo for the evolution of brain size differed considerably. For example, fragments of an *Australopithecus* skull dated to 3.9 million years old are virtually identical to the corresponding skull fragments a million years later. Evidently, once a viable bipedal adaptation was achieved, stabilizing selection took over, and there was little change for at least a few million years.

Then, 2.5 mya, change was again in the works, resulting in the branching out of new forms, including several robust species as well as the first appearance of the genus *Homo*. But again, from about 2.3 mya until robust

australopithecines became extinct around 1 mya, the robust forms underwent relatively little change.[19]

Evidently, the pattern in early human evolution has been relatively short periods of marked change with diversification, separated by prolonged periods of relative stasis or stability in the surviving species. While robust australopithecines continued this pattern, the new genus *Homo* began a steady course of brain expansion that continued over the next 2.3 million years until brain size reached its current state. With the appearance of this new larger-brained hominin, the first stone tools appear in the archaeological record.

Early Representatives of the Genus *Homo*

Just as the Leakeys thought, Olduvai Gorge with its stone tool assemblages was a good place to search for human ancestors. Part of what is now Olduvai Gorge was once a lake. Almost 2 mya, its shores were inhabited by numerous wild animals including a variety of bipeds. In 1959—when the Leakeys found the bones of the first specimen of robust *Australopithecus boisei* in association with some of these tools and the bones of birds, reptiles, antelopes, and pigs—they thought they had found the remains of one of the toolmakers. Fossils unearthed a few months later and a few feet below this first discovery led them to change their mind.

These fossil remains consisted of more than one individual, including a few cranial bones, a lower jaw, a clavicle, some finger bones (Figure 7.16), and the nearly complete left foot of an adult (Figure 7.17). Skull and jaw fragments indicated that these specimens represented a larger-brained biped without the specialized chewing apparatus of the robust australopithecines.

The Leakeys and colleagues named that contemporary *Homo habilis* (Latin for "handy man") and suggested that tool-wielding *H. habilis* may have eaten the animals and possibly had the *Australopithecus boisei* for dessert. Of course, we do not really know whether *A. boisei* from Olduvai Gorge met its end in this way, but we do know that cut marks from a stone tool are present on a 2.4-million-year-old australopithecine jaw bone from South Africa.[20] This was done, presumably, to remove the mandible, but for what purpose we do not know. In any event, it does lend credibility to the idea of *A. boisei* on occasion being dismembered by *H. habilis*.

Subsequent work at Olduvai has unearthed not only more skull fragments but other parts of the skeleton of

[19] Wood, B., Wood, C., & Konigsberg, L. (1994). *Paranthropus boisei*: An example of evolutionary stasis? *American Journal of Physical Anthropology 95*, 134.

[20] White, T. D., & Toth, N. (2000). Cutmarks on a Plio-Pleistocene hominid from Sterkfontein, South Africa. *American Journal of Physical Anthropology 111*, 579–584.

Juvenile gorilla　　Olduvai hominin　　Modern human

Figure 7.16 A comparison of hand bones of a juvenile gorilla, *Homo habilis* from Olduvai, and a modern human, highlights important differences in the structure of fingers and thumbs. In the top row are fingers, and in the second row are terminal (end) thumb bones. Although terminal finger bones are more human, lower finger bones are more curved and powerful. The bottom row compares thumb length and angle relative to the index finger.

Figure 7.17 A partial foot skeleton of *Homo habilis* (center) is compared with the same bones of a chimpanzee (left) and modern human (right). Note how *H. habilis'* bone at the base of the great toe is in line with the others, as in modern humans, making for effective walking but poor grasping.

H. habilis as well. Since the late 1960s, fossils of the genus *Homo* that are essentially contemporaneous with those from Olduvai have been found elsewhere in Africa, such as South Africa, Ethiopia, and several sites in Kenya.

The eastern shores of Lake Turkana, on the border between Kenya and Ethiopia, have been particularly rich with fossils from earliest *Homo*. One of the best of these fossils, known as KNM ER 1470, was discovered by the Leakeys' son Richard at Koobi Fora. (The letters KNM stand for Kenya National Museum; the ER, for East Rudolf, the name for Lake Turkana during the colonial era in Kenya.) The deposits in which it was found are about 1.9 million years old; these deposits, like those at Olduvai, also contain crude stone tools. The KNM ER 1470 skull is more modern in appearance than any *Australopithecus* skull and has a cranial capacity of 752 cubic centimeters (cc).

However, the large teeth and face of this specimen resemble the earlier australopithecines.

From this same site another well-preserved skull from the same time period (KNM ER 1813) possesses a cranial capacity of less than 600 cc but has the derived characteristics of a smaller, less projecting face and teeth (both of these specimens are shown in the photo on page 160). Though specimens attributed to *H. habilis* generally have cranial capacities greater than 600 cc, the cranial capacity of any individual is also in proportion to its body size. Therefore, many paleoanthropologists interpret KNM ER 1813 and ER 1470 as a female and male of a very sexually dimorphic species, with the smaller cranial capacity of KNM ER 1813 a reflection of her smaller body size (Figure 7.18).

Lumpers or Splitters?

Other paleoanthropologists do not agree with placing specimens as diverse as KNM ER 1813 and KNM ER 1470 in the single taxonomic group of *H. habilis*. Instead they feel that the diversity represented in these specimens warrants separating the fossils like the larger-brained KNM ER 1470 into a distinct coexisting group called *Homo*

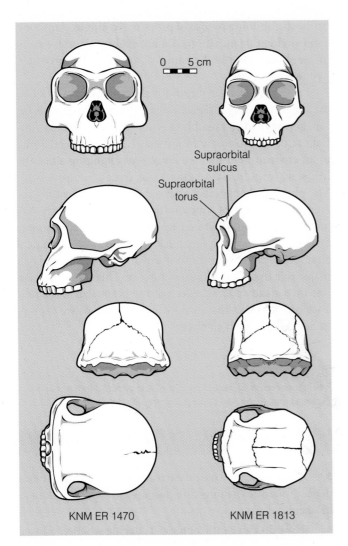

0   5 cm

Supraorbital
sulcus

Supraorbital
torus

KNM ER 1470   KNM ER 1813

Figure 7.18 The KNM ER 1470 skull—one of the most complete skulls of *Homo habilis*—is close to 2 million years old and is probably a male; it contrasts with the considerably smaller KNM ER 1813 skull, probably a female. Some paleoanthropologists feel this variation is too great to place these specimens in the same species.

rudolphensis. Whether one chooses to call these or any other contemporary fossils *Homo rudolphensis* or *Homo habilis* is more than a name game. Fossil names indicate researchers' perspectives about evolutionary relationships among groups. When specimens are given separate species names, it signifies that they form part of a reproductively isolated group.

Some paleoanthropologists approach the fossil record with the perspective that making such detailed biological determinations is arbitrary and that variability exists within any group.[21] Arguing that it is impossible to prove

whether a collection of ancient bones and teeth represents a distinct species, these paleoanthropologists tend to be "lumpers," placing similar-looking fossil specimens together in more inclusive groups. For example, gorillas show a degree of sexual dimorphism that lumpers attribute to *H. habilis.* "Splitters," by contrast, focus on the variation in the fossil record, interpreting minor differences in the shape of skeletons or skulls as evidence of distinct biological species with corresponding cultural capacities. Referring to the variable shape of the bony ridge above ancient eyes, South African paleoanthropologist Philip Tobias has quipped, "Splitters will create a new species at the drop of a brow ridge."[22] Splitting has the advantage of specificity while lumping has the advantage of simplicity. We will use a lumping approach throughout our discussion of the genus *Homo.*

Differences Between Early *Homo* and *Australopithecus*

By 2.4 mya, the evolution of the genus *Homo* was proceeding in a different direction from that of *Australopithecus.* In terms of body size, early *Homo* differs little from *Australopithecus.* Although early *Homo* had teeth that are large by modern standards—or even by those of a half-million years ago—they are smaller in relation to the size of the skull than those of any australopithecine. Early *Homo* also had undergone enlargement of the brain indicating that early *Homo's* mental abilities probably exceeded those of *Australopithecus.* Early *Homo* likely possessed a marked increase in ability to learn and to process information compared with australopithecines.

The later robust australopithecines from East and South Africa that coexisted with early *Homo* evolved into more specialized "grinding machines" with massive jaws and back teeth for processing plant foods. Robust australopithecine brain size did not change, nor is there firm evidence that they made stone tools. Thus in the period between 1 and 2.5 mya, two kinds of bipeds were headed in very different evolutionary directions: the robust australopithecines, specializing in plant foods and ultimately becoming extinct, and the genus *Homo,* with expanding cranial capacity, a varied diet that included meat, and the earliest evidence for stone tool making.

Without stone tools early *Homo* could eat few animals (only those that could be skinned by tooth or nail); therefore, their diet was limited in terms of animal protein. On the arid savannah, it is hard for a primate with a humanlike digestive system to satisfy its protein requirements from available plant resources. Moreover,

---

[21] Miller, J. M. A. (2000). Craniofacial variation in *Homo habilis:* An analysis of the evidence for multiple species. *American Journal of Physical Anthropology 112,* 122.

[22] Personal communication.

failure to do so has serious consequences: stunted growth, malnutrition, starvation, and death. Leaves and legumes (nitrogen-fixing plants, familiar modern examples being beans and peas) provide the most readily accessible plant sources of protein. The problem is that these raw plants are difficult for primates to digest; substances in the leaves and legumes cause proteins to pass right through the gut without being absorbed unless cooked.[23]

Chimpanzees have a similar problem when out on the savannah. Even with canine teeth far larger and sharper than ours or those of early *Homo,* chimpanzees frequently have trouble tearing through the skin of other animals.[24] In savannah environments, chimps spend about a third of their time foraging for insects (ants and termites), eggs, and small vertebrate animals. Such animal foods not only are easily digestible, but they provide high-quality proteins that contain all the essential amino

acids, the building blocks of protein. No single plant food can provide this nutritional balance. Only a combination of plants can supply the range of amino acids provided by meat alone.

Lacking long, sharp teeth for shearing meat, our earliest ancestors likely foraged for insects, but sharp tools for butchering made it possible to efficiently eat meat. The initial use of tools by early *Homo* may be related to adapting to an environment that we know was changing since the Miocene from forests to grasslands (recall Figure 7.14).[25] The physical changes that adapted bipeds for spending increasing amounts of time on the new grassy terrain may have encouraged tool making. Thus with the appearance of the genus *Homo,* a feedback loop between biological characteristics and cultural innovations began to play a major role in our evolutionary history. This set the human line on a steady course of increasing brain size and a reliance on culture as the means of adaptation, as we explore in detail in the next chapter.

---

[23] Stahl, A. B. (1984). Hominid dietary selection before fire. *Current Anthropology 25,* 151–168.

[24] Goodall, p. 372.

---

[25] Behrensmeyer, A. K., et al. (1997). Late Pliocene faunal turnover in the Turkana basin, Kenya, and Ethiopia. *Science 278,* 1589–1594.

Questions for Reflection

1.   The spectacular 4.4-million-year-old Ardi specimen has captured our collective imagination. Does the fact that this specimen has a name and a face change how you respond to the scientific facts? How do these ancient bones, which we know as the individual Ardi, challenge us to think about what it means to be human? How does the splash made by Ardi challenge our understanding of the nature of human origin studies?

2.   Describe the anatomy of bipedalism, providing examples from head to toe of how bipedalism can be "diagnosed" from a single bone. Do you think evidence from a single bone is enough to determine whether an organism from the past was bipedal?

3.   Who were the robust australopithecines? What evidence is used to demonstrate that they are an evolutionary dead end?

4.   How do paleoanthropologists decide whether a fossil specimen from the distant past is male or female? Do our cultural ideas about males and females in the present affect the interpretation of behavior in human evolutionary history?

5.   Do you think that members of the genera *Ardipithecus* and *Australopithecus* were tool users? What evidence would you use to support a case for tool use in these early bipeds?

Suggested Readings

Falk, D. (2004). *Braindance: New discoveries about human origins and brain evolution—revised and updated.* Gainesville: University Press of Florida.

In this updated and expanded version of her 1994 book, Falk presents her radiator theory to account for the lag between the appearance of bipedalism and the increase in the size of the brain over the course of human evolutionary history.

Johanson, D. C., Edgar, B., & Brill, D. (1996). *From Lucy to language.* New York: Simon & Schuster.

This coffee-table-sized book includes more than 200 color pictures of major fossil discoveries along with a readable, intelligent discussion of many of the key issues in paleoanthropology.

Johanson, D. C., & Wong, K. (2009). *Lucy's legacy: The quest for human origins*. New York: Harmony.

The adventures of fossil hunters and scientific debate both shine in this accessible book. While it begins with Johanson's own discovery of Lucy, the book is notable for its balance. It presents both sides of many of paleoanthropology's recent controversies along with interesting and engaging profiles of the international scientists who are weaving together the story of our evolution.

Larsen, C. S., Matter, R. M., & Gebo, D. L. (1998). *Human origins: The fossil record*. Long Grove, IL: Waveland.

This volume covers all the major fossil discoveries relevant to the study of human origins beginning with the Miocene apes. It has detailed drawings and clear, brief descriptions of each specimen, introducing the reader to the nature of the fossil evidence.

Zimmer, C. (2005). *Smithsonian intimate guide to human origins*. New York: HarperCollins.

This book by science writer Carl Zimmer is an intelligent and engaging presentation of the evidence of human evolution that includes discoveries up to 2005. It is also beautifully illustrated.

Challenge Issue With the appearance of the genus *Homo* 2.5 million years ago, our ancestors—with their increased brain size and emerging cultural repertoire—were better able to meet the challenges of survival. We know that without this brain expansion, reliance on culture could not have occurred, but we are not certain of the exact relationship between biological change and cultural capacity. Does each cultural innovation mark the appearance of a new species? Does a 20 percent increase in brain tissue do the same? And what about all the cultural changes that have occurred after brain size reached modern proportions? These fossils from Sima de los Huesos ("Pit of the Bones"), Sierra de Atapuerca, Spain, are an important part of the puzzle. They are the best collection of *Homo* fossils from a single site. Although the remains possess cranial capacities overlapping with the average size of contemporary humans, the scientists who discovered them place them in the species *Homo antecessor*. Dated to 400,000 years ago, these fossils fit into the complex period of our evolutionary history when brain size and cultural capability began to separate.

Early *Homo* and the Origins of Culture

Chapter Preview

When, Where, and How Did the Genus *Homo* Develop?

Since the late 1960s, a number of sites in South and East Africa have produced the fossil remains of lightly built bipeds all but indistinguishable from the earlier gracile australopithecines, except that the teeth are smaller and the brain is significantly larger relative to body size. The earliest fossils to exhibit these trends appeared around 2.5 million years ago (mya), along with the earliest evidence of stone tool making. *Homo habilis* or "handy man" was the name given to the first members of the genus as a reflection of their toolmaking capacities. While paleoanthropologists debate the number of species of early *Homo* existing during this time period, most concur that the genus *Homo* developed from one of the smaller-brained bipedal australopithecines in Africa by 2.5 mya. By 1.8 mya, brain size along with cultural capabilities increased considerably, marking the appearance of the species *Homo erectus,* a fossil group that appears to have descended through variational change from *H. habilis.* Equipped with larger brains and more sophisticated tools, *H. erectus* spread from Africa into previously uninhabited regions of Eurasia and distinct regional features appear in the fossil record. Paleoanthropologists debate whether this variation constitutes separate species and the relationship of these ancestral forms to modern *Homo sapiens.* The controversy intensifies when it comes to Neandertals, the large-brained, robust, muscular members of the genus *Homo* from Southwest Asia and Europe.

What Were the Cultural Capabilities of Our Ancestors?

The archaeological record, starting with the oldest known artifacts—stone tools dated to between 2.5 and 2.6 mya from Gona, Ethiopia—provides tangible evidence of *H. habilis'* culture in the distant past. These mark the start of the Lower Paleolithic or Lower Stone Age. With the appearance of *H. erectus,* more sophisticated stone tools included the hand axe and other tools of the Acheulean industry along with innovations such as the controlled use of fire (for light, warmth, protection, and cooking), travel across bodies of water, and hunting with specialized tools. The Middle Paleolithic that followed is marked by a diversification of tool types and more sophisticated methods of fabrication. The best-known industry of this period, the Mousterian, began around 166,000 years ago and was used by *all* people—Neandertals as well as other members of the genus *Homo* said to possess more anatomically modern skulls—in Europe, North Africa, and Southwest Asia up until 40,000 years ago.

What Is the Relationship Between Biological Change and Cultural Change in the Genus *Homo*?

Paleoanthropological reconstructions of the culture and behavior of our ancestors are based on evidence about the environment; archaeological remains of tools, hearths, and shelters; and biological data about teeth, musculature, brain size and structure. Paleoanthropologists attribute the cultural change of making stone tools with the biological change of increased brain size because both appear at the same time in archaeological remains and fossil evidence. The fabrication and use of stone tools needed to crack open bones of animals for marrow or to butcher dead animals required improved eye–hand coordination and a precision grip. These behavioral abilities depended on the capacity to learn *and* communicate, which depended on larger, more complex brains. Once the brain size of genus *Homo* reached modern proportions between 200,000 and 400,000 years ago, the clear relationship between cultural capabilities and brain size uncoupled. Some fossil skulls retained a number of ancestral features, as well as some specialized features typically not seen in modern *Homo sapiens.* Archaeological evidence shows that cultures throughout the globe had become rich and varied. These ancient peoples produced tools for specific purposes and objects for purely symbolic use; they also practiced ceremonial activities and cared for the old and disabled.

Paleoanthropologists are faced with evidence that is often scant, enigmatic, or full of misleading and even contradictory clues. The quest for the origin of modern humans from more ancient bipeds confronts mysteries, none of which has been completely resolved to this day.

Some of the mystery stems from the kind of evolutionary change that was set in motion with the appearance of the genus *Homo.* Beginning 2.5 mya, several million years after the appearance of bipedalism separated the human evolutionary line from those of the other African apes, brain size of our ancestors began to increase. Simultaneously, these early ancestors increased their cultural manipulation of the physical world through their use of stone tools. These new bipeds were the first members of the genus *Homo.* Over time, they increasingly relied on cultural adaptation as a rapid and effective way to adjust to the environment.

While the evolution of culture became critical for human survival, it was intricately tied to underlying biological capacities, specifically the evolution of the human brain. Over the course of the next 2.2 million years, increasing brain size and specialization of function (evidence preserved in fossilized skulls) permitted the development of language, planning, new technologies, and artistic expression. With the evolution of a brain that made versatile behavior possible, members of the genus *Homo* became biocultural beings.

Biological anthropologist Misia Landau has noted that the human being can be thought of as the hero in the narrative of human evolutionary history.[1] The hero, or evolving human, is faced with a series of natural challenges that cannot be overcome from a strictly biological standpoint. Endowed with the gift of intelligence, the hero can meet these challenges and become fully human. In this narrative, cultural capabilities increasingly separate humans from other evolving animals. But biological change and cultural change are very different phenomena. Cultural equipment and techniques can develop rapidly with innovations occurring during the lifetime of individuals. By contrast, because it depends upon heritable traits, biological change requires many generations.

---

[1] Landau, M. (1991). *Narratives of human evolution.* New Haven, CT: Yale University Press.

Homo The genus of bipeds that appeared 2.5 million years ago, characterized by increased brain size compared to earlier bipeds. The genus is divided into various species based on features such as brain size, skull shape, and cultural capabilities.

Oldowan tool tradition The first stone tool industry, beginning between 2.5 and 2.6 million years ago.

percussion method A technique of stone tool manufacture performed by striking the raw material with a hammerstone or by striking raw material against a stone anvil to remove flakes.

Paleoanthropologists consider whether an evident cultural change, such as a new type of stone tool, corresponds to a major biological change, such as the appearance of a new species. Reconciling the relation between biological and cultural change is often a source of debate within paleoanthropology.

The Discovery of the First Stone Toolmaker

The renowned paleoanthropologists Louis and Mary Leakey began their search for human origins at Olduvai Gorge, Tanzania, because of the presence of crude stone tools found there. The tools were found in deposits dating back to very early in the Pleistocene epoch, which began almost 2 mya. The oldest tools found at Olduvai Gorge defined the **Oldowan tool tradition.**

These earliest identifiable tools consist of a number of implements made using a system of manufacture called the **percussion method** (Figure 8.1). Sharp-edged flakes were obtained from a stone (often a large, waterworn cobble) either by using another stone as a hammer (a hammerstone) or by striking the cobble against a large rock (anvil) to remove the flakes. The finished flakes had

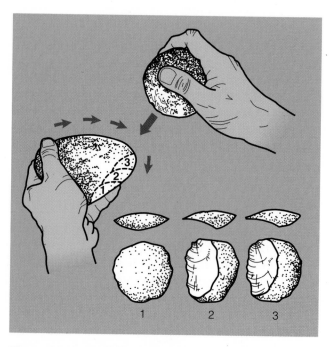

Figure 8.1 By 2.5 million years ago, early *Homo* in Africa had invented the percussion method of stone tool manufacture. This technological breakthrough, which is associated with a significant increase in brain size, made possible the butchering of meat from scavenged carcasses.

sharp edges, effective for cutting and scraping. Microscopic wear patterns show that these flakes were used for cutting meat, reeds, sedges, and grasses and for cutting and scraping wood. Small indentations on their surfaces suggest that the leftover cores were transformed into choppers for breaking open bones, and they may also have been employed to defend the user. The appearance of these tools marks the beginning of the **Lower Paleolithic,** the first part of the Old Stone Age.

The tools from Olduvai Gorge are not the oldest stone tools known. Paleoanthropologists have dated the start of the Lower Paleolithic to between 2.5 and 2.6 mya from similar assemblages recently discovered in Gona, Ethiopia. Lower Paleolithic tools have also been found in the vicinity of Lake Turkana in northwestern Kenya, in southern Ethiopia, as well as in other sites near Gona in the Afar Triangle of Ethiopia. Before this time, tool use among early bipeds probably consisted of heavy sticks to dig up roots or ward off animals, unshaped stones to throw for defense or to crack open nuts, and perhaps simple carrying devices made of knotted plant fibers. Perishable tools are not preserved in the archaeological record.

The makers of these early tools were highly skilled, consistently and efficiently producing many well-formed sharp-edged flakes from available raw materials with the least effort.[2] To do this the toolmaker had to have in mind an abstract idea of the tool to be made, as well as a specific set of steps to transform the raw material into finished product. Furthermore, the toolmaker would have to know which kinds of stone have the flaking properties that would allow the transformation to take place, as well as where such stone could be found.

Sometimes tool fabrication required the transport of raw materials over great distances. Such planning for the future undoubtedly was associated with natural selection favoring changes in brain structure. These changes mark the beginning of the genus *Homo.* As described in the previous chapter, **Homo habilis** was the name given to the oldest members of the genus by the Leakeys in 1959. With larger brains and the stone tools

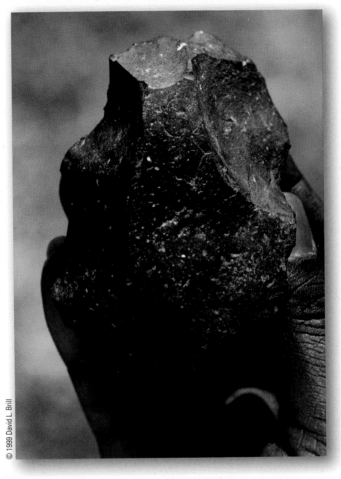

The oldest stone tools, dated to between 2.5 and 2.6 mya, were discovered in Gona, Ethiopia, by Ethiopian paleoanthropologist Sileshi Semaw.

© 1999 David L. Brill

preserved in the archaeological record, paleoanthropologists began to piece together a picture of the life of early *Homo.*

Sex, Gender, and the Behavior of Early *Homo*

When paleoanthropologists from the 1960s and 1970s depicted the lifeways of early *Homo,* they concentrated on "man the hunter," a tough guy with a killer instinct wielding tools on a savannah teeming with meat, while

Lower Paleolithic The first part of the Old Stone Age beginning with the earliest Oldowan tools spanning from about 200,000 or 250,000 to 2.6 million years ago.

Homo habilis "Handy man." The first fossil members of the genus *Homo* appearing 2.5 million years ago, with larger brains and smaller faces than australopithecines.

---

[2] Ambrose, S. H. (2001). Paleolithic technology and human evolution. *Science 291,* 1749.

In this artist's reconstruction separate roles are portrayed for males and females from early *Homo*. Do the roles depicted here derive from biological differences between the sexes or culturally established gender differences?

© The Field Museum Neg A102513C

the female members of the species stayed at home tending their young. Similarly, until the 1960s, most cultural anthropologists doing fieldwork among foragers stressed the role of male hunters and underreported the significance of female gatherers in providing food for

gender The cultural elaborations and meanings assigned to the biological differentiation between the sexes.

the community. Western notions of **gender,** the cultural elaborations and meanings assigned to the biological differentiation between the sexes, played a substantial role in creating these biases.

As anthropologists became aware of their own biases, they began to set the record straight, documenting the vital role of "woman the gatherer" in provisioning the social group in foraging cultures, past and present. (See this chapter's Biocultural Connection for the specific

---

Biocultural Connection

Sex, Gender, and Female Paleoanthropologists

Until the 1970s, the study of human evolution was permeated by a deep-seated bias reflecting the privileged status enjoyed by men in Western society. Beyond the obvious labeling of fossils as particular types of "men," irrespective of the sex of the individual represented, it took the form of portraying males as the active players in human evolution. Thus it was males who were seen as providers and innovators, using their wits to become ever-more effective suppliers of food and protection for passive females. The latter were seen as spending their time preparing food and caring for offspring, while the men were getting ahead by becoming ever smarter. Central to such thinking was the idea of "man the hunter," constantly honing his wits through the pursuit and killing of animals. Thus hunting by men was seen as the pivotal humanizing activity in evolution.

We now know that such ideas are culture-bound, reflecting the hopes and expectations of Euramerican culture in

the late 19th and early 20th centuries. This recognition came in the 1970s and was a direct consequence of the entry of a number of highly capable women into the profession of paleoanthropology.

Up until the 1960s, there were few women in any field of physical anthropology, but with the expansion of graduate programs and changing attitudes toward the role of women in society, increasing numbers of women went on to earn doctorates. One of these was Adrienne Zihlman, who earned her doctorate at the University of California at Berkeley in 1967. Subsequently, she authored a number of important papers critical of "man the hunter" scenarios. She was not the first to do so; as early as 1971, Sally Linton had published a preliminary paper on "woman the gatherer," but it was Zihlman who from 1976 on especially elaborated on the importance of female activities for human evolution. Others have joined in the effort, including Zihlman's companion in graduate school

and later colleague, Nancy Tanner, who wrote some papers with Zihlman and has produced important works of her own.

The work of Zihlman and her co-workers was crucial in forcing a reexamination of existing "man the hunter" scenarios; this produced recognition of the importance of scavenging in early human evolution as well as the value of female gathering and other activities.

Although there is still plenty to learn about human evolution, thanks to these women we now know that it was not a case of females being "uplifted" as a consequence of their association with progressively evolving males. Rather, the two sexes evolved together, with each making its own important contribution to the process.

BIOCULTURAL QUESTION

Can you think of any examples of how gender norms are influencing theories about the biological basis of male and female behavior today?

contributions of female paleoanthropologists.) The division of labor among contemporary food foragers, like all gender relations, does not conform to fixed boundaries defined through biologically based sex differences. Instead, it is influenced by cultural and environmental factors. It appears likely that the same principle applied to our human ancestors. Uncovering such biases is as important as any new discovery for interpreting the fossil record.

Evidence from chimpanzees and bonobos casts further doubt on the notion of a strict sex-based division of labor in human evolutionary history. As described in Chapter 4, female chimpanzees have been observed participating in hunting expeditions, even leading the behavior of hunting with spears. Meat gained from the successful hunt of a smaller mammal is shared within the group whether provided by a male or a female chimpanzee. Among bonobos, females hunt regularly and share meat as well as plant foods with one another. In other words, patterns of food sharing and hunting behaviors in these apes are variable, lending credit to the notion that culture plays a role in establishing these behaviors. Similarly, in our evolutionary history it is likely that culture—the shared learned behaviors of each early *Homo* group—played a role in food-sharing behaviors rather than strict biological differences between the sexes.

No evidence exists to establish definitively how procured foods may have been shared among our ancestors. When the evidence is fragmentary, as it is in all paleoanthropological reconstructions of behavior, gaps are all too easily filled in with behaviors that seem "natural" and familiar, such as the contemporary gender roles of the paleoanthropologist.

Hunters or Scavengers?

As biases in paleoanthropological interpretations were addressed, it became clear that early members of the genus *Homo* were not hunters of large game. Assemblages of Oldowan tools and broken animal bones tell us that both *H. habilis* and large carnivorous animals were active at these locations. In addition to marks on the bones made by slicing, scraping, and chopping with stone tools, there are tooth marks from gnawing. Some of the gnawing marks overlie the butcher marks, indicating that enough flesh remained on the bones after *Homo* was done with them to attract other carnivores. In other cases, though, the butcher marks overlie the tooth marks of carnivores, indicating that the animals got there first. This is what we would expect if *H. habilis* was scavenging the kills of other animals, rather than doing its own killing.

Further, areas that appear to be ancient butchering sites lack whole carcasses; apparently, only parts were transported away from the original location where they were obtained—again, the pattern that we would expect if they were "stolen" from the kill of some other animal. The stone tools, too, were made of raw material procured at distances of up to 60 kilometers from where they were used to process pieces of carcasses. Finally, the incredible density of bones at some of the sites and patterns of weathering indicate that the sites were used repeatedly for perhaps five to fifteen years.

By contrast, historically known and contemporary hunters typically bring whole carcasses back to camp or form camp around a large animal in order to fully process it. After processing, neither meat nor **marrow** (the fatty nutritious tissue inside long bones where blood cells are produced) are left. The bones themselves are broken up not just to get at the marrow (as at Oldowan sites) but to fabricate tools and other objects of bone (unlike at Oldowan sites).

The picture that emerges of our Oldowan forebears, then, is of scavengers, getting their meat from the Lower Paleolithic equivalent of modern-day roadkill, taking the spoils of their scavenging to particular places where tools, and the raw materials for making them (often procured from faraway sources), had been stockpiled in advance for the purpose of butchering. At the least, this may have required fabrication of carrying devices such as net bags and trail signs of the sort (described in Chapter 4) used by modern bonobos. Quite likely, *H. habilis* continued to sleep in trees or rocky cliffs, as do modern small-bodied terrestrial or semi-terrestrial primates, in order to be safe from predators.

Microscopic analysis of cut marks on bones has revealed that the earliest members of the genus *Homo* were actually **tertiary scavengers**—that is, third in line to get something from a carcass after a lion or leopard managed to kill some prey. After the initial kill, ferocious scavengers, such as hyenas and vultures, would swarm the rotting carcass. Next, our tool-wielding ancestors would scavenge for food, breaking open the shafts of long bones to get at the rich marrow inside. A small amount of marrow is a concentrated source of both protein and fat. Muscle alone, particularly from lean game animals, contains very little fat. Furthermore, as shown in the following Original Study, evolving humans may even have been prey themselves, and this selective pressure imposed by predators played a role in brain expansion.

marrow The tissue inside of long bones where blood cells are produced.

tertiary scavenger In a food chain, the third animal group (second to scavenge) to obtain meat from a kill made by a predator.

Humans as Prey   *by Donna Hart*

There's little doubt that humans, particularly those in Western cultures, think of themselves as the dominant form of life on earth. And we seldom question whether that view holds true for our species' distant past. . . . We swagger like the toughest kids on the block as we spread our technology over the landscape and irrevocably change it for other species.

. . . The vision of our utter superiority may even hold true for the last 500 years, but that's just the proverbial blink of an eye when compared to the 7 million years that our hominid ancestors wandered the planet.

"Where did we come from?" and "What were the first humans like?" are questions that have been asked since Darwin first proposed his theory of evolution. One commonly accepted answer is that our early ancestors were killers of other species and of their own kind, prone to violence and even cannibalism. In fact a club-swinging "Man the Hunter" is the stereotype of early humans that permeates literature, film, and even much scientific writing.

. . . Even the great paleontologist Louis S. B. Leakey endorsed it when he emphatically declared that we were not "cat food." Another legendary figure in the annals of paleontology, Raymond A. Dart, launched the killer-ape-man scenario in the mid-20th century. . . .

Dart had interpreted the finds in South African caves of fossilized bones from savannah herbivores together with damaged hominid skulls as evidence that our ancestors had been hunters. The fact that the skulls were battered in a peculiar fashion led to Dart's firm conviction that violence and cannibalism on the part of killer ape-men formed the stem from which our own species eventually flowered. In his 1953 article "The Predatory Transition from Ape to Man," Dart wrote that early hominids were "carnivorous creatures, that seized living quarries by violence, battered them to death, tore apart their broken bodies, [and] dismembered them limb from limb, . . . greedily devouring livid writhing flesh."

But what is the evidence for Man the Hunter? Could smallish, upright creatures with relatively tiny canine teeth and flat nails instead of claws, and with no tools or weapons in the earliest millennia, really have been deadly predators? Is it possible that our ancestors lacked the spirit of cooperation and desire for social harmony? We have only two reliable sources to consult for clues: the fossilized remains of the human family tree, and the behaviors and ecological relationships of our living primate relatives.

When we investigate those two sources, a different view of humankind emerges. First, consider the hominid fossils that have been discovered. Dart's first and most famous find, the cranium of an *Australopithecus* child who died over 2 million years ago (called the "Taung child" after the quarry in which the fossil was unearthed), has been reassessed by Lee Berger and Ron Clarke of the University of the Witwatersrand, in light of recent research on eagle predation. The same marks that occur on the Taung cranium are found on the remains of similarly sized African monkeys eaten today by crowned hawk eagles, known to clutch the monkeys' heads with their sharp talons.

C. K. Brain, a South African paleontologist like Dart, started the process of relabeling Man the Hunter as Man the Hunted when he slid the lower fangs of a fossil leopard into perfectly matched punctures in the skull of another australopithecine, who lived between 1 million and 2 million years ago. The paradigm change initiated by Brain continues to stimulate reassessment of hominid fossils.

The idea that our direct ancestor *Homo erectus* practiced cannibalism was based on the gruesome disfigurement of faces and brain-stem areas in a cache of skulls a half-million years old, found in the Zhoukoudian cave, in China. How else to explain these strange manipulations except as relics of Man the Hunter? But studies over the past few years by Noel T. Boaz and Russell L. Ciochon—of the Ross University School

Whether hunters or hunted, early *Homo* was in competition with formidable adversaries like hyenas. Communication and cooperation helped early *Homo* avoid carnivores that saw them as prey.

of Medicine and the University of Iowa, respectively—show that extinct giant hyenas could have left the marks as they crunched their way into the brains of their hominid prey.

The list of our ancestors' fossils showing evidence of predation continues to grow. A 1.75-million-year-old hominid skull unearthed in the Republic of Georgia shows punctures from the fangs of a saber-toothed cat. Another skull, about 900,000 years old, found in Kenya, exhibits carnivore bite marks on the brow ridge. . . . Those and other fossils provide rock-hard proof that a host of large, fierce animals preyed on human ancestors.

It is equally clear that, outside the West, no small amount of predation occurs today on modern humans. Although we are not likely to see these facts in American newspaper headlines, each year 3,000 people in sub-Saharan Africa are eaten by crocodiles, and 1,500 Tibetans are killed by bears about the size of grizzlies. In one Indian state between 1988 and 1998, over 200 people were attacked by leopards; 612 people were killed by tigers in the Sundarbans delta of India and Bangladesh between 1975 and 1985. The carnivore zoologist Hans Kruuk, of the University of Aberdeen, studied death records in eastern Europe and concluded that wolf predation on humans is still a fact of life in the region, as it was until the 19th century in western European countries like France and Holland.

The fact that humans and their ancestors are and were tasty meals for a wide range of predators is further supported by research on nonhuman primate species still in existence. My study of predation found that 178 species of predatory animals included primates in their diets. The predators ranged from tiny but fierce birds to 500-pound crocodiles, with a little of almost everything in between: tigers, lions, leopards, jaguars, jackals, hyenas, genets, civets, mongooses, Komodo dragons, pythons, eagles, hawks, owls, and even toucans.

Our closest genetic relatives, chimpanzees and gorillas, are prey to humans and other species. Who would have thought that gorillas, weighing as much as 400 pounds, would end up as cat food? Yet Michael Fay, a researcher with the Wildlife Conservation Society and the National Geographic Society, has found the remnants of a gorilla in leopard feces in the Central African Republic. Despite their obvious intelligence and strength, chimpanzees often fall victim to leopards and lions. In the Tai Forest in the Ivory Coast, Christophe Boesch, of the Max Planck Institute, found that over 5 percent of the chimp population in his study was consumed by leopards annually. Takahiro Tsukahara reported, in a 1993 article, that 6 percent of the chimpanzees in the Mahale Mountains National Park of Tanzania may fall victim to lions.

The theory of Man the Hunter as our archetypal ancestor isn't supported by archaeological evidence, either. Lewis R. Binford, one of the most influential figures in archaeology during the last half of the 20th century, dissented from the hunting theory on the ground that reconstructions of early humans as hunters were based on a priori positions and not on the archaeological record. Artifacts that would verify controlled fire and weapons, in particular, are lacking until relatively recent dates. . . .

And, of course, there's also the problem of how a small hominid could subdue a large herbivore. . . . Large-scale, systematic hunting of big herbivores for meat may not have occurred any earlier than 60,000 years ago—over 6 million years after the first hominids evolved.

What I am suggesting, then, is a less powerful, more ignominious beginning for our species. Consider this alternate image: smallish beings (adult females maybe weighing 60 pounds, with males a bit heavier), not overly analytical because their brain-to-body ratio was rather small, possessing the ability to stand and move upright, who basically spent millions of years as meat walking around on two legs. Rather than Man the Hunter, we may need to visualize ourselves as more like Giant Hyena Chow, or Protein on the Go.

Our species began as just one of many that had to be careful, to depend on other group members, and to communicate danger. We were quite simply small beasts within a large and complex ecosystem.

Is Man the Hunter a cultural construction of the West? Belief in a sinful, violent ancestor does fit nicely with Christian views of original sin and the necessity to be saved from our own awful, yet natural, desires. Other religions don't necessarily emphasize the ancient savage in the human past; indeed, modern-day hunter–gatherers, who have to live as part of nature, hold animistic beliefs in which humans are a part of the web of life, not superior creatures who dominate or ravage nature and each other.

Think of Man the Hunted, and you put a different face on our past. . . . We needed to live in groups (like most other primates) and work together to avoid predators. Thus an urge to cooperate can clearly be seen as a functional tool rather than a Pollyannaish nicety, and deadly competition among individuals or nations may be highly aberrant behavior, not hard-wired survival techniques. The same is true of our destructive domination of the earth by technological toys gone mad.

Raymond Dart declared that "the loathsome cruelty of mankind to man . . . is explicable only in terms of his carnivorous, and cannibalistic origin." But if our origin was not carnivorous and cannibalistic, we have no excuse for loathsome behavior. Our earliest evolutionary history is not pushing us to be awful bullies. Instead, our millions of years as prey suggest that we should be able to take our heritage of cooperation and interdependency to make a brighter future for ourselves and our planet.

Adapted from Hart, D. (2006, April 21). Humans as prey. Chronicle of Higher Education.

Whether as hunters or as the hunted, brain expansion and tool use played a significant role in the evolution of the genus *Homo*. The advanced preparation for meat processing implied by the storing of stone tools, and the raw materials for making them, attest to considerable foresight, an ability to plan ahead, and cooperation among our ancestors.

Brain Size and Diet

From its appearance 2.5 mya until about 200,000 years ago, the genus began a course of brain expansion through variational change (see Chapter 6) that continued until about 200,000 years ago. By this point, brain size had approximately tripled, reaching the proportion of contemporary people. The cranial capacity of the largely plant-eating *Australopithecus* ranged from 310 to 530 cubic centimeters (cc); that of the earliest known meat eater, *Homo habilis* from East Africa, ranged from 580 to 752 cc; whereas *Homo erectus*, who eventually hunted as well as scavenged for meat, possessed a cranial capacity of 775 to 1,225 cc.

Larger brains, in turn, required parallel improvements in diet. The energy demands of nerve tissue, of which the brain is made, are high—higher, in fact, than the demands of other types of tissue in the human body. Although a mere 2 percent of body weight, the brain accounts for about 20 to 25 percent of energy consumed at resting metabolic rate in modern human adults.[3] One can meet

---

[3] Leigh, S. R., & Park, P. B. (1998). Evolution of human growth prolongation. *American Journal of Physical Anthropology 107*, 347.

the brain's energy demands on a vegetarian diet, but the overall energy content of a given amount of plant food is generally less than that of the same amount of meat. Large animals that live on plant foods, such as gorillas, spend all day munching on plants to maintain their large bodies. Meat eaters, by contrast, have no need to eat so much, or so often. Consequently, meat-eating bipeds of both sexes may have had more leisure time available to explore and manipulate their environment.

The archaeological record provides us with a tangible record of our ancestors' cultural abilities that corresponds with the simultaneous biological expansion of the brain. Tool making itself puts a premium on manual dexterity, precision, and fine manipulation (Figure 8.2). Stone tools provide evidence of handedness that bespeaks specialization and lateralization of the brain associated with language.

Beginning with the appearance of the genus *Homo* in Africa 2.5 mya, increasing brain size and increasing cultural development each presumably acted to promote the other. The behaviors made possible by larger brains conferred advantages to large-brained individuals, increasing their reproductive success. Over time, large-brained individuals contributed more to successive generations, so that the population evolved to a larger-brained form. Natural selection for increases in learning ability thus led to the evolution of larger and more complex brains over about 2 million years.

Though it preceded increases in brain size by several million years, bipedalism set the stage for the evolution of large brains and human culture. It freed the hands for activities such as tool making and carrying of resources or infants. This new body plan, bipedalism, opened new opportunities for change.

Figure 8.2 A power grip (left) utilizes more of the hand while the precision grip (right) relies on the fingers for control, requiring corresponding organizational changes in the brain.

Homo erectus

In 1887, long before the discovery of *Australopithecus* and early *Homo* in Africa, the Dutch physician Eugenè Dubois set out to find the missing link between humans and apes. The presence of humanlike orangutans in the Dutch East Indies (now Indonesia) led him to start his search there. He joined the colonial service as an army surgeon and set sail.

When Dubois found fossilized remains consisting of a skull cap, a few teeth, and a thighbone at Trinil, on the island of Java, the features seemed to him part ape, part human. The flat skull with its low forehead and enormous brow ridges was like that of an ape; but at about 775 cubic centimeters it possessed a cranial capacity much larger than an ape's, even though small by modern human standards. The femur, or thighbone, was clearly human in shape, and its proportions indicated the creature was a biped. Believing that his specimens represented the missing link and that the thighbone indicated this creature was bipedal, Dubois named his find *Pithecanthropus erectus* (from the Greek *pithekos* meaning "ape," *anthropus* meaning "man") or "erect ape-man." Dubois used the genus name proposed in a paper by the German zoologist Ernst Haeckel, a strong supporter of Darwin's theory of evolution.

As with the Taung child, the first australopithecine discovered in the 1920s, many in the scientific community ridiculed and criticized Dubois's claim, suggesting instead that the apelike skull and humanlike femur came from different individuals. Controversy surrounded these specimens throughout Dubois's lifetime. He eventually retreated from the controversy, keeping the fossil specimens stored safely under the floorboards of his dining room. Ultimately, the discovery of more fossils provided enough evidence to fully support his claim. In the 1950s, the Trinil skull cap and similar specimens from Indonesia and China were assigned to the species *Homo erectus* because they were more human than apelike.

Fossils of *Homo erectus*

Until about 1.8 mya, Africa was the only home to the bipedal primates. It was on this continent that the first bipeds and the genus *Homo* originated. It was also in Africa that the first stone tools were invented. But by the time of *H. erectus*, members of the genus *Homo* had begun to spread far beyond their original homeland. Fossils of this species are now known from a number of localities not just in Africa, but in China, western Europe, Georgia (in the Caucasus Mountains), and India, as well as Java (Figure 8.3).

Although remains of *H. erectus* have been found in many different places in three continents, "lumpers," as discussed in the last chapter, emphasize that they are

Figure 8.3 Sites, with dates, at which *Homo erectus* remains have been found. The arrows indicate the proposed routes by which *Homo* spread from Africa to Eurasia.

unified by a number of shared characteristics. However, because the fossil evidence also suggests some differences within and among populations of *H. erectus* inhabiting discrete regions of Africa, Asia, and Europe, "splitters" prefer to divide *H. erectus* into multiple distinct groups, limiting the species *H. erectus* only to the specimens from Asia. In this taxonomic scheme *Homo ergaster* is used for African specimens from the early Pleistocene period that others describe as early *H. erectus* (Table 8.1).

Regardless of species designation, it is clear that beginning 1.8 mya these larger-brained members of the genus *Homo* not only lived in Africa but also had spread to Eurasia. Fossil specimens dating to 1.8 million years old have been recovered from Dmanisi, Georgia, as well as from Mojokerto, Indonesia. Many additional specimens have been found at a variety of sites in Europe and Asia.

Physical Characteristics of *Homo erectus*

Characteristic features of *H. erectus* are best known from the skull. Cranial capacity in *H. erectus* ranges from 600 to 1,225 cc (average about 1,000 cc). Thus cranial capacity overlaps with the nearly 2-million-year-old KNM ER 1470 skull from

Table 8.1	Alternate Species Designations for *Homo erectus* Fossils from Eurasia and Africa
Name	**Explanation**
Homo ergaster	Some paleoanthropologists feel that the large-brained successors to *H. habilis* from Africa and Asia are too different to be placed in the same species. Therefore, they use *H. ergaster* for the African specimens, saving *H. erectus* for the Asian fossils. Some paleoanthropologists place the recent discoveries from Dmanisi into this taxon.
Homo antecessor	This name was coined by "splitters" for the earliest *Homo* fossils from western Europe discovered in Spain; *antecessor* is Latin for "explorer" or "pioneer."
Homo heidelbergensis	Originally coined for the Mauer jaw (Mauer is not far from Heidelberg, Germany), this name is now used by some as a designation for all European fossils from about 500,000 years ago until the appearance of the Neandertals.

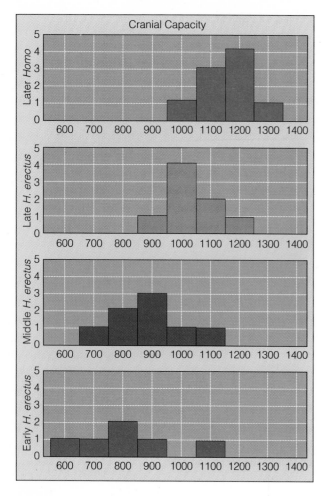

Figure 8.4 Cranial capacity in *Homo erectus* increased over time, as illustrated by these bar graphs, shown in cubic centimeters. The cranial capacity of late *Homo erectus* overlaps with the range seen in live humans.

East Africa (752 cc) and the 1,000 to 2,000 cc range (average 1,300 cc) for modern human skulls (Figure 8.4).

The cranium itself has a low vault (height of the dome of the skull top), and the head is long and narrow. When viewed from behind, its width is greater than its height, with its greatest width at the base. The skulls of modern humans when similarly viewed are higher than they are wide, with the widest dimension in the region above the ears. The shape of the inside of *H. erectus*' braincase shows near-modern development of the brain, especially in the speech area. Although some anthropologists argue that the vocal apparatus was not adequate for speech, others claim that asymmetries of the brain suggest the same pattern of right-handedness with left cerebral dominance that, in modern peoples, is correlated with the capacity for language.[4]

H. erectus possessed massive brow ridges (Figure 8.5). When viewed from above, a marked constriction or

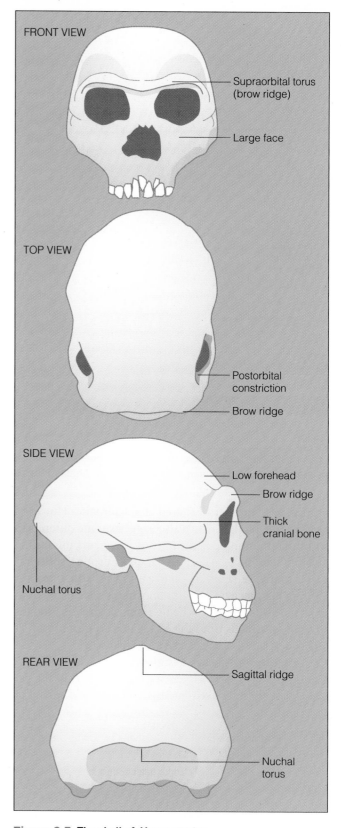

Figure 8.5 The skull of *Homo erectus.*

---

[4] Holloway, R. L. (1981). The Indonesian *Homo erectus* brain endocasts revisited. *American Journal of Physical Anthropology 55,* 521.

"pinching in" of the skull can be seen just behind the massive brow ridges. *H. erectus* also possessed a sloping forehead and a receding chin. Powerful jaws with large teeth, a protruding mouth, and huge neck muscles added to *H. erectus'* generally rugged appearance. Nevertheless, the face, teeth, and jaws of this species are smaller than those of *H. habilis*.

Apart from its skull, the skeleton of *H. erectus* differs only subtly from that of modern humans. Although its bodily proportions are like ours, it was more heavily muscled. Stature seems to have increased from the smaller size typical of the australopithecines and the earliest members of the genus *Homo*. The best evidence for this comes from a remarkably well-preserved skeleton of an adolescent male from Lake Turkana in Kenya. Sexual dimorphism in body size also appears to have decreased in *H. erectus* compared to earlier bipeds. A reduction in sexual dimorphism may be due to the increase in female size as an adaptation to childbirth.[5] The recent discovery of a capacious female *Homo erectus* pelvis in Gona, Ethiopia, supports this notion.[6]

Relationship among *Homo erectus, Homo habilis,* and Other Proposed Fossil Groups

The smaller teeth and larger brains of *Homo erectus* seem to mark the continuation of a trend first seen in *Homo habilis*. Increased body size, reduced sexual dimorphism, and more "human" body form of *H. erectus* are newly derived characteristics. Nonetheless, some skeletal resemblance to *H. habilis* exists, for example, in the long neck and low neck angle of the thighbone, the long low vault and marked constriction of the skull behind the eyes, and smaller brain size in the earliest *H. erectus* fossils.

Indeed, as already noted, it is very difficult to distinguish between the earliest *H. erectus* and the latest *H. habilis* fossils. Presumably the one form evolved from the other, fairly abruptly, around 1.8 to 1.9 mya. While the bones of Asian *H. erectus* are thicker and the brow ridges more pronounced compared to *H. erectus* from Africa,

detailed anatomical comparisons indicate levels of variation approximating those seen in *H. sapiens*.[7] Consistent with the notion of a single species is the observation that 1.8-million-year-old specimens from Dmanisi, in the Caucasus—a region that lies along the overland route between Africa and Eurasia—show a mix of characteristics seen in African and Asian *H. erectus* populations.[8]

Throughout the globe, the most recent fossils are more derived in appearance, and the oldest fossils (up to 1.8 million years old) display features reminiscent of earlier *H. habilis*. Indeed, distinguishing early *H. erectus* from late *H. habilis* is problematic—precisely what one would expect if the one evolved from the other. We will next explore the *H. erectus* finds by region.

Homo erectus from Africa

Although our samples of *H. erectus* fossils from Asia remain among the best, several important specimens are from Africa. Fossils now assigned to this species were discovered there as long ago as 1933, but the better-known finds have been made since 1960, at Olduvai Gorge and at Lake Turkana, Kenya. Among them is the most complete *H. erectus* skeleton ever found, that of an adolescent boy who died 1.6 mya. Paleoanthropologists infer the age of this specimen from his teeth (the 12-year molars are fully erupted) and the state of maturity of the bones. With a height of about 5 feet 3 inches at adolescence, this specimen was expected to attain a stature of about 6 feet by adulthood.

A trail of *H. erectus* footprints, like those from Laetoli, were also recently discovered along Lake Turkana. These footprints support the estimates of body mass (weight) and stature made from more fragmentary remains.

Homo erectus Entering Eurasia

Evidence of the spread of *H. erectus* from Africa into Eurasia is well preserved at the interesting site of Dmanisi in the Caucasus Mountains of Georgia. Dmanisi was first excavated as an archaeological site because of its importance as a crossroads for the caravan routes of Armenia, Persia, and Byzantium in medieval times. When Oldowan stone tools were found at this site in 1984, the hunt for fossil specimens began there as well.

[5] Hager, L. (1989). *The evolution of sex differences in the hominid bony pelvis*. PhD dissertation, University of California, Berkeley.

[6] Simpson, S. W., et al. (2008). A female *Homo erectus* pelvis from Gona, Ethiopia. *Science 322* (5904), 1089–1092.

[7] Rightmire, G. P. (1998). Evidence from facial morphology for similarity of Asian and African representatives of *Homo erectus. American Journal of Physical Anthropology 106*, 61.

[8] Rosas, A., & Bermudez de Castro, J. M. (1998). On the taxonomic affinities of the Dmanisi mandible (Georgia). *American Journal of Physical Anthropology 107*, 159.

One of the oldest and certainly one of the most complete *Homo erectus* fossils is the Nariokotome Boy from Lake Turkana, Kenya. The remains are those of a tall adolescent boy.

Since then, paleoanthropologists have recovered some remarkable remains that can be accurately dated to 1.8 mya through past volcanic activity in the region. In 1999, two well-preserved skulls, one with a partial face, were discovered. Thus the early habitation of this region by members of the genus *Homo* is supported at Dmanisi

with archaeological, anatomical, and geological evidence. Because rising sea levels since the Pleistocene make it impossible for paleoanthropologists to document coastal routes for the spread of *Homo* from Africa to Eurasia, the evidence from Georgia constitutes the only direct evidence of the spread of evolving humans from Africa to Europe and to Asia.

Homo erectus from Indonesia

While it took many years for the skull cap and thighbone discovered by Dubois to be accepted as part of the human line, these specimens are now considered typical Asian *H. erectus*. In the 1930s, a number of *H. erectus* fossils were discovered by German paleoanthropologist G. H. R. von Königswald at Sangiran, Java (see Figure 8.3). Von Königswald found a small skull that fluorine analysis and (later) potassium-argon dating assigned to the early Pleistocene. This indicated that these fossils were older than the Trinil skull cap found by Dubois, dating to approximately 500,000 to 700,000 years ago.

Since 1960, additional fossils have been found in Java, and we now have remains of around forty individuals. A long continuity of *H. erectus* populations in Southeast Asia is indicated, from 500,000 to 1.8 million years ago. Interestingly, the teeth and jaws of some of the earliest Javanese fossils are in many ways quite similar to those of *H. habilis*.[9] When considering the spread of *H. erectus* to Java, it is important to note that in the past, lower sea levels resulted in a continuous landmass between most of Indonesia and the Asian continent.

Homo erectus from China

In the mid-1920s another group of fossils from Asia, now known as *H. erectus,* was found by Davidson Black, a Canadian anatomist teaching at Peking Union Medical College. Black was led to this site after purchasing a few ancient humanlike teeth offered for their medicinal properties from a Beijing drugstore. He set out for the nearby

---

[9] Tobias, P. V., & von Königswald, G.H.R. (1964). A comparison between the Olduvai hominines and those of Java and some implications for hominid phylogeny. *Nature 204,* 515–518.

countryside to discover the "owner" of the teeth and perhaps a species of early human ancestor. At a place called Dragon Bone Hill in Zhoukoudian, 48 kilometers (30 miles) from Beijing, on the day before closing camp at the end of his first year of excavation, he found one molar tooth. Subsequently, Chinese paleoanthropologist W. C. Pei, who worked closely with Black, found a skull encased in limestone.

Between 1929 and 1934, the year of his death from silicosis—a lung disease caused by exposure to silica particles in the cave—Black labored along with Pei and French Jesuit paleontologist Pierre Teilhard de Chardin in the fossil-rich deposits of Zhoukoudian, uncovering fragment after fragment of ancient remains. On the basis of the anatomy of that first molar tooth, Black named these fossils *Sinanthropus pekinensis,* or "Chinese human of Peking" (Beijing), called "Peking Man" for short at the time. They are now recognized as an East Asian representative of *H. erectus.*

After Black's death, Franz Weidenreich, a German anatomist and paleoanthropologist, was sent to China by the Rockefeller Foundation to continue this work. As a Jew in Nazi Germany in the early 1930s, Weidenreich had sought refuge in the United States. By 1938, he and his colleagues recovered the remains of more than forty individuals, more than half of them women and children, from the limestone deposits of Zhoukoudian. Most fossils were fragmentary, represented by teeth, jawbones, and incomplete skulls. A spectacular composite specimen was reconstructed from the most complete remains. World War II (1939–1945) brought a halt to the digging, and the original Zhoukoudian specimens were lost during the Japanese occupation of China. The fossils had been carefully packed by Weidenreich and his team and placed with the U.S. Marines, but in the chaos of war, these precious fossils disappeared.

Fortunately, Weidenreich had made superb casts of most of the Zhoukoudian fossil specimens and sent them to the United States before the war. After the war, other specimens of *H. erectus* were discovered in China, at Zhoukoudian and a number of other localities (see Figure 8.3). The oldest skull is about 700,000 to 800,000 years old and comes from Lantian in central China. Even older is a fragment of a lower jaw from a cave in south-central China (Lunggupo) that is as old as the oldest Indonesian fossils. Like some of their Indonesian contemporaries, this Chinese fossil is reminiscent of African *H. habilis.* In contrast to these ancient remains, the original Zhoukoudian fossils appear to date between 300,000 and 600,000 years ago.

Although the two populations overlap in time, the majority of the Chinese fossils are, on the whole, not quite as old as those from Indonesia. Not surprisingly, Chinese *H. erectus* is less ancestral in appearance. Its average cranial capacity is about 1,000 cc, compared to 900 cc for Indonesian *H. erectus.* The smaller teeth and short jaw of the Chinese fossil specimens are further evidence of their more derived status.

© John Reader/Photo Researchers, Inc.

The original *Homo erectus* fossils from Zhoukoudian had been packed for shipment to the United States for safekeeping during World War II, but they mysteriously disappeared. Fortunately, excellent casts of the specimens and detailed anatomical descriptions (by Weidenreich) were made before the fossils were lost during the war.

Homo erectus from Western Europe

Although the fossil evidence indicates the presence of the genus *Homo* on the Eurasian landmass 1.8 mya (at Dmanisi, Georgia), the fossil evidence from western Europe dates to about 800,000 years ago. The evidence from the Grand Dolina site—in the Sierra de Atapuerca region of north-central Spain (see Table 8.1)—consists of fragments of four individuals dating to 800,000 years ago. A skull from Ceprano in Italy is thought to be approximately the same age if not older. Again, whether one lumps these specimens into the inclusive but varied species *H. erectus* or into several separate species differs according to the approach taken by paleoanthropologists with regard to the fossil record.

Some other fossils attributable to *H. erectus*—such as a robust shinbone from Boxgrove, England, and a large lower jaw from Mauer, Germany—are close to half a million years old. It is clear that the jaw came from a skull that was wide at the base, typical of *H. erectus.* These remains resemble *H. erectus* material from North Africa from the same time period. This observation and the fact that the earliest evidence of the genus *Homo* in western Europe comes from Spain and Italy suggest continued gene flow between this region and northern Africa.[10] At the time, a mere 6 or 7 kilometers separated Gibraltar from Morocco (compared to 13 kilometers today), and islands dotted the straits from Tunisia to Sicily. The only direct land connection between Africa and Eurasia is through the Middle East and into Turkey and the Caucasus.

The Culture of *Homo erectus*

As one might expect given its larger brain, *Homo erectus* outstripped its predecessors in cultural ability. *H. erectus* refined the technology of stone tool making and at some point began to use fire for light, protection, warmth, and cooking, though precisely when is still a matter for debate. Indirect evidence indicates that the organizational and planning abilities of *H. erectus*, or at least the later ones, were improved over those of their predecessors.

Acheulean Tool Tradition

Tools of the **Acheulean tradition** are associated with the remains of *H. erectus* in Africa, Europe, and southwestern Asia. Named for the stone tools first identified at St. Acheul, France, the signature piece of this tradition is the hand-axe: a teardrop-shaped tool pointed at one end with a sharp cutting edge all around (Figure 8.6).

The earliest hand-axes, from East Africa, are about 1.6 million years old. Those found in Europe are no older than about 500,000 years. At the same time that hand-axes appeared, archaeological sites in Europe became dramatically more common. This suggests an influx of individuals bringing Acheulean technology with them, implying continued gene flow into Europe. Because the spread of the genus *Homo* from Africa into Asia took place before the invention of the hand-axe, it is not surprising to find that different forms of tools were developed in East Asia.

The evidence from Olduvai Gorge shows that the Acheulean grew out of the Oldowan tradition: In lower strata, chopper tools were found along with remains of *H. habilis;* above, the first crude hand-axes were found intermingled with chopper tools; and in higher strata were found more finished-looking Acheulean hand-axes with *H. erectus* remains.

Early Acheulean tools represent a significant step beyond the generalized cutting, chopping, and scraping tools of the Oldowan tradition. The shapes of Oldowan tools were largely controlled by the original form, size, and mechanical

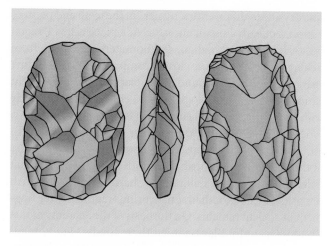

Figure 8.6 To fabricate this Acheulean hand-axe from flint, the toolmaker imposed a standardized arbitrary form on the naturally occurring raw material. The crafter made many separate strikes to create the sharp edge visible in profile.

properties of raw materials. The shapes of hand-axes and some other Acheulean tools, by contrast, were more standardized, apparently reflecting arbitrary preconceived designs imposed upon a diverse range of raw materials.[11] Overall, a sharper point and a more regular and larger cutting edge were produced from the same amount of stone.

During this part of the Lower Paleolithic tool kits began to diversify. Besides hand-axes, *H. erectus* used tools that functioned as cleavers (hand-axes with a straight, sharp edge where the point would otherwise be), picks and knives (variants of the hand-axe form), and flake tools (generally smaller tools made by hitting a flint core with a hammerstone, thus knocking off flakes with sharp edges). Many flake tools were byproducts of hand-axe and cleaver manufacture. Their sharp edges made them useful "as is," but many were retouched (modified again by ancient flint knappers) to make points, scrapers, borers, and other sorts of tools. Diversification of tool kits is also indicated by the smaller numbers of hand-axes in northern and eastern Europe where people relied on simple flaked choppers, a wide variety of unstandardized flakes, and supplementary tools made of bone, antler, and wood.

In eastern Asia, by contrast, people developed a variety of choppers, scrapers, points, and burins (chisel-like tools) different from those in southwestern Asia, Europe, and Africa. Besides direct percussion, anvil (striking the raw material against a stationary stone) and bipolar percussion (holding the raw material against an anvil, but striking it at the same time with a hammerstone) methods were used in tool manufacture. Although tens of thousands of stone tools have been found with *H. erectus* remains at Zhoukoudian, stone implements are not at all common in Southeast Asia. Here, favored materials likely were ones that do not preserve

---

[10] Balter, M. (2001). In search of the first Europeans. *Science 291,* 1724.

Acheulean tradition The tool-making tradition of *Homo erectus* in Africa, Europe, and southwestern Asia in which hand-axes were developed from the earlier Oldowan chopper.

---

[11] Ambrose, p. 1750.

well, such as bamboo and other local woods, from which excellent knives, scrapers, and so on can be made.

Use of Fire

With *H. erectus* came the first evidence of ancestral populations living outside the Old World tropics. Without controlled use of fire, it is unlikely that early humans could have moved successfully into regions where winter temperatures regularly dropped to temperate climate levels—as they must have in northern China, the mountain highlands of Central Asia, and most of Europe. Members of the genus *Homo* spread to these colder regions some 780,000 years ago.

The 700,000-year-old Kao Poh Nam rock shelter in Thailand provides compelling evidence for deliberate controlled use of fire. Here, a roughly circular arrangement of fire-cracked basalt cobbles was discovered in association with artifacts and animal bones. Because basalt rocks are not native to the rock shelter and are quite heavy, they were likely carried in by *H. erectus*. Limestone rocks, more readily available in the shelter, cannot be used for hearths because, when burned, limestone produces quicklime, a caustic substance that causes itching and burning skin rashes.[12] The hearth is associated with bones, showing clear evidence of cut marks from butchering as well as burning.

H. erectus may have been using fire even earlier, based on evidence from Swartkrans in South Africa. Here, in deposits estimated to date between 1 and 1.3 mya, bones have been found that had been heated to temperatures far in excess of what one would expect as the result of natural fires. Furthermore, the burned bones at Swartkrans do not occur in older, deeper deposits. If these fires were natural, they would be distributed among all archaeological layers. Because the bones indicate heating to such high temperatures that any meat on them would have been inedible, South African paleoanthropologists Andrew Sillen and C. K. Brain suggest that the Swartkrans fires functioned as protection from predators.[13]

Fire may also have been used by *H. erectus*, as it was by subsequent members of the genus *Homo*, not just for protection from animals out in the open but to frighten away cave-dwelling predators so that the fire users might

In regions where bamboo was readily available for the fabrication of effective tools, the same stone tool industries might not have developed. This contemporary scaffolding demonstrates bamboo's strength and versatility.

live in the caves themselves. In addition, fire could be used to provide warmth and light in these otherwise cold and dark habitations. While earlier bipeds likely used caves as part of their temperature regulation strategy as has been observed in nonhuman primates,[14] controlled use of fire expands the ability to regulate temperature considerably.

Not only did fire provide warmth, but it may have assisted in the quest for food. In places like central Europe and China, food would have been hard to come by in the long, cold winters when edible plants were unavailable and the large herds of animals dispersed and migrated. Our ancestors may have searched out the frozen carcasses of animals that had died naturally in the late fall and winter, using long wooden probes to locate them beneath the snow, wooden scoops to dig them out, and fire to thaw them so that they could be butchered and eaten.[15] Furthermore, such fire-assisted scavenging would have made available meat and hides of woolly mammoths, woolly rhinoceroses, and bison, which were probably beyond the ability of *H. erectus* to kill, at least until late in the species' career.

Perhaps it was the use of fire to thaw carcasses that led to the idea of cooking food. Some paleoanthropologists suggest that this behavioral change altered the forces of natural selection, which previously favored individuals

---

[12] Pope, G. G. (1989). Bamboo and human evolution. *Natural History 10,* 56.

[13] Sillen, A., & Brain, C. K. (1990). Old flame. *Natural History 4,* 10.

[14] Barrett, L., et al. (2004). Habitual cave use and thermoregulation in chacma baboons (*Papio hamadryas ursinus*). *Journal of Human Evolution 46* (2), 215–222.

[15] Gamble, C. (1986). *The Paleolithic settlement of Europe* (p. 387). Cambridge, England: Cambridge University Press.

with heavy jaws and large, sharp teeth (raw food is tougher and needs more chewing), favoring instead further reduction in tooth size along with supportive facial structure.

Alternatively, the reduction of tooth size and supporting structure may have occurred outside the context of adaptation. For example, the genetic changes responsible for increasing brain size may also have caused a reduction in tooth size as a secondary effect. The discovery of a genetic mutation, shared by all humans but absent in apes, that acts to prevent growth of powerful jaw muscles supports this hypothesis. Without heavy jaw muscles attached to the outside of the braincase, a significant constraint to brain growth was removed. In other words, humans may have developed large brains as an accidental byproduct of jaw-size reduction.[16]

Soft foods may have relaxed selection for massive jaws. But cooking does more than soften food. It detoxifies a number of otherwise poisonous plants; alters digestion-inhibiting substances so that important vitamins, minerals, and proteins can be absorbed while in the gut, rather than just passing through it unused; and makes high-energy complex carbohydrates like starch digestible. Cooking increased the nutritional resources available to humans and made them more secure.

The partial predigestion of food by cooking also may have allowed a reduction in the size of the digestive tract. To establish this biological change, paleoanthropologists do not have the benefit of fossilized digestive tracts. Instead they turn to comparative anatomy of the living hominoids. Despite its overall similarity of form to those of apes, the digestive tract of modern humans is substantially smaller. The advantage of this gut reduction is that it draws less energy to operate, thereby competing less with the high energy requirements of a larger brain.

Like tools, then, fire gave people more control over their environment. Fire modified the natural succession of day and night, perhaps encouraging *H. erectus* to stay up after dark to review the day's events and plan the next day's activities. Though we cannot know whether *H. erectus* enjoyed socializing and planning around campfires at night, we do have evidence at least of some planning behavior. Planning is implied by the existence of populations in temperate climates, where the ability to anticipate the needs of the winter season by advance preparation for the cold would have been crucial to survival.[17]

Although considerable variation exists, studies of modern humans indicate that most people can remain reasonably comfortable down to 50 degrees Fahrenheit (10 degrees Celsius) with minimal clothing so long as

they keep active. Below that temperature, hands and feet cool to the point of pain.[18] Clothing, like many other aspects of material culture, does not fossilize, so we have no direct evidence of the kind of clothing worn by *H. erectus*. We only know that it must have been more sophisticated than was required in warmer climates. In short, when our human ancestors learned to employ fire to warm and protect themselves and to cook their food, they dramatically increased their geographic range and nutritional options.

Hunting

Sites such as 400,000-year-old Ambrona and Torralba in Spain provide evidence that *H. erectus* developed the ability to organize in order to hunt large animals. The dismembered scattered remains of several elephants, horses, red deer, wild oxen, and rhinoceroses were preserved in an ancient swamp at Torralba. This finding, which cannot be explained as a result of any natural geologic process, indicates that these animals did not accidentally get mired in a swamp where they simply died and decayed.[19] In fact, the bones are closely associated with a variety of stone tools—a few thousand of them. Furthermore, the site contains very little evidence of carnivorous animal activity and none at all for the really big carnivores. Clearly, the genus *Homo* was involved—not just in butchering the animals but evidently in killing them as well.

It appears that the animals were actually driven into the swamp so that they could be easily killed. The remains of charcoal and carbon, widely but thinly scattered in the vicinity, raise the possibility that grassfires were used to drive the animals into the swamp. This evidence indicates more than opportunistic scavenging. Not only was *H. erectus* able to hunt, but considerable organizational and communicative skills are implied as well.

Other Evidence of Complex Thought

Other evidence of *H. erectus*' capabilities comes from the small island of Flores in Indonesia. Flores lies east of a deep-water strait that throughout the Pleistocene acted as a barrier to animals to and from Southeast Asia. Even at times of lowered sea levels, getting to Flores required crossing open water: at minimum 25 kilometers from Bali to Sumbawa, with an additional 19 kilometers to Flores. The presence

[16] Stedman, H. H., et al. (2004). Myosin gene mutation correlates with anatomical changes in the human lineage. *Nature 428*, 415–418.

[17] Goodenough, W. H. (1990). Evolution of the human capacity for beliefs. *American Anthropologist 92*, 601.

[18] Whiting, J. W. M., Sodergem, J. A., & Stigler, S. M. (1982). Winter temperature as a constraint to the migration of preindustrial peoples. *American Anthropologist 84*, 289.

[19] Freeman, L. G. (1992). *Ambrona and Torralba: New evidence and interpretation*. Paper presented at the 91st Annual Meeting, American Anthropological Association, San Francisco.

of 800,000-year-old stone tools on Flores indicates that somehow our ancestors navigated across the deep, fast-moving water.[20]

Evidence for a developing symbolic life is suggested by the increased standardization and refinement of Acheulean hand-axes over time. Moreover, at several sites in Europe, deliberately marked objects of stone, bone, and ivory have been found in Acheulean contexts. These include several objects from Bilzingsleben, Germany—among them a mastodon bone with a series of regular lines that appear to have been deliberately engraved. Similarly, the world's oldest known rock carvings are associated with Acheulean tools in a cave in India.[21] Though a far cry from the later Upper Paleolithic cave art of France and Spain, these are among the earliest Paleolithic artifacts that have no obvious utility or model in the natural world. Archaeologist Alexander Marshack argues that the use of such symbolic images requires some sort of spoken language, not only to assign meaning to the images but to maintain the tradition they seem to represent.[22]

The Question of Language

Though we do not have definitive evidence of *H. erectus'* linguistic abilities, indications of a developing symbolic life, as well as the need to plan for seasonal changes and to coordinate hunting activities (and cross stretches of open water), imply improving linguistic competence. Another interesting source of evidence for evolving humans' linguistic capability is found in the fossil record. There, it is apparent that the majority of the stone tools were made by right-handed individuals, supporting the theory of the increased specialization and lateralization of the evolving brain. In other primates and most mammals, the right and left sides of the brain duplicate each other's function; these animals use the right and left sides of their bodies equally and interchangeably. In humans, the emergence of handedness seems closely linked both developmentally (at about the age of 1 year) and evolutionarily with the appearance of language. Thus evidence of handedness in

Figure 8.7 Language areas in the left side of the brain. The right side of the human brain has different specialized functions.

Lower Paleolithic tools indicates that the kind of brain specialization required for language that is present in contemporary humans was well under way (Figure 8.7).

The vocal tract and brain of *H. erectus* are intermediate between those of *H. sapiens* and earlier *Australopithecus*. The **hypoglossal canal**—the passageway through the skull that accommodates the nerve that controls tongue movement, which is so important for spoken language—has taken on the characteristic large size seen in contemporary humans in fossil skulls dated to 500,000 years ago (Figure 8.8).[23]

Possibly, a changeover from reliance on gestural to spoken language was a driving force in these evolutionary changes. The reduction of tooth and jaw size, facilitating the ability to articulate speech sounds, may have also played a role. From an evolutionary standpoint, spoken language could be said to provide some advantages over a gestural one. Individuals do not have to stop whatever they are doing with their hands to "talk" (useful to a species increasingly dependent on tool use), and it is possible to talk in the dark, past opaque objects, or among people whose gaze is concentrated on something else (potential prey, for example).

[20] Gibbons, A. (1998). Ancient island tools suggest *Homo erectus* was a seafarer. *Science 279*, 1635.

[21] Bednarik, R. G. (1995). Concept-mediated marking in the Lower Paleolithic. *Current Anthropology 36*, 610–611.

[22] Marshack, A. (1976). Some implications of the Paleolithic symbolic evidence for the origin of language. *Current Anthropology 17*, 280.

[23] Cartmill, M. (1998). The gift of gab. *Discover 19* (11), 64.

hypoglossal canal The opening in the skull that accommodates the tongue-controlling hypoglossal nerve.

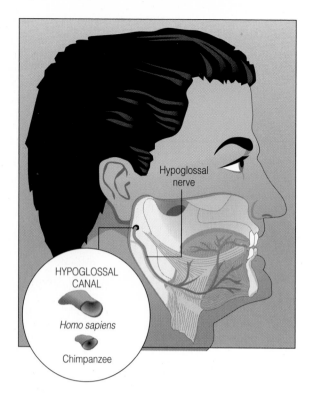

Figure 8.8 The size of the hypoglossal canal is much larger in humans than in chimpanzees. The nerve that passes through this canal controls tongue movement, and complex tongue movements are involved in spoken language. All members of the genus *Homo* after about 500,000 years ago have an enlarged hypoglossal canal.

With *H. erectus,* then, we find a clearer manifestation of the interplay among cultural, physical, and environmental factors than ever before. However slowly, social organization, technology, and communication developed in tandem with an increase in brain size and complexity. In fact, the cranial capacity of late *H. erectus* is 31 percent greater than the mean for early *H. erectus,* a rate of increase more rapid than the average fossil vertebrate rate.[24]

Archaic *Homo sapiens* and the Appearance of Modern-Sized Brains

Fossils from a number of sites in Africa, Asia, and Europe, dated to between 200,000 and 400,000 years ago, indicate that by this time cranial capacity reached modern proportions. Most fossil finds consist of parts of one or a very few individuals. The fossils from Sierra de Atapuerca in northern Spain (pictured in the chapter opener), are the only ones to exist as a population. Dated to 400,000 years ago,[25] the remains of at least twenty-eight individuals of both sexes and of various ages were deliberately dumped (after defleshing their skulls) by their contemporaries into a deep cave shaft known today as Sima de los Huesos ("Pit of the Bones"). The presence of animal bones in the same pit with humans raises the possibility that early humans simply used the site as a dump. Alternatively, the treatment of the dead at Atapuerca may have involved ritual activity that presaged burial of the dead, a practice that became common after 100,000 years ago.

As with any population, this one displays a significant degree of variation. Cranial capacity, for example, ranges from 1,125 to 1,390 cc, overlapping the upper end of the range for *H. erectus* and the average size of *H. sapiens* (1,300 cc). Overall, the bones display a mix of features, some typical of *H. erectus,* others of *H. sapiens,* including some incipient Neandertal characteristics. Despite this variation, the sample appears to show no more sexual dimorphism than displayed by modern humans.[26]

Other remains from Africa and Europe dating 200,000 to 400,000 years ago have shown a combination of *H. erectus* and *H. sapiens* features. Some—such as skulls from Ndutu in Tanzania, Swanscombe (England), and Steinheim (Germany)—have been classified as *H. sapiens,* while others—from Arago (France), Bilzingsleben (Germany), and Petralona (Greece), and several African sites—have been classified as *H. erectus.* Yet all have cranial capacities that fit within the range exhibited by the Sima de los Huesos skulls, which are classified as *H. antecessor.*

Comparisons of these skulls to those of living people or to *H. erectus* reflect their transitional nature. The Swanscombe and Steinheim skulls are large and robust, with their maximum breadth lower on the skull, more prominent brow ridges, larger faces, and bigger teeth. Similarly, the face of the Petralona skull from Greece resembles European Neandertals, while the back of the skull looks like *H. erectus.* Conversely, a skull from Salé in Morocco, which had a rather small brain for *H. sapiens* (930–960 cc), looks surprisingly modern from the back. Finally, various jaws from France and Morocco (in northern Africa) seem to combine features of *H. erectus* with those of the later European

[24] Wolpoff, M. H. (1993). Evolution in *Homo erectus:* The question of stasis. In R. L. Ciochon & J. G. Fleagle (Eds.), *The human evolution source book* (p. 396). Englewood Cliffs, NJ: Prentice-Hall.

[25] Parés, J. M., et al. (2000). On the age of hominid fossils at the Sima de los Huesos, Sierra de Atapuerca, Spain: Paleomagnetic evidence. *American Journal of Physical Anthropology 111,* 451–461.

[26] Lorenzo, C., et al. (1998). Intrapopulational body size variation and cranial capacity variation in middle Pleistocene humans: The Sima de los Huesos sample (Sierra de Atapuerca, Spain). *American Journal of Physical Anthropology 106,* 30.

Neandertals. A similar situation exists in East Asia, where skulls from several sites in China exhibit the same mix of *H. erectus* and *H. sapiens* characteristics.

"Lumpers" suggest that calling some of these early humans "late *H. erectus*" or "early *H. sapiens*" (or any of the other proposed species names within the genus *Homo*) serves no useful purpose and merely obscures their transitional status. They tend to lump these fossils into the **archaic *Homo sapiens*,** a category that reflects both their large brain size and the ancestral features on the skull. "Splitters" use a series of discrete names for specimens from this period that take into account some of the geographic and morphologic variation present in these fossils. Both approaches reflect their respective statements about evolutionary relationships among fossil groups.

Levalloisian Technique

With the appearance of large-brained members of the genus *Homo,* the pace of cultural change accelerated. A new method of flake manufacture was invented: the **Levalloisian technique,** so named after the French site where such tools were first excavated. Flake tools produced by this technique have been found widely in Africa, Europe, southwestern Asia, and even China along with Acheulean tools. In China, the technique could represent a case of independent invention, or it could indicate the spread of ideas from one part of the inhabited world to another.

The Levalloisian technique initially involves preparing a core by removing small flakes over the stone's surface. Following this, a striking platform is set up by a crosswise blow at one end of the core of stone (Figure 8.9). Striking the platform removes three or four long flakes, whose size and shape have been predetermined by the preceding preparation, leaving behind a nodule that looks like a tortoise shell. This method produces a longer edge for the same amount of flint than the previous ones used by evolving humans. Sharper edges can be produced in less time.

Other Cultural Innovations

At about the same time the Levalloisian technique was developed, our ancestors invented hafting—the fastening of small stone bifaces and flakes to handles of wood. Hafting led to the development of knives and more complex spears. Unlike the older handheld tools made simply by reduction (flaking of stone or working of wood), these new composite tools involved three components: a handle or shaft, a stone insert, and the materials to bind them. Manufacture involved planned sequences of actions that could be performed at different times and places.

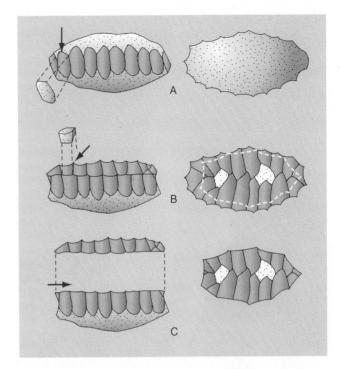

Figure 8.9 These drawings show side (left) and top (right) views of the steps in the Levalloisian technique. Drawing A shows the preparatory flaking of the stone core; B, the same on the top surface; and C, the final step of detaching a flake of a size and shape predetermined by the preceding steps.

With this new technology, regional stylistic and technological variants become more marked in the archaeological record, suggesting the emergence of distinct cultural traditions and culture areas. At the same time, the proportions of raw materials procured from faraway sources increased; whereas sources of stone for Acheulean tools were rarely more than 20 kilometers (12 miles) away, Levalloisian tools are found up to 320 kilometers (200 miles) from the sources of their stone.[27]

The use of yellow and red pigments of iron oxide, called ochre, a development first identified in Africa, became especially common by 130,000 years ago.[28] The use

---

[27] Ambrose, p. 1752.

[28] Barham, L. S. (1998). Possible early pigment use in South-Central Africa. *Current Anthropology 39,* 703–710.

---

archaic *Homo sapiens* A loosely defined group within the genus *Homo* that "lumpers" use for fossils with the combination of large brain size and ancestral features on the skull.

Levalloisian technique Tool-making technique by which three or four long triangular flakes were detached from a specially prepared core; developed by members of the genus *Homo* transitional from *H. erectus* to *H. sapiens*.

The practice of hafting, the fastening of small stone bifaces and flakes to handles of wood, was a major technological advance appearing in the archaeological record at about the same time as the invention of the Levalloisian technique.

of ochre may signal a rise in ritual activity, similar to the deliberate placement of the human remains in the Sima de los Huesos, Atapuerca, already noted. The use of red ochre in ancient burials may relate to its similarity to the color of blood as a powerful symbol of life.

The Neandertals

To many outside the field of anthropology, **Neandertals** are the quintessential caveman, portrayed by imaginative cartoonists as a slant-headed, stooped, dim-witted

Neandertals A distinct group within the genus *Homo* inhabiting Europe and southwestern Asia from approximately 30,000 to 125,000 years ago.

individual clad in animal skins and carrying a big club as he plods across the prehistoric landscape, perhaps dragging an unwilling female or a dead saber-toothed tiger. The stereotype has been perpetuated in novels and film. The popular image of Neandertals as brutish and incapable of spoken language, much less abstract or innovative thinking, may, in turn, have influenced the interpretation of the fossil and archaeological evidence. One of the most contentious issues in paleoanthropology today concerns whether the Neandertals represent an inferior side branch of human evolution that went extinct following the appearance of modern humans. Alternatively, descendents of the Neandertals may walk the earth today.

Neandertals were an extremely muscular people living from approximately 30,000 to 125,000 years ago in Europe and southwestern Asia. While having brains larger than the modern average size, Neandertals possessed faces distinctively different from those of modern humans. Their large noses and teeth projected forward. They had prominent bony brow ridges over their eyes. On the back of their skull, there was a bunlike bony mass for attachment of powerful neck muscles. These features, not in line with classic forms of Western beauty, may have contributed to the depiction of Neandertals as brutes. Their rude reputation may also derive from the timing of their discovery.

One of the first Neandertals was found in a cave in the Neander Valley ("tal" means "valley" in German, "thal" was the old, German spelling) near Düsseldorf, Germany, in 1856—well before scientific theories to account for human evolution had gained acceptance. (Darwin published *On the Origins of Species by Means of Natural Selection* three years later in 1859.)

Initially, experts were at a loss as to what to make of this discovery. Examination of the fossil skull, a few ribs, and some limb bones revealed that the individual was a human being, but it did not look "normal." Some people believed the bones were those of a sickly and deformed contemporary. Others thought the skeleton belonged to a soldier who had succumbed to "water on the brain" during the Napoleonic Wars earlier that century. One prominent anatomist thought the remains were those of an idiot suffering from malnutrition, whose violent temper had gotten him into many fights, flattening his forehead and making his brow ridges bumpy. Similarly, an analysis of a skeleton found in 1908 near La Chapelle-aux-Saints in France mistakenly concluded that the specimen's brain was apelike and that he walked like an ape.

The evidence indicates that Neandertals were nowhere near as brutish and apelike as originally portrayed, and some scholars now see them as the archaic *H. sapiens* of Europe and Southwest Asia, ancestral to

This early 20th-century portrayal of the La Chapelle-aux-Saints Neandertal, based on the research of French paleoanthropologist Marcellin Boule, makes a powerfully negative statement about the capabilities of this group as well as their distance from living humans. In looking at this sorry specimen, it is easy to forget that this portrayal is not derived directly from the fossil remains but from the collective imagination of early 20th-century Europeans. While paleoanthropologists uniformly recognize the inaccuracies and biases present in this engraving, present-day reconstructions of Neandertals still vary tremendously and reflect the conflicting scientific theories and beliefs about their place in our evolutionary history.

the more derived, anatomically modern populations of these regions of the last 30,000 years. For example, paleoanthropologist C. Loring Brace observed that "classic" Neandertal features (Figure 8.10) are commonly present in 10,000-year-old skulls from Denmark and Norway.[29]

Nevertheless, Neandertals are somewhat distinctive when compared to more recent populations. Although they held modern-sized brains (average cranial capacity 1,400 cc versus 1,300 cc for modern *H. sapiens*), Neandertal skulls are notable for the protruding appearance of the midfacial region. The wear patterns on their large front teeth indicate that they may have been heavily used for tasks other than chewing. In many individuals, front teeth were worn down to the root stub by 35 to 40 years of age. The large noses of Neandertals probably were necessary to warm, moisten, and clean the dry, dusty frigid air of the glacial climate, preventing damage to the lungs and brain as seen in cold-adapted people of recent times. At the back of the skull, the bunlike bony mass providing attachment for the powerful neck muscles counteracted the weight of a heavy face.

All Neandertal fossils indicate that both sexes were muscular, with extremely robust and dense limb bones. Relative to body mass, the limbs were short (as they are in modern humans native to especially cold climates). Their shoulder blades indicate the importance of overarm and downward thrusting movements. Their arms

[29] Ferrie, H. (1997). An interview with C. Loring Brace. *Current Anthropology 38*, 861.

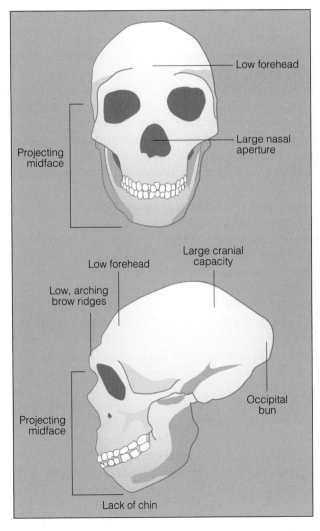

Figure 8.10 Features of the skull seen in "classic" Neandertals.

As this face-off between paleoanthropologist Milford Wolpoff and his reconstruction of a Neandertal shows, the latter did not differ all that much from modern humans of European descent.

were exceptionally powerful, and pronounced attachments on their hand bones attest to a remarkably strong grip. Science writer James Shreeve has suggested that a healthy Neandertal could lift an average North American football player over his head and throw him through the goalposts.[30] Their massive, dense foot and leg bones suggest high levels of strength and endurance, comparable to robust individuals who live today.

Because brain size is related to overall body mass, heavy robust Neandertal bodies account for the large average size of the Neandertal brain. With *H. habilis* and *H. erectus,* increasing brain size has been linked to increasing cultural capabilities. Because Neandertal brain size falls at the high end of the human size range, paleoanthropologists shift to debating whether changes in the *shape* of the skull and skeleton are associated with changes in cultural capabilities.

Though the interpretation of Neandertal fossils has changed dramatically compared to when first discovered, they are still surrounded by controversy. Those who propose that the Neandertal line went extinct emphasize a notion of Neandertal biological difference and cultural inferiority. Those who include Neandertals in our direct ancestry emphasize the sophistication of Neandertal culture, attributing differences in skull shape and body form to regional adaptation to an extremely cold climate and the retention of ancestral traits in a somewhat isolated population.

[30] Shreeve, J. (1995). *The Neandertal enigma: Solving the mystery of modern human origins* (p. 5). New York: William Morrow.

Javanese, African, and Chinese Archaic *Homo sapiens*

While the large-brained Neandertals inhabited Europe and Southwest Asia, other parts of the world were inhabited by variants of archaic *H. sapiens;* these lacked the extreme midfacial projection and massive muscle attachments on the back of the skull characteristic of the Neandertals. Skulls found in Java, Africa, and China date from roughly the same time period.

Eleven skulls found near the Solo River in Ngandong, Java, are a prime example. These skulls indicated modern-sized brains ranging from 1,013 to 1,252 cc, while retaining features of earlier Javanese *H. erectus.* When their dating was recently revised (to between 27,000 and 53,000 years ago) some researchers concluded that this proved a late survival of *H. erectus* in Asia, contemporary with *H. sapiens* elsewhere. But the Ngandong skulls remain what they always were: representatives of archaic *H. sapiens,* with modern-sized brains in otherwise ancient-looking skulls.

Fossils from various parts of Africa show a similar combination of ancient and modern traits. Equivalent remains have been found at several localities in China. Thus the Neandertals could be said to represent an extreme form of archaic *H. sapiens.* Elsewhere, the archaics look like robust versions of the early modern populations that lived in the same regions or like somewhat more derived versions of the *H. erectus* populations that preceded them. All appear to have contained modern-sized brains, with their skulls retaining some ancestral features.

The original Neandertal cranium discovered in the Neander Valley, Germany, in 1856 (the only one without a face) is depicted here with earlier fossils and a cranium from contemporary *Homo sapiens*. The other fossils, from the left, are a gracile australopithecine; *Homo habilis* (KNM ER 1470) discovered at Koobi Fora, Kenya; *Homo erectus* also from Koobi Fora; and an African archaic *Homo sapiens* from Kabwe, Zambia. Increasing cranial capacity over time is evident from this series as is the fact Neandertal brains are in the modern human range. Even without the Neandertal face, some of the differences in the shape of the skull compared to *H. sapiens* are evident. The African archaic *H. sapiens* is also quite different from the contemporary skeleton.

Middle Paleolithic Culture

Adaptations to the environment by *Homo* from the **Middle Paleolithic,** or middle part of the Old Stone Age, were both biological and cultural, but the capacity for cultural adaptation was predictably superior to what it had been in earlier members of the genus *Homo*. Possessing brains of modern size, these members of the genus *Homo* had, as we would expect, greater cultural capabilities than their ancestors. Such a brain played a role in technological innovations, conceptual thought of considerable sophistication, and, almost surely, communication through spoken language. In addition to the Levalloisian technique already described, the Middle Paleolithic also included the development of the Mousterian tool tradition.

Mousterian Tool Tradition

The **Mousterian** and Mousterian-like tool traditions of Europe, southwestern Asia, and northern Africa, dating between about 40,000 and 125,000 years ago, are the best known of these (Figure 8.1). Comparable traditions are found in China and Japan, where they likely arose independently from local tool-making traditions.

All these traditions represent a technological advance over preceding industries. For example, the 40 centimeters

Middle Paleolithic The middle part of the Old Stone Age characterized by the development of the Mousterian tradition of tool making and the earlier Levalloisian traditions.

Mousterian tradition The tool industry of the Neandertals and their contemporaries of Europe, southwestern Asia, and northern Africa from 40,000 to 125,000 years ago.

(16 inches) of working edge that an Acheulean flint worker could get from a kilogram (2.2-pound) core compares with the nearly 200 centimeters (6 feet) of working edge the Mousterian could obtain from the same core. Mousterian tools were used by *all* people—Neandertals as well as other members of the genus *Homo* said to possess

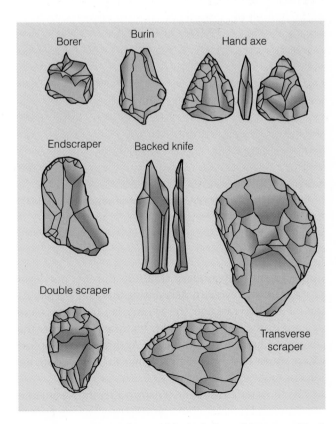

Figure 8.11 Mousterian tool kits include a wide range of tool types with specific functions along with finer workmanship.

Stone Tools for Modern Surgeons

When anthropologist Irven DeVore of Harvard University was to have some minor melanomas removed from his face, he did not leave it up to the surgeon to supply his own scalpels. Instead, he had graduate student John Shea make a scalpel. Making a blade of obsidian (a naturally occurring volcanic "glass") by the same techniques used by Upper Paleolithic people to make blades, he hafted this in a wooden handle, using melted pine resin as glue and then lashing it with sinew. After the procedure, the surgeon reported that the obsidian scalpel was superior to metal ones.[a]

DeVore was not the first to undergo surgery in which stone scalpels were used. In 1975, Don Crabtree, then at Idaho State University, prepared the scalpels that his surgeon would use in Crabtree's heart surgery. In 1980, Payson Sheets at the University of Colorado prepared obsidian scalpels that were

used successfully in eye surgery. And in 1986, David Pokotylo of the Museum of Anthropology at the University of British Columbia underwent reconstructive surgery on his hand with blades he himself had made (the hafting was done by his museum colleague, Len McFarlane).

The reason for these uses of scalpels modeled on ancient stone tools is that the anthropologists realized that obsidian is superior in almost every way to materials normally used to make scalpels: It is 210 to 1,050 times sharper than surgical steel, 100 to 500 times sharper than a razor blade, and three times sharper than a diamond blade (which not only costs much more but cannot be made with more than 3 mm of cutting edge).

Obsidian blades are easier to cut with and do less damage in the process (under a microscope, incisions made with the sharpest steel blades show torn ragged edges and are littered with bits

of displaced flesh).[b] As a consequence, the surgeon has better control over what she or he is doing, and the incisions heal faster with less scarring and pain. Because of the superiority of obsidian scalpels, Sheets went so far as to form a corporation in partnership with Boulder, Colorado, eye surgeon Dr. Firmon Hardenbergh. Together, they developed a means of producing cores of uniform size from molten glass, as well as a machine to detach blades from the cores.

---

[a] Shreeve, J. (1995). *The Neandertal enigma: Solving the mystery of modern human origins* (p. 134). New York: William Morrow.

[b] Sheets, P. D. (1987). Dawn of a New Stone Age in eye surgery. In R. J. Sharer & W. Ashmore (Eds.), *Archaeology: Discovering our past* (p. 231). Palo Alto, CA: Mayfield.

These electron micrographs of the tips of an obsidian blade (left) and a modern steel scalpel illustrate the superiority of the obsidian.

more anatomically modern skulls, in Europe, northern Africa, and southwestern Asia during this time period. At around 35,000 years ago, the Mousterian traditions were replaced by the Upper Paleolithic traditions, which are the subject of Chapter 9. However, the Anthropology Applied feature shows that stone tools continue to be important for humans today.

The Mousterian tradition is named after the Neandertal cave site of Le Moustier, in southern France. The presence of Acheulean hand-axes at Mousterian sites is one indication

that this culture was ultimately rooted in the older Acheulean tradition. Mousterian tools are generally lighter and smaller than those of earlier traditions. Whereas previously only two or three flakes could be obtained from the entire core, Mousterian toolmakers obtained many smaller flakes, which they skillfully retouched and sharpened. Their tool kits also contained a greater variety of types than the earlier ones: hand-axes, flakes, scrapers, borers, notched flakes for shaving wood, and many types of points that could be attached to wooden shafts to make spears. This variety of tools facilitated more effective use of food resources and enhanced the quality of clothing and shelter.

With the Mousterian cultural traditions, members of the genus *Homo* could cope with the nearly Arctic conditions that supervened in Eurasia as the glaciers expanded about 70,000 years ago. People likely came to live in cold climates as a result of a slow but steady population increase during the Pleistocene. Once there, they had little choice but to adapt as climates turned even colder.

Population expansion into previously uninhabited colder regions was made possible through a series of cultural adaptations to cold climate. Under such cold conditions, vegetable foods are only rarely or seasonally available, and meat becomes a critical staple. In particular, animal fats, rather than carbohydrates, become the chief source of energy. Energy-rich animal fat in the diets of cold-climate meat eaters provides them with the extra energy needed for hunting, as well as for keeping the body warm.

An abundance of associated animal bones, often clearly showing cut marks, indicates the importance of meat to Mousterian toolmakers. Frequently, the remains consist almost entirely of very large game—wild cattle (including the European bison known as the aurochs), wild horses, and even mammoths and woolly rhinoceroses. At several sites evidence indicates that particular species were singled out for the hunt. For example, at one site in the French Pyrenees, well over 90 percent of the faunal assemblage (representing at least 108 animals) consists of large members of the wild cattle family. These bones accumulated at the foot of a steep riverside escarpment, over which the animals were evidently stampeded. Evidence of similar cliff-fall hunting strategy is also found at La Quina in southwestern France and at a site in the Channel Islands just off the northwest coast of France.

Clearly, the Neandertals were not merely casual or opportunistic hunters but engaged in carefully planned and organized hunting of very large and potentially dangerous game.[31] The standardization of Mousterian hunting implements compared to household tools also reflects the importance of hunting for these ancient peoples. At the same time, the complexity of the tool kit needed for survival in a cold climate may have decreased the users' mobility. Decreased mobility is suggested by the greater depth of deposits and thus longer habitation at Mousterian sites compared with those from the earlier Lower Paleolithic. Such sites contain evidence of long production sequences, resharpening and discarding of tools, and large-scale butchering and cooking of game. Pebble paving, construction of simple walls, and the digging of post holes and artificial pits show how the inhabitants worked to improve living conditions in some caves and rock shelters. This evidence suggests that Mousterian sites were not simply stopovers in people's constant quest for food.

In addition, evidence suggests that Neandertal social organization had developed to the point of providing care for physically disabled members of the group. For the first time, the remains of old people are well represented in the fossil record. Furthermore, many elderly Neandertal skeletons show evidence of treatment for trauma, with extensive healing of wounds and little or no infection.[32]

One particularly dramatic example is Shanidar Cave in Iraq, which includes the remains of a partially blind man (the eye socket indicates serious injury) with a withered upper arm indicating loss of the arm from the elbow on down. Remains of another individual found at Krapina in Croatia suggests the possibility of surgical amputation of a hand. In La Chapelle, France, fossil remains indicate prolonged survival of a man badly crippled by arthritis. The earliest example comes from a 200,000-year-old site in France, where a toothless man was able to survive probably because others in his group processed or prechewed his food so he could swallow it. Whether this evidence indicates true compassion on the part of these early people is not clear, but it is certain that cultural factors helped ensure survival, allowing individuals to provide care for others.

The Symbolic Life of Neandertals

Indications of a rich symbolic life of Neandertals exist. For example, several sites contain clear evidence for deliberate burial of the dead. This is one reason for the relative abundance of reasonably complete Neandertal skeletons. The difficulty of digging an adult-sized grave without access to metal shovels suggests how important a social activity this was. Moreover, intentional positioning of dead bodies, whatever the specific reason may have been, constitutes evidence of symbolism.[33]

To date, at least seventeen sites in Europe, South Africa, and Southwest Asia include Middle Paleolithic burials. For example, at Kebara Cave in Israel, around 60,000 years ago, a Neandertal male between 25 and 35 years of age was placed in a pit on his back, with his arms folded over his chest and abdomen (Figure 8.12). Some time later, after complete decay of attaching ligaments, the grave was reopened and the skull removed (a practice that,

---

[31] Mellars, P. (1989). Major issues in the emergence of modern humans. *Current Anthropology 30*, 356–357.

[32] Conroy, G. C. (1997). *Reconstructing human origins: A modern synthesis* (p. 427). New York: Norton.

[33] Schepartz, L. A. (1993). Language and modern human origins. *Yearbook of Physical Anthropology 36*, 113.

Figure 8.12 The position of the body and the careful removal of the skull indicate that the fossil from Kebara Cave in Israel was deliberately buried there about 60,000 years ago.

interestingly, is sometimes seen in burials in the same region roughly 50,000 years later).

Shanidar Cave in Iraq provides evidence of a burial accompanied by what may have been a funeral ceremony. In the back of the cave a Neandertal was buried in a pit. Pollen analysis of the soil around the skeleton indicated that flowers had been placed below the body and in a wreath about the head. Because the key pollen types came from insect-pollinated flowers, few if any of the pollen grains could have found their way into the pit via air currents. The flowers in question consist solely of varieties valued in historic times for their medicinal properties.

Other evidence for symbolic behavior in Mousterian culture comes from the naturally occurring pigments: manganese dioxide and the red and yellow forms of ochre. Recovered chunks of these pigments reveal clear evidence of scraping to produce powder, as well as facets, like those that appear on a crayon, from use. A Mousterian artist also applied color to the carved and shaped section of a mammoth tooth about 50,000 years ago. This mammoth tooth may have been made for cultural symbolic purposes. Noteworthy is its similarity to ceremonial objects made of bone and ivory dated to the later

Upper Paleolithic and to the *churingas* made of wood by Australian Aborigines.

The mammoth tooth, which was once smeared with red ochre, has a highly polished face suggesting it was handled a lot. Microscopic examination reveals that it was never provided with a working edge for any utilitarian purpose. Such objects imply, as archaeologist Alexander Marshack has observed, "that the Neandertals did in fact have conceptual models and maps as well as problem-solving capacities comparable to, if not equal to, those found among anatomically modern humans."[34]

Evidence for symbolic activity on the part of Neandertals raises the possibility of the presence and use of musical instruments, such as a proposed bone flute from a Mousterian site in Slovenia in southern Europe. This object, consisting of a hollow bone with perforations, has sparked controversy. Some see it as nothing more than a cave bear bone that was chewed on by carnivores—hence the perforations. Its discoverer, French archaeologist Marcel Otte, on the other hand, sees it as a flute.

Unfortunately, the object is fragmentary; surviving are five holes, four on one side and one on the opposite side. The regular spacing of the four holes, fitting perfectly to the fingers of a human hand, and the location of the fifth hole at the base of the opposite side, at the natural location of the thumb, all lend credence to the flute hypothesis. While signs of gnawing by animals are present on this bone, they are superimposed on traces of human activity.[35] Were it found in an Upper Paleolithic context as was the flute discovered in Hohle Fels Cave in southwestern Germany, it would probably be accepted as a flute without argument. However, because its early date indicates it was made by a Neandertal, the interpretation of this object is tied to the larger controversy about Neandertals' cultural abilities and their place in human evolutionary history.

Speech and Language in the Middle Paleolithic

Among modern humans, the sharing of thoughts and ideas, as well as the transmission of culture from one generation to the next, is dependent upon language. Because the Neandertals and other Middle Paleolithic *Homo* had modern-sized brains and a sophisticated Mousterian

[34] Marshack, A. (1989). Evolution of the human capacity: The symbolic evidence. *Yearbook of Physical Anthropology 32*, 22.

[35] Otte, M. (2000). On the suggested bone flute from Slovenia. *Current Anthropology 41*, 271.

Courtesy of Marcel Otte

The first musical instrument? There is a strong possibility that this object, found in trash left by Neandertals, is the remains of a flute made of bone.

tool kit, it might be supposed that they had some form of language.

As pointed out by paleoanthropologist Stanley Ambrose, the Mousterian tool kit included composite tools involving the assembly of parts in different configurations to produce functionally different tools. He likens this ordered assembly of parts into tools to grammatical language, "because hierarchical assemblies of sounds produce meaningful phrases and sentences, and changing word order changes meaning."[36] Furthermore, "a composite tool may be analogous to a sentence, but explaining how to make one is the equivalent of a recipe or a short story."[37] In addition, the evidence for the manufacture of objects of symbolic significance supports the presence of language in Middle Paleolithic *Homo*. Objects such as the colored section of mammoth tooth already described would seem to have required some form of explanation through language.

While the archaeological evidence supports the symbolic thinking characteristic of language, specific anatomical features can be examined to determine whether this language was spoken or gestural. Some have argued that the Neandertals lacked the physical features necessary for speech. For example, an early 20th-century reconstruction of the angle at the base of the Neandertal skull was said to indicate that the larynx was higher in the throat than it is in modern humans, precluding humanlike speech. This reconstruction is now known to be faulty. Further, the

hyoid bone associated with the muscles of speech in the larynx is preserved from a skeleton from the Kebara Cave burial in Israel. Its shape is identical to that of contemporary humans, indicating that the vocal tract was adequate for speech.

With respect to the brain, paleoneurologists, working from endocranial casts, are agreed that Neandertals had the neural development necessary for spoken language. Indeed, they argue that the changes associated with language began even before the appearance of archaic *Homo sapiens*,[38] as described above. Consistent, too, is an expanded thoracic vertebral canal (the thorax is the upper part of the body), a feature Neandertals share with modern humans but not with early *Homo erectus* (or any other primate). This feature suggests the increased breath control required for speech.[39] This control enables production of long phrases or single expirations of breath, punctuated with quick inhalations at meaningful linguistic breaks.

Another argument—that a relatively flat base in Neandertal skulls would have prevented speech—has no merit, as some modern adults show as much flattening, yet have no trouble talking. Clearly, when the anatomical evidence is considered in its totality, there seems no compelling reason to deny Neandertals the ability to speak.

[36] Ambrose, p. 1751.
[37] Ibid.

[38] Schepartz, p. 98.
[39] MacLarnon, A. M., & Hewitt, G. P. (1999). The evolution of human speech: The role of enhanced breathing control. *American Journal of Physical Anthropology 109*, 341–363.

The discovery of a "language gene" by Swedish paleo-geneticist Svante Pääbo and colleagues at the Max Planck Institute for Evolutionary Anthropology in Leipzig, Germany, adds an interesting new dimension to the study of the evolution of language.[40] The gene, called FOXP2 found on chromosome 7, was identified through the analysis of a family in which members spanning several generations have severe language problems. Changes in the gene are hypothesized to control the ability to make fine movements of the mouth and larynx necessary for spoken language. The identification of this gene in humans allowed scientists to compare its structure to that found in other mammalian species.

The human FOXP2 gene differs from versions of the gene found in the chimpanzee, gorilla, orangutan, rhesus macaque, and mouse. While these differences among living species can be known, applying this knowledge to the earlier members of the genus *Homo* is far more difficult. We do not know precisely when in human evolution the human form of the FOXP2 gene appeared or whether this gene was associated with the formation of a new species of *Homo*.

In light of these genetic discoveries it is also interesting to consider the work done on language capacity in the great apes. For example, in her work with the bonobo named Kanzi, Sue Savage-Rumbaugh documented his ability to understand hundreds of spoken words and associate them with lexigrams (pictures of words) on a computer display while unable to create the sounds himself.[41] Speech and language are not identical.

[40] Lai, C. S. L., et al. (2001). A forkhead-domain gene is mutated in severe speech and language disorder. *Nature 413*, 519–523; Enard, W., et al. (2002). Molecular evolution of FOXP2, a gene involved in speech and language. *Nature 418*, 869–872.

[41] Savage-Rumbaugh, S., & Lewin, R. (1994). *Kanzi: The ape at the brink of the human mind.* New York: Wiley.

Culture, Skulls, and Modern Human Origins

For Middle Paleolithic *Homo*, cultural adaptive abilities relate to the fact that brain size was comparable to that of people living today. Archaeological evidence indicates sophisticated technology, as well as conceptual thought of considerable complexity, matching the increased cranial capacity. During this same time period, large-brained individuals with skulls with an anatomically modern shape began to appear. The earliest specimens with this skull shape—a more vertical forehead, diminished brow ridge, and a chin—appear first in Africa and later in Asia and Europe. Whether the derived features in the skull indicate the appearance of a new species with improved cultural capabilities remains a hotly debated question.

The transition from the Middle Paleolithic to the tools of the Upper Paleolithic occurred around 40,000 years ago, some 100,000 years or so after the appearance of the first anatomically modern specimens in Africa. The Upper Paleolithic is known not only for a veritable explosion of tool industries, but also for clear artistic expression preserved in representative sculptures, paintings, and engravings (see Chapter 9). But the earliest anatomically modern humans, like the Neandertals and other archaic forms, used tools of the Middle Paleolithic traditions.

The relationship between cultural developments of the Upper Paleolithic and underlying biological differences between anatomically modern humans and archaic forms remains one of the most contentious debates in paleoanthropology. Discussions concerning the fate of the Neandertals and their cultural abilities are integral to this debate. Whether or not a new kind of human—anatomically modern with correspondingly superior intellectual and creative abilities—is responsible for the cultural explosion of the Upper Paleolithic is considered in Chapter 9.

Questions for Reflection

1. Members of the genus *Homo* draw upon integrated biological and cultural capabilities to face the challenges of existence. How do these factors play into the designation of species in the fossil record?

2. Paleoanthropologists can be characterized as "lumpers" or "splitters" depending upon their approach to the identification of species in the fossil record. Which of these approaches do you prefer and why?

3. In his 1871 book *Descent of Man, and Selection in Relation to Sex,* Charles Darwin stated, "Thus man has ultimately become superior to woman. It is indeed fortunate that the law of equal transmission of characters prevails with mammals. Otherwise it is probable that man would have become as superior in mental endowment to woman as the peacock is in ornamental plumage to the peahen." How were the cultural norms of Darwin's time reflected in his statement? Can 21st-century paleoanthropologists speak about differences between the sexes in evolutionary contexts without introducing their own cultural biases?

4. Animals ranging from rabbits to plants have come to occupy new niches without the benefits of culture. Was the spread of *Homo* out of the African continent possible without the benefit of culture?

5. Though language itself does not "fossilize," the archaeological and fossil records provide some evidence of the linguistic capabilities of our ancestors. Using the evidence available, what sort of linguistic abilities do you think early *Homo* possessed?

Suggested Readings

Corballis, M. C. (2003). *From hand to mouth: The origins of human language.* Princeton, NJ: Princeton University Press.

This book, written by a psychologist, takes the position that facial and manual gestures rather than vocalization are key to the development of language. It brings data from linguistics, molecular genetics, animal behavior, psychology, and neurology to the anthropological question of when human language arose.

Delson, E., Tattersal, I., Brooks, A., & Van Couvering, J. (1999). *Encyclopedia of human evolution and prehistory.* New York: Garland.

Using an A to Z format, this user-friendly encyclopedia includes over 800 entries relating to human evolution and prehistory. It includes excellent diagrams, illustrations, and descriptions of key archaeological sites.

Potts, R. (1997). *Humanity's descent: The consequences of ecological instability.* New York: Avon.

Written by the director of the Smithsonian Institution's Human Origins Program, this book suggests that environmental instability was the unifying factor contributing to the acquisition of human language and culture.

Stanford, C. B. (2001). *The hunting apes: Meat eating and the origins of human behavior.* Princeton, NJ: Princeton University Press.

Though updated and less gender biased, this work revisits the old "man the hunter" hypothesis, suggesting that human intelligence is linked to the acquisition of meat and food sharing.

Walker, A., & Shipman, P. (1997). *The wisdom of the bones: In search of human origins.* New York: Vintage.

This book provides an engaging description of the discovery of the most complete *Homo erectus* specimen—the Nariokotome Boy from Lake Turkana, Kenya—as well as placing it within the context of the larger story of human evolution.

Zihlman, A. (2001). *The human evolution coloring book.* New York: Harper Resources.

Do not be deceived by the title or the book's visual hands-on format. This book provides an authoritative scientific approach to all aspects of the study of human evolution.

Challenge Issue This tiny 35,000-year-old "Venus" figurine (about the size and weight of a small cluster of grapes), recently discovered in the archaeologically rich Hohle Fels Cave in southwestern Germany and associated with the assumed earliest presence of undisputed *Homo sapiens* in Europe, changed paleoanthropological interpretations of the origins of figurative art. Prior to this discovery, the earliest figurative art had included only representations of animals; female figurines did not appear until about 30,000 years ago. The exaggerated breasts and vulva and stylized markings on this carving, as on similar prehistoric statuettes known as Venus figurines, indicate the importance of female fertility to our ancestors. Did our ancestors worship the power of females to give birth? Do these figurines represent our ancestors' attempts to connect groups of people to one another across time and space? Such creations suggest that humans, as a thoughtful and self-reflecting species, have always faced the challenge of understanding where and how we fit in the larger natural system of all life forms, past and present. In turn, these figurines challenge us to weigh whether a biological change was at the root of this creative expression, which would have separated these ancestors from the archaic *Homo sapiens* that came before them.

CHAPTER 9

The Global Expansion of *Homo sapiens* and Their Technology

Chapter Preview

When Did Anatomically Modern Forms of *Homo sapiens* Appear?

Although 160,000-year-old fossils from Ethiopia have been described as anatomically modern, the answer to this question is quite complex. Anatomical modernity refers to particular characteristics in the shape of the skull. While all humans today are members of a single species, and as such are equally "modern," some contemporary populations do not meet the definition of anatomical modernity used by some paleoanthropologists. To exclude contemporary humans from the species based on the shape of their skulls is an obvious impossibility. By extension, the application of this definition of anatomical modernity to the fossil record is a source of debate. Still, it is generally agreed that by 30,000 years ago, Upper Paleolithic populations in all parts of the inhabited world showed greater resemblance to more recent human populations than earlier large-brained *Homo*.

When and How Did Humans Spread to Australia and the Americas?

Around the time of the Upper Paleolithic, humans expanded into new regions, most dramatically Australia and the Americas. Expansion into Australia and New Guinea required crossing a deep, wide ocean channel and was thus dependent upon sophisticated watercraft. Spread to the Americas involved successful adaptation to Arctic conditions and movement over land through northeastern Asia to the Americas, along with the use of watercraft over even more extended distances. Anthropologists use archaeological, linguistic, and biological evidence to reconstruct the spread of humans into these new regions.

What Is the Relationship Between Middle Paleolithic *Homo* and Modern *Homo sapiens*?

Some paleoanthropologists propose that Neandertals, like other archaic forms, evolved into anatomically modern versions of *Homo sapiens* as different features of modern anatomy arising in other regional populations were carried to them through gene flow. In this framework, human populations throughout Africa, Europe, and Asia contributed to the making of modern humans. Other paleoanthropologists propose that anatomically modern humans with superior cultural capabilities appeared first in Africa about 200,000 years ago, replacing existing archaic forms as they spread from Africa to the rest of the world.

What Was the Culture of Upper Paleolithic Peoples Like?

Between 70,000 and 40,000 years ago the global archaeological record begins to become richer, not only with varied and sophisticated tool industries but also with evidence of increased human creativity, ingenuity, and problem solving. Upper Paleolithic cultures generally include a greater diversity of tools than previously, as well as a greater frequency of blade tools. Pressure-flaking techniques and the use of burins to fashion implements of bone and antler became widespread. In Europe, success of large game hunting increased with the invention of the spear-thrower, or atlatl, and nets aided in hunting of small game. In Africa the earliest small points appropriate for arrowheads appear during this time period. There was as well an explosion of creativity, represented by impressive works of art discovered in a variety of sites in Africa, Australia, Eurasia, and Australia.

The remains of ancient people who looked more like contemporary Europeans than Neandertals were first discovered in 1868 at Les Eyzies in France, in a rock shelter together with tools of the **Upper** (late) **Paleolithic.** Consisting of eight skeletons, they are commonly referred to as **Cro-Magnons,** after the rock shelter in which they were found. The name was extended to thirteen other specimens recovered between 1872 and 1902 in the caves of southwestern France and, since then, to other Upper Paleolithic skeletons discovered in other parts of Europe.

Because Cro-Magnons were found with Upper Paleolithic tools and seemed responsible for the production of impressive works of art, they were seen as particularly clever when compared with the Neandertals. The idea that Neandertals were dimwitted comfortably supported the prevailing stereotype of their supposedly brutish appearance. Their Mousterian tools were interpreted as evidence of cultural inferiority. Hence, Cro-Magnons were regarded as an anatomically modern people with a superior culture sweeping into Europe and replacing a primitive local population. This idea mirrored the European conquest of other parts of the world during the colonial expansion that was concurrent with the discovery of these fossils.

With the invention of reliable dating techniques in the 20th century, we now know that many Neandertal specimens of Europe and the later Cro-Magnon specimens date from different time periods. The Middle Paleolithic Mousterian technology is associated with earlier fossil specimens, Upper Paleolithic technology and art with later fossil specimens. Perhaps the most Eurocentric aspect of all is that historically this discussion focused on the European fossil evidence instead of incorporating evidence from throughout the globe. Recent fossil evidence for early anatomical modernity in Africa, evidence of regional continuity from Asia, and associated genetic studies allow paleoanthropologists to develop more comprehensive theories for the origins of modern humans.

Upper Paleolithic The last part (10,000 to 40,000 years ago) of the Old Stone Age, featuring tool industries characterized by long slim blades and an explosion of creative symbolic forms.

Cro-Magnon A European of the Upper Paleolithic after about 36,000 years ago.

Upper Paleolithic Peoples: The First Modern Humans

What do we mean by modernity? Paleoanthropologists look at both skull shape of and cultural practices. But still this is a difficult designation to make. While Cro-Magnons resemble later populations of modern Europeans—in braincase shape, high broad forehead, narrow nasal openings, and common presence of chins—their faces were on average shorter and broader than those of modern

In the novel and movie *Clan of the Cave Bear*, the anatomically modern heroine is depicted as a tall blonde beauty while Neandertals are depicted as dark and sloppy. These images conform both to the stereotypes about Neandertals and aesthetic standards in the Western dominant culture.

© David L. Brill

With a high forehead, the Cro-Magnon skull is more like contemporary Europeans compared to the prominent brow ridge and sloping forehead seen in the Neandertal skull. Whether these differences in skull shape account for their cultural differences rather than their relative age is hotly debated. The more recent Cro-Magnon skull even preserves evidence of cultural continuity in diet with local contemporary French people. This skull has evidence of a fungal infection, perhaps from eating tainted mushrooms. Mushrooms are a delicacy in this region of France to this day.

Europeans, their brow ridges were a bit more prominent, and their teeth and jaws were as large as those of Neandertals. Some (a skull from the original Cro-Magnon site, for instance) even display the distinctive occipital bun of the Neandertals on the back of the skull.[1] Nor were they particularly tall, as their height of 5 feet 7 or 8 inches (170–175 centimeters) does not fall outside the Neandertal range. Similarly, early Upper Paleolithic skulls from Brno, Mladec, and Predmosti, in the Czech Republic, retain heavy brow ridges and Neandertal-like muscle attachments on the back of the skull.[2]

Although the Cro-Magnons and Upper Paleolithic peoples from Africa and Asia are now routinely referred to as "anatomically modern," it is surprisingly difficult to be precise about what we mean by this. We think of people with brains the size of modern people, but this had already been achieved by archaic *H. sapiens.*

Average brain size actually peaked in Neandertals at 10 percent larger than the contemporary human average. The reduction to today's average size correlates with a reduction in brawn, as bodies have become less massive overall. Modern faces and jaws are, by and large, smaller as well, but there are exceptions. For example, anthropologists Milford Wolpoff and Rachel Caspari have pointed out that any definition of modernity that excludes Neandertals also excludes substantial numbers of recent and living Aborigines in Australia, although they are, quite obviously, a contemporary people. The fact is, no multidimensional diagnosis of anatomical modernity can be both exclusive of archaic populations and inclusive of all contemporary humans.[3]

Defining modernity in terms of culture also raises some questions. The appearance of modern-sized brains in archaic *Homo* was related to increased reliance on cultural adaptation, but the Upper Paleolithic was a time of great technological innovation. The emphasis on cultural adaptation led to the development of more complex tool kits; Upper Paleolithic tool kits are known for a preponderance of blade tools, with flint flakes at least twice as long as they are wide. The earliest blade tools come from sites in Africa, but these tools do not make up the majority of the tool types until well into the Upper Paleolithic. The Upper Paleolithic archaeological record also contains a proliferation of expressive arts.

Ultimately, technological improvements may also have reduced the intensity of selective pressures that had previously favored especially massive robust bodies, jaws, and teeth. With new emphasis on elongated tools having greater mechanical advantages, more effective techniques of hafting, a switch from thrusting to throwing spears, and development of net hunting, there was a marked reduction in overall muscularity. In addition, as the environment changed to milder conditions from the extreme cold that prevailed in Eurasia during the last Ice Age, selective pressure for short stature as an adaptation to conserve body heat may have also diminished.

The Human Origins Debate

On a biological level, the great human origins debate can be distilled to a question of whether one, some, or all populations of the archaic groups played a role in the evolution of modern *Homo sapiens.* Those supporting the multiregional hypothesis argue for a simultaneous local transition from *H. erectus* to modern *H. sapiens*

[1] Brace, C. L. (1997). Cro-Magnons "R" us? *Anthropology Newsletter 38* (8), 1.

[2] Bednarik, R. G. (1995). Concept-mediated marking in the Lower Paleolithic. *Current Anthropology 36,* 627; Minugh-Purvis, N. (1992). The inhabitants of Ice Age Europe. *Expedition 34* (3), 33–34.

[3] Wolpoff, M., & Caspari, R. (1997). *Race and human evolution: A fatal attraction* (pp. 344–345, 393). New York: Simon & Schuster.

throughout the parts of the world inhabited by members of the genus *Homo.* By contrast, those supporting a theory of recent African origins argue that all contemporary peoples are derived from one single population of archaic *H. sapiens* from Africa. This model proposes that the improved cultural capabilities of anatomically modern humans allowed this group to replace other archaic forms as they began to migrate out of Africa sometime after 100,000 years ago. Both theories are explored in detail below.

The Multiregional Hypothesis

As several anthropologists have noted, African, Chinese, and southeastern Asian fossils of archaic *Homo sapiens* imply continuity within these respective populations, from *H. erectus* through to modern *H. sapiens*;[4] this lends strong support to the interpretation that there was genetic continuity in these regions. For example, in China, Pleistocene fossils from the genus *Homo* consistently have small forward-facing cheeks and flatter faces than their contemporaries elsewhere, as is still true today. In Southeast Asia and Australia, by contrast, skulls are consistently robust, with huge cheeks and forward projection of the jaws.

In this model, gene flow among populations keeps the human species unified throughout the Pleistocene. No speciation events remove ancestral populations such as *H. erectus* or Neandertals from the line leading to *H. sapiens.* Although proponents of the **multiregional hypothesis** accept the idea of continuity from the earliest European fossils through the Neandertals to living people, many other paleoanthropologists reject the idea that Neandertals were involved in the ancestry of modern Europeans.

---

[4] Wolpoff, M. H., Wu, X. Z., & Thorne, A. G. (1984). Modern *Homo sapiens* origins: A general theory of hominid evolution involving fossil evidence from East Asia (pp. 411–483). In F. H. Smith & F. Spencer (Eds.), *The origins of modern humans.* New York: Alan R. Liss; Wolpoff & Caspari; Pope, G. G. (1992). Craniofacial evidence for the origin of modern humans in China. *Yearbook of Physical Anthropology 35,* 291.

multiregional hypothesis The hypothesis that modern humans originated through a process of simultaneous local transition from *Homo erectus* to *Homo sapiens* throughout the inhabited world.

recent African origins or "Eve" hypothesis The hypothesis that all modern people are derived from one single population of archaic *Homo sapiens* from Africa who migrated out of Africa after 100,000 years ago, replacing all other archaic forms due to their superior cultural capabilities; also called the out of Africa hypothesis.

The Recent African Origins or "Eve" Hypothesis

The **recent African origins or "Eve" hypothesis** (also called the *out of Africa hypothesis*) states that anatomically modern humans are descended from one specific population of *Homo sapiens,* replacing not just the Neandertals but other populations of archaic *H. sapiens* as our ancestors spread out of their original homeland. This idea did not originate from fossils, but from a relatively new technique that uses mitochondrial DNA (mtDNA) to reconstruct family trees.

Unlike nuclear DNA (in the cell nucleus), mtDNA is located in the mitochondria, the cellular structures that produce the energy needed to keep cells alive. Because sperm contribute virtually no mtDNA to the fertilized egg, mtDNA is inherited essentially from one's mother and is not subject to recombination through meiosis and fertilization with each succeeding generation as is nuclear DNA. Therefore, changes in mtDNA over time occur only through mutation. By comparing the mtDNA of living individuals from diverse geographic populations, anthropologists and molecular biologists seek to determine when and where modern *H. sapiens* originated (Figure 9.1).

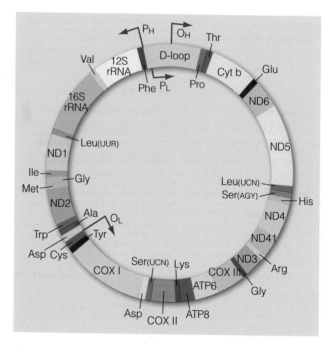

Figure 9.1 The 16,569 bases in mitochondrial DNA (mtDNA) are organized into circular chromosomes present in large numbers in every cell. The human mtDNA sequence has been entirely sequenced, with functional genes identified. Because mtDNA is maternally inherited and not subject to recombination, it can be used to establish evolutionary relationships. However, population size impacts the preservation of variation in the mtDNA genome and complicates using contemporary mtDNA variation to calibrate a molecular clock.

Visual Counterpoint

A comparison of the Neandertal (left) and the contemporary *H. sapiens* (right) shows that while both possess large brains there are distinct differences in the shape of the skull. The Neandertal has a large face, pronounced brow ridges, and a low, sloping forehead while the contemporary *H. sapiens* has a high forehead and a chin. The back of the Neandertal, though not visible from this angle, is robust (as seen in the Herto skull pictured below). In what other ways is Herto like these two specimens? How do these three skulls compare to the Cro Magnon skull pictured on page 205?

As widely reported in the popular press (including cover stories in *Newsweek* and *Time*), preliminary results suggest that the mitochondrial DNA of all living humans could be traced back to a "mitochondrial Eve" who lived in Africa some 200,000 years ago. If so, all other populations of archaic *H. sapiens,* as well as non-African *H. erectus,* would have to be ruled out of the ancestry of modern humans.

For many years, the recent African origins theory has been weakened by the lack of good fossil evidence from Africa. In 2003, however, skulls of two adults and one child, discovered in Ethiopia in East Africa in 1997, were described as anatomically modern and were reconstructed and dated to 160,000 years ago (see Anthropologists of Note).[5] The discoverers of these fossils called them *Homo sapiens idaltu* (meaning "elder" in the local Afar language). While conceding that the skulls are robust, they believe that these skulls have conclusively proved the recent African origins hypothesis, relegating Neandertals to a side branch of human evolution.

The recently discovered well-preserved specimens from Herto, Ethiopia, provide the best fossil evidence in support of the recent African origins hypothesis. Though these fossils unquestionably possess an anatomically modern appearance, they are still relatively robust. In addition, it is not clear whether the higher skull and forehead indicate superior cultural abilities.

Reconciling the Evidence

Though the recent African origins hypothesis is the majority position among Western paleoanthropologists, the theory does not prevail throughout the globe. Chinese

---

[5] White, T., et al. (2003). Pleistocene *Homo sapiens* from the Middle Awash, Ethiopia. *Nature 423,* 742–747.

Berhane Asfaw (b. 1953) ▪ Xinzhi Wu (b. 1930)

Born in Addis Ababa, Ethiopia, in 1953, **Berhane Asfaw** is a world-renowned paleoanthropologist leading major expeditions in Ethiopia. He is co-leader of the international Middle Awash Research Project, the research team responsible for the discovery of spectacular ancestral fossils dating from the entire 6-million-year course of human evolutionary history, including *Ardipithecus ramidus, Australopithecus afarensis, Australopithecus garhi, Homo erectus,* and, most recently, the *Homo sapiens idaltu* fossils from Herto, Ethiopia.

At the June 2003 press conference, organized by Teshome Toga, Ethiopia's minister of culture, Asfaw described the Herto specimens as the oldest "anatomically modern" humans, likening Ethiopia to the "Garden of Eden." This conference marked a shift in the Ethiopian government's stance toward the paleoanthropological research spanning Asfaw's career. Previous discoveries in the Middle Awash were also very important, but the government did not participate or support this research.

Asfaw entered the discipline of paleoanthropology through a program administered by the Leakey Foundation providing fellowships for Africans to pursue graduate studies in Europe and the United States. Since this program's inception in the late 1970s, the Leakey Foundation has awarded sixty-eight fellowships totaling $1.2 million to Kenyans, Ethiopians, and Tanzanians to pursue graduate education in paleoanthropology.

Asfaw, mentored by American paleoanthropologist Desmond Clark at the University of California, Berkeley, was among the earliest fellows in this program. They first met in 1979 when Asfaw was a senior studying geology in Addis Ababa. Asfaw obtained his doctorate in 1988 and returned to Ethiopia, where he had few Ethiopian anthropological colleagues, and the government had halted fossil exploration. Since that time, Asfaw has recruited and mentored many Ethiopian scholars, including Sileshi Semaw (see Chapter 8), and now has about a dozen on his team. Local scientists can protect the antiquities, keep fossils from disappearing, and mobilize government support. Asfaw's leadership in paleoanthropology has played a key role in helping the government recognize how important prehistory is for Ethiopia.

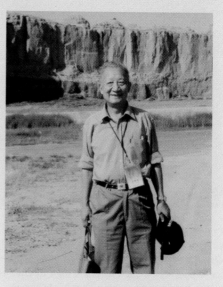

Xinzhi Wu is one of China's foremost paleoanthropological scholars, contributing to the development of the discipline for the past fifty years. As with many other paleoanthropologists, the study of human anatomy has been of vital importance to him.

He began his academic career with a degree from Shanghai Medical College followed by teaching in the Department of Human Anatomy at the Medical College in Dalian before beginning graduate studies in paleoanthropology. He is presently a professor at the Chinese Academy of Sciences Institute of Vertebrate Paleontology and Paleoanthropology in Beijing and the honorary president of the Chinese Society of Anatomical Sciences.

In addition to managing excavations in China and other parts of Asia, Wu has played a major role in the development of theories about modern human origins in cooperation with scholars internationally. He collaborated with Milford Wolpoff of the United States and Alan Thorne of Australia in the development of the theory of multiregional continuity for modern human origins. This theory fits well with the Asian fossil evidence proposing an important place for *Homo erectus* in modern human origins. Interestingly, it builds upon the model for human origins developed by Franz Weidenreich (see Chapter 8).

According to Wu, early humans from China are as old if not older than humans anyplace else. He suggests that the reason more fossils have been found in Africa recently is that Africa has been the site for more excavations.

Zhoukoudian remains a site of particular importance for Wu, as it documents continuous habitation of early humans and one of the earliest sites with evidence of controlled use of fire. Wu has predicted that more important discoveries will still be made at Zhoukoudian as a third of this site has still not been fully excavated. The Chinese government has responded to Wu's suggestions and is presently constructing a 2.4-square-kilometer "Peking Man" exhibition and paleoanthropology research area at Zhoukoudian.

Wu has welcomed many international scholars to China to study the Asian evidence. He also has led efforts to make descriptions of fossil material available in English. Collaborating with anthropologist Frank Poirier, he published the comprehensive volume *Human Evolution in China,* describing the fossil evidence and archaeological sites with great accuracy and detail.

© 1988 David L. Brill

paleoanthropologists, for example, favor the multiregional hypothesis because it fits well with the fossil discoveries from Asia and Australia. By contrast, the recent African origins hypothesis depends more upon the interpretation of fossils and cultural remains from Europe, Africa, and Southwest Asia. Three kinds of evidence are used to both support and critique each hypothesis for modern human origins: genetic, anatomical, and cultural.

The Genetic Evidence

Though genetic evidence has been the cornerstone of the recent African origins hypothesis, molecular evidence also provides grounds to challenge it. For example, upon reanalysis, the molecular evidence indicates that Africa was not the sole source of mtDNA in modern humans.[6] In addition, because both theories propose African origins for the human line, molecular data could be interpreted as evidence supporting the African origins of the genus *Homo,* rather than the more recent species *Homo sapiens.* Both models place ultimate human origins firmly in Africa.

Other assumptions made by DNA analysis are problematic. For example, it is assumed that rates of mutation are steady, when in fact they can be notoriously uneven. Another assumption is that mtDNA is not subject to selection, when in fact variants have been implicated in epilepsy and in a disease of the eye.[7] Another issue is that DNA is seen as traveling exclusively *from* Africa, when it is known that, over the past 10,000 years, there has been plenty of movement of humans *into* Africa as well. In fact, one study of DNA carried on the Y chromosome (the sex chromosome inherited exclusively in the male line) suggests that DNA on the Y chromosome of some Africans was introduced from Asia, where it originated some 200,000 years ago.[8] Nevertheless, recent work on the Y chromosome by anthropologist and geneticist Spencer Wells traces the human lineage to a single population living in Africa about 60,000 years ago.[9]

Despite the seeming conflict, all of these data indicate that gene flow has been an important aspect of human evolutionary history. The multiregional hypothesis and recent African origins hypothesis differ in terms of whether this gene flow occurred over the course of 200,000 or 2 million years.

Since 1997, studies of mitochondrial DNA have not been limited to living people. In that year, mtDNA was extracted from the original German Neandertal remains, and two other Neandertals have since been studied. Because the mtDNA of each of these differs substantially from modern Europeans, many have concluded that there can be no Neandertal ancestry in living humans and that Neandertals must constitute a separate species that went extinct.

But biological anthropologist John Relethford (a specialist in anthropological genetics) points out that these conclusions are premature.[10] For one thing, the average differences are not as great as those seen among living subspecies of the single species of chimpanzee. For another, differences between populations separated in time by tens of thousands of years tell us nothing about differences between populations contemporaneous with each other. More meaningful would be comparison of the DNA from a late Neandertal with an early anatomically modern European.

Finally, if we are to reject Neandertals in the ancestry of modern Europeans because their DNA cannot be detected in their supposed descendents, then we must also reject any connection between a 40,000- to 62,000-year-old skeleton from Australia (that everyone agrees is anatomically modern) and more recent native Australians. In this case, a mtDNA sequence present in an ancient human seems to have become extinct, in which case we must allow the same possibility for the Neandertals.[11] In short, it is definitely premature to use genetic evidence to remove from modern human ancestry all populations of archaic *H. sapiens* save those of Africa. Not even the Neandertals can be excluded.

The Anatomical Evidence

Though the recent fossil discoveries certainly provide evidence of the earliest anatomically modern specimens in Africa, they do not resolve the relationship between biological change in the shape of the skull and cultural change as preserved in the archaeological record. The changes in the archaeological record and the appearance of anatomically modern skulls are separated by some 100,000 years. The evidence from Southwest Asia is particularly interesting in this regard. Here, at a variety of sites dated to between 50,000 and 100,000 years ago, fossils described as both anatomically modern and Neandertal are present and associated with Mousterian technology.

Nevertheless, recent African origins proponents argue that anatomically modern peoples coexisted for a time with other archaic populations until the superior cultural capacities of the "moderns" resulted in extinction of the archaic peoples. Especially clear evidence of this is said to exist in Europe, where Neandertals and "moderns" are said to have coexisted in close proximity between 30,000 and 40,000 years ago. However, defining fossils as either Neandertals or "moderns" illustrates the difficulty with defining a distinct biological species, given the presence of variation found in humans.

---

[6] Templeton, A. R. (1995). The "Eve" hypothesis: A genetic critique and reanalysis. *American Anthropologist 95* (1), 51–72.

[7] Shreeve, J. (1995). *The Neandertal enigma: Solving the mystery of modern human origins* (p. 121). New York: William Morrow.

[8] Gibbons, A. (1997). Ideas on human origins evolve at anthropology gathering. *Science 276,* 535–536.

[9] Wells, S. (2002). *The journey of man: A genetic odyssey.* Princeton, NJ: Princeton University Press.

---

[10] Relethford, J. H. (2001). Absence of regional affinities of Neandertal DNA with living humans does not reject multiregional evolution. *American Journal of Physical Anthropology 115,* 95–98.

[11] Gibbons, A. (2001). The riddle of coexistence. *Science 291,* 1726.

If we think in terms of varied populations, as seen in living humans today,[12] we find that features reminiscent of modern humans can be discerned in some of the latest Neandertals. A specimen from Saint Césaire in France, for example, has a higher forehead and the presence of a chin. A number of other Neandertals, too, show incipient chin development as well as reduced facial protrusion and smaller brow ridges. Conversely, the earliest anatomically modern human skulls from Europe often exhibit features reminiscent of Neandertals (see Chapter 8). In addition, some typical Neandertal features such as the occipital bun are found in diverse living populations today such as Bushmen from southern Africa, Finns and Saami from Scandinavia, and Australian Aborigines. Accordingly, we might view the population of this region between 30,000 and 40,000 years ago as a varied one, with some individuals retaining a stronger Neandertal heritage than others, in whom modern characteristics are more prominent (Figure 9.2). If all these groups were members of the same species, gene flow would be expected, and individuals would express a mosaic of traits.

A mix of modern and Neandertal features is so strong in a child's skeleton recently found in Portugal as to lead several specialists to regard it as clear evidence of hybridization, or successful reproduction between the two

---

[12] Gould, S. J. (1996). *Full house: The spread of excellence from Plato to Darwin* (pp. 72–73). New York: Harmony.

Aurignacian tradition Tool-making tradition in Europe and western Asia at the beginning of the Upper Paleolithic.

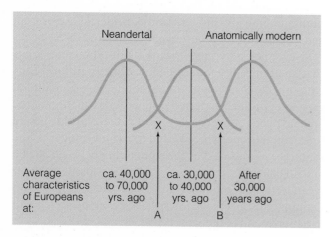

Neandertal   Anatomically modern

Average characteristics of Europeans at:

| ca. 40,000 to 70,000 yrs. ago | ca. 30,000 to 40,000 yrs. ago A | After 30,000 years ago B |

Figure 9.2 Graphically portrayed here is a shift in average characteristics of an otherwise varied population over time from Neandertal to more modern features. Between 30,000 and 40,000 years ago, we would expect to find individuals with characteristics such as those of the Saint Césaire Neandertal (A) and the almost (but not quite) modern Cro-Magnon (B).

groups.[13] This would mean that the two forms are of a single species, rather than separate ones. Others, of course, argue that features interpreted as Neandertal-like might instead be related to this child's "chunky" build.[14]

Scientists supporting the hypothesis that Neandertals are members of the species *Homo sapiens* suggest that the simplest explanation that accounts for all the evidence is that all of these fossils belong to a single varied population, with some individuals showing more typical Neandertal features than others. This accords with archaeological evidence that the intellectual abilities of "late Neandertals" were no different from those of "early moderns."[15]

The Cultural Evidence

Just as it is difficult to find evidence in the physical or mental makeup of Neandertals that would have prevented them from leading a typical Upper Paleolithic way of life, so too are there problems with using technology to distinguish Neandertals from their contemporaries. The Mousterian tool kits were used by Neandertals and anatomically modern humans alike during the Middle Paleolithic. At the time of the Upper Paleolithic transition, the latest Neandertals of Europe developed their own Upper Paleolithic technology (the Châtelperronian) comparable to the industries used by anatomically modern *H. sapiens*. No earlier than 36,500 years ago,[16] a new Upper Paleolithic technology, known as the **Aurignacian tradition**—named after Aurignac, France, where tools of this sort were first discovered—appeared in Europe (Figure 9.3).

Though commonly considered to have spread from southwestern Asia, a recent reanalysis failed to sustain this idea, suggesting instead that the Aurignacian is a distinctively European development.[17] Skeletal remains are rarely associated with Aurignacian tools, although anatomically modern humans are generally considered the makers of these tools. A notable exception to this notion is the central European site of Vindija, Croatia, where Neandertals are associated with an Aurignacian split-bone point.[18]

Some argue that the Upper Paleolithic technology of the Neandertals was a crude imitation of the true technological

---

[13] Holden, C. (1999). Ancient child burial uncovered in Portugal. *Science 283*, 169.

[14] Tattersall, I., & Schwartz, J. H. (1999). Hominids and hybrids: The place of Neanderthals in human evolution. *Proceedings of the National Academy of Science 96* (13), 7117–7119.

[15] d'Errico, F., et al. (1998). Neandertal acculturation in Western Europe? *Current Anthropology 39*, 521.

[16] Zilhão, J. (2000). Fate of the Neandertals. *Archaeology 53* (4), 30.

[17] Clark, G. A. (2002). Neandertal archaeology: Implications for our origins. *American Anthropologist 104* (1), 50–67.

[18] Karavani, I., & Smith, F. H. (2000). More on the Neanderthal problem: The Vindija case. *Current Anthropology 41*, 839.

Figure 9.3 Between 30,000 and 36,500 years ago, Upper Paleolithic industries developed from the Mousterian tradition by European Neandertals coexisted with the Aurignacian industry, usually associated with anatomically modern humans.

advancements practiced by anatomically modern humans. In some respects, however, Neandertals outdid their anatomically modern contemporaries, as in the use of red ochre, a substance less frequently used by Aurignacian peoples than by their late Neandertal neighbors.[19] This cannot be a case of borrowing ideas and techniques from Aurignacians, as these developments clearly predate the Aurignacian.[20]

Coexistence and Cultural Continuity

Neandertals and anatomically modern humans also coexisted in Southwest Asia long before the cultural innovations of the Upper Paleolithic (Figure 9.4). Here neither

the skeletal nor the archaeological evidence supports cultural difference between the fossil groups or absolute biological difference. Although Neandertal skeletons are clearly present at sites such as the caves of Kebara and Shanidar in Israel and Iraq, respectively, skeletons from some older sites have been described as anatomically modern.

At the cave site of Qafzeh near Nazareth in Israel, for example, 90,000-year-old skeletons are said to show none of the Neandertal hallmarks; although their faces and bodies are large and heavily built by today's standards, they are nonetheless claimed to be within the range of living peoples. Yet, a statistical study comparing a number of measurements from among Qafzeh, Upper Paleolithic, and Neandertal skulls found those from Qafzeh to fall in between the anatomically modern and

[19] Bednarik, p. 606.

[20] Zilhão, p. 40.

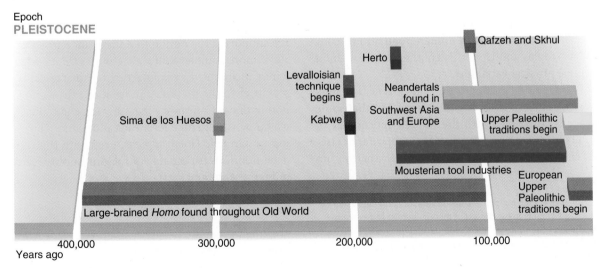

Figure 9.4 Around 400,000 years ago, large-brained members of the genus *Homo* began to be found throughout Africa and Eurasia; corresponding cultural changes are evident as well.

Neandertal norms, though slightly closer to the Neandertals.[21] Nor is the dentition functionally distinguishable when Qafzeh and Neandertal are compared.[22]

While skeletons from Skhul, a site on Mount Carmel of the same period, are similar to those from Qafzeh, they were also part of a population whose continuous range of variation included individuals with markedly Neandertal characteristics. Furthermore, the idea of two distinctly different but coexisting populations receives no support from the archaeological evidence. Individuals living at Skhul and Qafzeh were making and using the same Mousterian tools as those at Kebara and Shanidar, a fact that belies biologically distinct groups having different cultural abilities.

The examination of sites continuously inhabited throughout the Upper Pleistocene provides no significant evidence for behavioral differences between Middle Paleolithic and early Upper Paleolithic at these sites. For example, the Upper Paleolithic peoples who used Kebara Cave continued to live in exactly the same way as their Neandertal predecessors: They procured the same foods, processed them in the same way, used similar hearths, and disposed of their trash in the same way. The only evident difference is that the Neandertals did not use small stones or cobbles to bank their fires for warmth as did their Upper Paleolithic successors.[23]

Nevertheless, by 28,000 years ago, many of the extreme anatomical features seen in archaic groups like Neandertals seem to disappear from the fossil record in Europe and Southwest Asia. Instead, people with higher foreheads, smoother brow ridges, and distinct chins seemed to have Europe more or less to themselves. However, an examination of the full range of individual human variation across the globe and into the present reveals contemporary humans with skulls not meeting the anatomical definition of modernity proposed in the standard evolutionary arguments.[24] Similarly, many Neandertal features can be seen in living people today such as the occipital buns mentioned earlier. As is typical in human populations, contemporary peoples and Upper Paleolithic peoples exhibit considerable physical variability.

It is impossible to know just how much gene flow took place among ancient human populations, but that some took place is consistent with the sudden appearance of novel traits in one region later than their appearance elsewhere. For example, some Upper Paleolithic remains from

North Africa exhibit the kind of midfacial flatness previously seen only in East Asian fossils; similarly, various Cro-Magnon fossils from Europe show the short upper jaws, horizontally oriented cheek bones, and rectangular eye orbits previously seen in East Asians. Conversely, the round orbits, large frontal sinuses, and thin cranial bones seen in some archaic *H. sapiens* skulls from China represent the first appearance there of traits that have greater antiquity in Europe.[25] The movement of these physical traits has a complex genetic basis that depends upon gene flow among populations.

Not only is such gene flow consistent with the remarkable tendency humans have to "swap genes" between populations, even in the face of cultural barriers, but it is also consistent with the tendency of other primates to produce hybrids when two subspecies (and sometimes even species) come into contact.[26] Moreover, without such gene flow, evolution inevitably would have resulted in the appearance of multiple species of modern humans, something that clearly has not happened. In fact, the low level of genetic differentiation among modern human populations can be explained easily as a consequence of high levels of gene flow.[27]

Race and Human Evolution

The Neandertal question can be viewed as more than simply a fascinating discussion about interpreting the fossil evidence. It raises fundamental issues about the relationship between biological and cultural variation. Can a series of biological features indicate particular cultural abilities?

As we examined the fossil record throughout this chapter and others, we made inferences about the cultural capabilities of our ancestors based on biological features in combination with archaeological features. The increased brain size of *Homo habilis* noted around 2.5 million years ago supported the notion that these ancestors were capable of more complex cultural activities than australopithecines, including the manufacture of stone tools. When we get closer to the present, can we make the same kinds of assumptions? Can we say that only the anatomically modern humans, with high foreheads and reduced brow ridges, and not archaic *Homo sapiens,* even with their modern-sized brains, were capable of making sophisticated tools and representational art?

[21] Corruccini, R. S. (1992). Metrical reconsideration of the Skhul IV and IX and Border Cave I crania in the context of modern human origins. *American Journal of Physical Anthropology 87,* 433–445.

[22] Brace, C. L. (2000). *Evolution in an anthropological view* (p. 206). Walnut Creek, CA: Altamira.

[23] Corruccini, p. 436.

[24] Wolpoff & Caspari.

[25] Pope, pp. 287–288.

[26] Simons, E. L. (1989). Human origins. *Science 245,* 1349.

[27] Relethford, J. H., & Harpending, H. C. (1994). Craniometric variation, genetic theory, and modern human origins. *American Journal of Physical Anthropology 95,* 265.

Supporters of the multiregional hypothesis argue that we cannot.[28] They suggest that using a series of biological features to represent a type of human being (Neandertals) with certain cultural capacities (inferior) is like making assumptions about cultural capabilities of living humans based on their appearance. In living peoples, such an assumption would be considered stereotyping or even racism. Supporters of the recent African origins hypothesis counter that because their theory embraces African human origins, it could hardly be considered prejudicial.

While paleoanthropologists all acknowledge African origins for the first bipeds and the genus *Homo,* considerable disagreement exists with regard to the interpretation of the relationship between biological change and cultural change as we approach the present. The fossil and archaeological evidence from the Middle Paleolithic does not indicate a simple one-to-one correspondence between cultural innovations and a biological change preserved in the shape of the skull.

Upper Paleolithic Technology

In the Upper Paleolithic new techniques of core preparation allowed for more intensive production of highly standardized blades and permitted the proliferation of this tool type. The toolmaker formed a cylindrical core, struck the blade off near the edge of the core, and repeated this procedure, going around the core in one direction until finishing near its center (Figure 9.5). The procedure is analogous to peeling long leaves off an artichoke. With this **blade technique,** an Upper Paleolithic flint knapper could get 75 feet of working edge from a 2-pound core; a Mousterian knapper could get only 6 feet from the same sized core.

Other efficient techniques of tool manufacture also came into common use at this time. One such method was **pressure flaking,** in which a bone, antler, or wooden tool was used to press rather than strike off small flakes as the final step in stone tool manufacture (Figure 9.6). The advantage of this technique is that the toolmaker has greater control over the final shape of the tool than is possible with percussion flaking alone. The so-called Solutrean laurel leaf bifaces found in Spain and France are examples of this technique (see photo on page 214). The longest of these tools is 33 centimeters (13 inches) in length but less than a centimeter (about a quarter of an inch) thick. Through pressure flaking, tools could be worked with great precision into a variety of final forms, and worn tools could be effectively resharpened over and over until they were too small for further use.

Although invented in the Middle Paleolithic, the **burin,** a tool with a chisel-like edge, became more common in

Figure 9.5 During the Upper Paleolithic, a new technique was used to manufacture blades. The stone is worked to create a striking platform; long, almost parallel-sided flakes then are struck around the sides, providing sharp-edged blades.

Figure 9.6 Two methods used for pressure flaking in which a bone, antler, or wooden tool is used to press rather than strike off small flakes.

the Upper Paleolithic. Burins facilitated the working of bone, horn, antler, and ivory into such useful things as fishhooks, harpoons, and eyed needles. These implements made life easier for *Homo sapiens,* especially in colder

blade technique A technique of stone tool manufacture in which long, parallel-sided flakes are struck off the edges of a specially prepared core.

pressure flaking A technique of stone tool manufacture in which a bone, antler, or wooden tool is used to press, rather than strike off, small flakes from a piece of flint or similar stone.

burin A stone tool with chisel-like edges used for working bone and antler.

---

[28] Wolpoff & Caspari.

The techniques of the Upper Paleolithic allowed for the manufacture of a wide variety of tools. The finely wrought Solutrean bifaces of Europe (shaped like the leaf of a plant) were made using the pressure-flaking technique. Tools such as eyed needles and harpoons began to be manufactured out of bone as well.

northern regions where the ability to stitch together animal hides was particularly important for warmth.

The spear-thrower, also known by its Aztec name *atlatl,* appeared at this time as well. Atlatls are wooden devices, one end of which is gripped in the hunter's hand, while the other end has a hole or hook, in or against which the end of the spear is placed. It is held so as to effectively extend the length of the hunter's arm, thereby increasing the velocity of the spear when thrown. Using a spear-thrower greatly added to the efficiency of the spear as a hunting tool (Figure 9.7).

With handheld spears, hunters had to get close to their prey to make the kill. Because many of the animals they hunted were large and fierce, this was a dangerous business. The need to get within close striking range and the improbability of an instant kill exposed the hunter to considerable risk. But with the spear-thrower, the effective killing distance was increased; experiments demonstrate

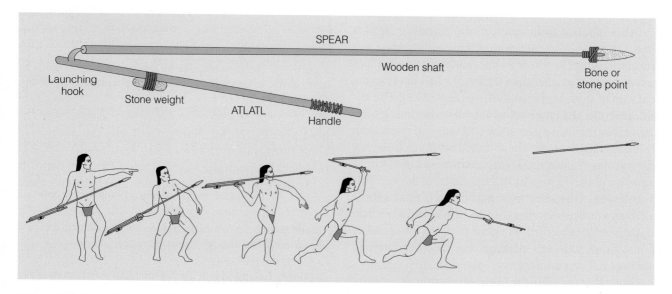

Figure 9.7 Spear-throwers (atlatls) allowed Upper Paleolithic individuals to throw spears at animals from a safe distance while still maintaining reasonable speed and accuracy. Upper Paleolithic artists frequently combined artistic expression with practical function, ornamenting their spear-throwers with animal figures.

that the effective killing distance of a spear when used with a spear-thrower is between 18 and 27 meters as opposed to significantly less without.[29]

Killing distance can be safely shortened when the kill is assured. The use of poison on spear tips, as employed by contemporary hunters such as the Hadza of Tanzania, will decrease the risk to a hunter at shorter range. It is not clear from the archaeological record when this innovation began, although the invention of tiny sharp stone blades for dart tips to provide a vehicle for poison delivery is clear. The earliest examples of these "microliths" began during the Upper Paleolithic in Africa, but did not become widespread until the Mesolithic or Middle Stone Age, as will be described in detail in Chapter 10.

Another important innovation, net hunting, appeared some time between 22,000 and 29,000 years ago.[30] Knotted nets, made from the fibers of wild plants such as hemp or nettle, left their impression on the clay floors of huts when people walked on them. When the huts later burned, these impressions, baked into the earth, provide evidence that nets existed. Their use accounts for the high number of hare, fox, and other small mammal and bird bones at archaeological sites. Like historically known and contemporary net hunters, such as the Mbuti of the Congo, everyone—men, women, and children—probably participated, frightening animals with loud noises to drive them to where hunters were stationed with their nets. In this way, large amounts of meat could be amassed without requiring great speed or strength on the part of the hunters.

A further improvement of hunting techniques came with the invention of the bow and arrow, which appeared first in Africa, but not until the end of the Upper Paleolithic in Europe. The greatest advantage of the bow is that it increases the distance between hunter and prey. Beyond 24 meters (79 feet), the accuracy and penetration of a spear thrown with a spear-thrower are not very good, whereas even a poor bow will shoot an arrow further, with greater accuracy and penetrating power. A good bow is effective even at nearly 91 meters (300 feet). Thus hunters were able to maintain more distance between themselves and dangerous prey, dramatically decreasing the risk to the hunter of being seriously injured by an animal fighting for survival as well as reducing the chance of startling an animal and triggering its flight.

Upper Paleolithic peoples not only had better tools but also a greater diversity of tool types than earlier peoples. The highly developed Upper Paleolithic kit included tools for use during different seasons, and regional variation in tool kits was greater than ever before. Thus it is really impossible to speak of a single Upper Paleolithic culture even in Europe, a relatively small and isolated region compared to Asia and Africa. For foot nomads, it was a formidable challenge to travel outside the region. Geologic features such as mountain ranges, oceans, and glaciers isolated groups of people from each other.

To understand the Upper Paleolithic, one must consider the many different traditions that made it possible for people to adapt ever more specifically to the various environments in which they were living. Just how proficient people had become at securing a livelihood is indicated by bone yards containing thousands of animal skeletons. At Solutré in France over a period of many years, for example, Upper Paleolithic hunters killed 10,000 horses; at Predmosti in the Czech Republic, they were responsible for the deaths of 1,000 mammoths. The favored big game of European hunters, however, was reindeer, which they killed in even greater numbers.

Upper Paleolithic Art

Although tools and weapons demonstrate the ingenuity of Upper Paleolithic peoples, artistic expression provides the best evidence of their creativity. Some have argued that artistic expression was made possible by a newly evolved biological ability to manipulate symbols and make images. However, the modern-sized brains of archaic *Homo sapiens* and increasingly compelling evidence of the presence of language or behaviors involving symbolism—such as burials—undercut this notion. Like agriculture, which came later (see Chapter 10), the artistic explosion may have been no more than a consequence of innovations made by a people who had the capacity to make them for tens of thousands of years already.

In fact, just as many of the distinctive tools that were commonly used in Upper Paleolithic times first appear in the Middle Paleolithic, so too do objects of art. In Southwest Asia, a crude figurine of volcanic tuff is some 250,000 years old.[31] While some scholars contest whether this was carved, those who believe it is state that it indicates that people had the ability to carve all sorts of things from wood, a substance easier to fashion than volcanic tuff but rarely preserved for long periods of time. Furthermore, ochre "crayons" from Middle Paleolithic contexts in various parts of the world must have been used to decorate or mark. In southern Africa, for example, regular use of yellow and red ochre goes back 130,000 years, with some

[29] Frayer, D. W. (1981). Body size, weapon use, and natural selection in the European Upper Paleolithic and Mesolithic. *American Anthropologist 83,* 58.

[30] Pringle, H. (1997). Ice Age communities may be earliest known net hunters. *Science 277,* 1203.

[31] Appenzeller, T. (1998). Art: Evolution or revolution? *Science 282,* 1452.

These 17,000-year-old images, painted on a wall in the multi-chambered Lascaux Cave in the Dordogne region of southwestern France, were discovered in 1940 by four teenage boys. In addition to the Ice Age animals depicted here—horses, wild ox, rhino, and bison—the chambers of Lascaux feature renderings of many other recognizable species. The carved and painted interiors of such caves were often deep underground and difficult to reach. Upper Paleolithic artists burned animal fat in sandstone lamps to light their way. In 1963 Lascaux Cave was closed to the public because carbon dioxide from the breath of thousands of visitors was damaging the ancient paintings. The French government built an exact replica of the cave so that visitors can still experience the wonder of these ancient works.

evidence as old as 200,000 years.[32] Perhaps pigments were used on people's bodies, as well as objects, as the 50,000-year-old mammoth-tooth *churinga* discussed in Chapter 8 might suggest. The timeline in Figure 9.8 shows some of the cultural events of the Upper Paleolithic.

Music

Evidence that music played a role in the lives of Upper Paleolithic peoples is documented through the presence of bone flutes and whistles in various sites, the most recently discovered dated to 35,000 years old. But again, such instruments may have their origin in Middle Paleolithic prototypes, such as the probable Neandertal flute discussed in

Chapter 8. Although we cannot be sure just where and when it happened, some genius discovered that bows could be used not just for killing, but to make music as well. Because the bow and arrow is an Upper Paleolithic invention, the musical bow likely is as well. We do know that the musical bow is the oldest of all stringed instruments, and its invention ultimately made possible the development of all of the stringed instruments with which we are familiar today.

Cave or Rock Art

The earliest evidence of cave art comes from Australia and dates back at least 45,000 years. This consists entirely of geometric patterns and repetitive motifs. Figurative

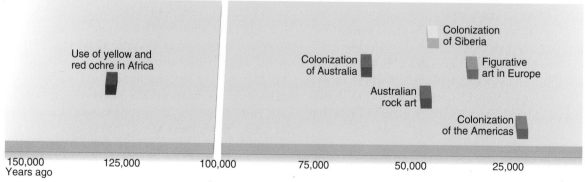

Figure 9.8 This timeline indicates the dates for some of the cultural innovations associated with the Upper Paleolithic.

© John Van Hasselt/Corbis Sygma

Rock art, like these paintings from Australia, depict things seen by dancers while in states of trance. Simple geometric designs such as zigzags, notches, dots, and spirals (as on the cave ceiling) as well as human and animal figures are common in these paintings.

pictures go back 35,000 years in Europe (the time of the Venus figurine of the chapter opener), although they do not become common until much later.

Pictorial art is probably equally old in Africa. Both engravings and paintings are known from many rock shelters and outcrops in southern Africa, where they continued to be made by Bushmen peoples until recently. Scenes feature both humans and animals, depicted with extraordinary skill, often in association with geometric and other abstract motifs. Some sites reveal that ancient peoples had the seemingly irresistible urge to add to existing rock paintings, while others used new sites for creating what we today call graffiti.

Because this rock art tradition continues unbroken into the present, it has been possible to discover what this art means. There is a close connection between the art and shamanism, and many scenes depict visions seen in states of trance. Distortions in the art, usually of human figures, represent sensations felt by individuals in a state of trance, whereas the geometric designs depict illusions that originate in the central nervous system in altered states of consciousness. These **entoptic phenomena** are luminous grids, dots, zigzags, and other designs that seem to shimmer, pulsate, rotate, and expand and are seen as one enters a state of trance. Sufferers of migraines experience similar hallucinations. Entopic phenomena are typical of the Australian cave art mentioned above.

In many recent cultures, geometric designs are used as symbolic expressions of genealogical patterns, records

of origins, and the afterlife.[33] The animals depicted in this art, often with startling realism, are not the ones most often eaten. Rather, they are powerful beasts like the eland (a large African antelope), and this power is important to shamans—individuals skilled at manipulating supernatural powers and spirits for human benefit—who try to harness it for their rain-making, healing, and other rituals.

The most famous Upper Paleolithic art is that of Europe, largely because most researchers of prehistoric art are themselves of European background. Though the earliest of this art took the form of sculpture and engravings—often portraying such animals as reindeer, horses, bears, and ibexes—figurative art abounds in the spectacular paintings on the walls of 200 or so caves in southern France and northern Spain. The oldest of these date from about 32,000 years ago. Visually accurate portrayals of Ice Age mammals—including bison, aurochs, horses, mammoths, and stags—were often painted one on top of another.

Although well represented in other media, humans are not commonly portrayed in cave paintings, nor are

[32] Barham, L. S. (1998). Possible early pigment use in South-Central Africa. *Current Anthropology 39,* 709.

[33] Schuster, C., & Carpenter, E. (1996). *Patterns that connect: Social symbolism in ancient and tribal art.* New York: Abrams.

entoptic phenomena   Bright pulsating forms that are generated by the central nervous system and seen in states of trance.

scenes or depictions of events at all common. Instead, the animals are often abstracted from nature and rendered two-dimensionally—no small achievement for these early artists. Sometimes the artists made use of bulges and other features of the rock to impart a more three-dimensional feeling. Frequently, the paintings are in hard-to-get-at places while suitable surfaces in more accessible places remain untouched. In some caves, the lamps by which the artists worked have been found; these are spoon-shaped objects of sandstone in which

animal fat was burned. Experimentation has shown that such lamps would have provided adequate illumination over several hours.

The techniques used by Upper Paleolithic peoples to create their cave paintings were unraveled a decade ago through the experimental work of Michel Lorblanchet. Interestingly, they turn out to be the same ones used by Aboriginal rock painters in Australia. Lorblanchet's experiments are described in the following Original Study by science writer Roger Lewin.

Original Study

Paleolithic Paint Job   *by Roger Lewin*

Lorblanchet's recent bid to re-create one of the most important Ice Age images in Europe was an affair of the heart as much as the head. "I tried to abandon my skin of a modern citizen, tried to experience the feeling of the artist, to enter the dialogue between the rock and the man," he explains. Every day for a week in the fall of 1990 he drove the 20 miles from his home in the medieval village of Cajarc into the hills above the river Lot. There, in a small, practically inaccessible cave, he transformed himself into an Upper Paleolithic painter.

And not just any Upper Paleolithic painter, but the one who 18,400 years ago crafted the dotted horses inside the famous cave of Pech Merle.

You can still see the original horses in Pech Merle's vast underground geologic splendor.

You enter through a narrow passageway and soon find yourself gazing across a grand cavern to where the painting seems to hang in the gloom. "Outside, the landscape is very different from the one the Upper Paleolithic people saw," says Lorblanchet. "But in here, the landscape is the same as it was more than 18,000 years ago. You see what the Upper Paleolithic people experienced." No matter where you look in this cavern, the eye is drawn back to the panel of horses.

The two horses face away from each other, rumps slightly overlapping, their outlines sketched in black. The animal on the right seems to come alive as it merges with a crook in the edge of the panel, the perfect natural shape for a horse's head. But the impression of naturalism quickly fades as the eye falls on the painting's dark dots. There are more than 200 of them, deliberately

distributed within and below the bodies and arcing around the right-hand horse's head and mane. More cryptic still are a smattering of red dots and half-circles and the floating outline of a fish. The surrealism is completed by six disembodied human hands stenciled above and below the animals.

Lorblanchet began thinking about recreating the horses after a research trip to Australia over a decade ago. Not only is Australia a treasure trove of rock art, but its aboriginal people are still creating it. "In Queensland I learned how people painted by spitting pigment onto the rock," he recalls. "They spat paint and used their hand, a piece of cloth, or a feather as a screen to create different lines and other effects. Elsewhere in Australia people used chewed twigs as paintbrushes, but in Queensland the spitting technique worked best." The rock surfaces there were too uneven for extensive brushwork, he adds—just as they are in Quercy.

When Lorblanchet returned home he looked at the Quercy paintings with a new eye. Sure enough, he began seeing the telltale signs of spit-painting—lines with edges that were sharply demarcated on one side and fuzzy on the other, as if they had been airbrushed—instead of the brushstrokes he and others had assumed were there. Could you produce lines that were crisp on both edges with the same technique, he wondered, and perhaps dots too? Archeologists had long recognized that hand stencils, which are common in prehistoric art,

© Jean Vertut

This spotted horse in the French cave of Pech Merle was painted by an Upper Paleolithic artist.

were produced by spitting paint around a hand held to the wall. But no one had thought that entire animal images could be created this way. Before he could test his ideas, however, Lorblanchet had to find a suitable rock face—the original horses were painted on a roughly vertical panel 13 feet across and 6 feet high. With the help of a speleologist, he eventually found a rock face in a remote cave high in the hills and set to work.

Following the aboriginal practices he had witnessed, Lorblanchet first made a light outline sketch of the horses with a charred stick. Then he prepared black pigment for the painting. "My intention had been to use manganese dioxide, as the Pech Merle painter did," says Lorblanchet, referring to one of the minerals ground up for paint by the early artists. "But I was advised that manganese is somewhat toxic, so I used wood charcoal instead." (Charcoal was used as pigment by Paleolithic painters in other caves, so Lorblanchet felt he could justify his concession to safety.) To turn the charcoal into paint, Lorblanchet ground it with a limestone block, put the powder in his mouth, and diluted it to the right consistency with saliva and water. For red pigment he used ochre from the local iron-rich clay.

He started with the dark mane of the right-hand horse. "I spat a series of dots and fused them together to represent tufts of hair," he says, unselfconsciously reproducing the spitting action as he talks. "Then I painted the horse's back by blowing the pigment below my hand held so"—he holds his hand flat against the rock with his thumb tucked in to form a straight line—"and used it like a stencil to produce a sharp upper edge and a diffused lower edge. You get an illusion of the animal's rounded flank this way."

He experimented as he went. "You see the angular rump?" he says, pointing to the original painting. "I reproduced that by holding my hand perpendicular to the rock, with my palm slightly bent, and I spat along the edge formed by my hand and the rock." He found he could produce sharp lines, such as those in the tail and in the upper hind leg, by spitting into the gap between parallel hands.

The belly demanded more ingenuity; he spat paint into a V-shape formed by his two splayed hands, rubbed it into a curved swath to shape the belly's outline, then finger-painted short protruding lines to suggest the animals' shaggy hair. Neatly outlined dots, he found, could not be made by blowing a thin jet of charcoal onto the wall. He had to spit pigment through a hole made in an animal skin. "I spent seven hours a day for a week," he says. "Puff . . . puff . . . puff. . . . It was exhausting, particularly because there was carbon monoxide in the cave. But you experience something special, painting like that. You feel you are breathing the image onto the rock—projecting your spirit from the deepest part of your body onto the rock surface."

Was that what the Paleolithic painter felt when creating this image? "Yes, I know it doesn't sound very scientific," Lorblanchet says of his highly personal style of investigation, "but the intellectual games of the structuralists haven't got us very far, have they? Studying rock art shouldn't be an intellectual game. It is about understanding humanity. That's why I believe the experimental approach is valid in this case."

Lewin, R. (1993). Paleolithic paint job. Discover 14 (7), 67–69. Copyright ©1993 The Walt Disney Co. Reprinted with permission of Discover Magazine.

Theories to account for the early European cave art are problematic because they often depend on conjectural and subjective interpretations. Some have argued that it is art for art's sake; but if that is so, why were animals often painted over one another, and why were they placed in inaccessible places? The latter might suggest that they were for ceremonial purposes and that the caves served as religious sanctuaries.

One suggestion is that the animals were drawn to ensure success in the hunt, another that their depiction was seen as a way to promote fertility and increase the size of the herds on which humans depended. In Altamira Cave in northern Spain, for example, the art shows a pervasive concern for the sexual reproduction of the bison.[34] In cave art generally, though, the animals painted show little relationship to those most frequently hunted. Furthermore, there are few depictions of animals being hunted or killed, nor are there depictions of animals copulating or with exaggerated sexual parts as there are in the Venus figures.[35]

Another suggestion is that initiation rites, such as those marking the transition to adulthood, took place in the painted galleries. In support of this idea, footprints, most of which are small, have been found in the clay floors of several caves, and in one they even circle a modeled clay bison. The painted animals, so this argument goes, may have had to do with knowledge being transmitted from the elders to the youths. Furthermore, the transmission of information might be implied by countless so-called signs, apparently abstract designs that accompany much Upper Paleolithic art. Some have interpreted these as tallies of animals killed, a reckoning of time according to a lunar calendar, or both.

These abstract designs, including such ones as the spots on the Pech Merle horses, suggest yet another possibility. For the most part, these are just like the entoptic designs seen by subjects in experiments dealing with altered states of consciousness and that are so consistently present in the rock art of southern Africa. Furthermore, the rock art of southern Africa shows the same painting of new

---

[34] Halverson, J. (1989). Review of the book *Altamira revisited and other essays on early art. American Antiquity 54,* 883.

[35] Conard, N. J. (2009). A female figurine from the basal Aurignacian deposits of Hohle Fels Cave in southwestern Germany. *Nature 459* (7244), 248.

images over older ones, as well as the same sort of fixation on large, powerful animals instead of the ones most often eaten. Thus the cave art of Europe may well represent the same depictions of trance experiences, painted after the fact. Consistent with this interpretation, the isolation of the cave and the shimmering light on the cave walls themselves are conducive to the sort of sensory distortion that can induce trance.

Ornamental Art

Artistic expression, whatever its purpose may have been, was not confined to rock surfaces and portable objects. Upper Paleolithic peoples also ornamented their bodies with necklaces of perforated animal teeth, shells, beads of bone, stone, and ivory, as well as rings, bracelets, and anklets. Clothing, too, was adorned with beads. Quite a lot of art was probably also executed in more delicate materials such as wood carving, painting on bark, and animal skins, which have not been preserved. Thus the rarity or absence of Upper Paleolithic art in some parts of the inhabited world may be due to the fact that some materials did not survive long in the archaeological record, not that they did not exist.

Gender and Art

As seen in the chapter opener, the Upper Paleolithic also includes numerous portrayals of voluptuous women with body parts often described as exaggerated. Many appear to be pregnant, and some are shown in birthing postures. These so-called Venus figures have been found at sites from southwestern France to as far as Siberia. Made of stone, ivory, antler, or baked clay, they differ little in style from place to place, testifying to the sharing of ideas over vast distances. Although some have interpreted the Venuses as objects associated with a fertility cult, others suggest that they may have been exchanged to cement alliances among groups.

Art historian LeRoy McDermott has suggested that the Venus figurines are "ordinary women's views of their own bodies" and the earliest examples of self-representation.[36] He suggests that the distortions and exaggerations of the female form visible in the Venus figurines derive from the ancient artist looking down over her own pregnant body. Paleolithic archaeologist Margaret Conkey opened the door to such interpretations through her work combining gender theory and feminist theory with the science of archaeology.

With a particular interest in the Upper Paleolithic art of Europe, Conkey has spent decades challenging the traditional notion that Paleolithic art was made by male artists as an expression of spiritual beliefs related to hunting activities. She emphasizes that many reconstructions of behavior in the past rely upon contemporary gender norms to fill in blanks left in the archaeological record. In other words, she is interested in the role of gender today in shaping the reconstruction of gender in the past. In the archaeological research she conducts, she seeks clues about gender in the deep past, evidence that is not shaped by gender stereotypes from the present.[37]

In this regard it is interesting to note that contemporary scientists describe Venus figurines largely in sexual terms rather than in terms of fertility and birth. For example, in a commentary in the prestigious journal *Nature* that accompanied the description of the the Hohle Fels Cave Venus, British archaeologist Paul Mellars states: "The figure is explicitly—and blatantly—that of a woman, with an exaggeration of sexual characteristics (large, projecting breasts, a greatly enlarged and explicit vulva, and bloated belly and thighs) that by twenty-first-century standards could be seen as bordering on the pornographic."[38]

Mellars's reaction to the Venus figurine reflects contemporary attitudes toward the nude female form rather than the intent of an ancient artist. Perhaps the artist was a female, looking at her own pregnant form or remembering the experience of giving birth. While the gender and the intention of the artist behind the Venus figurine cannot be known for sure, it is easy to imagine that pregnancy and the birth process were at least as awe-inspiring to Paleolithic peoples as were hunting experiences.

Human biology also provides us with some clues. Breasts and belly enlarge during pregnancy; the tissues around the vulva enlarge and stretch dramatically during the birth process. Breasts swell further with milk after a birth. Mellars's interpretation of the artistic depiction of these biological changes as "pornographic" derives from the gender norms of his particular culture. Many contemporary peoples with different worldviews would not react to the figurine in these terms.

Other Aspects of Upper Paleolithic Culture

Upper Paleolithic peoples lived not only in caves and rock shelters but also in structures built out in the open. In Ukraine, for example, the remains have been found of sizable settlements, in which huts were built on frameworks

[36] McDermott, L. (1996). Self-representation in Upper Paleolithic female figurines. *Current Anthropology 37*, 227–276.

[37] Gero, J. M., & Conkey, M. W. (Eds.). (1991). *Engendering archaeology: Women and prehistory*. New York: Wiley-Blackwell.

[38] Mellars, P. (2009). Archaeology: Origins of the female image. *Nature 459*, 176–177, at 176.

Reconstruction of an Upper Paleolithic hut with walls of interlocked mammoth mandibles.

of intricately stacked mammoth bones. Where the ground was frozen, cobblestones were heated and placed in the earth to sink in, thereby providing sturdy, dry floors. Their hearths, no longer shallow depressions or flat surfaces that radiated back little heat, were instead stone-lined pits that conserved heat for extended periods and made for more efficient cooking.

For the outdoors, they had the same sort of tailored clothing worn in historic times by Arctic and sub-Arctic peoples. And they engaged in long-distance trade, as indicated, for example, by the presence of seashells and Baltic amber at sites several hundred kilometers from the sources of these materials. Although Middle Paleolithic peoples also made use of rare and distant materials, they did not do so with the regularity seen in the Upper Paleolithic.

The Spread of Upper Paleolithic Peoples

Upper Paleolithic peoples expanded into regions previously uninhabited by their archaic forebears. Colonization of Siberia began about 42,000 years ago, although it took something like 10,000 years before humans reached the northeastern part of that region. While this spread did not involve crossing large bodies of water, this was the case for the spread to Greater Australia and the Americas.

The Sahul

Much earlier, possibly by at least 60,000 years ago, people managed to get to Australia, Tasmania, and New Guinea, then connected to one another in a single landmass called the **Sahul** (Figure 9.9).[39] To do this, they had to use some kind of watercraft because the Sahul was separated from the islands (which are geologically a part of the Asian landmass) of Java, Sumatra, Borneo, and Bali. At times of maximum glaciation and low sea levels, these islands were joined to one another in a single landmass called **Sunda,** but a deep ocean trench (called

---

[39] Rice, P. (2000). Paleoanthropology 2000—part 1. *General Anthropology 7* (1), 11; Zimmer, C. (1999). New date for the dawn of dream time. *Science 284,* 1243.

Sahul The greater Australian landmass including Australia, New Guinea, and Tasmania. At times of maximum glaciation and low sea levels, these areas were continuous.

Sunda The combined landmass of the contemporary islands of Java, Sumatra, Borneo, and Bali that was continuous with mainland Southeast Asia at times of low sea levels corresponding to maximum glaciation.

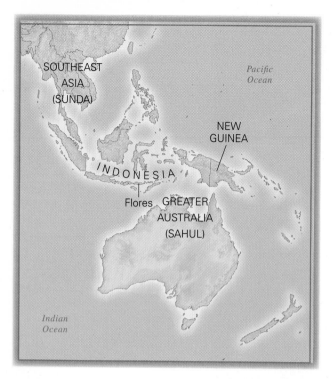

Figure 9.9 Habitation of Australia and New Guinea (joined together with Tasmania as a single landmass called Sahul) was dependent upon travel across the open ocean even at times of maximum glaciations when sea levels were low. This figure shows the coastlines of Sahul and Sunda (Southeast Asia plus the island of Java, Sumatra, Borneo, and Bali) now and in the past. As sea levels rose with melting glaciers, sites of early human habitation were submerged under water.

the Wallace Trench, after Alfred Russel Wallace, who, as described in Chapter 2, discovered natural selection at the same time as Charles Darwin) always separated Sunda and Sahul.

Anthropologist Joseph Birdsell suggested several routes of island hopping and seafaring to make the crossing between these landmasses.[40] Each of these routes still involves crossing open water without land visible on the horizon. The earliest known site in New Guinea dates to 40,000 years ago. Sites in Australia are dated to even earlier, but these dates are especially contentious because they involve the critical question of the relationship between anatomical modernity and the presence of humanlike culture. Early dates for habitation of the Sahul indicate that archaic *Homo* rather than anatomically modern forms possessed the cultural capacity for

oceanic navigation. Once in Australia, these people created some of the world's earliest sophisticated rock art, perhaps some 10,000 to 15,000 years earlier than the more famous European cave paintings.

Interestingly, considerable physical variation is seen in Australian fossil specimens from this period. Some specimens have the high forehead characteristic of anatomical modernity while others possess traits providing excellent evidence of continuity between living Aborigines and the earlier *Homo erectus* and archaic *Homo sapiens* fossils from Indonesia. Willandra Lakes—the fossil lake region of southeastern Australia, far from where the earliest archaeological evidence of human habitation of the continent was found—is particularly rich with fossils. The variation present in these fossils illustrates the problems inherent with making a one-to-one correspondence between the skull of a certain shape and cultural capabilities.

Other evidence for sophisticated ritual activity in early Australia is provided by the burial of a man at least 40,000 and possibly 60,000 years ago from the Willandra Lakes region. His body was positioned with his fingers intertwined around one another in the region of his penis, and red ochre had been scattered over the body. It may be that this pigment had more than symbolic value; for example, its iron salts have antiseptic and deodorizing properties, and there are recorded instances in which red ochre is associated with prolonging life and is used medicinally to treat particular conditions or infections. One historically known Aborigine society is reported to have used ochre to heal wounds, scars, and burns. A person with internal pain was covered with the substance and placed in the sun to promote sweating. See this chapter's Globalscape to learn about the importance of Willandra Lakes to global and local heritage today.

As in many parts of the world, paleoanthropologists conducting research on human evolution in Australia are essentially constructing a view of history that conflicts with the beliefs of Aborigines. The story of human evolution is utterly dependent on Western conceptions of time, relationships established through genetics, and a definition of what it means to be human. All of these concepts are at odds with Aboriginal beliefs about human origins. Still, while conducting their research on human evolution, paleoanthropologists working in Australia have advocated and supported the Aboriginal culture.

The Americas

While scientists concur that American Indian ancestry can be traced ultimately back to Asian origins, just when people arrived in the Americas has been a matter of lively debate. This debate draws upon geographical, cultural, and biological evidence.

[40] Birdsell, J. H. (1977). The recalibration of a paradigm for the first peopling of Greater Australia. In J. Allen, J. Golson, & R. Jones (Eds.), *Sunda and Sahul: Prehistoric studies in Southeast Asia, Melanesia, and Australia* (pp. 113–167). New York: Academic.

Globalscape

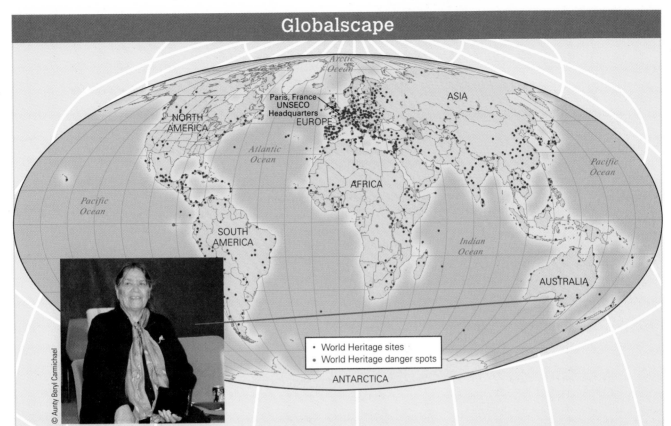

World Heritage sites
World Heritage danger spots

Whose Lakes Are These?

Paleoanthropologists regularly travel to early fossil sites and to museums where original fossil specimens are housed. Increasingly, these same destinations are becoming popular with tourists. Making sites accessible for everyone while protecting the sites requires considerable skill and knowledge. But most importantly, long before the advent of paleoanthropology or paleotourism, these sites were and are the homelands of living people.

Aboriginal people have lived along the shores of the Willandra Lakes region of Australia for at least 50,000 years. They have passed down their stories and cultural traditions even as the lakes dried up and a spectacular crescent-shaped, wind-formed dune (called a lunette) remained. The Mungo lunette has particular cultural significance to three Aboriginal tribal groups. Several major fossil finds from the region include cremated remains as well as an ochred burial, both dated to at least 40,000 years ago. Nearly 460 fossilized footprints dated to between 19,000 and 23,000 years ago were made by people of all ages who lived in the region when the Willandra Lakes were still full of water. How can a place

of local and global significance be appropriately preserved and honored?

Since 1972, UNESCO's World Heritage List has been an important part of maintaining places like Willandra Lakes, which was itself inscribed as a World Heritage Site in 1981. Individual states apply to UNESCO for site designation, and if approved they receive financial and political support for maintaining the site. When designated sites are threatened by natural disaster, war, pollution, or poorly managed tourism, they are placed on a danger list, indicated with a red dot on the map above, forcing the local governments to institute measures to protect the sites in order to continue receiving UNESCO support.

Each year approximately thirty new World Heritage sites are designated. In 2009 the list includes 890 properties: 176 natural preserves, 689 cultural sites, and 25 mixed sites. Fossil and archaeological sites are well represented on the World Heritage List. The Willandra Lakes site is recognized for both natural and cultural values.

While important to the world community, Willandra Lakes has particular meaning to the Aborigines. Aunty Beryl Carmichael, an elder of the Ngiyaampaa people, explains that this land is integrated with her culture:

Because when the old people would tell the stories, they'd just refer to them as "marrathal warkan," which means long, long time ago, when time first began for our people, as people on this land after creation. We have various sites around in our country, we call them the birthing places of all our stories. And of course, the stories are embedded with the lore that governs this whole land. The air, the land, the environment, the universe, the stars.[a]

Not only are Aunty Beryl's stories and the land around Willandra Lakes critical for the Ngiyaampaa and other Aboriginal groups, but their survival ultimately contributes to all of us.

On the next page are listed the sites considered endangered at the June 2009 meeting of the World Heritage Committee. Committee members included representatives from countries throughout the globe including: Australia, Bahrain, Barbados, Brazil, Canada, China, Cuba, Egypt, Israel, Jordan, Kenya, South Korea, Madagascar, Mauritius, Morocco, Nigeria, Peru, Spain, Sweden, Tunisia, and the United States.

Globalscape

These Word Heritage Sites in Danger are indicated with a red dot on the preceding page.

Afghanistan
Cultural landscape and archaeological remains of the Bamiyan Valley (2003)
Minaret and archaeological remains of Jam (2002)

Belize
Belize Barrier Reef reserve system (2009)

Central African Republic
Manovo-Gounda St. Floris National Park (1997)

Chile
Humberstone and Santa Laura Saltpeter Works (2005)

Colombia
Los Katíos National Park (2009)

Côte d'Ivoire
Comoé National Park (2003)
Mount Nimba Strict Nature Reserve (1992)

Democratic Republic of the Congo
Garamba National Park (1996)
Kahuzi-Biega National Park (1997)
Okapi Wildlife Reserve (1997)
Salonga National Park (1999)
Virunga National Park (1994)

Ecuador
Galápagos Islands (2007)

Egypt
Abu Mena (2001)

Ethiopia
Simien National Park (1996)

Georgia
Historical Monuments of Mtskheta (2009)

Guinea
Mount Nimba Strict Nature Reserve (1992)

India
Manas Wildlife Sanctuary (1992)

Iran
Bam and its cultural landscape (2004)

Iraq
Ashur (Qal'at Sherqat) (2003)
Samarra archaeological city (2007)

Jerusalem (site proposed by Jordan)
Old City of Jerusalem and its walls (1982)

Niger
Air and Ténéré Natural Reserves (1992)

Pakistan
Fort and Shalamar Gardens in Lahore (2000)

Peru
Chan Chan archaeological zone (1986)

Philippines
Rice terraces of the Philippine Cordilleras (2001)

Senegal
Niokolo-Koba National Park (2007)

Serbia
Medieval monuments in Kosovo (2006)

Tanzania
Ruins of Kilwa Kisiwani and ruins of Songo Mnara (2004)

Venezuela
Coro and its port (2005)

Yemen
Historic town of Zabid (2000)

Global Twister The listing of endangered sites brings global pressure on a state to find ways to protect the natural and cultural heritage contained within its boundaries. Do you think this method of global social pressure is effective?

[a] Australian Museum Archives.
http://australianmuseum.net.au/movie/Why-the-stories-are-told-Aunty-Beryl

The conventional wisdom has long been that the first people migrated into North America over dry land that connected Siberia to Alaska. This so-called land bridge was a consequence of the buildup of great continental glaciers. As these ice masses grew, there was a worldwide lowering of sea levels, causing an emergence of land in places like the Bering Strait where seas today are shallow. Thus Alaska became, in effect, an eastward extension of Siberia (Figure 9.10). Climatic patterns of the Ice Age kept this land bridge, known as Beringia or the Bering Land Bridge, relatively ice free and covered instead with lichens and mosses that could support herds of grazing animals. It is possible that Upper Paleolithic peoples could have come to the Americas simply by following herd animals. The latest genetic evidence indicates movement took place back and forth across Beringia.

According to geologists, conditions were right for ancient humans and herd animals to traverse Beringia between 11,000 and 25,000 years ago. Though this land bridge was also open between 40,000 and 75,000 years ago, there is no evidence that conclusively confirms human migration at these earlier dates. As with the Sahul, early dates open the possibility of spread to the Americas by archaic *Homo*.

Although ancient Siberians did indeed spread eastward, it is now clear that their way south was blocked by massive glaciers until 13,000 years ago at the earliest.[41] By then, people were already living further south in the Americas. Thus the question of how people first came to this hemisphere has been reopened. One possibility is that, like the first Australians, the first Americans may have come by boat or rafts, perhaps traveling between islands or ice-free pockets of coastline, from as far away as the Japanese islands and down North America's northwestern coast. Hints of such voyages are provided by a handful of North American skeletons (such as Kennewick Man) that bear a closer resemblance to the aboriginal Ainu people of northern Japan and their forebears than they do to other Asians or contemporary Native Americans. Unfortunately, because sea levels were lower than they are today, coastal sites used by early voyagers would now be under water.

Securely dated objects from Monte Verde, a site in south-central Chile, place people in southern South America by 12,500 years ago, if not earlier. Assuming the first

---

[41] Marshall, E. (2001). Preclovis sites fight for acceptance. *Science* 291, 1732.

Figure 9.10 The Arctic conditions and glaciers in northeastern Asia and northwestern North America provided opportunity and challenges for ancient people spreading to the Americas. On the one hand, the Arctic conditions provided a land bridge (Beringia) between the continents, but on the other hand, these harsh environmental conditions posed considerable challenges to humans. Ancient people may have also come to the Americas by sea. Once in North America, glaciers spanning a good portion of the continent determined the areas open to habitation.

populations spread from Siberia to Alaska, linguist Johanna Nichols suggests that the first people to arrive in North America did so by 20,000 years ago. She bases this estimate on the time it took various other languages to spread from their homelands—including Eskimo languages in the Arctic and Athabaskan languages from interior western Canada to New Mexico and Arizona (Navajo). Nichols's conclusion is that it would have taken at least 7,000 years for people to reach south-central Chile.[42] Others suggest people arrived in the Americas closer to 30,000 years ago or even earlier.

A recent genetic study using mtDNA indicates that two groups of migrants crossed Beringia between 15,000 and 17,000 years ago but then took different paths. One group traveled down the Pacific Coast and the other down the center of the continent. While the dates generated in this study are as early as others have suggested, these findings support the notion that distinct language groups made separate migrations.

The picture currently emerging, then, is of people, who may not have looked like modern Native Americans, arriving by boats or rafts and spreading southward and eastward over time. In fact, contact back and forth between North America and Siberia never stopped. In all probability, it became more common as the glaciers melted away. As a consequence, through gene flow as well as later arrivals of people from Asia, people living in the Americas came to have the broad faces, prominent cheekbones, and round cranial vaults that tend to characterize the skulls of many Native Americans today. Still, Native Americans, like all human populations, are physically variable. The Kennewick Man controversy described in Chapter 5 illustrates the complexities of establishing ethnic identity based on the shape of the skull. In order to trace the history of the peopling of the Americas, anthropologists must combine archaeological, linguistic, and cultural information with evidence of biological variation.

Although the earliest technologies in the Americas remain poorly known, they gave rise in North America, about 12,000 years ago, to the distinctive fluted spear points of **Paleoindian** hunters of big game, such as mammoths, mastodons, caribou, and now extinct forms of bison. Fluted points are finely made, with large channel flakes removed from one or both surfaces. This thinned section was inserted into the notched end of a spear shaft for a sturdy haft. Fluted points are found from the Atlantic seaboard to the Pacific Coast, and from Alaska down into Panama. The efficiency of the hunters who made and used these points may have hastened the extinction of the mammoth and other large Pleistocene mammals. By driving large numbers of animals over cliffs, they killed many more than they could possibly use, thus wasting huge amounts of meat.

Upper Paleolithic peoples in Australia and the Americas, like their counterparts in Africa and Eurasia, possessed sophisticated technology that was efficient and appropriate for the environments they inhabited. As in other parts of the world, when a technological innovation such as the fluted points begins, this technology is rapidly disseminated among the people inhabiting the region.

Major Paleolithic Trends

As we look at the larger picture, since the time the genus *Homo* appeared, evolving humans came to rely increasingly on cultural, as opposed to biological, adaptation. To handle environmental challenges, evolving humans developed appropriate tools, clothes, shelter, use of fire, and so forth rather than relying upon biological adaptation of the human organism. This was true whether human

---

[42] The first Americans, ca. 20,000. (1998). *Discover 19* (6), 24.

Paleoindians The earliest inhabitants of North America.

Biocultural Connection

Paleolithic Prescriptions for the Diseases of Civilization

Though increased life expectancy is often hailed as one of modern civilization's greatest accomplishments, in some ways we in the developed world lead far less healthy lifestyles than our ancestors. Throughout most of our evolutionary history, humans led more physically active lives and ate a more varied low-fat diet than we do now. Our ancestors did not drink or smoke. They spent their days scavenging or hunting for animal protein while gathering vegetable foods with some insects thrown in for good measure. They stayed fit through traveling great distances each day over the savannah and beyond.

Today we may survive longer, but in old age we are beset by chronic disease. Heart disease, diabetes, high blood pressure, and cancer shape the experience of old age in wealthy industrialized nations. The prevalence of these "diseases of civilization" has increased rapidly over the past sixty years. Anthropologists Melvin Konner and Marjorie Shostak and physician Boyd Eaton have suggested that our Paleolithic ancestors have provided a prescription for a cure. They propose that as "stone-agers in a fast lane," people's health will improve by returning to the lifestyle to which their bodies are adapted.[a] Such Paleolithic prescriptions are an example of evolutionary medicine—a branch of medical anthropology that uses evolutionary principles to contribute to human health.

Evolutionary medicine bases its prescriptions on the idea that rates of cultural change exceed the rates of biological change. Our food-forager physiology was shaped over millions of years, while the cultural changes leading to contemporary lifestyles have occurred rapidly.

Anthropologists George Armelagos and Mark Nathan Cohen suggest that the downward trajectory for human health began with the earliest human village settlements some 10,000 years ago.[b] When humans began farming rather than gathering, they often switched to single-crop diets. In addition, settlement into villages led directly to the increase in infectious disease. While the cultural invention of antibiotics has cured many infectious diseases, it also led to the increase in chronic diseases.

Our evolutionary history offers clues about the diet and lifestyle to which our bodies evolved. By returning to our ancient lifeways, we can make the diseases of civilization a thing of the past.

BIOCULTURAL QUESTION

What sort of Paleolithic prescriptions would our evolutionary history contribute toward behaviors such as childrearing practices, sleeping, and work patterns? Are there any ways that your culture or personal lifestyle is well aligned with past lifeways?

---

[a] Eaton, S. B., Konner, M., & Shostak, M. (1988). Stone-agers in the fast lane: Chronic degenerative diseases in evolutionary perspective. *American Journal of Medicine 84* (4), 739–749.

[b] Cohen, M. N., & Armelagos, G. J. (Eds.). (1984). *Paleopathology at the origins of agriculture*. Orlando: Academic.

---

populations lived in hot or cold, wet or dry, forest or grassland areas. Though culture is ultimately based on what might loosely be called brain power or, more formally, **cognitive capacity,** it is learned and not carried by genes. Therefore, cultural innovations may occur rapidly and can easily be transferred among individuals and groups.

Scientists have recently documented key differences in the proteins involved in brain metabolism in humans compared to other species that may account for some of this brain power. Unfortunately these metabolic changes are also associated with schizophrenia, indicating that there may have been some costs in the process. This study suggests that the cultural practice of cooking freed the body to devote more energy to brain metabolism.

While cooking was certainly an innovation of ancient *Homo,* the varied low-fat diet and high exercise of our ancestors were in general healthier than the dietary patterns prevailing in many parts of the world today. See this chapter's Biocultural Connection for a discussion of how a return to the diets of our forebears may improve human health.

Certain trends stand out from the information anthropologists have gathered about the Old Stone Age in most parts of the world. One was toward increasingly more sophisticated, varied, and specialized tool kits. Tools became progressively lighter and smaller, resulting in the conservation of raw materials and a better ratio between length of cutting edge and weight of stone. Tools became specialized according to region and function. Instead of crude all-purpose tools, more effective particularized devices were made to deal with the differing conditions of savannah, forest, and shore.

As humans came to rely increasingly on culture as a means to meet the challenges of existence, they were able to inhabit new environments. With more efficient tool technology, human population size could increase, allowing humans to spill over into more diverse environments. Improved cultural abilities may also have played a role in the reduction of heavy physical features, favoring instead decreased size and weight of face and teeth, the development of larger and more complex brains, and ultimately a reduction in body size and robustness. This dependence on intelligence rather than bulk provided the key for humans' increased reliance on cultural rather than physical adaptation. The development of conceptual thought can be seen in symbolic artifacts and signs of ritual activity throughout the world.

cognitive capacity A broad concept including intelligence, educability, concept formation, self-awareness, self-evaluation, attention span, sensitivity in discrimination, and creativity.

Through Paleolithic times, at least in the colder parts of the world, hunting became more important, and people became more proficient at it. Humans' intelligence enabled them to develop composite tools as well as the social organization and cooperation so important for survival and population growth. As discussed in the next chapter, this trend was reversed during the Mesolithic, when hunting lost its preeminence, and the gathering of wild plants and seafood became increasingly important.

As human populations grew and spread, cultural differences between regions also became more marked. While some indications of cultural contact and intercommunication are evident in the development of long-distance trade networks, tool assemblages developed in response to the specific challenges and resources of specific environments.

As Paleolithic peoples eventually spread over all the continents of the world, including Australia and the Americas, changes in climate and environment called for new kinds of adaptations. In forest environments, people needed tools for working wood; on the open savannah and plains, they came to use the bow and arrow to hunt the game they could not stalk closely; the people in settlements that grew up around lakes and along rivers and coasts developed harpoons and hooks; in the sub-Arctic regions, they needed tools to work the heavy skins of seals and caribou. The fact that culture is first and foremost a mechanism by which humans adapt means that as humans faced new challenges in the Paleolithic throughout the globe, their cultures differentiated regionally.

Questions for Reflection

1.   Upper Paleolithic art suggests that humans have always been challenged to understand where we fit in the larger system of life forms, past and present. What are your thoughts about how the impulse to create art relates to human efforts to make sense of our place in nature? What is your conception of the artist who might have made the Venus figurine in the chapter opening?

2.   What does it mean to be "modern," biologically or culturally? How should we define "human"?

3.   How do you feel personally about the possibility of having Neandertals as part of your ancestry? How might you relate the Neandertal debates to stereotyping or racism in contemporary society?

4.   Why do you think that most of the studies of prehistoric art have tended to focus on Europe? Do you think this focus reflects ethnocentrism or bias about the definition of art in Western cultures?

5.   Do you think that gender has played a role in anthropological interpretations of the behavior of our ancestors and the way that paleoanthropologists and archaeologists conduct their research? Do you believe that feminism has a role to play in the interpretation of the past?

Suggested Readings

Clottes, J., & Bennett, G. (2002). *World rock art* (conservation and cultural heritage series). San Francisco: Getty Trust Publication.

Written by Jean Clottes, a leading authority on rock art (and discoverer of the Upper Paleolithic cave art site Grotte de Chauvet), this book provides excellent descriptions and beautiful images of rock art throughout the world, beginning with the earliest examples from Australia to rock art from the 20th century.

Dillehay, T. D. (2001). *The settlement of the Americas.* New York: Basic.

In an engaging, clear style, Dillehay provides a detailed account of the evidence from South America that has recently challenged theories about the peopling of the Americas, with particular emphasis on the author's work in Chile.

Klein, R. (2002). *The dawn of human culture.* New York: Wiley.

While this book covers the entire history of human evolution, it provides a particular focus on the theory of recent African origins of the species *Homo sapiens* and associated cultural abilities.

White, R. (2003). *Prehistoric art: The symbolic journey of humankind.* New York: Abrams.

This sumptuously illustrated volume demonstrates the power of prehistoric imagery as well as providing a comprehensive overview of the theoretical approaches to studying prehistoric art. White presents a global survey of prehistoric art and demonstrates that Western notions of art have interfered with interpretations of prehistoric art.

Wolpoff, M., & Caspari, R. (1997). *Race and human evolution: A fatal attraction.* New York: Simon & Schuster.

This book is a detailed but readable presentation of the multiregional hypothesis of modern human origins. Among its strengths is a discussion of the problem of defining what "anatomically modern" means.

Challenge Issue This embroidery by Hmong artist Pangxiong Sirathasuk depicts not only her culture's story of the origins of farming—a way of life that first began as early as 10,000 years ago—but also some of the consequences of this shift from food foraging to food production. According to Hmong folklore, the vegetables started out walking into villages. But they became disgusted with human greed and walked back to the fields, stating that humans in the future would have to work very hard to receive the earth's bounty. Farming and the domestication of animals, along with settlement, mark the start of the Neolithic period. These cultural innovations solved some of the challenges of existence, but they also created new ones. Diets limited by reliance on single crops sometimes led to malnutrition and even famine when these crops failed. Crowded living conditions and close contact with animals in Neolithic villages promoted the spread of infectious disease. And as this embroidery shows, food production involves considerable labor. This artwork also demonstrates that the innovations from one part of the world disseminated globally. While the traditional Hmong homeland is in Southeast Asia, the pumpkins and corn depicted here are crops that were originally domesticated in the Americas. The development of permanent settlements and the domestication of animals and plants introduced new beliefs, daily routines, social relationships, and political structures that together continue to challenge humans globally.

CHAPTER 10

The Neolithic Revolution: The Domestication of Plants and Animals

Chapter Preview

When and Where Did the Change from Food Foraging to Food Production Begin?

Independent centers of early plant and animal domestication exist in Africa, China, Mesoamerica, North and South America, as well as Southwest and Southeast Asia. From these places, food production spread to most other parts of the world. Food production began independently at more or less the same time around 10,000 years ago in these different places—perhaps a bit earlier in Southwest Asia than elsewhere. Due to the breadth of changes induced by this transition, it is commonly referred to as the Neolithic revolution. Though farming has changed dramatically over the millennia, crops people rely on today, such as rice, wheat, and maize, originated with those earliest farmers.

Why Did the Change Take Place?

Though the Neolithic revolution can appear to be a cultural advancement because later cities and states developed from Neolithic villages, food production is not necessarily a more secure means of subsistence than food foraging. In the Neolithic, farming often limited the diversity of the human diet and required more work than hunting, gathering, and fishing. In addition, being sedentary created new vulnerability to disease. It may be that people did not become food producers due to clear-cut advantages of this way of life. Of various theories that have been proposed, the most likely is that food production came about as a consequence of a chance convergence of separate natural events and cultural developments.

What Were the Consequences of the Neolithic Revolution?

Although food production generally leaves less leisure time than food foraging, it does permit reallocation of the workload. Some people can produce enough food to support those who undertake other tasks, and so a number of technological developments, such as weaving and pottery making, generally accompany food production. In addition, a sedentary lifestyle in villages allows for the construction of more substantial housing. Finally, the new modes of work and resource allocation require new ways of organizing people, generally into lineages, clans, and common-interest associations.

Throughout the Paleolithic, people depended exclusively on wild sources of food for their survival. They hunted and trapped wild animals, fished, and gathered shellfish, eggs, berries, nuts, roots, and other plant foods, relying on their wits and muscles to acquire what nature provided. Whenever favored sources of food became scarce, people adjusted by increasing the variety of foods eaten and incorporating less desirable foods into their diets.

Over time, the subsistence practices of some people began to change in ways that radically transformed their way of life as they became food producers rather than food foragers.[1] For some human groups, food production was accompanied by a more sedentary existence, which in turn permitted a reorganization of the workload in society: Some individuals could be freed from the food quest to devote their energies to other tasks. Over the course of thousands of years, these changes brought about an unforeseen way of life. With good reason, the **Neolithic** (literally, the "New Stone" Age), when this change took place, has been characterized as revolutionary.

The Mesolithic Roots of Farming and Pastoralism

As seen in the previous chapter, by the end of the Paleolithic humans had spread throughout the globe. During this period much of the northern hemisphere was covered with glaciers. By 12,000 years ago, warmer climates prevailed, and these glaciers receded, causing changes in human habitats globally. As sea levels rose throughout the world, many areas that had been dry land during periods of glaciation—such as the Bering Strait, parts of the North Sea, and an extensive land area that had joined the eastern islands of Indonesia to mainland Asia—flooded.

---

[1] Rindos, D. (1984). *The origins of agriculture: An evolutionary perspective* (p. 99). Orlando: Academic.

Neolithic The New Stone Age; prehistoric period beginning about 10,000 years ago in which peoples possessed stone-based technologies and depended on domesticated plants and/or animals.

Mesolithic The Middle Stone Age period between the end of the Paleolithic and the start of the Neolithic; referred to as Archaic cultures in the Americas.

Archaic cultures Term used to refer to Mesolithic cultures in the Americas.

microlith A small blade of flint or similar stone, which were hafted together in handles or shafts made of wood, bone, or antler to make tools; widespread in the Mesolithic.

In some northern regions, warmer climates brought about particularly marked changes, allowing the replacement of barren tundra with forests. In the process, the herd animals—upon which northern Paleolithic peoples had depended for much of their food, clothing, and shelter—disappeared from many areas. Some, like the caribou and musk ox, moved to colder climates; others, like the mammoths, died out completely. In the new forests, animals were often more solitary in their habits. As a result, large cooperative hunts were less productive than before. Diets shifted to abundant plant foods as well as fish and other foods around lakeshores, bays, and rivers. In Europe, Asia, and Africa, this transitional period between the Paleolithic and the Neolithic is called the **Mesolithic,** or Middle Stone Age. In the Americas, comparable cultures are referred to as **Archaic cultures.**

New technologies accompanied the changed postglacial environment. Manufacture began of ground stone tools, shaped and sharpened by grinding the tool against sandstone, often using sand as an additional abrasive. These shaped, sharpened stones were set into wooden or sometimes antler handles to make effective axes and adzes, cutting tools with a sharp blade set at right angles to a handle. Though such implements take longer to make, they are less prone to breakage under heavy-duty usage than those made of chipped stone. Thus they were helpful in clearing forest areas and in the woodwork needed for the creation of dugout canoes and skin-covered boats. Evidence of seaworthy watercraft at Mesolithic sites indicates that human foraging for food took place on the open water as well as on land. Thus it was possible to make use of deep-water resources as well as those of coastal areas, rivers, and lakes.

The **microlith**—a small but hard, sharp blade—was the characteristic tool of the Mesolithic. Although a microlithic ("small stone") tool tradition existed in Central Africa by about 40,000 years ago,[2] such tools did not become common elsewhere until the Mesolithic. Microliths could be mass produced because they were small, easy to make, and could be fashioned from sections of blades. This small tool could be attached to an arrow or other tool shaft by using melted resin (from pine trees) as a binder.

Microliths provided Mesolithic people with an important advantage over their Upper Paleolithic forebears: The small size of the microlith enabled them to devise a wider array of composite tools made out of stone and wood or bone. Thus they could make sickles, harpoons, arrows, knives, and daggers by fitting microliths into slots in

---

[2] Bednarik, R. G. (1995). Concept-mediated marking in the Lower Paleolithic. *Current Anthropology 36,* 606.

wood, bone, or antler handles. Later experimentation with these forms led to more sophisticated tools and weapons such as bows to propel arrows.

Dwellings from the Mesolithic provide some evidence of a more sedentary lifestyle during this period. By contrast, most hunting peoples, and especially those depending on herd animals, are highly mobile. To be successful, hunters must follow migratory game. People subsisting on a diet of seafood and plants in the milder northern forested environments of this time period did not need to move regularly over large geographic areas.

In the warmer parts of the world, wild plant foods were more readily available, and so their collection complemented hunting in the Upper Paleolithic more than had been the case in the colder northern regions. Hence, in areas like Southwest Asia, the Mesolithic represents less of a changed way of life than was true in Europe. Here, the important **Natufian culture** flourished.

The Natufians lived between 10,200 and 12,500 years ago at the eastern end of the Mediterranean Sea in caves, rock shelters, and small villages with stone- and mud-walled houses. They are named after Wadi en-Natuf, a ravine near Jerusalem, Israel, where the remains of this culture were first found. They buried their dead in communal cemeteries, usually in shallow pits without any other objects or decorations. A small shrine is known from one of their villages—a 10,500-year-old settlement at Jericho in the Jordan River Valley. Basin-shaped depressions in the rocks found outside homes and plastered storage pits beneath the floors of the houses indicate that the Natufians were the earliest Mesolithic people known to have stored plant foods. Certain tools found among Natufian remains bear evidence of their use to cut grain. These Mesolithic sickles consisted of small stone blades set in straight handles of wood or bone.

The new way of life of the various Mesolithic and Archaic cultures generally provided supplies of food sufficiently abundant to permit people in some parts of the world to live in larger and more sedentary groups. They became village dwellers, and some of these settlements went on to expand into the first farming villages, towns, and ultimately cities.

The Neolithic Revolution

The Neolithic, or New Stone Age, derives its name from the polished stone tools that are characteristic of this period. But more important than the presence of these tools is the cultural transition from a foraging economy based on hunting, gathering, and fishing to one based on food production, representing a major change in the subsistence practices of early peoples. While many of the early food producers became village dwellers, other groups used Neolithic tools and settled in villages while still maintaining a foraging lifestyle as some groups do into the present. The **Neolithic revolution** was by no means smooth or instantaneous; in fact, the switch to food production spread over many centuries—even millennia—and was a direct outgrowth of the preceding Mesolithic. Where to draw the line between the two periods is not always clear.

The ultimate source of all cultural change is **innovation**: any new idea, method, or device that gains widespread acceptance in society. **Primary innovation** is the creation, invention, or discovery by chance of a completely new idea, method, or device. A chance discovery, such as the observation that clay permanently hardens when exposed to high temperatures, is the kind of primary innovation that likely took place around numerous ancient campfires. This perception allowed our ancestors to begin to make figurines of fired clay some 35,000 years ago.

A **secondary innovation** is a deliberate application or modification of an existing idea, method, or device. For example, ancient people applied the knowledge about fired clay to make pottery containers and cooking vessels. Recent evidence from Yuchanyan Cave, located in the southwest of China's Hunan Province, indicates the presence of the earliest pottery vessels; these are radio-carbon dated to between 15,430 and 18,300 years ago.

The transition to relatively complete reliance on domesticated plants and animals took several thousand years. While this transition has been particularly well studied in Southwest Asia, archaeological evidence for food production also

Pottery shards were recently discovered along with rice grains and stone tools at Yuchanyan Cave, located in China's Hunan Province, by a team of American, Israeli, and Chinese archaeologists. Bone fragments and charcoal found in association with the pottery allowed scientists to accurately date the pottery to between 17,500 and 18,300 years ago by measuring the fraction of carbon isotopes in these organic materials. The careful excavation at this site has provided important evidence that connects pottery making hunter-gatherers, who inhabited this cave, to the rice farmers that came to inhabit the nearby Yangzte River basin several thousand years later.

exists from other parts of the world such as China and Central America and the Andes at similar or somewhat younger dates. The critical point is not which region invented farming first, but rather the independent but more or less simultaneous invention of food production throughout the globe.

Domestication: What Is It?

Domestication is a process whereby humans modify, either intentionally or unintentionally, the genetic makeup of a population of plants or animals, sometimes to the extent that members of the population are unable to survive and/or reproduce without human assistance. Domestication is essentially a special case of interdependence between different species frequently seen in the natural world, where one species depends on another (that feeds upon it) for its protection and reproductive success.

> **domestication** An evolutionary process whereby humans modify, either intentionally or unintentionally, the genetic makeup of a population of plants or animals, sometimes to the extent that members of the population are unable to survive and/or reproduce without human assistance.

According to evolutionary biologist, geographer, and all-around theorist Jared Diamond, humans are not the only species known to domesticate another. Certain ants native to the American tropics grow fungi in their nests, and these fungi provide the ants with most of their nutrition. Like human farmers, the ants add manure to stimulate fungal growth and eliminate competing weeds, both mechanically and through use of antibiotic herbicides.[3] The fungi are protected and ensured reproductive success while providing the ants with a steady food supply.

In plant–human interactions, domestication ensures the plants' reproductive success while providing humans with food. Selective breeding eliminates thorns, toxins, and bad-tasting chemical compounds, which in the wild had served to ensure a plant species' survival, at the same time producing larger, tastier edible parts attractive to humans. Environmentalist Michael Pollan suggests that domesticated plant species successfully exploit human desires to out-compete other plant species and considers "agriculture as something grasses did to people to conquer trees."[4]

Evidence of Early Plant Domestication

Domesticated plants generally differ from their wild ancestors in ways favored by humans, including increased size, at least of edible parts; reduction or loss of natural means of seed dispersal; reduction or loss of protective devices such as husks or distasteful chemical compounds; loss of delayed seed germination (important to wild plants for survival in times of drought or other temporarily adverse conditions); and development of simultaneous ripening of the seed or fruit.

For example, wild cereals have a very fragile stem, whereas domesticated ones have a tough stem. Under natural conditions, plants with fragile stems scatter their seed for themselves, whereas those with tough stems do not. When the grain stalks were harvested, their soft stems would shatter at the touch of sickle or flail, and many of their seeds would be lost. Inevitably, though unintentionally, most of the seeds that people harvested would have been taken from the tough plants. Early domesticators probably also tended to select seed from plants having few husks or none at all—eventually breeding them out—because husking prior to pounding the grains into meal or flour required extra labor.

Many of the distinguishing characteristics of domesticated plants can be seen in remains from archaeological

---

[3] Diamond, J. (1998). Ants, crops, and history. *Science 281*, 1974–1975.

[4] Pollan, M. (2001). *The botany of desire: A plant's-eye view of the world.* New York: Random House.

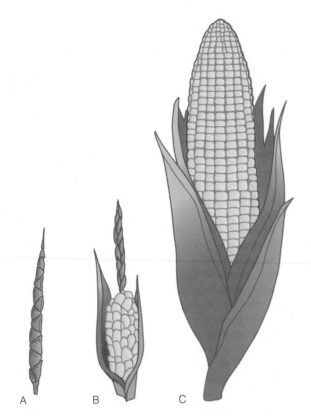

Figure 10.1 Teosinte (A), compared to 5,500-year-old maize (B) and modern maize (C). Teosinte, the wild grass from highland Mexico from which maize originated, is far less productive and does not taste very good. Like most plants that were domesticated, it was not a favored food for foraging people. Domestication transformed it into something highly desirable.

sites. Paleobotanists can often tell the fossil of a wild plant species from a domesticated one, for example, by studying the shape and size of various plant structures (Figure 10.1).[5]

Evidence of Early Animal Domestication

Domestication also produced changes in the skeletal structure of some animals. For example, the horns of wild goats and sheep differ from those of their domesticated counterparts. Some types of domesticated sheep have no horns altogether. Similarly, the size of an animal or its parts can vary with domestication as seen in the smaller size of certain teeth of domesticated pigs compared to those of wild ones.

A study of age and sex ratios of butchered animals at an archaeological site may indicate whether animal

domestication was practiced. Investigators have determined that if the age and/or sex ratios at the site differ from those in wild herds, the imbalances are due to domestication. Archaeologists documented a sharp rise in the number of young male goats killed at 10,000-year-old sites in the Zagros Mountains of Iran. Evidently people were slaughtering the young males for food and saving the females for breeding. Although such herd management does not prove that the goats were fully domesticated, it does indicate a step in that direction.[6] Similarly, archaeological sites in the Andean highlands, dating to around 6,300 years ago, contain evidence that these animals were penned up, indicating the beginning of domestication.

Why Humans Became Food Producers

Although it is tempting to think that a sudden flash of insight about the human ability to control plants and animals might have led ancient peoples to domestication, the evidence points us in different directions. As the following discussion illustrates, there are several false ideas about the motivation to becoming food producers.

Contemporary foragers show us that food production did not come about from discoveries, such as that seeds, if planted, grow into plants. These food foragers are perfectly aware of the role of seeds in plant growth, that plants grow better under certain conditions than others, and so forth. Jared Diamond aptly describes contemporary food foragers as "walking encyclopedias of natural history with individual names for as many as a thousand or more plant and animal species, and with detailed knowledge of those species' biological characteristics, distribution, and potential uses."[7] In addition, food foragers frequently apply their knowledge to actively manage the resources on which they depend. For example, indigenous people living in northern Australia deliberately alter the runoff channels of creeks to flood extensive tracts of land, converting them into fields of wild grain. Australian Aborigines choose to continue to forage while also managing the land.

Second, the switch from food foraging to food production does not free people from hard work. In fact, available ethnographic data indicate just the opposite—that

[5] Gould, S. J. (1991). *The flamingo's smile: Reflections in natural history* (p. 368). New York: Norton.

[6] Zeder, M. A., & Hesse, B. (2000). The initial domestication of goats (*Capra hircus*) in the Zagros Mountains 10,000 years ago. *Science 287*, 2254–2257.

[7] Diamond, J. (1997). *Guns, germs, and steel* (p. 143). New York: Norton.

Figure 10.2 The Fertile Crescent of Southwest Asia and the area of Natufian culture.

farmers, by and large, work far longer hours compared to most food foragers.

Finally, food production is not necessarily a more secure means of subsistence than food foraging. Seed crops in particular—of the sort originally domesticated in Southwest Asia, Central America, and the Andean highlands—are highly productive but not stable from an ecological perspective because of low species diversity. Without constant human attention, their productivity suffers.

For these reasons, it is little wonder that food foragers do not necessarily regard farming and animal husbandry as superior to hunting, gathering, or fishing. Thus some peoples in the world have continued as food foragers into the present. However, it has become increasingly difficult for them, because food-producing peoples (including postindustrial societies) have deprived them of more and more of the land base necessary for their way of life. As long as existing practices work well, there is no need for food foragers to abandon them, especially if they provide an eminently satisfactory way of life. Noting that food foragers have more time for play and relaxation than food producers, anthropologist Marshall Sahlins has labeled hunter-gatherers "the original affluent society."[8] Farming brings with it a whole new system of relationships that disturbs an age-old balance between humans and nature.

In view of what has been said so far, it is puzzling why any human beings abandoned food foraging in favor of food production. Several theories have been proposed to account for this change in human subsistence practices.

One older theory, championed by Australian archaeologist V. Gordon Childe, is the desiccation (from the Latin "to dry completely"), or oasis, theory, which is based on environmental determinism. Its proponents advanced the idea that the glacial cover over Europe and Asia caused a shift in rain patterns from Europe to northern Africa and southwestern Asia. When the glaciers retreated northward, so did the rain patterns. As a result, formerly lush regions of northern Africa and southwestern Asia became dryer, and people were forced to congregate at oases for water.

Because of the relative food scarcity in such an environment, necessity drove people to collect the wild grasses and seeds growing around the oases, congregating in a part of Southwest Asia known as the Fertile Crescent (Figure 10.2).

---

[8] Sahlins, M. (1972). *Stone age economics*. Chicago: Aldine.

Eventually they began to cultivate various plants to provide enough food for the community. According to this theory, animal domestication began because the oases attracted hungry animals, such as wild goats, sheep, and also cattle, which came to graze on the stubble of the grain fields and to drink. Finding that these animals were often too thin to kill for food, people began to fatten them up.

Although Childe's oasis theory can be critiqued on a number of grounds and many other theories have been proposed to account for the shift to domestication, it remains historically significant as the first scientifically testable explanation for the origins of food production. Childe's theory set the stage for the development of archaeology as a science. Later theories developed by archaeologists built on Childe's ideas and took into account the role of chance environmental circumstances of the specific region along with other specific cultural factors that may have driven change.

The Fertile Crescent

Present evidence indicates that the earliest plant domestication took place gradually in the Fertile Crescent, the long arc-shaped sweep of river valleys and coastal plains extending from the Upper Nile (Sudan) to the Lower Tigris (Iraq). Archaeological data suggest the domestication of rye as early as 13,000 years ago by people living at a site (Abu Hureyra) east of Aleppo, Syria, although wild plants and animals continued to be their major food sources. Over the next several millennia they became full-fledged farmers, cultivating rye and wheat.[9] By 10,300 years ago, others in the region were also growing crops.

This domestication process may have been the consequence of a chance convergence of independent natural events and other cultural developments.[10] The Natufians, whose culture we looked at earlier in this chapter, illustrate this process. These people lived at a time of dramatically changing climates in Southwest Asia. With the end of the last glaciation, temperatures became not only significantly warmer but markedly seasonal as well. Between 6,000 and 12,000 years ago, the region experienced the most extreme seasonality in its history, with dry summers significantly longer and hotter than today. As a consequence of increased evaporation, many shallow lakes dried up, leaving just three in the Jordan River Valley.

At the same time, the region's plant cover changed dramatically. Those plants best adapted to environmental instability and seasonal dryness were annuals, including wild cereal grains and legumes (such as peas, lentils, and chickpeas). Because they complete their life cycle in a single year, annuals can evolve very quickly under unstable conditions. Moreover, they store their reproductive abilities for the next wet season in abundant seeds, which can remain dormant for prolonged periods.

The Natufians, who lived where these conditions were especially severe, adapted by modifying their subsistence practices in two ways. First, they probably burned the landscape regularly to promote browsing by red deer and grazing by gazelles, the main focus of their hunting activities. Second, they placed greater emphasis on the collection of wild seeds from the annual plants that could be effectively stored to see people through the dry season. The importance of stored foods, coupled with the scarcity of reliable water sources, promoted more sedentary living patterns, reflected in the substantial villages of late Natufian times. The reliance upon seeds in Natufian subsistence was made possible by the fact that they already possessed sickles (originally used to cut reeds and sedges for baskets) for harvesting grain and grinding stones for processing a variety of wild foods.[11]

The use of sickles to harvest grain turned out to have important consequences, again unexpected, for the Natufians. In the course of harvesting, it was inevitable that many easily dispersed seeds would be lost at the harvest site, whereas those from plants that did not readily scatter their seeds would be mostly carried back to where people processed and stored them.[12]

The periodic burning of vegetation carried out to promote the deer and gazelle herds may have also affected the development of new genetic variation. Heat is known to affect mutation rates. Also, fire removes individuals from a population, which changes the genetic structure of a population drastically and quickly. With seeds for nondispersing variants being carried back to settlements, it was inevitable that some lost seeds would germinate and grow there on dump heaps and other disturbed sites (latrines, areas cleared of trees, or burned-over terrain).

Many of the plants that became domesticated were "colonizers," variants that do particularly well in disturbed habitats. Moreover, with people becoming increasingly sedentary, disturbed habitats became more extensive as resources closer to settlements were depleted over time. Thus, variants of plants particularly susceptible to human manipulation had more opportunities to

[9] Pringle, H. (1998). The slow birth of agriculture. *Science 282*, 1449.

[10] McCorriston, J., & Hole, F. (1991). The ecology of seasonal stress and the origins of agriculture in the Near East. *American Anthropologist 93*, 46–69.

[11] Olszewski, D. I. (1991). Comment. *Current Anthropology 32*, 43.

[12] Blumer, M. A., & Byrne, R. (1991). The ecological genetics and domestication and the origins of agriculture. *Current Anthropology 32*, 30.

flourish where people were living. Under such circumstances, it was inevitable that eventually people would begin to actively promote their growth, even by deliberately sowing them. Ultimately, people realized that they could play a more active role in the process by trying to breed the strains they preferred. With this, domestication shifted from an unintentional to an intentional process.

The development of animal domestication in Southwest Asia seems to have proceeded along somewhat similar lines in the hilly country of southeastern Turkey, northern Iraq, and the Zagros Mountains of Iran. Large herds of wild sheep and goats, as well as much environmental diversity, characterized these regions. From the flood plains of the valley of the Tigris and Euphrates Rivers, for example, travel to the north or east takes one into high country through three other zones: first steppe, then oak and pistachio woodlands, and finally high plateau country with grass, scrub, or desert vegetation. Valleys that run at right angles to the mountain ranges afford relatively easy access across these zones. Today, a number of peoples in the region still graze their herds of sheep and goats on the low steppe in the winter and move to high pastures on the plateaus in the summer.

Moving back in time prior to the domestication of plants and animals, we find the region inhabited by peoples whose subsistence pattern, like that of the Natufians, was one of food foraging. Different plants were found in different ecological zones, and because of the difference in altitude, plant foods matured at different times in different zones. Many animal species were hunted for meat and hides by these people, most notably the hoofed animals: deer, gazelles, wild goats, and wild sheep.

Their bones are far more common in human refuse piles than those of other animals. This is significant, for most of these animals naturally move back and forth from low winter pastures to high summer pastures. People followed these animals in their seasonal migrations, making use along the way of other wild foods in the zones through which they passed: palm dates in the lowlands; acorns, almonds, and pistachios higher up; apples and pears higher still; wild grains maturing at different times in different zones; woodland animals in the forested zone between summer and winter grazing lands. All in all, it was a rich, varied fare.

The archaeological record indicates that, at first, animals of all ages and sexes were hunted by the people of the Southwest Asian highlands. But, beginning about 11,000 years ago, the percentage of immature sheep eaten increased to about 50 percent of the total. At the same time, the percentage of females among animals eaten decreased. (Feasting on male lambs increases yields by sparing the females for breeding.)

This marks the beginning of human management of sheep. As this management of flocks became more efficient, sheep were increasingly shielded from the effects of natural selection, allowing variants preferred by humans to have increased reproductive success. Variants attractive to humans did not arise out of need but at random, as mutations do. But then humans selectively bred the varieties they favored. In such a way, those features characteristic of domestic sheep—such as greater fat and meat production, excess wool, and so on—began to develop.

By 9,000 years ago, the shape and size of the bones of domestic sheep had become distinguishable from those of wild sheep (Figure 10.3). At about the same

Figure 10.3 Domestication of sheep resulted in evolutionary changes that created more wool. Inset A shows a section, as seen through a microscope, of skin of wild sheep, showing the arrangement of primary (hair) and secondary (wool) follicles. Inset B shows a section of similarly enlarged skin of domestic sheep, showing the changed relationship and the change in size of follicles that accompanied the development of wool.

settlements. Without a notion of resource ownership, they suggest that hunters would not be likely to postpone the short-term gain of killing prey for the long-term gain of continued access to animals in the future.[15] Eventually, animal species domesticated in one area were introduced into areas outside their natural habitat.

To sum up, the domesticators of plants and animals sought only to maximize the food sources available to them. They were not aware of the long-term and revolutionary cultural consequences of their actions. But as the process continued, the productivity of the domestic species increased relative to wild species. Thus these domesticated species became increasingly important to subsistence, resulting in further domestication and further increases in productivity.

Other Centers of Domestication

In addition to Southwest Asia, the domestication of plants and, in some cases, animals took place independently in Southeast Asia, parts of the Americas (Central America, the Andean highlands, the tropical forests of South America, and eastern North America), northern China, and Africa (Figure 10.4). In China, domestication of rice was under way along the middle Yangtze River by about 11,000 years ago.[16] It was not until 4,000 years later, however, that domestic rice dominated wild rice to become the dietary staple.

In Southeast Asia, decorations on pottery depicting rice dated to between 5,000 and 8,800 years ago document it as the earliest species to be domesticated there. Nevertheless, the region is primarily known for the domestication of root crops, most notably yams and taro. Root crop farming, or **vegeculture,** typically involves the growing of many different species together in a single field. Because this approximates the complexity of the natural vegetation, vegeculture tends to be more stable than seed crop cultivation. Propagation or breeding of new plants typically occurs through vegetative means—the planting of cuttings—rather than the planting of seeds.

In the Americas, the domestication of plants began about as early as it did in these other regions. One species of domestic squash may have been grown as early as

© Sepp Seitz

Today, deliberate attempts to create new varieties of plants take place in many greenhouses, experiment stations, and labs. But when first begun, the creation of domestic plants was not deliberate; rather, it was the unforeseen outcome of traditional food-foraging activities. Today, genetically engineered crops are being created to survive massive applications of herbicides and pesticides. They are also engineered to *not* produce viable seeds, which solidifies corporate control of the food industry.

time, similar developments were taking place in southeastern Turkey and the lower Jordan River Valley, where pigs were the focus of attention.[13] The recent analysis of pottery vessels from the Near East and southeastern Europe indicates that people were using milk from domesticated cattle in a part of the Fertile Crescent by this time as well.[14]

Some researchers have recently linked animal domestication to the development of fixed territories and

[15] Alvard, M. S., & Kuznar, L. (2001). Deferred harvest: The transition from hunting to animal husbandry. *American Anthropologist 103* (2), 295–311.

[16] Pringle, p. 1449.

[13] Pringle, p. 1448.

[14] Evershed, R. P., et al. (2008). Earliest date for milk use in the Near East and southeastern Europe linked to cattle herding. *Nature.* doi:10.1038/nature07180.

vegeculture The cultivation of domesticated root crops, such as yams and taro.

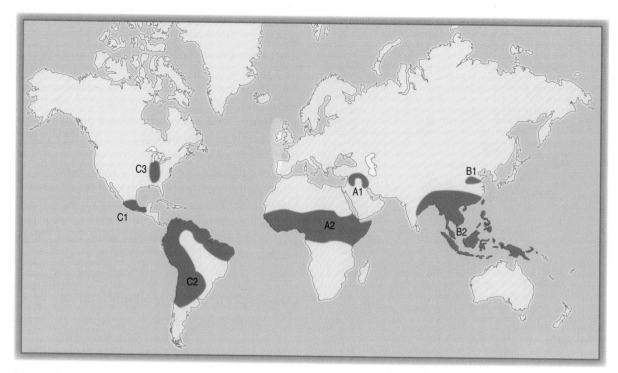

Figure 10.4 Early plant and animal domestication took place in such widely scattered areas as Southwest Asia (A1), Central Africa (A2), China (B1), Southeast Asia (B2), Central America (C1), South America (C2), and North America (C3).

The Dani people of New Guinea specialize in growing sweet potatoes, a crop introduced in the 17th century into a region with a long history of vegeculture. Today villagers grow more than seventy species of sweet potato and have incorporated this root crop into many important rituals. Here Dani women are roasting sweet potatoes on a fire as part of a ceremonial pig feast.

Globalscape

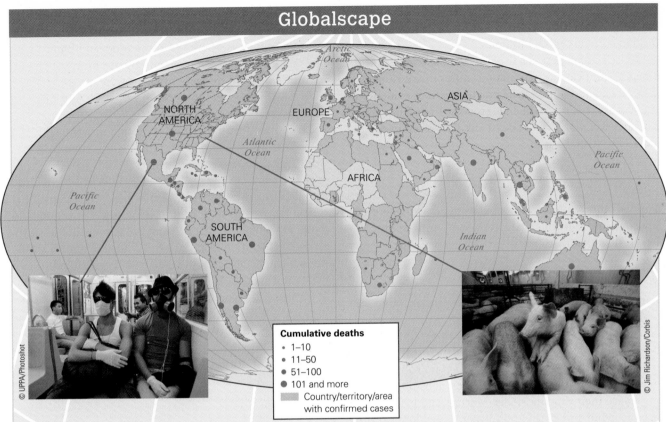

Cumulative deaths
- 1–10
- 11–50
- 51–100
- 101 and more
- Country/territory/area with confirmed cases

Factory Farming Fiasco?

In April 2009 protective masks and gloves were a common sight in Mexico City as the news of the first cases of swine flu pandemic appeared in the United States and Mexico. On June 11, 2009, the World Health Organization (WHO) made the pandemic official, and by July cases had been reported in three quarters of the states and territories the WHO monitors. Scientists across the world are examining the genetic makeup of the virus to determine its origins.

From the outset of the pandemic, many signs have pointed to a pig farming operation in Veracruz, Mexico, called Granjas Caroll, which is a subsidiary of Smithfield Foods, the world's largest pork producer. However, Ruben Donis, an expert virologist from the U.S. Centers for Disease Control and Prevention in Atlanta, Georgia, has come to a different conclusion based on genetic analysis. According to an article in the journal *Science,* Donis "suggests that the virus may have

originated in a U.S. pig that traveled to Asia as part of the hog trade. The virus may have infected a human there, who then traveled back to North America, where the virus perfected human-to-human spread, maybe even moving from the United States to Mexico."[a] Another report has linked the current strain of swine flu to a strain that ran through factory farms in North Carolina in 1998 and to the avian flu that killed over 50 million people in 1918.[b]

While scientists examine the genetic evidence for swine flu, a look at factory farming shows how these practices facilitate the proliferation of disease. For example, the pig population of North Carolina numbers about 10 million, and most of these pigs are crowded onto farms of over 5,000 animals. These pigs travel across the country as part of farming operations. A pig may be born in North Carolina, then travel to the heartland of the United States to fatten up before a final trip to the slaughterhouses in California.

The crowded conditions in pig farms mean that if the virus enters a farm it quickly can infect many pigs, which are then shipped to other places spreading the virus further, with many opportunities for the virus to pass between species. Health risks of global food distribution have long been a concern, and the swine flu outbreak elevates these concerns to a new level.

Global Twister   Do you think the swine flu pandemic should lead to changes in meat production and distribution globally?

---

[a] Cohen, J. (2009). Out of Mexico? Scientists ponder swine flu's origin. *Science 324* (5928), 700–702.

[b] Trifonov, V., et al. (2009). The origin of the recent swine influenza A (H1N1) virus infecting humans. *Eurosurveillance 14* (17). http://www.eurosurveillance.org/ViewArticle.aspx?ArticleId=19193.

courtyards. In addition to these houses, a stone tower that would have taken a hundred people over a hundred days to build was located inside one corner of the wall, near the spring. A staircase inside it probably led to a mud-brick building on top. This massive wall—near mud-brick storage facilities as well as peculiar structures of possible ceremonial significance—provides evidence of social changes in these early farming communities. A village cemetery also reflects the sedentary life of these early people; nomadic groups, with few exceptions, rarely buried their dead in a single central location.

Close contact between the farmers of Jericho and other villages is indicated by common features in art, ritual, use of prestige goods, and burial practices. Other evidence of trade consists of obsidian and turquoise from Sinai as well as marine shells from the coast, all discovered inside the walls of Jericho.

Neolithic Material Culture

Various innovations in the realms of tool making, pottery, housing, and clothing characterized life in Neolithic villages. All of these are examples of material culture.

TOOL MAKING

Early harvesting tools were made of wood or bone into which razor-sharp flint blades were inserted. Later tools continued to be made by chipping and flaking stone, but during the Neolithic period stone that was too hard to be chipped was ground and polished for tools. People developed sickles, scythes, forks, hoes, and simple plows to replace their digging sticks. Mortars and pestles were used to grind and crush grain. Later, when domesticated animals became available for use as draft animals, plows were redesigned. Along with the development of diverse technologies, individuals acquired specialized skills for creating a variety of implements, including leatherworks, weavings, and pottery.

POTTERY

Hard work on the part of those producing the food would also support other members of the society who could then apply their skills and energy to various craft specialties such as pottery. In the Neolithic, different forms of pottery were created for transporting and storing food, water, and various material possessions.

Because pottery vessels are impervious to damage by insects, rodents, and dampness, they could be used for storing small grain, seeds, and other materials. Moreover, food can be boiled in pottery vessels directly over the fire rather than by such ancient techniques as dropping stones heated directly in the fire into the food being cooked. Pottery was also used for pipes, ladles, lamps, and other objects, and some cultures used large vessels for disposal of the dead. Significantly, pottery containers remain important for much of humanity today.

Widespread use of pottery, which is made of clay and fired in very hot ovens, is a good, though not foolproof, indication of a sedentary community. It is found in abundance in all but a few of the earliest Neolithic settlements. Its fragility and weight make it less practical

for use by nomads and hunters, who more commonly use woven bags, baskets, and animal-hide containers. Nevertheless, there are some modern nomads who make and use pottery, just as there are farmers who do not. In fact, food foragers in Japan were making pottery by 13,000 years ago, long before it was being made in Southwest Asia.

The manufacture of pottery requires artful skill and considerable technological sophistication. To make a useful vessel requires knowledge of clay: how to remove impurities from it, how to shape it into desired forms, and how to dry it in a way that does not cause cracking. Proper firing is tricky as well; it must be heated to over 600 degrees Fahrenheit so that the clay will harden and resist future disintegration from moisture, but care must be taken to prevent the object from cracking or even exploding as it heats and later cools down.

Pottery is decorated in various ways. For example, designs can be engraved on the vessel before firing, or special rims, legs, bases, and other details may be made separately and fastened to the finished pot. Painting is the most common form of pottery decoration, and there are literally thousands of painted designs found among the pottery remains of ancient cultures.

HOUSING

Food production and the new sedentary lifestyle emphasized another technological development—permanent house building. Because they move frequently, most food foragers show little interest in permanent housing. Cave shelters, pits dug in the earth, and simple lean-tos made of hides and tree limbs serve the purpose of keeping the weather out. In the Neolithic, however, dwellings became more complex in design and more diverse in type. Some Neolithic peoples constructed houses of wood, while others built more elaborate shelters made of stone, sun-dried brick, or poles plastered together with mud or clay.

Although permanent housing frequently goes along with food production, there is evidence of substantial housing without domestication. For example, on the northwestern coast of North America, people lived in extensive houses made of heavy planks split from cedar logs, yet their food consisted entirely of wild plants and animals, especially salmon and sea mammals.

CLOTHING

During the Neolithic, for the first time in human history, clothing was made of woven textiles. The raw materials and technology necessary for the production of clothing came from several sources: flax and cotton from farming; wool from domesticated sheep, llamas, or goats; silk from silk worms. Human invention contributed the spindle for spinning and the loom for weaving.

© John Kerkhoven

Sometimes Neolithic villagers organized to carry out impressive communal works. Shown here is Stonehenge, the famous ceremonial and astronomical center in England, which dates back about 4,500 years. Used as a burial ground long before the massive stone circle was constructed, Stonehenge reflects the builders' understanding of the forces of nature and their impact on food production. For instance, the opening of the stone circles aligns precisely so that the sunlight passes through with the sunrise of the summer solstice and with the sunset of the winter solstice. This careful alignment indicates that the people of the Neolithic were paying close attention to the movements of the sun and the growing cycle of the seasons.

Neolithic Social Structure

Evidence of the economic and technological developments listed thus far has enabled archaeologists to make some inferences about the organization of Neolithic societies. For example, archaeological evidence reveals little in the way of a centrally organized and directed religious life, and burial sites exhibit no social differentiation. Early Neolithic graves tend not to be covered by stone slabs and rarely included elaborate objects. Burial practices tend to apply equally to all members of a community.

The small size of most villages and the absence of elaborate buildings suggest that the inhabitants knew one another very well and were even related; most of their relationships were probably highly personal ones, with equal emotional significance. Still, Neolithic people sometimes organized to carry out impressive communal works preserved in the archaeological record, such as the site of Stonehenge in England.

From all the evidence, it seems that Neolithic societies were relatively egalitarian with minimal division of labor, but they did develop some new and more specialized social roles. Villages appear to have been made up of several households, each providing for most of its own needs. The organizational needs of society beyond the household level were probably met by kinship groups.

Neolithic Culture in the Americas

In the Americas the shape and timing of the Neolithic revolution differed compared to other parts of the world. For example, Neolithic agricultural villages were common in Southwest Asia between 8,000 and 9,000 years ago, but similar villages did not appear in the Americas until about 4,500 years ago, in **Mesoamerica** (the region encompassing central and southern Mexico and northern Central America) and the Andean highlands. Moreover, pottery, which developed in Southwest Asia shortly after plant and animal domestication, did not emerge in the Americas until much later. The potter's wheel was

Mesoamerica The region encompassing central and southern Mexico and northern Central America.

not used by early Neolithic people in the Americas. Instead, elaborate pottery was manufactured by hand. Looms and the hand spindle appeared in the Americas about 3,000 years ago.

None of these absences indicate any backwardness on the part of Native American peoples, many of whom, as we have already seen, were highly sophisticated farmers and plant breeders. Rather, the effectiveness of existing practices was such that they continued to be satisfactory. When food production developed in Mesoamerica and the Andean highlands, it did so wholly independently of Europe and Asia, with different crops, animals, and technologies.

Outside Mesoamerica and the Andean highlands, hunting, fishing, and the gathering of wild plant foods remained important elements in the economy of Neolithic peoples in the Americas. Apparently, most American Indians chose not to entirely switch from a food-foraging to a food-producing mode of life, even though maize and other domestic crops came to be cultivated just about everywhere that climate permitted. The Indian lifeways were so effective, so well integrated into a complete cultural system, and so environmentally stable that for many of these groups the change to food production was unnecessary. The stable American Indian cultures were only disrupted by the arrival of European explorers who brought disease and devastation with them.

The Neolithic and Human Biology

Although we tend to think of the invention of food production in terms of its cultural impact, it obviously had a biological impact as well. From studies of human skeletons from Neolithic burials, physical anthropologists have found evidence for somewhat less mechanical stress on peoples' bodies and teeth. Although there are exceptions, the teeth of Neolithic peoples show less wear, their bones are less robust, and osteoarthritis (the result of stressed joint surfaces) is not as marked as in the skeletons of Paleolithic and Mesolithic peoples.

Though Neolithic teeth show less wear, recent discoveries from Pakistan provide the earliest evidence of human dentistry: tiny holes made in the molar teeth of ancient live humans, with fine flint drills.[24] Whether dentistry accompanied an increase in dental decay brought about by the dietary shift of this period remains to be seen. This would parallel the clear evidence for a marked overall deterioration in health and mortality during the Neolithic. Anthropologist Anna Roosevelt sums up our knowledge of this in the following Original Study.

---

[24] Coppa, A., et al. (2006). Early Neolithic tradition of dentistry. *Nature 440,* 755–756.

Original Study

History of Mortality and Physiological Stress   *by Anna Roosevelt*

Although there is a relative lack of evidence for the Paleolithic stage, enough skeletons have been studied that it seems clear that seasonal and periodic physiological stress regularly affected most prehistoric hunting-gathering populations, as evidenced by the presence of enamel hypoplasias [horizontal linear defects in tooth enamel] and Harris lines [horizontal lines near the ends of long bones].

What also seems clear is that severe and chronic stress, with high frequency of hypoplasias, infectious disease lesions, pathologies related to iron-deficiency anemia, and high mortality rates, is not characteristic of these early populations. There is no evidence of frequent, severe malnutrition, and so the diet must have been

© Alan H. Goodman, Hampshire College

Harris lines near the ends of these youthful thigh bones, found in a prehistoric farming community in Arizona, are indicative of recovery after growth arrest, caused by famine or disease.

adequate in calories and other nutrients most of the time.

During the Mesolithic, the proportion of starch in the diet rose, to judge from the increased occurrence of certain dental diseases, but not enough to create an impoverished

diet. At this time, diets seem to have been made up of a rather large number of foods, so that the failure of one food source would not be catastrophic. There is a possible slight tendency for Paleolithic people to be healthier and taller than Mesolithic people, but there is no apparent trend toward increasing physiological stress during the Mesolithic. Thus, it seems that both hunter-gatherers and incipient agriculturalists regularly underwent population pressure, but only to a moderate degree.

During the periods when effective agriculture first comes into use, there seems to be a temporary upturn in health and survival rates in a few regions: Europe, North America, and the eastern Mediterranean. At this stage, wild foods are still consumed periodically, and a variety of plants are cultivated, suggesting the availability of adequate amounts of different nutrients. Based on the increasing frequency of tooth disease related to high carbohydrate consumption, it seems that cultivated plants probably increased the storable calorie supply, removing for a time any seasonal or periodic problems in food supply. In most regions, however, the development of agriculture seems not to have had this effect, and there seems to have been a slight increase in physiological stress.

Stress, however, does not seem to have become common and widespread until after the development of high degrees of sedentism, population density, and reliance on intensive agriculture. At this stage in all regions the incidence of physiological stress increases greatly, and average mortality rates increase appreciably.

Most of these agricultural populations have high frequencies of porotic hyperostosis and cribra orbitalia [bone deformities indicative of chronic iron-deficiency anemia], and there is a substantial increase in the number and severity of enamel hypoplasias and pathologies associated with infectious disease. Stature in many populations appears to have been considerably lower than would be expected if genetically determined height maxima had been reached, which suggests that the growth arrests associated with pathologies were causing stunting.

Accompanying these indicators of poor health and nourishment, there is a universal drop in the occurrence of Harris lines, suggesting a poor rate of full recovery from the stress. Incidence of carbohydrate-related tooth disease increases, apparently because subsistence by this time is characterized by a heavy emphasis on a few starchy food crops. Populations seem to have grown beyond the point at which wild food resources could be a meaningful dietary supplement, and even domestic animal resources were commonly reserved for farm labor and transport rather than for diet supplementation.

It seems that a large proportion of most sedentary prehistoric populations under intensive agriculture underwent chronic and life-threatening malnutrition and disease, especially during infancy and childhood. The causes of the nutritional stress are likely to have been the poverty of the staple crops in most nutrients except calories, periodic famines caused by the instability of the agricultural system, and chronic lack of food due to both population growth and economic expropriation by elites. The increases in infectious disease probably reflect both a poorer diet and increased interpersonal contact in crowded settlements, and it is, in turn, likely to have aggravated nutritional problems.

Adapted from Roosevelt, A. C. (1984). Population, health, and the evolution of subsistence: Conclusions from the conference. In M. N. Cohen & G. J. Armelagos (Eds.), Paleopathology at the origins of agriculture (pp. 572–574). Orlando: Academic Press.

© Alan H. Goodman, Hampshire College

Enamel hypoplasias, such as those shown on these teeth, are indicative of arrested growth caused by famine or disease. These teeth are from an adult who lived in an ancient farming community in Arizona.

For the most part, the crops on which Neolithic peoples came to depend were selected for their higher productivity and storability rather than their nutritional value. Moreover, as already noted, their nutritional shortcomings would have been exacerbated by their susceptibility to periodic failure, particularly as populations grew in size. Thus the worsened health and mortality of Neolithic peoples are not surprising. Some have gone so far as to assert that the switch from food foraging to food production was the worst mistake that humans ever made.

Another key contributor to the increased incidence of disease and mortality was probably the new mode of life in Neolithic communities. Sedentary life in fixed villages brings with it sanitation problems as garbage and human waste accumulate. These are not a problem for small groups of people who move about from one campsite to another. Moreover, airborne diseases are more easily transmitted where people are gathered into villages. As discussed in Chapter 2, farming practices also created the ideal environment for the species of mosquito that spreads malaria.

Another factor, too, was the close association between humans and their domestic animals, a situation conducive to the transmission of diseases. A host of life-threatening diseases—including smallpox, chicken pox, swine flu, and many of those infectious diseases of childhood that were not overcome by medical science until the latter half of the 20th century—were transmitted to humans through their close association with domestic animals (Table 10.1). Higher mortality rates in Neolithic villages were offset by increased fertility, for population growth accelerated dramatically at precisely the moment that health and mortality worsened.

Table 10.1 Diseases Acquired from Domesticated Animals

Human Disease	Animal with Most Closely Related Pathogen	Deaths Globally According to WHO (Year)	Prevention Strategies
Measles	Cattle (rinderpest)	197,000 (2007)	Immunization
Tuberculosis	Cattle	1.6 million (2005)	Treatment of infected individuals to prevent spread
Smallpox	Cattle (cowpox) or other livestock with related pox viruses	Eradicated as of December 1979; between 1900 and eradication, smallpox killed 300–500 million people	Immunization
Influenza	Pigs, ducks	Several different types; all are seasonal and variable, with 250,000 to 500,000 deaths estimated annually	Immunization
Pertussis (whooping cough)	Pigs, dogs	297,000 (2000)	Immunization

Source: Diamond, J. (1997). *Guns, germs, and steel* (p. 207). New York: Norton; World Health Organization Fact Sheets.

The Neolithic and the Idea of Progress

Although the overall health of Neolithic peoples suffered as a consequence of this cultural shift, many view the transition from food foraging to food production as a great step upward on a ladder of progress. In part this interpretation is due to one of the more widely held beliefs of Western culture—that human history is basically a record of steady progress over time. To be sure, farming allowed people to increase the size of their populations, to live together in substantial sedentary communities, and to reorganize the workload in ways that permitted craft specialization. However, this idea of progress is the product of a set of cultural beliefs, not a universal truth. Each culture defines progress (if it does so at all) in its own terms.

Whatever the benefits of food production, however, a substantial price was paid.[25] As anthropologists Mark Cohen and George Armelagos put it, "Taken as a whole, indicators fairly clearly suggest an overall decline in the quality—and probably in the length—of human life associated with the adoption of agriculture."[26]

Rather than imposing ethnocentric notions of progress on the archaeological record, it is best to view the advent of food production as but one more factor contributing to the diversification of cultures, something that had begun in the Paleolithic. Although some societies continued to practice various forms of hunting, gathering, and fishing, others became horticultural, and some of those developed **agriculture.** Technologically more complex than horticultural societies, agriculturalists practice intensive crop cultivation, employing plows, fertilizers, and possibly irrigation. They may use a wooden or metal plow pulled by one or more harnessed draft animals, such as horses, oxen, or water buffaloes, to produce food on larger plots of land. The distinction between horticulturalist and intensive agriculturalist is not always an easy one to make. For example, the Hopi Indians of the North American Southwest traditionally employed irrigation in their farming while at the same time using basic hand tools.

Pastoralism arose in environments that were too dry, too grassy, too steep, too cold, or too hot for effective horticulture or intensive agriculture. Pastoralists breed and manage migratory herds of domesticated grazing animals, such as goats, sheep, cattle, llamas, or camels. For example, the Russian steppes, with their heavy grass cover, were not suitable to farming without a plow, but they were ideal for herding. Thus a number of peoples living in the arid grasslands and deserts that stretch from northwestern Africa into Central Asia kept large herds of domestic animals, relying on their neighbors for plant foods. Finally, some societies went on to develop civilizations—the subject of the next chapter.

---

[25] Cohen, M. N., & Armelagos, G. J. (1984). *Paleopathology at the origins of agriculture.* Orlando: Academic; Goodman, A., & Armelagos, G. J. (1985). Death and disease at Dr. Dickson's mounds. *Natural History 94* (9), 12–18.

agriculture The cultivation of food plants in soil prepared and maintained for crop production. Involves using technologies other than hand tools, such as irrigation, fertilizers, and the wooden or metal plow pulled by harnessed draft animals.

pastoralism Breeding and managing large herds of domesticated grazing and browsing animals, such as goats, sheep, cattle, horses, llamas, or camels.

---

[26] Cohen, M. N., & Armelagos, G. J. (1984). Paleopathology at the origins of agriculture: Editors' summation. In M. N. Cohen & G. J. Armelagos, *Paleopathology at the origins of agriculture* (p. 594). Orlando: Academic.

Questions for Reflection

1. The changed lifeways of the Neolithic included the domestication of plants and animals as well as settlement into villages. How did these cultural transformations solve the challenges of existence while at the same time create new problems? Did the Neolithic set into motion problems that are still with us today?

2. Why do you think some people of the past did not make the change from food foragers to food producers? What problems existing in today's world have their origins in the lifeways of the Neolithic?

3. Though human biology and culture are always interacting, the rates of biological change and cultural change uncoupled at some point in the history of our development. Think of examples of how the differences in these rates had consequences for humans in the Neolithic and in the present.

4. Why are the changes of the Neolithic sometimes mistakenly associated with progress? Why have the social forms that originated in the Neolithic come to dominate the earth?

5. Although the archaeological record indicates some differences in the timing of domestication of plants and animals in different parts of the world, why is it incorrect to say that one region was more advanced than another?

Suggested Readings

Childe, V. G. (1951). *Man makes himself.* New York: New American Library.

In this classic, originally published in 1936, Childe presented his concept of the Neolithic revolution. He places special emphasis on the technological inventions that helped transform humans from food gatherers to food producers.

Coe, S. D. (1994). *America's first cuisines.* Austin: University of Texas Press.

Writing in an accessible style, Coe discusses some of the more important crops grown by Native Americans and explores their early history and domestication. Following this she describes how these foods were prepared, served, and preserved by the Aztec, Maya, and Inca.

Diamond, J. (1997). *Guns, germs, and steel.* New York: Norton.

This Pulitzer Prize–winning bestseller addresses the question of the distribution of wealth and power in the world today. For Diamond, this answer requires an understanding of events associated with the origin and spread of food production. Although Diamond falls into various ethnocentric traps, he provides a great deal of solid information on the domestication and spread of crops and the biological consequences for humans.

Mann, C. C. (2005). *1491: New revelations of the Americas before Columbus.* New York: Knopf.

Mann dispels the myth of the Americas as an uninhabited wasteland before the arrival of Columbus and the European colonizers who followed him. He shows not only the richness of various Native American cultures but also the devastating effects of colonization.

Rindos, D. (1984). *The origins of agriculture: An evolutionary perspective.* Orlando: Academic.

This is one of the most important books on agricultural origins. After identifying the weaknesses of existing theories, Rindos presents his own evolutionary theory of agricultural origins.

Challenge Issue With the emergence of cities and states, human societies began to develop organized central governments and a concentration of power that made it possible to build monumental structures, such as the great pyramids of Egypt. But cities and states also ushered in a series of challenges, many of which city dwellers still face. For example, social stratification, in which a ruling elite controls the means of subsistence and many other aspects of daily life, exploits many city dwellers and poor people in outlying areas. While the people of stratified societies are interdependent, the elite classes have disproportionate access to and control of all resources, including human labor. In Cairo, as in other big cities, housing, for example, is dramatically different for different social classes. While the elite live in luxurious homes, 5 million urban poor live illegally in tomb rooms of cemeteries known as the City of the Dead.

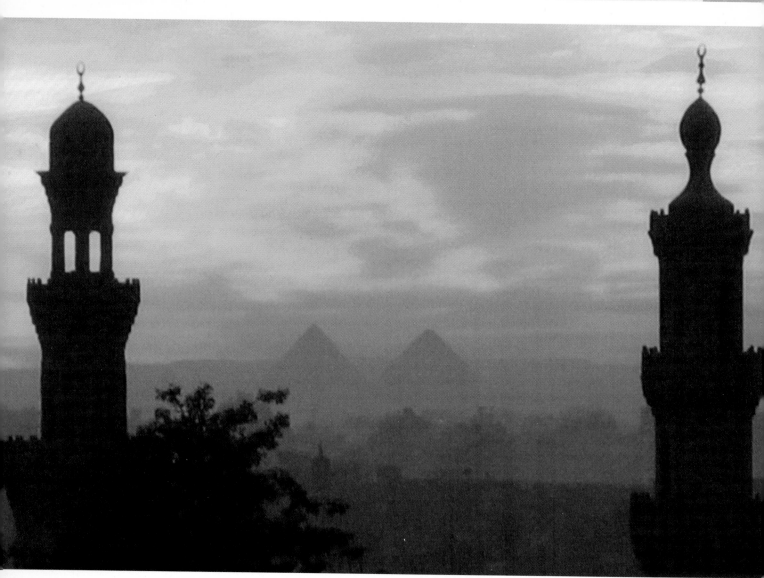

CHAPTER 11

The Emergence of Cities and States

Chapter Preview

When and Where Did the World's First Cities Develop?

Cities are urban settlements with well-defined centers and populations that are large, dense, and diversified both economically and socially. They are characteristic of civilizations that developed independently in Eurasia, Africa, and the Americas. Between 4,500 and 6,000 years ago, cities began to develop in China, the Indus and Nile Valleys, Mesopotamia, Mesoamerica, and the central Andes. The world's oldest cities were those of Mesopotamia, but one of the largest was located in Mesoamerica.

What Changes in Culture Accompanied the Rise of Cities?

Four basic cultural changes mark the transition from Neolithic village existence to life in urban centers: agricultural innovation, as new farming methods were developed; diversification of labor, as more people were freed from food production to pursue a variety of full-time craft specialties; the development of centralized governments to deal with the new problems of urban life; and the emergence of social classes, as people were ranked according to the work they did or the position of the families into which they were born.

Why Did Cities Develop into Civilizations?

Ancient cities developed into what anthropologists call civilizations: societies in which large numbers of people live in cities, are socially stratified, and are governed by centrally organized political systems called states. A number of theories have been proposed to explain why civilizations developed. For example, population growth led to competition for space and scarce resources. This competition favored the development of centralized authority to control resources and, incidentally, organized warfare. Some civilizations, though, appear to have developed as a result of unifying beliefs and values. In some cases, the self-promoting actions of powerful individuals may have played a role. Thus it may be that civilizations arose in different places for different reasons.

A walk down a busy street of a city such as New York or San Francisco brings us into contact with numerous activities essential to life in North American society. Sidewalks are crowded with people going to and from offices and stores. Heavy traffic of cars, buses, and trucks periodically comes to a standstill. A brief two-block stretch may contain a grocery store; sidewalk vendors; shops selling clothing, appliances, or books; a restaurant; a newsstand; a gas station; and a movie theater. Other features such as a museum, a police station, a school, a hospital, or a church distinguish some neighborhoods.

Each of these services or places of business is dependent on others from outside this two-block radius. A butcher shop, for instance, depends on slaughterhouses and beef ranches. A clothing store could not exist without designers, farmers who produce cotton and wool, and workers who manufacture synthetic fibers. Restaurants rely on refrigerated trucking and vegetable and dairy farmers. Hospitals need insurance companies, pharmaceutical companies, and medical equipment industries. All institutions, finally, depend on the public utilities—the telephone, gas, water, and electric companies. Although interdependence is not immediately apparent to the passerby, it is an important aspect of modern cities.

The interdependence of goods and services in a big city makes a variety of products readily available. But interdependence also creates vulnerability. If strikes, bad weather, or acts of violence cause one service to stop functioning, other services can deteriorate.

At the same time, cities are resilient in their response to stresses. When one service breaks down, others take over its functions. During a long newspaper strike in New York City in the 1960s, for example, several new magazines were launched, and television networks expanded their coverage of news and events. This phenomenon resembles the flourishing of reality television programs in the United States that took place during the 2007–2008 Hollywood writers' strike.

In many parts of the world the violence of war has caused extensive damage to basic infrastructure, leading to the development of alternative systems to cope with everything from procuring food to communicating within global political systems. The same is true for people coping with the aftermath of a natural disaster such as Hurricane Katrina in 2005 or the massive tsunami that hit the Pacific in 2004. With the interconnectedness of modern life due to the Internet and globalization, the interdependence of goods and services transcends far beyond city limits.

On the surface, city life seems so orderly that we take it for granted; but a moment's reflection reminds us that

© Getty Images

Since the American invasion in 2003, bombing and pillaging have damaged the infrastructure of Baghdad. Four days of heavy rain led to a collapse of the city's sewage system, which flooded the streets with contaminated water. Makeshift bridges were constructed and alternate routes were created to help people avoid waterborne disease.

the intricate fabric of city life did not always exist, and the concentrated availability of diverse goods is a very recent development in human history.

Defining Civilization

The word *civilization* comes from the Latin *civis*, which refers to one who is an inhabitant of a city, and *civitas*, which refers to the urban community in which one dwells. In everyday North American and European usage, the word *civilization* connotes refinement and progress and may imply ethnocentric judgments about cultures. In anthropology, by contrast, the term has a more precise meaning that avoids culture-bound notions. As used by anthropologists, **civilization** refers to societies in which large numbers of people live in cities, are socially stratified, and are

civilization In anthropology, a type of society marked by the presence of cities, social classes, and the state.

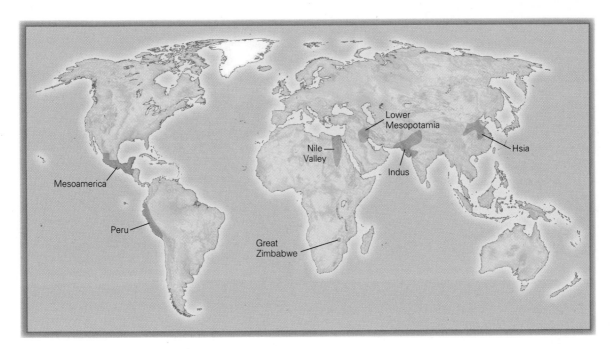

Figure 11.1 The major early civilizations sprang from Neolithic villages in various parts of the world. Those of the Americas developed wholly independently of those in Africa and Eurasia. Chinese civilization seems to have developed independently of Southwest Asia civilization, including the Nile and Indus civilizations.

governed by a ruling elite working through centrally organized political systems called states. We shall elaborate on all of these points in this chapter.

As Neolithic villages grew into towns, the world's first cities developed. This happened between 4,500 and 6,000 years ago—first in Mesopotamia (modern-day Iraq), then in Egypt's Nile Valley and India and Pakistan's Indus Valley. In China, civilization was under way by 5,000 years ago. Independent of these developments in Eurasia and Africa, the first American Indian cities appeared in Peru around 4,000 years ago and in Mesoamerica about 2,000 years ago (Figure 11.1).

What characterized these first cities? Why are they called the birthplaces of civilization? The first feature of cities—and of civilization—is their large size and population.

But cities are more than overgrown towns. Consider the case of Çatalhöyük, a compact 9,500-year-old settlement in south-central Turkey.[1] The tightly packed houses for its more than 5,000 inhabitants left no room for streets. People traversed the roofs of neighboring houses and dropped through a hole in the roof to get into their own home. While house walls were covered with paintings

and bas-reliefs, the houses were structurally similar to one another, and no known public architecture existed. People grew some crops and tended livestock but also collected significant amounts of food from wild plants and animals, never intensifying their agricultural practices. Evidence of a division of labor or of a centralized authority is minimal or nonexistent. It was as if several Neolithic villages were crammed together in one place at Çatalhöyük.

Archaeological evidence from early urban centers, by contrast, demonstrates organized planning by a central authority, technological intensification, and social stratification. For example, flood control and protection were vital components of the great ancient cities of the Indus River Valley, located in today's India and Pakistan. Mohenjo-Daro—an urban center at its peak some 4,500 years ago with a population of at least 20,000—was built on an artificial mound, safe from floodwaters. Further, the streets of this densely populated city were laid out in a grid pattern and included individual homes with sophisticated drainage systems.

---

[1] Material on Çatalhöyük is drawn from Balter, M. (1998). Why settle down? The mystery of communities. *Science 282*, 1442–1444; Balter, M. (1999). A long season puts Çatalhöyük in context. *Science 286*, 890–891; Balter, M. (2001). Did plaster hold Neolithic society together? *Science 294*, 2278–2281; Kunzig, R. (1999). A tale of two obsessed archaeologists, one ancient city and nagging doubts about whether science can ever hope to reveal the past. *Discover 20* (5), 84–92.

Visual Counterpoint

The view looking south down Teotihuacan's principal avenue, the Street of the Dead. This urban axis was unequaled in its scale until the construction of such modern-day avenues as the Champs-Élysées in Paris.

Ancient peoples incorporated their spiritual beliefs and social order into the cities they built. For example, the layout of the great Mesoamerican city Teotihuacan, founded 2,200 years ago, translated the solar calendar into a unified spatial pattern. The Street of the Dead—a grand north-south axis running from the Pyramid of the Moon and bordered by the Pyramid of the Sun and the royal palace compound—was deliberately oriented to an astronomical marker, east of true north. Ancient city planners even channeled the San Juan River to run through the city in conformity with the grid (Figure 11.2). Surrounding this core were thousands of apartment compounds, separated

Figure 11.2 The founders of Teotihuacan imposed an audacious plan on several square kilometers of landscape in central Mexico. At the center is the Street of the Dead, running from the Pyramid of the Moon (near top), past the Pyramid of the Sun, and, south of the San Juan River (Rio), the palace compound. Note the gridded layout of surrounding apartment compounds and the channeled San Juan River.

from one another by a grid of narrow streets, maintaining the east-of-north orientation throughout the city. It is estimated that over 100,000 people inhabited this great city until its sudden collapse possibly in the 7th century.

Finally, clear evidence for both social and economic diversity exists in Teotihuacan. Some six levels of society can be discerned through the varying size and quality of apartment rooms. Those at and near the top of the social scale lived on or near the Street of the Dead. The Pyramid of the Sun along this avenue was built above a cave, which was seen as a portal to the underworld and as the home of deities associated with death. Teotihuacan artisans worked on exotic goods and raw materials imported from afar, and at least two neighborhoods housed people with foreign affiliations—one with Oaxaca, the other (the "merchant's quarter") with the Gulf and Maya lowlands. Farmers, whose labor in fields (some of them irrigated) supplied the food to fellow city dwellers, also resided in the city.[2]

Mohenjo-Daro and Teotihuacan, like other early cities throughout the globe, were far more than expanded Neolithic villages. The changes that took place in the transition from village to city were so great that many consider the emergence of urban living to be one of the great developments in human culture. The following case study gives us a glimpse of another of the world's ancient cities, including how archaeologists have studied it and how it may have grown from a smaller farming community.

Tikal: A Case Study

The ancient city of Tikal, one of the largest lowland Maya centers in existence, is situated in Central America about 300 kilometers north of Guatemala City. Tikal was built on a broad limestone terrace in a rainforest. Here the Maya settled 3,000 years ago. Because the Maya calendar can be precisely correlated with our own, it is known that their civilization flourished until 1,100 years ago.

At its height, Tikal covered about 120 square kilometers (km²), and its center or nucleus was the Great Plaza, a large, paved area surrounded by about 300 major structures and thousands of houses (Figure 11.3). Starting from a small, dispersed population, Tikal swelled to at least 45,000 people. By 1,550 years ago, its population density had reached 600 to 700 people per square kilometer, which was three times that of the surrounding region.

Tikal and the surrounding region were intensively explored under the joint auspices of the University of Pennsylvania Museum and the Guatemalan government from 1956 through the 1960s. At the time, it was the most ambitious archaeological project undertaken in the western hemisphere.

In the first few years of the Tikal Project, archaeologists investigated only major temple and palace structures found in the vicinity of the Great Plaza, at the site's epicenter. But in 1959, aiming to gain a balanced view of Tikal's development and composition, they turned their attention to the hundreds of small mounds that surround larger buildings and were thought to be the remains of dwellings. In a sense, this represented a shift in the practice of archaeology toward studying the complexities of everyday life. Imagine how difficult it would be to get a realistic view of life in a major city such as Washington, DC, or Beijing by looking only at their monumental public buildings. Similarly, a realistic view of Tikal cannot be reconstructed without examining the full range of ruins in the area.

The excavation of small structures, most of which were probably houses, permitted the estimation of Tikal's population size and density. This information allowed archaeologists to test the conventional assumption that the Maya inhabitants' subsistence practices were inadequate to sustain large population concentrations.

Extensive excavation also provided a sound basis for a reconstruction of the everyday life and social organization of the Maya, a people who had been known almost entirely through the study of ceremonial remains. For example, differences in architecture, house construction, and associated artifacts and burials suggest differences in social class. Features of house distribution might reflect the existence of extended families or other types of kin groups. The excavation of both large and small structures revealed the social structure of the total population of Tikal.[3]

[2] Cowgill, G. L. (1997). State and society at Teotihuacan, Mexico. *Annual Review of Anthropology 26,* 129–161.

[3] Haviland, W. A. (2002). Settlement, society and demography at Tikal. In J. Sabloff (Ed.), *Tikal.* Santa Fe: School of American Research.

Figure 11.3 Tikal spreads far beyond the Great Plaza and the monumental buildings that have been excavated and are mapped here. Archaeologists used surveying techniques, test pits, and other strategies to fully define the city's boundaries and to understand the full spectrum of lifeways that took place there. The red outline in the center of the map delineates the royal court, royal burial ground, and central marketplace. In addition to what is pictured here, Tikal extends several kilometers outward in every direction. Those familiar with the original *Star Wars* movie will be interested to know that the aerial views of the rebel camp were filmed at Tikal, where monumental structures depicted in this map rise high above the forest canopy.

Surveying and Excavating the Site

Mapping crews surveyed 16 square kilometers of forested land surrounding the Great Plaza, providing a preliminary map to guide the small-structure excavation process.[4] Aerial photography could not be used for this mapping, because the tree canopy in this area is often 30 meters (about 100 feet) above the ground, obscuring all but the tallest temples. Many of the small ruins are practically invisible even to observers on the ground. Four years of mapping revealed that ancient Tikal was far larger than the original 16 km² surveyed. More time and money allowed continued surveying of the area to fully define the city's boundaries and calculate its overall size.[5]

The initial excavation of six structures, two plazas, and a platform revealed new structures not visible before excavation, the architectural complexity of the structures, and an enormous quantity of artifacts that had to be washed and catalogued. Some structures were partially excavated, and some remained uninvestigated. Following this initial work, the archaeological team excavated over a hundred additional small structures in different parts of the site in order to ensure investigation of a representative sample. The team also sank numerous test pits in various other small-structure groups to supplement the information gained from more extensive excavations.

---

[4] Haviland, W. A., et al. (1985). *Excavations in small residential groups of Tikal: Groups 4F-1 and 4F-2.* Philadelphia: University Museum.

[5] Puleston, D. E. (1983). *The settlement survey of Tikal.* Philadelphia: University Museum.

Evidence from the Excavation

Excavation at Tikal produced considerable information about the social organization, technology, and diversity in this ancient city, as well as the relationship between people in Tikal and other regions. For example, the site provided evidence of trade in nonperishable items. Granite, quartzite, hematite, pyrite, jade, slate, and obsidian all were imported, as either raw materials or finished products. Marine materials from Caribbean and Pacific coastal areas were found as well. Because Tikal is located on top of an abundant source of chert (a flintlike stone used to manufacture tools), this may have been exported in the form of raw material and finished objects. In addition, Tikal's location between two river systems may have facilitated an overland trade route. Evidence of trade in perishable goods—such as textiles, feathers, salt, and cacao—indicated that there were full-time traders among the Tikal Maya.

Technologically, specialized woodworking, pottery, obsidian, and shell workshops have been found. The skillful stone carving displayed on stone monuments suggests that occupational specialists did this work. The same is true of the fine artwork exhibited on ceramic vessels. Ancient artists had to envision what their work would look like after their pale, relatively colorless ceramics had been fired.

To control the large population, Tikal must have had some form of bureaucratic organization. From Maya written records (glyphs), we know that the government was headed by a hereditary ruling dynasty with sufficient power to organize massive construction and maintenance. This included a system of defensive ditches and embankments on the northern and southern edges of the city. The longest of these ran for a distance of perhaps 19 to 28 kilometers. Although we do not have direct evidence, there are clues to the existence of textile workers, dental workers, makers of bark cloth "paper," scribes, masons, astronomers, and other occupational specialists.

The religion of the Tikal Maya may have developed initially as a means to cope with the uncertainties of agriculture. Tikal soil is thin, and the only available water comes from rain that has been collected in reservoirs. Rain is abundant in season, but its onset tends to be unreliable. Conversely, the elevation of Tikal, high relative to surrounding terrain, may have caused it to be perceived as a "power place," especially suited for making contact with supernatural forces and beings.

The Maya priests tried not only to win over and please the deities in times of drought but also to honor them in times of plenty. Priests—experts on the Maya calendar—determined the most favorable time to plant

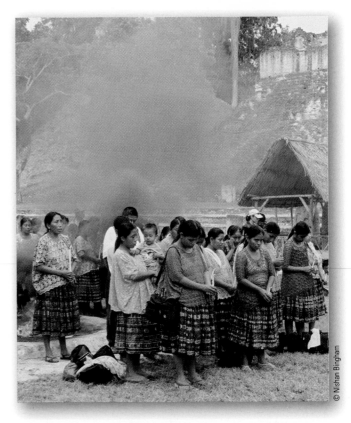

Archaeologists have proposed that Tikal may have emerged as an important site due to its relative altitude in the region. Today it is still an important religious center for local Maya, who gather in front of the acropolis for a traditional ceremony.

crops and were involved with other agricultural matters. This tended to keep people in or near the city so that they could receive guidance on their crops. The population in and around Tikal depended upon their priests to influence supernatural beings and forces on their behalf.

As the population increased, land for agriculture became scarce, forcing the Maya to find new methods of food production that could sustain the dense population concentrated at Tikal. They added the planting and tending of fruit trees and other crops that could be grown around their houses in soils enriched by human waste. (Unlike houses at Teotihuacan, those at Tikal were not built close to one another.) Along with increased reliance on household gardening, the Maya constructed artificially raised fields in areas that were flooded each rainy season. In these fields, crops could be intensively cultivated year after year, as long as they were carefully maintained. Measures were taken to maximize collection of water for the dry season—by converting low areas into reservoirs and constructing channels to carry runoff from plazas and other architecture into these reservoirs.

Carved monuments like this were commissioned by Tikal's rulers to commemorate important events in their regions. Portrayed on this one is a king who ruled about 1,220 years ago. Such skilled stone carving could only have been accomplished by a specialist. (For a translation of the inscription on the monument's left side, see Figure 11.7.)

As these changes were taking place, a class of artisans, craftspeople, and other occupational specialists emerged to serve the needs of an elite consisting of the priesthood and a ruling dynasty. The Maya built numerous temples, public buildings, and various kinds of houses appropriate to the distinct social classes of their society.

For several hundred years, Tikal was able to sustain its ever-growing population. When the pressure for food and land reached a critical point, population growth stopped. At the same time, warfare with other cities became increasingly destructive. These events are marked archaeologically by the abandonment of houses on prime land in rural areas, by the advent of nutritional problems visible in skeletons recovered from burials, and by the construction of the previously mentioned defensive ditches and embankments. In other words, a period of readjustment set in, which must have been directed by an already strong central authority. Activities then continued as before, but without further population growth for another 250 years or so.

As this case study shows, excavations at Tikal demonstrated the splendor, the social organization, the belief system, and the agricultural practices of the ancient Maya civilization, among other things. This chapter's Original Study illustrates a very different Maya site, just a day's walk from Tikal.

Original Study

Action Archaeology and the Community at El Pilar   *by Anabel Ford*

Resource management and conservation are palpable themes of the 21st century. Nowhere is this more keenly felt than in the tropics, seemingly our last terrestrial frontier. The Maya forest, one of the world's most biodiverse areas, is experiencing change at a rapid rate. Over the next two decades this area's population will double, threatening the integrity of the tropical ecosystems with contemporary development strategies that are at odds with the rich biodiversity of the region.

Curiously, in the past the Maya forest was home to a major civilization with at least three to nine times the current population of the region. The prosperity of the Classic Maya civilization

has been touted for the remarkable quality of their unique hieroglyphic writing; the beauty of their art expressed in stone, ceramics, and plaster; and the precision of their mathematics and astronomy. What was the secret of Maya conservation and prosperity? How can archaeology shed light on the conservation possibilities for the future? These are the questions I address in my research at El Pilar.

I began my work as an archaeologist in the Maya forest in 1972. Eschewing the monumental civic centers that draw tourist and scholar alike, I was interested in the everyday life of the Maya through the study of their cultural ecology—the multifaceted relationships of humans and their environment. Certainly, the glamorous archaeological centers intrigued me; they were testaments to the wealth of the Maya civilization. Yet, it seemed to me that an understanding of the ancient Maya landscape would tell us more about the relationship of the Maya and their forest than yet another major temple. After all, the Maya were an agrarian civilization.

The ancient Maya agricultural system must be the key to their growth and accomplishments. With more than a century of exploration of the temple centers, we know that the civic centers were made for the ceremonial use of the ruling elite, that the temples would hold tombs of the royals and would include dedications of some of the most astounding artworks of the ancient world. Centers, too, would present stone stele erected in commemoration of regal accomplishments with hieroglyphic writing that is increasingly understood as codification of the Mayan language. These facts about the Maya point to successful development founded in their land use strategies that supported the increasing populations, underwrote the affluent elite glamor, and allowed for the construction of major civic centers over 2 millennia. The Maya farmers were at the bottom of this astounding expansion, and that is where I thought there could be a real discovery.

Since agriculture figures so importantly in preindustrial agrarian societies, such as the Maya, we would expect that the majority of the settlements would be farming ones. But how can we understand the farming techniques and strategies? Our appreciation of the traditional land use methods has been subverted with technology and a European ecological imperialism that inhibits a full understanding of other land use systems.

During the conquest of the Maya area, Spaniards felt there was nothing to eat in the forest; presented with a staggering cornucopia of fruits and vegetables that could fill pages, they asserted they were starving, as there was no grain or cattle. Today, we use European terms to describe agricultural lands around the world that are in many ways inappropriate to describe traditional systems. The words *arable* specifically means "plowable" and is derived from the Egyptian word *Ard*, or "plow." *Arable* is equated with *cultivable* by the United Nations Food and Agriculture Organization,

and by doing so eliminates realms of land use and management that have a subtler impact on the environment. *Fallow* is loosely used to indicate abandoned fields, but really *fallow* means "unseeded plowed field." For European eyes, plowing was equivalent to cultivating, but in the New World cultivating embraced a much broader meaning that included fields of crops, selective succession, diverse orchards, and managed forests. In fact, it meant the entire landscape mosaic.

It is important to remember that the Maya, like all Native Americans prior to the tumultuous conquest 500 years ago, lived in the Stone Age without metal tools and largely without domesticated animals. This was not a hindrance, as it would seem today, but a fact that focused land use and intensification in other realms. Farmers were called upon to use their local skill and knowledge to provide for daily needs. And, as with all Native Americans, this skill would involve the landscape and most particularly the plants.

Reports of yields of grain from the Mesoamerican maize fields, or *milpas*, suggest that they were more than two to three times as productive as the fertile fields of the Seine River near Paris of the 16th century, the time of the conquest. The Maya farmed in cooperation with the natural environment. Like the Japanese rice farmer Masanubu Fukuoka describes in his book *One Straw Revolution*, Maya farmers today use their knowledge of the insects to insure pollination, their understanding of animals to promote propagation, their appreciation of water to determine planting, and their observations of change and nuance to increase their yields. This is not at all like the current agricultural development models that rely on increasingly complex techniques to raise production, disregarding nature in the process.

My focus on the patterns of the ancient Maya settlements has guided me along a path that I believe can provide important answers to questions of how the Maya achieved their success. The answers lie in finding where the everyday Maya lived, when they lived there, and what they did there. While popular notions would have you think that the Maya were a seething sea of humanity displacing the forest for their cities, I have discovered patterns on the landscape indicating that at their height in the Late Classic from 600 to 900 CE, the

Maya occupied less that two thirds of the landscape. More than 80 percent of the settlements were concentrated into less than 40 percent of the area, while another 40 percent of the region was largely unoccupied.

This diversity of land use intensity created a patchwork of stages of what traditional farmers see as a cycle from forest to field and from field to orchard and back to forest again. The result in the Maya forest garden was an economic landscape that supported the ancient Maya, fueled wealth in the colonial and independence eras with lumber, and underwrote capitalism with the natural gum chicle. Today more than 90 percent of the dominant trees of the forest are of economic value. The Maya constructed this valuable forest over the millennia.

Despite my interest in daily life in the forest, monumental buildings became a part of my work. While conducting a settlement survey in the forest, I uncovered and mapped El Pilar, a major ancient Maya urban center with enormous temples towering more than 22 meters high and plaza expanses greater than soccer fields. The whole center of civic buildings covers more than 50 hectares. El Pilar is the largest center in the Belize River area and is located only 50 km from Tikal. This center was bound to become a tourist destination, presenting an opportunity to explore new ways to tell the Maya story. My observation that the ancient Maya evolved a sustainable economy in the tropics of Mesoamerica led my approach to developing El Pilar.

Astride the contemporary border separating Belize from Guatemala, El Pilar has been the focus of a bold conservation design for an international peace park on a long-troubled border. The vision for El Pilar is founded on the preservation of cultural heritage in the context of the natural environment. With a collaborative and interdisciplinary team of local villagers, government administrators, and scientists, we have established the El Pilar Archaeological Reserve for Maya Flora and Fauna. Since 1993, the innovations of the El Pilar program have forged new ground in testing novel strategies for community participation in the conservation development of the El Pilar Archaeological Reserve.

This program touches major administrative themes of global importance: tourism, natural resources, foreign

CONTINUED

CONTINUED

affairs, agriculture, rural development, and education. Yet the program's impact goes further. Working with traditional forest gardeners affects agriculture, rural enterprise, and capacity building. There are few areas untouched by the program's inclusive sweep, and more arenas can contribute to its evolution.

At El Pilar, I practice what I call "action archaeology," a pioneering conservation model that draws on lessons learned from the recent and distant past to benefit contemporary populations. For example, the co-evolution of Maya society and the environment provide clues about sustainability in this region today. At El Pilar we have advanced programs that will simulate Maya forest gardens as an alternative to resource-diminishing plow-and-pasture farming methods. Working with the traditional farmers, school models are being established. These models will help to transfer knowledge to the younger generation and carry on important conservation strategies. The forest survives and demonstrates resilience to impacts brought on by human expansion. The ancient Maya lived with this forest for millennia, and the El Pilar program argues there are lessons to be learned from that past.

The El Pilar program recognizes the privilege it has enjoyed in forging an innovative community participatory process, in creating a unique management planning design, and in developing a new tourism destination. The success of local outreach at El Pilar can best be seen in the growth of the community organizations such as the El Pilar Forest Garden Network and Amigos de El Pilar (Friends of El Pilar). With groups based in both Belize and Guatemala working together, the El Pilar program can help build an inclusive relationship between the community and the reserve that is mutually beneficial. The development of this dynamic relationship lies at the heart of the El Pilar philosophy—resilient and with the potential to educate communities, reform local-level resource management, and inform conservation designs for the Maya forest.

© Rolox Awards for Excellence, Susan Gray

Anabel Ford is the Director of the Mesoamerican Research Center, University of California-Santa Barbara, and President of the nonprofit Exploring Solutions Past: The Maya Forest Alliance. http://www.marc.ucsb.edu/elpilar/

Cities and Cultural Change

If a person who grew up in a rural North American village today moved to Chicago, Montreal, or Los Angeles, she or he would experience a very different way of life. The same would be true for a Neolithic village dweller who moved into one of the world's first cities in Mesopotamia 5,500 years ago. Four basic changes mark the transition from Neolithic village life to life in the first urban centers: agricultural innovation, diversification of labor, central government, and social stratification.

Agricultural Innovation

Changes in farming methods distinguish early civilizations from Neolithic villages. The ancient Sumerians, for example, built an extensive system of dikes, canals, and reservoirs to irrigate their farmlands. With such a system, they could control water resources at will; water could be held and then run off into the fields as necessary.

Irrigation was important for crop yield, because not having to depend on the seasonal rain cycles allowed farmers to harvest more crops in one year. Increased crop yield, resulting from agricultural innovations, contributed to the high population densities of ancient civilizations.

Diversification of Labor

Diversified labor activity was also characteristic of early civilizations. In a Neolithic village without irrigation or plow farming, every family member participated in the raising of crops. But the high crop yields made possible by new farming methods and the increased population of cities permitted a sizable number of people to pursue nonagricultural activities on a full-time basis.

Ancient public records document a variety of specialized workers. For example, an early Mesopotamian document from the old Babylonian city of Lagash (modern Tell Al-Hiba, Iraq) lists the artisans, craftspeople, and others paid from crop surpluses stored in the temple granaries. These lists included coppersmiths, silversmiths, sculptors, merchants, potters, tanners, engravers, butchers, carpenters, spinners, barbers, cabinetmakers, bakers, clerks, and brewers.

With specialization came the expertise that led to the invention of new ways of making and doing things. In Eurasia and Africa, civilization ushered in what

Courtesy Andrew Snavely of Dobra Teas

While there is archaeological evidence suggestive of tea drinking by *Homo erectus* in China, according to legend, the mythical emperor Shen Nung (c. 3000 BCE) was the first to drink a cup after tea leaves fell into his pot of boiling water. What is certain is that this crop contributed to the development of early civilizations and trade networks across Asia. Today, tea is farmed by a combination of these ancient methods along with all the tools of modern science. Here, a delightful tea lady in the Gao Shan, high mountains of Nantou, Taiwan, hand picks leaves from plants cloned from original oolong plants in Fujian, China. Fresh oolong leaves are plucked during the spring and are processed by a variety of methods (from machine to foot rolling) to semi-oxidize the tea leaves. Taiwanese oolongs are best grown in altitudes of 1,500 to 2,800 meters (5,000–9,000 feet) where the air is thin and the sun is close, giving the teas a very vegetal, creamy tropical flavor.

archaeologists often refer to as the **Bronze Age,** a period marked by the production of tools and ornaments made of this metal alloy. Metals were in great demand for the manufacture of farmers' and artisans' tools, as well as for weapons. Copper and tin (the raw materials from which bronze is made) were smelted, or separated from their ores, then purified, and cast to make plows, swords, axes, and shields. Later, such tools were made from smelted iron. In violent disputes over borders or territory, stone knives, spears, and slings could not stand up against metal spears, arrowheads, swords, helmets, or other armor.

Bronze also allowed for a proliferation of ornamental objects that are found in museums around the world today (Figure 11.4). See this chapter's Globalscape for the story of the recovery of one artifact that was stolen from the Iraqi National Museum in Baghdad.

The indigenous civilizations of the Americas also used metals. In South America, copper, silver, and gold were used primarily for ceremonial and ornamental objects. The Aztec and Maya used the same soft metals for ceremonial and ornamental objects while continuing to rely on stone for their everyday tools. To those who assume that metal is inherently superior, this seems puzzling. However, the ready availability of obsidian (a glass formed by volcanic activity), its extreme sharpness (many times sharper than the finest steel), and the ease with which it could be worked made it perfectly suited to their needs. Moreover, unlike bronze—and especially iron—copper, silver, and gold are soft metals and have limited practical use. Obsidian tools provide some of the sharpest cutting edges ever made (recall the Anthropology Applied feature "Stone Tools for Modern Surgeons" in Chapter 8).

Early civilizations developed extensive trade systems to procure the raw materials needed for their technologies. In many parts of the world, boats provided greater access to trade centers, transporting large loads of imports and exports between cities at lower cost than if they had been carried overland. A one-way trip from the ancient Egyptian cities along the Nile River to the Mediterranean port city of Byblos in Phoenicia (not far from the present city of Beirut, Lebanon) took far less time by rowboat compared to the overland route. With a sailboat, it took even less time.

Egyptian kings, or pharaohs, sent expeditions south to Nubia (northern Sudan) for gold; east to the Sinai Peninsula for copper; to Arabia for spices and perfumes; to Asia for lapis lazuli (a blue semiprecious stone) and other jewels; north to Lebanon for cedar, wine, and funerary oils; and southwest to Central Africa for ivory, ebony, ostrich feathers, leopard skins, cattle, as well as for the people they enslaved. Evidence of trading from Great Zimbabwe in southern Africa indicates that by the 11th century these trading networks had extended throughout the Old World. Increased contact with foreign peoples through trade brought new information to trading economies, furthering the spread of innovations and bodies of knowledge such as geometry and astronomy.

Central Government

The emergence of a governing elite also characterized early civilizations. Because of their size and complexity, new cities required a strong central authority. The governing elite

Bronze Age In the Old World, the period marked by the production of tools and ornaments of bronze; began about 5,000 years ago in China and Southwest Asia and about 500 years earlier in Southeast Asia.

1. Artist fashions sculpture from wax.

2. The wax model is surrounded with clay.

3. This is heated so the clay hardens and the wax melts.
4. The now hollow mold is inverted and molten bronze metal is poured into it.

5. When the metal has cooled, the clay model is broken open to reveal a solid bronze sculpture.

Figure 11.4 **The same lost wax casting method used to create sculptures—such as the 3,000-year-old bronze Zeus, from the National Museum of Archaeology in Athens, Greece—is still used by artists today.**

These elliptical granite walls held together without any mortar at Great Zimbabwe in southern Zimbabwe, Africa, attest to the skill of the builders. When European explorers unwilling to accept the notion of civilization in sub-Saharan Africa discovered these magnificent ruins, they wrongly attributed them to white non-Africans. This false notion persisted until archaeologists demonstrated that these structures were part of a city with 12,000 to 20,000 inhabitants that served as the center of the Bantu state.

Globalscape

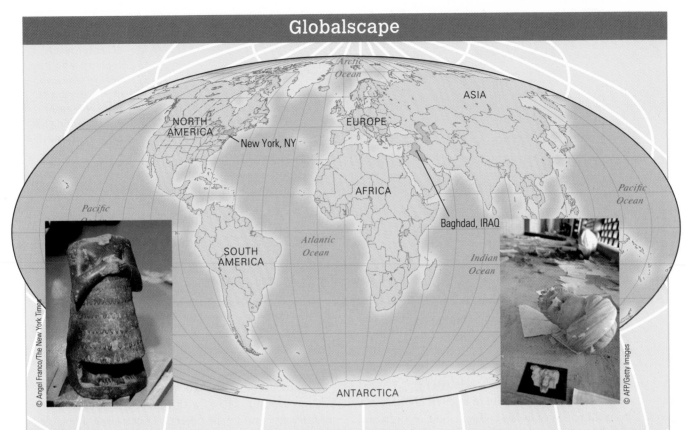

Iraqi Artifacts in New York City?

A clandestine operation carried out by the U.S. government led to the recovery in New York City of a priceless (though headless) 4,400-year-old stone statue of the Sumerian King Entemena of Lagash. The statue will be returned to its rightful place in the center of the Sumerian Hall of the Iraqi National Museum in Baghdad.

The modern-day state of Iraq, located in an area known as the cradle of civilization, is home to 10,000 archaeological sites preserving evidence of the earliest cities, laws, and civilizations. Though many Mesopotamian artifacts were brought to museums in Europe and the

United States in the 19th and early 20th centuries, the Iraqi National Museum in Baghdad still housed an extraordinary collection of priceless artifacts. That was the case until the weeks following the U.S. invasion in 2003, when several waves of looters removed tens of thousands of artifacts. According to Matthew Bogdanos, the Marine colonel who led the task force to track down and recover these artifacts, "The list of missing objects read like a 'who's who' of Near Eastern archaeology." Ironically, looting during the first Gulf War had led local archaeologists to move artifacts from regional museums to the National Museum of Baghdad for safekeeping.

This statue, like many other stolen artifacts, was first taken across the border into Syria and then made its way into the international black market in antiquities. Many artifacts have been returned to the museum through a no-questions-asked amnesty program. Others have required a combination of international cooperation and investigation, along with raids and seizures once artifacts have been tracked down.

Global Twister   If artifacts from ancient civilizations from throughout the world represent our shared global heritage, how can such treasures be kept safe from the chaos and desperation that result from war?

---

saw to it that different interest groups, such as farmers or craft specialists, provided their respective services and did not infringe on one another.

Just as they do today, governments of the past ensured that cities were safe from their enemies by constructing fortifications and raising an army. They levied taxes and appointed tax collectors so that construction workers, the army, and other public expenses could be paid. They saw to it that merchants, carpenters, or farmers who

made legal claims received justice according to standards of the legal system. They guaranteed safety for the lives and property of ordinary people and assured them that any harm done to one person by another would be justly handled. In addition, surplus food had to be stored for times of scarcity, and public works such as extensive irrigation systems or fortifications had to be supervised by competent, fair individuals. The mechanisms of government served all these functions.

Figure 11.5 The impermanence of spoken words contrasts with the relative permanence of written records. In all of human history, writing has been independently invented at least five times.

EVIDENCE OF CENTRALIZED AUTHORITY

Evidence of centralized authority in ancient civilizations comes from sources such as law codes, temple records, and royal chronicles. Excavation of the city structures themselves provides additional evidence because they can show definite signs of city planning. The precise astronomical layout of the Mesoamerican city Teotihuacan, described earlier, attests to strong, centralized control.

Monumental buildings and temples, palaces, and large sculptures are usually found in ancient civilizations. For example, the Great Pyramid for the tomb of Khufu, the Egyptian pharaoh, is 755 feet long (236 meters) and 481 feet high (147 meters); it contains about 2.3 million stone blocks, each with an average weight of 2.5 tons. The Greek historian Herodotus reports that it took 100,000 men twenty years to build this tomb. Such gigantic structures required a powerful central authority to harness the considerable labor force, engineering skills, and raw materials necessary for their construction.

Another indicator of the existence of centralized authority is writing, or some form of recorded information (Figure 11.5). With writing, central authorities could disseminate information and store, systematize, and deploy memory for political, religious, and economic purposes.

Scholars attribute the initial motive for the development of writing in Mesopotamia to record keeping of state affairs. Writing allowed early governments to track accounts of their food surplus, tribute records, and other business receipts. Some of the earliest documents appear to be just such records—accountings of bought and sold vegetables and animals, taxes, and storehouse inventories.

Before 5,500 years ago, records were comprised of tokens—ceramic pieces with different shapes indicative of different commercial objects. Thus a cone shape could represent a measure of grain, or a cylinder could be an animal. As the system developed, tokens became more sophisticated, representing different animals; processed foods such as oil, trussed ducks, or bread; and manufactured or imported goods such as textiles and metal.[6] Ultimately, clay tablets with impressed marks representing objects replaced these tokens.

By 5,000 years ago in the Mesopotamian city of Uruk in Iraq (which likely derives its modern name from this ancient place), a new writing technique emerged. Writers would use a reed stylus to make wedge-shaped markings on a tablet of damp clay. Originally, each marking stood for a word. Because most words in this language were monosyllabic, over time the markings came to stand for syllables (Figure 11.6).

Controversy surrounds the question of the earliest evidence of writing. Traditionally, the earliest writing was linked to Mesopotamia. However, in 2003 archaeologists working in the Henan Province of central China discovered signs carved into 8,600-year-old tortoise shells; these markings resemble later-written characters and predate the Mesopotamian evidence by about 2,000 years.[7]

---

[6] Lawler, A. (2001). Writing gets a rewrite. *Science 292*, 2419.

[7] Li, X., et al. (2003). The earliest writing? Sign use in the seventh millennium BC at Jiahu, Henan Province, China. *Antiquity 77*, 31–44.

Source: University of Pennsylvania Museum of Anthropology

Figure 11.6 Cuneiform writing developed from representational drawings of objects. Over time the drawings became simplified and more abstract, as well as being wedge-shaped so that they could be cut into a clay tablet with a stylus.

In the Americas, writing systems came into use among various Mesoamerican peoples, but the Maya system was particularly sophisticated. The Maya writing system, like other aspects of that culture, appears to have roots in the Olmec civilization,[8] though discoveries announced in 2006 of a stone tablet with a different writing system indicate that the Olmec had another form of writing distinct from Maya glyphs.[9]

The Maya hieroglyphic system had less to do with keeping track of state property than with extravagant celebrations of the accomplishments of their rulers. Maya lords glorified themselves by recording their dynastic genealogies, important conquests, and royal marriages; by using grandiose titles to refer to themselves; and by associating their actions with important astronomical events (Figure 11.7). Different though this may be from the recordkeeping of ancient Mesopotamia, all writing systems share a concern with political power and its maintenance.

THE EARLIEST GOVERNMENTS

A king and his advisors typically headed the earliest city governments. Of the many ancient kings known, one stands out as truly remarkable for the efficient government organization and highly developed legal system characterizing his reign. This is Hammurabi, the Babylonian king who lived in Mesopotamia (modern Iraq) sometime between 3,700 and 3,950 years ago. From Babylon, the

---

[8] Pohl, M.E.D., Pope, K. O., & von Nagy, C. (2002). Olmec origins of Mesoamerican writing, *Science 298,* 1984–1987.

[9] del Carmen Rodríguez Martínez, M. (2006). Oldest writing in the New World. *Science 313,* 1610–1614.

The day 13 Ahau
Eighteenth day of the month,
Cumku,

End of the seventeenth *katun.*
The completion of its period.

(part of the ruler's name?)
Chitam

In the dynastic line, lord of Tikal,
From Yax Moch Xoc
(an early Tikal king)

The ninth plus twenty,
In the count of the rulers

(successor to ?)
His lord father,

Yax Kin Caan Chac
(a probable title)

In the dynastic line, lord of Tikal,
In his fourth *katun* (period of 20 tuns,
or 360 day years)

The leader (*batab*)
Sixteen days plus one period
of twenty days,

Plus two tuns (back to),
The day 11 Kan,

Twelfth day of the month
of the parrot, Kayab,
He took the throne,

At the place of leadership,
He who scatters blessings.

Figure 11.7 The translation of the text on the monument shown on page 260 gives some indication of the importance of dynastic genealogy to Maya rulers. The "scattering" mentioned may refer to bloodletting as part of the ceremonies associated with the end of one twenty-year period, or *katun,* and the beginning of the next.

capital of his empire, he issued a set of laws now known as the Code of Hammurabi, notable for its thorough detail and standardization. It prescribed the correct form for legal procedures and determined penalties for perjury and false accusation. It contained laws applying to property rights, loans and debts, family rights, and even damages paid for malpractice by a physician. It defined fixed rates to be charged in various trades and branches of commerce and mechanisms to protect the poor, women, children, and slaves against injustice.

Officials ordered the code publicly displayed on huge stone slabs so that no one could plead ignorance. Even the poorest citizens were supposed to know their rights and responsibilities. Distinct social classes were clearly reflected in the code ("rule of law" does not necessarily mean "equality before the law"). For example, if an aristocrat put out the eye of a fellow aristocrat, the law required that his own eye be put out in turn; hence, the saying "an eye for an eye." However, if the aristocrat put out the eye of a commoner, the punishment was simply a payment of silver.[10]

While some civilizations flourished under a single ruler with extraordinary governing abilities, other civilizations possessed a widespread governing bureaucracy that was very efficient at every level. The government of the Inca empire is one such example.

The Inca civilization of Peru and its surrounding territories reached its peak 500 years ago, just before the arrival of the Spanish invaders. By 1525, it stretched 4,000 kilometers (2,500 miles) from north to south and 800 kilometers (500 miles) from east to west, making it one of the largest empires at the time. Its population, which numbered in the millions, was composed of people of many different ethnic groups. In the achievements of its government and political system, Inca civilization surpassed every other civilization of the Americas and most of those of Eurasia. An emperor, regarded as the divine son of the Sun God, headed the government. Under him came the royal family, the aristocracy, imperial administrators, and lower nobility, and below them the masses of artisans, craftspeople, and farmers.

The empire was divided into four administrative regions, further subdivided into provinces, and so on down to villages and families. Government agricultural and tax officials closely supervised farming activities such as planting, irrigation, and harvesting. Teams of professional relay runners could carry messages up to 400 kilometers (250 miles) in a single day over a network of roads and bridges that remains impressive even today.

Considering the complexity of the Inca civilization, it is surprising that they had no known form of conventional writing. Instead, public records and historical chronicles were maintained through an ingenious coding system of colored strings with knots.

Social Stratification

The rise of large, economically diversified populations presided over by centralized governing authorities brought with it the fourth cultural change characteristic of civilization: social stratification, or the emergence of social classes. For example, symbols of special status and privilege appeared in the ancient cities of Mesopotamia, where people were ranked according to the kind of work they did or the family into which they were born.

People who stood at or near the head of government were the earliest holders of high status. Although specialists of one sort or another—metalworkers, tanners, traders, or the like—generally outranked farmers, such specialization did not necessarily bring with it high status. Rather, people engaged in these kinds of economic activities were either members of the lower classes or outcasts.[11] Merchants in these societies could sometimes buy their way into a higher class. With time, the possession of wealth and the influence it could buy became in itself a requisite for high status, as it is in some contemporary cultures.

Archaeologists know that different social classes existed in ancient civilizations through evidence of laws and other written documents, as well as archaeological features including dwelling size and location. Social stratification is also revealed by burial customs. Graves excavated at early Neolithic sites are mostly simple pits dug in the ground, containing few, if any, grave goods. **Grave goods** consist of objects such as utensils, figurines, and personal possessions, symbolically placed in the grave for the deceased person's use in the afterlife. Early Neolithic grave sites reveal little variation, indicating essentially classless societies. Graves excavated in civilizations, by contrast, vary widely in size, mode of burial, and the number and variety of grave goods. This reflects a stratified society, divided into social classes. The graves of important people contain not only various artifacts made from precious materials, but sometimes, as in some early Egyptian burials, the remains of servants who were evidently killed to serve their master in the afterlife.

Skeletons from the burials may also provide evidence of stratification. Age at death as well as presence of certain

---

grave goods Items such as utensils, figurines, and personal possessions, symbolically placed in the grave for the deceased person's use in the afterlife.

---

[10] Moscati, S. (1962). *The face of the ancient orient* (p. 90). New York: Doubleday.

[11] Sjoberg, G. (1960). *The preindustrial city* (p. 325). New York: Free Press.

Grave goods frequently indicate the status of deceased individuals in stratified societies. For example, China's first emperor was buried with 7,000 life-size terra cotta figures of warriors.

© Tavid Rankin Bingham

diseases can be determined from skeletal remains. In stratified societies of the past, the dominant groups usually lived longer, ate better, and enjoyed an easier life than lower-ranking members of society, just as they do today.

The Making of States

From Africa to China to the South American Andes, ancient civilizations are almost always associated with magnificent palaces built high aboveground—with sculptures beautifully rendered using techniques that continue into the present and with vast, awe-inspiring engineering projects. These impressive accomplishments could indicate that civilization is better than other cultural forms, particularly when these societies came to dominate peoples with other social systems. But domination is more a reflection of aggression, size, and power than it is cultural superiority. In other words, the emergence of centralized governments, characteristic of civilizations, has allowed some cultures to dominate others and for civilizations to flourish. Anthropologists have proposed several theories to account for the transition from small, egalitarian farming villages to large urban centers in which population density, social inequality, and diversity of labor required a centralized government.

Ecological Theories

Ecological approaches emphasize the role of the environment in the development of states. Among these, the irrigation or **hydraulic theory** holds that civilizations developed

when Neolithic peoples realized that the best farming occurred in the fertile soils of river valleys, provided that they could control the periodic flooding.[12] The centralized effort to control the irrigation process blossomed into the first governing body, elite social class, and civilization.

Another theory suggests that in regions of ecological diversity, trade is necessary to procure scarce resources. In Mexico, for example, trade networks distributed chilies grown in the highlands, cotton and beans from intermediate elevations, and salt from the coasts to people throughout the region. Some form of centralized authority developed to organize trade for the procurement of these commodities and to redistribute them.

A third theory developed by anthropologist Robert Carneiro suggests that states develop where populations are hemmed in by such environmental barriers as mountains, deserts, seas, or other human populations as an outcome of warfare and conflict in these circumscribed regions.[13] As these populations grow, they have no space

---

[12] Wittfogel, K. A. (1957). *Oriental despotism, a comparative study of total power.* New Haven, CT: Yale University Press.

[13] Carneiro, R. L. (1970). A theory of the origin of the state. *Science 169,* 733–738.

hydraulic theory The theory that explains civilization's emergence as the result of the construction of elaborate irrigation systems, the functioning of which required full-time managers whose control blossomed into the first governing body and elite social class.

Tell It to the Marines: Teaching Troops about Cultural Heritage

by Jane C. Waldbaum

The need to protect ancient sites, museums, and antiquities in war-torn Iraq and Afghanistan has led the Archaeological Institute of America (AIA) to begin an innovative program to help educate troops soon to be sent to those countries. Conceived by AIA vice president C. Brian Rose, the program sends experienced lecturers to military bases to teach the basics of Middle Eastern archaeology and the importance of protecting the evidence of past cultures. The class, taken by both officers and enlisted men and women, is mandatory.

The effort is a supplement to the AIA's longstanding, nationwide lecture program in which scholars in archaeology and related fields present the latest research and developments to more than 102 local societies in the United States and Canada. The lectures for the troops focus specifically on the areas where military personnel will be deployed and on the specific sites, monuments,

museums, and artifacts that they might be called upon to protect.

The current lectures, funded in part by the Packard Humanities Institute, emphasize Mesopotamia's role in the development of writing, schools, libraries, law codes, calendars, and astronomy, as well as connections with familiar biblical figures such as Abraham and Daniel and ancient sites such as Ur and Babylon. Afghanistan's position as a crossroads of ancient civilizations and the route of Alexander the Great through the region is discussed. Troops also learn about basic archaeological techniques, the importance of preserving context, the necessity of working with archaeologists and conservators, and the most effective ways to protect sites against looters.

The first series of lectures was given at the Marine Corps base at Camp Lejeune, North Carolina, and there are plans to expand the program to other bases and services in the near future. "Many

of the officers have M.A. degrees; some are reservists and high-school history teachers," says Rose, who delivered the inaugural lectures last spring. "They care a great deal about the history of the areas in which they serve; some of them have actually lived in or near Babylon on earlier tours of duty. All of us have been struck by their thirst for knowledge during and after our lectures."

Many have helped get this program up and running, including U.S. Marine Colonel Matthew Bogdanos, who was instrumental in securing the return of many antiquities stolen from the Iraq Museum. "When it comes to clearing a building, neutralizing a land mine, or making a neighborhood safe for children, we know what to do," says Bogdanos. "When it comes to protecting a country's cultural heritage, we are just as eager to do the right thing—we just don't always know the best way to do it. This is where Brian Rose's groundbreaking program will pay dividends for generations."

in which to expand, and so they begin to compete for increasingly scarce resources. Internally, this may result in the development of social stratification, in which an elite controls important resources to which lower classes have limited access. Externally, this leads to warfare and even conquest, which, to be successful, require elaborate organization under a centralized authority. As this chapter's Anthropology Applied feature shows, in times of war centralized authorities such as the U.S. military are drawing upon archaeological expertise to protect cultural resources.

Problems exist with each of these ecological theories. Across the globe and through time, cultures can be found that do not fit these models. For example, some of the earliest large-scale irrigation systems developed in highland New Guinea, where strong centralized governments never emerged. North American Indians possessed trade networks that extended from Labrador in northeastern Canada to the Gulf of Mexico and the Yellowstone region of the Rocky Mountains and even to the Pacific—all without centralized control.[14] And in many of the cultures that

do not fit the theories of ecological determinism, neighboring cultures learned to coexist rather than pursuing warfare to the point of complete conquest.

Although few anthropologists would deny the importance of the human–environment relationship, many are dissatisfied with approaches that do not take into account human beliefs and values.[15] For example, as described in the case study of Tikal—while religion was tied to the earth in that the priests determined the most favorable time for planting crops—the beliefs and power relations that developed within Maya culture were not environmentally determined. Human societies past and present bring their beliefs and values into their interactions with the environment.

Action Theory

One criticism of the above theories is that they fail to recognize the capacity of aggressive, charismatic leaders to shape the course of human history. Accordingly, anthropologists Joyce Marcus and Kent Flannery have

[14] Haviland, W. A., & Power, M. W. (1994). *The original Vermonters* (2nd ed., chs. 3 & 4). Hanover, NH: University Press of New England.

[15] Adams, R. M. (2001). Scale and complexity in archaic states. *Latin American Antiquity 11*, 188.

The relative dearth of ancient monumental structures in North America has led some to assume the superiority of European civilization, rather than to acknowledge the successful nomadic cultural pattern of many North American Indian groups. Cities were present in precontact North America. Take for example Cahokia, located in Southern Illinois, a city with an estimated population of 40,000 people dating from 650 to 1400 CE. Cahokia's pyramid-shaped ceremonial mounds spanned an area larger than the great pyramids of Egypt. Until 1800, when Philadelphia surpassed it, Cahokia was the largest city in the land that is now the United States.

developed what they call **action theory.**[16] This theory acknowledges the relationship of society to the environment in shaping social and cultural behavior, but it also recognizes that forceful leaders strive to advance their positions through self-serving actions. In so doing, they may create change.

In the case of Maya history, for example, local leaders, who once relied on personal charisma for the economic and political support needed to sustain them in their positions, may have seized upon religion to solidify their power. Through religion they developed an ideology that endowed them and their descendants with supernatural ancestry and gave them privileged access to the gods, on which their followers depended. In this case, certain individuals could monopolize power and emerge as divine kings, using their power to subjugate any rivals.

As the above example makes clear, the context in which a forceful leader operates is critical. In the case of the Maya, the combination of existing cultural and ecological factors opened the way to the emergence of political dynasties. Thus explanations of civilization's emergence are likely to involve multiple causes, rather than just one. Furthermore, we may also have the cultural equivalent of what biologists call *convergence,* where similar societies come about in different ways. Consequently, a theory that accounts for the rise of civilization in one place may not account for its rise in another.

Civilization and Its Discontents

Living in the context of civilization ourselves, we are inclined to view its development as a great step up on a so-called ladder of progress. Whatever benefits civilization has brought, the cultural changes it represents have produced new problems. Among them is the problem of waste disposal. In fact, waste disposal probably began to be a problem in settled, farming communities even before civilizations emerged. But as villages grew into towns and towns grew into cities, the problem became far more serious, as crowded conditions and the buildup of garbage and sewage created optimal environments for infectious diseases such as bubonic plague, typhoid, and cholera. Early cities therefore tended to be disease-ridden places, with relatively high death rates.

Genetically based adaptation to diseases may also have influenced the course of civilization. In northern Europeans, for example, the mutation of a gene on chromosome 7

[16] Marcus, J., & Flannery, K. V. (1996). *Zapotec civilization: How urban society evolved in Mexico's Oaxaca Valley.* New York: Thames & Hudson.

action theory The theory that self-serving actions by forceful leaders play a role in civilization's emergence.

East of Naples, Italy, dumping of toxic waste and the sheer volume of normal garbage have become serious environmental threats. Organized crime syndicates provide illegal, less expensive ways to dispose of toxic waste, which has led to a contamination of the environment and the foods produced there. Dioxin, asbestos, and other toxins may have made their way into the food supply, including into water buffalo milk that is used to make the gourmet food buffalo mozzarella. In 2008, when the crime syndicate–run landfill reached capacity, garbage collectors went on strike leaving uncollected trash to pile up in the city.

© AFP/Getty Images

makes carriers resistant to cholera, typhoid, and other bacterial diarrheas.[17] Because of the mortality caused by these diseases, selection favored spread of this allele among the population. But, as with sickle-cell anemia, protection comes at a price. That price is cystic fibrosis—a usually fatal disease present in people who are homozygous for the altered gene.

The rise of towns and cities brought with it other acute, infectious diseases. In a small population, diseases such as chicken pox, influenza, measles, mumps, pertussis, polio, rubella, and smallpox will kill or immunize so high a proportion of the population that the virus cannot continue to propagate. Measles, for example, is likely to die out in any human population with fewer than half a million people.[18] Hence, such diseases, when introduced into small communities, spread immediately to the whole population and then die out. For these diseases to continue, they require a large population, such as is found in cities. Survivors possessed immunity to these deadly diseases.

The disease tuberculosis (TB) would not have become widespread without the development of cities. The bacteria that cause TB cannot survive in the presence of sunlight and fresh air. Before humans lived in dark, crowded urban centers, if an infected individual coughed and released the TB bacteria into the air, sunlight would prevent the spread of infection. Therefore, TB, like many other sicknesses, can be called a disease of civilization.

Social Stratification and Disease

Civilization affects disease in another powerful way. Social stratification is as much a determinant of disease as any bacterium, past and present. For example, Ashkenazi Jews of eastern Europe were forced into urban ghettos over several centuries, becoming especially vulnerable to the TB thriving in crowded, dark, confined neighborhoods. As we have seen with the genetic response to malaria (sickle cell and other abnormal hemoglobins) and bacterial diarrheas (the cystic fibrosis gene), TB triggered a genetic response in the form of the Tay-Sachs allele. Individuals heterozygous for the Tay-Sachs allele were protected from this disease.[19]

Unfortunately, homozygotes for the Tay-Sachs allele develop a lethal, degenerative condition that remains common in Ashkenazi Jews. Without the selective pressure of TB, the frequency of the Tay-Sachs allele would never have increased. Similarly, without the strict social

---

[17] Ridley, M. (1999). *Genome, the autobiography of a species in 23 chapters* (p. 142). New York: HarperCollins.

[18] Diamond, J. (1997). *Guns, germs, and steel* (p. 203). New York: Norton.

[19] Ridley, p. 191.

rules confining poor Jews to the ghettos (compounded by social and religious rules about marriage), the frequency of the Tay-Sachs allele would never have increased. In recent times, cultural mechanisms such as prenatal and premarital genetic testing have resulted in a decrease in the frequency of the Tay-Sachs allele.

Before the discovery of antibiotics in the early 20th century, individuals infected with the bacteria causing TB would invariably waste away and die. While antibiotics have reduced deaths from TB, resistant forms of the bacteria require an expensive regime of multiple drugs. Not only are poor individuals more likely to become infected with TB, they are also less likely to be able to afford expensive medicines required to treat this disease. For people in poor countries and for disadvantaged people in wealthier countries, TB—like AIDS—can be an incurable, fatal, infectious disease. As Holger Sawert from the World Health Organization has said, "Both TB and HIV thrive on poverty."[20] Before the social stratification accompanying the emergence of cities and states, as far as infectious microbes were concerned, all humans were the same.

Colonialism and Disease

Infectious disease played a major role in European colonization of the Americas. When Europeans with immunity to so-called Old World diseases came to the Americas for the first time, they brought these devastating diseases with them. Millions of Native Americans—who had never been exposed to influenza, smallpox, typhus, and measles—died as a result. The microbes causing these diseases and the human populations upon which they depend developed in tandem over thousands of years of urban life in Eurasia, and before that in village life with a variety of domesticated animal species. Thus anyone who survived acquired immunity in the process. See this chapter's Biocultural Connection for more on the death and disease Europeans brought with them when they colonized the Americas.

Very few diseases traveled back to Europe from the Americas. Instead, these colonizers brought back riches that they had pillaged and papers that gave them ownership of lands they had claimed. One rare exception is that Charles Darwin seems to have returned from his famous journey on the *H.M.S. Beagle* with Chagas disease, a parasitic infection caused by a bug bite.[21] Traditionally it was a disease of the rural poor, but today the large influx of poor farmers into urban centers in Mexico, Central America, and South America means that Chagas disease has become a problem in urban areas as well.

Anthropology and Cities of the Future

Not until relatively recent times did public health measures reduce the risk of living in cities, and had it not been for a constant influx of rural peoples, areas of high population density might not have persisted. Europe's urban population, for example, did not become self-sustaining until early in the 20th century.[22]

What led people to live in such unhealthy places? Most likely, people were attracted by the same things that lure people to cities today: They are vibrant, exciting places that provide people with new opportunities and protection in times of warfare. Of course, people's experience in the cities did not always live up to advance expectations, particularly for the poor.

In addition to health problems, many early cities faced social problems strikingly similar to those found in cities all over the world today. Dense population, inequalities of class systems, and oppressive centralized governments created internal stress. The poor saw that the wealthy had all the things that they themselves lacked. It was not just a question of luxury items; the poor did not have enough food or space in which to live with comfort, dignity, and health.

Evidence of warfare in early civilizations is common. Cities were fortified. Ancient documents list battles, raids, and wars between groups. Cylinder seals, paintings, and sculptures depict battle scenes, victorious kings, and captured prisoners of war. Increasing population and the accompanying scarcity of fertile farming land often led to boundary disputes and quarrels over land between civilized states or between so-called tribal peoples and a state. When war broke out, people crowded into walled cities for protection and for access to irrigation systems.

What we would call development today—the transformation of rural open spaces into densely populated and built-up environments—posed similar problems in the past. At the Maya city of Copan, in the present-day country of Honduras, much of the fertile bottom lands along the Copan River were paved over as the city grew, making the people more and more dependent on food grown in the fragile soils of the valley slopes. This ultimately led to catastrophic soil loss through erosion and a breakdown of food production. Similarly, in ancient Mesopotamia, evaporation of water from extensive irrigation works resulted in a buildup of salt in the soil, ruining it for agricultural use.

[20] Sawert, H. (2002). *TB and poverty in the context of global TB control.* World Health Organization. http://www.healthinitiative.org/html/Conf/satsymp/index.htm#2

[21] Adler, S. (1959). Darwin's illness. *Nature,* 1102–1103; Bernstein, R. E., et al. (1984). Darwin's illness: Chagas' disease resurgens. *Journal of the Royal Society of Medicine 77,* 608–609.

[22] Diamond, p. 203.

Perilous Pigs: The Introduction of Swine-Borne Disease to the Americas   *by Charles C. Mann*

On May 30, 1539, Hernando de Soto landed his private army near Tampa Bay, in Florida. . . . Half warrior, half venture capitalist, Soto had grown very rich very young by becoming a market leader in the nascent trade for Indian slaves. The profits had helped to fund Pizarro's seizure of the Incan empire, which had made Soto wealthier still. Looking quite literally for new worlds to conquer, he persuaded the Spanish Crown to let him loose in North America. . . . He came to Florida with 200 horses, 600 soldiers, and 300 pigs.

From today's perspective, it is difficult to imagine the ethical system that would justify Soto's actions. For four years his force, looking for gold, wandered through what is now Florida, Georgia, North and South Carolina, Tennessee, Alabama, Mississippi, Arkansas, and Texas, wrecking almost everything it touched. The inhabitants often fought back vigorously, but they had never before encountered an army with horses and guns. . . . Soto's men managed to rape, torture, enslave, and kill countless Indians. But the worst thing the Spaniards did, some researchers say, was entirely without malice—bring the pigs.

According to Charles Hudson, an anthropologist at the University of Georgia, . . . Soto crossed the Mississippi a few miles downstream from the present site of Memphis. . . . [T]he Spaniards were watched by several thousand Indian warriors. Utterly without fear, Soto brushed past the Indian force into what is now eastern Arkansas, through thickly settled land—"very well peopled with large towns," one of his men later recalled. . . . Eventually the Spaniards approached a cluster of small cities, each protected by earthen walls, sizeable moats, and deadeye archers. In his usual fashion, Soto brazenly marched in, stole food, and marched out.

After Soto left, no Europeans visited this part of the Mississippi Valley for more than a century. Early in 1682 whites appeared again, this time Frenchmen in canoes. . . . area[s] where Soto had found cities cheek by jowl . . . [were] deserted [without an] Indian village for 200 miles. About fifty settlements existed in this strip of the Mississippi when Soto showed up, according to Anne Ramenofsky, an anthropologist at the University of New

Mexico. . . . Soto "had a privileged glimpse" of an Indian world, Hudson says. "The window opened and slammed shut. When the French came in and the record opened up again, it was a transformed reality. A civilization crumbled. The question is, how did this happen?"

The question is even more complex than it may seem. Disaster of this magnitude suggests epidemic disease. In the view of Ramenofsky and Patricia Galloway, an anthropologist at the University of Texas, the source of the contagion was very likely not Soto's army but its ambulatory meat locker: his 300 pigs. Soto's force itself was too small to be an effective biological weapon. Sicknesses like measles and smallpox would have burned through his 600 soldiers long before they reached the Mississippi. But the same would not have held true for the pigs, which multiplied rapidly and were able to transmit their diseases to wildlife in the surrounding forest. When human beings and domesticated animals live close together, they trade microbes with abandon. Over time mutation spawns new diseases: Avian influenza becomes human influenza, bovine rinderpest becomes measles. Unlike Europeans, Indians did not live in close quarters with animals—they domesticated only the dog, the llama, the alpaca, the guinea pig, and, here and there, the turkey and the Muscovy duck. . . . [W]hat scientists call zoonotic disease was little known in the Americas. Swine alone can disseminate anthrax, brucellosis, leptospirosis, taeniasis, trichinosis, and tuberculosis. Pigs breed exuberantly and can transmit diseases to deer and turkeys. Only a few of Soto's pigs would have had to wander off to infect the forest.

Indeed, the calamity wrought by Soto apparently extended across the whole Southeast. The Coosa city-states, in western Georgia, and the Caddoan-speaking civilization, centered on the Texas-Arkansas border, disintegrated soon after Soto appeared. The Caddo had had a taste for monumental architecture: public plazas, ceremonial platforms, mausoleums. After Soto's army left, notes Timothy K. Perttula, an archaeological consultant in Austin, Texas, the Caddo stopped building community centers and began digging community cemeteries. . . . [After] Soto's . . . visit, Perttula believes, the Caddoan population fell from about

200,000 to about 8,500—a drop of nearly 96 percent. . . . "That's one reason whites think of Indians as nomadic hunters," says Russell Thornton, an anthropologist at the University of California at Los Angeles. "Everything else—all the heavily populated urbanized societies—was wiped out."

How could a few pigs truly wreak this much destruction? . . . One reason is that Indians were fresh territory for many plagues, not just one. Smallpox, typhoid, bubonic plague, influenza, mumps, measles, whooping cough—all rained down on the Americas in the century after Columbus. (Cholera, malaria, and scarlet fever came later.) Having little experience with epidemic diseases, Indians had no knowledge of how to combat them. In contrast, Europeans were well versed in the brutal logic of quarantine. They boarded up houses in which plague appeared and fled to the countryside. In Indian New England, Neal Salisbury, a historian at Smith College, wrote . . . [that] family and friends gathered with the shaman at the sufferer's bedside to wait out the illness—a practice that "could only have served to spread the disease more rapidly."

To Elizabeth Fenn, the smallpox historian, the squabble over numbers obscures a central fact. Whether one million or 10 million or 100 million died, . . . the pall of sorrow that engulfed the hemisphere was immeasurable. Languages, prayers, hopes, habits, and dreams—entire ways of life hissed away like steam. . . . In the long run, Fenn says, the consequential finding is not that many people died but that many people once lived. The Americas were filled with a stunningly diverse assortment of peoples who had knocked about the continents for millennia. "You have to wonder," Fenn says. "What were all those people *up* to in all that time?"

BIOCULTURAL QUESTION

Does the history of the decimation of American Indians through infectious disease have any parallels in the contemporary globalized world? Do infectious diseases impact all peoples equally?

Adapted from Mann, C. C. (2005). 1491: New revelations of the Americas before Columbus. New York: Knopf.

It is discouraging to note that many of the problems associated with the first civilizations are still with us. Waste disposal, pollution-related health problems, crowding, social inequities, and warfare continue to be serious problems. Through the study of past civilizations and through comparison of contemporary societies, we now stand a chance of understanding such problems. Such understanding represents a central part of the anthropologist's mission and can contribute to the ability of our species to transcend human-made problems.

Questions for Reflection

1. In large-scale societies of the past and present, people face the challenge of social stratification. Elite classes have disproportionate access to and control of all resources. Is social stratification an inevitable consequence of the emergence of cities and states? How can the study of social stratification in the past contribute to the resolution of contemporary issues of social justice?

2. In previous chapters it was emphasized that human evolutionary history should not be thought of as progress. Why is it similarly incorrect to think of the shift from village to city to state as progress?

3. What are some of the ways that differences in social stratification are expressed in your community? Does your community have any traditions surrounding death that serve to restate the social differentiation of individuals?

4. With today's global communication and economic networks, will it be possible to shift away from social systems involving centralized governments, or will a centralized authority have to control and protect resources for the entire world?

5. With many archaeological discoveries there is a value placed on "firsts," such as the earliest writing, the first city, or the earliest government. Given the history of the independent emergence of cities and states throughout the world, do you think that scientists should place more value on some of these events just because they are older?

Suggested Readings

Diamond, J. (1997). *Guns, germs, and steel*. New York: Norton.

Also recommended in Chapter 10, this book has an excellent discussion of the relation among diseases, social complexity, and social change.

Fagan, B. (2001). *The seventy great mysteries of the ancient world*. New York: Thames & Hudson.

Archaeologist Brian Fagan edited contributions from twenty-eight other archaeologists and historians about some of the great controversies in the field in this readable book.

Mann, C. C. (2005). *1491: New revelations of the Americas before Columbus*. New York: Knopf.

Also recommended in Chapter 10, this book demonstrates the devastation European colonizers brought to the Americas.

Marcus, J., & Flannery, K. V. (1996). *Zapotec civilization: How urban society evolved in Mexico's Oaxaca Valley*. New York: Thames & Hudson.

With its lavish illustrations, this looks like a coffee table book, but it is a thoughtful and serious work on the rise of a pristine civilization and a presentation of the authors' action theory.

McNeill W. (1992). *Plagues and people*. New York: Anchor.

This book offers an interpretation of world history through the impact of infectious disease. It documents the role disease played in the colonization of the Americas as well as continuing the investigation into the present with a social history of AIDS.

Sabloff, J. A. (1997). *The cities of ancient Mexico* (rev. ed.). New York: Thames & Hudson.

This well-written and lavishly illustrated book describes the major cities of the Olmecs, Zapotecs, Maya, Teotihuacans, Toltecs, and Aztecs. Following the descriptions, Sabloff discusses the question of origins, the problems of archaeological reconstruction, and the basis on which he provides vignettes of life in the ancient cities. The book concludes with a gazetteer of fifty sites in Mesoamerica.

Challenge Issue The people of the United States of America took a significant step toward redressing a history of slavery and racism with the election of Barack Hussein Obama as their forty-fourth president in 2008. This moment of extraordinary social and political significance challenges us to look at race and racism both in the past and in the present. It challenges us to recognize our common origins and to avoid oversimplification, discrimination, bigotry, and even bloodshed fueled by superficial differences. It requires us to recognize that racism feeds on folk beliefs that so-called racial groups are natural and separate divisions within our species based on visible physical differences. Biological evidence demonstrates that separate races do not exist. Broadly defined, geographic "racial" groupings differ from one another in only 7 percent of their genes. Having exchanged genes throughout evolutionary history, human populations continue to do so today. Instead of leading to the development of distinctive subspecies (biologically defined races), this genetic exchange has maintained all of humankind as a single species. Although race functions as a social and political category that promotes inequality in some societies, it is a cultural construct without an objective scientific basis.

CHAPTER 12

Modern Human Diversity: Race and Racism

Chapter Preview

What Is the History of Human Classification?

European scholars of the 18th through early 20th centuries classified humans into a series of subspecies based on geographic location and phenotypic features such as skin color, body size, head shape, and hair texture. Some scholars went a step farther and placed these types into a hierarchical framework in which the "white" race was considered to be superior to other races. With time, these efforts to classify humans into higher and lower forms were discredited for being racist and unscientific.

Is the Biological Concept of Race Useful for Studying Physical Variation in the Human Species?

No. Biologically defined, "race" refers to subspecies, and no subspecies exist within modern *Homo sapiens*. The vast majority of biological variation within our species occurs *within* populations rather than among them. Furthermore, the differences that do exist among populations occur in gradations from one neighboring population to another without sharp breaks. For these and other reasons, anthropologists have actively worked to expose the fallacy of race as a biological concept while at the same time acknowledging the existence of race as a cultural construct.

Is Studying Differences in Intelligence among Populations Valid?

These studies are flawed in many ways. First, studies attempting to document biological differences generally involve comparisons among races—a category that for humans is biologically false. Second, intelligence is a multifaceted phenomenon, and cultures vary in terms of which aspects of intelligence they value. Third, most instruments (tests) used to measure intelligence are biased toward the dominant culture of the people who created the test. Finally, as a complex set of traits, intelligence cannot be linked to discrete evolutionary forces acting in a particular environment.

What Are the Causes of Physical Variability?

Physical variability is a product of underlying genetic variation as it is expressed in a particular environment. Some physical traits are controlled by single genes, with variation present in alternate forms of the gene (alleles). Many physical characteristics like height, weight, or skin color are controlled by multiple genes and are thus expressed continuously, meaning this variation cannot be divided into discrete categories. Because evolutionary forces such as natural selection and random drift act on each physical trait independently, human biological variation can be studied only "one trait at a time."

From male to female, short to tall, light to dark, biological variation can be categorized in a number of ways, but in the end we are all members of the same species. Minute variations of our DNA give each of us a unique genetic fingerprint, yet this variation remains within the bounds of being genetically human. Visible differences are expressed within the framework of biological features shared throughout the species, and as a species, humans vary.

Human genetic variation generally is distributed across the globe in a continuous fashion. From a biological perspective, this variation sometimes follows a pattern imposed by interaction with the environment through the evolutionary process of natural selection. At other times, the variation results from random genetic drift. The significance we give our biological variation, however, is always patterned because the way we perceive variation—in fact, whether we perceive it at all—is determined by culture.

For example, in many Polynesian cultures, where skin color is not a determinant of social status, people pay little attention to this physical characteristic. By contrast, in countries such as the United States, Brazil, and South Africa, where skin color is a significant social and political category, it is one of the first things people notice. Furthermore, our brains appear to be hardwired for categorical thinking that, once learned, predisposes us to use these kinds of distinctions. We use different parts of our brain to think about people we consider to be like ourselves compared to the parts of the brain used when we are thinking about others. Biological diversity, therefore, cannot be studied without an awareness of the cultural dimensions that shape the questions asked about diversity as well as the history of how this knowledge has been used.

When European scholars first began their systematic study of worldwide human variation in the 18th century, they were concerned with documenting differences among human groups. Soon afterward, some began to divide these groups hierarchically into progressively "better types" of humans. Today, this hierarchical approach has been appropriately abandoned. Before exploring how contemporary biological variation is studied, we will examine the effects of social ideas about race and racial hierarchy on the interpretation of biological variation, past and present.

The History of Human Classification

Early European scholars tried to systematically classify *Homo sapiens* into subspecies, or races, based on geographic location and phenotypic features such as skin color, body size, head shape, and hair texture. The 18th-century Swedish naturalist Carolus Linnaeus originally divided humans into subspecies based on geographic location and classified all Europeans as "white," Africans as "black," American Indians as "red," and Asians as "yellow."

The German physician Johann Blumenbach (1752–1840) introduced some significant changes to this four-race scheme with the 1795 edition of his book *On the Natural Variety of Mankind*. Most notably, this book formally extended the notion of a hierarchy of human types. Based on a comparative examination of his human skull collection, Blumenbach judged as most beautiful the skull of a woman from the Caucasus Mountain range (located between the Black Sea and the Caspian Sea of southeastern Europe and southwestern Asia). The skull was more symmetrical than the others, and he saw it as a reflection of nature's ideal form: the circle. Surely, Blumenbach reasoned, this "perfect" specimen resembled God's original creation. Moreover, he thought that the living inhabitants of the Caucasus region were the most beautiful in the world. Based on these criteria, he concluded that this high mountain range, not far from the lands mentioned in the Bible, was the place of human origins.

Blumenbach concluded that all light-skinned peoples in Europe and adjacent parts of western Asia and northern Africa belonged to the same race. On this basis, he dropped the "European" race label and replaced it with "Caucasian." Although he continued to distinguish American Indians as a separate race, he regrouped dark-skinned Africans as "Ethiopian" and split those Asians not considered Caucasian into two separate races: "Mongolian" (referring to most inhabitants of Asia, including China and Japan) and "Malay" (indigenous Australians, Pacific Islanders, and others).

Convinced that Caucasians were closest to the original ideal humans supposedly created in God's image, Blumenbach ranked them as superior. The other races, he argued, were the result of "degeneration"; by moving away from their place of origin and adapting to different environments and climates, they had degenerated physically and morally into what many Europeans came to think of as inferior races.[1]

We now clearly recognize the factual errors and ethnocentric prejudices embedded in Blumenbach's work, as well as others, with respect to the concept of race. Especially disastrous is the notion of superior and inferior races, as this has been used to justify brutalities ranging from repression to slavery to mass murder to genocide.

---

[1] Gould, S. J. (1994). The geometer of race. *Discover 15* (11), 65–69.

Johann Blumenbach ordered humans into a hierarchical series with Caucasians (his own group) ranked the highest and created in God's image. He suggested that the variation seen in other races was a result of "degeneration" or movement away from this ideal type. (The five types he identified from left to right are: Mongolian, American Indian, Caucasian, Malay, and Ethiopian.) This view is both racist and an oversimplification of the way that human variation is expressed in the skeleton. While people from one part of the world might be more likely to possess a particular nuance of skull shape, within every population there is significant variation. Humans do not exist as discrete types.

It has also been employed to rationalize cruel mockery, as painfully illustrated in the tragic story of Ota Benga, an African Pygmy man who in the early 1900s was caged in a New York zoo with an orangutan.

Captured in a raid in Congo, Ota Benga came into the possession of a North American businessman, Samuel Verner, looking for exotic "savages" for exhibition in the United States. In 1904, Ota and a group of fellow Pygmies were shipped across the Atlantic and exhibited at the World's Fair in Saint Louis, Missouri. About 23 years old at the time, Ota was 4 feet 11 inches (150 centimeters) in height and weighed 103 pounds (47 kilograms). Throngs of visitors came to see displays of dozens of indigenous peoples from around the globe, shown in their traditional dress and living in replica villages doing their customary activities. The fair was a success for the organizers, and all the Pygmies survived to be shipped back to their homeland. Verner also returned to Congo and with Ota's help collected artifacts to be sold to the American Museum of Natural History in New York City.

In the summer of 1906, Ota came back to the United States with Verner, who soon went bankrupt and lost his entire collection. Left stranded in the big city, Ota was placed in the care of the museum and then taken to the Bronx Zoo and exhibited in the monkey house, with an orangutan as company. Ota's sharpened teeth (a cultural practice among his own people) were seen as evidence of

The placement of Ota Benga on display in the Bronx Zoo illustrates the depths of the racism in the early 20th century. Here's Ota Benga posing for the camera when he was part of the "African Exhibit" at the St. Louis World's Fair.

his supposedly cannibal nature. After intensive protest, zoo officials released Ota from his cage and during the day let him roam free in the park, where he was often harassed by teasing visitors. Ota (usually referred to as a "boy") was then turned over to an orphanage for African American children. In 1916, upon hearing that he would never return to his homeland, he took a revolver and shot himself through the heart.[2]

The racist display at the Bronx Zoo a century ago was by no means unique. Just the tip of the ethnocentric iceberg, it was the manifestation of a powerful ideology in which one small part of humanity sought to demonstrate and justify its claims of biological and cultural superiority. This had particular resonance in North America, where people of European descent colonized lands originally inhabited by Native Americans and then went on to exploit African slaves and Asians imported as a source of cheap labor. Indeed, such claims, based on false notions of race, have resulted in the oppression and genocide of millions of humans because of the color of their skin or the shape of their skull.

Fortunately, by the early 20th century, some scholars began to challenge the concept of racial hierarchies. Among the strongest critics was Franz Boas (1858–1942),

---

[2] Bradford, P. V., & Blume, H. (1992). *Ota Benga: The Pygmy in the zoo.* New York: St. Martin's.

a Jewish scientist who immigrated to the United States because of rising anti-Semitism in his German homeland and who became a founder of North America's four-field anthropology. As president of the American Association for the Advancement of Science, Boas criticized false claims of racial superiority in an important speech titled "Race and Progress," published in the prestigious journal *Science* in 1909. Boas's scholarship in both cultural and biological anthropology contributed to the depth of his critique.

Ashley Montagu (1905–1999), a student of Boas and one of the best-known anthropologists of his time, devoted much of his career to combating scientific racism. Born Israel Ehrenberg to a working-class Jewish family in England, he also felt the sting of anti-Semitism. After changing his name in the 1920s, he immigrated to the United States, where he went on to fight racism in his writing and in academic and public lectures. Of all his works, none is more important than his book *Man's Most Dangerous Myth: The Fallacy of Race.* Published in 1942, it debunked the concept of clearly bounded races as a "social myth." The book has since gone through many editions, the last in 2008. Montagu's once controversial ideas have now become mainstream, and his text remains one of the most comprehensive treatments of its subject. (For a contemporary approach to human biological variation, see this chapter's Anthropologist of Note.)

Generalized references to human types such as "Asiatic" or "Mongoloid," "European" or "Caucasoid," and "African"

Anthropologist of Note

Fatimah Jackson

While at first glance Fatimah Jackson's research areas seem quite diverse, they are unified by consistent representation of African American perspectives in biological anthropological research.

With a keen awareness of how culture determines the content of scientific questions, Jackson chooses hers carefully. One of her earliest areas of research concerned the use of common African plants as foods and medicines. She has examined the co-evolution of plants and humans and the ways plant compounds serve to attract and repel humans at various stages of ripeness. Through laboratory and field research, she has documented that cassava, a New World root crop providing the major source of dietary energy for over 500 million people, also guards against malaria. This crop has become a major food throughout Africa in areas where malaria is common.

© Courtesy of Robert T. Jackson

Jackson, who received her PhD from Cornell in 1981, is also the genetics group leader for the African Burial Ground Project (mentioned in Chapter 1). In a small area uncovered during a New York City construction project, scientists found the remains of thousands of Africans and people of African descent. Jackson

is recovering DNA from skeletal remains and attempting to match the dead with specific regions of Africa through the analysis of genetic markers in living African people.

Jackson, one of the early advocates for appropriate ethical treatment of minorities in the human genome project, is concerned with ensuring that the genetic work for the African Burial Ground Project is conducted with sensitivity to African people. She is therefore working to establish genetic laboratories and repositories in Africa. For Jackson, these laboratories are symbolic of the fact of human commonality and that all humans today have roots in Africa. As Director of the Institute of African American Research at the University of North Carolina, Chapel Hill, Jackson continues with her own research while connecting and advancing scholars from diverse academic disciplines.

or "Negroid" were at best mere statistical abstractions about populations in which certain physical features appeared in higher frequencies than in other populations; no example of "pure" racial types could be found. These categories turned out to be neither definitive nor particularly helpful. The visible traits were generally found to occur not in abrupt shifts from population to population but in a continuum that changed gradually, with few sharp breaks. To compound the problem, one trait might change gradually over a north-south gradient, whereas another might show a similar change from east to west. Human skin color, for instance, becomes progressively darker as one moves from northern Europe to Central Africa, whereas blood type B becomes progressively more common as one moves from western to eastern Europe.

Finally, there are many variations within each group, and those within groups are often greater than those between groups. In Africa, the light-brown skin color of someone from the Kalahari Desert might more closely resemble that of a person from Southeast Asia than the darkly pigmented person from southern Sudan who is supposed to be of the same race.

Race as a Biological Concept

To understand why the "racial" approach to human variation has been so unproductive and even damaging, we must first understand the race concept in strictly biological terms. In biology, a **race** is defined as a subspecies, or a population of a species differing geographically, morphologically, or genetically from other populations of the same species.

As straightforward as such a definition may seem, it has three very serious flaws. First, it is arbitrary; there is no agreement on how many differences it takes to make a race. For example, if one researcher emphasizes skin color while another emphasizes blood group differences, they will not classify people in the same way. Ultimately, it is impossible to reach agreement on the number of genes and precisely which ones are the most important for defining races.

The second weakness in the biological definition of race is that no one race has exclusive possession of any particular variant of any gene or genes. In human terms, the frequency of a trait like the type O blood group, for example, may be high in one population and low in another, but it is present in both. In other words, populations are genetically "open," meaning that genes flow between them. Because populations are genetically open, no fixed racial groups can exist. The only reproductive barriers that exist for humans are the cultural rules some societies impose regarding appropriate mates. As President Obama's family illustrates (Kenyan father and Euramerican mother, who, incidentally, was an anthropologist), these social barriers are changing.

Third, the biological definition of race does not apply to humans because the differences among individuals and within a so-called racial population are greater than the differences among populations. Evolutionary biologist Richard Lewontin demonstrated this through genetic analyses in the 1970s. He compared the amount of genetic variation within populations and among so-called racial types, finding a mere 7 percent of human variation existing among groups.[3] Instead, the vast majority of genetic variation exists *within* groups. As the science writer James Shreeve puts it, "most of what separates me genetically from a typical African or Eskimo also separates me from another average American of European ancestry."[4] This follows from the fact of genetic openness of races; no one race has an exclusive claim to any particular form of a gene or trait.

Considering the above, it is small wonder that most anthropologists have abandoned the race concept as being of utility in understanding human biological variation. Instead, they have found it more productive to study *clines*—the distribution and significance of single, specific, genetically based characteristics and continuous traits related to adaptation (see Chapter 2). They examine human variation within small breeding populations, the smallest units in which evolutionary change occurs.

© Laurence Dutton/Getty Images

Fingerprint patterns of loops, whorls, and arches are genetically determined. Grouping people on this basis would place most Europeans, sub-Saharan Africans, and East Asians together as "loops." Australian Aborigines and the people of Mongolia would be together as "whorls." The Bushmen of southern African would be grouped as "arches."

[3] Lewontin, R. C. (1972). The apportionment of human diversity. In T. Dobzhansky, et al. (Eds.), *Evolutionary biology* (pp. 381–398). New York: Plenum.

[4] Shreeve, J. (1994). Terms of estrangement. *Discover 15* (11), 60.

race In biology, a subspecies or a population of a species differing geographically, morphologically, or genetically from other populations of the same species; not applicable to people because the division of humans into discrete types does not represent the true nature of human biological variation. In some societies, race is an important social category.

Yao Ming, center for the Houston Rockets, receives his Special Olympics Global Ambassador jersey from athlete Xu Chuang (left) and Special Olympics East Asia President Dicken Yung. Standing side by side, these three individuals illustrate the wide range of variation seen within a single so-called racial category.

Conflation of the Biological into the Cultural Category of Race

While the biological race concept is not applicable to human variation, nevertheless race exists as a significant cultural category. Human groups frequently insert a false notion of biological difference into the cultural category of race to make it appear more factual and objective. In various ways, cultures define religious, linguistic, and ethnic groups as "races," thereby confusing linguistic and cultural traits with physical traits.

For example, in many Latin American countries, people are commonly classified as Indio (Indian), Mestizo (mixed), or Ladino (of Spanish descent). But despite the biological connotations of these terms, the criteria used for assigning individuals to these categories involve things such as whether they wear shoes, sandals, or go barefoot; speak Spanish or an Indian language; live in a thatched hut or a European-style house; and so forth. Thus an Indio—by speaking Spanish, wearing Western-style clothes, and living in a house in a non-Indio neighborhood—ceases to be an Indio, no matter how many "Indio genes" he or she may possess.

This sort of confusion of nonbiological characteristics with the biological notion of heredity is by no means limited to Latin American societies. To various extents, such confusion is found in most societies of Europe and North America. Take, for example, the fact that the racial categories used by the U.S. Census Bureau change with every census. Large catch-all categories (white, black, American Indian or Alaskan Native, Asian and Pacific Islander or native Hawaiian) include diverse peoples. Asian, for example, includes such different peoples as Chinese and East Indians, whereas native

In colonial Mexico, sixteen different *castas* ("castes") were named, giving specific labels to individuals who were various combinations of Spanish, Indian, and African ancestry. These paintings of *castas* are traditionally arranged from light to dark as a series and reflect an effort to impose hierarchy despite the fluid social system in place. In the United States the hierarchy was more rigid; the "one drop rule," also known as *hypodescent*, would ascribe the "lower" position to individuals if they had even one drop of blood from a grouping within the hierarchy.

Hawaiian and Alaskan are far more restrictive. The Census Bureau also asks people to identify Hispanic ethnicity, a category that includes people who, in their countries of origin, might be classified as Indio, Mestizo, or Ladino. The addition of categories for native Hawaiians, Middle Easterners, and people who consider themselves multiracial does nothing to improve the situation.

To compound the confusion, inclusion in one or another of these categories is usually based on self-identification, which means that these are not biological categories at all. The observation that the purported race of an individual can vary over the course of his or her lifetime speaks to the fact that cultural forces shape the designation of membership in a particular racial category.

Similarly, genetics research in medicine is regularly oversimplified according to the racial types defined in the 18th and 19th centuries. It remains to be seen whether this genetics research will avoid creating false genetic types that do not reflect the true nature of human variation. Recent claims of race-specific drugs and vaccines that are based on limited scientific data indicate that the social category of race may again be interfering with our understanding of the true nature of human genetic diversity.

To make matters worse, the confusion of social with biological factors is frequently combined with prejudices that then serve to exclude whole categories of people from certain roles or positions in society. For example, in colonial North America, a "racial" worldview, rooted in the unequal power relations between the English or Saxon "race" and the Irish or Celtic "race" in Europe, assigned American Indians and Africans imported as slaves to perpetual low status. A supposed biological inferiority

© blickwinkel/Alamy

These skulls, from the genocide war memorial in Rwanda, record some of the horror that took place in this Central African country in 1994. Over the course of only about a hundred days, a militia of the ruling Hutu majority brutally murdered close to 1 million ethnic Tutsis. With clear genocidal intent, systematic organization, and intense speed, Hutu actions, resembling those of the Nazi regime, remind us that genocide is far from a thing of the past. The global effects of the Rwandan genocide have been massive. Millions of Rwandans, both refugees and killers, now live in neighboring regions, disrupting the stability of these states. Through the United Nations and individual governments, the international community has recognized that it failed to act to prevent this genocide and collectively has taken steps toward maintaining peace in the region. The parallels between Rwanda and current conflicts in Congo, Burundi, and Sudan are chilling.

was used to justify this low status, whereas access to privilege, power, and wealth was reserved for favored groups of European descent.[5]

Because of the colonial association of lighter skin with greater power and higher social status, people whose history includes domination by lighter-skinned Europeans have sometimes valued this phenotype. In Haiti, for example, the "color question" has been the dominant force in social and political life. Skin texture, facial features, hair color, and socioeconomic class collectively play a role in the ranking. According to Haitian anthropologist Michel-Rolph Trouillot, "a rich black becomes a mulatto, a poor mulatto becomes black."[6]

The Nazis in Germany elevated a racialized worldview to state policy, with particularly evil consequences. The Nuremberg race laws of 1935 declared the superiority of the Aryan "race" and the inferiority of the Gypsy and Jewish "races." The Nazi doctrine justified, on supposed biological grounds, political repression and extermination. In all, 11 million people (Jews, Gypsies, homosexuals, and other so-called inferior people, as well as political opponents of the Nazi regime) were deliberately put to death.

Tragically, the Nazi Holocaust (from the Greek word for "wholly burnt" or "sacrificed by fire") is not unique in human history. Such genocides, programs of extermination of one group by another, have a long history that predates World War II and continues today. Recent and ongoing genocide in parts of South America, Africa, Europe, and Asia, like previous genocides, are accompanied by a rhetoric of dehumanization and a depiction of the people being exterminated as a lesser type of human.

The Social Significance of Race: Racism

Scientific facts, unfortunately, have been slow to change what people think about race. **Racism,** a doctrine of superiority by which one group justifies the dehumanization of others based on their distinctive physical characteristics, is not just about discriminatory ideas, values, or attitudes but

is also a political problem. Indeed, politicians have often exploited this concept as a means of mobilizing support, demonizing opponents, and eliminating rivals. Racial conflicts result from social stereotypes, not scientific facts.

Race and Behavior

The assumption that behavioral differences exist among so-called human races remains an issue to which many people still cling tenaciously. Throughout history, certain characteristics have been attributed to groups of people under a variety of names—national character, spirit, temperament—all of them vague and standing for a number of concepts unrelated to any biological phenomena. Common myths involve the "coldness" of Scandinavians or the "rudeness" of Americans or the "fierceness" of the Yanomami Indians. Such unjust characterizations rely upon a false notion of biological difference.

To date, no inborn behavioral characteristic can be attributed to any group of people (which the nonscientist might term a "race") that cannot be explained in terms of cultural practices. If the Chinese happen to exhibit exceptional visual-spatial skills, it is probably because reading Chinese characters requires a visual-spatial kind of learning, one that is not as necessary in mastering Western alphabets.[7] Similarly, the relative exclusion of "non-whites" from honors in the sport of golf (until Tiger Woods) had more to do with the social rules of country clubs and the sport's expense.[8] All such differences or characteristics can be explained in terms of culture.

In the same vein, high crime rates, alcoholism, and drug use among certain groups can be explained with reference to culture rather than biology. Individuals alienated and demoralized by poverty, injustice, and unequal opportunity tend to abandon the traditional paths to success of the dominant culture because these paths are blocked. In a racialized society, poverty and all its ill consequences affect some groups of people much more severely than others.

Race and Intelligence

A question frequently asked by those unfamiliar with the fallacy of biological race in humans is whether some "races" are inherently more intelligent than others. First we must ask, what do we mean by the term *intelligence*?

---

[5] American Anthropological Association. (1998). Statement on "race." Available: www.ameranthassn.org.

[6] Trouillot, M. R. (1996). Culture, color, and politics in Haiti. In S. Gregory & R. Sanjek (Eds.), *Race*. New Brunswick, NJ: Rutgers University Press.

racism A doctrine of superiority by which one group justifies the dehumanization of others based on their distinctive physical characteristics.

---

[7] Chan, J.W.C., & Vernon, P. E. (1988). Individual differences among the peoples of China. In J. W. Berry (Ed.), *Human abilities in cultural context* (pp. 340–357). Cambridge, England: Cambridge University Press.

[8] Before Tiger Woods came Charles Sifford (b. 1922), the first African American to win honors in golf. Sifford did so at a time when desegregating the sport meant being subjected to threats and racial abuse. In 2004, the World Golf Hall of Fame inducted him as their first African American member.

In the late 19th and early 20th centuries, "physiognomists" practiced a pseudo-science in which they associated particular facial or skull features with criminal behavior or insanity. Though these ideas may seem humorous and far-fetched to us today, they were only a step away from the racism embedded in the science of the time. Academic texts regularly use the terms "degraded" and "animalized" when describing the skulls and skeletons of non-whites. To challenge contemporary people to think about the boundary between science and pseudo-science, graphic artist W. David Powell has taken a series of these historical images as the subject of his artwork. The images and words he presents are taken directly from two books from that time: *Heads and Faces and How to Study Them: A Manual of Phrenology and Physiognomy for the People* (1885) by Nelson Sizer and H. S. Drayton; and *Vaught's Practical Character Reader* (1902) by Louis Allen Vaught. What signs of racism and stereotyping do you see in these images?

Unfortunately, there is no general agreement as to what abilities or talents actually make up what we call intelligence, even though some psychologists insist that it is a single quantifiable thing measured by IQ tests. Many more psychologists consider intelligence to be the product of the interaction of different sorts of cognitive abilities: verbal, mathematical-logical, spatial, linguistic, musical, bodily kinesthetic, social, and personal.[9] Each may be thought of as a particular kind of intelligence, unrelated to the others. This being so, these types of intelligence must be independently inherited (to the degree they are inherited), just as height, blood type, skin color, and so forth are independently inherited. Thus the various abilities that constitute intelligence are independently distributed like other phenotypic traits such as skin color and blood type.

But IQ tests themselves are not a fully valid measure of inborn intelligence. An IQ test measures performance (something that the individual does) rather than genetic disposition (something that the individual was born with). Performance reflects past experience and present motivational state, as well as innate ability.

Though IQ tests are not a reliable measure of inborn intelligence, using them to prove the existence of significant differences in intelligence among human populations has been going on for at least a century. In the United States systematic comparisons of intelligence between "whites" and "blacks" began in the early 20th century and were frequently combined with data gathered by physical anthropologists about skull shape and size.

During World War I, for example, a series of IQ tests, known as Alpha and Beta, were regularly given to draftees. The results showed that the average score attained by Euramericans was higher than that obtained by African Americans. Even though African Americans from the urban northern states scored higher than Euramericans from the rural South, and some African Americans scored

[9]Jacoby, R., & Glauberman, N. (Eds.). (1995). *The Bell Curve debate* (pp. 7, 55–56, 59). New York: Random House.

higher than most Euramericans, many people took this as proof of the intellectual superiority of "white" people. But all the tests really showed was that, on the average, "whites" outperformed "blacks" in the social situation of IQ testing. The tests did not measure intelligence per se, but the ability, conditioned by culture, of certain individuals to respond appropriately to certain questions conceived by Americans of European descent for comparable middle-class "whites." These tests frequently require knowledge of "white" middle-class values and linguistic behavior.

For such reasons, intelligence tests continue to be the subject of controversy. Many psychologists as well as anthropologists are convinced that they are of limited use, because they are applicable only to particular cultural settings. When researchers controlled for cultural and environmental factors, African and European Americans tended to score equally well.[10]

Nevertheless some researchers still insist that significant differences in intelligence exist among human populations.

---

[10] Sanday, P. R. (1975). On the causes of IQ differences between groups and implications for social policy. In M. F. A. Montagu (Ed.), *Race and IQ* (pp. 232–238). New York: Oxford.

Proponents of this view are Richard Herrnstein, a psychologist, and Charles Murray, a social scientist and former fellow of the American Enterprise Institute, a conservative U.S. think tank. Their argument, in a lengthy (and highly publicized) book entitled *The Bell Curve*, is that the difference in IQ scores between Americans of African, Asian, and European descent is primarily determined by genetic factors and therefore immutable.

Herrnstein and Murray's book has been criticized on many grounds, including violation of basic rules of statistics and their practice of utilizing studies, no matter how flawed, that appear to support their thesis while ignoring or barely mentioning those that contradict it. In addition, they are also wrong on purely theoretical grounds. Because genes are inherited independently of one another, whatever alleles that may be associated with intelligence bear no relationship with the ones for skin pigmentation or with any other aspect of human variation such as blood type.

Further, the expression of genes always occurs in an environment. Among humans, culture shapes all aspects of the environment. In the following Original Study, physical anthropologist Jonathan Marks extends the discussion of race and intelligence to stereotypes about athletic abilities of different so-called races.

Original Study

A Feckless Quest for the Basketball Gene   *by Jonathan Marks*

You know what they say about a little knowledge. Here's some: The greatest sprinters and basketball players are predominantly black. Here's some more: Nobel laureates in science are predominantly white.

What do we conclude? That blacks have natural running ability, and whites have natural science ability? Or perhaps that blacks have natural running ability, but whites don't have natural science ability, because that would be politically incorrect?

Or perhaps that we can draw no valid conclusions about the racial distribution of abilities on the basis of data like these.

That is what modern anthropology would say.

But it's not what a new book, *Taboo: Why Black Athletes Dominate Sports and Why We're Afraid to Talk about It*, says. It says that blacks dominate sports because of their genes and that we're afraid to talk about it on account of a cabal of high-ranking politically correct postmodern professors—myself, I am flattered to observe, among them.

The book is a piece of good old-fashioned American anti-intellectualism (those dang perfessers!) that plays to vulgar beliefs about group differences of the sort we recall from *The Bell Curve* six years ago. These are not, however, issues that anthropologists are "afraid to talk about"; we talk about them a lot. The author, journalist, and former television producer Jon Entine, simply doesn't like what we're saying. But to approach the subject with any degree of rigor, as anthropologists have been trying to do for nearly a century, requires recognizing that it consists of several related questions.

First, how can we infer a genetic basis for differences among people? The answer: Collect genetic data. There's no substitute. We could document consistent differences in physical features, acts, and accomplishments until the Second Coming and be entirely wrong in thinking they're genetically based. A thousand Nigerian Ibos and a thousand Danes will consistently be found to differ in complexion, language, and head shape. The first is genetic, the second isn't, and the third we simply don't understand.

What's clear is that, developmentally, the body is sufficiently plastic that subtle differences in the conditions of growth and life can affect it profoundly. Simple observation of difference is thus not a genetic argument.

Which brings us to the second question: How can we accept a genetic basis for athletic ability and reject it for intelligence? The answer: We can't. Both conclusions are based on the same standard of evidence. If we accept that blacks are genetically endowed jumpers because "they" jump so well, we are obliged to accept that they are genetically unendowed at schoolwork because "they" do so poorly.

In either case, we are faced with the scientifically impossible task of drawing conclusions from a mass of poorly controlled data. Controls are crucial in science: If every black schoolboy in America knows he's supposed to be good at basketball and bad at algebra, and we have no way to measure schoolboys outside the boundaries of such an expectation, how can we gauge their "natural" endowments? Lots of things go into the observation of excellence or failure, only one of which is genetic endowment.

But obviously humans differ. Thus, the last question: What's the relationship between patterns of human genetic variation and groups of people? The answer: It's complex.

All populations are heterogeneous and are built in some sense in opposition to other groups. Jew or Muslim, Hutu or Tutsi, Serb or Bosnian, Irish or English, Harvard or Yale—one thing we're certain of is that the groups of most significance to us don't correspond to much in nature.

Consider, then, the category "black athlete"—and let's limit ourselves to men here. It's broad enough to encompass Arthur Ashe, Mike Tyson, and Kobe Bryant.

When you read about the body of the black male athlete, whose body do you imagine? Whatever physical gift these men share is not immediately apparent from looking at them.

Black men of highly diverse builds enter athletics and excel.

Far more don't excel. In other words, there is a lot more to being black and to being a prominent athlete than mere biology. If professional excellence or overrepresentation could be regarded as evidence for genetic superiority, there would be strong implications for Jewish comedy genes and Irish policeman genes.

Inferring a group's excellence from the achievements of some members hangs on a crucial asymmetry: To accomplish something means that you had the ability to do it, but the failure to do it doesn't mean you didn't have the ability. And the existing genetic data testify that known DNA variations do not respect the boundaries of human groups.

To be an elite athlete, or elite anybody, presumably does require some kind of genetic gift. But those gifts must be immensely diverse, distributed broadly across the people of the world—at least to judge from the way that the erosion of social barriers consistently permits talent to manifest itself in different groups of people.

In an interview with *The Philadelphia Daily News* in February, Mr. Entine observed that Jews are overrepresented among critics of the views he espouses. But is that a significantly Jewish thing? Or is it simply a consequence of the fact that among any group of American intellectuals you'll find Jews overrepresented because they are a well-educated minority? There's certainly no shortage of non-Jews who find the ideas in *Taboo* to be demagogic quackery.

Of course, Jewish academics may sometimes be speaking as academics, not as Jews. Likewise black athletes may perform as athletes, not just as embodied blackness.

How easy it is to subvert Michael Jordan, the exceptional and extraordinary man, into merely the representative of the black athlete.

The problem with talking about the innate superiority of the black athlete is that it is make-believe genetics applied to naïvely conceptualized groups of people. It places a spotlight on imaginary natural differences that properly belongs on real social differences.

More important, it undermines the achievements of individuals as individuals. Whatever gifts we each have are far more likely, from what we know of genetics, to be unique individual constellations of genes than to be expressions of group endowments.

From Marks, J. (2000, April 8). A feckless quest for the basketball gene. New York Times. Copyright © 2000 by the New York Times Co. Reprinted by permission.

Separating genetic components of intelligence (or any other continuous trait) from environmental contributors poses enormous problems.[11] Most studies of intelligence rely on comparisons between identical twins: genetically identical individuals raised in the same or different environments. Twin studies are plagued by a host of problems: inadequate sample sizes, biased subjective judgments, failure to make sure that "separated twins" really were raised separately, unrepresentative samples of adoptees to serve as controls, untested assumptions about similarity of environments. In fact, children reared by the same mother resemble her in IQ to the same degree, whether or not they share her genes.[12] Clearly, the degree to which intelligence is inherited through genes is far from understood.[13]

Undoubtedly, the effects of social environment are important for intelligence. This should not surprise us, as other genetically determined traits are influenced by environmental factors. Height in humans, for example, has a genetic basis while also being dependent upon both nutrition and health status. (Severe illness in childhood arrests growth, and renewed growth never makes up for this loss.) While it is possible to see the effects of the environment on growth, the exact relative contributions of genetic and environmental factors on either the height or the intelligence of an individual are unknown.

Nevertheless, documentation of the importance of the environment in the expression of intelligence exposes further the problems with generalizations about IQ and "race." For example, IQ scores of all groups in the United States, as in most industrial and postindustrial countries, have risen some 15 points since World War II. In addition, the gap between Americans of African and European descent, for example, is narrower today than in the past. Other studies show impressive IQ scores for African American children born into socially deprived and economically disadvantaged backgrounds who have been adopted into highly educated and prosperous homes. It is now known that underprivileged children adopted into such privileged families can boost their IQs by 20 points.

---

[11] Andrews, L. B., & Nelkin, D. (1996). The Bell Curve: A statement. *Science 271,* 13.

[12] Lewontin, R. C., Rose, S., & Kamin, L. J. (1984). *Not in our genes* (pp. 100, 113, 116). New York: Pantheon.

[13] Ibid., pp. 9, 121.

ranking human beings with respect to their intelligence scores in terms of "racial" difference is doubly false.

Over the past 2.5 million years, all populations of the genus *Homo* have adapted primarily through culture—actively inventing solutions to the problems of survival, rather than relying only on biological adaptation. Thus we would expect a comparable degree of intelligence in all present-day human populations. The only way for individual human beings to develop their innate abilities and skills to the fullest is to ensure that they have access to the necessary resources and the opportunity to do so.

Studying Human Biological Diversity

Although the biological category of race is not valid when considering groups of humans, this is not to say that differences in various biological traits such as skin color do not exist. In fact, skin color provides an excellent example of the role of natural selection in shaping human variation.

The physical characteristics of both populations and individuals are a product of the interaction between genes and environments. For example, genes predispose people to a particular skin color, but an individual's skin color is also influenced by cultural and environmental factors. The skin of sailors, for example, is darkened or burned after many hours of exposure to the sun, depending on not only genetic predisposition but cultural practices regarding exposure to the sun. In other cases, such as A-B-O blood type, phenotypic expression closely reflects genotype.

For characteristics controlled by a single gene, different versions of that gene, known as alleles (see Chapter 2), also mediate variation. Such traits are called **polymorphic** (meaning "many shapes"). Our blood types—determined by the alleles for types A, B, and O blood—are an example of a polymorphism and may appear in any of four distinct phenotypic forms (A, B, O, and AB).

A species can also be considered polymorphic, meaning that there is wide variation among individuals (beyond differences between males and females). Here "polymorphic" refers to continuous phenotypic variation that may be genetically controlled by interactions among multiple different genes, in addition to the allelic variation described above. When a polymorphic species faces changing environmental conditions, the variation it has within its gene pool fosters survival of the species, since some of those individuals may possess traits that prove adaptive in the altered environment. Individuals whose physical characteristics enable them to do well in the new environment will usually reproduce more successfully, so that their

Differences in the growth process can lead to very different outcomes in terms of size as seen in these twins, who are genetically identical. Even starting from inside their mother's womb, twins may experience environmental differences in terms of blood and nutrient supply. This can impact not only size but cognitive development.

It is also well known that IQ scores rise in proportion to the test-takers' amount of schooling.

More such cases could be cited, but these three observations suffice to make the point. First, there is a bias in IQ testing based on social class. Second, the assertion that IQ is biologically fixed and immutable is clearly false. Third,

polymorphic Describing species with alternative forms (alleles) of particular genes.

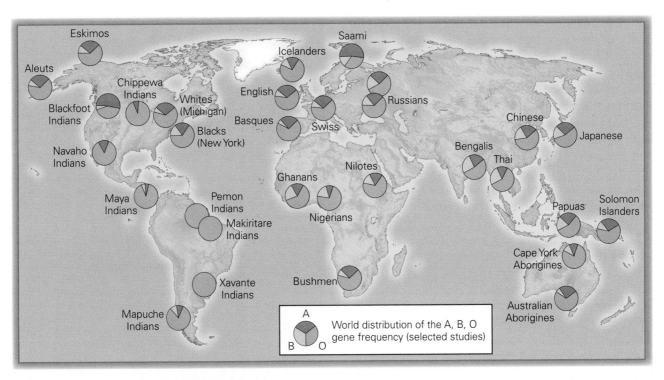

Figure 12.1 Frequencies of the three alleles for the A, B, and O blood groups for selected populations around the world illustrate the polytypic nature of *Homo sapiens*. The frequency of the alleles differs among populations.

genes become more common in subsequent generations. Similarly, the polymorphism of the human species has allowed us to thrive in a wide variety of environments.

When polymorphisms of a species are distributed into geographically dispersed populations, biologists describe this species as **polytypic** ("many types"); that is, genetic variability is unevenly distributed among populations. For example, in the distribution of the polymorphism for blood type (four distinct phenotypic groups: A, B, O, or AB), the human species is polytypic. The frequency of the O allele is highest in American Indians, especially among some populations native to South America; the highest frequencies of the allele for type A blood tend to be found among certain European populations (although the highest frequency is found among the Blackfoot Indians of the northern Plains in North America); the highest frequencies of the B allele are found in some Asian populations (Figure 12.1). Even though single traits may be grouped within specific geographic regions, when a greater number of traits are considered, specific human "types" cannot be identified. Instead each of these traits is independently subject to evolutionary forces.

As mentioned above, today anthropologists study biological diversity in terms of *clines,* or the continuous gradation over space in the form or frequency of a trait. As mentioned in Chapter 2, the spatial distribution or cline for the sickle-cell allele allowed anthropologists to identify the adaptive function of this gene in a malarial

environment. Clinal analysis of a continuous trait such as body shape, which is controlled by a series of genes, allows anthropologists to interpret human global variation in body build as an adaptation to climate.

Generally, people long native to regions with cold climates tend to have greater body bulk (not to be equated with fat) relative to their extremities (arms and legs) than do people native to regions with hot climates, who tend to be relatively long and slender. Interestingly, these differences show up as early as the time of *Homo erectus,* as described in Chapter 8. A person with larger body bulk and relatively shorter extremities may suffer more from summer heat than someone whose extremities are relatively long and whose body is slender. But they do conserve needed body heat under cold conditions. A bulky body tends to conserve more heat than a less bulky one, because it has less surface area relative to volume. In hot, open country, by contrast, people benefit from a long slender body that can get rid of excess heat quickly. A small slender body can also promote heat loss due to a high surface area-to-volume ratio.

In addition to very long-term effects that climate may have imposed on human variation, climate can also

polytypic Describing the expression of genetic variants in different frequencies in different populations of a species.

contribute to human variation through its impact on the process of growth and development (developmental adaptation). For example, some of the physiological mechanisms for withstanding cold or dissipating heat have been shown to vary depending upon the climate that an individual experiences as a child. Individuals who grow up in very cold climates develop circulatory system modifications that allow them to remain comfortable at temperatures that people from warmer climates cannot tolerate. Similarly, hot climate promotes the development of a higher density of sweat glands, creating a more efficient system for sweating to keep the body cool.

Cultural processes complicate studies of body build and climatic adaptation. For example, dietary differences particularly during childhood will cause variation in body shape through their effect on the growth process. Another complicating factor is clothing. Much of the way people adapt to cold is cultural rather than biological. For example, Inuit peoples of Arctic Canada live where it is very cold much of the year. To cope with this, they long ago developed efficient clothing to keep the body warm. Inside their clothing, the Inuit are provided with what amounts to an artificial tropical environment. Such cultural adaptations allow humans to inhabit the entire globe.

Some anthropologists have also suggested that variation in features such as face and eye shape relate to climate. For example, biological anthropologist Carleton Coon and his colleagues once proposed that the "Mongoloid face," common in populations native to East and Central Asia, as well as Arctic North America, exhibits features adapted to life in very cold environments.[14] The **epicanthic eye fold** (which minimizes the eye's exposure to the cold), a flat facial profile, and extensive fatty deposits may help to protect the face against frostbite.

Although experimental studies have failed to sustain the frostbite hypothesis, it is true that a flat facial profile generally goes with a round head. A significant percentage of body heat may be lost from the head. A round head, having less surface area relative to volume, loses less heat than a longer, more elliptical head. As one would predict from this, populations with more elliptical-shaped heads are generally found in hotter climates; those with rounder-shaped heads are more common in cold climates. However, these same features also could be present in populations due to genetic drift.

The epicanthic eye fold is common among people of East Asia. While some anthropologists have suggested that this feature might be an adaptation to cold, genetic drift could also be responsible for the frequency of this trait.

Culture and Biological Diversity

Although cultural adaptation has reduced the importance of biological adaptation and physical variation, at the same time cultural forces impose their own selective pressures. For example, take the reproductive fitness of individuals with diabetes—a disease with a known genetic predisposition. In North America and Europe today, where medication is relatively available, people with diabetes are as biologically fit as anyone else. However, if people with diabetes do not have access to the necessary medication, as is true in many parts of the world, their biological fitness is lost and they die out. Because financial status affects access to medical resources, one's biological fitness may be determined by this cultural factor.

Culture can also contribute directly to the development of disease. For example, one type of diabetes is very common among overweight individuals who get little exercise—a combination that describes 61 percent of people in the United States today. As peoples from traditional

---

[14] Coon, C. S. (1962). *The origins of races.* New York: Knopf.

epicanthic eye fold A fold of skin at the inner corner of the eye that covers the true corner of the eye; common in Asiatic populations.

Loss of traditional cultural practices brought about by forced reservation life has resulted in high rates of diabetes among American Indians. The Pima Indians of Arizona have the highest rates of diabetes in the world today. Diabetes was not a problem for the Pima before the plentiful high-carbohydrate diet and low activity patterns typical of U.S. culture replaced their traditional lifeways. Despite the sociopolitical roots of this disease in their community, the Pima have participated in government-funded research aimed at both understanding the genetic origins of diabetes and finding effective treatment for it. Here a Pima woman prepares to give herself an insulin injection.

consume milk or milk products. Only 10 to 30 percent of Americans of African descent and 0 to 30 percent of adult Asians are lactose tolerant.[15] By contrast, lactase retention and lactose tolerance are normal for over 80 percent of adults of northern European descent. Eastern Europeans, Arabs, and some East Africans are closer to northern Europeans in lactase retention than they are to Asians and other Africans.

Generally speaking, a high retention of lactase is found in populations with a long tradition of dairying. For them, fresh milk is an important dietary item. In such populations, selection in the past favored those individuals with the allele that confers the ability to assimilate lactose, selecting out those without this allele.

Because milk is associated with health in North American and European countries, powdered milk has long been a staple of economic aid to other countries. In fact, such practices work against the members of populations in which lactase is not commonly retained into adulthood. Those individuals who are not lactose tolerant are unable to utilize the many nutrients in milk. Frequently they also suffer diarrhea, abdominal cramping, and even bone degeneration, with serious results. In fact, the shipping of powdered milk to victims of South American earthquakes in the 1960s caused many deaths.

Among Europeans, lactose tolerance is linked with the evolution of a non-thrifty genotype as opposed to the thrifty genotype that characterized humans until about 6,000 years ago.[16] The **thrifty genotype** permits efficient storage of fat to draw on in times of food shortage. In times of scarcity, individuals with the thrifty genotype conserve glucose (a simple sugar) for use in brain and red blood cells (as opposed to other tissues such as muscle), as well as nitrogen (vital for growth and health).

Regular access to glucose through the lactose in milk led to selection for the non-thrifty genotype as protection against adult-onset diabetes, or at least its onset relatively late in life (at a nonreproductive age). Populations that are lactose intolerant retain the thrifty genotype. As a

cultures throughout the world adopt a Western high-sugar diet and low activity pattern, their incidence rates will rise for diabetes and obesity as well.

Another example of culture acting as an agent of biological selection is lactose tolerance: the ability to digest **lactose,** the primary constituent of fresh milk. To digest milk, the body has to make a particular enzyme—**lactase.** Most mammals as well as most human populations—especially Asian, Native Australian, Native American, and many (but not all) African populations—do not continue to produce lactase into adulthood. Adults with lactose intolerance suffer from gas pains and diarrhea when they

---

[15] Harrison, G. G. (1975). Primary adult lactase deficiency: A problem in anthropological genetics. *American Anthropologist 77,* 815–819.

[16] Allen, J. S., & Cheer, S. M. (1996). The non-thrifty genotype. *Current Anthropology 37,* 831–842.

lactose A sugar that is the primary constituent of fresh milk.

lactase An enzyme in the small intestine that enables humans to assimilate lactose.

thrifty genotype Human genotype that permits efficient storage of fat to draw on in times of food shortage and conservation of glucose and nitrogen.

Biocultural Connection

Beans, Enzymes, and Adaptation to Malaria

Some human adaptations to the deadly malarial parasite are biological while others are strictly tied to cultural practices such as local cuisine. The phenotype of the sickle-cell allele, for example, manifests specifically in red blood cells. Biological and dietary adaptations to malaria converge with the interaction between one form of the glucose-6-phosphate-dehydrogenase (G-6-PD) enzyme and fava bean consumption.

The fava bean is a broad flat bean (*Vivia faba*) that is a dietary staple

© Charles O. Cecil/Alamy

Fava beans, a dietary staple in the countries around the Mediterranean Sea, also provide some protection against malaria. However, in individuals with G-6-PD deficiency, the protective aspects of fava beans turn deadly. This dual role has led to a rich folklore surrounding fava beans.

in malaria-endemic areas along the Mediterranean coast. G-6-PD is an enzyme that serves to reduce one sugar, glucose-6-phosphate, to another sugar—in the process releasing an energy-rich molecule. The malaria parasite lives in red blood cells off of energy produced via G-6-PD. Individuals with a mutation in the G-6-PD gene, so-called G-6-PD-deficiency, produce energy by an alternate pathway not involving this enzyme that the parasite cannot use. Furthermore, G-6-PD-deficient red blood cells seem to turn over more quickly, thus allowing less time for the parasite to grow and multiply. While a different form of G-6-PD deficiency is also found in some sub-Saharan African populations, the form found in Mediterranean populations is at odds with an adaptation embedded in the cuisine of the region.

Enzymes naturally occurring in fava beans also contain substances that interfere with the development of the malarial parasite. In cultures around the Mediterranean Sea, where malaria is common, fava beans are incorporated into the diet through foods eaten at the height of the malaria season. However, if an individual with G-6-PD deficiency eats fava beans, the result is that the substances toxic to the parasite become toxic to humans. With G-6-PD deficiency, fava bean consumption leads to *hemolytic crisis* (Latin for "breaking of red blood cells") and a series of chemical reactions that release free radicals and hydrogen peroxide into the blood stream. This condition is known as *favism*.

The toxic effect of fava bean consumption in G-6-PD individuals has prompted a rich folklore around this simple food, including the ancient

Greek belief that fava beans contain the souls of the dead. The link between favism and G-6-PD deficiency has led parents of children with this condition to limit consumption of this favorite dietary staple.

Unfortunately, this has sometimes become a generalized elimination of many excellent sources of protein such as peanuts, lentils, chickpeas, soy beans, and nuts. Another biocultural connection is again at the root of this unnecessary deprivation. The Arabic name for fava beans is *foul* (pronounced "fool"), while the soy beans are called *foul-al-Soya,* and peanuts are *foul-al-Soudani*; in other words, the plants are linked linguistically even though they are unrelated biologically.[a]

An environmental stressor as potent as malaria has led to a number of human adaptations. In the case of fava beans and G-6-PD deficiency, these adaptations can work at cross purposes. Cultural knowledge of the biochemistry of these interactions will allow humans to adapt, regardless of their genotype.

BIOCULTURAL QUESTION

How does what you have learned from this chapter about the falsehood of the biological category of race relate to the way the varied adaptations to malaria described here work against one another?

---

[a]Babiker, M. A., et al. (1996). Unnecessary deprivation of common food items in glucose-6-phosphate dehydrogenase deficiency. *Annals of Saudi Arabia 16* (4), 462–463.

---

consequence, when they are introduced to Western-style diets (characterized by abundance, particularly of foods high in sugar content), the incidence of obesity and diabetes skyrockets. This chapter's Biocultural Connection describes another example of genetic and cultural adaptations working at cross purposes.

melanin The chemical responsible for dark skin pigmentation that helps protect against damage from ultraviolet radiation.

Skin Color: A Case Study in Adaptation

Generally, the notion of race is most commonly equated with skin color. Skin color is subject to great variation and is attributed to several key factors: the transparency or thickness of the skin; a copper-colored pigment called carotene; reflected color from the blood vessels (responsible for the rosy color of lightly pigmented people); and, most significantly, the amount of **melanin** (from *melas,* a Greek word meaning "black")—a dark pigment in the skin's outer layer. People with dark skin have more melanin-producing

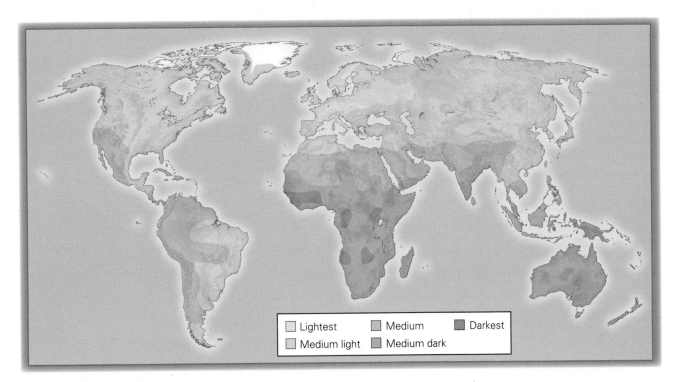

Figure 12.2 This map illustrates the distribution of dark and light human skin pigmentation before 1492. Medium-light skin color in Southeast Asia reflects the spread into that region of people from southern China, whereas the medium darkness of people native to southern Australia is a consequence of their tropical Southeast Asian ancestry. Lack of dark skin pigmentation among tropical populations of Native Americans reflects their more recent ancestry in northeastern Asia a mere 20,000 or so years ago.

cells than those with light skin, but everyone (except those with a condition called albinism) has a measure of melanin. Exposure to sunlight increases melanin production, causing skin color to deepen.

Melanin is known to protect skin against damaging ultraviolet solar radiation;[17] consequently, dark-skinned people are less susceptible to skin cancer and sunburn than are those with less melanin. They also seem to be less susceptible to destruction of certain vitamins under intense exposure to sunlight. Because the highest concentrations of dark-skinned people tend to be found in the tropical regions of the world, it appears that natural selection has favored heavily pigmented skin as a protection against exposure where ultraviolet radiation is most constant.

The inheritance of skin color involves several genes (rather than variants of a single gene), each with several alleles, thus creating a continuous range of phenotypic expression for this trait. In addition, the geographic distribution or cline of skin color, with few exceptions, tends to be continuous (Figures 12.2 and 12.3). The exceptions have to do with the historic movement of certain populations from their original homelands to other regions, or the practice of selective mating, or both.

Because skin cancer generally does not develop until later in life, it is less likely to have interfered with the reproductive success of lightly pigmented individuals in the tropics and so is probably not the agent of selection. On the other hand, severe sunburn, which is especially dangerous to infants, causes the body to overheat and interferes with its ability to sweat and rid itself of excess heat. Furthermore, it makes one susceptible to other kinds of infection. In addition to all this, decomposition of folate, an essential vitamin sensitive to heavy doses of ultraviolet radiation, can cause anemia, spontaneous abortion, and infertility.[18]

In northern latitudes, light skin has an adaptive advantage related to the skin's important biological function as the manufacturer of vitamin D through a chemical reaction dependent upon sunlight. Vitamin D is vital for maintaining the balance of calcium in the body. In northern climates with little sunshine, light skin allows enough sunlight to penetrate the skin so as to stimulate the

[17] Neer, R. M. (1975). The evolutionary significance of vitamin D, skin pigment, and ultraviolet light. *American Journal of Physical Anthropology 43*, 409–416.

[18] Branda, R. F., & Eatoil, J. W. (1978). Skin color and photolysis: An evolutionary hypothesis. *Science 201*, 625–626.

Figure 12.3 The east-west gradient in the frequency of type B blood in Europe contrasts with the north-south gradient in skin color shown in Figure 12.2. Just as the clines for skin color and blood type must be considered independently, so too must be whatever genes are involved in the complex of abilities known as "intelligence."

production of vitamin D, which is essential for healthy bones and for balance within the central nervous system. Without sufficient vitamin D, bone growth in children is impaired, resulting in misshapen, fragile bones, a condition known as rickets (Figure 12.4). There is an adult form of bone disease resulting from vitamin D deficiency as well. Dark pigmentation can interfere with vitamin D synthesis and with calcium balance when there is limited natural light.

Figure 12.4 Bone diseases such as osteomalacia and rickets caused by vitamin D deficiency can deform the birth canal of the pelvis to the degree that it can interfere with successful childbirth. Because sunshine is vital to the body's production of vitamin D, this disease was very common in the past among the poor in northern industrial cities because they had limited exposure to sunlight. Dietary supplements have reduced the impact of bone diseases, such as rickets, although they continue to be a problem in cultures that require women and girls to dress so that they are completely veiled from the sun.

The severe consequences of vitamin D deficiency can be avoided through cultural practices. Until recently, children in northern Europe and northern North America were regularly fed a spoonful of cod liver oil during the dark winter months. Today, pasteurized milk is often fortified with vitamin D.

Race and Human Evolution

Throughout this chapter we have explored the fallacy of the biological category of race when applied to the human species. Generalizations cannot be made about "types" of humans because no discrete types of humans exist. By contrast, the paleoanthropological analysis of the fossil record explored in previous chapters includes defining specific types of ancestors based on biological and cultural capacities that go hand in hand.

The increased brain size of *Homo habilis* noted around 2.5 million years ago supports the notion that these ancestors were capable of more complex cultural activities than australopithecines, including the manufacture of stone tools. Closer to the present, the same assumptions do not hold. At some point in our evolutionary history we became a single, unified global species. Bearing this in mind, we can frame the modern human origins debate in the terms of the content of this chapter.

Living people today such as this Aborigine do not meet the definition of anatomical modernity proposed in the recent African origins model. Some paleoanthropologists suggest that this proves that the definition is problematic because all living people are clearly full-fledged members of the species *Homo sapiens*.

The modern human origins debate hinges on the question of whether cultural abilities and intelligence can be inferred from details of skull and skeletal shape and size. Supporters of the multiregional hypothesis argue that they cannot.[19] They suggest that using a series of biological features to represent a type of human being (Neandertals) with certain cultural capacities (inferior) is like making assumptions about the cultural capabilities of living humans based on their appearance. In living people, such assumptions are considered stereotypes or racism. By arguing that ancient groups like Neandertals represent a distinct species, supporters of the recent African origins hypothesis bypass the potential prejudice inherent in these assumptions. Both theories embrace African human origins, and in doing so they confront the issue of skin color—the physical feature that has extreme political significance today.

At present, we clearly cannot make any assumptions about intelligence or behavior based on a single phenotypic trait such as skin color. Given what we know about the adaptive significance of human skin color and the fact that, until 800,000 years ago, the genus *Homo* exclusively inhabited the tropics, it is likely that lightly pigmented skins are a recent development in human history. Darkly pigmented skins are probably quite ancient. Consistent with humanity's African origins, the enzyme tyrosinase, which converts the amino acid tyrosine into the compound that forms melanin, is present in lightly pigmented peoples in sufficient quantity to make them very "black." The reason it does not is that they have genes that inactivate or inhibit it.[20]

Human skin, more liberally endowed with sweat glands and lacking heavy body hair compared to other primates, effectively eliminates excess body heat in a

[19] Ibid.

[20] Wills, C. (1994). The skin we're in. *Discover 15* (11), 79.

hot climate as described in Chapter 7. This would have been especially advantageous to our ancestors on the savannah, who could have avoided confrontations with carnivorous animals by carrying out most of their activities in the heat of the day. For the most part, large carnivores such as lions rest during this period, being active from dusk until early morning. Without much hair to cover their bodies, selection would have favored dark skins in our ancestors. All humans appear to have had a "black" ancestry, no matter how "white" some of them may appear to be today.

An interesting question is how long it took for light pigmentation to develop in populations living outside the tropics. Whether one subscribes to the multiregional continuity model or the recent African origins hypothesis, the settling of Greater Australia can be used to examine this question, as we know that the first people to reach Australia did so sometime between 40,000 and 60,000 years ago. These people came there from tropical Southeast Asia, spreading throughout Australia eventually to what is now the island of Tasmania, with a latitude and levels of ultraviolet radiation similar to New York City, Rome, or Beijing.

As Aboriginal Australians originally came from the tropics, we would expect them to have had darkly pigmented skin. In Australia, those populations that spread south of the tropics (where, as in northern latitudes, ultraviolet radiation is less intense) underwent some reduction of pigmentation. But for all that, their skin color is still far darker than that of Europeans or East Asians. Most of today's Southeast Asian population spread there from southern China following the invention of farming. This expansion of lighter-skinned populations effectively "swamped" the original populations of this region, except in a few out-of-the-way places like the Andaman Islands, in the Bay of Bengal between India and Thailand.[21] The obvious conclusion is that 40,000 to 60,000 years is not enough to produce significant depigmentation.[22] These observations also suggest that Europeans and East Asians may have lived outside the tropics for far longer than the people of Tasmania or that settlement in latitudes even more distant from the equator were required for depigmentation to occur.

One should not conclude that, because it is newer, lightly pigmented skin is better or more highly evolved than heavily pigmented skin. The latter is clearly better adapted to the conditions of life in the tropics, although with cultural adaptations like protective clothing, hats, and sunscreen lotions, very lightly pigmented peoples can survive there. Conversely, supplementary sources of vitamin D allow heavily pigmented peoples to do quite well away from the tropics. In both cases, culture has rendered skin color differences largely irrelevant from a biological perspective. With time, skin color may lose its social significance as well.

---

[21] Diamond, J. (1996). Empire of uniformity. *Discover 17* (3), 83–84.

[22] Ferrie, H. (1997). An interview with C. Loring Brace. *Current Anthropology 38*, 864.

Questions for Reflection

1. Humans are challenged to find ways to embrace and comprehend the range of biological diversity without succumbing to oversimplification, discrimination, and even bloodshed fueled by superficial differences. How do anthropological approaches to race contribute to meeting this challenge?

2. From an evolutionary perspective, why is human biological diversity a key component of our collective identity as a species?

3. Why do biological anthropologists and evolutionary biologists use clines to study human variation rather than the biological concept of subspecies? Can you imagine another species of animal, plant, or microorganism for which the subspecies concept makes sense?

4. How do you define the concept of intelligence? Do you think scientists will ever be able to discover the genetic basis of intelligence?

5. Globally, health statistics are gathered by country. In addition, some countries such as the United States gather health statistics by race. How are these two endeavors different and similar? Should health statistics be gathered by group?

Suggested Readings

Cohen, M. N. (1998). *Culture of intolerance: Chauvinism, class, and racism in the United States*. New Haven, CT: Yale University Press.

This very readable book summarizes what scientific data really say about biological differences among humans and exposes questionable assumptions in U.S. culture that promote intolerance and generate problems where none need exist.

Gould, S. J. (1996). *The mismeasure of man* (2nd ed.). New York: Norton.

This is an update of a classic critique of supposedly scientific studies that attempt to rank all people on a linear scale of intrinsic and unalterable mental worth. The revision was prompted by what Gould refers to as the "latest cyclic episode of biodeterminism" represented by the publication of the widely discussed book, *The Bell Curve*.

Graves, J. L. (2001). *The emperor's new clothes: Biological theories of race at the millennium*. New Brunswick, NJ: Rutgers University Press.

Graves, a laboratory geneticist, aims to show that there is no biological basis for separation of human beings into races and that the idea of race is a relatively recent social and political construction. His grasp of science is solid and up-to-date.

Jacoby, R., & Glauberman, N. (Eds.). (1995). *The Bell Curve debate*. New York: Random House.

This collection of articles by a wide variety of authors (biologists, anthropologists, psychologists, mathematicians, essayists) critically examines the claims raised in *The Bell Curve*. For anyone who hopes to understand the race and intelligence debate, this book is a must.

Marks, J. (1995). *Human biodiversity: Genes, race, and history*. Hawthorne, NY: Aldine.

In this book, Marks shows how genetics has undermined the fundamental assumptions of racial taxonomy. In addition to its presentation of the nature of human biodiversity, the book also deals with the history of cultural attitudes toward race and diversity.

Smedley, A. (1998). *Race in North America: Origin and evolution of a worldview*. Boulder, CO: Westview.

Audrey Smedley traces the cultural invention of the idea of race and how this false biological category has been used to rationalize inequality in North America.

Wolpoff, M., & Caspari, R. (1997). *Race and human evolution: A fatal attraction*. New York: Simon & Schuster.

Along with providing an excellent history of the pseudoscience of racial difference, this book is a detailed but readable presentation of the multiregional hypothesis of modern human origins. Among its strengths is a discussion of the problem of defining what "anatomically modern" means.

Challenge Issue Among the primate species, humans are the only ones capable of inhabiting the entire globe. Over the course of human evolutionary history, both our cultural and biological capabilities have contributed to our adaptability as a species. But today it seems that we are approaching the limits of our biological and cultural adaptability. The actions of human societies have changed the world on such a massive scale and at such a rapid pace that we, as a species, are facing novel challenges. If birth and death rates continue at current rates, global population size of 6.8 billion will double in less than fifty years, placing untenable pressures on the world's natural resources. As water, food, and fuel become impossibly scarce, how will humans adapt? Will this lead to warfare and to an impossible distance between the have-nots and the have-lots? Here, women in Mehdiganj, India, hold water urns called *gharas* with the words "Water Is Life" written on them to protest the nearby Coca-Cola bottling plant. As the plant uses up the local water, nearby farmers lose their livelihood and way of life. In a competition for resources such as this, global corporations like Coca-Cola have advantages over local inhabitants. But ultimately, for all of us to win, strategies must be implemented to ensure a planet in balance.

Lok Samiti (translation: People's Committee) of Mehdiganj, India. Photograph by Nandial Master.

CHAPTER 13

Human Adaptation to a Changing World

Chapter Preview

How Have Humans Adapted Biologically to Naturally Occurring Environmental Stressors?

When faced with an environmental stressor, the human species has responded biologically at three distinct levels: genetic, developmental, and physiological. Some genetic adaptations are expressed in terms of phenotypic variation of continuous traits. Even when the genetic bases to these adaptations are not precisely known, scientists can study them through comparative measurement of the associated phenotypic variation. In addition, the long period of human growth and development allows the environment to interact with genes and shape the human body. Short-term changes or physiological adaptations occur in response to a particular environmental stimulus. Today, the rapid rates at which cultural processes change human environments pose new biological challenges with important consequences for our species.

How Are Humans Adapting in the Face of Globalization?

The interconnectedness of humans to one another and to the environment is critical for understanding human adaptation and disease. Today, because local human environments are shaped by global political and economic systems, these features directly impact the distribution of health and disease. Simply describing disease in terms of biological processes, such as those associated with infection or malnutrition, leaves out the ultimate reasons that some individuals are likelier than others to become sick. Examination of the impact of political processes on disease can reveal its social causes, bringing us closer to finding long-lasting cures.

What Is Evolutionary Medicine?

Evolutionary medicine, a branch of medical anthropology, uses the principles of evolutionary theory to contribute to human health. Basic to this approach is framing health issues in terms of the relationship between biological change and cultural change. Biological evolution shaped humans slowly over millions of years while cultural change occurs relatively quickly. The resulting dissociation between human biology and current cultural practices may lead to disease. Also, because culture shapes even scientific interpretations of the human body, evolutionary medicine acknowledges that some physiological phenomena regarded as symptoms of disease can also be understood as naturally evolving defense mechanisms.

Throughout millions of years of human evolutionary history, biology and culture interacted to make humans the species we are today. The archaeological record and contemporary human variation reveal that biology and culture continue to shape all areas of human experience, including health and disease. Indeed, an inside joke among anthropologists is that if you do not know the answer to an exam question about biology and culture, the answer is either "both" or "malaria." Our current understanding of malaria, as explained in previous chapters, illustrates how answering "malaria" is just like answering "both." Farming practices (culture) of the past created the perfect environment for the malarial parasite. The genetic response (biology) to this environmental change was increased frequencies of the sickle-cell allele.

To add a few more biocultural layers closer to the present, think about how contemporary global inequalities contribute to the continued devastating effects of malaria in poorer countries today. For example, if malaria were a problem plaguing North America or Europe today, would most citizens of the countries with rampant malaria still be without adequate treatment or cure? Similarly, public health initiatives for genetic counseling to reduce frequencies of sickle-cell anemia in the United States have been met with distrust by African Americans who have experienced racism rooted in a false message of biological difference.[1] Would the average Euramerican

feel comfortable with genetic testing to eliminate a disease gene if he or she had experienced some of the wrongs underprivileged ethnic minorities have experienced in the name of science?

Consider, for example, the Tuskegee Syphilis Study, carried out by the U.S. Public Health Service in Macon County, Alabama, from 1932 to 1972. This study involved withholding syphilis medication from a group of poor African American men without their knowledge, so that the scientists could learn more about the biology of syphilis in the "Negro." These methods are now widely recognized as a moral breach that caused unnecessary pain and suffering to the men and their families. As a result of these unethical practices, the U.S. government changed its research policies involving the biological study of human subjects. In short, when examining a seemingly biological phenomenon such as disease, cultural factors must be considered at every level—from how that phenomenon is represented in each social group (reflected in this case in the false notion that the biology of syphilis would differ between people of different skin colors) to how biological research is conducted.

An integrated biocultural approach is one of the hallmarks of anthropology. In examples ranging from infant feeding and sleeping practices to the relationship between poverty and tuberculosis, biocultural connections have been emphasized throughout this book. In this chapter, we take a deeper look at this connection and examine some of the theoretical approaches biological and medical anthropologists use to examine the interaction of biology and culture.

---

[1] Tapper, M. (1999). *In the blood: Sickle-cell anemia and the politics of race.* Philadelphia: University of Pennsylvania Press.

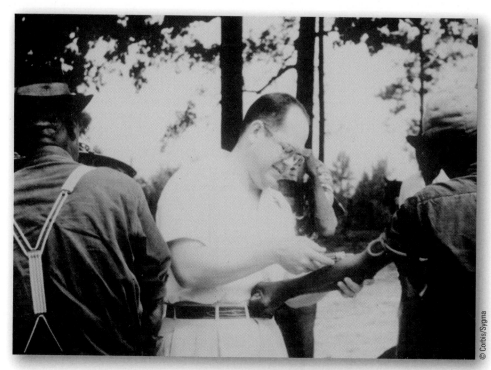

The Tuskegee Syphilis Study denied appropriate medical treatment to African American men in order to study the supposed differences in the biology of the disease in the "Negro." This human experimentation was not only false from a biological perspective but represents a moral breach in research conduct. Public outcry about this experiment led to regulations that protect all human subjects in biomedical research.

© Corbis/Sygma

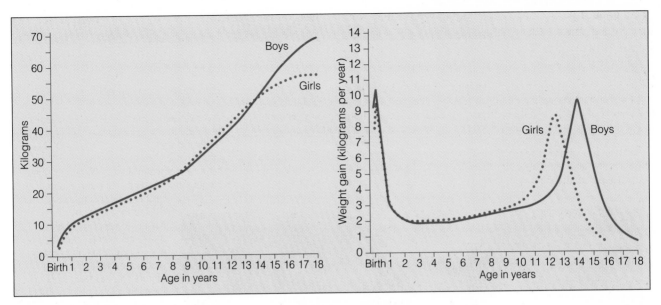

Figure 13.1 Franz Boas defined the features of the human growth curve. The graph on the left depicts distance, or the amount of growth attained over time, while the graph on the right shows the velocity, or rate of growth over time. These charts are widely used throughout the globe to determine the health status of children.

While humans possess a number of exquisite biological mechanisms through which they have adapted to the natural environment, these mechanisms can fall terribly short in today's globalizing world. Before turning to the challenges we face from the dramatic changes we have made in our environment today, we will explore the biological mechanisms humans have used over millennia to adapt to three naturally occurring environmental extremes: high altitude, cold, and heat.

Human Adaptation to Natural Environmental Stressors

Studies of human adaptation traditionally focus on the capacity of humans to adapt or adjust to their environment through biological and/or cultural mechanisms. Darwin's theory of natural selection accounts for discrete genetic changes built into the allele frequencies of populations, such as the various adaptations to malaria that we have examined. It also provides the mechanism for understanding that adaptations, evident in population variation of continuous phenotypic traits, depend upon multiple interacting genes. Even when the genetic bases to these adaptations (such as skin color or body build) are not precisely known, scientists can study them through comparative measurement of the associated phenotypic variation.

Humans possess two additional biological mechanisms through which they can adapt. The first of these, **developmental adaptation,** also produces permanent phenotypic variation as the environment shapes the expression of the genes each individual possesses. The extended period of growth and development characteristic of humans allows for a prolonged time period during which the environment can exert its effects on the developing organism.

The anthropological focus on growth and development has a long history dating back to the work of Franz Boas, the founder of American four-field anthropology. Boas is credited with discovering the features of the human growth curve (Figure 13.1). He demonstrated that the rate of human growth varies in typical patterns until adulthood, when physical growth ceases. Humans experience a period of very rapid growth after birth through infancy, followed by a gradually slower rate of growth during childhood. At adolescence, the rate of growth increases again during the adolescent growth spurt.

In addition to describing the long-term pattern of human growth, anthropologists have also demonstrated that within periods of growth, the actual growth process proceeds as a series of alternating bursts and relative quiet.[2]

---

[2] Lampl, M., Velhuis, J. D., & Johnson, M. L. (1992). Saltation and stasis: A model of human growth. *Science 258* (5083), 801–803.

developmental adaptation A permanent phenotypic variation derived from interaction between genes and the environment during the period of growth and development.

Peter Ellison

Reproductive biology and human health across cultures have been the focus of the work of biological anthropologist **Peter Ellison.** In the 1970s, Ellison first read Darwin's *Origin of Species* as a college student at St. John's College in Annapolis, Maryland. He found Darwin's text transformative and went to the University of Vermont to study biology; later he earned a doctorate in biological anthropology from Harvard, where he now runs a comprehensive program in reproductive ecology.

Ellison has pioneered techniques for hormonal analysis from saliva, and he uses this technique to monitor individuals' hormonal response to a variety of environmental stressors. This non-invasive technique has allowed Ellison to conduct hormonal studies throughout the world and to correlate hormonal levels with social events. People from long-term field sites in Congo, Poland, Japan, Nepal, and Paraguay have participated in this research, allowing Ellison to document the hormonal variation around biological events, such as egg implantation and breast-feeding, as well as cultural factors such as farm work or foraging.

He is especially interested in how behavior and social stimuli affect reproductive physiology. In Western societies, he has explored hormonal levels of males and females in response to stimuli, such as winning a championship or taking a stressful exam. He has also studied the relationship cancer development has to exercise and stress. In his recent book *On Fertile Ground,* Ellison illustrates how evolutionary forces have shaped human reproductive physiology into a system capable of precise responses to environmental stimuli.

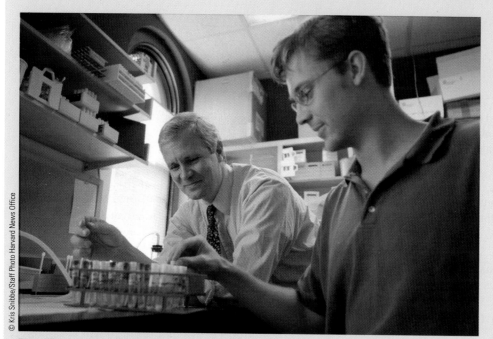

© Kris Snibbe/Staff Photo Harvard News Office

Peter Ellison (left) and Peter Gray discuss how male testosterone levels differ between married and single men and among men of different cultures.

When challenged by malnutrition, physical growth slows to permit immediate survival at the expense of height in adulthood. This adaptive mechanism may have negative consequences for subsequent generations as individuals who were malnourished as children have been shown to experience reduced reproductive success as adults.[3]

Boas also demonstrated differences in the growth of immigrant children in the United States compared to their parents. This work was the earliest documentation of the variable effects of different environments on the growth process. Presumably, immigrant children resemble their parents genetically; therefore, size differences between immigrant children and their parents could be attributed to the environment alone. This kind of difference, known as **a secular trend,** allows anthropologists to make inferences about environmental effects on growth and development.

For example, across the globe tremendous variation is seen in the age at menarche (first menstruation). Some of this variation can be attributed to genetically based population differences, while the remainder is due to environmental effects. The Bundi of New Guinea have the oldest average age (18) at menarche. An important theory accounting for the timing of sexual maturation ties age at menarche to the percentage of body fat possessed by growing individuals as a regulator of hormonal production. Hormones impact fertility into adulthood, but teasing apart the role of biology and culture with respect to hormones has proven to be complex. Take, for example, the case of androgen hormone levels, waist-to-hip ratio,

---

[3] Martorell, R. (1988). Body size, adaptation, and function. *GDP,* 335–347.

secular trend A physical difference among related people from distinct generations that allows anthropologists to make inferences about environmental effects on growth and development.

and fertility levels of women in high-powered careers. These women tend to have a more cylindrical shape, which could be because their bodies produce relatively more androgen than hourglass-shaped women. A higher androgen level, however, may be the reason for lower fertility among these women. High androgen levels may also represent a biological response to a specific work environment that ultimately impedes the fertility of women in high-powered careers.[4] The bottom line is that human hormonal systems are highly sensitive to a variety of environmental stimuli.

Over the past fifty years a secular trend of lower age at menarche has become evident in North America. Whether this secular trend is attributable to healthy or problematic environmental stimuli (such as childhood obesity or hormones in the environment) has yet to be determined. Biological anthropologist Peter Ellison works extensively on the connections between hormones and the environment—a subspecialty defined as reproductive ecology (see Anthropologist of Note).

While genetic and developmental adaptations are permanent parts of an adult's phenotype, **physiological adaptations,** short-term changes in response to a specific environmental stimulus, come and go. Along with cultural adaptations, these various biological mechanisms allow humans to be the only primate species to inhabit the entire globe. Over the course of our evolutionary history, most environmental stressors were climatic and geographic. Today, humans face a series of new environmental stressors of their own making.

Adaptation to High Altitude

High altitude differs from other natural environmental stressors because it is the least amenable to cultural adaptation. The major challenge of high altitude is the reduced availability of oxygen. Before the invention of oxygen masks and pressurized cabins in airplanes, there was no way to modify this environmental stressor.

When people speak of the air being "thinner" at high altitude, they are referring to the concentration (partial pressure) of oxygen available to the lungs, and so to the circulatory system. At high altitudes, the partial pressure of oxygen is sufficiently reduced so that most lowlanders experience severe oxygen deprivation (Figure 13.2).

Populations that have lived at high altitudes for generations, such as the Quechua Indians of the highlands of Peru and the Sherpa native to the Himalaya Mountains, possess a remarkable ability to tolerate oxygen deprivation, living and working at altitudes as high as 17,000 to 20,000 feet

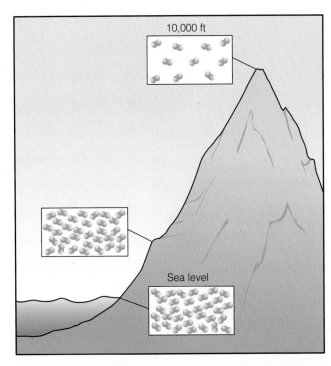

Figure 13.2 The amount of atmosphere above us determines the amount of pressure being exerted on oxygen molecules in the air. At sea level, the pressure of the atmosphere packs oxygen molecules more tightly together compared to the density of oxygen molecules at higher altitudes. This in turn impacts the ease at which oxygen can enter the lungs when we breathe.

above sea level. Physiological adaptation to the lower partial pressure of oxygen in the environment has rendered their body tissues resistant to oxygen deprivation.

Typical lowlanders can make both short- and long-term physiological adjustments to high altitude. In general, short-term changes help an individual avoid an immediate crisis, but the poor efficiency of these changes makes them difficult to sustain. Instead, long-term responses take over as the individual's physiological responses attain equilibrium with the environment. This process is known as **acclimatization.** Most lowlanders stepping off an airplane in Lima, Peru, will experience increased respiratory rate, cardiac output, and pulse rate. Their arteries will expand as blood pressure increases in order to get oxygen to the tissues. This kind of response cannot be maintained indefinitely. Instead, lowlanders acclimatize as their bodies begin to produce more red blood cells and hemoglobin in

physiological adaptation A short-term physiological change in response to a specific environmental stimulus. An immediate short-term response is not very efficient and is gradually replaced by a longer term response (see *acclimatization*).

acclimatization Long-term physiological adjustments made in order to attain an equilibrium with a specific environmental stimulus.

[4] Cashdan, E. (2008). Waist-to-hip ratio across cultures: Trade-offs between androgen- and estrogen-dependent traits. *Current Anthropology* 49 (6).

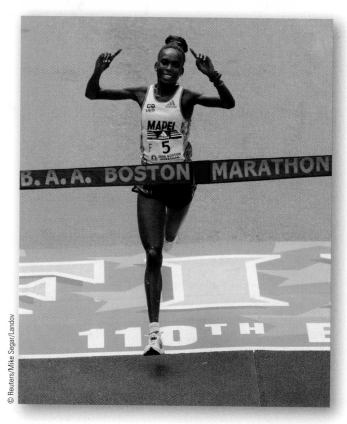

Observing that Kenyan runners, like Rita Jeptoo pictured here, have won most of the major marathon competitions over the past several decades, coaches have emulated the Kenyan approach. Adaptation to the hot, dry yet mountainous region leads to a long lean build (a product of the heat adaptation) and increased oxygen-carrying capacity. Although runners worldwide tend to be tall and lean, many athletes now train at high altitude so that when race day comes, their red blood cell count and hemoglobin levels allow them to carry more oxygen.

order to carry more oxygen. Because of differences in genetic makeup, individuals' physiological responses begin at varying altitudes.

Developmental adaptations are seen in individuals who spend their childhood period of growth and development at high altitude. Among the highland Quechua, for example, both the chest cavity and the right ventricle of the heart (which pushes blood to the lungs) are enlarged compared to lowland Quechua. This may have genetic underpinnings in that all Quechua experience a long period of growth and development compared to the average person in the United States.

Bergmann's rule The tendency for the bodies of mammals living in cold climates to be shorter and rounder than members of the same species living in warm climates.

Allen's rule The tendency for the bodies of mammals living in cold climates to have shorter appendages (arms and legs) than members of the same species living in warm climates.

Bergmann's Rule

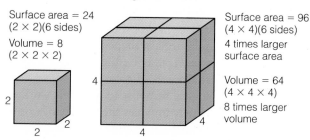

Surface area = 24
(2 × 2)(6 sides)
Volume = 8
(2 × 2 × 2)

Surface area = 96
(4 × 4)(6 sides)
4 times larger
surface area

Volume = 64
(4 × 4 × 4)
8 times larger
volume

Figure 13.3 Bergmann's rule refers to the observation that as overall body size increases, the amount of surface area increases less rapidly than the amount of volume. This accounts for the tendency for mammals living in cold climates to be more massive than members of the same species living in warmer climates. This allows for the conservation of heat in cold climates and its dissipation in warm climates.

The process of growth and development begins with reproduction, and high altitude exerts considerable effects on this process. For populations who have not adapted to high altitude, successful reproduction is not possible without some cultural interventions. For example, take the case of fertility among Spanish colonialists in the city of Potosi high in the Andes founded in order to mine the "mountain of silver" that towers above the community. For the first fifty-four years of this city's existence no Spanish child was born who survived childhood. Indigenous populations did not have these problems. To ensure reproductive success, Spanish women began the cultural practice of retreating to lower altitude for their pregnancies and the first year of their children's lives.[5]

At high altitudes cold stress is also a problem. As described in the previous chapter, a stocky body and short limbs help individuals conserve heat while the opposite facilitates heat loss. These phenomena have been formalized into two rules named after the naturalists who made such observations in mammals. **Bergmann's rule** refers to the tendency for the bodies of mammals living in cold climates to be more massive than members of the same species living in warm climates (Figure 13.3). **Allen's rule** refers to the tendency of mammals living in cold climates to have shorter appendages (arms and legs) than members of the same species living in warm climates (Figure 13.4).

Adaptation to Cold

Cold stress can exist without high altitude, as it does in the Arctic. In addition to the previously mentioned patterns of body and limb shape and size, other cold responses are also evident in Arctic populations.

---

[5] Wiley, A. S. (2004). *An ecology of high-altitude infancy: A biocultural perspective.* Cambridge, England: Cambridge University Press.

Allen's Rule

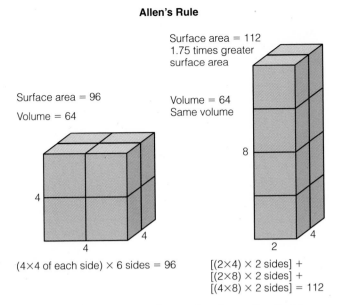

Surface area = 96
Volume = 64

Surface area = 112
1.75 times greater
surface area

Volume = 64
Same volume

8

4

4

4

2

4

(4×4 of each side) × 6 sides = 96

[(2×4) × 2 sides] +
[(2×8) × 2 sides] +
[(4×8) × 2 sides] = 112

Figure 13.4 Allen's rule refers to the observation that in two bodies that have the same volume, the one that is long and lean rather than short and squat will have a greater surface area. This accounts for the tendency for mammals living in cold climates to have shorter appendages (arms and legs) than the same species living in warmer climates. Heat can be dissipated through long limbs or conserved through short ones.

In extreme cold, the limbs need enough heat to prevent frostbite, but giving up heat to the periphery takes it away from the body core. Humans balance this through a cyclic expansion and contraction of the blood vessels of their limbs called the **hunting response**. Blood vessels oscillate between closing down to prevent heat loss and opening up to warm the hands and feet. When first exposed to cold as gloves are taken off, blood vessels immediately constrict. Initial alternations between open (warm) and shut (cold) and the corresponding temperature of the skin range dramatically. But the oscillations become smaller and more rapid, allowing a hunter to maintain the warmth-derived manual dexterity required for tying knots or positioning arrows.

Eskimos (including the Inuit) also deal with cold through a high metabolic rate: the rate at which their bodies burn energy. This may result from a diet high in protein and fat (whale blubber is the common food). In addition, genetic factors likely also contribute to Eskimos' high metabolic rate.

One short-term physiological response to cold is shivering. Shivering generates heat for the body quickly but cannot be maintained for long periods of time. Instead, as an individual acclimatizes to the cold, adjustments to diet, activity pattern, metabolic rate, and the circulatory system must occur.

Adaptation to Heat

The human body's primary physiological mechanism for coping with extreme heat is sweating or perspiring. Sweating is a process through which water released from sweat glands gives up body heat as the sweat evaporates. Therefore, water availability is a crucial aspect of adaptation to heat. Without drinking enough water to replace that which is lost through sweating, exposure to heat can be fatal.

Though there is some individual and population variation, each human has roughly 2 million sweat glands. These glands are spread out over a greater surface area on tall, thin bodies, facilitating water evaporation and heat loss. Thus Bergmann's and Allen's rules also apply to heat adaptation. The more surface area a body has, the more surface for the sweat glands. In addition, because heat is produced by unit of volume, having a high surface area-to-volume ratio is beneficial for heat loss. A long, slender body is best for dissipating heat. In a hot and humid environment such as a rainforest, water evaporation is a major challenge. In this environment, human populations have adapted to minimize heat production through a reduction in overall size while keeping a slender, lean build.

Human-Made Stressors of a Changing World

Traditionally, culture has played an important role in modifying natural stressors such as heat and cold. Housing, diet, and clothing traditions can alter such stressors considerably. But in today's globalizing world, the effects of culture are much more complex. Rather than alleviating physical stressors through simple cultural adaptations such as housing, diet, and clothing, cultural processes are *adding* stressors such as pollution, global warming, and exhaustion of the world's natural resources.

People cannot biologically adapt to these human-made stressors because biological change simply cannot keep pace with the rapid rate at which humans are changing the earth. Until human cultures cooperate to collectively address these global challenges, unnatural stressors will inevitably lead to sickness and suffering. An integrated, holistic anthropological perspective has much to contribute to alleviating if not eliminating these human-made stressors.

hunting response A cyclic expansion and contraction of the blood vessels of the limbs that balances releasing enough heat to prevent frostbite while maintaining heat in the body core.

Visual Counterpoint

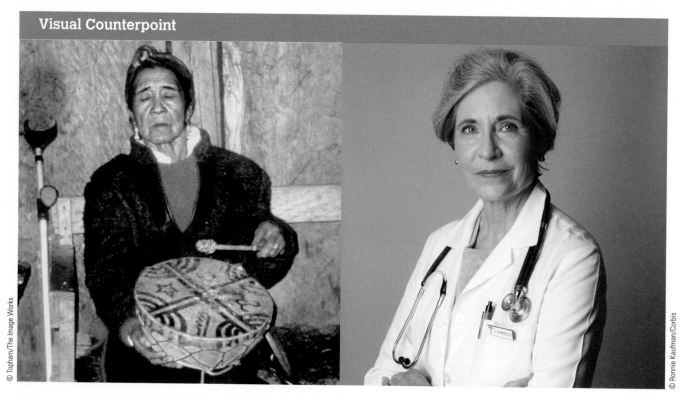

Shamans and biomedical doctors both rely upon manipulation of symbols to heal their patients. The physician's white coat is a powerful symbol of medical knowledge and authority that communicates to patients just as clearly as does the shaman's drum. Interestingly, medical schools in the United States are increasingly incorporating a "white coat" ceremony into medical education, conferring the power of the white coat onto new doctors.

The anthropological perspective holds that, beyond biology, cultural factors must be taken into account in any examination of human sickness and suffering. Human-made environments are shaped not only by local culture but by global political and economic systems. In short, anthropological perspectives are vital for successful adaptation to today's changing world.

The Development of Medical Anthropology

Medical anthropology, a specialization that cuts across all four fields of anthropology, contributes significantly to the understanding of sickness and suffering in the 21st century. Some of the earliest medical anthropologists were individuals trained as physicians and ethnographers who investigated the health beliefs and practices of peoples in "exotic"

places while also providing them with Western medicine. Medical anthropologists during this early period translated local experiences of sickness into the scientific language of Western biomedicine. Following a reevaluation of this ethnocentric approach in the 1970s, medical anthropology emerged as a specialization that brings theoretical and applied approaches from cultural and biological anthropology to the study of human health and sickness.

Medical anthropologists study **medical systems,** or patterned sets of ideas and practices relating to illness. Medical systems are cultural systems, similar to any other social institution. Medical anthropologists examine healing traditions and practices cross-culturally and the qualities all medical systems have in common. For example, the terms used by French cultural anthropologist Claude Lévi-Strauss to describe the healing powers of *shamans* (the name for indigenous healers, originally from Siberia, and now applied to many traditional healers) also apply to medical practices in Europe and North America.[6] In both situations, the healer has access to a world of restricted

medical system A patterned set of ideas and practices relating to illness.

[6] Lévi-Strauss, C. (1963). The sorcerer and his magic. In *Structural anthropology*. New York: Basic.

knowledge (spiritual or scientific) from which the average community member is excluded.

Medical anthropologists also use scientific models drawn from biological anthropology, such as evolutionary theory, to understand and improve human health. Moreover, they have turned their attention to the connections between human health and political and economic forces, both globally and locally. Because global flows of people, germs, cures, guns, and pollution underlie the distribution of sickness and health in the world today, a broad anthropological understanding of the origins of sickness is vital for alleviating human suffering.

Science, Illness, and Disease

During the course of medical anthropology's development as a distinct specialty within anthropology, the theoretical relationship between biological and cultural knowledge was transformed. The earliest research on medical systems was carried out by physician-anthropologists—individuals trained as medical doctors and as anthropologists who participated in the international public health movement emerging early in the 20th century. While delivering the medical care developed in Europe and North America, these physician-anthropologists simultaneously studied the health beliefs and practices of the cultures they were sent to help. Local cultural categories about sickness were translated into Western biomedical terms.

Initially, these Western approaches were thought to be culture-free depictions of human biology and were therefore used as an interpretive framework for examining the medical beliefs and practices of other cultures. Implicit in this work was the notion that the Western approach, with its supposed objectivity, was superior. Fieldwork conducted by cultural anthropologists, however, has shown that medical categories, like other aspects of a people's unique worldview, reflect the value system of their particular culture. For example, the Subinam people of Mindinao, one of the large islands of the Philippines, give different names to fungal infections of the skin depending on whether the infection is openly visible or hidden under clothes.[7] The biomedical and scientific categorization of fungal infections refers only to genus and species of the fungus.

In the 1970s the place of biological and cultural knowledge in medical anthropology was dramatically reorganized. The admission of mainland China to the United Nations in 1971, and the subsequent improvement of diplomatic and other relationships between that communist country and Western powers, played a role in this theoretical shift.[8] Cultural exchanges revealed a professional medical system in the East rivaling that of Western biomedicine in its scientific basis and technical feats. For example, the practice of open heart surgery in China, using only acupuncture needles as an anesthetic, challenged the assumption of biomedical superiority within anthropological thought. At this time scholars proposed that biomedicine is a cultural system, just like the medical systems in other cultures, and that it, too, is worthy of anthropological study.[9]

To effectively compare medical systems and health cross-culturally, medical anthropologists have made a theoretical distinction between the terms *disease* and *illness*. **Disease** refers to a specific pathology: a physical or biological abnormality. **Illness** refers to the meanings and elaborations given to particular physical states. Disease and illness do not necessarily overlap. An individual may experience illness without having a disease, or a disease may occur in the absence of illness.

In cultures with scientific medical systems, a key component of the social process of illness involves delineating human suffering in terms of biology. At times this extends to labeling an illness as a disease even though the biology is poorly understood. Think about alcoholism in the United States, for example. A person who is thought of as a drunk, partier, barfly, or boozer tends not to get sympathy from the rest of society. By contrast, a person struggling with the disease alcoholism receives cultural help from physicians, support from groups such as Alcoholics Anonymous, and financial aid from health insurance covering medical treatment. It matters little that the biology of this disease is still poorly understood and that alcoholism is treated through social support rather than expert manipulation of biology. By calling alcoholism a disease, it becomes a socially sanctioned and recognized illness within the dominant medical system of the United States. See this chapter's Globalscape for an innovative method of reducing the stigma and improving the health education of ordinary people in daily life.

---

[7] Frake, C. (1961). The diagnosis of disease among the Subinam of Mindinao. *American Anthropologist 63,* 113–132.

[8] Young, A. (1981). The creation of medical knowledge: Some problems in interpretation. *Social Science and Medicine 17,* 1205–1211.

[9] Kleinman, A. (1976). Concepts and a model for the comparison of medical systems as cultural systems. *Social Science and Medicine 12* (2B), 85–95.

disease A specific pathology; a physical or biological abnormality.

illness The meanings and elaborations given to a particular physical state.

Globalscape

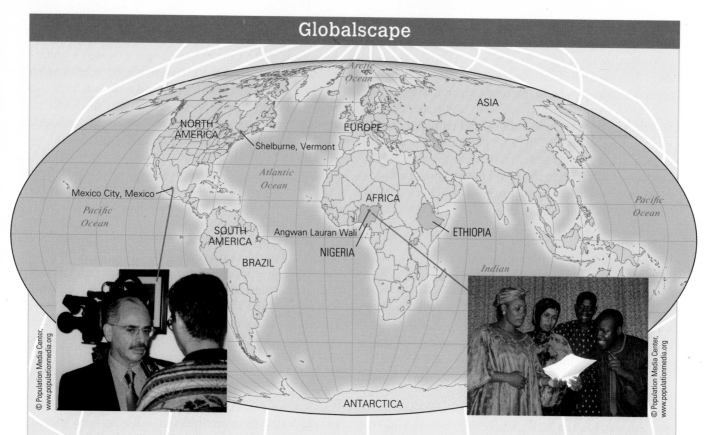

© Population Media Center, www.populationmedia.org

© Population Media Center, www.populationmedia.org

From Soap Opera to Clinic?

When Hajara Nasiru in Angwan Lauran Wali, Nigeria, listened to the radio soap opera *Gugar Goge* (*Tell It to Me Straight*), she learned something that changed her life. Created in Nigeria using a methodology developed originally in Mexico, the radio drama tells the story of 12-year-old Kande who is forced to marry a man more than twice her age. She soon becomes pregnant. After a prolonged labor, her baby dies, and Kande develops an obstetric fistula (a hole between either the rectum and vagina or the bladder and vagina) leading to incontinence, infection, and nerve damage. Kande's husband abandons her, but a neighbor brings her to the hospital in the nearby city of Zaira. After the fistula is repaired, Kande is able to return to her father's home in full health.

Like Kande, Hajara married young (at 15), and by the age of 25 she had experienced eight labors, lost five children, and developed a fistula with her last labor. After living with the debilitating discomfort for nine weeks, she invited her husband to listen to the soap opera too. *Gugar Goge* gave Hajara and her husband the information they needed. From the show, they learned that the fistula could be repaired and that Hajara need not suffer.

This radio drama is one of many created by the local branches of the Population Media Center (PMC), a U.S.-based international nongovernmental organization, headquartered in Shelburne, Vermont, that uses "entertainment-education for social change." PMC's methodology was developed by Mexican television producer Miguel Sabido, pictured above, whose *telenovelas* created dramatic social change across Mexico during the 1970s. For example, one program resulted in an eightfold increase in adult education and another led to a 50 percent increase in contraceptive use.

Population Media Center is bringing the Sabido methodology to the world, through work with local radio and television broadcasters, appropriate government ministries, and nongovernmental organizations. Their goal is to design and implement a comprehensive media strategy for addressing family and reproductive health issues. This collaborative process takes place locally with local constituents, identifying and addressing various health issues. These issues, once transformed into a radio drama such as *Gugar Goge,* are performed by professional local radio actors.

In addition to the individual success stories like Hajara's, success can be measured quantitatively at the country-wide level. For example, radio programs broadcast in Ethiopia in two different languages between 2002 and 2004 changed the reproductive health behavior in that region. The percentage of married women using contraception increased from 23 percent to 79 percent, and the birth rates for Ethiopia decreased by one whole child. Reduction in fertility is a vital part of the transition each society must make to achieve better overall health. In exit interviews at family planning clinics, a fourth of the 14,000 people surveyed cited the radio drama as their reason for coming.

Global Twister Would the Sabido method work in your community? Is it already at work? What health issues would you like to see embedded in soap operas?

Challenge Issue   Anthropologists take on the challenge of studying and describing cultures around the world and finding scientific explanations for their differences and similarities. Why do people think, feel, and act in certain ways—and find it wrong or impossible to do otherwise? Answers must come from fact-based knowledge about cultural diversity—knowledge that is not culture-bound and is widely recognized as significant. Over the years, anthropology has generated such knowledge through various theories and research methods. In particular, anthropologists obtain information through long-term, full-immersion fieldwork based on participant observation. Here we see anthropologist Lucas Bessire demonstrating his new handheld GPS receiver to Ayoreo Indian friends during a break in a hunting expedition in the dry forest of the Gran Chaco in Paraguay, South America—one involved moment among many in the all-engaging challenge of anthropological fieldwork.

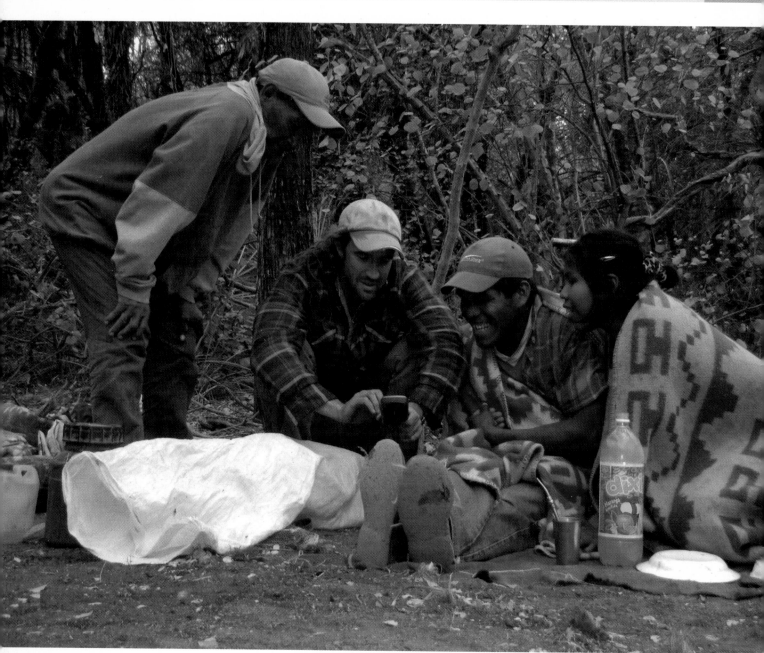

CHAPTER 15

Ethnographic Research: Its History, Methods, and Theories

Chapter Preview

How and Why Did Ethnographic Research Evolve?

In the early years of the discipline, many anthropologists documented traditional cultures they assumed would disappear due to disease, warfare, or acculturation imposed by colonialism, growing state power, or international market expansion. Some worked as government anthropologists, gathering data used to formulate policies concerning indigenous peoples or to help predict the behavior of enemies during wartime. After the colonial era ended in the 1960s, anthropologists established a code of ethics to ensure their research did not harm the groups they study. Today it is common for anthropologists to collaborate with minority groups and communities under siege and to assist in cultural revitalization efforts. Anthropological methods and knowledge are also applied to a range of globalization challenges, including economic development, conflict resolution, business, and politics. Finally, anthropologists do research to better understand what makes us tick and to explain cross-cultural differences and similarities.

How Is Research Related to Theory?

Data resulting from research, whether collected through fieldwork or another method, provide anthropologists with material needed to produce a comprehensive written (or filmed) ethnography, or description, of a culture. Moreover, they supply details that are fundamental to ethnology—cross-cultural comparisons and theories that explain different cultural beliefs and behaviors. Beyond offering explanations, theories help us frame new questions that deepen our understanding of cultural phenomena. Anthropologists have come up with a wide variety of theories, some of which have been replaced or improved by new information or better explanations. Gradually, much of what was puzzling or unknown about our complex species and its fascinating social and cultural diversity is exposed, revealed, or clarified through theoretically informed research.

What Are Ethnographic Research Methods?

Although anthropology relies on various research methods, its hallmark is extended fieldwork in a particular community or cultural group. This fieldwork features participant observation in which the researcher not only observes and documents the daily life of the community being studied but also participates in that life. Typically, an anthropologist's initial fieldwork is carried out solo and lasts a full year. However, some anthropologists work in teams, and some field stays may be briefer or longer. It is not uncommon for anthropologists to return to their field sites periodically over the course of several decades.

As briefly discussed in Chapter 1, cultural anthropology has two main scholarly components: *ethnography* and *ethnology*. Ethnography is a detailed description of a particular culture primarily based on fieldwork. Ethnology is the study and analysis of different cultures from a comparative or historical point of view, utilizing ethnographic accounts and developing anthropological theories that help explain why certain important differences or similarities occur among groups.

Historically, anthropology focused on non-Western traditional peoples whose languages were not written down—people whose communication was often direct and face to face, and whose knowledge about the past was based primarily on oral tradition. Even in societies where writing exists, not much of what is of interest to anthropologists is recorded in writing. Thus anthropologists have made a point of going to these places in person to observe and experience peoples and their cultures firsthand. This is called *fieldwork*.

Today, anthropological fieldwork takes place not only in small-scale communities in distant corners of the world, but also in modern urban neighborhoods in industrial or postindustrial societies. Anthropologists can be found doing fieldwork in a wide range of places and within a host of diverse groups and institutions, including global corporations, nongovernmental organizations (NGOs), migrant labor communities, and peoples scattered and dispersed because of natural or human-made catastrophes.

In our unsettled and globalizing world, where long-standing boundaries between cultures are being erased, new social networks and cultural constructs are emerging, made possible by long-distance mass transportation and communication technologies. Anthropologists today are adjusting their research methods to better describe, explain, and understand these complex but fascinating dynamics in the rapidly changing human condition of the 21st century.

History of Ethnographic Research and Its Uses

Anthropology emerged as a formal discipline during the heyday of colonialism (1870s–1950s) when many European anthropologists focused on the study of traditional peoples and their cultures in the colonies overseas. For instance, French anthropologists did most of their research in North and West Africa and Southeast Asia; British

anthropologists in southern and East Africa; Dutch anthropologists in what has become Indonesia, Western New Guinea, and Suriname; and Belgian anthropologists in Congo of Africa.

Meanwhile, anthropologists in North America focused primarily on their own countries' Native Indian and Eskimo communities—usually residing on tracts of land known as reservations, or in remote Arctic villages. Because these indigenous groups are surrounded by a dominant society that has settled on what used to be exclusively Native lands, and they are no longer completely independent from that larger society's national government, their reservations are sometimes described as *internal colonies*.

At one time it was common practice to compare peoples still pursuing traditional lifeways—based on hunting, fishing, gathering, and/or small-scale farming or herding—with the ancient prehistoric ancestors of Europeans and to categorize the cultures of these traditional peoples as "primitive." Although anthropologists have long abandoned such ethnocentric terminology, many others still think and speak of these traditional cultures as underdeveloped or even undeveloped. This misconception helped state societies, commercial enterprises, and other powerful outside groups justify expanding their activities and invading the lands belonging to these peoples, often exerting overwhelming pressure on them to change their ancestral ways.

Salvage Ethnography or Urgent Anthropology

In this disturbing and often violent historical context, the survival of thousands of traditional communities worldwide has been at stake. In fact, many of these threatened peoples have become physically extinct. Others survived but were forced to surrender their territories or their way of life. Although anthropologists have seldom been able to prevent such tragic events, they have tried to make a record of these cultural groups. This important early anthropological practice of documenting endangered cultures was initially called *salvage ethnography* and later became known as **urgent anthropology.**

By the late 1800s, many European and North American museums were sponsoring anthropological expeditions to collect cultural artifacts and other material remains (including skulls, bones, utensils, weapons, clothing, and ceremonial objects), as well as vocabularies, myths, and other relevant cultural data. Early anthropologists also began taking ethnographic photographs, and by the 1890s some began shooting documentary films or recording the speech, songs, and music of these so-called vanishing peoples.

urgent anthropology Ethnographic research that documents endangered cultures; also known as salvage ethnography.

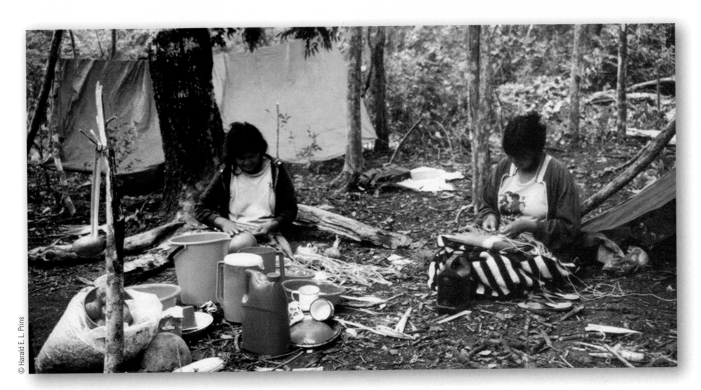

© Harald E. L. Prins

Until recently, Ayoreo Indian bands lived largely isolated in the Gran Chaco, a vast wilderness in South America's heartland. One by one, these migratory foragers have been forced to "come out" due to outside encroachment on their habitat. Today, most dispossessed Ayoreo Indians find themselves in different stages of acculturation. This photo shows Ayoreo women of Zapocó in Bolivia's forest. Dressed in Western hand-me-downs and surrounded by plastic from the modern society that is pressing in on them, they weave natural plant fibers into traditionally patterned bags to sell for cash, while men make money by cutting trees for logging companies.

Although the first generation of anthropologists often began their careers working for museums, those coming later were academically trained in the emerging discipline and became active in newly founded anthropology departments. In North America, most of the latter did their fieldwork on tribal reservations where indigenous communities were falling apart in the face of disease, poverty, and despair brought on by pressures of forced cultural change. These anthropologists interviewed American Indian elders still able to recall the ancestral way of life prior to the disruptions forced upon them. The researchers also collected oral histories, traditions, myths, legends, and other information, as well as old artifacts for research, preservation, and public display.

Beyond documenting social practices, beliefs, artifacts, and other disappearing cultural features, anthropologists also sought to reconstruct abandoned traditional lifeways remembered only by surviving elders. Although anthropological theories have come and gone during the past hundred years, the plight of indigenous peoples struggling for cultural survival endures. Anthropologists can and still do contribute to that effort, assisting in cultural preservation efforts. In that work, utilizing a variety of new methods, they can tap into and continue to build on

a professional legacy of salvage ethnography and urgent anthropology.

Acculturation Studies

Since the 1930s, anthropologists have been studying asymmetrical (sharply uneven) cultural contact or *acculturation*. This is the often disruptive process of cultural change occurring in traditional societies as they come in contact with more powerful state societies—in particular, industrialized or capitalist societies.

Typically, as the dominant (often foreign) power establishes its superiority, local indigenous cultures are made to appear inferior, ridiculous, or otherwise not worth preserving; and they are often forced to adopt the ways of the dominant society pressing in on them. Government-sponsored programs designed to compel indigenous groups to abandon their ancestral languages and cultural traditions for those of dominant society have ripped apart the unique cultural fabric of one group after another. These programs left many indigenous families impoverished, demoralized, and desperate.

One of the first anthropologists to study acculturation was Margaret Mead in her 1932 fieldwork among the Omaha Indians of Nebraska. In that research (one of many projects she undertook), she focused on community breakdown and cultural disintegration of this traditional American Indian tribe. In the course of the 20th century, numerous other anthropologists carried out acculturation studies in Asia, Africa, Australia, Oceania, the Americas, and even in parts of Europe, thereby greatly contributing to our knowledge of complex and often disturbing processes of cultural change.

Applied Anthropology

In identifying the disintegrating effects of asymmetrical cultural contact, acculturation studies gave birth to *applied anthropology*—the use of anthropological knowledge and methods to solve practical problems in communities confronting new challenges. For traditional groups in colonized territories or on reservations, government officials began looking at how anthropological research might help these communities struggling with imposed economic, social, and political changes. Voicing the need for an applied anthropology to address the negative effects of colonial policies, Polish-born British anthropologist Bronislaw Malinowski commented, "The anthropologist who is unable to register the tragic errors committed at times with the best intentions remains an antiquarian covered with academic dust and in fool's paradise."[1]

In 1937 the British government set up an anthropological research institute in what is now Zambia to study the impact of international markets on Central Africa's traditional societies. In the next decade, anthropologists worked on a number of problem-oriented studies throughout Africa, including the disruptive effects of the mining industry and labor migration on domestic economies and cultures.

Facing similar issues in North America, the U.S. Bureau of Indian Affairs (BIA), which oversees federally recognized tribes on Indian reservations, established an applied anthropology branch in the mid-1930s. Beyond studying the problems of acculturation, the handful of applied anthropologists hired by the BIA were to identify culturally appropriate ways for the U.S. government to introduce social and economic development programs to reduce poverty, promote literacy, and solve a host of other problems on the reservations.

In 1941, the international Society for Applied Anthropology was founded to promote scientific investigation of the principles controlling human relations and the encouragement of their practical application. Today, many academically trained anthropologists specialize in applied research, working for a variety of local, regional, national, and international institutions, in particular nongovernmental organizations (NGOs), and are active on numerous fronts in every corner of the world.

Studying Cultures at a Distance

During World War II (1939–1945) and the early years of the Cold War (over forty years of political hostility and sharp conflict in diplomacy, economics, and ideology between blocks of capitalist countries led by the United States and rival blocks of communist countries led by Russia), some anthropologists shifted their attention from small-scale traditional communities to modern state societies. Aiming to discover basic personality traits, or psychological profiles, shared by the majority of the people in modern state societies, several U.S. and British anthropologists became involved in a wartime government program of "national character" studies. Such studies were considered useful in efforts to better understand and deal with the newly declared enemy states of Japan and Germany (in World War II) and later Russia and others.

During wartime, on-location ethnographic fieldwork was impossible in enemy societies and challenging at best in most other foreign countries. So, Mead and her close friend Ruth Benedict (one of her former professors at Columbia University), along with several other anthropologists, developed innovative techniques for studying "culture at a distance." Their methods included the analysis of newspapers, literature, photographs, and popular films. They also collected information through structured interviews with immigrants and refugees from the enemy nations, as well as foreigners from other countries.[2]

For instance, the efforts of these anthropologists to portray the "national character" of peoples inhabiting distant countries included investigating topics such as child-rearing beliefs, attitudes, and practices, in conjunction with examining print or film materials for recurrent cultural themes and values. This cultural knowledge was also used for propaganda and psychological warfare. After the war, some of the information and insights based on such long-distance anthropological studies were found useful in temporarily governing the occupied territories and dealing with newly liberated populations in other parts of the world.

---

[1] In Mair, L. (1957). *An introduction to social anthropology* (p. 4). London: Oxford University Press. See also Malinowski, B. (1945). *The dynamics of culture change: An inquiry into race relations in Africa* (pp. 1–13). New Haven and London: Yale University Press.

[2] Mead, M., & Métraux, R. (Eds.). (1953). *The study of culture at a distance.* Chicago: University of Chicago Press.

Studying Contemporary State Societies

Although there were theoretical flaws in the national character studies and methodological problems in studying cultures at a distance, anthropological research on contemporary state societies was more than just a war-related endeavor. Even when anthropologists devoted themselves primarily to researching non-Western small-scale communities, they recognized that a generalized understanding of human relations, ideas, and behavior depends upon knowledge of *all* cultures and peoples, including those in complex, large-scale industrial societies organized in political states, such as modern France or the United States. Already during the years of the Great Depression (1930s) several anthropologists worked in their own countries in settings ranging from factories to farming communities and suburban neighborhoods.

One interesting example of an early anthropologist doing research on the home front is Hortense Powdermaker. Born in Philadelphia, Powdermaker went to London to study anthropology under Malinowski and did her first major ethnographic fieldwork among Melanesians in the southern Pacific. When she returned to the United States, she researched a racially segregated town in Mississippi in the 1930s.[3] During the next decade, she focused on combating U.S. dominant society's racism against African Americans and other ethnic minorities.

While in the South, Powdermaker became keenly aware of the importance of the mass media in shaping people's worldviews.[4] To further explore this ideological force in modern culture, she cast her critical eye on the domestic film industry and did a year of fieldwork in Hollywood (1946–1947).

As Powdermaker was wrapping up her Hollywood research, several other anthropologists were launching other kinds of studies in large-scale societies. Convinced that governments and colonial administrations, as well as new global institutions such as the United Nations (founded in 1945), could and should benefit from anthropological insights, Ruth Benedict and Margaret Mead initiated a team project in comparative research on contemporary cultures based at Columbia University in New York (1947–1952).

In 1950, Swiss anthropologist Alfred Métraux put together an international team of U.S., French, and Brazilian researchers to study contemporary race relations in Brazil. The project, sponsored by UNESCO (the United Nations Education, Science, and Culture Organization), was part of the UN's global campaign against racial prejudice and discrimination. Headquartered in Paris, Métraux selected this South American country as a research site primarily for comparative purposes. Like the United States, it was a former European colony with a large multi-ethnic population and a long history of black slavery. Brazil had abolished slavery twenty-five years later than the United States but had made much more progress in terms of its race relations. In contrast to the racially segregated United States, Brazil was believed to be an ideal example of harmonious, tolerant, and overall positive cross-racial relations. The research findings yielded unexpected results, showing that dark-skinned Brazilians of African descent did face systemic social and economic discrimination—albeit not in the political and legal form of racial segregation that pervaded the United States at the time.[5]

In 1956 and 1957, anthropologist Julian Steward left the United States to supervise an anthropological research team in developing countries such as Kenya, Nigeria, Peru, Mexico, Japan, Myanmar (Burma), Malaya, and Indonesia. His goal was to study the comparative impact of industrialization and urbanization upon these different populations. Other anthropologists launched similar projects in other parts of the world.

Peasant Studies

In the 1950s, as anthropologists widened their scope to consider the impact of complex state societies on the traditional indigenous groups central to early anthropological study, some zeroed in on peasant communities. Peasants represent an important social category, standing midway between modern industrial society and traditional subsistence foragers, herders, farmers, and fishers. Part of larger, more complex societies, peasant communities exist worldwide, and peasants number in the many hundreds of millions.

Peasantry represents the largest social category of our species so far. Because peasant unrest over economic and social problems fuels political instability in many developing countries, anthropological studies of these rural populations in Latin America, Africa, Asia, and elsewhere are considered significant and practical.[6] In addition to improving policies aimed at social and economic development in rural communities, anthropological peasant studies may offer insights into how to deal with peasants resisting challenges to their traditional way of life. Such anthropological research may be useful in promoting

[3] Powdermaker, H. (1939). *After freedom: A cultural study in the Deep South.* New York: Viking.

[4] Wolf, E. R., & Trager, G. L. (1971). Hortense Powdermaker 1900–1970. *American Anthropologist 73* (3), 784.

[5] Prins, H.E.L., & Krebs, E. (2006). Toward a land without evil: Alfred Métraux as UNESCO anthropologist 1948–1962. In *60 years of UNESCO history. Proceedings of the international symposium in Paris, 16–18 November 2005.* Paris: UNESCO.

[6] Redfield, R. (1953). *The primitive world and its transformations* (pp. 40–41). Ithaca, NY: Cornell University Press; Wolf, E. R. (1966). *Peasants* (p. 1). Englewood Cliffs, NJ: Prentice-Hall.

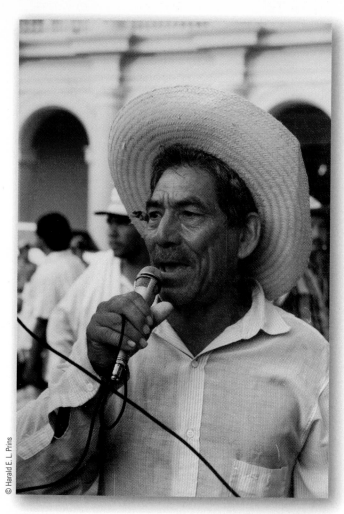

Peasant studies came to the fore during the 1950s as anthropologists began investigating rural peoples in state societies and the impact of capitalism on traditional small-scale communities. Here a Guarani-speaking peasant leader addresses a crowd in front of the presidential palace in Paraguay's capital city of Asunción at a massive protest rally against land dispossession.

social justice by helping to solve, manage, or avoid social conflicts and political violence, including rebellions and guerrilla warfare or insurgencies.[7]

Advocacy Anthropology and Studying Up

By the 1960s, European colonial powers had relinquished almost all of their overseas domains. Many anthropologists turned their attention to the newly independent countries in Africa and Asia, while others focused on South and Central America. However, as anti-Western sentiment and political upheaval seriously complicated fieldwork in many parts of the world, significant numbers of anthropologists investigated important issues of cultural change and conflict inside Europe and North America. Many of these issues, which remain focal points to this day, involve immigrants and refugees coming from places where anthropologists have conducted research.

Some anthropologists have gone beyond studying such groups to playing a role in helping them adjust to their new circumstances—an example of applied anthropology. Others have become advocates for peasant communities, ethnic or religious minorities, or indigenous groups struggling to hold onto their ancestral lands, natural resources, and customary ways of life. Both focus on identifying, preventing, or solving problems and challenges in groups that form part of complex societies and whose circumstances and affairs are conditioned or even determined by powerful outside institutions or corporations over which they generally have little or no control.

Although anthropologists have privately long championed the rights of indigenous peoples and other cultural groups under siege, one of the first anthropological research projects explicitly and publicly addressing the quest for social justice and cultural survival took place among the Meskwaki, or Fox Indians, on their reservation in the state of Iowa (1948–1959). Based on long-term fieldwork with this North American Indian community, anthropologist Sol Tax challenged government-sponsored applied anthropological research projects and proposed instead that researchers work directly with "disadvantaged, exploited, and oppressed communities [to help *them*] identify and solve their [*own*] problems."[8]

Over the past few decades, anthropologists committed to social justice and human rights have become actively and increasingly involved in efforts to assist indigenous groups, peasant communities, and ethnic minorities. Today, most anthropologists committed to community-based and politically involved research refer to their work as **advocacy anthropology.**

Anthropologist Robert Hitchcock has practiced advocacy anthropology for over three decades. Specializing in development issues, he has focused primarily on land rights, as well as the social, economic, and cultural rights, of indigenous peoples in southern Africa—especially Bushmen (San, Basarwa) groups in Botswana. Hitchcock's

---

[7] Firth, R. (1946). *Malay fishermen: Their peasant economy* (pp. ix–x). London: Kegan Paul; see also Wolf, E. R. (1969). *Peasant wars of the twentieth century* (pp. ix–xiii, 276–302). New York: Harper & Row.

advocacy anthropology Research that is community based and politically involved.

---

[8] Field, L. W. (2004). Beyond "applied" anthropology. In T. Biolsi (Ed.), *A companion to the anthropology of American Indians* (pp. 472–489). Oxford: Blackwell; see also Lurie, N. O. (1973). Action anthropology and the American Indian. In *Anthropology and the American Indian: A symposium* (p. 6). San Francisco: Indian Historical Press.

Dr. Rodolfo Stavenhagen, UN Special Rapporteur on the Situation of Human Rights and Fundamental Freedom of the Indigenous People. Here he appears with Victoria Tauli-Corpuz, chairperson of the UN Permanent Forum on Indigenous Issues, at a press conference near Manilla in the Phillipines in 2007.

work has involved helping Bushmen to ensure their rights to land—for foraging, pasturing, farming, and income-generation purposes—in the face of development projects aimed at setting aside land for the ranching, mining, or conservation interests of others. He helped draw up legislation on subsistence hunting in Botswana, making it the only country in Africa that allows broad-based hunting rights for indigenous peoples who forage for part of their livelihood.[9]

Today's most wide-ranging advocacy anthropologist is Rodolfo Stavenhagen, the UN's specialist on indigenous rights. A research professor at the Colegio de Mexico since 1965, he is founder and first president of the Mexican Academy of Human Rights. Stavenhagen leads investigations on the human rights and fundamental freedoms of indigenous peoples throughout the world.

Because of anthropology's mission to gain a more comprehensive understanding of the human condition in its full cross-cultural range and complexity, not just in distant places or at the margins of our own societies, some scholars have urged ethnographic research in the centers of political and economic power in the world's dominant societies. This widening of the anthropological scope is especially important for applied and advocacy anthropologists doing research on groups or communities embedded in larger and more complex processes of state-level politics

and economics or even transnational levels of global institutions and multinational corporations. Of particular note in this effort is anthropologist Laura Nader. Coining the term *study up,* she has called upon anthropologists to focus on Western elites, government bureaucracies, global corporations, philanthropic foundations, media empires, business clubs, and so on.

Studying up is easier said than done, because it is a formidable challenge to do participant observation in such well-guarded circles. And when these elites are confronted with research projects or findings not of their liking, they have the capacity and political power to stop or seriously obstruct the research or the dissemination of its results.

Globalization and Multi-Sited Ethnography

As noted in Chapter 1, the impact of globalization is everywhere. Distant localities are becoming linked in such a way that local events and situations are shaped by forces and activities occurring thousands of miles away, and vice versa. Connected by modern transportation, world trade, finance capital, transnational labor pools, and information superhighways, even the most geographically remote communities become increasingly interdependent. Indeed, all of humanity now exists in what we refer to in this text as a *globalscape*—a worldwide interconnected landscape with multiple intertwining and overlapping peoples and cultures on the move.

One consequence of globalization is the formation of *diasporic* populations (*diaspora* is a Greek word,

---

[9] Hitchcock, R. K., & Enghoff, M. (2004). *Capacity-building of first people of the Kalahari, Botswana: An evaluation.* Copenhagen: International Work Group for Indigenous Affairs.

originally meaning "scattering"), living and working far from their original homeland. Some diasporic groups feel uprooted and fragmented, but others are able to transcend vast distances and stay in touch with family and friends through communication technologies. With Internet access to blogs and other sources of news, combined with e-mail, text messaging, and a variety of social media platforms, geographically dispersed individuals spend more and more of their time in cyberspace.[10] This electronically mediated environment enables people who are far from home to remain informed, to maintain their social networks, and even to hold onto a historical sense of ethnic identity that culturally distinguishes them from those with whom they share their daily routines in actual geographic space..

Globalization has given rise to a new trend in anthropological research and analysis known as **multi-sited ethnography**—the investigation and documentation of peoples and cultures embedded in the larger structures of a globalizing world, utilizing a range of methods in various locations of time and space. Engaged in such mobile ethnography, researchers seek to capture the emerging dimension of the global by following individual actors, organizations, objects, images, stories, conflicts, and even pathogens as they move about in various interrelated transnational situations and locations.[11]

An example of multi-sited ethnographic research on a diasporic ethnic group is a recent study on transnational Han Chinese identities by Chinese American anthropologist Andrea Louie. Louie's fieldwork carried her to an array of locations in San Francisco, Hong Kong, and southern China—including her ancestral home in the Cantonese village Tiegang in Guangdong Province. Her paternal great-grandfather left the village in the 1840s, crossing the Pacific Ocean to work on railroad construction during the California Gold Rush. But other family members remained in their ancestral homeland. Here, Louie describes her research investigating Chinese identities from different and changing perspectives:

> My fieldwork on Chinese identities employed a type of mobile [ethnography] aimed at examining

Courtesy of Andrea Louie

A young girl born in China shares her China adoption workbook with anthropologist Andrea Louie at the child's home in St. Louis, Missouri. The interactive workbook encouraged the girl to draw a picture of what she imagined her birth mother looked like, to write down questions about her birth family, and to document the process of becoming a family through adoption. She received the book from her mother on her seventh "Gotcha Day," which marks the day that they first "got" each other in Wuhan, China. Andrea Louie helped film that important moment when she traveled to China with several adoptive parents on a fieldwork trip that was part of her larger multi-sited project on Chinese adoptee identities.

> various parts of a "relationship" being forged anew across national boundaries that draws on metaphors of shared heritage and place. In my investigation of "Chineseness" I conducted participant observation and interviews in San Francisco with Chinese American participants of the In Search of Roots program,[12] as well as later in China when they visited their ancestral villages and participated in government-sponsored Youth Festivals. . . . I interviewed people in their homes, and apartments; in cafes, culture centers, and McDonald's restaurants; and in rural Chinese villages and on jet planes, focusing on various moments and contexts of interaction within which multiple and often discrepant discourses of Chineseness are brought together.[13]

Also emerging in multi-sited ethnography are greater interdisciplinary approaches to fieldwork, bringing in theoretical ideas and research methods from cultural studies, media studies, and mass communication. One example is

---

[10] Appadurai, A. (1996). *Modernity at large: Cultural dimensions of globalization.* Minneapolis: University of Minnesota Press.

[11] Marcus, G. (1995). Ethnography in/of the world system: The emergence of multi-sited ethnography. *Annual review of anthropology 24,* 95–117; Robben, A.C.G.M., & Sluka, J. A. (Eds.). (2007). *Ethnographic fieldwork: An anthropological reader.* Malden, MA: Blackwell.

multi-sited ethnography The investigation and documentation of peoples and cultures embedded in the larger structures of a globalizing world, utilizing a range of methods in various locations of time and space.

[12] This program, run by organizations in Guangzhou and San Francisco, provides an opportunity for young adults (ages 17 to 25) of Cantonese descent to visit their ancestral villages in China.

[13] Louie, A. (2004). *Chineseness across borders: Renegotiating Chinese identities in China and the United States* (pp. 8–9). Durham and London: Duke University Press.

the emergence of ethnographic studies of online "imagined communities" or *cyberethnography.*

Even in the fast-changing, globalizing world of the 21st century, core ethnographic research methods developed about a century ago continue to be relevant and revealing. New technologies have been added to the anthropologist's tool kit, but the hallmarks of our discipline—holistic research through fieldwork with participant observation—is still a valued and productive tradition. Having presented a sweeping historical overview of shifting anthropological research challenges and strategies, we turn now to the topic of research methods.

Doing Ethnography

Every culture comprises underlying rules or standards that are rarely obvious. A major challenge to the anthropologist is to identify and analyze those rules. Fundamental to the effort is **ethnographic fieldwork**—extended on-location research to gather detailed and in-depth information on a society's customary ideas, values, and practices through participation in its collective social life.

While it is true that the scope of cultural anthropology has expanded to include urban life in complex industrial and postindustrial societies, ethnographic methods developed for fieldwork in traditional small-scale societies continue to be central to anthropological research in all types of communities. The methodology still includes personal observation of and participation in the everyday activities of the community, along with interviews, mapping, collection of genealogical data, and recording of sounds and visual images. It all begins with selecting a research site and a research problem or question.

Site Selection and Research Question

Anthropologists usually work outside their own culture, society, or ethnic group, most often in a foreign country. Although it has much to offer, anthropological study within one's own society may present special problems, as described by noted British anthropologist Sir Edmund Leach:

> Surprising though it may seem, fieldwork in a cultural context of which you already have intimate firsthand experience seems to be much more difficult than fieldwork which is approached from the naïve viewpoint of a total stranger. When anthropologists study facets of their own society their vision seems to become distorted by prejudices

which derive from private rather than public experience.[14]

For this reason, most successful anthropological studies of societies to which the researchers themselves belong are done by individuals who first worked in some other culture. The more one learns of other cultures, the more one gains a fresh and more revealing perspective on one's own.

But wherever the site, research requires advance planning that usually includes obtaining funding and securing permission from the community to be studied (and, where mandated, permission from government officials as well). If possible, researchers make a preliminary trip to the site to make these and other arrangements before moving there for more extended research. After exploring the local conditions and circumstances, they have the opportunity to better define their specific research question or problem. For instance, what is the psychological impact of a new highway on members of a traditionally isolated farming community? Or how does the introduction of new electronic media such as cell phones influence long-established gender relations in cultures with religious restrictions on social contact between men and women?

Preparatory Research

Before heading into the field, anthropologists do preparatory research. This includes delving into any existing written, visual, or sound information available about the people and place one has chosen to study. It may involve contacting and interviewing others who have some knowledge about or experience with the community, region, or country.

Because anthropologists must be able to communicate with the people they have chosen to study, they will also have to learn the language used in the community selected for fieldwork. Many of the more than 6,000 languages currently spoken in the world have now been recorded and written down, especially during the past century, so it is possible to learn some foreign languages prior to fieldwork. However, as in the early days of the discipline, some of today's anthropologists do research among peoples whose native languages have not

---

[14] Leach, E. (1982). *Social anthropology* (p. 124). Glasgow: Fontana.

ethnographic fieldwork Extended on-location research to gather detailed and in-depth information on a society's customary ideas, values, and practices through participation in its collective social life.

yet been written down. In this case, the researcher may be able to find someone who is minimally bilingual to help the anthropologist gain some proficiency with the language. Another possibility is to first learn an already recorded and closely related language, which provides some elementary communication skills during the early phase of the actual fieldwork.

Finally, anthropologists prepare for fieldwork by studying theoretical, historical, ethnographic, and other literature relevant to the research. For instance, anthropologists interested in understanding violence, both between and within groups, will read studies describing and theoretically explaining conflicts such as wars, insurgencies, raids, feuds, vengeance killings, and so on. Having delved into the existing literature, they may then formulate a theoretical framework and research question to guide them in their fieldwork. Such was the case when anthropologist Napoleon Chagnon applied sociobiological theory to his study of violence within Yanomami Indian communities in South America's tropical rainforest, suggesting that males with an aggressive reputation

as killers are reproductively more successful than those without such a status.[15]

Christopher Boehm took a different theoretical approach in his research on blood revenge among Slavic mountain people in Montenegro. He framed his research question in terms of the ecological function of this violent tradition, as it regulated relations between groups competing for survival in a harsh environment with scarce natural resources.[16]

Participant Observation: Ethnographic Tools and Aids

Once in the field, anthropologists rely on *participant observation*—a research method in which one learns about a group's behaviors and beliefs through social

---

[15] Chagnon, N. A. (1988). Life histories, blood revenge, and warfare in a tribal population. *Science 239*, 935–992.

[16] Boehm, C. (1984). *Blood revenge.* Lawrence: University of Kansas Press.

© Julia Jean

The hallmark research methodology for anthropologists is participant observation—illustrated by this photo of anthropologist Julia Jean (center), who is both observing *and* participating in a Hindu ritual at a temple for the Goddess Kamakhya in northeastern India.

involvement and personal observation within the community, as well as interviews and discussion with individual members of the group over an extended stay in the community. This work requires an ability to socially and psychologically adapt to a strange community with a different way of life. Keen personal observation skills are also essential, employing *all* the senses—sight, touch, smell, taste, and hearing—in order to perceive collective life in the other culture.

When participating in an unfamiliar culture, anthropologists are often helped by one or more generous individuals in the village or neighborhood. They may also be taken in by a family, and through participation in the daily routine of a household, they will gradually become familiar with the community's basic shared cultural features.

Anthropologists may also formally enlist the assistance of **key consultants**—members of the society being studied who provide information to help researchers understand the meaning of what they observe. (Early anthropologists referred to such individuals as *informants*.) Just as parents guide a child toward proper behavior, so do these insiders help researchers unravel the mysteries of what at first is a strange, puzzling, and unpredictable world. To compensate local individuals for their help in making anthropologists feel welcome in the community and gain access to the treasure troves of inside information, fieldworkers may thank them for their time and expertise with goods, services, or cash.

Beyond the skills and resources noted above, an anthropologist's most essential ethnographic tools in the field are notebooks, pen/pencil, camera, and sound and video recorders. Increasingly, researchers also use laptop computers equipped with data processing programs.

Although researchers may focus on a particular cultural aspect or issue, they will consider the culture as a whole for the sake of context. This holistic and integrative approach—a hallmark of anthropology—requires being tuned in to nearly countless details of daily life—both the ordinary and the extraordinary. By taking part in community life, anthropologists learn why and how events are organized and carried out. Through alert and sustained participation—carefully watching, questioning, listening, and analyzing over a period of time—they can usually identify, explain, and often predict a group's behavior.

Data Gathering:
The Ethnographer's Approach

Information collected by ethnographers falls into two main categories: quantitative and qualitative data. **Quantitative data** consist of statistical or measurable information, such as population density, demographic composition of people and animals, and the number and size of houses; the hours worked per day; the types and quantities of crops grown; the amount of carbohydrates or animal protein consumed per individual; the quantity of wood, dung, or other kinds of fuel used to cook food or heat dwellings; the number of children born out of wedlock; the ratio of spouses born and raised within or outside the community; and so on.

Qualitative data concern nonstatistical information about such features as settlement patterns, natural resources, social networks of kinship relations, customary beliefs and practices, personal life histories, and so on. Often, these nonquantifiable data are the most important part of ethnographic research because they capture the essence of a culture; this information provides us with deeper insights into the unique lives of different peoples, helping us truly understand what, why, and how they feel, think, and act in their own distinctive ways.

Beyond the generalities of participant observation, how exactly do ethnographers gather data? Field methods include formal and informal interviewing, mapping, collection of genealogical data, and recording sounds and images. Cultural anthropologists may also use surveys, but not in the way you might think. Below we touch on several key methods for collecting information.

TAKING SURVEYS

Unlike many other social scientists, anthropologists do not usually go into the field equipped with predetermined surveys or questionnaires; rather, they recognize that there are many things that can be discovered only by keeping an open mind while thoughtfully watching, listening, participating, and asking questions. As fieldwork proceeds, anthropologists sort their complex impressions and observations into a meaningful whole, sometimes by formulating and testing limited or low-level hypotheses, but just as often by making use of imagination or intuition and following up on hunches. What is important is that the results are constantly checked for accuracy and consistency, for if the parts fail to fit together in a way that is internally

---

key consultant A member of the society being studied who provides information that helps researchers understand the meaning of what they observe; early anthropologists referred to such individuals as informants.

quantitative data Statistical or measurable information, such as demographic composition, the types and quantities of crops grown, or the ratio of spouses born and raised within or outside the community.

qualitative data Nonstatistical information such as personal life stories and customary beliefs and practices.

During fieldwork, anthropologists use computers not only for recording and processing data, but as a means of communicating with the peoples being studied. Here we see ecologist James Kremer (pointing at the computer) and anthropologist Stephen Lansing (behind Kremer) who have researched the traditional rituals and network of water temples linked to the irrigation management of rice fields on the island of Bali in Indonesia. They are explaining a computer simulation of this system to the high priest of the Supreme Water Temple, as other temple priests look on. Located on the crater rim above the caldera and lake of Mount Batur, this temple is associated with the Goddess of the Crater Lake. Every year people from hundreds of villages bring offerings here, expressing gratitude to this deity for the gift of water.

coherent, it may be that a mistake has been made and further inquiry is necessary.

This is not to say that anthropologists do not conduct surveys. Some do. But these are just one part of a much larger research strategy that includes a considerable amount of qualitative data as well as quantitative. Also, in ethnographic fieldwork, surveys are usually carried out after one has spent enough time on location to have gained the community's confidence and to know how to compose a questionnaire with categories that are culturally relevant.

Two studies of a village in Peru illustrate the problem of gathering data through surveys alone. One was carried out by a sociologist who, after conducting the survey by questionnaire, concluded that people in the village invariably worked together on one another's privately owned plots of land. By contrast, a cultural anthropologist who lived in the village for over a year (including the brief period when the sociologist did his study) witnessed that particular practice only once. The anthropologist's long-term participant observation revealed that although the idea of labor exchange relations was important to the

people's sense of themselves, it was not a common economic practice.[17]

The point here is that questionnaires all too easily embody the concepts and categories of the researcher, who is an outsider, rather than those of the people being studied. Even where this is not a problem, questionnaires tend to concentrate on what is measurable, answerable, and acceptable as a question, rather than probing the less obvious and more complex qualitative aspects of society or culture.

Moreover, for a host of reasons—fear, ignorance, hostility, hope of reward—people may give false, incomplete, or biased information.[18] Keeping culture-bound ideas, which are often embedded in standardized questionnaires, out of research methods is an important point in all ethnographic research.

---

[17] Chambers, R. (1983). *Rural development: Putting the last first* (p. 51). New York: Longman.

[18] Sanjek, R. (1990). On ethnographic validity. In R. Sanjek (Ed.), *Field notes* (p. 395). Ithaca, NY: Cornell University Press.

INTERVIEWING

Asking questions is fundamental to ethnographic fieldwork and takes place in **informal interviews** (unstructured, open-ended conversations in everyday life) and **formal interviews** (structured question/answer sessions carefully noted as they occur and based on prepared questions). Informal interviews may be carried out at any time and in any place—on horseback, in a canoe, by a cooking fire, during ritual events, while walking through the community with a local inhabitant, and the list goes on. Such casual exchanges are essential, for it is often in these conversations that people share most freely. Moreover, questions put forth in formal interviews typically grow out of cultural knowledge and insights gained during informal ones.

Getting people to open up is an art born of a genuine interest in both the information and the person who is sharing it. It requires dropping all assumptions and cultivating the ability to *really* listen. It may even require a willingness to be the village idiot by asking simple questions to which the answers may seem obvious. Also, effective interviewers learn early on that numerous followup questions are vital since first answers may mask truth rather than reveal it. Questions generally fall into one of two categories: broad, *open-ended questions* (Can you tell me about your childhood?) and *closed questions* seeking specific pieces of information (Where and when were you born?).

In ethnographic fieldwork, interviews are used to collect a vast range of cultural information: from life histories, genealogies, and myths to craft techniques and midwife practices to beliefs concerning everything from illness to food taboos. Genealogical data can be especially useful, as they provide information about a range of social customs (such as cousin marriage), worldviews (such as ancestor worship), political relations (such as alliances), and economic arrangements (such as hunting or harvesting on clan-owned lands).

Researchers employ numerous **eliciting devices**—activities and objects used to draw out individuals and encourage them to recall and share information. There are countless examples of this: taking a walk with a local and asking about songs, legends, and place names linked to geographic features; sharing details about one's own family and neighborhood and inviting a telling in return; joining in a community activity and asking a local to explain the practice and why they are doing it; taking and sharing photographs of cultural objects or activities and asking locals to explain what they see in the pictures.

MAPPING

Many anthropologists have done fieldwork in remote places where there is little geographic documentation. Even if cartographers have mapped the region, standard maps seldom show geographic and spatial features that are culturally significant to the people living there. People inhabiting areas that form part of their ancestral homeland have a particular understanding of the area and their own names for local places. These native names may convey essential geographic information, describing the distinctive features of a locality such as its physical appearance, its specific dangers, or its precious resources.

Place names may derive from certain political realities such as headquarters, territorial boundaries, and so on. Others may make sense only in the cultural context of a local people's worldview as recounted in their myths, legends, songs, or other narrative traditions. Thus to truly understand the lay of the land, some anthropologists make their own detailed geographic maps documenting culturally relevant geographic features in the landscape inhabited by the people they study.

Especially since the early 1970s, anthropologists have become involved in indigenous land use and occupancy studies for various reasons, including the documentation of traditional land claims. Researchers constructing individual map biographies may gather information from a variety of sources: local oral histories; early written descriptions of explorers, traders, missionaries, and other visitors; and data obtained from archaeological excavations.

One such ethnogeographic research project took place in northwestern Canada, during the planning stage of the building of the Alaska Highway natural gas pipeline. Since the line would cut directly though Native lands, local indigenous community leaders and federal officials insisted that a study be done to determine how the new construction would affect indigenous inhabitants. Canadian anthropologist Hugh Brody, one of the researchers in this ethnogeographic study, explained: "These maps are the key to the studies and their greatest contribution. Hunters, trappers, fishermen, and berry-pickers mapped out all the land they had ever used in their lifetimes, encircling hunting areas species by species, marking gathering location and camping sites—everything their life on the land had entailed that could be marked on a map."[19]

In addition to mapping the local place names and geographic features, anthropologists may also map out

---

[19] Brody, H. (1981). *Maps and dreams* (p.147). New York: Pantheon.

informal interview An unstructured, open-ended conversation in everyday life.
formal interview A structured question/answer session carefully noted as it occurs and based on prepared questions.
eliciting device An activity or object used to draw out individuals and encourage them to recall and share information.

For anthropologist Michael Heckenberger, doing fieldwork among the Kuikuro people of the Upper Xingu River in the southern margins of the Amazon rainforest has become a collaborative undertaking. Together with other specialists on his research team, he has trained local tribespeople to help with the research project about their ancestral culture, which includes searching for the remains of ancient earthworks and mapping them. Here we see Laquai Kuikuro, one of the trained assistants, collecting GPS data (in this case, collecting points of a modern manioc field—manioc being a primary dietary staple of indigenous Amazonian communities in Brazil) and then reviewing the downloaded data. On the right is a map showing GPS-charted indigenous earthworks in the Upper Xingu superimposed over a Landsat satellite image.

information relevant to the local subsistence, such as animal migration routes, favorite fishing areas, places where medicinal plants can be harvested or firewood cut, and so on.

Today, by means of the technology known as global positioning system (GPS), researchers can measure precise distances by triangulating the travel time of radio signals from various orbiting satellites. They can create maps that pinpoint human settlement locations and the layout of dwellings, gardens, public spaces, watering holes, pastures, surrounding mountains, rivers, lakes, seashores, islands, swamps, forests, deserts, and any other relevant feature in the regional environment.

To store, edit, analyze, integrate, and display this geographically referenced spatial information, some anthropologists use cartographic digital technology, known as geographic information systems (GIS). GIS makes it possible to map the geographic features and natural resources in a certain environment—and to link these data to ethnographic information about population density and distribution, social networks of kinship relations, seasonal patterns of land use, private or collective claims of ownership, travel routes, sources of water, and so on. With GIS researchers can also integrate information about beliefs, myths, legends, songs, and other culturally relevant data associated with distinct locations. Moreover, they can create interactive inquiries for analysis

of research data as well as natural and cultural resource management.[20]

PHOTOGRAPHING AND FILMING

Most anthropologists use cameras for fieldwork, as well as notepads, computers, or sound recording devices to document their observations. Photography has been instrumental in anthropological research for more than a century. For instance, Franz Boas took photographs during his first fieldwork among the Inuit in the Canadian Arctic in the early 1880s. And just a few years after the invention of the moving picture camera in 1894, anthropologists began filming traditional dances by indigenous Australians and other ethnographic subjects of interest.

---

[20] Schoepfle, M. (2001). Ethnographic resource inventory and the National Park Service. *Cultural Resource Management 5*, 1–7.

Margaret Mead (1901–1978) ∎ *Gregory Bateson (1904–1980)*

From 1936 to 1938 **Margaret Mead** and **Gregory Bateson** did collaborative ethnographic fieldwork in Bali. Bateson, Mead's husband at the time, was a British anthropologist trained by Alfred C. Haddon, who led the 1898 Torres Strait expedition and is credited with making the first ethnographic film in the field. During their stay in Bali, Bateson took about 25,000 photographs and shot 22,000 feet of motion picture film. Afterward, the couple co-authored the photographic ethnography *Balinese Character: A Photographic Analysis* (1942).

That same year, Bateson worked as an anthropological film analyst studying German motion pictures. Soon Mead and a few other anthropologists became involved in thematic analysis of foreign fictional films. She later compiled a number of such visual anthropology studies in a co-edited volume titled *The Study of Culture at a Distance* (1953).

Mead became a tireless promoter of the scholarly use of ethnographic

Library of Congress

In 1938, after two years of fieldwork in Bali, Margaret Mead and Gregory Bateson began research in Papua New Guinea, where they staged this photograph of themselves to highlight the importance of cameras as part of the ethnographic tool kit. (Note camera on tripod behind Mead and other cameras atop the desk.)

photography and film. In 1960, the year the portable sync-sound film camera was invented, Mead was serving as president of the American Anthropology Association. In her presidential address at the association's annual gathering, she

pointed out what she saw as shortcomings in the discipline and urged anthropologists to use cameras more effectively.[a] Chiding her colleagues for not fully utilizing new technological developments, she complained that anthropology had come "to depend on words, and words, and words."

Mead's legacy is commemorated in numerous venues, including the Margaret Mead Film Festival hosted annually since 1977 by the American Museum of Natural History in New York City. Thus it was fitting that during the Margaret Mead Centennial celebrations in 2001 the American Anthropological Association endorsed a landmark visual media policy statement urging academic committees to consider ethnographic visuals—and not just ethnographic writing—when evaluating scholarly output of academics up for hiring, promotion, and tenure.

[a]Mead, M. (1960). Anthropology among the sciences. *American Anthropologist 63*, 475–482.

Especially following the invention of the portable synchronous-sound camera in 1960, ethnographic filmmaking took off. New technological developments made it increasingly obvious that visual media could serve a wide range of cross-cultural research purposes. Some anthropologists employed still photography in community surveys and elicitation techniques. Others turned to film to document and research traditional patterns of nonverbal communication such as body language and social space use. Cameras have also been (and continue to be) instrumental in documenting the disappearing world of traditional foragers, herders, and farmers surviving in remote places.

Since the digital revolution that began in the 1980s, we are witnessing an explosive growth in visual media all across the world. It is not unusual for anthropologists to arrive in remote villages where at least a few native inhabitants take their own pictures or record their own stories and music. For researchers in the field, native-made

audio-visual documents may represent a wealth of precious cultural information. The Anthropologists of Note feature details the long history of such equipment in anthropology.

Challenges of Ethnographic Fieldwork

While ethnographic fieldwork offers a range of opportunities to gain better and deeper insight into the community being studied, it comes with a Pandora's box of challenges. At the least, it usually requires researchers to step out of their cultural comfort zone into an unknown world that is sometimes unsettling. As touched upon in Chapter 1, anthropologists in the field are likely to face a wide array of challenges—physical, social, mental, political, and ethical.

While they are handling these challenges, they must be fully engaged in work and social activities with the community. In addition, they are doing a host of other things, such as interviewing, taking copious notes, and analyzing data. In the following paragraphs we offer details on some of the most common personal struggles anthropologists face in the field.

Social Acceptance

Having decided where to do ethnographic research and what to focus on, anthropologists embark on the journey to their field site. Because few choose to do research in their own home communities, most experience culture shock and loneliness at least during the initial stages of their work—work that requires them to establish social contacts with strangers who have little or no idea who they are, why they have come, or what they want from them. In short, a visiting anthropologist is as much a mystery to those she or he intends to study as the group is to the researcher.

Although there is no sure way of predicting how one will be received, it is certain that success in ethnographic fieldwork depends on mutual goodwill and the ability to develop friendships and other meaningful social relations. As New Zealand anthropologist Jeffrey Sluka notes, "The classic image of successful rapport and good fieldwork relations in cultural anthropology is that of the ethnographer who has been 'adopted' or named by the tribe or people he or she studies."[21]

Among the numerous ethnographic examples of anthropologists being adopted by a family, lineage, or clan is the case of Canadian anthropologist Richard Lee, adopted by a group of Ju/'hoansi (Bushmen) foragers in the Kalahari Desert. He describes the informal way in which this took place:

> One day in March 1964, I was visiting a !Xabe village, when Hwan//a, a woman about my age who was married to one of the Tswana Headman Isak's three sons, playfully began to call me, "Uncle, uncle, /Tontah, come see me."
>
> Puzzled, I drew closer; until that time the Ju had referred to me simply as the White Man (/Ton) or the bearded one. . . . Hwan//a smiled and said, "You are all alone here and I have no children, so I will name you /Tontah after my *tsu* /Tontah who is dead, and, as I have named you, you shall call me mother."
>
> . . . . The name stuck. Soon people all over the Dobe area were calling me /Tontah.[22]

Anthropologists adopted into networks of kinship relations not only gain social access and certain rights but also assume social obligations associated with their new kinship status. These relationships can be deep and enduring—as illustrated by Smithsonian anthropologist William Crocker's description of his 1991 return to the Canela tribal community after a twelve-year absence. He had lived among these Amazonian Indians in Brazil off and on for a total of sixty-six months from the 1950s through the 1970s. When he stepped out of the single-motor missionary plane that had brought him back in 1991, he was quickly surrounded by Canela:

> Once on the ground, I groped for names and terms of address while shaking many hands. Soon my Canela mother Tutkhwey (dove-woman), pulled me over to the shade of a plane's wing and pushed me down to a mat on the ground. She put both hands on my shoulders and, kneeling beside me, her head by mine, cried out words of mourning in a loud yodeling manner. Tears and phlegm dripped onto my shoulder and knees. According to a custom now abandoned by the younger women, she was crying for the loss of a grown daughter, Tsep-khwey (bat-woman), as well as for my return.[23]

Since that 1991 reunion, Crocker has visited the Canela community every other year—always receiving a warm welcome and staying with locals. Although many anthropologists are successful in gaining social acceptance and even adoption status in communities where they do participant observation, they rarely go completely native and abandon their own homeland—for even after long stays in a community, after learning to behave appropriately and communicate well, few become complete insiders.

Political Tension

Challenges during fieldwork include the possibility of being caught in political rivalries and used unwittingly by factions within the community; also, the anthropologist may be viewed with suspicion by government authorities who suspect the anthropologist of spying.

Anthropologist June Nash, for instance, has faced serious political and personal challenges doing fieldwork in various Latin American communities experiencing violent changes. As an outsider, Nash tried to avoid becoming embroiled in local conflicts but could not maintain her position as an impartial observer while researching a tin mining community in the Bolivian highlands. When the conflict between local

[21] Sluka, J. A. (2007). Fieldwork relations and rapport: Introduction. In A.C.G.M. Robben & J. A. Sluka (Eds.), *Ethnographic fieldwork: An anthropological reader* (p. 122). Malden, MA: Blackwell.

[22] Lee, R. B. (1993). *The Dobe Ju/'hoansi* (p. 61). Ft. Worth: Harcourt Brace.

[23] Crocker, W. H., & Crocker, J. G. (2004). *The Canela: Kinship, ritual, and sex in an Amazonian tribe* (p. 1). Belmont, CA: Wadsworth.

Anthropologist William Crocker did fieldwork among Canela Indians in Brazil over several decades. He still visits the community regularly. In this 1964 photograph, a Canela woman (M~i~i- kw'ej, or Alligator Woman) gives him a traditional haircut while other members of the community look on. She is the wife of his adoptive Canela "brother" and therefore a "wife" to Crocker in Canela kinship terms. Among the Canela, it is improper for a mother, sister, or daughter to cut a man's hair.

miners and bosses controlling the armed forces became violent, Nash found herself in a revolutionary setting in which miners viewed her tape recorder as an instrument of espionage and suspected her of being a CIA agent.[24]

All anthropologists face the overriding challenge of winning the trust that allows people to be themselves and share an unmasked version of their culture with a newcomer. Some do not succeed in meeting this challenge. So it was with anthropologist Lincoln Keiser in his difficult fieldwork in the remote town of Thull, situated in the Hindu Kush Mountains of northwestern Pakistan. Keiser ventured there to explore customary blood feuding among a Kohistani tribal community of 6,000 Muslims making their living by a mix of farming and herding in the rugged region. However, the people he had traveled so far to study did not appreciate his presence. As Keiser recounted, many of the fiercely independent tribesmen in this area, "where the AK-47 [sub-machine gun] symbolizes the violent quality of male social relations," treated him with great disdain and suspicion, as a foreign "infidel":

> Throughout my stay in Thull, many people remained convinced I was a creature sent by the devil to harm the community. . . . [Doing fieldwork there] was a test I failed, for a *jirga* [political council] of my most vocal opponents ultimately forced me to leave Thull three months before

I had planned. . . . Obviously, I have difficulty claiming the people of Thull as "my people" because so many of them never ceased to despise me. . . . Still, I learned from being hated.[25]

Gender, Age, Ideology, Ethnicity, and Skin Color

Keiser's fieldwork challenges stemmed in part from his non-Muslim religious identity, marking him as an outsider in the local community of the faithful. Gender, age, ethnicity, and skin color can also impact a researcher's access to a community. For instance, male ethnographers may face prohibitions or severe restrictions in interviewing women or observing certain women's activities. Similarly, a female researcher may not find ready reception among males in communities with gender-segregation traditions. With respect to skin color, African American anthropologist Norris Brock-Johnson encountered social obstacles while doing fieldwork in the American Midwest, but his dark skin helped him gain "admission to the world of black Caribbean shipwrights" on the island of Bequia where he studied traditional boatmaking.[26]

---

[24] Nash, J. (1976). Ethnology in a revolutionary setting. In M. A. Rynkiewich & J. P. Spradley (Eds.), *Ethics and anthropology: Dilemmas in fieldwork* (pp. 148–166). New York: Wiley.

[25] Keiser, L. (1991). *Friend by day, enemy by night: Organized vengeance in a Kohistani community* (p. 103). Fort Worth: Holt, Rinehart & Winston.

[26] Robben, A.C.G.M. (2007). Fieldwork identity: Introduction. In A.C.G.M. Robben & J. A. Sluka (Eds.), *Ethnographic fieldwork: An anthropological reader* (p. 61). Malden, MA: Blackwell; Johnson, N. B. (1984). Sex, color, and rites of passage in ethnographic research. *Human Organization* 43 (2), 108–120.

Subjectivity and Reflexivity

Whether working near home or abroad, when endeavoring to identify the rules that underlie each culture, ethnographers must grapple with the very real challenge of bias or subjectivity—his or her own and that of members in the community being studied. Because perceptions of reality may vary, an anthropologist must be extremely careful in describing a culture. To do so accurately, the researcher needs to seek out and consider three kinds of data:

1. The people's own understanding of their culture and the general rules they share—that is, their ideal sense of the way their own society ought to be.
2. The extent to which people believe they are observing those rules—that is, how they think they really behave.
3. The behavior that can be directly observed—that is, what the anthropologist actually sees happening.

Clearly, the way people think they *should* behave, the way in which they think they *do* behave, and the way in which they *actually* behave may be distinctly different. By carefully examining and comparing these elements, anthropologists can draw up a set of rules that may explain the acceptable range of behavior within a culture.

Beyond the possibility of drawing false conclusions based on a group's ideal sense of itself, anthropologists run the risk of misinterpretation due to personal feelings and biases shaped by their own culture, as well as gender and age. It is important to recognize this challenge and make every effort to overcome it, for otherwise one may seriously misconstrue what one sees.

A case in point is the story of how male bias in the Polish culture in which Malinowski was raised caused him to ignore or miss significant factors in his pioneering study of the Trobrianders. Unlike today, when anthropologists receive special training before going into the field, Malinowski set out to do fieldwork early in the 20th century with little formal preparation. The following Original Study, written by anthropologist Annette Weiner who ventured to the same islands sixty years after Malinowski, illustrates how gender can impact one's research findings—both in terms of the bias that may affect a researcher's outlook and in terms of what key consultants may feel comfortable sharing with a particular researcher.

In anthropology, researchers are expected to self-monitor through constantly checking their own personal or cultural biases and assumptions as they work. They must present these self-reflections along with their observations. This practice of critical self-examination is known as *reflexivity*.

Original Study

The Importance of Trobriand Women *by Annette B. Weiner*

Walking into a village at the beginning of fieldwork is entering a world without cultural guideposts. The task of learning values that others live by is never easy. The rigors of fieldwork involve listening and watching, learning a new language of speech and actions, and most of all, letting go of one's own cultural assumptions in order to understand the meanings others give to work, power, death, family, and friends. During my fieldwork in the Trobriand Islands of Papua New Guinea, I wrestled doggedly with each of these problems—and with the added challenge that I was working in the footsteps of a celebrated anthropological ancestor, Bronislaw Kasper Malinowski. . . .

In 1971, before my first trip to the Trobriands, I thought I understood many things about Trobriand customs and beliefs from having read Malinowski's exhaustive writings. Once there, however, I found that I had much more to discover about what I thought I already knew. For many months I worked with these discordant realities, always conscious of Malinowski's shadow, his words, his explanations. Although I found significant differences in areas of importance, I gradually came to understand how he reached certain conclusions. The answers we both received from informants were not so dissimilar, and I could actually trace how Malinowski had analyzed what his informants told him in a way that made sense and was scientifically significant—given what anthropologists generally then recognized about such societies. Sixty years separate our fieldwork, and any comparison of our studies illustrates not so much Malinowski's mistaken interpretations but the developments in anthropological knowledge and inquiry from his time to mine. . . .

My most significant point of departure from Malinowski's analyses was the attention I gave to women's productive work. In my original research plans, women were not the central focus of study, but on the first day I took up residence in a village I was taken by them to watch a distribution of their own wealth—bundles of banana leaves and banana fiber skirts—which they exchanged with other women in commemoration of someone who had recently died. Watching that event forced me to take women's economic roles more seriously than I would have from reading Malinowski's studies. Although Malinowski noted the high status of

Trobriand women, he attributed their importance to the fact that Trobrianders reckon descent through women, thereby giving them genealogical significance in a matrilineal society. Yet he never considered that this significance was underwritten by women's own wealth because he did not systematically investigate the women's productive activities. Although in his field notes he mentions Trobriand women making these seemingly useless banana bundles to be exchanged at a death, his published work only deals with men's wealth.

My taking seriously the importance of women's wealth not only brought women as the neglected half of society clearly into the ethnographic picture but also forced me to revise many of Malinowski's assumptions about Trobriand men. For example, Trobriand kinship as described by Malinowski has always been a subject of debate among anthropologists. For Malinowski, the basic relationships within a Trobriand family were guided by the matrilineal principle of "mother-right" and "father-love." A father was called "stranger" and had little authority over his own children. A woman's brother was the commanding figure and exercised control over his sister's sons because they were members of his matrilineage rather than their father's matrilineage. . . .

In my study of Trobriand women and men, a different configuration of matrilineal descent emerged. A Trobriand father is not a "stranger" in Malinowski's definition, nor is he a powerless figure as the third party to the relationship between a woman and her brother. The father is one of the most important persons in his child's life, and remains so even after his child grows up and marries. Even his procreative importance is incorporated into his child's growth and development. He gives his child many opportunities to gain things from his matrilineage, thereby adding to the available resources that he or she can draw upon.

At the same time, this giving creates obligations on the part of a man's children toward him that last even beyond his death. Thus, the roles that men and their children play in each other's lives are worked out through extensive cycles of exchanges, which define the strength of their relationships to each other and eventually benefit the other members of both their matrilineages. Central to these exchanges are women and their wealth.

That Malinowski never gave equal time to the women's side of things, given the deep significance of their role in societal and political life, is not surprising. Only recently have anthropologists begun to understand the importance of taking women's work seriously. . . . In the past, both women and men ethnographers generally analyzed the societies they studied from a male perspective. The "women's point of view" was largely ignored in the study of gender roles, since anthropologists generally perceived women as living in the shadows of men—occupying the private rather than the public sectors of society, rearing children rather than engaging in economic or political pursuits.

Estate of Annette B. Weiner

In the Trobriand Islands, women's wealth consists of banana leaves and banana-fiber skirts, large quantities of which must be given away on the death of a relative.

From Weiner, A. B. (1988). The Trobrianders of Papua New Guinea (pp. 4–7). New York: Holt, Rinehart & Winston.

Validation

As the Original Study makes clear, determining the accuracy of anthropological descriptions and conclusions can be difficult. In the natural sciences, one can replicate observations and experiments to try to establish the reliability of a researcher's conclusions. Thus one can see for oneself if one's colleague has "gotten it right." But validating ethnographic research is uniquely challenging because access to sites may be limited or barred altogether, due to a number of factors: insufficient funding, logistical difficulties in reaching the site, problems in obtaining permits, and changing cultural and environmental conditions. These factors mean that what could be observed in a certain context at a certain time cannot be observed at others. Thus one researcher cannot easily confirm the reliability or completeness of another's account.

For this reason, anthropologists bear a heavy responsibility for factual reporting, including disclosing key issues related to their research: Why was a particular location selected as a research site and for which research objectives? What were the local conditions during fieldwork? Who provided the key information and major insights? How were data collected and recorded? Without such background information, it is difficult to judge the validity of the account and the soundness of the researcher's conclusions.

Putting It All Together: Completing an Ethnography

After collecting ethnographic information, the next challenge is to piece together all that has been gathered into a coherent whole that accurately describes the culture. Traditionally, ethnographies are detailed written descriptions comprised of chapters on topics such as the circumstances and place of fieldwork itself; historical background; the community or group today; its natural environment; settlement patterns; subsistence practices; networks of kinship relations and other forms of social organization; marriage and sexuality; economic exchanges; political institutions; myths, sacred beliefs, and ceremonies; and current developments. These may be illustrated with photographs and accompanied by maps, kinship diagrams, and figures showing social and political organizational structures, settlement layout, floor plans of dwellings, seasonal cycles, and so on.

Visual Anthropology and Digital Media

Sometimes ethnographic research is documented not only in writing but also with sound recordings and on film. Visual records may be used for documentation and illustration as well as for analysis or as a means of gathering additional information in interviews. Moreover, footage shot for the sake of documentation and research may be edited into a documentary film. Not unlike a written ethnography, such a film is a structured whole composed of numerous selected sequences, visual montage, juxtaposition of sound and visual image, and narrative sequencing, all coherently edited into an accurate visual representation of the ethnographic subject.[27]

In recent years anthropologists have experimented with digital media.[28] With the emergence of **digital ethnography**—the use of digital technologies (audio and

visual) for the collection, analysis, and representation of ethnographic data—the potential for anthropological research, interpretation, and presentation is greater than ever before. Digital recording devices provide ethnographers with a wealth of material to analyze and utilize toward building hypotheses. They also open the door to sharing findings in new, varied, and interactive ways in the far-reaching digitalized realm of the Internet.[29] Digital ethnographers, having amassed a wealth of digital material while researching, are able to share their findings through DVDs, CD-ROMs, photo essays, podcasts, blogs, or vlogs (video blogging).

Ethnohistory

Ethnohistory is a kind of historical ethnography that studies cultures of the recent past through oral histories; the accounts of explorers, missionaries, and traders; and analysis of such records as land titles, birth and death records, and other archival materials. The ethnohistorical analysis of cultures is a valuable approach to understanding change and plays an important role in theory building.

---

[27] See Collier, J., & Collier, M. (1986). *Visual anthropology: Photography as a research method.* Albuquerque: University of New Mexico Press; El Guindi, F. (2004). *Visual anthropology: Essential method and theory.* Walnut Creek, CA: Altamira.

[28] See also Ginsburg, F. D., Abu-Lughod, L., & Larkin, B. (Eds.). (2009). *Media worlds: Anthropology on new terrain.* Berkeley: University California Press.

---

[29] Michael Wesch, personal communication.

Courtesy of Hu Tai-Li

Anthropologist-filmmaker Hu Tai-Li filming the Maleveq ceremony in the Paiwan village Kulalao, southern Taiwan. An award-winning pioneer of ethnographic films in Taiwan, Tai-Li is a research fellow at the Institute of Ethnology, Academia Sinica, a professor at National Chin-Hua University, and the president of the Taiwan International Ethnographic Film Festival. Since earning an undergraduate degree in history from the National Taiwan University and a PhD in anthropology from City University of New York, she has directed and produced a half-dozen documentaries on a range of topics—including traditional rituals and music, development issues, and national and ethnic identity.

---

digital ethnography The use of digital technologies (audio and visual) for the collection, analysis, and representation of ethnographic data.

ethnohistory A study of cultures of the recent past through oral histories; accounts of explorers, missionaries, and traders; and analysis of records such as land titles, birth and death records, and other archival materials.

Ethnology: From Description to Interpretation and Theory

Largely descriptive in nature, ethnography provides the basic data needed for *ethnology*—the branch of cultural anthropology that makes cross-cultural comparisons and develops theories that explain why certain important differences or similarities occur between groups. As noted in Chapter 1, the end product of anthropological research, if properly carried out, is a coherent statement about culture or human nature that provides an explanatory framework for understanding the ideas and actions of the people being studied. In short, such an explanation or interpretation supported by a reliable body of data is a **theory.** As discussed in Chapter 1, theory is distinct from *doctrine* or *dogma*—an assertion of opinion or belief formally handed down by an authority as indisputably true and accepted as a matter of faith.

Anthropologists do not claim that any one theory about culture is the absolute truth. Rather they judge or measure a theory's validity and soundness by varying degrees of probability; what is considered to be "true" is what is most probable. But while anthropologists are reluctant about making absolute statements about complex issues such as exactly how cultures function or change, they can and do provide fact-based evidence about whether assumptions have support or are unfounded and thus not true. Thus a theory, contrary to widespread misuse of the term, is much more than mere speculation; it is a critically examined explanation of observed reality.

Always open to future challenges born of new evidence or insights, scientific theory depends on demonstrable, fact-based evidence and repeated testing. So it is that, as our cross-cultural knowledge expands, the odds favor some anthropological theories over others. Old explanations or interpretations must sometimes be discarded as new theories based on better or more complete evidence are shown to be more effective or probable.

Ethnology and the Comparative Method

A single instance of any phenomenon is generally insufficient for supporting a plausible hypothesis. Without some basis for comparison, the hypothesis grounded in a single case may be no more than a hunch born of a unique happenstance or particular historical coincidence. Theories in anthropology may be generated from worldwide cross-cultural or historical comparisons or even comparisons with other species. For instance, anthropologists may examine a global sample of societies in order to discover whether a hypothesis proposed to explain certain phenomena is supported by fact-based evidence. Of necessity, the cross-cultural researcher depends upon evidence gathered by other scholars as well as his or her own.

A key resource that makes this possible is the **Human Relations Area Files (HRAF),** which is a vast collection of cross-indexed ethnographic and archaeological data catalogued by cultural characteristics and geographic location. This ever-growing data bank classifies more than 700 cultural characteristics and includes nearly 400 societies, past and present, from all around the world. Archived in about 300 libraries (on microfiche or online) and approaching a million pages of information, the HRAF facilitates comparative research on almost any cultural feature imaginable—warfare, subsistence practices, settlement patterns, marriage, rituals, and so on.

Among other things, anthropologists interested in finding explanations for certain social or cultural beliefs and practices can use HRAF to test their hypotheses. For example, Peggy Reeves Sanday examined a sample of 156 societies drawn from HRAF in an attempt to answer her comparative research questions concerning dominance and gender in different societies. Her study, published in 1981 (*Female Power and Male Dominance*), disproves the common misperception that women are universally subordinate to men, sheds light on the way men and women relate to each other, and ranks as a major landmark in the study of gender.

Cultural comparisons are not restricted to contemporary ethnographic data. Indeed, anthropologists frequently turn to archaeological or historical data to test hypotheses about cultural change. Cultural characteristics thought to be caused by certain specified conditions can be tested archaeologically by investigating similar situations where such conditions actually occurred. Also useful are data provided in ethnohistories.

Anthropology's Theoretical Perspectives: A Brief Overview

Entire books have been written about each of anthropology's numerous theoretical perspectives. Here we offer a general overview to convey the scope of anthropological theories and their role in explaining and interpreting cultures.

In the previous chapter, we presented the barrel model of culture as a dynamic system of adaptation in which social structure, infrastructure, and superstructure intricately

---

theory In science an explanation of natural phenomena, supported by a reliable body of data.

Human Relations Area Files (HRAF) A vast collection of cross-indexed ethnographic and archaeological data catalogued by cultural characteristics and geographic locations; archived in about 300 libraries (on microfiche or online).

interact. Helping us to imagine culture as an integrated whole, this model allows us to think about something very complex by reducing it to a highly simplified scheme or basic design.

Although most anthropologists generally conceptualize culture as holistic and integrative, they may have very different takes on the relative significance of different elements that make up the whole and exactly how they relate to one another. We touch on these contrasting perspectives below—in broad strokes.

Idealist

When analyzing a culture, some argue that humans act primarily on the basis of their ideas, concepts, or symbolic representations. In their research and analysis, these anthropologists usually emphasize that to understand or explain why humans behave as they do, one must first get into other people's heads and try to understand how they imagine, think, feel, and speak about the world in which they live. Because of the primacy of the superstructure (ideas, values), this is known as an **idealist perspective** (not to be confused with idealism in the sense of fantasy or hopeful imagination).

Examples of idealist perspectives include psychological and cognitive anthropology (culture and personality), ethnoscience, structuralism, and postmodernism, as well as symbolic and interpretive anthropology. The latter approach is most famously associated with anthropologist Clifford Geertz, who viewed humans primarily as "symbolizing, conceptualizing, and meaning-seeking" creatures. Drawing on words from German historical sociologist Max Weber, Geertz wrote: "Man is an animal suspended in webs of significance he himself has spun. I take culture to be those webs, and the analysis of it to be therefore not an experimental science in search of law but an interpretive one in search of meaning."[30] Geertz developed an artful ethnographic research strategy in which a culturally significant event or social drama (for instance, a Balinese cockfight) is chosen for observation and analysis as a form of "deep play" that may provide essential cultural insights. Peeling back layer upon layer of socially constructed meanings, the anthropologist offers what Geertz called a "thick description" of the event in a detailed ethnographic narrative.

---

[30] Geertz, C. (1973). *The interpretation of culture*. London: Hutchinson.

idealist perspective   A theoretical approach stressing the primacy of superstructure in cultural research and analysis.

materialist perspective   A theoretical approach stressing the primacy of infrastructure (material conditions) in cultural research and analysis.

Materialist

Many other anthropologists hold a theoretical perspective in which they stress explaining culture by first analyzing the material conditions that they see as determining people's lives. They may begin their research with an inventory of available natural resources for food and shelter, the number of mouths to feed and bodies to keep warm, the tools used in making a living, and so on. Anthropologists who highlight such environmental or economic factors as primary in shaping cultures basically share a **materialist perspective.**

Examples of materialist theoretical approaches include Marxism, neo-evolutionism, cultural ecology, sociobiology, and cultural materialism. In cultural ecology, anthropologists focus primarily on the subsistence mechanisms in a culture that enable a group to successfully adapt to its natural environment. Building on cultural ecology, some anthropologists include considerations of political economy such as industrial production, capitalist markets, wage labor, and finance capital. A political economy perspective is closely associated with Marxist theory, which essentially explains major change in society as the result of growing conflicts between opposing social classes, namely those who possess property and those who do not.

One result of widening the scope—combining cultural ecology and political economy to take into account the emerging world systems of international production and trade relations—is known as *political ecology*. Closely related is *cultural materialism*, a theoretical research strategy identified with Marvin Harris.[31] Placing primary emphasis on the role of environment, demography, technology, and economy in determining a culture's mental and social conditions, he argues that anthropologists can best explain ideas, values, and beliefs as adaptations to economic and environmental conditions (see the Biocultural Connection).

Structural-Functionalist

Not all anthropologists can be easily grouped in idealist or materialist camps. Giving primacy to social structure, many analyze a cultural group by first and foremost focusing on this middle layer in our barrel model. Although it is difficult to neatly pigeonhole various perspectives in this group, theoretical explanations worked out by pioneering French social thinkers like Emile Durkheim and his student Marcel Mauss influenced the development of *structural-functionalism*. Primarily associated with British anthropologists in the mid-1900s, this approach focuses on the underlying patterns or structures of social relationships, attributing functions to cultural institutions in terms of the contributions they make toward maintaining a group's social order.

---

[31] Harris, M. (1979). *Cultural materialism: The struggle for a science of culture*. New York: Random House.

Pig Lovers and Pig Haters *by Marvin Harris*

In the Old Testament of the Bible, the Israelite's God (Yahweh) denounced the pig as an unclean beast that pollutes if tasted or touched. Later, Allah conveyed the same basic message to his prophet Muhammad. Among millions of Jews and Muslims today, the pig remains an abomination, even though it can convert grains and tubers into high-grade fats and protein more efficiently than any other animal.

What prompted condemnation of an animal whose meat is relished by the greater part of humanity? For centuries, the most popular explanation was that the pig wallows in its own urine and eats excrement. But linking this to religious abhorrence leads to inconsistencies. Cows kept in a confined space also splash about in their own urine and feces.

These inconsistencies were recognized in the 12th century by Maimonides, a widely respected Jewish philosopher and physician in Egypt, who said God condemned swine as a public health measure because pork had "a bad and damaging effect upon the body." The mid-1800s discovery that eating undercooked pork caused trichinosis appeared to verify Maimonides's reasoning. Reform-minded Jews then renounced the taboo, convinced that if well-cooked pork did not endanger public health, eating it would not offend God. But others held to it.

Scholars have suggested this taboo stems from the idea that the animal was once considered divine—but this explanation falls short since sheep, goats, and cows were also once worshiped in the Middle East, and their meat is enjoyed by all religious groups in the region.

I think the real explanation lies in the fact that pig farming threatened the integrity of the basic cultural and natural ecosystems of the Middle East. Until their conquest of the Jordan Valley in Palestine over 3,000 years ago, the Israelites were nomadic herders, living almost entirely from sheep, goats, and cattle. Like all pastoralists, they maintained close relationships with sedentary farmers who held the oases and the great rivers. With this mixed farming and pastoral complex, the pork prohibition constituted a sound ecological strategy. The pastoralists could not raise pigs in their arid habitats, and among the semi-sedentary farming populations pigs were more of a threat than an asset.

The basic reason for this is that the world zones of pastoral nomadism correspond to unforested plains and hills that are too arid for rainfall agriculture and that cannot easily be irrigated. The domestic animals best adapted to these zones are ruminants (including cattle, sheep, and goats), which can digest grass, leaves, and other cellulose foods more effectively than other mammals.

The pig, however, is primarily a creature of forests and shaded riverbanks. Although it is omnivorous, its best weight gain is from foods low in cellulose (nuts, fruits, tubers, and especially grains), making it a direct competitor of man. It cannot subsist on grass alone and is ill-adapted to the hot, dry climate of the grasslands, mountains, and deserts in the Middle East. . . .

Among the ancient mixed farming and pastoralist communities of the Middle East, domestic animals were valued primarily as sources of milk, cheese, hides, dung, fiber, and traction for plowing. Goats, sheep, and cattle provided all of this, plus an occasional supplement of lean meat. From the beginning, therefore, pork must have been a luxury food, esteemed for its succulent, tender, and fatty qualities.

Between 4,000 and 9,000 years ago, the human population in the Middle East increased sixty-fold. Extensive deforestation accompanied this rise, largely due to damage caused by sheep and goat herds. Shade and water, the natural conditions appropriate for raising pigs, became ever more scarce, and pork became even more of a tempting luxury. . . . People find it difficult to resist such temptations on their own. Hence Yahweh and Allah were heard to say that swine were unclean—unfit to eat or touch.

In short, in the Middle East it was ecologically maladaptive . . . to raise pigs in substantial numbers, and small-scale production would only increase the temptation. Better then, to prohibit the consumption of pork entirely.

BIOCULTURAL CONNECTION

Consider a taboo you follow and come up with an explanation for it other than the conventional one that most people accept.

Adapted from Harris, M. (1989). Cows, pigs, wars, and witches: The riddles of culture *(pp. 35–60). New York: Vintage/ Random House.*

Beyond these three general groups, there are various other anthropological approaches. Some stress the importance of identifying general patterns or even discovering laws. Early anthropologists believed that they could discover such laws by means of the theory of *unilinear cultural evolution* of universal human progress, beginning with what was then called "savagery," followed by "barbarism," and gradually making progress toward a condition of human perfection known as "high civilization."[32]

Although anthropologists have long abandoned such sweeping generalizations as unscientific and ethnocentric, some continued to search for universal laws in the general development of human cultures by focusing on technological development as measured in the growing capacity for energy capture per capita of the population. This theoretical perspective is sometimes called *neo-evolutionism*. Others seek to explain recurring patterns in human social behavior in terms of laws of natural selection by focusing on possible relationships with human genetics, a theoretical perspective identified with sociobiology. Yet others stress that broad generalizations are impossible because each culture is distinct and can only be understood as resulting from unique historical processes and circumstances. Some even go a step further and focus on in-depth description and analysis of personal life histories of individual members in a group in order to reveal the work of a culture.

---

[32] Carneiro, R. L. (2003). *Evolutionism in cultural anthropology: A critical history.* Boulder, CO: Westview.

Beyond these cultural historical approaches, there are other theoretical perspectives that do not aim for laws or generalizations to explain culture. Theoretical perspectives that reject measuring and evaluating different cultures by means of some sort of universal standard, and stress that they can only be explained or interpreted in their own unique terms, are associated with the important anthropological principle known as *cultural relativism,* discussed in the previous chapter.

Ethical Responsibilities in Anthropological Research

As explained in this chapter, anthropologists obtain information about different peoples and their cultures through long-term, full-immersion fieldwork based on personal observation of and participation in the everyday activities of the community. Once they are admitted and allowed to stay, anthropologists are usually befriended and sometimes even adopted, gradually becoming familiar with the local social structures and cultural features and even with highly personal or politically sensitive details known only to trusted insiders.

Because the community is usually part of a larger and more powerful complex society, anthropological knowledge about how the locals live, what they own, what motivates them, and how they are organized has the potential to make the community vulnerable to exploitation and manipulation. In this context, it is good to be reminded of the ancient Latin maxim *scientia potentia est* ("knowledge is power"). In other words, anthropological knowledge may have far-reaching—and possibly negative—consequences for the peoples being studied.

This problematic relationship between knowledge and power is an uncomfortable one. Are there any rules that may guide anthropologists in their ethical decision making and help them judge right from wrong? This important issue is addressed in the American Anthropological Association's Code of Ethics (discussed in Chapter 1). First formalized in 1971 and modified in its current form in 1998, this document outlines the various ethical responsibilities and moral obligations of anthropologists, including this central maxim: "Anthropological researchers must do everything in their power to ensure that their research does not harm the safety, dignity, or privacy of the people with whom they work, conduct research, or perform other professional activities."

The first step in this endeavor is to communicate in advance the nature, purpose, and potential impact of the planned study to individuals who provide

U.S. Army

Former social science teacher Major Robert Holbert takes notes while drinking tea with local school administrators in a small Afghan town in 2007. Embedded with a U.S. Army brigade combat unit, the officer conducted sociocultural assessments as part of the "Human Terrain System" (HTS). Designed to improve the military's ability to understand the complexities of the "human terrain" (civilian population) as it applies to operations in war-torn Afghanistan, HTS has been part of a counterinsurgency strategy against Taliban guerillas since 2006. American social scientists, including anthropologists, participated in its development and implementation. Anthropological involvement in "the struggle for hearts and minds" has been controversial since the mid-1960s, sparking intense debates over ethical concerns that militarizing anthropology may harm communities.

information—and to obtain their informed consent or formal recorded agreement to participate in the research. But protecting the community one studies requires more than that; it demands constant vigilance and alertness. There are some situations where this is particularly challenging—such as working for a global business corporation, international bank, or government agency, such as the foreign service, police, or military.[33] Moreover, it may not be possible to fully anticipate all the cross-cultural and long-term consequences of publishing one's research findings. Navigating this ethical gray area is challenging, but it is the anthropologist's responsibility to be aware of moral responsibilities and to take every possible caution to ensure that one's research does not jeopardize the well-being of the people being studied.

[33]American Anthropological Association. (2007). Executive board statement on the Human Terrain System Project. http://www.aaanet.org/pdf/ EB_Resolution_110807.pdf; González, R. J. (2009). *American counterinsurgency: Human science and the human terrain.* Chicago: University of Chicago Press; McFate, M. (2007). *Role and effectiveness of socio-cultural knowledge for counterinsurgency.* Alexandria, VA: Institute for Defense Analysis.

Questions for Reflection

1. In describing and interpreting human cultures, anthropologists have long relied on ethnographic fieldwork, including participant observation. What makes this research method uniquely challenging and effective? Of what use might the findings be for meeting the unique challenges of our globalizing world?

2. Early anthropologists engaged in salvage ethnography (urgent anthropology) to create a reliable record of indigenous cultures once widely expected to vanish. Although many indigenous communities did lose customary practices due to acculturation, descendants of those cultures can now turn to anthropological records to revitalize their ancestral ways of life. Do you think this is a good thing? Why or why not?

3. In our globalizing world, a growing number of anthropologists carry out multi-sited ethnography rather than conduct research in a single community. If you would do such a multi-sited research project, what would you focus on, and where would you conduct your actual participant observations and interviews?

4. If you were invited to "study up," on which cultural group would you focus? How would you go about getting access to that group for participant observation, and what serious obstacles might you encounter?

5. In light of professional ethics, what moral dilemmas might anthropologists face in choosing to advise a government in exploring or implementing a nonviolent solution to a military conflict? How is military anthropology different from other forms of applied anthropology, such as working for the Foreign Service, the World Bank, the Roman Catholic Church, or an international business corporation such as IBM and Intel?

Suggested Readings

Bernard, H. R. (2002). *Research methods in anthropology: Qualitative and quantitative approaches* (3rd ed.). Walnut Creek, CA: Altamira.

Written in a conversational style and rich with examples, this extremely useful and accessible book has twenty chapters divided into three sections: preparing for fieldwork, data collection, and data analysis. It touches on all the basics, from literature search and research design to interviewing, field note management, multivariate analysis, ethics, and more.

Boškovic, A. (Ed.). (2009). *Other people's anthropologies: Ethnographic practice on the margins.* Oxford, England: Berghahn.

This volume with contributions from prominent and promising anthropologists from many different countries is based on a workshop of the European Association of Social Anthropologists held in Vienna in 2004. The collection offers fresh and alternative perspectives on a discipline historically dominated by scholars in the core of the world system, representing the so-called great traditions (Anglo-American, French, and German).

Dicks, B., et al (2005). *Qualitative research and hypermedia: Ethnography for the digital age (New technologies for social research).* Thousand Oaks, CA: Sage.

Introducing emerging ethnographic research methods that utilize new technologies, the authors explain how to conduct data collection, analysis, and representation using new technologies and hypermedia; they also discuss how digital technologies may transform ethnographic research.

Erickson, P. A., & Murphy, L. D. (2003). *A history of anthropological theory* (2nd ed.). Peterborough, Ontario: Broadview.

A clear and concise survey from antiquity to the modern era, effectively drawing the lines between the old and new. This edition features several new and expanded sections on topics including feminist anthropology, globalization, and medical anthropology.

Gordon, R., Lyons, H., and Lyons, A. (Eds.). (2010). *Fifty key anthropologists.* New York: Routledge.

A collection of engaging essays on some of the most significant figures who have shaped and defined the discipline of anthropology. The fifty anthropologists featured were selected based on their contributions to the discipline through theory, fieldwork, or institutional development.

Pink, S. (2001). *Doing visual ethnography: Images, media and representation in research.* Thousand Oaks, CA: Sage.

Exploring the use and potential of photography, video, and hypermedia in ethnographic and social research, this text offers a reflexive approach to the practical, theoretical, methodological, and ethical issues of using these media. Following each step of research, from planning to fieldwork to analysis and representation, the author suggests how visual images and technologies can be combined to form an integrated product..

Robben, A.C.G.M., & Sluka, J. A. (Eds.). (2007). *Ethnographic fieldwork: An anthropology reader.* Malden, MA: Blackwell.

This up-to-date text provides a comprehensive selection of classic and contemporary reflections, examining the tensions between self and other, the relationships between anthropologists and key consultants, conflicts and ethical challenges, various types of ethnographic research (including multi-sited fieldwork), and different styles of writing about fieldwork.

Challenge Issue As social creatures dependent upon one another for survival, humans face the challenge of communicating clearly in a multiplicity of situations about countless things connected to our well-being. We do this with a variety of distinctive gestures, sounds, touches, and body postures. Our most sophisticated means of sharing large amounts of complex information is through language—a foundation stone of every human culture. Today, as shown in this photo of a Tuareg nomad talking on his satellite phone while astride a camel in the Sahara Desert, modern technology enables people to communicate instantly from even the most remote corners of the earth. But to make sense of messages, they must share a language, no matter how sophisticated their electronic gadgets.

CHAPTER 16

Language and Communication

Chapter Preview

What Is Language?

A language is a system of symbolic communication using sounds and/or gestures that are put together according to rules, resulting in meanings that are based on agreement by a society and intelligible to all who share that language. Although humans rely heavily on spoken language, or speech, to communicate with one another, it is not their sole means of communication. Human language is embedded in an age-old gesture-call system in which body motions and facial expressions, along with vocal features such as tone and volume, play vital roles in conveying messages. The anthropological study of language can be divided into three key branches: descriptive linguistics, historical linguistics, and the investigation of language in relation to social and cultural settings.

How Is Language Related to Culture?

A culture consists of ideas and perceptions of the world that inform and are reflected in people's behavior. This complex of ideas and perceptions is encoded in a coherent system of symbols that serves as communication between members of a society. As such, language is fundamental to the functioning of human cultures. Social variables—such as age, gender, and economic status—may influence how people use language. Moreover, people communicate what is meaningful to them, and that is largely defined by their particular culture. Our use of language has an effect on, and is influenced by, our culture.

How Do Languages Change?

All languages are constantly transforming—new words are adopted or coined, others are dropped, and some shift in meaning. Languages change for various reasons, ranging from selective borrowing from another language to the need for new vocabulary to deal with technological innovations or altered social realities. On one hand, domination of one society by another may result in erosion or loss of a particular language. On the other, cultural revitalization may result in the resurgence or revival of a threatened or even extinct language. Today's global telecommunication revolution is transforming both written and spoken language all around the world.

The human ability to communicate through language rests squarely on our biological makeup. We are programmed for language, be it through sounds or gestures. (Sign languages, such as the American Sign Language—ASL—used by the hearing impaired, are fully developed languages in their own right.) Beyond the cries of babies, which are not learned but which do communicate, humans must learn their language. So it is that any normal child from anywhere in the world readily learns the language of his or her culture.

Language is a system of communication using sounds and/or gestures that are put together according to certain rules, resulting in meanings that are intelligible to all who share that language. These sounds and gestures are **symbols**—marks, sounds, gestures, motions, or other signs that are arbitrarily linked to something else and represent it *in a meaningful way*. For example, the word *crying* is a symbol, a combination of sounds to which we assign the meaning of a particular action and which we can use to communicate that meaning, whether or not anyone around us is actually crying.

Signals, unlike culturally learned symbols, or meaningful signs, are instinctive sounds and gestures that have a natural or self-evident meaning. Screams, sighs, and coughs, for example, are signals that convey some kind of emotional or physical state.

Today's language experts are not certain how much credit to give to animals, such as dolphins or chimpanzees, for the ability to use symbols as well as signals. But it has become evident that these animals and many others communicate in remarkable ways.[1] Apes have demonstrated an ability to understand language quite well, even using rudimentary grammar. Several chimpanzees, gorillas, and orangutans have been taught American Sign Language. Researchers have discovered that even vervet monkeys utilize distinct calls for communication. These calls go

beyond merely signaling levels of fear or arousal. Among other things, these small African monkeys have specific calls to signify the type of predator threatening the group. According to primatologist Allison Jolly,

> [The calls] include which direction to look in or where to run. There is an audience effect: calls are given when there is someone appropriate to listen . . . monkey calls are far more than involuntary expressions of emotion.[2]

What are the implications for our understanding of the nature and evolution of language? Before we can answer this, we need a better understanding of the various systems of animal communication. Meanwhile, even as debate continues over how human and animal communication relate to each other, we cannot dismiss communication among nonhuman species as a set of simple instinctive reflexes or fixed action patterns.[3]

A remarkable example of the many scientific efforts under way on this subject is the story of an orangutan named Chantek, featured in the following Original Study on the opposite page. Among other things, it illustrates the creative process of language development and the capacity of a nonhuman primate to recognize symbols.

While language studies such as the one involving Chantek are fascinating and reveal much about primate cognition, the fact remains that human culture is ultimately dependent on an elaborate system of communication far more complex than that of any other species—including our fellow primates. The reason for this is the sheer amount of knowledge that must be learned by each person from other individuals in order to fully participate in society. Of course, a significant amount of learning can and does take place in the absence of language by way of observation and imitation, guided by a limited number of meaningful signs or symbols. However, all known human cultures are so rich in content that they require communication systems that not only can give precise labels to various classes of phenomena but also permit people to think and talk about their own and others' experiences and expectations—past, present, and future.

The central and most highly developed human system of communication is language. Knowledge of the workings of language, then, is essential to a full understanding of what culture is about and how it operates.

---

[1] Among many references on this, see Bekoff, M., et al. (Eds.). (2002). *The cognitive animal: Empirical and theoretical perspectives on animal cognition.* Cambridge, MA: MIT Press; Patterson, F. G. P., & Gordon, W. (2002). Twenty-seven years of Project Koko and Michael. In B. Galdikas et al. (Eds.), *All apes great and small* (vol. 1): *Chimpanzees, bonobos, and gorillas* (pp. 165–176). New York: Kluwer Academic.

language A system of communication using sounds or gestures that are put together in meaningful ways according to a set of rules.

symbol A mark, sound, gesture, motion, or other sign that is arbitrarily linked to something else and represents it in a meaningful way.

signal An instinctive sound or gesture that has a natural or self-evident meaning.

---

[2] Jolly, A. (1991). Thinking like a vervet. *Science 251,* 574; see also Seyfarth, R. M., et al. (1980). Monkey responses to three different alarm calls: Evidence for predator classification and semantic communication. *Science 210,* 801–803.

[3] Armstrong, D. F., Stokoe, W. C., & Wilcox, S. E. (1993). Signs of the origin of syntax. *Current Anthropology 34,* 349–368; Burling, R. (1993). Primate calls, human language, and nonverbal communication. *Current Anthropology 34,* 25–53.

Language and the Intellectual Abilities of Orangutans   *by H. Lyn White Miles*

In 1978, after researchers began to use American Sign Language for the deaf to communicate with chimpanzees and gorillas, I began the first long-term study of the language ability of an orangutan named Chantek. There was criticism that symbol-using apes might just be imitating their human caregivers, but there is now growing agreement that orangutans, gorillas, and both chimpanzee species can develop language skills at the level of a 2- to 3-year-old human child.

© H. Lyn Miles, PhD, Chantek Foundation

Chantek beginning the sign for "tomato."

The goal of Project Chantek was to investigate the mind of an orangutan through a developmental study of his cognitive and linguistic skills. It was a great ethical and emotional responsibility to engage an orangutan in what anthropologists call "enculturation," since I would not only be teaching a form of communication, I would be teaching aspects of the culture upon which that language was based. . . .

A small group of caregivers at the University of Tennessee, Chattanooga, began raising Chantek when he was 9 months old. They communicated with him by using gestural signs based on the American Sign Language for the deaf. After a month, Chantek produced his own first sign and eventually learned to use approximately 150 different signs, forming a vocabulary similar to that of a very young child. Chantek learned names for people (LYN, JOHN), places (YARD, BROCK-HALL), things to eat (YOGURT, CHOCOLATE), actions (WORK, HUG), objects (SCREWDRIVER, MONEY), animals (DOG, APE), colors (RED, BLACK), pronouns (YOU, ME), location (UP, POINT), attributes (GOOD, HURT), and emphasis (MORE, TIME-TO-DO).

We found that Chantek's signing was spontaneous and nonrepetitious. He did not merely imitate his caregivers, but rather he actively used signs to initiate communications and meet his needs. Almost immediately, he began using signs in combinations and modulated their meanings with slight changes in how he articulated and arranged his signs. He commented "COKE DRINK" after drinking his coke, "PULL BEARD" while pulling a caregiver's hair through a fence, and "TIME HUG" while locked in his cage as his caregiver looked at her watch. But, beyond using signs in this way, could he use them as symbols, that is, more abstractly to represent a person, thing, action, or idea, even apart from its context or when it was not present?

One indication of the capacity of both deaf and hearing children to use symbolic language is the ability to point, which some researchers argued that apes could not do spontaneously. Chantek began to point to objects when he was 2 years old, somewhat later than human children. First, he showed and gave us objects, and then he began pointing where he wanted to be tickled and to where he wanted to be carried. Finally, he could answer questions like WHERE HAT? WHICH DIFFERENT? and WHAT WANT? by pointing to the correct object.

As Chantek's vocabulary increased, the ideas that he was expressing became more complex, such as when he signed BAD BIRD at noisy birds giving alarm calls, and WHITE CHEESE FOOD-EAT for cottage cheese. He understood that things had characteristics or attributes that could be described. He also created combinations of signs that we had never used before.

In the way that a child learns language, Chantek began to over- or under-extend the meaning of his signs, which gave us insight into his emotions and how he was beginning to classify his world. For example, he used the sign DOG for actual dogs, as well as for a picture of a dog in his Viewmaster, orangutans on television, barking noises on the radio, birds, horses, a tiger at the circus, a herd of cows, a picture of a cheetah, and a noisy helicopter that presumably sounded like it was barking. For Chantek, the sign BUG included crickets, cockroaches, a picture of a cockroach, beetles, slugs, small moths, spiders, worms, flies, a picture of a graph shaped like a butterfly, tiny brown pieces of cat food, and small bits of feces. He signed BREAK before he broke and shared pieces of crackers, and after he broke his toilet. He signed BAD to himself before he grabbed a cat, when he bit into a radish, and for a dead bird.

We also discovered that Chantek could comprehend our spoken English (after the first couple of years we used speech as well as signing). When he was 2 years old, Chantek began to sign for things that were not present. He frequently asked to go to places in his yard to look for animals, such as his pet squirrel and cat, who served as playmates. He also made requests for ICE CREAM, signing CAR RIDE and pulling us toward the parking lot for a trip to a local ice cream shop.

We learned that an orangutan can tell lies. Deception is an important indicator of language abilities since it requires a deliberate and intentional misrepresentation of reality. In order to deceive, you must be able to see events from the other person's perspective and negate his or her perception. Chantek began to deceive from a relatively early age, and we caught him in lies about three times a week. He learned that he could sign DIRTY to get into the bathroom to play with the washing machine, dryer, soap, and so on, instead of using the toilet. He also used his signs deceptively to gain social advantage in games, to divert attention in social interactions, and to avoid testing situations and to delay coming home after walks on campus.

CONTINUED

CONTINUED

On one occasion, Chantek stole a pencil eraser, pretended to swallow it, and "supported" his case by opening his mouth and signing FOOD-EAT, as if to say that he had swallowed it. However, he really held the eraser in his cheek, and later it was found in his bedroom where he commonly hid objects.

We carried out tests of Chantek's mental ability using measures developed for human children. Chantek reached a mental age equivalent to that of a 2- to 3-year-old child, with some skills of even older children. On some tasks done readily by children, such as using one object to represent another and pretend play, Chantek performed as well as children, but less frequently. He engaged in chase games in which he would look over his shoulder as he darted about, although no one was chasing him. He also signed to his toys and offered them food and drink.

By 4½ years of age, Chantek showed evidence of planning, creative simulation, and the use of objects in novel relations to one another to invent new meanings. For example, he simulated the context for food preparation by giving his caregiver two objects needed to prepare his milk formula

and staring at the location of the remaining ingredient.

Chantek was extremely curious and inventive. When he wanted to know the name of something, he offered his hands to be molded into the shape of the proper sign. But language is a creative process, so we were pleased to see that Chantek began to invent his own signs. He invented: NO-TEETH (to show us that he would not use his teeth during rough play); EYE-DRINK (for contact lens solution used by his caregivers); and DAVE-MISSING-FINGER (a name for a favorite university employee who had a hand injury). Like our ancestors, Chantek had become a creator of language.

(Adapted from Miles, H.L.W. (1993). Language and the orangutan: The old "person" of the forest. In P. Cavalieri & P. Singer (Eds.), The Great Ape Project (pp. 45–50). New York: St. Martin's Press.)

Update

My relationship and research with Chantek continue through the Chantek Foundation and Animal Nation, Inc. of Kennesaw, Georgia. Chantek now uses several hundred signs and has invented some new ones of his own—such as

KATSUP (by combining TOMATO and TOOTHPASTE). He uses a computer and makes stone tools, paintings, and other arts and crafts, including small percussion instruments used in my Native American rock band Animal Nation. Chantek also makes unique jewelry and found art assemblages of semi-precious stones for the foundation, which helps to fund the research.

As someone of Abenaki Indian heritage, I believe that animals are "persons of the nonhuman kind." There is a growing movement across the globe for recognition of the intelligence, personhood, and even legal protection of all great apes, based on their culture in natural settings and on what we have learned from Chantek's abilities. Plans are in the making for Chantek and other enculturated apes to live in culture-based preserves where they have more range of choices and learning opportunities than zoos or research centers are willing to provide. An exciting new project under the auspices of Animal Nation, Inc., will give great apes an opportunity to communicate with one another via the Internet. As rock musician Peter Gabriel says in his song "Animal Nation" about communicating with ages, "Who knows where this will end?" (For more information, see www.chantek.org.)

Linguistic Research and the Nature of Language

Any human language—Chinese, English, Swahili, or whatever—is obviously a means of transmitting information and sharing with others both collective and individual experiences. It is a system that enables us to translate our concerns, beliefs, and perceptions into symbols that can be understood and interpreted by others.

In spoken language, this is done by taking sounds—no language uses more than about fifty—and developing rules for putting them together in meaningful ways. Sign languages, such as American Sign Language, do the same with gestures rather than sounds. The vast array of languages in the world—some 7,000 or so different ones—may well astound and mystify us by their great variety and complexity, yet language experts have found that all languages, as far back as we can trace them, are organized in the same basic way.

The roots of **linguistics**—the systematic study of all aspects of language—go back a long way, to the works of

ancient language specialists in India more than 2,000 years ago. The European age of exploration, from the 16th through the 18th centuries, set the stage for a great leap forward in the scientific study of language. Explorers, invaders, and missionaries accumulated information about a huge diversity of languages from all around the world. More than 10,000 languages still existed when they began their inquiries.

Linguists in the 19th century, including anthropologists, made a significant contribution in comparative research—discovering patterns, relationships, and systems in the sounds and structures of different languages and tentatively formulating laws and principles concerning language. In the 20th century, while still collecting data, these researchers made considerable progress in unraveling the reasoning process behind language construction, testing and working from new and improved theories.

Insofar as theories and facts of language are verifiable by independent researchers looking at the same materials, it can now be said that we have a science of linguistics. This science has three main branches: descriptive linguistics, historical linguistics, and a third branch that focuses on language in relation to social and cultural settings.

linguistics The modern scientific study of all aspects of language.

For linguists studying language in the field, laptops and recording devices are indispensable tools. Here Tiffany Kershner of Kansas State University works with native Sukwa speakers in northern Malawi, Africa.

© Courtesy of Tiffany Kirschner

Descriptive Linguistics

How can an anthropologist, a trader, a missionary, a diplomat, or any other outsider research a foreign language that has not yet been described and analyzed, or for which there are no readily available written materials? There are hundreds of such undocumented languages in the world. Fortunately, effective methods have been developed to help with the task. Descriptive linguistics involves unraveling a language by recording, describing, and analyzing all of its features. It is a painstaking process, but it is ultimately rewarding in that it provides deeper understanding of a language—its structure, its unique linguistic repertoire (figures of speech, word plays, and so on), and its relationship to other languages.

The process of unlocking the underlying rules of a spoken language requires a trained ear and a thorough understanding of how multiple different speech sounds are produced. Without such know-how, it is extremely difficult to write out or make intelligent use of any data concerning a particular language. To satisfy this preliminary requirement, most people need special training in phonetics, discussed below.

Phonology

Rooted in the Greek word *phone* (meaning "sound"), **phonetics** is defined as the systematic identification and description of the distinctive sounds in a language. Phonetics is basic to **phonology,** the study of language sounds.

In order to analyze and describe any language, one needs first an inventory of all its distinctive sounds.

While some of the sounds used in other languages may seem very much like those of the researcher's own speech pattern, others may be unfamiliar. For example, the *th* sound common in English does not exist in the Dutch language and is difficult for most Dutch speakers to pronounce, just as the *r* sound used in numerous languages is tough for Japanese speakers. And the unique "click" sounds used in Bushman languages in southern Africa are difficult for speakers of just about every other language.

While collecting speech sounds or utterances, the linguist works to isolate the **phonemes**—the smallest units of sound that make a difference in meaning. This isolation and analysis may be done by a process called the *minimal-pair test.* The researcher tries to find two short words that appear to be exactly alike except for one sound, such as *bit* and *pit* in English. If the substitution of *b* for *p* in this minimal pair makes a difference in meaning, as it does in English, then those two sounds have been identified as distinct phonemes of the language and will require two different symbols to record. If, however, the linguist

> **phonetics** The systematic identification and description of distinctive speech sounds in a language.
> **phonology** The study of language sounds.
> **phonemes** The smallest units of sound that make a difference in meaning in a language.

finds two different pronunciations (as when "butter" is pronounced "budder") and then finds that there is no difference in their meaning for a native speaker, the sounds represented will be considered variants of the same phoneme. In such cases, for economy of representation only one of the two symbols will be used to record that sound wherever it is found.

Morphology, Syntax, and Grammar

While making and studying an inventory of distinctive sounds, linguists also look into **morphology,** the study of the patterns or rules of word formation in a language (including such things as rules concerning verb tense, pluralization, and compound words). They do this by marking out specific sounds and sound combinations that seem to have meaning. These are called **morphemes**—the smallest units of sound that carry a meaning in a language.

Morphemes are distinct from phonemes, which can alter meaning but have no meaning by themselves. For example, a linguist studying English in a North American farming community would soon learn that *cow* is a morpheme—a meaningful combination of the phonemes *c, o,* and *w*. Pointing to two of these animals, the linguist would elicit the word *cows* from local speakers. This would reveal yet another morpheme—the *s*—which can be added to the original morpheme to indicate plural.

The next step in unraveling a language is to identify its **syntax**—the patterns or rules by which morphemes are arranged into phrases and sentences. The **grammar** of the language will ultimately consist of all observations about its morphemes and syntax.

One of the strengths of modern descriptive linguistics is the objectivity of its methods. For example, English-speaking anthropologists who specialize in this will not approach a language with the idea that it must have nouns, verbs, prepositions, or any other of the form classes identifiable in English. Instead they see what turns up in the language and attempt to describe it in terms of its own inner workings. This allows for unanticipated discoveries. For instance, unlike many other languages, English does not distinguish between feminine and masculine nouns. So it

morphology The study of the patterns or rules of word formation in a language (including such things as rules concerning verb tense, pluralization, and compound words).

morphemes The smallest units of sound that carry a meaning in language. They are distinct from phonemes, which can alter meaning but have no meaning by themselves.

syntax The patterns or rules by which words are arranged into phrases and sentences.

grammar The entire formal structure of a language, including morphology and syntax.

is that English speakers use the definite article *the* in front of any noun, while French requires two types of such definite articles: *la* for feminine nouns and *le* for masculine—as in *la lune* (the moon) and *le soleil* (the sun).

German speakers go one step farther, utilizing three types of articles: *der* in front of masculine nouns, *die* for feminine, and *das* for neutral. It is also interesting to note that in contrast to their French neighbors, Germans consider the moon as masculine, so they say *der Mond*, and the sun as feminine, which makes it *die Sonne*. In another part of the world, the highlands of Peru and Bolivia in South America, indigenous peoples who speak Quechua are not concerned about whether nouns are gendered or neutral, for their language has no definite articles.

Historical Linguistics

While descriptive linguistics focuses on all features of a particular language at any one moment in time, historical linguistics deals with the fact that languages change. In addition to deciphering "dead" languages that are no longer spoken, specialists in this field investigate relationships between earlier and later forms of the same language, study older languages to track the processes of change into modern ones, and examine interrelationships among older languages. For example, they attempt to sort out the development of Latin (spoken almost 1,500 years ago in southern Europe) into the Romance languages of Italian, Spanish, Portuguese, French, and Romanian by identifying natural shifts in the original language and tracking modifications brought on by centuries of direct contact with Germanic-speaking invaders from northern Europe.

Historical linguists are not limited to the faraway past, for even modern languages are constantly transforming—adding new words, dropping others, or changing meaning. Technological breakthroughs resulting in new equipment and products prompt linguistic shifts. For instance, the electronic revolution that brought us radio, television, and computers has created entirely new vocabularies. Over the last decade or so, Internet use has widened the meaning of a host of already existing English words—from *hacking* and *surfing* to *spam*. Entirely new words, such as *blogging* and *vlogging* (video blogging), have been coined, leading to the creation of Internet dictionaries such as netlingo.com.

Increasing professional specialization is another driving force in language transformation. We see one of many examples in the field of biomedicine where today's students must learn the specialized vocabulary and idioms of the profession—over 6,000 new words in the first year of medical school.

Especially when focusing on long-term processes of change, historical linguists depend on written records of

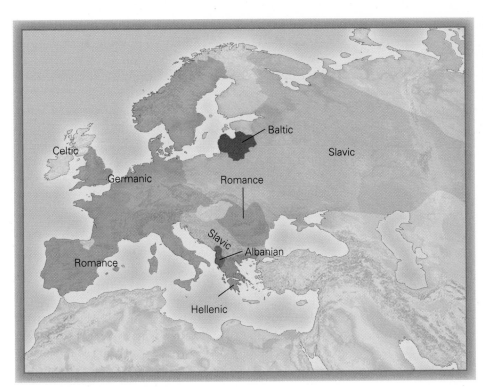

Figure 16.1 Indo-European language subgroups in Europe. Not all languages spoken in Europe are part of the Indo-European family. Basque, for example, is an ancient language still spoken in the French-Spanish borderland. Moreover, languages spoken by Hungarians, Estonians, Finns, Komi (in northeast Russia), and Saami (in northern Scandinavia) belong to the Uralic language family.

languages. They have achieved considerable success in working out the relationships among different languages, and these are reflected in schemes of classification. For example, English is one of approximately 140 languages classified in the larger Indo-European language family (Figure 16.1). A **language family** is a group of languages descended from a single ancestral language. This family is subdivided into some eleven subgroups (Germanic, Romance, and so on), indicating that there has been a long period (6,000 years or so) of **linguistic divergence** from an ancient unified language (reconstructed as Proto-Indo-European) into separate "daughter" languages. English is one of several languages in the Germanic subgroup (Figure 16.2), all of which are more closely related to one another than they are to the languages of any other subgroup of the Indo-European family.

So, despite the differences between them, the languages of one subgroup share certain features when compared to those of another. As an illustration, the word for "father" in the Germanic languages always starts with an *f* or closely related *v* sound (Dutch *vader,* German *Vater,* Gothic *Fadar*). Among the Romance languages, by contrast, the comparable word always starts with a *p*: French *père,* Spanish and Italian *padre*—all derived from the Latin *pater.* The original Indo-European word for "father" was *p'tēr,* so in this case, the Romance languages have retained the earlier pronunciation, whereas the Germanic languages have diverged. Thus many words that begin with *p* in the Romance languages, like Latin *piscis* and *pes,* become words like English *fish* and *foot* in the Germanic languages.

In addition to describing the changes that have taken place as languages have diverged from ancient parent languages, historical linguists have also developed methods to estimate when such divergences occurred. One such technique is known as **glottochronology,** a term derived from the Greek word *glottis,* which means "tongue" or "language." This method compares the **core vocabularies** of languages—pronouns, lower numerals, and names for body parts and natural objects. It is based on the assumption that these basic vocabularies change more slowly than other words and at a more or less constant rate of 14 to 19 percent per 1,000 years. That means that after about 1,000 years, two "sister languages" still share nearly 75 percent of the core vocabulary. (Linguists determined this rate by calculating changes documented in thirteen historic written languages.) By applying a mathematical formula to two related core vocabularies, one can roughly determine the approximate number of years since the languages separated.

language family A group of languages descended from a single ancestral language.

linguistic divergence The development of different languages from a single ancestral language.

glottochronology In linguistics, a method for identifying the approximate time that languages branched off from a common ancestor; based on analyzing core vocabularies.

core vocabulary The most basic and long-lasting words in any language—pronouns, lower numerals, and names for body parts and natural objects.

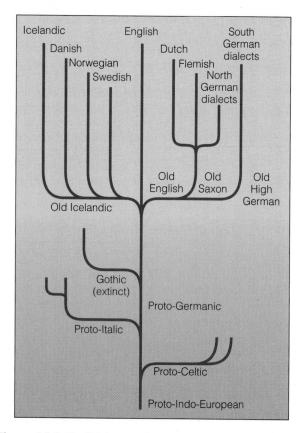

Figure 16.2 English is one of a group of languages in the Germanic subgroup of the Indo-European family. This diagram shows its relationship to other languages in the same subgroup. The root was Proto-Indo-European, an ancestral language originally spoken by early farmers and herders who spread north and west over Europe, bringing with them both their customs and their language.

Although not as precise we might like, glottochronology, in conjunction with other chronological dating methods such as those based on archaeological and genetic data, can help determine the time of linguistic divergence.

Processes of Linguistic Divergence

Studying modern languages in their specific cultural contexts can help us understand the processes of change that may have led to linguistic divergence. Clearly, one force for change is selective borrowing by one language from another. This is evident in the many French words present in the English language—and in the growing number of English words cropping up in languages all around the world due to globalization.

There is also a tendency for any group within a larger society to create its own unique vocabulary, whether it is a street gang, sorority, religious group, prison inmates, or platoon of soldiers. By changing the meaning of existing words or inventing new ones, members of the "in-group" can communicate with fellow members while effectively excluding outsiders who may be within hearing range.

Finally, there seems to be a human tendency to admire the person who comes up with a new and clever idiom, a useful word, or a particularly stylish pronunciation, as long as these do not seriously interfere with communication. All of this means that no language stands still.

Phonological differences among groups may be regarded in the same light as vocabulary differences. In a class-structured society, for example, members of the upper class may try to keep their pronunciation distinct from that of lower classes, or vice versa, as a means of reinforcing social boundaries.

Language Loss and Revival

Perhaps the most powerful force for linguistic change is the domination of one society over another, as demonstrated during 500 years of European colonialism. Such dominations persist today in many parts of the world, such as Taiwan's indigenous peoples being governed by Mandarin-speaking Chinese, Tarascan Indians by Spanish-speaking Mexicans, or Bushmen by English-speaking Namibians.

In many cases, foreign political control has resulted in linguistic erosion or even complete disappearance, sometimes leaving only a faint trace in old, indigenous names for geographic features such as hills and rivers. Over the last 500 years about 3,000 of the world's 10,000 or so languages have become extinct as a direct result of warfare, epidemics, and forced assimilation brought on by colonial powers and other aggressive outsiders. Most of the remaining 7,000 languages are spoken by very few people, and many of them are losing speakers rapidly due to globalization. Half have fewer than 10,000 speakers each, and a quarter have fewer than 1,000. Put another way, half of the world's languages are spoken by just 2 percent of the world's population.[4]

In North America, only 150 of the original 300 indigenous languages still exist, and many of these surviving tongues are moving toward extinction at an alarming rate. Thousands of indigenous languages elsewhere in the world are also threatened, such as Defaku, spoken by just 200 people in Nigeria. Fewer than ten people still speak N/u, a "click" language traditionally spoken in South Africa's Kalahari Desert. It is the only surviving member of the !Ui branch of the Tuu language family (previously called Southern Khoisan).

Anthropologists predict that the number of languages still spoken in the world today will be cut in half by the year 2100, in large part because children born into ethnic minority groups no longer use the ancestral language when they go to school, migrate to cities, join the larger workforce, and are exposed to printed and electronic media.

---

[4] Harrison, K. D. *Pop!Tech 2008: Scarcity and abundance: Global and local trends in language extinction.* www.poptech.org/ popcasts/k_david_harrison__poptech_2008

Collaborative efforts between community members and researchers to preserve fast-disappearing languages sometimes require creative solutions. Several linguistic anthropologists are collaborating on field research with speakers of endangered Khoisan "click" languages such as N|uu and !Xun in southern Africa. Using a portable ultrasound imaging machine, they capture the tongue movements of the click consonants. On the left, Johanna Brugman holds an ultrasound probe under the chin of one of the ten last remaining N|uu speakers, Ouma Katrina Esau, who is helping to document how click sounds are made. On the right, !Xun speaker Jenggu Rooi Fransisko wears a stabilization headset that anchors the probe under his chin. The blue tubes are Palatron sticks used to measure head and jaw movement in order to determine exactly how much movement is caused by the tongue alone. An image of the tongue appears on the ultrasound monitor. Clicks are produced by creating suction within a cavity formed between the front and back parts of the tongue—except in the case of bilabial clicks in which the cavity is made between the lips and the back of the tongue. N|uu is one of only three languages remaining in the world that use bilabial clicks as consonants.

Various media—the print press, radio, satellite television, Internet, and text messaging on cell phones—are driving the need for a shared language, and increasingly that is English. In the past 500 years, this language—originally spoken by about 2.5 million people living only in part of the British Isles in northwestern Europe—has spread around the world. Today some 375 million people (nearly 6 percent of the global population) claim English as their native tongue. Close to a billion others (about 15 percent of humanity) speak it as a second or foreign language.

While a common language allows people from different ethnic backgrounds to communicate, there is the risk that a global spread of one language may contribute to the disappearance of others. And with the extinction of each language, we lose "hundreds of generations of traditional knowledge encoded in these ancestral tongues"—a vast repository of knowledge about the natural world, plants, animals, ecosystems, and cultural traditions.[5] Among many examples is the inventory of 1,000 medicinal plants held in the threatened language of Kallawaya, an ancient "secret" language used by Indian herbal healers in the Bolivian highlands.

The United Nations Educational, Scientific, and Cultural Organization (UNESCO) recently marked out key factors used to assess the endangerment status of a language.[6] Beyond obvious points—such as declining numbers of

speakers, discriminatory governmental policies, illiteracy, and insufficient means for language education—a key issue is the impact electronic media such as the Internet have on language groups.

Today, Internet content exists in only a handful of languages, and 84 percent of Internet users are native speakers of just ten of the world's 7,000 languages. On one hand, there is the serious risk that the overwhelming presence of a few already dominant languages on the Internet further threatens endangered languages. On the other hand, the Internet offers a powerful tool for maintaining and revitalizing disappearing languages and the cultures to which they are tied—as indicated in the ever-growing number of indigenous groups developing computer programs to help teach their native tongues.

Ensuring digital access to local content is a new and important component in language preservation efforts. In 2001, UNESCO established Initiative B@bel, which uses information and communication technologies to support linguistic and cultural diversity. Promoting multilingualism on the Internet, this initiative aims to bridge the digital divide—to make access to Internet content and services more equitable for users worldwide (Figure 16.3).

Sometimes, in reaction to a real or perceived threat of cultural dominance by powerful foreign societies, ethnic groups and even entire countries may seek to maintain or reclaim their unique identity by purging their vocabularies of "foreign" terms. Emerging as a significant force

---

[5] www.livingtongues.org/background.html.

[6] www.unesco.org/webworld/babel.

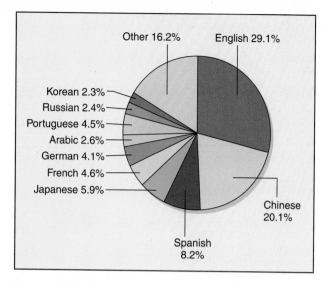

Figure 16.3 Although the world's digital divide is diminishing, it is still dramatic. As illustrated here, nearly 84 percent of today's 1.6 billion Internet users are native speakers of just ten of the world's 7,000 languages. Among the fastest-growing Internet language groups since 2005 are Arabic, Chinese, and Russian. (Source: www.internetworldstats.com, 2009)

for linguistic change, such **linguistic nationalism** is particularly characteristic of the former colonial countries of Africa and Asia today. It is by no means limited to those countries, however, as one can see by periodic French attempts to purge their language of such Americanisms as *le hamburger*. Another example of this is France's decision to substitute the word *e-mail* with the government-approved term *couriel*.

For many ethnic minorities, efforts to counter the threat of linguistic extinction or to resurrect already extinct languages form part of their struggle to maintain a sense of cultural identity and dignity. A prime means by which powerful groups try to assert their dominance over minorities living within their borders is to actively suppress their languages. Examples of this include 20th-century government-sanctioned efforts to repress Native American cultures in Canada and the United States and fully absorb them into mainstream society. Government policies included taking Indian children away from their parents and putting them in boarding schools where only English was allowed, and students were often punished for speaking their traditional

linguistic nationalism The attempt by ethnic minorities and even countries to proclaim independence by purging their language of foreign terms.

sociolinguistics The study of the relationship between language and society through examining how social categories (such as age, gender, ethnicity, religion, occupation, and class) influence the use and significance of distinctive styles of speech.

gendered speech Distinct male and female speech patterns, which vary across social and cultural settings.

languages. Upon returning to their homes, many could no longer communicate with their own close relatives and neighbors.

While now abolished, these institutions and the historical policies that shaped them did lasting damage to American Indian groups striving to maintain their cultural heritage. Especially over the past three decades many of these besieged indigenous communities have been actively involved in language revitalization efforts. Among numerous examples of this is the work of S. Neyooxet Greymorning, a Southern Arapaho, who has devoted three decades to developing and implementing ways to revive indigenous languages, including his own. Greymorning, a professor of anthropology and Native American studies at the University of Montana, tells his story in the Anthropology Applied feature.

Language in Its Social and Cultural Settings

As discussed in the section on descriptive linguistics, language is not simply a matter of combining sounds according to certain rules to come up with meaningful utterances. It is important to remember that languages are spoken by people who are members of distinct societies. In addition to the fact that most societies have their own unique cultures, individuals within each society tend to vary in the ways they use language based on social factors such as gender, age, class, and ethnicity.

We choose words and sentences to communicate meaning, and what is meaningful in one community or culture may not be in another. Our use of language reflects, and is reflected by, the rest of our culture. For that reason, linguistic anthropologists also research language in relation to its various distinctive social and cultural contexts. This third branch of linguistic study falls into two categories: sociolinguistics and ethnolinguistics.

Sociolinguistics

Sociolinguistics, the study of the relationship between language and society, examines how social categories (such as age, gender, ethnicity, religion, occupation, and class) influence the use and significance of distinctive styles of speech.

LANGUAGE AND GENDER

As a major factor in personal and social identity, gender is often reflected in language use, so it is not surprising that numerous thought-provoking sociolinguistic topics fall under the category of language and gender. These include research on **gendered speech**—distinct male and

When Bambi Spoke Arapaho: Preserving Indigenous Languages

by S. Neyooxet Greymorning

In life, there are experiences later recognized as defining moments. For me, a moment like that happened in my second year of college when some mysterious individual stood over me and asked, "What are you doing to help your people?" I remember getting up, going to the library, and walking along the stacks. Trailing my fingers over books, I randomly stopped and pulled one out. It was about the overall status of American Indian languages in the United States. Curious, I opened it, looked up Arapaho, and read that it was among the healthiest Native languages. Comforted by this, it didn't occur to me that a rapidly dwindling number of young Arapaho speakers was signaling the demise of my ancestral tongue. Years later when I told tribal Elder Francis Brown about this, he said, "The Elders called your name."

Perhaps they continued to call. When I went on to graduate school and studied anthropology, I felt driven to take almost every linguistic class available. By 1981, I understood that to lose a language is to lose aspects of how a people make sense of themselves and the world they live in, and the values that culturally and psychologically bind a people together shaping their identity. Feeling the need to do something, I decided to spend the summer on the Wind River Reservation in central Wyoming putting together an Arapaho dictionary. Then I learned that University of Massachusetts professor Dr. Zdeněk Salzmann, a Czech anthropologist who did linguistic work with the Arapaho, had the same idea. I called him, and he suggested we work together.

As a graduate student I dedicated myself to gaining the knowledge, skills, and experience that could contribute to revitalizing languages. Upon completing my doctorate, 1992, I was invited to direct a language and culture program on the Wind River Reservation where Arapaho language instruction had been introduced within the public school system in the late 1970s. By 1993, although Arapaho was taught from kindergarten–high school, my assessment revealed students were only able to say a few basic phrases and vocabulary words having to do with

Courtesy of S. Neyooxet Greymorning

food, animals, colors, and numbers—nothing near fluency and the goal of keeping Arapaho alive.

Recognizing the need for a different approach, I began laying the groundwork to establish one of the first full-day language immersion preschools on a reservation: Hinono'eitiino'oowu'—the Arapaho Language Lodge. The aim was for language "providers" to only speak Arapaho and use a multifaceted approach that included not only word and phrase acquisition, but also response exercises, visual association, and interaction with videos and audio cassettes of songs.

Around this time I contacted Disney Studios and convinced them to allow us to translate *Bambi* into Arapaho as a learning aid.[a] *Bambi* seemed like a good choice because it echoed traditional stories in which animals speak, it was a story that most children on the reservation knew, and as the story unfolds Bambi uses simple childlike language as he learns to talk.

However, even a multifaceted approach that included Bambi speaking Arapaho was not turning the tide of language demise, so I began to think through the challenges with increased focus. From 1996–2002 I gradually developed a new approach, Accelerated Second Language Acquisition (ASLA©™). During 2003, using

my children as language learners, I tested and honed ASLA into a workable methodology that helps re-tune the brain so people learn to visualize the language rather than continually translate back and forth in their minds between the language they know and the one they're learning.

In an effort to encourage language teachers on the reservation to adopt this approach, I have modeled teaching Arapaho through ASLA at the University of Montana with remarkable results. Beyond efforts to help preserve Arapaho, I'm regularly asked to give ASLA workshops for others who are committed to Indigenous language revitalization. To date, I have had contact with over 1,200 individual language instructors from more than 60 different communities in the US, Canada, and Australia, representing over 40 different languages.[b]

The challenge of preserving languages (and the countless keys to life that each one holds) is daunting in our age of globalization. But something my uncle told me during a boyhood visit with him encourages me to be counted among those who keep trying. He woke me at dawn and took me to a pond. There was no wind, and the water was like glass. After instructing me to pick up a small stone, he said, "Now drop it in the pond and tell me what you see." Releasing the stone, I watched it make ever-widening circles on the water. "I want you to always remember," said my uncle, "that nothing is so small that it can't put something larger than itself into motion."

[a]See Greymorning, S. N. (2001). Reflections on the Arapaho Language Project or, when Bambi spoke Arapaho and other tales of Arapaho language revitalization efforts. In K. Hale & L. Hinton, *The green book of language revitalization in practice* (pp. 287–297). New York: Academic.

[b]For video examples of students of ASLA speaking Arapaho, plus written comments from language instructors and students about ASLA, go to www.nsilc.org.

Makers of the feature film *Dances with Wolves* aimed for cultural authenticity by casting Native American actors and hiring a female language coach to teach Lakota to those who did not know how to speak it. However, the lessons did not include the "gendered speech" aspect of Lakota—the fact that females and males follow different rules of syntax. Consequently, when Native speakers of the language saw the film, they were amused to hear the actors who portrayed the Lakota warriors speaking like women.

© Orion Pictures Corporation/Everett Collection

female speech patterns, which vary across social and cultural settings.

One of the first in-depth studies in this vein, done in the early 1970s, asserted that neither language nor gender could be studied independently of the socially constructed communities in which we live. Exploring the relationship of gender and power, it addressed specific issues including social factors said to contribute to North American women exhibiting less decisive speech styles than men. This study and a subsequent wave of related scholarly works have produced new insights about language as a social speech "performance" in both private and public settings.[7]

Gendered speech research also includes the study of distinct male and female syntax exhibited in various languages around the world, such as the Lakota language, still spoken at the Pine Ridge and Rosebud Indian reservations in South Dakota. When a Lakota woman asks someone, "How are you?" she says, "Tonikt*hkahe*?" But when her brother poses the same question, he says, "Tonikt*ukahwo*?" As explained by Michael Two Horses, "Our language is gender-specific in the area of commands, queries, and a couple of other things."[8]

---

[7] See Lakoff, R. T. (2004). *Language and woman's place*. M. Bucholtz (Ed.). New York: Oxford University Press.

[8] Personal communication, April 2003.

dialects Varying forms of a language that reflect particular regions, occupations, or social classes and that are similar enough to be mutually intelligible.

SOCIAL DIALECTS

Sociolinguists are also interested in **dialects**—varying forms of a language that reflect particular regions, occupations, or social classes and that are similar enough to be mutually intelligible.

Distinguishing dialects from languages and revealing the relationship between power and language, the noted linguist-political activist Noam Chomsky often quoted the saying that a dialect is a language without an army.[9] Technically, all dialects are languages—there is nothing partial or sublinguistic about them—and the point at which two different dialects become distinctly different languages is roughly the point at which speakers of one are almost totally unable to communicate with speakers of the other.

Boundaries may be psychological, geographic, social, or economic, and they are not always very sharp. In the case of regional dialects, there is frequently a transitional territory, or perhaps a buffer zone, where features of both are found and understood, as between central and southern China. The fact is that if you learn the Chinese of Beijing, you will find that a Chinese person from Canton or Hong Kong will understand almost nothing of what you say, although both languages—or dialects—are usually lumped together as Chinese.

A classic example of the kind of dialect that may set one group apart from others within a single society is one

---

[9] See biographical entry for Chomsky in Shook, J. R., et al. (Eds.). (2004). *Dictionary of modern American philosophers, 1860–1960*. Bristol, England: Thoemmes Press. The saying is attributed to Yiddish linguist Max Weinreich.

spoken by many inner-city African Americans. Technically known as African American Vernacular English (AAVE), it has often been referred to as "black English" and "Ebonics." Unfortunately, there is a widespread misperception among non-AAVE speakers that this dialect is somehow substandard or defective. A basic principle of linguistics is that the selection of a so-called prestige dialect—in this case, what we may call Standard English as opposed to AAVE—is determined by social and historical forces such as wealth and power and is not dependent on virtues or shortcomings of the dialects themselves. In fact, AAVE is a highly structured mode of speech with patterned rules of sounds and sequences like any other language or dialect. Many of its distinctive features stem from the retention of sound patterns, grammatical rules concerning verbs, and even words of the West African languages spoken by the ancestors of present-day African Americans.[10]

In many societies where different dialects are spoken, individuals often become skilled at switching back and forth between them, depending on the situation in which they are speaking. Without being conscious of it, we all do the same sort of thing when we switch from formality to informality in our speech, depending upon where we are and to whom we are talking. The process of changing from one language mode to another as the situation demands, whether from one language to another or from one dialect of a language to another, is known as **code switching,** and it has been the subject of a number of sociolinguistic studies.

Ethnolinguistics

The study of the relationships between language and culture, and how they mutually influence and inform each other, is the domain of **ethnolinguistics.**

LINGUISTIC RELATIVITY

In this type of research, anthropologists may investigate how a language reflects the culturally significant aspects of a people's traditional natural environment. Among the Inuit in the Canadian Arctic, for instance, we find numerous words for different types of snow, whereas Americans in a city like Detroit most likely possess a rich vocabulary allowing them to precisely distinguish between many different types of cars, categorized by model, year, and manufacturer. This is an example of **linguistic relativity**—the idea that distinctions encoded in one language are unique to that language.

Another example concerns cultural categories of color. Languages have different ways of dividing and naming elements of the color spectrum, which is actually a continuum of multiple hues with no clear-cut boundaries between them. In English we speak of red, orange, yellow, green, blue, indigo, and violet, but other languages mark out different groupings. For instance, Indians in Mexico's northwestern mountains speaking Tarahumara have just one word for both "green" and "blue"—*siyoname.*

LINGUISTIC DETERMINISM

Related to linguistic relativity is the principle of **linguistic determinism**—the idea that language to some extent shapes the way in which people view and think about the world around them. An extreme version of this principle holds that language actually determines thought and thereby shapes behavior and culture itself. A more widely accepted view holds that thought is merely influenced by language.

Linguistic determinism is associated with the pioneering ethnolinguistic research of anthropologist Edward Sapir and his student Benjamin Lee Whorf during the 1930s and 1940s. Their research resulted in what is now known as the *Sapir-Whorf hypothesis:* Each language provides particular grooves of linguistic expression that predispose speakers of that language to perceive the world in a certain way. In Whorf's own words, "The structure of the language one habitually uses influences the manner in which one understands his environment. The picture of the universe shifts from tongue to tongue."[11]

Whorf gained many of these insights while translating English into Hopi, a North American Indian language still spoken in Arizona. Doing this work, he discovered that Hopi differs from English not only in vocabulary but also in terms of its grammatical categories such as nouns and

[11] Quoted in Hoebel, E. A. (1958). *Man in the primitive world: An introduction to anthropology* (p. 571). New York: McGraw-Hill.

code switching Changing from one mode of speech to another as the situation demands, whether from one language to another or from one dialect of a language to another.
ethnolinguistics A branch of linguistics that studies the relationships between language and culture and how they mutually influence and inform each other.
linguistic relativity The idea that distinctions encoded in one language are unique to that language.
linguistic determinism The idea that language to some extent shapes the way in which we view and think about the world around us.

[10] Monaghan, L., Hinton, L., & Kephart, R. (1997). Can't teach a dog to be a cat? The dialogue on ebonics. *Anthropology Newsletter 38* (3), 1, 8, 9.

verbs. For instance, Hopi use numbers for counting and measuring things that have physical existence, but they do not apply numbers in the same way to abstractions like time. They would have no problem translating an English sentence such as, "I see fifteen sheep grazing on three acres of grassland," but an equally simple sentence such as, "Three weeks ago, I enjoyed my fifteen minutes of fame" would require a much more complex translation into Hopi.

It is also of note that Hopi verbs express tenses differently than English verbs. Rather than marking past, present, and future, with -ed, -ing, or *will*, Hopi requires additional words to indicate if an event is completed, is still ongoing, or is expected to take place. So instead of saying, "Three strangers stayed for fifteen days in our village," a Hopi would say something like, "We remember three strangers stay in our village until the sixteenth day." In addition, Hopi verbs do not express tense by their forms. Unlike English verbs that change form to indicate past, present, and future, Hopi verbs distinguish among a statement of fact (if the speaker actually witnesses a certain event), a statement of expectation, and a statement that expresses regularity. For instance, when you ask an English-speaking athlete "Do you run?" he may answer "Yes," when in fact he may at that moment be sitting in an armchair watching TV. A Hopi athlete asked the same question in his own language might respond "No," because in Hopi the statement of fact "he runs" translates as *wari* ("running occurs"), whereas the statement that expresses regularity—"he runs" (such as, on the track team)—translates as *warikngwe* ("running occurs characteristically").

This shows that the Hopi language structures thinking and behavior with a focus on the present—on getting ready and carrying out what needs to be done right now. Whorf summed it up like this: "A characteristic of Hopi behavior is the emphasis on preparation. This includes announcing and getting ready for events well beforehand, elaborate precautions to insure persistence of desired conditions, and stress on good will as the preparer of good results."[12]

In the 1990s linguistic anthropologists devised new research strategies to actually test Sapir and Whorf's original hypothesis.[13] One study found that speakers of Swedish and Finnish (neighboring peoples who speak radically different languages) working at similar jobs in similar regions under similar laws and regulations show significantly different rates of on-the-job accidents. The rates are substantially lower among the Swedish speakers.

What emerges from comparison of the two languages is that Swedish (one of the Indo-European languages) emphasizes information about movement in three-dimensional space. Finnish (a Ural-Altaic language unrelated to Indo-European languages) emphasizes more static relations among coherent temporal entities. As a consequence, it seems that Finns organize the workplace in a way that favors the individual person over the temporal organization in the overall production process. This in turn leads to frequent production disruptions, haste, and (ultimately) accidents.

A more obvious ethnolinguistic observation is that language mirrors or reflects, rather than determines, cultural reality. Aymara Indians living in the Bolivian highlands, for example, depend on the potato (or *luki*) as their major source of food. Their language has over 200 words for potatoes, reflecting the many varieties they traditionally grow and the many different ways that they preserve and prepare this food. Similarly, anthropologists have noted that the language of the Nuer, a nomadic African people of southern Sudan, is rich in words and expressions having to do with cattle; not only are more than 400 words used to describe cattle, but Nuer boys actually take their names from them. By studying the language, we can determine the significance of cattle in Nuer culture and the whole etiquette of human and cattle relationships.

If language does mirror cultural reality, it would follow that changes in a culture will sooner or later be reflected in changes in the language. We see this happening all around the world today, including in the English language.

Linguists have found that although language is generally flexible and adaptable, established terminologies do tend to perpetuate themselves, reflecting and revealing the social structure and worldview of groups and people. For example, American English has a wide array of words having to do with conflict and warfare. It also features an abundance of militaristic metaphors, such as "conquering" space, "fighting" the "battle" of the bulge, carrying out a "war" against drugs, making a "killing" on the stock market, "shooting down" an argument, "torpedoing" a plan, "spearheading" a movement, "decapitating" a foreign government, or "bombing" on an exam, to mention just a few. An observer from a different and perhaps less aggressive culture, such as the Hopi in Arizona or the Jain in India, could gain considerable insight into the importance of open competition, winning, and military might in the United States simply by paying attention to such commonly used phrases.

---

[12] Carroll, J. B. (Ed.). (1956). *Language, thought and reality: Selected writings of Benjamin Lee Whorf* (p. 148). Cambridge, MA: MIT Press.

[13] Lucy, J. A. (1997). Linguistic relativity. *Annual Review of Anthropology* 26, 291–312.

with the appearance of neurological structures under-lying language in the earliest representatives of the genus *Homo* and steady enlargement of the human brain 200,000 to 2.5 million years ago. The soft tissues of the vocal tract related to speech are not preserved in the fossil record. But as outlined in the Biocultural Connection, a comparison of the vocal anatomy of chimps and humans allows paleoanthropologists to identify the anatomical differences responsible for human speech that appeared over the course of human evolution.[20]

---

[20] Leading evolutionary theorist Philip Lieberman argues that human language ability is the confluence of a succession of separate evolutionary developments rigged together by natural selection for an evolutionarily unique ability. See Lieberman, P. (2006). *Toward an evolutionary biology of language.* Cambridge, MA: Belknap.

Biocultural Connection

The Biology of Human Speech

While other primates have shown some capacity for language (a socially agreed upon code of communication), actual speech is unique to humans; this ability is linked to humans' distinct anatomical development of the vocal organs.

Of particular importance are the positions of the human larynx (voice box) and the epiglottis. The larynx, situated in the respiratory tract between the pharynx (throat) and trachea (wind pipe), contains the vocal chords. The epiglottis is the structure that separates the esophagus or food pipe from the wind pipe as food passes from the mouth to the stomach. (See the figure for comparative diagrams of the anatomy of this region in chimps and humans.)

As humans mature and develop the neurological and muscular coordination for speech, the larynx and epiglottis shift to a downward position. The human tongue bends at the back of the throat and is attached to the pharynx, the region of the throat where the food and airways share a common path. Sound occurs as air exhaled from the lungs passes over the vocal cords and causes them to vibrate.

Through continuous interactive movements of the tongue, pharynx, lips, and teeth, as well as nasal passages, the sounds are alternately modified to produce speech—the uniquely patterned sounds of a particular language. Based on longstanding socially learned patterns of speech, different languages stress certain distinctive types of sounds as significant and ignore others. For instance, languages belonging to the Iroquoian family, such as Mohawk, Seneca, and Cherokee, are among the few in the world that have no bilabial stops (*b* and *p* sounds). They also lack the labiodental spirants (*f* and *v* sounds), leaving the bilabial nasal *m* sound as the only consonant requiring lip articulation.

It takes many years of practice for people to master the muscular movements needed to produce the precise sounds of any particular language. But no human could produce the finely controlled speech sounds without a lowered position of the larynx and epiglottis.

BIOCULTURAL QUESTION
Sharing a capacity for speech, humans say and understand many thousands of words. Since macaws and other parrots also learn many words, do they have speech? And if so, do they actually think?

Nasal cavity
Palate
Tongue
Epiglottis
Larynx
Pharynx
Trachea

There are obvious advantages to spoken over gestural language for a species increasingly dependent on tool use for survival. To talk with one's hands, the person must stop whatever else he or she is doing with them; speech does not interfere with that. Other benefits include being able to talk in the dark, past opaque objects, or among speakers whose attention is diverted. Precisely when the changeover to spoken language took place is not known, although all would agree that spoken languages are at least as old as the species *Homo sapiens*.

Early anthropologists searched for a truly "primitive" language spoken by a living people that might show the processes of language just beginning or developing. That search has now been abandoned, for anthropologists have come to realize that there is no such thing as a "primitive" language in the world today, or even in the recent past. So far, all human languages that have been described and studied, even among people with something approximating a Stone Age technology, are highly developed, complex, and capable of expressing infinite meanings. Every language or dialect now known has a long history and has developed its own particular subtleties and complexities that reflect its speakers' way of life and what they want or need to communicate with others. Thus anthropologists recognize that all languages are more or less equally effective as systems of communication within their own particular cultural contexts.

From Speech to Writing

When anthropology developed as an academic discipline over a century ago, it concentrated its attention on small traditional communities that relied primarily on personal interaction and oral communication for survival. Cultures that depend on talking and listening often have rich traditions of storytelling and speechmaking, which play a central role in education, conflict resolution, political decision making, spiritual or supernatural practices, and many other aspects of life.

Traditional orators (from the Latin *orare*, "to speak") are usually trained from the time they are young. Their memorization skills are often enhanced by rhyme, rhythm, and melody. Orators may also employ special objects to help them remember—notched sticks, knotted strings, bands embroidered with shells, and so forth. Traditional Iroquois Indian orators often performed their formal speeches with wampum belts made of hemp string with white and bluish-purple shell beads woven into distinctive

patterns symbolizing important messages or agreements, including treaties with other nations.

Thousands of languages, past and present, have existed only in spoken form, but many others have been documented in visual graphic symbols of some sort. Over time, simplified pictures of things (pictographs) and ideas (ideographs) evolved into more stylized symbolic forms.

Although different peoples invented a variety of graphic styles, anthropologists distinguish an actual **writing system** as a set of visible or tactile signs used to represent units of language in a systematic way. Recently discovered symbols carved into 8,600-year-old tortoise shells found in western China may represent the world's earliest evidence of elementary writing.[21]

---

[21] Li, X., et al. (2003). The earliest writing? Sign use in the seventh millennium BC at Jiahu, Henan Province, China. *Antiquity 77*, 31–44.

Hendrick Tejonihokarawa ("Open the Door"), a Mohawk chief of the Iroquois Confederacy, holding a wampum belt made of hemp string and shell beads (quahog and whelk shells). Wampum designs were used to symbolize a variety of important messages or agreements, including treaties with other nations. (Painting is by the Dutch artist Johannes Verelst in 1710.)

writing system   A set of visible or tactile signs used to represent units of language in a systematic way.

A fully developed early writing system is Egyptian hieroglyphics, developed some 5,000 years ago and in use for about 3,500 years. Another very old system is *cuneiform,* an arrangement of wedge-shaped imprints developed primarily in Mesopotamia (southern Iraq), which lasted nearly as long. About two millennia after these systems were established, others began to appear, developing independently in distant locations around the world.[22]

Inscriptions discovered in Egypt's western desert suggest that our **alphabet** (a series of symbols representing the *sounds* of a language) was invented almost 4,000 years ago by Semitic-speaking peoples in that region. Inscriptions carved into a natural limestone wall alongside hundreds of Egyptian hieroglyphs show that these Semites adopted a limited number of hieroglyphs as symbols for sounds in their own language. For instance, they took the glyph for "ox" and determined that it would stand for the sound at the start of the Semitic word for "ox," which is *aleph.* (This symbol looks like the horned head of an ox—and like the letter *A* upside-down.) Likewise, they chose the Egyptian glyph for "house" to stand for the opening sound of the Semitic word for "house," which is *beth.* (This symbol looks like a two-room house—and like the letter *B* tipped back.) The result was a writing system with characters based on a selection of Egyptian glyphs but representing sounds in early Semitic. Over the next thousand years, Semitic-speaking peoples inhabiting the eastern Mediterranean, including Phoenicians, adopted this system and developed the script into a more linear form.[23]

Most of the alphabets used today descended from the Phoenician one. The Greeks adopted it about 2,800 years ago, modifying the characters to suit sounds in their own language. The word *alphabet* comes from the first two letters in the Greek writing system, *alpha* and *beta* (otherwise meaningless words in Greek). From Greece, the writing system spread to Rome. When Latin-speaking Romans expanded their empire throughout much of Europe, northern Africa, and western Asia, they used a modified Greek alphabet. From the 15th century onward, as European nations grew their trade networks and built colonial empires, the Latin alphabet spread far and wide, making it possible to mechanically reproduce writings in any human language.

Although other writing systems, such as Chinese (which routinely uses 4,000 characters, about 10 percent of the total), are used by hundreds of millions of people, modern inventions such as the Internet continue to expand the use of the Latin alphabet as a global writing system.

Literacy and Modern Telecommunication in Our Globalizing World

Thousands of years have passed since literacy first emerged, yet today more than 800 million adults worldwide cannot read and write. Illiteracy condemns already disadvantaged people to ongoing poverty—migrant rural workers, refugees, ethnic minorities, and those living in rural backlands and urban slums throughout the world. For example, a third of India's 1 billion inhabitants cannot read and write, and 75 million children around the world are not enrolled in school.[24]

Rural women are especially disadvantaged. Once again taking India as an example, less than half of the rural women there can read and write, and in some of the northeastern districts only one in five is literate. Yet, all across the globe, including India, literacy is rising more swiftly than ever. Declaring literacy a human right, the United Nations established September 8 as International Literacy Day and proclaimed the period 2003 to 2012 as the Literacy Decade with the objective of extending literacy to all humanity.[25]

Taking a historical look at the development of literacy in European nations, we find that in the 17th century, most English, French, and German adults were illiterate. And before that time, so few had mastered the skill of writing that, for long-distance communication, illiterate people relied on someone in town who for a fee would write a dictated note or letter, or read one that had been received. And even today, there are many adults in Europe and North America who have varying competencies in reading but little or none in writing—a more difficult skill.

While many people in the world still rely on others to write and read for them, the global telecommunication revolution has reached the most remote villagers on earth. The demand for cell phones is high, even among the

---

[24] UNESCO Institute for Statistics. (2007). http://stats.uis.unesco.org.

[25] www.unesco.org/education/litdecade.

---

[22] del Carmen Rodriguez Martinez, M., et al. (2006). Oldest writing in the New World. *Science 313* (5793), 1610–1614.

[23] Himmelfarb, E. J. (2000, January/February). First alphabet found in Egypt. Newsbrief. *Archaeology 53* (1).

alphabet A series of symbols representing the sounds of a language arranged in a traditional order.

poor in rural backlands and urban slums—and they make long-distance communication possible without literacy. Bypassing regular landline phone networks, which have not yet reached many locations, modern telecommunication systems are now transforming the cultural fabric everywhere—thanks to satellite phones and cell phone towers powered by fossil fuel, solar, or wind. Perhaps nowhere is this truer than in India, which has the fastest growing mobile phone market in the world.

Over the last two decades, the telecommunications revolution has expanded our acoustic space to global dimensions. Hundreds of millions of people now rely on mobile phones for communication beyond natural speaking range. Many, including those who are illiterate, use these phones only for voice calls. But others also use them to download e-mails, exchange text messages, and explore the Internet.

Beyond maintaining social networks, mobile phones are also used in everyday subsistence strategies. For example, they enable tens of millions of poor rural dwellers in developing countries to locate the best prices for their produce—making it possible for growers to deal directly with district markets rather than going through intermediaries.[26]

In today's fast-changing globalizing world, the mobile phone is more than a means of communication. It has become a survival tool—perhaps nowhere more so than in Japan, which now ranks as the world's top "cellular nation." On the move and surrounded by strangers, people use their mobiles to get and give information, to express their individuality, and to stay in touch—twittering instead of whistling to avoid feeling lost in the global jungle.

---

[26] See also Horst, H. A., & Miller, D. (Eds.). (2006). *The cell phone: An anthropology of communication*. New York: Berg.

© Charles Sturge/Alamy

The telecommunication revolution is reaching even the most remote places on earth thanks to satellite phones and cell phone towers powered by fossil fuel, the sun, or the wind. Those without phones of their own can often find mobile phone stands such as this one in Kampala, Uganda, in East Africa.

Questions for Reflection

1. In what ways do you feel prepared or unprepared to meet the challenge of communicating effectively in our increasingly globalized world?

2. Over 3,000 languages have disappeared over the last 500 years, most of them vanishing without a trace. Fewer than 7,000 remain. It is now estimated that about 30 languages per year will become extinct during the current century. Do you see this demise as positive or negative?

3. Applying the principle of linguistic determinism to your own language, consider how your perceptions of objective reality might have been shaped by your language. How might your sense of reality be different if you grew up speaking Hopi?

4. What distinguishes us from apes like Chantek the orangutan? What words might Chantek choose to tell us about his confined existence as a subject of scientific research?

5. Since much of our communication is nonverbal, how effective do you think text message codes like OJ (only joking), XD (excited), VSF (very sad face), or G (grin) are in digital communication when e-mailing or texting? Have your digital messages ever been misunderstood? If so, what do you think was at the root of the miscommunication, and how was it resolved?

Suggested Readings

Duranti, A. (2001). Linguistic anthropology: History, ideas, and issues. In A. Duranti (Ed.), *Linguistic anthropology: A reader* (pp. 1–38). Oxford, England: Blackwell.

A good summary of the development of the field of linguistic anthropology.

Gladdol, D. (2006). *English next.* London: British Council.

A fascinating overview of the rise of English as a global language—and the socioeconomic problems this spread presents to monolingual English-speaking people. (free PDF available online)

Harrison, K. D. (2008). *When languages die: The extinction of the world's languages and the erosion of human knowledge.* New York: Oxford University Press.

This compelling and thought-provoking catalogue of disappearing languages all around the world reveals, case by case, the great loss of human knowledge that accompanies their demise—knowledge about the natural world, cultural heritage, plus our understanding of the capacities of the human mind.

Lieberman, P. (2006). *Toward an evolutionary biology of language.* Cambridge, MA: Belknap.

A leading evolutionary theorist of language draws on evidence from evolutionary biology, genetics, physical anthropology, anatomy, and neuroscience.

Morse, D., et al. (1979). *Gestures: Their origins and distribution.* New York: Stein & Day.

This well-illustrated text explores the derivations and distributions of dozens of gestures, as well as the varied meanings they have in different parts of the world.

Yip, M. (2002). *Tone.* New York: Cambridge University Press.

A comprehensive and clearly organized introduction to tone and tonal phonology, covering the main types of tonal systems found in Africa, the Americas, and Asia.

Challenge Issue   Every society faces the challenge of humanizing its children, teaching them the values, social codes, and skills that will enable them to be functioning and contributing members in the community. This is vital, for it helps ensure that the society will perpetuate itself culturally as well as biologically. Most traditional communities raise children in ways that condition them for their future social status as adult men and women—making sure they have the appropriate appearance, apparel, attitude, and other culturally significant features that indicate gender differences. (A good number also provide cultural models for an alternative gender role.) This photo shows a Kazakh father and son setting out on a hunting expedition with a golden eagle in the Altai Mountains of western Mongolia. Kazakhs are semi-nomadic herders living in northern Central Asia (especially Kazakhstan, but also in western Mongolia and parts of Uzbekistan, China, and Russia). For centuries, they have trained golden eagles to partner them in hunting rabbit, marmot, fox, and even wolf—primarily for fur. They refer to this mighty bird of prey as a *berkut* and to the man who hunts with them as a *berkutchi*. Eagle hunting is a male tradition. Boys learn from their fathers and uncles how to capture, raise, train, and confidently handle an eagle from fledgling to maturity; how to ride high and proud on their horse stirrups with this huge raptor on their arm; when and how to release the bird to pursue the prey; and how to gallop across the steppes as fast as the wind to claim it.

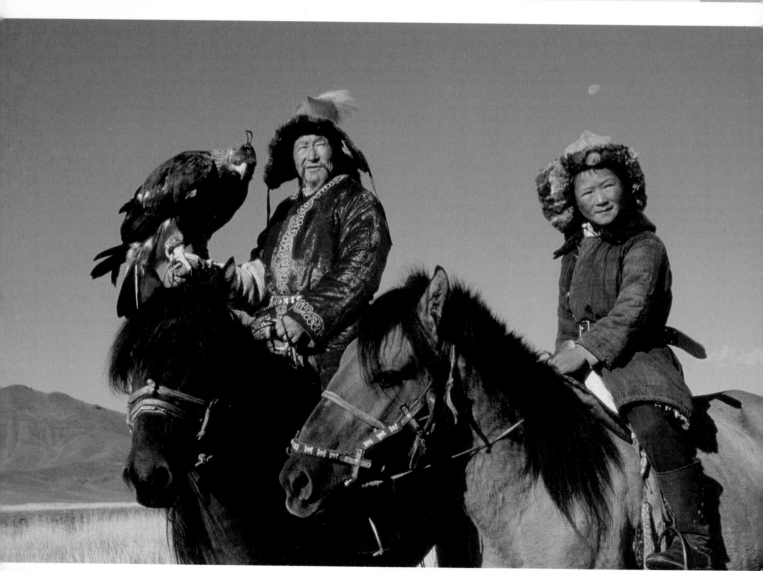

CHAPTER 17

Social Identity, Personality, and Gender

Chapter Preview

What Is Enculturation?

Enculturation is the process by which culture is passed from one generation to the next and through which individuals become members of their society. This process begins soon after birth with the development of self-awareness—the ability to perceive oneself as a unique being in time and space and to judge one's own actions. The way a person perceives and gets oriented to surrounding creatures and objects is specified by the culture in which he or she grows up. Along with object orientation, an individual's behavioral environment includes spatial, temporal, and normative orientations. In the past few decades, many cultures have rapidly transformed in response to technological advances, and individuals in these settings now experience a cyberspace reality as well as their material reality.

How Does Enculturation Influence Personality?

Studies suggest a relationship between enculturation and personality development. While each individual begins life with certain broad potentials and limitations that are genetically inherited, the distinct childrearing practices of each culture socialize children toward the particular norms and standards of their society and thereby impact personality. For example, childrearing practices in some cultures seem to promote the development of compliant personalities, while others seem to foster more independent, self-reliant personalities.

Are Different Personalities Characteristic of Different Cultures?

Each culture emphasizes certain personality traits as good and others as bad, and each has distinct ways of encouraging or discouraging those traits accordingly. Nonetheless, it is difficult to characterize cultures in terms of particular personalities. Of the several attempts made, the concept of modal personality is the most satisfactory. This recognizes that any human society has a range of individual personalities, but some will be more typical than others. Those that approximate the modal personality of a particular culture are thought of as normal. Since modal personalities may differ from one culture to another and since the acceptable range of variation from the standard may also differ per culture, it is clear that normal and abnormal are culturally relative concepts. This observation also applies to the range of socially acceptable gender expressions in different cultures.

In 1690 English philosopher John Locke presented the *tabula rasa* theory in his book *An Essay Concerning Human Understanding*. This notion holds that a newborn human is like a blank slate, and what the individual becomes in life is written on the slate by his or her life experiences. The implication is that at birth all individuals are basically the same in their potential for character development and that their adult personalities are exclusively the products of their postnatal experiences, which differ from culture to culture.

Locke's idea offered high hopes for the all-embracing impact of intellectual and moral instruction on a child's character formation, but it missed the mark, as we now know, for it did not take into consideration genetic contributions to human behavior. Based on recent breakthroughs in human genetic research, anthropologists have come to recognize that an identifiable portion of our behavior is genetically influenced.[1] This means each person is born with a particular set of inherited tendencies that help mark out his or her adult personality. While this genetic inheritance sets certain broad potentials and limitations, an individual's cultural environment, gender, social status, and unique life experiences, particularly in the early childhood years, also play a significant role in personality formation.

Since different cultures handle the raising and education of children in different ways, these practices and their effects on adult personalities are important subjects of anthropological inquiry. Such cross-cultural studies gave rise to the specialization of psychological anthropology and are the subjects of this chapter.

Enculturation: The Human Self and Social Identity

From the moment of birth, a person faces multiple survival challenges. Obviously, newborns cannot take care of their own biological needs. Only in myths and romantic fantasies do we encounter stories about children successfully coming of age alone in the wilderness or accomplishing this feat having been raised by animals in the wild. For example, Italians in Rome still celebrate the mythological founders of their city, the twin brothers Romulus and Remus, who according to legend were suckled as infants by a she-wolf. And millions of children around the world have been fascinated by stories about Tarzan and the apes or the jungle boy Mowgli and the wolves. Moreover, young

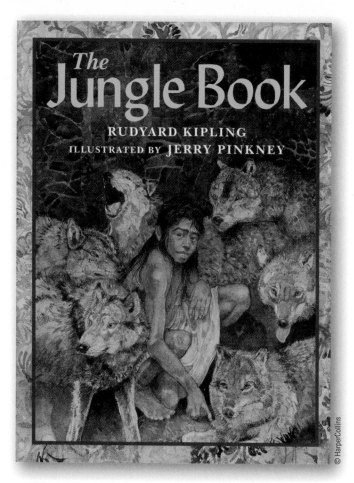

In 1916 the international Boy Scout movement expanded to include younger boys in a "cub scout" program inspired by Rudyard Kipling's *The Jungle Book* (1894). Born in former British India (1865), Kipling wrote this story about a young boy in India named Mowgli being raised by a wolf as one of her own cubs. Translated into some forty languages, including Hindi, Swahili, and Chinese, the book has been the subject of many cartoons and movies. Despite happy wild-child legends, human infants are biologically ill-equipped to survive successfully without culture.

and old alike have been captivated by newspaper hoaxes about "wild" children, such as a 10-year-old boy reported to have been found running among gazelles in the Syrian desert in 1946.

Fanciful imaginations aside, human children are biologically ill-equipped to survive without culture. This point has been driven home by several documented cases about feral children (*feral* comes from *fera*, which is Latin for "wild animal") who grew up deprived of human contact. None of them had a happy ending. For instance, there was nothing romantic about the girl Kamala, supposedly rescued from a wolf den in India in 1920: She moved about on all fours and could not feed herself. And everyone in Paris considered the naked "wild boy" captured in the woods outside Aveyron village in 1800 an incurable idiot. Clearly, the biological capacity for what we think of as human, which entails culture, must be nurtured to be realized.

[1] Harpending, H., & Cochran, G. (2002). In our genes. *Proceedings of the National Academy of Sciences USA 99* (1), 10–12.

Visual Counterpoint

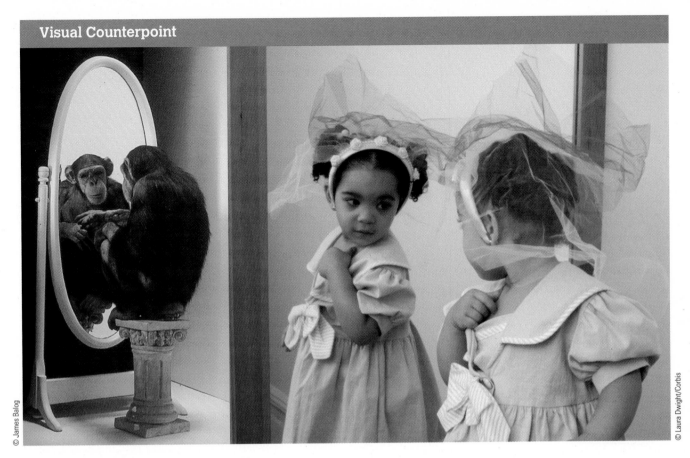

Self-awareness is not restricted to humans. This chimpanzee knows that the individual in the mirror is himself and not some other chimp, just as the girl recognizes herself.

Because culture is socially constructed and learned rather than biologically inherited, all societies must somehow ensure that culture is adequately transmitted from one generation to the next—a process we have already defined as *enculturation*. Since each group lives by a particular set of cultural rules, a child will have to learn the rules of his or her society in order to survive. Most of that learning takes place in the first few years when a child learns how to feel, think, speak, and, ultimately, act like an adult who embodies being Japanese, Kikuyu, Lakota, Norwegian, or whatever ethnic or national group into which it is born.

The first agents of enculturation in all societies are the members of the infant's household, especially the child's mother. (In fact, cultural factors are at work even before birth through what a pregnant mother eats, drinks, and inhales, as well as the sounds, rhythms, and activity patterns of her daily life.) Who the other members are depends on how households are structured in each particular society.

As the young person matures, individuals outside the household are brought into the enculturation process. These usually include other relatives and certainly the individual's peers. In some societies, professionals are brought into the process to provide formal instruction. In many societies, however, children are allowed to learn through observation and participation, at their own speed.

Self-Awareness

Enculturation begins with the development of **self-awareness**—the ability to identify oneself as an individual creature, to reflect on oneself, and to evaluate oneself. Humans do not have this cognitive ability at birth, even though it is essential for their successful social functioning. It is self-awareness that permits one to take social responsibility for one's conduct, to learn how to react to others, and to assume a variety of roles in society. An important aspect of self-awareness is the attachment of positive value to one's self. Without this, individuals cannot be motivated to act to their advantage.

self-awareness The ability to identify oneself as an individual, to reflect on oneself, and to evaluate oneself.

Self-awareness does not come all at once. In modern industrial and postindustrial societies, for example, self and non-self are not clearly distinguished until a child is about 2 years of age, lagging somewhat behind other cultures. Self-awareness develops in concert with neuromotor development, which is known to proceed at a slower rate in infants from industrial societies than in infants in many, perhaps even most, small-scale farming or foraging communities. The reasons for this slower rate are not yet clear, although the amount of human contact and stimulation that infants receive seems to play an important role.

As discussed in Chapter 1, infants in the United States, for example, generally do not sleep with their parents, most often being put in rooms of their own. This is seen as an important step in making them into individuals, "owners" of themselves and their capacities. As a consequence, they do not experience the steady stream of personal stimuli, including smell, movement, and warmth, that they would if co-sleeping. Private sleeping also takes away the opportunity for frequent nursing through the night.

In the majority of the world's societies, infants routinely sleep with their parents, or at least their mothers. Also, they are carried or held most other times, usually in an upright position. The mother typically responds to a cry or "fuss" within seconds, usually offering the infant her breast. So it is among traditional Ju/'hoansi (pronounced "zhutwasi") people of southern Africa's Kalahari Desert, whose infants breastfeed on demand in short frequent bouts—commonly nursing about four times an hour, for 1 or 2 minutes at a time. Overall, a 15-week-old Ju/'hoansi infant is in close contact with its mother about 70 percent of the time (compared to 20 percent for home-reared infants in the United States). Moreover, Ju/'hoansi babies usually have considerable contact with numerous other adults and children of all ages.

This steady stream of varied stimuli is significant, for recent studies show that stimulation plays a key role in the hardwiring of the brain; it is necessary for development of the neural circuitry. Looking at breastfeeding in particular, the longer a child is breastfed, the better his or her overall health, the higher he or she will score on cognitive tests, and the lower the risk of obesity, allergies, and attention deficit hyperactivity disorder.[2] Because our biological heritage as primates has programmed us to develop in response to social stimuli, it is not surprising that self-awareness and a variety of other beneficial qualities develop more rapidly in response to close contact with other humans.

Social Identity Through Personal Naming

Personal names are important devices for self-definition in all cultures. It is through naming that a social group acknowledges a child's birthright and establishes its social identity. Among the many cultural rules that exist in each society, those having to do with naming are unique because they individualize a person and at the same time identify one as a group member. In fact, names often express and represent multiple aspects of one's group identity—ethnic, gender, religious, political, or even rank, class, or caste. Without a name, an individual has no identity, no self. For this reason, many cultures consider name selection to be an important issue and mark the naming of a child with a special event or ritual known as a **naming ceremony**.

NAMING PRACTICES ACROSS CULTURES

Worldwide, there are countless contrasting approaches to naming. For instance, Aymara Indians in the Bolivian highland village of Laymi do not consider an infant truly human until they have given it a name. And naming does not happen until the child begins to speak the Aymara language, typically around the age of 2. Once the child shows the ability to speak like a human, he or she is considered fit to be recognized as such with a proper name. The naming ceremony marks the toddler's social transition from a state of "nature" to "culture" and consequently to full acceptance into the Laymi community.

Unlike the Aymara, Icelanders name babies at birth. Following ancient custom, Icelandic infants receive their father's personal given name as their last name. The suffix *sen* is added to a boy's name and *dottir* to a girl's name. Thus a brother and sister whose father is named Sven Olafsen would have the last names Svensen and Svendottir.

Among the Netsilik Inuit in Arctic Canada, a mother experiencing a difficult delivery would call out the names of deceased people of admirable character. The name being called at the moment of birth is thought to enter the infant's body and help the delivery, and the child would bear that name thereafter. Inuit parents may also name their children for deceased relatives in the belief that the spiritual identification will help shape their character.[3]

---

[2] Dettwyler, K. A. (1997, October). When to wean. *Natural History*, 49; World Health Organization. (2003). *Global strategy on infant and young child feeding*. Geneva: Author.

naming ceremony A special event or ritual to mark the naming of a child.

---

[3] Balikci, A. (1970). *The Netsilik Eskimo*. Garden City, NY: Natural History.

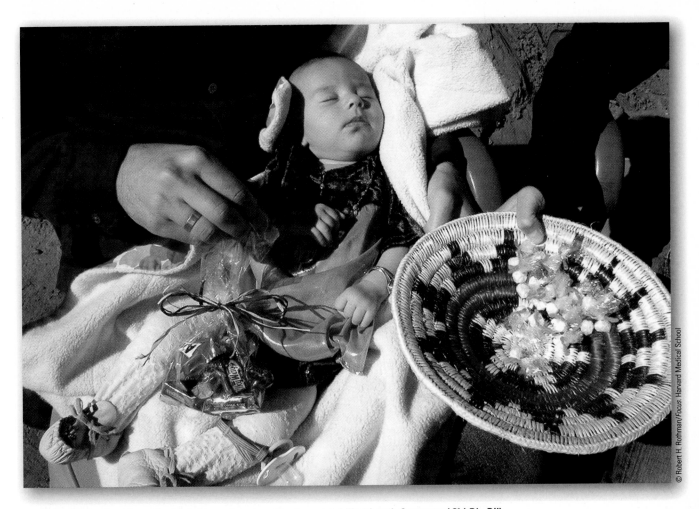

© Robert H. Rothman/*Focus*, Harvard Medical School

Navajo babies begin to learn the importance of community at a special First Laugh Ceremony (*Chi Dlo Dil*). At this event, the person who prompted an infant's first laugh teaches the child (and reminds the community) about the joy of generosity by helping the baby to give symbolic gifts of sweets and rock salt to each guest. Pictured here is the baby daughter of a pediatrician working at a remote clinic on the reservation. She celebrates her first laugh wearing a Navajo dress and jewelry given to her by her mother's Navajo patients.

In many cultures, a person receives a name soon after birth but may acquire new names during subsequent life phases. We see this in examples from two neighboring American Indian groups in the southwestern United States.

In the Hopi culture, on the twentieth day of a child's life, the father's sister gives the baby its name in a sunrise ceremony. At age 6, the child receives another name in a religious ceremony. Reaching adulthood, the person gets yet another name and keeps that one until the end of her or his life. Yet one more name is bestowed upon a Hopi at death, a name that is not to be mentioned after it is given.

In contrast, a Navajo child receives a name at birth. If born into a family that follows traditions, the baby is likely to be given an ancestral clan name soon after he or she laughs for the first time. Among the Navajo, laughter is seen as the earliest expression of human language, a signal that life as a social being has started. Thus it is an occasion for celebration. The person who prompted that very first laugh invites family and close friends to a First Laugh Ceremony. At the gathering, the party sponsor places rock salt in the baby's hand and helps slide the salt all over the little one's body. Representing tears—of both laughter and crying—the salt is said to provide strength and protection, leading to a long, happy life. Then the ancestral name is given. Next, because a central purpose of the occasion is to ensure that the child will become a generous person, the sponsor helps the baby give sweets and a piece of salt to each guest as they step forward to welcome the child into the embrace of the community. By accepting these symbolic gifts, guests also receive strength and protection. The ceremony reminds young and old alike of the importance of generosity and sharing.[4]

---

[4] Authors' participant observation at traditional Navajo First Laugh ceremony of Wesley Bitsie-Baldwin; personal communication, LaVerne Bitsie-Baldwin and Anjanette Bisie.

Name-giving customs play an important role in a person's life journey as a socially accepted member of a culture. But what about naming in multi-ethnic or pluralistic societies?

NAMING AND IDENTITY POLITICS

Because names symbolically express and represent an individual's cultural self, they may gain particular significance in personal and collective identity politics. For instance, when an ethnic group or nation falls under the control of a more powerful and expanding neighboring group, its members may be forced to assimilate and give up their cultural identity. One early indicator may be that families belonging to the subjugated or overwhelmed group decide to abandon their own ancestral naming traditions. Such was the case when Russia expanded its empire into Siberia and colonized the Turkic-speaking Xakas. Within a few generations, most Xakas had Russian names.[5]

The identity politics of personal naming practices can also be seen in North America, where cultural origins are rooted primarily in a British colonial past. The continent was long dominated by Anglo-Saxon Protestants who controlled the government, fashioned the collective cultural fabric, and pressed a political agenda of national assimilation in "melting pot" terms. For example, American Indian families, whether they lived on or off their tribal reservations, came under pressure to forgo their cultural traditions, including their customary personal and family names. As part of the assimilation process, many agreed or were compelled to have their indigenous names translated into English. In particular, those who became Christian converts adopted European names, at least for public identification and self-presentation.

Among countless examples of this is the personal story of Luther Standing Bear, a Sicangu (Brule Sioux) tribesman from the Rosebud Indian Reservation in South Dakota. In 1879, he and numerous other Lakota-speaking children were taken from the familiar grasslands of the Great Plains to a U.S. government-run boarding school in Pennsylvania "to learn the ways of white men." Years later he recalled the traumatic day when government agents took him from his family's tipi encampment at the recently established reservation:

> They wrote my name in a big book. At that time I was entered as "Oka Kte, or Plenty Kill, son of Standing Bear." After my name was in the book, all the white people shook hands with me and said something in the white man's language which I did not understand. . . .

> [After a long journey, we arrived at the Carlisle Indian school] where there was a lot of writing on one of the blackboards. We did not know what it meant, but our interpreter came into the room and said, "Do you see all these marks on the blackboard? Well, each word is a white man's name. They are going to give each one of you one of these names by which you will hereafter be known." None of the names were read or explained to us, so of course we did not know the sound or meaning of any of them.

> [Forbidden to speak our own languages, each of the Indian boys was handed a long stick and told to point to] any name he wanted. . . . I had selected the name "Luther"—not "Lutheran" as many people called me. . . . The teacher took a piece of white tape and wrote the name on it. Then she cut off a length of the tape and sewed it on the back of the boy's shirt. . . . Soon we all had the names of white men sewed on our backs."[6]

Name change stories are also common among immigrants hoping to avoid racial discrimination or ethnic stigmatization. For instance, it was not uncommon for Jewish immigrants and their U.S.-born children trying to "make it" in the entertainment industry to Americanize their names: Issur Danielovitch became Kirk Douglas, Jonathan Stuart Leibowitz switched to Jon Stewart, and Joyce Frankenberg turned into Jane Seymour.

A similar, more recent name shift example comes from U.S. President Barack Hussein Obama, born of (and named after) a Luo father from western Kenya and a Euramerican mother from Kansas. While studying in the United States, his East African father had "Americanized" his name into Barry, and the younger Obama did the same during his growing up years in Hawaii. Later, as a 19-year-old studying in New York, Barry found himself in an identity quest and reverted to Barack.[7]

In identity politics, naming can also be a resistance strategy by a minority group asserting its cultural pride or even rights of self-determination against a dominant society. For instance, a minority group in Bulgaria known as the Pomak defied the Bulgarian state and refused to convert to Eastern Orthodox Christianity. Moreover, in an act of cultural resistance, they held on to their own Turkish-Arabic naming traditions as an expression of their ethnic identity, no matter the political reality.[8]

[5] Butanayev, V. (n.d.). *Xooray attarì* [Xakas names]. Cited by Harrison, K. D. (2002). Naming practices and ethnic identity in Tuva. *Proceedings of the Chicago Linguistics Society 35* (2).

[6] Standing Bear, L. (1975). *My People the Sioux* (pp. 125, 137–138). Lincoln: University of Nebraska Press.

[7] Wolffe, R., Ramirez, J., & Bartholet, J. (2008, March 31). When Barry became Barack. *Newsweek.*

[8] See Harrison, K. D. (2002). Naming practices and ethnic identity in Tuva. *Proceedings of the Chicago Linguistics Society 35* (2).

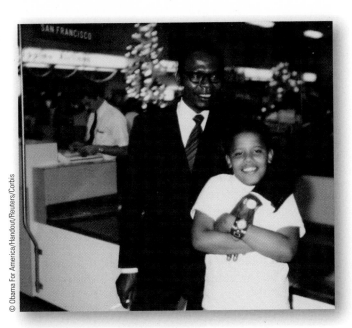

Barack Hussein Obama, Senior and Junior, 1971. Both American-ized their first name to Barry for a time. The father reverted to Barack when he returned to his home country of Kenya after studying in the United States. President Obama did the same at age 19 as an under-graduate in search of his identity.

In the United States, African Americans with inherited Christian names that were imposed upon their enslaved ancestors have, in growing numbers, rejected those names. Many have also abandoned the faith tradition represented by those names to become members of the Nation of Islam ("Black Muslims"). An enduringly famous example of this is champion boxer Cassius Clay, who converted to Islam in the mid-1960s. Like others, he rejected his "slave name" and adopted the name Muhammad Ali.

Among American Indians as well, name reversion has become quite common since the 1960s. For example, Lakota activist Russell Means of Pine Ridge Reservation recently announced that he wanted to be known as Oyate Wacinyapin ("Works for the People").

The Self and the Behavioral Environment

The development of self-awareness requires basic orientations that structure the psychological fields in which the self acts. These include object orientation, spatial orientation, temporal orientation, and normative orientation—discussed below.

Each individual must learn about a world of objects other than the self. Through this *object orientation*, each culture singles out for attention certain environmental features, while ignoring others or lumping them together into broad categories. A culture also explains the perceived

environment. This is important, for a cultural explanation of one's surroundings imposes a measure of order and provides the individual with a sense of direction needed to act meaningfully and effectively.

Behind this lies a powerful psychological drive to reduce uncertainty—part of the common human need for a balanced and integrated perspective on the relevant universe. When confronted with ambiguity and uncertainty, people invariably strive to clarify and give structure to the situation; they do this in ways that their particular culture deems appropriate. Thus our observations and explanations of the universe are largely culturally constructed and mediated symbolically through language. In fact, everything in the physical environment varies in the way it is perceived and experienced by humans. In short, we perceive the world around us through a cultural lens.

The behavioral environment in which the self acts also involves *spatial orientation,* or the ability to get from one object or place to another. Notably, when we speak of trying to *orient* ourselves, we are using an ancient word for "rising" that refers to the east where the sun comes up. Traditionally, place names commonly contain references to significant geographic features in the landscape. For instance, the name Mississippi in North America means literally "big river"; the English coastal city of Plymouth is located at the mouth of the river Plym; and the riverside city of Bamako, Mali, in West Africa translates as "crocodile river."

Finding your way to class, remembering where you left your car keys, directing someone to the nearest bus stop, and traveling through deep underground networks in subway tunnels are examples of highly complex cognitive tasks based on spatial orientation and memory. So is a desert nomad's ability to travel long distances from one remote oasis to another—determining the route by means of a mental map of the vast open landscape and gauging his location by the position of the sun in daytime, the stars at night, and even by the winds and smell of the air.

Technological revolutions in the 20th century have led to the invention of a newly created media environment, where we learn to orient ourselves in cyberspace. Without our spatial orientations, whether in natural or virtual reality, navigating through daily life would be impossible.

Temporal orientation, which gives people a sense of their place in time, is also part of the behavioral environment. Connecting past actions with those of the present and future provides a sense of self-continuity. This is the function of a calendar. Derived from the Latin word *kalendae,* which originally referred to a public announcement at the first day of a new month, or moon, such a chart gives people a framework for organizing their days, weeks, months, and even years. Just as the perceived environment of objects is organized in cultural terms, so too are time and space.

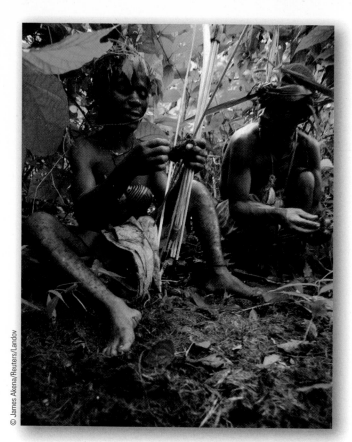

© James Akena/Reuters/Landov

Dark and foreboding to outsiders, the Ituri forest in the tropical heart of Africa is viewed with affection by the Mbuti foragers who live there. In their eyes, it is like a benevolent parent, providing them with all they ask for: sustenance, protection, and security.

A final aspect of the behavioral environment is the *normative orientation*. Moral values, ideals, and principles, which are purely cultural in origin, are as much a part of the individual's behavioral environment as are trees, rivers, and mountains. Without them people would have nothing by which to gauge their own actions or those of others. Normative orientation includes standards that indicate what ranges of behavior are acceptable for males, females, and whichever additional gender roles exist in a particular society.

Personality

In the process of enculturation, each individual is introduced to a society's natural and human-made environment along with a collective body of ideas about the self and others. The result is the creation of a kind of internalized

personality The distinctive way a person thinks, feels, and behaves.

cultural blueprint of the world in which the individual will feel, think, and act as a social being. It is his or her particular map of how to run the maze of life. When we speak of someone's personality, we are generalizing about that person's internalized map over time. Hence, personalities are products of enculturation, as experienced by individuals, each with his or her distinctive genetic makeup.

Personality does not lend itself to a formal definition, but we take it as the distinctive way a person thinks, feels, and behaves. Derived from the Latin word *persona*, meaning "mask," the term relates to the idea of learning to play one's role on the stage of daily life. Gradually, the "mask," as it is "placed" on the face of a child, begins to shape that person until there is little sense of the mask as a superimposed alien force. Instead it feels natural, as if one were born with it. The individual has successfully internalized the culture.

Personality Development

Although *what* one learns is important to personality development, most anthropologists assume that *how* one learns is no less important. Along with psychological theorists, anthropologists view childhood experiences as strongly influencing adult personality. Indeed, many pioneering psychological anthropologists have been attracted to Freudian psychoanalytic theory, while maintaining a critical eye.

Psychological literature tends to be long on speculative concepts, clinical data, and studies that are culture-bound. Anthropologists, for their part, are more interested in studies that seek to prove, modify, or at least shed light on the roles of different cultural influences in shaping personality. For example, traditionally the cultural ideal for the white middle class in Western societies has been for men to be tough, aggressive, assertive, dominant, and self-reliant, whereas women have been expected to be gentle, passive, obedient, and caring. To many, these personality contrasts between male and female seem so natural that they are thought to be biologically grounded and therefore fixed and universal. But are they? Have anthropologists identified any psychological or personality characteristics that universally differentiate the sexes?

ADOLESCENCE AND GENDER IDENTITY

Margaret Mead, a pioneer in anthropological study of gender identity and personality development, was a 24-year-old doctoral candidate when she set out for the Pacific Ocean island of Samoa. Mead wanted to test the theory (then widely accepted) that the biological changes of adolescence were always fraught with social, psychological, and emotional stress. Based on her fieldwork there, she later wrote the book *Coming of Age in Samoa: A Psychological Study of Primitive Youth for Western Civilization.*

In it she explained that adolescence does not have to be a time of stress and strain, but cultural conditions may make it so. Published in 1928, this book is generally credited with marking the beginning of psychological anthropology (culture and personality).

Pioneering works, however, are rarely without their faults, and *Coming of Age* is no exception. For one, Mead's time in the field (nine months) was not enough to understand fully the nuances of native speech and body language necessary to comprehend the innermost feelings of her informants. Furthermore, her sample of Samoan adolescents was a mere fifty, half of whom had not yet passed puberty.

Despite its faults, Mead's book stands as a landmark for several reasons: Not only was it a deliberate test of a Euramerican psychological hypothesis, but it also showed psychologists the value of modifying intelligence tests to make them appropriate for the population under study. Furthermore, by emphasizing the lesson to be drawn for Mead's own society, it laid the groundwork for the popularization of anthropology and advanced the cause of applied anthropology.

Other work by Mead has been equally foundational to the study of personality and gender. In the early 1930s she studied three ethnic groups in Papua New Guinea—the Arapesh, the Mundugamor, and the Tchambuli. This comparative research suggested that whatever biological differences exist between men and women, they are extremely malleable. In short, she concluded, biology is not destiny. Mead found that among the Arapesh, relations between men and women were expected to be equal, with both genders exhibiting what most North Americans traditionally consider feminine traits (cooperative, nurturing, and gentle).[9] She also discovered gender equality among the Mundugamor (now generally called Biwat); however, in that community both genders displayed supposedly masculine traits (individualistic, assertive, volatile, aggressive). Among the Tchambuli (now called Chambri), however, Mead found that women dominated men.

More recent anthropological research suggests that some of Mead's interpretations of gender roles were incorrect—for instance, neither do Chambri women dominate Chambri men nor vice versa. Yet, as with Mead's pioneering research in Samoa, her cross-cultural findings in Papua New Guinea remain valuable, despite their flaws, for they generated new insights into the human condition, showing that male dominance is not genetically fixed in our human "nature." Instead, it is socially constructed in the context of particular cultural adaptations and, consequently, alternative gender arrangements can be created. (See the Anthropologist of Note feature on Mead's teacher, colleague, and close friend Ruth Benedict for her pathbreaking work on personality as a cultural construct.) Although biological factors in male–female behavior do play a role (in fact, debate continues about the genetic and hormonal factors involved), it has nonetheless become clear that each culture provides different opportunities and has different expectations for ideal or acceptable behavior.[10]

CHILDREARING AND GENDER AMONG THE JU/'HOANSI

To understand the importance of childrearing practices for the development of gender-related personality characteristics, we may take another brief look at the already mentioned Ju/'hoansi, people native to the Kalahari Desert of Namibia and Botswana in southern Africa. The Ju/'hoansi are one of a number of groups traditionally referred to as Bushmen, who were once widespread through much of southern Africa.

Reo Fortune/Library of Congress

Anthropologist Margaret Mead in Pere, a small village on the island of Manus, now part of Papua New Guinea. Researching the thought processes of children through their drawings, she determined that what is considered childlike in thought varies according to the emphases of the culture. She published her findings in *Growing Up in New Guinea* (1930), a book written for a general audience.

[9] Mead, M. (1950). *Sex and temperament in three primitive societies*. New York: New American Library. (orig. 1935)

[10] Errington, F. K., & Gewertz, D. B. (2001). *Cultural alternatives and a feminist anthropology: An analysis of culturally constructed gender interests in Papua New Guinea*. Cambridge, England, and New York: Cambridge University Press.

Ruth Fulton Benedict (1887–1947)

Ruth Fulton Benedict came late to anthropology. After her graduation from Vassar College, she taught high school English, published poetry, and tried her hand at social work. At age 31, she began studying anthropology, first at the New School for Social Research in New York City, and then at Columbia University. Having earned her doctorate under Franz Boas, she joined his department. One of her first students was Margaret Mead.

As Benedict herself once said, the main purpose of anthropology is "to make the world safe for human differences." In anthropology, she developed the idea that culture was a collective projection of the personality of those who created it. In her most famous book *Patterns of Culture* (1934), she compared the cultures of three peoples—the Kwakiutl Indians of the Pacific Northwest coast in Canada, the Zuni Indians of the Arizona desert in the United States, and the Melanesians of Dobu Island off the southern shore of Papua New Guinea. She held that each was comparable to a great work of art, with an internal coherence and consistency of its own.

Seeing the Kwakiutl as egocentric, individualistic, and ecstatic in their rituals, she labeled their cultural

© The Granger Collection, New York

configuration "Dionysian" (named after the Greek god of wine and noisy feasting). The Zuni, whom she saw as living by the golden mean, wanting no part of excess or disruptive psychological states and distrusting of individualism, she characterized as "Apollonian" (named after the Greek god of poetry who exemplified beauty). The Dobuans, whose culture seemed to her magic-ridden, with everyone fearing and hating everyone else, she characterized as "paranoid."

Another theme of *Patterns of Culture* is that deviance should be understood as a conflict between an individual's personality and the norms of the culture to which the person belongs. Still in print today, *Patterns* has sold close to 2 million copies in a dozen languages. It had great influence on Mead during her cross-cultural gender studies among the Papuans in New Guinea.

Although *Patterns of Culture* still enjoys popularity in some nonanthropological circles, anthropologists have long since abandoned its approach as impressionistic. To compound the problem, Benedict's characterizations of cultures are misleading (the supposedly Apollonian Zunis, for example, indulge in such seemingly Dionysian practices as sword swallowing and walking over hot coals), and the use of such value-laden terms as "paranoid" prejudices others against the culture so labeled. Nonetheless, the book did have an enormous and valuable influence by focusing attention on the problem of the interrelation between culture and personality and by popularizing the reality of cultural variation.

Traditionally subsisting as nomadic hunter-gatherers (foragers), in the past three decades many Ju/'hoansi have been forced to settle down—tending small herds of goats, planting gardens for their livelihood, and engaging in occasional wage labor.[11]

Among those Ju/'hoansi who traditionally forage for a living, equality is stressed, and dominance and aggressiveness

are not tolerated in either gender. Men are as mild-mannered as the women, and women are as energetic and self-reliant as the men. By contrast, among the Ju/'hoansi who have recently settled in permanent villages, men and women exhibit personality characteristics resembling those traditionally thought of as typically masculine and feminine in North America and other industrial societies.

Among these food foragers, each newborn child receives extensive personal care from its mother during the first few years of life, for the space between births is typically four to five years. This is not to say that mothers are constantly with their children. For instance, when women go to collect wild plant foods in the bush, they do not always take their offspring along. At such times, the children are supervised by their fathers or other community adults, nearly half of whom are found in camp on any given day. Because these include men as well as women, children are as much habituated to the male as to the female presence.

Traditional Ju/'hoansi fathers spend much time with their offspring, interacting with them in nonauthoritarian

---

[11] Draper, P. (1975). !Kung women: Contrasts in sexual egalitarianism in foraging and sedentary contexts. In R. Reiter (Ed.), *Toward an anthropology of women* (pp. 77–109). New York: Monthly Review.

In traditional Ju/'hoansi society, fathers as well as mothers show great indulgence to children, who do not fear or respect men more than they do women.

ways. Although they may correct their children's behavior, so may women who neither defer to male authority nor use the threat of paternal punishment. Thus, among Ju/'hoansi foragers, no one grows up to respect or fear male authority any more than female authority. In fact, instead of being punished, a child who misbehaves will simply be carried away and introduced to some other more agreeable activity.

Children of both sexes do equally little work. Instead, they spend much of their time in playgroups that include boys and girls of widely different ages. And when it comes to older children keeping an eye out for the younger ones, this is done spontaneously rather than as an assigned task, and the burden does not fall more heavily on girls than boys. In short, Ju/'hoansi children in traditional foraging groups have few experiences that set one gender apart from the other.

The situation is different among Ju/'hoansi who have been forced to abandon their traditional life as foragers and now reside in permanent settlements: Women spend much of their time in and around the home preparing food, doing other domestic chores, and tending the children. Men, meanwhile, spend many hours outside the household growing crops, raising animals, or doing wage labor. As a result, children are less habituated to their presence. This remoteness of the men, combined with their greater knowledge of the outside world and their access to cash, tends to strengthen male influence in the household.

Within village households, gender typecasting begins early. As soon as girls are old enough, they are expected to attend to many of the needs of their younger siblings, thereby allowing their mothers time to deal with other domestic tasks. This not only shapes but also limits the behavior of girls, who cannot range as widely or explore as freely and independently as they could without little brothers and sisters in tow. Boys, by contrast, have little to do with babies and toddlers, and when they are assigned work, it generally takes them away from the household. Thus the space that village girls occupy becomes restricted, and they are trained in behaviors that promote passivity and nurturance, whereas village boys begin to learn the distant, controlling roles they will later play as adult men.

When comparing childrearing traditions in different cultures, we find that a group's economic organization and the social relations in its subsistence practices impact the way a child is brought up, and this, in turn, affects the adult personality. Cross-cultural comparisons also show that alternatives exist to the way that children are raised—which means that changing the societal conditions in which one's children grow up can alter significantly the way men and women act and interact.

With this in mind, we turn to a discussion about traditions of dependence and independence training. As you read, bear in mind that many cultures employ a mixture of these types of customary childrearing techniques.

DEPENDENCE TRAINING

Some years after Margaret Mead's pioneering comparative research on gender, psychological anthropologists carried out a significant and more wide-ranging series of cross-cultural studies on the effects of childrearing on personality. Among other things, their work showed that it is possible to distinguish between two general patterns of childrearing. These patterns stem from a number of practices that, regardless of the reason for their existence, have the effect of emphasizing dependence on the one hand and independence on the other. For convenience, we will call these "dependence training" and "independence training."[12]

Dependence training socializes people to think of themselves in terms of the larger whole. Its effect is to create community members whose idea of selfhood transcends individualism, promoting compliance in the

12 Whiting, J. W. M., & Child, I. L. (1953). *Child training and personality: A cross-cultural study.* New Haven, CT: Yale University Press.

dependence training   Childrearing practices that foster compliance in the performance of assigned tasks and dependence on the domestic group, rather than reliance on oneself.

performance of assigned tasks and keeping individuals within the group. This pattern is typically associated with extended families, which consist of several husband-wife-children units within the same household. It is most likely to be found in societies with an economy based on subsistence farming but also in foraging groups where several family groups may live together for at least part of the year. Big extended families are important, for they provide the labor force necessary to till the soil, tend whatever flocks are kept, and carry out other part-time economic pursuits considered necessary for existence.

These large families, however, have built into them certain potentially disruptive tensions. For example, important family decisions must be collectively accepted and followed. In addition, the in-marrying spouses—husbands and/or wives who come from other groups—must conform themselves to the group's will, something that may not be easy for them.

Dependence training helps to keep these potential problems under control and involves both supportive and corrective aspects. On the supportive side, parents are easygoing, and mothers yield to the desires of their young, particularly when it comes to breastfeeding, which is provided on demand and continues for several years. This may be interpreted as rewarding the child for seeking support within the family, the main agent in meeting the child's needs. Also on the supportive side, children at a relatively early age are assigned a number of child-care and domestic tasks, all of which make significant and obvious contributions to the family's welfare. Thus family members all actively work to help and support one another.

On the corrective side, behavior the adults interpret as aggressive or selfish is likely to be actively discouraged. Moreover, the adults tend to be insistent on overall obedience, which commonly inclines the individual toward being subordinate to the group. This combination of encouragement and discouragement in the socialization process teaches individuals to put the group's needs above their own—to be obedient, supportive, noncompetitive, and generally responsible, to stay within the fold and not do anything potentially disruptive. Indeed, a person's very definition of self comes from the individual being a part of a larger social whole rather than from his or her mere individual existence.

INDEPENDENCE TRAINING

Independence training fosters individual self-reliance and personal achievement. It is typically associated with societies in which a basic social unit consisting of parent(s) and offspring fends for itself. Independence training is particularly characteristic of mercantile (trading), industrial, and postindustrial societies where self-sufficiency and personal achievement are important traits for success, if not survival—especially for men, and increasingly for women.

This pattern of training involves both encouragement and discouragement. On the negative side, infant feeding is prompted more by schedule than demand. In North America, as noted above, babies are rarely nursed for more than a year, if that. Many parents resort to an artificial nipple or teething ring (pacifier) to satisfy the baby's sucking instincts—typically doing so to calm the child rather than out of an awareness that infants need sucking to strengthen and train coordination in the muscles used for feeding and speech.

North American parents are comparatively quick to start feeding infants baby food and even try to get them to feed themselves. Many are delighted if they can prop their infants up in the crib or playpen so that they can hold their own bottles. Moreover, as soon after birth as possible, children are commonly given their own private space, away from their parents.

Displays of individual will, assertiveness, and even aggression are encouraged or at least tolerated to a greater degree than where dependence training is the rule. In schools, and even in the family, competition and winning are emphasized. Schools in the United States, for example, devote considerable resources to competitive sports. Competition is fostered within the classroom as well—overtly through practices such as spelling bees and awards and covertly through customs such as grading on a curve. In addition, there are various popularity contests, such as crowning a prom queen and king or holding an election to choose the classmate who is "best looking" or "most likely to succeed." Thus by the time individuals have grown up in U.S. society, they have received a clear message: Life is about winning or losing, and losing is equal to failure.[13]

In sum, independence training generally encourages individuals to seek help and attention rather than to give it and to try to exert individual dominance. Such qualities are useful in societies with hierarchical social structures that emphasize personal achievement and where individuals are expected to look out for their own interests. Its socialization patterns match cultural values and expectations increasingly prevalent in the spread of global capitalism.

One kind of training—independence, dependence, or a combination of both—is not inherently better or worse

---

independence training Childrearing practices that foster independence, self-reliance, and personal achievement.

[13] Turnbull, C. M. (1983). *The human cycle* (p. 74). New York: Simon & Schuster.

than any other. If compliant adults who are accepting of authority are required, then independence training will not work well in that society. Nor will dependence training serve very well a society whose adults are expected to be self-reliant, questioning of authority, and ready to explore and embrace new ways of doing things. Building on this basic cross-cultural dichotomy in childrearing practices, comparative research by psychological anthropologists has greatly added to our increasingly sophisticated understanding of the complex relationship between culture and personality.

Group Personality

From the holistic perspective that anthropologists bring to the comparative study of childrearing, it is clear that these customary practices, personality development, and other aspects of culture are systemically interrelated. This insight has prompted research to explore whether whole societies might be analyzed in terms of particular personality types. Certainly, common sense suggests that personalities fitting for one culture may be less suitable for others. For example, an egocentric, aggressive personality would be out of place where self-effacement, cooperation, and sharing are the keys to success.

Unfortunately, common sense, like conventional wisdom in general, is not always true. Anthropologists asked themselves whether it would be possible to describe a group personality without falling into the trap of stereotyping. The answer is a qualified yes, especially with respect to traditional communities. The larger and more complex a society becomes, the greater its variegation in personalities. In an abstract way, we may speak of a generalized "cultural personality" for a society, as long as we do not expect to find a uniformity of personalities within that society.

Put another way, a person develops certain personality characteristics that, from common experience, resemble those of other people. Yet, each human being also acquires distinct personality traits because every individual is exposed to unique sets of experiences and may react to shared experiences in novel ways. Moreover, each person brings to these experiences a one-of-a-kind genetic potential (except in the case of identical twins) that plays a role in determining personality development.

Consider for example the Yanomami Indians, who subsist on foraging and horticulture in the tropical forests of northern Brazil and southern Venezuela. Commonly, Yanomami men strive to achieve a reputation for fierceness and aggressiveness, and they defend that reputation at the risk of serious personal injury and death. Yet, among the Yanomami there are men who have quiet and somewhat retiring personalities. It is all too easy for an outsider to overlook these individuals when other, more "typical" Yanomami are in the front row, pushing and demanding attention.

Modal Personality

Obviously, any productive approach to the problem of group personality must recognize that each individual is unique to a degree in both genetic inheritance and life experiences, and it must leave room for a range of different personality types in any society. In addition, personality traits that may be regarded as appropriate in men may not be so regarded in women, and vice versa. Given all this, we may focus our attention on the **modal personality**, defined as those character traits that occur with the highest frequency in a social group and are therefore the most representative of its culture.

Modal personality is a statistical concept rather than the personality of an average person in a particular society. As such, it opens up for investigation the questions of how more complex societies organize diversity and how diversity relates to cultural change. Such questions are easily missed if one associates a certain type of personality with one particular culture, as did some earlier anthropologists (see Ruth Benedict in Anthropologist of Note). At the same time, modal personalities of different groups can be compared.

Data on modal personality are best gathered by means of psychological tests (such as the Rorschach or "ink blot" test) administered to a sample of the population. In addition, observing and recording the frequency of certain behaviors, collecting and analyzing life histories and dreams, and analyzing popular tales, jokes, legends, and traditional myths can yield useful data on modal personality.

While having much to recommend it, the concept of modal personality as a means of dealing with group personality nevertheless presents certain difficulties. One is the complexity of the measurement techniques, which may be hard to do in the field. For instance, an adequate representative sample of subjects is necessary. The problem here is twofold: making sure the sample is really representative and having the time and personnel necessary to administer the tests, conduct interviews, and so on, all of which can be lengthy proceedings.

Also, the tests themselves constitute a problem, for those devised in one cultural setting may not be appropriate in another. Moreover, language differences or conflicting cultural values between the researcher and

modal personality Those character traits that occur with the highest frequency in a social group and are therefore the most representative of its culture.

the individuals being studied may inhibit communication and/or lead to misinterpretation. For example, just what is aggression? Does everyone define it the same way? Is it an elemental analytical concept, or does it involve other variables? In addition to the problem of test questions being culture-bound, it is worth noting that the concept of testing itself is culturally embedded, especially in hierarchically structured mass societies that value ranking systems based on people's potential capacity in production.

National Character

Several years ago, Italy's tourism minister publicly commented on "typical characteristics" of Germans, referring to them as "hyper-nationalistic blondes" and "beer-drinking slobs" holding "noisy burping contests" on Italy's beaches.[14] Outraged (and proud of his country's excellent beer), Germany's chancellor canceled his planned vacation to Italy and demanded an official apology. Of course, many Germans think of Italians as dark-eyed, hot-blooded spaghetti eaters. To say so in public, however, might cause an uproar.

Unflattering stereotypes about foreigners are deeply rooted in cultural traditions everywhere. Many Japanese believe Koreans are stingy, crude, and aggressive, while many Koreans see the Japanese as cold and arrogant. Similarly, we all have in mind some image, perhaps not well defined, of the typical citizen of Russia or Mexico or England. And Americans traveling abroad may be insulted that others in the world hold the negative image of loud, brash, and arrogant Yankees. Although these are simply stereotypes, we might ask if these stereotypes have any basis in fact. In reality, does such a thing as *national character* exist?

Some anthropologists once thought that the answer might be yes. So, they embarked on national character studies in the 1930s and 1940s, aiming to discover basic personality traits shared by the majority of the people of modern state societies. In what came to be known as the *culture and personality* movement, their research emphasized childrearing practices and education as the factors theoretically responsible for such characteristics.

Early on it was recognized that the national character studies were flawed, mainly because they made generalizations based on limited data, relatively small samples of informants, and questionable assumptions about developmental psychology. These flaws notwithstanding,

The collectively shared core values of Chinese culture promote the integration of the individual into a larger group, as we see in this large gathering of Taipei residents doing Tai Chi together.

national character studies were important in that they helped change the anthropological focus from traditional small-scale communities of foragers, herders, and farmers in exotic places to large-scale contemporary state societies. Moreover, they prompted new theoretical and methodological approaches to serious interdisciplinary group research.[15]

Core Values

An alternative approach to national character—one that allows for the fact that not all personalities will conform to cultural ideals—is that of Chinese American

---

[14] "Italy-Germany verbal war hots up." (2003, July 9). *Deccan Herald* (Bangalore, India).

[15] See Beeman, W. O. (2000). Introduction: Margaret Mead, cultural studies, and international understanding. In M. Mead & R. Métraux (Eds.), *The study of culture at a distance* (pp. xiv–xxxi). New York and Oxford: Berghahn.

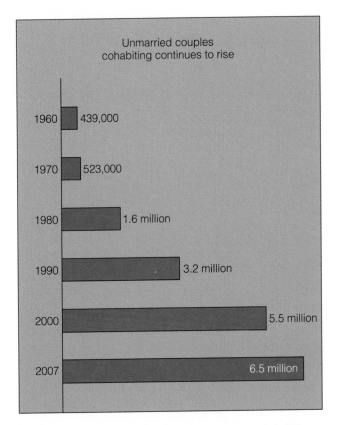

Unmarried couples
cohabiting continues to rise

Year	Value
1960	439,000
1970	523,000
1980	1.6 million
1990	3.2 million
2000	5.5 million
2007	6.5 million

Figure 17.1 **The number of opposite-sex couples cohabiting in the United States, by year. Cohabiting couples now make up almost 10 percent of all opposite-sex U.S. couples, married and unmarried.**
Source: U.S. Census Bureau, 2007.

anthropologist Francis Hsu. His approach is to study **core values** (values especially promoted by a particular culture) and related personality traits. The Chinese, he suggests, value kin ties and cooperation above all else. To them, mutual dependence is the very essence of personal relationships and has been for thousands of years. Compliance and subordination of one's will to that of family and kin transcend all else, while self-reliance is neither promoted nor a source of pride.

Perhaps the core value held in highest esteem by North Americans of European descent is rugged individualism. Each individual is supposed to be able to achieve anything he or she likes, given a willingness to work hard enough. From their earliest years, individuals are subjected to relentless pressures to excel, and as we have already noted, competition and winning are crucial to this. Undoubtedly, this contributes to the restlessness and drive seen as characteristic for much of North American society today—and increasingly common wherever people compete for survival, wealth, and power in the global market.

Also, to the degree that it motivates individuals to work hard and to go where the jobs are, this individualism fits well with the demands of a global market economy. Thus, while individuals in Chinese traditional society are firmly bound into a larger group to which they have lifelong obligations, most urban North Americans and western Europeans live isolated from relatives other than their young children and spouse—and even the commitment to marriage has lessened (Figure 17.1). Many people in western Europe, North America, and other industrial or postindustrial societies choose to remain single or postpone marriage. This growing individualism is also indicated by the declining rates of formal marriage and rising rates of divorce—with close to 50 percent of marriages now failing.[16]

Alternative Gender Models from a Cross-Cultural Perspective

As touched on earlier, the gender roles assigned to each sex vary from culture to culture and have an impact on personality formation. But what if the sex of an individual is not self-evident, as revealed in the following Original Study? Written when its author was an undergraduate student of philosophy at Bryn Mawr College in Pennsylvania, this narrative offers a compelling personal account of the emotional difficulties associated with intersexuality and gender ambiguity, while making the important point that attitudes toward gender vary cross-culturally. However, some of the cultural information is overly generalized and therefore not quite accurate, including the idea that all or most Native American spiritual-religious worldviews were and are nonhierarchical.[17]

[16] Observations on North American culture in this section are drawn primarily from Natadecha-Sponsal, P. (1993). The young, the rich and the famous: Individualism as an American cultural value. In P. R. DeVita & J. D. Armstrong (Eds.), *Distant mirrors: America as a foreign culture* (pp. 46–53). Belmont, CA: Wadsworth. See also Whitehead, B. D., & Popenoe, D. (2004). *The state of our unions: The social health of marriage in America 2004.* Rutgers, NJ: Rutgers University National Marriage Project; Noack, T. (2001). Cohabitation in Norway: An accepted and gradually more regulated way of living. *International Journal of Law, Policy, and the Family 15* (1), 102–117.

[17] For scholarly accounts of the issues presented here, readers may turn to several excellent books, including the one mentioned in the Original Study: Roscoe, W. (1991). *The Zuni man-woman.* Albuquerque: University of New Mexico Press.

core values Those values especially promoted by a particular culture.

The Blessed Curse   *by R. K. Williamson*

One morning not so long ago, a child was born. This birth, however, was no occasion for the customary celebration. Something was wrong: something very grave, very serious, very sinister. This child was born between sexes, an "intersexed" child. From the day of its birth, this child would be caught in a series of struggles involving virtually every aspect of its life. Things that required little thought under "ordinary" circumstances were, in this instance, extraordinarily difficult. Simple questions now had an air of complexity: "What is it, a girl or a boy?" "What do we name it?" "How shall we raise it?" "Who (or what) is to blame for this?"

A Foot in Both Worlds

The child referred to in the introductory paragraph is myself. As the great-granddaughter of a Cherokee woman, I was exposed to the Native American view of people who were born intersexed, and those who exhibited transgendered characteristics. This view, unlike the Euramerican one, sees such individuals in a very positive and affirming light. Yet my immediate family (mother, father, and brothers) were firmly fixed in a negative Christian Euramerican point of view. As a result, from a very early age I was presented with two different and conflicting views of myself. This resulted in a lot of confusion within me about what I was, how I came to be born the way I was, and what my intersexuality meant in terms of my spirituality as well as my place in society.

I remember, even as a small child, getting mixed messages about my worth as a human being. My grandmother, in keeping with Native American ways, would tell me stories about my birth. She would tell me how she knew when I was born that I had a special place in life, given to me by God, the Great Spirit, and that I had been given "a great strength that girls never have, yet a gentle tenderness that boys never know" and that I was "too pretty and beautiful to be a boy only and too strong to be a girl only." She rejoiced at this "special gift" and taught me that it meant that the Great Spirit had "something important for me to do in this life." I remember how good I felt inside when she told me these things and how I soberly contemplated, even at the young age of 5, that I must be diligent and try to learn and carry out the purpose designed just for me by the Great Spirit.

My parents, however, were so repulsed by my intersexuality that they would never speak of it directly. They would just refer to it as "the work of Satan." To them, I was not at all blessed with a "special gift" from some "Great Spirit," but was "cursed and given over to the Devil" by God. My father treated me with contempt, and my mother wavered between contempt and distant indifference. I was taken from one charismatic church to another in order to have the "demon of mixed sex" cast out of me. At some of these "deliverance" services I was even given a napkin to cough out the demon into!

In the end, no demon ever popped out of me. Still I grew up believing that there was something inherent within me that caused God to hate me, that my intersexuality was a punishment for this something, a mark of condemnation.

Whenever I stayed at my grandmother's house, my fears would be allayed, for she would once again remind me that I was fortunate to have been given this special gift. She was distraught that my parents were treating me cruelly and pleaded with them to let me live with her, but they would not let me stay at her home permanently. Nevertheless, they did let me spend a significant portion of my childhood with her. Had it not been for that, I might not have been able to survive the tremendous trials that awaited me in my walk through life.

Blessed Gift: The Native American View

It is now known that most, if not all, Native American societies had certain individuals that fell between the categories of "man" and "woman." The various nations had different names for such people, but a term broadly used and recognized is *berdache*, a word of French origin that designated a male, passive homosexual. [The preferred term today is *two-spirit*.] Some of these individuals were born physically intersexed. Others appeared to be anatomically normal males, but exhibited the character and the manners of women—or vice versa. The way native people treated such individuals reveals some interesting insights into Native American belief systems.

The Spirit

The extent to which Native Americans see spirituality is reflected in their belief that all things have a spirit: "Every object—plants, rocks, water, air, the moon, animals, humans, the earth itself—has a spirit. The spirit of one thing (including a human) is not superior to the spirit of any other. . . . The function of religion is not to try to condemn or to change what exists, but to accept the realities of the world and to appreciate their contributions to life. Everything that exists has a purpose."

This paradigm is the core of Native American thought and action. Because everything has a spirit, and no spirit is superior to that of another, there is no "above" or "below," no "superior" or "inferior," no "dominant" and "subordinate." These are only illusions that arise from unclear thinking. Thus, an intersexed child is not derided or viewed as a "freak of nature" in many traditional Native American cultures. Intersexuality (as well as masculinity in a female or effeminacy in a male) is seen as the manifestation of the spirit of the child, so an intersexed child is respected as much as a girl child or a boy child. It is the spirit of the child that determines what the gender of the child will ultimately be. According to a Lakota, Lame Deer, "the Great Spirit made them *winktes* [two-spirit], and we accepted them as such." In this sense, the child has no control over what her or his gender will be. It follows that where there is no choice, there can be no accountability on the part of the child. Indeed, the child who is given the spirit of a *winkte* is unable to resist becoming one.

> When an Omaha boy sees the Moon Being [a feminine Spirit] on his vision quest, the spirit holds in one hand a man's bow and arrow and in the other a woman's pack strap. . . . "When the youth tried to grasp the bow and arrows, the Moon Being crossed hands very quickly, and if the youth was not very careful he seized the pack strap instead of the bow and arrows, thereby fixing his lot in later life. In such a case he could not help acting [like a] woman, speaking, dressing, and working just as . . . women . . . do."

The Curse: The Euramerican View

In contrast to the view of respect and admiration of physical intersexuality and transgendered behavior traditionally held by Native Americans, the Europeans who came to "Turtle Island" (the Cherokee name for North America) brought with them their worldview, shaped by their Judeo-Christian beliefs. According to this religious perspective, there had to be, by mandate of God, a complete dichotomy of the sexes. . . .

Will Roscoe, in his book *The Zuni Man-Woman*, reports (pp. 172–173):

Spanish oppression of "homosexual" practices in the New World took brutal forms. In 1513, the explorer Balboa had some forty berdaches thrown to his dogs [to be eaten alive]—"a fine action by an honorable and Catholic Spaniard," as one Spanish historian commented. In Peru, the Spaniards burned "sodomites, . . . and in this way they frightened them in such a manner that they left this great sin."

It is abundantly clear that Christian Euramericans exerted every effort to destroy Native American culture:

In 1883, the U.S. Office of Indian Affairs issued a set of regulations

that came to be known as the Code of Religious Offenses, or Religious Crimes Code. . . . Indians who refused to adopt the habits of industry, or to engage in "civilized pursuits or employments" were subject to arrest and punishment. . . . By interfering with native sexuality [and culture], the agents of assimilation effectively undermined the social fabric of entire tribes. (Roscoe, p. 176)

A Personal Resolution

For me, the resolution to the dual message I was receiving was slow in coming, largely due to the fear and self-hatred instilled in me by Christianity. Eventually, though, the spirit wins out. I came to adopt my grandmother's teaching about my intersexuality. Through therapy, and a new, loving home environment, I was able to shed the constant fear of eternal punishment I felt for something I had no

control over. After all, I did not create myself.

Because of my own experience, and drawing on the teaching of my grandmother, I am now able to see myself as a wondrous creation of the Great Spirit—but not only me. All creation is wondrous. There is a purpose for everyone in the gender spectrum. Each person's spirit is unique in her or his or her-his own way. It is only by living true to the nature that was bestowed upon us by the Great Spirit, in my view, that we are able to be at peace with ourselves and be in harmony with our neighbor. This, to me, is the Great Meaning and the Great Purpose. . . .

Adapted from Williamson, R. K. (1995). The blessed curse: Spirituality and sexual difference as viewed by Euramerican and Native American cultures. The College News 18 (4). Reprinted with permission of the author.

The biological facts of human nature are not always as clear-cut as most people assume. At the level of chromosomes, biological sex is determined according to whether a person's 23rd chromosomal set is XX (female) or XY (male). Some of the genes on these chromosomes control sexual development. This standard biological package does not apply to all humans, and a considerable number are **intersexuals**—people who are born with reproductive organs, genitalia, and/or sex chromosomes that are not exclusively male or female. These individuals do not fit neatly into a binary gender standard.[18]

For example, some people are born with a genetic disorder that results in them having only one X chromosome instead of the usual two. A person with this chromosomal complex, known as Turner syndrome, develops female external genitalia but has nonfunctional ovaries and is therefore infertile. Other individuals are born with the XY sex chromosomes of a male but have an abnormality on the X chromosome that affects the body's sensitivity to androgens (male hormones). This is known as androgen insensitivity syndrome (AIS). An adult XY person with complete AIS appears fully female with a normal clitoris, labia, and breasts. Internally, these individuals possess testes (up in

the abdomen, rather than in their usual descended position in the scrotal sac), but they are otherwise born without a complete set of either male or female internal genital organs. They generally possess a short, blind-ended vagina.

"Hermaphrodites" make up a distinct category of intersexuality—although the terms "male pseudohermaphrodite" and "female pseudohermaphrodite" are often used to refer to a range of intersex conditions. The name, now objected to by many activists, comes from a figure in Greek mythology: Hermaphroditus (son of Hermes, messenger of the gods, and Aphrodite, goddess of beauty and love) who became half-male and half-female when he fell in love with a nymph and his body fused with hers.[19]

More obviously intersexed individuals ("true hermaphrodites") have both testicular and ovarian tissue. They may have a separate ovary and testis, but more commonly they have an ovotestis—a gonad containing both sorts of tissue. About 60 percent of hermaphrodites possess XX (female) sex chromosomes, and the remainder may have XY or a mosaic (a mixture). Their external genitalia may be ambiguous or female, and they may have a uterus or (more commonly) a hemi-uterus (half uterus).[20]

---

[18] This section is based on several sources: Chase, C. (1998). Hermaphrodites with attitude. *Gay and Lesbian Quarterly 4* (2), 189–211; Dumurat-Dreger, A. (1998, May/June). "Ambiguous sex" or ambivalent medicine? *The Hastings Center Report 28* (3), 2,435 (posted on the Intersex Society of North America website: www.isna.org); Fausto-Sterling, A. (1993). The five sexes: Why male and female are not enough. *The Sciences 33* (2), 20–24; the Mayo Clinic website: http://www.mayoclinic.com/.

[19] The Intersex Society of North America suggests using DSD (disorders of sexual development) rather than "hermaphrodites" as part of an effort to urge clinicians to shift from focusing on gender and genitals to the exclusion of the real medical problems people with DSD face.

[20] Fausto-Sterling, A. (2000, July). The five sexes revisited. *The Sciences*, 20–24.

intersexual A person born with reproductive organs, genitalia, and/or sex chromosomes that are not exclusively male or female.

Caster Semenya, an 18-year-old runner from the South African village of Limpopo. After winning the women's 800-meter race at the 2009 world championships in Berlin, Caster faced a barrage of media reports with headlines such as "Gold Awarded Amid Dispute Over Runner's Sex." Gender tests, subsequently ordered by the International Sports Federation, revealed that the runner has internal male sexual organs. Horrified by the way the issue has been handled, South African Sports Minister Makhenkesi Stofile told *Sports Illustrated,* "We think her human rights have been violated and her privacy invaded."

© AP Photo Anja Niedringhaus

Biologist Anne Fausto-Sterling, a specialist in this area, notes that the concept of intersexuality is rooted in "an idealized biological world in which our species is perfectly divided into two kinds:

> That idealized story papers over [that] some women have facial hair, some men have none; some women speak with deep voices, some men veritably squeak. Less well known is the fact that on close inspection, absolute dimorphism disintegrates even at the level of basic biology. Chromosomes, hormones, the internal sex structures, the gonads and external genitalia all vary more than most people realize. Those born outside of the . . . dimorphic mold are called intersexuals.[21]

Intersexuality may be unusual but is not uncommon. In fact, about 1 percent of all humans are intersexed in some (not necessarily visible) way—in other words, nearly 70 million people worldwide.[22] Until recently, it was rarely discussed publicly in many societies. Since the mid-20th century, individuals with financial means in technologically advanced parts of the world have had the option of reconstructive surgery and hormonal treatments to alter such conditions, and many parents faced with raising a visibly intersexed child in a culture intolerant of such minorities have chosen this option for their baby. However, there is a growing movement to put off such irreversible procedures indefinitely or until the child becomes old enough to be the one to make the choice. Obviously, a society's attitude toward these individuals can impact their personality—their fundamental sense of self and how they express it.

In addition to people who are biologically intersexed, throughout history some individuals have been subjected to a surgical removal of some of their sexual organs. In many cultures, male prisoners or war captives have undergone forced castration, a crushing or cutting of the testicles. While castration of adult males does not eliminate the sex drive or the possibility of having an erection, it does put an end to the production of sperm necessary for reproduction.

Archaeological evidence from ancient Egypt, Iraq, Iran, and China suggests that the cultural practice of castrating war captives may have begun several thousand years ago. Young boys captured during war or slave-raiding expeditions were often castrated before being sold and shipped off to serve in foreign households, including royal courts. In the Ottoman empire of the Turks, where these individuals could occupy a variety of important functions in the sultan's household from the

---

[21] Ibid.

[22] Fausto-Sterling, A. (2003, August 2). Personal e-mail communication from this recognized expert on the subject. For published statistics, see her article co-authored with Blackless, M., et al. (2000). How sexually dimorphic are we? Review and synthesis. *American Journal of Human Biology 12,* 151–166.

Biocultural Connection

A Cross-Cultural Perspective on Psychosomatic Symptoms and Mental Health

Biomedicine, the dominant medical system of Euramerican cultures, sometimes identifies physical ailments experienced by individuals as "psychosomatic"—a term derived from *psyche* ("mind") and *soma* ("body"). These ailments can be serious and painful, but because a precise physiological cause cannot be identified through scientific methods, the illness is viewed as something rooted in mental or emotional causes—and thus on some level not quite real.

Each culture possesses its own historically developed ideas about health, illness, and associated healing practices. While biomedicine is based in modern Western traditions of science, it is also steeped in the cultural beliefs and practices of the societies within which it operates. Fundamentally informed by a dualistic mind–body model, biomedicine represents the human body as a complex machine with parts that can be manipulated by experts. This approach has resulted in spectacular treatments, such as antibiotics that have eradicated certain infectious diseases.

Today, the remarkable breakthroughs of biomedicine are spreading rapidly throughout the world, and people from cultures with different healing systems are moving into countries where biomedicine dominates. This makes treating illnesses defined by biomedicine as psychosomatic disorders all the more difficult.

Indicative of our biocultural complexity, psychological factors such as emotional stress, worry, and anxiety may stem from cultural contexts and result in increased physiological agitation like irregular heart pounding or palpitations, heightened blood pressure, headaches, stomach and intestinal problems, muscle pains and tensions, rashes, appetite loss, insomnia, fatigue, and a range of other troubles. Indeed, when individuals are unable to deal successfully with stressful situations in daily life and do not get the opportunity for adequate mental rest and relaxation, even their natural immune systems may weaken, increasing their chances of getting a cold or some other infection. For people forced to adapt to a quickly changing way of life in their own country or immigrants adjusting to a foreign culture, these pressures may result in a range of disorders that are difficult to explain from the perspective of biomedicine.

Medical and psychological approaches developed in European and North American societies are often unsuccessful in dealing with these problems, for a number of reasons. For one, the various immigrant ethnic groups have different concepts of mind and body than do medical practitioners trained in Western (Euramerican) medicine. Among many Caribbean peoples, for example, a widely held belief is that spiritual forces are active in the world and that they influence human identity and behavior. For someone with a psychosomatic problem, it is normal to seek help from a local *curandero* or *curandera* ("folk healer"), a *santiguadora* ("herbalist"), or even a *santéro* (a Santéria priest) rather than a medical doctor or psychiatrist. Not only does the client not understand the symbols of Western psychiatry, but a psychiatric visit is often too expensive and may imply that the person is *loco*.

During the past few decades, however, anthropologists have become increasingly involved in cross-cultural medical mediation, challenging negative biases and correcting misinformation about non-Western indigenous perceptions of mind–body connections. The inclusion of culturally appropriate healing approaches has gained growing acceptance among the Western medical and psychological establishment in Europe, North America, and many other parts of the world.

BIOCULTURAL QUESTION

Given the cross-cultural differences in concepts of mind and body, should authorities in a pluralistic society apply the same standards to faith healers as to medical doctors?

---

of view, insanity is a culturally constructed mental illness, and people are considered insane when they fail to conform to a culturally defined range of normal behavior.

No matter how eccentric or bizarre certain behaviors might seem in a particular place and time, those behaviors are not necessarily abnormal in all cultures, and it is possible for the "abnormal" to become socially accepted in cultures that are changing. Such is the case with manic depression (now more properly called *bipolar disorder*) and attention deficit hyperactivity disorder (ADHD), both previously regarded as dreaded liabilities.

In western Europe and North America, the manic and hyperactivity aspects of these conditions have gradually become viewed as assets in the quest for success.[32] Just as social attitudes concerning a wide range of both psychological and physical differences change over time within a society, they also vary across cultures—as is evident in this chapter's Biocultural Connection.

CULTURAL RELATIVITY OF ABNORMALITY

Is "normal" is a meaningless concept when applied to personality? Within the context of a particular culture, the concept of normal personality is quite meaningful. Irving Hallowell, a major figure in the development of psychological anthropology, ironically observed that it is normal to share the delusions traditionally accepted by one's society. Abnormality involves the development of a delusional system of which the culture does not approve. The individual who is disturbed because he or she cannot adequately measure up to the norms of society and be happy may be termed "neurotic." When a person's delusional system is

---

[32] Martin, E. (1999). Flexible survivors. *Anthropology News 40* (6), 5–7.

so different that it in no way reflects his or her society's norms, the individual may be termed "psychotic."

If severe enough, culturally induced conflicts can produce psychosis and also determine its particular form. In a culture that encourages aggressiveness and suspicion, the insane person may be one who is passive and trusting. In a culture that encourages passivity and trust, the insane person may be the one who is aggressive and suspicious. Just as each society establishes its own norms, each individual is unique in his or her perceptions.

Although it is true that each particular culture defines what is and is not normal behavior, the situation is complicated by findings suggesting that major categories of mental disorders may be universal types of human affliction. Take, for example, schizophrenia—probably the most common of all psychoses and one that may be found in any culture, no matter how it may manifest itself. Individuals afflicted by schizophrenia experience distortions of reality that impair their ability to function adequately, so they often withdraw from the social world into their own psychological shell.

Although environmental factors play a role, evidence suggests that schizophrenia is caused by a biochemical disorder for which there is an inheritable tendency. One of its more severe forms is paranoid schizophrenia. Those suffering from it fear and mistrust nearly everyone. They hear voices that whisper dreadful things to them, and they are convinced that someone is "out to get them." Acting on this conviction, they engage in bizarre sorts of behaviors, which lead to their removal from society.

CULTURE-BOUND SYNDROME

A **culture-bound syndrome,** or ethnic psychosis, is a mental disorder specific to a particular cultural group (Table 17.1).[33] A historical example is Windigo psychosis, limited to northern Algonquian groups such as the Cree and Ojibwa. In their traditional belief systems, these Indians recognized the existence of cannibalistic monsters called Windigos. Individuals afflicted by the psychosis developed the delusion that, falling under the control of these monsters, they were themselves transformed into Windigos, with a craving for human flesh. As this happened, the psychotic individuals perceived people around them turning into edible animals—fat beavers, for instance. Although there are no known instances where sufferers of Windigo psychosis actually devoured humans, they were acutely afraid of doing so, and people around them feared that they might.

Windigo psychosis may seem different from clinical cases of paranoid schizophrenia found in Euramerican cultures, but a closer look suggests otherwise. The disorder was merely being expressed in ways compatible with traditional northern Algonquian cultures. Ideas of persecution, instead of being directed toward other humans, were directed toward supernatural beings (the Windigo monsters); cannibalistic panic replaced panic expressed in other forms.

Windigo behavior has seemed exotic and dramatic to Euramericans, but psychotic individuals draw upon whatever imagery and symbolism their culture has to offer. For instance, the delusions of Irish schizophrenics draw upon the images and symbols of Irish Catholicism and feature Virgin and Savior motifs. In short, the underlying biomedical structure of the mental disorder may be the same in all cases, but its expression is culturally specific.

A Western example of a culture-bound syndrome is "hysteria," expressed by fainting spells, choking fits, and even seizures and blindness. Identified in industrializing societies of 19th-century Europe and North America, this disorder was particularly associated with young urban women in well-to-do social circles. In fact, the term invented for this "nervous disease" is derived from the Greek word for uterus. Not only has the diagnosis of this disorder declined in the course of the 20th century, but the term itself was banished from the medical nomenclature.[34]

In more recent decades, we have seen the rise of two related culture-bound syndromes: *bulimia nervosa* and *anorexia nervosa.* Bulimia is characterized by frequent binge eating followed by vomiting or other frantic efforts to avoid gaining weight. Anorexia is an obsession to remain thin, evidenced in self-starvation that may result in death. This neurotic "fear of fatness" manifests itself in Western consumer societies where a growing percentage of the population is overweight or obese. Bulimia and anorexia are primarily diagnosed in female adolescents who reside in a culture that exalts thinness, even as fast food and leisure snacking are more prevalent. With the globalization of consumer society's fat-thin contradiction, its associated psychological eating disorders are also crossing borders.[35] Today, Japan is just behind the United States in deaths related to psychological eating disorders.[36]

---

[33] Simons, R. C., & Hughes, C. C. (Eds.). (1985). *The culture-bound syndromes: Folk illnesses of psychiatric and anthropological interest.* Dordrecht, Netherlands: Reidel.

culture-bound syndrome A mental disorder specific to a particular cultural group.

---

[34] Gordon, R. (2000). *Eating disorders: Anatomy of a social epidemic* (2nd ed.). New York: Wiley-Blackwell.

[35] Littlewood, R. (2004). Commentary: Globalization, culture, body image, and eating disorders. *Culture, Medicine, and Psychiatry 28* (4), 597–602.

[36] World Health Organization. (2004). Statistical information system. See also http://www.nationmaster.com/graph/mor_eat_dis-mortality-eating-disorders.

Table 17.1 Culture-Bound Syndromes

Name of Disorder	Culture	Description
Amok	Malaysia (also observed in Java, Philippines, Africa, and Tierra del Fuego)	A disorder characterized by sudden, wild outbursts of homicidal aggression in which the afflicted person may kill or injure others. The rage disorder is usually found in males who are rather withdrawn, quiet, and inoffensive prior to the onset of the disorder. Stress, sleep deprivation, extreme heat, and alcohol are among the conditions thought to precipitate the disorder. Several stages have been observed: Typically in the first stage the person becomes more withdrawn; then a period of brooding follows in which a loss of reality contact is evident. Ideas of persecution and anger predominate. Finally, a phase of automatism, or *amok*, occurs, in which the person jumps up, yells, grabs a knife, and stabs people or objects within reach. Exhaustion and depression usually follow, with amnesia for the rage.
Anorexia nervosa	Western countries (becoming global)	A disorder occurring most frequently among young women in which a preoccupation with thinness produces a refusal to eat. This condition can result in death.
Latah	Malaysia	A fear reaction often occurring in middle-aged women who are subservient and self-effacing. The disorder is precipitated by the word *snake* or by tickling. It is characterized by echolalia (repetition of the words and sentences of others). The disturbed individual may also react with negativism and the compulsive use of obscene language.
Koro	Southeast Asia (particularly Malaysia)	A fear reaction or anxiety in males in which the person fears that his penis will withdraw into his abdomen and he will die. This reaction may appear after sexual overindulgence or excessive masturbation. The anxiety is typically very intense and of sudden onset. The condition is "treated" by having the penis held firmly by the patient or by family members or friends. Often the penis is clamped to a wooden box.
Windigo	Algonquian Indians of Canada and northern United States	A fear reaction in which a hunter becomes anxious and agitated, convinced that he is bewitched. Fears center on his being turned into a cannibal by the power of a monster with an insatiable craving for human flesh.
Kitsunetsuki	Japan	A disorder in which victims believe that they are possessed by foxes and are said to change their facial expressions to resemble foxes. Entire families are often possessed and banned by the community.
Pibloktoq and other Arctic hysterias	Circumpolar peoples from Lapland eastward across Siberia, northern Alaska, and Canada to Greenland	A disorder brought on by fright, which is followed by a short period of bizarre behavior; victim may tear clothes off, jump in water or fire, roll in snow, try to walk on the ceiling, throw things, thrash about, and "speak in tongues." Outburst is followed by a return to normal behavior.

Source: Based on Carson, R. C., Butcher, J. N., & Coleman, J. C. (1990). *Abnormal psychology and modern life* (8th ed., p. 85). Glenview, IL: Scott Foresman.

Personal Identity and Mental Health in Globalizing Society

Anthropologists view childrearing, gender issues, social identity, and emotional and mental health issues in their cultural context; this perspective recognizes that each individual's unique personality, feelings of happiness, and overall sense of health are shaped or influenced by the particular culture within which the person is born and raised to function as a valued member of the community. These communities, however, are seldom stable.

As illustrated by the spread of consumer culture and its associated psychological disorders, people all across the world face sometimes bewildering challenges hurled at them by the forces of globalization. These forces impact how people raise their children, how their personalities are influenced, and how they maintain their individual and collective social, psychological, and mental health.

In the past few decades, medical and psychological anthropologists have made valuable contributions to improving health care, not only in so-called developing countries far away, but also in their own societies. However, mental health practices prevailing in Europe and North America remain ethnocentric when theorizing and treating psychological disorders—a problem reinforced by a reductionist biomedical mindset that largely ignores the role of cultural factors in the etiology, expression, course, and outcome of mental disorders. Furthermore, commercial pressures on the health-care establishment favor bioscience and pharmacotherapy, with drug companies providing a quick and cheap fix for the problem.[37]

---

[37] Luhrmann, T. M. (2001). *Of two minds: An anthropologist looks at American psychiatry*. New York: Vintage; Marsella, A. J., & White, G. (1982). *Cultural conceptions of mental health and therapy*. New York: Springer.

Informed by cultural relativist views on normality and deviance, anthropological perspectives on identity, mental health, and psychiatric disorders are especially useful in pluralistic societies where people from different ethnic groups, each with a distinctive culture, coexist and interact. Intensified by globalization, this multi-ethnic convergence drives home the need for a medical pluralism providing multiple healing modalities suited for the cultural dynamics of the 21st century.

Questions for Reflection

1. Every society faces the challenge of humanizing its children, teaching them the values and social codes that will enable them to be functioning, contributing members in the community. What childrearing practices did you experience that embody the values and social codes of your society?

2. Considering the cultural significance of naming ceremonies in so many societies, what do you think motivated your parents when they named you? Does that have any influence on your sense of self?

3. Margaret Mead's cross-cultural research on gender relations suggests that male dominance is a cultural construct and, consequently, that alternative gender arrangements can be created. Looking at your grandparents, parents, and siblings, do you see any changes in your own family? What about your own community? Do you think such changes are positive?

4. Given that nearly 70 million people in today's world are intersexed and in light of the fact that a very small fraction of these people have access to reconstructive surgery, what do you think of societies that have created cultural space for a third-gender option?

5. Do you know someone in your family, neighborhood, or school who is "abnormal"? What is the basis for that judgment, and do you think everyone shares that opinion? Can you imagine that personal habits you consider normal would be viewed as deviant in the past or in another country?

Suggested Readings

Barnouw, V. (1985). *Culture and personality* (4th ed.). Homewood, IL: Dorsey.

This is a revision of a well-respected text designed to introduce students to psychological anthropology.

Brettell, C. B., & Sargent, C. F. (Eds.). (2000). *Gender in cross-cultural perspective* (3rd ed.). Upper Saddle River, NJ: Prentice-Hall.

Classic and contemporary gender readings on a range of topics, including the cultural construction of femininity and masculinity and the impact of globalization on gender issues.

LaFont, S. (Ed.). (2003). *Constructing sexualities: Readings in sexuality, gender, and culture*. Upper Saddle River, NJ: Prentice-Hall.

A broad yet detailed look at sexuality and gender behavior. Statistics, ethnographic examples, and theoretical insights on numerous themes—from the biological basics and sex categories to sexual orientation and transsexuality.

Levine, R. A. (2007). Ethnographic studies of childhood: A historical overview. *American Anthropologist 109* (2), 247–260.

This article offers a succinct survey and discussion of the ethnographic literature on childhood studies in the 20th century, from psychoanalytically informed studies by Malinowski, Mead, and others in the 1920s and 1930s to comparative psychocultural studies launched by Whiting et al. in the 1950s, followed by diverse anthropological trends in infant studies from the 1960s onward.

Quinn, N. (2005). Universals of child rearing. *Anthropological Theory 5*, 475–514.

Based on cross-cultural comparisons of childrearing strategies, the author identifies four universal features of childrearing that together explain how every society so effectively enculturates children into valued adults.

Suárez-Orozoco, M. M., Spindler, G., & Spindler, L. (1994). *The making of psychological anthropology*, II. Fort Worth: Harcourt Brace.

This collection of articles consists of firsthand accounts of the objectives, accomplishments, and failures of well-known specialists in psychological anthropology.

Challenge Issue Facing the challenge of getting food, fuel, shelter, and other necessities, humans must gather, produce, or buy the means to satisfy such needs. During the span of human existence, this has been accomplished in a range of highly contrasting natural environments by different biological and cultural adaptations. Inventing and applying various technologies, humans have developed distinctive subsistence arrangements to harness energy and process required resources. Thus we may find hunters in Namibia's desert, fishers in Norway, manioc planters in Brazil's rainforest, goat herders in Iran's mountains, steel-mill laborers in South Korea, computer techs in India's cities, and poultry farmers in rural Alabama. While all human activities impact their environments, some are more invasive than others—as we see in this photo showing peasant farmers of Dazhai village practicing wet-rice cultivation on the mountainous slopes of Guangxi Province in southern China. They have created terraces to capture rainwater, prevent soil erosion, and increase food production.

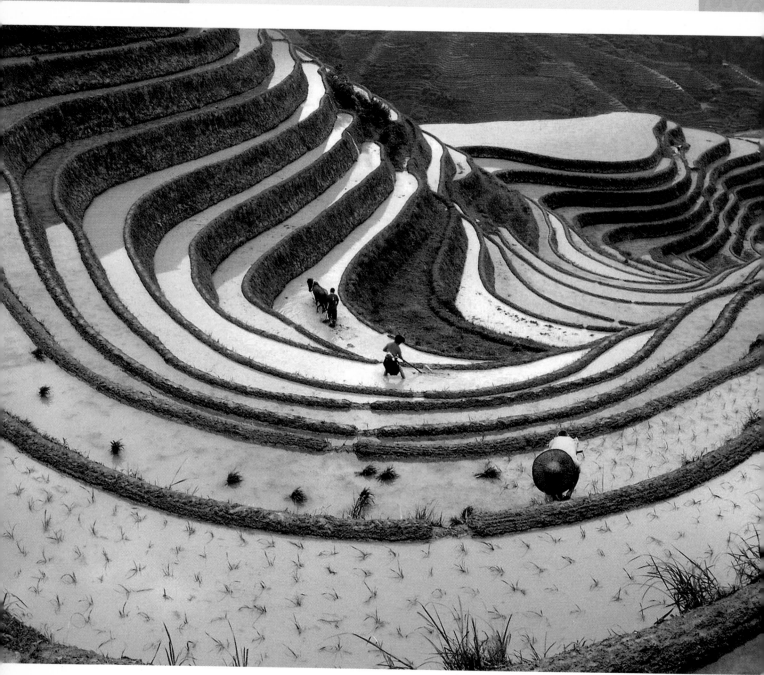

CHAPTER 18

Patterns of Subsistence

Chapter Preview

What Is Adaptation?

Adaptation refers to beneficial adjustments of organisms to their environment, a process that not only leads to changes in the organisms but also impacts their environment. Such dynamic interaction is necessary for the survival of all life forms, including human beings. The human species adapts not only biologically but culturally. In fact, in the course of evolution humans came to rely increasingly on cultural rather than biological change as a means of effectively adapting to different and changing environments.

How Do Humans Adapt Culturally?

Through cultural adaptation, humans develop ways of doing things that are compatible with the resources they have available to them and within the limitations of the various habitats in which they live. In a particular region, people living in similar environments tend to borrow from one another customs that work well in those settings. Once achieved, adaptations may be remarkably stable for long periods of time, even thousands of years. Humankind's unique creative capacity to adapt by means of culture has enabled our species to inhabit an extraordinary variety of environments.

What Cultural Adaptations Have Humans Achieved?

Food foraging is the oldest and most universal human adaptation and typically involves geographic mobility. Other adaptations, based on the domestication of plants and animals, began to develop in some parts of the world about 10,000 years ago. Horticulture (cultivating plants with hand tools) led to more permanent settlements (villages and towns) while pastoralism (herding grazing animals) required mobility to seek out pasture and water. Cities began to develop as early as 5,000 years ago in some world regions, as intensive agriculture and long-distance trading produced sufficient resources to support larger populations and various full-time specialists. And only about two centuries ago, a worldwide transition from an economy based on manual labor and draft animals toward one based on machines was set into motion by the industrial revolution, which radically transformed manufacturing, agriculture, mining, and transportation. These changes led to increasingly complex and large-scale social organizations—but did not necessarily improve the overall conditions of human existence. Two of the unanticipated negative consequences of a machine technology energized by fossil-fuel burning are environmental pollution and global warming, contributing to regional climate changes.

All living beings must satisfy certain basic needs to stay alive—including food, water, and shelter. Moreover, because these needs must be met on an ongoing basis, no creature could long survive if its relations with its environment were random and chaotic. All require regular access to a supply of food along with reliable means of obtaining and using it. A lion would die if all its prey disappeared, if its teeth and claws grew soft, or if its digestive system failed.

Although people face similar sorts of problems, they have an overwhelming advantage over other creatures: People have culture. If the rains do not come and the hot sun turns grassland into desert, we may pump water from deep wells, quenching our thirst, irrigating the pastures, and feeding our grazing animals. Conversely, if the rains do not end and our pastures turn into marshlands, we may choose to build earth mounds for our villages or dig canals to drain flooded fields. And to keep our food supplies from rotting, we can preserve them by drying or roasting and keep them in safe storage places for protection and future use. When our tools fail or are inadequate, we may choose to replace them or invent better ones. And if our stomachs are incapable of digesting a particular food, we can prepare it by cooking.

We are, nonetheless, subject to similar basic needs and pressures as are all other living creatures, and it is important to understand human survival from this point of view. The crucial concept that underlies such a perspective is adaptation: how humans adjust to and act upon the burdens and opportunities presented in daily life.

Adaptation

As discussed earlier in this book, *adaptation* is the process organisms undergo to achieve a beneficial adjustment to a particular environment. What makes human adaptation unique among all other species is our capacity to produce and reproduce culture, enabling us to creatively adapt to an extraordinary range of radically different environments. The biological underpinnings of this capacity include large brains and a long period of growth and development.

How humans adjust to the burdens and opportunities presented in daily life is the basic concern of all cultures. As defined earlier in the book, a people's *cultural adaptation* consists of a complex of ideas,

activities, and technologies that enable them to survive and even thrive; that adaptation, in turn, impacts their environment.

The process of adaptation establishes an ever-shifting balance between the needs of a population and the potential of its environment. This process can be illustrated by the Tsembaga people of Papua New Guinea, one of about twenty local groups of Maring speakers who support themselves chiefly through cultivating crops using simple hand tools such as digging sticks or hoes.[1] Although the Tsembaga also raise pigs, they eat them only under conditions of illness, injury, warfare, or celebration. At such times the pigs are sacrificed to ancestral spirits, and their flesh is ritually consumed. (This guarantees a supply of high-quality protein when it is most needed.)

Traditionally, the Tsembaga and their neighbors are bound together in a unique cycle of pig sacrifices that serves to mark the end of hostilities between groups. Hostilities are periodically fueled by ecological pressures in which pigs play a significant role. Because they fulfill important functions in the community, pigs are rarely slaughtered. Omnivorous eaters, they keep the village free of garbage and even human feces; moreover, they serve as status symbols for their owners who reserve them for important ritual feasts. But there are drawbacks to keeping the pigs alive and allowing them to multiply, since their numbers grow quickly. Invading the village gardens, the hungry pigs eat the sweet potatoes and other crops, leaving almost nothing for their human owners. In short, they become a problem.

The need to expand food cultivation in order to feed the prestigious but pesky pigs puts a strain on the land best suited for farming. Sooner or later, fighting breaks out between the Tsembaga and their neighbors. Hostilities usually end after several weeks, followed by a pig feast ritual. For this event, the Tsembaga butcher and roast almost all of their pigs and feast heartily on them with invited allies. By means of this feast, the Tsembaga not only pay their debts to their allies and gain prestige, but also eliminate a major source of irritation and complaint between neighbors. Moreover, the feast leaves everyone well fed and physically strengthened as a result of the animal protein intake. Even without hostilities over scarce land, such large pig feasts have been held whenever the pig population has become unmanageable—every five to ten years, depending on the groups' success in growing crops and raising animals. Thus the cycle of

[1] Rappaport, R. A. (1969). Ritual regulation of environmental relations among a New Guinea people. In A. P. Vayda (Ed.), *Environment and cultural behavior* (pp. 181–201). Garden City, NY: Natural History.

Biocultural Connection

Surviving in the Andes: Aymara Adaptation to High Altitude

However adaptable we are as a species through our diverse cultures, some natural environments pose such extreme climatic challenges that the human body must make physical adaptations to successfully survive. The central Andean highlands of Bolivia offer an interesting example of complex biocultural interaction, where a biologically adapted human body type has emerged due to natural selection.

Known as the *altiplano,* this high plateau has an average elevation of 4,000 meters (13,000 feet). Many thousands of years ago, small groups of human foragers in the warm lowlands climbed up the mountain slopes in search of game and other food. The higher they moved, the harder it became to breathe due to decreasing molecular concentration, or partial pressure, of oxygen in the inspired air. However, upon reaching the cold and treeless highlands, they found herds of llamas and hardy food plants, including potatoes—reasons to stay. Eventually (about 4,000 years ago) their descendants domesticated both the llamas and the potatoes and developed a new way of life as high-altitude agropastoralists.

The llamas provided meat and hides, as well as milk and wool. And the potatoes, a rich source of carbohydrates, became their staple food. In the course of many centuries, the Aymara selectively cultivated more than 200 varieties of these tubers on small family-owned tracts of land. They boiled them fresh for immediate consumption and also freeze-dried and preserved them as *chuño,* which is the Aymara's major source of nutrition to this day.

© Victor Englebert

Still surviving as highland subsistence farmers and herders, these Aymara Indians have adapted culturally and biologically to the cold and harsh conditions of Bolivia's altiplano. They live and go about their work at extremely high altitudes (up to 4,800 meters/15,600 feet), where partial pressure of oxygen in the air is far lower than that to which most humans are biologically accustomed.

Experiencing a marked hypoxemia (insufficient oxygenation of the blood), a person's normal physiological response to being active at such heights is quick and heavy breathing. Most outsiders visiting the altiplano typically need several days to acclimatize to these conditions. Going too high too quickly can cause *soroche* (mountain sickness), with physiological problems such as pulmonary hypertension, increased heart rates, shortness of breath, headaches, fever, lethargy, and nausea. These symptoms usually disappear when one becomes fully acclimated, but most people will still be quickly exhausted by otherwise normal physical exercise.

For the Aymara Indians whose ancestors have inhabited the altiplano for many thousands of years, the situation is different. Through generations of natural selection, their bodies have become biologically adapted to the low oxygen levels. Short-legged and barrel-chested, their small bodies have an unusually large thoracic volume compared to their tropical lowland neighbors and most other humans. Remarkably, their expanded heart and lungs possess about 30 percent greater pulmonary diffusing capacity to oxygenate blood. In short, the distinctly broad chests of the Aymara Indians are biological evidence of their adaptation to the low-oxygen atmosphere of a natural habitat in which they survive as high-altitude agropastoralists.

BIOCULTURAL QUESTION

If a group of Aymara Indians abandons their high-altitude homeland in the Bolivian altiplano and settles for a new life in the coastal lowlands, will their descendents still living in this low-altitude environment a dozen generations later have smaller chests?

For more information see Baker, P. (Ed.). (1978). The biology of high altitude peoples. London: Cambridge University Press; Rupert, J. L., & Hochachka, P. W. (2001). The evidence for hereditary factors contributing to high altitude adaptation in Andean natives: A review. High Altitude Medicine & Biology 2 (2), 235–256.

fighting and feasting keeps the ecological balance among humans, land, and animals.

Through their distinctive cultures, different human groups have managed to adapt to a very diverse range of natural environments—from Arctic snowfields to Polynesian coral islands, from the Sahara Desert to the Amazon rainforest. Adaptation occurs not only when humans make changes in their natural environment but also when they are biologically changed by their natural environment, as illustrated in this chapter's Biocultural Connection.

The Unit of Adaptation

The unit of adaptation includes both organisms and their environment. Organisms, including human beings, exist as members of a population; populations, in turn, must have the flexibility to cope with variability and change within the natural environment that sustains them. In biological terms, this flexibility means that different organisms within the population have somewhat differing genetic endowments. In cultural terms, it means that variation occurs among individual skills, knowledge, and personalities. Indeed, organisms and environments form dynamic interacting systems. And although environments do not determine culture, they do present certain possibilities and limitations: People might just as easily farm as fish, but we do not expect to find farmers in Siberia's frozen tundra or fishermen in the middle of North Africa's Sahara Desert.

Some anthropologists have adopted the ecologists' concept of **ecosystem,** defined as a system composed of both the natural environment and all the organisms living within it. The system is bound by the activities of the organisms, as well as by such physical processes as erosion and evaporation.

Adaptation in Cultural Evolution

Human groups adapt to their environments by means of their cultures. However, cultures may change over the course of time; they evolve. This is called **cultural evolution.** The process is sometimes confused with the idea of **progress**—the notion that humans are moving forward to a better, more advanced stage in their development toward perfection. Yet not all changes turn out to be positive in the long run, nor do they improve conditions for every member of a society even in the short run. Complex, urban societies are not more highly evolved than those of food foragers. Rather, both are highly evolved, but in quite different ways.

Cultural adaptation must also be understood from a historical point of view. To fit into an ecosystem, humans (like all organisms) must have the potential to adjust to or become a part of it. A good example of this is the Comanche, whose known history begins in the highlands of southern Idaho.[2] Living in that harsh,

---

[2] Wallace, E., & Hoebel, E. A. (1952). *The Comanches.* Norman: University of Oklahoma Press.

---

ecosystem A system, or a functioning whole, composed of both the natural environment and all the organisms living within it.

cultural evolution Cultural change over time; not to be confused with progress.

progress The notion that humans are moving forward to a better, more advanced stage in their cultural development toward perfection.

convergent evolution In cultural evolution, the development of similar cultural adaptations to similar environmental conditions by different peoples with different ancestral cultures.

arid region, these North American Indians traditionally subsisted on wild plants, small animals, and occasionally larger game. Their material equipment was simple and limited to what they (and their dogs) could carry or pull. The size of their groups was restricted, and what little social power could develop was in the hands of the shaman, who was a combination of healer and spiritual guide.

At some point in their nomadic history, the Comanche moved east onto the Great Plains, attracted by enormous bison herds. As much larger groups could be supported by the new and plentiful food supply, the Comanche needed a more complex political organization. Eventually they acquired horses and guns from European and neighboring Indian traders. This enhanced their hunting capabilities significantly and led to the emergence of powerful hunting chiefs.

The Comanche became raiders in order to get horses (which they did not breed for themselves), and their hunting chiefs evolved into war chiefs. The once materially unburdened and peaceful hunter-gatherers of the dry highlands became wealthy, and raiding became a way of life. In the late 18th and early 19th centuries, they dominated the southern Plains (now primarily Texas and Oklahoma). In moving from one regional environment to another and in adopting a new technology, the Comanche were able to take advantage of existing cultural capabilities to thrive in their new situation.

Sometimes societies that developed independently of one another find similar solutions to similar problems. For example, the Cheyenne Indians moved from the woodlands of the Great Lakes region to the Great Plains and took up a form of Plains Indian culture resembling that of the Comanche, even though the cultural historical backgrounds of the two groups differed significantly. (Before they transformed into horse-riding bison hunters, the Cheyenne had cultivated crops and gathered wild rice, which fostered a distinct set of social, political, and religious practices.) This is an example of **convergent evolution**—the development of similar cultural adaptations to similar environmental conditions by different peoples with different ancestral cultures. (See Figure 18.1 for a map of Native American culture areas.)

Especially interesting is that the Cheyenne gave up crop cultivation completely and focused exclusively on hunting and gathering after their move into the vast grasslands of the northern High Plains. Contrary to the popular notion of evolution as a progressive movement toward increased manipulation of the environment, this ethnographic example shows that cultural historical changes in subsistence practices do not always go from dependence on wild food to farming; they may go the other way as well.

A Comanche bison hunt as painted by artist George Catlin (1796–1872). Plains Indians such as the Comanche and Lakota developed similar cultures as they had to adapt to similar environmental conditions.

Related to the phenomenon of convergent evolution is **parallel evolution,** in which similar cultural adaptations to similar environmental conditions are achieved by peoples whose ancestral cultures were already somewhat alike. For example, the development of farming in Southwest Asia and Mesoamerica took place independently, as people in both regions, whose lifeways were already comparable, became dependent on a narrow range of plant foods that required human intervention for their protection and reproductive success. Both developed intensive forms of agriculture, built large cities, and created complex social and political organizations.

It is important to recognize that stability as well as change is involved in cultural adaptation and evolution; episodes of major adaptive change may be followed by long periods of relative stability in a cultural system. Moreover, not everybody benefits from changes, especially if change is forced upon them. As history painfully demonstrates, all too often humans have made changes that have had disastrous results, leading to the deaths of countless people—not to mention other creatures—and to the destruction of the natural environment.

Among the many examples of environmental destruction with catastrophic results is Easter Island in the southern Pacific. First settled by Polynesian seafarers about a thousand years ago, it became the homeland of the Rapanui people. Like other Polynesians, they subsisted on growing crops and raising chickens, as well as fishing, hunting, and gathering. Prospering, they produced surplus and formed chiefdoms. Success, however, did not last.

Within several generations, the energetic Rapanui had deforested their beautiful island, and their ecosystem began to collapse. Crop failure led to famines and social tensions, triggering violent conflicts leading to cycles of destruction. Warfare and disease decimated the population by about 75 percent. Their numbers had dropped to about 3,000 by the time Europeans first landed on their shores in the 18th century—bringing new diseases and other miseries that nearly wiped the Rapanui from the face of the earth.[3]

Environmental destruction on a much more massive scale has occurred in many other parts of the world, especially in the course of the 20th century, ruining the lives of millions. Considering such catastrophes, we must avoid falling into the ethnocentric trap of equating change with progress or with seeing everything as adaptive.

CULTURE AREAS

From early on, anthropologists recognized that ethnic groups living within the same broad habitat often share certain cultural traits. This reflects the fact that there

[3] Diamond, J. (2005). *Collapse: How societies choose to fail or succeed* (Ch. 2, pp. 79–119). New York: Penguin; Van Tilburg, J. A. (1994). *Easter Island archaeology, ecology and culture.* London: British Museum Press.

parallel evolution In cultural evolution, the development of similar cultural adaptations to similar environmental conditions by peoples whose ancestral cultures were already somewhat alike.

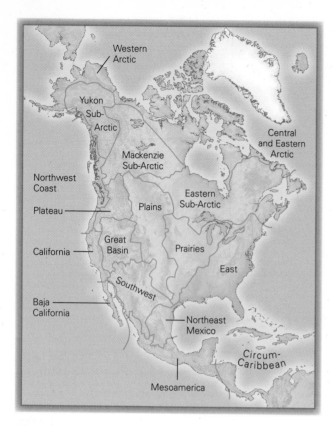

Figure 18.1 This map shows the major culture areas that have been identified for North and Central America. Within each, there is an overall similarity of Native cultures, as opposed to the differences that distinguish the cultures of one area from those of all others.

exists a basic relationship among their similar natural environment, available resources, and subsistence practices and that neighboring peoples are in contact and engage in exchange with one another.

Classifying groups according to their cultural traits, anthropologists have mapped geographic regions in which a number of societies have similar ways of life. Known as **culture areas,** such regions often correspond to ecological regions (Figure 18.1). In sub-Arctic North America, for example, migratory caribou herds graze across the vast tundra. For dozens of different groups that have made this area their home, these animals provide a major source of food as well as material for shelter and clothing. Adapting to more or less the same ecological resources in this sub-Arctic landscape, these groups have developed similar subsistence technologies and practices in the course of generations. They may speak very different languages, but they may all be said to form part of the same culture area.

culture area A geographic region in which a number of societies follow similar patterns of life.

Because of changes in the natural environment such as habitat destruction and the extinction of plant and animal species, culture areas are not always stable. Moreover, new species may be introduced and technologies may be invented or adopted from more distant cultures. Such was the case with the indigenous culture area of the Great Plains in North America (see Figure 18.1). For thousands of years, many indigenous groups with similar ways of life existed in this vast ecological area between the Mississippi River and the Rocky Mountains. Until the mid-1800s, when European immigrants invaded the region and almost completely annihilated the millions of free-ranging bison, these large grazing herds provided an obvious and practical source of food and materials for clothing and shelter.

The efficiency of indigenous groups in the southern grasslands increased greatly in the 1600s when they gained access to Spanish horses on the northern Mexican frontier and became mounted bison hunters. During the next century, the new horse complex spread northward to almost every indigenous group ranging in the Great Plains culture area. A total of thirty-one politically independent peoples, including the Cheyenne and Comanche just mentioned, reached a similar adaptation to this particular environment.

So it was that by the time of the Euramerican invasion of their vast hunting territories in the 19th century, the Indians of the Great Plains were all bison hunters, dependent on this animal for food, clothing, shelter, and bone tools. Each nation was organized into a number of warrior societies, and prestige came from hunting and fighting skills. Their villages were typically arranged in a distinctive circular pattern, and they shared many religious rituals, such as the Sun Dance.

During the 1870s and 1880s, railroads were built across the Great Plains, and mass slaughter of bison followed. More than 1 million of these animals were killed every year, mostly by non-Indians interested only in their hides and tongues (tongues were a luxury meat commodity, easily removed and compact to ship). With their herds almost exterminated, Indians of the Plains faced starvation, which made it impossible to effectively defend their homeland. This resulted in the near collapse of their traditional cultures from the 1890s onward.

CULTURE CORE

Environment and technology are not the only factors that determine a society's pattern of subsistence; social structure and political organization also influence how a society solves its food problem. For instance, if we wish to understand the rise of irrigation agriculture in the great centers of ancient civilization (such as in what are now Egypt, China, Peru, and Iraq), we need to know not only the technological and environmental factors that made the building of large-scale irrigation works possible but also the social structure and political organization that made it

In Bali, gatherings for rituals at water temples allowed farmers to arrange schedules for flooding their rice paddies.

© Joe Carini/The Image Works

feasible to mobilize the many workers necessary to build and maintain the systems and to grow and harvest the crops. For this understanding, we must examine the political elites and administrators that coordinated the work, decided where the water would be used, and determined how the agricultural products of this collective venture would be distributed.

The cultural features that are fundamental to the society's way of making its living are called its **culture core.** This includes the society's food-producing techniques, knowledge of available resources in its environment, and the work arrangements involved in applying those techniques to the local environment.

The culture core comprises other aspects of culture that bear on the production and distribution of food. Among these is worldview or ideology, evidenced in the ways religious beliefs sometimes prohibit the use of certain readily available and highly nutritious foods. For example, most Muslims and Jews abstain from eating pork because doing so is prohibited by their religion, and most Hindus do not eat beef because they revere cows as sacred animals. There are countless other food taboos, all varying across cultures: horse meat (regularly part of French fare but generally abhorred in England), dogs (not eaten by Europeans but a typical ingredient in Korean meals), monkeys (appreciated by Amazonian Indians but excluded from North American menus), insects (an important source of nutrition in many tropical cultures but considered creepy in most other parts of the world), and humans (not eaten by most humans).[4]

A number of anthropologists focus on identifying the principles behind native idea systems and how they inform a people about their environment. For example, on the Indonesian island of Bali, ritual meetings were held regularly at water temples, located at the forks of rivers. Part of the ritual included negotiating seasonal schedules for flooding the farmers' rice fields. Without the water temple rituals, irrigation coordination risks falling apart, resulting in water shortages, pest infestation, and lower productivity. In short, cultural beliefs, no matter how irrelevant they seem to uninformed outsiders, may offer the key to understanding another society's subsistence or any other long-established collective practice.

Modes of Subsistence

Human societies everywhere have developed a cultural infrastructure that is compatible with the natural resources they have available to them and within the limitations of their various habitats. Each mode of subsistence involves not only resources but also the technology required to effectively capture and utilize them, as well as the kinds of work arrangements that are developed to best suit a society's needs. In the next few pages,

culture core Cultural features that are fundamental in the society's way of making its living—including food-producing techniques, knowledge of available resources, and the work arrangements involved in applying those techniques to the local environment.

[4] Pelto, G. H., Goodman, A. H., & Dufour, D. L. (Eds.). (2000). *Nutritional anthropology: Biocultural perspectives on food and nutrition.* Mountain View, CA: Mayfield.

we will discuss the major types of cultural infrastructure, beginning with the oldest and most universal mode of subsistence: food foraging.

Food-Foraging Societies

Before the domestication of food plants and animals, all people supported themselves through **food foraging,** a mode of subsistence involving some combination of hunting, fishing, and gathering wild plant foods. When food foragers had the earth to themselves, they had their pick of the best environments. But gradually areas with rich soils and ample supplies of water were appropriated by farming societies and, more recently, by industrial and postindustrial societies. As a result, small foraging communities were edged out of their traditional habitats by these expanding groups.

Today at most a quarter of a million people (less then 0.005 percent of the world population of over 6.8 billion) still support themselves mainly as foragers. They are found only in the world's most marginal areas—frozen Arctic tundra, deserts, and inaccessible forests—and typically lead a migratory existence that makes it impractical to accumulate many material possessions. Because foraging

> **food foraging** Hunting, fishing, and gathering wild plant foods.

cultures have nearly disappeared in areas having a natural abundance of food and fuel resources, anthropologists are necessarily cautious when it comes to making generalizations about the ancient human past based on in-depth studies of still-existing foraging groups that have adapted to more marginal habitats.

Typically, foragers have ample and balanced diets and are less likely to experience severe famine than farmers. Their material possessions are limited, but so is their desire to amass things. Notably, they have plenty of leisure time for concentrating on family ties, social life, and spiritual development—apparently far more than people living in farming and industrial societies. Such findings clearly challenge the once widely held view that food foragers live a miserable existence.

It is important to note that present-day people who subsist by hunting, fishing, and wild plant collection are not following an ancient way of life because they do not know any better. Rather, they have been forced by circumstances into situations where foraging is the best means of survival or they simply prefer to live this way. In fact, foraging constitutes a rational response to particular ecological, economic, and sociopolitical realities. Moreover, for at least 2,000 years, hunters, fishers, and gatherers have met the demands for commodities such as furs, hides, feathers, ivory, pearls, fish, nuts, and honey within larger trading networks. Like everyone else, most food foragers are now part of a larger system with social, economic, and political relations extending far beyond regional, national, or even continental boundaries.

Human groups (including food foragers) do not exist in isolation except occasionally, and even then not for long. The bicycle this Bushman of southern Africa is riding is indicative of his links with the wider world. For 2,000 years, Bushmen have been interacting regularly with neighboring farmers and pastoralists. As well, food foragers have supplied much of the commodities desired by the rest of the world, such as the elephant ivory used for keyboards on pianos so widely sought in 19th-century North America.

Characteristics of Foraging Communities

The hallmarks of food-foraging societies (particularly those few that still or until recently survive in marginal areas that are not as naturally rich in food and fuel) include mobility, small group size, flexible division of labor by gender, food sharing, egalitarianism, communal property, and rarity of warfare.

Although much has been written on the theoretical importance of hunting for shaping the supposedly competitive and aggressive nature of the human species, most anthropologists are unconvinced by these arguments. To be sure, warlike behavior on the part of food-foraging peoples is known, but such behavior is a relatively recent phenomenon in response to pressure from expansionist states. In the absence of such pressures, food-foraging peoples are remarkably nonaggressive and place more emphasis on peacefulness and cooperation than they do on violent competition. We touch on each of the other characteristics below.

MOBILITY

Food foragers move as needed within a circumscribed region that is their home range to tap into naturally available food sources. Some groups, such as the Ju/'hoansi in the Kalahari Desert of southern Africa who depend on the reliable and highly drought-resistant mongongo nut, may keep to fairly fixed annual routes and cover only a restricted territory. Others, such as the traditional Shoshone in the western highlands of North America, had to cover a wider territory, their course determined by the local availability of the erratically productive pine nut.

A crucial factor in this mobility is availability of water. The distance between the food supply and water must not be so great that more energy is required to fetch water than can be obtained from the food.

SMALL GROUP SIZE

Another characteristic of the food-foraging adaptation is the small size of local groups, typically fewer than a hundred people. No completely satisfactory explanation for this has been offered, but both ecological and social factors are involved. Among the ecological factors is the **carrying capacity** of the land—the number of people that the available resources can support at a given level of food-getting techniques. This requires adjusting to seasonal and long-term changes in resource availability. Carrying capacity involves not only the immediate presence of food and water but also the tools and work necessary to secure them, as well as short- and long-term fluctuations in their availability.

In addition to seasonal or local adjustments, food foragers must make long-term adjustments to resources. Food-foraging populations usually stabilize at numbers well below the carrying capacity of their land. In fact, the home ranges of most food foragers can support from three to five times as many people as they typically do. In the long run, it may be more adaptive for a group to keep its numbers low rather than to expand indefinitely and risk destruction by a sudden and unexpected natural reduction in food resources. The population density of foraging groups surviving in marginal environments today rarely exceeds one person per square mile—a very low density.

How food-foraging peoples regulate population size relates to two things: how much body fat they accumulate and how they care for their children. Ovulation requires a certain minimum of body fat, and in traditional foraging societies, this is not achieved until early adulthood. Hence, female reproductive maturity typically occurs between the early and mid-20s, and teenage pregnancies—at least, successful ones—are virtually unknown.[5] Once a child is born, its mother nurses it several times each hour, even at night, and this continues over a period of four or five years. The constant stimulation of the mother's nipple suppresses the level of hormones that promote ovulation, making conception less likely, especially if work keeps the mother physically active and she does not have a large store of body fat to draw on for energy.[6] Continuing to nurse for several years, women give birth only at widely spaced intervals. Thus the total number of offspring remains low but sufficient to maintain stable population size.

FLEXIBLE DIVISION OF LABOR BY GENDER

Division of labor exists in all human societies and is probably as old as human culture. Among food foragers, the hunting and butchering of large game as well as the processing of hard or tough raw materials are almost universally masculine occupations. By contrast, women's

---

[5] Hrdy, S. B. (1999). Body fat and birth control. *Natural History 108* (8), 88; see also Frisch, R. (2002). *Female fertility and the body fat connection*. Chicago: University of Chicago Press.

[6] Small, M. F. (1997). Making connections. *American Scientist 85*, 503; see also Konner, M., & Worthman, C. (1980). Nursing frequency, gonadal function, and birth spacing among !Kung hunter-gatherers. *Science 207*, 788–791.

carrying capacity The number of people that the available resources can support at a given level of food-getting techniques.

Frequent nursing of children over four or five years acts to suppress ovulation among food foragers such as Ju/'hoansi. As a consequence, women give birth to relatively few offspring at widely spaced intervals.

work in foraging societies usually focuses on collecting and processing a variety of plant foods, as well as other domestic chores that can be fit to the demands of breast-feeding and that are more compatible with pregnancy and childbirth.

Among food foragers today, the work of women is no less arduous than that of men. Ju/'hoansi women, for example, may walk 12 miles a day, two or three times a week, to gather food, carrying not only their children but also, on the return home, between 15 and 33 pounds of food. Still, they do not have to travel quite as far as do men on the hunt, and their work is usually less dangerous. Also, their tasks require less rapid mobility, do not need complete and undivided attention, and are readily resumed after interruption.

All of this is compatible with those biological differences that remain between the sexes. Certainly women who are pregnant or have infants to nurse cannot travel long distances in pursuit of game as easily as men can. By

the same token, of course, women may have preferred and been better at the less risky task of gathering.

But, saying that differing gender roles among food foragers is compatible with the biological differences between men and women is *not* saying that these roles are biologically determined. Among the Great Plains Indians of North America, for example, there are quite a few reports of women who gained fame as hunters and warriors—both historically regarded as men's activities. In fact, the division of labor by gender is often far less rigid among food foragers than it is in most other types of society. Thus, Ju/'hoansi males, willingly and without embarrassment, as the occasion demands, will gather wild plant foods, build huts, and collect water, even though all are regarded as women's work.

Notably, the food-gathering activities of women play a major role in the survival of their group: Research shows that contemporary food foragers may obtain up to 60 or 70 percent of their diets from plant foods, with perhaps some fish and shellfish also provided primarily by women (the exceptions tend to be food foragers living in Arctic regions, where plant foods are not available for much of the year).

Although women in foraging societies commonly spend some time each day gathering plant foods, men rarely hunt on a daily basis. The amount of energy expended in hunting, especially in hot climates, is often greater than the energy return from the kill. Too much time spent searching out game might actually be counterproductive. Energy itself is derived primarily from plant carbohydrates, and it is usually the female gatherers who bring in the bulk of the calories. A certain amount of meat in the diet, though, guarantees high-quality protein that is less easily obtained from plant sources, for meat contains exactly the right balance of all of the amino acids (the building blocks of protein) the human body requires. No one plant food does this, and in order to get by without meat, people must hit on exactly the right combination of plants to provide the essential amino acids in the correct proportions.

FOOD SHARING

Another key feature of human social organization associated with food foraging is the sharing of food. Among the Ju/'hoansi, women have control over the food they collect and can share it with whomever they choose. Men, by contrast, are constrained by rules that specify how much meat is to be distributed and to whom. For the individual hunter, meat sharing is really a way of storing it for the future: His generosity, obligatory though it might be, gives him a claim on the future kills of other hunters. As a cultural trait, food sharing has the obvious survival value of distributing resources needed for subsistence.

Visual Counterpoint

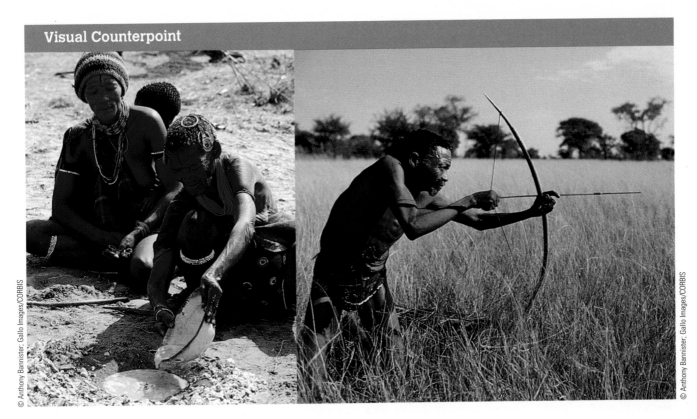

Typically, food foragers such as the Ju/'hoansi have a division of labor in which women gather and prepare "bush" food (here an ostrich egg omelet) and men usually do the hunting.

EGALITARIAN SOCIAL RELATIONS

An important characteristic of the food-foraging society is its egalitarianism. Because foragers are usually highly mobile and lack animal or mechanical transportation, they must be able to travel without many encumbrances, especially on food-getting expeditions. By necessity, the material goods they carry with them are limited to the barest essentials, which include implements for hunting, gathering, fishing, building, and cooking. (For example, the average weight of an individual's personal belongings among the Ju/'hoansi is just under 25 pounds.) In this context, it makes little sense for them to accumulate luxuries or surplus goods, and the fact that no one owns significantly more than another helps to limit status differences. Age and sex are usually the only sources of important status differences.

It is important to realize that status differences by themselves do not constitute inequality, a point that is easily misunderstood, especially where relations between men and women are concerned. In most traditional food-foraging societies, women did not and do not defer to men. To be sure, women may be excluded from some rituals in which males participate, but the reverse is also true. Moreover, the fruits of women's labor are controlled by them, not by men. Nor do women sacrifice their autonomy even in societies in which male hunting, rather than female gathering, brings in the bulk of the food.

Such was the case, for example, among the Innu (Montagnais) Indians of Labrador. Theirs was a society in which the hunt was of overwhelming importance. For their part, women manufactured clothing and other necessities, but provided much less of the food than is common among food foragers in most other natural environments. Until recently, women as well as men could be shamans. Nevertheless, women were excluded from ritual feasts having to do with hunting—but then, so were men excluded from ritual feasts held by women. Basically, each gender carried out its own activities, with neither meddling in those of the other. Early missionaries to the Innu hunting bands lamented that men had no inclination to make their wives obey them and worked long and hard to convince the Indians that civilization required men to impose their authority on women. But after 300 years of pressing this point, missionaries achieved only limited success.

Food foragers make no attempt to accumulate surplus foodstuffs, often an important source of status in agrarian societies. This does not mean that they live constantly on the verge of starvation, for their environment is their natural storehouse. Except in the coldest climates (where a surplus must be set aside to see people through the long, lean winter season) or in times of acute ecological disaster, some food can almost always be found in a group's territory. Because food resources are typically shared and distributed equally throughout the group (share and share alike is the order of the day), no one achieves the wealth or status that hoarding might bring. In such a society, having more than others is a sign of deviance rather than a desirable characteristic.

The food forager's concept of territory contributes as much to social equality as it does to the equal distribution of resources. Most groups have home ranges within which access to resources is open to all members. What is available to one is available to all. If an Mbuti Pygmy hunter living in the forests of Central Africa discovers a honey tree, he has first rights; but when he has taken his share, others have a turn. In the unlikely possibility that he does not take advantage of his discovery, others will. No individual within the community privately owns the tree; the system is first come, first served. Therefore, knowledge of the existence of food resources circulates quickly throughout the entire group.

How Technology Impacts Cultural Adaptations among Foragers

Like habitat, technology plays an important role in shaping the characteristics of the foraging life discussed above. The mobility of food-foraging groups may depend on the availability of water, as among the Ju/'hoansi, or of game animals and other seasonal resources, as among the Mbuti in the Democratic Republic of Congo in Central Africa. Different hunting technologies and techniques may also play a part in determining movement, as well as population size and division of labor by gender.

Consider, for example, the Mbuti Pygmies in the Ituri tropical forest. All Mbuti bands hunt elephants with spears. However, for other game, some of the bands use bows and others use large nets. Those equipped with nets have a cooperative division of labor in which

men, women, and children collaborate in driving antelope and other game into the net for the kill. Usually, this involves very long hours and movement over great distances as participants surround the animals and beat the woods noisily to chase the game in one direction toward the great nets. Since this sort of "beat-hunt" requires the cooperation of seven to thirty families, those using this method have relatively large camps. Among Mbuti bow hunters, on the other hand, only men go after the game. These archers tend to stay closer to the village for shorter periods of time and live in smaller groups, typically of no more than six families. While there is no significant difference in overall population density between net and bow hunting areas, archers generally harvest a greater diversity of animal species, including monkeys.[7]

Food-Producing Societies

Obviously, habitat and technology do not tell the whole story of how we humans feed ourselves. After the emergence of tool making, which enabled humans to consume significant amounts of meat as well as plant foods, the next truly momentous event in human history was the domestication of plants and animals. Over time, this achievement transformed cultural systems, with humans developing new economic arrangements, social structures, and ideological patterns based on plant cultivation, breeding and raising animals, or a mixture of both.

The transition from food foraging to food production first took place about 10,000 years ago in Southwest Asia (the Fertile Crescent, including the Jordan River Valley and neighboring regions in the Middle East). This was the beginning of the **Neolithic** or New Stone Age (from the Greek *neo* meaning "new" and *lith* meaning "stone"), in which people possessed stone-based technologies and depended on domesticated plants and/or animals. Within the next few thousand years, similar early transitions to agricultural economies took place independently in other parts of the world where human groups began to raise and (later) alter wild cereal plants such as wheat, maize (corn), and rice; legumes such as beans; gourds such as squash; and tubers such as potatoes. Doing the same with a number of wild animal species ranging in their hunting territories, they began to domesticate goats, sheep, pigs, cattle, and llamas (Figure 18.2).

Neolithic The New Stone Age; prehistoric period beginning about 10,000 years ago in which peoples possessed stone-based technologies and depended on domesticated plants and/or animals.

[7] Bailey, R. C., & Aunger, R. (1989). Net hunters vs. archers: Variation in women's subsistence strategies in the Ituri forest. *Human Ecology 17*, 273–297; Terashima, H. (1983). Mota and other hunting activities of the Mbuti archers: A socio-ecological study of subsistence technology. *African Studies Monograph* (Kyoto), 71–85.

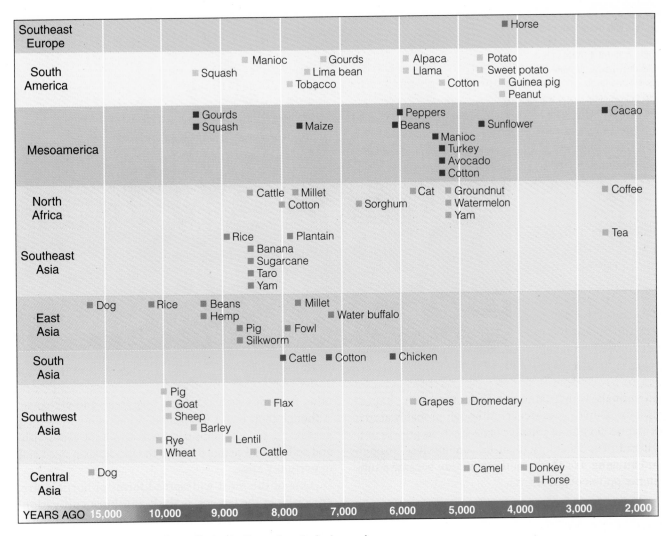

Figure 18.2 Appearance of domesticates in the archaeological record.

Because these activities brought about a radical transformation in almost every aspect of their cultural systems, Australian-born archaeologist Gordon Childe introduced the term **Neolithic revolution** to refer to the profound cultural change associated with the early domestication of plants and animals. As humans became increasingly dependent on domesticated crops, they mostly gave up their mobile way of life and settled down to till the soil, sow, weed, protect, harvest, and safely store their crops. No longer on the move, they could build more permanent dwellings and began to make pottery for storage of water, food, and so on.

Just why this change came about is one of the important questions in anthropology. Because food production requires more work than food foraging, is more monotonous, and is often a less secure means of subsistence, it is unlikely that people became food producers voluntarily.

Initially, it appears that food production arose as a largely unintended byproduct of existing food management practices. Among many examples, we may consider

the Paiute Indians, whose desert habitat in the western highlands of North America includes some oasis-like marshlands. These foragers discovered how to irrigate wild crops in their otherwise very dry homeland, thus increasing the quantity of wild seeds and bulbs to be harvested. Although their ecological intervention was very limited, it allowed them to settle down for longer periods in greater numbers than otherwise would have been possible.

Unlike the Paiute, who stopped just short of a Neolithic revolution, other groups elsewhere in the world continued to transform their landscapes in ways that favored the appearance of new varieties of particular plants

Neolithic revolution The profound cultural change beginning about 10,000 years ago and associated with the early domestication of plants and animals and settlement in permanent villages.

In preparation for new planting, this old, overgrown plot in the Amazon forest in Venezuela is burned. Although it looks destructive, if done properly, slash-and-burn cultivation is an ecologically sound way of growing crops in the tropics.

© Jacques Jangoux/Alamy

and animals, which came to take on increasing importance for people's subsistence. Although probably at first accidental, it became a matter of necessity as growth outstripped people's ability to sustain themselves through food foraging. For them, food production became a subsistence option of last resort.

Producing Food in Gardens: Horticulture

With the advent of plant domestication, some societies took up **horticulture** (from the Latin *hortus,* meaning "garden") in which small communities of gardeners cultivate crops with simple hand tools, using neither irrigation nor the plow. Typically, horticulturists cultivate several varieties of food plants together in small, hand-cleared gardens. Because they do not usually fertilize the soil, they use a given garden plot for only a few years before abandoning it in favor of a new one. Often, horticulturists grow enough food for their subsistence, and occasionally they produce a modest surplus that can be used for

other purposes such as inter-village feasts and exchange. Although their major food supplies may come from their gardens, many horticulturists will also hunt game, fish, and collect wild plants foods in the forest when need and opportunity arise.

One of the most widespread forms of horticulture, especially in the tropics, is **slash-and-burn cultivation,** or *swidden farming,* in which the natural vegetation is cut, the slash is subsequently burned, and crops are then planted among the ashes. This is an ecologically sophisticated and sustainable way of raising food, especially in the tropics, when carried out under the right conditions: low population densities and adequate amounts of land. It mimics the diversity of the natural ecosystem, growing several different crops in the same field. Mixed together, the crops are less vulnerable to pests and plant diseases than a single crop.

Not only is the system ecologically sound, but it is far more energy efficient than modern farming methods used in developed countries such as the United States, where natural resources such as land and fuel are still relatively cheap and abundant, and many farms operate with financial support in the form of government subsidies or tax breaks. While high-tech farming requires more energy input than it yields, slash-and-burn farming produces between 10 and 20 units of energy for every unit expended. A good example of how such a system works is provided by the Mekranoti Kayapo Indians of Brazil's Amazon forest, profiled in the following Original Study.

horticulture Cultivation of crops carried out with simple hand tools such as digging sticks or hoes.

slash-and-burn cultivation An extensive form of horticulture in which the natural vegetation is cut, the slash is subsequently burned, and crops are then planted among the ashes; also known as swidden farming.

Gardens of the Mekranoti Kayapo   *by Dennis Werner*

The planting of a Mekranoti garden always follows the same sequence. First, men clear the forest and then burn the debris. Then, in the ashes, both men and women plant sweet potatoes, manioc, bananas, corn, pumpkins, papaya, sugar cane, pineapple, cotton, tobacco, and annatto, whose seeds yield achiote, the red dye used for painting ornaments and people's bodies. Since the Mekranoti don't bother with weeding, the forest gradually invades the garden. After the second year, only manioc, sweet potatoes, and bananas remain. And after three years or so there is usually nothing left but bananas. Except for a few tree species that require hundreds of years to grow, the area will look like the original forest twenty-five to thirty years later.

This gardening technique, known as slash-and-burn, is one of the most common in the world. At one time critics condemned the technique as wasteful and ecologically destructive, but today we know that, especially in the humid tropics, slash-and-burn may be one of the best gardening techniques possible. Continuous high temperatures encourage the growth of the microorganisms that cause rot, so organic matter quickly breaks down into simple minerals. The heavy rains dissolve these valuable nutrients and carry them deep into the soils, out of the reach of plants. The tropical forest maintains its richness because the heavy foliage shades

the earth, cooling it and inhibiting the growth of the decomposers. A good deal of the rain is captured by leaves before ever reaching the ground.

When a tree falls in the forest and begins to rot, other plants quickly absorb the nutrients that are released. In contrast, with open-field agriculture, the sun heats the earth, the decomposers multiply, and the rains quickly leach the soils of their nutrients. In a few years a lush forest, if cleared for open one-crop agriculture, can be transformed into a barren wasteland.

A few months after the Mekranoti plant banana and papaya, these trees shade the soil, just as the larger forest trees do. The mixing of different kinds of plants in the same area means that minerals can be absorbed as soon as they are released; corn picks up nutrients very fast, while manioc is slow. Also, the small and temporary clearings mean that the forest can quickly reinvade its lost territory.

Because decomposers need moisture as well as warmth, the long Mekranoti dry season could alter this whole picture of soil ecology. But soil samples from recently burned Mekranoti fields and the adjacent forest floor showed that, as in most of the humid tropics, the high fertility of the Indians' garden plots comes from the trees that are burned there, not from the soil, as in temperate climates.

Getting a good burn is a tricky operation. Perhaps for this reason the more experienced and knowledgeable members of the community oversaw its timing. If done too early, the rains will leach out the minerals in the ash before planting time. If too late, the debris will be too wet to burn properly. Then, insects and weeds that could plague the plants will not die and few minerals will be released into the soil. If the winds are too weak, the burn will not cover the entire plot. If they are too strong, the fire can get out of hand.

Shortly after burning the plots and clearing away of some of the charred debris, people began the long job of planting, which took up all of September and lasted into October. In the center of the circular garden plot the women dug holes and threw in a few pieces of sweet potatoes. After covering the tubers with dirt, they usually asked a male to stomp on the mound and

make a ritual noise resembling a Bronx cheer—magic to ensure a large crop. Forming a large ring around the sweet potatoes, the Indians rapidly thrust pieces of manioc stems into the ground, one after the other.

When grown, manioc stems form a dense barrier to the sweet potato patch, and some of the plants must be cut down to gain entrance. Outside of the ring of manioc, the women planted yams, cotton, sugar cane, and annatto. Banana stalks and papaya trees, planted by simply throwing the seeds on the ground, form the outermost circle. The Indians also planted corn, pumpkins, watermelons, and pineapple throughout the garden. Rapid growers, they were harvested long before the manioc matured. The garden appeared to change magically from corn and pumpkins to sweet potatoes and manioc without replanting.

Mekranoti gardens grew well. A few Indians complained now and then about a peccary that had reduced their corn harvest or eaten a watermelon they had looked forward to enjoying, but in general the animals seemed to leave the crops alone. Even the leaf-cutting ants that are problems in other areas did not bother the Mekranoti. Occasionally a neighbor who had not planted a new garden would make off with a prized first-year crop, such as pumpkin, watermelon, or pineapple. But even these thefts were rare. In general, the Mekranoti could depend on harvesting whatever they planted.

Eventually, I wanted to calculate the productivity of Mekranoti gardens. Western agronomists knew very little about slash-and-burn crop cultivation. They were accustomed to experiments in which a field was given over to a single crop and the harvest happened all at once. Here, the plants were all mixed together, and people harvested piecemeal whenever they needed something. The manioc could stay in the ground, growing for several years before it was dug up.

I began measuring off areas of gardens to count how many manioc plants, ears of corn, or pumpkins were found there. The women thought it strange to see me struggling through the tangle of plants to measure off

CONTINUED

CONTINUED

areas, 10 meters by 10 meters, placing string along the borders, and then counting what was inside. Sometimes I asked a woman to dig up all of the sweet potatoes within the marked-off area. My requests were bizarre, but the women cooperated just the same, holding on to the ends of the measuring tapes, or sending their children to help. For some plants, like bananas, I simply counted the number of clumps of stalks in the garden, and the number of banana bunches I could see growing in various clumps. By watching how long it took the bananas to grow, from the time I could see them until they were harvested, I could

calculate a garden's total banana yield per year.

After returning from the field, I was able to combine the time allocation data with the garden productivities to get an idea of how hard the Mekranoti need to work to survive. The data showed that for every hour of gardening one Mekranoti adult produces almost 18,000 kilocalories of food. (As a basis for comparison, people in the United States consume approximately 3,000 kilocalories of food per day.) As insurance against bad years, and in case they receive visitors from other villages, they grow far more produce than they need. But even so, they don't need to work very hard to survive. A look at the average amount of time adults spend on different tasks every

week shows just how easygoing life in horticultural societies can be:

8.5 hours	Gardening
6.0 hours	Hunting
1.5 hours	Fishing
1.0 hour	Gathering wild foods
33.5 hours	All other jobs

Altogether, the Mekranoti need to work less than 51 hours a week, and this includes getting to and from work, cooking, repairing broken tools, and all of the other things we normally don't count as part of our work week.

From Werner, D. (1990). Amazon journey *(pp. 105–112). Englewood Cliffs, NJ: Prentice-Hall.*

Producing Food on Farms: Agriculture

In contrast to horticulture, **agriculture** (from the Latin *agri,* meaning "field") is growing food plants like grains, tubers, fruits, and vegetables in soil prepared and maintained for crop production. This form of more intensive food production involves using technologies other than hand tools, such as irrigation, fertilizers, and plows pulled by harnessed draft animals. In the so-called developed countries of the world, agriculture relies on fuel-powered tractors to produce food on large plots of land. But the ingenuity of some early agriculturalists is illustrated in this chapter's Anthropology Applied feature, highlighting an ecologically sound mountain terracing and irrigation system established 1,000 years ago.

Among agriculturists, surplus crop cultivation is generally substantial—providing food not only for their own needs but also for those of various full-time specialists and nonproducing consumers. This surplus may be traded or sold for cash, or it may be coerced out of the farmers through taxes, rent, or tribute (forced gifts acknowledging submission or protection) paid to landowners or other dominant groups. These landowners and specialists—such as traders, carpenters, blacksmiths, sculptors, basketmakers, and stonecutters—typically reside in substantial towns or cities, where political power is centralized in the hands

of a socially elite class. Dominated by more powerful groups and markets, much of what the farmers do is governed by political and economic forces over which they have little control.

It is not always easy to make the distinction between horticulture and agriculture. For example, the Hopi Indians of the North American Southwest, in addition to flood plain farming, also irrigate plots near springs, while using simple hand tools. Moreover, they produce for their own immediate needs and live in small towns without centralized political government.

Early food producers have developed several major crop complexes: two adapted to dry uplands and two to tropical wetlands. In the dry uplands of Southwest Asia, for example, farmers time their agricultural activities with the rhythm of the changing seasons, cultivating wheat, barley, oat, flax, rye, and millet. In the tropical wetlands of Southeast Asia, rice and tubers such as yams and taro are cultivated. In the Americas, people have adapted to natural environments similar to those of Africa and Eurasia, but have cultivated their own indigenous plants. Typically, maize, beans, squash, and the potato are grown in drier areas, whereas manioc is extensively grown in the tropical wetlands.

CHARACTERISTICS OF CROP-PRODUCING SOCIETIES

One of the most significant correlates of crop cultivation was the development of fixed settlements, in which farming families reside together near their cultivated fields. The task of food production lent itself to a different kind of social organization. Because the hard work of some members of the group could provide food for all, others became free to devote their time to inventing

agriculture The cultivation of food plants in soil prepared and maintained for crop production. Involves using technologies other than hand tools, such as irrigation, fertilizers, and the wooden or metal plow pulled by harnessed draft animals.

Agricultural Development and the Anthropologist

Gaining insight into the traditional practices of indigenous peoples, anthropologists have often been impressed by the ingenuity of their knowledge. This awareness has spread beyond the profession to the Western public at large, giving birth to the popular notion that indigenous groups invariably live in some sort of blissful oneness with the environment. But this was never the message of anthropologists, who know that traditional people are only human, and like all human beings, are capable of making mistakes. Just as we have much to learn from their successes, so can we learn from their failures.

Archaeologist Ann Kendall is doing just this in the Patacancha Valley in the Andes Mountains of southern Peru. Kendall is director and founder of the Cusichaca Trust, near Oxford, England, a rural development organization that revives ancient farming practices. In the late 1980s, after working for ten years on archaeological excavations and rural development projects, she invited botanist Alex Chepstow-Lusty of Cambridge University to investigate climatic change and paleoecological data. His findings, along with Kendall's, provided evidence of intensive farming in the Patacancha Valley, beginning about 4,000 years ago. The research showed that over time widespread clearing to establish and maintain farm plots, coupled with minimal terracing of the hillsides, had resulted in tremendous soil loss through erosion. By 1,900 years ago, soil degradation and a cooling climate had led to a dramatic reduction in farming. Then, about 1,000 years ago, farming was revived, this time with soil-sparing techniques.

Kendall's investigations have documented intensive irrigated terrace construction over two periods of occupation, including Inca development of the area. It was a sophisticated system, devised to counteract erosion and achieve maximum agricultural production. The effort required workers to haul load after load of soil up from the valley floor. In addition, they planted alder trees to stabilize the soil and to provide both firewood and building materials.

So successful was this farming system by Inca times that the number of people living in the valley quadrupled to some 4,000, about the same as it is now. However, yet another reversal of fortune occurred when the Spanish took over Peru and the terraces and trees here and elsewhere were allowed to deteriorate.

Armed with these research findings and information and insights gathered through interviews and meetings with locals, the Cusichaca Trust supported the restoration of the terraces and 5.8 kilometers of canal. The effort relied on local labor working with traditional methods and materials—clay (with a cactus mix to keep it moist), stone, and soil. Local families have replanted 160 hectares of the renovated pre-conquest terraces with maize, potatoes, and wheat, and the plots are up to ten times more productive than they were. Among other related accomplishments, twenty-one water systems have been installed, which reach more than 800 large families, and a traditional concept of home-based gardens has been adapted to introduce European-style vegetable gardens to improve diet and health and to facilitate market gardening. Since 1997, these projects have been under an independent local rural development organization known as ADESA.

The Cusichaca Trust has continued its pioneering work in areas of extreme poverty in Peru further to the north, such as Apurimac and Ayacucho, using tried and tested traditional technology in the restoration of ancient canal and terrace systems.

Adapted from Krajick, K. (1998). Greenfarming by the Incas? Science *281, 323. The 2003 update and elaboration by textbook authors are based on personal communication with Kendall and Cusichaca Trust reports. For more information, see www.cusichaca.org.*

and manufacturing the equipment needed for a new sedentary way of life. Tools for digging and harvesting, pottery for storage and cooking, clothing made of woven textiles, and housing made of stone, wood, or sun-dried bricks all came out of the new sedentary living conditions and the altered division of labor.

The Neolithic revolution also brought important changes in social structure. At first, social relations were egalitarian and hardly different from those that prevailed among food foragers. As settlements grew, however, and large numbers of people had to share important resources such as land and water, society became more elaborately organized.

Transhumance festival, Saint-Rémy-de-Provence, France. Before winter sets in, Saint-Rémy farmers lead their livestock from the high-altitude summer grazing grounds of the Alpilles Mountains to fields situated in the valley near the village. There the animals feed on the stubble of harvest crops, as well as hay (long and nutritious sun-dried grass harvested in the summer for winter feeding). In early summer, the animals are taken back to the cooler mountain pastures. Their seasonal comings and goings are often celebrated with festivals in which the herds are paraded through town.

Mixed Farming: Crop Growing and Animal Breeding

As noted above, indigenous food-producing cultures in the western hemisphere depended primarily on growing domesticated indigenous crops such as manioc, corn, and beans. With some exceptions, including the Aymara and Quechua, who traditionally also keep llamas and alpacas in their high-altitude homeland in the Andes Mountains of South America (see the Biocultural Connection feature), American Indians obtained sufficient meat, fat, leather, and wool from wild game.

On the other side of both oceans, however, Eurasian and African food-producing peoples often do not have an opportunity to obtain enough vitally important animal proteins from wild game, fish, or fowl (although they would not pass up a rare chance to catch some). Instead, many of these farming cultures have developed a mixed subsistence strategy and combine crop cultivation with animal husbandry. In addition to growing crops like cereals, tubers, or vegetables, they may also breed and raise animals for food and other purposes, including selling or trading. The variety of wild animals domesticated by humans in Africa and Eurasia includes chickens, ducks, geese, rabbits, pigs, goats, sheep, cattle, camels, dromedaries, donkeys, and horses.

Depending on cultural traditions, ecological circumstances, and animal habits, some species are kept in barns or fenced-off fields, while others may range quite freely in and around the settlement or designated pastures, albeit under supervision, branded or otherwise marked by their owners

as private property. For instance, in some English farming communities (not unlike Papua villages in New Guinea) historically it was not unusual to find ear-marked pigs freely roaming in the surrounding woodlands in search of acorns and any other food appealing to their omnivorous appetite.

Likewise, many ancient agricultural communities adapted to mountainous environments from the Alps to the Himalayas have traditionally herded livestock (cows, sheep, horses, and so on) in high summer pastures, leaving their narrow lowland valleys for alternative use—farming grains, keeping orchards, and growing vegetables and hay for animal winter food. After the crop harvest, before the weather turns cold and snow covers the higher pastures, those who left the village to tend the herds bring the animals back to the valley and settle in for the winter season. This "vertical" seasonal movement of herders and their livestock between high-altitude summer pastures and lowland valleys is an example of *transhumance* (*trans* means "across"; *humus* means "earth").

In contrast to transhumance, in which a number of men from the village annually move with their herds to seasonal pastures while other community members remain home in the settlement, there are also cultures in which the entire community migrates with the herds to their alternate grazing grounds—as described in the next section.[8]

---

[8] Cole, J. W., & Wolf, E. R. (1999). *The hidden frontier: Ecology and ethnicity in an alpine valley* (with a new introduction). Berkeley: University of California Press; see also Jones, S. (2005). Transhumance re-examined. *Journal of the Royal Anthropological Institute 11* (4), 841–842.

Herding Grazing Animals: Pastoralism

One of the more striking examples of human adaptation to the environment is **pastoralism**—breeding and managing large herds of domesticated herbivores (grazing and browsing animals), such as goats, sheep, cattle, horses, llamas, or camels. Unlike the forms of animal husbandry discussed above, pastoralism is a specialized way of life centered on breeding and herding animals.

Dependent on livestock for daily survival, families in pastoral cultures own herds of grazing animals whose need for food and drink determines the pastoralists' everyday routines. When a dozen or more herding families join together, their collective herds may number in the thousands and sometimes even a few hundred thousand. Unlike crop cultivators who need to remain close to their fields, pastoral peoples do not usually establish permanent settlements since they must follow or drive their large herds to new pastures on a regular basis. Like their herds, most pastoralists must be mobile and have adjusted their way of life accordingly.

CASE STUDY: BAKHTIARI HERDERS IN THE ZAGROS MOUNTAINS

Nomadic pastoralism is an effective way of living—far more so than sheep or cattle ranching—in environments that are too dry, cold, steep, or rocky for farming, such as the vast, arid grasslands that stretch eastward from North Africa through the Arabian Desert, across the plateau of Iran and into Turkistan and Mongolia. Today, in Africa and Asia alone, more than 21 million people are pastoralists, still migrating with their herds. These nomadic groups regard movement as a natural part of life.

Counted among the world's pastoral groups are the Bakhtiari, a fiercely independent people who live in the unforgiving Zagros Mountains of western Iran.[9] The Bakhtiari way of life, uniquely adapted to the seasonal fluctuations in their rugged mountainous environment, involves moving with their grazing animals from winter pastures in low steppe lands to summer pastures on high plateaus. For many thousands of years the Bakhtiari have tended herds of goats and fat-tailed sheep this way. Their lives revolve around these major seasonal migrations needed to provide good grazing lands for their flocks—hazardous journeys as long as 200 miles, over mountains as high as 12,000 feet, and through deep chasms and churning watercourses.

Each fall, before the harsh winter comes to the mountains, these nomads load their tents and other belongings on donkeys and drive their flocks down to the warm plains that border Iraq in the west. Here the grazing land is excellent and well watered during the winter months. In the spring, when the low-lying pastures dry up, the Bakhtiari return to the mountain valleys, where a new crop of grass is sprouting. For this trek, they split into five groups, each containing about 5,000 individuals and 50,000 animals.

The return trip north is especially dangerous because the mountain snows are melting and the gorges are full of turbulent, ice-cold water rushing down from the mountain peaks. This long trek is further burdened by the newborn spring lambs and goat kids. Where the watercourses are not very deep, the nomads ford them. Deeper channels, including one river that is a half-mile wide, are crossed with the help of inflatable goatskin rafts, on which they place infants and elderly or infirm family members, as well as lambs and kids. Men swim alongside the rafts, pushing them through the icy water. If they work from dawn to dusk, the nomads can get all of the people and animals across the river in five days. Not surprisingly, dozens of animals drown each day.

In the mountain passes, where a biting wind numbs the skin and brings tears to the eyes, the Bakhtiari trek a rugged slippery trail. Climbing the steep escarpments is dangerous, and often the stronger men must carry their children and the baby goats on their shoulders as they make their way over the ice and snow to the lush mountain valley that is their destination. During each migration the nomads may cover as many as 200 miles. The journey is familiar but not predictable. It can take weeks, for the flocks travel slowly and require constant attention. Men and older boys walk the route, driving the sheep and goats as they go. Women and children usually ride atop donkeys, along with tents and other equipment.

Reaching their destination, the Bakhtiari set up tents—traditionally black goat-hair shelters woven by the women. The tents are a fine example of adaptation to a changing environment. The goat-hair cloth retains heat and repels

[9] Material on the Bakhtiari is drawn mainly from Barth, F. (1960). Nomadism in the mountain and plateau areas of Southwest Asia. *The problems of the arid zone* (pp. 341–355). Paris: UNESCO; Coon, C. S. (1958). *Caravan: The story of the Middle East* (2nd ed., ch. 13). New York: Holt, Rinehart & Winston; Salzman, P. C. (1967). Political organization among nomadic peoples. *Proceedings of the American Philosophical Society 111*, 115–131.

pastoralism Breeding and managing large herds of domesticated grazing and browsing animals, such as goats, sheep, cattle, horses, llamas, or camels.

In the Zagros Mountains region of Iran, pastoral nomads follow seasonal pastures, migrating with their flocks over rugged terrain that includes perilously steep snowy passes and fast ice-cold rivers.

water during the winter and keeps out heat during the summer. These portable homes are easy to erect, take down, and transport. Inside, the furnishings are sparse and functional, but also artful. Heavy felt pads or elaborate wool rugs, also woven by the women, cover the ground, and pressed against the inside walls of the tent are stacks of blankets, goatskin containers, copper utensils, clay jugs, and bags of grain.

Central to Bakhtiari subsistence, sheep and goats provide milk, cheese, butter, meat, hides, and wool. Women and girls spend considerable time spinning wool into yarn—sometimes doing so while riding atop donkeys on the less rugged parts of their migration. They use the yarn to make not only rugs and tents, but also clothing, storage bags, and other essentials. With men owning and controlling the animals, which are of primary importance in Bakhtiari life, women generally have less economic and political power than their fathers, brothers, or husbands—but are by no means without influence.

The Bakhtiari live in the political state of Iran but have their own traditional system of justice, including laws and a penal code. They are governed by tribal leaders, or *khans,* men who are elected or inherit their office. Most Bakhtiari *khans* grew wealthy when oil was discovered in their homeland around the start of the 20th century, and many of them are well educated, having attended Iranian or foreign universities.

Despite this, and although some of them own houses in cities, the *khans* spend much of their lives among their people in the mountains. Such prominence of men in both economic and political affairs is common among pastoral nomads; theirs is very much a man's world. That said, elderly Bakhtiari women eventually may gain a good deal of power. And some women of all ages today are gaining a measure of economic control by selling their beautiful handmade rugs to traders, which brings in cash to their households.

While pastoral nomads like the Bakhtiari depend largely on their herds to meet their basic daily needs, they also trade surplus animals, leather, and wool (and various crafts such as woven rugs) with farmers or merchants in exchange for crops and valued commodities such as flour, dried fruit, spices, tea, metal knives, pots and kettles, cotton or linen textiles, guns, and (more recently) lightweight plastic containers, sheets, and so on. In other words, there are many ties that connect them to surrounding agricultural and industrial societies.

Intensive Agriculture: Urbanization and Peasantry

With the intensification of agriculture, some farming villages grew into towns and even cities (Figure 18.3). In these larger population centers, individuals who had previously

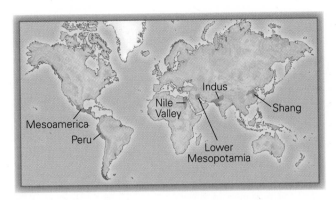

Figure 18.3 Locations of major early civilizations. Those of Central and South America developed wholly independently of those in Africa and Eurasia. Chinese civilization may have developed independently of those that developed earlier in Mesopotamia, the Egyptian Valley, and the Indus Valley.

been engaged in farming were freed to specialize in other activities. Thus craft specialists such as carpenters, blacksmiths, sculptors, basket makers, and stonecutters contribute to the vibrant, diversified life of the city.

Unlike horticulturists and pastoralists, city dwellers are only indirectly concerned with adapting to their natural environment. Far more important is the need to adapt to living and getting along with their fellow urbanites. Urbanization brings with it a new social order: Marked inequality develops as society becomes more complex, and people are ranked according to how much control they hold over resources, the kind of work they do, their gender, or the family they are born into. As social institutions cease to operate in simple, face-to-face groups of relatives, friends, and acquaintances, they become more formal and bureaucratic, with specialized political institutions.

With urbanization came a sharp increase in the tempo of human cultural change. Writing was created, trade intensified and expanded, the wheel and the sail were invented, and metallurgy and other crafts were developed. In many early cities, monumental buildings, such as royal palaces and temples, were built by thousands of men, often slaves taken in war. These feats of engineering still amaze modern architects and engineers. The inhabitants of these buildings—the ruling class composed of nobles and priests—formed a central government that dictated the social and religious rules to be followed and carried out by the merchants, craft specialists, warriors, servants, and other city dwellers.

Notably, these urbanized populations mostly depended for much of their daily food (such as bread, tortillas, vegetables, meat, fish, fruit, milk, butter, and cheese) and fuel (especially firewood for cooking and heating their dwellings) on what was produced or foraged in surrounding areas. For this reason, the urban ruling class sought to widen its territorial power and political control over rural populations. This is how farmers who raised their own crops and livestock as they saw fit, and who determined themselves if and how much surplus they would produce, lost that traditional self-determination.

Once a powerful group managed to dominate a community of farmers, it also imposed its rules on them, forcing them to work harder and obliging them to make payments in farm produce or labor services as fees for protection, as acknowledgment of submission, or other forms of exploitation. Thus burdened by taxes to feed those repressing them, these farmers were left with little to feed their own families and lost their independence. In short, subjected to an ever more dominant group, these farmers turned into **peasants.** One of the first anthropologists to study peasant communities was Eric Wolf, who defined them as "rural cultivators whose surpluses are transferred to a dominant group of rulers that uses the surpluses both to underwrite its own standard of living and to distribute the remainder to groups in society that do not farm but must be fed for their specific goods and services in turn."[10]

With their growing numbers trying to survive on less and less fertile land, and forced to pay tribute or taxes, the exploited peasant masses could expect little more than poverty. And so it continues in many parts of the world today. No matter how hard they work, most peasants possess too little land of their own to go beyond meeting the most basic needs of their families. Unable to produce enough of a surplus to sell for cash, they rarely have capital to buy the labor-saving equipment that could increase their production. Thus most peasants remain stuck in poverty, struggling to make ends meet. Meanwhile, big landowners and wealthy merchants have had the means to expand their holdings and invest in new machinery that leads to increased productivity and profitability.

Industrial Food Production

Until about 200 years ago, human societies all across the world had developed cultural infrastructures based on foraging, horticulture, agriculture, or pastoralism. This changed with the invention of the steam engine in England, which brought about an industrial revolution

---

[10] Wolf, E. R. (1966). *Peasants* (pp. 4–5). Englewood Cliffs, NJ: Prentice-Hall.

peasant A rural cultivator whose surpluses are transferred to a dominant group of rulers that uses the surpluses both to underwrite its own standard of living and to distribute the remainder to groups in society that do not farm but must be fed for their specific goods and services in turn.

Chickens ready for butchering are usually grabbed by their feet, stuffed in crates, and trucked off to the slaughterhouse. But some farmers use mechanical harvesters. Moving through a chicken barn, a harvester can pick up about 200 birds in 30 seconds. Once full, it places the birds in holding containers. From there, the chickens are mechanically transferred to a "packing unit," which automatically counts them and places them into drawers that are stacked, loaded onto a truck, and transported to a processing plant. There the chickens are mass-killed, cut up, and packaged.

© Anglia Autoflow Ltd.

that quickly spread to other parts of the globe. Replacing animal and human labor, as well as hand tools, new machines were invented, first powered by steam, then by biofuels (coal, gas, oil), sharply increasing factory production and boosting mass transportation.

Throughout the 1800s and 1900s, this resulted in large-scale industrialization of many societies. Technological inventions utilizing electricity and (since the 1940s) nuclear energy brought about more dramatic changes in social and economic organization on a worldwide scale.

Modern industrial technologies not only affect manufacturing but also impact food production. In contrast to traditional farms and plantations, which historically depended on human labor (often forced) and on animal power in many places, modern agriculture depends on newly invented labor-saving devices such as tractors, combines, milk machines, and so on. With large machines plowing, seeding, weeding, mowing, and harvesting crops, the need for farm hands and other rural workers is sharply diminished. This has also happened with livestock—in particular, hogs, cattle, and poultry.

Since the 1960s, food production in industrialized countries has become large-scale, enormously efficient,

agribusiness Large-scale businesses involved in food production, including farming, contract farming, seed supply, agrichemicals, farm machinery, distribution, processing, and marketing. Also known as corporate farming, it stands in contrast to smaller family-owned farms.

and often very profitable, especially for corporate owners and shareholders. Industrial food production has had far-reaching economic, social, and political consequences, not all of which are readily recognized as related and intertwined. Today, large food-producing corporations own enormous tracts of land on which they mass-produce tons of mechanically harvested crops and/or raise huge numbers of meat animals. Crops and animals alike are harvested, processed, packed, and shipped with ever-greater efficiency to supermarkets to feed largely urban masses.

Although meat, poultry, and other agricultural products are relatively cheap and thus affordable, even for millions of poorer people around the world, industrial food production by **agribusiness** has often been a disaster for millions of peasants and small farmers. Even medium-sized farms growing corn, wheat, or potatoes, or raising cows, hogs, and chickens can rarely compete without government subsidies. For that reason, the number of family-owned farms in western Europe and North America has dramatically declined in the past few decades. This process has led to huge drops in many rural populations, decimating many farming communities.

For the family farms that have managed to survive, there is seldom enough income to cover the costs of a large household, including education, health care, farm and household insurance, and taxes. This situation forces individuals to seek money-earning opportunities elsewhere, often far away. Ironically, some hire on as cheap wage laborers in poultry- or meat-packing plants where working conditions are distasteful and often dangerous.

Globalscape

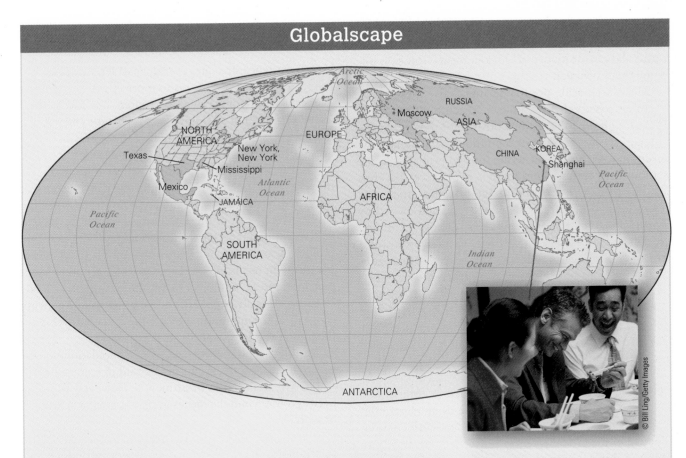

Chicken Out: Bush's Legs or Phoenix Talons?

Every evening in Moscow, Russians can be found enjoying a traditional dinner that may begin with *borscht* (beet soup) and *smetana* (sour cream), followed by a main course of *kotleta po-kievski* (boneless fried chicken breast)—or, if the budget is a bit tight, *nozhki busha* (chicken legs), baked, fried, or roasted—served with cabbage and potatoes.

Foreign visitors may recognize the breast entrée as chicken Kiev, but may be baffled to learn that the specialty *nozhki busha* translates as "Bush's legs." That is because these big meaty legs are imported from the United States and first appeared on Russian menus when the Soviet Union collapsed in 1991, during George H. W. Bush's

presidency (1989–1993). At the time, the Russian economy was dismal, and few people could afford beef or pork. Even chicken legs were too expensive for ordinary Russians. To help the transition to a capitalist democracy, the U.S. government promoted the advantages of free markets and global trade. What better propaganda than cheap chicken—especially since the American preference for white meat resulted in a surplus of dark meat legs. And so it was that the U.S. poultry industry entered the Russian market. Today, Russia imports more U.S. chicken than it produces on its own farms, especially legs—over a billion!

What happens with a typical 6-pound "broiler" chicken butchered by a Mexican immigrant working for minimum wage in a Mississippi poultry

plant? As we have seen, its legs are served up in Moscow, while its breasts end up on U.S. dining tables or on the menus of international airlines. And the rest of the bird? One of its frozen wings goes into a giant container shipped to Korea; the other to West Africa. The offal (neck, heart, liver, and guts) is transported to Jamaica where it is boiled and dished up in soup. The excess fat gets converted into biodiesel fuel at an experimental refinery in Texas. And what about its cute yellow feet? Both are exported to Shanghai, deep-fried, stewed, and served up as a delicacy called *fēngzhuâ*, or Phoenix talons, last seen being nibbled on by a visiting New York banker.

Global Twister What happens to the feathers?

Maximizing profits, agribusinesses are constantly streamlining food production and seeking ways to reduce labor costs by trimming the number of workers, minimizing employee benefits, and driving down wages. Pushing for market expansion beyond regional or even national boundaries, the largest among them have gone global. In the United States, for example, the poultry industry, which

requires vast quantities of corn and soy to feed the fast-growing roosters known as "broilers," now has a worldwide market in addition to growing domestic demand.

During the past half century, per capita consumption of chicken in the United States has increased tenfold to about 85 pounds per year. Considerably cheaper than pork or beef, it now represents nearly half of all meat eaten. Even so, U.S. consumption does not begin to match U.S. production, for the United States is the world's largest producer of chicken meat—some 36 billion pounds per year.

Most large-scale poultry farmers raise these broilers in enclosed "chicken houses." Each building is big enough to hold about 23,000 birds until they reach the butchering size (about 5 or 6 pounds), which takes just seven weeks. Chicken farms are located primarily in the southeastern states where there is ready access to corn and soy feed. The country's biggest broiler processing plant, located in Carthage, Mississippi, and owned by Tyson Food, is capable of slaughtering almost 2.5 million chickens per week. The $55-billion U.S. poultry business exports billions of tons of chicken annually to dozens of countries around the world. Nearly a quarter of its frozen chicken meat goes to Russia (over 900,000 tons comprised of more than a billion chicken legs). Another 400,000 tons go to China (primarily chicken feet, more than 1.2 billion of them). (See this chapter's Globalscape for more about chicken farming.)

Today's industrial food production and global marketing complex, involving a network of interlinked distribution centers, is made possible by an electronic-digital revolution that began in the late 20th century. That revolution is currently under way primarily in parts of North America, western Europe, Japan, and a few other wealthy countries where economies are increasingly based on the research and development of new knowledge and technologies, as well as providing information, services, and finance capital on a global scale.[11]

---

[11] Ritzer, G. (2007). *The coming of post-industrial society* (2nd ed.). New York: McGraw-Hill.

Concluding Remarks

New subsistence strategies over the past few centuries that use technological inventions to more effectively harness energy are commonly valued as progress. Yet, as discussed in this chapter, not all innovations turn out to be positive in the long run, nor do they improve the quality of life for every member of a society even in the short run.

Thousands of generations ago, our human ancestors emerged in Africa. They multiplied and dispersed, ultimately occupying every continent on earth. Adjusting as they went, each of these migrating groups developed its own cultural repertoire of ideas and practices to secure food, fuel, and safety for themselves and their offspring. Measured in terms of population growth, geographic expansion, and technological know-how, our species has been enormously successful in adapting itself to a wide range of different natural environments and developing the means required to satisfy its needs.

As long as the collective needs of a population remain within its means, the group can be said to enjoy a degree of relative abundance, or affluence. However, when its needs grow beyond the means available, it faces shortages, or scarcity.

Because abundance and shortage are based on the relationship between means and needs, affluence and scarcity are relative concepts. And for that reason, anthropologists tend to be cautious about the uncritical use of the term "progress" as applied to "economic development." Although there is no question that millions of people do enjoy a life of health and abundance, perhaps more so than their own ancestors, many must work harder and longer hours to put food on the table, and millions more live in poverty, are malnourished, and die too young. For them, the idea of human progress is unreal and difficult to swallow as truth.

Questions for Reflection

1. Since the beginning of human history, our species has met the challenge of survival by adapting to different environments. In capturing essential natural resources, we have also modified these environments. Do you know any examples of landscapes radically transformed for economic reasons? Who benefits from such environmental changes in the long run?

2. When buying a chicken breast sandwich in a deli, try to imagine where the food that fed your particular bird was cultivated; where the chicken was cooped up; how, where, and by whom it was slaughtered and packaged. And finally, while enjoying that breast stuck between slices of bread, ask yourself who might be chewing on the bird's feet somewhere on the other side of the world.

3. What was so radical about the domestication of plants and animals that led to it being referred to as the Neolithic *revolution*? Can you think of any equally radical changes in subsistence practices going on in the world today?

4. Consider the ideas of change and progress in light of the agricultural development project described in the Anthropology Applied feature. Come up with your own definition of progress that goes beyond the standard idea of technological and material advancement.

5. Technological development in industrial societies often results in highly productive machines effectively replacing animal and human workers. Think of a useful mechanical device and consider its benefits and costs, not only to you but also to others.

Suggested Readings

Bates, D. G. (2001). *Human adaptive strategies: Ecology, culture, and politics* (2nd ed.). Boston: Allyn & Bacon.

This book explores different adaptive practices and their correlative political structures. Theoretical issues are made accessible through the use of readable ethnographic case studies.

Bogucki, P. (1999). *The origins of human society.* Oxford, England: Blackwell.

The author provides a comprehensive global history of the human species, tracing the process of cultural evolution from our prehistoric beginnings as foragers to the creation of agricultural economies leading to complex societies and empires. As a record of human achievements, this book successfully incorporates the explosion in archaeological data accumulated since 1950.

Chatty, D. (1996). *Mobile pastoralists: Development planning and social change in Oman.* New York: Columbia University Press.

This study looks at the forces of modernization in a nomadic community and the resulting shift from herding to wage labor, as well as the changing role of women.

Lee, R. B., & Daly, R. H. (1999). *The Cambridge encyclopedia of hunters and gatherers.* New York: Cambridge University Press.

This is an essential reference text on foragers.

Pollan, M. (2008). *In defense of food: An eater's manifesto.* New York: Penguin.

This keen analysis of the American diet follows up on Pollan's *The Omnivore's Dilemma,* which firmly linked the industrialization of our food supply to the degradation of the environment. It chronicles how basic understanding of a balanced diet has been confused, complicated, and distorted by food industry marketers and nutritional scientists, who profit from the confusion. "Edible foodlike substances," writes Pollan, are often packaged with labels bearing health claims that are typically false or misleading, while "real food" is disappearing from the marketplace and is replaced by "nutrients," thereby ruining our health.

Challenge Issue   All humans face the challenge of securing resources needed for immediate and long-term survival. Whatever we lack, we may seek to get through exchange or trade. In today's capitalist societies people can exchange almost anything of value without ever actually meeting in person. But the market in traditional societies is a real location where people personally meet to exchange goods at designated times. So it is at this market in the Guatemalan highlands where Maya peasants meet. Growing more food than they need to feed their families, they barter the surplus for merchandise they do not grow or make themselves—from sugar and plastic containers to blue jeans, rubber boots, steel axes, knives, shovels, and machetes. They also sell their produce for money to pay for goods and services, such as medicine and the bus or truck that carries them to their villages. The distinctly embroidered blouse (*huipile*) worn by each of the Maya women reveals where she lives and whether she is single or married. All around the world, at marketplaces like this one, people from different places forge and affirm social networks of friends, neighbors, and allies needed for their safety and well-being.

CHAPTER 19

Economic Systems

Chapter Preview

How Do Anthropologists Study Economic Systems?

Anthropologists study the means by which goods are produced, distributed, and consumed in the context of the total culture of particular societies. Although they have adopted theories and concepts from economists, most anthropologists recognize that theoretical principles derived from the study of capitalist market economies have limited applicability to economic systems in societies that are not industrialized and where people do not produce and exchange goods for private profit. This is because, in these non-state societies, the economic sphere of behavior is not separate from the social, religious, and political spheres.

How Do Different Societies Organize Their Economic Resources and Labor?

In small-scale nonindustrial societies, land and other valuable resources are usually controlled by groups of relatives, and individual ownership is rare. Division of labor is by age and gender with some craft specialization. Production takes place in the quantity and at the time required, and most goods are consumed by the group that produces them. This is notably different from the economic arrangements in large-scale industrial and postindustrial societies where there is a much more complex division of labor, individuals or business corporations own property, producers and consumers rarely know each other, and transactions take place by means of money.

How and Why Are Goods Exchanged or Redistributed?

People exchange goods through reciprocity, redistribution, and/or market exchange. Reciprocity involves the exchange of goods and services of roughly equivalent value and is often undertaken for ritual or prestige purposes. Redistribution requires a government and/or religious elite to collect and reallocate resources, in the form of either goods or services. Leveling mechanisms ensure that no one accumulates significantly more goods than anyone else. Market exchange in nonindustrial societies takes place in designated locations where people trade goods, meet friends and strangers, and find entertainment. In modern societies, market exchange may be indirect, impersonal, and mediated by money or capital in the form of shares or stock. With the advent of digital technology, trading is also conducted on the Internet where individuals or corporations buy and sell "financial instruments" measured in minuscule percentages of large numbers with minute fluctuations on a global scale with lightning speed. The worldwide growth of mobile phone use also enables people in geographically remote or difficult to reach locations to be better informed economically and to engage directly in business transactions in larger markets.

An **economic system** is an organized arrangement for producing, distributing, and consuming goods. Since people, in pursuing a particular means of subsistence, necessarily produce, distribute, and consume things, our discussion of subsistence patterns in the previous chapter obviously involved economic matters. Yet economic systems encompass much more than we have covered so far. Now comes the rest of the story.

Economic Anthropology

Studying the economies of traditional small-scale societies, researchers from industrial and postindustrial capitalist societies run the risk of interpreting anthropological data in terms of their own technologies, their own values of work and property, and their own determination of what is rational. Take, for example, the following statement from a classic textbook in economics: "In all societies, the prevailing reality of life has been the inadequacy of output to fill the wants and needs of the people."[1]

This assertion fails to consider that in many societies people's wants and needs are maintained at levels that can be fully and continuously satisfied, and that without repressing or exploiting fellow human beings. In such societies, people gather or produce goods in the quantity and at the time required, and to do more than this makes no sense at all. No matter how hard they may work when hard work is called for, at other times they will have available hours, days, or even weeks on end to devote to "unproductive" (in the economic sense) activities.

To many observers enculturated in industrial or postindustrial societies, such people may seem lazy—and if they happen to be hunters and gatherers, even the skillful or strenuous work they do is likely to be misinterpreted. To those whose livelihoods depend on farming, trading, or factory or office work, hunting is typically defined as a sport. Hence, the male hunters in foraging societies are often perceived as spending virtually all of their time in recreational pursuits, while the female food gatherers are seen as working themselves to the bone.

To understand how the schedule of wants or demands of a given society is balanced against the supply of goods and services available, it is necessary to introduce a noneconomic variable: the anthropological variable of culture. In any given economic system, economic processes cannot be interpreted without culturally defining the demands and understanding the conventions that dictate how and when they are satisfied. The fact is, the economic sphere of behavior is *not* separate from the social, religious, and political spheres and thus is not completely free to follow its own purely economic logic. To be sure, economic behavior and institutions can be analyzed in strictly economic terms, but to do so is to ignore crucial noneconomic cultural considerations, which do, after all, have an impact on the way things are in real life. As a case in point, we may look briefly at yam production among the Trobriand Islanders, who inhabit a group of coral islands that lie in the southern Pacific Ocean off the eastern tip of New Guinea.[2]

Case Study: The Yam Complex in Trobriand Culture

Trobriand men spend a great deal of their time and energy raising yams—not for themselves or their own households, but to give to others, normally their sisters and married daughters. The purpose of cultivating these starchy edible roots is not to provision the households that receive them, because most of what people eat they grow for themselves in gardens where they plant taro, sweet potatoes, tapioca, greens, beans, and squash, as well as breadfruit and banana trees. The reason a man gives yams to a woman is to show his support for her husband and to enhance his own influence.

Once received by the woman, the gift yams are loaded into her husband's yam house, symbolizing his worth as a man of power and influence in his community. He may use some of these yams to purchase a variety of things, including arm shells, shell necklaces and earrings, betel nuts, pigs, chickens, and locally

[1] Heilbroner, R. L., & Thurow, L. C. (1981). *The economic problem* (6th ed., p. 327). Englewood Cliffs, NJ: Prentice-Hall.

economic system An organized arrangement for producing, distributing, and consuming goods.

[2] Weiner, A. B. (1988). *The Trobrianders of Papua New Guinea*. New York: Holt, Rinehart & Winston.

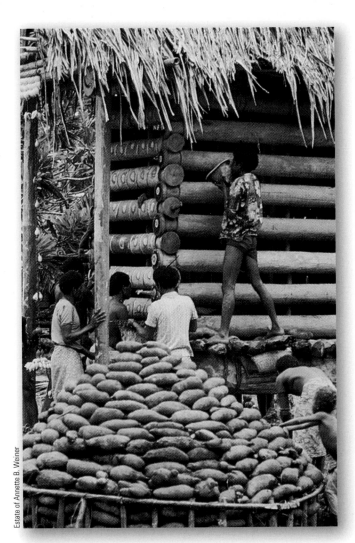

Estate of Annette B. Weiner

Trobriand Island men devote a great deal of time and energy to raising yams, not for themselves but to give to others. These yams, which have been raised by men related through marriage to a chief, are about to be loaded into the chief's yam house.

produced goods such as wooden bowls, combs, floor mats, lime pots, and even magic spells. Some he must use to fulfill social obligations. For instance, a man is expected to present yams to the relatives of his daughter's husband when she marries and again when death befalls a member of the husband's family. Finally, any man who aspires to high status and power is expected to show his worth by organizing a yam competition, during which he gives away huge quantities of yams to invited guests. As anthropologist Annette Weiner explains: "A yam house, then, is like a bank account; when full, a man is wealthy and powerful. Until yams are cooked or they rot, they may circulate as limited currency. That is why, once harvested, the usage of yams for daily food is avoided as much as possible."[3]

3 Ibid., p. 86.

By giving yams to his sister or daughter, a man not only expresses his confidence in the woman's husband, but also makes the latter indebted to him. Although the recipient rewards the gardener and his helpers by throwing a feast, at which they are fed cooked yams, taro, and—what everyone especially looks forward to—ample pieces of pork, this in no way pays off the debt. The debt can only be repaid in women's wealth, which consists of bundles of banana leaves and skirts made of the same material dyed red.

Although the banana leaf bundles are of no utilitarian value, extensive labor is invested in their production, and large quantities of them, along with skirts, are regarded as essential for paying off all the members of other family groups who were close to a recently deceased relative in life and who assisted with the funeral. Also, the wealth and vitality of the dead person's family group are measured by the quality and quantity of the bundles and skirts so distributed. Because a man has received yams from his wife's brother, he is obligated to provide his wife with yams for purchasing the necessary bundles and skirts, beyond those she has produced, to help with payments following the death of a member of her family. Because deaths are unpredictable and can occur at any time, a man must have yams available for his wife when she needs them. This, and the fact she may require all of his yams, acts as an effective check on a man's wealth.

Like people the world over, the Trobriand Islanders assign meanings to objects that make those objects worth far more than their cost in labor or materials. Yams, for example, establish long-term relationships that lead to other advantages, such as access to land, protection, assistance, and other kinds of wealth. Thus yam exchanges are as much social and political transactions as they are economic ones. Banana leaf bundles and skirts, for their part, are symbolic of the political status of families and of their immortality. In their distribution, which is related to rituals associated with death, we see how men in Trobriand society are ultimately dependent on women and their valuables.

So important are these matters to Trobrianders that even with the infiltration of Western culture—money, education, religion, and law—they remain committed to yam cultivation and to the production of women's wealth. Looked at in terms of modern capitalist economics, these activities appear meaningless, but viewed in terms of Trobriand values and concerns, they make a great deal of sense.

Production and Its Resources

In every society, particular customs and rules govern the kinds of work done, who does the work, attitudes toward the work, how it is accomplished, and who controls the resources necessary to produce desired goods, knowledge, and services. The primary resources in any culture are raw materials, technology, and labor. The rules directing the use of these are embedded in a people's culture and determine the way the economy operates within any given natural environment.

Land and Water Resources

All societies regulate allocation of valuable natural resources—especially land and water. Food foragers must determine who will hunt game and gather plants in their home range and where these activities take place. Groups that rely on fishing or growing crops need to make similar decisions concerning who carries out which task on which stretch of water or land. Farmers must have some means of determining title to land and access to water supplies for irrigation. Pastoralists require a system that determines rights to watering places and grazing land, as well as the right of access to land where they move their herds.

In Western capitalist societies, a system of private ownership of land and rights to natural resources generally prevails. Although elaborate laws have been enacted to regulate the buying, owning, and selling of land and water resources, if individuals wish to reallocate valuable farmland to some other purpose, for instance, they generally can.

In traditional nonindustrial societies, land is often controlled by kinship groups such as the family or band rather than by individuals. For example, among the Ju/'hoansi of the Kalahari Desert, each band of ten to thirty people lives on roughly 250 square miles of land, which they consider to be their territory— their own country. These territories are not defined by boundaries but in terms of water holes that are located within them. The land is said to be "owned" by those who have lived the longest in the band, usually a group of brothers and sisters or cousins. Their concept of landholding, however, is not something easily translated into modern Western terms

A Ju/'hoansi water hole. The practice of defining territories on the basis of core features such as water holes is typical of food foragers, such as these people of the Kalahari Desert in southern Africa.

of private ownership. Within their traditional worldview, no part of their homeland can be sold for money or traded away for goods. Outsiders must ask permission to enter the territory—but denying the request would be unthinkable.

The practice of defining territories on the basis of core features—be they water holes (as among the Ju/'hoansi), watercourses (as among Indians of the northeastern United States), unique sites in the landscape where ancestral spirits are thought to dwell (as among the Aborigines in Australia), or whatever—is typical of food foragers. Territorial boundaries tend to be rather vaguely defined, and to avoid friction, foragers may designate part of their territory as a buffer zone between them and their neighbors. The adaptive value of this is obvious: The size of band territories, as well as the size of the bands, can adjust to keep in balance with availability of resources in any given place. Such adjustment would be more difficult under a system of individual ownership of clearly bounded land.

Among some West African farming groups, a tributary system of land ownership prevails. All land is said to belong to the head chief, who allocates it to various subchiefs, who in turn distribute it to family groups. Then the family group leaders assign individual plots to each farmer. Just as in traditional Europe, these African people owe allegiance to the subchiefs (or nobles) and the head chief (or king). The people who work the land must pay tribute in the form of products or special services such as fighting for the king when necessary.

These people do not really own the land; rather, it is a kind of lease. Yet as long as the land is kept in use, rights to such use will pass to their heirs. No user, however, can give away, sell, or otherwise dispose of a plot of land without approval from the elder of the family group. When an individual no longer uses the allocated land, it reverts to the head of the large family group, who reallocates it to some other group member. The important operative principle here is that the system extends the individual's right to use land for an indefinite period, but the land is not "owned" outright. This serves to maintain the integrity of valuable farmland as such, preventing its loss through subdivision and conversion to other uses.

Technology Resources

All societies have some means of creating and allocating tools that are used to produce goods, as well as traditions for passing them on to succeeding generations. A society's **technology**—the number and types of tools employed, combined with knowledge about how to make and use them—is directly related to the lifestyles of its members. Food foragers and pastoral nomads who are frequently on the move are apt to have fewer and simpler tools than more settled peoples such as sedentary farmers. A great number of complex tools would hinder mobility. Thus, as noted in the previous chapter, the average weight of an individual's personal belongings among the Ju'hoansi is just under 25 pounds, limited to the barest essentials such as implements for hunting, gathering, fishing, building, and cooking. Pastoral nomads, aided by pack animals, typically have more material possessions than foragers, but still less than people who live in permanent settlements.

Food foragers make and use a variety of tools, many of which are ingenious in their effectiveness. Some of these they make for their individual use, but codes of generosity are such that a person may not refuse to give or loan what is requested. Tools may be given or loaned to others in exchange for the products resulting from their use. For example, a Ju/'hoansi who gives his arrow to another hunter has a right to a share in any animals the hunter kills. Game is considered to "belong" to the man whose arrow killed it, even when he is not present on the hunt. In this context, it makes little sense for them to accumulate luxuries or surplus goods, and the fact that no one owns significantly more than another helps to limit status differences.

Among horticulturists, the axe, digging stick, and hoe are the primary tools. Since these are relatively easy to produce, almost everyone can make them. Whoever makes a tool has first rights to it, but when he or she is not using it, any family member may ask to use it, and the request is rarely denied. Refusal would cause people to treat the tool owner with scorn for this singular lack of concern for others. If a relative helps raise the crop traded for a particular tool, that relative becomes part owner of the implement, and it may not be traded or given away without his or her permission.

In permanently settled agricultural communities, tools and other productive goods are more complex, heavier, and costlier to make. In such settings, individual ownership tends to be more absolute, as are the conditions under which people may borrow and use such equipment. It is easy to replace a knife lost by a relative during palm cultivation but much more difficult to replace an iron plow or a diesel-fueled harvesting machine. Rights to the ownership of complex tools are more rigidly applied; generally the person who has funded the purchase of a complex piece of machinery is considered the sole owner and may decide how and by whom it will be used.

Labor Resources and Patterns

In addition to raw materials and technology, labor is a key resource in any economic system. A look around the world reveals many different labor patterns, but two features are

technology Tools and other material equipment, together with the knowledge of how to make and use them.

Often, work that is considered inappropriate for women (or men) in one society is performed by them in another. Here we see female stone construction laborers in Bangalore, India, who carry concrete atop their heads.

© David Wells/The Image Works

almost always present in human cultures: a basic division of labor by gender and by age.

DIVISION OF LABOR BY GENDER

Anthropologists have studied extensively the social division of labor by gender in cultures of all sorts. Whether men or women do a particular job varies from group to group, but typically work has been and often continues to be divided into the tasks of either one or the other. For example, the practices most commonly regarded as "women's work" have tended to be those that can be carried out near home and that are easily resumed after interruption. The tasks historically often regarded as "men's work" have tended to be those requiring physical strength, rapid mobilization of high bursts of energy, frequent travel at some distance from home, and assumption of high levels of risk and danger.

Many exceptions occur, however, as in societies where women regularly carry burdensome loads or put in long hours of hard work cultivating crops in the fields. In some societies, women perform almost three quarters of all work, and in several societies they have served as warriors. For example, in the 19th-century West African kingdom of Dahomey (in what is now called Benin), thousands of women served in the armed forces of the Dahomean king, and some considered the women to be better fighters than their male counterparts. Also, there are references to female warriors in ancient Ireland, and archaeological evidence indicates their presence among Vikings.

During World War II in the early 1940s, some 58,000 Soviet women engaged in frontline combat defending their homeland against German invaders, and North Vietnamese women fought in mixed-gender army units during the Vietnam War in the 1960s and early 1970s. Today, women serve in the military of most countries, but only Canada, Denmark, France, Germany, and a few others permit them to join combat units.

Instead of looking for key biological factors to explain the social division of labor, a more useful strategy is to examine the kinds of work that men and women do in the context of specific societies to see how it relates to other cultural and historical factors. Researchers find a continuum of patterns, ranging from flexible integration of men and women to rigid segregation by gender.[4]

The *flexible/integrated pattern* is exemplified by the Ju/'hoansi discussed above and is seen most often among food foragers (as well as communities where crops are traditionally cultivated primarily for family consumption). In such societies, men and women perform up to 35 percent of activities with approximately equal participation, and tasks deemed especially appropriate for one gender may be performed by the other, without loss of face, as the situation warrants. Where these practices prevail, boys and

[4] Sanday, P. R. (1981). *Female power and male dominance: On the origins of sexual inequality* (pp. 79–80). Cambridge, England: Cambridge University Press.

girls grow up in much the same way, learn to value cooperation over competition, and become equally habituated to adult men and women, who interact with one another on a relatively equal basis.

Societies following a *segregated pattern* define almost all work as either masculine or feminine, so men and women rarely engage in joint efforts of any kind. In such societies, it is inconceivable that someone would even think of doing something considered the work of the opposite sex. This pattern is frequently seen in pastoral nomadic, intensive agricultural, and industrial societies, where men's work keeps them outside the home for much of the time. Typically, men in such societies are expected to be tough, aggressive, and competitive—and this often involves assertions of male superiority, and hence authority, over women. Historically, societies segregated by gender often have imposed their control on societies featuring integration, upsetting the egalitarian nature of the latter.

In the third pattern of labor division by gender, sometimes called the *dual sex configuration,* men and women carry out their work separately, as in societies segregated by gender, but the relationship between them is one of balanced complementarity rather than inequality. Although competition is a prevailing ethic, each gender manages its own affairs, and the interests of both men and women are represented at all levels. Thus, as in integrated societies, neither gender exerts dominance over the other. The dual sex orientation may be seen among certain American Indian peoples whose economies were based upon subsistence farming, as well as among several West African kingdoms, including that of the aforementioned Dahomeans.

In postindustrial societies, the division of labor by gender becomes blurred and even irrelevant, resembling the flexible/integrated pattern of traditional foragers briefly discussed above. Although gender preferences and discrimination in the workplace exist in societies making the economic transition, cultural ideas more fitting agricultural or industrial societies predictably change in due time, adjusting to postindustrial challenges and opportunities.

DIVISION OF LABOR BY AGE

Division of labor according to age is also typical of human societies. Among the Ju/'hoansi, for example, children are not expected to contribute significantly to subsistence until they reach their late teens. Indeed, until they possess adult levels of strength and endurance, many "bush" foods are tough for them to gather. Until that point, youngsters contribute primarily by taking care of their littlest siblings while grownups deal with subsistence needs.

The Ju/'hoansi equivalent of retirement comes somewhere around the age of 60. Elderly people, while they

will usually do some foraging for themselves, are not expected to contribute much food. However, older men and women alike play an essential role in spiritual matters. Freed from food taboos and other restrictions that apply to younger adults, they may handle ritual substances considered dangerous to those still involved with hunting or having children. By virtue of their old age, they have memories of customary practices and events that happened far in the past. Thus they are repositories of accumulated wisdom—the libraries of a nonliterate people—and are able to suggest solutions to problems younger adults have never before had to face. Considered useful for their knowledge, they are far from being unproductive members of society.

In some food-foraging societies, women do continue to make a significant contribution to provisioning in their later years. Among the Hadza of East Africa, the input of older women is critical to their daughters, whose foraging abilities are significantly hindered when they have new infants to nurse. The energy costs of lactation, along with the tasks of holding, carrying, and nursing an infant, all encumber the mother's foraging efficiency. Those most immediately affected by this are a woman's weaned children not yet old enough to forage effectively for themselves. The problem is solved by the foraging efforts of grandmothers.[5]

In many traditional farming societies, children as well as older people may make a greater contribution to the economy in terms of work and responsibility than is common in industrial or postindustrial societies. For instance, in Maya peasant communities in southern Mexico and Guatemala, children not only look after their younger brothers and sisters but also help with housework. Girls begin to make a substantial contribution to the work of the household by age 7 or 8. By age 11 they are constantly busy with an array of chores—grinding corn, making tortillas, fetching wood and water, sweeping, and so forth. Young boys have less to do but are given small tasks, such as bringing in the chickens or playing with a baby. However, by age 12 they are carrying toasted tortillas to the men out working in the fields and returning with loads of corn.[6]

Children also work in industrial societies, where poor families depend on every possible contribution to the household. There, however, economic desperation may easily lead to the cold exploitation of children in factory settings. The use of child labor has become a

[5] Hawkes, K., O'Connell, J. F., & Blurton Jones, N. G. (1997). Hadza women's time allocation, offspring, provisioning, and the evolution of long postmenopausal life spans. *Current Anthropology 38,* 551–577.

[6] Vogt, E. Z. (1990). *The Zinacantecos of Mexico, a modern Maya way of life* (2nd ed., pp. 83–87). Fort Worth: Holt, Rinehart & Winston.

This Hmong girl in a Thailand factory exemplifies the use of child labor in many parts of the world, often by large corporations. Even in Western countries, child labor plays a major economic role.

matter of increasing concern as large capitalist corporations rely more and more on the low-cost manufacture of goods in the world's poorer countries. Reliable figures are hard to come by, but it is estimated that there are some 200 million child laborers under age 14, almost all living in Third World countries where their families depend on the extra income they bring home. Many enter the labor force when they are only 6 or 7 years old, working full-time, from dawn to dusk, for extremely low wages, which helps keep the labor costs down.

Although the United States long ago passed laws prohibiting institutionalized child labor, the country imports at least $100 million worth of products manufactured by poorly paid children, ranging from rugs and carpets to clothing and soccer balls.[7]

COOPERATIVE LABOR

Cooperative work groups can be found everywhere—in foraging as well as food-producing and in nonindustrial as well as industrial societies. Often, if the effort involves the whole community, a festive spirit permeates the work. Jomo Kenyatta, a Kikuyu leader who was trained as an anthropologist before becoming Kenya's first president, described a happy moment in a communal workday of an East African farming village such as his own:

> If a stranger happens to pass by, he will have no idea that these people who are singing and dancing have completed their day's work. This is why most Europeans have erred by not realizing that the African in his own environment does not count hours or work by the movement of the clock, but works with good spirit and enthusiasm to complete the tasks before him.[8]

In some parts of East Africa, work parties begin with the display of a pot of millet beer to be consumed after the tasks have been finished. Home-brewed from millet, their major cereal crop, the beer is not really payment for the work; indeed, the labor involved is worth far more than the beer consumed. Rather, drinking the low-alcohol but highly nutritious beverage together is more of a symbolic activity to celebrate the spirit of friendship and mutual support, whereas recompense comes as individuals sooner or later participate in work parties for others. In rural areas all around the world, farmers commonly help one another during harvest and haying seasons, often sharing major pieces of equipment.

In most human societies, the basic unit within which cooperation takes place is the household. It is both a unit of production and consumption; only in industrial societies have these two things been separated.

TASK SPECIALIZATION

In contemporary industrial and postindustrial societies, there is a great diversity of specialized tasks to be performed, and no individual can even begin to know all of those customarily seen as fitting for his or her age and gender. However, although specialization has increased in these societies, modern technologies are making labor divisions based on gender less relevant. By contrast, in small-scale foraging and traditional crop-cultivating societies, where division of labor typically occurs along lines of age and gender, each person has knowledge and competence in all aspects of work appropriate to his or her age and gender. Yet, even in these nonindustrial societies there is a measure of specialization.

An example of task specialization can be found among the Afar people of the Danakil Depression in the borderlands of Eritrea and Ethiopia, one of the lowest and hottest places on earth.[9] The Danakil's desolate

[7] "It's the law: Child labor protection." (1997, November/December). *Peace and Justice News,* 11.

[8] Herskovits, M. (1952). *Economic anthropology: A study in comparative economics* (2nd ed., p. 103). New York: Knopf.

© Terry O'Sullivan

Scorching hot and dry, the Danakil Desert in northeastern Africa lies some 113 meters (370 feet) below sea level—remains of what was once part of the Red Sea—with enormous salt flats. Afar nomads and their pack camels periodically travel to this desert, cutting blocks of rock salt that they trade with peoples in the interior highlands. Here we see them preparing and packing their quarry for the long journey.

landscape features sulfur fields, smoking fissures, volcanic tremors, and vast salt plains. Since ancient times, groups of Afar men periodically mine the salt, hacking blocks from the plain's crust. The work is backbreaking, all the more so with temperatures soaring to 140 degrees Fahrenheit.

Along with the physical strength required for such work under the most trying conditions, successful mining demands specialized planning and organization skills for getting to and from the work site. Pack camels have to be fed in advance, since importing sufficient fodder for them interferes with their ability to carry out salt. Food and water, packed by Afar women at the desert's edge, must

be carried in for the miners, typically numbering thirty to forty per group. Travel is arranged for nighttime to avoid the scorching sun.[10]

In the past few decades, we have seen the emergence of new forms of task specialization in an international division of labor and in response to global markets of supply and demand. Many of these specializations are linked to tourism, now one of the largest industries in the world. Estimates vary, but in 2007 the industry employed some 230 million people and generated about $5 trillion— nearly 10 percent of the total value of goods and services produced worldwide. The recent global economic crisis beginning in 2008 slowed tourism's rapid rise, but the industry continues to grow, albeit at a slower space.[11] Some communities that still hold on to a natural habitat with a wealth of plant and animal life are able to tap into a specialized niche known as ecotourism, as detailed in this chapter's Anthropology Applied feature.

[9] Nesbitt, L. M. (1935). *Hell-hole of creation.* New York: Knopf.

[10] Mesghinua, H. M. (1966). Salt mining in Enderta. *Journal of Ethiopian Studies 4* (2); O'Mahoney, K. (1970). The salt trade. *Journal of Ethiopian Studies 8* (2).

[11] World Travel & Tourism Council: www.wttc.org. See also the UN's World Tourism Organization's annual report: www.unwto.org.

Anthropology Applied

Global Ecotourism and Local Indigenous Culture in Bolivia
by Amanda Stronza

We traveled in a small fleet of motorized canoes. As the sun dipped behind the trees one steamy afternoon in April 2002, we turned the last few bends of the Tuichi River and arrived to our destination, the Chalalán Ecolodge of northern Bolivia. Our group included eighteen indigenous leaders from various parts of the Amazon rainforest, a handful of regional tour operators, conservationists, environmental journalists, and me—an applied anthropologist studying the effects of ecotourism on local livelihoods, cultural traditions, and resource use. We had been navigating for nine hours through lowland rainforest to visit one of the first indigenous, community-run ecotourism lodges in the world.

As we wended our way, combing the riverbanks for caimans, capybaras, tapirs, and jaguars, our conversations meandered too. Mostly, the indigenous leaders shared stories of how ecotourism had affected their own forests and communities. They spoke of tourists who brought both opportunities and conflicts, and of their own efforts to balance conservation and development. They compared notes on wildlife in their regions, the kinds of visitors they had attracted, the profits they'd earned, the new skills they had gained, and the challenges they were facing as they sought to protect their lands and cultural traditions while also engaging with the global tourism industry.

Having studied ecotourism in the Amazon since 1993, I felt honored to be on board participating in these discussions. With support from the Critical Ecosystem Partnership Fund, I had the opportunity that year—the International Year of Ecotourism—to assemble leaders from three indigenous ecotourism projects in South America. All three were partnerships between local communities and private tour companies or nongovernmental organizations. For example, the lodge we were visiting, Chalalán, came about through a partnership between the Quechua-Tacana community of San José de Uchupiamonas, Bolivia, and two global organizations, Conservation International and the Inter-American Development Bank. Much of the $1,450,000 invested in Chalalán went toward preparing community members to assume full ownership and management of the lodge within five years. After a successful transfer in 2001, the lodge now belonged to San José's 600-member Quechua-Tacana community.

The indigenous leaders who gathered for this trip had keen, first-hand knowledge about the costs and benefits ecotourism can bring. They were former hunters, now leading tourists as birding and wildlife guides; small farmers and artisans making traditional handicrafts to sell to visitors; river-savvy fishermen supplementing their incomes by driving tour boats; and local leaders whose intimate knowledge of their communities helped them manage their own tour companies. Among them was Chalalán's general manager Guido Mamani, who recounted the benefits Chalalán had brought to the Tacana of San José. "Ten years ago," he recalled, "people were leaving San José because there were few ways to make a living. Today they are returning because of pride in the success of Chalalán. Now, they see opportunity here." As a result of their renewed pride in their mix of Quechua and Tacana histories, the community has begun hosting tourists for cultural tours in San José. "We want to give tourists presentations about the community and our customs," Mamani explained, "including our legends, dances, traditional music, the coca leaves, the traditional meals. We want to show our culture through special walks focusing on medicinal and other useful plants."

Mamani and the other indigenous ecotourism leaders characterized the success of their lodges in three ways: economic, social, and environmental. Chalalán, for example, counted its economic success in terms of employment and new income. It directly employs eighteen to twenty-four people at a time, and additional families supply farm produce and native fruits to the lodge. With artisans selling handicrafts to tourists, the community has gained regional fame for its wooden carved masks. The social benefits of Chalalán include new resources for education, health care, and communication. With their profits from tourism, the community built a school, a clinic, and a potable water system. They also purchased an antenna, solar panels, and a satellite dish to connect with the world from their remote forests along the Tuichi River.

Beyond these sorts of material improvements, ecotourism has catalyzed symbolic changes for the people of San José. "We have new solidarity in our cultural traditions," one woman noted, "and now we want to show who we are to the outside world." These experiences of Chalalan and similar projects suggest that ecotourism may be more than just a conservation and development idea—it may also be a source of pride, empowerment, and strengthened cultural identity among indigenous peoples.

Distribution and Exchange

In societies without a money economy, the rewards for labor are usually direct. The workers in a family group consume what they harvest, eat what the hunter or gatherer brings home, and use the tools they themselves make. But even where no formal medium of exchange such as money exists, some distribution of goods takes place.

Anthropologists often classify the cultural systems of distributing material goods into three modes: reciprocity, redistribution, and market exchange.[12]

---

[12] Polanyi, K. (1968). The economy as instituted process. In E. E. LeClair, Jr., & H. K. Schneider (Eds.), *Economic anthropology: Readings in theory and analysis* (pp. 127–138). New York: Holt, Rinehart & Winston.

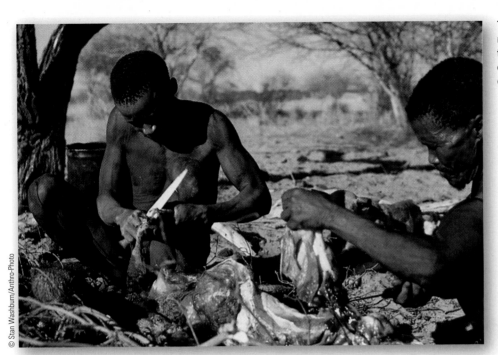

These Ju/'hoansi men are cutting up meat that will be shared by others in the camp. Food distribution practices of such food foragers are an example of generalized reciprocity.

Reciprocity

Reciprocity refers to the exchange of goods and services, of roughly equal value, between two parties. This may involve gift giving. Notably, individuals or groups in most cultures like to think that the main point of the transaction is the gift itself, yet what actually matters are the social ties that are created or reinforced between givers and receivers. Because reciprocity is about a relationship between the self and others, gift giving is seldom really selfless. The overriding (if unconscious) motive is to fulfill social obligations and perhaps to gain a bit of prestige in the process.

Cultural traditions dictate the manner and occasion of exchange. For example, when an animal is killed by a group of indigenous hunters in Australia, the meat is divided among the hunters' families and other relatives. Each person in the camp gets a share, the size depending on the nature of the person's kinship tie to the hunters. Typically, if the animal is a kangaroo, the left hind leg goes to the brother of the hunter, the tail to his father's brother's son, the loins and the fat to his father-in-law, the ribs to his mother-in-law, the forelegs to his father's younger sister, the head to his wife, and the entrails and the blood to the hunter. The hunter and his family seem to fare badly in this arrangement, but they have their turn when another man makes a kill. The giving and receiving are obligatory, as is the particularity of the distribution. Such sharing of food reinforces community bonds and ensures that everyone eats. By giving away part of a kill, the hunters get social credit for a similar amount of food in the future.

Reciprocity falls into several categories. The Australian food distribution example just noted constitutes an example of **generalized reciprocity**—exchange in which the value of what is given is not calculated, nor is the time of repayment specified. Gift giving, in the unselfish sense, also falls into this category. So, too, does the act of a kindhearted soul who stops to help a stranded motorist or someone else in distress and refuses payment with the admonition: "Pass it on to the next person in need."

Most generalized reciprocity, however, occurs among close kin or people who otherwise have very close ties with one another. Within such circles of intimacy, people give to others when they have the means and can count on receiving from others in time of need. Typically, participants will not consider such exchanges in economic terms but will couch them explicitly in terms of family and friendship social relations.

Balanced reciprocity differs in that it is not part of a long-term process. The giving and receiving, as well as the time involved, are more specific. One has a direct obligation to reciprocate promptly in equal value in order for the social relationship to continue. Examples of balanced reciprocity in contemporary North American society include such customary practices as hosting a

reciprocity The exchange of goods and services, of approximately equal value, between two parties.
generalized reciprocity A mode of exchange in which the value of what is given is not calculated, nor is the time of repayment specified.
balanced reciprocity A mode of exchange in which the giving and the receiving are specific as to the value of the goods and the time of their delivery.

Here we see a spectacular procession of the Three Wise Men or magician kings riding their camels into the Spanish city of Alcoi on the Eve of Epiphany. For this Roman Catholic holiday twelve days after Christmas, children write wish letters to these exotic kings from the east. Before going to bed on Epiphany night, youngsters place their shoes on the balcony or some other visible spot, along with food gifts for the kings' camels. Come morning, the children find presents left for them (supposedly) by the kings—a kind of ritualized gift "exchange" that represents balanced reciprocity.

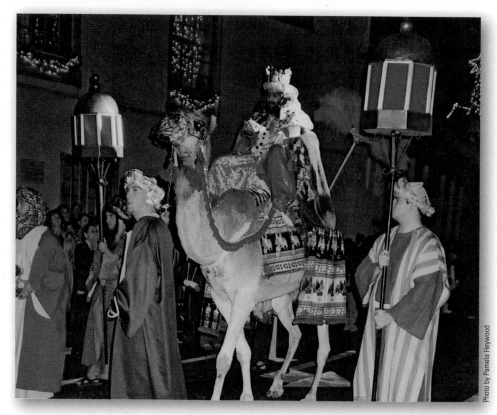

Photo by Pamela Heywood

baby shower for young friends expecting their first baby, giving presents at birthdays and various other culturally prescribed special occasions, and buying drinks when one's turn comes at a gathering of friends and associates.

Giving, receiving, and sharing as so far described constitute a form of social security or insurance. A family contributes to others when they have the means and can count on receiving from others in time of need—promoting an egalitarian distribution of wealth over the long run. Exchanges that occur within a group of relatives or between friends generally take the form of generalized or balanced reciprocity.

Negative reciprocity is a third form of exchange, in which the aim is to get something for as little as possible. The parties involved have opposing interests and are not usually closely related; they may be strangers or even enemies. They are people with whom exchanges are often neither fair nor balanced and are usually not expected to be such. This type of reciprocity may involve hard bargaining, manipulation, or outright cheating. An extreme form of negative reciprocity is to take something by force, while realizing that one's victim may seek compensation or retribution for losses.

negative reciprocity A form of exchange in which the aim is to get something for as little as possible. Neither fair nor balanced, it may involve hard bargaining, manipulation, and outright cheating.

Sometimes elements of negative as well as balanced reciprocity are present in an exchange. Such is often the case with political fundraising in the United States, where big contributors expect their generosity will buy influence with a candidate, resulting in benefits of equal value. The politician may seek to do as little as possible in return, but not so little as to jeopardize future donations. Those who accept too much and/or give too much in return risk legal repercussions.

TRADE AND BARTER

Trade refers to a transaction in which two or more people are involved in an exchange of something—a quantity of food, fuel, clothing, jewelry, animals, or money, for example—for something else of equal value. In such a transaction, the value of the trade goods can be fixed by previous agreements or negotiated on the spot by the trading partners. When there is no money involved in the transaction, and the parties negotiate a direct exchange of one trade good for another, we may speak of *barter*. In barter, arguing about the price and terms of the deal may well be in the form of negative reciprocity, with each party aiming to get the better end of the deal. Relative value is calculated, and despite an outward show of indifference, sharp dealing is generally the rule, when compared to the more balanced nature of exchanges within a group.

An arrangement that combines elements of balanced reciprocity as well as barter existed in India between the Kota and three neighboring peoples. The Kota, the musicians and blacksmiths for the region, were able to provide their neighbors with tools and with music considered essential for ceremonial occasions. In exchange, the Toda, with whom they had an amicable relationship, offered *ghee* (a kind of butter used for certain ceremonies) and buffalo used for funerals. For grain, the Kota relied on the Badaga farmers, with whom they had a competitive relationship that sometimes led to one-sided trading practices (in which the Kota usually came out ahead). The forest-dwelling Kurumba, who were renowned as sorcerers, had honey, cane, and occasionally fruit to offer, but their main contribution was protection against the supernatural. The Kota feared the Kurumba, and the Kurumba took advantage of this in their dealings, so that they always got more than they gave. Thus great latent hostility existed between these two peoples.

One interesting mechanism for facilitating exchange between potentially antagonist groups is **silent trade** in which no verbal communication takes place. In fact, it may involve no actual face-to-face contact at all. Such cases have often characterized the dealings between food-foraging peoples and their food-producing neighbors—such as the Veddah of Sri Lanka's tropical forest, who traditionally offer wild honey to Sinhalese in exchange for metal tools. Another example of silent trade occurs with the Mbuti Pygmy of Congo's Ituri forest, who trade bushmeat for plantains and other crops grown by Bantu villagers on small farms. It works like this: People from the forest leave trade goods in a clearing, then retreat and wait. Agriculturalists come to the spot, survey the goods, leave what they think is a fair exchange of their own wares, and then leave. The forest people return, and if satisfied with the offer, take it with them. If not, they leave it untouched, signifying that they expect more. In this way, for 2,000 or so years, foragers have supplied various commodities in demand in a wider economy.[13]

To speculate about the reasons for silent trade, in some situations it may be silent for lack of a common language. More often silent trade may serve to control situations of distrust so as to keep relations peaceful. Good relations are maintained by preventing direct contact. Another possibility that does not exclude the others is that it makes exchange possible where problems of status might make verbal communication unthinkable. In any event, it provides for the exchange of goods between groups despite potential barriers.

KULA RING: GIFT GIVING AND TRADING IN THE SOUTH PACIFIC

Balanced reciprocity can take more complicated forms, whereby mutual gift giving serves to facilitate social interaction, smoothing relations between traders wanting to do business. One classic ethnographic example of balanced reciprocity between trading partners seeking to be friends and do business at the same time is the **Kula ring** in the southwestern Pacific Ocean. This practice was first described by Bronislaw Malinowski and involves thousands of seafarers going to great lengths to establish and maintain good trade relations; this centuries-old ceremonial exchange system continues to this day.[14]

Kula participants are men of influence who travel to islands within the Trobriand ring to exchange prestige items—red shell necklaces (*soulava*), which are circulated around the ring of islands in a clockwise direction, and white shell armbands (*mwali*), which are carried in the opposite direction (Figure 19.1). Each man in the Kula is

[14] Malinowski, B. (1922). *Argonauts of the western Pacific* (p. 94). London: Routledge & Kegan Paul; and see Weiner, A. B. (1988). *The Trobrianders of Papua New Guinea* (p. 156). New York: Holt, Reinhart & Winston.

> **silent trade** A form of product exchange in which mutually distrusting ethnic groups avoid direct personal contact.
>
> **Kula ring** A form of balanced reciprocity that reinforces trade relations among the seafaring Trobriand Islanders and other Melanesians.

Figure 19.1 The ceremonial gift exchanges of shell necklaces and armbands in the Kula ring encourage trade and barter throughout the Melanesian islands.

[13] Turnbull. C. (1961). *The forest people.* New York: Simon & Schuster; Wilkie, D. S., & Curran, B. (1993). Historical trends in forager and farmer exchange in the Ituri rain forest of northeastern Zaïre. *Human Ecology* 21 (4), 389–417.

In Melanesia, men of influence paddle and sail within a large ring of islands in the southwestern Pacific off the eastern coast of Papua New Guinea to participate in the ceremonial trading of Kula shells, which smoothes trade relations and builds personal prestige.

© Irven DeVore/Anthro-Photo

linked to partners on the islands that neighbor his own. To a partner residing on an island in the clockwise direction, he offers a *soulava* and receives in return a *mwali*. He makes the reverse exchange of a *mwali* for a *soulava* to a partner living in the counterclockwise direction. Each of these trade partners eventually passes the object on to a Kula partner further along the chain of islands.

Soulava and *mwali* are ranked according to their size, their color, how finely they are polished, and their particular histories. Such is the fame of some that, when they appear in a village, they create a sensation.

Traditionally, men make their Kula journeys in elaborately carved dugout canoes, sailing and paddling these boats, which are 6 to 7.5 meters (20 to 25 feet) long, across open waters to shores some 100 kilometers (about 60 miles) or more away. The adventure is often dangerous and may take men away from their homes for several weeks, sometimes even months. Although men on Kula voyages may use the opportunity to trade for practical goods, acquiring such goods is not always the reason for these voyages—nor is Kula exchange a necessary part of regular trade expeditions.

Perhaps the best way to view the Kula is as an indigenous insurance policy in an economy fraught with danger and uncertainty. It establishes and reinforces social partnerships among traders doing business on distant shores, ensuring a welcome reception from people who have similar vested interests. This ceremonial exchange network does more than simply enhance the trade of foods and other goods essential for survival. Melanesians participating in the Kula ring have no doubt that

redistribution   A form of exchange in which goods flow into a central place, where they are sorted, counted, and reallocated.

their social position has to do with the company they keep, the circles in which they move. They derive their social prestige from the reputations of their partners and the valuables that they circulate. By giving and receiving armbands and necklaces that accumulate the histories of their travels and the names of those who have possessed them, men proclaim their individual fame and talent, gaining considerable influence for themselves in the process.

Like other forms of currency, *soulava* and *mwali* must flow from hand to hand; once they stop flowing, they may lose their value. A man who takes these valuables out of their inter-island circuit invites criticism. Not only might he lose prestige or social capital as a man of influence, but he might become a target of sorcery for unraveling the cultural fabric that holds the islands together as a functioning social and economic order.

As this example from the South Pacific illustrates, the potential tension among trading partners may be resolved or lessened by participation in a ritual of balanced reciprocity. As an elaborate complex of ceremony, political relationships, economic exchange, travel, magic, and social integration, the Kula ring illustrates the inseparability of economic matters from the rest of culture. Although perhaps difficult to recognize, this is just as true in modern industrial societies as it is in traditional Trobriand society—as is evident when heads of state engage in ceremonial gift exchanges at official visits.

Redistribution

Redistribution is a form of exchange in which goods flow into a central place where they are sorted, counted, and reallocated. Commonly, it involves an element of power. In societies with a sufficient surplus to support some sort of government, goods in the form of gifts, tribute, taxes, and the spoils of war are gathered into storehouses controlled by a chief or some other type of leader. From there they are handed out again. The leadership has three motives in redistributing this income: The first is to gain or maintain a position of power through a display of wealth and generosity; the second is to assure those who support the leadership an adequate standard of living by providing them with desired goods; and the third is to establish alliances with leaders of other groups by hosting them at lavish parties and giving them valuable goods.

The redistribution system of the ancient Inca empire in the Andean highlands of South America was one of the most efficient the world has ever known, both in the collection of tribute (obligatory contributions or gifts in the form of crops, goods, and services) and in its methods of administrative control.[15] Administrators kept inventories of resources and a census of the population, which at its peak reached 6 million. Each craft specialist had to produce a specific quota of goods from materials supplied by overseers. Required labor was used for some agricultural and mining work. Unpaid labor was also used in a program of public works that included a remarkable system of roads and bridges throughout the mountainous terrain, aqueducts that guaranteed a supply of water, temples for worship, and storehouses that held surplus food for times of famine.

Careful accounts were kept of income and expenditures. A central administration, regulated by the Inca emperor and his relatives, had the responsibility for ensuring that production was maintained and that commodities were distributed. Holding power over this command economy, the ruling elite lived in great luxury, but sufficient goods were redistributed to the common people to ensure that no one would be left in dire need or face the indignity of pauperism.

Taxes imposed by central governments of countries all around the world today are one form of redistribution—required payments typically based on a percentage of one's income and property value. Typically, a portion of the taxes goes toward supporting the government itself while the rest is redistributed either in cash (such as welfare payments and government loans or subsidies to businesses) or in the form of services (such as military defense, law enforcement, food and drug inspection, schools, highway construction, and the like). Tax codes vary greatly among countries. In many European countries, wealthy citizens are taxed at a considerably higher percentage of their income than are U.S. citizens.

SPENDING WEALTH TO GAIN PRESTIGE

In societies where people devote most of their time to subsistence activities, gradations of wealth are small, kept that way through various cultural mechanisms and systems of reciprocity that serve to spread quite fairly what little wealth exists. It is a different situation in ranked societies where substantial surpluses are produced, and the gap between the have-nots and the have-lots can be considerable. In these societies, showy display for social prestige—known as **conspicuous consumption**—is a strong motivator for the distribution of wealth.

Obviously, excessive efforts to impress others with one's wealth or status also play a prominent role in industrial and postindustrial societies, as individuals compete for prestige. Indeed, many North Americans and Europeans spend much of their lives trying to impress others. This requires the display of symbolic prestige items—designer clothes, substantial jewelry, mansions, expensive cars, private planes—and fits neatly into an economy based on consumer wants.

A form of conspicuous consumption also occurs in some crop-cultivating and foraging societies—as illustrated by potlatches hosted by the chiefs of various American Indian groups living along the Pacific Northwest coast, including the Tlingit, Haida, and Kwakwaka'wakw (Kwakiutl) peoples. A **potlatch** is a ceremonial event in which a village chief publicly gives away stockpiled food and other goods that signify wealth. (The term comes from the Chinook Indian word *patshatl*, which means "gift.")

Traditionally, a chief whose village had built up enough surplus to host such a feast for other villages in the region would give away large piles of sea otter furs, dried salmon, blankets, and other valuables while making boastful speeches about his generosity, greatness, and glorious ancestors. While other chiefs became indebted to him, he reaped the glory of successful and generous leadership and saw his prestige rise. In the future, his own village might face shortages, and he would find himself on the receiving end of a potlatch. Should that happen, he would have to listen to the self-serving and pompous speeches of rival chiefs. Obliged to receive, he would temporarily lose prestige and status.

In extreme displays of wealth, chiefs even destroyed some of their precious possessions. This occurred with some frequency in the second half of the 19th century, after European contact triggered a process of cultural change

conspicuous consumption A showy display of wealth for social prestige.

potlatch On the northwest coast of North America, a ceremonial event in which a village chief publicly gives away stockpiled food and other goods that signify wealth.

[15] Mason, J. A. (1957). *The ancient civilizations of Peru.* Baltimore: Penguin.

Among Native Americans living along the northwestern coast of North America, one gains prestige by giving away valuables at the potlatch feast. Here we see Tlingit clan members dressed in traditional Chilkat and Raven's Tail robes during a recent potlatch in Sitka, Alaska.

that included new trade wealth. Outsiders might view such grandiose displays as wasteful in the extreme. However, these extravagant giveaway ceremonies have played an ecologically adaptive role in a coastal region where villages alternately faced periods of scarcity and abundance and relied upon alliances and trade relations with one another for long-term survival. The potlatch provided a ceremonial opportunity to strategically redistribute surplus food and goods among allied villages in response to periodic fluctuations in fortune.

> **prestige economy**   Creation of a surplus for the express purpose of gaining prestige through a public display of wealth that is given away as gifts.
>
> **leveling mechanism**   A cultural obligation compelling prosperous members of a community to give away goods, host public feasts, provide free service, or otherwise demonstrate generosity so that no one permanently accumulates significantly more wealth than anyone else.

A strategy that features this sort of accumulation of surplus goods for the express purpose of displaying wealth and giving it away to raise one's status is known as a **prestige economy.** In contrast to conspicuous consumption in industrial and postindustrial societies, the emphasis is not on amassing goods that then become unavailable to others. Instead, it is on gaining wealth in order to give it away for the sake of prestige and status.

LEVELING MECHANISMS

The potlatch is an example of a **leveling mechanism**—a cultural obligation compelling prosperous members of a community to give away goods, host public feasts, provide free service, or otherwise demonstrate generosity so that no one permanently accumulates significantly more wealth than anyone else. With leveling mechanisms at work, greater wealth brings greater social pressure to spend and give generously. In exchange for such demonstrated altruism, a person not only increases his or her social standing in the community, but may also keep disruptive envy at bay.

Underscoring the value of collective well-being over individual self-interest, leveling mechanisms are important for the long-term survival of traditional communities. The potlatch is just one example of many cultural varieties of leveling mechanism.

By pressuring members into sharing their wealth in their own community rather than keeping it or privately investing it elsewhere, leveling mechanisms do more than keep resources in circulation. They also reduce social tensions among relatives, neighbors, and fellow town folk, promoting a collective sense of togetherness. An added practical benefit is that they ensure that necessary services within the community are performed.

Market Exchange

To an economist, **market exchange** has to do with the buying and selling of goods and services, with prices set by rules of supply and demand. Personal loyalties and moral values are not supposed to play a role, but they often do. Since the actual location of the transaction is not always relevant in today's world, we must distinguish between the *marketplace* and *market exchange*.

MARKETPLACE AND MARKET EXCHANGE

Typically, until well into the 20th century, market exchange was carried out in specific localities or marketplaces. This is still the case in much of the nonindustrial world and even in numerous centuries-old European and Asian towns and cities. In food-producing societies, marketplaces overseen by a centralized political authority provide the opportunity for farmers or peasants in the surrounding rural territories to exchange some of their livestock and produce for needed items manufactured in factories or in the workshops of craft specialists living (usually) in towns and cities. Thus markets require some sort of complex division of labor as well as centralized political organization.

The traditional market is local, specific, and contained. Prices are typically set on the basis of face-to-face bargaining rather than by unseen forces wholly removed from the transaction itself. Notably, sales do not necessarily involve money; instead, goods may be directly exchanged through some form of barter among the specific individuals involved.

In industrializing and industrial societies, many market transactions still take place in a specific identifiable location—including international trade fairs such as the semi-annual Canton Trade Fair in Guangzhou, China. In spring 2007, 13,000 Chinese enterprises participated in the event, offering 150,000 products and generating over $36 billion in export sales among 207,000 visitors. In 2009, reflecting the international financial crisis, sales dropped to $26 billion, but the event remains China's largest trade fair by far. Notably, despite the overall slump, the number of e-commerce visitors to the fair rose 2.5 percent.[16]

It is increasingly common for people living in technologically wired parts of the world to buy and sell everything from cattle to cars without ever being in the same city, let alone the same space. For example, think of Internet companies such as eBay where all buying and selling occur electronically and irrespective of geographic distance. When people talk about a market in today's industrial or postindustrial world, the particular geographic location where something is bought or sold is often not important at all.

The faceless market exchanges that take place in industrial and postindustrial societies stand in stark contrast to experiences in the marketplaces of nonindustrial societies, which have much of the excitement of a fair. Traditional exchange centers are colorful places where a host of sights, sounds, and smells awaken the senses. Typically, vendors and/or their family members produced the goods they are selling, thereby personalizing the transactions. Dancers and musicians may perform, and feasting and fighting may mark the end of the day. In these markets social relationships and personal interactions are key elements, and noneconomic activities may overshadow economic ones. In short, such markets are gathering places where people renew friendships, see relatives, gossip, and keep up with the world, while procuring needed goods they cannot produce for themselves.[17]

MONEY AS MEANS OF EXCHANGE

Although there have been marketplaces without money of any sort, money does facilitate trade. **Money** may be defined as something used to make payments for other goods and services as well as to measure their value. Its critical attributes are durability, transportability, divisibility, recognizability, and interchangeability. Items that have been used as money in various societies include salt, shells, precious stones, special beads, livestock, and valuable metals,

[16] Xinhua News Agency. (2009, May 9). Canton Fair wraps up with export orders down 17 percent. *China Daily*.

[17] Plattner, S. (1989). Markets and marketplaces. In S. Plattner (Ed.), *Economic anthropology* (p. 171). Stanford, CA: Stanford University Press.

market exchange The buying and selling of goods and services, with prices set by rules of supply and demand.
money Something used to make payments for other goods and services as well as to measure their value.

Visual Counterpoint

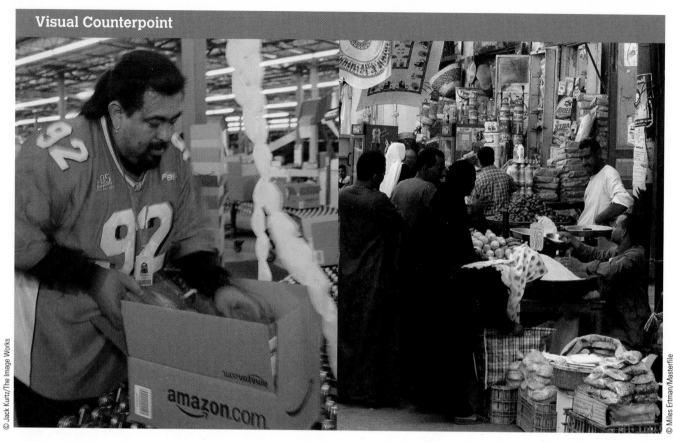

In many societies, particularly in developing countries, the market is an important focus of social as well as economic activity, as shown in the photo of a crowded outdoor market-place in Aswan, Egypt. In contrast, the packer pictured on the left works at an Amazon.com distribution center in Fernley, Nevada, preparing orders purchased on the Internet. With the advent of online shopping, people can buy and sell with no social interaction whatsoever.

such as iron, copper, silver, and gold. As revealed in this chapter's Biocultural Connection, cacao beans were also used as money—and more.

About 5,000 years ago, merchants and others in Mesopotamia (now part of Iraq) went beyond barter-ing in their trading activities and began using pieces of precious metal such as silver in their transactions. Once they agreed on the value of these pieces as a means of exchange (money), more complex commercial develop-ments followed. As the means of exchange was standard-ized in terms of value, it became easier to accumulate, lend, or borrow money for specified amounts and peri-ods against payment of interest. In due time, some mer-chants began to do business with money itself, and they became bankers.

As the use of money became widespread, the metal units were adapted to long-term use, easy storage, and long-distance transportation. In many cultures, such pieces of iron, copper, or silver were cast as miniature models of especially valuable implements like sword

blades, axes, or spades. But some 2,600 years ago in the ancient kingdom of Lydia (southwestern Turkey), they were molded into small flat discs conforming to different sizes and weights.[18] Over the next few centuries, metal coins were also standardized in terms of the metal's pu-rity and value, such as 100 units of copper equal 10 units of silver or 1 of gold.

By about 2,000 years ago, the commercial use of such coins was spreading throughout much of Europe and be-coming increasingly common in parts of Asia and Africa, especially along trade routes and in urban centers. Thus money set into motion radical economic changes in many traditional societies and introduced what has been called *merchant capitalism* in many parts of the world.[19]

---

[18] Davies, G. (2005). *A history of money from the earliest times to present day* (3rd ed.). Cardiff: University of Wales Press.

[19] See also Wolf, E. R. (1982). *Europe and the people without history* (pp. 135–141). Berkeley: University of California Press.

Biocultural Connection

Cacao: The Love Bean in the Money Tree

Several thousand years ago Indians in the tropical lowlands of southern Mexico discovered how to produce a hot brew from ground roasted beans. They collected these beans from melon-shaped fruit pods growing in trees identified by today's scientists as *Theobroma cacao*. By adding honey, vanilla, and some flowers for flavoring, they produced a beverage that made them feel good and believed that these beans were gifts from their gods.

Soon, cacao beans became part of long-distance trade networks and appeared in the Mexican highlands, where the Aztec elite adopted this drink brewed from *cacahuatl*, calling it *chocolatl*. In fact, these beans were so highly valued that Aztecs also used them as money. When Spanish invaders conquered Guatemala and Mexico in the 1520s, they adopted the region's practice of using cacao beans as currency inside their new colony. They also embraced the custom of drinking chocolate, which they introduced to Europe, where it became a luxury drink as well as a medicine.[a]

In the next 500 years, chocolate developed into a $14-billion global business, with the United States as the top importer of cacao beans or cacao products. Women buy 75 percent of the chocolate products, and on Valentine's Day more than $1 billion worth of chocolate is sold.

What is it about chocolate that makes it a natural love drug? Other than carbohydrates, minerals, and vitamins, it contains about 300 chemicals, including some with mood-altering effects. For instance, cacao beans contain several chemical components that trigger feelings of pleasure in the human brain. In addition to tryptophan, which increases serotonin levels, chocolate also contains phenylethylamine, an amphetaminelike substance that stimulates the body's own dopamine and has slight antidepressant effects. Chocolate contains anandamide (*anan* means "bliss" in Sanskrit), a messenger molecule that triggers the brain's pleasure center. Also naturally produced in the brain, anandamide's mood-enhancing effect is the same as that obtained from marijuana leaves.[b] Finally, chocolate also contains a mild stimulant called theobromine ("food of god"), which stimulates the human brain's production of natural opiates, reducing pain and increasing feelings of satisfaction and even euphoria.

These chemicals help explain why the last Aztec ruler Montezuma drank so much chocolate. A Spanish eyewitness, who visited his royal palace in the Aztec capital in 1519, later reported that Montezuma's servants sometimes brought their powerful lord "in cups of pure gold a drink made from the cocoa-plant, which they said he took before visiting his wives. . . . I saw them bring in a good fifty large jugs of this chocolate, all frothed up, of which he would drink a little. They always served it with great reverence."[c]

BIOCULTURAL QUESTION

Viewed as a divine gift by Mexican Indians, chocolate stimulates our brain's pleasure center. Why would women buy this natural love drug in much greater quantities than men?

[a]For an excellent cultural history of chocolate, see Coe, S. D., & Coe, M. D. (1996). *The true history of chocolate.* New York: Thames and Hudson; Grivetti, L. E. (2005). From aphrodisiac to health food: A cultural history of chocolate. *Karger Gazette* (68).
[b]Personal communication, Lawrence C. Davis, Kansas State University.
[c]del Castillo, B. D. (1963). *The conquest of New Spain* (pp. 226–227) (translation and introduction by J. M. Cohen). New York: Penguin.

Local Economies and Global Capitalism

Failing to overcome cultural biases can have serious economic consequences, especially in this era of globalization. For example, it has led prosperous countries to impose inappropriate development schemes in parts of the world that they regard as economically underdeveloped. Typically, these schemes focus on increasing the target country's gross national product through large-scale production that all too often boosts the well-being of a few but results in poverty, poor health, discontent, and a host of other ills for many.

Among many examples of this scenario is the global production of soy, which has increased greatly in many parts of the world. Of particular note is Paraguay, where big landowners, in cooperation with large agribusinesses (most of which are owned by neighboring Brazilians), produce genetically modified seeds, developed and marketed by foreign companies, especially the U.S.-based multinational corporation Monsanto. Although these landowners and agribusinesses possess just 1 percent of the total number of Paraguayan farms, they own almost 80 percent of the country's agricultural land. Exporting the soy, they make hefty profits because production costs are low and international demand is high for cattle feed and biofuel. But there are victims of their "progress": hundreds of thousands of small farmers, landless peasants, rural laborers, and their families. Traditionally growing much of their own food (plus a bit extra for the local market) on small plots, many locals have been edged out and forced to work for hunger wages or to migrate to the city, or even abroad, in order to survive. Those who stay face malnutrition and other hardships, for they lack enough fertile land to feed their families and do not earn enough to buy basic foodstuffs.[20]

[20] Fogel, R., & Riquelme, M. A. (2005). *Enclave sorjero. Merma de soberania y pobreza.* Ascuncion: Centro de Estudios Rurales Interdisciplinarias; Bodley, J. H. (1990). *Victims of progress* (3rd ed., p. 141). Mountain View, CA: Mayfield.

A crowd of protestors demonstrated against World Trade Organization (WTO) policies favoring rich countries over poor ones during an informal meeting of trade officials from 35 countries hosted by India in its capital city, New Delhi, September 2009. Established in 1995 and headquartered in Geneva, the WTO is the only global international organization with rules of trade among its 153 member countries.

© Associated Press/Mustafa Quraishi

Such are the failures of many foreign-imposed economic development schemes in which powerful institutions and corporations primarily representing outside interests disregard or ignore a key anthropological fact: A culture is not a random happening. It is an integrated system (as illustrated by the barrel model), and therefore a shift in the infrastructure, or economic base, impacts interlinked elements of the society's social structure and superstructure. As the ethnographic examples of the potlatch and the Kula ring show, economic activities in traditional cultures are intricately intertwined with social and political relations and even involve spiritual elements. Agribusinesses and other large-scale economic operations or development schemes that do not take such structural complexities into consideration may have unintended negative consequences on a society.

Fortunately, there is now a growing awareness on the part of development officials that future projects are unlikely to succeed without the expertise that anthropologically trained people can bring to bear. And, in some parts of the world anthropologists with indigenous roots are taking leading roles in shaping development agendas that build on rather than destroy tradition—as relayed in this chapter's Anthropologist of Note about Rosita Worl, a Tlingit from Juneau, Alaska.

Achieving a cross-cultural understanding of the economic organizations of other peoples that is not distorted or limited by the logic, hopes, and expectations of one's own society has also become important for corporate executives in today's world. Recognizing how the economic structures are intertwined with other aspects of a culture could help business corporations avoid problems of the sort experienced by Gerber, when it began selling baby food in Africa. As in the United States, Gerber's labels featured a picture of a smiling baby. Only later did company officials learn that, in Africa, businesses routinely put pictures of the products themselves on the outside label, since many people cannot read.[21]

As globalization increases so does corporate awareness of the cost of such cross-cultural miscues. So it is not surprising that business recruiters on college campuses in North America and elsewhere are now seeking job candidates with the kind of cross-cultural understanding of the world that anthropology provides.

When such work opportunities involve helping an enterprise more effectively exploit people for the sake of commercial gain, anthropologists have to deal with the profession's first ethical principle: Do no harm. It is important to note that powerful business corporations typically aim to make large profits. Their agenda is universally promoted through slogans such as "free trade," "free markets," and "free enterprise." The commercial success of such multinationals does not come without a price, and all too often that price is paid by still surviving indigenous foragers, small farmers, herders, fishermen, local artisans such as weavers and carpenters, and so on. From their viewpoint, such slogans of freedom have the ring of "savage capitalism," a term now often used in Latin America for a new world order in which the powerless feel condemned to misery.

Although political authorities in state-organized societies seek to govern and control economic activities for regulation and taxation purposes, they do not always

---

[21] "Madison Avenue relevance." (1999). *Anthropology Newsletter 40* (4), 32.

Rosita Worl

Alaskan anthropologist **Rosita Worl,** whose Tlingit names are *Yeidiklats'akw* and *Kaa hani,* belongs to the Thunderbird Clan from the ancient village of Klukwan in southeastern Alaska. During her growing-up years by the Chilkat River, elders taught her to speak loudly so her words could be heard above the sound of crashing water. And her mother, a cannery union organizer, took her along to meetings.

As a university student, Worl led a public protest for the first time—successfully challenging a development scheme in Juneau detrimental to local

Tlingit. When she decided to pursue her anthropology doctorate at Harvard, she did so with a strong sense of purpose: "You have to be analytical about your culture," she says. "At one time, before coming into contact with other societies, we were just able to live our culture, but now we have to be able to keep it intact while integrating it into modern institutions. We have to be able to communicate our cultural values to others and understand how those modern institutions impact those values."

Worl's graduate studies included fieldwork among the Iñupiat of Alaska's North Slope region—research that resulted in her becoming a spokesperson at state, national, and international levels for the protection of whaling practices and the indigenous subsistence lifestyle. For over three decades now, she has fought to safeguard traditional rights to natural resources essential for survival, for current and future generations, including her own children and grandchildren.

A recognized leader in sustainable, culturally informed economic development, Worl has held several major positions at the Sealaska Corporation, a large Native-owned business enterprise with almost 18,000 shareholders primarily of Tlingit and neighboring Haida and Tsimshian descent. Created under the 1971 Alaska Native Claims Settlement Act, Sealaska is now the largest private landholder in southeastern Alaska. Its subsidiaries collectively employ over a thousand people and include

timber harvesting, marketing wood products, land and forest resource management, construction, and information technology. Putting the holistic perspective and analytical tools of anthropology to practice, Worl has spearheaded efforts to incorporate the cultural values of southeast Alaska Natives into Sealaska—including shareholding opportunities for employees.

Currently, Worl serves as president of Sealaska Heritage Institute, a Native nonprofit organization that seeks to perpetuate and enhance Tlingit, Haida, and Tsimshian cultures, including language preservation and revitalization. Also on the faculty of the University of Alaska Southeast, she has written extensively about indigenous Alaska for academic and general audiences. She founded the journal *Alaska Native News* to educate Native Alaskans on a range of issues and is deeply involved in the implementation of the 1990 Native American Graves Protection and Repatriation Act.

Sought for her knowledge and expertise, Worl has served on the board of directors of the Smithsonian Institution's National Museum of the American Indian, as well as Cultural Survival, Inc. She has earned many honors for her work, including the American Anthropological Association's Solon T. Kimball Award for Public and Applied Anthropology, received in 2008 in recognition of her exemplary career in applying anthropology to public life in Alaska and beyond.

Photo: David Sheakley, Sealaska Heritage Institute.

succeed. Because of insufficient government resources, bureaucratic mismanagement, or official corruption, or because people are able to avoid government regulations and tax collectors, state-organized societies also possess a largely undocumented **informal economy**—a network of producing and circulating marketable commodities, labor, and services that for various reasons escapes government control (enumeration, regulation, or other types of public monitoring or auditing). Such enterprises may encompass a range of activities: house cleaning, child care, gardening, repair or construction work, making and selling alcoholic beverages, street peddling, money lending, begging, prostitution, gambling, drug dealing, pick-pocketing, and labor by illegal foreign workers, to mention just a few.

These off-the-books or black market activities have been known for a long time but generally have been

dismissed by economists as of marginal importance. Yet, in many countries of the world, the informal economy is, in fact, more important than the formal economy. In many places, large numbers of under- and unemployed people who have only limited access to the formal economic sector in effect improvise, "getting by" on scant resources. Meanwhile, more affluent members of society may dodge various regulations in order to maximize returns and/or to vent their frustrations at their perceived loss of self-determination in the face of increasing government regulation.

informal economy A network of producing and circulating marketable commodities, labor, and services that for various reasons escapes government control.

Globalscape

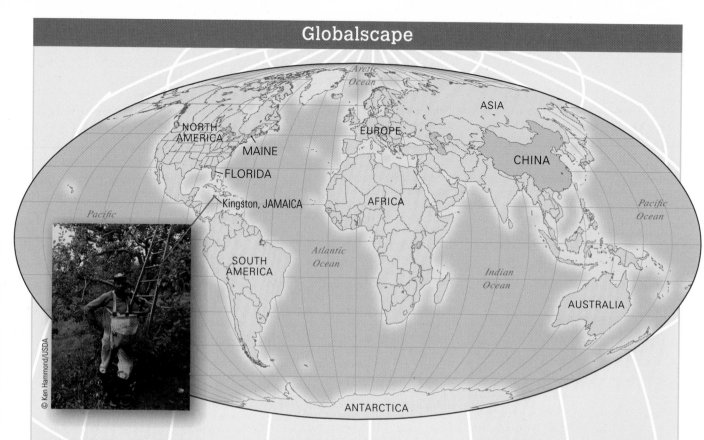

How Much for a Red Delicious?
Each fall, about 600 Jamaicans migrate to Maine for the apple harvest.[a] While plucking the trees with speed and skill, they listen to reggae music that reminds them of home. Calling each other "brother," they go by nicknames like "Rasta." Most are poor peasants from mountain villages in the Caribbean where they grow yams. But their villages do not produce enough to feed their families, so they go elsewhere to earn cash.

Before leaving Jamaica, they must cut their dreadlocks and shave their beards. Screened and contracted by a labor recruiter in Kingston, they receive a temporary foreign farm workers visa from the U.S. embassy and then fly to Miami. Traveling northward by bus, many work on tobacco farms en route to Maine's orchards (and in Florida's

sugar cane fields on the way home). Earning the minimum hourly wage as regulated by the federal H-2A program for "temporary agricultural workers," they work seven days a week, up to 10 hours daily. Orchard owners value these foreigners, for they are twice as productive as local pickers. Moreover, hand-picked apples graded "extra fancy" earn farmers eight times the price of apples destined for processing.

While in the United States, the Jamaicans remain quite isolated, trying to save as much as they can to send more money home. Just before leaving the country, Rasta and his "brothers" buy things like a television, refrigerator, clothes, and shoes to take home as gifts or as goods to be resold for profit. Lately, their cash-earning opportunities in Maine are disappearing due to a tide of cheaper illegal

workers and a diminished demand for U.S.-grown apples due to increasing Chinese competition.

Although rural labor conditions for seasonal migrant workers in the United States have been likened to indentured service (causing some critics to call the federal H-2A program "rent-a-slave"), for Jamaicans like Rasta, it is an opportunity to escape from the dismal poverty on their Caribbean island.

Global Twister   When you take a big bite from your next apple, think of a brother like Rasta. What do you think is "fair value" anyway?

---
[a] See Rathke, L. (1989). To Maine for apples. *Salt Magazine 9* (4), 24–47.

Adult men and women from poor regions in the world may be forced to search for income far away from home. Those who cannot find a paying job within their own country seek cash-earning opportunities abroad. For multiple reasons such as visa requirements, most laborers who cross international borders legally get temporary work permits as "guest workers" but are not immigrants in that foreign country.

North Africa and Southwest Asia are cheap foreign labor reservoirs for the wealthy industrialized countries of western Europe, while Latin America and the Caribbean provide workers for the United States, which draws more migrant laborers than any other country in the world. These workers often send *remittances* (a portion of their earnings) to their families back in their home village or town abroad. A significant percentage of remittances flows through informal systems rather than through banks, so the sum total of these global transfers is unknown, but it is estimated to be well over $100 billion per year.

For a very poor country such as Jamaica, the total annual inflow of remittances is ten times greater than the foreign aid received and makes up almost 15 percent of that Caribbean island's income. Over a quarter of Jamaicans receive remittances from relatives working abroad, and the average value of such cash transfers for a typical Jamaican household is higher than the average per capita gross domestic product (GDP) in that island nation. For a specific example, see this chapter's Globalscape.

Concluding Remarks

Now that globalization is connecting national, regional, and local markets in which natural resources, commodities, and human labor are bought and sold, people everywhere in the world face new economic opportunities and confront new challenges. Not only are natural environments more quickly and radically transformed by means of new powerful technologies, but long-established subsistence practices, economic arrangements, social organizations, and associated ideas, beliefs, and values are also under enormous pressure.

Questions for Reflection

1. Imagine that you have gone to live with a group of nomadic foragers who meet the challenges of survival by hunting, fishing, and gathering, rather than by shopping. How would that way of life challenge your current attitude about social relations, possessions, and the natural environment?

2. Consider the differences between reciprocity and market exchange. What role does each play in your own society?

3. As the potlatch ceremony shows, prestige may be gained by giving away wealth. Does such a prestige-building mechanism exist in your own society? If so, how does it work?

4. When shopping for groceries in a supermarket, think of this chapter's Globalscape and try to imagine the great chain of human hands involved in getting something as simple as a nice red apple from a distant orchard to your own mouth. How many people do you think handled the fruit to get it to you?

5. Economic relations in traditional cultures are usually wrapped up in social, political, and even spiritual issues. Can you think of any examples in your own society in which the economic sphere is inextricably intertwined with other structures in the cultural system?

Suggested Readings

Blumberg, R. L. (1991). *Gender, family, and the economy: The triple overlap.* Newbury Park, CA: Sage.

The author presents a look at the interrelationship of gender, domestic life, and the economy.

Dalton, G. (1971). *Traditional tribal and peasant economies: An introductory survey of economic anthropology.* Reading, MA: Addison-Wesley.

This is just what the title says it is, by a major specialist in economic anthropology.

Mauss, M. (2000). *The gift: The form and reason for exchange in archaic societies* (translation by W. D. Halls and foreword by M. Douglas). New York: Norton.

Originally published as *Essai sur le don* in the French journal *Année Sociologique* (1923–1924), this short book remains the classic on reciprocity and traditional gift exchange.

Plattner, S. (Ed.). (1989). *Economic anthropology.* Stanford, CA: Stanford University Press.

This is a collection of essays from twelve scholars in the field concerning a variety of issues. These include economic behavior in various cultures, gender roles and common property resources, informal economics in industrial societies, and mass marketing in urban areas.

Wilk, R. R. (1996). *Economics and cultures: An introduction to economic anthropology.* Boulder, CO: Westview.

This lively primer traces the history of the dialogue between anthropology and economics and identifies the subdiscipline's basic practical and theoretical problems.

Challenge Issue   All around the world humans face the challenge of managing sexual relations and establishing social alliances essential to the survival of individuals and their offspring. Adjusting to particular natural environments and facing distinct economic and political challenges, each group establishes its own specific social arrangements in terms of childrearing tasks, gender relations, household and family structures, and residence patterns. Because marriage and family, in various forms, play a fundamental role in determining these arrangements, wedding rituals are especially important cultural events. Whether private or public, sacred or secular, weddings reveal, confirm, and underscore important ideas and values of culture. Symbolically rich, they usually feature particular speech rituals, along with prescribed apparel, postures and gestures, food and drink, songs and dances—all passed down (with occasional alterations) through many generations. Here we see a traditional Japanese wedding at Tokyo's sacred Meiji shrine. Conforming to the ancient tradition of Shinto ("the way of the spirits"), the bride wears a white silk kimono as a profession of purity. Her white hood symbolically hides "horns of jealousy" from her new mother-in-law, who will have authority over her in the household she is joining.

CHAPTER 20

Sex, Marriage, and Family

Chapter Preview

What Is Marriage?

A nonethnocentric definition of marriage is a culturally sanctioned union between two or more people that establishes certain rights and obligations between the people, between them and their children, and between them and their in-laws. Although most marriages around the world involve unions between one woman and one man, numerous other arrangements exist. For example, many cultures not only permit but encourage marriage of one man to multiple wives. The specific form marriage takes is related to who has rights and obligations to offspring that may result from the marital union, as well as how property is distributed. In contrast to mating—the sexual bonding that all animal species do—marriage is a cultural institution, backed by economic, social, legal, and ideological forces.

What Is the Difference Between Family and Household?

Households are task-oriented residential units within which economic production, consumption, inheritance, childrearing, and shelter are organized and accomplished. In the vast majority of human societies, a household consists of a family or part of a family or their core members, even though some household members may not be relatives of the family around which it is built. In some societies, families may be less important to people than the households in which they live.

What Is the Family?

Although the idea of family means different things to different people, in anthropological terms it is a group of two or more people related by blood, marriage, or adoption. The family may take many forms, ranging from a single parent with one or more children, to a married couple or polygamous spouses with offspring, to several generations of parents and their children. The particular form family takes within a society is related to distinct social, historical, and ecological circumstances.

In contrast to individuals raised in traditional Shinto Japanese families featured in this chapter's opening photo, young people in the Trobriand Islands of the southern Pacific are traditionally unconstrained in premarital sexual explorations. By age 7 or 8, they begin playing erotic games and imitating adult seductive attitudes. Within another four or five years they start pursuing sexual partners in earnest—experimenting erotically with a variety of individuals.

Since attracting sexual partners is an important matter among young Trobrianders, they spend a great deal of time making themselves look attractive and seductive. Their daily conversations are loaded with sexual hints, and magical spells as well as small gifts are employed to entice a prospective sex partner to the beach at night or to the house in which boys sleep apart from their parents. Because girls, too, sleep apart from their parents, youths and adolescents have considerable freedom in arranging their erotic escapades. Boys and girls play this game as equals, with neither having an advantage over the other.

By the time Trobrianders are in their mid-teens, meetings between lovers may take up most of the night, and affairs are apt to last for several months. Ultimately, a young islander begins to meet the same partner again and again, rejecting the advances of others. When the couple is ready, they appear together one morning outside the young man's house as a way of announcing their intention to be married.

Until the latter part of the 20th century, the Trobriand attitude toward adolescent sexuality was in marked contrast to that of most Western cultures in Europe and North America where individuals were not supposed to have sexual relations before or outside of marriage. Since then, practices in much of Europe and North America have converged toward those of the Trobrianders, even though the traditional ideal of premarital abstinence has not been abandoned entirely.

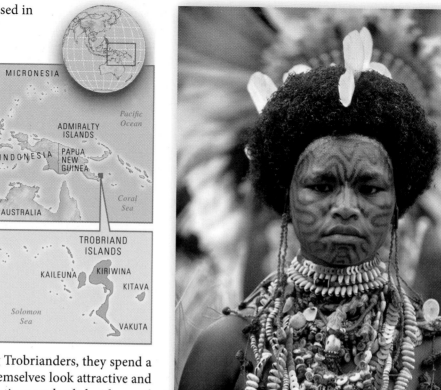

To attract lovers, young Trobriand women and men must look as attractive and seductive as possible. This woman's beauty has been enhanced by face painting and adornments given by her father.

Control of Sexual Relations

In the absence of effective birth control, the usual outcome of sexual activity between fertile individuals of the opposite sex is that, sooner or later, the woman becomes pregnant. Given the intricate array of social responsibilities involved in rearing the children that are born of sexual relations—and the potential for violent conflict resulting from unregulated sexual competition—it is not surprising that all societies have cultural rules that seek to regulate those relations.

However, the rules concerning when, how, and between whom sex takes place vary across cultures. For instance, in some societies, sexual intercourse during pregnancy is taboo, while in others it is looked upon positively as something that promotes the growth of the fetus. And while some cultures sharply condemn same-sex acts or relations, many others are indifferent and do not even have a special term to distinguish homosexuality as significant in its own right. In several cultures same-sex acts are not only accepted but even prescribed. Such is the case in some Papua societies in New Guinea, for example, where certain prescribed male-to-male sexual acts are part of initiation rituals required of all

Visual Counterpoint

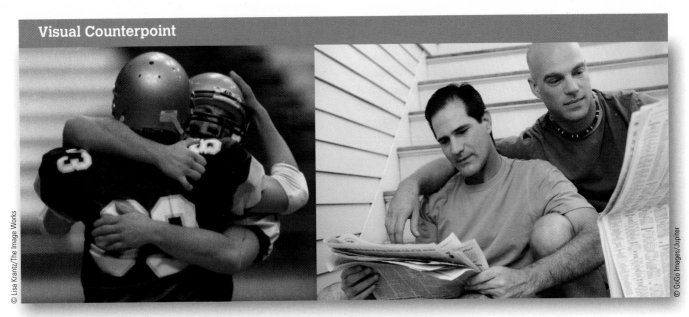

Although homosexuality is a widespread phenomenon, in some societies homosexuals confront repression or ridicule. In parts of the United States, for example, public displays of same-sex affection between men in particular are often looked upon as distasteful or even disgusting. One nationwide exception is the football field, where an extreme measure of rough-and-tumble masculine behavior makes it possible for players to pat each other on the behind, exchange celebratory hugs, and even leap into each other's arms without bringing their sexual orientation into question.

boys to become respected adult men.[1] In those cultures, people traditionally see the transmission of semen from older to younger boys, through oral sex, as vital for building up the strength needed to protect against the supposedly debilitating effects of adult heterosexual intercourse.[2]

Despite longstanding culture-based opposition to homosexuality in many areas of the world, this sexual orientation exists within the wider range of human sexual relations, emotional attractions, and social identities, and it is far from uncommon. Homosexuality is found in diverse contexts—from lifelong loving relationships to casual sexual encounters, and from being fully open to being utterly private and secretive. During the past few decades, public denigration and condemnation of homosexuality have diminished in numerous countries, and same-sex relationships have become a publicly accepted part of the cosmopolitan lifestyle in metropolitan centers such as Amsterdam, Paris, Rio de Janeiro, and San Francisco. As recently as 2009, India decriminalized

homosexuality.[3] Clearly, the social rules and cultural meanings of all sexual behavior are subject to great variability not only across cultures but also across time.

Marriage and the Regulation of Sexual Relations

In much of Europe and North America, the traditional ideal was (and in some communities still is) that all sexual activity outside of marriage was taboo. Individuals were expected to establish a family through marriage, by which one gains an exclusive right of sexual access to another person. And while forbidding or disapproving of *premarital* sexual relations, these societies often criminalized *extramarital* affairs as adultery. According to strict Judeo-Christian law, as prescribed in the Book of Leviticus (20:10), adultery was punishable by death: "And the man that committeth adultery with another man's wife . . . , the adulterer and the adulteress shall surely be put to death." Deuteronomy (22:24) adds: "Then ye shall bring them

---

[1] Kirkpatrick, R. C. (2000). The evolution of human homosexual behavior. *Current Anthropology 41,* 385.

[2] Herdt, G. H. (1993). Semen transactions in Sambia culture. In D. N. Suggs & A. W. Mirade (Eds.), *Culture and human sexuality* (pp. 298–327). Pacific Grove, CA: Brooks/Cole.

[3] Timmons, H., & Kumar, H. (2009, July 3). Indian court overturns gay sex ban. *New York Times.*

both out unto the gate of that city, and ye shall stone them with stones that they die."

Many centuries later, among Christian fundamentalist colonists in 17th- and 18th-century New England, adultery by women remained a serious crime. While it did not lead to stoning, women so accused were shunned by the community and could even be imprisoned. As recounted in *The Scarlet Letter* by Nathaniel Hawthorne, the adulteress was forced to have the letter "A" stitched on her dress, publicly signifying her transgression.

Such restrictions exist today in many traditional Muslim societies in northern Africa and western Asia, where age-old Shariah law continues or has been reinstated to regulate social behavior in strict accordance with religious standards of morality. Under this law, women found guilty of having sexual relations outside marriage can be sentenced to death by stoning. In northern Nigeria, for example, a Muslim woman who committed adultery and had a child outside marriage was sentenced to death in 2002. Her sentence was ultimately overturned by an Islamic appeals court, but it nonetheless drove home the rule of Shariah law. Turning legal transgressions into a public spectacle, authorities reinforce public awareness of the rules of social conduct.

A positive side effect of such restrictive rules of sexual behavior is that they may limit the spread of sexually transmitted diseases. For instance, the global epidemic of HIV/AIDS has had dramatically less impact in North Africa's Muslim countries than in the non-Muslim states of sub-Saharan Africa, where the average infection rate among adults is almost 17 times higher. The statistics vividly illustrate the impact of religious and cultural prohibitions: The reported percentage of adults infected by the virus is 0.1 percent in Algeria, Morocco, and Tunisia, in contrast to 18.8 percent in South Africa, 24.1 percent in Botswana, and 33.8 percent in Swaziland.[4] Communities devastated by this sexually transmitted disease not only confront a serious public health problem but also face a cultural challenge in that they must create a new public awareness and adjust attitudes about sexual pleasure so that they do not endanger their collective well-being.

Yet most cultures in the world do not sharply regulate an individual's personal habits, including sexual practices.

Indeed, a majority of all cultures are considered sexually permissive or semi-permissive (the former having few or no restrictions on sexual experimentation before marriage, the latter allowing some experimentation but less openly). A minority of known societies—about 15 percent—have rules requiring that sexual involvement take place only within marriage.

This brings us to an anthropological definition of **marriage**—a culturally sanctioned union between two or more people that establishes certain rights and obligations between the people, between them and their children, and between them and their in-laws. Such marriage rights and obligations most often include, but are not limited to, sex, labor, property, childrearing, exchange, and status. Thus defined, marriage is universal. Notably, our definition of marriage refers to "people" rather than "a man and a woman" because in some countries same-sex marriages are socially acceptable and allowed by law, even though opposite-sex marriages are far more common. We will return to this point later in the chapter.

In many cultures, marriage is considered the central and most important social institution. In such cultures, people will spend considerable time and energy on maintaining this institution. They may do so in various ways, including highlighting the ritual moment when the wedding takes place, festively memorializing the event at designated times such as anniversaries, and making it difficult to divorce.

In some societies, however, marriage is a relatively marginal institution and is not considered central to the establishing and maintenance of family life and society. For instance, marriage has lost much of its traditional significance in the Scandinavian societies of Iceland, Norway, Sweden, and Denmark, in part due to changes in the political economy, more balanced gender relations, and shared public benefits of these capitalist welfare states.

Sexual and Marriage Practices among the Nayar

The relative unimportance of marriage as the major defining institution for establishing a family is not unique to wealthy European nations. For instance, historically, marriage has been of marginal significance in the family life of the Nayar people of Kerala in southwestern India. A landowning warrior caste, their estates are traditionally held by corporations made up of kinsmen related in the female line. These blood relatives live together in a large household, with the eldest male serving as manager.

Like Trobriand Islanders and contemporary Scandinavians noted above, the Nayar are a sexually permissive culture.[5] A classic anthropological study describes three

---

[4] AIDS Epidemic Update. (2007), p. 7. Geneva: Joint United Nations Program on HIV/AIDS (USAID) and World Health Organization. www.unaids.org; see also Gray, P. B. (2004, May). HIV and Islam: Is HIV prevalence lower among Muslims? *Social Science & Medicine* 58 (9), 1751–1756.

marriage A culturally sanctioned union between two or more people that establishes certain rights and obligations between the people, between them and their children, and between them and their in-laws. Such marriage rights and obligations most often include, but are not limited to, sex, labor, property, childrearing, exchange, and status.

---

[5] Our interpretation of the Nayar follows Goodenough, W. H. (1970). *Description and comparison in cultural anthropology* (pp. 6–11). Chicago: Aldine.

transactions related to customary Nayar sexual and marriage practices.[6] (Note that many of the practices described here have changed since the mid-20th century.) The first, taking place shortly before a girl experiences her first menstruation, involves a ceremony that joins her with a "ritual husband" in a temporary union. This union, which does not necessarily involve sexual

relations, lasts for a few days and then breaks up. (Neither individual has any further obligation, although later, when the girl becomes a woman, she and her children typically participate in ritual mourning for the man when he dies.) This temporary union establishes the girl as an adult ready for motherhood and eligible for sexual activity with men approved by her household.

The second transaction takes place when a young Nayar woman enters into a continuing sexual liaison with a man approved by her family. This is a formal relationship that requires the man to present her with gifts three times each year until the relationship is terminated. In return, the man can spend nights with her. In spite of continuing sexual privileges, however, this "visiting husband" has no obligation to support his sex partner economically, nor is her home regarded as his home. In fact, she may have such an arrangement with more than one man at the same time. Regardless of the number of men with whom she is involved, this second transaction, the Nayar version of marriage, clearly specifies who has sexual rights to whom and includes rules that deter conflicts between the men.

If a Nayar woman becomes pregnant, one of the men with whom she has a relationship (who may or may not be the biological father) must formally acknowledge paternity. This third transaction, marked by the man giving gifts to the woman and the midwife, establishes the child's birth rights. In this sense, it is the counterpart of the registration of birth in Western societies, which clearly establishes motherhood and fatherhood. However, once a man has formally acknowledged fatherhood by gift giving, he may continue to take interest in the child, but he has no further obligations. Support and education for the child are the responsibility of the mother and her brothers with whom she and her offspring live.

Indeed, unlike most other cultural groups in the world, the traditional Nayar household includes only the mother,

her children, and her other blood relatives, technically known as **consanguineal kin.** It does not include any of the "husbands" or other people related through marriage—technically known as **affinal kin.** In other words, sisters and their offspring all live together with their brothers and their mother and her brothers. Historically, this arrangement addressed the need for security in a cultural group where warfare was common.

Among the Nayar, sexual relations are forbidden between consanguineal relatives and thus are permitted only with individuals who live in other households. This brings us to another human universal: the incest taboo.

The Incest Taboo

Just as marriage in its various forms is found in all cultures, so is the **incest taboo**—the prohibition of sexual contact between certain close relatives. But, what is defined as "close" is not the same in all cultures. Moreover, such definitions may be subject to change over time. While the scope and details of the taboo vary across cultures and time, almost all societies past and present strongly forbid sexual relations at least between parents and children and nearly always between siblings. In some societies the taboo extends to other close relatives, such as cousins, and even some relatives linked through marriage.

Anthropologists have long been fascinated by the incest taboo and have proposed many explanations for its cross-cultural existence and variation. The simplest explanation, based on the idea of "human nature," is that our species has an "instinctive" repulsion for incest. It has been documented that human beings raised together have less sexual attraction for one another. However, by itself this "familiarity breeds contempt" argument may simply substitute the result for the cause. The incest taboo ensures that children and their parents, who are constantly in close contact, avoid regarding one another as sexual objects. Besides this, if an instinctive horror of incest exists, how do we account for the far from rare violations of the incest taboo? (In the United States, for instance, an estimated 10 to 14 percent of children under 18 years of age have been involved in incestuous relations.[7])

---

[7] Whelehan, P. (1985). Review of incest, a biosocial view. *American Anthropologist 87*, 678; see also U.S. Department of Health and Human Services, Administration on Children, Youth, and Families. (2005). *Child maltreatment 2003*. Washington, DC: U.S. Government Printing Office.

---

consanguineal kin Biologically related relatives, commonly referred to as blood relatives.

affinal kin People related through marriage.

incest taboo The prohibition of sexual relations between specified individuals, usually parent and child and sibling relations at a minimum.

---

[6] Gough, K. (1959). The Nayars and the definition of marriage. *Journal of the Royal Anthropological Institute of Great Britain and Ireland 89*, 23–34.

Charles Darwin (founder of the theory of natural selection) and his first-cousin wife, Emma Wedgewood. Before proposing, Charles made a "pros and cons" list about marrying Emma. It said nothing about their close familial relationship. Rather, his concerns centered on the question of whether supporting a wife and children would compromise his scientific career. Ultimately, the idea of a "constant companion (& friend in old age) who will feel interested in one" won out. During their three-month engagement he wrote to her: "I think you will humanize me, & soon teach me there is greater happiness, than building theories, & accumulating facts in silence & solitude. . . ." Bonds of real affection linked the couple throughout their long lives.

Moreover, so-called instinctive repulsion does not explain institutionalized incest, such as a requirement that the divine ruler of the Inca empire in ancient Peru be married to his own (half) sister. Sharing the same father, both siblings belonged to the political dynasty that derived its sacred right to rule the empire from Inti, its ancestral Sun God. And by virtue of this royal lineage's godly origin, their children could claim the same sacred political status as their human-divine father and mother. Ancient emperors in Egypt also practiced such religiously prescribed incest based on a similar claim to godly status.

Early students of genetics argued that the incest taboo prevents the harmful effects of inbreeding. While this is so, it is also true that, as with domestic animals, inbreeding can increase desired characteristics as well as detrimental ones. Furthermore, undesirable effects will show up sooner than without inbreeding, so whatever genes are responsible for them are quickly eliminated from the population. That said, a preference for a genetically different mate does tend to maintain a higher level of genetic diversity within a population, and in evolution this variation works to a species' advantage. Without genetic diversity a species cannot adapt biologically to environmental change.

The inbreeding or biological-avoidance theory of incest can be challenged on several fronts. For instance, detailed census records made in Roman Egypt about 2,000 years ago show that brother–sister marriages were not uncommon in farming villages, and we have no evidence for linking this cultural practice to any biological imperatives.[8] To the contrary, some anthropologists have argued that the incest taboo exists as a cultural means to preserve the stability and integrity of the family, which is essential to maintaining social order. Sexual relations between members other than the husband and wife would introduce competition, destroying the harmony of a social unit fundamental to societal order. A truly convincing explanation of the incest taboo has yet to be advanced.[9]

Endogamy and Exogamy

Whatever its cause, the utility of the incest taboo can be seen by examining its effects on social structure. Closely related to prohibitions against incest are cultural rules against **endogamy** (from Greek *endon*, "within," and *gamos*, "marriage"), or marriage within a particular group of individuals (cousins and in-laws, for example). If the group is defined as one's immediate family alone, then societies generally prohibit or at least discourage endogamy, thereby promoting **exogamy** (*exo* is Greek for "outside"), or marriage outside the group. Yet, a society that practices exogamy at one level may practice endogamy at another. Among the Trobriand Islanders, for example, each

---

[8] Leavitt, G. C. (1990). Sociobiological explanations of incest avoidance: A critical review of evidential claims. *American Anthropologist 92*, 982.

[9] In a sample of 129 societies, anthropologist Nancy Thornhill (1993) found that only fifty-seven had specific rules against parent–child or sibling incest. Twice that number (114) had explicit rules to control activity with cousins, in-laws, or both (quoted in Haviland, W. A., & Gordon, R. J. (Eds.), *Talking about people* (p. 127). Mountain View, CA: Mayfield). Absence of specific incest rules, however, does not mean sexual relations with close relatives were either common or condoned.

---

endogamy Marriage within a particular group or category of individuals.

exogamy Marriage outside the group.

Biocultural Connection

Marriage Prohibitions in the United States   *by Martin Ottenheimer*

In the United States, every state has laws prohibiting the marriage of some relatives. Every state forbids parent–child and sibling marriages, but there is considerable variation in prohibitions concerning more distant relatives. For example, although the majority of states ban marriage between first cousins, nineteen states allow it and others permit it under certain conditions. Notably, the United States is the only country in the Western world that has prohibitions against first-cousin marriage.

Many people in the United States believe that laws forbidding marriage between family members exist because parents who are too close biologically run the risk of producing children with mental and physical defects. Convinced that first cousins fall within this "too close" category, they believe laws against first-cousin marriage were established to protect families from the effects of harmful genes.

There are two major problems with this belief: First, cousin prohibitions were enacted in the United States long before the discovery of the genetic mechanisms of disease. Second, genetic research has shown that offspring of

first-cousin couples do not have any significantly greater risk of negative results than offspring of very distantly related parents.

Why, then, do some North Americans maintain this belief? To answer this question, it helps to know that laws against first-cousin marriage first appeared in the United States right after the mid-1800s when evolutionary models of human behavior became fashionable. In particular, a pre-Darwinian model that explained social evolution as dependent upon biological factors gained popularity. It supposed that "progress from savagery to civilization" was possible when humans ceased inbreeding. Cousin marriage was thought to be characteristic of savagery, the lowest form of human social life, and it was believed to inhibit the intellectual and social development of humans. It became associated with "primitive" behavior and dreaded as a threat to a civilized America.

Thus, a powerful myth emerged in American popular culture, which has since become embedded in law. That myth is held and defended to this day, sometimes with great emotion despite being based on a discredited social

evolutionary theory and contradicted by the results of modern genetic research.

Recently, a group of geneticists published the result of a study of consanguineous unions, estimating that there is "about a 1.7–2.8% increased risk for congenital defects above the population background risk."[a] Not only is this a high estimate, it is also well within the bounds of the margin of statistical error. But even so, it is a lower risk than that associated with offspring from women over the age of 40—who are not forbidden by the government to marry or bear children.

BIOCULTURAL QUESTION

What do you think is the underlying cultural logic that makes some societies traditionally forbid first cousins from marrying each other, whereas others, equally unfamiliar with genetics, accept or even prefer such marriages?

[a]Bennett, R. L., et al. (2002, April). Genetic counseling and screening of consanguineous couples and their offspring: Recommendations of the National Society of Genetic Counselors. *Journal of Genetic Counseling 11* (2), 97–119.

---

individual has to marry outside of his or her own clan and lineage (exogamy). However, since eligible sex partners are to be found within one's own community, village endogamy is commonly practiced.

Interestingly, societies vary widely concerning which relatives are or are not covered by rules of exogamy. For example, first cousins are prohibited from marrying each other in many countries where the Roman Catholic Church has long been a dominant institution. In the United States, laws against such marriages exist in thirty-one states, and there is a general assumption nationwide that these laws are rooted in genetics. Yet, in numerous other societies around the world, first cousins are preferred spouses,[10] and a recent report in the *Journal of Genetic Counseling* concludes that "cousins can have children together without running much greater risk than a 'normal' couple of their children having genetic

abnormalities."[11] (See a discussion of U.S. marriage prohibitions in the Biocultural Connection.)

Early anthropologists suggested that our ancestors discovered the advantage of intermarriage as a means of creating bonds of friendship. French anthropologist Claude Lévi-Strauss elaborated on this idea. He saw exogamy as a form of intergroup social exchange in which "wife-giving" and "wife-taking" (or, as happens in communities with female-headed households, husband-giving and husband-taking) created social networks and alliances between distinct communities. By widening the human network, a larger number of people could pool natural resources and cultural information, including technology and other useful knowledge. (For more on this, see Anthropologist of Note.)

Building on the theory advanced by Lévi-Strauss, other anthropologists have proposed that exogamy is an

---

[10] Ottenheimer, M. (1996). *Forbidden relatives: The American myth of cousin marriage* (pp. 116–133). Champaign: University of Illinois Press.

[11] Grossman, J. (2002). Should the law be kinder to kissin' cousins? A genetic report should cause a rethinking of incest laws. *Find Law.* (accessed October 16, 2009)

Claude Lévi-Strauss (1908–2009)

Claude Lévi-Strauss lived to be 100. When he died, he was the most celebrated anthropologist in the world. Born in Belgium, where his father briefly worked as a portrait painter, he grew up in Paris. As a boy during World War I, Claude lived with his grandfather, a rabbi of Versailles.

He studied law and philosophy at the Sorbonne, married a young anthropologist named Dina Dreyfus, and became a philosophy teacher. In 1935 the couple ventured across the ocean to Brazil's University of São Paulo, where his wife taught anthropology and he sociology. Influenced by 18th-century romantic philosopher Rousseau and fascinated by historical accounts of Brazilian Indians, he preferred ethnographic research and lectured on tribal social organizations.

In 1937, he and his wife organized an expedition into the Amazon forest, visiting Bororo and other tribal villages and collecting artifacts for museums. In 1938, they made another journey and researched recently contacted Nambikwara Indians. Back in Paris together

Renowned French anthropologist Claude Lévi-Strauss at age 100 in his home library.

Bibliothèque nationale de France. © Marc Rochette

in 1939, their marriage dissolved. That same year, the Second World War erupted, and the French army mobilized its soldiers, including Lévi-Strauss.

A year after Nazi Germany conquered France in 1940, Lévi-Strauss escaped to New York City, where he became an anthropology professor at the New School for Social Research. Teaching courses on South American Indians during the war years, he befriended other European exiles, including the linguist Roman Jakobson who pioneered the structural analysis of language.

After the war, Lévi-Strauss became French cultural consul in the United States, based in New York. Maintaining ties with the academic community, including anthropologist Margaret Mead, he completed his two-part doctoral thesis: *The Elementary Structures of Kinship* and *The Family and Social Life of the Nambikwara Indians*. Theoretically influenced by Jakobson's structural linguistics, his thesis analyzed the logical structures underlying the social relations of kin-ordered societies.

Building on Marcel Mauss's 1925 study of gift exchange as a means to build or maintain a social relationship, he applied the concept of reciprocity to kinship, arguing that marriage is based on the exchange relationship between kin-groups of "wife-givers" and "wife-takers."

Returning to France in late 1947, he became associate director of the ethnographic museum in Paris and successfully defended his thesis at the Sorbonne. His structural analysis was recognized as a pioneering study in kinship and marriage.

In 1949 Lévi-Strauss joined an international body of experts invited by UNESCO to discuss and define the "race" concept, a disputed term associated with discrimination and genocide. Three years later, he authored *Race and History,* a book that became instrumental in UNESCO's worldwide campaign against racism and ethnocentrism. By then, he had become an anthropology professor at the École Pratique des Hautes Études in Paris. Continuing his prolific writing, he published *Tristes Tropiques* (1955). This memoir about his ethnographic adventures among Amazonian Indians won him international fame. His next book, *Structural Anthropology* (1958), also became a classic. It presented his theoretical perspective that the human mind produces logical structures, classifying reality in terms of binary oppositions (such as light–dark, good–evil, nature–culture, and male–female) and that all humans share a mental demand for order expressed in a drive toward classification.

In 1959 Lévi-Strauss was appointed to a chair in social anthropology at the Collège de France and founded his own institute there. Specializing in the comparative study of religion, he undertook a massive comparative study and structural analysis of myths, resulting in a series of instantaneously classic books. In 1973, he was elected to the centuries-old Académie Française, a prestigious institution with just forty members known as "immortals." Countless other honors from around the world followed. Now, survived by his wife Monique and two sons, he lies in a small rural cemetery in Burgundy, near his old mansion where he liked to reflect on the human condition.

important means of creating and maintaining political alliances and promoting trade between groups, thereby ensuring mutual protection and access to needed goods and resources not otherwise available. Forging wider kinship networks, exogamy also functions to integrate distinctive groups and thus potentially reduces violent conflict.

Distinction Between Marriage and Mating

Having defined marriage, in part, in terms of sexual access, we must make clear the distinction between marriage and mating. All animals, including humans, mate for

breeding—some for life and some not, some with a single individual and some with several or many. Among humans, mates are secured and held solely through personal effort and mutual consent.

In contrast to mating, which occurs when individuals join for purposes of sexual relations, marriage is a socially binding and culturally recognized relationship. Only marriage is backed by social, political, and ideological factors that regulate sexual relations as well as reproductive rights and obligations. Even among the Nayar, discussed above, where marriage seems to involve little other than a sexual relationship, a woman's husband is legally obligated to provide her with gifts at specified intervals. Nor may a

Nayar woman legally have sex with a man to whom she is not married.

Thus while mating is biological, marriage is cultural. This is evident when we consider the various forms of marriage around the world.

Forms of Marriage

Within societies, and all the more so across cultures, we see contrasts in the constructs and contracts of marriage. Indeed, as is evident in the definition of marriage given above, this institution comes in various forms—and these forms are distinct in terms of the number and gender of spouses involved.

Monogamy

Monogamy—marriage in which both partners have just one spouse—is the most common form of marriage worldwide. In North America and most of Europe, it is the only legally recognized form of marriage. In these places, not only are other forms prohibited, but systems of inheritance, whereby property and wealth are transferred from one generation to the next, are based on the institution of monogamous marriage. In some parts of the world (including Europe and North America), where divorce rates are high and people who have been divorced remarry, an increasingly common form of marriage is **serial monogamy,** whereby an individual marries a series of partners in succession.

Polygamy

Monogamy is the most common marriage form worldwide, but it is not the most culturally preferred. That distinction goes to **polygamy** (one individual having multiple spouses)—specifically to **polygyny,** in which a man is married to more than one woman (*gyne* is Greek for "woman" and "wife"). Favored in about 80 to 85 percent of the world's cultures, polygyny is commonly practiced in parts of Asia and much of sub-Saharan Africa.[12]

Although polygyny is the favored marriage form in these places, monogamy exceeds it, and the reason for this is economic rather than moral. In many polygynous societies, where a groom is usually expected to compensate a bride's family in cash or kind, a man must be

fairly wealthy to be able to afford more than one wife. Recent multiple surveys of twenty-five sub-Saharan African countries where polygyny is common show that it declined by about half between the 1970s and 2001. This dramatic decline has many reasons, one of which is related to families making an economic transition from traditional farming and herding to wage labor in cities. Nonetheless, polygyny remains highly significant with an overall average of 25 percent of married women in such unions.[13]

Polygyny is particularly common in traditional food-producing societies that support themselves by herding grazing animals or growing crops and where women do the bulk of cultivation. Under these conditions, women are valued both as workers and as child bearers. Because the labor of wives in polygynous households generates wealth and little support is required from husbands, the wives have a strong bargaining position within the household. Often, they have considerable freedom of movement and some economic independence from the sale of crafts or crops. Wealth-generating polygyny is found in its fullest elaboration in parts of sub-Saharan Africa and southwestern Asia, though it is known elsewhere as well.[14]

In societies practicing wealth-generating polygyny, most men and women do enter into polygynous marriages, although some are able to do so earlier in life than others. This is made possible by a female-biased sex ratio and/or a mean age at marriage for females that is significantly below that for males. In fact, this marriage pattern is frequently found in societies where violence, including war, is common and where many young males lose their lives in fighting. Their high combat mortality results in a population where women outnumber men.

By contrast, in societies where men are more heavily involved in productive work, generally only a small minority of marriages are polygynous. Under these circumstances,

---

[13] Ibid.

[14] White, D. R. (1988). Rethinking polygyny: Co-wives, codes, and cultural systems. *Current Anthropology 29,* 529–572.

---

monogamy Marriage in which both partners have just one spouse.

serial monogamy A marriage form in which a man or a woman marries or lives with a series of partners in succession.

polygamy One individual having multiple spouses at the same time; from the Greek words *poly* ("many") and *gamos* ("marriage").

polygyny Marriage of a man to two or more women at the same time; a form of polygamy.

---

[12] Lloyd, C. B. (Ed.). (2005). *Growing up global: The changing transitions to adulthood in developing countries* (pp. 450–453). Washington, DC: National Academies Press, Committee on Population, National Research Council, and Institute of Medicine of the National Academies.

Visual Counterpoint

A Christian polygamist with his three wives and children in front of their dormitory-style home in Utah, and a Baranarana man of Upper Guinea with his two wives and children.

women are more dependent on men for support, so they are valued as child bearers more than for the work they do. This is commonly the case in pastoral nomadic societies where men are the primary owners and tenders of livestock. This makes women especially vulnerable if they prove incapable of bearing children, which is one reason a man may seek another wife.

Another reason for a man to take on secondary wives is to demonstrate his high position in society. But where men do most of the productive work, they must work extremely hard to support more than one wife, and few actually do so. Usually, it is the exceptional hunter or male shaman ("medicine man") in a food-foraging society or a particularly wealthy man in a horticultural, agricultural, or pastoral society who is most apt to practice polygyny. When he does, it is usually of the *sororal* type, with the co-wives being sisters. Having lived their lives together before marriage, the sisters continue to do so with their husband, instead of occupying separate dwellings of their own.

Polygyny also occurs in a few places in Europe. In 1972, for example, English laws concerning marriage changed to accommodate immigrants who traditionally practiced polygyny. Since that time polygamous marriages have been legal in England for some specific religious minorities, including Muslims and Sephardic Jews. According to one family law specialist, the real impetus behind this law change was a growing concern that "destitute immigrant wives, abandoned by their husbands, [were] overburdening the welfare state."[15]

Even in the United States where it is illegal, somewhere between 20,000 and 60,000 people in the Rocky Mountain states live in households made up of a man with two or more wives.[16] Most consider themselves Mormons, even though the official Mormon Church does not approve of the practice. A growing minority, however, call themselves "Christian polygamists," citing the Bible as justification.[17] Despite its illegality and concerns that the practice can jeopardize the rights and well-being of young women, regional law enforcement officials have adopted a "live and let live" attitude toward religious-based polygyny in their region. Women involved in the practice are sometimes outspoken in defending it. One woman—a lawyer and one

[15] Cretney, S. (2003). *Family law in the twentieth century: A history* (pp. 72–73). New York: Oxford University Press.

[16] Egan, T. (1999, February 28). The persistence of polygamy. *New York Times Magazine,* 52.

[17] Wolfson, H. (2000, January 22). Polygamists make the Christian connection. *Burlington Free Press,* 2c.

of nine co-wives—expresses her attitude toward polygyny as follows:

> I see it as the ideal way for a woman to have a career and children. In our family, the women can help each other care for the children. Women in monogamous relationships don't have that luxury. As I see it, if this lifestyle didn't already exist, it would have to be invented to accommodate career women.[18]

In some societies, if a man dies, leaving behind a wife and children, it is customary that one of his brothers marries the widowed sister-in-law—but this obligation does not preclude the brother having another wife then or in the future. This custom, called the *levirate* (from the Latin *levir*, which means "husband's brother"), not only provides security for the widow (and her children) but also is a way for the husband's family to maintain the established relationship with her family and their rights over her sexuality and her future children: It acts to preserve kin relationships between families previously established. The levirate also ensures that the deceased man's lineage will be perpetuated, as all children born to his remarried widow are formally acknowledged as *his* legitimate offspring, even though his brother is their biological father.

A related marriage tradition is the *sororate* (Latin *soror* means "sister"), in which a man has the right to marry a (usually younger) sister of his deceased wife. In some societies, the sororate also applies to a man who has married a woman who is unable to bear children. This custom entitles a man to a replacement wife from his in-laws. In societies that have the levirate and sororate—customary in many traditional foraging, farming, and herding cultures—the in-law relationship between the two families is maintained even after the spouse's death and secures an established alliance between two groups.

Although monogamy and polygyny are the most common forms of marriage in the world today, other forms do occur. **Polyandry,** the marriage of one woman to two or more men simultaneously, is known in only a few societies, perhaps in part because a woman's life expectancy is usually longer than a man's, and female infant mortality is somewhat lower, so a surplus of women in a society is likely.

Fewer than a dozen societies are known to have favored this form of marriage, but they involve people as widely separated as eastern Inuit (Eskimos) in Canada, Marquesan Islanders of Polynesia, and Tibetans in Central Asia. In Tibet, where inheritance is in the male line and arable land is limited, the marriage of brothers to a single woman (*fraternal polyandry*) keeps the land together by preventing it from being repeatedly subdivided among sons from one generation to the next. Unlike monogamy, it also holds down population growth, thereby avoiding increased pressures on resources. Finally, among Tibetans who practice a mixed economy of farming, herding, and trading in the Trans Himalayas, fraternal polyandry provides the household with an adequate pool of male labor for all three subsistence activities.[19]

Other Forms of Marriage

There are several other marriage forms, each with its own particular cultural expressions and reasons for being. For instance, the social practice of **group marriage** occurs in a few societies. Also known as *co-marriage,* this is a rare arrangement in which several men and women have sexual access to one another. Until a few decades ago, Iñupiat Eskimos in northern Alaska, for instance, engaged in "spouse exchange" (*nuliaqatigiit*) between non-kin, with two conjugal husband–wife couples being united by shared sexual access. Highly institutionalized arrangements, these intimate relationships implied ties of mutual aid and support across territorial boundaries and were expected to last throughout the lifetime of the participants.[20] The ties between the couples were so strong that their children retained a recognized relationship to one another.[21]

In contrast to group marriage, there are also arrangements anthropologists categorize as **fictive marriage**—marriage by proxy to the symbols of someone

---

[19] Levine, N. E., & Silk, J. B. (1997). Why polyandry fails. *Current Anthropology 38,* 375–398.

[20] Chance, N. A. (1990). *The Iñupiat and Arctic Alaska: An ethnography of development* (pp.110–111). New York: Harcourt.

[21] Spencer, R. F. (1984). North Alaska Coast Eskimo. In D. Damas (Ed.), *Arctic: Handbook of North American Indians* (Vol. 5, pp. 320–337). Washington, DC: Smithsonian Institution.

polyandry Marriage of a woman to two or more men at one time; a form of polygamy.

group marriage Marriage in which several men and women have sexual access to one another; also called co-marriage.

fictive marriage Marriage by proxy to the symbols of someone not physically present to establish the social status of a spouse and heirs.

---

[18] Johnson, D. (1996). Polygamists emerge from secrecy, seeking not just peace but respect. In W. A. Haviland & R. J. Gordon (Eds.), *Talking about people* (2nd ed., pp. 129–131). Mountain View, CA: Mayfield.

not physically present in order to establish a social status for a spouse and heirs. One major reason for such a marriage is to control rights to property in the next generation. One type of fictive marriage occurs in several traditional African societies, most famously among Nuer cattle herders of southern Sudan, where a woman can marry a man who has died without heirs. In such situations the deceased man's brother may become his stand-in, or proxy, and marry a woman on his behalf. As in the case of the marriage custom of the sororate, discussed above, the biological offspring will be considered as having been fathered by the dead man's spirit. Recognized as his legitimate children, they are his rightful heirs. Because such spouses are absent in the flesh yet believed to exist in spirit form, anthropologists refer to these fictive unions as *ghost marriages*.[22]

Fictive marriage variations also exist outside Africa. For instance, a form of ghost marriage can be found in traditional Christianity, in particular Roman Catholic monasteries, where women who remain virgins devote their lives to religious service. When a young woman decides to become a nun, she may enter a religious order as a novice. Being promised in spiritual marriage to Jesus Christ, deemed to be the divine bridegroom, she makes vows of celibacy and chastity, abstaining from regular marriage and renouncing all sexual pleasures. In a special marriage by proxy ceremony, such women are "wedded" as spouses of Christ, who they believe died as a human but lives on as divine spirit in heaven. Veiled and clothed as divine spouses, these nuns also receive a new name, thus completely shedding their old social identities.[23]

Other cultural forms of wedding by proxy can be found throughout the world. In the Netherlands, for example, there is the legal custom known as "marriage with the glove" (*huwelijk met de handschoen*). In this official ceremony, just one of the marriage partners appears before the civil authorities—the other is represented symbolically by an imaginary glove and physically by someone formally authorized as a legal proxy. Traditionally, such proxy marriage ceremonies accommodated physically separated partners such as Dutch seafarers or nationals residing in remote territories.

In several places in the United States, including Colorado and Texas, we find yet another example of marriage by proxy. These marriages involve citizens who are incarcerated, deployed in the military, residing in a foreign country, or otherwise prevented from being physically present at the formal ceremony. In California, this wedding option became legal in 2004 but is restricted to members of the U.S. armed forces in wartime or to those who are deployed in combat operations abroad. Since the 1860s, a *double-proxy marriage* has been possible in Montana, where partners may become legally married in a civil wedding ceremony with neither party appearing before the official authorities.

The U.S. government recognizes legal proxy marriages, and as a result these ceremonies are becoming more common in the military, especially among troops deployed in dangerous overseas operations. In cases of injury or death, a military person married in a proxy wedding ceremony may leave a partner (with or without children) with full military benefits. Those who survive and return home may opt to celebrate their already legal marriage in a religious or otherwise meaningful ceremony with family and friends.[24]

Choice of Spouse

The Western egalitarian ideal that an individual should be free to marry whomever he or she chooses is a distinct arrangement, certainly not universally embraced. In many societies, marriage and the establishment of a family are considered far too important to be left to the whims of young people. The individual relationship of two people who are expected to spend their lives together and raise their children together is viewed as incidental to the more serious matter of making allies of two families through the marriage bond. Marriage involves a transfer of rights between families, including rights to property and rights over children, as well as sexual rights. Thus marriages tend to be arranged for the economic and political advantage of the family unit.

Although arranged marriages are rare in North American society, they do occur. Among ethnic minorities, they may serve to preserve traditional values that people fear might otherwise be lost. Among families of wealth and power, marriages may be arranged by segregating their children in private schools and carefully steering them toward appropriate spouses. The following Original Study illustrates how marriages may be arranged in cultures where such traditional practices remain commonplace.

[22] Evans-Pritchard, E. E. (1951). *Kinship and marriage among the Nuer.* New York: Oxford University Press.

[23] See also Pope Pius XII. (1954). *Sacra Virginitas. Encyclical on consecrated virginity.* The Catholic Encyclopedia Online: www.newadvent.org.

[24] Shane, L., III. (2005). Happy couple both no-show wedding: Deployed troops make use of double-proxy ceremony. *Stars & Stripes 3* (17), 6; see also www.MarriageByProxy.com.

Arranging Marriage in India   *by Serena Nanda*

Six years [after my first field trip to India] I returned to do fieldwork among the middle class in Bombay, a modern, sophisticated city. From the experience of my earlier visit, I decided to include a study of arranged marriages in my project. By this time I had met many Indian couples whose marriages had been arranged and who seemed very happy. Particularly in contrast to the fate of many of my married friends in the United States who were already in the process of divorce, the positive aspects of arranged marriages appeared to me to outweigh the negatives. In fact, I thought I might even participate in arranging a marriage myself. I had been fairly successful in the United States in "fixing up" many of my friends, and I was confident that my matchmaking skills could be easily applied to this new situation, once I learned the basic rules. "After all," I thought, "how complicated can it be?"

An opportunity presented itself almost immediately. A friend from my previous Indian trip was in the process of arranging for the marriage of her eldest son. Since my friend's family was eminently respectable and the boy himself personable, well educated, and nice looking, I was sure that by the end of my year's fieldwork, we would have found a match.

The basic rule seems to be that a family's reputation is most important. It is understood that matches would be arranged only within the same caste and general social class, although some crossing of subcastes is permissible if the class positions of the bride's and groom's families are similar. Although dowry is now prohibited by law in India, extensive gift exchanges took place with every marriage. Even when the boy's family does not "make demands," every girl's family nevertheless feels the obligation to give the traditional gifts—to the girl, to the boy, and to the boy's family. Particularly when the couple would be living in the joint family—that is, with the boy's parents and his married brothers and their families, as well as with unmarried siblings, which is still very common even among the urban, upper-middle class in India—the girl's parents are anxious to establish smooth relations between their family and that of the boy. Offering the proper gifts, even when not called "dowry," is often an important factor in influencing the relationship between the bride's and groom's families and perhaps, also, the treatment of the bride in her new home.

In a society where divorce is still a scandal and where, in fact, the divorce rate is exceedingly low, an arranged marriage is the beginning of a lifetime relationship not just between the bride and groom but between their families as well. Thus, while a girl's looks are important, her character is even more so, for she is being judged as a prospective daughter-in-law as much as a prospective bride. . . .

My friend is a highly esteemed wife, mother, and daughter-in-law. She is religious, soft-spoken, modest, and deferential. She rarely gossips and never quarrels, two qualities highly desirable in a woman. A family that has the reputation for gossip and conflict among its womenfolk will not find it easy to get good wives for their sons. . . .

Originally from North India, my friend's family had lived for forty years in Bombay, where her husband owned a business. The family had delayed in seeking a match for their eldest son because he had been an air force pilot for several years, stationed in such remote places that it had seemed fruitless to try to find a girl who would be willing to

accompany him. In their social class, a military career, despite its economic security, has little prestige and is considered a drawback in finding a suitable bride. . . .

The son had recently left the military and joined his father's business. Since he was a college graduate, modern, and well traveled, from such a good family, and, I thought, quite handsome, it seemed to me that he, or rather his family, was in a position to pick and choose. I said as much to my friend. While she agreed that there were many advantages on their side, she also said, "We must keep in mind that my son is both short and dark; these are drawbacks in finding the right match." . . .

An important source of contacts in trying to arrange her son's marriage was my friend's social club in Bombay. Many of the women had daughters of the right age, and some had already expressed an interest in my friend's son. I was most enthusiastic about the possibilities of one particular family who had five daughters, all of whom were pretty, demure, and well educated. Their mother had told my friend, "You can have your pick for your son, whichever one of my daughters appeals to you most." I saw a match in sight. "Surely," I said to my friend, "we will find one there. Let's go visit and make our choice." But my friend held back; she did not seem to share my enthusiasm, for reasons I could not then fathom.

When I kept pressing for an explanation of her reluctance, she admitted, "See, Serena, here is the problem. The family has so many daughters, how will they be able to provide nicely for any of them? . . . Since this is our eldest son, it's best if we marry him to a girl who is the only daughter, then the wedding will truly be a gala affair." I argued that surely the quality of the girls themselves made up for any deficiency in the elaborateness of the wedding. My friend admitted this point but still seemed reluctant to proceed.

Is there something else," I asked her, "some factor I have missed?" "Well," she finally said, "there is one other thing. They have one daughter already married and living in Bombay. The mother is always complaining to me that

CONTINUED

CONTINUED

the girl's in-laws don't let her visit her own family often enough. So it makes me wonder, will she be that kind of mother who always wants her daughter at her own home? This will prevent the girl from adjusting to our house. It is not a good thing." And so, this family of five daughters was dropped as a possibility.

Somewhat disappointed, I nevertheless respected my friend's reasoning and geared up for the next prospect. This was also the daughter of a woman in my friend's social club. There was clear interest in this family and I could see why. The family's reputation was excellent; in fact, they came from a subcaste slightly higher than my friend's own. The girl, who was an only daughter, was pretty and well educated and had a brother studying in the United States. Yet, after expressing an interest to me in this family, all talk of them suddenly died down and the search began elsewhere.

"What happened to that girl as a prospect?" I asked one day. "You never mention her anymore. She is so pretty and so educated, what did you find wrong?"

"She is too educated. We've decided against it. My husband's father saw the girl on the bus the other day and thought her forward. A girl who 'roams about' the city by herself is not the girl for our family." My disappointment this time was even greater, as I thought the son would have liked the girl very much. . . . I learned that if the family of the girl has even a slightly higher social status than the family of the boy, the bride may think herself too good for them, and this too will cause problems. . . .

After one more candidate, who my friend decided was not attractive enough for her son, almost six months had passed and I had become anxious. My friend laughed at my impatience:

"Don't be so much in a hurry," she said. "You Americans want everything done so quickly. You get married quickly and then just as quickly get divorced. Here we take marriage more seriously. We must take all the factors into account. It is not enough for us to learn by our mistakes. This is too serious a business. If a mistake is made we have not only ruined the life of our son or daughter, but we have spoiled the reputation of our family as well. And that will make it much harder for their brothers and sisters to get married. So we must be very careful."

What she said was true and I promised myself to be more patient. I had really hoped and expected that the match would be made before my year in India was up. But it was not to be. When I left India my friend seemed no further along in finding a suitable match for her son than when I had arrived.

Two years later, I returned to India and still my friend had not found a girl for her son. By this time, he was close to 30, and I think she was a little worried. Since she knew I had friends all over India, and I was going to be there for a year, she asked me to "help her in this work" and keep an eye out for someone suitable. . . .

It was almost at the end of my year's stay in India that I met a family with a marriageable daughter whom I felt might be a good possibility for my friend's son. . . . This new family had a successful business in a medium-sized city in central India and were from the same subcaste as my friend. The daughter was pretty and chic; in fact, she had studied fashion design in college. Her parents would not allow her to go off by herself to any of the major cities in India where she could make a career, but they had compromised with her wish to work by allowing her to run a small dress-making

boutique from their home. In spite of her desire to have a career, the daughter was both modest and home-loving and had had a traditional, sheltered upbringing.

I mentioned the possibility of a match with my friend's son. The girl's parents were most interested. Although their daughter was not eager to marry just yet, the idea of living in Bombay—a sophisticated, extremely fashion-conscious city where she could continue her education in clothing design—was a great inducement. I gave the girl's father my friend's address and suggested that when they went to Bombay on some business or whatever, they look up the boy's family.

Returning to Bombay on my way to New York, I told my friend of this newly discovered possibility. She seemed to feel there was potential but, in spite of my urging, would not make any moves herself. She rather preferred to wait for the girl's family to call upon them.

A year later I received a letter from my friend. The family had indeed come to visit Bombay, and their daughter and my friend's daughter, who were near in age, had become very good friends. During that year, the two girls had frequently visited each other. I thought things looked promising.

Last week I received an invitation to a wedding: My friend's son and the girl were getting married. Since I had found the match, my presence was particularly requested at the wedding. I was thrilled. Success at last! As I prepared to leave for India, I began thinking, "Now, my friend's younger son, who do I know who has a nice girl for him . . . ?"

From Nanda, S. (1992). Arranging a marriage in India. In P. R. De Vita (Ed.). The naked anthropologist (pp. 139–143). Belmont, CA: Wadsworth.

Cousin Marriage

While cousin marriage is prohibited in some societies, certain cousins are the preferred marriage partners in others. A **parallel cousin** is the child of a father's brother or a mother's sister (Figure 20.1). In some societies, the preferred spouse for a man is his father's brother's daughter

(or, from the woman's point of view, her father's brother's son). This is known as *patrilateral parallel-cousin marriage.*

Although not obligatory, such marriages have been favored historically among Arabs, the ancient Israelites, and the ancient Greeks. All of these societies are (or were) hierarchical in nature—that is, some people are ranked higher than others because they have more power and property—and although male dominance and descent are emphasized, property of value to men is inherited by daughters as well as sons. When a man marries his father's brother's daughter (or a woman marries her father's

parallel cousin Child of a father's brother or a mother's sister.

Figure 20.1 Anthropologists use diagrams of this sort to illustrate kinship relationships. This one shows the distinction between cross cousins and parallel cousins. In such diagrams, males are always shown as triangles, females as circles, marital ties by an equal sign (=), sibling relationships as a horizontal line, and parent–child relationships as a vertical line. Terms are given from the perspective of the individual labeled EGO, who can be male or female.

brother's son), property is retained within the single male line of descent. In these societies, generally speaking, the greater the property, the more this form of parallel-cousin marriage is apt to occur.

A **cross cousin** is the child of a mother's brother or a father's sister (see Figure 20.1). Some societies favor *matrilateral cross-cousin marriage*—marriage of a man to his mother's brother's daughter or a woman to her father's sister's son. This preference exists among food foragers (such as the Aborigines of Australia) and some farming cultures (including various peoples of South India). Among food foragers, who inherit relatively little in the way of property, such marriages help establish and maintain ties of solidarity between social groups. In agricultural societies, however, the transmission of property is an important determinant. In societies that trace descent exclusively in the female line, for instance, property and other important rights usually pass from a man to his sister's son; under cross-cousin marriage, the sister's son is also the man's daughter's husband.

Same-Sex Marriage

As noted earlier in this chapter, our definition of marriage refers to a union between "people" rather than "a man and a woman" because in some societies same-sex marriages are socially acceptable and officially allowed by law. Marriages between individuals of the same sex may provide a way of dealing with problems for which opposite-sex marriage offers no satisfactory solution. This is the case with woman–woman marriage, a practice permitted in many societies of sub-Saharan Africa, although in none does it involve more than a small minority of all women.

Details differ from one society to another, but woman–woman marriages among the Nandi people living in the highlands of the Rift Valley Province of western Kenya may

be taken as representative of such practices in Africa.[25] The Nandi are a pastoral people who also do considerable farming. Control of most significant property and the primary means of production—livestock and land—is exclusively in the hands of men and may only be transmitted to their male heirs, usually their sons. Since polygyny is the preferred form of marriage, a man's property is normally divided equally among his wives for their sons to inherit. Within the household, each wife has her own home in which she lives with her children, but all are under the authority of the husband, who is a remote and aloof figure within the household. In such situations, the position of a woman who bears no sons is difficult; not only does she not help perpetuate her husband's male line—a major concern among the Nandi—but also she has no one to inherit the proper share of her husband's property.

To get around these problems, a woman of advanced age who bore no sons may become a female husband by marrying a young woman. The purpose of this

[25] The following is based on Obler, R. S. (1982). Is the female husband a man? Woman/woman marriage among the Nandi of Kenya. *Ethnology 19*, 69–88.

cross cousin Child of a mother's brother or a father's sister.

arrangement is for the young wife to provide the male heirs her female husband could not. To accomplish this, the woman's wife enters into a sexual relationship with a man other than her female husband's male husband; usually it is one of his male relatives. No other obligations exist between this woman and her male sex partner, and her female husband is recognized as the social and legal father of any children born under these conditions.

In keeping with her role as female husband, this woman is expected to abandon her female gender identity and, ideally, dress and behave as a man. In practice, the ideal is not completely achieved, for the habits of a lifetime are difficult to reverse. Generally, it is in the context of domestic activities, which are most highly symbolic of female identity, that female husbands most completely assume a male identity.

The individuals who are parties to woman–woman marriages enjoy several advantages. By assuming male identity, a barren or sonless woman raises her status considerably and even achieves near equality with men, who otherwise occupy a far more favored position in Nandi society than women. A woman who marries a female husband is usually one who is unable to make a good marriage, often because she (the female husband's wife) has lost face as a consequence of premarital pregnancy. By marrying a female husband, she too raises her status and also secures legitimacy for her children. Moreover, a female husband is usually less harsh and demanding, spends more time with her, and allows her a greater say in decision making than a male husband does. The one thing she may not do is engage in sexual activity with her marriage partner. In fact, female husbands are expected to abandon sexual activity altogether, including with their male husbands to whom they remain married even though the women now have their own wives.

In contrast to woman–woman marriages among the Nandi are same-sex marriages that include sexual activity between partners. Over the past decade, the legal recognition of such unions has become a matter of vigorous debate in some parts of the world. Several countries—including Belgium, Canada, the Netherlands, Norway, South Africa, Spain, and Sweden—have passed laws legalizing gay marriages. Meanwhile, numerous U.S. states have adopted constitutional amendments barring same-sex marriage, while others—including Connecticut, Iowa, Massachusetts, New Hampshire, and Vermont—now legally recognize these unions. Additional states recognize same-sex marriage but do not allow official gay wedding ceremonies to take place within their boundaries. The issue of same-sex marriage remains unsettled in many parts of the world, with official policies sometimes swinging back and forth—evidence of the fact that cultures are dynamic and capable of change. In addition, close to a dozen U.S. states and about two dozen countries around the world recognize civil unions (also known as civil or domestic partnerships), which offer a varying range of marriage benefits.

The arguments most commonly marshaled by opponents of same-sex unions are, first, that marriage has always been between males and females—but as we have just seen, this is not true. Same-sex marriages have been documented not only for a number of societies in Africa but in other parts of the world as well. As among the Nandi, they provide acceptable positions in society for individuals who might otherwise be marginalized.

A second argument against same-sex unions is that they legitimize gays and lesbians, whose sexual orientations have been widely regarded as unnatural. But again, as discussed in earlier chapters, neither cross-cultural studies nor studies of other animal species suggest that homosexual behavior is unnatural.

A third argument, that the function of marriage is to produce children, is at best a partial truth, as marriage involves economic, political, and legal considerations as well. Moreover, it is increasingly common for same-sex partners (and growing numbers of heterosexual couples) to have children through adoption or by turning to modern reproductive technologies. There is also the fact that in many societies, such as the Nandi, there is a separation between the sexual and the reproductive attributes of women.

Marriage and Economic Exchange

In the Trobriand Islands, when a young couple decides to get married, they sit in public on the veranda of the young man's adolescent retreat, where all may see them. Here they remain until the bride's mother brings the couple cooked yams, which they then eat together, making their marriage official. A day later the bride is presented with three long skirts by the husband's sister, a symbol of the fact that the sexual freedom of adolescence is now over for the newlywed woman. This is followed by a large presentation of uncooked yams by the bride's father and her mother's brother, who represent both her father's lineage and her own.

Meanwhile, the groom's father and mother's brother collect such valuables as stone axe blades, clay pots, money, and the occasional Kula shell (see previous chapter) to present to the young wife's maternal kin and father. After the first year of the marriage, during which the bride's mother continues to provide the couple's meals of cooked yams, each of the young husband's relatives, who provided

In some societies, when a woman marries she receives her share of the family inheritance (her dowry), which she brings to her new family (unlike bride-price, which passes from the groom's family to the bride's family). Shown here are Slovakian women in a traditional farming village each carrying a trousseau (*výbava nevesty*)—consisting of the bride's clothes, linen, bedding, and other objects of her dowry—in a festive procession to her new home. Traditionally, the bride keeps her finer linen in a beautifully carved or painted dowry chest. In addition, her birth family contributes some livestock, land, or other form of wealth, which Slovaks call *veno*, to the new household. Held in her name, this property provides the woman with a measure of independence from her husband.

valuables for his father and mother's brother to present to the bride's relatives, will receive yams from her maternal relatives and father. All of this gift giving back and forth between the husband's and wife's lineages, as well as those of their fathers, serves to bind the four parties together in a way that makes people respect and honor the marriage and that creates obligations on the part of the woman's kin to take care of her husband in the future.

As among the Trobriand Islanders, marriages in many human societies are formalized by some sort of economic exchange. Among the Trobrianders, this takes the form of a gift exchange, as just described. Far more common is **bridewealth** (sometimes called *bride-price*), which involves payments of money or valuable goods to a bride's parents or other close kin. This usually happens in patrilineal societies where the bride will become a member of the household where her husband grew up; this household will benefit from her labor as well as from the offspring she produces. Thus her family must be compensated for their loss.

Not only is bride-price not a simple "buying and selling" of women, but the bride's parents may use the money to purchase jewelry or household furnishings for her or to finance an elaborate and costly wedding celebration. It also contributes to the stability of the marriage, because it usually must

be refunded if the couple separates. Other forms of compensation are an exchange of women between families— "My son will marry your daughter if your son will marry my daughter." Yet another is **bride service**, a period of time during which the groom works for the bride's family.

In a number of societies more or less restricted to the western, southern, and eastern margins of Eurasia, where the economy is based on agriculture, women often bring a **dowry** with them at marriage. A form of dowry in the United States is the custom of the bride's family paying the wedding expenses. Another example is that a Roman Catholic woman joining a religious order as a consecrated nun, and thus entering into a spiritual marriage as discussed earlier, also traditionally brings a dowry (*dos religiosa*) to that institution. In effect, a dowry

bridewealth Money or valuable goods paid by the groom or his family to the bride's family upon marriage; also called bride-price.

bride service A designated period of time when the groom works for the bride's family.

dowry Payment of a woman's inheritance at the time of her marriage, either to her or to her husband.

is a woman's share of parental property that, instead of passing to her upon her parents' death, is distributed to her at the time of her marriage. This does not mean that she retains control of this property after marriage. In some European countries, for example, a woman's property traditionally falls exclusively under her husband's control. Having benefited by what she has brought to the marriage, however, he is obligated to look out for her future well-being, including her security after his death.

One of the functions of dowry is to ensure a woman's support in widowhood (or after divorce), an important consideration in a society where men carry out the bulk of productive work, and women are valued for their reproductive potential rather than for the work they do. In such societies, women incapable of bearing children are especially vulnerable, but the dowry they bring with them at marriage helps protect them against desertion. Another function of dowry is to reflect the economic status of the woman in societies where differences in wealth are important. It also permits women, with the aid of their parents and kin, to compete through dowry for desirable (that is, wealthy) husbands.

Divorce

Like marriage, divorce in most societies is a matter of great concern to the couple's families as it impacts not only the individuals dissolving their marital relationship but also offspring, in-laws, other relatives, and sometimes entire communities. Indeed, divorce may have social, political, and economic consequences far beyond the breakup of a couple and their household.

Across cultures, divorce arrangements can be made for a variety of reasons and with varying degrees of difficulty. Among the Gusii farmers of western Kenya, for instance, sterility and impotence are grounds for a divorce. Among certain aboriginal peoples in northern Canada and Chenchu foragers in central India, divorce is traditionally discouraged after children are born; couples usually are urged by their families to adjust their differences. By contrast, in the southwestern United States, a traditional Hopi Indian woman in Arizona could divorce her husband at any time merely by placing his belongings outside the door to indicate he is no longer welcome. Among the most common reasons for

divorce across cultures are infidelity, sterility, cruelty, and desertion.[26]

An adult unmarried woman is very rare in most non-Western societies where a divorced woman usually soon remarries. In many societies, economic considerations are often the strongest motivation to wed. On the island of New Guinea, a man does not marry because of sexual needs, which he can readily satisfy out of wedlock, but because there it is important to have a female partner to carry out tasks that traditionally fall to women—making pots and cooking his meals, fabricating nets, and weeding his plantings. Likewise, women in communities that depend for security upon males capable of fighting need husbands who are raised to be able warriors as well as good hunters.

Although divorce rates may be high in various parts of the world, they have become so high in Western industrial and postindustrial societies that many worry about the future of what they view as traditional and familiar forms of marriage and the family. It is interesting to note that although divorce was next to impossible in Western societies between 1000 and 1800, for the many generations in those centuries few marriages lasted more than about ten or twenty years, due to high mortality rates caused in part by inadequate health care and medical expertise.[27] For instance, women dying young in childbirth ended many marriages. With increased longevity, separation by death has diminished, and separation by legal action has grown. In the United States today, some 50 percent of first marriages end in divorce—twice the 1960 divorce rate but slightly less than the high point in the early 1980s.[28]

Family and Household

Dependence on group living for survival is a basic human characteristic. We have inherited this from primate ancestors, although we have developed it in our own distinctly human way—through culture. However each culture may define what constitutes a family, this social unit forms the basic cooperative structure that ensures an individual's primary needs and provides the necessary care for children to develop as healthy and productive members of the group and thereby help ensure its future.

Comparative historical and cross-cultural studies reveal a wide variety of family patterns, and these patterns may change over time. Thus the definition of **family** is

---

family Two or more people related by blood, marriage, or adoption. The family may take many forms, ranging from a single parent with one or more children, to a married couple or polygamous spouses with or without offspring, to several generations of parents and their children.

[26] Goodwin, R. (1999). *Personal relationships across cultures* (pp. 86–89). New York: Routledge; see also Betzig, L. (1989). Causes of conjugal dissolution: A cross-cultural study. *Current Anthropology 30*, 654–676.

[27] Stone, L. (1998). *Kinship and gender: An introduction* (p. 235). Boulder, CO: Westview.

[28] Whitehead, B. D., & Popenoe, D. (2004). *The state of our unions: The social health of marriage in America 2004*. Rutgers, NJ: Rutgers University National Marriage Project.

This is a celebration at the palace in the Yoruba City of Oyo, Nigeria. As is usual in societies with royalty, the Yoruba royal household includes many individuals not related to the ruler, as well as the royal family.

necessarily broad: two or more people related by blood, marriage, or adoption. The family may take many forms, ranging from a single parent with one or more children, to a married couple or polygamous spouses with offspring, to several generations of parents and their children.

In all known cultures, past and present, gender plays at least some role in determining the division of labor. An effective way to facilitate economic cooperation between men and women and simultaneously provide for a close bond between mother and child is by establishing residential groups that include adults of both sexes. The differing nature of male and female roles, as defined by different cultures, makes it advantageous in many cultures for a child to have an adult of the same sex available to serve as a proper model for the appropriate adult role. The presence of adult men and women in the same residential group provides for this. The men, however, need not be the women's husbands. In some societies they are the women's brothers—as in the case of the Nayar, discussed earlier in this chapter, where sisters and their children live together with their brothers and their mother and her brothers.

For purposes of cross-cultural comparison, anthropologists define the **household** as the basic residential unit where economic production, consumption, inheritance, childrearing, and shelter are organized and carried out. In the vast majority of human societies, most households are made up of families, but there are many other arrangements. For instance, among the Mundurucu Indians, a horticultural people living in the center of Brazil's Amazon rainforest, married men and women are members of separate households, meeting periodically for sexual activity. At age 13 boys join their fathers in the men's house. Meanwhile, their sisters continue to live with

their mothers and the younger boys in two or three houses grouped around the men's house. Thus the men's house constitutes one household inhabited by adult males and their sexually mature sons, and the women's houses, inhabited by adult women and prepubescent boys and girls, constitute others.

An array of other domestic arrangements can be found in other parts of the world, including situations in which co-residents of a household are not related biologically or by marriage—such as the service personnel in an elaborate royal household, apprentices in the household of craft specialists, low-status clients in the household of rich and powerful patrons, or groups of children being raised by paired teams of adult male and female community members in an Israeli kibbutz (a collectively owned and operated agricultural settlement). So it is that *family* and *household* are not always synonymous.

Forms of the Family

To discuss the various forms families take in response to particular social, historical, and ecological circumstances, we must, at the outset, make a distinction between a **conjugal family** (in Latin *conjugere* means "to join together"),

household The basic residential unit where economic production, consumption, inheritance, childrearing, and shelter are organized and carried out.
conjugal family A family established through marriage.

which is formed on the basis of marital ties, and a **consanguineal family** (based on the Latin word *consanguineus*, literally meaning "of the same blood"), which consists of related women, their brothers, and the women's offspring.

Consanguineal families are not common, but there are more examples than the classic case of the Nayar described earlier in the chapter. Among these are the Musuo of southwestern China and the Tory Islanders—a Roman Catholic, Gaelic-speaking fisherfolk living off the coast of Ireland. The Tory Islanders, who do not marry until they are in their late 20s or early 30s, look at it this way:

> Oh well, you get married at that age, it's too late to break up arrangements that you have already known for a long time. . . . You know, I have my sisters and brothers to look after, why should I leave home to go live with a husband? After all, he's got his sisters and his brothers looking after him.[29]

Because the Tory Island community numbers but a few hundred people, husbands and wives are within easy commuting distance of each other.

According to a cross-cultural survey of family types in 192 cultures around the world, the extended family is most common, present in about 48 percent of those cultures, compared to the nuclear family at 25 percent, and polygamy at 22 percent.[30] Each of these is discussed below.

The Nuclear Family

The smallest family unit is known as the **nuclear family**, a group consisting of one or two parents and dependent offspring, which may include a stepparent, stepsiblings, and adopted children (Figure 20.2). Until recently, the term *nuclear family* referred solely to the mother, father, and child(ren) unit—the family form that most North Americans, Europeans, and many others now regard as the normal or natural nucleus of larger family units. In the United States father–mother–child(ren) nuclear family households reached their highest frequency around 1950, when 60 percent of all households conformed to this model.[31] Today such families make up less than a quarter

Figure 20.2 This diagram shows the relationships in a traditional nuclear family, a form that is common but declining in North America and much of Europe.

of U.S. households,[32] and the term *nuclear family* is used to cover the social reality of several types of small parent–child units, including single parents with children and same-sex couples with children.

Industrialization and market capitalism have played a historical role in shaping the nuclear family most of us are familiar with today. One reason for this is that factories, mining and transportation companies, warehouses, shops, and other businesses generally only pay individual wage earners for the jobs they are hired to do. Whether these workers are single, married, divorced, or have siblings or children is really not a concern to the profit-seeking companies. Because jobs may come and go, individual wage earners must remain mobile to adapt to the labor markets. And since few wage earners have the financial resources to support large numbers of relatives without incomes of their own, industrial or postindustrial societies do not favor the continuance of larger extended families (discussed below), which are standard in most societies traditionally dependent on pastoral nomadism, agriculture, or horticulture.

Interestingly, the nuclear family is also likely to be prominent in traditional foraging societies such as that of the Eskimo people who live in the barren Arctic environments of eastern Siberia (Russia), Alaska, Greenland, and Canada (where Eskimos are now known as Inuit). In the winter the traditional

---

[29] Fox, R. (1981, December 3). [Interview]. Coast Telecourses, Inc., Los Angeles.

[30] Winick, C. (Ed.). (1970). *Dictionary of anthropology* (p. 202). Totowa, NJ: Littlefield, Adams.

[31] Stacey, J. (1990). *Brave new families* (pp. 5, 10). New York: Basic.

consanguineal family A family of "blood relatives" consisting of related women, their brothers, and the women's offspring.

nuclear family A group consisting of one or two parents and dependent offspring, which may include a stepparent, stepsiblings, and adopted children. Until recently this term referred only to the father, mother, and child(ren) unit.

---

[32] Irvine, M. (1999, November 24). Mom-and-pop houses grow rare. *Burlington Free Press*; see also U.S. Census Bureau. (2008). *American Community Survey, 2006–2008*.

Among Inuit people in Canada who still hunt for much of their food, nuclear families, such as the one shown here, are typical. Their isolation from other relatives is usually temporary. Much of the time they are found in groups of at least a few related families.

Inuit husband and wife, with their children, roam the vast Arctic Canadian snowscape in their quest for food. The husband hunts and makes shelters. The wife cooks, is responsible for the children, and makes the clothing and keeps it in good repair. One of a wife's traditional chores is to chew her husband's boots to soften the leather for the next day so that he can resume his quest for game. The wife and her children could not survive without the husband, and life for a man is unimaginable without a wife.

Similar to nuclear families in industrial societies, those living under especially harsh environmental conditions must be prepared to fend for themselves. Such isolation comes with its own set of challenges, including the difficulties of rearing children without multigenerational support and a lack of familial care for the elderly. Nonetheless, this form of family is well adapted to a mode of subsistence that requires a high degree of geographic mobility. For the Inuit in Canada, this mobility permits the hunt for food; for other North Americans, the hunt for jobs and improved social status requires a mobile form of family unit.

Not even among the Inuit, however, is the nuclear family as independent from other kin as it has become among most non-Native North Americans. When Inuit families are off by themselves, it is regarded as a matter of temporary expediency; most of the time, they are found in groups of at least a few families together, with members of one family having relatives in all of the others.[33] Thus families cooperate with one another on a daily basis, sharing food and other resources, looking out for one another's children, and sometimes eating together.

The sense of shared responsibility for one another's children and for the general welfare in Inuit multifamily groups contrasts with families in the United States, which are basically "on their own." Here, individual families are responsible for their own child care and for the welfare of their own family members, with little assistance from outside.[34] To be sure, families can and often do help one another out, but they are under no obligation to do so; and even if they wish to, they may find it impossible due to geographic separation born of high mobility. In fact, once children reach the age of majority (18), parents have no further legal obligation to them, nor do the children to their parents.

The Extended Family

When two or more closely related nuclear families cluster together in a large domestic group, they form a unit known as the **extended family.** This larger family unit, common in traditional horticultural, agricultural, and pastoral societies around the world, typically consists of siblings with their spouses and offspring, and often their parents. All of these kin, some related by blood and some by marriage, live and work together for the common good and deal with outsiders as a single unit.

Because members of the younger generation bring their husbands or wives to live in the family, extended

---

[33] Graburn, N.H.H. (1969). *Eskimos without igloos: Social and economic development in Sugluk* (pp. 56–58). Boston: Little, Brown.

[34] Collier, J., Rosaldo, M. Z., & Yanagisako, S. (1982). Is there a family? New anthropological views. In B. Thorne & M. Yalom (Eds.), *Rethinking the family: Some feminist questions* (pp. 34–35). New York: Longman.

extended family Two or more closely related nuclear families clustered together in a large domestic group.

Extended family households exist in many parts of the world, including among the Maya people of Central America and Mexico.[35] In many of their communities, sons bring their wives to live in houses built on the edges of a small open plaza, on one edge of which their father's house already stands. Numerous household activities are carried out on this plaza—children play while adults weave, do some other productive work, or socialize with guests. The head of the family is the sons' father, who makes most of the important decisions. All members of the family work together for the common good and deal with outsiders as a single unit.

© Joe Cavanaugh/DDB Stock Photo

families have continuity through time. As older members die off, new members are born into the family. Extended families have built into them particular challenges. Among these are difficulties that the in-marrying spouse is likely to have in adjusting to his or her spouse's family.

In North America, extended families can still be found on many American Indian reservations. They also exist in some non-Indian communities, for example along the Maine coast,[36] where they developed in response to a unique economy featuring a mix of farming and seafaring, coupled with an ideal of self-sufficiency. Because family farms were incapable of providing self-sufficiency, seafaring was taken up as an economic alternative. Seagoing commerce, however, was periodically afflicted by depression, so family farming remained important as a cushion against hard economic times. The need for a sufficient labor pool to tend the farm—while at the same time furnish officers, crew, or both for locally owned vessels—was satisfied by the practice of a newly married couple settling on the farm of either the bride's or the groom's parents. Thus most people spent their lives cooperating on a day-to-day basis in economic activities with close relatives, all of whom lived together (even if in separate houses) on the same farm.

Nontraditional Families and Non-Family Households

In North America and parts of Europe, increasing numbers of people live in non-family households, either alone or with people who are not relatives. In fact, nearly 34 percent of households in the United States fall into this category[37] (Figure 20.3). Many others live as members of what are often called *nontraditional families*.

Increasingly common are *cohabitation* households, made up of unmarried couples. Since 1960, such households have increased in number dramatically especially among young couples in their 20s and early 30s in North America and parts of Europe. In Norway, over half of all live births now occur outside marriage. One reason for this is that Norwegian "cohabiting couples who have children together or have lived together for minimum two years will have many of the same rights and obligations to social security, pensions and taxation as their married counterparts."[38] For many others, however, cohabitation represents a relatively short-term domestic arrangement, since most cohabiting couples either marry or separate within two years.[39]

Cohabitation breakup has contributed to the growing number of single-parent households—as have increases in divorce, sexual activity outside marriage, declining marriage rates among women of childbearing age, and the number of women preferring single motherhood. In the United States, more than a third of all births occur outside of marriage.[40] There, the percentage of single-parent households has grown to nearly 10 percent, while the

---

[35] Vogt, E. Z. (1990). *The Zinacantecos of Mexico, A modern Maya way of life* (2nd ed., pp. 30–34). Fort Worth: Holt, Rinehart & Winston.

[36] Haviland, W. A. (1974). Farming, seafaring and bilocal residence on the coast of Maine. *Man in the Northeast 6,* 31–44.

[37] U.S. Census Bureau. (2008). *American Community Survey, 2006–2008.*

[38] Noack, T. (2001). Cohabitation in Norway: An accepted and gradually more regulated way of living. *International Journal of Law, Policy, and the Family 15* (1), 102–117.

[39] Forste, R. (2008). *Prelude to marriage, or alternative to marriage? A social demographic look at cohabitation in the U.S.* Working paper. Social Science Electronic Publishing, Inc. http://papers.ssrn.com/sol3/papers.cfm?abstract_id=269172.

[40] Stein, R., & St. George, D. (2009, May 13). Babies increasingly born to unwed mothers. *Washington Post.*

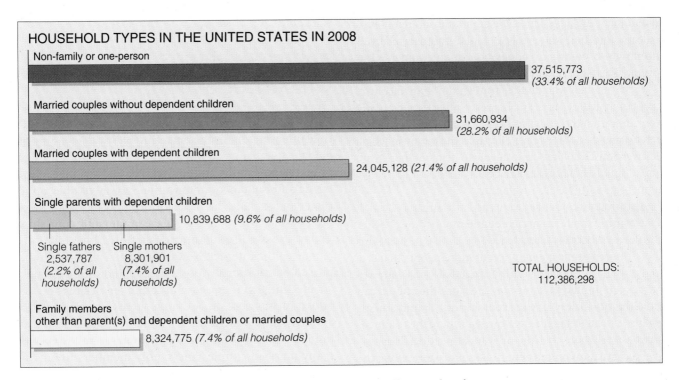

Figure 20.3 Household types in the United States, based on U.S. Census Bureau, *American Community Survey, 2006–2008.*

number comprised of married couples with children has dropped to just below 22 percent. Although single-parent households account for about 10 percent of all U.S. households, they are home to 30 percent of all children (under 18 years of age) in the country.[41]

In the vast majority of cases, a child in a single-parent household lives with the mother. Also significant today are the high numbers of *blended families,* comprised of a married couple together raising children from previous unions.

Single-parent households headed by women are neither new nor restricted to industrial or postindustrial societies. They have been known and studied for a long time in the countries of the Caribbean Sea, where men historically have been exploited as a cheap source of labor for sugar, coffee, or banana plantations. In more recent decades, many of these men are now also working as temporary migrant laborers in foreign countries, primarily in the United States—often living in temporary households comprised of fellow laborers.

Residence Patterns

Where some form of conjugal or extended family is the norm, family exogamy requires that either the husband or wife, if not both, must move to a new household upon marriage. There are several common patterns of residence that a newly married couple may adopt—the prime determinant

being ecological circumstances, although other factors enter in as well. Thus postmarital residence arrangements, far from being arbitrary, are adaptive in character. Here we will mention only the four most common patterns.

Patrilocal residence is when a married couple lives in the husband's father's place of residence. This arrangement is favorable in situations where men play a predominant role in subsistence, particularly if they own property that can be accumulated, if polygyny is customary, if warfare is prominent enough to make cooperation among men especially important, and if an elaborate political organization exists in which men wield authority. These conditions are most often found together in societies that rely on animal husbandry and/or intensive agriculture for their subsistence. Where patrilocal residence is customary, the bride often must move to a different band or community. In such cases, her parents' family is not only losing the services of a useful family member, but they are losing her potential offspring as well. Hence, some kind of compensation to her family, most commonly bride-price, is usual.

Matrilocal residence, in which a married couple lives in the wife's mother's place of residence, is likely if cultural ecological circumstances make the role of the woman

---

[41] U.S. Census Bureau. (2008). *American Community Survey, 2006–2008.*

patrilocal residence A residence pattern in which a married couple lives in the husband's father's place of residence.

matrilocal residence A residence pattern in which a married couple lives in the wife's mother's place of residence.

predominant for subsistence. It is found most often in horticultural societies, where political organization is relatively uncentralized and where cooperation among women is important. The Hopi Indians provide one example. Although it is the Hopi men who do the farming, the women control access to land and "own" the harvest. Indeed, men are not even allowed in the granaries. Under matrilocal residence, men usually do not move very far from the family in which they were raised so they are available to help out there from time to time. Therefore, marriage usually does not involve compensation to the groom's family.

Ambilocal residence (*ambi* in Latin means "both"), a pattern in which a married couple may choose either matrilocal or patrilocal residence, is adaptive in situations where the economic cooperation of more people than are available in the nuclear family is needed but where resources are limited in some way. Because the couple can join either the bride's or the groom's family, family membership is flexible, and the two can live where the resources look best or where their labor is most needed. This was once the situation on the peninsulas and islands along the coast of Maine, where, as already noted, extended family households were based upon ambilocal residence.

The same residential pattern is particularly common among food-foraging peoples, as among the Mbuti Pygmies of Africa's Ituri forest. Typically, a Mbuti marries someone from another band, so that one spouse always has in-laws who live elsewhere. If foraging is bad in their part of the tropical rainforest, the couple has somewhere else to go where food may be more readily available. Ambilocality greatly enhances the Mbutis' opportunity to find food. It also provides a place to go if a dispute breaks out with someone in the band where the couple is currently living. Consequently, Mbuti camps are constantly changing their composition as people split off to go live with their in-laws, while others are joining from other groups. For a people like food foragers, who find their food in nature and who maintain an egalitarian social order, ambilocal residence can be a crucial factor in both survival and conflict resolution.

Under **neolocal residence,** a married couple forms a household in a separate location. This occurs where the independence of the nuclear family is emphasized. In industrial societies such as the United States, where most economic activity occurs outside rather than inside the family and where it is important for individuals to be able to move where jobs can be found, neolocal residence is better suited than any of the other patterns.

---

ambilocal residence A residence pattern in which a married couple may choose either matrilocal or patrilocal residence.
neolocal residence A pattern in which a married couple establishes the household in a location apart from either the husband's or the wife's relatives.

Marriage, Family, and Households in a Globalized World

Large-scale emigration, modern technology, and multiple other factors in the emerging political economy of global capitalism also impact the cross-cultural mosaic of marriage, family, and household. For instance, electronic and digital communication by way of fiber optic cables and satellites has transformed how individuals express sexual attraction and engage in romantic courtship. Today, cross-cultural and transnational love relations bloom via the Internet. New technologies also permit the pursuit of traditionally prohibited relationships through clandestine text messaging of forbidden desires and tabooed intimacies—for example, across castes in India and between young unmarried men and women in traditional Muslim communities. Beyond sex and romance, many married couples and family members living far apart depend on satellite communications technology to stay in touch.

Adoption and New Reproductive Technologies

Although it has not been uncommon for childless couples in many cultures throughout human history to adopt children, including orphans and even captives, today it is a transnational practice for adults from industrial and postindustrial countries to travel across the world in search of infants to adopt, regardless of their ethnic heritage (see this chapter's Globalscape). Also increasingly common is open adoption, which makes it possible for a child to have a relationship with both the biological and the adoptive parents.

Among other contributing factors to today's diversity of families and households are *new reproductive technologies* (NRTs), including various forms of *in vitro fertilization* (IVF) in which an egg is fertilized in a laboratory. The embryo is then transferred into the uterus to begin a pregnancy or is frozen for future use. In cases of IVF with a surrogate mother using donor egg and sperm, a newborn essentially has five parents: the birth parents who provided the egg and sperm, the surrogate mother who carried the baby, and the parents who will raise the baby.

Migrant Workforces

Also of note in terms of new residential patterns is the ever-growing number of households comprised of temporary and migrant workers. Today, China alone has 114 million

Globalscape

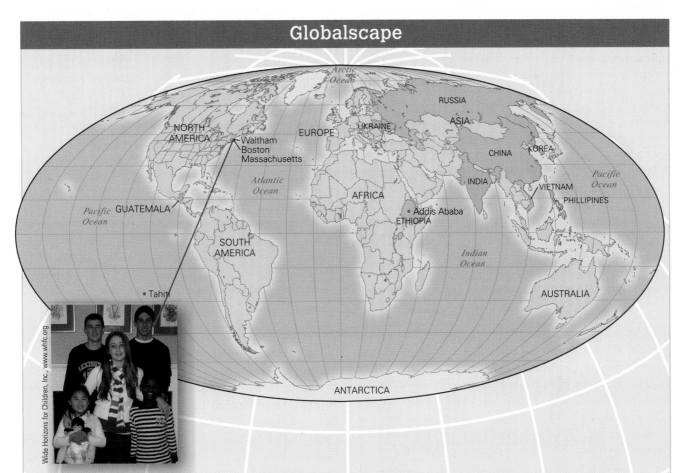

Wide Horizons for Children, Inc., www.whfc.org

Transnational Child Exchange?

Settling into her seat for the flight to Boston, Kathryn cradled the sleepy head of her newly adopted son, Mesay. As the plane lifted away from African soil and presented a sweeping view of Ethiopia's capital, tears slid down her cheeks. Were the tears for Ethiopia's loss of a boy, a boy's loss of Ethiopia, or her profound joy for the gift of adoption?

Child exchange is a universal phenomenon, taking place across the world and throughout human history. Just as marriage and kinship mean different things in different cultures, so does child exchange, referred to in the English language as "adoption." In some cultures, adoption is quite rare, while in others, such as in Polynesian communities in the Pacific Islands, it is very common. For instance, in a small village in Tahiti it was found that over 25 percent of children were raised by adoptive parents.

A cross-cultural understanding of adoption is vital now that child exchange has become part of the global flow, especially from poor countries in Africa, Latin America, Southeast Asia, and eastern Europe, to affluent countries in North America and western Europe. The global exchange of children initially involved war orphans after World War II. In recent decades, extreme poverty has become a major factor, as mothers confronting serious deprivation may feel forced to abandon, give away, or sometimes sell their children. Whether brokered by government or nongovernmental agencies, by for-profit or non-profit enterprises, global child exchange has become a big business—legal and illegal, moral and amoral, happifying and horrifying. This is especially true in poor countries where most workers earn less than a dollar a day, and a foreign adoption nets $12,000 to $35,000 in broker fees.

Since the early 1970s, about 500,000 foreign children have been adopted into families in the United States alone. A nearly equal number ended up in other wealthy countries. The global flow to the United States peaked in 2004 when nearly 23,000 arrived—most from China (30%), Russia (25%), Guatemala (14%), and Korea (7%), with 5,500 flown in from other poor countries such as India, Philippines, Ukraine, and Vietnam. Statistics vary (and shift) according to adoption rules. Some countries have shut the door on foreign adoptions due to accusations of "exporting" or even "selling" children. Others restrict or prohibit it for religious reasons. Sudan, for example, forbids foreign adoption of Muslim children and automatically classifies religiously unidentified orphans as Muslim.

A country that does not discriminate on the basis of religion is its neighbor, Ethiopia, which has gained popularity as an infant-provider country. One of six U.S. agencies officially approved to do foreign adoptions from Ethiopia is Wide Horizons for Children in Waltham, Massachusetts, which has placed many Ethiopian children with U.S. families. Among them is Mesay, now settled into his new life with Kathryn, her husband, and their four other children, including a sister about his age, adopted from China as an infant.

Global Twister How do you compare a European or North American woman who accepts a surrogate pregnancy fee of $115,000 to $150,000 to cover all costs of bearing a child for someone else to a Third World mother living in poverty, who decides to give up her child for adoption for a price?

© Edward Burtynsky

Many of China's 114 million migrant laborers work in factories and live in factory dormitories such as the one shown here.

of them, mostly young people who have quit the peasant villages of their childhood and traveled to fast-growing cities to work in factories, shops, restaurants, and other such places. Some pile into apartments with friends or co-workers; others live in factory dormitories—new, single-generation households that stand in stark contrast to the multigeneration extended family households in which they were raised. Similar scenes are repeated all around the world as individuals in this transient workforce set up house together far away from home in order to make a living.

Although many countries have passed legislation intended to provide migrants with protections concerning housing—as well as work conditions and pay, such as the 1983 Migrant and Seasonal Agricultural Worker Protection Act in the United States—living conditions for these workers are often miserable.[42]

As the various ethnographic examples in this chapter illustrate, our species has invented a wide variety of marriage, family, and household forms, each in correspondence with related features in the social structure and conforming to the larger cultural system. In the face of new challenges, we explore and tinker in search of solutions, sometimes resulting in finding completely new forms, and other times returning to time-tested formulas of more traditional varieties.

---

[42] Chang, L. (2005, June 9). A migrant worker sees rural home in new light. *Wall Street Journal*.

Questions for Reflection

1. According to Shinto tradition in traditional Japanese society, a white wedding dress symbolizes the bride's purity. Many women living in less sexually restrictive societies also choose white bridal gowns. What do you think is the reason behind this—and the fact that the prescribed dress colors for Japanese grooms are black and gray? Does your culture have a similar color code?

2. Members of traditional communities in countries where the state is either weak or absent depend on consanguineal and affinal relatives to help meet the basic challenges of survival. In such traditional societies, why would it be risky to choose marriage partners exclusively on the basis of romantic love? Can you imagine other factors playing a role if the long-term survival of your community is at stake?

3. Although most women in Europe and North America probably view polygyny as a marriage practice exclusively benefiting men, women in cultures where such marriages are traditional may stress more positive sides of sharing a husband with several co-wives. Under which conditions do you think polygyny could be considered as relatively beneficial for women?

4. Many children in Europe and North America are raised in single-parent households. In contrast to the United States, where most children living with their unmarried mothers grow up in economically disadvantaged households, relatively few children raised by unmarried mothers in Norway face poverty. Why do you think that is?

5. Does your own society have cultural rules about alternative sexual orientations and sexual relations before or outside marriage? Have the rules become looser or tighter since your parents' generation? Do you expect economic and social changes will further alter ideas and attitudes toward sex and marriage? And if so, will they become more or less restrictive?

Suggested Readings

Coontz, S. (2005). *Marriage, a history: From obedience to intimacy, or how love conquered marriage*. New York: Viking Adult.

Challenging the idea that marriage is in crisis due to rising divorce rates, out-of-wedlock births, and same-sex unions, Coontz argues that marriage has always been in a state of flux and that "almost every marital and sexual arrangement we have seen in recent years . . . has been tried somewhere before." Placing current concepts of marriage in broad historical context, Coontz explains marriage as a political tool, a means of ensuring a domestic labor force, and a flexible reflection of changing social standards.

Hirsch, J. S., & Wardlow, H. (Eds.). (2006). *Modern loves: The anthropology of romantic courtship and companionate marriage*. Ann Arbor: University of Michigan Press.

This volume offers a political and economic understanding of changing ideals of romantic love, courtship, and marriage in the context of globalization. Through a cross-cultural sample of ethnographically rich descriptions, the book traces some of the sources of these shifts in mass media, missionization, and the spread of individualism.

Holy, L. (1996). *Anthropological perspectives on kinship*. London: Pluto.

Holy investigates changes in the conceptualization of kinship brought about by new reproductive technologies and the growing interest in culturally specific notions of personhood and gender. Considering the extent to which Western assumptions have guided anthropological studies of kinship, the author offers critical reflection on cultural bias in approaches to the subject.

Hutter, M. (Ed.). (2003). *The family experience: A reader in cultural diversity* (4th ed.). Boston: Allyn & Bacon.

This readable anthology examines the cultural diversity of the North American family by providing relevant articles integrating race, class, gender, and ethnicity. Taken as a whole, these readings reveal both historical trends and unique variations that widen our understanding of the diversity, patterns, and dynamics of the U.S. family.

Modell, J. (1994). *Kinship with strangers: Adoption and interpretations of kinship in American culture*. Berkeley: University of California Press.

The author, an adopter and an anthropologist, analyzes the "core symbols" of kinship in American culture—birth, biology, and blood—and examines their impact on people who experience the "fictive" kinship of adoption.

Stockard, J. E. (2002). *Marriage in culture: Practice and meaning across diverse societies*. Ft. Worth: Harcourt College.

This innovative, accessible text explores the meaning of marriage in different cultures, using compelling ethnographic accounts of the Ju/'hoansi (Bushmen), Chinese, Iroquois, and Tibetan societies to familiarize students with anthropologists' unique perspective on marriage in culture. Each chapter explores the ways in which different economic, political, family, and gender systems shape the practice and meaning of marriage.

Stone, L. (2005). *Kinship and gender: An introduction* (3rd ed.). Boulder, CO: Westview.

Focusing on gender, Stone considers the cross-cultural variations in marriage practices in the broader context of kinship studies. A particular strength is the inclusion of specific case studies to illustrate general principles. The book ends with a thought-provoking discussion of new reproductive technologies and their repercussions for both kinship and gender. This revised and updated edition features new case studies on primate kinship, U.S. kinship, and new reproductive technologies.

© Li Jianhui/The Image Works

Challenge Issue All humans face the challenge of creating and maintaining a social network that reaches beyond the capabilities of immediate family or household to provide security and support. On a basic level that network is arranged by kinship and may extend to distantly related individuals who claim descent from the same ancestor—living or long-deceased. Kin-groups are defined differently across cultures. For example, among the Han, the dominant ethnic majority in China, almost all ancestral temples, or clan houses, are dedicated to male forebears, reflecting the country's long-established patrilineal rules of descent and cultural values. Clan members affirm their place in the kin-group by making offerings to the ancestors in special ancestral halls or temples such as the one pictured here, located in a family home in Taishun, Zhejiang Province.

CHAPTER 21

Kinship and Descent

Chapter Preview

What Is Kinship?

Kinship is a social network of relatives within which individuals possess certain mutual rights and obligations. One's place in this network, or kinship status, determines what these rights and obligations are. Providing groups of relatives with a social structure, kinship helps shield them from the dangers of disorganization and fracture. Kinship is especially important in societies where a centralized government, a professional military, or financial institutions are absent or do not function effectively. In such societies, individuals must depend on a wide network of relatives for support and protection.

What Are Descent Groups?

A descent group is a kind of kinship group in which being in the direct line of descent from a particular real or mythical ancestor is a criterion of membership. Descent may be traced exclusively through men or women, or through either at the discretion of the individual. Two different means of tracing descent may be used at the same time to assign individuals to different groups for different purposes. In societies without descent groups, such as many food-foraging as well as industrial and postindustrial societies, people rely instead on the kindred: an individual's close blood relatives on the maternal and paternal sides of his or her family. Because each kindred is an ego-centered family group, it is a less stable social unit than the descent group.

What Are the Functions of Kin-Ordered Groups?

Kin-ordered groups are social networks of relatives organized to deal with specific challenges that commonly confront human societies: maintaining the integrity of resources that cannot be divided without being destroyed; providing workforces for tasks that require a labor pool larger than households can provide; and rallying support for purposes of self-defense or offensive attack. Kin-ordered organizations such as descent groups arise from extended family organization. Kinship terminology is affected by and adjusts to the kinds of descent or other kinship groups that are important in a society.

All societies rely on some form of family and/or household organization to meet basic human needs: securing food, shelter, and protection against danger, coordinating work, regulating sexual activities, and organizing childrearing. As efficient and flexible as family and household organization may be for meeting such challenges, many societies confront problems that are beyond the coping ability of family and household organization.

For example, members of one independent local group often need some means of interacting with people outside their immediate circle for defense against natural disasters or outside aggressors and for securing vitally important natural resources for food, fuel, and shelter. A wider circle may also be necessary in forming a cooperative workforce for tasks that require more participants than households alone can provide.

Humans have come up with many ways to widen their circles of support to meet such challenges. One is through a formal political system, with personnel to make and enforce laws, keep the peace, allocate resources, and perform other regulatory and societal functions. But the predominant way to build this support in societies that are not organized as political states—especially foraging, crop-cultivating, and pastoral

kinship A network of relatives within which individuals possess certain mutual rights and obligations.

descent group Any kin-ordered social group with a membership in the direct line of descent from a real (historical) or fictional common ancestor.

societies—is by means of **kinship,** a social network of relatives within which individuals possess certain mutual rights and obligations.

Descent Groups

A common way of organizing a society along kinship lines is by creating what anthropologists call descent groups. Found in many societies, a **descent group** is any kin-ordered social group with a membership in the direct line of descent from a real (historical) or fictional common ancestor. Members of such a group trace their shared connections back to such an ancestor through a chain of parent–child links. The addition of a few culturally meaningful obligations and taboos acts as a kind of glue to help hold the structured social group together.

Membership in a descent group provides individuals with a wider social network of relatives without whom it is difficult or even impossible to effectively deal with the multiple challenges of survival humans face, including securing vitally important natural resources for food, fuel, shelter, and other necessities. Although many important functions of the descent group are taken over by other institutions when a society becomes politically organized as a state, elements of such kin-ordered groups may continue. We see this with many traditional indigenous societies that have become part of larger state societies yet endure as distinctive kin-ordered communities.

So it is with the Maori of New Zealand, featured in this chapter's Biocultural Connection. Retaining key elements of their traditional social structure, they are still organized in about thirty large descent groups known

Biocultural Connection

Maori Origins: Ancestral Genes and Mythical Canoes

Anthropologists have been fascinated to find that the oral traditions of Maori people in New Zealand fit quite well with scientific findings. New Zealand, an island country whose dramatic geography served as the setting for the *Lord of the Rings* film trilogy, lies in a remote corner of the Pacific Ocean about 1,900 kilometers (1,200 miles) southeast of Australia. Named by Dutch seafarers who landed on its shores in 1642, it was claimed by the British as a colony about 150 years later. Maori, the country's indigenous people, fought back but were outgunned, outnumbered, and forced to lay down their arms in the

early 1870s. Today, nearly 600,000 of New Zealand's 4.1 million citizens claim some Maori ancestry.

Maori have an age-old legend about how they came to Aotearoa ("Land of the Long White Cloud"), their name for New Zealand: More than twenty-five generations ago, their Polynesian ancestors arrived in a great fleet of sailing canoes from Hawaiki, their mythical homeland sometimes identified with Tahiti where the native language closely resembles their own. According to chants and genealogies passed down through the ages, this fleet consisted of at least seven (perhaps up to thirteen) seafaring

Indeed, while women in matrilineal societies may have considerable power, they do not hold exclusive authority in the descent group. They share it with men. Usually, these are the brothers, rather than the husbands, of the women through whom descent is traced. Apparently, a function of matrilineal systems is to provide continuous female solidarity within the female work group. Matrilineal systems are usually found in horticultural societies in which women perform much of the work in the house and nearby gardens. Matrilineal descent in part prevails because women's labor as crop cultivators is regarded as so important to the society.

In a matrilineal system, brothers and sisters belong to the descent group of the mother, the mother's mother, the mother's siblings, and the mother's sisters' children. Thus every male belongs to the same descent group as his mother, and a man's own children belong to his wife's descent group, not his.

Although not true of all matrilineal systems, a common feature is the relative weakness of the social tie between wife and husband. A woman's husband lacks authority in the household they share. Her brother, and not the husband-father, distributes goods, organizes work, settles disputes, supervises rituals, and administers inheritance and succession rules. Meanwhile, her husband fulfills the same role in his own sister's household. Furthermore, his property and status are inherited by his sister's son rather than his son. Thus brothers and sisters maintain lifelong ties with one another, whereas marital ties are easily severed. In matrilineal societies, unsatisfactory marriages are more easily ended than in patrilineal societies.

Among Hopi Indians, a farming people whose ancestors have lived in *pueblos* ("villages") in northeastern Arizona for many centuries, society is divided into a number of clans based strictly on matrilineal descent.[4] (This is also true of many other Native American groups, such as the White Mountain Apache living just south of the Hopi.) At birth, every Hopi is assigned to his or her mother's clan. This

affiliation is so important that, in a very real sense, a person has no social identity in the community apart from it. Two or more clans together constitute larger supraclan units, which anthropologists refer to as *phratries* (discussed later in this chapter). There are nine phratries in Hopi society, and within each phratry member clans are expected to support one another and observe strict exogamy. Because people from all nine phratries can be found living in any given Hopi village, marriage partners usually can be found in one's home community. This same dispersal of membership provides individuals with rights of entry into villages other than their own.

Although phratries and clans are the major kinship units in Hopi culture, the actual functional social units consist of lineages, and there are several in each village. Each Hopi lineage is headed by a senior woman (usually the eldest), although it is her brother or mother's brother who keeps the sacred "medicine bundle" (objects of spiritual power considered essential for peoples' well-being) and plays an active role in running lineage affairs. However, the senior woman is no mere figurehead. She may act as mediator to help resolve disputes among group members. Also, although her brother and mother's brother have the right to offer her advice and criticism, they are equally obligated to listen to what she has to say, and she does not yield her authority to them.

Most female authority, however, is exerted within the household, which is the smallest distinct unit of Hopi society, and here men clearly take second place. These households consist of the women of the lineage with their husbands and unmarried sons, all of whom used to live in sets of adjacent rooms in single large buildings. Nowadays, nuclear families often live (frequently with a maternal relative or two) in separate houses, but motorized vehicles enable related households to maintain close contact and cooperation as before.

Hopi lineages function as landholding corporations, allocating land for the support of member households. These lands are farmed by "outsiders," the husbands of the women whose lineage owns the land, and the harvest belongs to these women. Thus Hopi men spend their lives laboring for their wives' lineages, and in return they are given food and shelter. Although sons learn from their fathers how to farm, a man has no real authority over his son. This is because a man's own children belong to his wife's lineage while his sister's children form part of his. When parents have difficulty with an unruly child, the mother's brother is called upon to mete out discipline. A man's loyalties are therefore divided between his wife's household on the one hand and his sisters' on the other. According to tradition, if a man is perceived as being an unsatisfactory husband, his wife merely has to place his

---

[4] Most of the following is from Connelly, J. C. (1979). Hopi social organization. In A. Ortiz (Ed.), *Handbook of North American Indians, Vol. 9, Southwest* (pp. 539–553). Washington, DC: Smithsonian Institution.

White Mountain Apaches in Arizona, like their Hopi neighbors, are organized in matrilineal clans. Closely related through the maternal line, small groups of these Apache Indian women traditionally live and work together, farming on stream banks in the mountains and gathering wild foods in ancestral territories. They trace their ancestry to *Is dzán naadleeshe'* (Changing Woman), a mythological founding mother. This photo shows three generations in prayer during a traditional puberty ceremony known as *na'ii'ees* ("getting her ready"), also called a Sunrise Dance. During this event, marking a girl's transition into womanhood, the sacred power of her clan's founding mother ritually passes to her.

personal belongings outside the door, and the marriage is over.

In addition to their economic and legal functions, lineages play a role in Hopi ceremonial activities. Although membership in the associations that actually perform ceremonies is open to all who have the proper qualifications, clans own and manage all the associations, and in each village a leading lineage acts as its clan's representative. This lineage owns a special house where the clan's religious paraphernalia are stored and cared for by the "clan mother." Together with her brother, the clan's "big uncle," she helps manage ceremonial activities.

Traditionally, each Hopi village is politically autonomous, with its own chief and all-male village council. Here again, however, descent group organization makes itself felt, for the council is made up of men who inherit their positions through their clans. Moreover, the powers of the chief and his council are limited; the chief's major job is to maintain harmony between his village and the spiritual world, and whatever authority he and his council wield is directed at coordination of community effort, not enforcement of official decrees. Decisions are made on a consensual basis, and women's views have to be considered, as well as those of men.

Once again, although men hold positions of authority, women have considerable control over their decisions in a behind-the-scenes way. These men, after all, live in households women control, and their positions within them depend largely on how well they get along with the senior women. Outside the household, women's refusal to play their part in the performance of ceremonies gives them

veto power. Small wonder, then, that Hopi men readily admit that "women usually get their way."[5]

Other Forms of Descent

Among Samoan Islanders (and numerous other cultures in the Pacific as well as in Southeast Asia) a person has the option of affiliating with either the mother's or the father's descent group. Known as *ambilineal descent,* such a kin-ordered system provides a measure of flexibility. However, this flexibility also introduces a possibility of dispute and conflict as unilineal groups compete for members.

This problem does not arise under *double descent,* or double unilineal descent, a very rare system in which descent is matrilineal for some purposes and patrilineal for others.

Generally, where double descent is traced, the matrilineal and patrilineal groups take action in different spheres of society. For example, among the Yakö of eastern Nigeria, property is divided into both patrilineal possessions and matrilineal possessions.[6] The patrilineage owns

---

[5] Schlegel, A. (1977). Male and female in Hopi thought and action. In A. Schlegel (Ed.), *Sexual stratification* (p. 254). New York: Columbia University Press.

[6] Forde, C. D. (1968). Double descent among the Yakö. In P. Bohannan & J. Middleton (Eds.), *Kinship and social organization* (pp. 179–191). Garden City, NY: Natural History.

perpetual productive resources, such as land, whereas the matrilineage owns consumable property, such as livestock. The legally weaker matriline is somewhat more important in religious matters than the patriline. Through double descent, a Yakö might inherit grazing lands from the father's patrilineal group and certain ritual privileges from the mother's matrilineal group.

Finally, when descent derives from both the mother's and father's families equally, anthropologists use the term *bilateral descent*. In such a system people trace their descent from all ancestors, regardless of their gender or side of the family. We may recognize bilateral descent when individuals apply the same genealogical terms to identify similarly related individuals on both sides of the family. For instance, when they speak of a "grandmother" or "grandfather," no indication is given whether these relatives are on the paternal or maternal side of the family.

Bilateral descent exists in various foraging cultures and is also quite common in many contemporary state societies with agricultural, industrial, or postindustrial economies. For example, although most people in Europe, Australia, and North America typically inherit their father's family name (indicative of a culture's history in which patrilineal descent is the norm), they usually consider themselves as much a member of their mother's as their father's family.

Descent Within the Larger Cultural System

There is a close relationship between the descent system and a cultural system's infrastructure. Generally, patrilineal descent predominates where male labor is considered of prime importance, as among pastoralists and agriculturalists. Matrilineal descent predominates mainly among horticulturalists in societies where female work in subsistence is especially important. Numerous matrilineal societies are found in southern Asia, one of the earliest cradles of food production in the world. They are also prominent in parts of indigenous North America, South America's tropical lowlands, and parts of Africa.

Regardless of how descent is traced, descent groups are usually more than mere sets of relatives providing emotional support and a sense of belonging. In nonindustrial societies they are tightly organized working units providing security and services in what can be a difficult, uncertain life. The tasks descent groups perform are manifold. Besides acting as economic units providing mutual aid to their members, they may act to support the aged and

infirm and help with marriages and deaths. Often, they play a role in determining whom an individual may or may not marry.

In many societies an individual has no legal or political status except as a lineage member. Since "citizenship" is derived from lineage membership and legal status depends on it, political powers are derived from it as well. Because a lineage endures after the deaths of members with new members continually born into it, it has a continuing existence that enables it to act like a corporation, as in owning property, organizing productive activities, distributing goods and labor power, assigning status, and regulating relations with other groups. The descent group also may act as a repository of religious traditions. Ancestor worship, for example, is often a powerful force acting to enhance group solidarity. Thus it is a strong, effective base of social organization.

Whatever form of descent predominates, the kin of both mother and father are important components of the social structure in all societies. Just because descent may be traced patrilineally this does not mean that matrilineal relatives are necessarily unimportant. It simply means that, for purposes of group membership, the mother's relatives are excluded. Similarly, under matrilineal descent, the father's relatives are excluded for purposes of group membership.

By way of example, among the matrilineal Trobriand Islanders in the southern Pacific, discussed in previous chapters, children belong to their mother's descent groups, yet fathers play an important role in their upbringing. Upon marriage, the bride and groom's paternal relatives contribute to the exchange of gifts, and, throughout life, a man may expect his paternal kin to help him improve his economic and political position in society. Eventually, sons may expect to inherit personal property from their fathers.

As a traditional institution in a kin-ordered society, the descent group often endures in state-organized societies where political institutions are ineffective or weakly developed. Such is the case in many countries of the world today, especially in remote mountain or desert villages difficult to reach by state authorities.

Also, because the cultural ideas, values, and practices associated with traditional descent groups may be deeply embedded, such patterns of culture often endure in *diasporic communities* (among immigrants who have relocated from their ancestral homelands and retain their distinct cultural identities as ethnic minority groups in their new host countries). In such situations, it is not uncommon for people to seek familiar, kin-ordered cultural solutions to challenges faced in unfamiliar state-organized settings. We see an example of this in the following Original Study on "honor killing" by a young female anthropologist in the Netherlands.

Honor Killings in the Netherlands   *by Clementine van Eck*

When I first told my anthropology professors I wanted to write my dissertation on honor killing among Turkish immigrants in the Netherlands, they told me no way. It was the mid-1990s, and everyone seemed to feel that writing negative things about struggling immigrants was discriminatory. Better to choose a subject that would help them deal with the challenges of settling in Dutch society, such as the problems they experienced as foreigners in school or at work. But I was quite determined to investigate this issue and finally found a professor who shared my interest—Dr. Anton Blok. He himself was specialized in Italian mafia,[a] so quite used to violence of the cultural sort.

Before getting into some of the details of my research, I need to set the stage. Until the 1960s, the Netherlands was a relatively homogeneous society (despite its colonial past). The major differences among its people were not ethnic but religious, namely their distinct ties to Catholicism or Protestantism (of various kinds). The country's population makeup began to change dramatically after the economic boom of the 1960s created a need for cheap labor and led to an influx of migrants from poor areas in Mediterranean countries seeking wage-earning opportunities.

These newcomers came not as immigrants but as "guest laborers" (*gastarbeiders*) expected to return to their countries of origin, including Italy, Yugoslavia, Turkey, and Morocco. While

many did go back home, numerous others did not. In contrast to most of the guest workers from southern European nations, those from Turkey and Morocco are mainly Muslim. And unlike southern European workers who stayed on as immigrants and successfully assimilated into Dutch society, many of the Muslim newcomers formed isolated, diasporic communities.

During the past three decades, these communities have expanded in size and are concentrated in certain areas of various cities. Today, the Turkish population in the Netherlands is about 350,000. Most of them have become Dutch citizens, but they maintain some key cultural features of their historical "honor-and-shame" traditions. And this is what is at stake when we are dealing with the problem of honor killing.

Anthropologists have identified honor-and-shame traditions in many parts of the world, especially in remote traditional herding and farming societies where the power of the political state is either absent or ineffective. People in such areas, my professor, Dr. Blok, explained,

> cannot depend on stable centers of political control for the protection of life and patrimony. In the absence of effective state control, they have to rely on their own forces—on various forms of self-help. These conditions . . . put a premium on self-assertive qualities in men, involving the readiness and capacity to use physical force in order to guarantee the immunity of life and property, including women as the most precious and vulnerable part of the patrimony of men. The extremes of this sense of honour are reached when even merely glancing at a woman is felt as an affront, an incursion into a male domain, touching off a violent response.[b]

Beyond serving as a means of social control in isolated areas, honor-and-shame traditions may be used in situations where state mechanisms are alien to a certain group of people, as among some Turkish and Moroccan migrants in the Netherlands. Focusing on the latter, I tried to make sense of certain cultural practices that often baffle indigenous

Dutch citizens accustomed to a highly organized bureaucratic state where our personal security and justice are effectively managed by social workers, police, courts, and so on. Most of all, I wanted to understand honor killings.

Honor killings are murders in the form of a ritual and they are carried out to purify tarnished honor—specifically honor having to do with something Turks refer to as *namus*. Both men and women possess *namus*. For women and girls *namus* means chastity, while for men it means having chaste family members. A man is therefore dependent for his *namus* on the conduct of the womenfolk in his family. This means in effect that women and girls must not have illicit contact with a member of the opposite sex and must avoid becoming the subject of gossip, since gossip alone can impugn *namus*. The victim of an honor killing can be the girl or woman who tarnished her honor, or the man who did this to her (usually her boyfriend). The girl or woman is killed by her family members, the man is killed by the family of the girl/woman whose honor he has violated.

As I was wrapping up my PhD in 2000, Dutch society still didn't seem quite ready to acknowledge the phenomenon of honor killing. That year a Kurdish boy whose parents were born in Turkey tried to shoot the boyfriend of his sister. Because the attempt took place in a high school and resulted in injury to several students and a teacher, authorities focused on the issue of school safety rather than on the cultural reasons behind the murder attempt.

A shift in government and public awareness of honor killing took place in 2004. That year three Muslim Turkish women were killed by their former husbands on the street. Coming in quick succession, one after the other, these murders did not escape the attention of government officials or the media. Finally, honor killing was on the national agenda. In November of that year I was appointed as cultural anthropologist at the Dutch police force in The Hague district and began working with law enforcers on honor killing cases there (and soon in other areas of the country).

On 2 November 2004, the day I gave an opening speech about honor killings to colleagues at my new job, a radical Muslim migrant from Morocco shot the famous Dutch author and film director Theo van Gogh, well known for his critical, often mocking, views on Islam. Although his murder was not an honor killing, it had key elements of that cleansing ritual: It occurred in a public place (on the street) in front of many people, the victim had to die (injury would not suffice), the killer used many shots (or knife thrusts), the killing was planned (it was not the product of a sudden outburst), and the killer had no remorse.

Let me tell you about a recent and quite typical case. On a Friday evening the local police in an eastern Dutch community called in the help of our police team. A 17-year-old Turkish girl had run away to the family home of her Dutch boyfriend, also 17. Her father, who had discovered that this boy had a police record, telephoned his parents and asked them to send the daughter home. The parents tried to calm him down and told him his daughter was safe at their house. But as he saw it, she was in the most unsafe place in the world,

for she was with the boy she loved. This could only mean that her virginity was in jeopardy and therefore the *namus* of the whole family.

My colleagues and I concluded that the girl had to be taken out of her boyfriend's home that same night: the father knew the place, he didn't want the boy as a son-in-law, and he believed his daughter not mature enough to make a decision about something as important as marriage. ("Just having a boyfriend" was not allowed. You either marry or you don't have a boyfriend, at least not an obvious one.) Because of my honor killing research, I was well aware of similar situations that ended in honor killings. To leave the girl where she was would invite disaster.

After we persuaded the prosecutor that intervention was necessary, the girl was taken from her boyfriend's house and brought to a guarded shelter to prevent her from fleeing back to him the next day. This is anthropology-in-action. You cannot always just wait and see what will happen (although I admit that as a scholar this is very tempting); you have to take responsibility and take

action if you're convinced that a human life is at stake.

When I took up the study of cultural anthropology, I did so just because it intrigued me. I never imagined that what I learned might become really useful. So, what I would like to say to anthropology students is: Never give up on an interesting subject. One day it might just matter that you have become an expert in that area. At this moment I am analyzing all kinds of threatening cases and drawing up genealogies of the families involved—all in the effort to deepen our understanding of and help prevent honor killings.

[a] Blok, A. (1974). *The mafia of a Sicilian village 1860–1960*. New York: Harper & Row.
[b] Blok, A. (1981). Rams and billy-goats: A key to the Mediterranean code of honour. *Man, New Series 16* (3), 427–440. See also Van Eck, C. (2003). *Purified by blood: honour killings amongst Turks in the Netherlands*. Amsterdam: Amsterdam University Press.

Lineage Exogamy

A common characteristic of lineages is *exogamy*. As defined in the previous chapter, this means that lineage members must find their marriage partners in other lineages. One advantage of exogamy is that competition for desirable spouses within the group is curbed, promoting the group's internal cohesiveness. Lineage exogamy means that each marriage is more than a union between two individuals; it is also a new alliance between lineages. This helps to maintain them as components of larger social systems. Finally, lineage exogamy promotes open communication within a society, facilitating the diffusion of knowledge from one lineage to another.

In contemporary North American Indian communities, kinship and descent play an essential role in tribal membership—as illustrated in this chapter's Anthropology Applied.

From Lineage to Clan

In the course of time, as generation succeeds generation and new members are born into the lineage, the kinship group's membership may become too large to manage or may outgrow the lineage's resources. When this happens, as we have seen with the Chinese *tsu*, **fission** occurs; that

is, the original lineage splits into new, smaller lineages. Usually the members of the new lineages continue to recognize their original relationship to one another. The result of this process is the appearance of a larger kind of descent group: the clan.

As already noted, a clan—typically consisting of several lineages—is an extended unilineal descent group whose members claim common descent from a distant ancestor (usually legendary or mythological) but are unable to trace the precise genealogical links back to that ancestor. This stems from the great genealogical depth of the clan, whose founding ancestor lived so far in the past that the links must be assumed rather than known in detail. A clan differs from a lineage in another respect: It lacks the residential unity that is generally, although not always, characteristic of a lineage's core members. As with the lineage, descent may be patrilineal, matrilineal, or ambilineal.

Because clan membership is dispersed rather than localized, it usually does not involve a shared holding of tangible property. Instead, it involves shared participation in

fission The splitting of a descent group into two or more new descent groups.

Resolving a Native American Tribal Membership Dispute

by Harald E. L. Prins

In autumn 1998, I received a call from the tribal chief of the Aroostook band of Micmacs in northern Maine asking for help in resolving a bitter tribal membership dispute. The conflict centered on the fact that several hundred individuals had become tribal members without proper certification of their Micmac kinship status. Traditionalists in the community argued that their tribe's organization was being taken over by "non-Indians." With the formal status of so many members in question, the tribal administration could not properly determine who was entitled to benefit from the available health, housing, and education programs. After some hostile confrontations between the factions, tribal elders requested a formal inquiry into the membership controversy, and I was called in as a neutral party with a long history of working with the band.

My involvement as an advocacy anthropologist began in 1981, when these Micmacs (also spelled Mi'kmaq) first employed me, along with Bunny McBride, to help them achieve U.S. government recognition of their Indian status. At the time, the Micmacs formed a poor and landless community not yet officially recognized as a tribe. During that decade, we helped the band define its political strategies, which included petitioning for federal recognition of their Indian status; claiming their traditional rights to hunt, trap, and fish; and even demanding return of lost ancestral lands.

To generate popular support for the effort, I co-produced a film about the community (*Our Lives in Our Hands*, 1986). Most important, we gathered oral histories and detailed archival documentation to address kinship issues and other government criteria for tribal recognition. The latter included important genealogical records showing that most Micmac adults in the region were at least "half-blood" (having two of their grandparents officially recorded as Indians).

Based on this evidence, we effectively argued that Aroostook Micmacs could claim aboriginal title to lands in the region. Also, we were able to convince politicians in Washington, DC, to introduce a special bill to acknowledge their tribal status and settle their land claims. When

formal hearings were held in 1990, I testified in the U.S. Senate as an expert witness for the Micmacs. The following year, the Aroostook Band of Micmacs Settlement Act became federal law. This made the band eligible for the financial assistance (health, housing, education, and child welfare) and economic development loans that are available to all federally recognized tribes in the United States. Moreover, the law provided the band with funding to buy a 5,000-acre territorial base in Maine.

Flush with federal funding and rapidly expanding its activities, the 500-member band became overwhelmed by complex bureaucratic regulations now governing their existence. Without formally established ground rules determining who could apply for tribal membership, and overlooking federally imposed regulations, hundreds of new names were rather casually added to its tribal rolls.

By 1997, the Aroostook band population had ballooned to almost 1,200 members, and Micmac traditionalists were questioning the legitimacy of many whose names had been added to the band roster. With mounting tension threatening to destroy the band, the tribal chief invited me to evaluate critically the membership claims of more than half the tribe. In early 1999, I reviewed the kinship records submitted by hundreds of individuals whose membership on the tribal rolls was in question. Several months later, I offered my final report to the Micmac community.

After traditional prayers, sweetgrass burning, drumming, and a traditional meal of salmon and moose, I formally presented my findings. Based on the official criteria, about 100 lineal descendants of the original members and just over 150 newcomers met the minimum required qualifications for membership; several hundred others would have to be removed from the tribal roster. After singing, drumming, and closing prayers, the Micmac gathering dispersed.

Today, the band numbers about 850 members and is doing well. It has purchased several tracts of land (collectively over 600 acres), including a small residential reservation near Presque Isle, now home to about 200 Micmacs. Also located here are new tribal administration offices, a health clinic, and a cultural center.

© David Sanipass

The Sanipass-Lafford family cluster in Chapman, Maine, represents a traditional Micmac residential kin-group. Such extended families typically include grandchildren and bilaterally related family members such as in-laws, uncles, and aunts. Taken from the Sanipass family album, this picture shows a handful of members in the mid-1980s: Marline Sanipass Morey with two of her nephews and uncles.

© Lawrence Migdale/PIX

Tsimishian people of Metlakatla, Alaska, raise a memorial totem pole gifted to the community by noted carver David Boxley, a member of the Eagle clan. The tradition of erecting totem poles to commemorate special events endures in several Native American communities in the Pacific Northwest. Carved from tall cedar trees, these spectacular monuments display a clan or lineage's ceremonial property and are prominently positioned as frontal house posts, as markers at grave sites, or at some other place of significance. Often depicting legendary ancestors and mythological animals, the painted carvings symbolically represent a descent group's cultural status and associated privileges in the community.

ceremonial and political matters. Only on special occasions will the membership gather together for specific purposes.

Clans, however, may handle important integrative functions. Like lineages, they may regulate marriage through exogamy. Because of their dispersed membership, clans give individuals the right of entry into associated local groups no matter where they are. Members usually are expected to give protection and hospitality to others in the clan. Hence, these can be expected in any local group that includes people who belong to a single clan.

Clans, lacking the residential unity of lineages, frequently depend on symbols—of animals, plants, natural forces, colors, and special objects—to provide members with solidarity and a ready means of identification. These symbols, called *totems,* often are associated with the clan's mythical origin and reinforce clan members' awareness of their common descent.

The word *totem* comes from the Ojibwa American Indian word *ototeman,* meaning "he is a relative of mine." **Totemism** was defined by the British anthropologist A. R. Radcliffe-Brown as a set of customary beliefs and practices that set up a special system of relations between the society and the plants, animals, and other natural objects that are important.[7]

Totemism varies among cultures. For example, Iroquois Indian matrilineal clans in New York carry such totemic names as Wolf, Bear, and Turtle. Families belonging to these clans can be found in different villages of the Mohawk or any other of the six Iroquois nations, and they act toward each other as if they are related as "brothers," "sisters," "sons," or "daughters." By this device, members of, say, a Bear clan in a Mohawk village can traditionally travel to a nearby Oneida village, or to more distant Onondaga, Cayuga, Tuscarora, or even Seneca villages some 200 miles west of their homeland, and be welcomed and hosted in any of these Iroquois settlements by members of local Bear clans.

In addition to the above-mentioned matrilineal clans (or matriclans), there are also patrilineal clans (or patriclans) tracing descent exclusively through men from a founding ancestor. Historically, a few dozen such clans existed in the Scottish highlands, often identified with the prefix "Mac" or "Mc" (from an old Celtic word meaning "son of"). During the past few hundred years, large Scottish clans such as McGregor and Mackenzie broke apart as many members moved away in search of economic opportunity. Today, their descendants are dispersed all across the globe, especially in Australia, Canada, England,

---

[7] Radcliffe-Brown, A. R. (1931). Social organization of Australian tribes. *Oceana Monographs 1,* 29.

totemism The belief that people are related to particular animals, plants, or natural objects by virtue of descent from common ancestral spirits.

In the highlands of Scotland, as among many traditional peoples around the world, large kinship groups known as clans have been important units of social organization. Now dispersed all over the world, clan members gather and express their kinship with one another by wearing a tartan skirt, or kilt, with a distinct plaid identifying clan membership. Pictured here is a "parade of tartans"—a festive expression of group identity and ethnic pride during a gathering of the clans at Grandfather Mountain in North Carolina.

Clans among the Six Nations of the Iroquois confederacy in New York State are a kinship construct that, traditionally, facilitated free travel of clan members to multiple member villages. This portrait, made in 1710, shows Sa Ga Yeath Qua Pieth Tow, a chief of the Mohawk Nation. Behind him stands a bear, which represents his clan.

New Zealand, and the United States. During the past few decades, widely scattered descendants have sought to reestablish their kinship ties to ancestral clans, and many travel great distances to attend the annual gathering of their clan, preferably in their traditional ancient homeland in the highlands of Scotland. These clan members express their kinship with one another by wearing woolen shawls, kilts, or other pieces of clothing made of their clan tartan—a distinct plaid pattern and color identifying their particular clan membership.

A reductive variation of totemism may be found in contemporary industrial and postindustrial societies, where sports teams are often given the names of such powerful wild animals as bears, lions, and wildcats. In the United States, this extends to the Democratic Party's donkey and the Republican Party's elephant, and to the Elks, the Lions, and other fraternal and social organizations. These animal emblems, or mascots, however, do not involve the notion of biological descent and the strong sense of kinship that they symbolize for clans, nor are they linked with the traditional ritual observances associated with clan totems.

Phratries and Moieties

Larger kinds of descent groups are phratries and moieties (Figure 21.3). A **phratry** (after the Greek word for "brotherhood") is a unilineal descent group composed of

phratry A unilineal descent group composed of at least two clans that supposedly share a common ancestry, whether or not they really do.

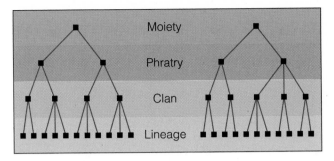

Figure 21.3 This diagram shows how lineages, clans, phratries, and moieties form an organizational hierarchy. Each moiety is subdivided into phratries, each phratry into clans, and each clan into lineages.

at least two clans that supposedly share a common ancestry, whether or not they really do. Like individuals in the clan, phratry members cannot trace precisely their descent links to a common ancestor, although they firmly believe such an ancestor existed.

If the entire society is divided into only two major descent groups, whether they are equivalent to clans or phratries, each group is called a **moiety** (after the French word *moitié,* for "half"). Members of the moiety believe themselves to share a common ancestor but cannot prove it through definite genealogical links. As a rule, the feelings of kinship among members of lineages and clans are stronger than those of members of phratries and moieties. This may be due to the much larger size and more diffuse nature of the latter groups.

Since feelings of kinship are often weaker between people from different clans, the moiety system is a cultural invention that keeps clan-based communities together by

binding the clans into a social network of obligatory giving and receiving. That is to say, by institutionalizing reciprocity between groups of clans, the moiety system joins together families who otherwise would not be sufficiently invested in maintaining the commonwealth.

Like lineages and clans, phratries and moieties are often exogamous, and so these different kin-groups are bound together by marriages between their members. And like clans, they provide members rights of access to other communities, as among the Hopi. In a community that does not include one's clan members, one's phratry members are still there to turn to for hospitality. Finally, moieties may perform reciprocal services for one another. Among them, individuals turn to members of the opposite "half" in their community for the necessary mourning rituals when a member of their own moiety dies. Such interdependence between moieties, again, serves to maintain the cohesion of the entire society.

The principle of institutionalized reciprocity between groups of matrilineal clans organized into two equal halves, or moieties, is beautifully illustrated in the circular settlement pattern of many traditional Indian villages in the tropical forest of South America's Amazon region. Dwellings located in one-half of the village are those of clans belonging to one exogamous moiety, and those on the opposite side are the dwellings of clans belonging to the other. Since their clans are often matrilineal, the institutionalized rules of reciprocity in this kin-ordered

> **moiety** Each group that results from a division of a society into two halves on the basis of descent.

Many Amazonian Indians in South America's tropical woodlands traditionally live in circular villages socially divided into moieties. Here we see the Canela Indians' Escalvado village as it was in 1970. (Behind it is a smaller abandoned village where part of the tribe lived before uniting under one chief.) The village is 300 meters (165 feet) wide. The community's "upper" moiety meets in the western part. Nearly all 1,800 members of the Canela tribe reside in the village during festival seasons, but otherwise they are largely dispersed into their smaller, farm-centered circular villages. (Missionaries built the landing strip.)

Figure 21.4 **EGO** and his or her kindred. The kindred designates a person's exact degree of being related by blood to other relatives in the family. This degree of blood relatedness determines not only one's social obligations toward relatives, but also one's rights. For instance, when a wealthy, widowed, and childless woman dies without a will, specific surviving members of her kindred will be legally entitled to inherit from her.

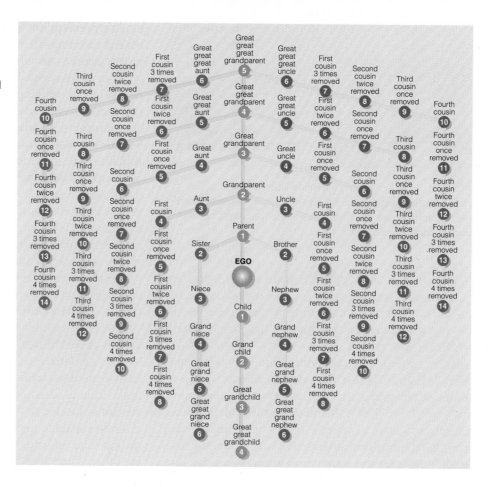

community traditionally require that a woman marry a man from a clan house on the opposite side of the village, who then moves into her ancestral clan house. Their son, however, will one day have to find a wife from his father's original moiety and will have to move to his father's mother's side of the village. That is to say, the moiety system of institutionalized reciprocity functions like a social "zipper" between clans engaged in a repetitive cycle of exchange relations.

Bilateral Kinship and the Kindred

Important though descent groups are in many societies, they are not found in all societies, nor are they the only kinds of extended kinship groups to be found. *Bilateral*

kindred An individual's close blood relatives on the maternal and paternal sides of his or her family.

EGO The central person from whom the degree of each relationship is traced.

kinship, a characteristic of most contemporary European and American societies as well as a number of food-foraging cultures, affiliates a person with genetically close relatives (but not in-laws) through both sexes. In other words, the individual traces descent through both parents, all four grandparents, and so forth, recognizing multiple ancestors. Theoretically, one is associated equally with all "blood" relatives on both the mother's and father's sides of the family. Thus this principle relates an individual lineally to all eight great-grandparents and laterally to all third and fourth cousins.

Since such a huge group is too big to be socially practical, it is usually reduced to a smaller circle of paternal and maternal relatives, called the kindred. The **kindred** may be defined as an individual's close blood relatives on the maternal and paternal side of his or her family. Since the kindred is laterally rather than lineally organized—that is, **EGO,** or the central person from whom the degree of each relationship is traced, is the center of the group — it is not a true descent group (Figure 21.4).

Most North Americans are familiar with the kindred; those who belong are simply referred to as relatives. It includes those blood relatives on both sides of the family who are seen on important occasions, such as family weddings, reunions, and funerals. In the United States, for example, nearly everyone can identify the members of their kindred up to grandparents and first cousins, and quite a few can also name their great grandparents.

Because of its bilateral structure, a kindred is never the same for any two people except siblings (brothers and sisters). And it is not self-perpetuating—it ceases with EGO's death. It has no constant leader, nor can it easily hold, administer, or pass on property. Because of its vagueness, temporary nature, and changing affiliation, the kindred cannot function as a group except in relation to EGO. In most cases, it cannot organize work, nor can it easily administer justice or assign status.

It can, however, be turned to for aid. In non-Western societies, for example, raiding or trading parties may be composed of kindreds. The group comes together to perform some particular function, shares the results, and then disbands. It also can act as a ceremonial group for rites of passage—initiation rituals and the like. Traditionally, the kindred is also of importance in many European cultures, where it may serve to help raise bail, compensate a victim's family, or carry out revenge for the murder or injury of a someone in one's kindred. Finally, kindreds also can regulate marriage through exogamy.

Kindreds are frequently found in industrial and postindustrial state societies where capitalist wage labor conditions promote mobility and individualism, thereby weakening the importance of a strong kinship organization. In societies where small domestic units—nuclear families or single-parent households—are of primary importance, bilateral kinship and kindred organization are likely to result. This can be seen in modern industrial and postindustrial societies, in newly emerging societies in the "underdeveloped" world, and in still-existing food-foraging societies throughout the world.

Kinship Terminology and Kinship Groups

Any system of organizing people who are relatives into different kinds of groups—whether kindreds, lineages, or clans—influences how relatives are labeled. Kinship terminology systems vary considerably across cultures, reflecting the positions individuals occupy within their respective societies and helping to differentiate one relative from another. Distinguishing factors include gender, generational differences, or genealogical differences. In the various systems of kinship terminology, any one of these factors may be emphasized at the expense of others.

By looking at the terms a particular society uses for their relatives, an anthropologist can tell how kinship groups are structured, what relationships are considered especially important, and sometimes what the prevailing attitudes are concerning various relationships. For instance, a number of languages use the same term to identify a brother and a cousin, and others have a single word for cousin, niece, and nephew. Some cultures find it useful to distinguish an oldest brother from his younger brothers and have different words for these brothers. And unlike English, many languages distinguish between an aunt who is a mother's sister and one who is a father's sister.

Regardless of the factors emphasized, all kinship terminologies accomplish two important tasks. First, they classify similar kinds of individuals into single specific categories; second, they separate different kinds of individuals into distinct categories. Generally, two or more kin are merged under the same term when the individuals have more or less the same rights and obligations with respect to the person referring to them as such. This is the case among most English-speaking North Americans, for instance, when someone refers to a mother's sister and a father's sister both as an "aunt." As far as the speaker is concerned, both relatives possess a similar status.

Several different systems of kinship terminology result from the application of the above principles just mentioned, including the Eskimo, Hawaiian, Iroquois, Crow, Omaha, Sudanese, Kariera, and Aranda systems, each named after the ethnographic example first or best described by anthropologists. The latter five of these systems are fascinating in their complexity and are found among only a few of the world's societies. However, to illustrate some of the basic principles involved, we will focus our attention on the first three systems.

Eskimo System

The Eskimo system, comparatively rare among all the world's systems, is the one used by Euramericans, as well as by a number of food-foraging peoples (including the Inuit and other Eskimos; hence the name). Sometimes referred to as the *lineal system*, the **Eskimo system** emphasizes the nuclear family by specifically identifying mother, father, brother, and sister while lumping together all other relatives into a few large categories (Figure 21.5). For example, the father is distinguished from the father's brother (uncle), but the father's brother

Eskimo system Kinship reckoning in which the nuclear family is emphasized by specifically identifying the mother, father, brother, and sister, while lumping together all other relatives into broad categories such as uncle, aunt, and cousin; also known as a lineal system.

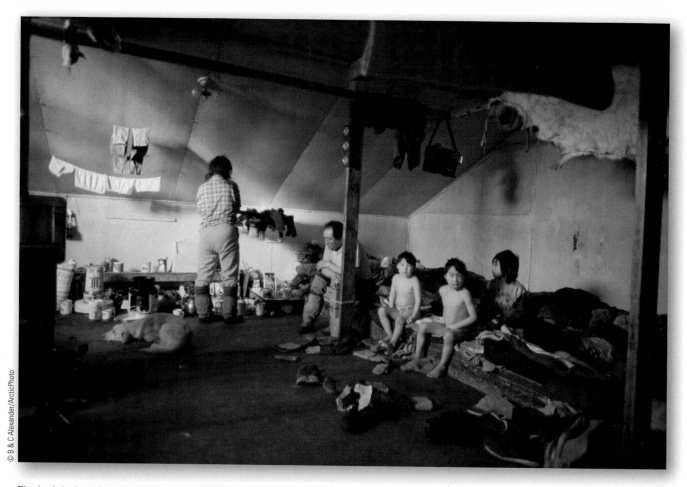

The Inuit in Canada are one of several large Eskimo groups inhabiting Arctic regions from Greenland to Alaska and eastern Siberia. Although they speak different languages and dialects, they share a traditional way of life primarily based on hunting and fishing in which the nuclear family is the primary social unit. As such, their kinship terminology system specifically identifies EGO's father, mother, brother, and sister and lumps all other relatives into a few broad categories that do not distinguish the side of the family from which they derive. Here we see the Taqqaugaq family in their outpost camp home at Iglurjuat on Baffin Island, Nunavut, Canada.

Figure 21.5 The Eskimo system of kinship terminology emphasizes the nuclear family (circled). EGO's father and mother are distinguished from EGO's aunts and uncles, as are siblings from cousins.

is not distinguished from the mother's brother (both are called "uncle"). The mother's sister and father's sister are treated similarly, both called "aunt." In addition, all the sons and daughters of aunts and uncles are called "cousin," thereby making a generational distinction but without indicating the side of the family to which they belong or even their gender.

Unlike other terminologies, the Eskimo system provides separate and distinct terms for the nuclear family members. This is probably because the Eskimo system is generally found in bilateral societies where the dominant kin-group is the kindred, in which only immediate family members are important in day-to-day affairs. This is especially true of modern North American societies, where many families are independent, living apart from, and not directly involved with, other relatives except on special occasions. Thus most North Americans (and others) generally distinguish between their closest kin (parents and siblings) but lump together (as aunts, uncles, cousins) other kin on both sides of the family.

Hawaiian System

The **Hawaiian system** of kinship terminology, common (as its name implies) in Hawaii and other islands in the southern central Pacific Ocean but found elsewhere as well, is the least complex system, in that it uses the fewest terms. The Hawaiian system is also called the *generational system,* since all relatives of the same generation and sex are referred to by the same term (Figure 21.6). For example, in one's parents' generation, the term used to refer to one's father is used as well for the father's brother and mother's brother. Similarly, one's mother, mother's sister, and father's sister are all lumped together under a single term. In EGO's generation, male and female cousins are distinguished by gender and are equated with brothers and sisters.

> **Hawaiian system** Kinship reckoning in which all relatives of the same sex and generation are referred to by the same term.

Figure 21.6 In the Hawaiian kinship system the men numbered 2 and 6 are called by the same term as father (3) by EGO; the women numbered 1 and 5 are called by the same term as mother (4). All cousins' of EGO's own generation (7–16) are considered brothers (B) and sisters (Z).

Polynesian societies throughout the Pacific Ocean are traditionally structured according to the Hawaiian system of kinship terminology. With so many relatives identified as their fathers and mothers, children growing up in hamlets on islands such as Hawaii, as well as Tahiti, Samoa, Tonga, or Figi, are welcome in many homes where they share meals and find a place to sleep like other brothers and sisters.

© Erica Heider

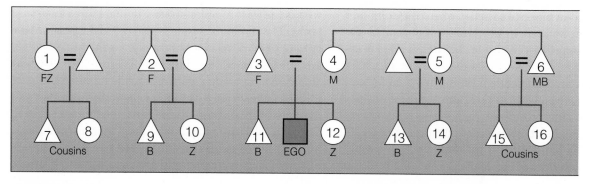

Figure 21.7 According to the Iroquois system of kinship terminology, EGO's father's brother (2) is called by the same term as the father (3); the mother's sister (5) is called by the same term as the mother (4); but the people numbered 1 and 6 are each referred to by a distinct term. Those people numbered 9 to 14 are all considered siblings, but 7, 8, 15, and 16 are considered cousins.

The Hawaiian system reflects the absence of strong unilineal descent, and members on both the father's and the mother's sides are viewed as more or less equal. The siblings of EGO's father and mother are all recognized as being similar relations and are merged under a single term appropriate for their gender. In like manner, the children belonging to the siblings of EGO's parents are related to EGO in the same way the brother and sister are. Falling under the incest taboo, they are ruled out as potential marriage partners.

Iroquois System

In the **Iroquois system** of kinship terminology, the father and father's brother are referred to by a single term, as are the mother and mother's sister; however, the father's sister and mother's brother are given separate terms (Figure 21.7). In one's own generation, brothers, sisters, and parallel cousins (offspring of parental siblings of the same sex—that is, the children of the mother's sister or father's brother) of the same sex are referred to by the same terms, which is logical enough considering that they are the offspring of people who are classified in the same category as EGO's actual mother and father. Cross cousins (offspring of parental siblings of opposite sex—that is, the children of the mother's brother or father's sister) are distinguished by terms that set them apart from all other

kin. In fact, cross cousins are often preferred as spouses, for marriage to them reaffirms alliances between related lineages or clans.

Iroquois terminology, named for the Iroquoian Indians of North America's woodlands, is in fact very widespread and is usually found with unilineal descent groups. It was, for example, the terminology in use until recently in rural Chinese Han society.

Making Relatives

In every culture—from kin-ordered foraging, herding, or farming communities to state-organized capitalist societies—people have developed ideas about the status of relatives. These ideas concern how someone becomes one of "us"—whether by birth, paternal recognition, or some other means. And although many languages may stress the biological, as the English term "blood relative" demonstrates, what ultimately matters is the *culturally defined social status* of a person who is recognized as kin, with all the specific rights and obligations that come with being a daughter, son, brother, or sister to someone else in that kin-group. That is what "being related" is all about and what gives it symbolic meaning with practical consequences. Each kin term marks out a specific set of rights and obligations for individuals socially identified by such a cultural label. In state societies governed by law, these rights may even be legally spelled out in detail.

Fictive Kin by Ritual Adoption

One example of "making relatives" of individuals who are not biologically related is adoption—as discussed in the previous chapter's Globalscape on the transnational

---

Iroquois system Kinship reckoning in which a father and father's brother are referred to by a single term, as are a mother and mother's sister, but a father's sister and mother's brother are given separate terms. Parallel cousins are classified with brothers and sisters, while cross cousins are classified separately but not equated with relatives of some other generation.

adoption of children. Adoption is a longstanding and widespread cultural practice in many societies all across the world. For instance, it is not uncommon in kin-ordered tribal communities for the head of a clan or family to adopt an outsider, especially when such an individual is valued as a contributing member because of unique skills or contacts with the outside world.

Historically, families and clans facing exceptional challenges to their survival sometimes went to war to obtain human captives from other societies—sometimes young men, but especially women and children. These captives would then be adopted. This occurred among Iroquois Indians in northeastern America. In the 17th and 18th centuries, they often incorporated specially selected war captives and other valued strangers, including European colonists, into their kin-groups in order to make up for population losses due to warfare and disease. As soon as these newcomers were ceremonially naturalized, they acquired essentially the same birthright status as those actually born into one of the families and were henceforth identified by the same kin term as the member being replaced.

Today, it is still not uncommon in traditional societies, especially in kin-ordered communities, for the head of a clan or family to adopt an outsider, especially when such an individual is valued as a contributing member because of unique skills or contacts with the outside world. This may also befall an anthropologist, as noted in our fieldwork chapter, when she or he is doing long-term participant observation in a culture where such ritual incorporation into a kin-group is customary. As an outsider committed to learning the language and culture, the anthropologist may also offer valuable services in return, bringing useful gifts such as steel axes or machetes. As an adopted member of a family or clan, such an out/insider provides a useful linkage with powerful external forces, including international organizations with a mission to protect human rights.

A form of ritual adoption traditionally practiced in many parts of Europe—and spreading to other parts of the world through European colonization or settlement—is the institution of god-parenthood. Generally, this involves a mother and/or father of a newborn child inviting another adult, whether already a relative or not, to become the godfather or godmother to their newborn when it is baptized and formally named. One of the many variations of this institution is *compadrazgo,* or "co-parenthood." Especially common in Latin America, *compadrazgo* involves a child's father and/or mother and godfather and/or godmother becoming linked to each other through the ritual of a Roman Catholic baptism; they thereby agree to certain mutual rights and obligations. In *compadrazgo,* the main emphasis is placed not on the child–godparent relationship but on the fictive kinship between the child's parents and the sponsor who becomes a ritual co-parent, or *compadre.* Historically common in South Europe and Latin America, such quasi-kinship is

> a pact for mutual support between the two *compadres,* co-parents, involved. Such a pact can be entered into between two *compadres* who are each other's equals in social and economic standing. Very often, however, it is formed between people, of whom one is wealthier, of higher social standing and more powerful politically than the other.[8]

Kinship and New Reproductive Technologies

Today's advances in reproductive technologies also pose new opportunities for kin-making. As defined in the previous chapter, *new reproductive technologies* (NRTs) are alternative means of reproduction such as surrogate motherhood and in vitro fertilization. Since 1978, when the world's first "test-tube baby" was created, thousands of babies have been created outside the womb, without sexual intercourse—and all kinds of new technologies have become part of the reproductive repertoire.

These technologies have opened up a mind-boggling array of reproductive possibilities and social relations. For example, if a child is conceived from a donor egg, implanted in another woman's womb, to be raised by yet another woman, who is its mother? To complicate matters even further, the egg may have been fertilized by sperm from a donor not married to, or in a sexual relationship with, any of these women. Indeed, it has been suggested that about a dozen different modern kin-type categories are embraced in the concepts of mother and father in today's changing societies.[9]

Clearly, NRTs challenge previously held notions of parenthood and kinship. They force us to rethink what being biologically "related" to others really means. Moreover, they drive home the point that the human capacity for securing relatives is not only impressive and ingenious but also fascinating.

---

[8] Wolf, E. R., & Hansen, E. C. (1972). *The human condition in Latin America* (pp. 131–132). New York: Oxford University Press.

[9] Stone, L. (1998). *Kinship and gender* (p. 272). Boulder, CO: Westview.

Questions for Reflection

1.   Have you, for reasons of support and security, created and maintained a social network of relatives beyond your immediate family or household? How so?

2.   People in modern industrial and postindustrial societies generally treasure ideas of personal freedom, individuality, and privacy as essential to their happiness. Considering the social functions of kinship relations in traditional non-state societies, why do you think that such ideas may be considered unsociable and even dangerously selfish?

3.   Why do you think that one of the simplest kinship terminology systems imaginable, namely the Eskimo system, is functionally adequate for most Europeans, North Americans, Australians, and others living in complex modern societies?

4.   One major reason anthropologists are so interested in understanding a culture's kinship terminology system is that it offers a quick but crucially important insight into a group's social structure. Why do you think this is especially true for traditional communities of foragers, herders, and farmers but is less so for urban neighborhoods in industrial and postindustrial societies?

5.   Why do you think that religious institutions such as the Roman Catholic Church and criminal associations such as the Mafia use kinship terms such as "father," "mother," "brother," "sister," "son," and "daughter" for members who are not relatives?

Suggested Readings

Carsten, J. (Ed.). (2008). *Cultures of relatedness: New approaches to the study of kinship*. Cambridge, England: Cambridge University Press.

A cross-cultural examination of what it means to be a relative at a time when established ideas about kinship are being transformed by radical changes in marriage arrangements and gender relations, as well as new reproductive technologies. This collection of contemporary studies—including cultures in Alaska, China, India, Madagascar, and Sudan—shows why we can no longer take it for granted that our most fundamental social relationships are grounded in biology or nature.

Finkler, K. (2000). *Experiencing the new genetics: Family and kinship on the medical frontier*. Philadelphia: University of Pennsylvania Press.

An exploration of medical and genetic aspects of kinship and debates concerning the social impact of modern medical and genetic knowledge and practices.

Fox, R. (1968). *Kinship and marriage in an anthropological perspective*. Baltimore: Penguin.

This classic book outlines some of the methods of analysis used in the anthropological treatment of kinship and marriage. It updates Radcliffe-Brown's *African Systems of Kinship and Marriage* and features a perspective focused on kinship groups and social organization.

Parkin, R. (1997). *Kinship: An introduction to basic concepts*. Cambridge, MA: Blackwell.

A solid, useful, readable text on the basics of kinship study.

Schusky, E. L. (1983). *Manual for kinship analysis* (2nd ed.). Lanham, MD: University Press of America.

This useful book discusses the elements of kinship, diagramming, systems classification, and descent with specific examples.

Challenge Issue   Beyond ties of kinship and household, people extend their social networks to cope with multiple challenges of human survival. These networks may take the form of groups based on gender, age, common interest, and social class. The latter—tied to ranking differences in wealth, status, and power—may range from relatively open to closed social classes such as estates, castes, or "races." Societies traditionally depending on armed self-defense for their security may meet this challenge by forming groups of young men who are mature enough to fight but still unmarried and childless. Such is the case among various East African herding societies, including the Samburu of Kenya, pictured here. Male teenagers of the same age set are collectively initiated as warriors, serving together for fifteen years in protecting their community and livestock from wild animals and enemies. Their long braids of hair, treated with red ochre clay, and ornaments distinguish them from other Samburu.

Anthropologists and Social Impact Assessment

Anthropologists frequently do a type of policy research called a *social impact assessment*, which entails collecting data about a community or neighborhood for planners of development projects. Such an assessment seeks to determine a project's effect by determining how and upon whom its impact will fall and whether the impact is likely to be positive or negative.

In the United States, any project requiring a federal permit or license, or using federal funds, by law must be preceded by a social impact assessment as part of the environmental review process. Examples of such projects include highway construction, urban renewal, water diversion schemes, and land reclamation. Often, such projects are sited so that their impact falls most heavily on neighborhoods or communities inhabited by people in low socioeconomic strata—sometimes because the projects are viewed as a way of improving the lives of poor people and sometimes because the poor people have less political power to block these proposals.

As an illustration of this kind of work, anthropologist Sue Ellen Jacobs was hired to do a social impact assessment of a water diversion project in New Mexico planned by the Bureau of Land Reclamation in cooperation with the Bureau

of Indian Affairs. This project proposed construction of a diversion dam and an extensive canal system for irrigation on the Rio Grande. The project would affect twenty-two communities inhabited by primarily Hispanic Americans, as well as two Indian pueblos. Unemployment was high in the region, and the project was seen as a way to promote urbanization, which theoretically would be associated with industrial development, while bringing new land into production for intensive agriculture.

What the planners failed to take into account was that both the Hispanic and Indian populations were heavily committed to farming for household consumption (with some surpluses raised for the market), using a system of irrigation canals that had been established for 300 years. These canals are maintained by elected supervisors familiar with the communities and knowledgeable about water laws, ditch management, and sustainable crop production. Such individuals can resolve conflicts concerning water allocation and land use—and often other issues as well. Under the proposed project, this system was to be given up in favor of one in which fewer people would control larger tracts of land, and water allocation would be in the hands of a government technocrat.

One of the strongest measures of local government would be lost.

Not surprisingly, Jacobs discovered widespread community opposition to this project, and her report helped convince Congress that any positive impact was far outweighed by negative effects. One of the major objections to the construction project was that it would obliterate the centuries-old irrigation system. Project planners did not seem to recognize the antiquity and cultural significance of these traditional irrigation structures, referring to them as "temporary diversion structures." The fact that the old dams associated with the ditches were attached to local descent groups was simply not acknowledged in the government documents.

Beyond infringing on local control, the project threatened the community with a range of negative side effects: problems linked to population growth and relocation, a loss of fishing and other river-related resources, and new health hazards, including increased threat of drowning, insect breeding, and airborne dust.

Adapted from van Willigen, J. (1986). Applied anthropology (p. 169). South Hadley, MA: Bergin & Garvey.

divided and ranked into social strata, or layers, and do not share equally in the basic resources that support income, status, and power. Members of the bottom strata typically have fewer resources, lower status, and less power than those in top-ranked strata. In addition, the restrictions and obligations imposed on those in the lowest-ranked strata are usually more strenuous or oppressive, and they must work harder for far less financial reward.

In short, social stratification amounts to culturally institutionalized inequality. In the United States, Hispanic, African American, and American Indian groups are among those who have struggled with their positions in the low-ranked strata. As profiled in this chapter's Anthropology Applied feature, their needs are often ignored in development efforts.

Stratified societies stand in sharp contrast to **egalitarian societies,** in which everyone has about equal rank, access to, and power over basic resources. In these societies, social values of communal sharing are culturally emphasized and approved; wealth hoarding and elitist pretensions are despised, belittled, or ridiculed. As we saw in earlier chapters,

foraging societies are characteristically egalitarian, although there are some exceptions.

Social Class and Caste

A **social class** may be defined as a category of individuals in a stratified society who enjoy equal or nearly equal prestige according to the system of evaluation. The qualification "nearly equal" is important, for a certain amount of inequality may occur even within a given class. Class distinctions are not always clear-cut and obvious in societies that have a wide and continuous range of differential privileges.

egalitarian society A society in which everyone has about equal rank, access to, and power over the basic resources that support survival, influence, and prestige.

social class A category of individuals in a stratified society who enjoy equal or nearly equal prestige according to the system of evaluation.

A **caste** is a closed social class in a stratified society in which membership is determined by birth and fixed for life. The opposite of the principle that all humans are born equal, the caste system is based on the principle that humans neither are nor can be equal. Castes are strongly endogamous, and offspring are automatically members of their parents' caste.

TRADITIONAL HINDU CASTE SYSTEM

The classic ethnographic example of a caste system is the traditional Hindu caste system of India (also found in other parts of Asia, including Nepal and Bali). Perhaps the world's longest surviving social hierarchy, it encompasses a complex ranking of social groups on the basis of "ritual purity." Each of some 2,000 different castes considers itself as a distinct community higher or lower than other castes, although their particular ranking varies among geographic regions and over time.

The different castes are associated with specific occupations and customs, such as food habits and styles of dress, along with rituals involving notions of purity and pollution. Traditional Hindus are taught to follow the ritual path of duty, or *dharma*, of the specific caste into which they are born, and learn to avoid everyone and everything considered taboo to their caste. For this reason, castes are always endogamous. Differences in caste rankings are traditionally justified by the Hindu religious doctrine of the transmigration of the soul, or *karma*, a belief that one's place in life is determined by one's deeds in previous lifetimes.

All of these castes, or *jatis*, are organized into four ranked orders, or *varnas* (literally meaning "colors"), distinguished partly by occupation and ranked in order of descending religious status of purity (Figure 22.1). The religious foundation for this social hierarchy is found in a sacred text known as the Laws of Manu, an ancient work about 2,000 years old and considered by traditional Hindus as the highest authority on their cultural institutions. It defines the Brahmans as the purest and therefore highest *varna*. As priests and lawgivers, Brahmans represent the world of religion and learning. Next come the fighters and rulers, known as the Kshatriyas. Below them are the Vaisyas (merchants and traders), who are engaged in commercial, agricultural, and pastoral pursuits. At the bottom are the Sudras (artisans and laborers), an order required to serve the other three *varnas* and who also make a living by handicrafts.

Falling outside the *varna* system is a fifth category of degraded individuals known as "Untouchables." These

"outcastes" are tasked with doing the "dirty work" in society—collecting garbage, removing animal carcasses, cleaning streets, and disposing of dung, sewage, and other refuse. Commonly associated with filth and discriminated against by fellow Hindus as ritually impure, Untouchables were historically prohibited from owning land or the tools of their trade. Brahmans (who view themselves as the most pure) and members of other *varnas* avoid direct contact with these Untouchables, due to the belief that touching or accepting food from such "dirty" persons—let alone having sexual relations with them—would result in ritual pollution.

Untouchables constitute a large pool of cheap labor at the beck and call of those controlling economic and political affairs. In an effort to bestow some dignity on these poverty-stricken victims of the caste system, Hindu nationalist leader Mahatma Gandhi renamed them *harijan* or "children of God."

Although India's national constitution of 1950 sought to abolish caste discrimination and the practice of Untouchability, the caste system remains deeply entrenched in Hindu culture and is still widespread throughout southern Asia, especially in rural India. In what has been called India's "hidden apartheid," entire villages in many Indian states remain completely segregated by caste. Traditionally powerless and desperately poor, members of this religious inferior underclass endure near complete social isolation, humiliation, and discrimination based exclusively on their birth status. Even the shadow of an Untouchable is believed to pollute the higher-ranking castes. They may not cross the line dividing their part of the village from that occupied by higher castes, drink water from public wells, or visit the same temples as the higher castes. Their children are still often made to sit at the back of classrooms, and in rural areas huge numbers still lack access to education altogether.[9] Over the past five decades, Untouchables,

---

caste A closed social class in a stratified society in which membership is determined by birth and fixed for life.

[9] Committee on the Elimination of Racial Discrimination, India. (2007, March). Consideration of reports submitted by states parties under Article 9 of the International Convention on the Elimination of All Forms of Racial Discrimination, 70th Session (p. 3). www2.ohchr.org/english/bodies/cerd/cerds70.htm; see also "Hidden apartheid: Caste discrimination against India's Untouchables." (2007). Human Rights Watch and the Center for Human Rights and Global Justice.

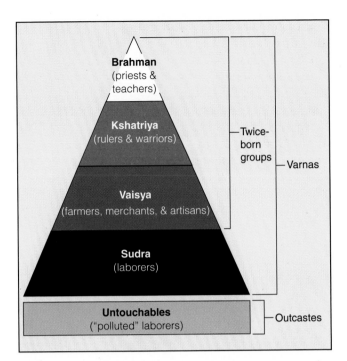

Figure 22.1 Hindu castes are organized into four "grades of being" called *varnas* ("colors"), which determine what members are permitted to do, touch, or eat; where they live; how they dress; and who they can marry. The highest-ranking order Brahman is associated with the color white, below which are the Kshatriya (red) and Vaisya (brown). Members born into these *varnas* are all believed to have been reincarnated from a morally correct earlier life in a lower-ranked order. Below these three are the Sudra (black), who make a living as laborers. Lower still are the "polluted" laborers—the Untouchables who are charged with cleaning the streets and with the collection and disposal of garbage, animal carcasses, and sewage. Brahmans and members of other *varnas* avoid direct contact with Untouchables, believing that touching or accepting food from them would result in ritual pollution.

in concert with the lowest-ranking Sudra castes, have built a civil rights movement—described later in this chapter.

Castelike situations are found in other places in the world. In Bolivia, Ecuador, and several other South and Central American countries, for example, the wealthy upper class is almost exclusively white and rarely intermarries with people of non-European descent. In contrast, the lower class of working poor in those countries is primarily made up of American Indian laborers and peasants. Likewise, most European stratified societies were historically organized in closed social classes known as *estates*—ranked as clergy, nobility, and citizens and each with distinctive political rights (privileges). These were hierarchically identified by titles and forms of address, and they

were publicly identified by distinctive dress and codes of behavior.

Historical Racial Segregation in South Africa and the United States

Other than social class, caste, and estate, the hierarchy in a stratified society may be based on ethnic origin or skin color. For instance, dark-skinned individuals culturally classified as "colored" or "black" may encounter social rules excluding them from certain jobs or neighborhoods and making it difficult if not impossible to befriend or marry someone with a lighter skin color.

One of the best-known historical examples of a pluralistic country with social stratification based on the notion of "race" is South Africa. From 1948 to 1994, a minority of 4.5 million people of European descent imposed a political regime of racial segregation and discrimination on 25 million indigenous Zulu, Sotho, Tswana, Xhosas, Khoi (Hottentot), Bushmen, and other ethnic groups. Known as *apartheid* (an Afrikaans-Dutch term meaning "segregation" or "separation"), this white superiority ideology officially relegated indigenous dark-skinned Africans to a low-ranking stratum. Similar to the Hindu caste system with its concepts of ritual purity and pollution, South African whites feared pollution of their purity through improper contact with blacks.

Until the mid-20th century, institutionalized racial segregation officially prevailed in the United States, where the country's ruling upper class was historically comprised exclusively of individuals of European ("Caucasian" or "white") descent. After the American Revolution, several states in New England joined Virginia and other southern states and made it illegal for whites to marry blacks or American Indians. After the federal government officially abolished slavery in 1863, these miscegenation laws remained in force in many states from Maine to Florida for decades.

In 1924, Virginia's General Assembly passed the Racial Integrity Act to prevent light-skinned individuals with some African ancestry from "passing" as whites. Known as the *one drop rule,* it codified the idea of white racial purity by classifying individuals as black if just one of their multiple ancestors was of African origin ("one drop of Negro blood").

However light-skinned, they were subject to a wide range of discriminatory practices not applicable to whites. Such institutionalized racial discrimination continued for a century after slavery was abolished, and today self-segregation exists in many parts of the United States.

Despite U.S. civil rights laws passed in the 1960s (prohibiting discrimination in accommodations, schools, employment, and voting for reasons of color, "race," religion, or national origin), economic inequality persists as the

During South Africa's apartheid regime (1948–1994), the white minority of European descent imposed strict racial segregation in that country, which not only dictated where "blacks" and "coloreds" were allowed to live or work, but also prohibited who they could marry, where they could worship and socialize, and even where they could swim.

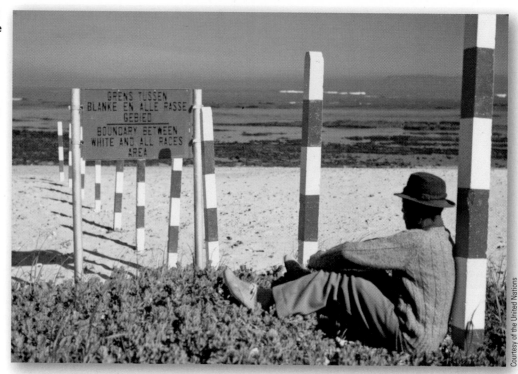

Courtesy of the United Nations

typical African American household has 54 cents of income and 12 cents of wealth for every corresponding dollar in the typical white American household.[10] And, despite laws against it, discrimination continues, especially in former slave-holding states such as North Carolina. Recent research on that state's legal system showed that the life of a "white" person is more highly valued than a "non-white," as defendants whose victims are "white" are 3.5 times more likely to be sentenced to death than those with "non-white" victims.[11]

Indicators of Social Status

Social status in a stratified society, whether divided in open or closed classes, is manifested in several ways. One is through *verbal evaluation*—what people say about others in their own society. For this, anything can be singled out for attention and spoken of favorably or unfavorably: from a person's physical features, dress, social manners, and speech to his or her circle of friends, economic activities, political affiliations, church membership, and material possessions such as houses, cars, and so on. Cultures evaluate such identifying features differently, and what may be spoken of favorably in one may be spoken of unfavorably in another and ignored in a third.

Furthermore, cultural values may change, so that something regarded favorably at one time may not be so regarded at another. This is one reason why a researcher may be misled by verbal evaluation, for what people say may not correspond completely with social reality. As an example, the official language of Egypt is Classical Arabic, the language of the Koran (the holiest of Islamic texts). Though it is highly valued, no one in Egypt uses this language in daily interaction; rather, it is used for official documents or on formal occasions. Those most proficient in it are not of the upper class but, rather, of the lower middle classes. These are the people educated in the public schools (where Classical Arabic is the language of schooling) and who hold jobs in the government bureaucracy (which requires the most use of Classical Arabic). Upper-class Egyptians, by contrast, go to private schools, where they learn the foreign languages essential for success in diplomacy and in the global economy of business and industry.[12]

[10] Boshara, R. (2003, January/February). Wealth inequality: The $6,000 solution. *Atlantic Monthly*. See also Kennickell, A. B. (2003, November). *A rolling tide: Changes in the distribution of wealth in the U.S. 1989–2001.* Levy Economics Institute.

[11] Unah, I., & Boger, C. (2001, April). *Race and the death penalty in North Carolina.* www.common-sense.org/pdfs/NCDeathPenaltyReport2001.pdf.

[12] Haeri, N. (1997). The reproduction of symbolic capital: Language, state, and class in Egypt. *Current Anthropology 38,* 795–816.

Social status in a stratified society is also indicated through *patterns of association*—not just who interacts with whom but how and in what context. In Western society, informal, friendly relations take place mostly within one's own class. Relations with members of other classes tend to be more formal and occur in the context of specific situations. For example, a corporate executive and a janitor normally are members of different social classes. They may have frequent contact with each other, but it occurs in the setting of the corporate offices and usually requires certain stereotyped behavior patterns.

A third way social status is manifested is through *symbolic indicators*. For example, in the United States certain activities and possessions are indicative of class: occupation (a garbage collector has different class status than a medical specialist); wealth (rich people are generally in a higher social class than poor people); dress ("white collar" versus "blue collar"); form of recreation (people of the upper class are expected to play golf rather than shoot pool down at the pool hall—but they can shoot pool at home or in a club); residential location (people of the upper class do not ordinarily live in slums); kind of car; and so on. All sorts of status symbols are indicative of class position, including measures such as the number of bathrooms in a person's house. That said, class rankings do not fully correlate with economic status or pay scales. The local garbage collector or unionized factory laborer typically makes more money than an average college professor with a doctorate.

Symbolic indicators involve factors of lifestyle, but differences in life chances may also signal differences in class standing. Life is apt to be less hard for members of an upper class as opposed to a lower class. This shows up in a tendency for lower infant mortality and longer life expectancy for the upper class. There is also a tendency for greater physical stature and robustness among people of the upper class—the result of better diet and protection from serious illness in their growing-up years (see the Biocultural Connection).

Maintaining Stratification

In any system of stratification, those who dominate proclaim their supposedly superior status by means of a powerful ideology, commonly asserting it through intimidation or propaganda (in the form of gossip, media, religious doctrine, and so forth) that presents their position as normal, natural, divinely guided, or at least well-deserved. As anthropologist Laura Nader points out, "Systems of thought develop over time and reflect the interests of certain classes or groups in the society who manage to universalize their beliefs and values."[13]

So it is with certain religious ideologies that effectively assert that the social order is divinely fixed and therefore not to be questioned. With the aid of culturally institutionalized thought structures, religious and otherwise, those in power hope that members of the lower classes will thereby "know their place" and not contest their domination by the "chosen elite." If, however, this domination is contested, the elite usually control the power of the state and use its institutions to protect their privileged position.

In India, for example, Hindu belief in reincarnation and an incorruptible supernatural power that assigns people to a particular caste position, as a reward or punishment for the deeds and misdeeds of past lives, justifies one's position in this life. If, however, individuals faithfully perform the duties appropriate to their caste in this lifetime, then they can expect to be reborn into a higher caste in a future existence.

In the minds of orthodox Hindus, one's caste position is something earned rather than the accident of birth as it appears to outside observers. In contrast to India's traditional caste system, which explicitly recognizes (and accepts as legitimate) inequality among people, the principle of human equality is fundamental to the American worldview in the Unites States—despite the country's history of racial and gender discrimination and its stark disparities in wealth, status, and power.

Social Mobility

Most stratified societies offer at least some **social mobility**—upward or downward change in one's social class position. The prospects of improving status and wealth help to ease the strains inherent in any system of inequality.

Social mobility is most common in societies made up of independent nuclear families where the individual is closely tied to fewer people—especially when neolocal residence is the norm and it is assumed that individuals will leave their family of birth when they become adults. In such social settings—through hard work, occupational success, opportune marriage, and disassociation from the lower-class family in which they grew up—individuals can more easily move up in status and rank.

In societies where the extended family is the usual form, mobility tends to be more difficult, because each individual is strongly tied to many relatives. Typically,

[13] Nader, L. (1997). Controlling processes: Tracing the dynamic components of power. *Current Anthropology 38*, 271.

social mobility Upward or downward change in one's social class position in a stratified society.

Biocultural Connection

African Burial Ground Project   *by Michael Blakey*

In 1991, construction workers in lower Manhattan unearthed what turned out to be an African burial ground, the final resting place of some 10,000 enslaved African captives brought to New York in the 17th and 18th centuries to build the city and provide the labor for its thriving economy. The discovery sparked controversy as the African American public held protests and prayer vigils to stop the part of a federal building project that nearly destroyed the site.

As a biological anthropologist and African American, I had a unique opportunity to work together with the descendant African American community to develop a plan that included both extensive biocultural research and the humane retention of the sacred nature of the site, ultimately through reburial and the creation of a fitting memorial. The research also involved archaeological and historical studies that used a broad African diasporic context for understanding the lifetime experiences of these people who were enslaved and buried in New York.

Studying a sample population of 419 individuals from the burial ground, our team used an exhaustive range of skeletal biological methods, producing a database containing more than 200,000 observations of genetics, morphology, age, sex, growth and development, muscle development, trauma, nutrition, and disease. The bones revealed an unmistakable biocultural connection: physical wear and tear of an entire community brought on by the social institution of slavery.

We now know, based on this study, that life for Africans in colonial New York was characterized by poor nutrition, grueling physical labor that enlarged and often tore muscles, and death rates that were unusually high for 15- to 25-year-olds. Many of these young adults died soon after arriving on slaving ships. Few Africans lived past 40 years of age, and less than 2 percent lived beyond 55. Church records show strikingly different mortality trends for the Europeans of New York: About eight times as many English as Africans lived past 55 years of age, and mortality in adolescence and the early 20s was relatively low.

Skeletal research also showed that those Africans who died as children and were most likely to have been born in New York exhibited stunted and disrupted growth and exposure to high levels of lead pollution—unlike those who had been born in Africa (and were distinguishable because they had filed teeth). Fertility was very low among enslaved women in New York, and infant mortality was high. In these respects, this northern colonial city was very similar to South Carolina and the Caribbean to which its economy was tied—regions where conditions for African captives were among the harshest.

Individuals in this deeply troubling burial ground came from warring African states including Calibar, Asante, Benin, Dahomey, Congo, Madagascar, and many others—states that wrestled with the European demand for human chattel. They resisted their enslavement through rebellion, and they resisted their dehumanization by carefully burying their dead and preserving what they could of their cultures.

BIOCULTURAL QUESTION

Although few will question that slavery is an inhuman system of labor exploitation, was it economically rational for slave owners to mistreat their "human chattel," as indicated by the poor health, low fertility, and high mortality of African slaves in colonial New York?

Excavation of the African Burial Ground in lower Manhattan, New York City. The site is now a National Monument featuring a distinctive memorial that commemorates and communicates the story of this all-important historical archaeological project. The memorial is operated by the National Park Service.

© A. J. Giordano/Corbis SABA

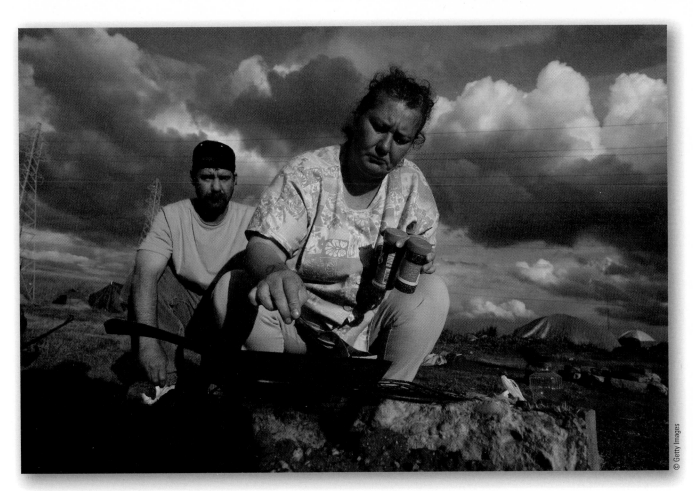

Stratified societies are hierarchically structured into social classes that can be closed, like Hindu castes in traditional India, or open, as in the United States and most other industrialized societies based on capitalist economies. Either way, people ranking at the bottom of the social order tend to be powerless and poor. The open class system of the United States allows individuals to move upward in social rank and become one of the have-lots, but they may also slide down the social ladder and end up as have-nots. Today, almost 40 million women, men, and children (over 13 percent) in the United States are officially classified as "in poverty." About 3.5 million of these poor periodically experience being homeless in any given year, and about 150,000 are chronically homeless. A disproportionate number (40 percent) is African American, but most are Americans of European descent. Homelessness is growing due to a worsening global economy that has spiked unemployment and home foreclosures. Here we see a newly homeless couple cooking potatoes over a campfire at a homeless tent city in Sacramento, California.

if a person in such a society moves up to a higher social class, it is expected that he or she will help the rest of the family move up as well. In all likelihood, the extended families of the highly successful Ivory Coast soccer players described in this chapter's Globalscape have experienced upward social mobility through their ties to these athletes.

Societies that permit a great deal of upward and downward mobility are referred to as *open-class societies*— although the openness is apt to be less in practice than members hope or believe. In the United States, despite its rags-to-riches ideology, most mobility involves a move up or down only a notch; however, if this continues in a family over several generations, it may add up to a major change. Nonetheless, U.S. society makes much of the relatively rare examples of great upward mobility consistent with its cultural values and tends to overlook the numerous cases of little or no upward (not to mention downward) mobility.

Caste societies exemplify *closed-class societies* because of their severe institutionalized limits on social mobility. Yet, even the Hindu caste system, with its guiding ideology that all social hierarchies within it are eternally fixed, has a degree of flexibility and mobility. Although individuals cannot move up or down the caste hierarchy, whole groups can do so depending on claims they assert for higher ranking and on how well they can convince or manipulate others into acknowledging their claims.

Globalscape

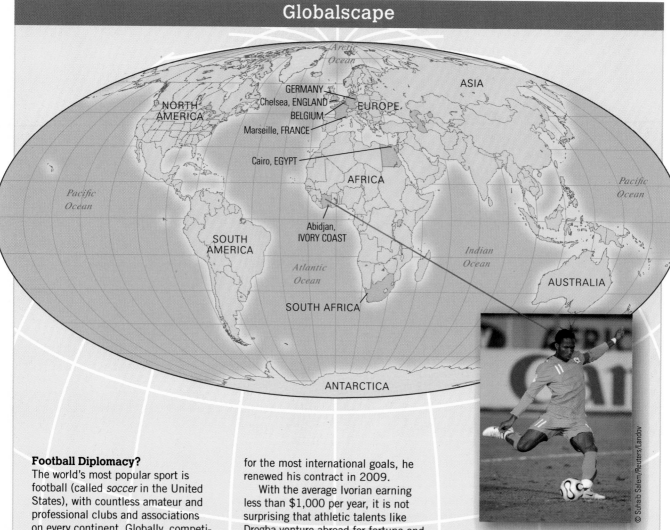

Football Diplomacy?

The world's most popular sport is football (called *soccer* in the United States), with countless amateur and professional clubs and associations on every continent. Globally, competitions are organized by the Federation Internationale de Football Association (FIFA), which organizes the World Cup every four years.

Football is a ticket to upward social mobility for many thousands of gifted, hardworking, and lucky players, including Didier Drogba, who plays for England's Chelsea Football Club and for his own country—the Ivory Coast national team, nicknamed "the Elephants." Born in Abidjan, the major city in this former French West African colony, Drogba is a southerner belonging to the Bete, one of the country's sixty-five ethnic groups. Recruited at an early age for a Belgian club and becoming a powerful striker, he was drafted by a French club in Marseille for $8 million. Chosen French Player of the Year in 2004, after just one season, he signed with England's champion team, Chelsea, for a record $42-million multi-year contract (not counting endorsements). Holding the team's record

for the most international goals, he renewed his contract in 2009.

With the average Ivorian earning less than $1,000 per year, it is not surprising that athletic talents like Drogba venture abroad for fortune and fame. In fact, all twenty-three members of the Ivory Coast national football team normally play abroad, most for wealthy European clubs. For the 2006 World Cup in Berlin, Germany, they trained together in Egypt, under a French coach. Meanwhile, their home country was wracked by a brutal civil war pitting southern ethnic groups against northern ones.

Ninety percent of the Ivory Coast's foreign exchange earnings come from cocoa beans. As a world-renowned sports star, Drogba appears in ads promoting the international sale of Ivorian chocolate. He also promotes peace: During the 2006 games, enthusiastically watched on television by millions of fellow Ivorians back home, team captain Drogba and his teammates (representing both southern and northern Ivory Coast) pleaded that the unity of the Elephants in the stadium would inspire fellow Ivorians to settle their conflict and reunite as a country. In 2007, a tentative

peace agreement was reached. That same year, Drogba became a Goodwill Ambassador for the United Nations Development Program, helping efforts to end extreme poverty in Africa.

Recently Drogba gained yet another opportunity to contribute to positive change: After years of facing anti-apartheid sporting boycotts, South Africa is proud to host the 2010 World Cup. Expected to draw a cumulative worldwide audience of 30 billion (more than the last Olympics), it promises to be the most spectacular sporting event of the year—and could be Drogba's biggest forum ever for inspiring international goodwill.

Global Twister How realistic is Drogba's idea that a national multi-ethnic soccer team competing for the World Cup can help unite its country's rival factions in a lasting way?

© Barcroft/Fame Pictures

Members of India's Gulabi Gang, sometimes referred to as "pink vigilantes." Poor rural woman, most of whom are Dalits (Untouchables and members of the lowest castes), they are collectively challenging the repressive status quo. Banding together, they demand justice—shaming and intimidating abusive men as well as corrupt officials who deny them equal access to water, farming supplies, and other resources.

During the past half century, political activism has stirred among members of India's vast underclass of Untouchables (outcasts) and lowest Sudra castes—collectively known as *Dalits*, a Sanskrit name meaning "crushed" or "suppressed." Historically discriminated against and economically exploited, they now number about 200 million scattered all across this vast South Asian country of 1.15 billion people. A growing political force, Dalits are now organizing themselves on local, regional, and even national levels. Their movement for civil rights is facilitated by increased access to digital communication technology.

Within the vast underclass of Dalits, women and children are especially vulnerable, barely surviving at the very bottom of Indian society. In recent years, however, Dalit women in many parts of India have joined hands with the intention of claiming social justice. Perhaps best known among them is a group in India's northern province of Uttar Pradesh who vigorously protest government discrimination and official corruption and strive to create opportunities for women. Dressed in vibrant pink saris and wielding traditional Indian fighting sticks known as

lathi, they are known as the Gulabi ("Pink") Gang. They demand justice—shaming and intimidating abusive men and corrupt officials who deny them equal access to water, farming supplies, and other resources. As one of these "pink vigilantes" puts it, "On my own I have no rights, but together, as the Gulabi Gang, we have power."[14]

The Dalit women's movement in India illustrates that even long-established and culturally entrenched hierarchical orders are not immune from being challenged, reformed, or even overthrown. Great disparities in wealth, power, and privilege may persist and even grow in many parts of the world, but there are notable social changes in the opposite direction. In the course of the 19th century, slavery was abolished and declared illegal nearly everywhere in the world. And in the last century, civil rights, women's rights, and other human rights movements resulted in social and legal reforms, as well as changes in ideas and values regarding hierarchical social orders in many countries.

---

[14] Dunbar, P. (2008, January 19). The pink vigilantes. www.dailymail.co.uk.

Questions for Reflection

1. When young adults leave their parental home to go to college or find employment in a distant part of the country, they face the challenge of establishing new social relationships—ones that are not based on kinship but on common interest. To which common-interest associations do you belong and why?

2. Do you use a networking platform such as Facebook or Twitter to stay in touch with relatives, friends, schoolmates, or colleagues? Where are these individuals in your digital social network geographically located? How often do you see them in real space, and is your interaction with them different in person than online?

3. Do you think that members of an upper class or caste in a socially stratified system have a greater vested interest in the idea of law and order than those forced to exist on the bottom of such societies? Why or why not?

4. Slavery in the United States was officially abolished in 1863, caste-based discrimination of Untouchables was constitutionally outlawed in India in 1950, and race-based segregation in South Africa officially ended with the abolition of apartheid in 1993. Considering these important political changes, do you think that social repression against these groups has now ended for good?

5. In your own life, have you personally seen and experienced grouping by gender, age, and social status? What do you see as the positive and negative aspects of these groupings?

Suggested Readings

Bernardi, B. (1985). *Age class systems: Social institutions and policies based on age.* New York: Cambridge University Press.

This is a cross-cultural analysis of age as a device for organizing society and seeing to the distribution and rotation of power.

Bradfield, R. M. (1998). *A natural history of associations* (2nd ed.). New York: International Universities Press.

First published in 1973, this major anthropological study of common-interest associations attempts to provide a comprehensive theory of the origin of associations and their role in kin-based societies.

De Mott, B. (1990). *The imperial middle: Why Americans can't think straight about class.* New York: Morrow.

This critical commentary on the myth that the United States is a classless society demonstrates the great social and political costs of buying into that idea.

Price, T. D., & Feinman, G. M. (Eds.). (1995). *Foundations of social inequality.* New York: Plenum.

A collection of essays by various contributors examining the emergence of social inequality.

Sanday, P. R. (1981). *Female power and male dominance: On the origins of sexual inequality.* Cambridge, England: Cambridge University Press.

A cross-cultural study of various ways that male–female relations are organized in human societies. Demonstrating that male dominance is not inherent in those relations, the author suggests that dominance emerges in situations of stress as a result of chronic food shortages, migration, and colonial domination.

Smedley, A. (2007). *Race in North America: Origin and evolution of a worldview. Boulder*, CO: Westview.

A cultural historical analysis of the invention and development of the idea of race and the political ideological context from which it emerged. Smedley considers in this latest edition whether race is a universal concept, offers interpretations of the human genome, analyzes new racial categories on the U.S. census, including "mixed-race," and deftly counters claims of scientific racism.

Steady, F. C. (2005). *Women and collective action in Africa.* New York: Palgrave Macmillan.

This examination of women's movements and collective action in Africa begins in precolonial times and moves through to the present. It identifies and discusses the various arenas in which collective action has influenced and can influence, including women's traditional, mutual-aid, and religious associations.

Challenge Issue In all societies, from the largest to the smallest, people face the challenge of who gets what, when, where, and how. This is the challenge of politics and involves mobilizing, contesting, and controlling power. In the political process, coalitions of individuals and groups defend or dispute an established social and economic order as they fight or negotiate with rival factions and foreign neighbors. Political organization takes many forms, of which the state is just one. State-organized societies are complex, large-scale, and stratified, with a centralized government supported by administrative bureaucracies largely paid for by society members or subjects. In traditional kin-ordered societies, such as tribes, political power is neither centralized nor monopolized, but shared by social networks of extended families, lineages, or clans. Representing their kinfolk, leaders gather periodically to discuss and resolve collective challenges. Among the Pashtun of Afghanistan and Pakistan, such a political assembly is known as a *jirga*—as shown in this photo of tribal elders attending a Loya Jirga (Grand Assembly) in Afghanistan's capital city of Kabul. Representing many different tribal communities, these elders are delegated to settle disputes, decide on treaties, discuss trade issues, and deal with other important political matters such as law and order in their war-torn homelands.

CHAPTER 23

Politics, Power, and Violence

Chapter Preview

How Are Power and Political Organization Different?

All human relations involve power, which refers to the ability of individuals or groups to impose their will upon others and make them do things even against their own wants or wishes. Power—from persuasion to violence—also operates on the societal level. The ability to impose or maintain order and to resolve conflicts requires political organization, which refers to the means by which a society maintains order internally and manages its affairs with other societies externally. It may be relatively uncentralized and informal, as in bands and tribes, or more centralized and formal, as in chiefdoms and states.

How Are Social and Political Order Formed and Maintained?

Social controls may be internalized—in cultural values that are "built into" individuals—or externalized, in the form of sanctions. Positive sanctions encourage approved behavior, while negative sanctions discourage unacceptable behavior. Negative sanctions are called laws if they are formalized and enforced by an authorized political agency. Force or violence may be employed to impose or maintain order within a society or between groups. Although states and chiefdoms frequently practice warfare as a means of achieving political objectives, some groups condemn or avoid such organized violence.

How Do Political Systems Obtain Support and Legitimacy?

In uncentralized systems, people depend primarily upon their kin-ordered local networks for support and protection. Politically represented by personally known leaders, they give loyalty and cooperation freely because there is power sharing in the political decision-making process. Centralized systems, by contrast, rely more heavily on institutionalized power, authority, and even coercion. Political organizations all over the world seek to justify their power as popularly mandated, divinely ordained, naturally given, or otherwise ideologically authorized.

Ironically, the social ties that facilitate human coexistence and cooperation also create the dynamics that may lead to social tension and possible violent conflict within and between groups. We see this in a wide range of situations: in riots among fans rooting for different soccer teams, in the gang violence in many North American cities, and in bloody conflicts between neighboring religious or ethnic groups such as Hindu Tamils and Buddhist Sinhalese, Muslim Palestinians and Jewish Israelis, and Roman Catholic Croats and Eastern Orthodox Serbs in southern Europe.

Therefore, every society must have ways and means for resolving internal conflicts and preventing a breakdown of its social order. Moreover, each society must possess the capacity to deal with neighboring societies in peaceful or troubled times. To meet these internal and external challenges, individuals and groups form coalitions capable of defending or contesting an established social and/or economic order and, if necessary, fighting or settling conflicts with rival factions and foreign neighbors. This is the business of *politics* (derived from the Greek word *polis*, referring to a self-governing "city").

Complex political structures known as *states* first began to emerge over 5,000 years ago. Commonly unstable, many have disappeared in the course of history, some temporarily and others forever. Some were annexed by other states, and others collapsed or fragmented into smaller political units. Although some present-day states are very old—such as Japan, which has endured as a state for almost 1,500 years—few are older than the United States, an independent country since 1783.

Despite the predominance of state societies today, there are still groups where political organization consists of flexible and informal kinship systems whose leaders lack real **power**—the ability of individuals or groups to impose their will upon others and make them do things even against their own wants or wishes. Between these two polarities of kin-ordered and state-organized political systems lies a world of variety.

power The ability of individuals or groups to impose their will upon others and make them do things even against their own wants or wishes.

political organization The way power is accumulated, arranged, executed, and structurally distributed and embedded in society; the means through which a society creates and maintains social order.

band A relatively small and loosely organized kin-ordered group that inhabits a common territory and that may split periodically into smaller extended family groups that are politically and economically independent.

Systems of Political Organization

The term **political organization** refers to the way power is accumulated, arranged, executed, and structurally embedded in society, whether in organizing a whale hunt, managing irrigated farmlands, staging a religious festival, or raising an army. In short, it is the means through which a society creates and maintains social order. It assumes a variety of forms among the peoples of the world, but anthropologists have simplified this complex subject by identifying four basic kinds of political systems: bands, tribes, chiefdoms, and states (Figure 23.1). The first two are uncentralized systems; the latter two are centralized.

Uncentralized Political Systems

Until recently, many non-Western peoples have had neither chiefs with established rights and duties nor any fixed form of government, as those who live in modern states understand the term. Instead, marriage and kinship have formed their principal means of social organization. The economies of these societies are primarily of a subsistence type, and populations are typically small.

Leaders do not have real power to force compliance with the society's customs or rules, but if individuals do not conform, they may become targets of scorn and gossip or even be banished. Important decisions are usually made in a collective manner by agreement among adults. Dissenting members may decide to act with the majority, or they may choose to adopt some other course of action, including leaving the group.

This egalitarian form of political organization provides great flexibility, which in many situations offers an adaptive advantage. Since power in these kin-ordered communities is shared, with nobody exercising exclusive control over collective resources or public affairs, individuals typically enjoy much more freedom than those who are part of larger and more complex political systems.

BANDS

The **band** is a relatively small and loosely organized kin-ordered group that inhabits a common territory and that may split periodically into smaller family groups that are politically and economically independent. Typically, bands are found among food foragers and other small-scale migratory communities where families organize into politically autonomous extended family groups that usually camp together as long as environmental and subsistence circumstances are favorable. Bands periodically break up into smaller groups to forage for food or visit other relatives. The band is probably the oldest form of political

TYPES OF POLITICAL ORGANIZATION
The symbol → indicates that the attribute varies between less and more complex societies of that type.

	BAND	TRIBE	CHIEFDOM	STATE
MEMBERSHIP Number of people	Dozens and up	Hundreds and up	Thousands and up	Tens of thousands and up
Settlement pattern	Mobile	Mobile or fixed: 1 or more villages	Fixed: 2 or more villages	Fixed: Many villages and cities
Basis of relationships	Kin	Kin, descent groups	Kin, rank, and residence	Class and residence
Ethnicities and languages	1	1	1	1 or more
GOVERNMENT Decision making, leadership	"Egalitarian"	"Egalitarian" or Big Man	Centralized, hereditary	Centralized
Bureaucracy	None	None	None, or 1 or 2 levels	Many levels
Monopoly of force and information	No	No	No → Yes	Yes
Conflict resolution	Informal	Informal	Centralized	Laws, judges
Hierarchy of settlement	No	No	No → Paramount village or head town	Capital
ECONOMY Food production	No	No → Yes	Yes → Intensive	Intensive
Labor specialization	No	No	No → Yes	Yes
Exchanges	Reciprocal	Reciprocal	Redistributive ("tribute")	Redistributive ("taxes")
Control of land	Band	Descent group	Chief	Various
SOCIETY Stratified	No	No	Yes, ranked by kin	Yes, by class or caste
Slavery	No	No	Some, small-scale	Some, large-scale
Luxury goods for elite	No	No	Yes	Yes
Public architecture	No	No	No → Yes	Yes
Indigenous literacy	No	No	No → Some	Often

Figure 23.1 This figure outlines the four basic types of political systems: bands, tribes, chiefdoms, and states. Bands and tribes are uncentralized political organizations; chiefdoms and states are centralized political organizations.

organization, since all humans were once food foragers and remained so until the development of farming and pastoralism over the past 10,000 years.

Since bands are egalitarian and small, numbering at most a few hundred people, no real need exists for formal, centralized political systems. Because everyone is related to—and knows on a personal basis—everyone else with whom dealings are required, there is high value placed on "getting along." Conflicts that do arise are usually settled informally through gossip, ridicule, direct negotiation, or mediation. When negotiation or mediation is used, the focus is on reaching a solution considered fair by all concerned parties, rather than on conforming to some abstract law or rule. Where all else fails, disgruntled individuals have the option of leaving to go live in another band where they have relatives or trying to establish a new community of their own.

Decisions affecting a band are made with the participation of all its adult members, with an emphasis on achieving consensus—a collective agreement—rather than a simple majority. Individuals become leaders by virtue of their abilities and serve in that capacity only as long as they retain the confidence of the community. They have no real power to force people to abide by their decisions. A leader who exceeds what people are willing to accept quickly loses followers.

An example of the informal nature of band leadership is found among the Ju/'hoansi Bushmen of the Kalahari Desert mentioned in earlier chapters. Each Ju/'hoansi band is composed of a group of families that live together, linked through kinship to one another and to the headman (or, less often, headwoman). Although each band has rights to the territory it occupies and the resources within it, two or more bands may range over the same land.

Documentary Educational Resources

Toma, a Ju/'hoansi headman, is known to many people worldwide through the classic ethnographic film *The Hunters.*

The head, called the *kxau,* or "owner," is the focal point for the band's claims on the territory. He or she does not personally own the land or resources but symbolically represents the rights of band members to them. If the head leaves the area to live elsewhere, people turn to someone else to lead them.

The head coordinates band migration when resources are no longer adequate for subsistence in a particular habitat. This leader's major duty is to plan when and where the group will move, and when the move begins his or her position is at the head of the line. The leader selects the site for the new settlement and has the first choice of a spot for his or her own fire.

There are few other material rewards or duties. For example, a Ju/'hoansi head is not a judge and does not punish other band members. Wrongdoers are judged and held accountable by public opinion, usually expressed by gossip—which can play an important role in curbing socially unacceptable behavior. In small-scale communities where everyone is interdependent, public scolding or open expression of irritation may escalate into serious anger and lead to splits that jeopardize everyone's security.

Through gossip—talking behind someone's back and spreading rumors about behavior considered disruptive, shameful, or ridiculous—people accomplish several

tribe In anthropology, refers to a range of kin-ordered groups that are politically integrated by some unifying factor and whose members share a common ancestry, identity, culture, language, and territory.

objectives while avoiding the potential disruption of open confrontation. First, gossip underscores and reinforces the cultural standards of "normal" people who abide by the unwritten rules of proper conduct. At the same time, the gossip discredits those who violate standards of socially acceptable behavior. Furthermore, since gossip can damage a person's reputation and is often fueled by hidden jealousy or a secret desire to retaliate against someone considered too accomplished or successful, it may function like a leveling mechanism to reduce a real or perceived threat of someone becoming too dominant.

Another prime technique in small-scale societies for resolving disputes, or even avoiding them in the first place, is mobility. Those unable to get along with others of their group may feel pressured to move to another group where existing kinship ties give them rights of entry.

TRIBES

The second type of uncentralized authority system is the tribe. In anthropology, the term **tribe** refers to a wide range of kin-ordered groups that are politically integrated by some unifying factor and whose members share a common ancestry, identity, culture, language, and territory. Tribes may develop when a number of culturally related bands join together, peacefully settle disputes, participate in periodic visiting and communal feasting, and intermarry, for purposes of economic exchange and/or collective self-defense against common enemies.

Typically, though not invariably, a tribe has an economy based on some form of crop cultivation or herding. Since these subsistence methods usually yield more food than those of the food-foraging band, tribal membership is usually larger than band membership. While band population densities are usually less than one person per square mile, tribal population densities generally exceed that and may be as high as 250 per square mile. Greater population density brings a new set of problems to be solved as opportunities for bickering, begging, adultery, and theft increase markedly, especially among people living in permanent villages.

Each tribe consists of one or more self-supporting and self-governing local communities (including smaller kin-groups earlier discussed as bands) that may then form alliances with others for various purposes. As in the band, political organization in the tribe is informal and temporary. Whenever a situation requiring political integration of all or several groups within the tribe arises—perhaps for defense, to carry out a raid, to pool resources in times of scarcity, or to capitalize on a windfall that must be distributed quickly lest it spoil—groups come together to deal with the situation in a cooperative manner. When the problem is satisfactorily solved, each group then resumes autonomy.

In many tribal societies the organizing unit and seat of political authority is the clan, comprised of people

Shown here is a meeting of the Navajo Tribal Council, a nontraditional governing body created in response to requirements set by the U.S. government in order for the Navajo to exercise national sovereignty. Calling themselves *Dineh* ("the people"), the Navajo were traditionally organized in self-governing communities led by respected clan leaders known as *naat'aanii* ("the ones who orate"). These clan leaders led the collective decision-making process by their wise guidance and consensus building.

who consider themselves descended from a common ancestor. Within the clan, elders or headmen and/or headwomen regulate members' affairs and represent their clan in interactions with other clans. As a group, the elders of all the clans may form a council that acts within the community or for the community in dealings with outsiders. Because clan members usually do not all live together in a single community, clan organization facilitates joint action with members of related communities when necessary.

Leadership in tribal societies is also relatively informal, as is evident in a wide array of past and present examples. The Navajo Indians in the southwestern United States, for example, traditionally did not think of government as something fixed and all-powerful, and leadership was not vested in a central authority. A local leader was a man respected for his age, integrity, and wisdom. Therefore, people sought his advice frequently, but he had no formal means of control and could not force any decision on those who asked for his help. Group decisions were made by public consensus, although the most influential man usually played a key role in reaching a decision. Social mechanisms that induced members to abide by group decisions included gossip, criticism, withdrawal of cooperation, and the belief that antisocial actions caused sickness and other misfortune.

Another example of tribal leadership is the "Big Man." Common in the South Pacific, such men are leaders of localized descent groups or of a territorial group. The Big Man combines a measure of interest in his community's welfare with a great deal of cunning and calculation for his own personal gain. His political status is personal; he does not come to a position of power in any formal sense, nor is he elected. His prestige is the result of strategic acts that contribute to his political capital, raise him above most other tribe members, and attract to him a number of loyal followers who benefit from or depend on his success.

The Kapauku of Western New Guinea typify this form of political organization. Among them, the Big Man is called the *tonowi* or "rich one." To achieve this status, one must be male, wealthy, generous, and eloquent. Physical bravery and an ability to deal with the supernatural are also common *tonowi* characteristics, but they are not essential.

The *tonowi* functions as the headman of the village unit in a wide variety of situations within and beyond the community. He represents his group in dealing with outsiders and other villages and acts as negotiator and/or judge when disputes break out among his followers.

Because Kapauku culture places a high value on wealth, a well-to-do man is considered successful and admirable—provided he is also generous when it comes to making loans. Those who refuse to lend money to other

This Big Man from New Guinea is wearing his official regalia.

© George Holton/Photo Researchers, Inc.

for a *tonowi* to lose his fortune rapidly due to poor management or bad luck with his pigs. Thus the Kapauku political structure shifts frequently; as one man loses wealth and consequently power, another gains it and becomes a *tonowi*. By virtue of this flexibility in the political organization, no one *tonowi* accumulates much political capital or holds on to political power for too long.

Although it is far more common for tribal chiefs to be men, in some cultures women serve in such leadership positions, as discussed later in this chapter.

POLITICAL INTEGRATION BEYOND THE KIN-GROUP

Age sets, age grades, and common-interest groups discussed in the previous chapter are among the political integration mechanisms used by tribal societies. Cutting across territorial and kin-groupings, these organizations link members from different lineages and clans.

For example, among the Tiriki of East Africa (mentioned in the previous chapter) the Warrior age grade guards the village and grazing lands, while Judicial Elders resolve disputes. The oldest age grade, the Ritual Elders, advise on matters involving the well-being of all the Tiriki people. With the tribe's political affairs in the hands of the various age grades and their officers, this type of organization enables the largely independent kin-groups to solve conflicts and sometimes even avoid feuding between the lineages.

Another system of political integration found among tribes in many parts of the world is the common-interest association, also discussed in the previous chapter. For example, among many Indian peoples inhabiting North America's Great Plains in the 19th century, the band comprised the basic territorial and political unit within a tribe or ethnic group. In addition, however, there were a number of military societies or warrior clubs.

Among the Cheyenne, for instance, there were seven of these military societies. A boy might be invited to join one of these clubs when he achieved warrior status, whereupon he became familiar with the society's particular insignia, songs, and rituals. Beyond military functions, the warrior societies also had ceremonial and social functions.

The Cheyenne warriors' daily tasks consisted of overseeing activities in the village, protecting families on the move to the next camping site, and enforcing buffalo hunting rules. In addition, each warrior club had its own repertoire of dances, performed on special ceremonial occasions. Since each Cheyenne band had identical military societies bearing identical names, the societies served to integrate the entire tribe for military and political purposes.[1]

villagers may be ostracized, ridiculed, and, in extreme cases, actually executed by a group of warriors. Such responses to tightfistedness ensure that economic wealth is distributed throughout the group.

The *tonowi* acquires political power through his loans. Other villagers comply with his requests because they are in his debt (often interest-free) and they do not want to have to repay their loans. Those who have not yet borrowed from him may wish to do so in the future, so they, too, want to keep his goodwill.

The *tonowi* gains further support by taking into his household young male apprentices who receive business training along with food and shelter. He also gives them a loan that enables them to marry when the apprenticeship ends. In return, they act as messengers and bodyguards. After leaving, they remain tied to the *tonowi* by bonds of affection and gratitude. Political support also comes from the *tonowi*'s kinsmen, whose relationship brings with it varying obligations.

As discussed in an earlier chapter, the *tonowi*'s wealth comes from his success at breeding pigs, which is the focus of the entire Kapauku economy. It is not uncommon

---

[1] Hoebel, E. A. (1960). *The Cheyennes: Indians of the Great Plains.* New York: Holt, Rinehart & Winston.

Centralized Political Systems

In bands and tribes, political authority is not centralized, and each group is economically and politically autonomous. Political organization is vested in kinship, age, and common-interest groups. Populations are small and relatively homogeneous, with people engaged for the most part in the same sorts of activities throughout their lives.

However, as a society's social life becomes more complex—as population rises, technology becomes more intricate, and specialization of labor and trade networks produce surplus goods—the opportunity increases for some individuals or groups to exercise control at the expense of others. In such societies, political authority and power are concentrated in a single individual (the chief) or in a body of individuals (the state).

CHIEFDOMS

A **chiefdom** is a regional polity (a politically organized society) in which two or more local groups are organized under a single ruling individual—the chief—who is at the head of a ranked hierarchy of people. An individual's status in such a polity is determined by the closeness of his or her relationship to the chief. Those closest are officially superior and receive deferential treatment from those of lower ranks.

The office of the chief is usually for life and often hereditary. Typically, it passes from a man to his son or his sister's son, depending on whether descent is traced patrilineally or matrilineally.

Unlike the headman or headwoman in bands and tribes, the leader of a chiefdom is generally a true authority figure, whose right to make final decisions, give commands, and enforce obedience serves to unite members in all affairs and at all times. For example, a chief can distribute land among community members and recruit people into military service.

Chiefdoms have a recognized hierarchy consisting of major and minor authorities who control major and minor subdivisions. Such an arrangement is, in effect, a chain of command, linking leaders at every level. It serves to bind groups in the heartland to the chief's headquarters, be it a mud and dung hut or a marble palace. Although leaders of chiefdoms are almost always men, in some cultures a politically astute wife, sister, or single daughter of a deceased male chief could inherit such a powerful position as well.

Chiefs usually control the economic activities of those who fall under their political rule. Typically, chiefdoms involve redistributive systems, and the chief has control over surplus goods and perhaps even over the community's labor force. Thus, he (and sometimes she) may demand a quota of rice from farmers, which will then be redistributed to the entire community. Similarly, laborers may be recruited to build irrigation works, a palace, or a temple.

The chief may also amass a great amount of personal wealth and pass it on to offspring. Land, cattle, and luxury goods produced by specialists can be collected by the chief and become part of the power base. Moreover, high-ranking families of the chiefdom may engage in the same practice and use their possessions as evidence of noble status.

An example of this form of political organization may be seen among the Kpelle of Liberia in West Africa.[2] Among them is a class of *paramount chiefs,* each of whom presides over one of the Kpelle chiefdoms (each chiefdom is now a district of the Liberian state). The paramount chiefs' traditional tasks are hearing disputes, preserving order, seeing to the upkeep of trails, and performing various other supervisory functions. In addition, they are now salaried officials of the Liberian government, mediating between it and their own people.

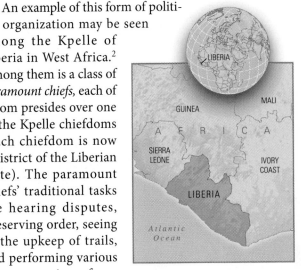

Also, a paramount chief receives government commissions on taxes and court fees collected within his chiefdom, plus a commission for providing laborers for the rubber plantations. Moreover, he gets a stipulated amount of rice from each household and gifts from people who come to request favors and intercessions. In keeping with his exalted station in life, a paramount chief has at his disposal uniformed messengers, a literate clerk, and the symbols of wealth: many wives, embroidered gowns, and freedom from manual labor.

In a ranked hierarchy beneath each Kpelle paramount chief are several lesser chiefs: one for each district within the chiefdom, one for each town within a district, and one for each quarter of all but the smallest towns. Each acts as a kind of lieutenant for his chief of the next higher rank and also serves as a liaison between him and those of lower rank. Unlike paramount or district chiefs, who are comparatively remote, town and quarter chiefs are readily accessible to people at the local level.

---

[2] Gibbs, J. L., Jr. (1965). The Kpelle of Liberia. In J. L. Gibbs, Jr. (Ed.), *Peoples of Africa* (pp. 216–218). New York: Holt, Rinehart & Winston.

chiefdom A regional polity in which two or more local groups are organized under a single chief, who is at the head of a ranked hierarchy of people.

A Kpelle chief in Liberia, West Africa, listens to a dispute in his district. Settling disputes is one of several ongoing traditional tasks that fall to paramount chiefs among Kpelle people.

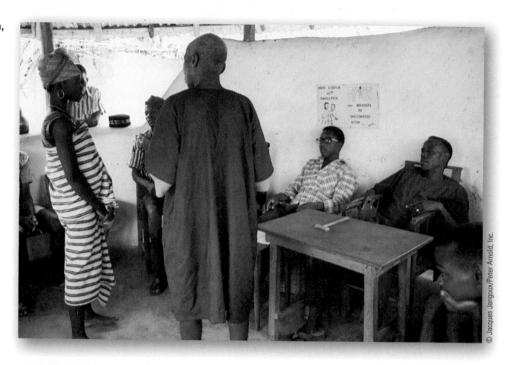

Traditionally, chiefdoms in all parts of the world have been highly unstable, with lesser chiefs trying to take power from higher-ranking chiefs or paramount chiefs vying with one another for supreme power. In precolonial Hawaii, for example, war was the way to gain territory and maintain power; great chiefs set out to conquer one another in an effort to become paramount chief of all the islands. When one chief conquered another, the loser and all his nobles were dispossessed of all property and were lucky if they escaped alive. The new chief then appointed his own supporters to positions of political power. As a consequence, there was very little continuity of government or religious administration.

STATES

The **state** is a political institution established to manage and defend a complex, socially stratified society occupying a defined territory. The most formal of political systems, the state is organized and directed by a government that has the capacity and authority to make laws and to use military force to defend or expand its territories. Some of the smallest states today measure less than 2.59 square kilometers (1 square mile), while the largest cover over 15.5 million square kilometers (6 million square miles).

Often states are ruled by coalitions of well-connected and wealthy individuals or groups that have accumulated and fought over power. Possessing the resources (including

state In anthropology, a political institution established to manage and defend a complex, socially stratified society occupying a defined territory.

money, weapons, and manpower), these ruling elites exercise power by institutional means, such as a government and bureaucracy, which allow them to arrange and rearrange a society's social and economical order.

A large population in a state-organized society requires increased food production and wider distribution networks. Together, these lead to a transformation of the landscape by way of irrigation and terracing, carefully managed crop rotation cycles, and intensive competition for resources—such as clearly demarcated lands, roads, and enough farmers and other rural workers to support market systems and a specialized urban sector. Under such conditions, corporate groups that stress exclusive membership proliferate, ethnic differentiation and ethnocentrism become more pronounced, and the potential for social conflict increases dramatically. Given these circumstances, state institutions, which minimally involve a bureaucracy, a military, and (usually) an official religion, provide the means for numerous and diverse groups to function together as an integrated whole.

Every state, whatever its population, claims sovereign power over its subjects, controls social tension, represses or punishes violent protest by angry factions, and protects its territorial borders against hostile forces, including neighboring states. Throughout history, neighboring states have often had conflicts over territorial boundaries.

Since their first appearance some 5,000 years ago, political states have been anything but permanent. They are often unstable, and many have disappeared in the course of time, some temporarily and others forever. Some were annexed by other states, and others collapsed or fragmented into smaller political units. As already noted, while some present-day states are very old—such as Japan, which has

After the British empire pulled out of South Asia over sixty years ago, that subcontinent erupted in warfare between Muslims and Hindus. The region was then carved up along religious lines into Pakistan and India. Since then, these countries have fought three wars against each other. The tense political relations between these nuclear-armed rivals are symbolically displayed in the military border-closing ritual at Wagah, pictured here. Every evening, Pakistani Pathan guards, dressed in black uniforms and fan-tailed headgear of the same color, face India's border guards, dressed in khaki uniforms and hats adorned with scarlet fan-tails. Brandishing rifles and parading in goose-step, they greet each other, lock gates, and lower their national flags.

been a state for almost 1,500 years—few are older than the United States. Nowhere have states even begun to show the staying power of less centralized political systems.[3]

From the perspective of the political elite in control, the state's formation and endurance are something positive—evidence of progress. This view is not necessarily shared by those who are not represented in the political decision-making process or who fail to benefit from the system. This is especially the case when subjects of the state are forced to pay for the maintenance of the bureaucracy and public works in the form of state-imposed taxes or tribute payments in goods or labor services.

An important distinction to make at this point is between state and nation. As noted in Chapter 1, a **nation** is a people who share a collective identity based on a common culture, language, territorial base, and history.[4] Today, there are roughly 200 internationally recognized states in the world, most of which did not exist before the end of World War II (1945). By contrast, there are about 5,000 nations (including tribes), many of which have existed since time immemorial. Rarely do state and nation coincide, as they do, for example, in Iceland, Japan, and Swaziland.

About 73 percent of the world's states are *pluralistic societies,* defined in an earlier chapter as societies in which two or more ethnic groups or nationalities are politically organized into one territorial state but maintain their cultural differences.[5] Often, smaller nations (including tribes) and other groups find themselves at the mercy of one or more dominant nations or ethnic groups controlling the state. Frequently facing discrimination or repression, some minority nations seek to improve their political position by founding an independent state. In the process, they usually encounter stiff opposition, with sometimes violent confrontations.

So it is with the Chechens, a small Sunni Muslim nation within the Russian Federation, for example, or the Palestinians (Sunni Muslims and Christians), who continue to struggle for political independence as a nation against the Jewish state of Israel, which dominates their homeland. And so it is with the Kurds, an Iranian-speaking Sunni Muslim nation whose homeland is subdivided between the modern states of Turkey, Iraq, and Iran. As members of a cross-border nation, many Kurds are willing to fight for political autonomy or even national independence,

[3] Diamond, J. (2005). *Collapse: How societies choose to fail or succeed.* New York: Viking Penguin.

[4] Clay, J. W. (1996). What's a nation? In W. A. Haviland & R. J. Gordon (Eds.), *Talking about people* (2nd ed., p. 188). Mountain View, CA: Mayfield.

[5] van den Berghe, P. L. (1992). The modern state: Nation builder or nation killer? *International Journal of Group Tensions 92* (3), 193.

nation A people who share a collective identity based on a common culture, language, territorial base, and history.

Figure 23.2 The Kurds—most of whom live in Turkey, Iran, and Iraq—are an example of a nation without a state. With a population of about 27 million, they are much more numerous than Australians, for example. In fact, the total population of the four Scandinavian countries—Denmark, Finland, Norway, and Sweden—is less than that of the Kurds who have no independent country of their own.

but they are forced to accept their minority status in these three neighboring states.

Covering almost 200,000 square kilometers (77 square miles), the cross-border region known as Kurdistan was historically organized in several semi-independent chiefdoms or principalities called *emirates*. After a series of long wars between the Safavid Iranian and Ottoman Turkish empires in the 16th century, these powerful rivals split the Kurdish homeland between them. After the First World War, several new states, including Iraq and Syria, were carved out of the collapsed Ottoman empire and split from what is now the Republic of Turkey. Kurds as well as Arabs, Armenians, Turks, and other minorities, and Muslims as well as Christians, coexist in Kurdistan (Figure 23.2).

Forming a new state is a political challenge. Violent confrontation is typically the way that some nations have forged their own state. Such armed struggle recently made it possible for Bosnia, a southern European country primarily inhabited by Sunni Muslims, to split from Serb-dominated Yugoslavia. But other nations have been able to peacefully establish statehood, as exemplified by Papua New Guinea in the southern Pacific, which became an independent state in 1975.

An important aspect of the state is its delegation of authority to maintain order within and outside its borders.

Police, foreign ministries, war ministries, and other bureaucracies function to control and punish disruptive acts of crime, dissension, and rebellion. By such agencies the state asserts authority impersonally and in a consistent, predictable manner. Western forms of government, like that of the United States, of course, are state governments, and their organization and workings are undoubtedly familiar to most everyone.

An example of a not-so-familiar state is Swaziland in southern Africa. One of the world's few true nation-states, it is home to the Swazi—a Bantu-speaking people.[6] Although the Swazi are primarily farmers, cattle raising is also practiced—and highly esteemed. In fact, the ritual, wealth, and power of their authority system are all intricately linked with cattle.

The traditional Swazi authority system was characterized by a highly developed dual monarchy (now a thing of the past), a hereditary aristocracy, and elaborate kinship rituals, as well as by statewide age sets. The king and his mother were the central figures of national activity, linking all the people of the Swazi state: They presided over higher courts, summoned national gatherings, controlled age classes, allocated land, disbursed national wealth, took precedence in ritual, and helped organize important social events.

Advising the king were the senior princes, who were usually his uncles and half-brothers. Between the king and the princes were two specially created *tinsila*, or blood brothers, who were chosen from certain common clans. These men were his shields, protecting him from evildoers and serving him in intimate personal situations. In addition, the king was guided by two *tindvuna*, or counselors, one civil and one military. The people of the state made their opinions known through two councils: the *liqoqo*, or privy council (dissolved in 1986), composed of senior princes, and the *libanda*, or council of state, composed of chiefs and headmen and open to all adult males of the state. The *liqoqo* could advise the king, make decisions, and carry them out. For example, they could rule on questions about land, education, traditional ritual, court procedure, and transport.

---

[6] Kuper, H. (1965). The Swazi of Swaziland. In J. L. Gibbs, Jr. (Ed.), *Peoples of Africa* (pp. 475–512). New York: Holt, Rinehart & Winston.

Swazi government extended from the smallest local unit—the homestead—upward to the central administration. The head of a homestead had legal and administrative powers; he was responsible for the crimes of those under him, controlled their property, and spoke for them before his superiors. On the district level, political organization was similar to that of the central government. The relationship between a district chief, however, and his subjects was personal and familiar; he knew all the families in his district. To prevent a district chief from becoming too autocratic, his subjects could easily transfer their allegiance to a more responsive chief. Swazi officials held their positions for life and were dismissed only for treason or witchcraft. Incompetence, drunkenness, and stupidity were frowned upon, but they were not considered to be sufficient grounds for dismissal.

Political Systems and the Question of Legitimacy

Whatever a society's political system, it must find some way to obtain and retain the people's allegiance. In uncentralized systems, where every adult participates in all decision making, loyalty and cooperation are freely given because each person is considered a part of the political system. As the group grows larger, however, and the organization becomes more formal, the problem of obtaining and keeping public support becomes more complicated.

Centralized political systems may rely upon coercion as a means of social control. This, however, carries a measure of risk since the personnel needed to apply force often must be numerous and may grow to be a political power. Also, the emphasis on force typically creates resentment and may lessen cooperation. Thus police states are generally short-lived; most societies choose less extreme forms of social coercion. In the United States, this tendency is reflected in the increasing emphasis placed on cultural controls, as we discuss later in this chapter. Laura Nader (see Anthropologist of Note) is well known for her anthropological research concerning issues of power, including social and cultural control.

Also basic to the political process is the concept of **legitimacy**, or the right of political leaders to govern—to hold, use, and allocate power. Legitimacy is a form of support for a political system; unlike force, legitimacy is based on the socially accepted customs, rules, or laws that bind and hold a people together as a collective whole. For example, among the Kapauku of Western New Guinea discussed a few pages back, the legitimacy of the *tonowi's*

power comes from his wealth; the head of the traditional Dahomey state in what is now Benin, West Africa, acquired legitimacy through his age, as he was always the oldest living male; and the kings of Hawaii and of France (before its bloody revolution in 1789) and the emperor of Japan (before being defeated by the Allies in 1945) were thought to have a divine right to rule.

Power based on legitimacy results in *authority*. It is distinct from power based solely on force: Obedience to authority results from the belief that obedience is "right"; compliance to power based on force results from fear of being deprived of liberty, physical well-being, life, or material property. Thus power based on legitimacy is symbolic and depends upon the positive expectations of those who recognize and accept it. If the expectations are not met regularly (if the head of state fails to deliver economic prosperity or the leader is continuously unsuccessful in preventing or dealing with calamities), the legitimacy of the recognized power figure erodes or may collapse altogether.

Politics and Religion

Religion is often intricately connected with politics. Frequently it is religion that legitimizes the political order and leadership. Religious beliefs may influence or provide authoritative approval to customary rules and laws. For example, acts that people believe to be sinful, such as murder, are often illegal as well.

In both industrial and nonindustrial societies, belief in the supernatural is important and is reflected in people's political institutions. One place where the effect of religion on politics was well exemplified was in medieval Europe: Holy wars were fought over the smallest matter; labor was mobilized to build immense cathedrals in honor of the Virgin Mary and other saints; kings and queens ruled by "divine right" and (in the West) pledged allegiance to the pope and asked his blessing in all important ventures, whether marital or martial.

In Peru, the divine ruler of the Inca empire proclaimed absolute authority based on the proposition that he was descended from the Sun God. Mexico's ancient Aztec state was also a politico-religious one, having a divine ruler and engaging in nearly constant warfare

legitimacy The right of political leaders to govern—to hold, use, and allocate power—on the socially accepted customs, rules, or laws that bind and hold a people together as a collective whole.

Laura Nader (b. 1930)

Courtesy of Dr. Laura Nader

Laura Nader has stood out among her peers from the start of her career in 1960, when she became the first woman faculty member in the anthropology department at the University of California, Berkeley.

Nader and her three siblings grew up in Winsted, Connecticut, children of immigrants from Lebanon. As she recalls, "My dad left Lebanon for political reasons, and when he came to the land of the free, he took it seriously. So we were raised to believe that you should be involved in public issues." They were also taught to question assumptions. Both Nader and her younger brother Ralph have made careers of doing this. She is an anthropologist noted for her cross-cultural research on law, justice, and social control and their connection to power structures. He is a consumer advocate and frequent U.S. presidential candidate who is a watchdog on issues of public health and the safety and quality of life.

Laura Nader's undergraduate studies included a study-abroad year in Mexico. Later, while earning her doctorate in anthropology at Radcliffe College, she returned to Mexico to do fieldwork in a Zapotec Indian peasant village in the Sierra Madre Mountains of Oaxaca. Reflecting on this and subsequent research, she says, "In the 1950s, when I went to southern Mexico, I was studying how the Zapotec organize their lives, what they do with their problems, what they do when they go to court. And when I came back to this country, I started looking at American equivalents, at how Americans solve their consumer and service complaints."

Nader's first decade of teaching at Berkeley coincided with the Vietnam War, an era when the campus was in a perpetual state of turmoil with students demonstrating for peace and civil rights. Turning into a scholaractivist, she called upon colleagues to "study up" and do research on the world's power elite. "The study of man," she wrote in 1972, "is confronted with an unprecedented situation: Never before have a few, by their actions and inactions, had the power of life and death over so many members of the species."

To date, the results of Nader's own research have appeared in over a hundred publications. Among these are her numerous books, including *Naked Science—Anthropological Inquiry into Boundaries, Power, and Knowledge* (1996) and *The Life of the Law: Anthropological Projects* (2002).

Playing a leading role in the development of the anthropology of law, Nader has taken on specialists in the fields of law, children's issues, nuclear energy, and science (including her own profession), critically questioning the basic assumptions ("central dogmas") under which these experts operate. She presses her students to do the same—to think critically, question authority, and break free from the "controlling processes" of the power elite. In 2000, Nader accepted one of the highest honors of the American Anthropological Association—an invitation to give the distinguished lecture at its annual gathering.

Adapted from "Interview with Laura Nader." (2000, November). California Monthly.

to procure captives for human sacrifices thought necessary to assuage or please the gods. Modern Iran was proclaimed an "Islamic republic" in the 1979 revolution that toppled the authoritarian regime of the shah, and its first head of state, Ayatollah Ruhollah Khomeini, was the most holy of all Shiite Muslim holy men. As the highest-ranking religious and political authority of the country, he was proclaimed its supreme leader, a position he held until his death ten years later. Since then, Iran remains a theocratic republic with a high-ranking Shia Muslim cleric, or ayatollah, as its most powerful authority. The country's democratically elected parliament and president are subordinate to the ayatollah.

The fact that the president of the United States takes the oath of office by swearing on the Bible is another instance of the use of religion to legitimize political power, as is the phrase "one nation, under God" in the Pledge of Allegiance. On U.S. coins is the phrase "In God We Trust," many meetings of government bodies begin with a prayer or invocation, and the phrase "so help me God" is routinely used in legal proceedings. Despite an official separation of church and state, religious legitimization of government lingers.

Political Leadership and Gender

Irrespective of cultural configuration or type of political organization, women hold important positions of political leadership far less often than men. Furthermore, when they do occupy publicly recognized offices, their power and authority rarely exceed those of men. But significant exceptions occur. Historically, one might cite the female chiefs, or *sachems,* of Algonquian Indian

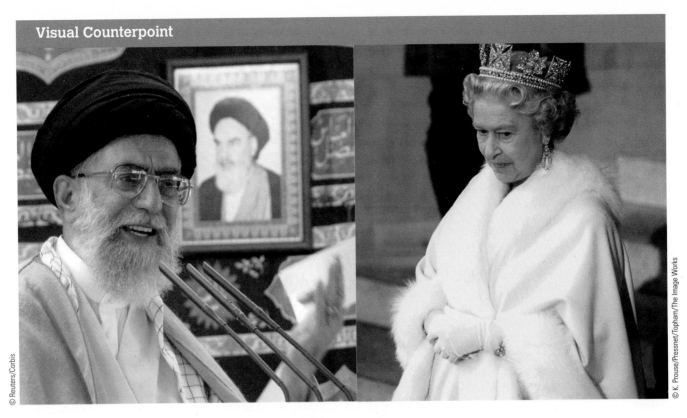

Visual Counterpoint

In contrast to countries such as the United States, where religion and state are constitution-ally separated, countries such as Iran and Great Britain permit a much closer relationship be-tween political and religious affairs. For instance, Iran's current religious leader, **Ayatollah Ali Khamenei,** is not only the supreme spiritual leader but also his country's highest political au-thority. In England, **Queen Elizabeth** is not only her country's nominal head of state but also "the Supreme Governor" of the Church of England, which entitles her to appoint the Anglican bishops in that state.

communities in southern New England, as well as pow-erful queens in several Asian, African, and European monarchies.

Perhaps most notable is Queen Victoria, the long-reigning queen of England, Scotland, Wales, and Ireland. Also recognized as monarch in a host of colonies all over the world, Victoria even acquired the title "Empress of In-dia" and became the world's wealthiest and most powerful leader. During her reign from 1837 until 1901, the Brit-ish empire encompassed 20 percent of the land area of the world and even more of its population. London, its capital, was the world's financial center.

In addition to inheriting high positions of political leadership, a growing number of women have also been elected as presidents, chancellors, or prime ministers. Countries with elected female heads of state now or in recent years include Argentina, Indonesia, Ireland, Sri Lanka, Norway, India, Liberia, Chile, Germany, and the Philippines, to mention just a few. While such high-profile female leadership is still relatively rare, women regularly

enjoy as much political power as men in a number of so-cieties. In band societies, for example, it is common for fe-males to have as much of a say in public affairs as males, even though more often than not men are the nominal leaders of their groups.

Among the Iroquois nations of New York State, all leader-ship positions above the household and clan levels were, with-out exception, filled by men. Thus men held all positions on the village and tribal councils, as well as on the great council of the Iroquois Confederacy. However, they were completely beholden to women, for only women could nominate men to high office. Moreover, women actively lobbied the men on the councils and could have someone removed from office whenever it suited them.

Lower visibility in politics does not necessarily indi-cate that women lack power in political affairs. And just as there are various ways in which women play a role behind the scenes, so it is when they have more visible roles, as in the traditional dual-sex system of the Igbo in Nigeria, West Africa. Among the Igbo, each political unit had separate political institutions for men and women, so that both had an autonomous sphere of authority, as well as an area of shared responsibility.[7] At the head of each political unit was a male *obi*, considered the head of government although in fact he presided over the male community, and a female *omu*, the acknowledged mother of the whole community but in practice concerned with the female section. Unlike a queen (though both she and the *obi* were crowned), the *omu* was neither the *obi's* wife nor the previous *obi's* daughter.

Just as the *obi* had a council of dignitaries to advise him and act as a check against any arbitrary exercise of power, the *omu* was served by a council of women in equal number to the *obi's* male councilors. The duties of the *omu* and her councilors involved such tasks as establishing rules and regulations for the community market (marketing was a woman's activity) and hearing cases involving women brought to her from throughout the town or village. If such cases also involved men, then she and her council would cooperate with the *obi* and his council.

In the Igbo system, then, women managed their own affairs, and their interests were represented at all levels of government. Moreover, they had the right to enforce their decisions and rules with sanctions similar to those employed by men, including strikes, boycotts, and "sitting on" someone, including a man:

> To "sit on" or "make war on" a man involved gathering at his compound, sometimes late at night, dancing, singing scurrilous songs which detailed the women's grievances against him and often called his manhood into question, banging on his hut with the pestles women used for pounding yams, and perhaps demolishing his hut or plastering it with mud and roughing him up a bit. A man might be sanctioned in this way for mistreating his wife, for violating the women's market rules, or for letting his cows eat the women's crops. The women would stay at his hut throughout the day, and late into the night if necessary, until he repented and promised to mend his ways.[8]

When the British imposed colonial rule on the Igbo in the late 1800s, they failed to recognize the autonomy and power of the women. One reason for that oversight

---

[7] Okonjo, K. (1976). The dual-sex political system in operation: Igbo women and community politics in midwestern Nigeria. In N. Hafkin & E. Bay (Eds.), *Women in Africa*. Stanford, CA: Stanford University Press.

[8] Van Allen, J. (1997). Sitting on a man: Colonialism and the lost political institutions of Igbo women. In R. Grinker & C. Steiner (Eds.), *Perspectives on Africa* (p. 450). Boston: Blackwell.

Liberian President Ellen Johnson Sirleaf inspects members of the Liberian police after taking the presidential oath in January 2006. The first female president on the African continent, Sirleaf is a Harvard-educated economist who took the world by surprise when she won the top office in her war-torn and poverty-stricken country. Since becoming president, she has managed to eliminate most of Liberia's international debt, promote investment in the country, and significantly increase its economic output. Serious challenges continue, but she has done much to change Liberia's course.

© AFP/Getty Images

was that the British were blinded by the cultural values of their own male-dominated society, in which the domestic sphere was seen as the ideal place for women. Ironically, as mentioned earlier, the powerful ruler of the British empire at the time was Queen Victoria. Nevertheless, the British introduced "reforms" that destroyed traditional forms of female autonomy and power without providing alternative forms in exchange. As a result, Igbo women lost much of their traditional equality and became subordinate to men.

Political Organization and the Maintenance of Order

Political organization always includes means of maintaining order that ensure people behave in acceptable ways and define what action will be taken when they do not. In chiefdoms and states, some sort of authority has the power to regulate the affairs of society. In bands and tribes, however, people behave generally as they are expected to, without the direct intervention of any centralized political authority. To a large degree, gossip, criticism, fear of supernatural forces, and the like serve as effective deterrents to antisocial behavior.

Internalized Controls

Individuals who are well-socialized and enculturated members of their own society typically acquire an internalized set of shared beliefs and values about what is proper and what is not. These values are so deeply ingrained that each person becomes personally responsible for his or her own conduct. **Cultural control** may be thought of as an internalized form of self-control, as opposed to **social control,** which involves external enforcement through open coercion.

Cultural controls are embedded in our consciousness and may rely on deterrents such as fear of supernatural punishment—ancestral spirits sabotaging the hunting, for example—and magical retaliation. Like the devout Christian who avoids sinning for fear of hell, the individual expects some sort of punishment, even though no one in the community may be aware of the wrongdoing.

Cultural controls can also be framed in positive terms, with customary ways and means that encourage individual sacrifice for the common good. For example, many cultures honor traditions of giving to, or volunteering for, charitable or humanitarian institutions. Performed out of a desire to help those in need, such personal sacrifices (from the Latin *sacer*, "holy," and *facere*, "making") may be motivated by a spiritual or religious worldview. Often deeply rooted in basic ideas of a wider community and reciprocity, they are also cultural controls against self-seeking, self-serving, greedy opportunism that threatens the well-being of a larger community.

INTERNALIZED CONTROLS AMONG THE WAPE OF PAPUA NEW GUINEA

As an example of how internalized controls serve to keep people in line, we may look at the Wape people of Papua New Guinea, who believe the spirits of deceased ancestors roam lineage lands, protecting them from trespassers and helping their hunting descendants by driving game their way.[9] These ancestral spirits also punish those who have wronged them or their descendants by preventing hunters from finding game or causing them to miss their shots, thereby depriving people of much needed meat.

Nowadays, the Wape hunt with shotguns, which the community purchases for the use of one man, whose job it is to hunt for all the others. The cartridges used in the hunt, however, are invariably supplied by individual community members. Thus if the gunman shoots and misses, it is not viewed as his failing. Rather, it is because the owner of the fired shell, or some close relative, has quarreled or wronged another person whose deceased relative is securing revenge by causing the hunter to miss. Or, if the gunman cannot even find game, it is because vengeful ancestors have chased the animals away. As a proxy hunter for the villagers, the gunman is potentially subject to sanctions by ancestral spirits in response to collective wrongs by those for whom he hunts.

For the Wape, then, successful hunting depends upon avoiding quarrels and maintaining tranquility within the community so as not to antagonize anybody's deceased ancestor. Unfortunately, complete harmony is impossible to achieve in any human community, and the Wape are no exception. When hunting is poor, the gunman must discover what quarrels and wrongs have occurred within his village to identify the proper ancestral spirits to appeal to for renewed success. Usually, this is done in a special meeting where confessions of wrongdoing may be forthcoming. If not, questioning accusations are bandied about until resolution occurs, but even with no resolution, the meeting must end amicably to prevent new antagonisms. In this way, everyone's behavior comes under public scrutiny, reminding all of what is expected of them and encouraging villagers to avoid acts that will cast them in an unfavorable light.

---

[9] Mitchell, W. E. (1973, December). A new weapon stirs up old ghosts. *Natural History Magazine,* 77–84.

cultural control Control through beliefs and values deeply internalized in the minds of individuals.
social control External control through open coercion.

Formal sanctions may involve some form of regulated combat, seen here as armed dancers near Mount Hagen in New Guinea demand redress for murder.

Externalized Controls

Because internalized controls are not wholly sufficient even in bands and tribes, every society develops externalized social controls known as **sanctions** designed to encourage conformity to social norms. Operating within social groups of all sizes and involving a mix of cultural and social controls, sanctions may vary significantly within a given society, but they fall into one of two categories: positive or negative. Positive sanctions consist of incentives to conformity such as awards, titles, and recognition by one's neighbors. Negative sanctions consist of threats such as imprisonment, fines, corporal punishment, or ostracism from the community for violation of social norms.

For sanctions to be effective, they must be applied consistently, and they must be generally known among members of the society. Even if some individuals are not convinced of the advantages of social conformity, they are still more likely to obey society's rules than to accept the consequences of not doing so.

Sanctions may also be either formal or informal, depending on whether or not a legal statute is involved. In the United States, the man who goes shirtless in shorts to a church service may be subject to a variety of informal sanctions, ranging from disapproving glances from the

clergy to the chuckling of other parishioners. If, however, he were to show up without any clothing at all, he would be subject to the formal negative sanction of arrest for indecent exposure. Only in the second instance would he have been guilty of breaking the law.

Formal sanctions, such as laws, are always organized, because they attempt to precisely and explicitly regulate people's behavior, whether they are peacefully trading with others or confronting others on a battlefield. Other examples of organized sanctions include, on the positive side, military decorations and monetary rewards. On the negative side are loss of face, exclusion from social life and its privileges, seizure of property, imprisonment, and even bodily mutilation or death.

Informal sanctions emphasize cultural control and are diffuse in nature, involving spontaneous expressions of approval or disapproval by members of the group or community. They are, nonetheless, very effective in enforcing a large number of seemingly unimportant customs. Because most people want to be accepted, they are willing to acquiesce to the rules that govern dress, eating, and conversation, even in the absence of actual laws.

Social Control Through Witchcraft

In societies with or without centralized political systems, witchcraft sometimes functions as an agent of social control and involves both internal and external controls. An individual will think twice before offending a neighbor if

sanction An externalized social control designed to encourage conformity to social norms.

convinced that the neighbor could retaliate by resorting to black magic. Similarly, individuals may not wish to be accused of practicing witchcraft, and so they behave with greater circumspection.

Among the Azande of the Sudan, people who think they have been bewitched may consult an oracle, who, after performing the appropriate mystical rites, then may establish or confirm the identity of the offending witch.[10] Confronted with this evidence, the witch will usually agree to cooperate in order to avoid any additional trouble. Should the victim die, the relatives of the deceased may choose to make magic against the witch, ultimately accepting the death of some villager as evidence of both guilt and the efficacy of their magic.

For the Azande, witchcraft provides not only a sanction against antisocial behavior but also a means of dealing with natural hostilities and death. No one wishes to be thought of as a witch, and surely no one wishes to be victimized by one. By institutionalizing their emotional responses, the Azande successfully maintain social order.

Social Control Through Law

In Western society, someone who commits an offense against another person may become subject to a series of complex legal proceedings. In criminal cases the primary concern is to assign and punish guilt rather than to help out the victim. The offender will be arrested by the police; tried before a judge and perhaps a jury; and,

---

[10] Evans-Pritchard, E. E. (1937). *Witchcraft, oracles and magic among the Azande.* London: Oxford University Press.

depending on the severity of the crime, may be fined, imprisoned, or even executed. Rarely does the victim receive restitution or compensation. Throughout this chain of events, the accused party is dealt with by police, judges, jurors, and jailers, who may have no personal acquaintance whatsoever with the plaintiff or the defendant.

By contrast, among traditional Inuit in northern Canada, all offenses are considered to involve disputes between individuals; thus, they must be settled between the disputants themselves. A traditional way of doing this is through a *song duel,* in which the individuals involved heap insults upon one another in songs specially composed for the occasion. Although society does not intervene, its interests are represented by spectators, whose applause determines the outcome. If, however, social harmony cannot be restored—and that is the goal, rather than assigning and punishing guilt—one or the other disputant may move to another band. Ultimately, there is no binding legal authority.

DEFINITION OF LAW

Once two Inuit settle a dispute by engaging in a singing contest, the affair is considered closed; no further action is expected. Would we choose to describe the outcome of such a contest as a *legal* decision? If every law is a sanction but not every sanction is a law, how are we to distinguish between social sanctions in general and those to which we apply the label "law"?

According to anthropologist E. Adamson Hoebel, an important pioneer in the cross-cultural study of law, "A social norm is legal if its neglect or infraction is regularly met, in threat or in fact, by the application of physical force by an individual or group possessing the socially recognized

Having a song duel is the traditional approach to dispute resolution among the Inuit of northern Canada.

© Bryan & Cherry Alexander/Arcticphoto

privilege of so acting."[11] In stressing the legitimate use of physical coercion, Hoebel deemphasized the traditional association of law with a centralized court system.

Although rules enacted by an authorized legislative body and enforced by the judicial mechanisms of the state are fundamental features of Western jurisprudence, they are not the universal backbone of human law. Can any concept of law be applied to societies for whom the notion of a centralized judiciary is virtually meaningless? How shall we categorize Inuit song duels and other socially condoned forms of dispute resolution that seem to meet some but not all of the criteria of law?

Ultimately, it is always of greatest value to consider each case within its cultural context. After all, law reflects a society's basic postulates, so to understand any society's laws, one must understand the underlying values and assumptions. Nonetheless, a working definition of law is useful for purposes of discussion and cross-cultural comparison, and for this, **law** is adequately characterized as formal rules of conduct that, when violated, lead to negative sanctions.

FUNCTIONS OF LAW

Anthropologists recognize several basic functions of law, in particular the following three: First, it defines relationships among society's members and marks out proper behavior under specified circumstances. Knowledge of the law permits each person to know his or her rights and duties with respect to every other member of society.

Second, law allocates the authority to employ coercion in the enforcement of sanctions. In societies with centralized political systems, such authority is generally vested in the government and its judiciary system. In societies that lack centralized political control, the authority to employ force may be allocated directly to the injured party.

Third, law functions to redefine social relations and to ensure social flexibility. As new situations arise, law must determine whether old rules and assumptions retain their validity and to what extent they must be altered. Law, if it is to operate efficiently, must allow room for change.

---

[11] Hoebel, E. A. (1954). *The law of primitive man: A study in comparative legal dynamics* (p. 28). Cambridge, MA: Harvard University Press.

---

law Formal rules of conduct that, when violated, effectuate negative sanctions.

negotiation The use of direct argument and compromise by the parties to a dispute to arrive voluntarily at a mutually satisfactory agreement.

mediation Settlement of a dispute through negotiation assisted by an unbiased third party.

In practice, law is never as neat as a written description about it. In any given society, people are usually members of various subgroups—and fall under the varied dictates of these diverse groups. For example, among the Kapauku of Papua New Guinea, discussed earlier in this chapter, each individual is simultaneously a member of a family, a household, a sublineage, and a confederacy—and is subject to all the (sometimes conflicting) rules and regulations of each. Furthermore, the power to employ sanctions may vary from level to level within a given society. Thus the head of a Kapauku household in Papua New Guinea may punish a household member by slapping or beating, but the authority to confiscate property is vested exclusively in the headman of the lineage. Analogous distinctions exist in the United States among municipal, state, and federal jurisdictions. The complexity of legal jurisdiction within each society makes it difficult to generalize about law.

Punishing Crimes and Settling Disputes

As we have observed, an important function of negative sanctions, legal or otherwise, is to discourage the breach of social norms. A person contemplating theft is aware of the possibility of being caught and punished. Yet, even in the face of severe sanctions, individuals in every society sometimes violate the norms and subject themselves to the consequences of their behavior.

In Western societies a clear distinction is made between offenses against the state and offenses against an individual. However, in non-state societies such as bands and tribes, all offenses are viewed as transgressions against individuals or kin-groups (families, lineages, clans, and so on).

Disputes between individuals or kin-groups may seriously disrupt the social order, especially in small groups where the number of disputants, though small in absolute numbers, may be a large percentage of the total population. For example, although the Inuit traditionally have no effective domestic or economic unit beyond the family, a dispute between two people will interfere with the ability of members of separate families to come to one another's aid when necessary and is consequently a matter of wider social concern. The goal of judicial proceedings in such instances is restoring social harmony rather than punishing an offender. When distinguishing between offenses of concern to the community as a whole and those of concern only to a few individuals, we may refer to them as *collective* or *personal*.

Basically, disputes are settled in one of two ways. First, disputing parties may, through argument and compromise, voluntarily arrive at a mutually satisfactory agreement. This form of settlement is referred to as **negotiation** or, if it involves the assistance of an unbiased third party, **mediation.** In bands and tribes a third-party mediator has no coercive power and thus cannot force disputants to abide by such a decision, but as a person who commands great personal respect, the mediator frequently may help bring about a settlement.

Second, in chiefdoms and states, an authorized third party may issue a binding decision that the disputing parties will be compelled to respect. This process is referred to as **adjudication.** The difference between mediation and adjudication is basically a difference in authorization. In a dispute settled by adjudication, the disputing parties present their positions as compellingly as they can to an authority with the requisite legal power right to hear the case, but they do not participate in the ultimate decision making. Although the adjudication process is not universally characteristic, every society employs some form of negotiation to settle disputes.

Often negotiation acts as a prerequisite or an alternative to adjudication. For example, in the resolution of U.S. labor disputes, striking workers may first negotiate with management, often with the mediation of a third party. If the state decides the strike constitutes a threat to the public welfare, the disputing parties may be forced to submit to adjudication. In this case, the responsibility for resolving the dispute is transferred to a presumably impartial judge.

The judge's work is difficult and complex. In addition to sifting through evidence presented, he or she must consider a wide range of norms, values, and earlier rulings to arrive at a decision intended to be considered just not only by the disputing parties but by the public and other judges as well.

In many politically centralized societies, incorruptible supernatural, or at least nonhuman, powers are thought to make judgments through a "trial by ordeal." For example, among the Kpelle of Liberia discussed earlier in this chapter, when guilt is in doubt an "ordeal operator" licensed by the government may apply a hot knife to a suspect's leg. If the leg is burned, the suspect is guilty; if not, innocence is assumed. But the operator does not merely heat the knife and apply it. After massaging the suspect's legs and determining the knife is hot enough, the operator then strokes his own leg with it without being burned, demonstrating that the innocent will escape injury. The knife is then applied to the suspect.

Up to this point—consciously or unconsciously—the operator has read the suspect's nonverbal cues: gestures, the degree of muscular tension, amount of perspiration, and so forth. From this the operator can judge whether or not the accused is showing so much anxiety as to indicate probable guilt; in effect, a psychological stress evaluation has been made. As the knife is applied, it is manipulated to either burn or not burn the suspect, once this judgment has been made. The operator does this manipulation easily by controlling how long the knife is in the fire, as well as the pressure and angle at which it is pressed against the leg.[12]

Similar to this is the use of the lie detector (polygraph) in the United States, although the guiding ideology is scientific rather than supernaturalistic. Nevertheless, an incorruptible nonhuman agency is thought to establish who is lying and who is not, whereas in reality the polygraph operator cannot just "read" the needles of the machine. He or she must judge whether or not they are registering a high level of anxiety brought on by the testing situation, as opposed to the stress of guilt. Thus the polygraph operator has much in common with the Kpelle ordeal operator.

Restorative Justice and Conflict Resolution

Punitive justice, such as imprisonment, may be the most common approach to justice in North America, but it has not proven to be an effective way of changing criminal behavior. There are cultural alternatives.

Indigenous communities in Canada successfully urged their federal government to reform justice services to make them more consistent with indigenous values and traditions.[13] In particular, they have pressed for restorative justice techniques such as the Talking Circle, traditionally used in various forms by several Native American groups. For this, parties involved in a conflict come together in a circle with equal opportunity to express their views—one at a time, free of interruption. Usually, a "talking stick" (or an eagle feather or some other symbolic object) is held by whoever is speaking to signal that she or he has the right to talk at that moment and others have the responsibility to listen.

In North America over the past three decades there has been significant movement away from the courts in favor of outside negotiation and mediation to resolve a wide variety of disputes. Many jurists see this as a means to clear overloaded court dockets so as to concentrate on more important cases.

Today, leaders in the field of dispute resolution are finding effective ways to bring about balanced resolutions to conflict. An example of this appears in the Anthropology Applied feature.

---

[12] Gibbs, J. L., Jr. (1983). [Interview]. *Faces of culture: Program 18.* Fountain Valley, CA: Coast Telecourses.

[13] Criminal Code of Canada, §718.2(e).

---

adjudication Mediation with an unbiased third party making the ultimate decision.

Dispute Resolution and the Anthropologist

In an era when the consequences of violent approaches to dispute resolution are more far-reaching than ever, conflict management is of growing importance. A world leader in this profession is anthropologist William L. Ury, an independent negotiations specialist.

In his first year at graduate school, Ury began looking for ways to apply anthropology to practical problems, including conflicts of all dimensions. He wrote a paper about the role of anthropology in peacemaking and on a whim sent it to Roger Fisher, a law professor noted for his work in negotiation and world affairs. Fisher, in turn, invited the young graduate student to co-author a kind of how-to book for international mediators. The book they researched and wrote together turned out to have a far wider audience, for it presented basic principles of negotiation that could be applied to household spats, management–employee conflicts, or international crises. Titled *Getting to Yes: Negotiating Agreement Without Giving In* (1981), it sold millions of copies, was translated into twenty-one languages, and earned the nickname "the negotiator's bible."

While working on *Getting to Yes*, Ury and Fisher co-founded the Program on Negotiation (PON) at Harvard Law School, pulling together an interdisciplinary group of academics interested in new approaches to and applications of the negotiation process. Today this applied research center is a multiuniversity consortium that trains mediators, businesspeople, and government officials in negotiation skills. It has four key goals: (1) design, implement, and evaluate better dispute resolution practices; (2) promote collaboration among practitioners and scholars; (3) develop education programs and materials for instruction in negotiation and dispute resolution; (4) increase public awareness and understanding of successful conflict resolution efforts.

In 1982, Ury earned his doctorate in anthropology from Harvard with a dissertation titled "Talk Out or Walk Out: The Role and Control of Conflict in a Kentucky Coal Mine." Afterward, he taught for several years while maintaining a leadership role at PON. In particular, he devoted himself to PON's Global Negotiation Project (initially known as the Project on Avoiding War). Today, having left his teaching post at Harvard, Ury continues to serve as director of the Global Negotiation Project, writing, consulting, and running regular workshops on dealing with difficult people and situations.

Utilizing a cross-cultural perspective sharpened through years of anthropological research, he specializes in ethnic and secessionist disputes, including those between white and black South Africans, Serbs and Croats, Turks and Kurds, Catholics and Protestants in Northern Ireland, and Russians and Chechens in the former Soviet Union.

Among the most effective tools in Ury's applied anthropology work are the books he continues to write on dispute resolution—from his 1993 *Getting Past No* to his 2007 title, *The Power of a Positive No*. His 1999 book, *Getting to Peace: Transforming Conflict at Home, at Work, and in the World*, examines what he calls the "third side," which is the role that the surrounding community can play in preventing, resolving, and containing destructive conflict between two parties.[a]

His 2002 edited volume *Must We Fight?* challenges entrenched ideas that violence and war are inevitable and presents convincing evidence that human beings have as much inherent potential for cooperation and coexistence as they do for violent conflict. The key point in this book is that violence is a choice. In Ury's words, "Conflict is not going to end, but violence can."[b]

What Ury and others in this field are doing is helping create a culture of negotiation in a world where adversarial, win–lose attitudes are out of step with the increasingly interdependent relations between people.

---

[a]Pease, T. (2000, Spring). Taking the third side. *Andover Bulletin.*

[b]Ury, W. (2002, Winter). A global immune system. *Andover Bulletin*; see also www.pon.harvard.edu/

Violent Conflict and Warfare

Although the regulation of a society's internal affairs is an important function of any political system, it is by no means the sole function. Another is the management of its external affairs—relations not just among different states but among different bands, lineages, clans, or whatever the largest autonomous political unit may be. And just as force, threatened or actual, may be used to maintain or restore order within a society, such powerful pressures are also used in the conduct of external affairs.

Humans have a horrific track record when it comes to violence. Far more lethal than spontaneous and individual outbursts of aggression, organized violence in the form of war is responsible for enormous suffering and deliberate destruction of life and property. In the past 5,000 years or so, some 14,000 wars have been fought, resulting in many hundreds of millions of casualties. In the 20th century alone, an estimated 150 million people lost their lives due to human violence.

The scope of violent conflict is wide, ranging from individual fights, local feuds, raids, and piracy (see the Globalscape) to formally declared international wars fought by professional armed forces. In addition, we may distinguish among various civil wars (in which armies from different geographic areas, ethnic or religious groups, or political parties within the same state are pitted against each other), rebellions, and guerrilla warfare involving small-scale hit-and-run tactical operations instead of pitched battles.

Why War?

In addition to the varying scales and methods of warfare, there are different motives, strategic objectives, and political or moral justifications for it. Some societies engage in

Globalscape

Badri Media/epa/Corbis

Pirate Pursuits in Puntland?

Abshir Boya, a towering Somali pirate, is active in coastal waters off the Horn of Africa, which juts deep into the Arabian Sea. He lives in the old fishing port of Eyl in Puntland, an autonomous territory in Somalia. By 2009, Eyl had become a pirate haven, holding a dozen hijacked foreign ships and their multinational crews.

Like Boyah, most of the few hundred other pirates based in Puntland are Darod clansmen pressed out of their traditional fisheries by foreign commercial fleets polluting their coasts and depleting their fish stocks. Since 1991, Somalia has been splintered by rebellions, clan rivalries, and foreign armed interventions. It no longer has a centralized power system maintaining law and order for its citizens, who survive on an average annual income of $600. With a national

economy in tatters, Boyah and his clansmen spied the wealth passing through the Arabian Sea and decided to grab a share.

Bankrolled by emigrated Somali investors living in cities such as Melbourne, Dubai, Nairobi, London, Toronto, and Minneapolis, pirate gangs are equipped with radios, cell phones, and GPS, plus semi-automatic pistols, assault rifles, and rocket-propelled grenade launchers bought in Yemen. Speeding across open sea in skiffs, they chase cargo ships, oil tankers, and cruise ships from around the world, including the U.S., Canada, Denmark, France, Saudi Arabia, India, and China.

Some pirate captains have banked success, including Boyah who claims to have led over twenty-five hijackings. Ship owners pay huge ransoms, frequently topping $1 million per ship. Somali sea bandits—about a thousand

in total—collectively net between $80 and $150 million annually. They are obliged to pay their backers and share earnings with many poor relatives in their large clan. Far bigger profits go to Lloyd's of London, which earns an extra $400 million a year on piracy insurance for ships plying these dangerous waters.

The United Nations has called on nations with vessels in the area to repress piracy with military force. Today, a dozen navies patrol a million square miles of sea. Numerous Somali pirates have been killed or captured. Criminal prosecution of piracy in international waters is a big problem due to questions over jurisdiction, but many are now in jails in half a dozen foreign countries.

Global Twister What is justice for Somali fishermen pressed into piracy?

---

defensive wars only and avoid armed confrontations with others unless seriously threatened or actually attacked. Others initiate aggressive wars to pursue particular strategic goals, including material benefits in the form of precious resources such as slaves, gold, or oil, as well as territorial expansion or control over trade routes. In some cultures, aggressive wars are waged for ideological reasons,

such as spreading one's own worldview or religion and defeating "evil" ideas or heresies elsewhere.

Beyond such explanations for warfare, is there something in our genetic makeup that makes it inevitable? Some argue that males of the human species are naturally aggressive. As evidence they point to aggressive group behavior exhibited by chimpanzees in Tanzania where researchers observed one group systematically destroy another and take over their territory. Also, they cite the "fierce" behavior of people such as the Yanomami Indians who inhabit the Amazon rainforest on either side of the border between Brazil and Venezuela. These tropical horticulturalists and foragers have been described as living in a chronic state of war, and some scientists suggest this exemplifies the way all humans once behaved.

Occasionally, archaeologists have discovered stone spear points embedded in ancient human skeletons. Also, here is ample evidence that armed conflicts in the form of deadly feuds and raids have long existed in stateless societies such as foraging bands, horticultural villagers, or nomadic herders. However, warfare among humans is likely to be situation specific rather than an unavoidable expression of genetic predisposition for violent behavior (see this chapter's Biocultural Connection).

Moreover, war is not a universal phenomenon, for in various parts of the world there are societies that do not practice warfare as we know it. Examples include people as diverse as the Ju/'hoansi Bushmen and Pygmy peoples of southern Africa, the Arapesh of New Guinea, and the Jain of India, as well as the Amish of North America. Among societies that do practice warfare, levels of violence may differ dramatically.

Biocultural Connection

Sex, Gender, and Human Violence

At the start of the 21st century, war and violence are no longer the strictly male domains that they were in many societies in the past. War has become embedded in civilian life in many parts of the world, and it impacts the daily lives of women and children. Moreover, women now serve in the military forces of several states, although their participation in combat is often limited. Some female soldiers in the United States argue that gender should not limit their participation in combat as they consider themselves as strong, capable, and well trained as their male counterparts. Others believe that biologically based sex differences make war a particularly male domain.

Scientists have long argued that males are more suited to combat because natural selection has made them on average larger and stronger than females. This idea, known as sexual selection, was first put forth by Darwin in the 19th century. At that time he proposed that the physical specializations of males in animal species—such as horns, vibrant plumage, and, in the case of humans, intelligence and tool use—demonstrate selection acting upon males to aid in the competition for mates. In these scenarios, male reproductive success is thought to be optimized through a strategy of "spreading seed"—in other words, by being sexually active with as many females as possible.

Females, on the other hand, are considered gatekeepers who optimize their reproductive success through caring for individual offspring. According to this theory of sexual selection, in species where male–male competition is high,

males will be considerably larger than females, and aggression will serve males well. In monogamous species, males and females will be of similar sizes.

Primatologist Richard Wrangham has taken the idea of sexual selection even further. In his book *Demonic Males,* he explores the idea that both male aggression and patriarchy have an evolutionary basis. He states that humans, like our close cousins the chimpanzees, are "party gang" species characterized by strong bonds among groups of males who have dominion over an expandable territory. These features "suffice to account for natural selection's ugly legacy, the tendency to look for killing opportunities when hostile neighbors meet."[a] Violence in turn generates a male-dominated social order: "Patriarchy comes from biology in the sense that it emerges from men's temperaments out of their evolutionarily derived efforts to control women and at the same time have solidarity with fellow males in competition against outsiders."[b] While Wrangham allows that evolutionary forces have shaped women as well, he suggests that females' evolutionary interests cannot be met without cooperation with males.

Feminist scholars have pointed out that these scientific models are "gendered" in that they incorporate the norms derived from the scientists' culture. Darwin's original model of sexual selection incorporated the Victorian gender norms of the passive female and active male. Primatologist Laura Fedigan suggests that in Darwinian models women evolved in positive directions only by a "coat tails" process whereby females were "pulled along"

toward improved biological states by virtue of the progress of the genes they shared with males.[c] Wrangham's more recent *Demonic Males* theory is similarly shaped by culture. It incorporates the dominant world order (military states) and the gender norms (aggressive males) it values. In both cases, the putatively scientific theory has created a natural basis for a series of social conventions.

This does not mean that biological differences between the sexes cannot be studied in the natural world. Instead, scientists studying sex differences must be especially sensitive to how they may project cultural beliefs onto nature. Meanwhile, the attitudes of some women soldiers continue to challenge generalizations regarding "military specialization" by gender.

BIOCULTURAL QUESTION

All across the world, males are far more likely to serve as warriors than females and, consequently, are far more likely to lose their lives on the battlefield. Do you think that there is any structural relationship between high male combat mortality rates and polgyny as the preferred marriage type in most traditional cultures?

---

[a]Wrangham, R., & Peterson, D. (1996). *Demonic males* (p. 168). Boston: Houghton Mifflin.

[b]Ibid., p. 125.

[c]Fedigan, L. M. (1986). The changing role of women in models of human evolution. *Annual Review of Anthropology 15,* 25–66.

We have ample reason to suppose that war—not to be confused with more limited forms of deadly violence such as raids—has become a problem only in the last 10,000 years, since the invention of food-production techniques and especially since the formation of centralized states 5,000 years ago. It has reached crisis proportions in the past 200 years, with the invention of modern weaponry and increased direction of violence against civilian populations.

Beginning in 1917 with military use of mustard gas—a chemical poison that causes blindness, large blisters on exposed skin, and (if inhaled) bleeding and blistering in mouth, throat, and lungs—the development of weapons of mass destruction has been horrendously effective. Today, the chemical, biological, and nuclear weapons arsenals stockpiled by many states are sufficient to wipe out all life on the planet, many times over.

Not surprisingly, given this development in the technology of death, casualties not just of civilians but also of *children* far outnumber those of soldiers. Indeed, because dangerous poisons, such as the anthrax bacterium or the nerve gas Sarin, are easy to produce and cheap, non-state groups, including terrorists, also seek to gain access to these modern weapons of mass destruction, if only to threaten to use them against more powerful opponents. Thus warfare on this level is not so much an age-old problem as it is a relatively recent one.

Among food foragers, with their uncentralized political systems, violence may erupt sporadically, but warfare was all but unknown until recent times. There are several reasons for this. First of all, since territorial boundaries and membership among food-foraging bands are usually fluid and loosely defined, a man who hunts with one band today may hunt with a neighboring band next month. This renders warfare impractical.

So, too, does the systematic exchange of marriage partners among food-foraging groups, which makes it likely that someone in each band will have a sibling, parent, or cousin in a neighboring band. Moreover, the absence of a food surplus among foragers makes prolonged combat difficult. In sum, where populations are small, food surpluses are absent, property ownership minimal, and no state organization exists, the likelihood of organized violence by one group against another is small.[14]

Despite the traditional view of the gardener or farmer as a gentle tiller of the soil, it is among such people, along with pastoralists, that warfare becomes prominent. One reason may be that food-producing peoples are much more likely to experience significant population growth, as opposed to food foragers whose numbers are generally maintained well below carrying capacity (the number of people that the available resources can support at a given level of food-getting techniques). This population growth, if unchecked, can lead to resource depletion, one solution to which may be seizure of some other people's resources.

In addition, the commitment to a fixed piece of land inherent in farming makes such societies somewhat less fluid in their membership than those of food foragers. Instead of marrying distantly, farmers marry locally, depriving them of long-distance kin networks. In rigidly matrilocal or patrilocal societies, each new generation is bound to the same territory, no matter how small it may be or how large the group trying to live within it.

The availability of unoccupied lands may not serve as a sufficient detriment to the outbreak of war. Among swidden farmers, for example, competition for land cleared of old-growth forest frequently leads to hostility and armed conflict. The centralization of political control and the possession of valuable property among farming people provide many more stimuli for warfare.

It is among such peoples, especially those organized into states, where the violence of warfare is most apt to result in indiscriminate mass killing. This development has reached its peak in modern states. Indeed, much (but not all) of the warfare that has been observed in recent stateless societies (so-called tribal warfare) has been provoked by aggressively expanding states.[15]

Although competition for scarce resources may turn violent and lead to war, the motivations and justifications for war are often embedded in a society's worldview—the collective body of ideas that members of a culture generally share concerning the ultimate shape and substance of their reality. There are many historical examples of wars inspired or justified by religious ideas, ranging from the Crusades to Aztec Indian wars. More recently, the *jihad*—an Arabic word meaning "struggle" or Holy War—by Muslim fundamentalists called the Taliban in Afghanistan and Pakistan seeks to expel infidels (nonbelievers) from ancestral soil. An instructive comparison can be made between the two historical examples that follow.

Fighting for Worldview: The Crusades and Aztec Warfare

In 1095 the Roman Catholic Pope Urban II launched the first Crusade ("War of the Cross"), with a speech urging the Christian nobles of Europe to end their ceaseless wars against one another and instead direct their hostilities toward the infidels—in this case, Muslim Turks and Arabs in the Middle East. In the same speech the pope also alluded to the economic benefits to be realized by seizing

---

[14] Knauft, B. M. (1991). Violence and sociality in human evolution. *Current Anthropology 32*, 391–409.

[15] Whitehead, N. L., & Ferguson, R. B. (1993, November). Deceptive stereotypes about tribal warfare. *Chronicle of Higher Education*, A48.

the resources of the infidels. Although clearly the Crusades were motivated by more than religious ideology, they were justified as a holy war to liberate Jerusalem and the Holy Land from Muslims. However, the success of the Crusades was limited, and twenty years after the ninth and final Crusade (1271–1272), the last Christian stronghold in Palestine surrendered to a Muslim army.

Within the next few centuries, however, Europe's Christian powers turned their attention to state building and colonial expansion in other parts of the world. Along with this growth and outward expansion came advances in the technology and organization of warfare. With the emergence of states (not just in Europe but in other parts of the world as well) has come a dramatic increase in the scale of warfare. This is not surprising, given the state's acceptance of force as a legitimate tool for regulating human affairs and its ability to organize large numbers of people.

Consider, for example, the Aztec state in the central Mexican highlands, which engaged in continuous warfare from the mid-1400s until its demise in the early 1520s. By way of battle, the state collected tribute and achieved regional dominance. Moreover, by waging war against their neighbors, Aztecs obtained prisoners to use as offerings for their gods; the Aztecs believed their gods required human sacrifice to maintain the cosmic order: "The warrior slated for sacrifice was a *teomiqui*, 'he who dies in god-like fashion,' and would feed the sun so that it might shine upon the world and keep it in motion."[16]

Among Aztecs, this worldview justified, even sanctified, perpetual aggression. In fact, according to the noted anthropologist Eric Wolf, priests bearing the images of the Aztec war god Huitilopochtli and other deities walked ahead of the army and gave the signal to commence combat by lighting a fire and blowing on shell trumpets. The victory that followed, Wolf wrote, "always had the same results: Long lines of captives, wooden collars about their necks, made the long journey to Tenochtitlán to be offered upon the altars of the gods."[17]

Several thousand captives could be sacrificed after one of these Aztec military campaigns, and within a single year as many as 20,000 may have been offered to the gods in that capital city of the Aztec state. In fact, one major motive for the Aztecs to wage war against rival states was to obtain war captives for sacrificial rituals.

---

[16] Keen, B. (1971). *The Aztec image in Western thought* (p. 13). New Brunswick, NJ: Rutgers University Press.

[17] Wolf, E. R. (1999). *Envisioning power: Ideologies of dominance and crisis* (p. 263). Berkeley: University of California Press.

genocide The physical extermination of one people by another, either as a deliberate act or as the accidental outcome of activities carried out by one people with little regard for their impact on others.

War was glorified and associated with the beauty of flowers. Warriors were called "dancing flowers," and captives were known as "flowers of the heart," with the blood of warriors called "flower-water." Success in capturing warriors destined for sacrifice made an Aztec war hero "rich in flowers." For this reason, military expeditions to obtain war captives were known as "flowery wars."

The Aztec flowery wars and the Christian Crusades are just two of many examples of how religious motivations and ideological justifications for war are embedded in a society's worldview. We will discuss other aspects of worldview in the following chapter, which focuses on religion and the supernatural.

Genocide

As these cross-cultural examples of violent conflicts indicate, warfare often involves a complex dynamic of economic, political, and ideological interests. Such is especially the case when violence escalates into **genocide**—the physical extermination of one people by another, either as a deliberate act or as the accidental outcome of activities carried out by one people with little regard for their impact on others.

Genocide is not a new phenomenon. One of the most infamous 19th-century acts of genocide was the systematic killing of the indigenous inhabitants of Tasmania, a large island just south of Australia. British wool growers wanted the indigenous peoples removed so that they could take control of the sheep on the island. The government advanced their interests through military campaigns against the natives.

These campaigns failed to achieve the complete elimination of the Tasmanians, but what the military could not achieve was done by George Augustus Robinson, a British Protestant missionary. Rounding up the surviving natives, he brought them to his mission station, where they died from the combination of psychological depression and lack of resistance to European disease. Robinson retired to Britain to contemplate the horrible if unintended consequences of his actions, which secured Tasmania for the British commercial wool industry: the demise of the last full-blooded Tasmanians.

There are examples of genocide all across the world and throughout history. In North America, for example, European settlers massacred numerous indigenous communities from the 1500s up until the late 1800s in California. Among the many Californian Indian groups now extinct are the Yahi, a small tribe of foragers traditionally ranging the Sierra Nevada. Defending their territory from invading gold miners and settlers, most lost their lives. After a massacre in 1865, only thirty survived and went into hiding in the remote mountain wilderness. Some of them were killed by cattlemen, others died of other causes in the next forty years, until only one tribesman was left. Lonely, he straggled out and was discovered in a cattle

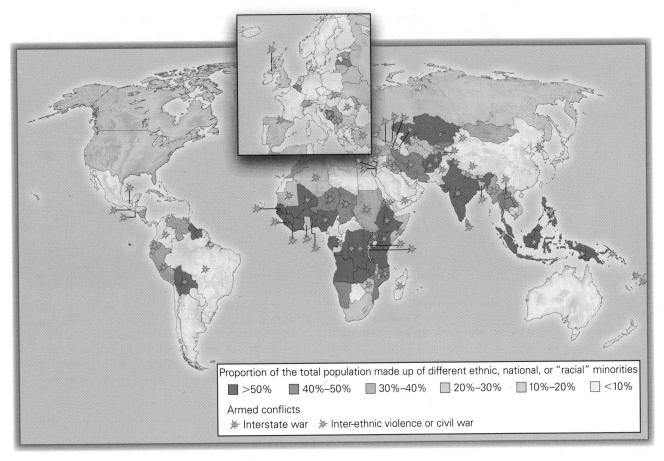

Proportion of the total population made up of different ethnic, national, or "racial" minorities

■ >50% ■ 40%–50% ■ 30%–40% ■ 20%–30% ■ 10%–20% □ <10%

Armed conflicts
✳ Interstate war   ✳ Inter-ethnic violence or civil war

Figure 23.3 In pluralistic societies in which two or more ethnic groups or nationalities form part of the same political state, violent conflict between neighboring groups is not uncommon.

corral in the summer of 1911. Causing a sensation as the "last wild Indian," he was taken to the University of California in San Francisco. Never revealing his name because of a cultural taboo, he became known as Ishi, the word for "man" in his native language.[18]

The most widely known act of genocide in recent history was the attempt of the Nazis during World War II to wipe out European Jews and Roma (Gypsies) in the name of racial superiority and improvement of the human species. Unfortunately, referring to this atrocity as "*the* Holocaust"— as if it were something unique or at least exceptional—tends to blind us to the fact that this thoroughly monstrous act is but one example of an all-too-common phenomenon.

Among numerous more contemporary examples of mass murder, Khmer Rouge soldiers in Cambodia killed 1.7 million fellow citizens, or 20 percent of that country's population, between 1975 and 1979. During the next decade, government-sponsored terrorism against indigenous communities in Guatemala reached its height, and Saddam Hussein's government used poison gas against the Kurdish ethnic minority in northern Iraq. In 1994, more

than half a million Tutsi people were slaughtered by their Hutu neighbors in the African country of Rwanda.[19] Estimates vary, but during the 20th century as many as 83 million people have died of genocide.[20] The horrors continue in our current century with, among others, the genocidal campaign against the non-Arab black peoples in the Darfur desert region of western Sudan.

Wars Today

Currently, there are numerous wars going on in the world (Figure 23.3). They occur not only *between* countries but also *within* states where the political leadership and government bureaucracy are corrupt, repressive, ineffective, or without popular support. Notably, many armies around the world recruit not only adult men, but also women and children. Today, more than 250,000 child soldiers, many as young as 12 years old, are participating in armed conflicts around the world.[21]

---

[18] Starn, O. (2005). *Ishi's brain: In search of America's last "wild" Indian.* New York: Norton.

[19] www.hrw.org/reports/1999/rwanda.

[20] White, M. (2001). *Historical atlas of the twentieth century.* http://users. erols.com/mwhite28/20centry.htm; see also van den Berghe, p. 198.

[21] "Study estimates 250,000 active child soldiers." (2006, July 26). Associated Press.

Congo is one of Africa's failed states, the consequence of a century of ruthless colonial exploitation, many decades of government mismanagement, and an ill-equipped bureaucracy. With a wealth of precious natural resources—including gold, diamonds, and uranium, especially in the eastern frontier provinces far from the capital—the country risks splintering. Since 1998, a gruesome war has devastated the peoples living in eastern Congo. In addition to the deaths of almost 6 million people, millions more are homeless. Here we see a small part of the 200,000 refugees fleeing from the horrors of mass murder, pillage, famine, and rape.

The following examples offer some specific data on wars from the last decade of the 20th century to today. In the 1990s, between 2 and 3 million died due to separatist warfare in the southern Sudan. And since warfare erupted in eastern Congo in 1998, almost 6 million people have died and millions more have been forced to flee their home villages. Involving eight African states and about twenty-five armed forces, this gruesome war with mass murder and mass rape is also known as Africa's World War. Clashes between various government troops, ethnic rebel groups, and freelancing militias continue in Congo's lawless borderlands.

Moreover, the Middle East remains mired in political turmoil and violent strife, especially since the U.S.-led military invasion of Afghanistan in 2001, where a Muslim fundamentalist regime was removed from power as it provided a territorial base for an international terrorist organization. Two years later, the U.S. launched an invasion of Iraq, unseating Saddam Hussein whose dictatorship was deemed hostile to U.S. strategic interests in the oil-rich region. In addition to many tens of thousands of fatalities in both Iraq and Afghanistan, the vast majority of whom are noncombatants—children, women, and elders—there has also been massive destruction of roads, bridges, buildings, and livelihoods. Without a political leadership capable of effectively governing these pluralistic countries, providing security, and maintaining law and order, both war-torn countries seem doomed to be failed states.

Beyond these wars, there are numerous so-called low-intensity wars involving guerrilla organizations, rebel armies, resistance movements, terrorist cells, and a host of other armed groups engaged in violent conflict with official state-controlled armed forces. Every year, confrontations result in hundreds of hot spots and violent flashpoints, most of which are never reported in Western news media.[22]

As the above cross-cultural examples show, the causes of warfare are complex, involving economic, political, and ideological factors. The challenge of eliminating human warfare has never been greater than it is in today's world—nor has the cost of *not* finding a way to do so. In the First World War a new term, "crimes against humanity," was coined to identify inhumane acts such as the systematic persecution of one ethnic group by another, massive deportation or massacre of noncombatants, and other gruesome atrocities. Since 1945, the United Nations has been charged with the prosecution of this crime, albeit with mixed success.

In 2002, a permanent tribunal to prosecute crimes against humanity, genocide, and war crimes was established in The Hague, the Netherlands, called the International Criminal Court. So far, 110 states are members of this court, including all of South America, most of Europe, and about half the countries in Africa. Another forty-eight countries have signed but not ratified this international treaty. Some countries, however, refuse to join, including China, India, Israel, Russia, Sudan, and the United States. Nevertheless, the establishment of this court shows that almost a century after the start of the First World War, and more than half a century after the founding of the United Nations, issues of crime and punishment are now also recognized as global affairs.

---

[22] icasualties.org.

Questions for Reflection

1.   In Afghanistan, a pluralistic society with many ethnic groups and tribes, the central government is so weak and has so little power that it cannot effectively manage, let alone protect, the country and its highly diverse population. Yet political ties among tribal communities are periodically reinforced by an ancient institution called the Loya Jirga, or Grand Council. Considering the geographic, political, economic, and cross-cultural challenges this poor Asian country faces, do you think Afghanistan has a better chance as a decentralized state, in which each region has considerable autonomy and is governed by tribal councils, than as a state with a centralized government?

2.   Considering the comparative historical examples of the Crusades by European Christian armies and Aztec Indian warfare in Mexico, do you think there is a relationship between a profitable arms industry, promoting military dominance, and the pursuit of war as a means of solving conflicts? If so, what is the role of an ideology that asserts national and/or religious righteousness?

3.   If political organization functions to impose or maintain order and to resolve conflicts, why do you think that a government in a country such as yours is so interested in legitimizing its power? What happens when a government loses such legitimacy?

4.   Which nationalities or ethnic groups do you know that are dominant, and which can you identify that are in a minority position or are repressed? What is the basis for this inequality?

5.   When your own government declares war against another country, on which basis does it seek to justify its decision to send soldiers into battle?

Suggested Readings

Cheater, A. (2005). *The anthropology of power.* London: Routledge.

The author presents case studies from a wide range of societies to examine the issues surrounding power and whether power can actually be transferred to the powerless. The book explores how traditionally disempowered groups gain influence in postcolonial and multicultural settings. Also, it surveys the relationships between empowerment and economic development, gender, and environmentalism.

Kertzer, D. I. (1989). *Ritual, politics, and power.* New Haven, CT: Yale University Press.

Using numerous examples from traditional and modern societies and writing in clear accessible prose, the author argues that political symbols manifested through rituals explain much of the political life of modern nations, contrary to the usual rational, utilitarian, and interest-group explanations. He discusses how elites use rituals to support the existing order, while revolutionaries use them to replace it.

Nader, L. (2002). *The life of the law: Anthropological projects.* Berkeley: University of California Press.

A renowned legal anthropologist, Nader presents a historical overview of the development of this specialization and explores the role of the law in the struggle for social and economic justice. Considering the profound impact of globalization on both the law and anthropology, she discusses the growing dominance of capitalist corporations and the prominence of neoliberal ideology and practice. Linking the growing popularity of the alternative dispute resolution movement, this critical theorist argues that mediation as an approach to conflict resolution is structured to favor powerful capitalist interests.

Ury, W. (Ed.). (2002). *Must we fight? From the battlefield to the schoolyard—A new perspective on violent conflict and its prevention.* Hoboken, NJ: Jossey-Bass.

This fresh exploration of the question of whether violence and war are inevitable presents evidence from leading anthropologists and other scholars that human beings have as much inherent potential for cooperation and coexistence as they do for violent conflict.

Vincent, J. (2002). *The anthropology of politics: A reader in ethnography, theory, and critique.* Boston: Blackwell.

This sweeping historical and theoretical introduction to the field features readings from noted anthropologists past and present, enriched by Vincent's insightful headnotes.

Whitehead, N., & Ferguson, R. B. (Eds.). (1992). *War in the tribal zone.* Santa Fe: School of American Research Press.

The central point of this book is that the transformation and intensification of war, as well as the formation of tribes, result from complex interaction in the "tribal zone" that begins where centralized authority makes contact with stateless people it does not rule. In such zones, newly introduced plants, animals, diseases, and technologies often spread widely, even before colonizers appear. These and other changes disrupt existing social and political relationships, fostering new alliances and creating conflicts.

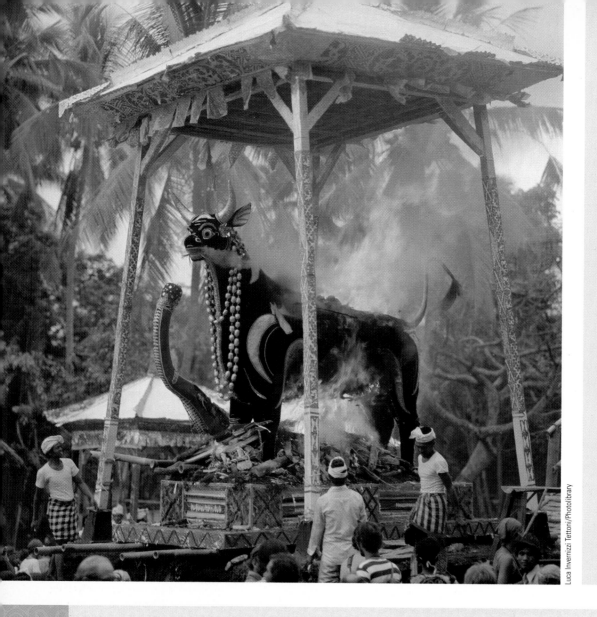

Challenge Issue As self-aware and self-reflecting beings, humans face emotional and intellectual challenges born of the need to make sense of our place in the universe. We puzzle over human origin and destiny and truly big questions about time and space, as we wrestle with existential questions about our own fate, life, and death. Throughout time and across the globe, humans have creatively addressed these ponderings and worked out answers articulated in sacred narratives and associated ceremonies, rituals, and other cultural forms of religious or spiritual expression. One spectacular cultural example of people coming to terms with death is the Hindu cremation ceremony (*ngaben*) on the Indonesian island of Bali. After a death, relatives, friends, and neighbors transform emotional grief into a theatrical ceremony; everyone joyfully participates by making food and presenting offerings for the *ngaben*. For this dramatic ritual, the dead body is placed inside a wooden sarcophagus built in the shape of a bull (a sacred animal according to Hindu religion) and then set afire. Through cremation, the person's *roh* (spirit or soul) is believed to be ritually purified and freed from its material remains. As the *roh* takes wing and migrates to its next existence, the physical body continues to burn. Later, when the bones are no longer hot, they are collected and ground up while a priest chants prayers. The ashes are then taken to the island's coast and ceremonially released into the sea.

CHAPTER 24

Spirituality, Religion, and the Supernatural

Chapter Preview

What Are Religion and Spirituality?

Religion and spirituality form part of a cultural system's superstructure, which comprises a society's worldview. Religion is an organized system of ideas about spiritual reality, or the supernatural, along with associated beliefs and ceremonial practices. Spirituality, which also concerns the supernatural, involves less formalized beliefs and practices and is often individual rather than collective. Humans rely on both religion and spirituality to give meaning to the world and their place in it and to deal with problems that defy ordinary explanation or simple and direct solutions. To overcome these challenges, people appeal to, or seek to influence and even manipulate, spiritual or supernatural beings and powers.

What Are the Identifying Features of Religion and Spirituality?

Religion (and spiritual practices in general) consists of various beliefs and rituals—prayers, songs, dances, offerings, and sacrifices—that people use to interpret, appeal to, and manipulate supernatural beings and powers to their advantage. These beings and powers may be gods and goddesses, ancestral and other spirits, or impersonal powers, either by themselves or in various combinations. In all societies certain individuals are especially skilled at dealing with these beings and powers and assist other members of society in their ritual activities. A body of myths rationalizes or explains the system in a manner consistent with people's experience in the world in which they live. In many cultures, efforts to control supernatural powers include witchcraft and magic.

What Functions Do Religion and Spirituality Serve?

All religions serve a number of important social, psychological, and emotional functions, as well as ideological purposes: They help maintain social solidarity; they feature rituals that may be used to enhance the learning of oral traditions; they reduce anxieties by explaining the unknown; and they offer comfort with the belief that supernatural aid is available for healing and emotional relief in times of crisis. Religious systems also provide guidance about right and wrong, setting precedents for acceptable behavior and transferring the burden of decision making from individuals to supernatural powers. Spirituality also serves emotional, psychological, and social functions, but it tends to be fitted to more personal preferences, and its form and expression are often uniquely creative.

From an anthropological point of view, spirituality and religion are part of a cultural system's superstructure, earlier defined as the collective body of ideas, beliefs, and values by which a group of people makes sense of the world and their place in it. In contrast to other disciplines such as theology, for example, which may focus on questions concerning the nature of God or the idea of divine spirit and the interpretation of ancient sacred texts, anthropology examines spirituality and religion in terms of a society's **worldview**—the collective body of ideas that members of a culture generally share concerning the ultimate shape and substance of their reality. In their cross-cultural studies of different religious and spiritual beliefs and practices, anthropologists seek to remain unbiased regarding any particular historical tradition, belief, or ritual considered sacred by the people they study.

The Role of Religion and Spirituality

Among people in all cultures, particular spiritual or religious beliefs and practices fulfill numerous social and psychological needs, such as reducing anxiety by presenting an orderly view of the universe and answers to existential questions, including those concerning suffering and death. They can provide the path by which people transcend their burdensome and mortal existence and attain, if only momentarily, spiritual hope and relief.

In addition, a shared religion reinforces group norms, provides moral sanctions for individual conduct, and furnishes the ideology of common purpose and values that support the well-being of the community. Also of note, people often turn to religion or spirituality in the hope of reaching a specific goal, such as the healing of physical, emotional, or social ills.

Perhaps it is because they fulfill these and numerous other social and psychological needs shared by humans across cultures that supernatural beliefs are universal. While recognizing that not all individuals believe in a supernatural force or entity, anthropologists know of no group of people anywhere on the face of the earth who, at any time over the past 100,000 years, has been without some manifestation of spirituality or religion. Not even in countries such as China and North Korea, where atheism remains the communist state dogma and where powerful regimes have long suppressed religious institutions, did religion entirely disappear.

In the 19th century, the European intellectual tradition gave rise to the idea that modern science would ultimately replace religion by showing people the irrationality of their spiritual beliefs and practices. The expectation was that as valid scientific explanations became available, people would abandon their religious beliefs and rituals as superstitious myths and false worship. Although it is true that in wealthy northwestern European states such as Sweden the percentage of inhabitants who consider themselves atheist, agnostic, or simply non-believers in God is now the highest in the world, that secularist trend is by no means universal.[1] In fact, in many places, the opposite trend seems to prevail.

Far from causing religion's demise, and despite the enormous growth of scientific knowledge, modernization does not always lead to greater rationality or predictability in rapidly changing societies. In fact, globalization often leads to a destabilization of the established order. The upheaval in ordinary people's lives often produces new anxieties and raises new questions about human existence.

Although traditional, mainline Christian religions have shown some decline, nondenominational spirituality is on the rise. Also on the rise are fundamentalist religions, which often take a strong antiscience position. Examples include Islamic fundamentalism in countries such as Afghanistan, Algeria, and Iran; Jewish fundamentalism in Israel and the United States; and Hindu fundamentalism

---

[1] Zuckerman, P. (2005). Atheism: Contemporary rates and patterns. In M. Martin (Ed.), *The Cambridge companion to atheism.* Cambridge, England: Cambridge University Press.

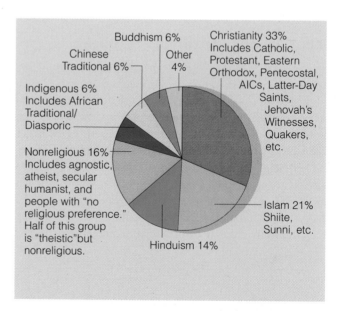

Figure 24.1 The major religions of the world with their percentages of believers. Note that the total adds up to more than 100 percent due to rounding and due to the upper-bound estimates used for each group. As we go to press, more recent comparative figures for all these groups are not available. However, a 2009 study by the Pew Research Center reports that the number of Muslims has grown to 1.57 billion, representing about 23 percent of the total global population. Sources: adherents.com; Pew Research Center, 2009.

Members of the Church of Zion, an indigenous Christian church with a primarily Zulu congregation, perform a baptism in the Indian Ocean near Durban, South Africa. Over half of all Christian church members in South Africa belong to indigenous churches that combine some elements of their traditional African beliefs and rituals with those of Christianity.

© Ed Kashi/Corbis

in India. Christian fundamentalism is represented in the dramatic growth of evangelical denominations in the United States, Central America, and sub-Saharan Africa.

Among the fastest-growing religious communities in the world are the indigenous churches of Africa. Over the last half century, the number of registered indigenous denominations in southern Africa alone has doubled from about 5,000 to 10,000. There, it is estimated that more than half of Christian church members belong to indigenous churches, like the Amanazaretha Church founded by a Zulu prophet and popular among fellow Zulus in Natal.[2]

Within the United States, non-Christian religions are also growing: Islam (3 to 5 million followers—up from 527,000 in 1990), Buddhism (2 to 3 million—up from 401,000 in 1990), and Hinduism (1.28 million—up from 227,000 in 1990), not to mention various new age options such as Wicca (a modern, nature-oriented religion that draws upon ancient western European and pre-Christian beliefs and now counts about 310,000 adherents).[3]

Notably, just 16 percent of the adult population throughout the world claim to be nonreligious (Figure 24.1). This is not to say that those classified as nonreligious are all atheists, because this miscellaneous "negative" category actually includes many millions of individuals in dozens of countries who may reject or not fit under the label of any organized religion but who are metaphysically involved in creative arrangements of spiritual beliefs and practices of their own choosing.

Spiritual and religious beliefs do often change over time, but in whichever cultural form, faith in supernatural powers remains a dominant and dynamic force in most contemporary societies. It is not the responsibility of anthropologists to rank or pass judgment on the metaphysical truth of any particular faith system, but it is their task to show how each embodies a number of revealing facts about humans and the particular cultural superstructure within which these religious or spiritual beliefs are ideologically embedded.

The Anthropological Approach to Religion and Spirituality

Although people in different cultures—each with their own beliefs about the ultimate shape and substance of the supernatural—may have particular ideas about religion and spirituality, we offer a basic definition of both: **Religion is** an organized system of ideas about the spiritual sphere or the supernatural, along with associated

---

[2] Kunnie, J. (2007). *Umoya: The spirit in Africa.* Self-produced DVD, available at www.coh.arizona.edu/aas/aas.htm.

[3] U.S. Census 2000; www.adherents.com. See also *World almanac.* (2004). New York: Press Publishing.; and pluralism.org (the Pluralism Project, Harvard University).

religion An organized system of ideas about the spiritual sphere or the supernatural, along with associated ceremonial practices by which people try to interpret and/or influence aspects of the universe otherwise beyond their control.

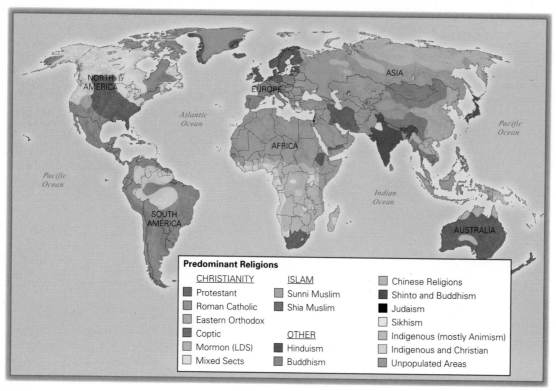

Predominant Religions

CHRISTIANITY
- Protestant
- Roman Catholic
- Eastern Orthodox
- Coptic
- Mormon (LDS)
- Mixed Sects

ISLAM
- Sunni Muslim
- Shia Muslim

OTHER
- Hinduism
- Buddhism

- Chinese Religions
- Shinto and Buddhism
- Judaism
- Sikhism
- Indigenous (mostly Animism)
- Indigenous and Christian
- Unpopulated Areas

Figure 24.2 A half-page map cannot begin to convey the thousands of different religions and belief systems in the world or the complex dynamics of sectarian splinter groups. This one offers only a broad-stroke look at the global distribution of major religions, indicating where they are the majority. In some areas, the mixture of different religions is such that no single faith is shared by most of that region's inhabitants. Notably, this map is not detailed enough to depict geographic pockets with significant numbers of a particular faith. For instance, even though New York City is the second largest Jewish population center in the world and its 1.75 million Jewish adherents count for close to 10 percent of the total metropolitan area population, the city, like New York State, comprises mainly Roman Catholics (38 percent) and members of various Christian Protestant religions (30 percent). And many other significant religious groups are not individually represented here, such as Sikhism, with over 23 million members, Jehovah's Witnesses (7 million), Cao Dai in Vietnam (5 million), and Aladura in Nigeria (1 million).

ceremonial practices by which people try to interpret and/or influence aspects of the universe otherwise beyond their control. Similar to religion, **spirituality** is also concerned with the sacred, as distinguished from material matters, but it is often individual rather than collective and does not require a distinctive format or traditional organization. Both are indicators that many aspects of the human experience are thought to be beyond scientific or empirical explanation.

Since no known culture, including those of modern industrial and postindustrial societies, has achieved complete certainty in controlling existing or future conditions and circumstances, spirituality and/or religion play a role

spirituality Concern with the sacred, as distinguished from material matters. In contrast to religion, spirituality is often individual rather than collective and does not require a distinctive format or traditional organization.

in all known cultures. However, considerable variability exists globally (Figure 24.2).

At one end of the spectrum are food-foraging peoples, whose technological ability to manipulate their environment is limited and who tend to see themselves as part of, rather than masters of, nature. This may be referred to as a *naturalistic worldview*. Among food foragers religion is likely to be inseparable from the rest of daily life. It also mirrors and confirms the egalitarian nature of social relations in their societies, in that individuals do not plead with high-ranking deities for aid the way members of stratified societies do.

At the other end of the spectrum is Western civilization, with its ideological commitment to overcoming problems through technological and organizational skills. Here religion is less a part of daily activities and is restricted to more specific occasions. Moreover, with its hierarchy of supernatural beings—for instance, God and (in some religions) the angels, saints, or holy people—it reflects and confirms the stratified nature of the society in which it is embedded.

Religious activity may be less prominent in the lives of social elites, who may see themselves as more in control of their own destinies, than it is in the lives of peasants or members of lower classes. Among the latter, religion may afford some compensation for a dependent position in society. Yet religion is still important to elite members of society, in that it rationalizes the system in such a way that less advantaged people are not as likely to question the existing social order as they might otherwise be. With hope for a better existence after death, one may be more willing to put up with a disadvantaged position in life. Thus religious beliefs serve to influence and perpetuate certain ideas about the relationships, if not the actual relations, between different classes of people.

Spiritual Forces and Supernatural Beings

A hallmark of religion is belief in spiritual forces and supernatural beings. In attempting to control by religious means what cannot be controlled in other ways, humans turn to prayer, sacrifice, and other religious or spiritual rituals. These presuppose the existence of spiritual forces that can be tapped into, or supernatural beings interested in human affairs and available for aid. In many cultures, these metaphysical forces or beings are associated with unique places such as extraordinary rocks, lakes, wells, waterfalls, or other special geographic locations valued as sacred sites.

Beginning with supernatural beings, we may divide them into three categories: major deities (gods and goddesses), ancestral spirits, and other sorts of spirit beings. Although the variety of deities and spirits recognized by the world's cultures is tremendous, it is possible to make certain generalizations about them.

Gods and Goddesses

Gods and goddesses are major deities, and as such they are more remote than other spirit beings. They are usually seen as controlling the universe. If more than one is recognized (known as **polytheism**), each has charge of a particular part of the universe. Such was the case with the gods and goddesses of ancient Greece: Zeus was lord of the sky, Poseidon was ruler of the sea, and Hades was lord of the underworld and ruler of the dead.

In addition to these three brothers, Greek mythology features a host of other deities, female as well as male, each similarly concerned with specific aspects of life and the universe. A **pantheon,** or the collection of gods and goddesses such as in Greek mythology, is common in non-Western

states as well. Since states typically have grown through conquest, often their pantheons have expanded as local deities of conquered peoples were incorporated into the official state pantheon.

Another frequent though not invariable feature of pantheons is the presence of a supreme deity, who may be all but totally ignored by humans. The Aztecs of the Mexican highlands, for instance, recognized a supreme pair to whom they paid little attention. After all, being so remote, this divine duo was unlikely to be interested in human affairs. The sensible practice, then, was to focus attention on less remote deities who were more directly concerned with human activities.

Whether or not a people recognize gods, goddesses, or both has to do with how men and women relate to each other in everyday life. Generally speaking, societies that subordinate women to men define the supreme deity in masculine terms. For instance, in traditional Christian religions believers speak of God as a "father" who had a divine "son" but do not entertain thoughts of God as a "mother" or of a divine "daughter." Such male-privileging religions developed in traditional societies with economies based on the herding of animals or intensive agriculture carried out or controlled by men, who are dominating figures to their children.

Goddesses, by contrast, are likely to be most prominent in societies where women play a significant role in the economy, where women enjoy relative equality with men, and where men are less controlling figures to their wives and children. Such societies are most often those that depend on crop cultivation carried out solely or mostly by women.

As an illustration, the early Israelites, like other pastoral nomadic groups of the Middle East, described their god in masculine, authoritarian terms. By contrast, goddesses played central roles in religious ritual and in the popular imagination of the region's farming peoples. Associated with these goddesses were concepts of light, fertility, and procreation. About 3,200 years ago, the Israelite tribes crossed the Jordan River and entered the land of Canaan (Palestine) where they began to till the soil and grow crops, requiring them to establish a new kind of relationship with the land. As they settled down and became sedentary, dependent upon rainfall and concerned about seasonal cycles and soil fertility (as the region's Canaanites already were), they adopted many of the region's already established Canaanite goddess cults. Although diametrically opposed to the original Israelite supreme male deity

---

polytheism Belief in several gods and/or goddesses (as contrasted with monotheism—belief in one god or goddess).

pantheon The several gods and goddesses of a people.

The patriarchal nature of traditional Euramerican society is culturally articulated and ideologically justified by its Judeo-Christian theology, in which a supreme male deity gives life to the first man, as depicted here on the ceiling of the Sistine Chapel in Rome. Only later is the first woman created—out of the rib of the first man.

cult, worship of these Canaanite female deities appealed to the farming people's desire for security by seeking to control the forces of fertility.

Later, when the Israelite tribes sought national unity in the face of a military threat by neighboring nations and when they ethnocentrically strengthened their own identity as a supernaturally "chosen people," the goddess cults lost out to followers of the old masculine tribal god. This ancient masculine-authoritarian concept of god has been perpetuated down to the present, not just in the Judaic tradition but also by most Christians and Muslims, whose religions stem from the old Israelite religion. As a consequence, this masculine-authoritarian model has played an important role in perpetuating a relationship between men and women in which the latter traditionally have been expected to submit to the rule of men at every level of Jewish, Christian, and Islamic society.

Ancestral Spirits

A belief in ancestral spirits is consistent with the widespread notion that human beings are made up of two closely intertwined parts: a physical body and a mental component or spiritual self. For example, traditional belief of the Penobscot Indians in Maine holds that each person has a vital spirit capable of traveling apart from the body. Given such a concept, the idea of a spirit being freed from the body in trance and dreams or by death, and having an existence thereafter, seems quite reasonable. Frequently, where a belief in ancestral spirits exists, these beings are seen as retaining an active interest and even participation in society.

Belief in ancestral spirits of one sort or another is found in many parts of the world, especially among people having unilineal descent systems with their associated ancestor orientation. In several such African societies, the concept is highly elaborate. Here one

frequently finds ancestral spirits behaving just like humans. They are able to feel hot, cold, and pain, and they may be capable of dying a second death by drowning or burning. They even may participate in family and lineage affairs, and seats will be provided for them, even though the spirits are invisible. If they are annoyed, they may send sickness or death. Eventually, they are reborn as new members of their lineage, and, in societies that hold such beliefs, adults need to observe infants closely to determine just who has been reborn. Such beliefs provide a strong sense of continuity that links the past, present, and future.

Ancestor spirits played an important role in the patrilineal society of traditional China. For the gift of life, a boy was forever indebted to his parents, owing them obedience, deference, and a comfortable old age. Even after their death, he had to provide for them in the spirit world, offering them food, money, and incense on the anniversaries of their births and deaths. In addition, people collectively worshiped all lineage ancestors periodically throughout the year. Giving birth to sons was regarded as an obligation to the ancestors, because boys inherited their father's ancestral duties.

To fulfill his ancestors' needs for descendants (and his own need to be respectable in a culture that demanded satisfying the needs of one's ancestors), a man would go so far as to marry a girl who had been adopted into his family as an infant so she could be raised as a dutiful wife for him, even when this arrangement went against the wishes of both parties. Furthermore, a father readily would force his daughter to marry a man against her will. In fact, a female child raised to be cast out by her natal family might not find acceptance in her husband's family for years. Not until after death, when her vital spirit was carried in a tablet and placed in the shrine of her husband's family, was she an official member of it. As a consequence, once a son was born to her, a woman worked long and hard to establish the strongest possible tie between herself and her son to ensure she would be looked after in life.

Strong beliefs in ancestral spirits are particularly appropriate in a society of descent-based groups with their associated ancestor orientation. But, more than this, as noted above, these beliefs provide a strong sense of continuity that links the past, present, and future.

Other Types of Spiritual Forces and Supernatural Beings

ANIMISM

One of the most widespread concepts concerning supernatural beings is **animism,** a belief that nature is animated (enlivened or energized) by distinct personalized spirit beings separable from bodies. Spirits such as souls and ghosts are thought to dwell in humans and animals but also in human-made artifacts, plants, stones, mountains, wells, and other natural features. So too the woods may be full of a variety of unattached or free-ranging spirits.

The various spirit beings involved are a highly diverse lot. Generally speaking, though, they are less remote than gods and goddesses and are more involved in people's daily affairs. They may be benevolent, malevolent, or just plain neutral. They also may be awesome, terrifying, lovable, or mischievous. Since they may be pleased or irritated by human actions, people are obliged to be concerned about them.

Animism, a concept theoretically developed by the pioneering British anthropologist Sir Edward B. Tylor (1832–1917), is typical of those who see themselves as being a part of nature rather than superior to it. This includes most food foragers, as well as those food-producing peoples who acknowledge little qualitative difference between a human life and any living entity from turtles to trees, or even rivers and mountains. In such societies, gods and goddesses are relatively unimportant, but the woods are full of spirits. Gods and goddesses, if they exist at all, may be seen as having created the world and perhaps making it fit to live in; but in animism, spirits are the ones to beseech when ill, the ones to help or hinder the shaman, and the ones whom the ordinary hunter may meet when off in the woods.

ANIMATISM

Although supernatural power is often thought of as being vested in supernatural beings, it does not have to be. Such is the case with **animatism**—the belief that nature is enlivened or energized by an impersonal spiritual power or supernatural energy, which may make itself manifest in any special place, thing, or living creature. Although this concept is not universal, it is found in cultures on every continent.

The Melanesians, for example, think of *mana* as a spiritual force inherent in all objects—not unlike the idea of a cosmic energy passing into and through everything, affecting living and nonliving matter alike (similar to "the Force" in the *Star Wars* films). It is not in itself physical, but it can reveal itself physically. A warrior's success in fighting is not attributed to his own strength but to the *mana* contained in an amulet that hangs around his neck. Similarly, a farmer may know a great deal about horticulture, soil conditioning, and the correct time for sowing and harvesting but nevertheless depend upon *mana* for a successful crop, often building a simple altar to this power at one end of the field. If the crop is good, it is a sign that the farmer has in some way appropriated the necessary *mana*. Far from being a personalized spirit power, *mana* is abstract in the extreme, a spiritual force or metaphysical energy lying always just beyond reach of the senses.

This concept of impersonal potency or energy was widespread among North American Indians. The Algonquins called it *manitou*; to the Mohawk it was *orenda*; to the Lakota, *wakonda*. For instance, as discussed in the upcoming section on sacred sites, Bear Butte in the Black Hills is a mountain where Lakota believers feel a strong presence of spirit power, or *wakonda*.

In some cultures this impersonal spirit power, or metaphysical energy, is turned to for healing purposes. Notably, *animism* (as a belief in distinct spirit beings) and *animatism* (which lacks particular substance or individual form) are not mutually exclusive. They are often found in the same culture, as in Melanesian societies and also in the North American Indian societies just mentioned.

People trying to comprehend beliefs in the supernatural beings and powers that others recognize frequently ask how such beliefs are maintained. In part, the answer is through manifestations of power. Given a belief in animatism and/or the powers of supernatural beings, one is predisposed to see what appear to be results of the application of such powers. For example, if a Melanesian warrior is convinced of his power because he possesses the necessary *mana* and he is successful, he is likely to interpret this success as proof of the power of *mana*. Beyond this, because of his confidence in his *mana*, he may be willing to take more chances in his fighting, and this indeed could mean the difference between success or failure.

Failures, of course, do occur, but they can be explained. Perhaps one's prayer was not answered because a deity or spirit was still angry about some past insult. Or perhaps

> **animism** A belief that nature is animated (enlivened or energized) by distinct personalized spirit beings separable from bodies.
>
> **animatism** A belief that nature is enlivened or energized by an impersonal spiritual power or supernatural potency.

An example of animism exists among Inuit of Arctic Canada, who believed that nature is animated by supernatural beings separable from the physical body or material substance they inhabit. Referring to such spirits as *anirniit* (singular *anirniq,* meaning "breath"), traditional Inuit still obey certain taboos and perform rituals when killing seal and other game animals and dividing the meat. This is to avoid offending the animal's spirit (which lives on and may take revenge on the hunter). Today, most Inuit are Christians and their concept of *anirniq* is akin to "soul." But traditional food rituals continue. In this photo, Inuit at Baffin Island, Nunavut, pray before a shared Easter feast of fish and seal meat.

B&C Alexander/ArcticPhoto

the Melanesian warrior lost his battle because he was not as successful in bringing *mana* to bear or his opponent had more of it. In any case, humans generally emphasize successes over failures, and long after many of the latter have been forgotten, tales will still be told of the workings of supernatural powers.

Beliefs are also maintained through myths—explanatory narratives that rationalize and reinforce religious beliefs and practices. We will discuss myths in more detail later in this chapter.

Sacred Places

In addition to revering special supernatural figures such as deities, ancestral spirits, and other special beings, some religious traditions consider certain geographic places to be spiritually significant or even sacred. Typically, such sites are rivers, lakes, waterfalls, islands, forests, caves, and—especially—mountains. Often, their status is due to some unique shape or outstanding feature, such as a conical volcano capped with snow. Numerous mountains around the world fall into this category. Often they are associated with origin myths as splendid abodes of the gods. Or they are revered as dwelling places for the spirits of the dead, heights where prophets received their divine directions, or retreats for prayer, meditation, and vision quests.

Three sacred mountains are shared by the Jewish, Christian, and Muslim traditions: Mount Ararat in the Caucasus Mountains, a multinational region between Russia and Turkey where the ark of the ancient patriarch Noah is said to have landed after the Great Flood; Mount Horeb, the

"mountain of God" in the Sinai Desert where the prophet Moses received the stone tablets from his god with the ten sacred rules of behavior; and Mount Moriah, also known as the Temple Mount, at the old city of Jerusalem. According to Jewish tradition, it was from this hilltop that God gathered "the dust of the ground" to create Adam, the ancestor of all human beings today. And it was there that Solomon, the Israelite king, is believed to have been divinely ordered to build the Great Temple almost 3,000 years ago.

Almost 1,500 years later, the prophet Muhammad came to this place on a mystic night journey in company with the angel Gabriel and riding a winged horse. After a prayer meeting with the prophets Abraham, Moses, and Jesus, Muhammad was led by Gabriel to the top of the rock and ascended on a ladder of golden light to heaven where Allah gave him his divine instructions. On this holy spot, the sacred shrine *Masjid Qubbat As-Sakhrah* ("Dome of the Rock") was built for Muslim pilgrims. Completed in 691 AD, it is the oldest Muslim building in existence and the third holiest site in Islam.

Similar traditions exist in many other cultures. For instance, the Japanese view the snow-capped perfect volcanic cone of Mount Fuji ("ever-lasting life") as a sacred place. Aztecs held several snow-capped volcanoes sacred, including Popocatepetl ("Smoking Mountain") just outside Mexico City. And the same can be said for Kirinyaga (Mount Kenya) in East Africa. Straddling the equator, it is seen as a holy place by the Kikuyu people who believe this "Mountain of Brightness" to be the earthly dwelling place of their creator god Ngai. Likewise, the ancient Greeks considered Mount Olympus to be the mythological abode of Zeus, the king of all their gods. In some religious traditions, such as among the Aymara of the Bolivian highlands, a volcanic mountain like Kaata is not only considered sacred, but is actually deified and worshiped as a living god.

Symbolic of the supreme being, or associated with various important deities or ancestral spirits, sacred mountains may feature in religious ceremonies or spiritual rituals. In some religious traditions, these towering geographic features are places of worship, like shrines, or are sacred destinations for spiritual journeys or pilgrimages. For example, as mentioned above, dozens of American Indian nations in the Great Plains consider Bear Butte in the Black Hills of South Dakota to be of great spiritual significance. They come to this domed mountain for meditation, prayers, and sacred vision quests. For outsiders

unfamiliar with (or unsympathetic to) the indigenous traditions, these sacred mountains may be valued for commercial or recreational purposes, thus leading to bitter controversies and unfortunate consequences.

Religious Specialists

Much of religion's value comes from the activities called for by its prescriptions and rules. Participation in religious ceremonies may bring a sense of personal lift—a wave of reassurance, a feeling of overwhelming joy, and even a sense of moving into a trancelike state—or a feeling of closeness to fellow participants. The beliefs and ceremonies of religions vary considerably, as do the individuals who guide others in these religious practices.

All human societies include individuals who guide and supplement the religious practices of others. Such individuals are seen to be highly skilled at contacting and influencing supernatural beings and manipulating or connecting to supernatural forces. Often their qualification is that they have undergone special training. In addition, they may display certain distinctive personality traits that make them particularly well suited to perform these tasks.

Priests and Priestesses

In societies with the resources to support a full-time occupational specialist, a **priest or priestess** will have the role of guiding religious practices and influencing the supernatural. He or she is the socially initiated, ceremonially inducted member of a recognized religious organization, with a rank and function that belong to him or her as the holder of a position others have held before. The sources of power are the society and the institution within which the priest or priestess functions.

The priest, if not the priestess, is a familiar figure in Western societies; he is the priest, minister, imam, lama, rabbi, or whatever the official title may be in an organized religion. With their god defined historically in masculine, authoritarian terms, it is not surprising that, in the Judaic, Christian, and Islamic religions, the most important positions traditionally have been filled by men. Female religious specialists are likely to be found only in societies where women are acknowledged to contribute in a major way to the economy and where gods

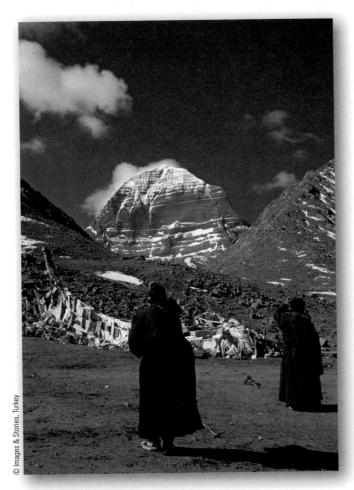

Pilgrims at Mount Kailash in Tibet. Rising 6,700 meters (about 22,000 feet), this mountain has been held sacred for thousands of years by Hindus, Buddhists, Jains, and followers of Bön (Tibet's indigenous religion). They do not deify this peak, but they believe it to be the sacred abode of Lord Shiva, a member of the supreme divine trinity—so sacred that they would not even dream of trying to climb it. Year after year, thousands of pilgrims follow the ancient tradition of circling the mountain on foot. The rugged, 52-kilometer (32-mile) trek, known as *parikarma*, is seen as a holy ritual that removes sins and brings good fortune.

priest or priestess A full-time religious specialist formally recognized for his or her role in guiding the religious practices of others and for contacting and influencing supernatural powers.

Change Your Karma and Change Your Sex?   *by Hillary Crane*

As Mahayana Buddhists, Taiwanese Chan (Zen) monastics believe that all humans are able to reach enlightenment and be released from reincarnation. But they believe it is easier for some because of the situation into which they are born—for example, if one is born in a country where Buddhism is practiced, in a family that teaches proper behavior, or with exceptional mental or physical gifts.

Chan monastics view contrasting human circumstances as the result of the karma accrued in previous lives. They believe certain behavior—such

as diligently practicing Buddhism—improves karma and the chances of attaining spiritual goals in this lifetime or coming back in a better birth. Other behavior—such as killing a living being, eating meat, desiring or becoming attached to things or people—accrues bad karma.

One way karma manifests itself is in one's sex. Taiwanese Buddhists believe that being born female makes it harder to attain spiritual goals. This idea comes, in part, from the inferior status of women in Taiwan and the belief that their "complicated bodies" and monthly menstruation cycles can distract them. Moreover, they believe, women are more enmeshed in their families than men and their emotional ties keep them focused on worldly rather than spiritual tasks.

Taiwanese Buddhists who decide to become monks and nuns must break from their families to enter a monastery. Since women are thought to be more attached to their families than are men, leaving home is seen as a particularly big step for nuns and a sign that they are more like men than most women. In fact, a nun's character is considered masculine, unlike the frightened, indecisive, and emotional traits usually associated with women in Taiwan. When they leave home nuns even stop referring to themselves as women and call one another *shixiong* ("dharma brother"). They use this linguistic change to signal that they identify themselves as men and to

remind one another to behave like men, particularly like the monks at the temple.

Monastics also reduce their attachments to worldly things like music and food. Nuns usually emphasize forsaking food and eat as little as possible. Their appearance, already quite masculine because they shave their heads and wear loose, gray clothing, becomes even more so when they lose weight—particularly in their hips, breasts, and thighs. Also, after becoming monastics, they often experience a slowing or stopping of their menses. Although these physical changes can be attributed to change in diet and lifestyle, the nuns point to them as signs they are becoming men, making progress toward their spiritual goals, and improving their karma.

BIOCULTURAL QUESTION

The Zen Buddhist ideal of enlightenment, realized when the soul is released from reincarnation, prescribes an extreme ascetic lifestyle for nuns that makes them physically incapable of biological reproduction. Do you think that their infertility allows these female monastics to emotionally adapt to a way of life that denies them motherhood?

For a more detailed treatment of this topic, see Crane, H (2001). Men in spirit: The masculinization of Taiwanese Buddhist nuns. *Doctoral dissertation, Brown University.*

---

and goddesses are both recognized. In western Europe and North America, for instance, where women are now wage earners in almost every profession and occupy leadership positions in the workforce, they have an increasing presence in the leadership of many Judeo-Christian religious groups.[4]

Although women still do not occupy the highest-ranking religious leadership positions in the Roman Catholic Church (headed by a male pope and his all-male council, the College of Cardinals), this Christian religion does recognize important female saints. Most significant among these is the Virgin Mary, held to be the human mother of God's son. In many places where Roman Catholicism has spread, worshipers have created cults around this female

saint. Moreover, all around the world women devoted to a religious life have formed their own places for religious exclusion as nuns jointly belonging to a cloister or convent, headed by an abbess.

Such all-female religious institutions are not unique to Roman Catholicism. Convents of nuns are also part of Buddhist religious traditions. They can be found in several places around the world—in particular, Asian countries, including Thailand, as described by anthropologist Hillary Crane in this chapter's Biocultural Connection.

Shamans

Societies that lack full-time occupational specialization have existed far longer than those with such specialization, and they have always included individuals with special powers and skills that enable them to connect with and manipulate supernatural beings and forces. These powers

---

[4] Lehman, E. C., Jr. (2002, Fall). Women's path into the ministry. *Pulpit & Pew Research Reports 1, 4.*

have come to them through some personal experience, usually in solitude. In an altered state of consciousness, they receive a vision that empowers them to heal the sick, change the weather, control the movements of animals, and foretell the future. As they perfect these and related skills, they assume the role of shaman.

The word *shaman* originally referred to medical-religious specialists, or spiritual guides, among the Tungus and other Siberian pastoral nomads with animist beliefs. By means of various techniques such as fasting, drumming, chanting, or dancing, as well as hallucinogenic mushrooms, these Siberian shamans enter into a trance, or altered state of consciousness. While in this waking dream state, they experience visions of an alternate reality inhabited by spirit beings such as guardian animal spirits who may assist in the healing.

Cross-cultural research of shamanism shows that similar medical-religious healing practices also exist in traditional cultures outside Siberia. For that reason, the term *shaman* has also been applied to a variety of part-time spiritual leaders and traditional healers ("medicine men") active in North and South American indigenous communities and beyond.

As defined by anthropologist Michael Harner, famous for his participant observation among Shuar (or Jivaro) Indian shamans in the Amazon rainforest, a **shaman** is "a man or woman who enters an altered state of consciousness—at will—to contact and utilize an ordinarily hidden reality in order to acquire knowledge, power, and to help other persons. The shaman has at least one, and usually more, 'spirits' in his or her personal service."[5]

The term *shaman* has become so popular in recent decades that any non-Western local priest, healer, or diviner is often loosely referred to as one.[6] In the United States millions of people learned something about shamans through the popular autobiography of Black Elk, a traditional Lakota Indian holy man. Numerous other publications on shamanism have appeared over the past four decades, and some Euramericans have gone into practice as shamans, a development that has triggered considerable resentment among some Native Americans. ("They stole our land, now they are stealing our religion.") In addition to so-called new age enthusiasts, among whom shamanism is particularly popular, faith healers and other evangelists among fundamentalist Christians share many of the characteristics of shamanism.

Typically, one becomes a shaman by passing through stages of learning and practical experience, often involving

psychological and emotional ordeals brought about by isolation, fasting, physical torture, sensory deprivation, and/or hallucinations. These hallucinations (derived from the Latin word for "mental wandering") occur when the shaman is in a trance, which may occur spontaneously but can also be induced by drumming or consuming mind-altering drugs such as psychoactive vines or mushrooms.

Among the Penobscot Indians in northern New England, for example, any person could become a shaman, since no formal institution provided rules and regulations to guide religious consciousness. The search for shamanic visions was pursued by most adult Penobscot males, who would go off alone and—through meditation, sensory deprivation, and hyperventilation—induce an altered state of consciousness in which they hoped to receive a vision. Not all were successful, but failure did not result in social disgrace. Those who did achieve success experienced a sense of being freed from their bodily existence in which they established a special relationship with a particular animal spirit that appeared in their trance state. This became the shaman's animal helper—a common element in shamanism—who thereafter would assist the individual in performing shamanic tasks.

Because shamanism is rooted in altered states of consciousness and the nervous system that produces these trance states is universal, individuals involved in shamanism experience similarly structured visual, auditory, somatic (touch), olfactory (smell), and gustatory (taste) hallucinations. The widespread occurrence of shamanism and the remarkable similarities among shamanic traditions everywhere are consequences of this universal neurological inheritance. At the same time, the meanings ascribed to sensations experienced in altered states and made of their content are culturally determined; hence, despite their overall similarities, local traditions always vary in their details.

The shaman is essentially a religious go-between who acts on behalf of some human client, often to bring about healing or to foretell some future event. To do so, the shaman intervenes to influence or impose his or her will on supernatural powers. The shaman can be contrasted with the priest or priestess, whose "clients" are the deities. Priests and priestesses frequently tell people what to do; the shaman tells supernatural beings what to do. In return for services rendered, the shaman may collect a fee—fresh meat, yams, or a favorite possession. In some cases, the added prestige, authority, and

[5] Harner, M. (1980). *The way of the shaman: A guide to power and healing* (p. 20). San Francisco: Harper & Row.

[6] Kehoe, A. (2000). *Shamans and religion: An anthropological exploration in critical thinking.* Prospect Heights, IL: Waveland.

shaman A person who enters an altered state of consciousness—at will—to contact and utilize an ordinarily hidden reality in order to acquire knowledge, power, and to help others.

Visual Counterpoint

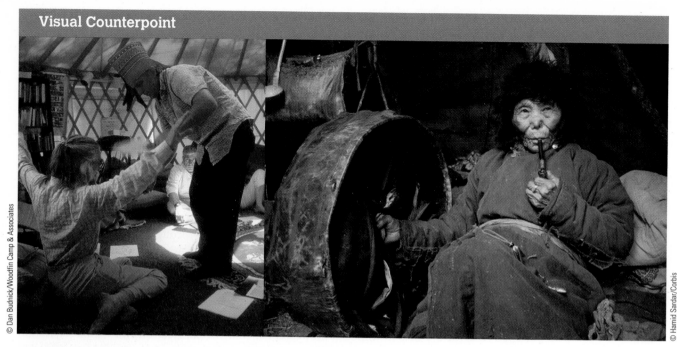

Shamanism is by no means absent in modern industrial societies. Here we see a new age shaman in North America (left) and a traditional shaman in Mongolia. The Mongolian shaman's drum is crafted from the wood of a tree struck by lightning and covered with leather made from a female red deer. It is believed that when the shaman goes into a trance, her drum transforms into a magic steed that carries her into the dark sky of her ancestors.

social power attached to the shaman's status are reward enough.

When a shaman acts on behalf of a client, he or she may put on something of a show—one that heightens the basic drama with a sense of danger. Typically, the shaman enters a trance state, in which he or she experiences the sensation of traveling to the alternate world and seeing and interacting with spirit beings. The shaman tries to impose his or her will upon these spirits, an inherently dangerous contest, considering the superhuman powers that spirits are thought to possess.

An example of this can be seen in the trance dances of the Ju/'hoansi Bushmen of southern Africa's Kalahari Desert. Traditional Ju/'hoansi belief holds that illness and misfortune are caused by invisible arrows shot by spirits. The arrows can be removed by healers, men and women who possess the powerful healing force called *n/um* (the Ju/'hoansi equivalent of *mana*). Some healers can activate *n/um* by solo singing or instrument playing, but more often this is accomplished

through the medicinal curing ceremony or trance dance. To the sound of undulating melodies sung by women, healers dance around the fire, sometimes for hours. The music, the strenuous dancing, the smoke, the heat of the fire, and the healers' intense concentration cause their

n/um to heat up. When it comes to a boil, trance is achieved and *n/um* is available as a powerful healing force to serve the entire community. In trance, a healer lays hands on and ritually cures everyone sitting around the fire.[7]

In many human societies, sleight-of-hand tricks and ventriloquism occur at the same time as trancing. Among Arctic peoples, for example, a shaman may summon spirits in the dark and produce flapping noises and strange voices to impress the audience. Some Western observers regard this kind of trickery as evidence of the fraudulent nature of shamanism. However, those who have studied shamanic practices agree that even though shamans know perfectly well that they are manipulating people with their tricks, they really believe in their power to deal with supernatural forces and spirit beings. Their power, verified by the trance experience, gives them the right as well as the ability to manipulate people in minor technical matters. In short, the shaman regards his or her ability to perform extraordinary tricks as further proof of superior powers.

---

[7] Shostak, M. (1983). *Nisa: The life and words of a !Kung woman* (pp. 291–293). New York: Vintage.

Ju/'hoansi shaman healer and helper in trance dance.

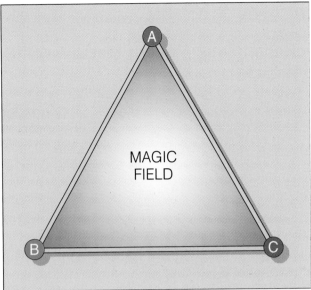

Figure 24.3 The shamanic complex. Shamanic healing takes place within a "magic field" created when the shaman (A) and patient (B), as well as their community (C), are all convinced that the shaman is a genuine healing master using appropriate techniques that are effective and beneficial. Similar psychological processes are involved in Western medical treatments.

The importance of shamanism in a society should not be underestimated. It promotes, through the drama of performance, a trancelike feeling and a release of tension. And it provides psychological assurance that prevailing upon supernatural powers and spirits otherwise beyond human control can bring about invulnerability from attack, success at love, or the return of health. In fact, a frequent reason for a shamanic performance is poor health—a concept that is difficult to define effectively in cross-cultural terms. Not only do people in diverse cultures recognize and experience different types of illnesses, they may also view and explain them in different terms. The culturally defined diagnosis of an illness, in turn, determines how the patient will be treated according to the beliefs of the culture, in order to achieve healing.

Although the psychological effects of the shamanic treatment are not known, the connection between mind and body may contribute to the patient's recovery. From an anthropological perspective, shamanic healings can be understood by means of a three-cornered model: the *shamanic complex* (Figure 24.3). This triangle is created by the relationships among the shaman and the patient and the community to which both belong.

For healing to take place, the shaman needs to be convinced of the effectiveness of his or her spiritual powers and techniques. Likewise, the patient must see the shaman as a genuine healing master using appropriate techniques. Finally, to close the triangle's "magic field," the community within which the shaman operates on the patient must view the healing ceremony and its practitioner as potentially effective and beneficial.

Such dynamics are not unique to shamanic healing ceremonies, for similar social psychological processes are involved in Western medical treatments as well. Consider, for example, the *placebo effect*—the beneficial result a patient experiences after a particular treatment, due to his or her expectations concerning the treatment rather than from the treatment itself. Notably, some people involved in modern medicine work collaboratively with practitioners

Reconciling Modern Medicine with Traditional Beliefs in Swaziland

by Edward C. Green

Although the biomedical germ theory is generally known and accepted in Western societies today, this is not the case in many other societies around the world. In southern Africa's Swaziland, for example, many illnesses are generally thought to be caused by sorcery or by loss of ancestral protection. (Sexually transmitted diseases—STDs—and other contagious diseases are exceptions to these beliefs.)

Even where the effectiveness of Western medicine is recognized, the ultimate question remains: Why did a disease come to a particular person in the first place? Thus, for the treatment of disease, the Swazi have traditionally relied upon herbalists, diviner mediums through whom ancestor spirits are thought to work, and (more recently) Christian faith healers. Unfortunately, such individuals have usually been regarded as quacks and charlatans by the medical establishment. Yet, the herbal medicines used by traditional healers are effective in several ways, and the reassurance provided patient and family alike through rituals that reduce stress and anxiety plays an important role in the patient's recovery. In a country where there is one traditional healer for every 110 people, but only one physician for every 10,000, the potential benefit of cooperation between physicians and healers seems self-evident. Nevertheless, it was largely unrecognized until proposed by anthropologists D. M. Warren (in Ghana) and later, myself.

It was in 1981, when I was a Washington-based independent consultant, that I first went to Swaziland as a researcher for the Rural Water-Borne Disease Control Project, funded by the United States Agency for International Development. Assigned the task of finding out about knowledge, attitudes, and practices related to water and sanitation, and aware of the serious deficiencies of conventional surveys that rely on pre-coded questionnaires, I used instead the traditional anthropological techniques of open-ended interviews with key informants, along with participant observation. The key informants were traditional healers, their patients, and rural health motivators (women chosen by communities to receive eight weeks of training in preventive health care in regional clinics). Without such anthropological research, it would have been impossible to design and interpret a reliable survey instrument, but the added payoff was that I learned a great deal about Swazi theories of illness and its treatment.

Disposed at the outset to recognize the positive value of many traditional practices, I could also see how cooperation with physicians might be achieved. For example, traditional healers already recognized the utility of Western medicines for treatment of diseases considered not indigenous to Africa, and traditional preventive medicines were routinely given to children through inhalation, something like childhood vaccinations. Thus, nontraditional medicines and vaccinations might be accepted, if presented in ways that resembled traditional medicine.

Realizing the suspicion existing on both sides, I and my Swazi associate Lydia Makhubu (a chemist who had studied the properties of indigenous medicines) recommended to the minister of health a cooperative project focusing on a problem of concern to both health professionals and native healers: infant diarrheal diseases. These had recently become a health problem of high concern to the general public; healers wanted a means to prevent such diseases, and a means of treatment existed—oral rehydration therapy—that was compatible with traditional treatments for diarrhea (herbal preparations taken orally over a period of time). Packets of oral rehydration salts, along with instructions, were provided to healers in a pilot project, with positive results. This helped convince health professionals of the benefits of cooperation, while the healers saw the distribution of packets to them as a gesture of trust and cooperation on the part of their government.

Since then, further steps toward cooperation have been taken, such as work in prevention of AIDS, STDs, and TB. All of this demonstrates the importance of finding how to work in ways compatible with existing belief systems. Directly challenging traditional beliefs, as all too often happens, does little more than create stress, confusion, and resentment among people.

Adapted from Green, E. C. (1987). The planning of health education strategies in Swaziland, and the integration of modern and traditional health sectors in Swaziland. In R. M. Wulff & S. J. Fiske (Eds.), Anthropological praxis: Translating knowledge into action (pp. 15–25, 87–97). Boulder, CO: Westview.

of traditional belief systems toward the healing of various illnesses—as illustrated in this chapter's Anthropology Applied feature.

Sacred Performances: Rituals and Ceremonies

Rituals or ceremonial acts are not all religious in nature (consider, for example, college graduation ceremonies in North America), but those that are play a crucial role in religious activity. Religious ritual is the means through which people relate to the supernatural; it is religion in action. Ritual serves to relieve social tensions and reinforce a group's collective bonds. More than this, it provides a means of marking many important events and lessening the social disruption and individual suffering of crises, such as death.

Anthropologists have classified several different types of ritual. These include rituals of purity, rites of passage, and rites of intensification. We begin with rituals of purity, which illustrate not only how members of a social group are bound together, but also how they reinforce the boundaries between the group and outsiders by means of cultural prohibitions known as taboos. Next come rituals

Exiled Tibetan monks at Drepunk Loseling monastery in India patiently create a mandala. Using narrow metal funnels, they spend many days placing millions of grains of fine colored sand into a geometric design that has deep spiritual significance in their Buddhist worldview. An ancient Sanskrit word, *mandala* means "circle-circumference" or "completion," referring to the enlightened mind of the Buddha. The ritual provides a visual framework for meditation toward establishing the radiant mental state. It is a tool for spiritual teaching, trance induction, and blessing the earth and all its creatures. Once complete, the sacred work is dismantled, and the sand is disseminated (usually in a body of running water) to spread the blessings.

for when individuals change their social status within their group. And finally, we briefly discuss rituals that allow members of a social group to strengthen their common identity in times of crisis.

Taboos: Cultural Prohibitions and Rituals of Purification

In many societies people follow certain culturally prescribed rules about what they can or cannot eat or drink, touch, or talk about. Many millions of Hindus, for example, eat pork but avoid beef because they regard the cow as a sacred animal. On the other hand, many millions of Muslims consume beef but avoid pork because in their religion swine is considered unclean. They share this pork taboo with Jews, both evoking the will of God (called Allah by Muslims and Yahweh by Jews) to justify their dietary laws. Christians accept the first books of the Bible as sacred and foundational, but ignore its laws prohibiting the eating of swine: "Their flesh you shall not eat, and their carcasses you shall not touch."[8] And although Hindus, Muslims, Jews, and Christians all consider cannibalism offensive and even inhuman, there are societies that do not prohibit eating human flesh and provide certain cultural rules that categorize which types of human flesh can be consumed when, where, and how.

Taboo, the word used to describe these traditional prohibitions, is derived from the Polynesian term *tabu* (or *tapu*). Among Pacific Islanders such as Maoris or Samoans, this term refers to something that has supernatural power and is to be avoided. It can apply to an object (such as food), a person (such as a high-ranking noble), or a place (a shrine or temple). Especially applied to blood

---

[8] Deuteronomy 14: 3, 8. See also Leviticus 11: 7, 11.

taboo A prohibition, which, if not observed, leads to a penalty inflicted by magic, spiritual force, or religion.

and anything associated with sickness and death, taboos are taken very seriously. When a taboo is violated, believers expect supernatural punishment will follow. This penalty may come in magic form as misfortune—an unlucky accident, resulting in loss, sickness, or death. It is also possible that the taboo breaker will be punished by designated members in the community and may be ordered to undergo a purification ritual and make a sacrifice. Sometimes, the ultimate sacrifice is demanded and the offender is executed.

In the previous chapter, we discussed how the traditional hierarchy in the Hindu caste society is religiously reinforced by strict rules against ritual pollution that govern the lives of members of the different *varnas*. As members of the highest-ranking "grade of being," Brahmans are especially concerned about maintaining their "purity," which is symbolically associated with the color white and publicly visible in their dress. Like other traditional Hindus, they dutifully follow their ritually prescribed rules of conduct, known as *dharma* and thus avoid becoming "unclean." If they break a taboo, they are believed to have violated the fundamental Hindu principles of the cosmic order. And for someone who believes in reincarnation, such misconduct has consequences for one's *karma*, the soul's destiny or fate when it is reincarnated (literally, "returns into flesh") in the next life. Clearly, rules of ritual purity and pollution are embedded in this society's worldview and, as such, form part of a culture's superstructure.

Anthropologists specializing in comparative religion have been intrigued by the cross-cultural variation in cultural categories, classifying certain animals, plants, objects, or acts as unclean or "dirty," and others as dangerous or taboo.[9] Why do people make such prohibitions and deny themselves what others may enjoy as pleasures in life? In her classic study *Purity and Danger: An Analysis of Concepts of Pollution and Taboo*, British anthropologist Mary Douglas offers many insights originally based on her

research among the Lele in Congo: "Reflection on dirt involves reflection on the relation of order to disorder, being to non being, form to formlessness, life to death."[10]

Relating taboos involving rituals of purity to cultural classifications of the cosmic order, Douglas explains

> Dirt is essentially disorder. There is no such thing as absolute dirt: it exists in the eyes of the beholder. If we shun dirt, it is not because of craven fear, still less of dread of holy terror. . . . Dirt offends against order. Eliminating it is not a negative movement, but a positive effort to organise the environment. [Rituals] of purity and impurity create unity in experience. [By] their means, symbolic patterns are worked out and publicly displayed.[11]

Informed by their religious beliefs about the cosmic order and the laws that maintain its structure as a functioning system, members of a culture learn to find their proper place in society. Rules maintaining social order within the group, as well as defining these groups from others, are reinforced by rituals of purity and associated taboos. As such, these rituals not only serve to more effectively integrate individuals into that complex whole we call "culture," but also to help avoid mix-ups and mistakes that can cause chaos and thereby endanger the survival of the group.

Rites of Passage

Rites of passage are rituals that mark important stages in an individual's life cycle. In one of anthropology's classic works, German-French ethnographer Arnold van Gennep analyzed the rites of passage that mark an individual's crossing over from one social status to another. Such rituals help members of a society through the major social transitions or crucial crises in their lives, such as birth, puberty, graduation, marriage, parenthood, advancement to a higher official rank, and death.[12] Comparing these social transitions with "a territorial passage" in which travelers leave a country, cross its border (or limit), and enter another, he found it useful to divide ceremonies for all of these status transitions or life crises into three phases: pre-liminary (of separation), liminary (of marginality), and post-liminary (of admission). In anthropology today, this scheme is presented as three stages: **separation, transition,** and **incorporation;** the first being ritual removal of the individual from everyday society, followed by

---

[9] See, among others, Durkheim, E., & Mauss, M. (1963). *Primitive classification.* Chicago: University of Chicago Press. (orig. 1902); Lévi-Strauss, C. (1969). *The raw and the cooked.* New York: Harper & Row; Leach, E. (1964). Anthropological aspects of language: Animal categories and verbal abuse. In W. Lessa & E. Vogt (Eds.), *Reader in comparative religion* (4th ed.). New York: Harper & Row.

rite of passage A ritual that marks an important stage in an individual's life cycle, such as birth, marriage, and death.

separation In a rite of passage, the ritual removal of the individual from society.

transition In a rite of passage, isolation of the individual following separation and prior to incorporation into society.

incorporation In a rite of passage, reincorporation of the individual into society in his or her new status.

---

[10] Douglas, M. (1966). *Purity and danger: An analysis of concepts of pollution and taboo* (p. 6). London: Routledge & Kegan Paul.

[11] Ibid., pp. 2–3.

[12] Van Gennep, A. (1960). *The rites of passage.* Chicago: University of Chicago Press. (orig. [1909]. *Les rites de passage.* Paris: Émile Nourry)

a period of isolation, and, finally, formal return and read-mission back into society in his or her new status.

This sequence of stages is something that takes place in many forms in all cultures around the world, from military boot camps to college fraternity and sorority initiation ceremonies in the United States to a global array of puberty ceremonies that mark the transition from childhood to adulthood.

MALE INITIATION RITES

The Aborigines of Australia provide an example of a male initiation rite into manhood. When the elders decide the time for initiation, the boys are taken from the village (separation), while the women cry and make a ritual show of resistance. At a place distant from the camp, groups of men from many villages gather. The elders sing and dance, while the initiates act as though they are dead. The climax of this part of the ritual is a bodily operation, such as circumcision or the knocking out of a tooth. Australian anthropologist A. P. Elkin comments:

> This is partly a continuation of the drama of death. The tooth-knocking, circumcision or other symbolical act "killed" the novice; after this he does not return to the general camp and normally may not be seen by any woman. He is dead to the ordinary life of the tribe.[13]

In this transitional stage, the novice may be shown secret ceremonies and receive some instruction, but the most significant element is his complete removal from society. In the course of these Australian puberty rites, the initiate must learn the lore that all adult men are expected to know. The trauma of the occasion is a pedagogical technique that ensures he will learn and remember everything; in a nonliterate society the perpetuation of cultural traditions requires no less, and so effective teaching methods are necessary.

On his return to society (incorporation), the novice is welcomed with ceremonies, as though he had returned from the dead. This alerts the society at large to the individual's new status—people can expect him to act in certain ways, and in return they must act in the appropriate ways toward him. The individual's new rights and duties are thus clearly defined. He is spared, for example, the problems of a teenager in North America, whose status is ill defined as neither adult nor child.

In the Australian case just cited, boys are prepared not just for adulthood but also for manhood. In their society, for example, courage and endurance are considered important masculine virtues, and the pain of tooth-knocking and circumcision helps instill these in initiates.

FEMALE INITIATION RITES

In a similar way to the male initiation rite described above, female initiation rites help prepare Mende girls in West Africa for womanhood. After they have begun to menstruate, the girls are removed from society to spend weeks, or even months, in seclusion. There, they discard the clothes of childhood, smear their bodies with white clay, and dress in short skirts and many strands of beads.

Shortly after entering this transitional stage, the girls undergo clitoridectomy, a removal of the clitoris, viewed as the feminine version of the penis. The girls (and Mende in general) believe this form of female circumcision enhances their reproductive potential. While secluded, they are trained in the moral and practical responsibilities of potential child bearers by experienced women. With the training comes a good deal of singing, dancing, storytelling, and food—and a strong sense of sisterhood. The pain and danger of the surgery, endured in the context of intense social support from other women, serve as a metaphor for childbirth, which may well take place in the same place of seclusion, again with the support of experienced women. They emerge from their initiation as women in knowledgeable control of their sexuality, eligible for marriage and childbearing. Having gone through this ritual, a traditional Mende woman knows she is "all woman."

In recent decades, various activist groups in North America and western Europe, in particular, have identified clitoridectomy as one of several forms of female genital mutilation (FGM). Practiced in Africa and Asia especially, FGM has been condemned as a human rights violation, and committees to end the practice have been set up in twenty-two African countries.[14] Notably, women's breast implant surgery has been compared to FGM as Western industrialized society's version of what it takes to be "all woman."[15] The Original Study in the final chapter of this book addresses this issue in detail.

Rites of Intensification

Rites of intensification are rituals that take place during a crisis in the life of the group and serve to bind individuals together. Whatever the precise nature of the crisis—a

---

[13] Elkin, A. P. (1964). *The Australian Aborigines.* Garden City, NY: Doubleday/Anchor.

[14] "Female genital mutilation." (2000). Fact sheet no. 241. World Health Organization; Dirie, W., & Miller, C. (1998). *Desert flower: The extraordinary journey of a desert nomad* (pp. 218, 219). New York: Morrow.

[15] MacCormack, C. P. (1977). Biological events and cultural control. *Signs 3*, 98.

rite of intensification A ritual that takes place during a crisis in the life of the group and serves to bind individuals together.

drought that threatens crops, the sudden appearance of an enemy war party, the onset of an epidemic—mass ceremonies are performed to ease the sense of danger. This unites people in a common effort so that fear and confusion yield to collective action and a degree of optimism. The balance in the relations of all concerned is restored to normal, and the community's values are celebrated and affirmed.

While an individual's death might be regarded as the ultimate crisis in that person's life, it is, as well, a crisis for the entire group, particularly if the group is small. A member of the community has been removed, so its composition has been seriously altered. The survivors, therefore, must readjust and restore balance. They also need to reconcile themselves to the loss of someone to whom they were emotionally tied.

A remarkable cultural example of a rite of intensification is the Hindu cremation ceremony in Bali, depicted in this chapter's opening photograph. Sharing a worldview with a religious belief in the reincarnation of a deceased person's soul, the Balinese deal with death by turning what could be a painful emotional experience of grief and loss into a joyous celebration of life's progressive continuity by being reborn in a future existence. At the same time, as a social reminder of Hindu caste differences in Balinese stratified society, the family of a deceased relative uses this elaborate public ceremony to display its wealth and social rank. Everyone can see that some funeral pyres are bigger and more beautiful than others (such as those built for members of a noble or royal family on the island).

Funerary ceremonies, then, can be regarded as rites of intensification that permit the living to express in nondisruptive ways their upset over the death while providing for social readjustment. Frequently such ceremonies feature ambivalence toward the dead person. For example, one part of the funerary rites of certain Melanesians was the eating of the dead person's flesh. This ritual cannibalism, witnessed by anthropologist Bronislaw Malinowski, was performed with "extreme repugnance and dread and usually followed by a violent vomiting fit. At the same time it is felt to be a supreme act of reverence, love, and devotion."[16]

This custom and the emotions accompanying it clearly reveal ambivalence toward death: On the one hand, there is the survivors' desire to maintain the tie to the dead person, and, on the other hand, they feel disgust and fear at

Ritual cannibalism appears in various societies in diverse forms. In Christianity, it is symbolic rather than actual, although millions of orthodox believers subscribe to the doctrine of transubstantiation, which holds that in Holy Communion the consecrated red wine and wafer or bread actually change into the divine blood and flesh of Christ, the Son of God.

the transformation wrought by death. According to Malinowski, funeral ceremonies provide an approved collective means for individuals to express these feelings while maintaining social cohesiveness and preventing disruption of society.

Rites of intensification do not have to be limited to times of overt crisis. In regions with marked differences in seasons where human activities must change accordingly, these rites will take the form of annual ceremonies. These are particularly common among horticultural and agricultural peoples, with their planting and harvest ceremonies. Because these are critical times for such cultures, the ceremonies express reverence toward nature's generation and fertility upon which people's very existence depends.

Participation in rituals of reverence and celebration during planting and harvest seasons reinforces group involvement. It also serves as a kind of dress rehearsal for

---

[16] Malinowski, B. (1954). *Magic, science, and religion* (p. 50). Garden City, NY: Doubleday.

crisis situations by promoting the habit of relying on supernatural forces—a habit that may make a crucial difference under stressful circumstances when it is important not to give way to fear and despair.

Magic

Among the most fascinating of ritual practices is the belief that supernatural powers can be compelled to act in certain ways for good or evil purposes by recourse to specified formulas. This is a classical anthropological notion of magic. Many societies have magical rituals to ensure good crops, the replenishment of game, the fertility of domestic animals, and the avoidance or healing of illness.

Although many Western peoples today—seeking to objectify and demythologize their world—have tried to suppress magic mysteries in their own consciousness, they continue to be fascinated by them. Not only are books and films about demonic possession and witchcraft avidly devoured and discussed, but horoscope columns are a regular feature of daily newspapers in the United States. And magical rituals are still commonly practiced by many Westerners seeking some luck where the outcome is in doubt or beyond factual influence—from lighting a votive candle for someone going through a hard time, to wearing lucky boxers on a hot date, to the curious gesturing baseball pitchers perform before each throw.

In the 19th century British anthropologist Sir James George Frazer made a useful distinction between two fundamental principles of magic. The first principle, that "like produces like," he named **imitative magic** (sometimes called *sympathetic magic*). In Myanmar (Burma) in Southeast Asia, for example, a rejected lover might engage a sorcerer to make an image of his would-be love. If this image were tossed into water, to the accompaniment of certain charms, it was expected that the hapless girl would go mad. Thus the girl would suffer a fate similar to that of her image.

Frazer called the second principle of thought on which magic is based **contagious magic**—the idea that things or persons once in contact can influence each other after the contact is broken. The most common example of contagious magic is the permanent relationship between an individual and any part of his or her body, such as hair, fingernails, or teeth. Frazer cited the Basutos of Lesotho in southern Africa, who were careful to conceal their extracted teeth because these might fall into the hands of certain mythical beings who could harm the owners of the teeth by working magic on them. Related to this is the custom, in Western

A 100-year-old fetish from Congo in Central Africa, believed to possess harmful spirit power. Known as a *nkondi*, the power of the wooden carving comes in part from magic herbs hidden behind the mirror. During a special ritual (reflecting the principle of imitative magic), iron nails were driven into this figure to activate its power to destroy hostile evil spirits or hunt down wrongdoers and take vengeance.

societies, of treasuring things that have been touched by special people. Such things range from a saint's relics to possessions of other admired or idolized individuals, from rock stars to sport heroes to spiritual gurus.

imitative magic Magic based on the principle that like produces like; sometimes called sympathetic magic.

contagious magic Magic based on the principle that things or persons once in contact can influence each other after the contact is broken.

Witchcraft

In Salem, Massachusetts, 200 innocent citizens suspected of being witches were arrested in 1692; of these, thirteen women and six men were hanged, and one 80-year-old farmer was tortured to death. Despite awarding damages to descendants of some of the victims nineteen years later, it was not until 1957 that the last of the Salem witches were exonerated by the Massachusetts legislature. **Witchcraft** is an explanation of events based on the belief that certain individuals possess an innate psychic power capable of causing harm, including sickness and death.

> **witchcraft** An explanation of events based on the belief that certain individuals possess an innate psychic power capable of causing harm, including sickness and death.

In North America, interest in and practice of witchcraft have grown significantly over the past four decades, with the rise of Wicca among highly educated segments of society. Contrary to popular belief, witchcraft is *not* concerned exclusively, or even primarily, with working evil.

Although many North Americans suppose it to be something that belongs to a less enlightened past, witchcraft is alive and well in the United States today. Indeed, starting in the 1960s, a "witch cult" known as Wicca began to gain popularity, including among highly educated segments of U.S. society. Inspired by various pre-Christian western European beliefs, in particular the idea of a sacred Mother Earth, Wicca is a nature-centered religion. And, contrary to widespread but false rumor, its self-styled "witches" do not worship Satan and are not concerned with "working evil." In fact, Wicca's core ethical statement, known as the Wiccan Rede, states that it can "harm none, do what you will."

Ibibio Witchcraft

North Americans are not alone in having a contemporary interest in witchcraft. For example, as the Ibibio of Nigeria have become increasingly exposed to modern education and scientific training, their reliance on witchcraft as an explanation for misfortune has increased.[17] Furthermore, it is often the younger, more educated members of Ibibio society who accuse others of bewitching them. Frequently, the accused are older, more traditional members of society; thus we have an expression of the intergenerational hostility that often exists in fast-changing traditional societies.

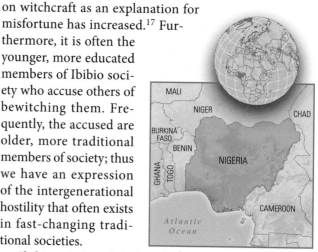

Ibibio witchcraft beliefs are highly developed and longstanding—as they are among most traditional peoples of sub-Saharan Africa. A rat that eats a person's crops is not really a rat but a witch that changed into one. If a young and enterprising man cannot get a job or fails an exam, he has been bewitched. If someone's money is wasted or if the person becomes sick, is bitten by a snake, or is struck by lightning, the reason is always the same—witchcraft.

Indeed, traditional Ibibio attribute virtually all misfortune, illness, or death to the malevolent activity of witches. The modern Ibibio's knowledge about the role of microorganisms in disease has little impact; after all, it says nothing about why these microorganisms were sent to the afflicted individual. Although Ibibio religious beliefs provide alternative explanations for misfortune, those carry

[17] Offiong, D. (1985). Witchcraft among the Ibibio of Nigeria. In A. C. Lehmann & J. E. Myers (Eds.), *Magic, witchcraft, and religion* (pp. 152–165). Palo Alto, CA: Mayfield.

negative connotations and do not elicit nearly as much sympathy from others. If evil befalls a person, witchcraft is a far more satisfying explanation than something such as offspring disobedience or violation of a taboo.

Ibibio witches are thought to be men or women who have within them a special substance acquired from another established witch. From swallowing this substance—made up of needles, colored threads, and other ingredients—one is believed to become endowed with a special psychic power that causes injury, even death, to others regardless of whether its possessor intends harm or not. It is believed to give them the ability to transform into animals and travel any distance at incredible speed to get at their unsuspecting victims, whom they may torture or kill by transferring the victim's soul or vital spirit into an animal, which is then eaten.

To identify a witch, an Ibibio looks for any person living in the region whose behavior is considered odd, out of the ordinary, immoral, or unsocial. Any combination of the following may cause someone to be labeled a witch: not being fond of greeting people; living alone in a place apart from others; charging too high a price for something; enjoying adultery or committing incest; walking about at night; not showing sufficient grief upon the death of a relative or other member of the community; taking improper care of one's parents, children, or wives; and being cold-hearted. Witches are apt to look and act mean and to be socially disruptive people in the sense that their behavior exceeds the range of variance considered acceptable.

The Ibibio make a distinction between *sorcerers,* whose acts are especially diabolical and destructive, and benign *witches,* whose witchcraft is relatively harmless, even though their powers are thought to be greater than those of their malevolent counterparts. Sorcerers are the very embodiment of a society's conception of evil—beings that flout the rules of sexual behavior and disregard every other standard of decency. Benign witches are often the community's nonconformists. Typically, they are morose, arrogant, and unfriendly people who keep to themselves but otherwise cause little disturbance. Such witches are thought to be dangerous when offended—likely to retaliate by causing sickness, death, crop failure, cattle disease, or any number of lesser ills. Not surprisingly, people viewed as witches are usually treated with considerable caution, respect, and even fear.[18]

Functions of Witchcraft

Why witchcraft? We might better ask, why not? In a world where there are few proven techniques for dealing with everyday crises, especially sickness, a belief in witches is not foolish; it is indispensable.[19] No one wants to resign oneself to illness, and if the malady is caused by a witch's curse, then magical countermeasures should cure it.

Not only does the idea of personalized evil answer the problem of unmerited suffering, but it also provides an explanation for many happenings for which no cause can be discovered. Witchcraft, then, cannot be refuted. Even if we could convince a person that his or her illness was due to natural causes, the victim would still ask, as the Ibibio do, Why me? Why now? Such a view leaves no room for pure chance; everything must be assigned a cause or meaning. Witchcraft offers an explanation and, in so doing, also provides both the basis and the means for taking counteraction.

Nor is witchcraft always entirely harmful. Its positive functions are noted in many African societies where people traditionally believe sickness, death, or other harm may be caused by witches. If people in the community agree that evildoing magic is in play, the ensuing search for the perpetrator of the misfortune becomes, in effect, a communal probe into dysfunctional social behavior. A witch-hunt is, in fact, a systematic investigation, through a public hearing, into all social relationships involving the victim of the sickness or death. Was a husband or wife unfaithful or a son lacking in the performance of his duties? Were an individual's friends uncooperative, or was the victim guilty of any of these wrongs? Accusations are reciprocal, and before long just about every unsocial or hostile act that has occurred in that society since the last outbreak of witchcraft (as manifested in sickness, death, or some other misfortune) is brought into the open.[20]

Through such periodic public scrutiny of behavior, people are reminded of what their society regards as both strengths and weaknesses of character. This encourages individuals to suppress as best they can those personality traits that are looked upon with disapproval, for if they do not, they at some time may be accused of being a witch. A belief in witchcraft thus serves as a broad control on antisocial behavior.

Witchcraft among the Navajo

Widely known among American Indians are the Navajo of the southwestern United States, who possess a highly developed concept of witchcraft. Several types of witchcraft are distinguished. Witchery encompasses the practices of witches, who are said to meet at night to practice cannibalism and kill people at a distance. Sorcery is distinguished from witchery only by the methods used by the sorcerer, who casts spells on individuals using the victim's

---

[18] See Mair, L. (1969). *Witchcraft* (p. 37). New York: McGraw-Hill.
[19] Ibid.

[20] Turnbull, C. M. (1983). *The human cycle* (p. 181). New York: Simon & Schuster.

fingernails, hair, or discarded clothing. Wizardry is not distinguished so much by its effects as by its manner of working: Wizards kill by injecting a cursed substance, such as a tooth from a corpse, into the victim's body.

Whether or not a particular illness results from Navajo witchcraft is determined by **divination**—a magical procedure or spiritual ritual designed to find out what is not knowable by ordinary means. Once a person is charged with witchcraft, he or she is publicly interrogated—in the past, possibly even tortured until there is a confession. It is believed the witch's own curse will turn against the witch once this happens, so it is expected that the witch will die within a year. Some confessed witches have been allowed to live in exile.

Navajo witchcraft serves to channel anxieties, tensions, and frustrations caused by the pressures from Euramericans.[21] The rigid rules of proper behavior among the Navajo allow little means for expression of hostility, except through accusations of witchcraft. Such accusations funnel pent-up negative emotions against individuals without upsetting the wider society. Another function of witchcraft accusations is that they permit direct expression of hostile feelings against people toward whom one ordinarily would be unable to express anger.

On a more positive note, individuals strive to behave in ways that will prevent them from being accused of witchcraft. Since excessive wealth is believed to result from witchcraft, individuals are encouraged to redistribute their assets among friends and relatives, thereby leveling economic differences. Similarly, because the Navajo believe elders, if neglected, will turn into witches, people are strongly motivated to take care of aged relatives. And because leaders are thought to be witches, people are understandably reluctant to go against their wishes, lest they suffer supernatural retribution.

The Consequences of Witchcraft

Anthropological research suggests that witchcraft, despite its often negative image, frequently functions in a very positive way to manage tensions within a society. Nonetheless, events may get out of hand, particularly in crisis situations, when widespread accusations may cause great

---

[21] Kluckhohn, C. (1944). Navajo witchcraft. *Papers of the Peabody Museum of American Archaeology and Ethnology 22* (2).

divination A magical procedure or spiritual ritual designed to find out what is not knowable by ordinary means, such as foretelling the future by interpreting omens.

suffering. This certainly was the case in the Salem witch trials, but even those pale in comparison to the half a million individuals executed as witches in Europe from the 15th through the 17th centuries. This was a time of profound change in European societies, marked by a good deal of political and religious conflict. At such times, it is all too easy to search out scapegoats to blame for what people believe are undesirable changes.

The Functions of Religion

Just as belief in witchcraft may serve a variety of psychological and social functions, so too do religious beliefs and practices in general. Here we may summarize these functions in a somewhat more systematic way.

One psychological function is to provide a model of the universe, which plays a key role in establishing orderly human behavior. Through special stories, or myths, people find answers to important questions such as: What does the universe look like, how does it work, and what is my place in it? To many Euramericans, the word *myth* conjures up the idea of an invented story about imaginary events, something that did not factually happen. This is not true for those people for whom a particular myth comprises part of their worldview. To them myths are sacred and true stories, not unlike historical documents in contemporary European or North American culture. And even in these literate societies, myths exist, such as the accounts of creation in the Book of Genesis. Invariably, myths are full of accounts about the doings of various supernatural beings and thus serve to reinforce beliefs in them.

Beyond this, by explaining the unknown and making it understandable, religion reduces the fears and anxieties of individuals. As we have seen, these explanations typically assume the existence of supernatural beings and powers, which people may potentially appeal to or manipulate as a means for dealing with crises. Thus at least theoretically, divine aid is available when all else fails.

A social function of religion is to prompt reflection concerning conduct. In this context, religion plays a role in social control, which, as we saw in the last chapter, does not rely on law alone. This is done through notions of right and wrong, good and evil. Right actions earn the approval of whatever supernatural powers are recognized by a particular culture. Wrong actions may cause revenge or punishment through supernatural agencies. In short, by deliberately raising people's feelings of guilt and anxiety about their actions, religion helps keep them in line.

Religion does more than this, though; it sets guidelines for acceptable behavior. We have noted already the

© AP/Ed Wray

Many Bugis of Sulawesi—the third largest island in Indonesia, historically known as Celebes—are seafarers. Famous for their oceangoing schooners, these Muslims are excellent sailors who have long plied the trade routes between Australia and Malaysia and beyond, delivering spice and cargo to and from the thousands of islands to the major trading centers. Life at sea brings many risks—sudden storms, piracy, and other mishaps that may cause anxiety. Sustained by their faith, religion provides these mariners with a measure of psychological security. Here we see Bugis sailors praying in front of their schooners in the harbor of Jakarta on a holiday marking the end of Ramadan, the Islamic month of fasting, when Muslims refrain from eating, drinking, smoking, and sexual activities, from sunrise to sunset. This taboo serves to purify thought and build restraint for the sake of Allah.

connection between myths and religion. Usually, myths feature tales of extraordinary or supernatural beings that in various ways illustrate the society's ethical code in action. So it is that Gluskabe, the Penobscot Indian cultural hero, is portrayed in that society's traditions as tricking and punishing those who lie, mock others, behave greedily, overreact, or engage in other behaviors deemed inappropriate in Penobscot culture.

Moreover, the specific situations relayed in myths serve as guidelines for human behavior in similar circumstances. The Old and New Testaments of the Bible are rich in the same sort of material, as is the Koran. Related to this, by the models and morals it sets forth and advocates, religion serves to justify and perpetuate a particular social order. Thus in the Jewish, Christian, and Islamic traditions, a masculine-authoritarian godhead along with a creation story that portrays a woman as responsible for a fall from grace serve to justify a social order in which men exercise control over women.

A psychological function also is tied up in this. A society's moral code, since it is considered to be divinely ordained, lifts the burden of responsibility from the shoulders of the society's individual members, at least in important situations. It can be a tremendous relief to individuals to know that the responsibility for the way things are rests with the gods or spirit forces rather than with themselves.

Another social function of religion is its role in the maintenance of social solidarity. In our discussion of shamans, we saw how such individuals provide a focus, thus

A Sufi *sema* (prayer dance) in Istanbul, Turkey. Sufism, a mystical Muslim movement that emerged in the late 10th century, borrowing ideas from Buddhism, Christianity, and Neoplatonism, emphasizes the surrender of individual ego and attachment to worldly things in order to be receptive to God's grace. Known as "Whirling Dervishes," these Sufi dancers are part of the Mevlevi brotherhood founded by Mevlana Rumi in the 13th century. According to Mevlevi tradition, during the *sema* the soul is freed from earthly ties and able to jubilantly commune with the divine. (*Dervish* literally means "doorway" and is thought to be an entrance from the material world to the spiritual.) The felt hat represents personal ego's tombstone, and the wide skirt symbolizes its shroud.

supplying one ingredient to help maintain group unity. In addition, common participation in rituals and a basic uniformity of beliefs bind people together and reinforce their identification with the group. Rituals are particularly effective for enhancing group solidarity, as the atmosphere is charged with emotion. The ecstatic feelings people experience in such circumstances positively reinforce their participation. Here, once again, we find religion providing psychological assurance while fulfilling the needs of society.

One other area in which religion serves a social function is education. In our discussion of rites of passage, we noted that puberty rituals of Aborigines in Australia served as a kind of crash course in traditional lore. By providing a memorable occasion, initiation rites can enhance learning and so help ensure the perpetuation of a nonliterate culture. And as we saw in the female initiation rites among the Mende, these girls will have the knowledge they will need to fulfill their adult roles in society.

Rites of intensification can also be educational. Frequently, such rites involve dramas that portray matters of cultural importance. For example, among a food-foraging people, dances may imitate the movement of game and techniques of hunting. Among farmers a fixed round of ceremonies may emphasize the steps necessary for successful crops. All of this helps preserve knowledge important to a people's material well-being, gives expression to their worldview, and thereby reinforces their collective self-understanding. Finally, as noted earlier in this chapter, people often turn to established religion or follow prophets—spiritual leaders believed to be divinely inspired—in the hope of reaching a specific goal, such as the healing of physical, emotional, or social ills.

Religion in Cultural Change: Revitalization Movements

No anthropological consideration of religion is complete without some mention of **revitalization movements**—movements for radical cultural reform in response to widespread social disruption and collective feelings of great stress and despair. Many such movements developed in indigenous societies where European colonial exploitation caused enormous upheaval.

Among the various types of revitalization movements is the **cargo cult**—a spiritual movement (especially noted

revitalization movement A movement for radical cultural reform in response to widespread social disruption and collective feelings of great stress and despair.

cargo cult A spiritual movement (especially noted in Melanesia) in reaction to disruptive contact with Western capitalism, promising resurrection of deceased relatives, destruction or enslavement sf white foreigners, and the magical arrival of utopian riches.

in Melanesia in the Southwest Pacific) in reaction to disruptive contact with Western capitalism, promising resurrection of deceased relatives, destruction or enslavement of white foreigners, and the magical arrival of utopian riches. Indigenous Melanesians referred to the white man's wealth as "cargo" (pidgin English for European trade goods). In times of great social stress, native prophets emerged, predicting that the time of suffering would come to an end and a new paradise on earth would soon arrive. Their deceased ancestors would return to life, and the rich white man would magically disappear—swallowed by an earthquake or swept away by a huge wave. However, their cargo would be left for the prophets and their cult followers who performed rituals to hasten this supernatural redistribution of wealth.[22]

One of many cargo cults took place in 1931 at Buka, in the Solomon Islands in the Pacific Ocean. A native religious movement suddenly emerged there when prophets predicted that a deluge would soon engulf all whites and a ship would then arrive filled with Western industrial commodities. The prophets told their followers to construct a storehouse for the goods and to prepare themselves to repulse the colonial police. They also spread word that the ship would come only after the natives had used up all their own supplies, and for this reason believers ceased working in the fields. Although the leaders of the movement were arrested, the cult continued for some years.

As deliberate efforts to construct a more satisfying culture, revitalization movements aim to reform not just the religious sphere of activity but an entire cultural system. Such drastic measures are taken when a group's anxiety and frustration have become so intense that the only way to reduce the stress is to overturn the entire social system and replace it with a new one. From the cargo cults of Melanesia to the 1890 Ghost Dance of many North American Indians to the Mau Mau of the Kikuyu in Kenya in the 1950s, extreme and sometimes violent religious reactions to European domination are so common that anthropologists have sought to formulate their underlying causes and general characteristics.

Revitalization movements are by no means restricted to the colonial world, and in the United States alone hundreds of them have sprung up. These range from Mormonism, which began in the 19th century, to the more recent Unification Church led by Reverend Sun Myung Moon, the Branch Davidians led by Seventh-Day Adventist prophet David Koresh, and the Black Muslims led by Prophet Elijah Muhammad. Recent U.S. revitalization movements also include the American Indian revival of the spectacular Sun Dance ceremony, now held each summer at various reservations in the Great Plains.

Anthropologists now recognize a sequence common to all expressions of the revitalization process.[23] First is the normal state of society, in which stress is not too great and sufficient cultural means exist to satisfy needs. Under certain conditions, such as domination by a more powerful group or severe economic depression, stress and frustration are steadily amplified; this ushers in the second phase, or period of increased individual stress. If there are no significant adaptive changes, a period of cultural distortion follows in which stress becomes so chronic that socially approved methods of releasing tension begin to break down. This steady deterioration of the culture may be checked by a period of revitalization, during which a dynamic cult or religious movement grips a sizable portion of the population.

Sometimes the movement will be so out of touch with existing circumstances that it is doomed to failure from the beginning. This was the case with the Heaven's Gate cult, which mixed bits and pieces of apocalyptic Christian beliefs predicting destruction of the world at the end of the millennium with folk myths of contemporary North American culture, in particular those having to do with UFOs (alien spaceships). Its followers committed mass suicide out of a conviction that their spiritual essences would reunite with higher extraterrestrial beings in a spaceship that awaited them behind the tail of the Hale-Bopp comet, ready to take them "home."

More rarely, a movement may tap long-dormant adaptive forces underlying a culture, and an enduring religion may result. Such was the case with Mormonism. Though heavily persecuted at first and hounded from place to place, Mormons adapted to the point that their religion thrives in the United States today. Indeed, revitalization movements lie at the root of all known religions—Judaism, Christianity, and Islam included.

In Africa, during and following the period of foreign colonization and missionization, indigenous groups resisted or creatively revised Christian teachings and formed culturally appropriate religious movements. Since the 1970s, thousands of indigenous Christian churches have been founded. These churches are often born of alternative theological interpretations, new divinely inspired revelations, or cultural disagreements between African Christians and European or North American missionaries over inclusion of some traditional African practices, such as animism, ancestor worship, and polygyny. Today the African continent is as religiously and spiritually diverse

[22] For more on cargo cults, see Lindstrom, L. (1993). *Cargo cult: Strange stories of desire from Melanesia and beyond.* Honolulu: University of Hawaii Press; and Worsley, P. (1957). *The trumpet shall sound: A study of "cargo" cults in Melanesia.* London: Macgibbon & Kee.

[23] Wallace, A.F.C. (1970). *Culture and personality* (2nd ed., pp. 191–196). New York: Random House.

as ever. Although at least 40 percent of the population is Christian and more than another 40 percent is Muslim, African indigenous religions persist and are often merged with Christianity or Islam.

The Persistence of Religion

Interestingly, millions of people caught up by the radical upheaval of globalization are turning to religious precepts and practices to allay the anxiety of a world fraught with dangers and uncertainties. The need to find deeper meaning in life and to make sense of an increasingly complex, uncharted, and often confusing, even frightening world continues to drive human beings to explore not only scientifically, but also religiously and spiritually. As chronicled in this chapter, this quest for metaphysical explanations and revelations occurs all around the globe. These signs are apparent from massive religious gatherings to the recurrent rise of new spiritual leaders and religious movements, growing interest and participation in pilgrimages and spiritual healing ceremonies, and persistent desires to safeguard certain buildings and natural places that people have designated as sacred sites.

However, the cultural boundary between the sacred and the ordinary is not always obvious. Indeed, one of the social functions of organized religion (and, in less formalized ways, spirituality) is that it provides ethical principles and guidelines for the faithful or inspired on how to morally conduct themselves in their daily social interactions, including business dealings. The following Original Study on Shariah-compliant banking demonstrates this point and closes our chapter.

Original Study

Sacred Law in Global Capitalism *by Bill Maurer*

I will never forget my introduction to Islamic banking. It happened at a 1998 conference when I happened into a darkened room where the founder of an Islamic investment firm was showing a clip from the old Hollywood classic movie, *It's a Wonderful Life*. On the screen, George Bailey, played by Jimmy Stewart, faces an anxious crowd of Bedford Falls citizens, who have rushed into his Building and Loan, passbooks in hand, desperate to get their money. There is about to be a run on the bank.

One of the townspeople says he wants his money, *now*. George protests, "But you're thinking of this place all wrong—as if I had the money back in a safe. The money's not *here*. Why, your money's in Joe's house that's right next to yours, and in the Kennedy house, and Mrs. Macklin's house, and in a hundred others. You're lending them the money to build and then they're gonna pay it back to you as best they can. . . . Now, we can get through this thing all right. We've got to stick together, though. We've got to have faith in each other." The people cry, "I've got doctor's bills to pay!" "Can't feed my kids on faith!"

Then Mary, George's newlywed bride, shouts from behind the counter, "I've got two thousand dollars!" and holds up a wad of bills. It is the money for their honeymoon. George chimes in, "This'll tide us over until the bank reopens tomorrow." He proceeds to disburse money based on people's stated needs ("Could I have $17.50?" one woman asks meekly) and guaranteed only by his trust in them.

Seconds before six o'clock, the last client leaves. George has just two dollars left. He, Mary, his Uncle Billy, and two cousins count down the seconds and then lock the doors. They have managed to stay in business for one more day. They place the two remaining dollars in a tray, and George offers a toast: "To Mama Dollar and to Papa Dollar, and if you want this old Building and Loan to stay in business you better have a family real quick." "I wish they were rabbits," says Cousin Tilly.

At this point in the film, the conference host paused the video and said, "This is the first *lariba* movie." A murmur went through the crowd. No one quite knew what he meant. Most of the audience was Muslim; this was a Christmas movie. What was our host trying to say?

I now know that *lariba* is Arabic for "no increase." The Koran invokes the term *riba* (increase) twenty times, and the term is often translated as interest or usury (excessive interest). Islamic banking and finance aim to avoid *riba* through profit-and-loss sharing, leasing, or other forms of equity- or asset-based financing.

We are all aware of the recent global financial crisis, which led to the collapse of major corporations, the nationalization of big banks and car companies, massive unemployment, and unnerving insecurity for many people in the United States and around the world. One of the leading causes of the crisis was the marketing of debt to people who probably could not repay, and the packaging of those debts into complicated financial instruments that were supposed to curb risk but instead increased it.

What, you might ask, does anthropology have to contribute to the study of the financial markets, money, and the wider economy? Quite a lot, actually. Among other things, anthropologists have repeatedly demonstrated that economic decisions thought to be purely rational and self-interested are actually deeply embedded in social relationships, cultural values, and religious beliefs.

Take securitized debt instruments, for example—loans like mortgages, chopped up and rebundled together into salable commodities. When they started to go sour, many commentators blamed the instruments' complexity, and called for a return to an economy based on real things instead of abstract tradable debt. However, we know from our research across the globe that peoples in different cultures do not always differentiate the real from the abstract in the same way. A person's reputation might be deemed more solid and real than a piece of gold. And a piece of gold only has real value because people agree to it, as a convention.

After that 1998 conference, I began my study of global Islamic banking, including the efforts of American Muslims to create a new kind of "Islamic" mortgage that enables devout Muslims to buy a home in accordance with Islam's prohibition of interest. Instead of financing a home purchase with interest-bearing debt, Islamic alternatives rely on either leasing contracts (a sort of rent-to-own arrangement where the bank owns the house and the purchaser buys out the bank's share over time) or a partnership arrangement (like a joint business venture). Rather than having debt and interest at the center of the mortgage, as in a conventional loan, the house itself and its fair market rental value are at the center. The purchaser buys out the bank's share over time. At the center is the asset—the real thing—not the debt.

Of course, there is no reason why a joint partnership to own a piece of property is any more "real" or less "abstract" than bundling together debt. It depends on one's point of view, and one's precommitments to certain values—prohibiting interest and sharing risk, for example, or distributing risk onto others. In Islamic finance, the former is seen as "Shariah compliant," or in accord with Islamic law; and the latter, as unjust, for it offloads one's own share of risk onto others.

At the same time, Islamic mortgages often require relatively large down payments; this excludes poorer people from achieving the American dream of homeownership. So, we need to ask ourselves whether the virtues of adherence to the precepts of one's religion outweigh broader social goals of financial inclusion.

Global Islamic banking today owes much to the immigration of Middle Eastern and South Asian students and professionals to the United States and western Europe since the 1970s, and the consolidation of large U.S. Muslim organizations. The oil boom in the Middle East during the 1970s, which sparked renewed interest in Islamic banking in many Muslim-majority countries, also encouraged the development of a loosely knit interconnected network of Muslim international businessmen, who, working for oil and chemical companies as well as financial firms, gained experience in Western regulatory and business environments.

Islamic home financing expanded greatly after the 2001 terrorist attack on New York's World Trade Center and the Pentagon; these attacks sent shockwaves through the capitalist world system dominated by Wall Street. First of all, Americans in general, Muslims included, took their money out of the

stock market after the attack and started investing in real estate, buoyed by low interest rates and feeding the speculative real estate bubble. Second, Islamic mutual funds had been able to maintain their "Islamicity" in part by contributing a portion of their profits to charity in order to religiously "cleanse" the funds; however, as charities came under governmental suspicion for terrorist money laundering, many Muslims withdrew their investments from these funds. Third, home financing, American Muslims told me, is the cornerstone of the "American dream," and they were eager to demonstrate their commitment to that dream.

People involved in Islamic banking and finance are continually engaged in an effort to define precisely what their field is. Is *riba* simply Arabic for "interest," or does *riba* only refer to "excessive interest" or usury? Does the prohibition say something about justice, or does it moralize about proper market relationships? Like any aspect of culture—economy included—Islamic banking is always a field of debate. And more debate, not less, may help us all to find just, peaceful, and profitable ways out of the various catastrophes we continually make for ourselves, as we create the abstractions and realities that mutually determine our lives together.

Palani Mohan /The New York Times/Redux

Until the early 1990s, millions of Muslims throughout the world had few investment opportunities due to the ethics derived from Shariah law. Since then, hundreds of Islamic financial institutions have emerged in over fifty countries. Big American and European banks, including Citibank, have also entered the Islamic banking business in order to tap into the rising oil wealth. Today, Shariah-compliant banks manage well over $750 billion globally. Here we see three Muslim women in Kualu Lumpur, Malaysia.

Questions for Reflection

1. Beyond biological survival, humans need to find meaning in their existence. Do you ever ponder questions such as the meaning of your life and big issues such as the origin or destiny of the human species? How does your culture, including your religious or spiritual beliefs, offer you guidance in finding meaningful answers to such big questions?

2. Revitalization movements occur in reaction to the upheavals caused by rapid colonization and modernization. Do you think that the rise of Christian fundamentalism in the North American Bible Belt today is a response to such upheavals as well?

3. You have read about female genital mutilation as a rite of passage in some cultures. Do you know of any genital mutilation practices in your society? Why are so many boys in the United States circumcised immediately after their birth?

4. Do the basic dynamics of the shamanic complex also apply to preachers or priests in modern churches and medical doctors working in modern hospitals? Can you think of some similarities among the shaman, preacher, and medical doctor in terms of their respective fields of operation?

5. In postindustrial societies such as western Europe, the United States, and Canada, there is growing interest in shamanism and alternative healing techniques. Is there any relationship between globalization and this phenomenon?

Suggested Readings

Behrend, H., & Luig, U. (Eds.). (2000). *Spirit possession, modernity, and power in Africa.* Madison: University of Wisconsin Press.

This fascinating collection investigates how African spirit possession cults respond to local circumstances in a globalizing world. Contributors focus on power, histories, gender roles, and images of the other in shaping these beliefs and practices, introducing pantheons of new holy spirits—such as spirits of airplanes and guitars in Central Africa or Christian spirits with names like "Hitler" fighting against the government of Uganda.

Bowen, J. R. (2004). *Religions in practice: An approach to the anthropology of religion* (3rd ed.). Boston: Allyn & Bacon.

This author investigates how people from an array of spiritual traditions engage in special and everyday religious practices (prayer, sacrifice, pilgrimage, dress, rituals related to death) and discusses major issues of gender, states, and laws with respect to religion. The book also includes a review of religious studies theories from Hegel and Tylor to Geertz.

Bowie, F. (2006). *The anthropology of religion: An introduction* (2nd ed.). Malden, MA: Blackwell.

This readable introductory text presents the central theoretical ideas in the anthropology of religion, illustrating them with specific case studies. This edition features new chapters on mythology and pilgrimage, plus coverage of topics such as spirit possession and cargo cults.

Geertz, C. (2004). Religion as a cultural system. In M. Banton (Ed.), *Anthropological approaches to the study of religion* (pp. 1–46). London: Routledge. (orig. 1966)

In this gracefully written essay, Geertz describes religion as a cultural system of guidance, meaning, and authority in human affairs. Often cited in other disciplines as well, this is now regarded as a classic statement of the interpretive perspective on culture.

Lambek, M. (2002). *A reader in the anthropology of religion.* London: Blackwell.

This ambitious reader encompasses the breadth, depth, and complexity of anthropology's investigations into religion—and aims to create a conversation between Western and non-Western cultures, as well as between anthropology and other disciplines in the social sciences and humanities. It features a general introduction, a comprehensive range of classical and recent readings, and an extensive bibliography that is indexed according to both ethnographic region and religious topics and practices.

Tedlock, B. (2005). *The woman in the shaman's body: Reclaiming the feminine in religion and medicine.* New York: Random House.

Tracing the history of shamanism around the globe and illuminating the roles of women, the author integrates scholarship and her personal experience as a practicing shaman.

Challenge Issue   Humans in all cultures throughout time face the challenge of creatively articulating their feelings and ideas about themselves and the world around them. Although not all societies distinguish art as a special cultural domain, people everywhere have developed aesthetic forms—musical, visual, verbal, movement, and so on—to symbolically express, appreciate, and share sensations of beauty in all its variety. Art may be individual and personal. But it may also symbolically articulate, stimulate, and reinforce experiences and feelings of collective social identity, reminding and inspiring participants and observers alike of cultural values and ideals they share as members of a community. We see this when people join in a song of praise or devotion to an institution to which they belong, as in a national anthem. On such special occasions, processions may be staged in which people wear artfully designed clothing, carry banners, and march or dance to music, expressing important ideas and values. Such is the case here where we see the national army band of the small Buddhist kingdom of Bhutan. Band members wear traditional dress, but their instruments have been more recently adopted as a result of British colonial influence in South Asia. In addition to bagpipers shown here, the band features a brass section, which leads the way for singing the national anthem *Druk tsendhen* ("The Thunder Dragon Kingdom"), honoring the traditional *Druk Gylapo* (Dragon King) who serves as head of state.

CHAPTER 25

The Arts

Chapter Preview

What Is Art?

Although difficult to define, art may be understood as the creative use of the human imagination to aesthetically interpret, express, and engage life, modifying experienced reality in the process. Many contemporary Western peoples consider art as exclusively aesthetic, serving no practical purpose, but most societies past and present have used art to give meaningful expression to almost every part of their culture, including ideas about religion, kinship, and ethnic identity. Almost anything can become an object of artistic creativity—skin, hair, dress, dwellings, vehicles, weapons, utensils, and so on.

Why Do Anthropologists Study Art?

Anthropologists have found that art often reflects a society's collective ideas, values, and concerns. From myths, songs, dances, paintings, carvings, and so on, anthropologists may learn how a people imagine their reality and understand themselves as well as other beings around them. Through the cross-cultural study of art and creativity, we discover much about different worldviews, religious beliefs, political ideas, social values, kinship structures, economic relations, and historical memory.

What Are the Functions of Art?

Aside from adding beauty and pleasure to everyday life, art serves a number of functions. Myths, for example, may offer basic explanations about the world and set cultural standards for right behavior. The verbal arts generally transmit and preserve a culture's customs and values. Songs, too, may do this within the structures imposed by musical form. And any art form, to the degree that it is characteristic of a particular society, may contribute to the cohesiveness or solidarity of that society. Yet, art may also express political themes and be used to influence events and create social change. Often it is created for religious purposes, to honor or beseech the aid of a divine power, a sacred being, an ancestral spirit, or an animal spirit.

Humans in all cultures throughout time have expressed feelings and ideas about themselves and the world around them through **art**—the creative use of the human imagination to aesthetically interpret, express, and engage life, modifying experienced reality in the process. Art comes in many forms: visual, verbal, musical, dance, and so on. Most societies, past and present, have used art to symbolically express almost every part of their culture, including ideas about religion, kinship, and ethnic identity.

In North America, the arts often are seen as a luxury, an aesthetic pleasure that people engage in for personal or collective enjoyment quite apart from more useful or productive pursuits. This attitude becomes apparent whenever public funds are in short supply. On the local level, for example, in battles over school budgets, art programs are often the first to be cut. On the national level, fiscal conservatives repeatedly seek to curb funds for theater performances, museum exhibits, concerts, and other fine arts to be enjoyed by the general public on the premise that these lack the practical importance of roads, sewers, police, warplanes, office bureaucracies, and other government priorities.

Indeed, a significant portion of the society views artists and their supporters as an elite group subsidized at the expense of "practical" tax-paying citizens. This is due in large part to the rather recent Western concept of fine art as a distinct cultural category of art for art's sake, unrelated to society at large but relished by specialists and wealthy collectors who chatter about, purchase, or even commission works of art for enjoyment in the privacy of their homes or showings in selective galleries and museums.

The idea of art serving purely aesthetic but impractical purposes seems firmly entrenched in the thinking of many contemporary Western peoples. Today, for example, the objects from the ancient tomb of the young Egyptian King Tutankhamen are on display in a museum, where they may be seen and admired as the exquisite works of art that they are. They were made, however, not for human eyes but to guarantee the eternal life of the king and protect him from evil forces that might enter his body and gain control over it.

Similarly, we may listen to the singing of a sea chantey purely for aesthetic pleasure, as a form of entertainment. But, in fact, in the days of sailing by wind power alone, sea chanteys served very useful and practical purposes. They set the appropriate rhythm for the performance of specific shipboard tasks such as hoisting or reefing sails, and the same qualities that make them pleasurable to listen to today served to coordinate these tasks and to relieve boredom.

art The creative use of the human imagination to aesthetically interpret, express, and engage life, modifying experienced reality in the process.

Such links between art and other aspects of everyday life are common in human societies around the world. This can also be seen in the way that art has been incorporated into everyday, functional objects—from pottery and baskets used to carry or store food to carpets and mats woven by nomadic herders to cover the ground inside their portable tent dwellings. Designs painted on or woven or carved into such objects typically express ideas, values, and things that have meaning to an entire community.

All of this goes to show that artistic expression is as basic to human beings as talking and is by no means limited to a special category of people called "artists." For example, all human beings adorn their bodies in certain ways and by doing so make a statement about who they are, both as individuals and as members of society. Similarly, people in all cultures tell stories in which they express their values, hopes, and concerns and in the process reveal much about themselves and the nature of the world as they see it. In short, all peoples engage in artistic expression. And, they have been doing this in countless ways for at least 40,000 years—from fashioning and playing bone flutes to painting animals on ancient rock walls to digital music jamming on iPhones.

Far from being a luxury to be afforded or appreciated by a minority of sophisticated experts or frivolous lovers of art, creativity is a necessary activity in which everyone participates in one way or another.

Whether a particular work of art is intended to be appreciated purely for beauty or to serve some practical purpose, it requires the same special combination of symbolic representation of form and expression of feeling that constitute the creative imagination. Because human creativity and the ability to symbolize are universal, art is an important subject for anthropological study.

The Anthropological Study of Art

Anthropologists have found that art often reflects a society's collective ideas, values, and concerns. Indeed, through the cross-cultural study of art—myths, songs, dances, paintings, carvings, designs, and so on—we may discover much about different worldviews and religious beliefs, as well as political ideas, social values, kinship structures, economic relations, and historical memory.

In approaching art as a cultural phenomenon, anthropologists have the pleasant task of cataloguing, photographing, recording, describing, and analyzing all possible forms of imaginative activity in any particular culture. An enormous variety of forms and modes of artistic expression exists in the world. Because people everywhere

Visual Counterpoint

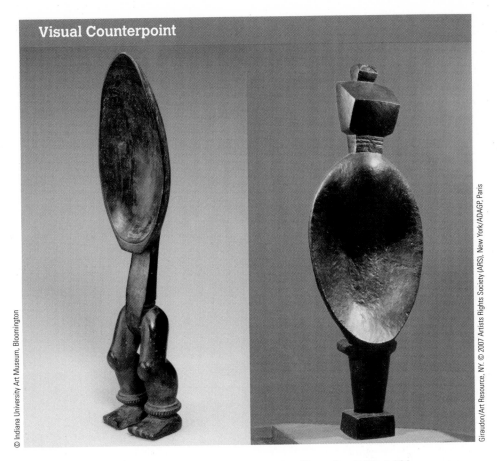

On the left is a wooden spoon used by the Dan people of Ivory Coast, West Africa, carver unknown. On the right is a bronze sculpture, *Spoon Woman*, created by the Italian artist Alberto Giacometti in 1926. Both may be beautiful, but one is functional and the other purely aesthetic. Usually, traditional utilitarian objects, no matter how exquisite, are identified only in terms of the "primitive" or "tribal" cultures in which they were made. In contrast, "works of art" created for the sake of art itself are typically tied to the name of the person who made them. How curious it is that this great modern piece credited to the famous Giacometti was inspired by a now-nameless West African.

continue to create and develop in ever-new ways, there is no end to the interesting process of collecting and describing the world's ornaments, ceremonial masks, body decorations, clothing variations, blanket and rug designs, pottery and basket styles, monuments, architectural embellishments, legends, work songs, dances, and other art forms—many of them rich with religious symbolism.

To study and analyze art, anthropologists employ a combination of aesthetic, narrative, and interpretive approaches. The distinctions among these methods can be illustrated through a brief look at a famous work of Western art, Leonardo da Vinci's painting *The Last Supper*.[1] A non-Christian viewing this late 15th-century mural in

Italy will see thirteen people at a table, apparently enjoying a meal. Although one of the men clutches a bag of money and appears to have knocked over a dish of salt, nothing else in the scene seems out of the ordinary.

Aesthetically, our non-Christian observer may admire the way the composition fits the space available, how the attitudes of the men are depicted, and the means by which the artist conveys a sense of movement. As narrative, the painting may be seen as a record of customs, table manners, dress, and architecture. But to interpret this picture—to perceive its real meaning—the viewer must be aware that in Western culture money symbolizes the root of all evil, and spilling the salt symbolizes impending disaster. But even this is not enough; to fully understand this work of art, one must know something of the beliefs of Christianity. In other words, moving to the interpretive level of studying art requires knowledge of the symbols and beliefs of the people responsible for the art.

[1] This example is drawn from Lewis-Williams, J. D. (1990). *Discovering southern African rock art* (p. 9). Cape Town and Johannesburg: David Philip.

Detail of *The Last Supper* **by the famous Italian artist Leonardo da Vinci (1452–1519). To really understand this painting, one must know something about Christianity and about the general cultural symbols and beliefs of the artist's place and time.**

A good way to deepen our insight into the relationship between art and the rest of culture is to examine critically some of the generalizations that have already been made about specific art forms. Since it is impossible to cover all art forms in the space of a single chapter, we shall concentrate on just a few—visual, verbal, and musical—in that order.

Visual Art

For many people, the first thing that springs to mind in connection with the word *art* is some sort of visual image, be it a painting, drawing, sketch, or whatever. And indeed, in many parts of the world, people have been making pictures in one way or another for a very long time—etching in bone; engraving in rock; painting on cave walls and rock surfaces; carving and painting on wood, gourds, and clay pots; or painting on textiles, bark cloth, animal hide, or even their own bodies. Some form of visual art is a part of every historically known human culture, and extraordinary examples have been found at prehistoric sites dating back more than 35,000 years.

As a type of symbolic expression, visual art may be representational (imitating closely the forms of nature) or abstract (drawing from natural forms but representing only their basic patterns or arrangements). In some of the Indian art of North America's northwest coast, for example, animal figures may be so highly stylized as to be difficult for an outsider to identify. Although the art appears abstract, the artist has created it based on nature, even though he or she has exaggerated and deliberately transformed various shapes to express a particular feeling toward the animals. Because artists do these exaggerations and transformations according to the aesthetic principles of their Indian culture, their meanings are understood not just by the artist but by other members of the community as well.

This collective understanding of symbols is a hallmark in traditional art. Unlike modern Western art, which is judged in large part on its creative originality and the unique vision of an individual artist, traditional art is all about community and shared symbolism. Consider, for example symbols related to kinship. As discussed in earlier chapters, small-scale traditional societies—hunter-gatherers, nomadic herders, slash-and-burn horticulturists—are profoundly interested in kinship relations. In such societies, kinship may be symbolically expressed in stylized motifs and colorful designs etched or painted on human skin, animal hides or bones, pottery, wood, rocks, or almost any other surface

Outstretched Limbs | Curved Limbs | Stepped Limbs

Hanging Limbs | Hourglass | Hocker

In the figure at left, the two rows of diagrams at the top show the stylized human figures that are the basic bricks used in the construction of genealogical patterns. Each figure is designed to be joined limb-and-limb with adjacent figures to illustrate descent or other kin relationships. The diagrams in the two bottom rows show how these basic figures are linked arm-and-leg with diagonally adjacent figures to depict descent. For thousands of years people all over the world have linked such figures together, creating the familiar geometric patterns that we see in countless art forms, from pottery to sculpture to weaving—patterns that informed eyes recognize as genealogical.

imaginable. To cultural outsiders these designs appear to be purely decorative, ornamental, or abstract, but they can actually be decoded in terms of genealogical iconography primarily illustrating social relations of marriage and descent.[2]

Shared symbolism has also been fundamental to the traditional art of tattooing—although that is changing in some parts of the world, as discussed in the following Original Study.

[2] Schuster, C., & Carpenter, E. (1996). *Patterns that connect: Social symbolism in ancient and tribal art.* New York: Abrams; see also Prins, H.E.L. (1998). Book review of Schuster, C., & Carpenter, E. *American Anthropologist 100* (3), 841.

Original Study

The Modern Tattoo Community *by Margo DeMello*

As an anthropology graduate student in the early 1990s, I had no idea what (or, more accurately, whom) to study for my field research. Working as an animal advocate, I had a house full of creatures to care for, which left me in no position for long-term travel to a far-off field site.

Then one of my professors suggested a topic that was literally under my nose—tattooing. I myself had several tattoos and spent quite a bit of time with other tattooed people, including my husband who had just become a professional tattooist.

Early on in my research, I, along with my husband, strove to find a way to "join" what is known as the "tattoo community," finding that it was not as friendly and open as we had imagined it to be. As an anthropologist, I came to see that the sense of exclusion we felt reflected the fact that we were on the lower rungs of a highly stratified social group in which an artist's status is based on such features as class, geography, and professional and artistic credentials, and a "fan" might be judged on the type and extent of his or her tattoos, the artist(s) who created them, the level of media coverage achieved, and more. This awareness led to one of the major

CONTINUED

CONTINUED

focuses of my work: how class and status increasingly came to define this once working-class art form.

Ultimately, I spent almost five years studying and writing about tattooing, finding my "community" wherever tattooed people talked about themselves and each other—within the pages of tattoo magazines and mainstream newspapers, on Internet newsgroups, and at tattoo-oriented events across the country. I spent countless hours in tattoo shops watching the artists work; I collected what I call "tattoo narratives," which are often elaborate, sometimes spiritual, stories that people tell about their tattoos; and I followed the careers of seminal artists. I even learned to tattoo a bit myself, placing a few particularly ugly images on my patient husband's body.

Tattoos are created by inserting ink or some other pigment through the epidermis (outer skin) into the dermis (the second layer of skin) through the use of needles. They may be beautiful as designs in and of themselves, but they can also express a multitude of meanings about the wearer and his or her place within the social group. Whether used in an overt punitive fashion (as in the tattooing of slaves or prisoners) or to mark clan or cult membership, religious or tribal affiliation, social status, or marital position, tattoos have historically been a social sign. They have long been one of the simplest ways of establishing humans as social beings. In fact, tattooing is one of the most persistent and universal forms of body art and may date back as far as the Upper Paleolithic era (10,000–40,000 years ago).

Tattoos as signs derive their communicative power from more than a simple sign-to-meaning correspondence: They also communicate through color, style, manner of execution, and location on the body. Traditionally inscribed on easily viewable parts of the body, tattoos were designed to be "read" by others and were part of a collectively understood system of inscription. However, for many middle-class North Americans today tattoos are more about private statement than public sign, and these individuals, especially women, tend to favor smaller tattoos in private spots.

The process by which tattooing has expanded in the United States from a working-class folk art into a more widespread and often refined aesthetic practice is related to a number of shifts in North American culture that occurred during the 1970s and 1980s. This time period saw the introduction of finely trained artists into tattooing, bringing with them radically different backgrounds and artistic sensibilities to draw from. More and more middle-class men and women began getting tattooed, attracted by the expanded artistic choices and the new, more spiritual context of body decoration.

Tattoos have been partially transformed into fine art by a process of redefinition and framing based on formal qualities (that is, the skill of the artist, the iconic content of the tattoo, the style in which the tattoo is executed, and so on) and ideological qualities (the discourses that surround "artistic" tattoos, discourses that point to some higher reality on which the tattoo is based). When it is judged that a tattoo has certain formal artistic qualities as well as expresses a higher, often spiritual, reality, then it is seen as art.

While it may seem as though tattoos are not good candidates to be defined as art, due to their lack of permanence (the body, after all, ages and dies) and their seeming inability to be displayed within a gallery setting, modern tattoo art shows get around these problems by photographing tattoos and displaying them in a way that showcases the "art" and often minimizes the body. By both literally and figuratively "framing" tattoos in a museum or gallery setting, or within an art book, the tattoo is removed from its social function and remade into art.

The basic working-class American tattoo designs (such as "Mother" or "Donna" inscribed alongside a heart) have been relegated to the bottom rung of today's tattoo hierarchy in the United States. Such tattoos are now seen by middle-class artists and fans as too literal, too transparently obvious, and too grounded in everyday experience and social life to qualify as art.

The modern, artistic tattoos that have increasingly gained favor are less "readable" and no longer have an easily recognizable function. Often derived from foreign (or "exotic") cultures (such as Polynesia) and custom-drawn for the wearer, they tend to eliminate the social aspect in favor of the highly individualistic. Some are purely decorative, and those that are intended to signify meaning often do so only for the individual or those in his or her intimate circle.

Tattoos in the United States have traveled a long way from the tattoo of old: brought to North America by way of British Captain James Cook's 18th-century explorations of the Pacific, moving, over time, from a mark of affiliation to a highly individual statement of personal identity, losing and regaining function, meaning, and content along the way. In our increasingly global world, tattoo designs and motifs move swiftly and easily across cultural boundaries. As this happens, their original, communal meanings are often lost—but they are not meaningless. An animal crest tattoo traditionally worn by Indians on the northwest coast of North America to signify clan membership may now be worn by a non-Native in Boston as an artful, often private, sign of rebellion against Western "coat and tie" consumer culture.

For more on this topic, see DeMello, M. (2000). Bodies of inscription: A cultural history of the modern tattoo community. (2000). Durham, NC: Duke University Press.

© Michael M. Phillips

For many U.S. Marines in Iraq, memorial tattoos have provided a way to give ink-and-skin permanence to fallen friends. In memory of fellow Marine Lance Cpl. Michael Torres, Curt Stiver of Oshkosh, Wisconsin, had a tattoo artist copy onto his left chest a photograph taken of Torres in infantry school.

Rock Art from Southern Africa

Rock art—paintings and engravings made on the faces of rock outcrops and on the interior walls of rock shelters—is one of the world's oldest art traditions. Bushmen in southern Africa practiced this art continually from at least 27,000 years ago until the beginning of the 20th century when European colonization led to the demise of their societies. Their art depicted humans and animals in highly sophisticated ways, sometimes in static poses but often in highly animated scenes. It also featured what appear to be abstract signs—dots, zigzags, nested curves, and the like. Until fairly recently, the significance of these abstract features puzzled non-Bushmen, as did the fact that new pictures were quite often created directly over existing images.

Because Bushman rock art, especially the paintings, are generally seen as beautiful and pleasurable to look at, it is not surprising that the specialists who first studied them took the aesthetic approach—analyzing how things were depicted. Investigating the various colored pigments, they found that the Bushmen had used charcoal and specularite (hematite mineral) for black; silica, china clay, and gypsum for white; and ferric oxide for red and reddish-brown hues—and that they had mixed the colors with fat, blood, and perhaps water. The paint had been applied to the rough rock with great skill. Indeed, the effectiveness of line and the way shading was used to suggest the contours of the animals' bodies elicit admiration, as does the realistic rendering of details such as the twist of an eland's horns or the black line running along its back.

Specialists also analyze Bushman rock art as "narrative," investigating *what* it depicts. Certainly, aspects of Bushman life are shown, as in several hunting scenes of men with bows, arrows, quivers, and hunting bags. Some depictions show hunting nets and also fish traps. Women are also portrayed—identifiable by their visible sexual characteristics and the stone-weighted digging sticks they carry.

In addition to aesthetic and narrative approaches, researchers study Bushman rock art from an interpretive angle—looking at it in light of contemporary ethnographic research among modern-day Bushman communities. Doing so, we see that certain designs relate to the shamanic trance dance. These include fly whisks, which are used to extract invisible arrows of sickness, and designs of hand-clapping women surrounding dancing men whose bodies are bent forward in the distinctive posture caused by the cramping of abdominal muscles as they go into trance. The designs also show dancers' arms outstretched behind their backs, which present-day Bushmen do to catch more *n/um*—supernatural power.

However, for a more complete interpretation of this scene, anthropologists have to go beyond ethnographic observation and description of the trance dance and learn about altered states of consciousness. Laboratory research shows that humans typically move through three stages when entering a trance. In the first stage, the nervous system generates images of luminous, pulsating, revolving, and constantly shifting geometric patterns known as *entoptic phenomena*—similar to images seen during a migraine headache. Usually these include dots, zigzags, grids, filigrees, nested curves, and parallel lines, often in a spiral pattern.

In the second stage, the brain tries to make sense of these abstract forms (a process known as *construal*). Here,

Bushmen in southern Africa created rock paintings and engravings depicting animals they believed possessed great supernatural powers, especially the eland. Many of these renderings also featured trance dancing, with shamans transforming into birds, appearing elongated and weightless as in flight or water—imagery based on altered states of consciousness experienced in trance.

Peyote Art: Divine Visions among the Huichol

For generations, Huichol Indians living in Mexico's mountainous western Sierra Madre region have created art remarkable for its vibrant colors. They are especially noted for their spectacular beadwork and embroidery. Although many people far and wide appreciate the intricate beauty of Huichol art, most are probably unaware that the colorful designs express a religious worldview tied to the chemical substance of a sacred plant: a small cactus "button" known as peyote (*Lophophora williamsii*).[a]

Among the many Huichol gods and goddesses, all addressed in kinship terms, is Our Grandfather Fire. His principal spirit helper is Our Elder Brother Deer, a messenger between the gods and humans. Serving the Huichol as their spiritual guide, this divine deer is also the peyote cactus itself. Huichol Indians refer to peyote as *yawéi hikuri,* the "divine flesh of Elder Brother Deer." Guided by their shamans on a pilgrimage to harvest peyote, they "hunt" this "deer" in Wirikúta, the sacred desert highlands where their ancestor deities dwell. Having found and "shot" the first cactus button with an arrow, they gather many more, later to be consumed in fresh, dried, or liquid form.

Participating in a holy communion with the creator god, Huichol shamans

© Russell Cobb/Dallas Observer

Huichol artist Olivia Carrillo makes peyote-inspired art in Real de Catorce, a town in the mountains of central Mexico. About an hour's horseback ride away from the Huichol sacred mountain Wirikúta, the town is located in the peyote heartland.

consume peyote (the divine flesh) as a sacrament. Doing so, they enter into an ecstatic trance. With the help of peyote, their spiritual guide, they become hawks or eagles soaring high in the sky. Having visions extending far across the world, they interact directly with their gods and seek advice on behalf of those who need help in dealing with illness and other misfortunes.

From a purely chemical point of view, peyote contains a psychotropic substance identified by scientists as an alkaloid. By consuming some of this toxic organic substance, the

Huichol move into an altered state of consciousness. In this dreamlike psychological state, which is also profoundly emotional, they experience religiously inspired, brilliantly colored visions from their spirit world.

These are reflected in Huichol art, such as the piece pictured here in which a stylized peyote button and deer have been rendered in rainbow-hued beadwork by Huichol artist Olivia Carrillo, who lives in the peyote heartland of central Mexico. The sacred cactus, with its flower- or starlike shape, is the most prominent symbolic design in Huichol art, beaded onto fabric and objects of all kinds or embroidered on clothing.

BIOCULTURAL QUESTION

In Huichol Indian art we often find vibrantly colored peyote buttons, articulating shamanic visions induced by this psychotropic cactus. What inspired traditional European artists painting Christian holy men and women with a halo—a silver- or gold-colored ring around or above their heads?

---

[a]Schaeffer, S. B., & Furst, P. T. (Eds.). (1996). *People of the peyote: Huichol Indian history, religion, and survival.* Albuquerque: University of New Mexico Press.

---

cultural influences come into play, so a trancing Bushman in southern Africa's Kalahari is likely to construe a grid pattern as markings on the skin of a giraffe, nested curves as a honeycomb (honey is a delicacy in the region), and so forth. A New York City police officer or a Chinese priest would construe the patterns in very different ways.

During the third and deepest trance stage, people tend to feel as if they are at one with their visions, passing into a rotating tunnel or vortex. Typically, the tunnel has lattice-like sides where **iconic images** of animals,

humans, and monsters appear, merging with the entoptic forms of the early trance stages. Because these iconic images are culture specific, individuals usually see things that have high significance within their culture. Thus Bushmen often see the eland, a massive antelope they believe carries supernatural powers for making rain. So, one of the things shamans try to do in trance is to "capture" these envisioned elands ("rain animals") for purposes of making rain.

All of this helps us understand why elands are so prominent in the Bushman rock art. Moreover, it reveals the significance of the zigzags, dots, grids, and so forth that are so often a part of the compositions. It also leads to an understanding of other puzzling features of the art. For example, the third trance stage includes such sensations

iconic images Culturally specific people, animals, and monsters seen in the deepest stage of trance.

as being stretched out or elongated, weightlessness as in flight or in the water, and difficulty breathing as when under water. Hence we find depictions in the art of humans who appear to be abnormally long, as well as individuals who appear to be swimming or flying.

Another well-documented trance phenomenon is the sensation of being transformed into some sort of animal. Such experiences are triggered in the deepest stage of trance if the individual sees or thinks of an animal. This sensation accounts for the part human–part animal (therianthrope) images in the art.

Finally, we are able to comprehend the layering of one work of art over another with the interpretative approach; not only are the visions seen in trance commonly superimposed on one another as they rotate and move, but if the trancer stares at a painting or engraving of an earlier vision, the new one will appear as if projected on the old.

The interpretive approach makes clear, then, that the rock art of southern Africa—even in the case of compositions that otherwise might appear to be scenes of everyday life—is intimately connected with the practices and beliefs of shamanism. After shamans came out of trance and reflected on their visions, they proceeded to paint or engrave their recollections on the rock faces. But these were more than records of important visions; they had their own innate power, owing to their supposed supernatural origin. This being so, when the need arose for a new trance experience, it might be held where the old vision was recorded to draw power from it.

A similar interpretive analysis is needed to fully understand the art of Huichol Indians living in Mexico, as profiled in this chapter's Biocultural Connection feature.

Verbal Art

The verbal arts include narratives, dramas, poetry, incantations, proverbs, riddles, word games—as well as naming procedures, compliments, and insults, when these take structured and special forms. Narratives, in particular, have received considerable attention from linguists and anthropologists.

In the 19th century, when the industrial revolution triggered a series of radical changes in the national cultural fabric of state societies, the pressures of modernization were also transforming the way of life in traditional communities of peasants and other rural folk. Although many folk communities still preserved their own unique historical heritage, their distinctive local customs—including legends, songs, dances, dress, and crafts—began to disappear without a trace. Alarmed about these vanishing traditions, some amateur scholars and professional academics began collecting the unwritten popular stories (and other artistic traditions) of rural peoples. They coined the word **folklore** to distinguish between "folk art" and the "fine art" of the

elite. Today, many linguists and anthropologists prefer to speak of a culture's oral traditions and verbal arts rather than its folklore and folktales, recognizing that the distinction between folk and fine art is a projection imposed by Western elites.

Generally, the narratives that make up the verbal arts have been divided into several basic and recurring categories, including myth, legend, and tale.

Myth

Derived from the Greek word *mythos,* meaning "speech" or "story," a **myth** is a sacred narrative that explains the fundamentals of human existence—where we and everything in our world came from, why we are here, and where we are going. Beyond this explanatory function, a myth provides a rationale for religious beliefs and practices and sets cultural standards for proper behavior. A typical creation or origin myth, traditional with the western Abenaki of northwestern New England and southern Quebec, goes as follows:

> In the beginning, *Tabaldak,* "The Owner," created all living things but one—the spirit being who was to accomplish the final transformation of the earth. *Tabaldak* made man and woman out of a piece of stone, but he didn't like the result, their hearts being cold and hard. So, he broke them up, and their remains today can be seen in the many stones that litter the landscape of the Abenaki homeland. Then *Tabaldak* tried again, this time using living wood, and from this came all later Abenakis. Like the trees from which the wood came, these people were rooted in the earth and could dance as gracefully as trees swaying in the wind.
>
> The one living thing not created by *Tabaldak* was *Odzihózo,* "He Makes Himself from Something." This transformer created himself out of dust, but he wasn't able to accomplish it all at once. At first, he managed only his head, body, and arms; the legs came later, growing slowly as legs do on a tadpole. Not waiting until his legs were grown, he set out to transform the shape of the earth. He dragged his body about with his hands, gouging channels that became the rivers. To make the mountains, he piled dirt up with his hands. Once his legs grew, *Odzihózo's* task was made easier; by merely extending his legs, he made the tributaries of the main stream. . . .

folklore A term coined by 19th-century scholars studying the unwritten stories and other artistic traditions of rural peoples to distinguish between "folk art" and the "fine art" of the literate elite.

myth A sacred narrative that explains the fundamentals of human existence—where we and everything in our world came from, why we are here, and where we are going.

The last work he made was Lake Champlain and liked it so well that he climbed onto a rock in Burlington Bay and changed himself into stone so he could sit there and enjoy his masterpiece through the ages. He is still there and he is still given offerings of tobacco as Abenakis pass this way. The Abenaki call the rock *Odzihózo,* since it is the Transformer himself.[3]

Such a myth, insofar as it is believed, accepted, and perpetuated in a culture, expresses part of a people's traditional worldview. This Abenaki myth accounts for the existence of rivers, mountains, lakes, and other features of the landscape, as well as of humans and all other living things. It also sanctions particular attitudes and behaviors. It is a product of creative imagination and is a work of art, as well as a potentially religious statement.

Extrapolating from the details of this particular Abenaki myth, we may conclude that these people recognize a kinship among all living things; after all, they were all part of the same creation, and humans even were made from living wood.

This idea of closeness among all living things led the Abenaki to show special respect to the animals they hunted in order to sustain their own lives. For example, before eating meat, they placed an offering of grease on the fire to thank Tabaldak.

A characteristic of myths such as this one is that the unknown is simplified and explained in terms of the known. The analysis of myths has been carried to great lengths, becoming a field of study almost unto itself. Myth making is an extremely significant kind of human creativity, and studying the myth-making process and its results can give valuable clues to the way people perceive and think about their world.

Legend

A **legend** is a story about a memorable event or figure handed down by tradition and told as true but without historical evidence. An example of a modern urban legend in the United States is one that was often told by Ronald Reagan when he was president, about an African American woman on welfare in Chicago. Supposedly, her ability to collect something like 103 welfare checks under different names enabled her to live lavishly. Although proved to

be false, the story was told as if true (by the president even after he was informed that it was not true) as legends are.

This particular legend illustrates a number of features all such narratives share: They cannot be attributed to any known author; they always exist in multiple versions, but, in spite of variation, they are told with sufficient detail to be plausible; and they tell us something about the cultures in which they are found. In this case, we learn something about popular anger against wasteful government spending of taxpayer dollars ("big government" policies to help the poor), mainstream society's views on self-reliant individualism and hard work (distrust, if not dislike, of the poor), and, last but not least, enduring racism in U.S. society (the story is told by whites, who identify the woman as African American).

Clearly, legends (no more than myths) are not confined to nonliterate, nonindustrialized societies. Legends commonly consist of pseudo-historical narratives that account for the deeds of heroes, the movements of peoples, and the establishment of local customs, typically with a mixture of realism and the supernatural or extraordinary. As stories, they are not necessarily believed or disbelieved, but they usually serve to entertain as well as to instruct and to inspire or bolster pride in family, community, or nation. Legends all around the world tell us something about the cultures in which they are found.

To a degree, in literate societies, the function of legends has been taken over by history. The trouble is that history does not always tell people what they want to hear about themselves, or, conversely, it tells them things that they would prefer not to hear. By projecting their culture's hopes and expectations onto the record of the past, they seize upon and even exaggerate some past events while ignoring or giving scant attention to others. Although this often takes place unconsciously, so strong is the motivation to transform history into legend that states have even gone so far as to deliberately rewrite it.

Not surprisingly, different groups often recall and recount the same historical event in highly contrasting ways. For instance, white colonists and their descendants who settled in New England portrayed the region's 17th-century Indian rebellion, led by Chief Metacomet (better known in American history books as King Philip), as a treacherous uprising and described the Indian defeat as a divinely guided military victory over heathen savages. In this violent conflict, thousands on both sides lost their lives. Although many Indian survivors found refuge among neighboring indigenous nations, hundreds of Indian captives were sold as slaves and died in foreign lands. Unable to resist English colonial land grabs and repression, Indians who were allowed to remain in their homeland were confined to small reservations where they came under the administrative control of white agents.

In public commemorations and written historical accounts, the Indian side of this conflict remains largely

---

[3] Haviland, W. A., & Power, M. W. (1994). *The original Vermonters: Native inhabitants, past and present* (2nd ed., p. 193). Hanover, NH: University Press of New England.

legend A story about a memorable event or figure handed down by tradition and told as true but without historical evidence.

unvoiced and unknown to the general public.[4] For this reason, American Indians sometimes joke bitterly about such one-sided versions of the past as "his story," and scholars attempting to separate historical fact from fiction frequently incur the wrath of people who refuse to abandon what they wish to believe is true, whether or not it really is.

A long, dramatic narrative recounting the celebrated deeds of a historic or legendary hero—often sung or recited in poetic language—is known as an **epic.** In parts of western and Central Africa, people hold remarkably elaborate and formalized recitations of extremely long legends, lasting several hours and even days. These long narratives have been described as veritable encyclopedias of a culture's most diverse aspects, with direct and indirect statements about history, institutions, relationships, values, and ideas. Epics are typically found in nonliterate societies with some form of state political organization; they serve to transmit and preserve a culture's legal and political precedents and practices.

Legends may incorporate mythological details, especially when they make an appeal to the supernatural, and are therefore not always clearly distinct from myth. Legends may also incorporate proverbs and incidental tales and thus be related to other forms of verbal art as well.

For the anthropologist, a major significance of the secular and apparently realistic portions of legends, whether long or short, is the clues they provide as to what constitutes a culture's approved or ideal ethical behavior. The subject matter of legends is essentially problem solving and mentoring, and the content is likely to include physical and psychological trials of many kinds. Certain questions may be answered explicitly or implicitly. In what circumstances, if any, does the culture permit homicide? What kinds of behavior are considered heroic or cowardly? Does the culture stress forgiveness over retaliation as an admirable trait?

Tale

A third type of creative narrative, the **tale,** is recognized as fiction that is for entertainment but may also draw a moral or teach a practical lesson. Consider this brief summary of a tale from Ghana in West Africa, known as "Father, Son, and Donkey":

> A father and his son farmed their corn, sold it, and spent part of the profit on a donkey. When the hot season came, they harvested their yams and prepared to take them to storage, using their donkey. The father mounted the donkey and they

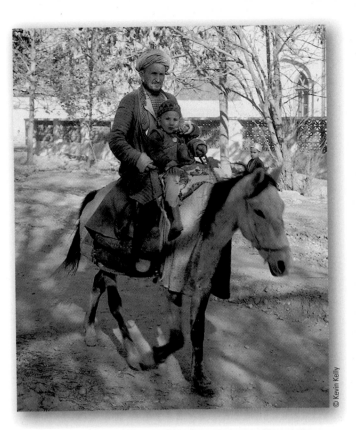

© Kevin Kelly

A scene such as this may bring to mind the internationally popular "Father, Son, and Donkey" tale. Told in different versions featuring localized draft animals, this tale conveys a basic motif or story situation—father and son trying in vain to please everyone.

all three proceeded on their way until they met some people. "What? You lazy man!" the people said to the father. "You let your young son walk barefoot on this hot ground while you ride on a donkey? For shame!" The father yielded his place to the son, and they proceeded until they came to an old woman. "What? You useless boy!" said the old woman. "You ride on the donkey and let your poor father walk barefoot on this hot ground? For shame!" The son dismounted, and both father and son walked on the road, leading the donkey behind them until they came to an old man. "What? You foolish people!" said the old man. "You have a donkey and you walk barefoot on the hot ground instead of riding?" And so it goes. Listen: when you are doing something and other people come along, just keep on doing what you like.

epic A long, dramatic narrative recounting the celebrated deeds of a historic or legendary hero—often sung or recited in poetic language.

tale A creative narrative that is recognized as fiction for entertainment but may also draw a moral or teach a practical lesson.

[4] Calloway, C. (1997). Introduction: Surviving the dark ages. In C. G. Calloway (Ed.), *After King Philip's war: Presence and persistence in Indian New England* (pp. 1–28). Hanover, NH: University Press of New England.

This is precisely the kind of tale that is of special interest in traditional folklore studies. It is an internationally popular "numbskull" tale. Versions of it have been recorded in India, Southwest Asia, southern and western Europe, and North America, as well as in West Africa. It is classified or catalogued as exhibiting a basic **motif** or story situation—father and son trying to please everyone—one of the many thousands that have been found to recur in tales around the world. Despite variations in detail, every version follows the same basic structure in the sequence of events, sometimes called the syntax of the tale: A peasant father and son work together, a beast of burden is purchased, the three set out on a short excursion, the father rides and is criticized, the son rides and is criticized, both walk and are criticized, and a conclusion is drawn.

Tales of this sort (not to mention myths and legends) that are found to have wide geographic distribution raise the question: Where did they originate? Did the story arise only once and then pass from one culture to another (diffusion)? Or did the stories arise independently (independent invention) in response to like causes in similar settings, or perhaps as a consequence of inherited mental preferences and images deeply embedded in the evolutionary construction of the human brain? Or is it merely that there are logical limits to the structure of stories, so that, by coincidence, different cultures are bound to come up with similar motifs and syntax?[5]

A surprisingly large number of motifs in European and African tales are traceable to ancient sources in India, evidence of diffusion of tales. Of course, purely local tales also exist. Within any particular culture, anthropologists usually can categorize local types of tales: animal, human experience, trickster, dilemma, ghost, moral, scatological, nonsense tales, and so on. In West Africa, for example, there is a remarkable prevalence of stories with animal protagonists. Many were carried to the slaveholding areas of the Americas; the Uncle Remus stories about Brer Rabbit and Brer Fox may be part of this tradition.

The significance of tales for the anthropologist rests partly in this matter of their distribution. They provide evidence of either cultural contacts or cultural isolation and of limits of influence and cultural cohesion.

Anthropologists are interested, however, in more than these questions of distribution. Like legends, tales very often illustrate local solutions to universal human ethical problems, and in some sense they state a moral philosophy. Anthropologists recognize that regardless of where the tale of the father, the son, and the donkey originated, the very fact it is told in West Africa suggests that it states something valid for that culture. The tale's lesson of a necessary degree of self-confidence in the face of arbitrary social criticism is therefore something that can be found in the culture's values and beliefs.

Other Verbal Art

Myths, legends, and tales, prominent as they are in anthropological studies, in many cultures turn out to be no more important than many other verbal arts. In the culture of the Awlad 'Ali Bedouins of Egypt's western desert, for example, poetry is a lively and active verbal art, especially as a vehicle for personal expression and private communication. These Bedouins use two forms of poetry. One is the elaborately structured and heroic poems men chant or recite only on ceremonial occasions and in specific public contexts. The other is the *ghinnawas* or "little songs" that punctuate everyday conversations, especially of women. Simple in structure, these deal with personal matters and feelings more appropriate to informal social situations, and older men regard them as the unimportant productions of women and youths.

Despite this official devaluation in the male-dominated Bedouin society, however, "little songs" play a vital part in people's daily lives. In these poems individuals are shielded from the consequences of making statements and expressing sentiments that contravene the moral system. Paradoxically, by sharing these "immoral" sentiments only with intimates and veiling them in impersonal traditional formulas, those who recite them demonstrate that they have a certain control, which actually enhances their moral standing. As is often true of folklore in general, the "little songs" of the Awlad 'Ali provide a culturally appropriate outlet for otherwise taboo thoughts or opinions.[6] Disaster jokes are an example of this in contemporary North American society.

In all cultures the words of songs constitute a kind of poetry. Poetry and stories recited with gesture, movement, and props become drama. Drama combined with dance,

---

[5] Gould, S. J. (2000). The narthex of San Marco and the pangenetic paradigm. *Natural History 109* (6), 29.

motif A story situation in a tale.

[6] Abu-Lughod, L. (1986). *Veiled sentiments: Honor and poetry in a Bedouin society* (p. 252). Berkeley: University of California Press.

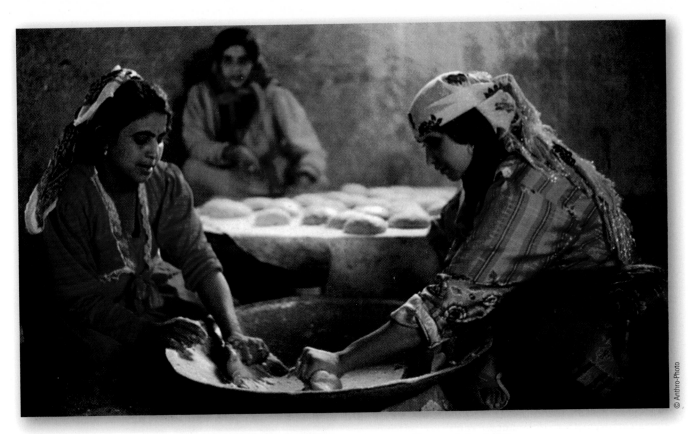

The *ghinnawas* or "little songs" of the Awlad 'Ali Bedouins in Egypt punctuate conversations carried out while the people perform everyday chores, such as making bread, as these young women are doing. Through these "little songs," they can express what otherwise are taboo subjects.

music, and spectacle becomes a public celebration. The more we look at the individual arts, the clearer it becomes that they often are interrelated and interdependent. The verbal arts are, in fact, simply differing manifestations of the same creative imagination that produces music and the other arts.

Musical Art

Evidence of humans making music reaches far back in time. Bone flutes and whistles that date back some 40,000 years and resemble today's recorders have been found by archaeologists. And historically known food-foraging peoples were not without music. In the Kalahari Desert, for example, a Ju/'hoansi hunter off by himself would play a tune on his bow simply to help wile away the time. (Long before anyone thought of beating swords into plowshares, some genius discovered that bows could be used not just to kill but to make music as well.) In northern New England, Abenaki shamans used cedar flutes to call game, lure enemies, and attract women. In addition, shamans would use

a drum—over which two rawhide strings were stretched to produce a buzzing sound, representing singing—to allow communication with the spirit world.

The study of music in specific cultural settings, or **ethnomusicology,** began in the 19th century with the collection of folksongs and has developed into a specialized subfield of anthropological study. Ethnomusicology studies the world's musics in their cultural contexts from a comparative and relativistic perspective.[7] Although early ethnomusicologists primarily focused on non-Western musical traditions in tribal cultures, some now also study folk music or music played and enjoyed in different ethnic communities within industrialized modern states.

---

[7] See Nettl, B. (2005). The study of ethnomusicology: Thirty-one issues and concepts (pp. 12–13). Chicago: University of Illinois Press.

ethnomusicology The study of a society's music in terms of its cultural setting.

What is of primary importance when distinguishing music from other modes of expression? Music to one person may be merely noise to another. Music is a form of communication that includes a nonverbal auditory component. The information it transmits is often abstract and emotional rather than concrete ideas and is experienced in a variety of ways by different listeners. Such factors make music tough to define. In fact, no single definition of music can be agreed upon, because different peoples may include or exclude different ideas within that category. Ethnomusicologists often distinguish between "music" and that which is "musical."

Much of the historical development of ethnomusicology has been based on musicology, which is primarily the study of European music. As a result of this history, music has been discussed in terms of elements considered important in European music (especially tonality, rhythm, melody), when these may be of little importance to the practitioner. European music is defined, primarily, in terms of the presence of melody and rhythm. Melody is a function of tonality, and rhythm is an organizing concept involving tempo, stress, and measured repetition. Although these can be addressed in non-European music, they may not be the defining characteristics of a performance.

In general, human music is said to differ from natural music—the songs of birds, wolves, and whales, for example—by being almost everywhere perceived in terms of a repertoire of tones at fixed or regular intervals: in other words, a scale. Scale systems and their modifications make up what is known as **tonality** in music. These vary cross-culturally, so it is not surprising that something that sounds musical to one group of people may come across as noise to another.

Humans make closed systems out of a formless range of possible sounds by dividing the distance between a tone and its first overtone or sympathetic vibration (which always has exactly twice as many vibrations as the basic tone) into a series of measured steps. In the Western or European system, the distance between the basic tone and the first overtone is called the *octave*; it consists of seven steps—five whole tones and two semitones. The whole tones are further divided into semitones for a total working scale of twelve tones. Interestingly, some birds pitch their songs to the same scale as Western music,[8] perhaps influencing the way these people developed their scale.

One of the most common alternatives to the semitonal system is the *pentatonic* (five-tone) system, which divides the scale into five nearly equidistant tones. Such scales may be found all over the world, including in much European folk music. Arabic and Persian music has smaller units of a third of a tone with scales of seventeen and twenty-four steps in the octave. Even quarter-tone scales are used in large parts of South Asia, North Africa, and the Middle East with subtleties of shading that are nearly indistinguishable to most Western ears. Small wonder, then, that even when Westerners can hear what sounds like melody and rhythm in these systems, the total result may sound peculiar to them, or "out of tune."

Like so many other cultural elements, musical instruments and even styles of playing and singing are now circulating around the globe, as are the artists themselves. One such example is West African musician Saliou "Zale" Seck, known for his "funky crisscrossing rhythms." A member of the Lébou tribe, Zale was born in the old fishing town of Yoff, just north of Senegal's capital city of Dakar. He performs Wolof percussive music on traditional skin-covered *djembe* (hand drum) and *sabar* (played with one hand and a stick). Coming from a long line of *griots* (oral historians-traditional storytellers), he transmits his people's memory through lyrics of love and humanity. Fluent in French (his country was a French colony for many years), he has toured Europe and played on radio and television in France. Recently, Zale relocated to the French-speaking Canadian city of Quebec to further pursue his musical career.

---

[8] Gray, P. M., et al. (2001). The music of nature and the nature of music. *Science 291,* 52.

tonality In music, scale systems and their modifications.

Another organizing factor in music is rhythm. Involving tempo, stress, and measured repetition, it may be more important than tonality. One reason for this may be our constant exposure to natural pulses, such as our own heartbeat and rhythms of breathing and walking. Even before we are born, we are exposed to our mother's heartbeat and to the rhythms of her movements, and as infants we experience rhythmic touching, petting, stroking, and rocking.[9]

The rhythms of traditional European music are most often measured into recurrent patterns of two, three, and four beats, with combinations of weak and strong beats to mark the division and form patterns. Non-European music is likely to move in patterns of five, seven, or eleven beats, with complex arrangements of internal beats and sometimes *polyrhythms*: one instrument or singer using a pattern of three beats, for example, while another uses a pattern of five or seven. Polyrhythms are frequent in the drum music of West Africa, which shows remarkable precision in the overlapping of rhythmic lines. Non-European music also may contain *shifting rhythms*: a pattern of three beats, for example, followed by a pattern of two or five beats with little or no regular recurrence or repetition of any one pattern, although the patterns are fixed and identifiable as units.

Melody involves both tonality and rhythm, for it is a rhythmical succession of musical tones organized as a distinct phrase or sequence of phrases.

Functions of Art

Art in all its many forms has countless functions beyond providing aesthetic pleasure. For anthropologists and others seeking to understand cultures beyond their own, art offers insights into a culture's worldview, giving clues about everything from gender and kinship relations to religious beliefs, political ideas, historical memory, and so on.

For those within a society, art may serve to display social status, spiritual identity, and political power. An example of this can be seen in the totem poles of Indians living along North America's northwest coast. Erected in front of the homes of chiefs, these poles are inscribed with symbols that are visual reminders of the social hierarchy. Similarly, art is used to mark kinship ties, as seen in Scottish tartans designed to identify clan affiliation. It can also affirm group solidarity and identity beyond kinship lines, as evidenced in national emblems such as the dragon (Bhutan), bald eagle (United States), maple leaf (Canada), crescent moon (Turkey), and cedar tree (Lebanon) that typically appear on coins, government buildings, and so on. Sometimes art is employed to express political themes and influence events, as in the counter-culture rock and folk music of the 1960s in the United States. Other times it is used to transmit traditional culture and ancestral ties, as in epic poems passed down from generation to generation.

As an activity or behavior that contributes to human well-being and that helps give shape and significance to life, art is often intricately intertwined with religion and spirituality. Shamans drum to help create a trance state, Buddhist monks chant to focus their meditation, and Christians sing hymns to praise God. And in some parts of the world, artisans create funerary boxes that are so creative that they find their way into museums as art (see the Globalscape feature). In elaborate ceremonies involving ornamentation, masks, costumes, songs, dances, and effigies, it is not easy to say precisely where art stops and religion begins.

Furthermore, music, dance, and other arts may be used, like magic, to "enchant"—to take advantage of the emotional or psychological predispositions of another person or group so as to cause them to perceive reality in a way favorable to the interests of the "enchanter." Often it is created to honor or beseech the aid of a deity, an ancestral spirit, or an animal spirit. Indeed, the arts may be used to manipulate a seemingly inexhaustible list of human passions, including desire, terror, wonder, love, fantasy, and vanity.[10] (Marketing specialists, of course, are well aware of this, which is why they routinely employ certain music and images in their advertising.)

Clearly, art in all its varied forms is used in a vast number of ways for a great array of purposes. To simplify our discussion of its numerous functions, we will consider a particular art form as embedded in a cultural system: music.

Functions of Music

Music is a powerful identifier. Many marginalized groups have used it for purposes of self-identification—as a means of building group solidarity and distinguishing themselves from dominant culture and sometimes as a channel for direct social and political commentary. Examples of this range from ethnic groups sponsoring music festivals to rock bands such as Britain's Rolling Stones, Coldplay, and Radiohead to North American rap artists Kanye West, Eminem, and Jay-Z. Music plays an important role in

[9] Dissanayake, E. (2000). Birth of the arts. *Natural History 109* (10), 89.

[10] Gell, A. (1988). Technology and magic. *Anthropology Today 4* (2), 7; Lewis-Williams, J. D. (1997). Agency, art and altered consciousness: A motif in French (Quercy) upper Paleolithic parietal art. *Antiquity 71*, 810–830.

Globalscape

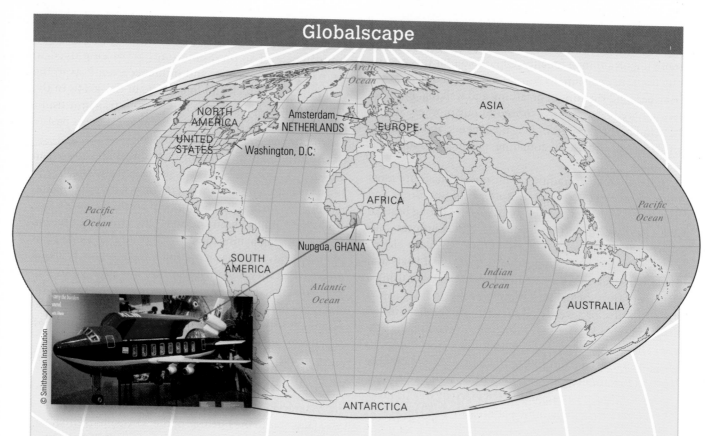

© Smithsonian Institution

Do Coffins Fly?

In his workshop in Nungua, Ghana, master carpenter Paa Joe makes unique painted wooden coffins for his clients in his Ga society and beyond. Some are spectacular, representing richly colored tropical fish or even luxury cars, such as Mercedes-Benz. Celebrating the life accomplishments of the deceased, these designer coffins show off the family's prominent status and wealth.

As a collective expression of culturally shared ideas about the afterlife, a Ga funeral ceremony reminds the mourners of important values embodied in the departed individual. Seeing the deceased off on a journey to the afterlife, Ga mourners call out praises to this person, and some may even pour schnapps on the coffin. Henceforth, the deceased will continue to be ritually honored as an ancestor by descendants.

The 747 jumbo jet coffin pictured here confers upon the deceased the prestige and mystique of air travel. Its colors, blue and white, are those of the KLM Royal Dutch Airline, a long-time provider of air service between this West African country and the rest of the world. Its creator, Paa Joe, began working at age 15 for his cousin Kane Quaye, a carpenter known for designer coffins. Later, Joe started his own workshop, and before too long he began receiving orders from other parts of the world—not only from individuals but also from museums. Using wood, enamel paint, satin, and Christmas wrapping paper, Joe created this KLM airplane coffin in 1997 for the Smithsonian National Museum of Natural History in Washington, DC, where millions of visitors from all over the globe now admire this Ghanian funereal ritual object.

Global Twister When the Smithsonian Museum purchased one of Paa Joe's remarkable coffins for public display, did this West African funereal ritual object transform into a work of art?

Based on script for African Voices exhibition at NMNH, Smithsonian courtesy of Dr. Mari Jo Arnoldi.

Native American potlatches and powwows where Native American groups gather to reaffirm and celebrate their ethnic identities. And Scottish gatherings would not be Scottish without the sound of the highland bagpipes and the fiddle.

This power of music to shape identity has had varying consequences. The English understood that the bagpipes created a strong sense of identity among the highland regiments of the British army and encouraged it within certain bounds, even as they suppressed piping in Scotland itself under the Disarming Act. Over time, the British military piping tradition was assimilated into the Scottish piping tradition and so was accepted and spread by Scottish pipers. As a result, much of the supposedly

Scottish piping one hears today consists of marches written within the conventions of the musical tradition of England, though shaped to fit the physical constraints of the instrument. Less often heard is the "classical" music known in Scottish Gaelic as Pibroch ("pipering") or, as some prefer to call traditional pipe music, Ceòl Mòr ("great music"). This more traditional Scottish pipe music has been revived over the past century and is now often romantically associated with rising cultural pride and even nationalist sentiment.

The English adoption of the highland bagpipe into Scottish regiments is an instance of those in authority employing music to further a political agenda. So, too, in Spain, former dictator Francisco Franco (who came to power in the 1930s) established community choruses in even the smallest towns to promote the singing of patriotic songs. Similarly, in Ireland Comhaltas Ceoltoiri Eireann has promoted the collection and performance of traditional Irish music, and in Brittany and Galicia, music is playing an important role in attempts to revive the spirits of the indigenous Celtic cultures in these regions of France and Spain.

The social function of music is perhaps most obvious in song, since these contain verbal text. Like other verbal forms, songs often express a group's values, beliefs, and concerns, but they do so with an increased formalism resulting from adherence to the systematic rules or conventions of pitch, rhythm, timbre, and musical genre. For this reason, music plays an important part in the cultural preservation and revitalization efforts of indigenous peoples around the world whose traditions were repressed or nearly exterminated through colonialism.

Work songs have played an important part in manual labor, serving to coordinate efforts in heavy or dangerous labor (such as weighing anchor and furling sail on board ships), to synchronize axe or hammer strokes, and to pass time and relieve tedium as with oyster-shucking songs. Songs also have been used to soothe babies to sleep, to charm animals into giving more milk, to keep witchcraft at bay, and to advertise goods. Songs may also serve social and political purposes, spreading particular ideas swiftly and effectively by giving them a special form involving poetic language and rhythm and by attaching a pleasing and appropriate tune, be it solemn or light.

In the United States numerous examples exist of marginalized social and ethnic groups attempting to gain a larger audience and more compassion for their plight through song. Perhaps no better example exists than African Americans, whose ancestors were captured and carried across the Atlantic Ocean to be sold as slaves. Out

Laborers in Mali, West Africa, working to the beat of a drum, which serves to set the pace of work, unify the workforce, and relieve boredom.

Visual Counterpoint

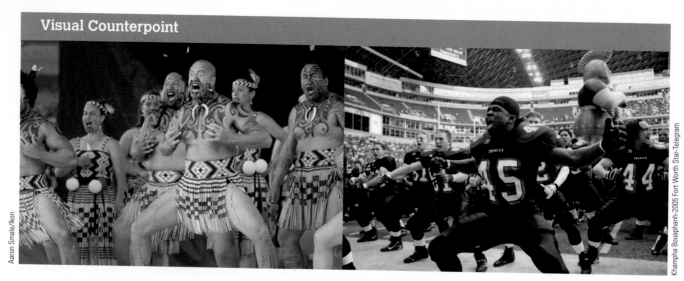

In cultures all across the world, people are not only concerned with making a living, but also with defending themselves against hostile outsiders. Those traditionally sent off to battle rely not only on their strength and weapons but may boost their own collective fighting spirits and intimidate and inspire fear in their rivals through musical rituals. Some of these traditional war rituals have been preserved and adapted for performance in theater or competitive male team sports. One spectacular example is the *haka,* a war dance (and song) originally performed by Maori warriors in New Zealand and now performed by rival rugby and football teams from many Pacific Ocean island nations. Opposite the photo showing Maori dancers performing the *haka* on stage, members of the Texas Trinity Trojans high school football team do it on the field. The Trojans have several outstanding players from Tonga, a large group of islands south of Samoa. Their families migrated to the United States for employment opportunities but maintain close contact and frequently visit home. For the Tongans and their teammates in Texas, jointly performing the *haka* minutes before the game makes them feel proud and inspires them to win. Among the first college football players from the Pacific to act out the war dance before a game were Samoan athletes at Kansas State University in the early 1980s.

of their experience emerged spirituals and, ultimately, gospel, jazz, blues, rock and roll, and rap. These forms all found their way into the North American mainstream, and white performers such as Elvis Presley and Benny Goodman (the latter with integrated bands—unusual in the 1930s) presented their own versions of this music to white audiences. Even composers of so-called serious music—ranging from Leonard Bernstein to George Gershwin to Antonin Dvořák to Francis Poulenc—were influenced by the music of African Americans. In short, music of a marginalized group of former slaves eventually captivated the entire world, even while the descendants of those slaves have had to struggle continually to escape their subordinate status.

In the 1950s and 1960s performers such as Pete Seeger and Joan Baez gained great visibility when supporting civil and human rights causes in the United States. Indeed, both performers' celebrity status led to the broader dissemination of their social and political beliefs. Such celebrity status comes from skill in performing and communicating with the intended audience. So powerful a force was music in the civil rights and peace movements of the time that Seeger was targeted by right-wing Senator Joseph McCarthy's anticommunist crusade, which aimed to discredit the political left as anti-American and unpatriotic. Seeger became one of many performers blacklisted by the entertainment industry due to this political witch-hunt.

In Australia, certain ceremonial songs of the Aborigines have taken on a new legal function, as they are being introduced into court as evidence of early settlement patterns. These songs recount ancient adventures of mythic ancestors who lived in "Dreamtime" and created water holes, mountains, valleys, and other significant features in the landscape. The ancestors' tracks are known as *songlines,* and through ceremonial songs countless generations of Aborigines have passed on sacred ecological knowledge.

This oral tradition helps Aborigines to claim extensive indigenous land ownership, thus allowing them greater authority to use the land, as well as to negotiate and profit from the sale of natural resources. This had been impossible before. The British, upon their annexation of Australia, declared the land ownerless (*Terra Nullius*). Although the Aborigines had preserved their records of ownership in song and story, these were not admissible in the British courts.

In the early 1970s, however, the Aborigines exposed the injustice of the situation, and the Australian government began responding in a more favorable, if still limited, fashion, granting the claims of traditional ownership to groups in the Northern Territory. In 1992 the legitimacy of the concept of *Terra Nullius* was overturned, and native claims are now being presented in the other territories as well. These newer claimants are granted equal partnership with developers and others. Sacred sites are being recognized, and profits are being shared with the traditional owners. Proof of native ownership includes recordings of Aborigine songs indicative of traditional patterns of settlement, travel, and land use.[11]

Music gives basic human ideas a concrete form, made memorable and attractive with melody and rhythm. Whether a song's content is didactic, satiric, inspirational, religious, political, or purely emotional, the formless has been given form, and feelings hard to express in words alone are communicated in a symbolic and memorable way that can be repeated and shared. This, in turn, shapes and gives meaning to the community.

Art, Globalization, and Cultural Survival

Clearly, there is more to art than meets the eye or ear (not to mention the nose and tongue—consider how burning incense or tobacco is part of the artfulness of sacred ceremonies and imagine the cross-cultural array of smells and tastes in the cooking arts). In fact, art is such a significant part of any culture that many indigenous groups around the world whose lifeways have been threatened—first by colonialism and now by globalization—are using aesthetic expressions as part of a cultural survival strategy. They are finding that a traditional art form—a dance, a song, a dress, a basket, a carving, or anything that is distinctly beautiful and well made or performed—can serve as a powerful symbol that conveys the vital message, "We're still here, and we're still a culturally distinct people with our own particular beliefs and values."

There are many examples of art playing a role in indigenous rights efforts. Consider the Native rights case of the Aroostook band of Micmac Indians in northern Maine, described in the Anthropology Applied feature in the kinship and descent chapter. Building support for this particular case involved making a documentary film to inform politicians and the general public about the band's cultural identity and tribulations.[12] At the time, only a dozen or so families in this band still practiced traditional wood-splint basketry. However, it had been a common livelihood for many generations, and almost every band member had parents or grandparents who had made baskets.

Emblematic of Micmac identity, including their stubborn desire for self-determination, basketry became a focal point of the film, which ultimately played a key role in the success of the band's Native rights case. More than this, the film helped create a wider market for Micmac baskets, and by conveying the diligence and real skill involved in making them, it justified raising the prices of the baskets to levels that make the craft a viable livelihood. This, in turn, has prompted young people to take up basketry and strengthened their relationships with Micmac elders who are now passing on the age-old art to a new generation. A great array of similar examples of the link between art and cultural survival can be found all around the world. One of them is featured in the following Anthropology Applied feature, which closes out this chapter.

---

[11] Koch, G. (1997). Songs, land rights, and archives in Australia. *Cultural Survival Quarterly 20* (4). See also Berndt, R. M., & Berndt, C. H. (1989). *The speaking land: Myth and story in Aboriginal Australia*. New York: Penguin.

[12] Prins, H.E.L., & Carter, K. (1986). *Our lives in our hands*. Video and 16mm. Color. 50 min. Distributed by Watertown, MA: Documentary Educational Resources and Bucksport, ME: Northeast Historic Film; see also Prins, H.E.L. (2002). Visual media and the primitivist perplex: Colonial fantasies, indigenous imagination, and advocacy in North America. In F. D. Ginsburg et al. (Eds.), *Media worlds: Anthropology on new terrain* (pp. 58–74). Berkeley: University of California Press.

Bringing Back the Past   *by Jennifer Sapiel Neptune*

Near the turn of the 20th century, a young Penobscot woman sat for a photograph, wearing a very old and elaborately beaded ceremonial chief's collar. She was the daughter of Joseph and Elizabeth Nicola and the descendant of a long line of tribal leaders. Her name was Florence Nicola, and she would go on to live a long life, marry Leo Shay, raise a family, and be remembered as a fine basketmaker and dedicated advocate for our tribe. Her efforts brought increased educational opportunities, the right for Native people in the state of Maine to vote in state and federal elections, and the first bridge that would connect our small village of Indian Island in the Penobscot River to the mainland.

Now, over one hundred years later, the photograph has resurfaced and found its way back to her son, Charles Shay. Charles brought the photograph of his mother to our tribal historian who recognized the collar as one he had seen in the book *Penobscot Man* by Frank G. Speck, and he was then able to trace it to the collections of the Smithsonian Institution's Museum of the American Indian.

In the late part of the nineteenth century the idea of the "vanishing Indian" took hold in anthropology—leading to a specialized field known as "salvage ethnography," which sought to save traditional knowledge, life ways, and material culture. Collecting examples of material culture to be sold into museum collections had become a business for some—which was how the collar Florence wore in the photograph came to be purchased by George Heye sometime before 1905 and then joined the collections of the museum. I have always found it ironic that we as a people and culture did not vanish; but during this time many of our tribes' most precious material objects did.

Bangor Daily News/Bridget Brown

Penobscot artist and cultural anthropologist Jennifer Neptune hugs tribal elder Charles Shay after giving him the traditional collar he commissioned. Modeled after a collar owned by his ancestors and now in the Smithsonian Institution's National Museum of the American Indian, the piece took Neptune more than 300 hours to make.

As a teenager I spent a lot of time in the library at the University of Maine looking through photographs in books of Penobscot beadwork, appliqué ribbon work, basketry, and carvings that were now in museums all over the world. I dreamed of being able to visit these objects, to study them up close, and to be able to find a way to bring them back into our world. It was for this reason that I went into anthropology, to learn how to research and write about my own culture. I started doing reproductions of the old beadwork designs, became a basketmaker, consulted on museum exhibitions, sold my own artwork, and worked with the Maine Indian Basketmakers Alliance promoting the work of basketmakers and artists from the four tribes in Maine.

In the spring of 2006 Charles showed me the photograph of his mother and asked me if I could make a reproduction of the collar for him.

As I worked on the collar, I was struck by how so much had changed since the late 18th century when the original collar was made. Back then the wool, silk ribbon, and beads its maker used had come by ship, horse, and foot from trade or treaty annuities; my materials were ordered over the Internet and came by UPS and FedEx. She worked by the light of the sun or fire; I worked mostly in the evenings with electric lights. Her world had northern forests still untouched by logging and filled with caribou and wolves; my world had airplanes, cars, and motor boats.

As I worked some more, I thought about what had stayed the same. We had lived and watched the sun rise and set on the same island our ancestors had for over 7,000 years. I wondered if we had stitched the same prayers into our work and if we used the same medicinal plants to soothe our aching hands and shoulders at the end of the day.

There are no words that can express how gratifying it was to hand over the finished collar to Charles—and to have played a part in returning to him, his family, and our tribe a part our history.

One hundred years ago when the collar left my community, anthropology seemed to be about taking objects, stories, and information away. As an anthropologist and artist I believe that I have a responsibility to use what I have learned to give back to my community. I have been so fortunate to be able to have spent time in museum collections visiting objects that most of my own people will never have the opportunity to see. What I learned from my time with the collar was that the objects that left still have a relationship with us today; they have a story that wants to be told, and they are waiting for someone to listen.

Questions for Reflection

1. All across the world and throughout human history, people have creatively expressed ideas and feelings through art, whether in music, dance, imagery, or sculpture. Do you know any specific forms of art originally created for, and performed by, or in, your own community? Do these art forms have any cultural meaning or social function?

2. Among the Maori in New Zealand, tattooing is a traditional form of skin art, and their tattoo designs are typically based on cultural symbols understood by all members in the community. Are the tattoo designs in your culture based on traditional motifs that have a shared symbolic meaning?

3. Because kinship relations are important in small-scale traditional societies, these relationships are often symbolically represented in artistic designs and motifs. What are some of the major concerns in your society, and are these concerns reflected in any of your culture's art forms?

4. In some cultures art is produced not to be preserved and enjoyed by the living but to be buried along with the dead. In fact, in some cultures highly valued art objects may also be burned or otherwise destroyed. Can you think of any reason for such seemingly irrational cultural practices?

5. Many museums and private collectors in Europe and North America are interested in so-called tribal art, such as African statues or American Indian masks originally used in sacred rituals. Are there sacred objects such as paintings or carvings in your religion that might also be collected, bought, or sold as art?

Suggested Readings

Buckland, T. J. (Ed.). (2007). *Dancing from past to present: Nation, culture, identities*. Madison: University of Wisconsin Press.

In this wide-ranging collection of ethnographic and historical essays, the reader will enjoy learning about the cultural significance and social role of dance in many different societies in all parts of the world—from England to India, Java, Korea, Macedonia, New Mexico, and Tonga in the southern Pacific.

Dundes, A. (1980). *Interpreting folklore*. Bloomington: Indiana University Press.

A collection of articles that assesses the materials folklorists have amassed and classified, this book seeks to broaden and refine traditional assumptions about the proper subject matter and methods of folklore.

Layton, R. (1991). *The anthropology of art* (2nd ed.). Cambridge, England: Cambridge University Press.

This readable introduction to the diversity of non-Western art deals with questions of aesthetic appreciation, the use of art, and the big question: What *is* art?

Morphy, H., & Perkins, M. (Eds.). (2006). *Anthropology of art: A reader*. Boston: Blackwell.

This illustrated anthology explores the art of different cultures at different times, covering the essential theoretical debates in the anthropology of art—including definitions of art and aesthetics, the nature of authenticity and representational processes, the primitivism controversy, and the history of trade and commodification.

Seeger, A. (2004). *Why Suyá sing: A musical anthropology*. Champaign: University of Illinois Press.

Examining the myth telling, speech making, and singing of Suyá Indians in Mato Grosso, Brazil, Seeger considers why music is important for them—and by extension for other groups. He reveals how Suyá singing creates euphoria out of silence, a village community out of a collection of houses, a socialized adult out of a boy, and contributes to the formation of ideas about time, space, and social identity.

Venbrux, E., Rosi, P. S., & Welsch, R. L. (Eds.). (2006). *Exploring world art*. Long Grove, IL: Waveland.

Ethnographic case studies examine the contemporary art world from local and comparative global perspectives, spanning topics such as artistic agency, new art forms and media, arenas of cultural production, and the role of gender in these innovative traditions.

Challenge Issue For long-term survival, human cultures must adapt to different environments and shifting circumstances. Today's technological and other major changes challenge us to adjust at an ever-faster pace. The challenge is all the more unsettling in traditional communities where changes are often imposed by powerful outside forces undermining customary ways of life. However, some cultures confront change on their own terms, even welcoming new ideas, products, and practices into their lives as improvements. This harbor scene in the small kingdom of Bahrain reflects the rapid changes occurring in many non-Western countries today. Strategically situated in the Persian Gulf, Bahrain has long been an international trading center. A former British protectorate, it is a multi-ethnic and multilingual country, historically dominated by Arab Muslims. Over half the workforce hails from Egypt, India, Iran, Pakistan, and beyond, consisting primarily of unskilled migrant laborers. Here we see the traditional Arab sailing *dhows* that share this busy sea lane with high-tech warships and the huge oil tankers that export this region's black liquid wealth. The splendid skyline behind them features ultra-modern buildings, including the Bahrain World Trade Center on the right, designed to resemble the silhouette of *dhows*. Its hi-tech, sail-shaped twin towers funnel sea breeze into turbines that produce 15 percent of the power needed to operate the offices of these 50-story buildings.

CHAPTER 26

Processes of Change

Chapter Preview

Why Do Cultures Change?

All cultures change at one time or another for a variety of reasons. Although people may deliberately alter their ways in response to problems or challenges, much change is unforeseen, unplanned, and undirected. Changes in existing values and behavior may also come about due to contact with other peoples who introduce new ideas or tools. This sometimes involves the massive imposition of foreign ideas and practices through conquest of one group by another. Through cultural change, societies can adapt to altered conditions; however, not all change is positive or adaptive.

What Is Modernization?

Modernization is a problematic term referring to a process of change by which traditional, nonindustrial societies acquire characteristics of technologically complex societies. Accelerated modernization interconnecting all parts of the world is known as globalization. Although commonly assumed to be a good thing, modernization has also led to the destruction of treasured customs and values, leaving many people unsettled, disoriented, and demoralized.

How Do Cultures Change?

The mechanisms of cultural change include innovation, diffusion, cultural loss, and acculturation. Innovation is the discovery or creation of something that is then accepted by fellow members in a society. Diffusion is the borrowing of something from another group, and cultural loss is the abandonment of an existing practice or trait, with or without replacement. Acculturation is a massive change that comes about in a group due to intensive firsthand contact with another, usually more powerful, group. Typically, it occurs when dominant societies forcefully expand their activities beyond their borders, pressuring other societies to abandon their traditional culture and replace it with the foreign one.

Culture has become the primary medium through which the human species adapts to changes and solves the problems of existence. Various cultural institutions—such as religion, kinship, marriage, and political and economic organization—mesh to form an integrated cultural system. Because systems generally work to maintain stability, cultures are often fairly steady and remain so unless there is a critical change in one or more significant factors such as natural environment, technology, population density—or in people's perceptions of the various conditions to which they are adapted.

Archaeological studies reveal how elements of a culture may persist for long periods. In northeastern North America, for example, the cultures of indigenous inhabitants remained relatively consistent over thousands of years because they successfully adapted to relatively minor fluctuations in their social conditions and natural environments, making changes from time to time in tools, utensils, and other material support.

Although stability may be a striking feature of many traditional cultures, all cultures are capable of adapting to changing conditions—climatic, economic, political, or ideological. Adaptation is a consequence of change that happens to work favorably for a population.

However, not all change is positive or adaptive, and not all cultures are equally well equipped for making the necessary adjustments in a timely fashion. In a stable society, change may occur gently and gradually, without altering in any fundamental way the culture's underlying structures, as was the case in much of North America before the European invasion several centuries ago. Sometimes, though, the pace of change may increase dramatically, to the point of destabilizing or even breaking up a cultural system. The modern world is full of examples of such radical changes, from the disintegration of the Soviet Union to the utter devastation of many indigenous communities in the Amazon caused by state efforts to develop Indian homelands and capitalize on the rainforest's natural resources.

The causes of change are many, including accidental discoveries, deliberate attempts to solve a perceived problem, and interaction with other peoples who introduce—or force—new ideas or tools or ways of life. Sometimes change is caused by the unexpected outcome of particular actions or events. Among countless examples is the establishment of European colonies in the homelands of Algonquian-speaking Natives in northeastern America nearly 500 years ago. Many people today assume this came about because the culture of the newcomers was better or more advanced than that of the region's original inhabitants. However, one could just as well argue that it was the reverse, for at the time these Indians had higher quality diets, enjoyed better health, and experienced less violence in their lives than did most Europeans.[1]

A deeper look at American history shows that the colonial settlements in New England were actually the outcome of a series of unrelated historical events that happened to coincide at a critical time. In the 1500s, economic and political developments in England drove large numbers of small farmers off the land during a period of population growth, thereby forcing an outward migration. By pure chance, this took place shortly after the European discovery of the Americas. Seeing the New World as an answer to its overpopulation, the English attempted to establish overseas colonies in lands they claimed and renamed New England. Early efforts failed, until an epidemic of unprecedented scope resulted in the sudden death of 75 to 90 percent of the indigenous inhabitants.

This devastating epidemic occurred because the region's Native communities were exposed to a host of foreign diseases through contact with European fishermen and traders. It left the weakened remnants of indigenous survivors with few defenses against aggressive colonizers, many of whom possessed natural immunity to the diseases. For centuries, Europeans had been living under conditions that were ideal for the incubation and spread of infectious diseases, which periodically killed off up to 80 percent of local populations. Since those who survived had a higher resistance to the diseases than those who succumbed, such resistance became more common in European populations over time. Indians at the time of the European invasion, by contrast, lacked all resistance to these diseases.

Although the crucial issue of immunity played a huge role in England's North American colonization efforts, it is unlikely the English could have dispossessed the surviving indigenous peoples from their land were it not for one other important factor: They crossed the Atlantic Ocean equipped with the political and military techniques for dominating other peoples—tactics previously used to impose rule over the Scots, Irish, and Welsh. In addition, they came with the ideology of a "just war," which they believed justified dispossessing America's indigenous peoples who fought back in defense.

Change imposed upon one group by another continues in much of the world today as culture contact intensifies between societies unequal in power. Among those who have the power to drive and direct change in their favor, it is typically referred to as "progress," which literally translates as "to move forward"—that is, in a positive direction. But progress is a relative term that implies improvement *as defined by the people who profit or otherwise benefit from the changes set into motion.* In other words, progress is in the eye of the beholder, for not everyone benefits from change. In fact, countless peoples (including traditional foraging, herding, and peasant communities in many parts of the world) have become the victims of progress, seeing their lives destroyed by powerful others focused on plucking almost all of the fruits for themselves.

[1] Stannard, D. E. (1992). *American holocaust* (pp. 57–67). Oxford, England: Oxford University Press.

Eric R. Wolf (1923–1999)

Like the millions of peasants about whom he wrote, **Eric Wolf** personally experienced radical upheaval in his life due to powerful outside political forces. A war refugee in his teens, he survived the battlefields and mass murders of Nazi-occupied Europe. Driven by the inequities and atrocities he witnessed during World War II, he turned to anthropology to sort through issues of power. Viewing anthropology as the most scientific of the humanities and the most humane of the sciences, he became famous for his comparative historical studies on peasants, power, and the transforming impact of capitalism on traditional nations.

Wolf's life began in Austria shortly after the First World War. During that terrible conflict, his Austrian father had been a prisoner of war in Siberia, where he met Wolf's mother, a Russian exile. When peace returned, the couple married and settled in Vienna, where Eric was born in 1923. Growing up in Austria's capital and then (because of his father's job) in Sudetenland in what is now the Czech Republic, young Eric enjoyed a life of relative ease. He relished summers spent in the Alps among local peasants in exotic costumes, and he drank in his mother's tales about her father's adventures with Siberian nomads.

Life changed for Eric in 1938 when Adolf Hitler grabbed power in Germany, annexed Austria and Sudetenland, and threatened Jews like the Wolfs. Seeking security for their 15-year-old son,

© Sydel Silverman

Eric's parents sent him to high school in England. In 1940, a year after World War II broke out, British authorities believed invasion was imminent and ordered aliens, including Eric, into an internment camp. There he met other refugees from Nazi-occupied Europe and had his first exposure to Marxist theories. Soon, he left England for New York City and enrolled at Queens College, where Professor Hortense Powdermaker, a former student of Malinowski, introduced him to anthropology.

In 1943, the 20-year-old refugee enlisted in the U.S. Army's 10th Mountain Division. Fighting in the mountains of Tuscany, Italy, he won a Silver Star for combat bravery. At the war's end, Wolf returned to the United States, completed his bachelor's degree, and

went on to graduate school at Columbia University, studying anthropology under Julian Steward and Ruth Benedict. After earning his doctorate in 1951, based on fieldwork in Puerto Rico, he did extensive research on Mexican peasants.

Following short stints at various U.S. universities, he became a professor at the University of Michigan in 1961. A prolific writer, Wolf gained tremendous recognition for his fourth book, *Peasant Wars of the Twentieth Century,* published in 1969 during the height of the Vietnam War. Against that war, he headed a newly founded ethics committee in the American Anthropological Association and helped expose counter-insurgency uses of anthropological research in Southeast Asia.

Wolf left Michigan in 1971, accepting a distinguished professorship at Lehman College in the Bronx, New York. There his classes were filled with working-class students of all ethnic backgrounds, including many who took the courses he taught in Spanish. In addition, he taught anthropology at the Graduate School of the City University of New York. After many more publications, Wolf wrote his award-winning book, *Europe and the People Without History* (1982). In 1990, he received a MacArthur "genius" prize. Shortly before his death of cancer in 1999, he published *Envisioning Power: Ideologies of Dominance and Crisis,* which explores how ideas and power are connected though the medium of culture.

In recent decades, some anthropologists have focused on the historical impact European capitalist expansionism has had on indigenous cultures around the world, radically changing or even destroying them. One of the first and most prominent among these anthropologists was Eric Wolf, who personally experienced the global havoc and upheaval of the 20th century (see Anthropologist of Note).

Mechanisms of Change

Anthropologists are not only interested in the structures of cultures as systems of adaptation, which help us understand how a population maintains itself in a certain habitat, but also in explaining processes of cultural change.

Some of the major mechanisms involved in cultural change are innovation, diffusion, and cultural loss. These types of change are typically voluntary and are not imposed on a population by outside forces.

Innovation

The ultimate source of all cultural change is innovation: any new idea, method, or device that gains widespread acceptance in society. **Primary innovation** is the creation, invention, or chance discovery of a completely new idea,

primary innovation The creation, invention, or chance discovery of a completely new idea, method, or device.

A Hopi Indian woman firing pottery vessels. The earliest discovery that firing clay vessels makes them more durable took place in Asia, probably when clay-lined basins next to cooking fires were accidentally fired. Later, a similar innovation took place in the Americas.

© Stephen Trimble

method, or device. A **secondary innovation** is a deliberate application or modification of an existing idea, method, or device.

An example of a primary innovation is the discovery that firing clay makes it permanently hard. Presumably, accidental firing of clay occurred frequently in ancient cooking fires—but a chance occurrence is of no consequence unless someone perceives an application for it. This discovery took place about 25,000 years ago, when people began making figurines of fired clay. However, it was not until about 10,000 years later that people recognized a highly practical application of fired clay and began using it to make pottery containers and cooking vessels— a secondary innovation.

The earliest known pottery was recently found in Yuchanyan Cave, an Upper Paleolithic site in southern China, where broken pieces of coarse, thick-walled, and low-fired ceramic vessels were dated to between 15,000 and 18,000 years ago.[2] Meanwhile, almost everywhere else in the world, people continued using baskets, animal-hide bags, and stone or wooden bowls for containers.

Scholarly reconstruction of the development of pottery suggests that it probably came about in the following way:[3] Thousands of years ago, people in parts of Asia were familiar with the working of clay, using it to build houses, line storage pits, and model figurines. In addition, their cooking areas included clay-lined basins built into the floor and clay ovens and hearths, making the accidental firing of clay inevitable. Once the significance of fired clay—the primary innovation—was understood, then the application of known techniques to it—secondary innovation— became possible. Clay could be modeled in the familiar way but now into the known shapes of existing containers. It could then be fired, either in an open fire or in the same facilities used for cooking food. Early pottery imitated leather and stone containers, but over time potters developed shapes and decorative techniques specifically suited to the new technology.

Archaeological research shows that the earliest known clay vessels produced were initially handmade, and the earliest furnaces or kilns were the same ovens used for cooking. As people became more adept at making pottery, they refined the technology. To aid in production, the clay could be modeled on a mat or other surface that could be turned as work progressed. Hence, the potter could sit in one place while working, without having to get up to move around the clay. A further refinement was to mount the

[2] Boaretto, E., et al. (2009, June 16). Radiocarbon dating of charcoal and bone collagen associated with early pottery at Yuchanyan Cave, Hunan Province, China. *Proceedings of the National Academy of Sciences, USA* 106 (24), 9595–9600.

secondary innovation The deliberate application or modification of an existing idea, method, or device.

[3] Amiran, R. (1965). The beginnings of pottery-making in the Near East. In F. R. Matson (Ed.), *Ceramics and man* (pp. 240–247). Viking Fund Publications in Anthropology, 41.

Lefthand driving on London Bridge in England. Once one's reflexes become habituated to doing something one way, it becomes difficult to do it differently. An example is the custom of driving a vehicle on a particular side of the highway. Which is the correct side? About a third of the world's population is used to traveling on the left, while the rest is accustomed to the right. When a British, Australian, Indonesian, or Japanese tourist visits the United States, France, or Mexico, the experience of driving on the opposite ("wrong") side of the road is challenging and often disorienting.

movable surface on a vertical rotating shaft—an application of a known principle used for drills—creating the potter's wheel and permitting mass production. Kilns, too, were modified for better heat circulation by separating the firing chamber from the fire itself. By chance, these improved kilns produced enough heat to smelt metal ores such as copper, tin, gold, silver, and lead. Presumably, this discovery was made by accident—another primary innovation—and set the stage for the eventual development of the forced-draft furnace out of the earlier pottery kiln.

The accidental discoveries responsible for primary innovations are not generated by environmental change or some other need, nor are they necessarily adaptive. They are, however, given structure by the cultural context. Thus the outcome of the discovery of fired clay by migratory food foragers 25,000 years ago was very different from what it was when discovered later by more sedentary farmers in Southwest Asia, where it set off a cultural chain reaction as one invention led to another. Indeed, given particular sets of cultural goals, values, and knowledge, certain innovations are nearly inevitable.

Although a culture's internal dynamics may encourage particular innovative tendencies, they may discourage or remain neutral about others. Indeed, Polish astronomer Nicolaus Copernicus's discovery in the early 1500s of the rotation of the planets around the sun and the discovery of the basic laws of heredity in the early 1860s by Austrian botanist Gregor Mendel are instances of genuine creative insights out of step with the established needs, values, and goals of their times and places. In fact, Mendel's pioneering experiments in genetics remained obscure until sixteen years after his death, when three scientists working

independently rediscovered, all in the same year (1900), the same laws of heredity. In the context of turn-of-the-century Western culture, Mendel's laws were bound to be discovered, even if Mendel's botanical experiments had not revealed them earlier.

Although an innovation must be reasonably consistent with a society's needs, values, and goals in order to gain acceptance, it takes more than this. Force of custom or habit tends to obstruct ready acceptance of the new or unfamiliar, for people typically stick with what they are used to rather than adopt something strange that requires adjustment on their part.

Obviously, an innovation is not assured of acceptance simply because it is notably better than the thing, method, or idea it might replace. Much depends on the prestige of the innovator and potential adopters. If the innovator's prestige is high, this will help gain more general acceptance for the innovation. If it is low, acceptance is less likely, unless the innovator can attract a sponsor who has high prestige.

Diffusion

The spread of certain ideas, customs, or practices from one culture to another is known as **diffusion.** So common is cross-cultural borrowing that North American anthropologist Ralph Linton suggested that it accounts for as much as

diffusion The spread of certain ideas, customs, or practices from one culture to another.

Change, whether generated within a society or introduced from the outside, may encounter unexpected cultural obstacles. Such obstacles are often ideologically embedded in religious faith-based traditions, such as some conservative Mennonite sects in North America rejecting motorized vehicles in their rural communities. In several Asian and African countries primarily inhabited by Muslims, orthodox religious groups oppose modern development and the spread of what they consider immoral foreign influences. Instead, they seek to return to or maintain a society based on Muslim traditions. Here we see a class of traditional Muslim students in Lahore, Pakistan, studying the holy scriptures of the Koran at a *madrasah* (religious school).

90 percent of any culture's content. People are creative about their borrowing, however, picking and choosing from multiple possibilities and sources. Usually their selections are limited to those compatible with the existing culture.

In Guatemala in the 1960s, for example, Maya Indians, who then (as now) made up more than half of that country's population, would adopt Western ways if the practical advantage of what they adopted was self-evident and did not conflict with deeply rooted traditional values and customs. The use of metal hoes, shovels, and machetes became standard early on, for they are superior to stone tools and yet compatible with the cultivation of corn in the traditional way by men using hand tools.

Yet, other modern practices that might seem advantageous to the Maya were resisted if they were perceived to be in conflict with Indian tradition. Pursuing these practices could make one a social outcast. This happened to a young farmer who tried using chemical fertilizers and pesticides to grow cash crops of vegetables not eaten by the Maya to sell in the city. He found he could not secure a "good" woman for a wife—a "good" woman (in his cultural context) being one who has never had sex with another man and is hard-working, skilled at domestic chores, and willing to attend

to her husband's needs. However, after abandoning his unorthodox ways, he gained acceptance in his community as a "real" man—one who provides for his household by working steadily at farming and making charcoal in the traditional ways. No longer conspicuous as someone different from other local men, he married well within a short time.[4]

An awareness of the extent of cultural borrowing can be eye opening. Take, for example, the numerous things that people all around the globe have borrowed from American Indians. Domestic plants developed ("invented") by the Indians—potatoes, avocados, beans, squash, tomatoes, peanuts, manioc, chili peppers, chocolate, sweet potatoes, and corn (maize), to name a few—furnish a major portion of the world's food supply. In fact, American Indians are recognized as primary contributors to the world's varied cuisine and credited with developing the largest array of nutritious foods.[5]

---

[4] Reina, R. E. (1966). *The law of the saints* (pp. 65–68). Indianapolis: Bobbs-Merrill.

[5] Weatherford, J. (1988). *Indian givers: How the Indians of the Americas transformed the New World* (p. 115). New York: Ballantine.

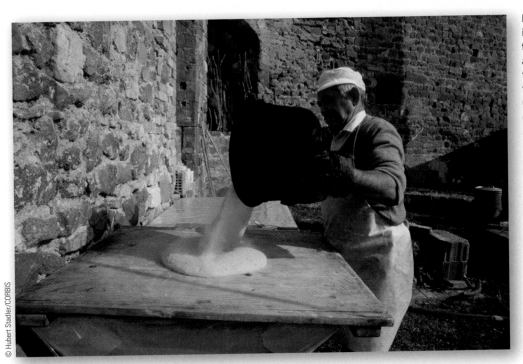

© Hubert Stadler/CORBIS

Having spread from the tropics of the Mexican highlands to much of the rest of North and South America, corn diffused rapidly to the rest of the world after Italian explorer Christopher Columbus first crossed the Atlantic in 1492. A favorite dish in Italy is polenta (a thick mush made of cornmeal). Here we see it being made the traditional way: boiled in a big copper cauldron over a fire of hot coals and then spread out and cooled to firmness on a wooden or stone slab.

Take corn, for instance, also known as maize (derived from a Caribbean Indian word *maíz*). The English originally referred to this Native American cereal plant as "Indian corn." First cultivated by indigenous peoples in the Mexican highlands over 7,000 years ago, this food crop diffused to much of the rest of North, Central, and South America over the next few millennia. In 1493, the explorer Columbus returned from America to Spain with a sampling of maize. First planted in kitchen gardens in Andalusia, in the course of several decades maize spread to other parts of Spain and Portugal. From there it diffused southwest, reaching France and northern Italy by the late 1530s. Producing more calories per acre than traditional European crops, it was initially grown as green fodder to feed pigs and other livestock. However, forced by poverty and famine, peasants and other poor folk in southern Europe accepted this new food as cornmeal cakes or thick porridge. Portuguese traders introduced maize to western Africa and across the Indian Ocean to South Asia from where it spread to China before the mid-1500s.

Diffusing across the globe, maize has become one of the world's major staple foods and culturally incorporated under many different names. This dietary revolution not only completely altered people's lives but is also responsible for enormous population growth, especially since the 18th century.[6] Today, a greater weight of maize is produced each year than rice, wheat, or any other grain—about 800 million tons, with over half of the global production taking place in the United States and China.

In recent years, an enormous quantity of maize has been grown for biomass fuel, such as ethanol, as an alternative to nonrenewable fossil fuels such as oil. Moreover, the production of genetically engineered maize (manipulated with herbicide or drought-resistant genes) has been gaining ground, especially in the United States and many developing countries, but this practice is resisted by European farmers and consumers.

Another remarkable example of diffusion—across multiple language barriers and despite long-held local traditions—is the metric system for measuring length, weight, capacity, currency, and temperature. Based on a classification in which standard units of measurement are multiplied or divided by 10 in order to produce larger or smaller units, this rational system has simplified calculations and is practical on many levels of accounting and management. In 1795, three centuries after an engineer in the Netherlands first proposed the use of decimal fractions for measures, weights, and currency in everyday life, and just a few years after the French revolution toppled the monarchy, the French First Republic adopted the metric system as its official system of measurement. As a result of French military expansion under Napoleon, this system was forced upon conquered neighboring countries, standardizing a bewildering array of regional and local systems of measurement that had been traditionally used for generations.

---

[6] Braudel, F. (1979). *The structures of everyday life: Civilization and capitalism 15th–18th century* (vol. 1, pp. 163–167). New York: Harper & Row.

During the 1800s, the metric system gained acceptance in most of Europe and various other parts of the world, and by 1900 about forty countries had officially adopted it. The system continued to spread over the next century, despite initial reluctance or even resistance in some countries, such as Great Britain. Since the early 1970s, that country and most of its former colonies have made a full transition to the metric system. British law now defines each "Imperial unit" in terms of the metric equivalent, having adjusted the traditional currency system of pence (penny), sixpence, shilling (12-pence), and pound (20 shillings) by doing away with the sixpence and shilling and making the pound equivalent to 100 pence. Likewise, Imperial units of length—measured in terms of the inch, foot (12 inches), yard (36 inches), mile (63,360 inches), and league (190,080 inches)—were also officially declared obsolete (although many older Britons still hold on to traditional measurements in daily life). Today, at least officially, the metric system is almost universal, with the exception of Myanmar (Burma), Liberia, and, most notably, the United States.[7]

Despite the obvious importance of diffusion, an innovation from another culture probably faces more obstacles when it comes to being accepted than does one that is "homegrown." In the United States, for example, this is one reason why people have been so reluctant to abandon the cumbersome English system of weights and measures for the far more logical metric system. While all other countries in the world have essentially converted to metric, in the United States the switchover is still less than about 50 percent. Hence, ethnocentrism may act as a barrier to cultural diffusion.

Cultural Loss

Most often people look at cultural change as an accumulation of innovations. Frequently, however, the acceptance of a new innovation results in **cultural loss**—the abandonment of an existing practice or trait. For example, in ancient times chariots and carts were used widely in northern Africa and southwestern Asia, but wheeled vehicles virtually disappeared from Morocco to Afghanistan about 1,500 years ago. They were replaced by camels, not because of some reversion to the past but because camels used as pack animals worked better. The old Roman empire roads had deteriorated, and these sturdy animals traveled well with or without roads. Their endurance, longevity, and ability to ford rivers and traverse rough ground made pack camels admirably suited for the region. Plus, they were economical in terms of labor: A wagon required a man for every two draft animals, but a single person could manage up to six pack camels.

Reflecting on this, paleontologist Stephen Jay Gould commented that this surprises most Westerners because

> Wheels have come to symbolize in our culture . . . intelligent exploitation and technological progress. . . . The success of camels reemphasizes a fundamental theme. . . . Adaptation, be it biological or cultural, represents a better fit to specific, local environments, not an inevitable stage in a ladder of progress. Wheels were a formidable invention, and their uses are manifold. . . . But camels may work better in some circumstances. Wheels, like wings, fins, and brains, are exquisite devices for certain purposes, not signs of intrinsic superiority.[8]

Often overlooked is another facet of losing apparently useful traits: loss without replacement. An example of this is the historical absence of boats among the indigenous inhabitants of the Canary Islands, a group of small islands isolated off North Africa's Atlantic coastline. The ancestors of these people must have had boats, for without them they could never have transported themselves and their domestic livestock to the islands in the first place. Later, without boats, they had no way to communicate with other islands or with the mainland. This loss of something useful came about due to the islands' lack of stone suitable for making polished stone axes, which in turn limited the islanders' carpentry.[9]

Repressive Change

Innovation, diffusion, and cultural loss all may take place among peoples who are free to decide for themselves what changes they will or will not accept. Not always, however, do people have the liberty to make their own choices. Frequently, changes they would not willingly make have

---

[7] Cardarelli, F. (2003). *Encyclopaedia of scientific units, weights, and measures: Their SI equivalences and origins.* London: Springer.

cultural loss The abandonment of an existing practice or trait.

[8] Gould, S. J. (1983). *Hens' teeth and horses' toes* (p. 159). New York: Norton.

[9] Coon, C. S. (1954). *The story of man* (p. 174). New York: Knopf.

Until a few decades ago, these Ache Indians survived as traditional hunters and gatherers in the deep tropical forest of eastern Paraguay. Not unlike the Ju/'hoansi of southern Africa, they were organized in small migratory bands and rarely had contact with outsiders. Armed with spears and bows and arrows, they could not defend their homeland against large numbers of foreign invaders equipped with chainsaws, bulldozers, and firearms. Massacres and foreign diseases, coupled with massive deforestation of their hunting territories, almost annihilated these people in the 1950s and 1960s. Since then, they have been exposed to intensive acculturation. Here we see the break up of an Ache encampment in the middle of Asunción, Paraguay's capital city, where they lived during many weeks of protest against government policies.

been forced upon them by some other group, usually in the course of conquest and colonialism. A direct outcome in many cases is repressive change to a culture, which anthropologists call acculturation. The most radical form of repressive change is ethnocide.

Acculturation and Ethnocide

Acculturation is the massive culture change that occurs in a society when it experiences intensive firsthand contact with a more powerful society. It always involves an element of force, either directly, as in conquests, or indirectly, as in the implicit or explicit threat that force will be used if people refuse to make the demanded changes. Other variables include degree of cultural difference; circumstances, intensity, frequency, and hostility of contact; relative status of the agents of contact; who is dominant and who is submissive; and whether the nature of

the flow is reciprocal or nonreciprocal. *Acculturation* and *diffusion* are not equivalent terms; one culture can borrow from another without being in the least forced into change.

In the course of cultural contact, any number of things may happen. Merger or fusion occurs when two cultures lose their separate identities and form a single culture, as historically expressed by the melting pot ideology of English-speaking, Protestant Euramerican culture in the United States. Sometimes, though, one of the cultures loses its autonomy but retains its identity as a subculture in the form of a caste, class, or ethnic group.

acculturation Massive culture change that occurs in a society when it experiences intensive firsthand contact with a more powerful society.

© Harald E. L. Prins

This is typical of conquest or slavery situations, and the United States has examples of this despite its melting pot ideology—we need look no further than the nearest American Indian reservation.

Acculturation may occur as a result of military conquest, political and economic expansion, or massive invasion and breaking up of cultural structures by dominant newcomers who know or care nothing about the traditional beliefs and practices of the people they seek to control. Under the sway of powerful outsiders—and unable to effectively resist imposed changes and obstructed in carrying out many of their own social, religious, and economic activities—subordinated groups are forced into new social and cultural practices that tend to isolate individuals and destroy the integrity of their traditional communities.

In virtually all parts of the world today, people are faced with the tragedy of forced removal from their traditional homelands, as entire communities are uprooted to make way for hydroelectric projects, grazing lands for cattle, mining operations, or highway construction. In Brazil's rush to develop the vast Amazon rainforest, for instance, entire indigenous communities have been relocated to "national parks," where resources are inadequate for the number of people and where former enemies are often forced to live in close proximity.

Ethnocide, the violent eradication of an ethnic group's collective cultural identity as a distinctive people, occurs when a dominant society deliberately sets out to destroy another society's cultural heritage. This may take place when a powerful nation aggressively expands its territorial control by annexing neighboring peoples and their territories, incorporating the conquered groups as subjects. A policy of ethnocide typically includes forbidding a subjugated nation's ancestral language, criminalizing their traditional customs, destroying their religion and demolishing sacred places and practices, breaking up their social organizations, and dispossessing or removing the survivors from their homelands—in essence, stopping short of physical extermination while removing all traces of their unique culture.

One tragic current example is Tibet, which could not defend itself against an invasion by the Chinese communist army in 1950. The Chinese government then initiated its ethnocidal policies by means of systematic attacks against traditional Tibetan culture. Seeking to stamp out deeply rooted religious beliefs and practices, it ordered the demolition of most Buddhist temples and monasteries. Following a mass uprising, hundreds of thousands of Tibetans were killed or forced into exile abroad. Seeking to annihilate Tibetan identity, China sought to turn the surviving Tibetans into political subjects who would culturally identify themselves as Chinese nationals.[10]

Ethnocide may also take place when so many carriers of a culture die that those who manage to survive become refugees, living among peoples of different cultures. Examples of this may be seen in many parts of the world today (Figure 26.1). A particularly well-documented case occurred in Brazil's Amazon basin in 1968, when developers hired killers to wipe out several Indian groups, using arsenic, dynamite, and machine guns from light planes.

Violence continues to be used in Brazil as a means of dealing with indigenous peoples. For example, according to conservative estimates, at least 1,500 Yanomami Indians died in the 1980s, many the victims of deliberate massacres, as cattle ranchers and gold miners poured into northern Brazil. By 1990, 70 percent of Yanomami land in Brazil had been illegally expropriated; fish supplies were poisoned by mercury contamination of rivers; and malaria, venereal disease, and tuberculosis were running rampant. The Yanomami were dying at the rate of 10 percent a year, and their fertility had dropped to near zero. Many villages were left with no children or old people, and the survivors awaited their fate with a profound terror of extinction.[11]

The typical attitude of many Brazilians toward such situations is illustrated by their government's reaction to a diplomatic journey that two Kayapó Indian leaders and an anthropologist made to the United States. They ventured north to speak with World Bank authorities and

---

[10] www.savetibet.org/tibet/us/proceedings/senatefrmauramoynihan.php. See also Avedon, J. F. (1997). *In exile from the land of snows: The definitive account of the Dalai Lama and Tibet since the Chinese conquest.* New York: Harper.

[11] Turner, T. (1991). Major shift in Brazilian Yanomami policy. *Anthropology Newsletter 32* (5), 1, 46.

ethnocide The violent eradication of an ethnic group's collective cultural identity as a distinctive people; occurs when a dominant society deliberately sets out to destroy another society's cultural heritage.

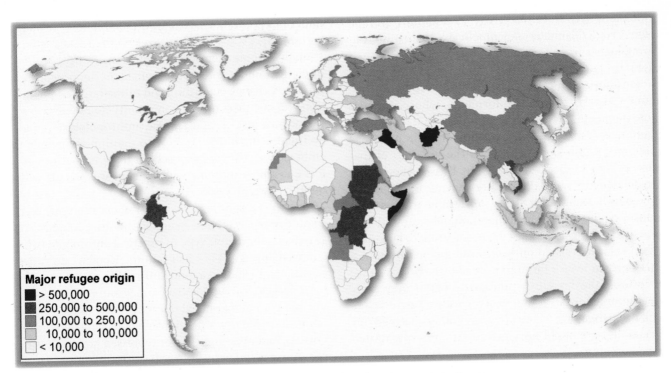

Figure 26.1 Maps and numbers cannot capture the plight of the 42 million forcibly displaced people in the world, most escaping violent conflict in pluralistic societies. Sixteen million have fled their homelands and many are now stuck in cramped and squalid refugee camps. One out of four refugees in the world escaped from Afghanistan (2.8 million). Today, Afghans are located in 69 different asylum countries. Iraqis are the second largest refugee group, with 1.9 million having sought refuge mainly in neighboring countries, in particular Syria.
Source: United Nations Refugee Agency.

Major refugee origin
- ■ > 500,000
- 250,000 to 500,000
- 100,000 to 250,000
- 10,000 to 100,000
- □ < 10,000

various government officials in the U.S. Congress and State Department concerning the destruction of their land and way of life caused by internationally financed development projects. All three were charged with violating Brazil's Foreign Sedition Act, which prohibits foreigners from secretly stirring up discontent, resistance, or revolt against the government in power. This charge and other relevant atrocities provoked international outrage, which in turn prompted Brazilian authorities to recommend policy changes that could favorably impact the country's indigenous peoples. However, whether their recommendations will be sufficient to effect positive change, or will even be acted upon fully, remains to be seen.

Directed Change

Although the process of acculturation often unfolds without planning, powerful elites may devise and enforce programs of cultural change, directing immigrant or subordinated groups into learning and accepting dominant society's cultural beliefs and practices. So it was with the Ju/'hoansi of southern Africa. Rounded up by government

officials in the early 1960s, these Bushmen were confined to a reservation in Tsumkwe where they could not possibly provide for their own needs. The government supplied them with rations, but these were insufficient to meet basic nutritional needs.

In poor health and prevented from developing meaningful alternatives to traditional activities, the Ju/'hoansi became embittered and depressed, and their death rate came to exceed the birthrate. Within the next few years, however, surviving Ju/'hoansi began to take matters into their own hands. They returned to water holes in their traditional homeland, where, assisted by anthropologists and others concerned with their welfare, they are trying to sustain themselves by raising livestock. Whether this will succeed remains to be seen, as there are still many obstacles to overcome.

One byproduct of colonial dealings with indigenous peoples has been the growth of *applied anthropology,* originally concerned with the use of anthropological techniques and knowledge for the purpose of advising in government programs of directed cultural change and solving practical problems. For example, in the United States, the Bureau of American Ethnology was founded in 1876 to gather reliable data the government might use to formulate Indian policies. At the time, anthropologists were convinced of the practicality of their discipline, and many who did ethnographic work among Indians devoted a great deal of time, energy, and even money to assisting their informants, whose interests were frequently at risk.

In the 20th century, the scope and intent of applied anthropology expanded. In the first part of that century, the applied work of Franz Boas—who almost singlehandedly trained an entire generation of anthropologists in the United States—proved instrumental in reforming the country's immigration policies. With impressive statistical data based on comparative skull measurements and related physical anthropological studies, this German Jewish immigrant challenged popular race theories of the day. He demonstrated that theories privileging non-Jewish immigrants from western Europe and discrimination against Jews and others deemed undesirable were based not on fact but on deeply rooted racial prejudice.

In the 1930s, anthropologists with clearly pragmatic objectives did a number of studies in industrial and other institutional settings in the United States. With World War II came increased involvement in colonial administration beyond U.S. borders, especially in the Pacific, by American officers trained in anthropology. The rapid postwar recovery of Japan was due in no small measure to the influence of anthropologists in structuring the U.S. occupation. Anthropologists continue to play an active role today in administering U.S. trust territories in the Pacific.

All too often, however, states and other powerful institutions directly intervening in the affairs of different ethnic groups or foreign societies fail to seek professional advice from anthropologists who possess relevant cross-cultural expertise and deeper insights. Such failures have contributed to a host of avoidable errors in planning and executing nation-building programs in ethnically divided countries such as Iraq and Afghanistan, both of which are now devastated by war and violence.

Today, applied anthropologists are in growing demand in the field of international development because of their specialized knowledge of social structure, value systems, and the functional interrelatedness of cultures targeted for development. Those working in this arena face a particular challenge: As anthropologists, they are bound to respect other peoples' dignity and cultural integrity, yet they are asked for advice on how to change certain aspects of those cultures. If the request comes from the people themselves, that is one thing, but more often than not, it comes from outsiders. Supposedly, the proposed change is for the good of the targeted population, yet members of that community do not always see it that way. Just how far applied anthropologists should go in advising outsiders how to manipulate people to embrace the changes proposed for them is a serious ethical question, especially when it concerns people without the power to resist.

In direct response to such critical questions concerning the application and benefits of anthropological research, an alternative type of practical anthropology has emerged during the last half century. Known by a variety of names—including action anthropology and committed, engaged, involved, and advocacy anthropology—this involves community-based research and action in collaboration and solidarity with indigenous societies, ethnic minorities, and other besieged or repressed groups. In sum, not only are the practical applications of anthropology necessary, but there is a growing demand for anthropologically informed pragmatic solutions.

Reactions to Repressive Change

The reactions of indigenous peoples to the changes outsiders have thrust upon them have varied considerably. Some have responded by moving to the nearest available forest, desert, or other remote place in hopes of being left alone. In Brazil, a number of communities once located near the coast took this option a few hundred years ago and were successful until the great push to develop the Amazon forest began in the 1960s. Others, like many Indians of North America, took up arms to fight back but were ultimately forced to sign treaties and surrender much of their ancestral lands, after which they were reduced to an impoverished underclass in their own land. Today, they continue to fight through nonviolent means to retain their identities as distinct peoples and to regain control over natural resources on their lands.

In addition, ethnic groups may try to retain their distinctive identities by maintaining cultural boundaries such as holding on to traditional language, festive ceremonies, customary dress, ritual songs and dances, unique food, and so on. Indeed, when facing modernization, people often seek emotional comfort from **tradition**—customary ideas and practices passed on from generation to generation, which in a modernizing society may form an obstacle to new ways of doing things.

tradition Customary ideas and practices passed on from generation to generation, which in a modernizing society may form an obstacle to new ways of doing things.

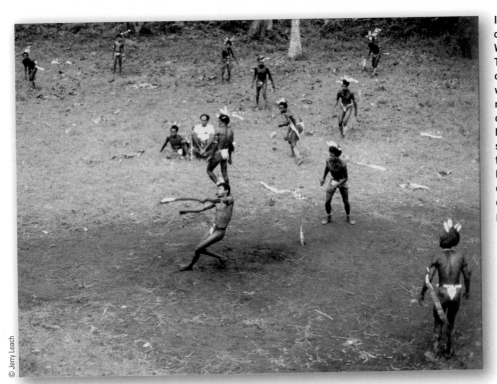

Indigenous peoples have reacted to colonialism in many different ways. When British missionaries pressed Trobriand Islanders of Melanesia to celebrate their regular yam harvests with a game of "civilized" cricket rather than traditional "wild" erotic dances, Trobrianders responded by transforming the staid British sport into an exuberant event that featured sexual chants and dances between innings. This is an example of syncretism—the creative blending of indigenous and foreign beliefs and practices into new cultural forms.

© Jerry Leach

Syncretism

When people are able to hold on to some of their traditions in the face of powerful outside domination, the result may be **syncretism**—the creative blending of indigenous and foreign beliefs and practices into new cultural forms. A fine illustration of this is the game of cricket as played by the Trobriand Islanders of Melanesia, some of whose practices we looked at in earlier chapters. When Trobrianders were under British rule, missionaries introduced them to this rather reserved British game to replace the erotic dancing and open sexuality that normally followed the yam harvests. Traditionally, this was the season when chiefs sought to spread their fame by hosting nights of dancing, providing food for the hundreds of young married people who participated. For several months, there would be night after night of provocative dancing, accompanied by chanting and shouting full of sexual innuendo, each night ending as couples disappeared into the bush together.

Since no chief wished to be outdone by any other (being outdone brought into question the strength of one's magic), the dancing had a strong competitive element, and fighting sometimes erupted. To the British Protestant missionaries, cricket seemed a good way to end all of this in a way that would encourage conformity to "civilized" comportment in dress, religion, and sportsmanship. The Trobrianders, however, were determined to "rubbish" (throw out) the British rules of the game. They did this by turning it into the same kind of distinctly Trobriand event that their thrilling dance competitions had once been.

Making cricket their own, Trobrianders added battle dress and battle magic and incorporated erotic dancing into the game. Instead of inviting dancers each night, chiefs now arrange cricket matches. Pitching has been modified from the British style to one closer to their old way of throwing a spear. Following the game, they hold massive feasts, where wealth is displayed to enhance their prestige.

Cricket, in its altered form, has been made to serve traditional systems of prestige and exchange. Neither primitive nor passively accepted in its original form, Trobriand cricket was thoughtfully and creatively adapted into a sophisticated activity reflecting the importance of basic indigenous cultural premises. Exuberance and pride are displayed by everyone associated with the sport, and the players are as much concerned with conveying the full meaning of who they are as with scoring well. From the sensual dressing in preparation for the game to the team chanting songs full of sexual metaphors to the erotic chorus-line dancing between the innings, it is clear that each participant is playing for his own importance, for the fame of his team, and for the hundreds of attractive young women who watch the game.

syncretism In acculturation, the creative blending of indigenous and foreign beliefs and practices into new cultural forms.

Revitalization Movements

Another common reaction to repressive change is revitalization. As noted in the chapter on religion and spirituality, *revitalization movements* are efforts for radical cultural reform in response to widespread social disruption and collective feelings of anxiety and despair. They are often, but not always, religiously or spiritually based. When primary ties of culture, social relationships, and activities are broken, and meaningless activity is imposed by outside forces, individuals and groups characteristically react by rejecting newly introduced cultural elements and reclaiming historical roots and traditional identity, along with a measure of spiritual imagination.

In the United States, revitalization movements have occurred often—whenever significant segments of the population have found their conditions in life to be at odds with the values of the American Dream. For example, the 1960s saw the emergence of revitalization movements among young people of middle-class and even upper-class families. In their case, the professed cultural values of peace, equality, and individual freedom were seen to be at odds with the realities of persistent war, poverty, and constraints on individual action imposed by a variety of impersonal institutions. Youths countered these realities by advocating free love, joining hippie communes, celebrating new forms of rock and folk music, using mind-altering drugs, challenging authority, growing their hair long, and wearing unconventional clothes.

By the 1980s revitalization movements were becoming prominent even among older, more affluent segments of U.S. society, as in the rise of the so-called religious right. In these cases, the reaction is not so much against a perceived failure of the American Dream as it is against perceived threats to that dream by dissenters and activists within their society, by foreign governments, by new ideas that challenge other ideas they prefer to believe, and by the sheer complexity of modern life.

Clearly, when value systems are out of step with existing realities, a condition of cultural crisis is likely to build up that may breed reactive movements. Not all suppressed, conquered, or colonized people eventually rebel against established authority, although why they do not is debatable. When they do, however, cultural resistance may take one of several forms, all of which are varieties of revitalization movements. Some of these revitalization movements take on a revolutionary character, as did the Taliban in Afghanistan.

rebellion Organized armed resistance to an established government or authority in power.

The 2006 inauguration of Bolivia's first indigenous president, Evo Morales, shown here flanked by native spiritual leaders. The ceremony took place at the archaeological site of Tiwanaku, the ancient capital of a large indigenous empire in the Bolivian highlands surrounding Lake Titicaca. Wearing traditional royal clothing and speaking in his native Aymara tongue, Morales proclaimed, "Today begins a new era for the native peoples of the world." He chose this symbolic event to officially launch an indigenous cultural revitalization movement in a country where most citizens are Aymara, Quechua, or members of other indigenous nations. Long repressed, often dispossessed, and struggling against poverty, more than a dozen generations of Bolivian Indians have seen their ancestral traditions marginalized by Spanish-speaking European invaders and their descendants. True to his vow to establish a fairer distribution of wealth in South America's poorest country, Morales nationalized many companies and used the income to finance social programs. He won reelection in December 2009.

Rebellion and Revolution

When the scale of discontent within a society reaches a certain level, the possibilities are high for **rebellion**—organized armed resistance to an established government or authority in power. There have been many peasant rebellions around the world in the course of history. Often, such rebellions are triggered by repressive regimes imposing new taxes on the already struggling small farmers unable to feed their families under such unacceptable levels of exploitation.

© AFP/Getty Images

One current example is the Zapatista Maya Indian uprising in southern Mexico, which began in the mid-1990s and has not yet been resolved. This rebellion involves thousands of poor Indian farmers whose livelihoods have been threatened by the disruptive changes imposed on them and whose human rights under the Mexican constitution have never been fully implemented.

In contrast to rebellions, which have rather limited objectives, a **revolution**—a radical change in a society or culture—involves a more dramatic transformation. Revolutions occur when the level of discontent in a society is very high. In the political arena, revolution involves the forced overthrow of an old government and the establishment of a completely new one.

Such was the case when Muslim fundamentalists in Iran toppled the imperial regime of the shah in 1979 and replaced him with Ayatollah Khomeini, a high-ranking Shiite Muslim religious leader. Returning to his homeland from exile and becoming Iran's new leader, he instituted a new social and political order based on Islamic fundamentalist principles.

The question of why revolutions erupt, as well as why they frequently fail to live up to the expectations of the people initiating them, is unsolved. It is clear, however, that the colonial policies of countries such as Britain, France, Spain, Portugal, and the United States during the 19th and early 20th centuries have created a worldwide situation in which revolution is nearly inevitable. Despite the political independence most colonies have gained since World War II, powerful countries continue to exploit many of these "underdeveloped" countries for their natural resources and cheap labor, causing a deep resentment of rulers beholden to foreign powers. Further discontent has been caused as governing elites in newly independent states try to assert their control over peoples living within their boundaries. By virtue of a common ancestry, possession of distinct cultures, persistent occupation of their own territories, and traditions

> **revolution** Radical change in a society or culture. In the political arena, it involves the forced overthrow of an old government and establishment of a completely new one.

On New Year's Day 1994, when the North American Free Trade Agreement (NAFTA) went into effect, 3,000 armed peasants belonging to the Zapatista revolutionary movement invaded towns in southern Mexico. Mostly Maya Indians, they declared war on the Mexican government, claiming that globalization was destroying their rural communities. Strong Internet presence helped them build an international network of political support. Now committed to nonviolent resistance to Mexican state control, Zapatistas have created 32 self-governing municipalities and established their own local health, justice, and education services.

In China, women's labor has become critical to economic expansion. Much of this labor is controlled by male heads of families, who act as agents of the state in allocating labor.

© A. Ramey/PhotoEdit

of self-determination, the peoples they aim to control identify themselves as distinct nations and refuse to recognize the legitimacy of what they regard as a foreign government.

Thus in many a former colony, large numbers of people have taken up arms to resist annexation and absorption by imposed state governments run by people of other nationalities. As they attempt to make their multi-ethnic states into unified countries, ruling elites of one nationality set about stripping the peoples of other nations within their states of their lands, resources, and particular cultural identities. The phenomenon is so common that Belgian sociologist Pierre van den Berghe has renamed what modern states refer to as "nation building" as, in fact, "nation killing."[12]

One of the most important facts of our time is that the vast majority of the distinct peoples of the world have never consented to rule by the governments of states within which they find themselves living.[13] In many newly emerging countries, such peoples feel they have no other option than to take up weapons in armed protest and fight.

Apart from rebellions against authoritarian regimes, such as in the Chinese, French, and Russian revolutions, many revolutions in modern times have been insurgencies against political rule imposed by foreign powers. Such resistance usually takes the form of national independence movements that wage campaigns of armed defiance against colonial or imperial dominance. The Mexican war of liberation against Spain in the early 1800s and the Algerian struggle for independence from France in the 1950s are relevant examples.

Of the hundreds of armed conflicts in the world today, almost all are in the economically poor countries of Africa, Asia, and Latin America, many of which were at one time under European colonial domination. Of these wars, the majority are between the state and one or more nations or ethnic groups within the state's borders. These groups are seeking to maintain or regain control of their personal lives, communities, lands, and resources in the face of what they regard as repression or subjugation by a foreign power.[14]

Revolutions do not always accomplish what they set out to do. One of the stated goals of the 1949 Chinese communist revolution, for example, was to liberate women from the oppression of a strongly patriarchal society in which a woman owed lifelong obedience to some male relative—first her father, later her husband, and, after his death, her oldest son. Although changes were and continue to be made, the transformation overall has been frustrated by the cultural lens through which the revolutionaries viewed their work. A tradition of deeply rooted patriarchy extending back at least 2,200 years is not easily overcome and has influenced many of the decisions made by communist China's leaders since the revolution.

Despite the current rapid changes taking place in China today, in many rural parts of the country a woman's life is still largely determined by her relationship to a man—be it her father, husband, or son—rather than by

[12] van den Berghe, P. (1992). The modern state: Nation builder or nation killer? *International Journal of Group Tensions 22* (3), 191–207.

[13] Nietschmann, B. (1987). The third world war. *Cultural Survival Quarterly 11* (3), 3.

[14] Ibid.

her own efforts or failures. Moreover, many rural women face official local policies that identify their primary roles as wives and mothers. When they do work outside the house, it is generally at jobs with low pay, low status, and no benefits. Indeed, the 1990s saw a major outbreak of the abduction and sale of women from rural areas as brides and workers. Women's no-wage home labor (and low-wage outside labor) for their husbands' households have been essential to China's economic expansion, which relies on the allocation of labor by the heads of patrilineal households.[15]

This situation shows that the undermining of revolutionary goals, if it occurs, is not necessarily by political opponents. Rather, it may be a consequence of the revolutionaries' own traditional cultural background. In rural China, as long as women marry out and their labor is controlled by male heads of families, women will be seen as commodities.

It should be understood that revolution is a relatively recent phenomenon, occurring only during the past 5,000 years or so. The reason is that political rebellion requires a centralized political authority to rebel against, and states did not exist before 5,000 years ago. Obviously, then, in kin-ordered societies organized as tribes and bands, without a centralized government, there could be no rebellion or political revolution.

Modernization

One of the most frequently used terms to describe social and cultural changes as they are occurring today is **modernization.** This is most clearly defined as an all-encompassing and global process of political and socioeconomic change, whereby developing societies acquire some of the cultural characteristics common to Western industrial societies.

Derived from the Latin word *modo* ("just now"), modernization literally refers to something "in the present time." The dominant idea behind this concept is that "becoming modern" is becoming like European, North American, and other wealthy industrial or postindustrial societies, with the very clear implication that not to do so is to be stuck in the past—backward, inferior, and needing to be improved. It is unfortunate that the term modernization continues to be so widely used. Since we seem to be stuck with it, the best we can do at the moment is to recognize its problematic one-sidedness, even as we continue to use it.

The process of modernization may be best understood as consisting of five subprocesses, all interrelated with no fixed order of appearance:

- *Technological development:* In the course of modernization, traditional knowledge and techniques give way to the application of scientific knowledge and techniques borrowed mainly from the industrialized West.
- *Agricultural development:* This is represented by a shift in emphasis from subsistence farming to commercial farming. Instead of raising crops and livestock for their own use, people turn with growing frequency to the production of cash crops, with increased reliance on a cash economy and on global markets for selling farm products and purchasing goods.
- *Urbanization:* This subprocess is marked particularly by population movements from rural settlements into cities.
- *Industrialization:* Here human and animal power become less important, and greater emphasis is placed on material forms of energy—especially fossil fuels—to drive machines.
- *Telecommunication:* The fifth and most recent subprocess involves electronic and digital media processing and sharing of news, commodity prices, fashions, and entertainment, as well as political and religious opinions. Information is widely dispersed to a mass audience, far across national borders.

As modernization proceeds, other changes are likely to follow. In the political realm, political parties and some sort of electoral apparatus frequently appear, along with the development of an administrative bureaucracy. In formal education, institutional learning opportunities expand, literacy increases, and an indigenous educated elite develops. Formalized religion becomes less important in many areas of thought and behavior, as traditional beliefs and practices are undermined. Many long-held rights and duties connected with kinship are altered, if not eliminated, especially where distant relatives are concerned. Finally, where social stratification is a factor, social mobility increases as ascribed status becomes less important and personal achievement counts for more.

Self-Determination

A closer examination of traditional cultures that have felt the impact of modernization or other cultural changes will help to illustrate some of the problems such cultures have met. We will focus here on the Shuar Indians of Ecuador

[15] Gates, H. (1996). Buying brides in China—again. *Anthropology Today 12* (4), 10.

modernization The process of political and socioeconomic change, whereby developing societies acquire some of the cultural characteristics of Western industrial societies.

and the Skolt Lapps, one of several groups of Saami people living in the Arctic and sub-Arctic tundra of northwest Russia and Scandinavia.

SAAMI HERDERS: THE SNOWMOBILE REVOLUTION AND ITS UNINTENDED CONSEQUENCES

In the 1960s Saami reindeer herders in Scandinavia eagerly adopted snowmobiles, expecting that the new technology would make herding physically easier and economically more advantageous. The choice to modernize was essentially theirs, but in Finland it backfired. As snowmobile technology replaced traditional skills, the ability of the Saami (historically also known as Lapps) to creatively survive on their own diminished, and their dependency on the outside world grew.

Given the high cost of buying, maintaining, and fueling the machines, they faced a sharp rise in their need for money. To obtain cash, men began going outside their communities for wage labor more than just occasionally, as had previously been the case.

One might argue that dependency on the larger economy and the need for cash are prices worth paying for an improved system of reindeer herding. However, snowmobiles contributed in a significant way to a disastrous decline in reindeer herding in some Saami communities, such as among the Skolt Lapps of northern Finland. Traditionally Skolt men tended the animals, moving about on wooden skis and associating closely with the herds—intensively from November to January and periodically from January to April. But once snowmobiles were introduced, the familiar, prolonged, and largely peaceful relationship between herder and beast changed into a noisy, traumatic one. The humans that reindeer encountered came speeding out of the woods on noisy, smelly machines that invariably chased the animals, often for long distances. Instead of helping the reindeer in their winter food quest, aiding does with their calves, and protecting the herd from predators, men appeared periodically, either to slaughter or to castrate the animals.

The reindeer became wary of people, resulting in de-domestication, with reindeer scattering and running off

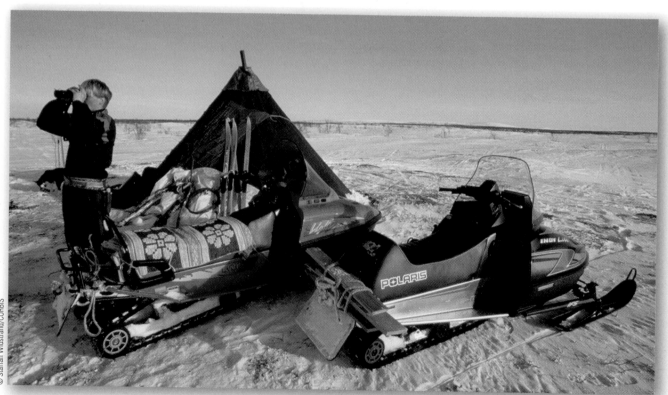

© Staffan Widstrand/CORBIS

In the 1960s, Saami reindeer herders in Scandinavia's Arctic tundra adopted newly invented snowmobiles, convinced that these modern machines would make traditional herding physically easier and economically more advantageous. Here a young Saami man stands beside his tent and snowmobile, searching for his reindeer with binoculars.

to less accessible areas. In addition, snowmobile harassment seemed to adversely affect birthing and the survival of calves. Within a decade the average size of the family herd among the Skolts had dropped from fifty to twelve—a number that is not economically viable.

This is a classic illustration that change, even when initiated by a community on its own volition, is not always advantageous. The financial cost of mechanized herding and the decline in domesticated herd size have led many to abandon herding altogether. Now, the majority of men are no longer herders at all. This constitutes a serious economic problem, since few local subsistence alternatives are available.[16]

SHUAR INDIANS AND CATTLE IN THE AMAZON: A SUCCESSFUL EXPERIMENT IN CONTROLLED ADAPTATION

In contrast to the Saami in northern Europe, the Shuar Indians of Ecuador's tropical forest deliberately avoided modernization until they felt that they had no other option, having seen whole societies destroyed elsewhere in the Amazon basin. Traditionally organized in small autonomous groups that engaged in constant feuding, the Shuar (historically better known as Jivaro) survived on a mixed subsistence strategy of foraging and gardening. In 1964, threatened with the loss of their land base as more and more Ecuadoran colonists intruded into their territory, leaders from the many, widely scattered Shuar communities came together and founded a fully independent ethnic organization—the Shuar Federation—to take control over their own future.

Recognized by Ecuador's government, albeit reluctantly, the federation is officially dedicated to promotion of the social, economic, and moral advancement of the growing Shuar population and to coordinating development with official government agencies. Since its founding, the federation has secured title to more than 96,000 hectares of communal land; established a cattle herd of more than 15,000 head as the people's primary source of income; taken control of their own education, using their own language and mostly Shuar teachers; and established their own bilingual radio station and a bilingual newspaper.

Obviously, all of this has transformed daily life among the Shuar, but they have been able to maintain a variety of distinctive cultural markers, including their language, communal land tenure, cooperative production and distribution, a basically egalitarian economy, and kin-based communities that retain maximum autonomy. For all the changes, they feel they are still Shuar and distinct from other Ecuadorans.[17]

The Shuar case shows that indigenous peoples are capable of taking control of their own destinies even in the face of intense outside pressures, *if* allowed to do so. Unfortunately, until recently, few have had that option. Prior to European invasions of the Amazon rainforest, more than 700 distinct ethnic groups inhabited this vast region. By 1900 in Brazil, the number was down to 270, and today something like 180 remain.[18] Many of these survivors find themselves in situations not unlike that of the Yanomami, described earlier in this chapter. Nevertheless, some are showing resourcefulness in resisting the outside forces of destruction arrayed against them. Some receive help from anthropologists, as discussed in the Anthropology Applied feature on the next page.

Globalization in the "Underdeveloped" World

Throughout the so-called underdeveloped world, in Africa, Asia, Latin America, and elsewhere, whole countries are in the throes of radical political and economic change and overall cultural transformation. In fact, inventions and major advances in industrial production, mass transportation, and communication and information technologies are transforming societies in Europe and North America as well. As discussed in Chapter 1, this worldwide process of accelerated modernization in which all parts of the earth are becoming interconnected in one vast interrelated and all-encompassing system is known as *globalization,* evidenced in global movements of natural resources, trade goods, human labor, finance capital, information, and infectious diseases.

All around the globe we are witnessing the removal of economic activities—or at least their control—from the family and community setting. And we are seeing the altered structure of the family in the face of the changing labor market: young children relying increasingly on parents alone for affection, instead of on the extended family; parental authority generally declining; schools replacing the family as the primary educational unit; old people spending their last days in nursing homes rather than with family members; and many other changes.

In many societies, this modernization process is now happening very fast, often without the necessary time to adjust. Changes that took generations to accomplish in Europe and North America are attempted within the span

[16] Pelto, P. J. (1973). *The snowmobile revolution: Technology and social change in the Arctic.* Menlo Park, CA: Cummings.

[17] Bodley, J. H. (1990). *Victims of progress* (3rd ed., pp. 160–162). Mountain View, CA: Mayfield.

[18] *Cultural Survival Quarterly.* (1991). *15* (4), 38.

Development Anthropology and Dams

Over a 35-year career in scholarly and applied work, Michael M. Horowitz, president and executive director of the Institute for Development Anthropology (IDA) and distinguished professor of anthropology at the State University of New York at Binghamton, has made pioneering contributions to applied anthropology. His work has focused on achieving equitable economic growth, environmental sustainability, conflict resolution, and participatory government in the former colonial world.

Since co-founding IDA in 1976, Horowitz has been its principal leader. He has played a key role in bringing anthropology forward as an applied science in international development organizations such as the World Bank, the United Nations Fund for Women, and the U.S. Agency for International Development (USAID), as well as nongovernmental organizations (NGOs) such as Oxfam and the International Union for the Conservation of Nature. He has mentored several generations of young scholars and professionals—paying particular attention to those from developing countries—encouraging the application of anthropology's comparative and holistic methodologies and theories to empower low-income majorities in the so-called underdeveloped world.

Horowitz's work with pastoralists and floodplain dwellers has had substantial positive impact on the well-being of small producers and landholders in developing countries. A clear example of this is the impact of his work on the lives and livelihoods of people living downstream of a hydropower dam in West Africa. Beginning in the 1980s, he and his IDA team carried out rigorous anthropological research along the Senegal River, which flows through Mali, Senegal, and Mauritania. Their study showed that traditional, pre-dam, flood-recession farming yielded better results than irrigated agriculture and was better for the environment.

This finding influenced decisions made by these countries and affiliated NGOs to manage the system with a controlled release from the Manatali Dam in Mali in order to reproduce as nearly as possible the pre-dam flow system. Horowitz's long-term field research demonstrated that seasonal flooding would provide economic, environmental, and sociocultural benefits for nearly a million small producers.

Recognized by national governments, NGOs, and development funding agencies, the work of Horowitz and his IDA colleagues on the Senegal River Basin Monitoring Activity (SRBMA) was a breakthrough in the concepts of resettlement and river management, and it continues to influence development policy. Prior to IDA's work in West Africa, no hydropower dam had ever been managed with a controlled flood. Since then, IDA has been asked to help apply the SRMBA model to other parts of the world, including the lower Zambezi River in Mozambique and the Mekong River in Laos, Cambodia, and Vietnam.

Visible from space, China's Three Gorges hydroelectric dam is the world's biggest and most powerful hydroelectric dam. About 2,300 meters (7,700 feet) long and 185 meters (330 feet) high, it controls the Yangtze, the world's third largest river. After fifteen years of construction with a price tag of $22 billion, it became operational in 2009. The dam was built to provide a clean energy alternative to coal and to control flooding along the Yangtze River. However, it has been controversial since its inception, flooding ancient archaeological and cultural sites, displacing more than 1.4 million people, and causing significant ecological changes, including risks of landslides that threaten some 4 million people. Unlike the dam described in this Anthropology Applied feature, not one social scientist was consulted in the planning and assessment phase of Three Gorges Dam.

Adapted from Young, W. (Ed.). (2000). Kimball Award winner. Anthropology News 41(8), 29, with update based on personal communication with IDA, November 2003.

of a single generation in developing countries. In the process cultures frequently face unforeseen disruptions and a rapid erosion of dearly held values they had no intention of giving up. Anthropologists doing fieldwork in distant communities throughout the world witness how these traditional cultures have been impacted, and often destroyed, by powerful global forces.

Commonly, the burden of modernization falls most heavily on women. For example, the commercialization of agriculture often involves land reforms that overlook or ignore women's traditional land rights. This reduces their control of and access to resources at the same time that mechanization of food production and processing drastically reduces their opportunities for employment. As a consequence, women are confined more and more to traditional domestic tasks, which are increasingly devalued as commercial production becomes the dominant concern.

Moreover, the domestic workload tends to increase, because men are less available to help out, while tasks such as fuel gathering and water collection are made more difficult as common land and resources come to be privately owned and as woodlands are reserved for commercial exploitation. As well, the growing of nonfood crops—such as cotton and sisal or luxury crops such as tea, coffee, and cacao (source of chocolate)—for the world market makes households vulnerable to wide price fluctuations. As a result, people cannot afford the high-quality diet that subsistence farming provided,

and they become malnourished. In short, with modernization, women frequently find themselves in an increasingly inferior position. As their workload increases, the value assigned to the work they do declines, as does their relative educational status, not to mention their health and nutrition.

Globalization: Must It Be Painful?

Most anthropologists see the radical changes that affect traditional non-Western peoples caught up in the modern technological world as an ordeal. Yet, the more common attitude in the industrial West has been that modernization is both inevitable and good—that however disagreeable the "medicine" may be, it is worth it for the "backward" people to become just like people in the West. (For a serious look at the consequences of these changes, see the Biocultural Connection.)

Biocultural Connection

Studying the Emergence of New Diseases

Since the Neolithic, humans have had to cope with a host of new diseases that began as a consequence of changes in human behavior. Recently, this has become a renewed source of concern following the resurgence of infectious diseases and the spread of a host of new and lethal diseases.[a]

All told, more than thirty diseases new to medicine have emerged in the past thirty years. Perhaps the best known of these is AIDS, which has become a top killer among infectious diseases. Since 1981, more than 25 million people have died of AIDS, and today some 33 million people around the world are living with AIDS/HIV.[b] But there are others—like Ebola hemorrhagic fever, which causes victims to bleed to death; other hemorrhagic fevers like dengue fever, Lassa fever, and hantavirus; invasive streptococcus A, which consumes the victims' flesh; Legionnaire's disease; and Lyme disease.

What has sparked the appearance and spread of these new diseases remains a mystery, but one theory is that some are the result of human activities. In particular, the intrusion of people into new ecological settings, such as rainforests, along with construction of roads and worldwide shipping and airplane traffic, allows viruses and other infectious microbes to spread rapidly to large numbers of people. It is now generally accepted that the HIV virus responsible for AIDS transferred to humans from chimpanzees in the tropical forests of the Democratic Republic of Congo as a

consequence of hunting and butchering these animals for food. For the first thirty years, few people were affected; it was not until people began congregating in quickly growing cities like Kinshasa that conditions were ripe for an epidemic.

In recognition of her research to gain a better understanding of the interplay between ecological disturbance and the emergence of new diseases, medical anthropologist Carol Jenkins received a MacArthur Foundation grant in 1993. From her base at the Papua New Guinea Institute of Medical Research, she has been tracking the health of local people in the wake of a massive logging operation, work that provides insights on questions such as how disease organisms spread from animal hosts to humans.

Since most of the "new" viruses that have suddenly afflicted humans are in fact old ones that have been present in animals like monkeys (monkey pox), rodents (hantavirus), deer (Lyme disease), and insects (West Nile virus), it appears that something new has enabled them to jump from their animal hosts to humans.

A recent example comes from Congo. Here civil war created a situation where villagers in the central part of the country were faced with starvation. Their response was to increase the hunting of animals, including monkeys, squirrels, and rats that carry a disease called monkey pox. Related to smallpox, the disease transfers easily to humans, resulting in the largest outbreak of this disease ever seen among humans. What

makes this outbreak even more serious is an apparently new strain of the infection, enabling it to spread from person to person, instead of only from an animal host.[c]

Large-scale habitat disturbance is an obvious candidate for such disease transfers. So far, however, it is hard to make more than a circumstantial case by looking back after a disease outbreak. The work of Jenkins and her team is unique in that she was able to get baseline health data on local people before their environment was disturbed. Thus she is in a position to follow events as they unfold.

It will be some time before conclusions can be drawn from Jenkins's study. Its importance is obvious; in an era of globalization, as air travel allows diseases to spread worldwide, we need a fuller understanding of how pathogens interact with their hosts if we are to devise effective preventive and therapeutic strategies to deal with them.

BIOCULTURAL QUESTION

Since some new viruses and bacteria are fast-spreading and lethal, what do you think of government-funded research and development of killer diseases for purposes of biological warfare?

---

[a]Gibbons, A. (1993). Where are new diseases born? *Science 261*, 680–681.

[b]See www.avert.org/worldstats.htm.

[c]Cohen, J. (1997). Is an old virus up to new tricks? *Science 277*, 312–313.

This Western view has little to do with the cold political and economic realities of the contemporary world. It overlooks the stark fact that the standard of middle- and upper-class living throughout the industrialized world (and increasingly in metropolitan areas worldwide) is based on a rate of consumption of nonrenewable resources whereby a small fraction of the world's population uses the vast majority of these precious resources. The imbalance continues, suggesting that it is impossible for most peoples of the world to achieve a material standard of living at all comparable to the majority of people in wealthy countries in the near future. At the very least, the peoples of the industrial and postindustrial parts of the world would have to cut drastically their unrelenting and often wasteful consumption of resources. So far, few have shown a willingness to seriously adjust their standard of living in order to do this.

In large part due to the influence of global media, along with mass tourism, countless people around the world today have been led to aspire to a material standard of living like that commonly enjoyed by people in industrialized and postindustrialized countries, even as the gap between rich and poor continues to widen among and within countries. Every year, many millions of people slide below the poverty level.[19] This has led to what has been called a "culture of discontent" in which aspirations far exceed the bounds of local opportunities.

No longer satisfied with traditional values and often unable to sustain themselves in the rural backlands, people all over the world are moving to the large cities to find a better life. All too often they live out their days in poor, congested, and diseased slums while attempting to achieve what is usually beyond their reach. Unfortunately, despite rosy predictions about a better future, hundreds of millions of people in our world remain trapped in a wretched reality, struggling against poverty, hunger, poor health, and other dangers. In the next and final chapter of this book, we further explore the underlying structures and deeper causes of these problems and look at the role anthropology can and does play in helping to meet these challenges.

---

[19] Paul Magnarella, cited in Kurth, P. (1998, October 14). Capitol crimes. *Seven Days*, 7.

Questions for Reflection

1. Globalization radically challenges most of us to adjust at an ever-faster pace within increasingly complex transnational settings. Do you feel that these changes are good for everyone? As exemplified by Bahrain, described in the chapter opener, which groups benefit the most, and which the least, from globalization?

2. Taking a close look at your clothing and your meals today, can you identify the places of geographic origin of any of the raw materials in what you wear and consume?

3. On a regular basis, the news media are reporting about violent uprisings or rebellion and armed conflicts that result in death and destruction. Why do you think many people feel the need to fight?

4. When societies become involved in the modernizing process, all levels of their cultural systems are affected by these changes. Do you think that people are fully aware of the long-term consequences of the changes they themselves may have welcomed? Can you come up with any examples of unforeseen changes in your own community or neighborhood?

5. In many Muslim countries, orthodox religious groups oppose modern developments that they associate with moral corruption and seek to maintain or return to a way of life more strictly based on Islamic traditions. Do you know Christian or Jewish fundamentalist groups having similar conservative values and ideals? What would be the future of your own family or community if a religious fundamentalist group became large enough to gain political power and rule the country?

Suggested Readings

Bodley, J. H. (2008). *Victims of progress* (5th ed.). Lanham, MD: Alta Mira.

In this compelling account of the effect of technology and development on "victims of progress," the author reviews major issues, including health and disease, oil development, global warming, and ecocide. He also discusses the political struggle for self-determination by indigenous peoples.

Inda, J. X., & Renato, R. (Eds.). (2001). *The anthropology of globalization: A reader.* Malden, MA, and Oxford: Blackwell.

This wide-ranging reader focuses simultaneously on the large-scale processes through which various cultures are increasingly interconnected and on the ways that people around the world—from Africa and Asia to the Caribbean and North America—mediate these processes in culturally specific ways.

Maybury-Lewis, D. (2001). *Indigenous peoples, ethnic groups, and the state* (2nd ed.). Boston: Allyn & Bacon.

The author, who founded the organization Cultural Survival, summarizes modernization's effect on "tribalism and ethnic parochialism." Revealing the peculiar situation of indigenous peoples as ethnic minorities alien to the states in which they live, he describes the worldwide proliferation of ethnic conflicts and the growing demand for indigenous rights. The book stands on its own, while serving as introduction to a series of individual ethnographies on indigenous peoples and their struggles.

Prins, H.E.L. (1996). *The Mi'kmaq: Resistance, accommodation, and cultural survival.* Belmont, CA: Wadsworth.

This content-rich case study spans 500 years of history, chronicling the endurance of a tribal nation—its ordeals in the face of colonialism, and its current struggle for self-determination and cultural revitalization. Rare for its multi-vocality.

Spindler, G., & Stockard, J. E. (Eds.). (2006). *Globalization and change in fifteen cultures.* Belmont, CA: Wadsworth.

This collection of original articles reflects a world changed by globalization and an anthropology committed to documenting the effects of the vast cultural flows of people, information, goods, and technology. Spindler and Stockard's introduction frames the topic of cultural change, and the fifteen anthropologists in the anthology take readers on a return visit to their original field sites, asking questions for a new era and writing of peoples familiar to them yet transformed by global forces.

Stannard, D. E. (1992). *American holocaust.* Oxford, England: Oxford University Press.

Stannard deals with 500 years of cultural change in the Americas arising from contact between European and Native cultures. In doing so, he focuses on genocide, relates it to the Holocaust of World War II, and demonstrates how deeply rooted the phenomenon is in Western culture and Christianity.

Andreas Valentin/LatinContent/Getty Images

Challenge Issue   For at least 10,000 years humans have met the challenges of survival not only by adapting to their natural environment but by transforming it to fit their needs. They have turned deserts, forests, swamps, and mountainsides into pastures, farmlands, and industrial centers, creating new survival opportunities (and often some unanticipated new challenges) for an ever-growing population. In the course of history thousands of cities have been built, and during the past half century the world's urban population has more than tripled, rising from 750 million to 2.9 billion. In 2000 there were nearly 400 cities in the world with 1 million or more residents. Urban areas are gaining about 67 million people per year—about 1.3 million every week. As the global population grows, the number of big cities will grow substantially, with the majority located in coastal areas of developing countries. One of the world's largest and most violent cities is Rio de Janeiro, a metropolitan area in coastal Brazil. Almost half of its multi-ethnic population of 14 million is poor, living in crowded slums and shantytowns with unsanitary conditions and inadequate health care. Remarkably, even in the face of hardship, humans find ways to celebrate. In Rio, citizens from all walks of life participate in the annual carnival, forgetting the challenges of survival during a few days of abundant feasting and revelry before Lent. With the motto "Everyone is free," hundreds of thousands of people, citizens and tourists alike, sing and dance around multicolored parade floats, carried away by Afro-Brazilian drumming and music and briefly enjoying a happy feeling of community.

CHAPTER 27

Global Challenges, Local Responses, and the Role of Anthropology

Chapter Preview

What Can Anthropologists Tell Us of the Future?

Although anthropologists cannot entirely predict future cultural forms, they can identify patterns and trends and foresee some of their consequences if they continue. Moreover, they can shed light on already identified problems by showing how they relate to each other and to cultural features and structures that may not be obvious to experts in other disciplines. This ability to systematically consider cultural facts and their underlying structures in a wider context and from a comparative perspective is a recognized anthropological specialty.

What Are the Cultural Trends in Today's World?

One major cultural trend is globalization, including worldwide adoption of the products, technologies, ideas, and cultural practices of powerful Western countries. This move toward a homogenized, global culture is countered by an opposite trend of ethnic and religious groups all over the world reasserting their distinctive cultural identities and emphasizing their unique historical traditions. A third trend is the growing concern that rising populations, spiraling energy use, and expanding consumption are devastating our natural resources, overwhelming us with waste, and poisoning our environment.

What Problems Must Be Solved for Humans to Have a Viable Future?

Creative, effective, and responsible solutions need to be found to deal with a host of serious problems posed by vanishing natural resources, environmental destruction, ever-more powerful technologies, and unequal distribution of wealth. Today's huge demographic shifts are also problematic—explosive population growth in many poorer parts of the world, lowering birth rates leading to population decline in some of the wealthiest countries, and movements of individuals or entire families escaping poverty or violence in their homelands. Many people fail to recognize that most of the problems facing us are interconnected. Anthropology provides us with a critical and realistic understanding of the emergence of a global cultural system and its radical impact on local communities. Its cross-cultural and historically informed perspective is essential for solving problems and ensuring a future in which all peoples enjoy basic human rights.

Anthropology is superficially described by those who know little about it as an exotic discipline interested mainly in what happened long ago and far away. The most common popular stereotype is that anthropologists devote all of their attention to digging up the past and describing the last surviving tribal peoples with traditional ways of life. Yet, as noted throughout this book, anthropologists also investigate the ways and workings of industrial and postindustrial societies. Indeed, anthropologists are interested in the entire range of human cultures past and present—in their similarities and differences and in the multiple ways they influence one another.

In this era, marked by rapid and radical change all around the world, many anthropologists wonder what today's globalizing processes will create and what will be transformed, disrupted, or damaged beyond repair. When traditional communities are exposed to intense contact with more powerful groups, their cultures may change with unprecedented speed, often for the worse, becoming disintegrated and less supportive. Since globalization seems unstoppable, we are compelled to ask: How can the thousands of different societies, having existed for centuries if not millennia, maintain their distinctive cultural identities and deal successfully with the multiple challenges hurled at them?

The Future of Humanity

To comprehend anthropology's role in understanding and solving problems in times to come, we must look at flaws frequently seen in publications and planning efforts focused on the future, especially in the 21st century. First of all, given the current speed and complexity of worldwide changes, it is nearly impossible to predict and plan for more than about fifty years ahead. Even that time span is tricky since projections of future trends are usually based on recent historical trajectories and cannot factor in all the possible inventions or events (including catastrophes) that determine the course of human history. While we must try to anticipate and plan for future needs and challenges, long-term predictions are bound to be problematic. As one anthropologist quipped: "It is worth recalling the story of the person who leaped from a very tall building and on being asked how things were going as he passed the 20th floor replied 'Fine, so far.' "[1]

A second flaw typical in futurist projections is a tendency to treat subjects in isolation, without reference to pertinent trends outside an expert's field of competence. For example,

agricultural planning is often based on the assumption that a certain amount of water is available for irrigation, whether or not urban planners or others have designs upon that same water. Thus people may be counting on natural resources in the future that will not, in fact, be available.

This brings us to a third flaw common among futurists: The tendency to project the hopes and expectations of one's own group or culture into the future interferes with the scientific objectivity necessary to see and address emerging problems. A recent example is the war in Iraq, where the goals of the official U.S. and British planners blinded them to the complex problems that would emerge.

Against this background, anthropology's contribution to our understanding of the future is clear. Anthropologists bring a perspective that is not only long term, but also holistic, integrative, and comparative. With more than a hundred years of cross-cultural research behind them—based on ancient archaeological finds, linguistic information, biological data, as well as participant observation within living cultures—anthropologists have a comprehensive view on short-term trends and recognize culture-bound assertions when they encounter them. Moreover, they are familiar with alternative ways of dealing with a wide variety of problems.

A Global, Transnational Culture?

Despite vast geographic distance, human populations have always interacted. The interaction intensified about 500 years ago, when the first sailing ship successfully circumnavigated the entire globe—an almost three-year journey that was completed in 1522, but at great cost. Four of the five Spanish ships perished, as did most of the crew, as well as the seafarer Ferdinand Magellan who led this epic voyage of discovery.

Since then, peoples inhabiting every far-flung corner of the world have come in contact with one another, directly or indirectly. Many benefited from the new opportunities and prospered, enjoying the new commodities, such as sugar, spices, tobacco, silk, and other exotic luxuries. Millions, however, died in terrible epidemics or brutal warfare. Millions more were forced into slave labor or lost their independence and self-determination under colonial rule.

About two centuries ago, the invention of steam engines and other machinery brought about the industrial revolution, with large-scale factory production and an expanding transportation network of steam-powered trains and ships. Modern mass transportation, along with recent revolutions in telecommunication technology—from print media to telegraph and telephone to radio, television, satellites, and the Internet—makes it possible to exchange more information with more people faster and over greater distances. Obviously, this global flow of

---

[1] Cowgill, G. L. (1980). Letter. *Science 210*, 1305.

Reuters/China Photo

When McDonald's was first introduced to Hong Kong in 1975, the Chinese name for this fast-food restaurant was *Mai-Dang-Nu*, chosen to phonetically approximate the English brand name. However, since this translates "wheat-becomes-slaves," the U.S.-based global corporation altered it slightly to *Mai-Dang-Lao* when opening franchises in Taiwan and mainland China. This also caused confusion as it means "wheat-becomes-work." By 2009, McDonald's had more than 2,000 restaurants in China and plans to launch hundreds more in the next few years. Many people see the worldwide spread of giants like McDonald's, Kentucky Fried Chicken, Pepsi, and Coca-Cola as a sign of a homogeneous global culture.

humans, their products, and their ideas plays a major role in culture change.

A popular belief since the mid-1900s has been that humanity's future will feature a single homogenous global culture. This idea is based largely on the observation that technological developments in communication, transportation, and trade are causing peoples of the world to increasingly watch the same television programs, read the same newspapers, eat the same foods, wear the same types of clothes, and communicate via satellites and the Internet.

The continuation of such trends, so this thinking goes, would mean that North Americans who travel a hundred years from now to Botswana, Colombia, or Denmark would find the local inhabitants living in a manner identical or similar to theirs. Yet, as we look at ethnic conflicts around the world, this forecast seems unlikely.

Certainly it is striking—the extent to which such items as Western-style fast food, soft drinks, clothing, music, and movies have spread to virtually all parts of the world. Daily serving nearly 50 million customers in 31,000 restaurants in almost 120 countries, the U.S.-based global corporation McDonald's operates the world's largest fast-food chain. Famous for its "Big Mac" hamburger, it has become emblematic of the homogenizing of the world's different cultures in the age of globalization, sometimes referred to as the "McDonaldization" of societies.[2] And

many countries—Costa Rica or Japan, for example—appear to have gone a long way toward becoming Westernized. Moreover, looking at the past 5,000 years of human history, we see that political units have tended to become larger, more all-encompassing, and fewer in number. The logical outcome of this trend would be a further reduction of autonomous political units into a single one taking in the entire globe.

However, anthropologists call attention to something that all large states throughout time have had in common: a tendency to come apart. Not only have the great empires of the past, without exception, broken up into numbers of smaller independent states, but states in virtually all parts of the world today show this same tendency to fragment, usually along major geographic and ethnic divisions.

The threat of political collapse is ever-present in multi-ethnic states, especially when these countries are large, difficult to travel in, and lack unifying cultural features such as a common national language. Such has been the case, for instance, with Afghanistan. This vast, mountainous country is inhabited by several major ethnic groups, including Pashtun who live mainly in the south, and Tajik, Uzbek, Hazara, and Turkmen who live mainly in the north. Although the Pashtun are greatest in number and most dominant in the past 200 years, they have never been able to successfully impose their political will on the other ethnic groups who maintain a great deal of independence. Nor have they succeeded in making their own native tongue, Pashto, the country's national language.

The tendency of multi-ethnic states to break apart has been especially noteworthy since the end of the Cold War between the United States and the former Soviet Union

---

[2] Referring to the "process by which institutions in society become standardized and focused on efficiency and predictability," this term was first coined by George Ritzer in his 1983 article "The McDonaldization of Society," *Journal of American Culture* 6 (1), 100–107. Since the 1990s, this term has also been used by antiglobalization activists seeking to safeguard their traditional cultures against the onslaught of modernization.

after the fall of the Berlin Wall in 1989. For example, 1991 saw the dramatic breakup of the Soviet Union into about a dozen independent republics—Russia, Armenia, Belarus, Estonia, Ukraine, and Georgia, among others. In 2008, about seventeen years after Georgia gained its own independence as an internationally recognized state, this multi-ethnic republic diminished in size when two of its ethnically distinct regions, South Ossetia and Abkhazia, officially split after years of separatist pressure. Declaring independence, Abkhazia and South Ossetia both seek international recognition as small sovereign republics. While Russia and a few allies now recognize both mini republics as independent states, most other UN member countries do not.

The splintering tendency of multi-ethnic states can also be seen in separatist movements such as that of French-speaking peoples in Canada, Basques in Spain, Tibetans in China, Karen in Myanmar (Burma), Kurds in Turkey and Iraq, and so on—this list is far from exhaustive. Nor is the United States immune, as can be seen in Native American nations seeking to secure greater political self-determination on their reservations. We may have reached the point where the tendency for political units to grow in size while decreasing in number is being canceled out by their tendency to fragment into a greater number of smaller ones.

Despite these examples, there are also a few instances of reunification. Best known among these is the 1990 reunification of Germany, divided since the end of World War II as East and West Germany, into one large federal republic. Another notable exception is the recent integration of twenty-seven European countries into the European Union—however hindered by linguistic differences, distinctive cultural traditions, and bureaucratic red tape.

Also, many global integrative mechanisms have been developed to counteract the centrifugal forces at work. These include international sporting events from Wimbledon to the Olympics, plus organizations ranging from UNESCO to Rotary Clubs, Boy Scouts, and Girl Guides, as well as humanitarian aid organizations such as Doctors Without Borders and Save the Children. Notably, while such mechanisms connect people all around the world, they do not represent a global transnational culture.

The Problem of a Global Culture

The idea of a shared global culture may have a degree of popular appeal in certain circles. A common language, for instance, would greatly facilitate international exchange, and a shared ideology (with everyone having similar political ideals and religious beliefs) might lessen cross-cultural misunderstandings and conflicting viewpoints that have led so often to violence over the past several hundred years.

However, anthropologists greet this prognosis with skepticism, suspecting that distinctive worldviews will persist, even in the face of massive changes. Moreover, new worldviews are emerging, and those that are changing are not necessarily changing in the same fashion. In fact, given the intensified interactions among people in the world today, especially where competing interests are involved, it is more likely that the potential for serious conflict is actually growing.

Although the forces of globalization impact almost every society, not all peoples react the same way to the changes on their doorstep. Those who are willing and

Olympic Games are unique among the many strands in today's global web. Inspired by the ancient Greek sporting event held at Olympia 2,000 years ago, the games have become a global spectacle, with thousands of athletes from all around the world competing in a different country every four years. In today's world—where powerful states have conquered and destroyed many smaller nations and tens of millions have been killed in warfare worldwide—this global sports gathering is a crucial ritual, celebrating international peace in a friendly rivalry for medals and prestige. Pictured here is the opening ceremony of the 2008 Olympics in China.

Paul Gilham/Getty Images

able to make the required adjustments may actually benefit from the transformation in their cultures, whereas others less well positioned for the changes may resist and/or have a deeply troubling experience. In short, globalization is a complex and dynamic process with a vast range of national, regional, and even local cultural reactions and adjustments.

Some have argued that perhaps a generalized world culture would be desirable in the future, because some traditional cultures may be too specialized to adjust to a changed environment. For instance, when Amazonian Indians pursuing traditional ways of life that are well adapted to South America's tropical rainforest are confronted with sudden, radical changes brought on by foreign invaders, their long-established cultures often collapse. The reason for this, it is argued, is that the forest-dwellers' traditions and political and social organizations are not adapted to modern ways and that they are naturally destined to give way to the new. The problem with this argument is that, far from being unable to adapt, such traditional peoples have been robbed repeatedly of the opportunity to work out their own adaptations according to their own priorities. Their demise is caused not by laws of nature but rather by the political and economic choices of powerful outside forces.

Pluralistic Societies and Multiculturalism

If a single homogenous global culture is not necessarily the wave of the future, what is? Some predict a world in which ethnic groups will become more nationalistic in response to globalization, each group stressing its unique cultural heritage and emphasizing differences with neighboring groups. But not all ethnic groups organize themselves politically as distinctive sovereign nations with their own independent state. In fact, it has been common for two or more neighboring ethnic groups or nations to draw together in a loose political union while maintaining their particular cultural identities. One complex example is Russia. Geographically the largest country in the world, it is a federation consisting of twenty-one autonomous republics. Representing territories of non-Russian ethnicity, such as Tatarstan and Yakutia, these republics may have their own national language.

However, because such *pluralistic societies* lack a common cultural identity and heritage, and often do not share the same language or religion, political relationships between them can be fraught with tension. When feelings of ethnonationalism are not far from the surface, political pressure may build up and result in separation and independence. For instance, over the past two decades Chechen nationalists have waged wars and insurgencies to split the republic of Chechnya (an area in the northern Caucasus Mountains primarily inhabited by Sunni Muslim Chechens) from the Russian Federation.

One way of curbing divisive pressures in pluralistic or multi-ethnic societies is the adoption of a public policy based on mutual respect and tolerance for cultural differences. Known as **multiculturalism,** such an official policy asserts the value of different cultures coexisting within a country and stresses the reciprocal responsibility of all citizens to accept the rights of others to freely express their views and values. In contrast to state policies in which a dominant ethnic group uses its power to impose its own culture as the national standard, forcing other groups within the same state to assimilate, multiculturalism involves a public policy for managing a society's cultural diversity. Examples of long-established multiculturalism may be seen in states such as Switzerland (where German-, French-, Italian-, and Romansh-speaking peoples coexist under the same government) and Canada (where French- and English-speaking Canadians as well as dozens of indigenous nations live side by side).

Although cultural pluralism is still more common than multiculturalism, several multi-ethnic countries have recently changed their official melting pot ideology and associated policies of assimilation. One example of a country that is moving toward multiculturalism is the United States, which now has over 120 different ethnic groups within its borders, in addition to hundreds of federally recognized American Indian groups. Another is Australia, now counting over a hundred ethnic groups and with eighty languages spoken within its territorial boundaries. Similar changes are also under way in many European countries where millions of foreign immigrants have settled during the past few decades. Such changes are not easy, however, and often engender protests along the way.

We cannot ignore the fact that what historically has been called "nation building" in all parts of the world almost always involves attempts to subordinate or even destroy the cultures of peoples whose nationalities differ from those in control of the government.[3] During the last two decades of the 20th century, states were borrowing more money to fight peoples within their own boundaries than for all other programs combined. Nearly all state debt in Africa and

---

[3] van den Berghe, P. (1992). The modern state: Nation builder or nation killer? *International Journal of Group Tensions* 22 (3), 194–198.

multiculturalism Public policy for managing cultural diversity in a multi-ethnic society, officially stressing mutual respect and tolerance for cultural differences within a country's borders.

John Moore/Getty Images

Although South Africa's apartheid regime was abolished in 1993 and that pluralistic country is no longer politically dominated by a white minority, social tensions between different ethnic groups remain. With few opportunities to earn money, many of the 8 million people living in Johannesburg's squalid townships and squatter camps are unemployed and impoverished, and they blame foreign immigrants for their misery. This *xenophobia* ("fear of strangers") has frequently turned violent, resulting in bloody assaults against foreigners, many of whom are from poor neighboring countries such as Zimbabwe and Mozambique. Dozens have been killed, hundreds cruelly beaten and butchered, and thousands forced to flee. But there is a counter voice: Here we see a demonstration of South Africans and immigrants protesting the brutal murder of forty foreign laborers in Johannesburg in 2008.

nearly half of all other debt in "underdeveloped" countries comes from the cost of weapons purchased by states to fight their own citizens.[4] The more divergent cultural traditions are, the more difficult it is to make pluralism work.

Pluralistic Societies and Ethnocentrism

A major obstacle to the successful functioning of a pluralistic society is the loyalty each ethnic group has toward its distinctive language and unique cultural traditions, from which its members derive psychological support and a firm social bond to their community. Such ethnic pride is often tied to ethnocentrism, the belief that the ways of one's own culture are the only proper ones. To overcome this cultural superiority complex, a pluralistic society may have to develop a common superstructure with an ideology that binds different peoples together in a collective identity and destiny.

As illustrated again and again in this book, ethnic pride and loyalty are often turned into an ethnocentric charter

for denigrating people with different cultural practices and exploiting them for the benefit of one's own group. Although this is not an inevitable result, when it does occur, unrest, hostility, and violence commonly ensue.[5] This is evident in a growing nationalist intolerance toward foreign laborers and recent immigrants in many parts of the world today, especially where economies are in decline and local populations become agitated about survival and security.

Transnational Cultural Flows in a Global Environment

Anthropologist Arjun Appadurai, born in India, has developed theoretical concepts to help us understand the complex and largely unpredictable processes currently rearranging human relations and restructuring cultural

---

[4] *Cultural Survival Quarterly* (1991). *15* (4), 38.

[5] Nieftagodien, N. (2008, June 18). Incoherent response to crisis. *The Star,* Johannesburg. http://web.wits.ac.za/NewsRoom/NewsItems/Noor+Nieftag odien+xenophobia+opinion.htm

systems worldwide. Although most people in today's world still function within geographically defined communities, Appadurai points out that territorial borders have become increasingly irrelevant given the "cultural flows" in our emerging global environment. He marks out five global spaces or dimensions in which transnational cultural flows occur, identifying them as "scapes" (meaning something crafted, configured, or transformed by humans):

- *Ethnoscapes:* the fluid and shifting landscape of migrants, refugees, exiles, tourists, and other moving groups and people.
- *Technoscapes:* the global configuration of technologies moving at high speeds across previously restrictive borders.
- *Financescapes:* the global crossroads of currency speculation and financial transfers.
- *Mediascapes:* the distribution of electronic media capabilities to produce and spread information, plus the large complex repertoire of narratives and visual images generated by these media.
- *Ideoscapes:* ideologies produced by the state and alternative ideologies developed by non-state and counter-hegemonic forces, around which societies organize their political cultures and collective cultural identities.

Each of these "scapes" plays a significant role in structural power, the topic of our next section.[6] Notably, Appadurai's "scape" concept inspired the Globalscape feature in this textbook.

Structural Power in the Age of Globalization

A new form of expansive international capitalism has emerged since the mid-1900s. Operating under the banner of globalization, it builds on earlier cultural structures of worldwide trade networks, and it is the successor to a system of colonialism in which a handful of powerful, mainly European, capitalist states ruled and exploited foreign nations inhabiting distant territories.

Enormously complex and turbulent, globalization is a dynamically structured process in which individuals, business corporations, and political institutions actively rearrange and restructure the political field to their own competitive advantage, vying for increasingly scarce

natural resources, cheap labor, new commercial markets, and ever-larger profits. This restructuring occurs in a vast arena spanning the entire globe. Doing this, of course, requires a great deal of power.

As discussed previously, power refers to the ability of individuals or groups to impose their will upon others and make them do things even against their own wants or wishes. Power plays a major role in coordinating and regulating collective behavior toward imposing or maintaining law and order within—and beyond—a particular community or society.

There are different levels of power within societies, as well as among societies. Anthropologist Eric Wolf pointed out the importance of understanding a macro level of power that he referred to as **structural power**—power that organizes and orchestrates the systemic interaction within and among societies, directing economic and political forces on the one hand and ideological forces that shape public ideas, values, and beliefs on the other.[7] The concept of structural power applies not only to regional political organizations such as chiefdoms or states but also captures the complex new cultural formations currently restructuring and transfiguring societies and environments everywhere on earth.

Joseph Nye—a political scientist, international security specialist, and former assistant secretary of defense in the U.S. government—refers to these two major interacting forces in the worldwide arena as "hard power" and "soft power."[8] **Hard power** is the kind of coercive power that is backed up by economic and military force. **Soft power** is cooptive rather than coercive, pressing others through attraction and persuasion to change their ideas, beliefs, values, and behaviors. Although propaganda is a form of soft power, the exercise of ideological influence (the global struggle for hearts and minds) also operates through more subtle means, such as foreign aid, international diplomacy,

---

[7] Wolf, E. (1999). *Envisioning power: Ideologies of dominance and crisis* (p. 5). Berkeley: University of California Press.

[8] Nye, J. (2002). *The paradox of American power: Why the world's only superpower can't go it alone.* New York: Oxford University Press.

structural power Power that organizes and orchestrates the systemic interaction within and among societies, directing economic and political forces on the one hand and ideological forces that shape public ideas, values, and beliefs on the other.

hard power Coercive power that is backed up by economic and military force.

soft power Cooptive power that presses others through attraction and persuasion to change their ideas, beliefs, values, and behaviors.

---

[6] Appadurai, A. (1990). Disjuncture and difference in the global cultural economy. *Public Culture 2,* 1–24.

news media, sports, entertainment, museum exhibits, and academic exchanges.

Military Hard Power

Today the United States has more hard power at its disposal than any of its allies or rivals worldwide. It is the global leader in military expenditure, spending $711 billion in 2008, followed by Europe ($289 billion), and China ($122 billion). In fact, as the world's still-dominant superpower, the United States is responsible for almost half of the $1.473 trillion spent on arms worldwide[9] (Figure 27.1).

Moreover, although there are seven other nuclear weapons states (Britain, France, and China, as well as Israel, India, Pakistan, and North Korea, collectively possessing nearly 900 active nuclear warheads), Russia and the United States have by far the largest nuclear arsenals at their disposal—minimally 5,830 and 5,735 operational warheads, respectively. (There are also nearly 16,000 intact but nonoperational warheads, almost all in the hands of the United States and Russia.)[10]

In addition to military might, hard power involves using economic strength as a political instrument of coercion or intimidation in the global structuring process. Among other things, this means that economic size and productivity, technological capability, and finance capital

---

[9] www.globalissue.org.

[10] Norris, R. S., & Kristensen, H. M. (2006, July/August). Global nuclear stockpiles, 1945–2006. *Bulletin of the Atomic Scientists 62* (4), 64–66.

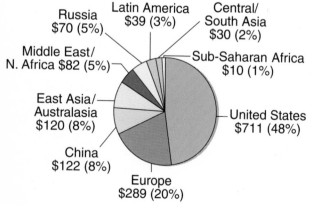

U.S. Military Spending vs. the World, 2008 (in billions of U.S. dollars)

Figure 27.1 The United States is responsible for nearly half of the $1.473 trillion spent on arms worldwide.
Source: Center for Arms Control and Non-Proliferation, 2008.

may be brought to bear on the global market, forcing less powerful states to weaken the systems protecting their workers, natural resources, and local markets.

As the world's largest economy and leading exporter, the United States has long pushed for free trade for its corporations doing business on a global scale. Sometimes it uses military power to impose changes on a foreign political landscape by means of armed interventions or full-scale invasions. For instance, when the United Fruit Company (later bought by Del Monte), owner of enormous banana plantations in Guatemala, saw its economic interests threatened by that country's democratically elected government, the U.S. government engineered a military coup in 1954 that resulted in a dictatorship favorable to U.S.-based corporations.

Through history, the United States (like several other powerful countries, including Russia, Britain, and France) has engaged in such military interventions around the world. Because of this, many see the United States as an ever-present threat, apt to use overwhelming military force in order to benefit its corporate interests from fruit to fuel, from microchips to automobiles. The corporations, in turn, wield enormous political and financial power over governments and international organizations, including the World Trade Organization, headquartered in Geneva, and global banking institutions such as the International Monetary Fund (IMF) and World Bank, both based in Washington, DC.

The IMF is a specialized agency of the United Nations, but it functions virtually independently of UN control. Specializing in short-term loans to assist poor or developing countries, its financial resources weigh in at more than $500 billion. The five wealthiest countries in the world (United States, Japan, Germany, France, and Britain) control 40 percent of this global fund and dominate its executive board. As the global lender of last resort, the IMF's structural power is evident not only in which development projects and policies it chooses to support financially, but also in its surveillance practices, which involve monitoring a borrower's economic and financial developments.

The World Bank is an independent specialized agency of the UN as well as a member and observer in many UN bodies. It makes long-term loans ($20 billion annually) for economic development projects such as roads, schools, and health systems to reduce poverty in about a hundred developing countries. Like the IMF, it is largely controlled by a handful of powerful capitalist states. Operating under geopolitical constraints, these global banking institutions strategically direct capital flows to projects in certain parts of the world, financially supporting some governments and withholding capital from others.

Both the IMF and the World Bank have been accused of being insensitive to the political and cultural consequences of the projects they support. For example, in the 1990s the World Bank provided loans to a hydropower project in southern Chile to build dams in the upper Bio-Bio River without considering the human rights of local Pehuenche Indians. The dam flooded a large part of the Pehuenche's ancestral lands, forcing hundreds to be resettled against their own will.

Likewise, the World Bank approved a $40-million loan to the Chinese government to relocate almost 60,000 poor Han Chinese farmers to more fertile land in Qinghai, territory that Tibetans consider part of their homeland. Pro-Tibetan groups around the world protested that the bank was supporting China's effort to weaken the Tibetan ethnic minority population in that region. Due to these protests, the bank delayed funding, pending investigation. When the investigative panel concluded that regulations had been violated, the Chinese government took offense and withdrew its loan application from the Bank, declaring that it would use its own financial resources to implement the Qinghai component of the China Western Poverty Reduction Project.

Globalization does more than create a worldwide arena in which megacorporations reap megaprofits. It also wreaks havoc in many traditional cultures and disrupts long-established social organizations everywhere. By the early 21st century, the global trend of economic inequality has become quite clear: The poor are becoming poorer, and the rich are becoming richer.

Home to more global corporations than any other country, the United States is endeavoring to protect its interests by investing in what it refers to as a "global security environment." Numerous other countries, unable to afford expensive weapons systems or blocked from developing or acquiring them, have invested in biological or chemical weaponry. Still others, including relatively powerless political groups, have resorted to insurgencies, guerrilla tactics, or even terrorism.

Economic Hard Power

Global corporations, rare before the latter half of the 20th century, now are a far-reaching economic and political force in the world. Modern-day business giants such as General Electric, Shell, and Toyota are actually clusters of several corporations joined by ties of common ownership and responsive to a common management strategy. Usually tightly controlled by a head office in one country, megacorporations organize and integrate production across the international boundaries of different countries for interests formulated in corporate boardrooms, irrespective of whether these are consistent with the interests of people in the countries where they operate. These megacorporations are the products of the technological revolution, for without mass transportation, sophisticated data processing equipment, and telecommunication, they could not conduct or manage their transnational capitalist operations.

Though typically thought of as responding impersonally to outside market forces, megacorporations are in fact controlled by an increasingly smaller number of wealthy capitalists who benefit directly from their operations. Yet, unlike political leaders, the world's largest individual stockholders and most powerful directors are virtually unknown to the general public. For that matter, most people cannot even name the world's ten leading global corporations, which include Wal-Mart, Shell, and Toyota (Figure 27.2). Each of the top ten business giants currently generates annual revenues well over $200 billion, and three of them top the $400 billion mark.[11]

So great is the power of large businesses operating all across the globe that they increasingly thwart the wishes of national governments or international organizations such as the United Nations, Red Cross, and the International Court of Justice. Because megacorporations restrict information about their operations, it can be difficult for governments to make informed policy decisions. It took years for the U.S. Congress to extract information from tobacco companies to decide what to do about tobacco legislation, and it is nearly as slow-going today getting energy and media companies to provide data needed for regulatory purposes.

Beyond this, global corporations have repeatedly shown they can overrule foreign policy decisions. While some might see this as a hopeful signal for getting beyond ethnocentric motivations, it raises the unsettling issue of whether the global arena should be controlled by immense powerful private corporations interested only in financial profits. According to one market research organization:

> Today, the top 100 companies control 33 percent of the world's assets, but employ only one percent of the world's workforce. General Motors is larger than Denmark, Wal-Mart bigger than South Africa. The mega-corporations roam freely around the globe, lobbying legislators, bankrolling elections and playing governments off against each other to get the best deals. Their private hands control the bulk of the world's news and information flows.[12]

---

[11] Forbes International 500 List for 2008.

[12] www.adbusters.org. See also Hertz, N. (2001). *The silent takeover: Global capitalism and the death of democracy* (p. 43). New York: Arrow.

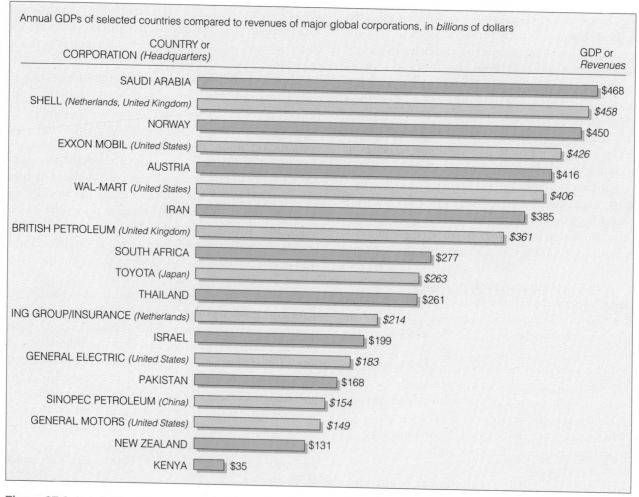

Annual GDPs of selected countries compared to revenues of major global corporations, in *billions* of dollars

COUNTRY or CORPORATION (Headquarters) — GDP or Revenues

Country or Corporation	GDP or Revenues
SAUDI ARABIA	$468
SHELL (Netherlands, United Kingdom)	$458
NORWAY	$450
EXXON MOBIL (United States)	$426
AUSTRIA	$416
WAL-MART (United States)	$406
IRAN	$385
BRITISH PETROLEUM (United Kingdom)	$361
SOUTH AFRICA	$277
TOYOTA (Japan)	$263
THAILAND	$261
ING GROUP/INSURANCE (Netherlands)	$214
ISRAEL	$199
GENERAL ELECTRIC (United States)	$183
PAKISTAN	$168
SINOPEC PETROLEUM (China)	$154
GENERAL MOTORS (United States)	$149
NEW ZEALAND	$131
KENYA	$35

Figure 27.2 In today's consumer-driven world, it is not uncommon for the yearly revenues of large multinational corporations to equal and even exceed the total value of all goods and services produced within many countries per year, known as a country's gross domestic product (GDP). This graph shows the annual GDPs of selected countries alongside the annual revenues of leading global corporations. Notably, Shell revenues exceed the GDPs of 172 of the world's 195 countries. Not shown here are the countries with the highest and lowest GDPs. About half have GDPs under $18 billion, and thirty fall below $1 billion. Only fourteen countries surpass $1 trillion, including the United States at $14 trillion, with Japan in second place at nearly $5 trillion. (Note: GDP says nothing about the unequal distribution of wealth within a country.)

Source: Based on the global 500 sales figures for 2008 listed on www.forbes.com and the 2008 GDP figures provided on www.worldbank.org.

Global corporations are changing the shape of the world and the lives of individuals from every walk of life, including those they employ. In the never-ending search for cheap labor, these megacorporations have returned to a practice once common in the textile mills of 19th-century Britain and New England, but now on a much larger scale. More than ever before, they have come to favor women for low-skilled assembly jobs. In so-called underdeveloped countries, as subsistence farming gives way to mechanized agriculture for production of crops for export, women are less able to contribute to their families'

survival. Together with the devaluation of domestic work, women are pressured to seek jobs outside the household to contribute to its support. Since most women in these countries do not have the time or resources to get an education or to develop special job skills, only low-paying jobs are open to them.

Big business has created problems for consumers as well as workers. In a ten-year intensive study of relations between producers and consumers of products and services, anthropologist Laura Nader found repeated, documented offenses by North American businesses that could not be handled by existing complaint mechanisms, either in or out of court.[13]

Faceless relations between producers and consumers, among whom there is a grossly unequal distribution of power, have exacted a high cost: a terrible sense of indifference, apathy, even a loss of faith in the dehumanized system itself. When workers do not trust their bosses and bosses do not trust one another, production and trade relations on every level are damaged or ruined. This alienation may ultimately lead to a systemic breakdown. With production, trading, and banking operations on a global scale, the breakdown in one part of the system may trigger a worldwide chain reaction of failures. Such was the global crisis triggered by the bankruptcy of a handful of mismanaged Wall Street firms in 2008.[14]

Soft Power: A Global Media Environment

In addition to reliance on military and economic hard power in the global quest for dominance and profit, competing states and corporations utilize the ideological persuasion of soft power as transmitted through electronic and digital media, communication satellites, and other information technology. One of the major tasks of soft power is to sell the general idea of globalization as something positive and progressive (as "freedom," "free" trade, "free" market) and to frame or brand anything that opposes capitalism in negative terms.

The far-reaching capabilities of modern electronic and digital technologies have led to the creation of a global media environment that plays a major role in how individuals and even societies view themselves and their place in the world. Together with radio and television, the Internet is now the dominant means of mass communication around the world. The global flow of information made possible by fiber optic cables and communication satellites orbiting the earth is almost entirely digital-electronic, taking place in a new boundless cultural space identified earlier in this chapter as a "global mediascape."

In recent years, the power of corporations has become all the greater through media expansion. Over the past two decades, a global commercial media system has developed, dominated by a few megacorporations (such as

The poorest people in the world, such as this Maka Indian woman in Paraguay, often wear clothing discarded by those who are better off—and people from all walks of life can be found wearing clothes with corporate logos. The power that big business (such as the Disney media corporation) has over individuals is illustrated by the ability of corporations to get consumers to pay for goods that advertise corporate products.

General Electric and Disney), most based in the United States. Control of television and other media, as well as the advertising industry, gives global corporations enormous influence on the ideas and behavior of hundreds of millions of ordinary people across the world.

Consider, for example, the powerful marketing messages that shape cultural standards concerning the ideal human body. The widespread nature of this concern is evident in the abundance of TV infomercials selling workout equipment and "age-defying" cosmetic products, as well as in the highly popular TV drama *Nip/Tuck* and the much-watched reality program *Dr. 90210* (which follows the stories of plastic surgery patients and doctors in Beverly Hills, California). The following Original Study offers details on what has become a lucrative cosmetic surgery industry.

[13] Nader, L. (Ed.). (1981). *No access to law: Alternatives to the American judicial system.* New York: Academic.

[14] Notably, as Brazilian anthropologist Gustavo Lins Ribeiro points out, today even informal economies, burgeoning in Latin America and elsewhere, are globalized. See Ribeiro, G. L. (2009). Non-hegemonic globalizations: Alternative transnational processes and agents. *Anthropological Theory 9* (3), 297–329.

Standardizing the Body: The Question of Choice   *by Laura Nader*

The question of choice is central to the story of how medicine and business generate controlling processes in the shaping of women's bodies. Images of the body appear natural within their specific cultural milieus. For example, breast implants are not seen as odd within the cultural milieu of the United States, and female circumcision and infibulation (also known as female genital mutilation or FGM) are not considered odd among people from the Sudan and several other African countries. However, many feminist writers differentiate FGM from breast implantation by arguing that North American women *choose* to have breast implants whereas in Africa women are presumably subject to indoctrination since they experience circumcision as young girls.

One of the most heated debates arising from the public health concern over breast implants is whether the recipients are freely situated—that is, whether their decision is voluntary or whether control is disguised as free will.

An informed response to the free choice argument requires knowing how the beauty-industrial complex works. Toward this end, corporate accountability researcher Linda Coco carried out fieldwork in multiple sites, gaining insights into the inner workings of a multibillion-dollar industry that segments the female body and manufactures commodities of and for the body.

Coco's research shows how some women get caught in the official beauty ideology, and in the case of silicone-gel breast implants some hundreds of thousands of women have been ensnared. But who gets caught and when are important to an understanding of the ecology of power. The average age of a woman having breast implantation is 36 years, and she has an average of two children. She is the beauty industry's insecure consumer recast as a patient

with an illness the industry defines as hypertrophy (small breasts).

Coco quotes a past president of the American Society of Plastic and Reconstructive Surgery (ASPRS):

> There is substantial and enlarging medical knowledge to the effect that these deformities [small breasts] are really a disease which result in the patient's feelings of inadequacies, lack of self-confidence, distortion of body image, and a total lack of well-being due to a lack of self-perceived femininity. . . .

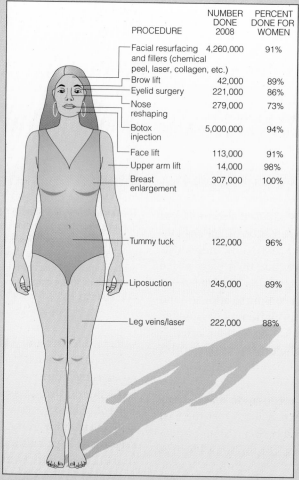

PROCEDURE	NUMBER DONE 2008	PERCENT DONE FOR WOMEN
Facial resurfacing and fillers (chemical peel, laser, collagen, etc.)	4,260,000	91%
Brow lift	42,000	89%
Eyelid surgery	221,000	86%
Nose reshaping	279,000	73%
Botox injection	5,000,000	94%
Face lift	113,000	91%
Upper arm lift	14,000	98%
Breast enlargement	307,000	100%
Tummy tuck	122,000	96%
Liposuction	245,000	89%
Leg veins/laser	222,000	88%

Selected cosmetic surgical and nonsurgical procedures in the United States (2008) and the percentage carried out for women. In total 1.7 million cosmetic surgeries were done and 10.4 million nonsurgical procedures (chemical peels, laser treatments, Botox injections, and so on) at a total cost of about $10.3 billion. Overall, the number of procedures is up 882 percent since 1992, and 63 percent since 2000.

Enlargement . . . is therefore . . . necessary to ensure the quality of life for the patient.

In other words, cosmetic surgery is necessary to the patient's psychological health.

The plastic surgeon regards the construction of the official breast as art, the aim being to reform the female body according to the ideals of classic Western art. One surgeon pioneering procedures for correcting deformity took as his ideal female figure that of ancient Greek statues, which he carefully measured, noticing the exact size and shape of the breasts, their vertical location between the third and seventh ribs, the horizontal between the line of the sternal (breast bone) border and the anterior axillary line, and so forth. In Coco's analysis the exercise of the plastic surgeon's technoart recreates a particular static, official breast shape and applies this creation ostensibly to relieve women's mental suffering. The surgeon becomes a psychological healer as well as an artist.

Along with art and psychology, there is, of course, the business of organized plastic surgery, which responds to the demands and opportunities of market economics [see figure]. By the late 1970s and early 1980s there was a glut of plastic surgeons. The ASPRS began to operate like a commercial enterprise instead of a medical society, saturating the media with ads and even providing low-cost financing. The discourse became a sales pitch. Women "seek" breast implants to keep their husbands or their jobs, to attract men, or to become socially acceptable. Coco calls this "patriarchal capitalism" and questions whether this is free choice or "mind colonization."

Understanding "choice" led Coco to an examination of the power both in the doctor–patient relationship and in the control of information.

She found that women "were told by the media, plastic surgeons, women's magazines, other women, and the business world that they could enhance their lives by enhancing their bust lines . . . the social imperative for appearance was personalized, psychologized, and normalized." Social surveys indicate that, to the extent that women internalize the social imperative, they feel they are making the decision on their own.

Not surprisingly, women whose surgery resulted in medical complications often came to recognize the external processes of coercive persuasion that had led them to seek implants. In some ways, they resembled former cult members who had been deprogrammed: Their disillusionment caused them to question the system that had encouraged them to make the decision in the first place. The result was a gradual building of protest against the industry, expressed in networks, newsletters, support groups, workshops, and seminars. As have some former cult members, women have brought suit, testified before lawmakers, and challenged in other

ways some of the largest corporations and insurance companies in the land.

The choice of implants, they learn, is part of a matrix of controlling processes in which women are subjects. Given the right circumstances it could happen to anyone. In the Sudan, the young girl is told that FGM procedures are done for her and not to her. In the United States the mutilation of natural breasts is also done for the recreation of femininity. Although power is exercised differently in these two cases, Coco notes the similarity: "The operation on the female breast in [North] America holds much of the same social symbolism and expression of cultural mandate as does FGM in Sudan. Thus, the question of why women choose breast augmentation becomes moot."

Breast implantation is now spreading elsewhere, most notably to China. Will it become a functional equivalent to foot-binding in China as part of the competition between patriarchies East and West? Whatever the answer, many social thinkers agree that people are always more vulnerable to intense persuasion

during periods of historical dislocation— a break with structures and symbols familiar to the life cycle—in which the media can bring us images and ideas originating in past, contemporary, or even imaginary worlds.

Feminist researchers have sought to crack controlling paradigms such as those that define women's capacities and those that construct a standardized body shape and determine what is beautiful in women. Some of their writings are attempts to free the mind from the beauty constructions of cosmetic industries and fashion magazines. Others relay how the one model of Western beauty is affecting members of ethnic groups who aspire to look the way advertisements say they should. Choice is an illusion, since the restructuring of taste is inextricably linked to shifts in the organization of consumption.

Adapted from Nader, L. (1997). Controlling processes: Tracing the dynamics of power. Current Anthropology 38, 715–717.

Problems of Structural Violence

Structural power and its associated concepts of hard and soft power enable us to better understand the global arena in which local communities throughout the world are now compelled to operate and the unequal the distribution of wealth, health, and power in today's world. When structural power undermines the well-being of others, we may speak of **structural violence**—physical and/or psychological harm (including repression, environmental destruction, poverty, hunger, illness, and premature death) caused by impersonal, exploitative, and unjust social, political, and economic systems.[15]

A useful baseline for identifying structural violence is provided by the Universal Declaration of Human Rights, officially adopted by all members of the United Nations in 1948. Anthropologists played a key role in drafting this important document. The declaration's preamble begins with the statement that "recognition of the inherent dignity and of the equal and inalienable rights of all members of the human family is the foundation of freedom, justice, and peace in the world."[16] Generally speaking, structural

violence concerns the impersonal systemic violation of the human rights of individuals and communities to a healthy, peaceful, and dignified life.

Although human rights abuses are nothing new, globalization has enormously expanded and intensified structural violence. For instance, it is leading to an ever-widening gap between the wealthiest and poorest peoples, the powerful and powerless. In 1960 the average income for the twenty wealthiest countries in the world was fifteen times that of the twenty poorest. Today it is thirty times higher.[17]

Notably, these figures fail to indicate that some of the poorest countries in the world have a small number of very rich citizens, and that very wealthy countries include many poor inhabitants. In fact, the income disparity between rich and poor within many countries has been widening in recent years—as evident in the "income inequality index" annually posted by the United Nations. The index ranges from 0 to 100, with 0 corresponding to perfect equality (where everyone has the same income) and 100 corresponding to perfect inequality (where one person has all the income and everyone else has zero

[17] www.worldbank.org/poverty. (2005 statistics).

[15] See Farmer, P. (1996). On suffering and structural violence: A view from below. *Daedelus 125 (1),* 261–283.

[16] Universal Declaration of Human Rights. www.ccnmtl.columbia.edu/projects/mmt/udhr.

structural violence Physical and/or psychological harm (including repression, environmental destruction, poverty, hunger, illness, and premature death) caused by impersonal, exploitative, and unjust social, political, and economic systems.

income). Measuring the gap between the richest and poorest 10 percent of the population in China, for example, the income inequality index shows that the world's largest communist country is even more unequal (21.5) than the United States, the world's largest capitalist country (15.9). By comparison, other wealthy industrialized countries have a much more equal income distribution, including Germany (6.9) and Japan (4.5).

On the other hand, the greatest income disparities between the richest and poorest 10 percent can be found in some of the poorest countries, including Paraguay (65.4), the Central African Republic (69.2), and Haiti (71.7).[18] However, the United States now has the highest income inequality in the wealthy industrialized world, and the big gap between rich and poor is widening.

Measured on a global scale, the wealth of the ultra-rich has reached stratospheric proportions. Today, the world's 225 richest individuals have a combined wealth equal to the annual income of the poorest 47 percent of the entire world population. In dramatic contrast, nearly half of all people in the world get by on less than $2.50 per day. Measuring the gap in another way reveals that the richest 20 percent of the human population enjoys 77 percent of all goods and services in the world. The other 80 percent of humanity has the benefit of only 23 percent—and the poorest 20 percent gets a mere 1.5 percent of those goods and services.[19]

Structural violence has countless manifestations in addition to widespread poverty. These range from the cultural destruction already indicated to hunger and obesity, and environmental degradation, all discussed in the remaining pages of this chapter.

Overpopulation and Poverty

In 1750, 1 billion people lived on earth. Over the next two centuries our numbers climbed to nearly 2.5 billion. And between 1950 and 2000 the world population soared above 6 billion. Today, India and China each have more than 1 billion inhabitants. Such increases are highly significant because population growth increases the scale of hunger and pollution—and the many problems tied to these two big issues. Although controlling population growth does not eliminate the other problems, we are unlikely to be able to solve them unless population growth is stopped or even reversed.

For a population to hold steady, there must be a balance between birthrates and death rates. In other words, people must produce only enough offspring to replace themselves when they die. This is known as **replacement reproduction.** Prior to 1976, birthrates around the world generally exceeded death rates, with the exception of European and North American populations. Poor people, in particular, have tended to have large families because children have been their main resource. Children can provide a needed labor pool to work farms, and they are the only source of security for the elderly. Historically, people were apt to limit the size of their families only when they became wealthy enough that their money replaced children as their main resource; at that point, children actually *cost* them money. Given this, we can see why birthrates remained high for so long in the world's poorer countries. To those who live in poverty, children are seen as potentially valuable contributors to the household income.

Since the mid-1970s, birthrates have dropped below replacement level (which is about 2.1 children per woman) in virtually every industrialized country and also in nineteen developing countries—including China, the world's most populous country. Even in much of Africa, as well as South Asia and Central and South America (home to most of the world's poorer nations), birthrates have also declined but far less dramatically.[20]

Despite progress, the worldwide population continues to grow. Projections are extremely tricky, given variables such as AIDS, but current estimates suggest that global population will peak around 2050 at about 9.37 billion people. The severity of the situation becomes clear with the realization that the present world population of more than 6 billion people can be sustained only by using up nonrenewable resources such as oil, which is like living off income-producing capital. It works for a time, but once the capital is gone, so is the possibility of even having an income to live on.

Hunger and Obesity

As frequently dramatized in media reports, hundreds of millions of people face hunger on a regular basis, leading to a variety of health problems, premature death, and other forms of suffering. Today, over a quarter of the world's countries do not produce enough food to feed their populations and cannot afford to import what is

---

[18] http://en.wikipedia.org/wiki/List_of_countries_by_income_equality.This site features a list of countries by income inequality, drawing wealth figures from various sources, including the United Nations and the U.S. Central Intelligence Agency. See also: Davies, J. B., et al. (2007). *The world distribution of household wealth.* University of California, Santa Cruz, Mapping Global Inequalities, Center for Global, International, and Regional Studies.

[19] Kurth, P. (1998, October 14). Capital crimes. *Seven Days,* 7; Swaminathan, M. S. (2000). Science in response to basic human needs. *Science 287,* 425. See also World Bank Development Indicators, 2008, and Human Development Report 2002, *Deepening democracy in a fragmented world,* United Nations Development Program.

replacement reproduction The point at which birthrates and death rates are in equilibrium; people producing only enough offspring to replace themselves when they die.

[20] Bongaarts, J. (1998). Demographic consequences of declining fertility. *Science 282,* 419; Wattenberg, B. J. (1997, November 23). The population explosion is over. *New York Times Magazine,* 60.

The Gila River Indian community canal. In the 19th century Pima Indians in southwest Arizona, who call themselves *Akimel O'otham,* or "river people," lost the river that had for generations sustained their farming culture when white farmers upstream siphoned it off. The theft of the river—combined with U.S. federal government rations of lard (pig fat), canned meats, and sugary processed foods—unhinged traditional Pima life and conspired with genetic anomalies to sow an obesity epidemic that has left this reservation community with among the highest diabetes rates in the world. In 2004, after decades of litigation, the Pima and neighboring Maricopa Indians achieved the largest Indian water rights settlement ever. Water is once again beginning to flow by way of irrigation canals, making it possible to reestablish vegetable farms with the hope of boosting Pima economy and restoring a healthier lifestyle. The question is whether this can repair the damage of generations of structural violence.

needed. In fact, our species has now reached a disturbing historic milestone with well over 1 billion humans going hungry every day. Most (almost 650 million) of these unfortunates live in Asia and the Pacific islands. Next comes sub-Saharan Africa with about 265 million, followed by the Middle East and North Africa with 53 million, and another 15 million in the world's wealthy countries.[21]

Hunger is caused not only by drought and pests, but also by violent ethnic, religious, or political conflicts that uproot families and by a food production and distribution system geared to satisfy the demands of the world's most powerful countries. During the 20th century, 44 million people died due to human-made famine.[22] For example, in several sub-Saharan African countries plagued by chronic civil strife, it has been almost impossible to raise and harvest crops, for hordes of hungry refugees, roaming militias, and underpaid soldiers constantly raid fields.

Without adequate nutrition, humans lose their ability to resist disease. And without access to adequate health care, many of the poverty-stricken sick have little chance to survive. For the poor—especially in refugee camps, slums, and other places with miserable living conditions—suffering is a normal condition of life, and death looms everywhere. Such is the case, for example, in Sudan's ethnic war-torn Darfur region. Since 2003, the conflict in Sudan has claimed a half-million lives and chased more than 2.5 million people from their homes to camps where hunger, thirst, and disease are daily threats.

Today, nearly one out of every six human beings experiences chronic hunger. Every year, famine claims the lives of some 6 million children aged 5 and under, and those who survive it often suffer from physical and mental impairment.[23] These are victims of structural violence, because the increasing rate of starvation is not only due to environmental calamities or warfare, but also to the collapse of local markets caused by foreign imports, massive job cuts, and growing poverty rates.

[21] Food and Agriculture Organization (FAO), United Nations. (2009). *1.02 billion people hungry: One sixth of humanity undernourished—more than ever before.* http://www.fao.org/news/story/en/item/20568/icode/

[22] Hunger Project. (2003). www.thp.org; White, M. (2001). *Historical atlas of the twentieth century.* http://users.erols.com/mwhite28/20century.htm.

[23] Hunger Project; Swaminathan.

The high cost of western farming practices, such as spraying chemicals to increase yields and decrease various pests and blights, is prohibitive for the world's small-scale farmers. Moreover, the practice trades short-term benefits for long-term pollution and health problems.

Another problem is that millions of acres in Africa, Asia, and Latin America once devoted to subsistence farming have been given over to the raising of cash crops for export. This has enriched members of elite social classes in these parts of the world, while satisfying the appetites of people in developed countries for coffee, tea, chocolate, bananas, and beef. Those who used to farm the land for their own food needs have been relocated—either to urban areas, where all too often there is no employment for them, or to areas ecologically unsuited for farming.

In Africa, such lands are often occupied seasonally by pastoral nomads, and turning them over to cultivation has reduced pasture available for livestock and led to overgrazing. The increase in cleared land, coupled with overgrazing, has depleted both soil and water, with disastrous consequences to nomad and farmer alike. So it is that more than 250 million people can no longer grow crops on their farms, and 1 billion people in about a hundred countries are in danger of losing their ability to grow crops.[24]

One strategy urged upon so-called underdeveloped countries, especially by government officials and development advisors from Europe and the United States, has been to adopt practices that have made agriculture in industrialized societies incredibly productive. However, this strategy ignores the crucial fact that these large-scale, commercial farming practices require a financial investment that small farmers and poor countries cannot afford—a substantial outlay of cash for chemical fertilizers, pesticides, and herbicides, not to mention fossil fuels needed to run all the mechanized equipment. Despite its spectacular short-term success, serious questions arise about whether such a profligate food production system can be sustained over the centuries, even in North America.

Yet another problem with the idea of copying U.S. farming styles has to do with subsidies. Despite official rhetoric about free markets, governments of the wealthiest capitalist states in North America and western Europe spend between $100 billion and $300 billion annually on agriculture subsidies. In the United States, the world's largest agricultural exporter, 75 percent of these go to the wealthiest 10 percent of the farmers and large agricultural corporations.

Small farmers in poor countries cannot compete with subsidized agribusinesses that are selling mass-produced and often genetically engineered crops. Many small farmers have been forced to quit farming, leave their villages, and seek work in cities or as migrant workers abroad.

Such is the fate of many Maya Indians today. Since the early 1980s, when so many fled Guatemala's violence and poverty, thousands have made their way to places like southeastern Florida and taken low-paying jobs as illegal immigrants. Because of endemic poverty in their homeland where they would face starvation, these victims of structural violence have no choice but to remain where they are, condemned to an uncertain life in exile as cheap laborers without civil rights, Social Security, or health insurance.

Ironically, while many millions are starving in some parts of the world, many millions of others are overeating—quite literally eating themselves to death. In

---

[24] Godfrey, T. (2000, December 27). Biotech threatening biodiversity. *Burlington Free Press*, 10A.

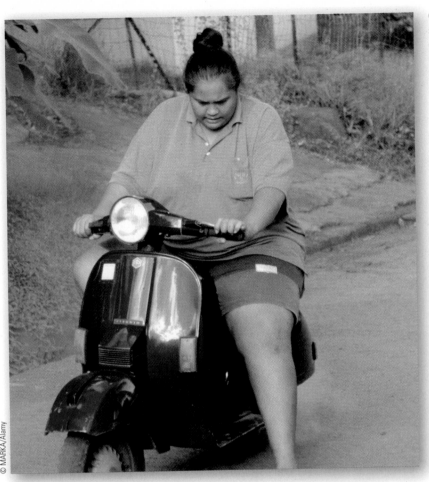

On the South Pacific island of Nauru, the world's smallest independent republic, about 80 percent of the 14,000 inhabitants are now classified as obese. This island nation in Micronesia also has the world's highest rate of diabetes.

© MARKA/Alamy

fact, the number of overfed people now exceeds those who are underfed. According to the World Watch Institute in Washington, DC, more than 1.1 billion people worldwide are now overweight. And over 350 million of these are obese, but still often malnourished in that their diets lack certain nutrients.

Seriously concerned about the sharp rise in associated health problems (including stroke, diabetes, cancer, and heart disease), the World Health Organization classifies obesity as a global epidemic. Overeating is particularly dangerous for individuals living in societies where machines have eased the physical burdens of work and other human activities, which helps explain why more than half of the people in some industrial and postindustrial countries are overweight.

However, the obesity epidemic is not due solely to excessive eating and lack of physical activity. A key factor is the high sugar and fat content of mass-marketed foods. Thus in Japan, where food habits differ significantly from those in the United States, obesity plagues just over 3 percent of the population, compared to the U.S. rate of 32 percent. In fact, U.S. obesity figures have doubled over the past three decades, placing it at the top of the obesity chart among wealthy industrialized countries. Obesity rates differ between men and women, higher and lower income groups, and among various ethnic groups. The highest U.S. rate is among African American women, half of whom suffer obesity.[25]

The problem of obesity has become a serious concern even in some developing countries, especially where people have switched to a diet based on processed or canned fast food. The highest obesity rates worldwide can now be found among Pacific Island nations such as Fiji, Samoa, and Tonga, where being fat is traditionally associated with cultural ideals of beauty, good health, and high status.

Topping the world's obesity prevalence list is the island of Nauru, formerly known as Pleasant Island. Traditionally, Nauruans valued food as a symbol of well-being and social pride, considered fat as a sign of beauty, and associated large body size with strength and prosperity.[26] In the days when Nauruans still depended largely on fishing and gathering for most of their food, obesity was not a medical

25 Centers for Disease Control and Prevention. (2009). Differences in prevalence of obesity among black, white, and Hispanic adults—United States, 2006–2008. *Morbidity and Mortality Weekly Report 58* (27), 740–744. Drewnowski, A., & Specter, S. E. (2004). Poverty and obesity: the role of energy density and energy costs. *American Journal of Clinical Nutrition 79* (1), 6–16.

26 Pollock, N. J. (1995). Social fattening patterns in the Pacific—the positive side of obesity. A Nauru case study. In I. DeGarine & N. J. Pollock (Eds.), *Social aspects of obesity* (pp. 87–109). London: Routledge.

problem. However, when royalties from phosphate mining provided each family with large amounts of cash, their diets and lifestyles changed radically for the worse. Today, phosphate wealth has disappeared, but the junk food diet remains, and 80 percent of the indigenous population of this small island republic in Micronesia has become obese; about 30 percent of them now have diabetes.[27]

Pollution and Global Warming

The effects of corporate agribusiness practices are part of larger problems of environmental degradation in which pollution is tolerated for the sake of higher profits that benefit specific individuals and societies. Industrial activities are producing highly toxic waste at unprecedented rates, and factory emissions are poisoning the air. For example, smokestack gases are clearly implicated in acid rain, which

is damaging lakes and forests all over northeastern North America. Air containing water vapor with a high acid content is, of course, harmful to the lungs, but the health hazard is greater than this. As ground and surface water becomes more acidic, the solubility of lead, cadmium, mercury, and aluminum, all of them toxic, rises sharply. For instance, aluminum contamination is high enough on 17 percent of the world's farmland to be toxic to plants—and has been linked to senile dementia, Alzheimer's, and Parkinson's diseases, three major health problems in industrial countries.

Finding their way into the world's oceans, toxic substances also create hazards for seafood consumers. For instance, Canadian Inuit face health problems related to eating fish and sea mammals that feed in waters contaminated by industrial chemical waste such as polychlorinated biphenyls (PCBs) (see the Biocultural Connection).[28] Obviously, environmental poisoning affects peoples all across the globe (Figure 27.3).

---

[27] That said, not all people who are overweight or obese are so because they eat too much junk food and do too little exercise. In addition to cultural factors, being overweight or obese can also have genetic or other biological causes.

[28] Inuit Tapiirit Kanatami. http://www.tapirisat.ca/english_text/ itk/ departments/enviro/ncp.

Land areas with significant acid precipitation and atmospheric pollution

Land areas with significant atmospheric pollution

Land areas with significant acid precipitation

Land areas of secondary atmospheric pollution

Air pollution plume: average wind direction and force

(Wind blows in the direction of the tapered end of the air pollution plume and the force of the wind is indicated by the size of the plume.)

Figure 27.3 Almost all processes of physical geography begin and end with flows of energy and matter among land, sea, and air. Because of the primacy of the atmosphere in this exchange system, air pollution is potentially one of the most dangerous human modifications in environmental systems. Pollutants such as various oxides of nitrogen or sulfur cause the development of acid precipitation, which damages soil, vegetation, and wildlife. Air pollution in the form of smog is often dangerous for human health. And most atmospheric scientists believe that the efficiency of the atmosphere in retaining heat—the greenhouse effect—is being enhanced by increased carbon dioxide, methane, and other gases produced by industrial and agricultural activities. The result, a period of global warming, threatens to dramatically alter climates in all parts of the world.
Source: *Student Atlas of Anthropology* by J. L. Allen & A. C. Shalinsky, p. 132. ©2003 McGraw-Hill/Dushkin Publishing.

Toxic Breast Milk Threatens Arctic Culture

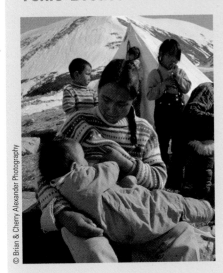

© Brian & Cherry Alexander Photography

Asked to picture the Inuit people inhabiting the Arctic coasts of Canada, Greenland, and Labrador, you are likely to envision them dressed in fur parkas and moving across a pristine, snow-covered landscape on dogsleds—perhaps coming home from hunting seal, walrus, or whale.

Such imaginings are still true—except for the pristine part. Although Inuit live nearer to the North Pole than to any city, factory, or farm, they are not isolated from the pollutants of modern society. Chemicals originating in the cities and farms of North America, Europe, and Asia travel thousands of miles to Inuit territories via winds, rivers, and ocean currents. These toxins have a long life in the Arctic, breaking down very slowly due to icy temperatures and low sunlight. Ingested by zooplankton, the chemicals spread through the seafood chain as one species consumes another. The result is alarming levels of pesticides, mercury, and industrial chemicals in Arctic animals—and in the Inuit people who rely on fishing and hunting for food.

Of particular note are toxic chemicals known as PCBs (polychlorinated biphenyls), used widely over several decades for numerous purposes, such as industrial lubricants, insulating materials, and paint stabilizers. Research shows a widespread presence of PCBs in the breast milk of women around the globe. But nowhere on earth is the concentration higher than among the Inuit—on average seven times that of nursing mothers in Canada's biggest cities.[a]

PCBs have been linked to a wide range of health problems, from liver damage to weakened immune systems to cancer. Studies of children exposed to PCBs in the womb and through breast milk show impaired learning and memory functions. Beyond having a destructive impact on the health of humans (and other animal species), PCBs are impacting the economy, social organization, and psychological well-being of Arctic peoples. Nowhere is this more true than among the 450 Inuit living on Broughton Island, near Canada's Baffin Island. Here, word of skyrocketing PCB levels cost the community its valuable market for Arctic char fish. Other Inuits refer to them as "PCB people," and it is said that Inuit men now avoid marrying women from the island.[b]

The suggestion that the answer to these problems is a change of diet is soundly rejected by Inuit people, who have no real alternatives for affordable food. Abandoning the consumption of traditional seafood would destroy a 4,000-year-old culture based on hunting and fishing. Countless aspects of traditional Inuit culture—from worldview and social arrangements to vocabularies and myths—are linked to Arctic animals and the skills it takes to rely on them for food and so many other things. As one Inuit put it: "Our foods do more than nourish our bodies. They feed our souls. When I eat Inuit foods, I know who I am."[c]

The manufacture of PCBs is now banned in many Western countries (including the United States), and PCB levels are gradually declining worldwide. However, because of their persistence (and widespread presence in remnant industrial goods such as fluorescent lighting fixtures and electrical appliances), they are still the highest-concentration toxins in breast milk, even among mothers born after the ban.

And even as PCBs decline, other commercial chemicals are finding their way northward. To date, about 200 hazardous compounds originating in industrialized regions have been detected in the bodies of Arctic peoples.[d] Global warming is fueling the problem, because as glaciers and snow melt, long-stored toxins are released.

BIOCULTURAL QUESTION

Since corporations are able to profit from large-scale and long-distance commercial activities, we should not be surprised that their operations may also cause serious damage to fellow humans in remote natural environments. What do you think of the profiteering of structural violence?

---

[a] Colborn, T., et al. (1997). *Our stolen future* (pp. 107–108). New York: Plume/Penguin.

[b] Arctic Monitoring Assessment Project (AMAP). (2003). *AMAP assessment 2002: Human health in the Arctic* (pp. xii–xiii, 22–23). Oslo: Author.

[c] Ingmar Egede, quoted in Cone, M. (2005). *Silent snow: The slow poisoning of the Arctic* (p. 1). New York: Grove.

[d] Additional sources: Johansen, B. E. (2002). The Inuit's struggle with dioxins and other organic pollutants. *American Indian Quarterly 26* (3), 479–490; Natural Resources Defense Council. (2005, March 25). Healthy milk, healthy baby: Chemical pollution and mother's milk. www.NRDC.org; Williams, F. (2005, January 9). Toxic breast milk? *New York Times Magazine.*

Added to this is the problem of climatic change, in particular global warming—the greenhouse effect—caused primarily by the burning of fossil fuels (oil, gas, and coal). During the past 200 years, global cultural development has relied on burning increasing quantities of these fuels, with dire results: massive deforestation and desertification, along with severe air, water, and soil pollution threatening the health of all life. Fossil fuel use has dramatically increased carbon dioxide levels, trapping more heat in the earth's atmosphere. Rising temperatures are causing more

Malé is one of many low-lying islands threatened by rising sea levels brought on by global warming. It is the capital island of the Maldives, an Indian Ocean archipelago comprised of 1,200 low-lying islands (199 inhabited), home to about 375,000 people. Climate change and rising sea levels are of great concern to the Maldivians, since their country is only 2.4 meters (8 feet) above sea level at its highest point. As global warming causes the polar ice caps to melt and sea levels to rise, the entire country could disappear. In recent years, the government had a $60-million sea-wall built around Malé and undertook the construction of a nearby artificial island where the land and buildings are several feet higher than the rest of the Maldives.

and greater storms, droughts, and heat waves, devastating populations in vulnerable areas. And if the massive meltdown of Arctic ice now under way continues, rising sea levels will inundate low coastal areas worldwide. Entire islands may soon disappear, including thousands of villages and even large cities.

Although much is unknown about the extent of global warming, scientists now overwhelmingly agree it is real and poses a serious challenge. Experts predict that it will lead to an expansion of the geographic ranges of tropical diseases and increase the incidence of respiratory diseases due to additional smog caused by warmer temperatures. Also, they expect an increase in deaths due to heat waves, as witnessed in the 52,000 deaths attributed to the 2003 heat wave in Europe.[29]

Structural violence also manifests itself in the shifting of manufacturing and hazardous waste disposal from developed to developing countries. In the late 1980s, a tightening of environmental regulations in industrialized countries led to a dramatic rise in the cost of hazardous waste disposal. Seeking cheaper ways to get rid of the wastes, "toxic traders" began shipping hazardous waste to eastern Europe and especially to poor and underdeveloped countries in western Africa (see the Globalscape). When news of this became public, international outrage about the poisoning of soil, air, and water in these poor countries led to the drafting and adoption of the Basel Convention to prohibit the export of hazardous wastes and to minimize their generation.

Today, the scope of the convention is severely limited by the fact that the United States, the largest toxic residue producer in the world, has not ratified the agreement.[30] Moreover, unscrupulous entrepreneurs and corrupt government officials have found ways to circumvent international treaty obligations.

Whereas a small number of wealthy countries—primarily in western Europe and North America—have reaped many economic benefits of early industrialization and global trade, they are also responsible for an estimated two-thirds of the atmospheric buildup of heat-trapping carbon dioxide (CO_2). By contrast, all of Africa, a huge continent three times larger than all of Europe, is responsible for less than 3 percent of the global CO_2 emissions in the past hundred years. Measuring the inequality in human terms, each person in North America adds, on average, 20 tons of carbon dioxide (a greenhouse gas) a year to the atmosphere. In "underdeveloped" countries, less than 3 tons per person are emitted.[31] And one North American consumes hundreds of times the resources of a single African, with all that implies with respect to waste disposal and environmental degradation (Figure 27.4). According to botanist Peter Raven, "if everyone lived like Americans, you'd need three planet earths . . . to sustain that level of consumption."[32]

[29] Larsen, J. (2006, July 28). *Setting the record straight.* Earth Policy Institute, Eco-economy updates.

[30] "Hazardous waste trafficking." www.Choike.org.

[31] Broecker, W. S. (1992, April). Global warming on trial. *Natural History,* 14.

[32] Quoted in Becker, J. (2004, March). *National Geographic,* 90.

Globalscape

Probo Koala's Dirty Secrets?

One day in 2006, the *Probo Koala* unloaded a cargo of processed fuel in Nigeria, West Africa. Then the tanker sailed to Amsterdam where a Dutch treatment plant was to process its 400 tons of leftover toxic sludge. Navigating the oceans under the Panamanian flag, this ship's all-Russian crew serves under a Greek captain. Managed and operated by a Greek maritime company, the ship's registered owner is based in Norway. For this journey, it was chartered by a Dutch subsidiary of Trafigura, a multinational company headquartered in Switzerland that specializes in transporting oil and mineral products.

When port authorities in Amsterdam discovered that the *Probo Koala*'s captain had underreported the poison levels in his cargo, the cost of treating the waste jumped to $600,000. Unwilling to pay the higher fee, the captain ordered his ship back

to West Africa in search of a cheap place to dispose of the waste. Finding unscrupulous businessmen and corrupt officials in Ivory Coast, he negotiated a dumping fee of about $18,000. Deposited in open-air waste pits on the edge of Abidjan (population 5 million), the substance gave off toxic gas that burned lungs and skin and caused severe headaches and vomiting—injuring at least 30,000 people and killing seventeen.

The *Probo Koala* forms part of a profitable global business network capitalizing on the more than 350 million tons of hazardous waste generated annually, primarily by industrial societies. Although most of this waste is now properly disposed, some companies avoid environmental regulations and high treatment costs within Europe and North America, seeking cheap (possibly illegal) options—including dumping at sea. Many millions of tons of hazardous waste

are transported across the oceans to underdeveloped countries.

In a 2009 out-of-court settlement, Trafigura agreed to pay a total of $43,000 to cover all claims, but many see this as a slap on the hand that does not begin to match the gravity of the crime. Greenpeace has determined to take the company to court, claiming that Trafigura knew the toxicity and illegality of the dump.

Global Twister Although hazardous waste dumping by the *Probo Koala* resulted in the arrest of several African businessmen in Ivory Coast, should the other participants in this global crime be judged and punished? If so, under which laws?

Yet, millions of peasants, herders, fishermen, and other folk inhabiting the world's developing countries in Africa, Asia, and Latin America find themselves paying for the progress enjoyed by fellow human beings who have reaped the benefits of industrialization for several generations. They now suffer from global-induced droughts and floods, but lack the capital to effectively deal with them. As President Yoweri Mueseveni of Uganda told an African Union

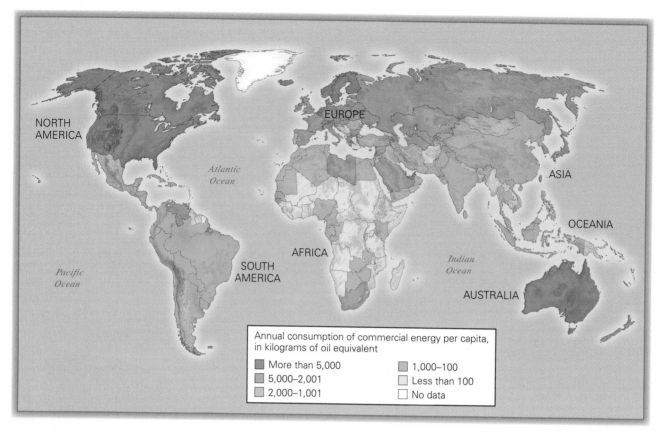

Figure 27.4 Most of the world's highest energy consumers are in North America and western Europe where at least 100 gigajoules of commercial energy per year are consumed by each person. (A gigajoule is the equivalent of about 3.5 metric tons of coal.) In some of these countries, such as the United States and Canada, the consumption rates are in the 300-gigajoule range. At the other end of the scale are low-income countries, whose consumption rates are often less than 1 percent of those in the United States. These figures do not include the consumption of noncommercial energy—the traditional fuels of firewood, animal dung, and other organic matter widely used in the less developed parts of the world.

Source: *Student Atlas of Anthropology* by J. L. Allen & A. C. Shalinsky, p. 126. ©2004, McGraw-Hill/Dushkin Publishing.

summit in Ethiopia in 2007, "We have a message here to tell these [wealthy industrialized] countries, that you are causing aggression to us by causing global warming."[33]

Reactions to Globalization

No matter how effectively a dominant state or corporation combines its hard and soft power, globalization does run into opposition. Pockets of resistance exist within the wealthy industrial and postindustrial states as well as elsewhere in the world. This resistance may be manifested in the rise of traditionalism and revitalization movements—efforts to return to life as it was (or how people think it was) before the familiar order became unhinged and people became unsettled. Some of these reactionary movements may take the form of resurgent ethnonationalism or religious fundamentalist movements. Others may find expression in alternative grassroots movements from radical environmental groups to peace groups.

While it is true that states and big corporations have expanded their power and influence through electronic communication technologies, it is also true that these same technologies present opportunities to those who have traditionally been powerless. They provide a means of distributing information and promoting activities that are distinct from or in opposition to those of dominant society.

One striking case of a cultural reaction to globalization is the Taliban, a group of Muslim religious fundamentalists

[33] UN's Intergovernmental Panel on Climate Change in 2007. Cited by Friedman, T. (2007, April). *New York Times.*

in Afghanistan. The Taliban (the Pashto word for "students," specifically of Islam) helped to force the Russian army out of their country and end the subsequent civil war; then they rose to power in the 1990s and imposed a radical version of traditional Islamic law (Shariah) in an effort to create an Islamic republic based on strict religious values.

In the United States, there has been a similar, though less radical, reaction against modernity. "Born again" and other fundamentalist citizens seek to shape or transform not only their towns but also states and even the entire country by electing politicians committed to forging a national culture based on what they see as American patriotism, English-only legislation, and traditional Christian values.[34]

Ethnic Minorities and Indigenous Peoples: Struggles for Human Rights

Throughout this book, we have discussed a wide range of cultures all across the globe. Many of our examples involve peoples who see themselves as members of distinct nations by virtue of their birth and their cultural and territorial heritage—nations over whom peoples of some other ethnic background have tried to assert political control. An estimated 5,000 such national groups exist in the world today, as opposed to a mere 192 states formally admitted as members of the United Nations (nearly four times the original fifty-one members at its founding in 1945).[35] Although some of these national or ethnic groups are small in population and area—100 or so people living on a few acres—many others are quite large. The Karen people inhabiting southern Myanmar (Burma), for example, number some 4.5 to 5 million, exceeding the population of nearly half of the countries in the world. And Kurds, living in Turkey, Iran, and Iraq, number about 30 million.

The reactions of such groups to forced annexation and domination by state regimes controlled by people of other nations range all the way from the nonviolence of the Saami in Scandinavia, Inuit of Nunavut in northern Canada, or Maori of New Zealand to bloody fights for national independence by Basque separatists in Spain, Karen in eastern Myanmar (Burma), Chechens in southern Russia, or Palestinians in the Middle East. In pursuit of self-determination, national autonomy, independence, or whatever their political objectives, some struggles have been going on for decades.

Since the mid-1900s, global institutions such as the United Nations have tried to address the problem of discrimination, repression, and crimes against humanity, in particular genocide. For example, even though it often fails to act on it, the UN General Assembly's 1966 Covenant of Human Rights states unequivocally:

> In those states in which ethnic, religious or linguistic minorities exist, persons belonging to such minorities shall not be denied the rights, in community with the other members of their group, to enjoy their own culture, to profess and practice their own religion or to use their own language.[36]

This covenant applies not only to minority groups, but also to the world's indigenous peoples, who make up about 5 percent of humanity's population. Nearly all indigenous groups are relatively small nations. Typically, they have suffered repression or discrimination by ethnically different, more powerful, and almost always more heavily populated groups that have gained control over their ancestral homelands.

In the early 1970s indigenous peoples began to organize self-determination movements, resisting acculturation and challenging violations of their human rights. Joining forces across international borders, they established the World Council of Indigenous Peoples in 1975.

In 2007, after many years of popular media campaigns, political lobbying, and diplomatic pressure by hundreds of indigenous leaders and other activists all around the globe, the UN General Assembly finally adopted the Declaration of the Rights of Indigenous Peoples. A foundational document in the global human rights struggle, it contains some 150 articles urging respect for indigenous cultural heritages, calling for official recognition of indigenous land titles and rights of self-determination, and demanding an end to all forms of oppression and discrimination as a principle of international law.

Global Migrations: Refugees, Migrants, and Diasporic Communities

Structural power and structural violence may both be involved in human migration. Throughout human history, individuals, families, and sometimes entire communities have migrated in pursuit of food, safety, and opportunity. Migration has always had a significant effect on world social geography, contributing to cultural change and development, to the diffusion of ideas and innovations, and to

---

[34] Marsella, A. J. (1982). Pulling it together: Discussion and comments. In S. Pastner & W. A. Haviland (Eds.), *Confronting the creationists* (pp. 79–80). *Northeaster Anthropological Association, Occasional Proceedings* 1.

[35] *Cultural Survival Quarterly.* (1992). *15*(4), 38.

[36] Quoted in Bodley, J. H. (1990). *Victims of progress* (3rd ed., p. 99). Mountain View, CA: Mayfield.

In 1982 the UN Sub-Commission on the Promotion and Protection of Human Rights established a Working Group on Indigenous Populations (WGIP). Eleven years later WGIP completed a draft of the Declaration of the Rights of Indigenous Peoples, ratified in 2007. Here we see delegates from Japan's ethnic Ainu community in the UN assembly hall at a recent WGIP gathering.

© EPA/Laurent Gilleron/Corbis

the complex mixture of peoples and cultures found in the world today.

Internal migration occurs within the boundaries of a country. Unable to sustain themselves in the rural backlands, people all over the world continue to move to large urban areas, hoping to find a better life. All too often they live out their days in poor, congested, and diseased slums while attempting to achieve what is usually beyond their reach.

External migration is movement from one country to another. Such migration may be voluntary (people seeking better conditions and opportunities), but all too often it may be involuntary, forced, or imposed—people who have been taken as slaves or prisoners, or driven from their homelands by war, political unrest, religious persecution, or environment disasters. Figure 27.5 shows the patterns of worldwide migration.

Today, about 42 million people in almost half of the world's countries are either internally displaced or have crossed international borders as refugees. Some 9 million of these people have been forced outside their countries, most of them suffering in makeshift camps where they cannot make a living. In some cases, large numbers of an

ethnic group are forced to abandon their homes and flee for their lives. For instance, some 18 million Africans are currently uprooted. In war-torn Sudan alone, more than 2.5 million people have been driven from their homes.

In addition to such forced displacements, tens of thousands of people migrate to wealthy countries every year in search of wage labor and a better future for themselves and their offspring. While most cross international borders as legal immigrants, seeking work permits and ultimately citizenship in their new homeland, untold numbers of others are illegal and do not enjoy many important rights and benefits.

Legal or not, many of these immigrants face great challenges as poor newcomers in these societies—all the more so because they may encounter racism and discrimination. As a consequence, many newcomers form or join communities of people who have come from the same part of the world. Modern transportation and telecommunication technology make it possible for these *diasporic communities,* which exist all across the globe, to remain in contact with relatives and friends who have settled elsewhere, as well as with their country of origin. Indicative of this aspect of globalization is that today about 200 million people (almost 3 percent of the world's population) live outside their countries of birth—not as refugees or immigrants, but as transnationals who earn their living in one country while remaining citizens of another.[37]

internal migration Movement within the boundaries of a country.

external migration Movement from one country to another. It may be voluntary or involuntary.

_____

[37] UN. Global Commission on International Migration, 2005.

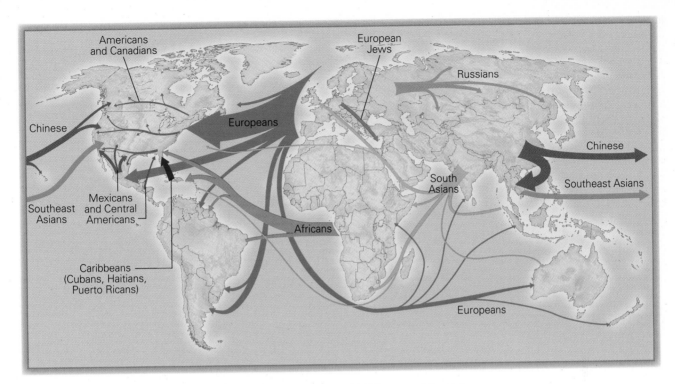

Figure 27.5 Migration has had and continues to have a significant effect on world social geography, contributing to cultural change and development, to the diffusion of ideas and innovations, and to the complex mixture of people and cultures found in the world today. Internal migration occurs within the boundaries of a country; external migration is movement from one country or region to another. **Not shown here are recent migration waves from Africa and Turkey to Europe.**

Source: From *Student Atlas of Anthropology* by J. L. Allen & A. C. Shalinsky, p. 73. Copyright © 2003 McGraw-Hill/ Dushkin Publishing.

Over the past few decades, mass migration across international borders has dramatically changed the ethnic composition of affluent societies in western Europe and North America. Since indigenous peoples such as the Cree or Navajo (just to mention two of more than 500 remaining tribal nations) are the original inhabitants of North America, nearly everyone else (almost 99 percent) is either immigrant offspring or a more recent newcomer. The 13 million Mexicans residing in the United States represent about one fourth of all foreign-born newcomers. As the largest and fastest-growing group of immigrants in the United States, they are settled primarily in California and Texas where many form Spanish-speaking ethnic enclaves. In addition there are over 25 million other immigrants from Asian countries, such as China and India, and African countries, such as Nigeria and Ethiopia. Today, almost 2 million African immigrants live in the United States, a 55-fold increase since the 1960s, with large clusters of different nationalities from that continent concentrated in Washington, DC, New York City, Atlanta, and other major metropolitan areas.

In contrast to former European colonies such as the settler societies of Australia, Canada, and the United States, in which indigenous peoples make up a very small proportion of the population, countries such as Germany, England, and France are traditionally inhabited by closely related ethnic groups historically unified and culturally integrated as nations. Accordingly, massive immigration into Europe by foreigners primarily from Asia and Africa has resulted in considerable upheaval, with the host countries facing unfamiliar problems with cultural integration. Such is the case with Germany, where almost 4 million people of Turkish origin now live and work.

Initially needed as cheap, unskilled laborers, Turks were hired as "guest workers" in highly industrialized urban areas. Since most of them remained, the authorities instituted a family reunification policy, which resulted in hundreds of thousands of Turkish relatives entering the country. Even after several decades in Germany, the vast majority of German Turks do not possess citizenship and have not become culturally integrated into

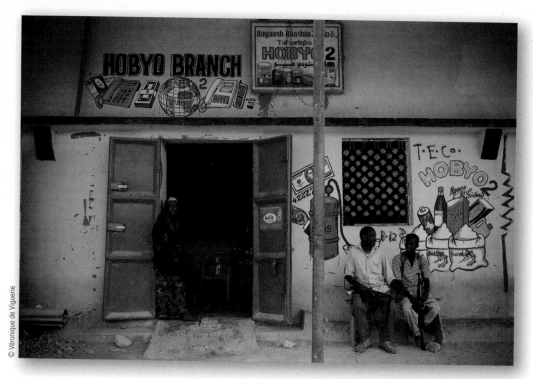

Two decades of clan feuds, violence, and warfare have wreaked havoc on the Republic of Somalia in East Africa. Its weakened central government is powerless to safeguard coastal waters from foreign trawlers depriving Somali fishermen of their livelihood. Nor can it stop local fishermen from turning to piracy for subsistence. Many Somali citizens rely on foreign aid, along with a flow of cash from fellow clan members living abroad, some of whom invest in piracy for profit. Piracy is a booming, multimillion-dollar enterprise in the country's informal economy. Pirates based in the coastal village of Hobyo get supplies 200 kilometers (125 miles) inland at this shop in Gaalkacyo. Its façade features symbols that reflect the globalized business of piracy in this region. Pirates call in their orders by cell phone, and the owner sends them out by truck, charging twice the normal price.

German society. Turkish, spoken by Germany's largest ethnic minority, has become that country's second language.

The ethnic composition in France has also dramatically changed in the past few decades. About 1.5 million Africans and another 2 million people from other parts of the world, mainly from former colonial territories, now live in that country. As with the Turks in Germany, many of these foreigners come in search of economic opportunity but do not become culturally integrated into French society. The same is true for England, now home to over 1.5 million South Asians, plus another 1.3 million people of African descent who hail primarily from the former British colonies.

Although migrants may experience *xenophobia* ("fear of strangers"), hostility, hardship, disappointment, and sometimes failure in their new countries, those who remain trapped in their troubled homelands often face worse challenges: malnutrition, hunger, chronic disease, and violence, resulting in a low life expectancy for many.

As mentioned in an earlier chapter, one fascinating aspect of this global movement of wage-earning workers is the electronic transfer of money in the form of remittances to relatives and friends still living in ancestral cities or villages abroad. For example, Mexicans working in the United States send an estimated $26 billion of their yearly

U.S. earnings by means of money transfers to relatives left behind in their home regions. Without these payments, many local communities throughout Mexico would face major economic problems. Worldwide, remittances total some $330 billion per year.[38] While still high, remittances have declined due to the global recession, causing real hardship in the impoverished communities that have come to depend on them.

Concluding Remarks

As defined in Chapter 1, anthropology is the comparative study of humankind everywhere and throughout time. It seeks to produce reliable knowledge about different peoples and cultures, their ideas and behaviors. Since the beginning of the discipline in the mid-1800s, generations of anthropologists have studied our species in all its cultural and biological variation. In the process, they described in great detail an enormous number and range of different cultures, and they collected a staggering volume of biological data

---

[38] www.worldbank.org/prospects/migrationandremittances.

© Véronique de Viguerie

and ethnographic artifacts while documenting and recording the sounds and sights of hundreds of different cultures.

Today, many of the cultures studied by the earliest anthropologists more than a century ago have changed profoundly in response to powerful outside influences and internal dynamics. Others have disappeared as a result of deadly epidemics, violent conflicts, acculturation, ethnocide, or genocide. All too often, the only detailed records we now possess of these altered and vanished cultures are those that some visiting anthropologist was able to document before it was too late.

But anthropologists do much more than try to preserve precious information about distinctive peoples and cultures. As chronicled in the pages of this book, they also try to explain why cultures are similar or different, why and how they did or did not change. Moreover, they try to identify the particular knowledge and insights that each culture holds concerning the human condition—including contrasting views about humankind's place in the world, how natural resources are used and treated, and how one relates to fellow humans and other species.

Anthropologists are trained to understand and explain economic, social, political, and ideological factors, as well as biological and environmental features and processes, as parts of interrelated dynamic systems. Theoretical models and concepts, such as structural power and structural violence, indicate how remote and seemingly unrelated factors and processes are connected in complex and significant ways.

A holistic and integrative perspective, as developed and tested by several generations of anthropologists in the course of more than a century of cross-cultural research in all parts of the world, has become essential to our understanding of such troubling problems as overpopulation, poverty, food shortages, environmental destruction, and disease in the age of globalization. Especially now that the world's societies, large and small, are becoming more interdependent, these structural dynamics play out on a global scale.

We now recognize that successful economic development in some regions of the world is not always beneficial to peoples in other parts of the world. Considering such systemic relationships, we must question whether a relentless accumulation of wealth and ruthless pursuit of power by strategically positioned individuals and groups come at the expense of the world's small, poor, marginal, or subordinate peoples. Since the victims of repression and exploitation may riot in angry protest against those held responsible for their misery and suffering, structural violence can lead to dangerous destabilization. This, in turn, may spawn political extremism and even threaten global peace and security.[39]

Critically evaluating the global process of economic progress, anthropologists also question whether well-being is adequately measured in financial terms such as per capita annual income, as growth may come at the cost of a decline in the overall quality of life. Although people in different cultures define their personal and collective sense of happiness in their own terms, all member states of the United Nations officially subscribe to the ideal of universal human rights, which include the pursuit of happiness. Indeed, this is all the more important if we realize that not only does our happiness depend on a combination of physical, mental, emotional, and social well-being, but individual and collective human health does as well.

Because of their traditional research focus on non-Western traditional peoples and cultures—many of which are confronting radical environmental problems, physical challenges, political repression, acculturation, and worse— "anthropologists have written more about the dark sides of humanity than about the more joyful aspects of human existence."[40] This much is clear: The greater the repression, exploitation, and structural violence, the less probable it is for a people to overcome problems born of poverty, scarcity, illness, discord, violence, and environmental degradation. Conversely, the greater the opportunities to secure a livelihood in plenty and freedom, the likelier a people will experience health, happiness, and overall well-being.[41]

The value of a global, cross-cultural, and critical perspective is increasingly recognized and affirmed by international organizations that now employ anthropologists for their ethnographic observational skills and analytical insights. For example, after a series of ill-conceived and mismanaged development projects that harmed more than helped local populations, the World Bank contracted dozens of anthropologists for projects all around the world. The same is true for other international organizations, as well as some global corporations and state government agencies.

Beyond studying different cultures, some anthropologists reach out to assist besieged groups struggling to survive in today's rapidly changing world. In so doing,

---

[39] "UN food agency warns G8 ministers of unparalleled hunger crisis as funding falls." (2009, June 12). http://www.un.org/apps/news/story.asp?NewsID=31116&Cr=WFP&Cr1=hunger

[40] Blok, A. (1992). Beyond the bounds of anthropology. In J. Abbink & H. Vermeulen (Eds.), *History and culture: Essays on the work of Eric R. Wolf* (pp. 5–20, quote at 15). Amsterdam: Het Spinhuis.

[41] Almost thirty years ago, Eric Wolf noted that "an anthropology of happiness" had not yet been invented (see McBride, B. [1980]. *Eric. R. Wolf interview. Between subjectivity and objectivity.* Unpublished master's thesis, Anthropology Department, Columbia University). Since then, there have been studies on that subject, including Matthews, G. (2006). Happiness and the pursuit of a life worth living: An anthropological approach. In Y. K. Ng & L. S. Ho (Eds.), *Happiness and public policy* (pp. 147–168). Hampshire, England: Palgrave Macmillan; Thin, N. (2007). "Realising the substance of their happiness": How anthropology forgot about *homo gauisus*. In A. C. Jimenez (Ed.), *Culture and the politics of freedom: The anthropology of well-being*. London: Pluto; Veenhoven, R. (1993). *Happiness in nations: Subjective appreciation of life in 56 nations 1946–1992.* Rotterdam: RISBO.

they seek to put into practice their own knowledge about humankind—knowledge deepened through the comparative perspective of anthropology, which is cross-culturally, historically, and biologically informed.

Because anthropological research is fascinating and also has the potential to help solve practical problems, a unique group of people have been drawn to the discipline. Among them is Paul Farmer, a world-renowned medical doctor, anthropologist, and human rights activist (see the Anthropologist of Note). Many anthropologists are inspired by the old but still valid idea that anthropology must aim to live up to its ideal as the most liberating of the sciences. As stated by noted anthropologist Margaret Mead, "Never doubt that a small group of committed people can change the world; indeed it is the only thing that ever has."

Anthropologist of Note

Paul Farmer (b. 1959)

Medical anthropologist **Paul Farmer**—doctor, Harvard professor, world-renowned infectious disease specialist, and recipient of a MacArthur "genius" grant—grew up in a trailer park in Florida without running water.[a] Admitted to Duke University on scholarship, he majored in anthropology and labored alongside poor Haitian farm workers in North Carolina's tobacco fields. After getting his bachelor's degree in 1982, he spent a year in Haiti and found his life's calling: to diagnose and cure infectious diseases and transform health care on a global scale by focusing on the world's poorest communities. Returning to the United States, Farmer earned both an MD and a doctorate in anthropology from Harvard in 1990.

While still a graduate student, Farmer returned frequently to Haiti. Increasingly involved in health issues in the area of Cange, a remote village in Haiti's destitute Central Plateau region, he (with a trio of fellow activists) formed a group called Zanmi Lasante (Haitian Kreyol for "Partners in Health"). In 1985,

the Zanmi Lasante group established a clinic with financial support from a Boston philanthropist. Two years later they founded the Boston-based Partners in Health (PIH) foundation to support their growing endeavor to help the poorest of the poor deal with infectious diseases, especially AIDS and tuberculosis.

The endeavor includes research (ethnographic as well as medical) needed to carry the work forward with a clear vision. As an applied anthropologist aiming to ease human suffering, Farmer bases his activism on holistic and interpretive ethnographic analysis that includes "a historical understanding of the large-scale social and economic structures in which affliction is embedded." Issues of structural violence are fundamental in his research and practice. Noting that social and economic inequalities "have powerfully sculpted not only the [demographic] distribution of infectious diseases but also the course of health outcomes among the afflicted," he concludes, "Inequality itself constitutes our modern plague."[b]

Since its founding, Zanmi Lasante has expanded its one-room clinic to a multiservice health complex that includes a primary school, an infirmary, a surgery wing, a training program for health outreach workers, a 104-bed hospital, a women's clinic, and a pediatric care facility. Moreover, it has pioneered the treatment of multidrug-resistant tuberculosis and HIV in Haiti. And Partners in Health, now funded by a wide range of organizations, has expanded its reach to include Lesotho, Malawi, and Rwanda in Africa, as well as Peru, Mexico, Russia, and the United States. The foundation's reach continues to grow, fueled by Farmer's passionate conviction that "health is a human right."

In concert with his active and extensive work with PIH around the globe, Farmer is a professor of medical anthropology in Harvard University's Department of Social Medicine and maintains an active practice in infectious diseases and as chief of the Division of Social Medicine and Health Inequalities at Brigham and Women's Hospital in Boston. Among numerous honors, he has received the Margaret Mead Award from the American Anthropological Association and is the subject of the Pulitzer Prize–winning book by Tracy Kidder (see footnote below).

[a] This profile draws from numerous sources, including: Kidder, T. (2003). *Mountains beyond mountains: The quest of Dr. Paul Farmer, a man who would cure the world.* New York: Random House; Farmer, P. (2004, June). An anthropology of structural violence. *Current Anthropology 45,* 3. Farmer, P. (1996). On suffering and structural violence: A view from below. *Daedelus 125* (1), 261–283.

[b] Farmer, P. (2001). *Infections and inequalities: the modern plagues.* Berkeley: University of California Press.

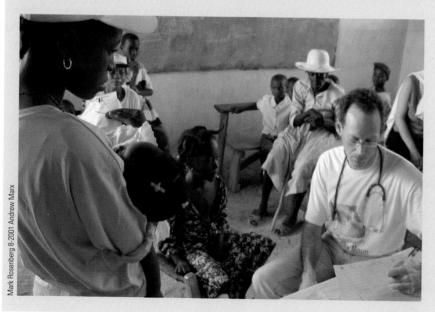

Mark Rosenberg 8-2001 Andrew Marx

Questions for Reflection

1. Given that the number of big cities is growing worldwide, especially in developing countries, do you know of any public festival other than carnival that brings people together from all walks of life for a few hours or a day? Can you think of any social integrative functions of such as public feast?

2. Reflecting on the human condition past and present, and the challenges facing your own family in the age of globalization, do you imagine the future in terms of continued progress? How do you measure that and by which cultural standard?

3. Considering the relationship between structural power and structural violence, does your own lifestyle in terms of buying clothes and food, driving cars, and so on reflect or have an effect on the globalization process?

4. In the global mediascape, television viewers and Internet users are not only consumers of news and entertainment but are also exposed to soft power. Can you think of an example of soft power in your daily life? And at which point does such influence turn into propaganda or manipulation?

5. The World Health Organization, UNESCO, Oxfam, and Amnesty International are global institutions concerned with structural violence and human rights violations. Confronted with genocidal conflicts, famines, epidemics, and torture of political prisoners, people active in these organizations try to improve the human condition. Why do you think that an anthropological perspective on such worldwide problems might be of practical use? Can you think of an example?

Suggested Readings

Appadurai, A. (1996). *Modernity at large: Cultural dimensions of globalization.* Minneapolis: University of Minnesota Press.

In this fundamental contribution to how globalization works, a leading anthropologist discusses how forces such as migration and electronic mediation acquire shaping roles in the production of contemporary culture.

Bodley, J. H. (2007). *Anthropology and contemporary human problems* (5th ed.). Lanham, MD: Alta Mira.

Anthropologist Bodley examines some of the most serious problems in the world today: overconsumption, resource depletion, hunger and starvation, overpopulation, violence, and war.

Farmer, P. (2003). *Pathologies of power: Health, human rights, and the new war on the poor.* Berkeley: University of California Press.

Farmer argues that promoting the social and economic rights of the world's poor is the most important human rights struggle of our time. Based on eyewitness accounts from Russian prisons and poor peasant communities in Haiti, Mexico, and Peru, his book exposes relationships between political and economic injustice and the suffering of the powerless. Linking the painful experiences of individual victims to a broader analysis of structural violence, Farmer hopes that new medical and social technologies will develop in conjunction with a more informed sense of social justice.

Ginsburg, F. D., Abu-Lughod, L., & Larkin, B. (Eds.). (2009). *Media worlds: Anthropology on new terrain.* Berkeley: University of California Press.

Groundbreaking essays by pioneers of media studies in anthropology, discussing the place and function of film, video, radio, television, and cinema in different cultures and showing that contemporary peoples and cultures cannot be understood without the mediascapes they inhabit.

Lewellen, T. C. (2002). *The anthropology of globalization: Cultural anthropology enters the 21st century.* Westport, CT: Greenwood.

Readable introduction, summary, and critique of globalization with telling and timely ethnographic examples.

Ong, A. (1999). *Flexible citizenship: The cultural logics of transnationality.* Durham, NC: Duke University Press.

Ong demonstrates how the Chinese transnational community confounds notions of peripheral non-Westerners and argues that the contemporary world is creating the context for the rise of China.

Trouillot, M. R. (2003). *Global transformations: Anthropology and the modern world.* New York: Palgrave Macmillan.

Examining anthropology's history and discussing future possibilities for the discipline, the author challenges colleagues to question dominant narratives of globalization and to radically rethink key concepts of anthropology.

Glossary

abduction Movement away from midline of the body or from the center of the hand or foot.

absolute or chronometric dating In archaeology and paleoanthropology, dates for recovered material based on solar years, centuries, or other units of absolute time.

acclimatization Long-term physiological adjustments made in order to attain an equilibrium with a specific environmental stimulus.

acculturation Massive culture change that occurs in a society when it experiences intensive firsthand contact with a more powerful society.

Acheulean tradition The tool-making tradition of *Homo erectus* in Africa, Europe, and southwestern Asia in which hand-axes were developed from the earlier Oldowan chopper.

action theory The theory that self-serving actions by forceful leaders play a role in civilization's emergence.

adaptation A series of beneficial adjustments to the environment.

adaptive radiation Rapid diversification of an evolving population as it adapts to a variety of available niches.

adduction Movement toward the midline of the body or to the center of the hand or foot.

adjudication Mediation with an unbiased third party making the ultimate decision.

advocacy anthropology Research that is community based and politically involved.

affiliative Tending to promote social cohesion.

affinal kin People related through marriage.

age grade An organized category of people based on age; every individual passes through a series of such categories over his or her lifetime.

age set A formally established group of people born during a certain time span who move through the series of age-grade categories together.

agribusiness Large-scale businesses involved in food production, including farming, contract farming, seed supply, agrichemicals, farm machinery, distribution, processing, and marketing. Also known as corporate farming, it stands in contrast to smaller family-owned farms.

agriculture The cultivation of food plants in soil prepared and maintained for crop production. Involves using technologies other than hand tools, such as irrigation, fertilizers, and the wooden or metal plow pulled by harnessed draft animals.

alleles Alternate forms of a single gene.

Allen's rule The tendency for the bodies of mammals living in cold climates to have shorter appendages (arms and legs) than members of the same species living in warm climates.

alphabet A series of symbols representing the sounds of a language arranged in a traditional order.

altruism Concern for the welfare of others expressed as increased risk undertaken by individuals for the good of the group.

ambilocal residence A residence pattern in which a married couple may choose either matrilocal or patrilocal residence.

anagenesis A sustained directional shift in a population's average characteristics.

analogies In biology, structures possessed by different organisms that are superficially similar due to similar function; without sharing a common developmental pathway or structure.

ancestral Characteristics that define a group of organisms that are due to shared ancestry.

animatism A belief that nature is enlivened or energized by an impersonal spiritual power or supernatural potency.

animism A belief that nature is animated (enlivened or energized) by distinct personalized spirit beings separable from bodies.

Anthropoidea A suborder of the primates that includes New World monkeys, Old World monkeys, and apes (including humans).

anthropology The study of humankind in all times and places.

applied anthropology The use of anthropological knowledge and methods to solve practical problems, often for a specific client.

arboreal Living in the trees.

arboreal hypothesis A theory for primate evolution that proposes that life in the trees was responsible for enhanced visual acuity and manual dexterity in primates.

archaeology The study of human cultures through the recovery and analysis of material remains and environmental data.

Archaic cultures Mesolithic cultures in the Americas.

archaic *Homo sapiens* A loosely defined group within the genus *Homo* that "lumpers" use for fossils with the combination of large brain size and ancestral features on the skull.

Ardipithecus ramidus One of the earliest bipeds that lived in eastern Africa about 4.4 million years ago.

art The creative use of the human imagination to aesthetically interpret, express, and engage life, modifying experienced reality in the process.

artifact Any object fashioned or altered by humans.

Aurignacian tradition Tool-making tradition in Europe and western Asia at the beginning of the Upper Paleolithic.

Australopithecus The genus including several species of early bipeds from East, South, and Central Africa living between about 1.1 and 4.3 million years ago, one of whom was directly ancestral to humans.

balanced reciprocity A mode of exchange in which the giving and the receiving are specific as to the value of the goods and the time of their delivery.

band A relatively small and loosely organized kin-ordered group that inhabits a common territory and that may split periodically into smaller extended family groups that are politically and economically independent.

Bergmann's rule The tendency for the bodies of mammals living in cold climates to be shorter and rounder than members of the same species living in warm climates.

binocular vision Vision with increased depth perception from two eyes set next to each other allowing their visual fields to overlap.

bioarchaeology The archaeological study of human remains emphasizing the preservation of cultural and social processes in the skeleton.

biocultural Focusing on the interaction of biology and culture.

bipedalism The mode of locomotion in which an organism walks upright on its two hind legs characteristic of humans and their ancestors; also called bipedality.

blade technique A technique of stone tool manufacture by which long, parallel-sided flakes are struck off the edges of a specially prepared core.

brachiation Using the arms to move from branch to branch, with the body hanging suspended beneath the arms.

bride service A designated period of time when the groom works for the bride's family.

bridewealth Money or valuable goods paid by the groom or his family to the bride's family upon marriage; also called bride-price.

Bronze Age In the Old World, the period marked by the production of tools and ornaments of bronze; began about 5,000 years ago in China and Southwest Asia and about 500 years earlier in Southeast Asia.

burin A stone tool with chisel-like edges used for working bone and antler.

cargo cult A spiritual movement (especially noted in Melanesia) in reaction to disruptive contact with Western capitalism, promising resurrection of deceased relatives, destruction or enslavement of white foreigners, and the magical arrival of utopian riches.

carrying capacity The number of people that the available resources can support at a given level of food-getting techniques.

caste A closed social class in a stratified society in which membership is determined by birth and fixed for life.

Catarrhini An anthropoid infraorder that includes Old World monkeys, apes, and humans.

chiefdom A regional polity in which two or more local groups are organized under a single chief, who is at the head of a ranked hierarchy of people.

chromatid One half of the "X" shape of chromosomes visible once replication is complete. Sister chromatids are exact copies of each other.

chromosomes In the cell nucleus, the structures visible during cellular division containing long strands of DNA combined with a protein.

civilization In anthropology, a type of society marked by the presence of cities, social classes, and the state.

clade A taxonomic grouping that contains a single common ancestor and all of its descendants.

cladogenesis Speciation through a branching mechanism whereby an ancestral population gives rise to two or more descendant populations.

clan An extended unilineal kinship group, often consisting of several lineages, whose members claim common descent from a remote ancestor, usually legendary or mythological.

clavicle The collarbone connecting the sternum (breastbone) with the scapula (shoulder blade).

clines Gradual changes in the frequency of an allele or trait over space.

code switching Changing from one mode of speech to another as the situation demands, whether from one language to another or from one dialect of a language to another.

codon Three-base sequence of a gene that specifies a particular amino acid for inclusion in a protein.

cognitive capacity A broad concept including intelligence, educability, concept formation, self-awareness, self-evaluation, attention span, sensitivity in discrimination, and creativity.

common-interest association An association that results from an act of joining based on sharing particular activities, objectives, values, or beliefs, sometimes rooted in common ethnic, religious, or regional background.

community A unit of primate social organization composed of fifty or more individuals who inhabit a large geographic area together.

conjugal family A family established through marriage.

consanguineal family A family of "blood relatives" consisting of related women, their brothers, and the women's offspring.

consanguineal kin Biologically related relatives, commonly referred to as blood relatives.

conspicuous consumption A showy display of wealth for social prestige.

contagious magic Magic based on the principle that things or persons once in contact can influence each other after the contact is broken.

continental drift According to the theory of plate tectonics, the movement of continents embedded in underlying plates on the earth's surface in relation to one another over the history of life on earth.

convergent evolution In biological evolution, a process by which unrelated populations develop similarities to one another due to similar function rather than shared ancestry.

convergent evolution In cultural evolution, the development of similar cultural adaptations to similar environmental conditions by different peoples with different ancestral cultures.

coprolites Preserved fecal material providing evidence of the diet and health of past organisms.

core values Those values especially promoted by a particular culture.

core vocabulary The most basic and long-lasting words in any language—pronouns, lower numerals, and names for body parts and natural objects.

cranium The braincase of the skull.

Cro-Magnon A European of the Upper Paleolithic after about 36,000 years ago.

cross cousin Child of a mother's brother or a father's sister.

cultural adaptation A complex of ideas, activities, and technologies that enable people to survive and even thrive in their environment.

cultural anthropology The study of customary patterns in human behavior, thought, and feelings. It focuses on humans as culture-producing and culture-reproducing creatures. Also known as social or sociocultural anthropology.

cultural control Control through beliefs and values deeply internalized in the minds of individuals.

cultural evolution Cultural change over time; not to be confused with progress.

cultural loss The abandonment of an existing practice or trait.

cultural relativism The idea that one must suspend judgment of other people's practices in order to understand them in their own cultural terms.

cultural resource management A branch of archaeology tied to government policies for the protection of cultural resources and involving surveying and/or excavating archaeological and historical remains threatened by construction or development.

culture A society's shared and socially transmitted ideas, values, and perceptions, which are used to make sense of experience and generate behavior and are reflected in that behavior.

culture area A geographic region in which a number of societies follow similar patterns of life.

culture-bound Theories about the world and reality based on the assumptions and values of one's own culture.

culture-bound syndrome A mental disorder specific to a particular cultural group.

culture core Cultural features that are fundamental in the society's way of making its living—including food-producing techniques, knowledge of available resources, and the work arrangements involved in applying those techniques to the local environment.

datum point The starting point, or reference, for a grid system.

demographics Population characteristics such as the number of individuals of each age and sex.

dendrochronology In archaeology and paleoanthropology, a technique of chronometric dating based on the number of rings of growth found in a tree trunk.

dental formula The number of each tooth type (incisors, canines, premolars, and molars) on one half of each jaw. Unlike other mammals, primates possess equal numbers on their upper and lower jaws so the dental formula for the species is a single series of numbers.

dependence training Childrearing practices that foster compliance in the performance of assigned tasks and dependence on the domestic group, rather than reliance on oneself.

derived Characteristics that define a group of organisms and that did not exist in ancestral populations.

descent group Any kin-ordered social group with a membership in the direct line of descent from a real (historical) or fictional common ancestor.

developmental adaptation A permanent phenotypic variation derived from interaction between genes and the environment during the period of growth and development.

dialects Varying forms of a language that reflect particular regions, occupations, or social classes and that are similar enough to be mutually intelligible.

diastema A space between the canines and other teeth allowing the large projecting canines to fit within the jaw.

diffusion The spread of certain ideas, customs, or practices from one culture to another.

digital ethnography The use of digital technologies (audio and visual) for the collection, analysis, and representation of ethnographic data.

discourse An extended communication on a particular subject.

disease Refers to a specific pathology; a physical or biological abnormality.

displacement Referring to things and events removed in time and space.

diurnal Active during the day and at rest at night.

divination A magical procedure or spiritual ritual designed to find out what is not knowable by ordinary means, such as foretelling the future by interpreting omens.

DNA Deoxyribonucleic acid. The genetic material consisting of a complex molecule whose base structure directs the synthesis of proteins.

doctrine An assertion of opinion or belief formally handed down by an authority as true and indisputable.

domestication An evolutionary process whereby humans modify, either intentionally or unintentionally, the genetic makeup of a population of plants or animals, sometimes to the extent that members of the population are unable to survive and/or reproduce without human assistance.

dominance The ability of one allele for a trait to mask the presence of another allele.

dominance hierarchies An observed ranking system in primate societies ordering individuals from high (alpha) to low standing corresponding to predictable behavioral interactions including domination.

dowry Payment of a woman's inheritance at the time of her marriage, either to her or to her husband.

ecofact The natural remains of plants and animals found in the archaeological record.

ecological niche A species' way of life considered in the full context of its environment, including factors such as diet, activity, terrain, vegetation, predators, prey, and climate.

economic system An organized arrangement for producing, distributing, and consuming goods.

ecosystem A system, or a functioning whole, composed of both the natural environment and all the organisms living within it.

egalitarian society A society in which everyone has about equal rank, access to, and power over the basic resources that support survival, influence, and prestige.

EGO The central person from whom the degree of each relationship is traced.

eliciting device An activity or object used to draw out individuals and encourage them to recall and share information.

empirical Based on observations of the world rather than on intuition or faith.

enculturation The process by which a society's culture is passed on from one generation to the next and individuals become members of their society.

endemic The public health term for a disease that is widespread in a population.

endocast A cast of the inside of a skull; used to help determine the size and shape of the brain.

endogamy Marriage within a particular group or category of individuals.

entoptic phenomena Bright pulsating forms that are generated by the central nervous system and seen in states of trance.

enzyme Protein that initiates and directs chemical reactions.

epic A long, dramatic narrative recounting the celebrated deeds of a historic or legendary hero—often sung or recited in poetic language.

Eskimo system Kinship reckoning in which the nuclear family is emphasized by specifically identifying the mother, father, brother, and sister, while lumping together all other relatives into broad categories such as uncle, aunt, and cousin; also known as a lineal system.

estrus In some primate females, the time of sexual receptivity during which ovulation is visibly displayed.

ethnic group People who collectively and publicly identify themselves as a distinct group based on cultural features such as common origin, language, customs, and traditional beliefs.

ethnicity This term, rooted in the Greek word *ethnikos* ("nation") and related to *ethnos* ("custom"), is the expression of the set of cultural ideas held by an ethnic group.

ethnocentrism The belief that the ways of one's own culture are the only proper ones.

ethnocide The violent eradication of an ethnic group's collective cultural identity as a distinctive people; occurs when a dominant society deliberately sets out to destroy another society's cultural heritage.

ethnographic fieldwork Extended on-location research to gather detailed and in-depth information on a society's customary ideas, values, and practices through participation in its collective social life.

ethnography A detailed description of a particular culture primarily based on fieldwork.

ethnohistory A study of cultures of the recent past through oral histories; accounts of explorers, missionaries, and traders; and through analysis of records such as land titles, birth and death records, and other archival materials.

ethnolinguistics A branch of linguistics that studies the relationships between language and culture and how they mutually influence and inform each other.

ethnology The study and analysis of different cultures from a comparative or historical point of view, utilizing ethnographic accounts and developing anthropological theories that help explain why certain important differences or similarities occur among groups.

ethnomusicology The study of a society's music in terms of its cultural setting.

evolution Changes in allele frequencies in populations; also known as microevolution.

evolutionary medicine An approach to human sickness and health combining principles of evolutionary theory and human evolutionary history.

exogamy Marriage outside the group.

extended family Two or more closely related nuclear families clustered together into a large domestic group.

external migration Movement from one country to another. It may be voluntary or involuntary.

family Two or more people related by blood, marriage, or adoption. The family may take many forms, ranging from a single parent with one or more children, to a married couple or polygamous spouses with or without offspring, to several generations of parents and their children.

feature A non-portable element such as a hearth or an architectural element such as a wall that is preserved in the archaeological record.

fictive marriage Marriage by proxy to the symbols of someone not physically present to establish the social status of a spouse and heirs.

fieldwork The term anthropologists use for on-location research.

fission The splitting of a descent group into two or more new descent groups.

flotation An archaeological technique employed to recover very tiny objects by immersion of soil samples in water to separate heavy from light particles.

fluorine dating In archaeology or paleoanthropology, a technique for relative dating based on the fact that the amount of fluorine in bones is proportional to their age.

folklore A term coined by 19th-century scholars studying the unwritten stories and other artistic traditions of rural peoples to distinguish between "folk art" and the "fine art" of the literate elite.

food foraging Hunting, fishing, and gathering wild plant foods.

foramen magnum A large opening in the skull through which the spinal cord passes and connects to the brain.

forensic anthropology Applied subfield of physical anthropology that specializes in the identification of human skeletal remains for legal purposes.

formal interview A structured question/answer session carefully notated as it occurs and based on prepared questions.

fossil Any mineralized trace or impression of an organism that has been preserved in the earth's crust from past geologic time.

founder effects A particular form of genetic drift deriving from a small founding population not possessing all the alleles present in the original population.

fovea centralis A shallow pit in the retina of the eye that enables an animal to focus on an object while maintaining visual contact with its surroundings.

gender The cultural elaborations and meanings assigned to the biological differentiation between the sexes.

gendered speech Distinct male and female speech patterns, which vary across social and cultural settings.

gene A portion of the DNA molecule containing a sequence of base pairs that is the fundamental physical and functional unit of heredity.

gene flow The introduction of alleles from the gene pool of one population into that of another.

gene pool All the genetic variants possessed by members of a population.

generalized reciprocity A mode of exchange in which the value of what is given is not calculated, nor is the time of repayment specified.

genetic code The sequence of three bases (a codon) that specifies the sequence of amino acids in protein synthesis.

genetic drift Chance fluctuations of allele frequencies in the gene pool of a population.

genocide The physical extermination of one people by another, either as a deliberate act or as the accidental outcome of activities carried out by one people with little regard for their impact on others.

genome The complete structure sequence of DNA for a species.

genotype The alleles possessed for a particular gene.

genus (genera, pl.) In the system of plant and animal classification, a group of like species.

gesture Facial expressions and body postures and motions that convey intended as well as subconscious messages.

globalization Worldwide interconnectedness, evidenced in global movements of natural resources, trade goods, human labor, finance capital, information, and infectious diseases.

glottochronology In linguistics, a method for identifying the approximate time that languages branched off from a common ancestor; based on analyzing core vocabularies.

gracile australopithecines Members of the genus *Australopithecus* possessing a more lightly built chewing apparatus; likely had a diet that included more meat than that of the robust australopithecines; best represented by the South African species *A. africanus*.

grade A general level of biological organization seen among a group of species; useful for constructing evolutionary relationships.

grammar The entire formal structure of a language, including morphology and syntax.

grave goods Items such as utensils, figurines, and personal possessions, symbolically placed in the grave for the deceased person's use in the afterlife.

grid system A system for recording data in three dimensions for an archaeological excavation.

grooming The ritual cleaning of another animal's coat to remove parasites and other matter.

group marriage Marriage in which several men and women have sexual access to one another; also called co-marriage.

Haplorhini In the alternate primate taxonomy, the suborder that includes tarsiers, monkeys, apes, and humans.

hard power Coercive power that is backed up by economic and military force.

Hardy-Weinberg principle Demonstrates algebraically that the percentage of individuals that are homozygous for the dominant allele, homozygous for the recessive allele, and heterozygous should remain constant from one generation to the next, provided that certain specified conditions are met.

Hawaiian system Kinship reckoning in which all relatives of the same sex and generation are referred to by the same term.

health disparity A difference in the health status between the wealthy elite and the poor in stratified societies.

hemoglobin The protein that carries oxygen in red blood cells.

heterochrony Change in the timing of developmental events that is often responsible for changes in the shape or size of a body part.

heterozygous Refers to a chromosome pair that bears different alleles for a single gene.

holistic perspective A fundamental principle of anthropology: that the various parts of human culture and biology must be viewed in the broadest possible context in order to understand their interconnections and interdependence.

homeobox gene A gene responsible for large-scale effects on growth and development that are frequently responsible for major reorganization of body plans in organisms.

homeotherm An animal that maintains a relatively constant body temperature despite environmental fluctuations.

home range The geographic area within which a group of primates usually moves.

hominid African hominoid family that includes humans and their ancestors. Some scientists, recognizing the close relationship of humans, chimps, bonobos, and gorillas, use the term *hominid* to refer to all African hominoids. They then divide the hominid family into two subfamilies: the Paninae (chimps, bonobos, and gorillas) and the Homininae (humans and their ancestors).

hominin The taxonomic subfamily or tribe within the primates that includes humans and our ancestors.

hominoid The taxonomic division superfamily within the Old World primates that includes gibbons, siamangs, orangutans, gorillas, chimpanzees, bonobos, and humans.

Homo The genus of bipeds that appeared 2.5 million years ago characterized by increasing brain size compared to earlier bipeds. The genus is divided into various species based on features such as brain size, skull shape, and cultural capabilities.

Homo habilis "Handy man." The first fossil members of the genus *Homo* appearing 2.5 million years ago, with larger brains and smaller faces than australopithecines.

homologies In biology, structures possessed by two different organisms that arise in similar fashion and pass through similar stages during embryonic development though they may possess different functions.

homozygous Refers to a chromosome pair that bears identical alleles for a single gene.

horticulture Cultivation of crops carried out with simple hand tools such as digging sticks or hoes.

household The basic residential unit where economic production, consumption, inheritance, childrearing, and shelter are organized and carried out.

Human Relations Area Files (HRAF) A vast collection of cross-indexed ethnographic and archaeological data catalogued by cultural characteristics and geographic locations; archived in about 300 libraries (on microfiche or online).

hunting response A cyclic expansion and contraction of the blood vessels of the limbs that balance releasing enough heat to prevent frostbite with maintaining heat in the body core.

hydraulic theory The theory that explains civilization's emergence as the result of the construction of elaborate irrigation systems, the functioning of which required full-time managers whose control blossomed into the first governing body and elite social class.

hypoglossal canal The opening in the skull that accommodates the tongue-controlling hypoglossal nerve.

hypothesis A tentative explanation of the relation between certain phenomena.

iconic images Culturally specific people, animals, and monsters seen in the deepest stage of trance.

idealist perspective A theoretical approach stressing the primacy of superstructure in cultural research and analysis.

illness The meanings and elaborations given to a particular physical state.

imitative magic Magic based on the principle that like produces like; sometimes called sympathetic magic.

incest taboo The prohibition of sexual relations between specified individuals, usually parent and child and sibling relations at a minimum.

incorporation In a rite of passage, reincorporation of the individual into society in his or her new status.

independence training Childrearing practices that foster independence, self-reliance, and personal achievement.

informal economy A network of producing and circulating marketable commodities, labor, and services that for various reasons escape government control.

informal interview An unstructured, open-ended conversation in everyday life.

informed consent Formal recorded agreement to participate in research; federally mandated for all research in the United States and Europe.

infrastructure The economic foundation of a society, including its subsistence practices and the tools and other material equipment used to make a living.

innovation Any new idea, method, or device that gains widespread acceptance in society.

internal migration Movement within the boundaries of a country.

intersexual A person born with reproductive organs, genitalia, and/or sex chromosomes that are not exclusively male or female.

Iroquois system Kinship reckoning in which a father and father's brother are referred to by a single term, as are a mother and mother's sister, but a father's sister and mother's brother are given separate terms. Parallel cousins are classified with brothers and sisters, while cross cousins are classified separately but not equated with relatives of some other generation.

ischial callosities Hardened, nerveless pads on the buttocks that allow baboons and other primates to sit for long periods of time.

isolating mechanism A factor that separates breeding populations, thereby preventing gene flow, creating divergent subspecies, and ultimately (if maintained) divergent species.

isotherm An animal whose body temperature rises or falls according to the temperature of the surrounding environment.

Kenyanthropus platyops A proposed genus and species of biped contemporary with early australopithecines; may not be a separate genus.

key consultant A member of the society being studied who provides information that helps researchers understand the meaning of what they observe; early anthropologists referred to such individuals as informants.

kindred An individual's close blood relatives on the maternal and paternal sides of his or her family.

kinesics A system of notating and analyzing postures, facial expressions, and body motions that convey messages.

kinship A network of relatives within which individuals possess certain mutual rights and obligations.

k-selected Reproduction involving the production of relatively few offspring with high parental investment in each.

Kula ring A form of balanced reciprocity that reinforces trade relations among the seafaring Trobriand Islanders and other Melanesians.

lactase An enzyme in the small intestine that enables humans to assimilate lactose.

lactose A sugar that is the primary constituent of fresh milk.

language A system of communication using sounds or gestures that are put together in meaningful ways according to a set of rules.

language family A group of languages descended from a single ancestral language.

law Formal rules of conduct that, when violated, effectuate negative sanctions.

law of competitive exclusion When two closely related species compete for the same niche, one will out-compete the other, bringing about the latter's extinction.

law of independent assortment The Mendelian principle that genes controlling different traits are inherited independently of one another.

law of segregation The Mendelian principle that variants of genes for a particular trait retain their separate identities through the generations.

legend A story about a memorable event or figure handed down by tradition and told as true but without historical evidence.

legitimacy The right of political leaders to govern—to hold, use, and allocate power—on the socially accepted customs, rules, or laws that bind and hold a people together as a collective whole.

Levalloisian technique Tool-making technique by which three or four long triangular flakes were detached from a specially prepared core; developed by members of the genus *Homo* transitional from *H. erectus* to *H. sapiens*.

leveling mechanism A cultural obligation compelling prosperous members of a community to give away goods, host public feasts, provide free service, or otherwise demonstrate generosity so that no one permanently accumulates significantly more wealth than anyone else.

lineage A unilineal kinship group descended from a common ancestor or founder who lived four to six generations ago, and in which relationships among members can be exactly stated in genealogical terms.

linguistic anthropology The study of human languages—looking at their structure, history, and relation to social and cultural contexts.

linguistic determinism The idea that language to some extent shapes the way in which we view and think about the world around us.

linguistic divergence The development of different languages from a single ancestral language.

linguistic nationalism The attempt by ethnic minorities and even countries to proclaim independence by purging their language of foreign terms.

linguistic relativity The idea that distinctions encoded in one language are unique to that language.

linguistics The modern scientific study of all aspects of language.

Lower Paleolithic The first part of the Old Stone Age beginning with the earliest Oldowan tools spanning from about 200,000 or 250,000 to 2.6 million years ago.

macroevolution Evolution above the species level.

mammal The class of vertebrate animals distinguished by bodies covered with fur, self-regulating temperature, and, in females, milk-producing mammary glands.

market exchange The buying and selling of goods and services, with prices set by rules of supply and demand.

marriage A culturally sanctioned union between two or more people that establishes certain rights and obligations between the people, between them and their children, and between them and their in-laws. Such marriage rights and obligations most often include, but are not limited to, sex, labor, property, childrearing, exchange, and status.

marrow The tissue inside of long bones where blood cells are produced.

material culture The durable aspects of culture such as tools, structures, and art.

materialist perspective A theoretical approach stressing the primacy of infrastructure (material conditions) in cultural research and analysis.

matrilineal descent Descent traced exclusively through the female line to establish group membership.

matrilocal residence A residence pattern in which a married couple lives in the wife's mother's place of residence.

mediation Settlement of a dispute through negotiation assisted by an unbiased third party.

medical anthropology A specialization in anthropology that combines theoretical and applied approaches from cultural and biological anthropology with the study of human health and disease.

medical pluralism The presence of multiple medical systems, each with its own practices and beliefs in a society.

medical system A patterned set of ideas and practices relating to illness.

meiosis A kind of cell division that produces the sex cells, each of which has half the number of chromosomes found in other cells of the organism.

melanin The chemical responsible for dark skin pigmentation that helps protect against damage from ultraviolet radiation.

Mesoamerica The region encompassing central and southern Mexico and northern Central America.

Mesolithic The Middle Stone Age period between the end of the Paleolithic and the start of the Neolithic; referred to as Archaic cultures in the Americas.

microlith A small blade of flint or similar stone, several of which were hafted together in wooden handles to make tools; widespread in the Mesolithic.

middens A refuse or garbage disposal area in an archaeological site.

Middle Paleolithic The middle part of the Old Stone Age characterized by the development of the Mousterian tradition of tool making and the earlier Levalloisian traditions.

mitosis A kind of cell division that produces new cells having exactly the same number of chromosome pairs, and hence copies of genes, as the parent cell.

modal personality Those character traits that occur with the highest frequency in a social group and are therefore the most representative of its culture.

modernization The process of political and socioeconomic change, whereby developing societies acquire some of the cultural characteristics of Western industrial societies.

moiety Each group that results from a division of a society into two halves on the basis of descent.

molecular anthropology A branch of biological anthropology that uses genetic and biochemical techniques to test hypotheses about human evolution, adaptation, and variation.

molecular clock The hypothesis that dates of divergences among related species can be calculated through an examination of the genetic mutations that have accrued since the divergence.

money Something used to make payments for other goods and services as well as to measure their value.

monogamous Mating for life with a single individual of the opposite sex.

monogamy Marriage in which both partners have just one spouse.

morphemes The smallest units of sound that carry a meaning in language. They are distinct from phonemes, which can alter meaning but have no meaning by themselves.

morphology The study of the patterns or rules of word formation in a language (including such things as rules concerning verb tense, pluralization, and compound words).

Mousterian tradition The tool industry of the Neandertals and their contemporaries of Europe, southwestern Asia, and northern Africa from 40,000 to 125,000 years ago.

motif A story situation in a tale.

multiculturalism Public policy for managing cultural diversity in a multi-ethnic society, officially stressing mutual respect and tolerance for cultural differences within a country's borders.

multiregional hypothesis The hypothesis that modern humans originated through a process of simultaneous local transition from *Homo erectus* to *Homo sapiens* throughout the inhabited world.

multi-sited ethnography The investigation and documentation of peoples and cultures embedded in the larger structures of a globalizing world, utilizing a range of methods in various locations of time and space.

mutation Chance alteration of genetic material that produces new variation.

myth A sacred narrative that explains the fundamentals of human existence—where we and everything in our world came from, why we are here, and where we are going.

naming ceremony A special event or ritual to mark the naming of a child.

natal group The group or the community an animal has inhabited since birth.

nation A people who share a collective identity based on a common culture, language, territorial base, and history.

Natufian culture A Mesolithic culture living in the lands that are now Israel, Lebanon, and western Syria, between about 10,200 and 12,500 years ago.

natural selection The evolutionary process through which factors in the environment exert pressure, favoring some individuals over others to produce the next generation.

Neandertals A distinct group within the genus *Homo* inhabiting Europe and southwestern Asia from approximately 30,000 to 125,000 years ago.

negative reciprocity A form of exchange in which the aim is to get something for as little as possible. Neither fair nor balanced, it may involve hard bargaining, manipulation, and outright cheating.

negotiation The use of direct argument and compromise by the parties to a dispute to arrive voluntarily at a mutually satisfactory agreement.

Neolithic The New Stone Age; prehistoric period beginning about 10,000 years ago in which peoples possessed stone-based technologies and depended on domesticated plants and/or animals.

Neolithic revolution The profound cultural change beginning about 10,000 years ago and associated with the early domestication of plants and animals and settlement in permanent villages. Sometimes referred to as the Neolithic transition.

neolocal residence A pattern in which a married couple establishes the household in a location apart from either the husband's or the wife's relatives.

nocturnal Active at night and at rest during the day.

notochord A rodlike structure of cartilage that, in vertebrates, is replaced by the vertebral column.

nuclear family A group consisting of one or two parents and dependent offspring, which may include a stepparent, stepsiblings, and adopted children. Until recently this term referred only to the father, mother, and child(ren) unit.

Oldowan tool tradition The first stone tool industry, beginning between 2.5 and 2.6 million years ago.

opposable Able to bring the thumb or big toe in contact with the tips of the other digits on the same hand or foot in order to grasp objects.

paleoanthropology The study of the origins and predecessors of the present human species; the study of human evolution.

Paleoindians The earliest inhabitants of North America.

palynology In archaeology and paleoanthropology, a technique of relative dating based on changes in fossil pollen over time.

pantheon The several gods and goddesses of a people.

paralanguage Voice effects that accompany language and convey meaning. These include vocalizations such as giggling, groaning, or sighing, as well as voice qualities such as pitch and tempo.

parallel cousin Child of a father's brother or a mother's sister.

parallel evolution In cultural evolution, the development of similar cultural adaptations to similar environmental conditions by peoples whose ancestral cultures were already somewhat alike.

participant observation In ethnography, the technique of learning a people's culture through social participation and personal observation within the community being studied, as well as interviews and discussion with individual members of the group over an extended period of time.

pastoralism Breeding and managing large herds of domesticated grazing and browsing animals, such as goats, sheep, cattle, horses, llamas, or camels.

patrilineal descent Descent traced exclusively through the male line to establish group membership; also known as agnatic or male descent.

patrilocal residence A residence pattern in which a married couple lives in the husband's father's place of residence.

peasant A rural cultivator whose surpluses are transferred to a dominant group of rulers that uses the surpluses both to underwrite its own standard of living and to distribute the remainder to groups in society that do not farm but must be fed for their specific goods and services in turn.

percussion method A technique of stone tool manufacture performed by striking the raw material with a hammerstone or by striking raw material against a stone anvil to remove flakes.

personality The distinctive way a person thinks, feels, and behaves.

phenotype The observable characteristic of an organism that may or may not reflect a particular genotype due to the variable expression of dominant and recessive alleles.

phonemes The smallest units of sound that make a difference in meaning in a language.

phonetics The systematic identification and description of distinctive speech sounds in a language.

phonology The study of language sounds.

phratry A unilineal descent group composed of at least two clans that supposedly share a common ancestry, whether or not they really do.

physical anthropology The systematic study of humans as biological organisms; also known as biological anthropology.

physiological adaptation A short-term physiological change in response to a specific environmental stimulus. An immediate short-term response is not very efficient and is gradually replaced by a longer term response (see *acclimatization*).

Platyrrhini An anthropoid infraorder that includes New World monkeys.

pluralistic society A society in which two or more ethnic groups or nationalities are politically organized into one territorial state but maintain their cultural differences.

political organization The way power is accumulated, arranged, executed, and structurally distributed and embedded in society; the means through which a society creates and maintains social order.

polyandry Marriage of a woman to two or more men at one time; a form of polygamy.

polygamy One individual having multiple spouses at the same time; from the Greek words *poly* ("many") and *gamos* ("marriage").

polygenetic inheritance When two or more genes contribute to the phenotypic expression of a single characteristic.

polygyny Marriage of a man to two or more women at the same time; a form of polygamy.

polymerase chain reaction (PCR) A technique for amplifying or creating multiple copies of fragments of DNA so that they can be studied in the laboratory.

polymorphic Describing species with alternative forms (alleles) of particular genes.

polytheism Belief in several gods and/or goddesses (as contrasted with monotheism—belief in one god or goddess).

polytypic Describing the expression of genetic variants in different frequencies in different populations of a species.

population In biology, a group of similar individuals that can and do interbreed.

potassium-argon dating In archaeology and paleoanthropology, a technique of chronometric dating that measures the ratio of radioactive potassium to argon in volcanic debris associated with human remains.

potlatch On the northwest coast of North America, a ceremonial event in which a village chief publicly gives away stockpiled food and other goods that signify wealth.

power The ability of individuals or groups to impose their will upon others and make them do things even against their own wants or wishes.

preadapted Possessing characteristics that, by chance, are advantageous in future environmental conditions.

prehensile Having the ability to grasp.

prehistory A conventional term used to refer to the period of time before the appearance of written records; does not deny the existence of history, merely of *written* history.

pressure flaking A technique of stone tool manufacture in which a bone, antler, or wooden tool is used to press, rather than strike off, small flakes from a piece of flint or similar stone.

prestige economy Creation of a surplus for the express purpose of gaining prestige through a public display of wealth that is given away as gifts.

priest or priestess A full-time religious specialist formally recognized for his or her role in guiding the religious practices of others and for contacting and influencing supernatural powers.

primary innovation The creation, invention, or chance discovery of a completely new idea, method, or device.

primate The group of mammals that includes lemurs, lorises, tarsiers, monkeys, apes, and humans.

primatology The study of living and fossil primates.

prion An infectious protein lacking any genetic material but capable of causing the reorganization and destruction of other proteins.

progress The notion that humans are moving forward to a better, more advanced stage in their cultural development toward perfection.

Prosimii A suborder of the primates that includes lemurs, lorises, and tarsiers.

proxemics The cross-cultural study of people's perception and use of space.

punctuated equilibria A model of macroevolutionary change that suggests evolution occurs via long periods of stability or stasis punctuated by periods of rapid change.

qualitative data Nonstatistical information such as personal life stories and customary beliefs and practices.

quantitative data Statistical or measurable information, such as demographic composition, the types and quantities of crops grown, or the ratio of spouses born and raised within or outside the community.

race In biology, a subspecies or a population of a species differing geographically, morphologically, or genetically from other populations of the same species; not applicable to people because the division of humans into discrete types does not represent the true nature of human biological variation. In some societies, race is an important social category.

racism A doctrine of superiority by which one group justifies the dehumanization of others based on their distinctive physical characteristics.

radiocarbon dating In archaeology and paleoanthropology, a technique of chronometric dating based on measuring the amount of radioactive carbon (^{14}C) left in organic materials found in archaeological sites.

rebellion Organized armed resistance to an established government or authority in power.

recent African origins or "Eve" hypothesis The hypothesis that all modern people are derived from one single population of archaic *Homo sapiens* from Africa who migrated out of Africa after 100,000 years ago, replacing all other archaic forms due to their superior cultural capabilities; also called the out of Africa hypothesis.

recessive Refers to an allele for a trait whose expression is masked by the presence of a dominant allele.

reciprocity The exchange of goods and services, of approximately equal value, between two parties.

redistribution A form of exchange in which goods flow into a central place, where they are sorted, counted, and reallocated.

relative dating In archaeology and paleoanthropology, designating an event, object, or fossil as being older or younger than another.

religion An organized system of ideas about the spiritual sphere or the supernatural, along with associated ceremonial practices by which people try to interpret and/or influence aspects of the universe otherwise beyond their control.

replacement reproduction The point at which birthrates and death rates are in equilibrium; people producing only enough offspring to replace themselves when they die.

reproductive success The relative production of fertile offspring by a genotype. In practical terms, the number of offspring produced by individual members of a population is tallied and compared to that of others.

revitalization movement A movement for radical cultural reform in response to widespread social disruption and collective feelings of great stress and despair.

revolution Radical change in a society or culture. In the political arena, it involves the forced overthrow of an old government and establishment of a completely new one.

ribosomes Structures in the cell where translation occurs.

rite of intensification A ritual that takes place during a crisis in the life of the group and serves to bind individuals together.

rite of passage A ritual that marks an important stage in an individual's life cycle, such as birth, marriage, and death.

RNA Ribonucleic acid; similar to DNA but with uracil substituted for the base thymine. Transcribes and carries instructions from DNA from the nucleus to the ribosomes where it directs protein synthesis. Some simple life forms contain RNA only.

robust australopithecines Several species within the genus *Australopithecus*, who lived from 2.5 to 1.1 million years ago in eastern and southern Africa; known for the rugged nature of their chewing apparatus (large back teeth, large chewing muscles, and a bony ridge on their skull tops for the insertion of these large muscles).

r-selected Reproduction involving the production of large numbers of offspring with relatively low parental investment in each.

sagittal crest A crest running from front to back on the top of the skull along the midline to provide a surface of bone for the attachment of the large temporal muscles for chewing.

Sahul The greater Australian landmass including Australia, New Guinea, and Tasmania. At times of maximum glaciation and low sea levels, these areas were continuous.

sanction An externalized social control designed to encourage conformity to social norms.

savannah Semi-arid plains environment as in eastern Africa.

scapula The shoulder blade.

secondary innovation The deliberate application or modification of an existing idea, method, or device.

secular trend A physical difference among related people from distinct generations that allows anthropologists to make inferences about environmental effects on growth and development.

self-awareness The ability to identify oneself as an individual, to reflect on oneself, and to evaluate oneself.

separation In a rite of passage, the ritual removal of the individual from society.

serial monogamy A marriage form in which a man or a woman marries or lives with a series of partners in succession.

seriation In archaeology and paleoanthropology, a technique for relative dating based on putting groups of objects into a sequence in relation to one another.

sexual dimorphism Within a single species, differences in the shape or size of a feature for males and females in body features not directly related to reproduction such as body size or canine tooth shape and size.

shaman A person who enters an altered state of consciousness—at will—to contact and utilize an ordinarily hidden reality in order to acquire knowledge and power, and to help others.

sickle-cell anemia An inherited form of anemia caused by a mutation in the hemoglobin protein that causes the red blood cells to assume a sickle shape.

signal An instinctive sound or gesture that has a natural or self-evident meaning.

silent trade A form of product exchange in which mutually distrusting ethnic groups avoid direct personal contact.

slash-and-burn cultivation An extensive form of horticulture in which the natural vegetation is cut, the slash is subsequently burned, and crops are then planted among the ashes; also known as swidden farming.

social class A category of individuals in a stratified society who enjoy equal or nearly equal prestige according to the system of evaluation.

social control External control through open coercion.

social mobility Upward or downward change in one's social class position in a stratified society.

social structure The rule-governed relationships—with all their rights and obligations—that hold members of a society together. This includes households, families, associations, and power relations, including politics.

society An organized group or groups of interdependent people who generally share a common territory, language, and culture and who act together for collective survival and well-being.

sociolinguistics The study of the relationship between language and society through examining how social categories (such as age, gender, ethnicity, religion, occupation, and class) influence the use and significance of distinctive styles of speech.

soft power Cooptive power that presses others through attraction and persuasion to change their ideas, beliefs, values, and behaviors.

soil mark A stain that shows up on the surface of recently plowed fields that reveals an archaeological site.

speciation The process of forming new species.

species The smallest working unit in the system of classification. Among living organisms, species are populations or groups of populations capable of interbreeding and producing fertile viable offspring.

spirituality Concern with the sacred, as distinguished from material matters. In contrast to religion, spirituality is often individual rather than collective and does not require a distinctive format or traditional organization.

stabilizing selection Natural selection acting to promote stability rather than change in a population's gene pool.

state In anthropology, a political institution established to manage and defend a complex, socially stratified society occupying a defined territory.

stereoscopic vision Complete three-dimensional vision (or depth perception) from binocular vision and nerve connections that run from each eye to both sides of the brain, allowing nerve cells to integrate the images derived from each eye.

stratified Layered; term used to describe archaeological sites where the remains lie in layers, one upon another.

stratified society A society in which people are hierarchically divided and ranked into social strata, or layers, and do not share equally in the basic resources that support survival, influence, and prestige.

stratigraphy In archaeology and paleoanthropology, the most reliable method of relative dating by means of strata.

Strepsirhini In the alternate primate taxonomy, the suborder that includes the lemurs and lorises without the tarsiers.

structural power Power that organizes and orchestrates the systemic interaction within and among societies, directing economic and political forces on the one hand and ideological forces that shape public ideas, values, and beliefs on the other.

structural violence Physical and/or psychological harm (including repression, environmental destruction, poverty, hunger, illness, and premature death) caused by impersonal, exploitative, and unjust social, political, and economic systems.

Conroy, G. C. (1997). *Reconstructing human origins: A modern synthesis.* New York: Norton.

Coon, C. S. (1954). *The story of man.* New York: Knopf.

Coon, C. S. (1958). *Caravan: The story of the Middle East* (2nd ed.). New York: Holt, Rinehart & Winston.

Coon, C. S. (1962). *The origins of races.* New York: Knopf.

Coontz, S. (2005). *Marriage, a history: From obedience to intimacy, or how love conquered marriage.* New York: Viking Adult.

Cooper, A., Poinar, H. N., Pääbo, S., Radovci, C. J., Debénath, A., Caparros, M., Barroso-Ruiz, C., Bertranpetit, J., Nielsen-March, C., Hedges, R.E.M., & Sykes, B. (1997). Neanderthal genetics. *Science 277,* 1021–1024.

Coppa, A., et al. (2006). Early Neolithic tradition of dentistry. *Nature 440,* 755–756.

Coppens, Y., Howell, F. C., Isaac, G. L., & Leakey, R.E.F. (Eds.). (1976). *Earliest man and environments in the Lake Rudolf Basin: Stratigraphy, paleoecology, and evolution.* Chicago: University of Chicago Press.

Corballis, M. C. (2003). *From hand to mouth: The origins of human language.* Princeton, NJ: Princeton University Press.

Corbey, R. (1995). Introduction: Missing links, or the ape's place in nature. In R. Corbey & B. Theunissen (Eds.), *Ape, man, apeman: Changing views since 1600* (p.1). Leiden: Department of Prehistory, Leiden University.

Cornwell, T. (1995, November 10). Skeleton staff. *Times Higher Education,* 20. http://www.timeshighereducation.co.uk/story.asp?storyCode=96035&sectioncode=26

Corruccini, R. S. (1992). Metrical reconsideration of the Skhul IV and IX and Border Cave I crania in the context of modern human origins. *American Journal of Physical Anthropology 87,* 433–445.

Cotte, M. (2008). *Journal of Analytical Atomic Spectrometry.* doi: 10.1039/b801358f.

Cowgill, G. L. (1980). Letter. *Science 210,* 1305.

Cowgill, G. L. (1997). State and society at Teotihuacan, Mexico. *Annual Review of Anthropology 26,* 129–161.

Crane, H. (2001). *Men in spirit: The masculinization of Taiwanese Buddhist nuns.* Doctoral dissertation, Brown University.

Crane, L. B., Yeager, E., & Whitman, R. L. (1981). *An introduction to linguistics.* Boston: Little, Brown.

Cretney, S. (2003). *Family law in the twentieth century: A history.* New York: Oxford University Press.

Crocker, W. H., & Crocker, J. G. (1994). *The Canela, bonding through kinship, ritual, and sex.* Fort Worth: Harcourt Brace.

Crocker, W. H., & Crocker, J. G. (2004). *The Canela: Kinship, ritual, and sex in an Amazonian tribe.* Belmont, CA: Wadsworth.

Culbert, T. P. (Ed.). (1973). *The Classic Maya collapse.* Albuquerque: University of New Mexico Press.

Culotta, E. (1995). Asian hominids grow older. *Science 270,* 1116–1117.

Culotta, E. (1995). New finds rekindle debate over anthropoid origins. *Science 268,* 1851.

Culotta, E., & Koshland, D. E., Jr. (1994). DNA repair works its way to the top. *Science 266,* 1926.

Cultural Survival Quarterly. (1991). *15* (4).

D'Adesky, A.-C. (2004). *Moving mountains: The race to treat global AIDS.* New York: Verso.

Dalton, G. (Ed.). (1967). *Tribal and peasant economics: Readings in economic anthropology.* Garden City, NY: Natural History.

Dalton, G. (1971). *Traditional tribal and peasant economics: An introductory survey of economic anthropology.* Reading, MA: Addison-Wesley.

Daniel, G. (1970). *The first civilizations: The archaeology of their origins.* New York: Apollo Editions.

Dalton, G. (1971). *Traditional tribal and peasant economics: An introductory survey of economic anthropology.* Reading, MA: Addison-Wesley.

Darwin, C. (1887). *Autobiography.* Reprinted in F. Darwin (Ed.), (1902), *The life and letters of Charles Darwin.* London: John Murray.

Darwin, C. (1936). *The descent of man and selection in relation to sex.* New York: Random House (Modern Library). (orig. 1871)

Darwin, C. (2007). *On the origin of species by means of natural selection, or the preservation of favoured races in the struggle for life.* New York: Cosimo. (orig. 1859)

Davenport, W. (1959). Linear descent and descent groups. *American Anthropologist 61,* 557–573.

Davies, G. (2005). *A history of money from the earliest times to present day* (3rd ed.). Cardiff: University of Wales Press.

Davies, J. B., et al. (2007). *The world distribution of household wealth.* University of California, Santa Cruz, Mapping Global Inequalities, Center for Global, International, and Regional Studies.

Davis, S. H. (1982). *Victims of the miracle.* Cambridge, England: Cambridge University Press.

Deetz, J. (1977). *In small things forgotten: The archaeology of early American life.* Garden City, NY: Anchor/Doubleday.

de la Torre, S., & Snowden, C. T. (2009). Dialects in pygmy marmosets? Population variation in call structure. *American Journal of Primatology 71* (4), 333–342.

del Carmen Rodríguez Martínez, M., et al. (2006). Oldest writing in the New World. *Science 313* (5793), 1610–1614.

del Castillo, B. D. (1963). *The conquest of New Spain* (translation and introduction by J. M. Cohen). New York: Penguin.

Delson, E., Tattersal, I., Brooks, A., & Van Couvering, J. (1999). *Encyclopedia of human evolution and prehistory.* New York: Garland.

DeMello, M. (2000). *Bodies of inscription: A cultural history of the modern tattoo community.* Durham: Duke University Press.

De Mott, B. (1990). *The imperial middle: Why Americans can't think straight about class.* New York: Morrow.

d'Errico, F., Zilhão, J., Julien, M., Baffier, D., & Pelegrin, J. (1998). Neandertal acculturation in western Europe? *Current Anthropology 39,* 521.

DeSilva, J. M. (2009). Functional morphology of the ankle and the likelihood of climbing in early hominins. *Proceedings of the National Academy of Sciences, USA 106,* 6567–6572.

Desowitz, R. S. (1987). *New Guinea tapeworms and Jewish grandmothers.* New York: Norton.

Dettwyler, K. A. (1994). *Dancing skeletons: Life and death in West Africa.* Prospect Heights, IL: Waveland.

Dettwyler, K. A. (1997, October). When to wean. *Natural History,* 49.

DeVore, I. (Ed.). (1965). *Primate behavior: Field studies of monkeys and apes.* New York: Holt, Rinehart & Winston.

de Waal, F.B.M. (1998). Comment. *Current Anthropology 39,* 407.

de Waal, F.B.M. (2000). Primates—A natural heritage of conflict resolution. *Science 28,* 586–590.

de Waal, F.B.M. (2001). *The ape and the sushi master.* New York: Basic.

de Waal, F.B.M. (2001). Sing the song of evolution. *Natural History 110* (8), 77.

de Waal, F.B.M. (2003). *My family album: Thirty years of primate photography.* Berkeley: University of California Press.

de Waal, F.B.M., & Johanowicz, D. L. (1993). Modification of reconciliation behavior through social experience: An experiment with two macaque species. *Child Development 64,* 897–908.

de Waal, F.B.M., Kano, T., & Parish, A. R. (1998). Comments. *Current Anthropology 39,* 408, 410, 413.

de Waal, F.B.M., & Lanting F. (1998). *Bonobo: The forgotten ape.* Berkeley: University of California Press.

Diamond, J. (1996). Empire of uniformity. *Discover 17* (3), 83–84.

Diamond, J. (1997). *Guns, germs, and steel.* New York: Norton.

Diamond, J. (1998). Ants, crops, and history. *Science 281,* 1974–1975.

Diamond, J. (2005). *Collapse: How societies choose to fail or succeed.* New York: Penguin.

Dicks, B., et al. (2005). *Qualitative research and hypermedia: Ethnography for the digital age (New technologies for social research).* Thousand Oaks, CA: Sage.

Dillehay, T. D. (2001). *The settlement of the Americas.* New York: Basic.

Dirie, W., & Miller, C. (1998). *Desert flower: The extraordinary journey of a desert nomad.* New York: Morrow.

Dissanayake, E. (2000). Birth of the arts. *Natural History 109* (10), 89.

Dixon, J. E., Cann, J. R., & Renfrew, C. (1968). Obsidian and the origins of trade. *Scientific American 218,* 38–46.

Dobyns, H. F., Doughty, P. L., & Lasswell, H. D. (Eds.). (1971). *Peasants, power, and applied social change.* London: Sage.

Dobzhansky, T. (1962). *Mankind evolving.* New Haven, CT: Yale University Press.

Dorit, R. (1997). Molecular evolution and scientific inquiry, misperceived. *American Scientist 85,* 474–475.

Douglas, M. (1966). *Purity and danger: An analysis of concepts of pollution and taboo.* London: Routledge & Kegan Paul.

Dozier, E. (1970). *The Pueblo Indians of North America.* New York: Holt, Rinehart & Winston.

Draper, P. (1975). !Kung women: Contrasts in sexual egalitarianism in foraging and sedentary contexts. In R. Reiter (Ed.), *Toward an anthropology of women* (pp. 77–109). New York: Monthly Review.

Drewnowski, A., & Specter, S. E. (2004). Poverty and obesity: the role of energy density and energy costs. *American Journal of Clinical Nutrition 79* (1), 6–16.

Driver, H. (1964). *Indians of North America.* Chicago: University of Chicago Press.

Dubos, R. (1968). *So human an animal.* New York: Scribner.

Dumurat-Dreger, A. (1998, May/June). "Ambiguous sex" or ambivalent medicine? *Hastings Center Report 28* (3), 2435 (posted on the website for Intersex Society of North America: www.isna.org)

Dunbar, P. (2008, January 19). The pink vigilantes. www.dailymail.co.uk

Duncan, A. S., Kappelman, J., & Shapiro, L. J. (1994). Metasophalangeal joint function and positional behavior in *Australopithecus afarensis. American Journal of Physical Anthropology 93,* 67–81.

Dundes, A. (1980). *Interpreting folklore.* Bloomington: Indiana University Press.

Durant, J. C. (2000, April 23). Everybody into the gene pool. *New York Times Book Review,* 11.

Duranti, A. (2001). Linguistic anthropology: History, ideas, and issues. In A. Duranti (Ed.), *Linguistic anthropology: A reader* (pp. 1–38). Oxford: Blackwell.

Durkheim, E. (1964). *The division of labor in society.* New York: Free Press. (orig. 1893)

Durkheim, E. (1965). *The elementary forms of the religious life.* New York: Free Press. (orig. 1912)

Durkheim, E., & Mauss, M. (1963). *Primitive classification.* Chicago: University of Chicago Press. (orig. 1902)

duToit, B. M. (1991). *Human sexuality: Cross cultural readings.* New York: McGraw-Hill.

Eastman, C. M. (1990). *Aspects of language and culture* (2nd ed.). Novato, CA: Chandler & Sharp.

Eaton, S. B., Konner, M., & Shostak, M. (1988). Stone-agers in the fast lane: Chronic degenerative diseases in evolutionary perspective. *American Journal of Medicine 84* (4), 739–749.

Edwards, J. (Ed.). (1999). *Technologies of procreation: Kinship in the age of assisted conception.* New York: Routledge.

Edwards, S. W. (1978). Nonutilitarian activities on the Lower Paleolithic: A look at the two kinds of evidence. *Current Anthropology 19* (l), 135–137.

Egan, T. (1999, February 28). The persistence of polygamy. *New York Times Magazine,* 52.

Ehrlich, P. R., & Ehrlich, A. H. (2008). *The dominant animal: Human evolution and the environment.* Washington, DC: Island.

Eiseley, L. (1958). *Darwin's century: Evolution and the men who discovered it.* New York: Doubleday.

Eisenstadt, S. N. (1956). *From generation to generation: Age groups and social structure.* New York: Free Press.

El Guindi, F. (2004). *Visual anthropology: Essential method and theory.* Walnut Creek, CA: Altamira.

Elkin, A. P. (1964). *The Australian Aborigines.* Garden City, NY: Doubleday/Anchor.

Ellis, C. (2006). *A dancing people: Powwow culture on the southern plains.* Lawrence: University Press of Kansas.

Ellison, P. T. (1990). Human ovarian function and reproductive ecology: New hypotheses. *American Anthropologist 92,* 933–952.

Ellison, P. T. (2003). *On fertile ground: A natural history of human reproduction.* Cambridge, MA: Harvard University Press.

Ember, C. R., & Ember, M. (1996). What have we learned from cross-cultural research? *General Anthropology 2* (2), 5.

Enard, W., et al. (2002). Molecular evolution of FOXP2, a gene involved in speech and language. *Nature 418,* 869–872.

Erickson, P. A., & Murphy, L. D. (2003). *A history of anthropological theory* (2nd ed.). Peterborough, Ontario: Broadview.

Errington, F. K., & Gewertz, D. B. (2001). *Cultural alternatives and a feminist anthropology: An analysis of culturally constructed gender interests in Papua New Guinea.* Cambridge, England, and New York: Cambridge University Press.

Ervin-Tripp, S. (1973). *Language acquisition and communicative choice.* Stanford, CA: Stanford University Press.

Esber, G. S. (1987). Designing Apache houses with Apaches. In R. M. Wulff & S. J. Fiske (Eds.), *Anthropological praxis: Translating knowledge into action* (pp. 187–196). Boulder, CO: Westview.

Eugenides, J. (2002). *Middlesex: A novel.* New York: Farrar, Straus and Giroux.

Evans-Pritchard, E. E. (1937). *Witchcraft, oracles and magic among the Azande.* London: Oxford University Press.

Evans-Pritchard, E. E. (1951). *Kinship and marriage among the Nuer.* New York: Oxford University Press.

Evans-Pritchard, E. E. (1968). *The Nuer: A description of the modes of livelihood and political institutions of a Nilotic people.* London: Oxford University Press.

Evershed, R. P., et al. (2008). Earliest date for milk use in the Near East and southeastern Europe linked to cattle herding. *Nature.* doi:10.1038/nature07180.

Fagan, B. M. (1995). *People of the earth* (8th ed.). New York: HarperCollins.

Fagan, B. M. (2000). *Ancient lives: An introduction to archaeology.* Englewood Cliffs, NJ: Prentice-Hall.

Fagan, B. (2001). *The seventy great mysteries of the ancient world.* New York: Thames & Hudson.

Fagan, B. M. (2005). *Archaeology: A brief introduction* (9th ed.). New York: Longman.

Fagan, B. M., Beck, C., & Silberman, N. A. (1998). *The Oxford companion to archaeology.* New York: Oxford University Press.

Falk, D. (1975). Comparative anatomy of the larynx in man and the chimpanzee: Implications for language in Neanderthal. *American Journal of Physical Anthropology 43* (1), 123–132.

Falk, D. (1989). Apelike endocast of "ape-man" Taung. *American Journal of Physical Anthropology 80,* 335–339.

Falk, D. (1993). A good brain is hard to cool. *Natural History 102* (8), 65.

Falk, D. (1993). Hominid paleoneurology. In R. L. Ciochon & J. G. Fleagle (Eds.), *The human evolution source book.* Englewood Cliffs, NJ: Prentice-Hall.

Falk, D. (2004). *Braindance: New discoveries about human origins and brain evolution—revised and updated.* Gainesville: University Press of Florida.

Falk, D., et al. (2005). The brain of LB1, *Homo floresiensis. Science 308,* 242–245.

Farmer, P. (1992). *AIDS and accusation: Haiti and the geography of blame.* Berkeley: University of California Press.

Farmer, P. (1996). On suffering and structural violence: A view from below. *Daedelus 125* (1), 261–283.

Farmer, P. (2001). *Infections and inequalities: The modern plagues.* Berkeley: University of California Press.

Farmer, P. (2003). *Pathologies of power: Health, human rights, and the new war on the poor.* Berkeley: University of California Press.

Farmer, P. (2004, June). An anthropology of structural violence. *Current Anthropology 45,* 3.

Farnell, B. (1995). *Do you see what I mean? Plains Indian sign talk and the embodiment of action.* Austin: University of Texas Press.

Fausto-Sterling, A. (1993, March/April). The five sexes: Why male and female are not enough. *The Sciences 33* (2), 20–24.

Fausto-Sterling, A. (2000, July/August). The five sexes revisited. *The Sciences 40* (4), 19–24.

Fausto-Sterling, A. (2003, August 2). Personal e-mail communication.

Feder, K. L. (2008). *Frauds, myths, and mysteries: Science and pseudoscience in archaeology* (6th ed.). New York: McGraw-Hill.

Fedigan, L. M. (1986). The changing role of women in models of human evolution. *Annual Review of Anthropology 15,* 25–56.

Fedigan, L. M. (1992). *Primate paradigms: Sex roles and social bonds.* Chicago: University of Chicago Press.

"Female genital mutilation." (2000). Fact sheet no. 241. World Health Organization.

Fernandez-Carriba, S., & Loeches, A. (2001). Fruit smearing by captive chimpanzees: A newly observed food-processing behavior. *Current Anthropology 42,* 143–147.

Ferrie, H. (1997). An interview with C. Loring Brace. *Current Anthropology 38,* 851–869.

Field, L. W. (2004). Beyond "applied" anthropology. In T. Biolsi (Ed.), *A companion to the anthropology of American Indians* (pp. 472–489). Oxford: Blackwell.

Finkler, K. (2000). *Experiencing the new genetics: Family and kinship on the medical frontier.* Philadelphia: University of Pennsylvania Press.

"The first Americans, ca. 20,000 B.C." (1998). *Discover 19* (6), 24.

Firth, R. (1946). *Malay fishermen: Their peasant economy.* London: Kegan Paul.

Firth, R. (1952). *Elements of social organization.* London: Watts.

Firth, R. (1957). *Man and culture: An evaluation of Bronislaw Malinowski.* London: Routledge.

Firth, R. (Ed.). (1967). *Themes in economic anthropology.* London: Tavistock.

Fisher, R., & Ury, W. L. (1991). *Getting to yes: Negotiating agreement without giving in* (2nd ed.). Boston: Houghton Mifflin.

Flannery, K. V. (1973). The origins of agriculture. In B. J. Siegel, A. R. Beals, & S. A. Tyler (Eds.), *Annual Review of Anthropology* (Vol. 2, pp. 271–310). Palo Alto, CA: Annual Reviews.

Flannery, K. V. (Ed.). (1976). *The Mesoamerican village.* New York: Seminar.

Fleagle, J. (1998). *Primate adaptation and evolution.* New York: Academic.

Fogel, R, & Riquelme, M. A. (2005). *Enclave sorjero. Merma de soberania y pobreza.* Ascuncion: Centro de Estudios Rurales Interdisciplinarias.

Folger, T. (1993). The naked and the bipedal. *Discover 14* (11), 34–35.

Food and Agriculture Organization (FAO), United Nations. (2009). *1.02 billion people hungry: One sixth of humanity undernourished—more than ever before.* http://www.fao.org/news/story/en/item/20568/icode/

Forbes, J. D. (1964). *The Indian in America's past.* Englewood Cliffs, NJ: Prentice-Hall.

Forbes International 500 List. (2008).

Forde, C. D. (1955). The Nupe. In D. Forde (Ed.), *Peoples of the Niger-Benue confluence.* London: International African Institute (Ethnographic Survey of Africa. Western Africa, part 10).

Forde, C. D. (1968). Double descent among the Yakö. In P. Bohannan & J. Middleton (Eds.), *Kinship and social organization* (pp. 179–191). Garden City, NY: Natural History.

Forste, R. (2008). *Prelude to marriage, or alternative to marriage? A social demographic look at cohabitation in the U.S.* Working paper. Social Science Electronic Publishing, Inc. http://papers.ssrn.com/sol3/papers.cfm?abstract_id=269172.

Fortes, M. (1950). Kinship and marriage among the Ashanti. In A. R. Radcliffe-Brown & C. D. Forde (Eds.), *African systems of kinship and marriage.* London: Oxford University Press.

Fortes, M. (1969). *Kinship and the social order: The legacy of Lewis Henry Morgan.* Chicago: Aldine.

Fortes, M., & Evans-Prichard, E. E. (Eds.). (1962). *African political systems.* London: Oxford University Press. (orig. 1940)

Fossey, D. (1983). *Gorillas in the mist.* Burlington, MA: Houghton Mifflin.

Foster, G. M. (1955). Peasant society and the image of the limited good. *American Anthropologist 67,* 293–315.

Fountain, H. (2000, January 30). Now the ancient ways are less mysterious. *New York Times,* 5.

"4.1 billion mobile phone subscribers worldwide." (2009, March 27). www.mocom2020.com/2009/03/41-billion-mobile-phone-subscribers-worldwide/

Fouts, R. S., & Waters, G. (2001). Chimpanzee sign language and Darwinian continuity: Evidence for a neurology continuity of language. *Neurological Research 23,* 787–794.

Fox, R. (1968). *Encounter with anthropology.* New York: Dell.

Fox, R. (1968). *Kinship and marriage in an anthropological perspective.* Baltimore: Penguin.

Fox, R. (1981, December 3). [Interview]. Coast Telecourses, Inc., Los Angeles.

Frake, C. (1961). The diagnosis of disease among the Subinam of Mindinao. *American Anthropologist 63,*113–132.

Frake, C. O. (1992). Lessons of the Mayan sky. In A. F. Aveni (Ed.), *The sky in Mayan literature* (pp. 274–291). New York: Oxford University Press.

Franzen, J. L., Gingerich, P. D., Habersetzer, J., Hurum, J. H., von Koenigswald, W., et al. (2009). Complete primate skeleton from the middle Eocene of Messel in Germany: Morphology and paleobiology. *PLoS ONE 4* (5), e5723.

Fraser, D. (Ed.). (1966). *The many faces of primitive art: A critical anthology.* Englewood Cliffs, NJ: Prentice-Hall.

Frayer, D. W. (1981). Body size, weapon use, and natural selection in the European Upper Paleolithic and Mesolithic. *American Anthropologist 83,* 57–73.

Frazer, Sir J. G. (1961 reissue). *The new golden bough.* New York: Doubleday, Anchor.

Freeman, J. D. (1960). The Iban of western Borneo. In G. P. Murdock (Ed.), *Social structure in Southeast Asia.* Chicago: Quadrangle.

Freeman, L. G. (1992). *Ambrona and Torralba: New evidence and interpretation.* Paper presented at the 91st Annual Meeting, American Anthropological Association.

Fried, M. (1967). *The evolution of political society: An essay in political anthropology.* New York: Random House.

Fried, M., Harris, M., & Murphy, R. (1968). *War: The anthropology of armed conflict and aggression.* Garden City, NY: Natural History.

Friedl, E. (1975). *Women and men: An anthropologist's view.* New York: Holt, Rinehart & Winston.

Friedman, J. (Ed.). (2003). *Globalization, the state, and violence.* Walnut Creek, CA: Altamira.

Friedman, T. (2007, April). *New York Times.*

Frisch, R. (2002). *Female fertility and the body fat connection.* Chicago: University of Chicago Press.

Frye, D. P. (2000). Conflict management in cross-cultural perspective. In F. Aureli & F.B.M. de Waal (Eds.), *Natural conflict resolution* (pp. 334–351). Berkeley: University of California Press.

Furst, P. T. (1976). *Hallucinogens and culture* (p. 7). Novato, CA: Chandler & Sharp.

Galdikas, B. (1995). *Reflections on Eden: My years with the orangutans of Borneo.* New York: Little, Brown.

Gamble, C. (1986). *The Paleolithic settlement of Europe.* Cambridge, England: Cambridge University Press.

Gardner, R. A., Gardner, B. T., & Van Cantfort, T. E. (Eds.). (1989). *Teaching sign language to chimpanzees.* Albany: State University of New York Press.

Garn, S. M. (1970). *Human races* (3rd ed.). Springfield, IL: Thomas.

Gates, H. (1996). Buying brides in China—again. *Anthropology Today 12* (4), 10.

Gebo, D. L., Dagosto, D., Beard, K. C., & Tao, Q. (2001). Middle Eocene primate tarsals from China: Implications for haplorhine evolution. *American Journal of Physical Anthropology 116,* 83–107.

Geertz, C. (1965). The impact of the concept of culture on the concept of man. In J. R. Platt (Ed.), *New views of man.* Chicago: University of Chicago Press.

Geertz, C. (1973). *The interpretation of culture.* London: Hutchinson.

Geertz, C. (1984). Distinguished lecture: Anti anti-relativism. *American Anthropologist 86,* 263–278.

Geertz, C. (2004). Religion as a cultural system. In M. Banton (Ed.), *Anthropological approaches to the study of religion* (pp. 1–46). London: Routledge. (orig. 1966)

Gell, A. (1988). Technology and magic. *Anthropology Today 4* (2), 6–9.

"Gene study suggests Polynesians came from Taiwan." (2005, July 4). Reuters.

Gero, J. M., & Conkey, M. W. (Eds.). (1991). *Engendering archaeology: Women and prehistory.* New York: Wiley-Blackwell.

Gibbons, A. (1993). Where are new diseases born? *Science 261,* 680–681.

Gibbons, A. (1997). Ideas on human origins evolve at anthropology gathering. *Science 276,* 535–536.

Gibbons, A. (1998). Ancient island tools suggest *Homo erectus* was a seafarer. *Science 279,* 1635.

Gibbons, A. (2001). The riddle of coexistence. *Science 291,* 1726.

Gibbons, A. (2001). Studying humans—and their cousins and parasites. *Science 292,* 627.

Gibbs, J. L., Jr. (1965). The Kpelle of Liberia. In J. L. Gibbs, Jr. (Ed.), *Peoples of Africa* (pp. 216–218). New York: Holt, Rinehart & Winston.

Gibbs, J. L., Jr. (1983). [Interview]. *Faces of culture: Program 18.* Fountain Valley, CA: Coast Telecourses.

Giddens, A. (1990). *The consequences of modernity.* Stanford, CA: Stanford University Press.

Ginsburg, F. D., Abu-Lughod, L., & Larkin, B. (Eds.). (2009). *Media worlds: Anthropology on new terrain.* Berkeley: University of California Press.

Gladdol, D. (2006). *English next.* London: British Council.

Gledhill, J. (2000). *Power and its disguises: Anthropological perspectives on politics* (2nd ed.). Boulder, CO: Pluto.

Godfrey, T. (2000, December 27). Biotech threatening biodiversity. *Burlington Free Press,* 10A.

Godlier, M. (1971). Salt currency and the circulation of commodities among the Baruya of New Guinea. In G. Dalton (Ed.), *Studies in economic anthropology.* Washington, DC: American Anthropological Association (Anthropological Studies No. 7).

González, R. J. (2009). *American counterinsurgency: Human science and the human terrain.* Chicago: University of Chicago Press.

Goodall, J. (1986). *The chimpanzees of Gombe: Patterns of behavior.* Cambridge, MA: Belknap.

Goodall, J. (1990). *Through a window: My thirty years with the chimpanzees of Gombe.* Boston: Houghton Mifflin.

Goodall, J. (2000). *Reason for hope: A spiritual journey.* New York: Warner.

Goodenough, W. (Ed.). (1964). *Explorations in cultural anthropology: Essays in honor of George Murdock.* New York: McGraw–Hill.

Goodenough, W. (1965). Rethinking status and role: Toward a general model of the cultural organization of social relationships. In M. Benton (Ed.), *The relevance of models for social anthropology.* New York: Praeger.

Goodenough, W. H. (1970). *Description and comparison in cultural anthropology.* Chicago: Aldine.

Goodenough, W. H. (1990). Evolution of the human capacity for beliefs. *American Anthropologist 92,* 601.

Goodman, A., & Armelagos, G. J. (1985). Death and disease at Dr. Dickson's mounds. *Natural History 94* (9), 12–18.

Goodman, M., Bailey, W. J., Hayasaka, K., Stanhope, M. J., Slightom J., & Czelusniak, J. (1994). Molecular evidence on primate phylogeny from DNA sequences. *American Journal of Physical Anthropology 94,* 7.

Goodwin, R. (1999). *Personal relationships across cultures.* New York: Routledge.

Goody, J. (1969). *Comparative studies in kinship.* Stanford, CA: Stanford University Press.

Goody, J. (1976). *Production and reproduction: A comparative study of the domestic domain.* Cambridge, MA: Cambridge University Press.

Goody, J. (1983). *The development of the family and marriage in Europe.* Cambridge, MA: Cambridge University Press.

Gordon, R. (2000). *Eating disorders: Anatomy of a social epidemic* (2nd ed.). New York: Wiley-Blackwell.

Gordon, R., Lyons, H., & Lyons, A. (Eds.). (2010). *Fifty key anthropologists.* New York: Routledge.

Gordon, R. J. (1992). *The Bushman myth: The making of a Namibian underclass.* Boulder, CO: Westview.

Gordon, R. J., & Megitt, M. J. (1985). *Law and order in the New Guinea highlands.* Hanover, NH: University Press of New England.

Gough, K. (1959). The Nayars and the definition of marriage. *Journal of the Royal Anthropological Institute of Great Britain and Ireland 89,* 23–34.

Gould, S. J. (1983). *Hen's teeth and horses' toes.* New York: Norton.

Gould, S. J. (1985). *The flamingo's smile: Reflections in natural history.* New York: Norton.

Gould, S. J. (1989). *Wonderful life.* New York: Norton.

Gould, S. J. (1991). *Bully for brontosaurus.* New York: Norton.

Gould, S. J. (1994). The geometer of race. *Discover 15* (11), 65–69.

Gould, S. J. (1996). *Full house: The spread of excellence from Plato to Darwin.* New York: Harmony.

Gould, S. J. (1996). *The mismeasure of man* (2nd ed.). New York: Norton.

Gould, S. J. (2000). The narthex of San Marco and the pangenetic paradigm. *Natural History 109* (6), 29.

Gould, S. J. (2000). What does the dreaded "E" word mean anyway? *Natural History 109* (1), 34–36.

Graburn, N.H.H. (1969). *Eskimos without igloos: Social and economic development in Sugluk.* Boston: Little, Brown.

Graburn, N. H. (1971). *Readings in kinship and social structure.* New York: Harper & Row.

Graves, J. L. (2001). *The emperor's new clothes: Biological theories of race at the millennium.* New Brunswick, NJ: Rutgers University Press.

Graves, P. (1991). New models and metaphors for the Neanderthal debate. *Current Anthropology 32*(5), 513–543.

Gray, P. B. (2004, May). HIV and Islam: Is HIV prevalence lower among Muslims? *Social Science & Medicine 58* (9), 1751–1756.

Gray, P. M., Krause, B., Atema, J., Payne, R., Krumhansl, C., & Baptista, L. (2001). The music of nature and the nature of music. *Science 291,* 52.

Green, E. C. (1987). The planning of health education strategies in Swaziland, and the integration of modern and traditional health sectors in Swaziland. In R. M. Wulff & S. J. Fiske (Eds.), *Anthropological praxis: Translating knowledge into action* (pp. 15–25, 87–97). Boulder, CO: Westview.

Greenberg, J. H. (1968). *Anthropological linguistics: An introduction.* New York: Random House.

Greymorning, S. N. (2001). Reflections on the Arapaho Language Project or, when Bambi spoke Arapaho and other tales of Arapaho language revitalization efforts. In K. Hale & L. Hinton (Eds.), *The green book of language revitalization in practice* (pp. 287–297). New York: Academic.

Grine, F. E. (1993). Australopithecine taxonomy and phylogeny: Historical background and recent interpretation. In R. L. Ciochon & J. G. Fleagle (Eds.), *The human evolution source book.* Englewood Cliffs, NJ: Prentice-Hall.

Grivetti, L. E. (2005). From aphrodisiac to health food: A cultural history of chocolate. *Karger Gazette,* 68.

Grossman, J. (2002). Should the law be kinder to kissin' cousins? A genetic report should cause a rethinking of incest laws. *Find Law.* (accessed October 16, 2009)

Grün, R., & Thorne, A. (1997). Dating the Ngandong humans. *Science 276,* 1575.

Guillette, E. A., et al. (1998, June). An anthropological approach to the evaluation of preschool children exposed to pesticides in Mexico. *Environmental Health Perspectives 106,* 347.

Guthrie, S. (1993). *Faces in the clouds: A new theory of religions.* New York: Oxford University Press.

Gutin, J. A. (1995). Do Kenya tools root birth of modern thought in Africa? *Science 270,* 1118–1119.

Haeri, N. (1997). The reproduction of symbolic capital: Language, state and class in Egypt. *Current Anthropology 38,* 795–816.

Hafkin, N., & Bay, E. (Eds.). (1976). *Women in Africa.* Stanford, CA: Stanford University Press.

Hager, L. (1989). *The evolution of sex differences in the hominid bony pelvis.* Ph.D. dissertation, University of California, Berkeley.

Haglund, W. D., Conner, M., & Scott, D. D. (2001). The archaeology of contemporary mass graves. *Historical Archaeology 35* (1), 57–69.

Hahn, R. A. (1992). The state of federal health statistics on racial and ethnic groups. *Journal of the American Medica Association 267* (2), 268–271.

Hall, E. T. (1959). *The silent language.* Garden City, NY: Anchor/Doubleday.

Hall, E. T., & Hall, M. R. (1986). The sounds of silence. In E. Angeloni (Ed.), *Anthropology 86/87* (pp. 65–70). Guilford, CT: Dushkin.

Hall, K.R.L., & DeVore, I. (1965). Baboon social behavior. In I. DeVore (Ed.), *Primate behavior.* New York: Holt, Rinehart & Winston.

Hallowell, A. I. (1955). *Culture and experience.* Philadelphia: University of Pennsylvania Press.

Halperin, R. H. (1994). *Cultural economies: Past and present.* Austin: University of Texas Press.

Halverson, J. (1989). Review of the book *Altamira Revisited and other essays on early art. American Antiquity 54,* 883.

Handwerk, B. (2005, March 8). King Tut not murdered violently, CT scans show. *National Geographic News,* 2.

Hannah, J. L. (1988). *Dance, sex and gender.* Chicago: University of Chicago Press.

Hanson, A. (1989). The making of the Maori: Culture invention and its logic. *American Anthropologist 91* (4), 890–902.

Harcourt-Smith, W.E.H., & Aiello, L. C. (2004). Fossils, feet and the evolution of human bipedal locomotion. *Journal of Anatomy 204,* 403–416.

Harlow, H. F. (1962). Social deprivation in monkeys. *Scientific America 206,* 1–10.

Harner, M. (1980). *The way of the shaman: A guide to power and healing.* San Francisco: Harper & Row.

Harpending, H., & Cochran, G. (2002). In our genes. *Proceedings of the National Academy of Sciences, USA 99* (1), 10–12.

Harpending, J. H., & Harpending, H. C. (1995). Ancient differences in population can mimic a recent African origin of modern humans. *Current Anthropology 36,* 667–674.

Harris, M. (1965). The cultural ecology of India's sacred cattle. *Current Anthropology 7,* 51–66.

Harris, M. (1968). *The rise of anthropological theory: A history of theories of culture.* New York: Crowell.

Harris, M. (1979). *Cultural materialism: The struggle for a science of culture.* New York: Random House.

Harris, M. (1989). *Cows, pigs, wars, and witches: The riddles of culture.* New York: Vintage/Random House.

Harrison, G. G. (1975). Primary adult lactase deficiency: A problem in anthropological genetics. *American Anthropologist 77,* 815–819.

Harrison, K. D. (2008). *When languages die: The extinction of the world's languages and the erosion of human knowledge.* New York: Oxford University Press.

Harrison, K. D. *Pop!Tech 2008: Scarcity and abundance: Global and local trends in language extinction.* www.poptech.org/popcasts/k_david_harrison__poptech_2008

Hart, C. W., Pilling, A. R., & Goodale, J. (1988). *Tiwi of North Australia* (3rd ed.). New York: Holt, Rinehart & Winston.

Hart, D. (2006, April 21). Humans as prey. *Chronicle of Higher Education.*

Hart, D., & Sussman, R. W. (2005). *Man the hunted: Primates, predators, and human evolution.* Boulder, CO: Westview.

Hartwig, W. C. (2002). *The primate fossil record.* New York: Cambridge University Press.

Hartwig, W. C., & Doneski, K. (1998). Evolution of the hominid hand and toolmaking behavior. *American Journal of Physical Anthropology 106,* 401–402.

Hatch, E. (1983). *Culture and morality: The relativity of values in anthropology.* New York: Columbia University Press.

Hatcher, E. P. (1985). *Art as culture, an introduction to the anthropology of art.* New York: University Press of America.

Haviland, W. A. (1967). Stature at Tikal, Guatemala: Implications for ancient Maya, demography, and social organization. *American Antiquity 32,* 316–325.

Haviland, W. A. (1970). Tikal, Guatemala and Mesoamerican urbanism. *World Archaeology 2,* 186–198.

Haviland, W. A. (1972). A new look at Classic Maya social organization at Tikal. *Ceramica de Cultura Maya 8,* 1–16.

Haviland, W. A. (1974). Farming, seafaring and bilocal residence on the coast of Maine. *Man in the Northeast 6,* 31–44.

Haviland, W. A. (1997). Cleansing young minds, or what should we be doing in introductory anthropology? In C. P. Kottak, J. J. White, R. H. Furlow, & P. C. Rice (Eds.), *The teaching of anthropology: Problems, issues, and decisions* (p. 35). Mountain View, CA: Mayfield.

Haviland, W. A. (1997). The rise and fall of sexual inequality: Death and gender at Tikal, Guatemala. *Ancient Mesoamerica 8,* 1–12.

Haviland, W. A. (2002). Settlement, society and demography at Tikal. In J. Sabloff (Ed.), *Tikal.* Santa Fe: School of American Research.

Haviland, W. A. (2003). *Tikal, Guatemala: A Maya way to urbanism.* Paper prepared for 3rd INAH/Penn State Conference on Mesoamerican Urbanism.

Haviland, W. A., & Gordon, R. J. (Eds.). (1993). *Talking about people.* Mountain View, CA: Mayfield.

Haviland, W. A., et al. (1985). *Excavations in small residential groups of Tikal: Groups 4F-1 and 4F-2.* Philadelphia: University Museum.

Haviland, W. A., & Moholy-Nagy, H. (1992). Distinguishing the high and mighty from the hoi polloi at Tikal, Guatemala. In A. F. Chase & D. Z. Chase (Eds.), *Mesoamerican elites: An archaeological assessment.* Norman: Oklahoma University Press.

Haviland, W. A., & Power, M. W. (1994). *The original Vermonters: Native inhabitants, past and present* (2nd ed.). Hanover, NH: University Press of New England.

Hawkes, K., O'Connell, J. F., & Blurton Jones, N. G. (1997). Hadza women's time allocation, offspring, provisioning, and the evolution of long postmenopausal life spans. *Current Anthropology 38,* 551–577.

Hawks, J. (2006, July 21). Neandertal Genome Project. http://johnhawks.net/weblog.

"Hazardous waste trafficking." www.Choike.org

Heilbroner, R. L., & Thurow, L. C. (1981). *The economic problem* (6th ed.). Englewood Cliffs, NJ: Prentice-Hall.

Heita, K. (1999). Imanishi's world view. *Journal of Japanese Trade and Industry 18* (2), 15.

Heitzman, J., & Wordem, R. L. (Eds.). (2006). *India: A country study* (sect. 2, 5th ed.). Washington, DC: Federal Research Division, Library of Congress.

Helm, J. (1962). The ecological approach in anthropology. *American Journal of Sociology 67,* 630–649.

Helman, C. B. (2003). *Culture, health, and illness: An introduction for health professionals.* New York: Butterworth Heinemann Medical.

Henry, D. O., et al. (2004). Human behavioral organization in the Middle Paleolithic: Were Neandertals different? *American Anthropologist 107* (1), 17–31.

Henry, J. (1974). A theory for an anthropological analysis of American culture. In J. G. Jorgensen & M. Truzzi (Eds.), *Anthropology and American life.* Englewood Cliffs, NJ: Prentice-Hall.

Herdt, G. (Ed.). (1996). *Third sex, third gender: Beyond sexual dimorphism in culture and history.* New York: Zone.

Herdt, G. H. (1993). Semen transactions in Sambia culture. In D. N. Suggs & A. W. Mirade (Eds.), *Culture and human sexuality* (pp. 298–327). Pacific Grove, CA: Brooks/Cole.

Herskovits, M. J. (1952). *Economic anthropology: A study in comparative economics* (2nd ed.). New York: Knopf.

Hertz, N. (2001). *The silent takeover: Global capitalism and the death of democracy.* New York: Arrow.

Hewes, G. W. (1973). Primate communication and the gestural origin of language. *Current Anthropology 14,* 5–24.

"Hidden apartheid: Caste discrimination against India's Untouchables." (2007). Human Rights Watch and the Center for Human Rights and Global Justice.

Himmelfarb, E. J. (2000, January/February). First alphabet found in Egypt. Newsbrief. *Archaeology 53* (1).

Hirsch, J. S., & Wardlow, H. (Eds.). (2006). *Modern loves: The anthropology of romantic courtship and companionate marriage.* Ann Arbor: University of Michigan Press.

Historical atlas of the twentieth century. http://users.erols.com/mwhite28/20centry.htm

Hitchcock, R. K., & Enghoff, M. (2004). *Capacity-building of first people of the Kalahari, Botswana: An evaluation.* Copenhagen: International Work Group for Indigenous Affairs.

Hodgen, M. (1964). *Early anthropology in the sixteenth and seventeenth centuries.* Philadelphia: University of Pennsylvania Press.

Hoebel, E. A. (1954). *The law of primitive man: A study in comparative legal dynamics.* Cambridge, MA: Harvard University Press.

Hoebel, E. A. (1958). *Man in the primitive world: An introduction to anthropology.* New York: McGraw-Hill.

Hoebel, E. A. (1960). *The Cheyennes: Indians of the Great Plains.* New York: Holt, Rinehart & Winston.

Holden, C. (1996). Missing link for Miocene apes. *Science 271,* 151.

Holden, C. (1999). Ancient child burial uncovered in Portugal. *Science 283,* 169.

Hole, F. (1966). Investigating the origins of Mesopotamian civilization. *Science 153,* 605–611.

Hole, F., & Heizer, R. F. (1969). *An introduction to prehistoric archeology.* New York: Holt, Rinehart & Winston.

Holloway, R. L. (1980). The O. H. 7 (Olduvai Gorge, Tanzania) hominid partial brain endocast revisited. *American Journal of Physical Anthropology 53,* 267–274.

Holloway, R. L. (1981). The Indonesian *Homo erectus* brain endocast revisited. *American Journal of Physical Anthropology 55,* 503–521.

Holloway, R. L. (1981). Volumetric and asymmetry determinations on recent hominid endocasts: Spy I and II, Djebel Jhroud 1, and the Salb *Homo erectus* specimens, with some notes on Neanderthal brain size. *American Journal of Physical Anthropology 55,* 385–393.

Holloway, R. L., & de LaCoste-Lareymondie, M. C. (1982). Brain endocast asymmetry in pongids and hominids: Some preliminary findings on the paleontology of cerebral dominance. *American Journal of Physical Anthropology 58,* 101–110.

Holmes, L. D. (2000). *Paradise bent* (film review). *American Anthropologist 102* (3), 604–605.

Holy, L. (1996). *Anthropological perspectives on kinship.* London: Pluto.

Horst, H. A., & Miller, D. (Eds.). (2006). *The cell phone: An anthropology of communication.* New York: Berg.

Hostetler, J., & Huntington, G. (1971). *Children in Amish society.* New York: Holt, Rinehart & Winston.

Houle, A. (1999). The origin of platyrrhines: An evaluation of the Antarctic scenario and the floating island model. *American Journal of Physical Anthropology 109,* 554–556.

Howell, F. C. (1970). *Early man.* New York: Time-Life.

Hrdy, S. B. (1999). Body fat and birth control. *Natural History 108* (8), 88.

Hsiaotung, F. (1939). *Peasant life in China.* London: Kegan, Paul.

Hsu, F. L. (1961). *Psychological anthropology: Approaches to culture and personality.* Homewood, IL: Dorsey.

Hsu, F.L.K. (1979). The cultural problems of the cultural anthropologist. *American Anthropologist 81,* 517–532.

Hubert, H., & Mauss, M. (1964). *Sacrifice.* Chicago: University of Chicago Press.

Human development report. (2002). *Deepening democracy in a fragmented world.* United Nations Development Program.

Hunger Project. (2003). www.thp.org

Hunt, R. C. (Ed.). (1967). *Personalities and cultures: Readings in psychological anthropology.* Garden City, NY: Natural History.

Hutter, M. (Ed.). (2003). *The family experience: A reader in cultural diversity* (4th ed.). Boston: Allyn & Bacon.

Hymes, D. (1964). *Language in culture and society: A reader in linguistics and anthropology.* New York: Harper & Row.

Hymes, D. (Ed.). (1972). *Reinventing anthropology.* New York: Pantheon. icasualties.org.

Hymes, D. (1974). *Foundations in sociolinguistics: An ethnographic approach.* Philadelphia: University of Pennsylvania Press.

Imanishi, K., & Asquith, P. (2002). *Japanese view of nature: The world of living things.* New York: Routledge/Curzon.

Inda, J. X., & Rosaldo, R. (Eds.). (2001). *The anthropology of globalization: A reader.* Malden, MA, and Oxford: Blackwell.

Ingmanson, E. J. (1998). Comment. *Current Anthropology 39,* 409.

Inkeles, A., & Levinson, D. J. (1954). National character: The study of modal personality and socio-cultural systems. In G. Lindzey (Ed.), *Handbook of social psychology.* Reading, MA: Addison-Wesley.

International Lesbian, Gay, Bisexual, Trans and Intersex Association (ILGA). (2009). The *2009 report on state-sponsored homophobia.*

Internet World Stats. (2009). www.internetworldstats.com

"Interview with Laura Nader." (2000, November). *California Monthly.*

Inuit Tapiirit Katami. http://www.taprisat.ca/english- text/itk/departments/enviro/ncp

Irvine, M. (1999, November 24). Mom-and-pop houses grow rare. *Burlington Free Press.*

"Italy-Germany verbal war hots up." (2003, July 9). *Deccan Herald* (Bangalore, India).

"It's the law: Child labor protection." (1997, November/December). *Peace and Justice News,* 11.

Jacobs, S. E. (1994). Native American two-spirits. *Anthropology Newsletter 35* (8), 7.

Jacoby, R., & Glauberman, N. (Eds.). (1995). *The Bell Curve debate.* New York: Random House.

Jane Goodall Institute. http://www.janegoodall.org/jane/study-corner/Jane/bio.asp (accessed June 16, 2009)

Jenkins, A. C., Macrae, C. N., & Mitchell, J. P. (2008). Repetition suppression of ventromedial prefrontal activity during judgments of self and others. *Proceedings of the National Academy of Sciences, 105* (11), 4507–4512.

Jennings, F. (1976). *The invasion of America.* New York: Norton.

Jennings, J. D. (1974). *Prehistory of North America* (2nd ed.). New York: McGraw-Hill.

Johansen, B. E. (2002). The Inuit's struggle with dioxins and other organic pollutants. *American Indian Quarterly 26* (3), 479–490.

Johanson, D., & Shreeve, J. (1989). *Lucy's child: The discovery of a human ancestor.* New York: Avon.

Johanson, D. C., & Edey, M. (1981). *Lucy, the beginnings of humankind.* New York: Simon & Schuster.

Johanson, D. C, Edgar, B., & Brill, D. (1996). *From Lucy to language.* New York: Simon & Schuster.

Johanson, D. C., & White, T. D. (1979). A systematic assessment of early African hominids. *Science 203,* 321–330.

Johanson, D. C., & Wong, K. (2009). *Lucy's legacy: The quest for human origins.* New York: Harmony.

John, V. (1971). Whose is the failure? In C. L. Brace, G. R. Gamble, & J. T. Bond (Eds.), *Race*

and intelligence. Washington, DC: American Anthropological Association.

Johnson, A. (1989). Horticulturalists: Economic behavior in tribes. In S. Plattner (Ed.), *Economic anthropology* (pp. 49–77). Stanford, CA: Stanford University Press.

Johnson, A. W., & Earle, T. (1987). *The evolution of human societies, from foraging group to agrarian state.* Stanford, CA: Stanford University Press.

Johnson, D. (1996). Polygamists emerge from secrecy, seeking not just peace but respect. In W. A. Haviland & R. J. Gordon (Eds.), *Talking about people* (2nd ed., pp. 129–131). Mountain View, CA: Mayfield.

Johnson, N. B. (1984). Sex, color, and rites of passage in ethnographic research. *Human Organization 43* (2), 108–120.

Jolly, A. (1985). *The evolution of primate behavior* (2nd ed.). New York: Macmillan.

Jolly, A. (1991). Thinking like a vervet. *Science 251,* 574.

Jolly, C. J. (1970). The seed eaters: A new model of hominid differentiation based on a baboon analogy. *Man 5,* 5–26.

Jones, S. (2005). Transhumance re-examined. *Journal of the Royal Anthropological Institute 11* (4), 841–842.

Jones, S., Martin, R., & Pilbeam, D. (Eds.). (1994). *The Cambridge encyclopedia of human evolution.* New York: Cambridge University Press.

Jorgensen, J. (1972). *The sun dance religion.* Chicago: University of Chicago Press.

Joukowsky, M. A. (1980). *A complete field manual of archaeology: Tools and techniques of field work for archaeologists.* Englewood Cliffs, NJ: Prentice-Hall.

Kaiser, J. (1994). A new theory of insect wing origins takes off. *Science 266,* 363.

Kalwet, H. (1988). *Dreamtime and inner space: The world of the shaman.* New York: Random House.

Kaplan, D. (1972). *Culture theory.* Englewood Cliffs, NJ: Prentice-Hall (Foundations of Modern Anthropology).

Kaplan, D. (2000). The darker side of the original affluent society. *Journal of Anthropological Research 53*(3), 301–324.

Kaplan, M. (2008, August 5). Almost half of primate species face extinction. doi: 10.1038/news.2008.1013.

Karavani, I., & Smith, F. H. (2000). More on the Neanderthal problem: The Vindija case. *Current Anthropology 41,* 839.

Kawamura S. (1959). The process of sub-culture propagation among Japanese macaques. *Primates 2,* 43–60.

Kay, R. F., Fleagle, J. G., & Simons, E. L. (1981). A revision of the Oligocene apes of the Fayum Province, Egypt. *American Journal of Physical Anthropology 55,* 293–322.

Kay, R. F., Ross, C., & Williams, B. A. (1997). Anthropoid origins. *Science 275,* 797–804.

Kay, R. F., Theweissen, J.G.M., & Yoder, A. D. (1992). Cranial anatomy of *Ignacius graybullianus* and the affinities of the plesiadapiformes. *American Journal of Physical Anthropology 89* (4), 477–498.

Kedia, S., & Van Willigen, J. (2005). *Applied anthropology: Domains of application.* New York: Praeger.

Keen, B. (1971). *The Aztec image in western thought.* New Brunswick, NJ: Rutgers University Press.

Kehoe, A. (1989). *The ghost dance: Ethno-history and revitalization.* Fort Worth: Holt, Rinehart & Winston.

Kehoe, A. (2000). *Shamans and religion: An anthropological exploration in critical thinking.* Prospect Heights, IL: Waveland.

Keiser, L. (1991). *Friend by day, enemy by night: Organized vengeance in a Kohistani community*. Fort Worth: Holt, Rinehart & Winston.

Kelly, T. L. (2006). *Sadhus, the great renouncers*. Photography exhibit, Indigo Gallery, Naxal, Kathmandu, Nepal. www.asianart.com/exhibitions/sadhus/index.html

Kendall, L. (1990, October). In the company of witches. *Natural History*, 92.

Kennickell, A. B. (2003, November). *A rolling tide: Changes in the distribution of wealth in the U.S. 1989–2001*. Levy Economics Institute.

Kertzer, D. I. (1989). *Ritual, politics, and power*. New Haven, CT: Yale University Press.

Key, M. R. (1975). *Paralanguage and kinesics: Nonverbal communication*. Metuchen, NJ: Scarecrow.

Khaitovich, P., Lockstone, H. E., Wayland, M. T., Tsang, T. M., Jayatilaka, S. D., Guo, A. J., Zhou, J., Somel, M., Harris, L. W., Holmes, E., Pääbo, S., & Bahn, S. (2008). Metabolic changes in schizophrenia and human brain evolution. *Genome Biology* 9 (8), R124.

Kidder, T. (2003). *Mountains beyond mountains: The quest of Dr. Paul Farmer, a man who would cure the world*. New York: Random House.

Kirkpatrick, R. C. (2000). The evolution of human homosexual behavior. *Current Anthropology 41*, 384.

Klass, M. (1995). *Ordered universes: Approaches to the anthropology of religion*. Boulder, CO: Westview.

Klass, M., & Weisgrau, M. (Eds.). (1999). *Across the boundaries of belief: Contemporary issues in the anthropology of religion*. Boulder, CO: Westview.

Klein, R. (2002). *The dawn of human culture*. New York: Wiley.

Klein, R. G., & Edgar, B. (2002). *The dawn of human culture*. New York: Wiley.

Kleinman, A. (1976). Concepts and a model for the comparison of medical systems as cultural systems. *Social Science and Medicine 12* (2B), 85–95.

Kluckhohn, C. (1970). *Mirror for man*. Greenwich, CT: Fawcett.

Kluckhohn, C. (1994). Navajo witchcraft. *Papers of the Peabody Museum of American Archaeology and Ethnology 22* (2).

Knauft, B. M. (1991). Violence and sociality in human evolution. *Current Anthropology 32*, 391–409.

Koch, G. (1997). Songs, land rights, and archives in Australia. *Cultural Survival Quarterly 20* (4).

Komai, T., & Fukuoka, G. (1934, October). Postnatal growth disparity in monozygotic twins. *Journal of Heredity 25*, 423–430.

Konner, M., & Worthman, C. (1980). Nursing frequency, gonadal function, and birth spacing among !Kung hunter-gatherers. *Science 207*, 788–791.

Koufos, G. (1993). Mandible of *Ouranopithecus macedoniensis* (hominidae: primates) from a new late Miocene locality in Macedonia (Greece). *American Journal of Physical Anthropology 91*, 225–234.

Krader, L. (1968). *Formation of the state*. Englewood Cliffs, NJ: Prentice-Hall.

Krajick, K. (1998). Greenfarming by the Incas? *Science 281*, 323.

Kramer, P. A. (1998). The costs of human locomotion: Maternal investment in child transport. *American Journal of Physical Anthropology 107*, 71–85.

Kraybill, D. B. (2001). *The riddle of Amish culture*. Baltimore: Johns Hopkins University Press.

Kroeber, A. (1958). Totem and taboo: An ethnologic psycho-analysis. In W. Lessa & E. Z. Vogt (Eds.), *Reader in comparative religion: An anthropological approach*. New York: Harper & Row.

Kroeber, A. L. (1939). Cultural and natural areas of native North America. *American Archaeology and Ethnology* (Vol. 38). Berkeley: University of California Press.

Kroeber, A. L. (1963). *Anthropology: Cultural processes and patterns*. New York: Harcourt.

Kroeber, A. L., & Kluckhohn, C. (1952). *Culture: A critical review of concepts and definitions*. Cambridge, MA: Harvard University Press (*Papers of the Peabody Museum of American Archaeology and Ethnology, 47*).

Kruger, J., et al. (2005, December). Egocentrism over e-mail: Can people communicate as well as they think? *Journal of Personality and Social Psychology 89* (6), 925–936.

Kummer, H. (1971). *Primate societies: Group techniques of ecological adaptation*. Chicago: Aldine.

Kunnie, J. (2003). Africa's fast growing indigenous churches. http://coh.arizona.edu/newandnotable/kunnie/kunnie.html

Kunnie, J. (2007). *Umoya: The spirit in Africa*. Self-produced DVD, available at www.coh.arizona.edu/aas/aas.htm

Kunzig, R. (1999). A tale of two obsessed archaeologists, one ancient city and nagging doubts about whether science can ever hope to reveal the past. *Discover 20* (5), 84–92.

Kuper, H. (1965). The Swazi of Swaziland. In J. L. Gibbs (Ed.), *Peoples of Africa* (pp. 479–511). New York: Holt, Rinehart & Winston.

Kurth, P. (1998, October 14). Capital crimes. *Seven Days*, 7.

Kurtz, D. V. (2001). *Political anthropology: Paradigms and power*. Boulder, CO: Westview.

Kushner, G. (1969). *Anthropology of complex societies*. Stanford, CA: Stanford University Press.

LaFont, S. (Ed.). (2003). *Constructing sexualities: Readings in sexuality, gender, and culture*. Upper Saddle River, NJ: Prentice-Hall.

Lai, C.S.L., et al. (2001). A forkhead-domain gene is mutated in severe speech and language disorder. *Nature 413*, 519–523.

Lakoff, R. T. (2004). *Language and woman's place*. M. Bucholtz (Ed.). New York: Oxford University Press.

Lambek, M. (2002). *A reader in the anthropology of religion*. London: Blackwell.

Lampl, M., Velhuis, J. D., & Johnson, M. L. (1992). Saltation and stasis: A model of human growth. *Science 258* (5083), 801–803.

Lancaster, J. B. (1975). *Primate behavior and the emergence of human culture*. New York: Holt, Rinehart & Winston.

Landau, M. (1991). *Narratives of human evolution*. New Haven, CT: Yale University Press.

Lang, I. A., et al. (2008). Association of urinary bisphenol A concentration with medical disorders and laboratory abnormalities in adults. *Journal of the American Medical Association 300* (11), 1303–1310.

Langan, P., & Harlow, C. (1994). *Child rape victims, 1992*. Washington, DC: Bureau of Justice Statistics, U.S. Department of Justice.

Lanning, E. P. (1967). *Peru before the Incas*. Englewood Cliffs, NJ: Prentice-Hall.

Larsen, C. S., Matter, R. M., & Gebo, D. L. (1998). *Human origins: The fossil record*. Long Grove, IL: Waveland.

Larsen, J. (2006, July 28). *Setting the record straight*. Earth Policy Institute, Eco-economy updates.

Latimer, B., Ohman, J. C., & Lovejoy, C. O. (1987). Talocrural joint in African hominoids: Implications for *Australopithecus afarensis*. *American Journal of Physical Anthropology 74*, 155–175.

Lawler, A. (2001). Writing gets a rewrite. *Science 292*, 2419.

Layton, R. (1991). *The anthropology of art* (2nd ed.). Cambridge, MA: Cambridge University Press.

Leach, E. (1961). *Rethinking anthropology*. London: Athlone.

Leach, E. (1962). The determinants of differential cross-cousin marriage. *Man 62*, 238.

Leach, E. (1962). On certain unconsidered aspects of double descent systems. *Man 214*, 13–34.

Leach, E. (1964). Anthropological aspects of language: Animal categories and verbal abuse. In W. Lessa & E. Vogt (Eds.), *Reader in comparative religion* (4th ed.). New York: Harper & Row.

Leach, E. (1982). *Social anthropology*. Glasgow: Fontana.

Leacock, E. (1981). *Myths of male dominance: Collected articles on women cross culturally*. New York: Monthly Review.

Leacock, E. (1981). Women's status in egalitarian society: Implications for social evolution. In *Myths of male dominance: Collected articles on women cross culturally*. New York: Monthly Review.

Leakey, L.S.B. (1965). *Olduvai Gorge, 1951–1961* (Vol. 1). London: Cambridge University Press.

Leakey, L.S.B., Tobias, P. B., & Napier, J. R. (1964). A new species of the genus *Homo* from Olduvai Gorge. *Nature 202*, 7–9.

Leakey, M. D. (1971). *Olduvai Gorge: Excavations in Beds I and II. 1960–1963*. London and New York: Cambridge University Press.

Leakey, M. G., Spoor, F., Brown, F. H., Gathogo, P. N., Kiare, C., Leakey, L. N., & McDougal, I. (2001). New hominin genus from eastern Africa shows diverse middle Pliocene lineages. *Nature 410*, 433–440.

Leap, W. L. (1987). Tribally controlled culture change: The Northern Ute language revival project. In R. M. Wulff & S. J. Fiske (Eds.), *Anthropological praxis: Translating knowledge into action* (pp. 197–211). Boulder, CO: Westview.

Leavitt, G. C. (1990). Sociobiological explanations of incest avoidance: A critical review of evidential claims. *American Anthropologist 92*, 982.

Leclerc-Madlala, S. (2002). Bodies and politics: Healing rituals in the democratic South Africa. In V. Faure (Ed.), *Les cahiers de l'IFAS*, No. 2. Johannesburg: French Institute.

Lee, R. B. (1993). *The Dobe Ju/'hoansi*. Ft. Worth: Harcourt Brace.

Lee, R. B., & Daly, R. H. (1999). *The Cambridge encyclopedia of hunters and gatherers*. New York: Cambridge University Press.

Lee, R. B., & DeVore, I. (Eds.). (1968). *Man the hunter*. Chicago: Aldine.

Lees, R. (1953). The basis of glottochronology. *Language 29*, 113–127.

Lehman, E. C., Jr. (2002, Fall). Women's path into the ministry. *Pulpit & Pew Research Reports 1*, 4.

Lehmann, A. C., & Myers, J. E. (Eds.). (2000). *Magic, witchcraft, and religion: An anthropological study of the supernatural* (5th ed.). Mountain View, CA: Mayfield.

Lehmann, J., & Joseph, S. (2009). *Biochar for environmental management: Science and technology*. London: Earthscan.

Leigh, S. R., & Park, P. B. (1998). Evolution of human growth prolongation. *American Journal of Physical Anthropology 107*, 331–350.

Leinhardt, G. (1964). *Social anthropology.* London: Oxford University Press.

LeMay, M. (1975). The language capability of Neanderthal man. *American Journal of Physical Anthropology 43* (1), 9–14.

Lenski, G. (1966). *Power and privilege: A theory of social stratification.* New York: McGraw-Hill.

Leroi-Gourhan, A. (1968). The evolution of Paleolithic art. *Scientific American 218,* 58*ff.*

Lestel, D. (1998). How chimpanzees have domesticated humans. *Anthropology Today 12* (3).

Leth, P. M. (2007).The use of CT scanning in forensic autopsy. *Forensic Science, Medicine, and Pathology 3* (1), 65–69.

Levine, N. E., & Silk, J. B. (1997). Why polyandry fails. *Current Anthropology 38,* 375–398.

Levine, R. A. (2007). Ethnographic studies of childhood: A historical overview. *American Anthropologist 109* (2), 247–260.

Lévi-Strauss, C. (1963). The sorcerer and his magic. In *Structural anthropology.* New York: Basic.

Lévi-Strauss, C. (1969). *The raw and the cooked.* New York: Harper & Row.

Lewellen, T. C. (2002). *The anthropology of globalization: Cultural anthropology enters the 21st century.* Westport, CT: Greenwood.

Lewin, R. (1987). Four legs bad, two legs good. *Science 235,* 969.

Lewin, R. (1993). Paleolithic paint job. *Discover 14* (7), 64–70.

Lewis, I. M. (1976). *Social anthropology in perspective.* Harmondsworth, England: Penguin.

Lewis-Williams, J. D. (1990). *Discovering southern African rock art.* Cape Town and Johannesburg: David Philip.

Lewis-Williams, J. D. (1997). Agency, art, and altered consciousness: A motif in French (Quercy) Upper Paleolithic parietal art. *Antiquity 71,* 810–830.

Lewis-Williams, J. D., & Dowson, T. A. (1988). Signs of all times: Entoptic phenomena in Upper Paleolithic art. *Current Anthropology 29,* 201–245.

Lewis-Williams, J. D., & Dowson, T. A. (1993). On vision and power in the Neolithic: Evidence from the decorated monuments. *Current Anthropology 34,* 55–65.

Lewis-Williams, J. D., Dowson, T. A., & Deacon, J. (1993). Rock art and changing perceptions of Southern Africa's past: Ezeljagdspoort reviewed. *Antiquity 67,* 273–291.

Lewontin, R. C. (1972). The apportionment of human diversity. In T. Dobzhansky et al. (Eds.), *Evolutionary biology* (pp. 381–398). New York: Plenum.

Lewontin, R. C., Rose, S., & Kamin, L. J. (1984). *Not in our genes.* New York: Pantheon.

Li, X., Harbottle, G., Zhang, J., & Wang, C. (2003).The earliest writing? Sign use in the seventh millennium bc at Jiahu, Henan Province, China. *Antiquity 77,* 31–44.

Lieberman, P. (2006). *Toward an evolutionary biology of language.* Cambridge, MA: Belknap.

Lindenbaum, S. (1978). *Kuru sorcery: Disease and danger in the New Guinea highlands.* New York: McGraw-Hill.

Lindstrom, L. (1993). *Cargo cult: Strange stories of desire from Melanesia and beyond.* Honolulu: University of Hawaii Press.

Little, K. L. (1973). *African women in towns: An aspect of Africa's social revolution.* New York: Cambridge University Press.

Littlewood, R. (2004). Commentary: Globalization, culture, body image, and eating disorders. *Culture, Medicine, and Psychiatry 28* (4), 597–602.

Livingstone, F. B. (1973). The distribution of abnormal hemoglobin genes and their significance for human evolution. In C. Loring

Brace & J. Metress (Eds.), *Man in evolutionary perspective.* New York: Wiley.

Living Tongues. www.livingtongues.org/background.html

Lloyd, C. B. (Ed.). (2005). *Growing up global: The changing transitions to adulthood in developing countries* (pp. 450–453). Washington, DC: National Academies Press, Committee on Population, National Research Council, and Institute of Medicine of the National Academies.

Lock, M. (2001). *Twice dead: Organ transplants and the reinvention of death.* Berkeley: University of California Press.

Lorenzo, C., Carretero, J. M., Arsuaga, J. L., Gracia, A., & Martinez, I. (1998). Intrapopulational body size variation and cranial capacity variation in middle Pleistocene humans: The Sima de los Huesos sample (Sierra de Atapuerca, Spain). *American Journal of Physical Anthropology 106,* 19–33.

Loubser, J.H.N. (2003). *Archaeology: The comic.* Lanham, MD: Altamira.

Louckey, J., & Carlsen, R. (1991). Massacre in Santiago Atitlán. *Cultural Survival Quarterly 15* (3), 70.

Louie, A. (2004). *Chineseness across borders: Renegotiating Chinese identities in China and the United States.* Durham and London: Duke University Press.

Lounsbury, F. (1964). The structural analysis of kinship semantics. In H. G. Lunt (Ed.), *Proceedings of the Ninth International Congress of Linguists.* The Hague: Mouton.

Lovejoy, C. O. (1981). Origin of man. *Science 211,* 341–350.

Lowie, R. H. (1948). *Social organization.* New York: Holt, Rinehart & Winston.

Lowie, R. H. (1956). *Crow Indians.* New York: Holt, Rinehart & Winston. (orig. 1935)

Lucy, J. A. (1997). Linguistic relativity. *Annual Review of Anthropology 26,* 291–312.

Luhrmann, T. M. (2001). *Of two minds: An anthropologist looks at American psychiatry.* New York: Vintage.

Lurie, N. O. (1973). Action anthropology and the American Indian. In *Anthropology and the American Indian: A symposium.* San Francisco: Indian Historical.

MacCormack, C. P. (1977). Biological events and cultural control. *Signs 3,* 93–100.

MacLarnon, A. M., & Hewitt, G. P. (1999). The evolution of human speech: The role of enhanced breathing control. *American Journal of Physical Anthropology 109,* 341–363.

MacNeish, R. S. (1992). *The origins of agriculture and settled life.* Norman: University of Oklahoma Press.

"Madison Avenue relevance." (1999). *Anthropology Newsletter 40* (4), 32.

Maggioncalda, A. N., & Sapolsky, R. M. (2002). Disturbing behaviors of the orangutan. *Scientific American 286* (6), 60–65.

Mair, L. (1957). *An introduction to social anthropology.* London: Oxford University Press.

Mair, L. (1969). *Witchcraft.* New York: McGraw-Hill.

Mair, L. (1971). *Marriage.* Baltimore: Penguin.

Malefijt, A. de W. (1969). *Religion and culture: An introduction to anthropology of religion.* London: Macmillan.

Malinowski, B. (1945). *The dynamics of culture change: An inquiry into race relations in Africa.* New Haven, CT: Yale University Press.

Malinowski, B. (1951). *Crime and custom in savage society.* London: Routledge.

Malinowski, B. (1954). *Magic, science, and religion.* Garden City, NY: Doubleday.

Malinowski, B. (1961). *Argonauts of the western Pacific.* New York: Dutton. (orig. 1922)

Mann, A., Lampl, M., & Monge, J. (1990). Patterns of ontogeny in human evolution: Evidence from dental development. *Yearbook of Physical Anthropology 33,* 111–150.

Mann, C. C. (2000). Misconduct alleged in Yanomamo studies. *Science 289* (2), 253.

Mann, C. C. (2002).The real dirt on rainforest fertility. *Science 297,* 920–923.

Mann, C. C. (2005). *1491: New revelations of the Americas before Columbus.* New York: Knopf.

Marcus, G. (1995). Ethnography in/of the world system: The emergence of multi-sited ethnography. *Annual Review of Anthropology 24,* 95–117.

Marcus, J., & Flannery, K. V. (1996). *Zapotec civilization: How urban society evolved in Mexico's Oaxaca Valley.* New York: Thames & Hudson.

Marks, J. (1995). *Human biodiversity: Genes, race and history.* Hawthorne, NY: Aldine.

Marks, J. (2000, April 8). A feckless quest for the basketball gene. *New York Times.*

Marks, J. (2000, May 12). 98% alike (what our similarity to apes tells us about our understanding of genetics). *Chronicle of Higher Education,* B7.

Marks, J. (2002). *What it means to be 98 percent chimpanzee: Apes, people, and their genes.* Berkeley: University of California Press.

Marks, J. (2009). *Why I am not a scientist: Anthropology and modern knowledge.* Berkeley: University of California Press.

Marsella, A. J. (1982). Pulling it together: Discussion and comments. In S. Pastner & W. A. Haviland (Eds.), *Confronting the creationists* (pp. 79–80). *Northeastern Anthropological Association, Occasional Proceedings 1.*

Marsella, A. J., & White, G. (1982). *Cultural conceptions of mental health and therapy.* New York: Springer.

Marshack, A. (1976). Some implications of the Paleolithic symbolic evidence for the origin of language. *Current Anthropology 17* (2), 274–282.

Marshack, A. (1989). Evolution of the human capacity: The symbolic evidence. *Yearbook of Physical Anthropology 32,* 1–34.

Marshall, E. (2001). Preclovis sites fight for acceptance. *Science 291,* 1732.

Marshall, L. (1961). Sharing, talking and giving: Relief of social tensions among !Kung bushmen. *Africa 31,* 231–249.

Marshall, M. (1990). Two tales from the Trukese taproom. In P. R. DeVita (Ed.), *The humbled anthropologist* (pp. 12–17). Belmont, CA: Wadsworth.

Martin, E. (1994). *Flexible bodies: Tracking immunity in American culture—from the days of polio to the age of AIDS.* Boston: Beacon.

Martin, E. (1999). Flexible survivors. *Anthropology News 40* (6), 5–7.

Martorell, R. (1988). Body size, adaptation, and function. *GDP,* 335–347.

Mascia-Lees, F. E., & Black, N. J. (2000). *Gender and anthropology.* Prospect Heights, IL: Waveland.

Mason, J. A. (1957). *The ancient civilizations of Peru.* Baltimore: Penguin.

Mathieu, C. (2003). *A history and anthropological study of the ancient kingdoms of the Sino-Tibetan borderland—Naxi and Mosuo.* New York: Mellen.

Matthews, G. (2006). Happiness and the pursuit of a life worth living: An anthropological approach. In Y.-K. Ng & L. S. Ho (Eds.), *Happiness and public policy* (pp. 147–168). Hampshire, England: Palgrave Macmillan.

Mauss, M. (2000). *The gift: The form and reason for exchange in archaic societies* (translation by W. D. Halls and foreword by M. Douglas). New York: Norton.

May, R. (2000). Melding heart and head. *Beyond 2000*. New York: United Nations Environment Programme. http://www.unep.org/ourplanet/imgversn/111/may.html

Maybury-Lewis, D. (1960). Parallel descent and the Apinaye anomaly. *Southwestern Journal of Anthropology 16*, 191–216.

Maybury-Lewis, D. (1984). The prospects for plural societies. *1982 Proceedings of the American Ethnological Society.*

Maybury-Lewis, D. (1993, fall). A new world dilemma: The Indian question in the Americas. *Symbols*, 17–23.

Maybury-Lewis, D. (2001). *Indigenous peoples, ethnic groups, and the state* (2nd ed.). Boston: Allyn & Bacon.

Maybury-Lewis, D.H.P. (1993). A special sort of pleading. In W. A. Haviland & R. J. Gordon (Eds.), *Talking about people* (2nd ed., p. 17). Mountain View, CA: Mayfield.

Mayo Clinic. http://www.mayoclinic.com/

Mayr, E., & Diamond, J. (2002). *What evolution is*. New York: Basic.

McBride, B. (1980). *Eric. R. Wolf interview. Between subjectivity and objectivity*. Unpublished masters thesis, anthropology department, Columbia University.

McCorriston, J., & Hole, F. (1991). The ecology of seasonal stress and the origins of agriculture in the Near East. *American Anthropologist 93*, 46–69.

McDermott, L. (1996). Self-representation in Upper Paleolithic female figurines. *Current Anthropology 37*, 227–276.

McElroy, A., & Townsend, P. K. (2003). *Medical anthropology in ecological perspective*. Boulder, CO: Westview.

McFate, M. (2007). *Role and effectiveness of sociocultural knowledge for counterinsurgency*. Alexandria, VA: Institute for Defense Analysis.

McFee, M. (1972). *Modern Blackfeet: Montanans on a reservation*. New York: Holt, Rinehart & Winston.

McGrew, W. C. (2000). Dental care in chimps. *Science 288*, 1747.

McHenry, H. (1975). Fossils and the mosaic nature of human evolution. *Science 190*, 524–431.

McHenry, H. M. (1992). Body size and proportions in early hominids. *American Journal of Physical Anthropology 87*, 407–431.

McHenry, H. M., & Jones, A. L. (2006). Hallucial convergence in early hominids. *Journal of Human Evolution 50*, 534–539.

McKenna, J. J. (1999). Co-sleeping and SIDS. In W. Trevathan, E. O. Smith, & J. J. McKenna (Eds.), *Evolutionary medicine*. London: Oxford University Press.

McKenna, J. J. (2002, September–October). Breastfeeding and bedsharing. *Mothering*, 28–37.

McKenna, J. J., & McDade, T. (2005, June). Why babies should never sleep alone: A review of the co-sleeping controversy in relation to SIDS, bedsharing, and breast feeding. *Pediatric Respiratory Reviews 6* (2), 134–152.

McNeill, W. (1992). *Plagues and people*. New York: Anchor.

Mead, A.T.P. (1996). Genealogy, sacredness, and the commodities market. *Cultural Survival Quarterly 20* (2).

Mead, M. (1928). *Coming of age in Samoa: A psychological study of primitive youth for western civilization*. New York: Morrow.

Mead, M. (1960). Anthropology among the sciences. *American Anthropologist 63*, 475–482.

Mead, M. (1963). *Sex and temperament in three primitive societies* (3rd ed.). New York: Morrow. (orig. 1935)

Mead, M., & Metraux, R. (Eds.). (1953). *The study of culture at a distance*. Chicago: University of Chicago Press.

Medicine, B. (1994). Gender. In M. B. Davis (Ed.), *Native America in the twentieth century*. New York: Garland.

Melaart, J. (1967). *Catal Hüyük: A Neolithic town in Anatolia*. London: Thames & Hudson.

Mellars, P. (1989). Major issues in the emergence of modern humans. *Current Anthropology 30*, 356–357.

Mellars, P. (2009). Archaeology: Origins of the female image. *Nature 459*, 176–177.

Meltzer, D., Fowler, D., & Sabloff, J. (Eds.). (1986). *American archaeology: Past & future*. Washington, DC: Smithsonian Institution.

Merin, Y. (2002). *Equality for same-sex couples: The legal recognition of gay partnerships in Europe and the United States*. Chicago: University of Chicago Press.

Merriam, A. P. (1964). *The anthropology of music*. Chicago: Northwestern University Press.

Mesghinua, H. M. (1966). Salt mining in Enderta. *Journal of Ethiopian Studies 4* (2).

Métraux, A. (1953). Applied anthropology in government: United Nations. In A. A. Kroeber (Ed.), *Anthropology today: An encyclopedic inventory* (pp. 880–894).Chicago: University of Chicago Press.

Meyer, J. (2008). Typology and acoustic strategies of whistled languages: Phonetic comparison and perceptual cues of whistled vowels. *Journal of the International Phonetic Association 38*, 69–94.

Meyer J., & Gautheron, B. (2006). Whistled speech and whistled languages. In K. Brown (Ed.), *Encyclopedia of language & linguistics* (2nd ed., vol. 13, pp. 573–576). Oxford, England: Elsevier.

Meyer, J., Meunier, F., & Dentel, L. (2007). Identification of natural whistled vowels by non-whistlers. *Proceedings of Interspeech 2007* (pp. 1593–1596). Antwerpen, Belgium.

Miles, H.L.W. (1993). Language and the orangutan: The "old person" of the forest. In P. Cavalieri & P. Singer (Eds.), *The Great Ape Project* (pp. 45–50). New York: St. Martin's.

Miller, J.M.A. (2000). Craniofacial variation in *Homo habilis*: An analysis of the evidence for multiple species. *American Journal of Physical Anthropology 112*, 122.

Millon, R. (1973). *Urbanization of Teotihuacán, Mexico: Vol. 1, Part 1. The Teotihuacán map*. Austin: University of Texas Press.

Mintz, S. (1996). A taste of history. In W. A. Haviland & R. J. Gordon (Eds.), *Talking about people* (2nd ed., pp. 81–82). Mountain View, CA: Mayfield.

Minugh-Purvis, N. (1992). The inhabitants of Ice Age Europe. *Expedition 34* (3), 23–36.

Mitchell, W. E. (1973, December). A new weapon stirs up old ghosts. *Natural History*, 77–84.

Modell, J. (1994). *Kinship with strangers: Adoption and interpretations of kinship in American culture*. Berkeley: University of California Press.

Molnar, S. (1992). *Human variation: Races, types and ethnic groups* (3rd ed.). Englewood Cliffs, NJ: Prentice-Hall.

Monaghan, L., Hinton, L., & Kephart, R. (1997). Can't teach a dog to be a cat? The dialogue on ebonics. *Anthropology Newsletter 38* (3), 1, 8, 9.

Montagu, A. (1964). *The concept of race*. London: Macmillan.

Montagu, A. (1964). *Man's most dangerous myth: The fallacy of race* (4th ed.) New York: World Publishing.

Montagu, A. (1975). *Race and IQ*. New York: Oxford University Press.

Moore, J. (1998). Comment. *Current Anthropology 39*, 412.

Morgan, L. H. (1877). *Ancient society*. New York: World Publishing.

Morphy, H., & Perkins, M. (Eds.). (2006). *Anthropology of art: A reader*. Boston: Blackwell.

Morse, D., et al. (1979). *Gestures: Their origins and distribution*. New York: Stein & Day.

Moscati, S. (1962). *The face of the ancient orient*. New York: Doubleday.

Murdock, G. P. (1960). Cognatic forms of social organization. In G. P. Murdock (Ed.), *Social structure in Southeast Asia* (pp. 1–14). Chicago: Quadrangle Books.

Murdock, G. P. (1965). *Social structure*. New York: Free Press.

Murphy, R. (1971). *The dialectics of social life: Alarms and excursions in anthropological theory*. New York: Basic.

Murphy, R., & Kasdan, L. (1959). The structure of parallel cousin marriage. *American Anthropologist 61*, 17–29.

Mydens, S. (2001, August 12). He's not hairy, he's my brother. *New York Times*, sec. 4, 5.

Myrdal, G. (1974). Challenge to affluence: The emergence of an "under-class." In J. G. Jorgensen & M. Truzzi (Eds.), *Anthropology and American life*. Englewood Cliffs, NJ: Prentice-Hall.

Nader, L. (Ed.). (1965). The ethnography of law, part II. *American Anthropologist 67* (6).

Nader, L. (Ed.). (1969). *Law in culture and society*. Chicago: Aldine.

Nader, L. (Ed). (1981). *No access to law: Alternatives to the American judicial system*. New York: Academic.

Nader, L. (Ed.). (1996). *Naked science: Anthropological inquiry into boundaries, power, and knowledge*. New York: Routledge.

Nader, L. (1997). Controlling processes: Tracing the dynamics of power. *Current Anthropology 38*, 715–717.

Nader, L. (Ed.). (1997). *Law in culture and society*. Berkeley: University of California Press.

Nader, L. (2002). *The life of the law: Anthropological projects*. Berkeley: University of California Press.

Nader, L., & Todd, Jr., H. F. (1978). *The disputing process: Law in ten societies*. New York: Columbia University Press.

Nanda, S. (1990). *Neither man nor woman: The hijras of India*. Belmont, CA: Wadsworth.

Nanda, S. (1992). Arranging a marriage in India. In P. R. De Vita (Ed.), *The naked anthropologist* (pp. 139–143). Belmont, CA: Wadsworth.

Nash, J. (1976). Ethnology in a revolutionary setting. In M. A. Rynkiewich & J. P. Spradley (Eds.), *Ethics and anthropology: Dilemmas in fieldwork* (pp. 148–166). New York: Wiley.

Natadecha-Sponsal, P. (1993). The young, the rich and the famous: Individualism as an American cultural value. In P. R. DeVita & J. D. Armstrong (Eds.), *Distant mirrors: America as a foreign culture* (pp. 46–53). Belmont, CA: Wadsworth.

NationMaster.com. http://www.nationmaster.com/graph/mor_eat_dis-mortality-eating-disorders

Natural Resources Defense Council. (2005, March 25). Healthy milk, healthy baby: Chemical pollution and mother's milk. www.NRDC.org

Needham, R. (Ed.). (1971). *Rethinking kinship and marriage*. London: Tavistock.

Needham, R. (1972). *Belief, language and experience*. Chicago: University of Chicago Press.

Neer, R. M. (1975). The evolutionary significance of vitamin D, skin pigment, and ultraviolet light. *American Journal of Physical Anthropology 43,* 409–416.

Nesbitt, L. M. (1935). *Hell-hole of creation.* New York: Knopf.

Nesse, R. M., & Williams, G. C. (1996). *Why we get sick.* New York: Vintage.

Netting, R. M., Wilk, R. R., & Arnould, E. J. (Eds.). (1984). *Households: Comparative and historical studies of the domestic group.* Berkeley: University of California Press.

Nettl, B. (2005). *The study of ethnomusicology: Thirty-one issues and concepts.* Chicago: University of Illinois Press.

Nieftagodien, N. (2008, June 18). Incoherent response to crisis. *The Star,* Johannesburg. http://web.wits.ac.za/NewsRoom/NewsItems/Noor+Nieftagodien+xenophobia+opinion.htm

Nietschmann, B. (1987). The third world war. *Cultural Survival Quarterly 11* (3), 1–16.

Nishinda T. (1987). Local traditions and cultural transmission (pp. 462–474). In B. B. Smuts et al. (Eds.), *Primate society.* Chicago: University of Chicago Press.

Noack, T. (2001). Cohabitation in Norway: An accepted and gradually more regulated way of living. *International Journal of Law, Policy, and the Family 15* (1), 102–117.

Normile, D. (1998). Habitat seen as playing larger role in shaping behavior. *Science 279,* 1454.

Norris, R. S., & Kristensen, H. M. (2006, July/August). Global nuclear stockpiles, 1945–2006. *Bulletin of the Atomic Scientists 62* (4), 64–66.

Nunney, L. (1998). Are we selfish, are we nice, or are we nice because we are selfish? *Science 281,* 1619.

Nye, J. (2002). *The paradox of American power: Why the world's only superpower can't go it alone.* New York: Oxford University Press.

Oakley, K. P. (1964). *Man the tool-maker.* Chicago: University of Chicago Press.

O'Barr, W. M., & Conley, J. M. (1993). When a juror watches a lawyer. In W. A. Haviland & R. J. Gordon (Eds.), *Talking about people* (2nd ed., pp. 42– 45). Mountain View, CA: Mayfield.

Obler, R. S. (1982). Is the female husband a man? Woman/woman marriage among the Nandi of Kenya. *Ethnology 19,* 69–88.

O'Carroll, E. (2008, June 27). Spain to grant some human rights to apes. *Christian Science Monitor.*

Offiong, D. (1985). Witchcraft among the Ibibio of Nigeria. In A. C. Lehmann & J. E. Myers (Eds.), *Magic, witchcraft, and religion* (pp. 152–165). Palo Alto, CA: Mayfield.

Okonjo, K. (1976). The dual-sex political system in operation: Igbo women and community politics in midwestern Nigeria. In N. Hafkin & E. Bay (Eds.), *Women in Africa.* Stanford, CA: Stanford University Press.

Olszewski, D. I. (1991). Comment. *Current Anthropology 32,* 43.

O'Mahoney, K. (1970). The salt trade. *Journal of Ethiopian Studies 8* (2).

Ong, A. (1999). *Flexible citizenship: The cultural logics of transnationality.* Durham, NC: Duke University Press.

Orlando, L., et al. (6 June 2006). Correspondence: Revisiting Neandertal diversity with a 100,000 year old mtDNA sequence. *Current Biology 16,* 400–402.

Oswalt, W. H. (1972). *Habitat and technology.* New York: Holt, Rinehart & Winston.

Otte, M. (2000). On the suggested bone flute from Slovenia. *Current Anthropology 41,* 271.

Otten, C. M. (1971). *Anthropology and art: Readings in cross-cultural aesthetics.* Garden City, NY: Natural History.

Ottenberg, P. (1965). The Afikpo Ibo of eastern Nigeria. In J. L. Gibbs (Ed.), *Peoples of Africa.* New York: Holt, Rinehart & Winston.

Ottenheimer, M. (1996). *Forbidden relatives: The American myth of cousin marriage.* Chicago: University of Illinois Press.

Otterbein, K. F. (1971). *The evolution of war.* New Haven, CT: HRAF Press.

Pandian, J. (1998). *Culture, religion, and the sacred self: A critical introduction to the anthropological study of religion.* Englewood Cliffs, NJ: Prentice-Hall.

Paredes, J. A., & Purdum, E. D. (1990). "Bye, bye Ted . . . " *Anthropology Today 6* (2), 9.

Parés, J. M., Perez-Gonzalez, A., Weil, A. B., & Arsuaga, J. L. (2000). On the age of hominid fossils at the Sima de los Huesos, Sierra de Atapuerca, Spain: Paleomagnetic evidence. *American Journal of Physical Anthropology 111,* 451–461.

Parish, A. R. (1998). Comment. *Current Anthropology 39,* 414.

Parker, R. G. (1991). *Bodies, pleasures, and passions: Sexual culture in contemporary Brazil.* Boston: Beacon.

Parkin, R. (1997). *Kinship: An introduction to basic concepts.* Cambridge, MA: Blackwell.

Parnell, R. (1999). Gorilla exposé. *Natural History 108* (8), 43.

Partridge, W. (Ed.). (1984). *Training manual in development anthropology.* Washington, DC: American Anthropological Association.

Patterson, F.G.P., & Gordon, W. (2002). Twenty-seven years of Project Koko and Michael. In B. Galdikas et al. (Eds.), *All apes great and small* (vol. 1): *Chimpanzees, bonobos, and gorillas* (pp. 165–176). New York: Kluwer Academic.

Patterson, F., & Linden, E. (1981). *The education of Koko.* New York: Holt, Rinehart & Winston.

Peacock, J. L. (2002). *The anthropological lens: Harsh light, soft focus* (2nd ed.). New York: Cambridge University Press.

Pease, T. (2000, Spring). Taking the third side. *Andover Bulletin.*

Pelto, G. H., Goodman, A. H., & Dufour, D. L. (Eds.). (2000). *Nutritional anthropology: Biocultural perspectives on food and nutrition.* Mountain View, CA: Mayfield.

Pelto, P. J. (1973). *The snowmobile revolution: Technology and social change in the Arctic.* Menlo Park, CA: Cummings.

Pennisi, E. (1999). Genetic study shakes up out of Africa theory. *Science 283,* 1828.

Perego, U. A., Achilli, A., Angerhofer, N., Accetturo, M., Pala, M., Olivieri, A., Kashani, B. H., Ritchie, K. H., Scozzari, R., Kong, P., Myres, N. M., Salas, A., Semino, O., Bandelt, H-J., Woodward, S. R., & Torroni, A. (2009). Distinctive Paleo-Indian migration routes from Beringia marked by two rare mtDNA haplogroups. *Current Biology 19* (1), 1–8, 13.

Peters, C. R. (1979). Toward an ecological model of African Plio-Pleistocene hominid adaptations. *American Anthropologist 81*(2), 261–278.

Petersen J. B., Neuves, E., & Heckenberger, M. J. (2001). Gift from the past: *Terra preta* and prehistoric American occupation in Amazonia. In C. McEwan and C. Barreo (Eds.), *Unknown Amazon* (pp. 86–105). London: British Museum.

Pew Research Center. (2007). *Global attitudes survey.*

Pew Research Center. (2009). Mapping the global Muslim population: A report on the size and distribution of the world's Muslim population. http://pewforum.org/newassets/images/reports/Muslimpopulation/Muslimpopulation.pdf

Pfeiffer, J. E. (1978). *The emergence of man.* New York: Harper & Row.

Pfeiffer, J. E. (1985). *The creative explosion.* Ithaca, NY: Cornell University Press.

Piddocke, S. (1965). The potlatch system of the southern Kwakiutl: A new perspective. *Southwestern Journal of Anthropology 21,* 244–264.

Piggott, S. (1965). *Ancient Europe.* Chicago: Aldine.

Pilbeam, D. R. (1987). Rethinking human origins. In R. L. Ciochon & J. G. Fleagle (Eds.), *Primate evolution and human origins* (p. 217). Hawthorne, NY: Aldine.

Pimentel, D. (1991). Response. *Science 252,* 358.

Pimentel, D., Hurd, L. E., Bellotti, A. C., Forster, M. J., Oka, I. N., Sholes, O. D., & Whitman, R. J. (1973). Food production and the energy crisis. *Science, 182.*

Pink, S. (2001). *Doing visual ethnography: Images, media and representation in research.* Thousand Oaks, CA: Sage.

Pinker, S. (1994). *The language instinct: How the mind creates language.* New York: Morrow.

Piperno, D. R., & Fritz, G. J. (1994). On the emergence of agriculture in the new world. *Current Anthropology 35,* 637–643.

Pitts, V. (2003). *In the flesh: The cultural politics of body modification.* New York: Palgrave Macmillan.

Plane, A. M. (1996). Putting a face on colonization: Factionalism and gender politics in the life history of Awashunkes, the "Squaw Sachem" of Saconnet. In R. S. Grumet (Ed.), *Northeastern Indian lives, 1632–1816* (pp.140–175). Amherst: University of Massachusetts Press.

Plattner, S. (Ed.). (1989). *Economic anthropology.* Stanford, CA: Stanford University Press.

Plattner, S. (1989). Markets and marketplaces. In S. Plattner (Ed.), *Economic anthropology.* Stanford, CA: Stanford University Press.

Pluralism Project, Harvard University. pluralism.org

Pohl, M.E.D., Pope, K. O., & von Nagy, C. (2002). Olmec origins of Mesoamerican writing. *Science 298,* 1984–1987.

Polanyi, K. (1968). The economy as instituted process. In E. E. LeClair, Jr., & H. K. Schneider (Eds.), *Economic anthropology: Readings in theory and analysis* (pp. 127–138). New York: Holt, Rinehart & Winston.

Pollan, M. (2001). *The botany of desire: A plant's-eye view of the world.* New York: Random House.

Pollan, M. (2008). *In defense of food: An eater's manifesto.* New York: Penguin.

Pollock, N. J. (1995). Social fattening patterns in the Pacific—the positive side of obesity. A Nauru case study. In I. DeGarine & N. J. Pollock (Eds.), *Social aspects of obesity* (pp. 87–109). London: Routledge.

Pope, G. G. (1989, October). Bamboo and human evolution. *Natural History 98,* 48–57.

Pope, G. G. (1992). Craniofacial evidence for the origin of modern humans in China. *Yearbook of Physical Anthropology 35,* 243–298.

Pope Pius XII. (1954). *Sacra Virginitas. Encyclical on consecrated virginity.* The Catholic Encyclopedia Online: www.newadvent.org

Pospisil, L. (1963). *The Kapauku Papuans of west New Guinea.* New York: Holt, Rinehart & Winston.

Pospisil, L. (1971). *Anthropology of law: A comparative theory.* New York: Harper & Row.

Potts, R. (1997). *Humanity's descent: The consequences of ecological instability.* New York: Avon.

Powdermaker, H. (1939). *After freedom: A cultural study in the Deep South.* New York: Viking.

Powdermaker, H. (1976). *Stranger and friend: The way of an anthropologist.* London: Secker and Warburg.

Power, M. G. (1995). Gombe revisited: Are chimpanzees violent and hierarchical in the free state? *General Anthropology 2* (1), 5–9.

Premack, A. J., & Premack, D. (1972). Teaching language to an ape. *Scientific American 277*(4), 92–99.

Price, T. D., & Feinman, G. M. (Eds.). (1995). *Foundations of social inequality.* New York: Plenum.

Pringle, H. (1997). Ice Age communities may be earliest known net hunters. *Science 277,* 1203–1204.

Pringle, H. (1998). The slow birth of agriculture. *Science 282,* 1449.

Prins, A.H.J. (1953). *East African class systems.* Groningen, the Netherlands: J. B. Wolters.

Prins, H.E.L. (1996). *The Mi'kmaq: Resistance, accommodation, and cultural survival* (p. 106). Orlando: Harcourt Brace.

Prins, H.E.L. (1998). Book review of Schuster, C., & Carpenter, E. *American Anthropologist 100* (3), 841.

Prins, H.E.L. (2002). Visual media and the primitivist perplex: Colonial fantasies, indigenous imagination, and advocacy in North America. In F. D. Ginsburg et al. (Eds.), *Media worlds: Anthropology on new terrain* (pp. 58–74). Berkeley: University of California Press.

Prins, H.E.L., & Carter, K. (1986). *Our lives in our hands.* Video and 16mm. Color. 50 min. Distributed by Watertown, MA: Documentary Educational Resources and Bucksport, ME: Northeast Historic Film

Prins, H.E.L., & Krebs, E. (2006). Toward a land without evil: Alfred Métraux a UNESCO anthropologist 1948–1962. In *60 years of UNESCO history. Proceedings of the international symposium in Paris, 16–18 November 2005.* Paris: UNESCO.

Profet, M. (1991). The function of allergy: Immunological defense against toxins. *Quarterly Review of Biology 66* (1), 23–62.

Profet, M. (1995). *Protecting your baby to be.* New York: Addison Wesley.

Pruetz, J. D., & Bertolani, P. (2007, March 6).Savanna chimpanzees, *Pan troglodytes verus,* hunt with tools. *Current Biology 17,* 412–417.

Puleston, D. E. (1983). *The settlement survey of Tikal.* Philadelphia: University Museum.

Quinn, N. (2005). Universals of child rearing. *Anthropological Theory 5,* 475–514.

Radcliffe-Brown, A. R. (1931). Social organization of Australian tribes. *Oceana Monographs 1,* 29.

Radcliffe-Brown, A. R., & Forde, C. D. (Eds.). (1950). *African systems of kinship and marriage.* London: Oxford University Press.

Radin, P. (1923). The Winnebago tribe. In *37th annual report of the Bureau of American Ethnology, 1915–1916* (pp. 33–550). Washington, DC: Government Printing Office.

Rapp, R. (1999). *Testing women, testing the fetus: The social impact of amniocentesis in America.* New York: Routledge.

Rappaport, R. A. (1969). Ritual regulation of environmental relations among a New Guinea people. In A. P. Vayda (Ed.), *Environment and cultural behavior* (pp. 181–201). Garden City, NY. Natural History.

Rappaport, R. A. (1984). *Pigs for the ancestors* (Enl. ed.). New Haven, CT: Yale University Press.

Rappaport, R. A. (1999). *Holiness and humanity: Ritual in the making of religious life.* New York: Cambridge University Press.

Rathje, W. L. (1974). The garbage project: A new way of looking at the problems of archaeology. *Archaeology 27,* 236–241.

Rathje, W. L. (1993). Rubbish! In W. A. Haviland & R. J. Gordon (Eds.), *Talking about people:*

Readings in contemporary cultural anthropology. Mountain View, CA: Mayfield.

Rathke, L. (1989). To Maine for apples. *Salt Magazine 9* (4), 24–47.

Read-Martin, C. E., & Read, D. W. (1975). Australopithecine scavenging and human evolution: An approach from faunal analysis. *Current Anthropology 16* (3), 359–368.

Recent demographic developments in Europe—2000. Council of Europe.

Recer, P. (1998, February 16). Apes shown to communicate in the wild. *Burlington Free Press,* 12A.

Redfield, R. (1953). *The primitive world and its transformations.* Ithaca, NY: Cornell University Press.

Redman, C. L. (1978). *The rise of civilization: From early farmers to urban society in the ancient Near East.* San Francisco: Freeman.

Reid, J. J., Schiffer, M. B., & Rathje, W. L. (1975). Behavioral archaeology: Four strategies. *American Anthropologist 77,* 864–869.

Reina, R. E. (1966). *The law of the saints.* Indianapolis: Bobbs-Merrill.

Relethford, J. H. (2001). Absence of regional affinities of Neandertal DNA with living humans does not reject multiregional evolution. *American Journal of Physical Anthropology 115,* 95–98.

Relethford, J. H., & Harpending, H. C. (1994). Craniometric variation, genetic theory, and modern human origins. *American Journal of Physical Anthropology 95,* 249–270.

Renfrew, C. (1973). *Before civilization: The radiocarbon revolution and prehistoric Europe.* London: Jonathan Cape.

"Return to the African Burial Ground: An interview with physical anthropologist Michael L. Blakey." (2003, November 20). *Archaeology.* http://www.archaeology.org/online/interviews/blakey/

Reynolds, V. (1994). Primates in the field, primates in the lab. *Anthropology Today 10* (2), 4.

Ribeiro, G. L. (2009). Non-hegemonic globalizations: Alternative transnational processes and agents. *Anthropological Theory 9* (3), 297–329.

Rice, P. (2000). Paleoanthropology 2000—part 1. *General Anthropology 7* (1), 11.

Richmond, B. G., Fleagle, J. K., & Swisher III, C. C. (1998). First Hominoid elbow from the Miocene of Ethiopia and the evolution of the Catarrhine elbow. *American Journal of Physical Anthropology 105,* 257–277.

Richter, C. A., et al. (2007). In vivo effects of bisphenol A in laboratory rodent studies. *Reproductive Toxicology 24* (2), 199–224.

Ridley, M. (1999). *Genome: The autobiography of a species in 23 chapters.* New York: HarperCollins.

Rightmire, G. P. (1990). *The evolution of Homo erectus: Comparative anatomical studies of an extinct human species.* Cambridge, MA: Cambridge University Press.

Rightmire, G. P. (1998). Evidence from facial morphology for similarity of Asian and African representatives of *Homo erectus. American Journal of Physical Anthropology 106,* 61–85.

Rindos, D. (1984). *The origins of agriculture: An evolutionary perspective.* Orlando: Academic.

Ritzer, G. (1983). The McDonaldization of society, *Journal of American Culture 6* (1), 100–107.

Ritzer, G. (2007). *The coming of post-industrial society* (2nd ed.). New York: McGraw-Hill.

Robben, A.C.G.M. (2007). Fieldwork identity: Introduction. In A.C.G.M. Robben & J. A. Sluka (Eds.), *Ethnographic fieldwork: An anthropological reader* (pp. 59–63). Malden, MA: Blackwell.

Robben, A.C.G.M. (2007). Reflexive ethnography: Introduction. In A.C.G.M. Robben & J. A. Sluka (Eds.), *Ethnographic fieldwork: An anthropological reader* (pp. 443–446). Malden, MA: Blackwell.

Robben, A.C.G.M., & Sluka, J. A. (Eds.). (2007). *Ethnographic fieldwork: An anthropological reader.* Malden, MA: Blackwell.

Rogers, J. (1994). Levels of the genealogical hierarchy and the problem of hominid phylogeny. *American Journal of Physical Anthropology 94,* 81–88.

Romer, A. S. (1945). *Vertebrate paleontology.* Chicago: University of Chicago Press.

Roosevelt, A. C. (1984). Population, health, and the evolution of subsistence: Conclusions from the conference. In M. N. Cohen & G. J. Armelagos (Eds.), *Paleopathology at the origins of agriculture* (pp. 572–574). Orlando: Academic.

Rosas, A., & Bermdez de Castro, J. M. (1998). On the taxonomic affinities of the Dmanisi mandible (Georgia). *American Journal of Physical Anthropology 107,* 145–162.

Roscoe, P. B. (1995). The perils of "positivism" in cultural anthropology. *American Anthropologist 97,* 497.

Roscoe, W. (1991). *Zuni man-woman.* Albuquerque: University of New Mexico Press.

Rowe, N., & Mittermeier, R. A. (1996). *The pictorial guide to the living primates.* East Hampton, NY: Pogonias.

Ruhlen, M. (1994). *The origin of language: Tracing the evolution of the mother tongue.* New York: Wiley.

Rupert, J. L., & Hochachka, P. W. (2001). The evidence for hereditary factors contributing to high altitude adaptation in Andean natives: A review. *High Altitude Medicine & Biology 2* (2), 235–256.

Ruvdo, M. (1994). Molecular evolutionary processes and conflicting gene trees: The hominoid case. *American Journal of Physical Anthropology 94,* 89–113.

Sabloff, J. A. (1997). *The cities of ancient Mexico* (rev. ed.). New York: Thames & Hudson.

Sabloff, J. A., & Lambert-Karlovsky, C. C. (Eds.). (1974). *The rise and fall of civilizations, modern archaeological approaches to ancient cultures.* Menlo Park, CA: Cummings.

Sacks, O. (1998). *Island of the colorblind.* New York: Knopf.

Sahlins, M. (1961). The segmentary lineage: An organization of predatory expansion. *American Anthropologist 63,* 322–343.

Sahlins, M. (1968). *Tribesmen.* Englewood Cliffs, NJ: Prentice-Hall (Foundations of Modern Anthropology).

Sahlins, M. (1972). *Stone age economics.* Chicago: Aldine.

Salzman, P. C. (1967). Political organization among nomadic peoples. *Proceedings of the American Philosophical Society 111,* 115–131.

Sanday, P. R. (1975). On the causes of IQ differences among groups and implications for social policy. In M.F.A. Montagu (Ed.), *Race and IQ* (pp. 232–238). New York: Oxford.

Sanday, P. R. (1981). *Female power and male dominance: On the origins of sexual inequality.* Cambridge, England: Cambridge University Press.

Sanday, P. R. (2002). *Women at the center: Life in a modern matriarchy.* Ithaca: Cornell University Press.

Sangree, W. H. (1965). The Bantu Tiriki of western Kenya. In J. L. Gibbs, Jr. (Ed.), *Peoples of Africa* (pp. 69–72). New York: Holt, Rinehart & Winston.

Sanjek, R. (1990). On ethnographic validity. In R. Sanjek (Ed.), *Field notes.* Ithaca, NY: Cornell University Press.

Sapir, E. (1921). *Language.* New York: Harcourt.

Sapolsky, R. (2002). *A primate's memoir: Love, death, and baboons in East Africa.* New York: Vintage.

Savage-Rumbaugh, S., & Lewin, R. (1994). *Kanzi: The ape at the brink of the human mind.* New York: Wiley.

Sawert, H. (2002). *TB and poverty in the context of global TB control.* World Health Organization. http://www.healthinitiative.org/html/Conf/satsymp/index.htm#2

Scaglion, R. (1987). Contemporary law development in Papua New Guinea. In R. M. Wulff & S. J. Fiske (Eds.), *Anthropological praxis: Translating knowledge into action.* Boulder, CO: Westview.

Schaeffer, S. B., & Furst, P. T. (Eds.). (1996). *People of the peyote: Huichol Indian history, religion, and survival.* Albuquerque: University of New Mexico Press.

Scheflen, A. E. (1972). *Body language and the social order.* Englewood Cliffs, NJ: Prentice-Hall.

Schepartz, L.A. (1993). Language and human origins. *Yearbook of Physical Anthropology 36,* 91–126.

Scheper-Hughes, N., & Waquant, L. (2002). *Commodifying bodies.* London: Sage (Theory, Culture, and Society series).

Schlegel, A. (1977). Male and female in Hopi thought and action. In A. Schlegel (Ed.), *Sexual stratification* (pp. 245–269). New York: Columbia University Press.

Schoepfle, M. (2001). Ethnographic resource inventory and the National Park Service. *Cultural Resource Management 5,* 1–7.

Schrire, C. (Ed.) (1984). *Past and present in hunter-gatherer studies.* Orlando: Academic.

Schusky, E. L. (1983). *Manual for kinship analysis* (2nd ed.). Lanham, MD: University Press of America.

Schuster, C., & Carpenter, E. (1996). *Patterns that connect: Social symbolism in ancient and tribal art.* New York: Abrams.

Schuster, G., Smits, W., & Ullal, J. (2008). *Thinkers of the jungle: The orangutan report.* H. F. Uhlmann.

Schwartz, J. H. (1984). Hominoid evolution: A review and a reassessment. *Current Anthropology 25* (5), 655–672.

Schwartz, M. (1997). *A history of dogs in the early Americas.* New Haven: Yale University Press.

Scully, T. (2008). Online anthropology draws protest from aboriginal group. *Nature 453,* 1155.

Scupin, R. (Ed.). (2000). *Religion and culture: An anthropological focus.* Upper Saddle River, NJ: Prentice-Hall.

Seeger, A. (2004). *Why Suyá sing: A musical anthropology.* Champaign: University of Illinois Press.

Sellen, D. W., & Mace, R. (1997). Fertility and mode of subsistence: A phylogenetic analysis. *Current Anthropology 38,* 886.

Semenov, S. A. (1964). *Prehistoric technology.* New York: Barnes & Noble.

Senut, B., Pickford, M., Gommery, D., Mein, P., Cheboi, K., & Coppens, Y. (2001). First hominid from the Miocene (Lukeino Formation, Kenya). *Comptes Rendus de l'Académie de Sciences 332,* 137–144.

Seyfarth, R. M., Cheney, D. L., & Marler, P. (1980). Vervet monkey alarm calls: Semantic communication in a free-ranging primate. *Animal Behavior 28* (4),1070–1094.

Seyfarth, R. M., et al. (1980). Monkey responses to three different alarm calls: Evidence for predator classification and semantic communication. *Science 210,* 801–803.

Seymour, D. Z. (1986). Black children, black speech. In P. Escholz, A. Rosa, & V. Clark (Eds.), *Language awareness* (4th ed.). New York: St. Martin's.

Shane, L., III. (2005). Happy couple both no-show wedding: Deployed troops make use of double-proxy ceremony. *Stars & Stripes 3* (17), 6.

Shapiro, H. (Ed.). (1971). *Man, culture and society* (2nd ed.). New York: Oxford University Press.

Sharer, R. J., & Ashmore, W. (2007). *Archaeology: Discovering our past* (4th ed.). New York: McGraw-Hill.

Shaw, D. G. (1984). A light at the end of the tunnel: Anthropological contributions toward global competence. *Anthropology Newsletter 25,* 16.

Shearer, R. R., & Gould, S. J. (1999). Of two minds and one nature. *Science 286,* 1093.

Sheets, P. D. (1993). Dawn of a new Stone Age in eye surgery. In R. J. Sharer & W. Ashmore (Eds.), *Archaeology: Discovering our past* (2nd ed.). Palo Alto, CA: Mayfield.

Shipman, P. (1993). *Life history of a fossil: An introduction to taphonomy and paleoecology.* Cambridge, MA: Harvard University Press.

Shook, J. R., et al. (Eds.). (2004). *Dictionary of modern American philosophers, 1860–1960.* Bristol, England: Thoemmes.

Shore, B. (1996). *Culture in mind: Meaning, construction, and cultural cognition.* New York: Oxford University Press.

Shostak, M. (1983). *Nisa: The life and words of a !Kung woman.* New York: Vintage.

Shreeve, J. (1994). Terms of estrangement. *Discover 15* (11), 60.

Shreeve, J. (1995). *The Neandertal enigma: Solving the mystery of modern human origins.* New York: William Morrow.

Shuey, A. M. (1966). *The testing of Negro intelligence.* New York: Social Science.

Sillen, A., & Brain, C. K. (1990). Old flame. *Natural History 4,* 6–10.

Simons, E. L. (1972). *Primate evolution.* New York: Macmillan.

Simons, E. L. (1989) Human origins. *Science 245,* 1349.

Simons, E. L. (1995). Skulls and anterior teeth of *Catopithecus* (Primates: Anthropoidea) from the Eocene and anthropoid origins. *Science 268,* 1885–1888.

Simons, E. L., Rasmussen, D. T., & Gebo, D. L. (1987). A new species of *Propliopithecus* from the Fayum, Egypt. *American Journal of Physical Anthropology 73,* 139–147.

Simons, R. C., & Hughes, C. C. (Eds.). (1985). *The culture-bound syndromes: Folk illnesses of psychiatric and anthropological interest.* Dordrecht, Netherlands: Reidel.

Simpson, G. G. (1949). *The meaning of evolution.* New Haven, CT: Yale University Press.

Simpson, S. (1995, April). Whispers from the ice. *Alaska,* 23–28.

Simpson, S. W., Quade, J., Levin, N. E., Butler, R., Dupont-Nivet, G., Everett, M., & Semaw, S. (2008). A female *Homo erectus* pelvis from Gona, Ethiopia. *Science 322* (5904), 1089–1092.

Sjoberg, G. (1960). *The preindustrial city.* New York: Free Press.

Sluka, J. A. (2007). Fieldwork relations and rapport: Introduction. In A.C.G.M. Robben & J. A. Sluka (Eds.), *Ethnographic fieldwork: An anthropological reader.* Malden, MA: Blackwell.

Small, M. F. (1997). Making connections. *American Scientist 85,* 503.

Small, M. F. (2000). Kinship envy. *Natural History 109* (2), 88.

Small, M. F. (2008, August 15). Why red is such a potent color. *Live Science.* http://www.livescience.com/culture/080815-hn-color-red.html

Small, M. F. (2009, May 15). Why "Ida" inspires navel-gazing at our ancestry. *Live Science.* http://www.livescience.com/history/090520-hn-ida.html

Smedley, A. (2007). *Race in North America: Origin and evolution of a worldview.* Boulder, CO: Westview.

Smith, B. H. (1994). Patterns of dental development in *Homo, Australopithecus, Pan,* and gorilla. *American Journal of Physical Anthropology 94,* 307–325.

Smith, F. H., & Raynard, G. C. (1980). Evolution of the supraorbital region in Upper Pleistocene fossil hominids from South-Central Europe. *American Journal of Physical Anthropology 53,* 589–610.

Smith, P.E.L. (1976). *Food production and its consequences* (2nd ed.). Menlo Park, CA: Cummings.

Snowden, C. T. (1990). Language capabilities of nonhuman animals. *Yearbook of Physical Anthropology 33,* 215–243.

Speck, F. G. (1920). Penobscot shamanism. *Memoirs of the American Anthropological Association 6,* 239–288.

Speck, F. G. (1970). *Penobscot man: The life history of a forest tribe in Maine.* New York: Octagon.

Spencer, F., & Smith, F. H. (1981). The significance of Ales Hrdlicka's "Neanderthal phase of man": A historical and current assessment. *American Journal of Physical Anthropology 56,* 435–459.

Spencer, H. (1896). *Principles of sociology.* New York: Appleton.

Spencer, R. F. (1984). North Alaska Coast Eskimo. In D. Damas (Ed.), *Arctic: Handbook of North American Indians* (Vol. 5, pp. 320–337). Washington, DC: Smithsonian Institution.

Spindler, G., & Stockard, J. E. (Eds.). (2006). *Globalization and change in fifteen cultures.* Belmont, CA: Wadsworth.

Spradley, J. P. (1979). *The ethnographic interview.* New York: Holt, Rinehart & Winston.

Spradley, J. P. (1980). *Participant observation.* New York: Holt, Rinehart & Winston.

Springen, K. (2008, September 15). What it means to be a woman: How women around the world cope with infertility. *Newsweek Web Exclusive.* http://www.newsweek.com/id/158625

Stacey, J. (1990). *Brave new families.* New York: Basic.

Stahl, A. B. (1984). Hominid dietary selection before fire. *Current Anthropology 25,* 151–168.

Standing Bear, L. (1975). *My people the Sioux.* Lincoln: University of Nebraska Press.

Stanford, C. B. (2001). *Chimpanzee and red colobus: The ecology of predator and prey.* Cambridge, MA: Harvard University Press.

Stanford, C. B. (2001). *The hunting apes: Meat eating and the origins of human behavior.* Princeton, NJ: Princeton University Press.

Stannard, D. E. (1992). *American holocaust.* Oxford, England: Oxford University Press.

Starn, O. (2005). *Ishi's brain: In search of America's last "wild" Indian.* New York: Norton.

Steady, F. C. (2001). *Women and the Amistad connection, Sierra Leone Krio Society.* Rochester, VT: Schenkman.

Steady, F. C. (2005). *Women and collective action in Africa.* New York: Palgrave Macmillan.

Stedman, H. H., et al. (2004). Myosin gene mutation correlates with anatomical changes in the human lineage. *Nature 428,* 415–418.

Stein, R., & St. George, D. (2009, May 13). Babies increasingly born to unwed mothers. *Washington Post.*

Stein, R. L., & Stein, P. L. (2004). *Anthropology of religion, magic, and witchcraft*. Boston: Allyn & Bacon.

Steward, J. H. (1972). *Theory of culture change: The methodology of multilinear evolution.* Urbana: University of Illinois Press.

Stiglitz, J. E. (2003). *Globalization and its discontents.* New York: Norton.

Stiles, D. (1979). Early Acheulean and developed Oldowan. *Current Anthropology 20* (l), 126–129.

Stockard, J. E. (2002). *Marriage in culture: Practice and meaning across diverse societies.* Ft. Worth: Harcourt College.

Stocking, G. W., Jr. (1968). *Race, culture and evolution: Essays in the history of anthropology.* New York: Free Press.

Stone, L. (2005). *Kinship and gender: An introduction* (3rd ed.). Boulder, CO: Westview.

Stone, R. (1995). If the mercury soars, so may health hazards. *Science 267,* 958.

Straus, W. L., & Cave, A.J.E. (1957). Pathology and the posture of Neanderthal man. *Quarterly Review of Biology, 32.*

Strier, K. (1993, March). Menu for a monkey. *Natural History, 42.*

Stringer, C. B., & McKie, R. (1996). *African exodus: The origins of modern humanity.* London: Jonathan Cape.

Strum, S., & Mitchell, W. (1987). Baboon models and muddles. In W. Kinsey (Ed.), *The evolution of human behavior: Primate models.* Albany: State University of New York Press.

Stuart-MacAdam, P., & Dettwyler, K. A. (Eds.). (1995). *Breastfeeding: Biocultural perspectives.* New York: Aldine.

"Study estimates 250,000 active child soldiers."(2006, July 26). Associated Press.

Suarez-Orozoco, M. M., Spindler, G., & Spindler, L. (1994). *The making of psychological anthropology, II.* Fort Worth: Harcourt Brace.

Susman, R. L. (1988). Hand of *Paranthropus robustus* from Member 1, Swartkrans: Fossil evidence for tool behavior. *Science 240,* 781–784.

Suwa, G., et al. (2007, August 23). A new species of great ape from the late Miocene epoch in Ethiopia. *Nature 448,* 921–924.

Swadesh, M. (1959). Linguistics as an instrument of prehistory. *Southwestern Journal of Anthropology 15,* 20–35.

Swaminathan, M. S. (2000). Science in response to basic human needs. *Science 287,* 425.

Swisher III, C. C., Curtis, G. H., Jacob, T., Getty, A. G., Suprijo, A., & Widiasmoro. (1994). Age of the earliest known hominids in Java, Indonesia. *Science 263,* 1118–1121.

Tapper, M. (1999). *In the blood: Sickle-cell anemia and the politics of race.* Philadelphia: University of Pennsylvania Press.

Tattersal, I. (1998). *Becoming human: Evolution and human uniqueness.* New York: Harcourt Brace.

Tattersall, I., & Schwartz, J. H. (1999). Hominids and hybrids: The place of Neanderthals in human evolution. *Proceedings of the National Academy of Science 96* (13), 7117–7119.

Tax, S. (1953). *Penny capitalism: A Guatemalan Indian economy.* Washington, DC: Smithsonian Institution, Institute of Social Anthropology, Pub. No. 16.

Taylor, G. (2000). *Castration: Abbreviated history of western manhood.* New York: Routledge.

Tedlock, B. (2005). *The woman in the shaman's body: Reclaiming the feminine in religion and medicine.* New York: Random House.

Templeton, A. R. (1994). Eve: Hypothesis compatibility versus hypothesis testing. *American Anthropologist 96* (1), 141–147.

Templeton, A. R. (1995). The "Eve" hypothesis: A genetic critique and re-analysis. *American Anthropologist 95* (1), 51–72.

Terashima, H. (1983). Mota and other hunting activities of the Mbuti archers: A socio-ecological study of subsistence technology. *African Studies Monograph* (Kyoto), 71–85.

Thin, N. (2007). "Realising the substance of their happiness": How anthropology forgot about *Homo gauius.* In A. C. Jimenez (Ed.), *Culture and the politics of freedom: The anthropology of well-being.* London: Pluto

Thomas, E. M. (1994). *The tribe of the tiger: Cats and their culture* (pp. 109–186). New York: Simon & Schuster.

Thompson, P. (2009, March 6). Sign of the times: Jobless pitch "tent city" in Sacramento. *Mail Online* (London). http://obrag.org/?p=5008

Thomson, K. S. (1997). Natural selection and evolution's smoking gun. *American Scientist 85,* 516–518.

Thorne, A. G., & Wolpoff, M.D.H. (1981). Regional continuity in Australasian Pleistocene hominid evolution. *American Journal of Physical Anthropology 55,* 337–349.

Thornhill, N. (1993). Quoted in W. A. Haviland & R. J. Gordon (Eds.), *Talking about people* (p. 127). Mountain View, CA: Mayfield.

Timmons, H., & Kumar, H. (2009, July 3). Indian court overturns gay sex ban. *New York Times.*

Tobias, P. V., & von Konigswald, G.H.R. (1964). A comparison between the Olduvai hominines and those of Java and some implications for hominid phylogeny. *Nature 204,* 515–518.

Toth, N., Schick, K. D., Savage-Rumbaugh, E. S., Sevcik, R. A., & Rumbaugh, D. M. (1993–2001). Pan the tool-maker: Investigations into the stone tool-making and tool-using capabilities of a bonobo (*Pan panisicus*). *Journal of Archaeological Science 20* (1), 81–91.

Tracy, J. L., & Matsumoto, D. (2008). The spontaneous expression of pride and shame: Evidence for biologically innate nonverbal displays. *Proceedings of the National Academy of Sciences 105* (33), 11655–11660.

Trevathan, W., Smith, E. O., & McKenna, J. J. (Eds.). (1999). *Evolutionary medicine.* London: Oxford University Press.

Trifonov, V., et al. (2009). The origin of the recent swine influenza A (H1N1) virus infecting humans. *Eurosurveillance 14* (17). http://www.eurosurveillance.org/ViewArticle.aspx?ArticleId=19193

Trinkaus, E. (1986). The Neanderthals and modern human origins. *Annual Review of Anthropology 15,* 197.

Trinkaus, E., & Shipman, P. (1992). *The Neandertals: Changing the image of mankind.* New York: Knopf.

Trouillot, M. R. (1996). Culture, color, and politics in Haiti. In S. Gregory & R. Sanjek (Eds.), *Race.* New Brunswick, NJ: Rutgers University Press.

Trouillot, M. R. (2003). *Global transformations: Anthropology and the modern world.* New York: Palgrave Macmillan.

Tumin, M. M. (1967). *Social stratification: The forms and functions of inequality.* Englewood Cliffs, NJ: Prentice-Hall (Foundations of Modern Sociology).

Turnbull, C. M. (1961). *The forest people.* New York: Simon & Schuster.

Turnbull, C. M. (1983). *The human cycle.* New York: Simon & Schuster.

Turnbull, C. M. (1983). *Mbuti Pygmies: Change and adaptation.* New York: Holt, Rinehart & Winston.

Turner, T. (1991). Major shift in Brazilian Yanomami policy. *Anthropology Newsletter 32* (5), 1, 46.

Turner, V. W. (1957). *Schism and continuity in an African society.* Manchester, England: University Press.

Turner, V. W. (1969). *The ritual process.* Chicago: Aldine.

Tylor, E. B. (1871). *Primitive culture: Researches into the development of mythology, philosophy, religion, language, art and customs.* London: Murray.

Tylor, Sir E. B. (1931). Animism. In V. F. Calverton (Ed.), *The making of man: An outline of anthropology.* New York: Modern Library.

Unah, I., & Boger, C. (2001, April). *Race and the death penalty in North Carolina.* www.commonsense.org/pdfs/NCDeathPenaltyReport2001.pdf

UNESCO. www.unesco.org/webworld/babel

UNESCO. www.unesco.org/education/litdecade

UNESCO Institute for Statistics. (2007). http://stats.uis.unesco.org

"UN food agency warns G8 ministers of unparalleled hunger crisis as funding falls." (2009, June 12). http://www.un.org/apps/news/story.asp?NewsID=31116&Cr=WFP&Cr1=hunger

United Nations, World Tourism Organization. www.unwto.org

Universal Declaration of Human Rights. www.ccnmtl.columbia.edu/projects/mmt/udhr

Urban, G. (2001). *Metaculture: How cultures move through the modern world.* Westport, CT: Greenwood.

Ury, W. L. (1993). *Getting past no: Negotiating your way from confrontation.* New York: Bantam.

Ury, W. L. (1999). *Getting to peace: Transforming conflict at home, at work, and in the world.* New York: Viking.

Ury, W. (2002, Winter). A global immune system. *Andover Bulletin.*

Ury, W. (Ed.). (2002). *Must we fight? From the battlefield to the schoolyard—A new perspective on violent conflict and its prevention.* Hoboken, NJ: Jossey-Bass.

U.S. Census Bureau. (2002). *Current population survey.*

U.S. Census Bureau. (2008). *American Community Survey, 2006–2008.*

U.S. Census Bureau News. (2004, March 18).

U.S. Department of Health and Human Services, Administration on Children, Youth, and Families. (2005). *Child maltreatment 2003.* Washington, DC: U.S. Government Printing Office.

Van Allen, J. (1997). Sitting on a man: Colonialism and the lost political institutions of Igbo women. In R. Grinker & C. Steiner (Eds.), *Perspectives on Africa* (p. 450). Boston: Blackwell.

van den Berghe, P. (1992). The modern state: Nation builder or nation killer? *International Journal of Group Tensions 22* (3), 191–207.

Van Eck, C. (2003). *Purified by blood: Honour killings amongst Turks in the Netherlands.* Amsterdam: Amsterdam University Press.

Van Gennep, A. (1960). *The rites of passage.* Chicago: University of Chicago Press. (orig. [1909]. *Les rites de passage.* Paris: Émile Nourry)

Van Tilburg, J. A. (1994). *Easter Island: Archaeology, ecology, and culture.* London: British Museum.

Van Willigen, J. (1986). *Applied anthropology.* South Hadley, MA: Bergin & Garvey.

Veenhoven, R. (1993). *Happiness in nations: Subjective appreciation of life in 56 nations 1946–1992.* Rotterdam: RISBO.

Venbrux, E., Rosi, P. S., & Welsch, R. L. (Eds.). (2006). *Exploring world art.* Longrove, IL: Waveland.

Vincent, J. (2002). *The anthropology of politics: A reader in ethnography, theory, and critique.* Boston: Blackwell.

Vogt, E. Z. (1990). *The Zinacantecos of Mexico: A modern Maya way of life* (2nd ed.). Fort Worth: Holt, Rinehart & Winston.

vom Saal, F. S., & Myers, J. P. (2008). Bisphenol A and risk of metabolic disorders. *Journal of the American Medical Association, 300* (11), 1353–1355.

Waldbaum, J. C. (2005, November/December). Tell it to the Marines: Teaching troops about cultural heritage. *Archaeology 58* (6).

Walker, A., & Shipman, P. (1997). *The wisdom of the bones: In search of human origins.* New York: Vintage.

Wallace, A.F.C. (1956). Revitalization movements. *American Anthropologist 58,* 264–281.

Wallace, A.F.C. (1966). *Religion: An anthropological view.* New York: Random House.

Wallace, A.F.C. (1970). *Culture and personality* (2nd ed.). New York: Random House.

Wallace, E., & Hoebel, E. A. (1952). *The Comanches.* Norman: University of Oklahoma Press.

Walrath, D. (2002). Decoding the discourses: Feminism and science, review essay. *American Anthropology 104* (1), 327–330.

Walrath, D. (2003). Rethinking pelvic typologies and the human birth mechanism. *Current Anthropology 44* (1), 5–31.

Walrath, D. (2006). Gender, genes, and the evolution of human birth. In P. L. Geller & M. K. Stockett (Eds.), *Feminist anthropology: Past, present, and future.* Philadelphia: University of Pennsylvania Press.

Ward, C. V., Walker, A., Teaford, M. F., & Odhiambo, I. (1993). Partial skeleton of Proconsul nyanzae from Mfangano Island, Kenya. *American Journal of Physical Anthropology 90,* 77–111.

Washburn, S. L., & Moore, R. (1980). *Ape into human: A study of human evolution* (2nd ed.). Boston: Little, Brown.

Wattenberg, B. J. (1997, November 23). The population explosion is over. *New York Times Magazine,* 60.

Weatherford, J. (1988). *Indian givers: How the Indians of the Americas transformed the world.* New York: Ballantine.

Weiner, A. B. (1977). Review of Trobriand cricket: An ingenious response to colonialism. *American Anthropologist 79,* 506.

Weiner, A. B. (1988). *The Trobrianders of Papua New Guinea.* New York: Holt, Rinehart & Winston.

Weiner, J. S. (1955). *The Piltdown forgery.* Oxford, England: Oxford University Press.

Weiss, M. L., & Mann, A. E. (1990). *Human biology and behavior* (5th ed.). Boston: Little, Brown.

Wells, S. (2002). *The journey of man: A genetic odyssey.* Princeton, NJ: Princeton University Press.

Werner, D. (1990). *Amazon journey.* Englewood Cliffs, NJ: Prentice-Hall.

Wheeler, P. (1993). Human ancestors walked tall, stayed cool. *Natural History 102* (8), 65–66.

Whelehan, P. (1985). Review of incest, a biosocial view. *American Anthropologist 87,* 678.

White, D. R. (1988). Rethinking polygyny: Co-wives, codes, and cultural systems. *Current Anthropology 29,* 529–572.

White, L. (1949). *The science of culture: A study of man and civilization.* New York: Farrar, Straus.

White, L. (1959). *The evolution of culture: The development of civilization to the fall of Rome.* New York: McGraw-Hill.

White, M. (2001). *Historical atlas of the twentieth century.* http://users.erols.com/mwhite28/20centry.htm

White, R. (2003). *Prehistoric art: The symbolic journey of humankind.* New York: Abrams.

White, T., Asfaw, B., Degusta, D., Gilbert, H., Richards, G., Suwa, G., & Howell, F. C. (2003). Pleistocene *Homo sapiens* from the Middle Awash, Ethiopia. *Nature 423,* 742–747.

White, T. D. (1979). Evolutionary implications of Pliocene hominid footprints. *Science 208,* 175–176.

White, T. D. (2003). Early hominids—diversity or distortion? *Science 299,* 1994–1997.

White, T. D., Asfaw, B., Beyne, Y., Haile-Selassie, Y., Lovejoy, C. O., Suwa, G., & Wolde Gabriel, G. (2009, October). *Ardipithecus ramidus* and the paleobiology of early hominids. *Science 326* (5949), 64, 75–86.

White, T. D., & Toth, N. (2000). Cutmarks on a Plio-Pleistocene hominid from Sterkfontein, South Africa. *American Journal of Physical Anthropology 111,* 579–584.

Whitehead, B. D., & Popenoe, D. (2004). *The state of our unions: The social health of marriage in America 2004.* Rutgers, NJ: Rutgers University National Marriage Project.

Whitehead, N., & Ferguson, R. B. (Eds.). (1992). *War in the tribal zone.* Santa Fe: School of American Research.

Whitehead, N. L., & Ferguson, R. B. (1993, November). Deceptive stereotypes about tribal warfare. *Chronicle of Higher Education,* A48.

Whiting, B. B. (Ed.). (1963). *Six cultures: Studies of child rearing.* New York: Wiley.

Whiting, J.W.M., & Child, I. L. (1953). *Child training and personality: A cross-cultural study.* New Haven, CT: Yale University Press.

Whiting, J.W.M., Sodergem, J. A., & Stigler, S. M. (1982). Winter temperature as a constraint to the migration of preindustrial peoples. *American Anthropologist 84,* 289.

Whorf, B. (1941). The relation of habitual thought and behavior to language. In L. Spier, A. I. Hallowell, & S. S. Newman (Eds.), *Language, culture, and personality: Essays in memory of Edward Sapir* (pp. 75–93). Menasha, WI: Sapir Memorial Publication Fund.

Whyte, A.L.H. (2005). Human evolution in Polynesia. *Human Biology 77* (2), 157–177.

Wiley, A. S. (2004). *An ecology of high-altitude infancy: A biocultural perspective.* Cambridge, England: Cambridge University Press.

Wilk, R. R. (1996). *Economics and cultures: An introduction to economic anthropology.* Boulder, CO: Westview.

Wilkie, D. S., & Curran, B. (1993). Historical trends in forager and farmer exchange in the Ituri rain forest of northeastern Zaïre. *Human Ecology 21* (4), 389–417.

Willey, G. R. (1966). *An introduction to American archaeology: Vol. 1. North America.* Englewood Cliffs, NJ: Prentice-Hall.

Willey, G. R. (1971). *An introduction to American archaeology, Vol. 2: South America.* Englewood Cliffs, NJ: Prentice-Hall.

Williams, F. (2005, January 9). Toxic breast milk? *New York Times Magazine.*

Williamson, R. K. (1995). The blessed curse: Spirituality and sexual difference as viewed by Euramerican and Native American cultures. *The College News 18* (4).

Wills, C. (1994). The skin we're in. *Discover 15* (11), 79.

Wilson, A. K., & Sarich, V. M. (1969). A molecular time scale for human evolution. *Proceedings of the National Academy of Science 63,* 1,089–1,093.

Wingert, P. (1965). *Primitive art: Its tradition and styles.* New York: World.

Winick, C. (Ed.). (1970). *Dictionary of anthropology.* Totowa, NJ: Littlefield, Adams.

Wirsing, R. L. (1985). The health of traditional societies and the effects of acculturation. *Current Anthropology 26* (3), 303–322.

Wittfogel, K. A. (1957). *Oriental despotism, a comparative study of total power.* New Haven, CT: Yale University Press.

Wolf, E. R. (1966). *Peasants.* Englewood Cliffs, NJ: Prentice-Hall.

Wolf, E. R. (1969). *Peasant wars of the twentieth century.* New York: Harper & Row.

Wolf, E. R. (1982). *Europe and the people without history.* Berkeley: University of California Press.

Wolf, E. R. (1999). *Envisioning power: Ideologies of dominance and crisis.* Berkeley: University of California Press.

Wolf, E. R., & Hansen, E. C. (1972). *The human condition in Latin America.* New York: Oxford University Press.

Wolf, E. R., & Trager, G. L. (1971). Hortense Powdermaker 1900–1970. *American Anthropologist 73* (3), 784.

Wolf, M. (1985). *Revolution postponed: Women in contemporary China.* Stanford, CA: Stanford University Press.

Wolffe, R., Ramirez, J., & Bartholet, J. (2008, March 31). *Newsweek.*

Wolfson, H. (2000, January 22). Polygamists make the Christian connection. *Burlington Free Press,* 2c.

Wolpoff, M. H. (1993). Evolution in *Homo erectus:* The question of stasis. In R. L. Ciochon & J. G. Fleagle (Eds.), *The human evolution source book.* Englewood Cliffs, NJ: Prentice-Hall.

Wolpoff, M. H. (1993). Multiregional evolution: The fossil alternative to Eden. In R. L. Ciochon & J. G. Fleagle (Eds.), *The human evolution source book.* Englewood Cliffs, NJ: Prentice-Hall.

Wolpoff, M. (1996). *Australopithecus:* A new look at an old ancestor. *General Anthropology 3* (1), 2.

Wolpoff, M., & Caspari, R. (1997). *Race and human evolution: A fatal attraction.* New York: Simon & Schuster.

Wolpoff, M. H., Wu, X. Z., & Thorne, A. G. (1984). Modern *Homo sapiens* origins: A general theory of hominid evolution involving fossil evidence from east Asia. In F. H. Smith and F. Spencer (Eds.), *The origins of modern humans* (pp. 411–483). New York: Alan R. Liss.

Wood, B., & Aiello, L. C. (1998). Taxonomic and functional implications of mandibular scaling in early hominines. *American Journal of Physical Anthropology 105,* 523–538.

Wood, B., Wood, C., & Konigsberg, L. (1994). *Paranthropus boisei:* An example of evolutionary stasis? *American Journal of Physical Anthropology 95,* 117–136.

Woolfson, P. (1972). Language, thought, and culture. In V. P. Clark, P. A. Escholz, & A. F. Rosa (Eds.), *Language.* New York: St. Martin's.

World almanac. (2004). New York: Press Publishing.

World Bank. www.worldbank.org/poverty

World Bank Development Indicators. (2008).

World Health Organization. http://www.who.int/about/definition/en

World Health Organization. (2003). *Global strategy on infant and young child feeding.* Geneva: Author.

World Health Organization. (2004). Statistical information system.

World Meteorological Organization. (2003). Increasing heat waves and other health hazards. greenpeaceusa.org/climate/index.fpl/7096/article/907.html

World Travel & Tourism Council. www.wttc.org

Worsley, P. (1957). *The trumpet shall sound: A study of "cargo" cults in Melanesia.* London: Macgibbon & Kee.

Worsley, P. (1959). Cargo cults. *Scientific American 200* (May), 117–128.

Wrangham, R., & Peterson, D. (1996). *Demonic males.* Boston: Houghton Mifflin.

Wulff, R. M., & Fiske, S. J. (1987). *Anthropological praxis: Translating knowledge into action.* Boulder, CO: Westview.

Xinhua News Agency. (2009, May 9). Canton Fair wraps up with export orders down 17 percent. *China Daily.*

Yip, M. (2002). *Tone.* New York: Cambridge University Press.

Young, A. (1981). The creation of medical knowledge: Some problems in interpretation. *Social Science and Medicine 17,* 1205–1211.

Young, W. (Ed.). (2000). Kimball award winner. *Anthropology News 41* (8), 29.

Zeder, M. A., & Hesse, B. (2000). The initial domestication of goats (*Capra hircus*) in the Zagros Mountains 10,000 years ago. *Science 287,* 2254–2257.

Zeresenay, A., Spoor, F., Kimbel, W. H., Bobe, R., Geraads, D., Reed, D., & Wynn, J. G. (2006). A juvenile early hominin skeleton from Dikika, Ethiopia. *Nature 443,* 296–301.

Zihlman, A. (2001). *The human evolution coloring book.* New York: Harper Resources.

Zilhão, J. (2000). Fate of the Neandertals. *Archaeology 53* (4), 30.

Zimmer, C. (1999). New date for the dawn of dream time. *Science 284,* 1243.

Zimmer, C. (2001). *Evolution: The triumph of an idea.* New York: HarperCollins.

Zimmer, C. (2005) *Smithsonian intimate guide to human origins.* New York: HarperCollins.

Zohary, D., & Hopf, M. (1993). *Domestication of plants in the Old World* (2nd ed.). Oxford: Clarenden.

Zuckerman, P. (2005). Atheism: Contemporary rates and patterns. In M. Martin (Ed.), *The Cambridge companion to atheism.* Cambridge, England: Cambridge University Press.

Photo Credits

CHAPTER 1

p. 2: © New York Times/Stephanie Sinclair/VII Photo Agency; **p. 4:** © Documentary Educational Resources; **p. 6 (left):** © Michael Newman/ PhotoEdit; **p. 6 (right):** © Marie-Stenzel/National Geographic Image Collection; **p. 9:** © Associated Press; **p. 10:** © AP Photo/Rodrigo Abd; **p. 12:** © Jeff Schonberg 2009; **p. 14:** © Living Tongues Institute; **p. 17 (above right):** National Anthropological Archives Smithsonian Museum 1895 Neg # 02871000; **p. 17 (below left):** Bildarchiv Preussischer Kulturbesitz/Art Resource, NY; **p. 19:** © Kerry Cullinan; **p. 22:** © The Canadian Press/ Kevin Frayer; **p. 23 (left):** © Associated Press; **p. 23 (right):** © K. Bhagya Prakash in *Frontline* Vol 19, issue 7, March 30–April 12, 2002

CHAPTER 2

p. 26: © Imagemore Co., Ltd./Corbis; **p. 29:** From Lindauer Bilderbogen no. 5 edited by Frederich Boer, Jan Thorbecke Verlag Sigmaringen West Germany; **p. 30 (left):** © Yvette Pigeon; **p. 30 (right):** © BIOS Huguet Pierre/Peter Arnold, Inc.; **p. 31 (left):** © Fritz Polking/Peter Arnold, Inc.; **p. 31 (right):** © Dana Walrath; **p. 33:** © Vittorio Luzzati/National Portrait Gallery, London; **p. 36:** Courtesy of Rayna Rapp; **p. 40:** By Jonathan Marks (2000) "98% Alike: What Our Similarity to Apes Tell Us about Our Understanding Genetics." *The Chronicle of Higher Education,* May 12; **p. 42:** 20th Century Fox/The Kobal Collection/Hayes, Kerry; **p. 44:** © Marcia Inhorn; **p. 46:** © Camille Tokerud/Getty Images; **p. 47:** Otorohanga Zoological Society; **p. 48:** © Meckes/ Ottawa/Photo Researchers, Inc.

CHAPTER 3

p. 52: © Steve Bloom Images/Alamy; **p. 55:** Courtesy of Michele L. Goldsmith; Photograph © Katherine Hope; **p. 57:** © Peter Arnold, Inc.; **p. 62:** © Tom Brakefield/Corbis; **p. 63:** © Cheng Min/Xinhua/Landov; **p. 66 (left):** © blickwirkel/ Alamy; **p. 66 (right):** © Kevin Schafer/Peter Arnold, Inc.; **p. 67:** © Danita Delimont/Alamy; **p. 68:** © Inga Arndt/Minden Pictures; **p. 69:** © dbimages/Alamy; **p. 70:** © Gerard Lacz/Peter Arnold, Inc.; **p. 71:** © Jay Ullal; **p. 72 (left):** © 2005 Jim West/The Image Works; **p. 72 (right):** © Population Media Center, www. populationmedia.org; **p. 73:** © Martin Bennett/ Alamy; **p. 74:** © AWF/Paul Thomson

CHAPTER 4

p. 76: Courtesy of Save the Chimps, the world's largest sanctuary for rescued chimpanzees. (www.savethechimps.org); **p. 79:** © Paul van Gaalen/zefa/Corbis; **p. 81 (left):** © Michael Nichols/National Geographic Image Collection;

p. 81 (right): Bunataro Imanishi; **p. 82:** © Amy Parish/Anthro-Photo; **p. 84:** © Gunter Ziesler/ Peter Arnold, Inc.; **p. 85:** © Biosphere/Gunther Michel/Peter Arnold, Inc.; **p. 86 (left):** © John Guistina; **p. 86 (right):** © Danita Delimont/ Alamy; **p. 89:** © Tim Davis/Corbis; **p. 90:** © Bob Willingham; **p. 91:** The Great Ape Trust, photo courtesy of Sue Savage-Rumbaugh; **p. 92:** © age footstock/SuperStock; **p. 93:** © Martin Harvey/ Peter Arnold, Inc.

CHAPTER 5

p. 98: © John Warburton-Lee Photography/ Alamy; **p. 101:** © AP Images; **p. 102:** © Javier Trueba/Madrid Scientific Films; **p. 104:** Courtesy of Anne Jensen and Glenn Sheehan; **p. 106 (left):** © Charles Walker/Topfoto/The Image Works; **p. 106 (right):** © WaterFrame/Alamy; **p. 108:** © John Crock; **p. 111 (above):** © British Museum/Art Resource, NY; **p. 111 (below):** © University of Pennsylvania Museum From *Tikal, A Handbook of the Ancient Maya Ruins* by William R. Coe, 1967 #153371; **p. 112:** © AFP/ Getty Images; **p. 113:** © Kenneth Garrett/National Geographic Image Collection; **p. 115:** © Eurelios/ Photo Researchers, Inc.; **p. 117:** © University of Pennsylvania Museum # CX61-4-123

CHAPTER 6

p. 122: Courtesy of PLoS; **p. 125 (left):** © David Bygott/Kibuyu Partners; **p. 125 (right):** © Nishan Bingham; **p. 126:** © David Scharf/Photo Researchers, Inc.; **p. 128 (left):** © Wolfgang Kaehler/Corbis; **p. 128 (right):** © Pete Saloutos/ Corbis; **p. 132 (left):** The Kobal Collection/ Hammer; **p. 132 (right):** © Nishan Bingham; **p. 135:** Courtesy of PLoS; **p. 137 (right):** © David Begun; **p. 138:** The Natural History Museum, London; **p. 139:** Roger Ressmeyer/Corbis; **p. 141 (left):** Michel Brunet; **p. 141 (right):** © Orban, Thierry/Corbis Sygma

CHAPTER 7

p. 144: © T. White Inc.; **p. 147 (left):** Andrew Hill/ Anthro-Photo; **p. 148:** © T. White, Inc.; **p. 149:** © Melville Bell Grosvenor/National Geographic Image Collection; **p. 150:** Pascal Goetgheluck/ Photo Researchers, Inc.; **p. 151:** Discovery of the Pittdown Man in 1911, Cooke, Arthur Clarke (1867–1951)/Geological Society, London, UK/ The Bridgeman Art Library; **p. 153:** AP Photo/ Richard Drew; **p. 155:** VILEM BISCHOF/AFP/ Getty Images; **p. 156:** © Kristin Mosher/Danita Delimont. All Rights Reserved; **p. 158:** © Dr. Fred Spoon/National Museums of Kenya; **p. 160:** © John Reader/Photo Researchers, Inc.; **p. 161:** © T. White, 1998; **p. 165:** Aztec Tlazolteotl. Photographed by Man Ray (1890–1976) © Artists Rights

Society (ARS), NY. Statuette of Ixcuina, Mexican Goddess of Maternity. 1890–1941. Gelatin silver print, 9-1/16 × 6-7/8″ (23 × 17.4 cm). Gift of James Thrall Soby (204.1991) Digital image © The Museum of Modern Art/Licensed by SCALA/Art Resource, NY

CHAPTER 8

p. 172: © Javier Trueba/Madrid Scientific Films; **p. 175:** © 1999 David L. Brill; **p. 176:** © The Field Museum Neg A102513c; **p. 178:** © J & B Photos/ Animals, Animals; **p. 184:** National Museums of Kenya; **p. 185:** © John Reader/Photo Researchers, Inc.; **p. 187:** © Michael S. Yamashita/Corbis; **p. 192:** © PhotoDisc/Getty Images; **p. 193:** Mary Evans Picture Library/Alamy; **p. 194:** © Paul Jaminski/UM Photo Services; **p. 195:** © The Natural History Museum, London; **p. 196 (left & right):** © William A. Haviland; **p. 199:** Courtesy of Marcel Otte

CHAPTER 9

p. 202: Photographer: H. Jensen/Copyright © University of Tubingen; **p. 204:** Jonesfilm/ Warner Bros/The Kobal Collection; **p. 205:** © David L. Brill; **p. 207 (above):** Pascal Goetgheluck/Photo Researchers, Inc.; **p. 207 (below):** © 2001 David L. Brill/Brill Atlanta; **p. 208 (below):** © 1988 David L. Brill; **p. 214 (left):** Gianni Dagli Orti/Corbis; **p. 214 (right):** Réunion de Musées Nationaux/Art Resource, NY; **p. 216:** Rock painting of a bull and horses, c. 17,000 BC, Prehistoric/Caves of Lascaux, Dordogne, France/The Bridgeman Art Library/ copyright status: out of copyright; **p. 217:** © John van Hasselt/Corbis Sygma; **p. 218:** © Jean Vertut; **p. 221:** © Goran Burenhult; **p. 223:** © Aunty Beryl Carmichael

CHAPTER 10

p. 228: © Tavid Bingham and Amory Ledyard; **p. 232:** © Tian chao—Imaginechina/AP Images; **p. 237:** © Sepp Seitz; **p. 238:** © maggiegowan. co.uk/Alamy; **p. 239:** © Harvey Finkle; **p. 241:** © Dr. Bruno Glaser Universitat Bayreuth; **p. 242:** © Bettmann/Corbis; **p. 243 (left):** © Dennis MacDonald/PhotoEdit; **p. 243 (right):** © Irven DeVore/Anthro/Photo; **p. 245 (left):** © UPPA/ Photoshot; **p. 245 (right):** © Jim Richardson/ Corbis; **p. 247:** © John Kerkhoven; **pp. 248 & 249:** © Alan H. Goodman, Hampshire College

CHAPTER 11

p. 252: © Aladin Abdel Naby/Reuters/Landov; **p. 254:** © Getty Images; **p. 256 (left):** © William A. Haviland; **p. 256 (right):** © Image Source/ Getty Images; **p. 259:** © Nishan Bingham;

Index

Italic page numbers indicate charts, figures, and maps.

80025 75540

80025 75540